Ref 920
Encyclope   P9-DYP-268
biography. Supplement

ENCYCLOPEDIA OF WORLD BIOGRAPHY
SUPPLEMENT

27

ENCYCLOPEDIA OF WORLD BIOGRAPHY

SUPPLEMENT

A / Z **27**

THOMSON

GALE

Detroit • New York • San Francisco • New Haven, Conn. • Waterville, Maine • London

THOMSON
✳
GALE™

Encyclopedia of World Biography Supplement, Volume 27

Project Editor
Tracie Ratiner

Editorial Support Services
Andrea Lopeman

Rights and Acquisitions Management
Jackie Jones, Ronald Montgomery,
Sue Rudolph

Imaging and Multimedia
Lezlie Light

Image Research and Acquisitions
Leitha Etheridge-Sims

Manufacturing
Drew Kalasky

LIBRARY OF CONGRESS CATALOGING-IN-PUBLICATION DATA
ISBN 13: 978-1-4144-1892-6
ISBN 10: 1-4144-1892-2
ISSN 1099-7326

This title is also available as an e-book.
ISBN 978-1-4144-2928-1

Printed in the United States of America

10 9 8 7 6 5 4 3 2 1

CONTENTS

INTRODUCTION

The study of biography has always held an important, if not explicitly stated, place in school curricula. The absence in schools of a class specifically devoted to studying the lives of the giants of human history belies the focus most courses have always had on people. From ancient times to the present, the world has been shaped by the decisions, philosophies, inventions, discoveries, artistic creations, medical breakthroughs, and written works of its myriad personalities. Librarians, teachers, and students alike recognize that our lives are immensely enriched when we learn about those individuals who have made their mark on the world we live in today.

Encyclopedia of World Biography Supplement, Volume 27, provides biographical information on 175 individuals not covered in the 17-volume second edition of *Encyclopedia of World Biography (EWB)* and its supplements, Volumes 18, 19, 20, 21, 22, 23, 24, 25 and 26. Like other volumes in the *EWB* series, this supplement represents a unique, comprehensive source for biographical information on those people who, for their contributions to human culture and society, have reputations that stand the test of time. Each original article ends with a bibliographic section. There is also an index to names and subjects, which cumulates all persons appearing as main entries in the *EWB* second edition, the Volume 18, 19, 20, 21, 22, 23, 24, 25 and 26 supplements, and this supplement—more than 8,000 people!

Articles. Arranged alphabetically following the letter-by-letter convention (spaces and hyphens have been ignored), articles begin with the full name of the person profiled in large, bold type. Next is a boldfaced, descriptive paragraph that includes birth and death years in parentheses. It provides a capsule identification and a statement of the person's significance. The essay that follows is approximately 2,000 words in length and offers a substantial treatment of the person's life. Some of the essays proceed chronologically while others confine biographical data to a paragraph or two and move on to a consideration and evaluation of the subject's work. Where very few biographical facts are known, the article is necessarily devoted to an analysis of the subject's contribution.

Following the essay is a bibliographic section arranged by source type. Citations include books, periodicals, and online Internet addresses for World Wide Web pages, where current information can be found.

Portraits accompany many of the articles and provide either an authentic likeness, contemporaneous with the subject, or a later representation of artistic merit. For artists, occasionally self-portraits have been included. Of the ancient figures, there are depictions from coins, engravings, and sculptures; of the moderns, there are many portrait photographs.

Index. The *EWB Supplement* index is a useful key to the encyclopedia. Persons, places, battles, treaties, institutions, buildings, inventions, books, works of art, ideas, philosophies, styles, movements—all are indexed for quick reference just as in a general encyclopedia. The index entry for a person includes a brief identification with birth and death dates *and* is cumulative so that any person for whom an article was written who appears in the second edition of *EWB* (volumes 1–16) and its supplements (volumes 18–27) can be located. The subject terms within the index, however, apply only to volume 27. Every index reference includes the title of the article to which the reader is being directed as well as the volume and page numbers.

Because *EWB Supplement,* Volume 27, is an encyclopedia of biography, its index differs in important ways from the indexes to other encyclopedias. Basically, this is an index of people, and that fact has several interesting consequences. First, the information to which the index refers the reader on a particular topic is always about people associated with that topic. Thus the entry "Quantum theory (physics)" lists articles on people associated with quantum theory. Each article may discuss a person's contribution to quantum theory, but no single article or group of articles is intended to provide a comprehensive treatment of quantum theory as such. Second, the index is rich in classified entries. All persons who are subjects of articles in the encyclopedia, for example, are listed in one or more classifications in the index—abolitionists, astronomers, engineers, philosophers, zoologists, etc.

The index, together with the biographical articles, make *EWB Supplement* an enduring and valuable source for biographical information. As school course work changes to reflect advances in technology and further revelations about the universe, the life stories of the people who have risen above the ordinary and earned a place in the annals of human history will continue to fascinate students of all ages.

We Welcome Your Suggestions. Mail your comments and suggestions for enhancing and improving the *Encyclopedia of World Biography Supplement* to:

The Editors
Encyclopedia of World Biography Supplement
The Gale Group
27500 Drake Road
Farmington Hills, MI 48331-3535
Phone: (800) 347-4253

ADVISORY BOARD

Photographs and illustrations appearing in the *Encyclopedia of World Biography Supplement,* Volume 27, have been used with the permission of the following sources:

AMERICAN BROADCASTING COMPANIES: Mal Goode.

AP/WIDE WORLD PHOTOS: Mahmoud Abbas, Mahmoud Ahmadinejad, Eddie Arcaro, Ban Ki-Moon, Agatha Barbara, Baruj Benacerraf, Elmer Bernstein, Art Blakey, John "Jack" Buck, Mary Bunting-Smith, Elaine Chao, Jean-Michel Cousteau, Guy Fawkes, Steve Irwin, Andrea Jung, Joseph Kabila, Kirk Kerkorian, Ken Kesey, AQ Khan, Walter S. G. Kohn, John Agyekum Kufuor, Ricardo Lagos, Hedy Lamarr, Richard Lane, Jong-Wook Lee, Alan Lomax, Maas Peter, Alice Sheets Marriott, Deepa Mehta, Mae Questel, Elizabeth Tilberis, Pramoedya Ananta Toer, PL Travers, Klaus von Klitzing, Yimou Zhang.

CAMERA PRESS LONDON: Martina Arroyo.

CORBIS: Bonnie Cashin, Wendell Chino, Paul Crutzen, Martha Gellhorn, Edward Said.

GETTY IMAGES: Rudolfo Anaya, Kjell Magne Bondevik, Art Buchwald, Paul Cadmus, Jackie Chan, Rosemary Clooney, Thomas De Quincey, John Denver, Gerard Depardieu, Gerald M. Edelman, Oriana Fallaci, Eileen Farrell, Serge Gainsbourg, Stan Getz, Carlos Ghosn, Gunther von Hagens, Stephen Harper, Heloise, Myra Hess, Sir William Jones, Aleksander Kwasniewski, Georges Melies, Anne Murray, Arthur Murray, Indra K. Nooyi, Donny and Marie Osmond, Catherine Parr, Molly Picon, Artur Schnabel, Rudolf Steiner, Iva Toguri d'Aquino, Michel Tremblay, Dorothy West, Narcissa Whitman, Susilo Bambang Yudhoyono, Zinedine Zidane.

LANDOV: Red Auerbach, Santiago Calatrava, Felipe Calderon, June Carter Cash, Roger A. Enrico, Richard R. Ernst, Victor Jara, Athanasius Kircher, Stanislaw Lem, Luiz Inacio Lula da Silva, John Peel, Anna Politkovskaya, Emma Thompson, Dieter Zetsche, Slavoj Zizek.

OBITUARIES

The following people, appearing in volumes 1–26 of the *Encyclopedia of World Biography,* have died since the publication of the second edition and its supplements. Each entry lists the volume where the full biography can be found.

ALTMAN, ROBERT (born 1925), American filmmaker, died of complications of cancer in Los Angeles, California, on November 21, 2006 (Vol. 20).

ANDREWS, BENNY (born 1930), African American artist, died of cancer at his home in Brooklyn, New York, on November 10, 2006 (Vol. 25).

BENTSEN, LLOYD (born 1921), American senator and Democratic vice-presidential candidate in 1988, died of complications from a stroke in Houston, Texas, on May 23, 2006 (Vol. 2).

BOTHA, PETER WILLEM (born 1916), South African prime minister and first executive state president of the Republic, died at his home in Western Cape, South Africa, on October 31, 2006 (Vol. 2).

BRADLEY, ED (born 1941), African American broadcast journalist, died of leukemia in New York City, on November 9, 2006 (Vol. 2).

BROWN, JAMES (born c. 1933), African American singer, died of congestive heart failure in Atlanta, Georgia, on December 25, 2006 (Vol. 3).

COFFIN, WILLIAM SLOANE, JR. (born 1924), American anti-war activist and university chaplain, died of congestive heart failure in Strafford, Vermont, on April 12, 2006 (Vol. 4).

DUNHAM, KATHERINE (born 1910), African American dancer, choreographer and anthropologist, died in New York, New York, on May 21, 2006 (Vol. 5).

ECEVIT, BÜLENT (born 1925), Turkish statesman and prime minister, died in Ankara, Turkey, on November 5, 2006 (Vol. 5).

FORD, GERALD (born 1913), U.S Republican vice president (1973) and president (1974-1976), died in Rancho Mirage, California, on December 26, 2006 (Vol. 6).

FRIEDMAN, MILTON (born 1912), American economist, died of heart failure in San Francisco, California, on November 16, 2006 (Vol. 6).

GALBRAITH, JOHN KENNETH (born 1908), Economist and scholar of the American Institutionalist school, died of natural causes in Cambridge, Massachusetts, on April 29, 2006 (Vol. 6).

GEERTZ, CLIFFORD (born 1926), American cultural anthropologist, died of complications after heart surgery in Philadelphia, Pennsylvania, on October 30, 2006 (Vol. 6).

HARAWI, ILYAS AL- (born 1925), President of Lebanon, died of cancer in Beirut, Lebanon, on July 7, 2006 (Vol. 23).

HUSSEIN, SADDAM (born 1937), socialist president of the Iraqi Republic and strongman of the ruling Ba'th regime, died by hanging in Baghdad, Iraq, on December 30, 2006 (Vol. 13).

IMAMURA, SHOHEI (born 1926), Japanese film director and producer, died of liver cancer in Tokyo, Japan, on May 30, 2006 (Vol. 25).

KIRKPATRICK, JEANE J. (born 1926), Professor and first woman U.S. ambassador to the United Nations, died of congestive heart failure in Bethesda, Maryland, on December 7, 2006 (Vol. 9).

KUNITZ, STANLEY JASSPON (born 1905), American poet laureate, died of pneumonia in New York, New York, on May 14, 2006 (Vol. 22).

LIGETI, GYÖRGY Austrian composer, died in Vienna, Austria, on June 12, 2006 (Vol. 9).

LIND, JAKOV (Heinz Landwirth; born 1927), Austrian autobiographer, short-story writer, novelist and playwright, died in London, England, on February 16, 2007 (Vol. 9).

ENCYCLOPEDIA OF WORLD BIOGRAPHY

MAHFUZ, NAJIB (Naguib Mahfouz; born 1911), Egyptian novelist, died of complication of a fall in Cairo, Egypt, on August 30, 2006 (Vol. 10).

MATHIAS, BOB (born 1930), American track and field star, died of cancer in Fresno, California, on September 2, 2006 (Vol. 21).

MENOTTI, GIAN CARLO (born 1911), Italian-born American composer, died in Monaco, on February 1, 2007 (Vol. 10).

OLSEN, TILLIE (nee Tillie Lerner; born 1913), American author, died in Oakland, California, on January 1, 2007 (Vol. 20).

PEP, WILLIE (William Guiglermo Papaleo; born 1922), American boxer, died of Alzheimer's disease in Rocky Hill, Connecticut, on November 24, 2006 (Vol. 21).

PINOCHET UGARTE, AUGUSTO (born 1915), Chilean military leader and dictator, died in Santiago, Chile, on December 10, 2006 (Vol. 12).

RICHARDS, ANN WILLIS (born 1933), Democratic governor of Texas, died of esophageal cancer at her home in Austin, Texas, on September 13, 2006 (Vol. 13).

SCHLESINGER, ARTHUR MEIER, JR. (born 1917), American historian and Democratic party activist, died of a heart attack in New York, New York, on February 28, 2007 (Vol. 14).

SCHWARZKOPF, ELISABETH (born 1915), German opera singer, died at her home in Schruns, Austria, on August 3, 2006 (Vol. 25).

SERVAN-SCHREIBER, JEAN-JACQUES (born 1924), French journalist and writer on public affairs, died of complications from bronchitis, in Fécamp, France, on November 7, 2006 (Vol. 14).

SPARK, MURIEL SARAH (born 1918), British author, died in Florence, Italy, on April 14, 2006 (Vol. 14).

STROESSNER, ALFREDO (born 1912), Paraguayan statesman, died of complication from hernia surgery in Brasilia, Brazil, on August 16, 2006 (Vol. 14).

STYRON, WILLIAM (born 1925), American southern writer of novels and articles, died of pneumonia in Martha's Vineyard, Massachusetts, on November 1, 2006 (Vol. 15).

THARP, MARIE (born 1920), American geologist and oceanographic cartologist, died of cancer in Nyack, New York, on August 23, 2006 (Vol. 15).

THOMSON, KENNETH R. (born 1923), Canadian print and broadcast journalism magnate, died of a heart attack in Toronto, Ontario, on June 12, 2006 (Vol. 15).

A

Mahmoud Abbas

Mahmoud Abbas (born 1935) became chairman of the Palestine Liberation Organization (PLO) after Yasir Arafat died in November of 2004, and two months later was easily elected president of the Palestinian Authority. He is the leader of Fatah, the nationalist Palestinian political wing whose principal rival, the Islamic Hamas, gained legislative control of the Authority early in 2006. The United States and Great Britain support Abbas, seen as a moderate, instead of Hamas, which has refused to recognize Israel.

His leadership "was meant to open a new, post–Yasir Afarat chapter in Israeli–Palestinian relations in which the peace plan known as the roadmap was meant to lead both sides towards resolution," the British Broadcasting Corporation wrote on its BBC News website. "But, on one side the bitter struggle between Israel and Hamas has left him on the sidelines. On the other, the power struggle with Arafat—who had refused to hand over crucial powers to Mr. Abbas—limited his ability to act and took up much of his time." Abbas met late in 2006 with Israeli Prime Minister Ehud Olmert to discuss peace plans and planned to meet with U.S. Secretary of State Condoleezza Rice in 2007.

Family Fled to Syria

Abbas, known widely as Abu Mazen, or "Father of Mazen," was born in 1935 in Safed, British Mandate Palestine. His family moved to Syria in 1948, during the Arab–Israeli war that erupted after the United Nations recognized Israel by dividing Palestine into Jewish and Arab states. He worked variously as a laborer and schoolteacher before obtaining his bachelor of arts degree from Damascus University. After studying law in Egypt, he earned his Ph.D. from Oriental College in Moscow. Abbas co-founded Fatah with Arafat in the 1950s while in exile in Qatar, where he was a personnel director in the civil service. He helped recruit several Palestinians who would become important PLO operatives. In addition, he accompanied the PLO leader in Jordan, Tunisia, and Lebanon. "In the early days of the movement, he became respected for his clean and simple living," BBC News wrote. Abbas has also been a member of the Palestine National Council since 1968.

Over the years Abbas worked best behind the scenes. "Mahmoud Abbas always kept to the background, but also built up a network of powerful contacts that included Arab leaders and heads of intelligence services," according to BBC News. He raised considerable money for the organization in the 1970s and was also a security operative. In 1980 Arafat named him head of the PLO's subdivision for national and international relations.

"Abbas has long been considered an exponent of a peaceful solution to the Palestinian–Israeli conflict," the website MidEast Web wrote. "He advocated negotiations with Israelis and negotiated a dialogue with Jewish and pacifist movements in the 1970s." Some Jewish groups, however, have widely criticized Abbas, in particular for his 1984 book *The Other Side: The Secret Relationship Between Nazism and Zionism,* that evolved from his doctorate. Critics said he understated the number of Jewish deaths during the Holocaust and accused some Jews of working with the Nazi regime. According to BBC News, Abbas denied those charges in a 2003 interview with the Israeli daily newspaper *Haaretz.*

1

Abbas drew widespread praise for his role in the Oslo talks that resulted in the 1993 accord in which Israelis and the PLO agreed on mutual recognition. He accompanied Arafat to the White House for the signing of the Oslo Declaration of Principles at a ceremony with U.S. President Bill Clinton. Abbas has overseen the PLO's negotiating affairs department since 1994. "In the light of his origins in Safed in Galilee—which is now northern Israel—he is said to hold strong views about the right of return of Palestinian refugees," BBC News wrote. In 1996 the PLO elevated him to second in command behind Arafat.

First Head of Palestinian Authority

In March of 2003, Arafat, under pressure from the administration of U.S. President George W. Bush, appointed Abbas as the first prime minister of the Palestinian Authority. The White House had frozen Arafat out of peace talks. Craig Nelson, in the Australian-based newspaper *The Age,* summarized the degree of difficulty in Abbas's juggling act. "Your boss is Yasir Arafat, who tries to undercut you at every turn. The president of the United States is pressing you to stop Islamic militant groups from carrying out suicide bombings. The man sitting across from you at the negotiating table—the hawkish, settlement-building Israeli prime minister, Ariel Sharon—represents everything you have fought against during your career," Nelson wrote in a profile on Abbas. "Compounding your difficulties is the fact that you are not elected." While Abbas never criticized Arafat publicly while the latter was alive, they argued heatedly many times in private.

Abbas quit as prime minister after four months of struggles with Arafat over control of Palestinian security forces. Ahmed Qurei succeeded him. Abbas became PLO chairman after Arafat died in November of 2004, and two months later he was easily elected Palestinian Authority president.

Battled Frequently with Hamas

The United States and Israel looked favorably upon Abbas, who distanced himself from the terror groups and was one of the first Palestinian leaders to recognize Israel's right to exist. But in 2005 and 2006, Abbas's internal struggles intensified. While Fatah, through Abbas, controlled the presidency, Hamas took legislative control of the Palestinian Authority in January of 2006. The following December, Abbas said he would call early elections, including that of his own office, as a way of settling the political disputes that had escalated into violence during the year. "We shall not continue this vicious circle," Abbas, as quoted in the *Washington Post,* told legislators, religious leaders, and political supporters in Ramallah, West Bank. "Let us go back to the people and let them have their say."

Hamas officials, however, said they would not agree to a new election so early in the four-year term, and questioned Abbas's right to call such an election. "If the president is willing to go to early elections, he can resign and enter an early presidential election," Hamas official Fawzi Barhoun told the *Washington Post.* "We were elected by the Palestinians, and we are not willing to go through with this experiment. The president's call is illegitimate."

Some observers said Abbas's move was crafted to pressure Hamas to renew stalled talks about a coalition government. But Robert Malley and Henry Siegman in the *International Herald Tribune* called such a strategy unworkable. It is predicated, they said, on several variables, including the Bush administration earmarking considerable time on the Israeli-Palesntinian conflict and negotiating concessions out of Israel. "None of this is likely to happen, even if Abbas's Fatah group were somehow to replace Hamas in this Western-scripted fantasy, Abbas would be handed his third betrayal by the United States and Israel," Malley and Siegman wrote. They cited Abbas's appointment as prime minister and election as president. "On both occasions, promises were made. At the time of writing, Palestinians are still waiting," they wrote.

British Prime Minister Tony Blair visited the West Bank and Israel in December of 2006 on behalf of Palestinian moderates. "The next few weeks should be a critical time for the Middle East," Blair said, after meeting with Abbas in Ramallah. "If the international community really means what it says about supporting people who share the vision of a two-state solution, who are moderate, who are prepared to shoulder their responsibilities, then now is the time for the international community to respond." Violence, meanwhile, continued to escalate. Five days before Blair spoke, gunmen ambushed the entourage of Prime Minister Ismail Haniyeh of Hamas, wounding his son. In addition, a security official working for Abbas was seriously wounded in another shooting. Killings continued despite an announced ceasefire. Abbas stood by his call for early elections. "I want the people to choose," he said, according to United Press International.

Hamas has nearly two–thirds of the seats in the Legislative Council. According to the UPI, a poll conducted by the Palestinian Center for Policy and Survey Research in December of 2006 said if an election were held then, Fatah would get 42 percent of the votes and Hamas 36 percent— and the gap had been widening of late. In addition, the poll said, a presidential election would be too close to call, with Abbas receiving 46 percent, Haniyeh 45 percent, and about nine percent undecided. The UPI's Joshua Brilliant wrote: "One wonders whether Abbas would really order early elections when Fatah and his own lead are so small. Abbas's tactic in threatening to call early elections was to prove Hamsas's policies hurt the Palestinians."

Held Summit with Olmert

On December 23, 2006, Abbas and Israeli Prime Minister Ehud Olmert held their first meeting, in Jerusalem, and Olmert promised him during the two–hour session to release $100 million in Palestinian funds that Israel had frozen, and remove some West Bank checkpoints. Olmert had taken over as prime minister after Sharon suffered an incapacitating stroke the previous January. It was the first meeting between Israeli and Palestinian leaders in nearly two years. "Olmert and Abbas, weakened by political troubles at home, are seeking to bolster their positions by showing progress in peace efforts," Joel Greenberg wrote in the *Chicago Tribune.* Olmert's office, according to the newspaper, released a statement saying the pair had agreed to meet more frequently, and agreed "the time has come to advance the peace process via concrete steps."

The two parties, however, had still not agreed on a prisoner release, a major contention point. Olmert would not free Palestinian prisoners unless the Palestinians would do likewise with Israeli soldier Corporal Gilad Shalit, who has been detained in the Gaza Strip since Hamas militants and two affiliated groups corralled him in a raid the previous June.

Old Guard Would Not Let Go

Abbas announced that Rice would visit the Middle East in January of 2007, as a follow-up to her meetings with Abbas and Olmert late in 2006. He said he would float the idea of a "back channel" for negotiations with Israel. Abbas and Egypt, a pivotal moderator, favor bypassing the prescribed U.S. "road map" for Middle East peace.

Khaled Abu Toameh, in the *Jerusalem Post,* said Fatah would be beatable in another election. Toameh added: "Ever since Fatah lost the election about one year ago, its leaders have been too busy searching for ways to return to power at any cost."

The majority of Palestinians, Steven Erlanger wrote in the *New York Times,* perceive Abbas as a "great disappointment." Erlanger quoted Palestinian political analyst Khaled Duzdar as saying Abbas has not declared a state of emergency in the Palestinian territories because he cannot implement one. "Abbas today is a weak reed, with little power to carry out his decrees or his will," Erlanger wrote.

Abbas and his wife, Amina, have three sons, Mazen, Yaser, and Tareq. Abbas also has seven grandchildren. Abbas once had surgery in the United States for prostate cancer.

Online

"Analysis: Blair Tries to Help PA Moderates," United Press International, December 19, 2006, http://www.upi.com/ InternationalIntelligence/view.php?StoryID = 20 (December 19, 2006).

"Analysis: Same Old Fatah Means Victory for Hamas," *Jerusalem Post,* December 19, 2006, http://www.jpost.com/servlet/ Satellite?pagename = JPost%2FJPArticle%2FShowFull&cid; = 1164881888715 (December 19, 2006).

"Biography of Mahmoud Abbas," MidEast Web, http://www .mideastweb.org/bio-mabbas.htm (December 27, 2006).

"Bio: Mahmoud Abbas," Fox News, November 20, 2004, http://www.foxnews.com/story/0,2933,85531,00.html (December 15, 2006).

"Hamas Rejects Plan by Abbas to Call Elections," *Washington Post,* December 17, 2006, http://www.washingtonpost.com/ wp-dyn/content/article/2006/12/16/AR2006121600436.html (December 19, 2006).

"In Abbas, Western Hopes Hang on Thin Reed," *New York Times,* December 18, 2006, http://www.nytimes.com/2006/ 12/19/world/middleeast/19assess.html (December 19, 2006).

"Mahmoud Abbas," Biography Resource Center, http://www .galenet.galegroup.com/servlet/BioRC?vrsn = 149&OP; = contains&locID; = galetrial&srchtp; = name&ca; = 2&AI; = U13002306&NA; = Mahmoud + Abbas&ste; = 4&tbst; = prp&n; = 10 (December 5, 2006).

"Profile: Mahmoud Abbas," BBC News, January 10, 2005, http://www.news.bbc.co.uk/2/hi/middle_east/1933453.stm (December 27, 2006).

"Rice to Visit in the Mideast Next Month: Abbas," *Washington Post,* December 27, 2006, http://www.washingtonpost.com/ wp-dyn/content/article/2006/12/27/AR2006122700675.html (December 27, 2006). □

Edward Abbey

The controversial writings on the American West by American essayist and novelist Edward Abbey (1927–1989) exerted a strong influence on the development of the modern environmental movement in both its mainstream and radical forms.

Abbey's voluminous writings, mostly about or set in the Western deserts, ranged from intensely detailed descriptions of the natural world to angry or satirical commentaries on effects of modern civilization on American wildlands. One of Abbey's most widely quoted aphorisms, first appearing in the essay collection *Desert Solitaire,* held that "Growth for the sake of growth is the ideology of the cancer cell." Abbey held anarchist convictions, and he viewed government and industry as collaborators in the destruction of the natural environment. *Desert Solitaire* and Abbey's comic novel *The Monkey Wrench Gang* achieved mass success, winning Abbey a strong following among members of the counterculture of the

1970s and beyond. The overarching emphasis of Abbey's writing, however, was personal and philosophical; like the 19th-century New England essayist Henry David Thoreau, to whom he has sometimes been compared, Abbey viewed the natural world in almost mystical terms.

Family Suffered Hard Times

The oldest of five children, Abbey sometimes suggested that he had been born in a farmhouse in a tiny community with the idyllic name of Home, Pennsylvania. In fact his birth occurred on January 29, 1927, in a hospital in Indiana, Pennsylvania, a considerably larger town nearby. His tendency toward unconventional attitudes was partly shaped by his father, Paul Revere Abbey, a committed socialist who subscribed to *Soviet Life* magazine for many years. A rootless, searching quality in Edward Abbey's life may also have had its beginnings in his childhood: the family was hard hit by the economic depression of the early 1930s, moving from place to place as Paul Abbey searched for work as a real estate agent and camping out during several stretches when money was at its tightest.

Abbey's family made the best of their situation; his mother, Mildred Postlewaite Abbey, instilled in him an appreciation of nature. In 1941 the family moved to a farm, located near Home, that Abbey dubbed the Old Lonesome Briar Patch. His creative energy began to show itself early on when he began to write and draw little comic books for which he would demand series subscriptions from siblings and friends. In high school he did well in English classes and was thought of as highly intelligent but as something of an intimidating loner.

This perception changed in 1944, for that summer, between his junior and senior years at Indiana High School, Abbey lived out a dream held by many young people: he took off from home and traveled around the country, relying mostly on hitchhiking and freight trains for transportation. The trip, described in an essay called "Hallelujah on the Bum" included in Abbey's book *The Journey Home: Some Words in Defense of the American West,* took him through Chicago and Yellowstone National Park to Seattle, San Francisco, and the desert Southwest in the middle of summer. He had all his possessions and money stolen by one driver who gave him a ride, and in Flagstaff, Arizona, he spent a night on the floor of a jail cell with a group of drunks after being arrested for vagrancy. He also fell in love with the West. "I became a Westerner at the age of 17, in the summer of 1944, while hitchhiking around the USA," Abbey later wrote (as quoted by biographer James Cahalan). "For me it was love at first sight—a total passion which has never left me." And he began to write about that passion in articles published in his high school newspaper, the *High Arrow.*

For the next several years, Abbey's life resembled those of many other young American men. Drafted into the U.S. Army in the summer of 1945 after graduating from high school, he was sent to Italy and served as a clerk and military motorcycle police officer. Honorably discharged in 1947, he used the stipends he received as a result of the so-called G.I. Bill (Servicemen's Readjustment Act) to attend college, first at Indiana University in Pennsylvania, and then at the University of New Mexico, where he graduated with a philosophy degree in 1951. He married a college sweetheart, Jean Schmechel, in 1950.

Published First Novel

Underneath these activities, however, brewed various ideas of a nonconformist cast. As an undergraduate, he had already run into trouble when he adorned the cover of a student literary journal with a controversial quotation ascribed to the 18th-century French philosopher Denis Diderot—"Mankind will never be free until the last king is strangled with the entrails of the last priest"—and then compounded the insult by attributing the line to *Little Women* author Louisa May Alcott. Abbey found himself drawn toward creative writing. In 1954 he finished a novel, *Jonathan Troy.* He later disparaged the work, which drew heavily on the locale of his Pennsylvania boyhood, but the book landed with a major publisher (Dodd, Mead) and successfully launched his long literary career. Later critics found much to admire in this early effort, and in 1956 Abbey found a ready market for his second novel, *The Brave Cowboy: An Old Tale in a New Time.* The book, which dealt with the doomed heroics of an old-time cowboy in the modern world, was adapted to screen in the 1962 film *Lonely Are the Brave* with actor Kirk Douglas in the lead role of Jack Burns. Douglas insisted on making the film over studio objections.

Abbey also took steps that brought him closer to the desert he loved. For many years between 1956 and 1971 he took temporary jobs with the U.S. National Park Service as a ranger and fire lookout. For his first two summers he worked at Utah's Arches National Monument (later Arches National Park). A compulsive journal-keeper by this time, he wrote voluminously about the awe-inspiring rock formations that gave the park its name, about the ecology of the area, and about the future Abbey saw coming—a future in which fragile natural areas would be overrun with hordes of tourist automobiles. Abbey's journals later became the basis for one of his most celebrated books, *Desert Solitaire: A Season in the Wilderness.*

For much of the 1950s and 1960s, Abbey's life was restless. His first marriage quickly ended in divorce, but in 1952 he married New York–born New Mexico art student Rita Deanin, and the couple had two sons. Abbey enrolled in a master's program in philosophy at Yale University in 1953 but hated his symbolic logic class and left. The family bounced back and forth between the New York area, where Abbey held various jobs (he was a technical writer, factory employee, and at one point a welfare caseworker) and Albuquerque, where he received a master's degree in philosophy at the University of New Mexico in 1959. His thesis was entitled *Anarchism and the Morality of Violence.* Around that time, Abbey and some like-minded friends began to commit occasional acts of sabotage against development projects in the West—they would, for example, pour sugar syrup into the oil tanks of construction equipment, thus putting it out of commission. He continued to write fiction; his third novel, *Fire on the Mountain,* was drawn on the real-life story of a rancher who refused to turn over land to the government for a missile test site.

In 1965 Abbey's marriage to Deanin, long on the rocks, came to an end. Close to 40 years old, with few stable employment prospects, he seemed to have hit a career stall. But with the publication of *Desert Solitaire* in 1968 (by the McGraw-Hill house) his fortunes as a writer turned around for good. Abbey alternated chapters on parks development and on such topics as water in the Western ecosystem with grand philosophical themes, and the mixture caught on among young readers in whom an environmental consciousness was just beginning to awaken. The book was reprinted well over a dozen times, and by the mid-1970s Abbey was able to augment his income from his books and his park ranger work with writing professorships at several schools. Chief among these was the University of Arizona, which provided Abbey with a base for his work in his later years.

Inspired Radical Environmentalists

Always productive as a writer, Abbey was distracted from his work by the death of his third wife, Judith Pepper, from leukemia in 1970. With Pepper Abbey had a third child, Susannah. A fourth marriage, to Renee Dowling, lasted from 1974 to 1980, and a fifth, to Clarke Cartwright, began in 1982 and endured for the rest of Abbey's life. Two more children, Rebecca and Benjamin, were born to Abbey and Cartwright. Abbey published a novel, *Black Sun,* in 1971, and he furnished text for several large-format books of Southwest photographs, including the Time-Life series volume *Cactus Country* in 1973. His most important book of the 1970s, however, was 1975's *The Monkey Wrench Gang,* a comic novel drawing on Abbey's development-sabotage activities. Not strongly promoted by its publisher, Lippincott, the book was reported to have sold 500,000 copies thanks mostly to word-of-mouth publicity. The activities of the loosely knit Earth First! group were sometimes modeled on those in Abbey's novel, and the term "monkeywrenching" entered the vocabulary of radical environmentalism.

Abbey discouraged violence and remained ambivalent about the more radical applications of his ideas. He characterized *The Monkey Wrench Gang* as something of a rant, inspired by anger over such events as the inundation of a spectacular stretch of Colorado River scenery after the river was impounded by the Glen Canyon Dam in the 1960s. Abbey was never afraid to stir controversy, however, and he alienated some of his allies within the environmental movement with various positions he took in the 1970s and 1980s. He advocated closing the U.S.–Mexican border to Mexican immigration, for example. And he was unsympathetic to the feminist movement; critics complained that the female characters in some of his novels were little more than thin stereotypes. In the West, Abbey had admirers and detractors on all points of the political spectrum. He was defended by fellow antidevelopment activist Wendell Berry in an influential 1985 essay entitled "A Few Words in Favor of Edward Abbey." Arguing that Abbey had never claimed the environmentalist mantle, Berry asked, "If Mr. Abbey is not an

environmentalist, what is he? He is, I think, at least in the essays, an autobiographer." Indeed, Abbey's larger-than-life personality showed through in everything he wrote, whether fiction, nonfiction, or the poetry that was published at the end of his life.

In poor health in the 1980s, Abbey was at one point given a terminal cancer diagnosis and told he had six months to live. The diagnosis proved erroneous, however, and Abbey lived to complete several more books—essay collections and several novels, including the autobiographical *The Fool's Progress* and the posthumously published *Hayduke Lives!* (1990, featuring characters from *The Monkey Wrench Gang*). Abbey's journals and essays provided material for a steady stream of publications that appeared after his death. Suffering from increasingly serious esophageal bleeding, Abbey laid plans to die in the open, under the desert skies. He and several friends went out into the desert in early March of 1989, but he rallied and was brought back to his cabin in Oracle, Arizona, near Tucson, where he died on March 14, 1989. His friends buried him, illegally, at an unspecified location said to be on federal land, and the legend of his burial, together with the outlaw mystique and the philosophical vigor of his writings, continued to strengthen his reputation in the years after he passed away.

Books

Bishop, James, Jr., *Epitaph for a Desert Anarchist: The Life and Legacy of Edward Abbey,* Atheneum, 1994.

Cahalan, James M., *Edward Abbey: A Life,* University of Arizona Press, 2001.

Dictionary of Literary Biography, Volume 256: Twentieth-Century American Western Writers (Gale Group, 2002); Volume 275: Twentieth-Century American Nature Writers (Gale Group, 2003).

Periodicals

Independent (London, England), March 27, 1989, Gazette section.

New York Times, May 7, 1989.

St. Petersburg Times (St. Petersburg, FL), March 19, 1989.

Online

Berry, Wendell, "A Few Words in Favor of Edward Abbey," http://home.btconnect.com/tipiglen/abbey.html (September 23, 2006).

"Biography," http://www.abbeyweb.net (September 23, 2006). □

Muhammad Ibn Abd al-Wahhab

Among the least understood of the thinkers and leaders who have shaped the modern world is Muhammad ibn Abd al-Wahhab (c. 1702–c. 1791), the founder of the fundamentalist branch of Islamic thought and practice known as Wahhabism.

bn Abd al-Wahhab's life and beliefs are a source of controversy, both within Islam and in the Western non-Islamic world. Even the term "Wahabbism" is controversial, for within Ibn Abd al-Wahhab's own lifetime it (and its Arabic equivalents) were used primarily by Ibn Abd al-Wahhab's opponents; his followers called themselves *Muwahiddun* or Unitarians, believers in a unity. His writings and actions are susceptible to multiple interpretations. But it can be said that Ibn Abd al-Wahhab was essentially a puritan—not in the contemporary sense of that word, which now tends to refer exclusively to restrictions on sexual activity and its depiction in cultural products, but in the word's older sense, used by early American colonists and indicating a return to the basic tenets of a religion, in this case Islam. Ibn Abd al-Wahhab's influence was closely bound up with the emergence of Saudi Arabia as a state, and his ideas continue to flourish there, a fact of immense importance in contemporary world affairs.

Family Schooled in Conservative Tradition

The facts of Ibn Abd al-Wahhab's life, transmitted to posterity mostly by a circle of close followers, are not always clear. He was born in 1702 or 1703 in the town of al-Uyaynah in the Najd region of the Arabian peninsula, now in northern Saudi Arabia. His family, at least as far back as a grandfather who was a famous judge in religious maters, contained scholars in the conservative Hanbali tradition, one of the main schools of legal thinking in Sunni Islam. By the time he was ten he had memorized the Quran, and he made the required hajj or pilgrimage to Mecca as a teenager. Soon after that he traveled to the religious center of Medina, studying with noted religious scholars in addition to his own father.

By that time he had already begun preaching in his hometown, and it had become apparent that he was controversial from the start. His teachings were based directly on the Quran itself and on the *hadith* tradition of teachings associated with the Prophet Muhammad. He rejected the influence of local religious scholars known as *ulama*, who in turn worked to minimize his influence. He was forced to leave al-Uyaynah, marking the first of several occasions in which he ran afoul of powerful figures. It was at this point that he traveled to Mecca and Medina. Among the figures with whom he studied was Muhammad Hayat al-Sindi, a figure from the Indian subcontinent who had witnessed the deterioration of the Mughal Empire, and who inculcated in Ibn Abd al-Wahhab the idea that pure forms of Islam could regenerate lost political glories.

Ibn Abd al-Wahhab also studied in Basra in what is now Iraq. By this time he was considered an erudite young scholar, and his teacher, Muhammad al-Mujmui, allowed his own children to study with Ibn Abd al-Wahhab. In Basra Ibn Abd al-Wahhab probably encountered scholars from the rival Shia branch of Islam, which he denounced in one treatise. But his quarrel was not primarily with Shia Islam, or with the mystic Sufi sect that he sometimes denounced. Rather, Ibn Abd al-Wahhab was motivated above all by the principle of *tawhid* or montheism, a belief in one God,

called Allah in Arabic. He rejected belief in any idol, and he did not accept that any earthly object could be associated with the divine. Ibn Abd al-Wahhab made his way back to the Arabian peninsula, staying in his hometown and then in Al-Ahsa, and finally moving to Huraymila, where his father had taken up residence.

In Huraymila, Ibn Abd al-Wahhab wrote the best known of his roughly 15 treatises, *Kitab al-Tawhid,* or *The Book of Monotheism.* It was at this time that he began to attract supporters in large numbers, with two local tribes joining forces to accept him as a religious leader. He also gained detractors in equal numbers, apparently stirring up anger among a group of slaves with his strict fulminations against sexual immorality. Members of this group mounted an assassination attempt against Ibn Abd al-Wahhab, but it was unsuccessful. Once more, he returned to his hometown of al-Uyaynah.

Gained Secular Patron

Ibn Abd al-Wahhab found military protection from the area's new ruler, Uthman ibn Hamid ibn Muammar. The alliance foreshadowed Ibn Abd al-Wahhab's later partnership with Muhammad ibn Saud, the founder of Saudi Arabia, and it brought Ibn Abd al-Wahhab new power and influence. It was during this period that he undertook three controversial actions designed to offer graphic demonstrations of his beliefs. These were controversial in Ibn Abd al-Wahhab's own time and remain so, providing famous images of the strict form of Islam he espoused.

The first involved a group of trees that the inhabitants of al-Uyaynah considered sacred and invested with quasi-magical powers. Much to Ibn Abd al-Wahhab's dismay, they would hang various items in the branches of the trees in the hope that they would bring blessings or good luck. For Ibn Abd al-Wahhab, this was a direct violation of the *tawhid* principle that blessings could come only from God. He took direct action to stamp out this example of popular religious belief: he and his followers cut down the grove of sacred trees, with Ibn Abd al-Wahhab himself taking the ax to the most venerated tree of all.

Ibn Abd al-Wahhab's second well-publicized move in al-Uyaynah took aim not at popular superstition but at an icon of Islam itself: a monument built over the tomb of Zayd ibn al-Khattab, an early associate of the Prophet Muhammad himself. Ibn Abd al-Wahhab and his followers destroyed the monument because it violated a central tenet of the *hadith* stating that Muhammad had commanded the destruction of such shrines, because they tended to promote worship of human beings rather than the unitary divine. Ibn Abd al-Wahhab was worried about the strength of the local population's attachment to the monument and asked ibn Muammar for a guard of six hundred men as he destroyed it.

The third event at al-Uyaynah involved a woman who had confessed to Ibn Abd al-Wahhab that she had committed adultery. After she repeated the act several times, Ibn Abd al-Wahhab ordered that she be stoned to death. In that instance he followed the advice of the local *ulama* or Islamic scholars, but in many other instances he came into conflict with these figures. Natana J. Delong-Bas wrote in

Wahhabi Islam that Ibn Abd al-Wahhab faced "opposition by local religious scholars and political leaders who feared a threat to their own power bases." His campaign to purify Sunni Islam was also in part an attempt to confront corruption in the secular world.

Exiled from Al-Uyaynah

As a result of these events and of his growing influence, local Islamic scholars in al-Uyaynah mounted a campaign against Ibn Abd al-Wahhab. Their allegations, which included the charge that he espoused violence against those who did not subscribe to his interpretation of Islam, reached the ears of the leader of the powerful local Bani Khalid tribe, who demanded that Ibn Abd al-Wahhab's protector, Ibn Muammar, either have Ibn Abd al-Wahhab killed or exile him from the region. Ibn Abd al-Wahhab told Ibn Muammar that this situation represented a test of faith, but Ibn Muammar eventually gave in and sent Ibn Abd al-Wahhab into the desert with a pair of horsemen, who may have had instructions to kill him, but did not.

Ibn Abd al-Wahhab landed in the town of al-Diriyah, near Riyadh, and once again his religious fervor attracted a powerful patron—this time one who would become the most powerful Arabian ruler of all. After preaching to small groups, he succeeded in obtaining an introduction to Muhammad ibn Saud, the founder of the modern House of Saud that unified the nation of Saudi Arabia and continues to rule there. In 1744 Ibn Abd al-Wahhab and Muhammad ibn Saud formed a sort of partnership of mutual non-interference, in which Ibn Abd al-Wahhab pledged not to impede Ibn Saud's plans to conquer the Arabian peninsula, while the ruler agreed to back Ibn Abd al-Wahhab's brand of Islam. The basic outlines of the agreement persist today; although adherents of Ibn Abd al-Wahhab's thinking are a minority within the Kingdom of Saudi Arabia, the philosophy dominates Saudi life, and its more restrictive aspects are visible in everyday affairs.

Ibn Saud conquered Riyadh over a period of 27 years and consolidated his hold over other Arabian cities. The degree to which this campaign represented a holy war has been debated. Sometimes Ibn Abd al-Wahhab absented himself from Ibn Saud's more far-flung campaigns, not opposing them but also not offering them religious legitimacy. Conflict continued for much of the eighteenth century, not only on the battlefield but also on the field of religious ideas, as Islamic scholars continued to mount opposition to Ibn Abd al-Wahhab. At times he directed actual warfare against his opponents, perhaps defensive in nature. Meanwhile, the power and wealth of the Saud family increased, especially under Ibn Saud's son, Abd al-Aziz. Ibn Abd al-Wahhab counseled the newly prosperous inhabitants of lands conquered by the Saud rulers to obey the Prophet's injunction that they donate 2.5 percent of their income to charity and to follow the strict tenets of his teaching, but he was disturbed by the growing atmosphere of luxury that surrounded him.

Finally, after the conquest of Riyadh in 1773, Ibn Abd al-Wahhab withdrew from public life. He even gave up the title of imam, or prayer leader, devoting his last years to prayer, reflection, teaching, and the study of religious texts. Ibn Abd al-Wahhab died in 1791 or 1792, just as the power of the House of Saud was reaching its long zenith. Controversy over his legacy has persisted to the present time. Some have alleged that his strict interpretation of Islam has motivated terrorist activities generally and has specifically formed the basis for the militant Islam of terrorist mastermind Osama bin Laden, a Saudi follower of Wahhabism. During his own lifetime, however, Ibn Abd al-Wahhab favored debate and religious instruction over violent campaigns as methods of persuasion, and the proposed link between bin Laden and Wahhab's thought has encountered strenuous objections.

Books

DeLong-Bas, Natana J., *Wahhabi Islam: From Revival and Reform to Global Jihad,* Oxford, 2004.
Martin, Richard C., ed., *Encyclopedia of Islam and the Muslim World,* Macmillan, 2004.
Schwartz, Stephen, *The Two Faces of Islam: The House of Sa'ud from Tradition to Terror,* Doubleday, 2002.

Periodicals

History: Review of New Books, Winter 2005.

Online

"Muhammad Ibn Abd al-Wahab," Jaringan Islam Liberal (Indonesia), http://www.islamlib.com (January 30, 2007). □

Mahmoud Ahmadinejad

After his election as president of the Islamic Republic of Iran on June 24, 2005, Mahmoud Ahmadinejad (born 1956) emerged as one of the world's most controversial, and in some quarters most feared, political leaders.

With a hard-line attitude and a devout, almost mystical Islamic faith forged partly in Iran's earlier conflicts with Iraq and with the United States, Ahmadinejad defied Western demands that Iran halt the development of its nuclear energy program, which in the view of many Western leaders was intended to put Iran on the path toward acquisition of nuclear weapons. That possibility alarmed no one more than the leaders of Israel, whose legitimacy as a state Ahmadinejad repeatedly questioned. According to *U.S. News & World Report* as well as other news outlets, he even stated that "Israel must be wiped off the map." Ahmadinejad had critics within Iran as well, but he was a charismatic politician with a strong base of support at home, especially among Iranians who had shared his modest origins. Even in the West, Ahmadinejad became an instantly recognizable figure in his characteristic loafers and light-colored cotton jackets.

Son of Blacksmith

Mahmoud Ahmadinejad (mah-MOOD ah-mah-dih-nee-ZHAHD) was born Mahmoud Saborjhian on October 28, 1956, the fourth son among seven children of a blacksmith in the town of Aradan, Iran, near the larger city of Garmsar. When he was one year old, the family moved to the Iranian capital of Tehran and took the more religious surname of Ahmadinejad. He grew up in a country under the sway of Western influence: three years before he was born, the U.S. Central Intelligence Agency had sponsored a coup that installed the pro-Western Shah Mohammed Reza Pahlavi as Iran's head of state. Many Iranians, led by the country's hierarchy of Islamic clerics, resented the Western incursion into Iranian culture and politics.

That resentment reached a peak during Ahmadinejad's college years. His chance to pursue higher education was a direct result of his scholastic accomplishments; in 1975 he finished 130th among students in the entire country who took university entrance exams that year, and he was admitted as a civil engineering student at Tehran's University of Science and Technology. Ahmadinejad would eventually go on for master's and doctoral degrees in engineering, but in the late 1970s political activities took first place in his life. Islamic activism was repressed by the Shah, but Ahmadinejad turned out anti-Shah leaflets on a hidden printing press, and he and some friends issued a protest magazine called *Jiq va Dad* (Scream and Shout). He joined a student group called the Office for Strengthening Unity Between Universities and Theological Seminaries.

This group of religious students was involved with the seizure of the American embassy in Tehran in the fall of 1979 and the subsequent imprisonment of embassy staff as hostages. An Iranian official who was a friend of Ahmadinejad's at the time told *Newsweek* that Ahmadinejad participated in planning sessions but actually argued against the embassy takeover. The Global Security website, however, reported that Ahmadinejad had advocated a simultaneous attack on both the U.S. and Soviet Union embassies. After Ahmadinejad's election as president, some former U.S. hostages alleged that he had been among the actual hostage-takers. Ahmadinejad has denied the allegation, and U.S. intelligence agencies have generally supported his denials.

Whatever his actual involvement in the plot, the devoutly religious Ahmadinejad devoted his energies to supporting the government of the new Islamic Republic of Iran under the spiritual leadership of Ayatollah Ruhollah Khomeini, and he soon became active in the inner circles of the regime's military arm. After Iraqi leader Saddam Hussein ordered an invasion of Iran in 1980, Ahmadinejad volunteered to fight the Iraqis in western Iran, home to many members of the Kurdish ethnic group. By 1986 he was a senior member of Iran's elite Special Brigade of Revolutionary Guards. He participated in covert operations near the city of Kirkuk and worked to counter not only the Iraqi incursion but also the political aspirations of the stateless Kurds. Ahmadinejad was placed in charge of two Iranian cities, Maku and Khoy, and he served as an advisor to the governor-general of Iran's Kurdistan province.

Mixed Academic and Political Activities

Later, during his political career, Ahmadinejad would often invoke the names of his many comrades-in-arms who had fallen on the battlefield. He was part of a generation that lived through both the Islamic Revolution and the Iran-Iraq war, a generation that would come to dominate Iranian life. In the late 1980s Ahmadinejad's life was outwardly uneventful, but he continued to maintain his ties to the country's revolutionary leadership. In 1986 he was admitted into a master's degree program in engineering at the University of Science and Technology. He married another university professor and had two sons and a daughter

In 1989 Ahmadinejad joined the civil engineering faculty at the University of Science and Technology. He continued his political and military activities, however. A member of Austria's parliament, citing unnamed Iranian sources, charged that Ahmadinejad participated, as a lookout, in the assassination of Kurdish leader Abdul Rahman Ghassemlou in Vienna in 1989. *Newsweek* reported that U.S. intelligence agents had found no evidence of this, but Austrian authorities were investigating the charge as of 2006. In 1993 Ahmadinejad joined the Iranian government as advisor for cultural affairs to the minister of culture and higher education, and later that year he was named governor general of Ardabil province.

It has been reported that Ahmadinejad received a doctoral degree in transportation engineering in 1987, but his own website biography gives the date of that degree as 1997. The later date corresponds with a period during which Ahmadinejad's hard-line faction was out of power in Iran—he was removed from his governorship after the election of moderate reformer Mohammad Khatami as Iranian president that year. Ahmadinejad returned to his teaching job, wearing the black-and-white kaffiyeh scarf associated with Palestinian leader Yasser Arafat as he walked around campus. He was out of political life until 2003, when he was named mayor of Tehran by the city's conservative-dominated municipal council.

Ahmadinejad was still little known nationally and internationally, but his charisma and political skills first became evident during his tenure as Tehran's mayor. He imposed new cultural restrictions favored by the mullahs, or Islamic religious leaders, who really held the reins of power in Iran, shutting down Western fast-food restaurants and ordering the covering of billboard advertisements featuring English soccer star David Beckham. But as significant as his actual policies was the bond Ahmadinejad formed with Tehran's deeply religious working class. At one point he donned a street sweeper's uniform to earn the support of city workers, and he shunned limousine transportation in favor of a 1977 Peugeot automobile he had owned for many years.

Earned Reputation as Incorruptible

Ahmadinejad's own working class speech patterns were ridiculed by Tehran's political elite, but ordinary Iranians saw him as a rather spiritual figure untouched by the political corruption that was dragging down the country's economy despite its vast reserves of oil. The suave interview subject, who later became known to American audiences with his appearance on the *60 Minutes* television program, made an impression on Iranians as well. His calm demeanor, Brown University professor William Beeman told Thomas Omestad of *U.S. News & World Report,* reflected "a Sufi-like detachment from desire. This plays fantastically in Iran."

In 2005 Ahmadinejad, still not a familiar name internationally, entered the race for president of Iran. Contrary to the predictions of observers, he snared one of two spots in the June runoff against the moderate, well-established, and personally wealthy Islamic cleric Hashemi Rafsanjani. Ahmadinejad employed displays of personal piety, visiting a shrine in the town of Jamarkan, where many Iranians believed that the Mahdi, a religious leader from early in the history of Islam's Shiite branch, would miraculously reappear. He combined this pious message with promises of new social programs, and on June 24 he won a convincing victory over Rafsanjani in the runoff, winning 17,046,441 votes to Rafsanjani's 9,841,346. Western governments, and even Shiite religious leaders in neighboring Iraq, had little idea of who he was.

They soon found out a great deal more. Ahmadinejad followed through on campaign pledges to increase social spending and, confounding predictions that he would impose Islamic dress codes on Iranian women, he actually liberalized regulations pertaining to women's attendance at sporting events. But what gained attention in the West was Ahmadinejad's confrontational foreign policy stance. Alarmed by a litany of anti-Israeli rhetoric in Ahmadinejad's

public speeches, U.S. president George W. Bush demanded that Iran halt its civilian nuclear power program, which was widely viewed in the West as a possible prelude to the acquisition of nuclear weapons. Through 2005 and 2006, Iran resisted United Nations attempts—supported even by Russia and China—to slow its nuclear program. Ahmadinejad steadfastly denied that the research had military aims, telling Weymouth that "our religion prohibits us from having nuclear arms."

As some in Israel and in the U.S. administration were reportedly considering a difficult campaign of direct military action against Iran, commentators disagreed over the nature of the threat Ahmedinejad posed. Many were unnerved by his combination of militancy and religious fervor. But Fareed Zakaria, writing in *Newsweek,* believed that "as long as the [international anti-Iranian-nuclear] alliance is patient, united, and smart—and keeps the focus on Tehran's actions, not Washington's bellicosity—the odds favor America."

In 2006 Ahmadinejad took his case directly to America's leadership and to its people—the former in a rambling, 18-page letter sent to President Bush that attacked American foreign policy, and the latter in the new medium of the blog (or weblog). He established his own website and posted a "Message to the American People" that asked, "Is it not possible to put wealth and power in the service of peace, stability, prosperity, and the happiness of all peoples through a commitment to justice and respect for the rights of all nations, instead of aggression and war?" By late 2006, although the conflict over Iran's nuclear program was still very much alive, former Secretary of State Henry Kissinger had joined other top-level American leaders in urging that Iran be brought into negotiations over Iraq's future. Ahmadinejad's international reputation declined further in December of that year when Iran hosted a conference of scholars who questioned the historical veracity of the Holocaust during World War II. The long-term implications of Ahmadinejad's rising international influence remained unclear.

Books

Newsmakers, Issue 1, Thomson Gale, 2007.

Periodicals

National Review, May 8, 2006.
New Statesman, December 5, 2005.
New Yorker, May 29, 2006.
Newsweek, July 4, 2005; September 26, 2005; February 13, 2006; September 11, 2006.
San Diego Union Tribune, January 19, 2007.
Time, July 4, 2005; April 3, 2006; September 25, 2006.
U.S. News & World Report, November 7, 2005; October 2, 2006.

Online

"Biography of H.E. Dr. Ahmadi Nejad, Honourable President of Islamic Republic of Iran," Presidency of the Islamic Republic of Iran, http://www.president.ir/eng/ahmadinejad/bio (December 1, 2006).

"Message to the American People," Mahmoud Ahmedinejad Official Website, http://www.ahmadinejad.ir (December 1, 2006). □

Elsie Allen

Renowned Pomo weaver Elsie Allen (1899–1990) is credited with saving Pomo weaving from cultural extinction by breaking with tradition and teaching the traditional basket weaving techniques to non-Indians and native individuals outside her immediate family.

A Pomo Childhood

Elsie Allen was born September 22, 1899, amid the neat rows of a hop field outside what is now Santa Rosa, California. Her parents were George (of the Ukiah Pomo) and Annie (of the Cloverdale Pomo) Comanche. Allen's father died when she was just a girl; at age eight she went to live with her maternal grandmother in the village of the Cloverdale Pomo. This early phase of her life was idyllic. One website dedicated to Allen's history painted a picture of a little girl who "made dolls for herself of cattail grass . . . [and] gave bushes, trees [and] willows names. They were persons and playmates in her imagination."

Pomo weaving skills were essentially matrilineal—passed down from mother to daughter. Men wove fish traps, infant cradles and other rudimentary items, but it was the female tribe members who raised the skill to an art form, producing elegant and vibrant baskets that proved as functional as they were beautiful. Allen learned basket-making basics from her grandmother and her mother, spending her days steeped in the traditions of her people and speaking only the native Pomo language. Allen's mother, Annie, remarried a man of half-Pomo heritage named Richard Burke and bore him a son and a daughter. After her mother remarried, Allen moved with these new siblings to the village of the Hopland Pomo, but by then the encroachment of white culture was actively pushing the Pomo ways aside. Parents hid their children in fear of abduction in the name of cultural assimilation when whites visited, and most families, Allen's included, worked as laborers on farms owned by non-Indians in order to survive.

Education

The days of innocent hunting and gathering had long since passed for the Pomo, however, and Allen was no exception. She began working as a field hand at the age of ten. At age 11 she was forced by authorities to attend a boarding school for Indians in Covelo, California, more than 80 miles from her home. The months that followed were some of the most miserable in Allen's long life. The artist's biographical entry in *Notable Native Americans* explained how "her inability to speak English—the only language spoken at the school—made life there very difficult. In addition, soon after arriving in Covelo, Allen lost all her belongings in a fire. Forced to wear boys' clothes, perform seemingly meaningless activities, and abandon her native tongue, she had little incentive for learning." Allen left the boarding school as soon as she was able and returned home to attend a local day school in her village, where she learned to read, write and speak English. At 18, Allen moved to San Francisco and took a job as a domestic maid, a position in which she experienced her share of racial discrimination. She worked her way into a custodial job at St. Joseph's Hospital in 1918, thanks to a labor shortage at the close of the World War I.

Trouble with Tradition

Allen married Arthur Allen of the Pinoleville Pomo tribe in 1919. They had two girls and two boys. In 1924 Allen's grandmother died and the family's baskets were buried with her according to Pomo tradition, leaving Elsie Allen with few materials and samples to work from. Allen's mother, however, continued weaving and used her own determination and hard labor to build the family basket collection back up throughout her own lifetime. A website that chronicled Allen's life quoted Allen as she describes the frustration she experienced at the hands of the Pomo burial traditions, "In the first few years of my married life . . . I made a basket that was buried with my grandmother. My next basket was buried with my great uncle. A third basket was passed all around to relatives . . . [and was finally] buried with my brother-in-law. I didn't have a good feeling about making baskets after that."

Allen's disappointment was understandable, considering that most baskets took years to make. Time had to be spent trudging through marsh and muck to gather plant materials like willow, sedge roots, bulrush roots, and redbud bark, and then more time was spent to cure and prepare the materials. All this preparation was then followed by hours of weaving that could stretch into months and even years before the work was complete. To make matters even more difficult, by Allen's time the plants used for traditional basket making were considered weeds, and often aggressively eradicated by pesticides as the California land was developed. As a result, weaving materials became increasingly scarce.

Pomo Weaving

The Pomo were one of California's biggest, most celebrated tribes, with lands that spread across modern-day Sonoma, Mendocino, and Lake counties. The tribe's main foods were acorns and other seeds gathered by women in baskets they wove according to a traditional method. Baskets and weaving were essential to the Pomo, who did not have access to clay for pottery. They made and used giant baskets on stilts to store acorns, woven seed beaters to thrash seeds loose from wild grasses and grains, and baskets with head straps to gather them. Acorn meal was mixed and cooked using hot stones in water–tight baskets with exceptionally snug weaves that allowed them to withstand both the heat of the stones and the moisture. The men also hunted using fish traps of woven willow. Even the houses were woven around bent pole frames and were said to have looked like upside-down baskets. When they traveled to gather food, they wove great mats that they attached to poles to create temporary shelters. The woman's skirts were often made of woven rushes or shredded bark, and they wove reeds to make rafts that they used on the lakes and rivers for crossing and fishing.

Mary Worthylake's book *The Pomo* explained how "Pomo basket-makers were unusual in their use of twining and coiling. The finest baskets, made for show or for gifts, were coiled. ... Thirty wrappings to an inch make a fine basket, but Pomo baskets sometimes had sixty or even more wrappings. The variety of patterns, the feathers and beads, and the fine workmanship show that Pomo women were excellent artists." The Pomo also played a game—later called *lacrosse* by French settlers—using sticks with baskets at the end for catching and throwing a ball.

A Mother's Wish

When Allen's mother, Annie Burke, was on her deathbed she ignored the fact that tradition insisted a Pomo woman be buried with the baskets she had made, and demanded that Allen keep the family baskets so that Pomo artistry would not die out. Allen's biographical entry in *Native American Women* stated that her mother promised that keeping and sharing the baskets would "take Allen traveling, bring people enjoyment, and create an understanding that the Pomo weren't 'dumb.'" In 1962 Allen respected her mother's dying wish and loaned the family baskets to the Mendocino County Museum in Willets, California. The collection was named the "Elsie Allen Collection," and displays 131 baskets made by Allen and her relatives.

A Woman Among Women

Pomo culture honored and respected female authority, traditionally placing a female chief in charge of women's concerns. Allen maintained aspects of this dynamic through her work in women's groups like the Pomo Women's Club (founded in 1940 and disbanded in 1957), which successfully fought prejudicial bans against Indians sitting on the main floors of local theatres, and the Hintil Women's Club, which dispensed charity and provided financial scholarships for local Native individuals. Allen made and sold baskets to help raise funds for these organizations, as well as lending her voice and valued opinion on important matters.

Allen spent most of her life unable to find enough time to gather materials or do a significant amount of weaving. She cared for her family and remained socially active in the affairs and wellbeing of her people in a time when racial prejudice was rampant in California. It was not unusual for establishments to post signs declaring that dogs and Indians were not allowed. When Allen turned 62, her children had grown and she was free to return her attention and skills to basket weaving. She remembered her mother's dying wish, and regularly demonstrated the traditional Pomo weaving

methods she had learned in her youth for substantial audiences. Her book, *Pomo Basketmaking: A Supreme Art for the Weaver,* was published in 1972 and introduced a wide readership to the art of Pomo basket weaving. Allen's book is described by reviewer Paula Giese as "a Native woman's personal history woven into ... an art and a craft that is more in harmony with nature, more environmentally-centered—because of its use of living plants—than any other." Giese claimed that "The Pomo basketmaker is, of necessity, a natural scientist, and the necessities of the late 20th century force her to be an environmentalist too, if her art is to survive."

As if in support of Giese's claim, Allen also spent three years (1979–1981) as a valuable consultant to the Warm Springs Cultural Resources Study, a Sonoma State University project with the goal of detailing the history and cultures of the Dry Creek and Cloverdale Pomo tribes. The reason behind the study lay in the U.S. Army Engineer Corps' intention to build a dam at Warm Springs that would create Lake Sonoma by flooding a valley in which a large majority of weaving plants grew wild. Allen and other concerned experts were consulted about the native plants in the area, and they succeeded in organizing a re-planting of endangered plant species that would be destroyed by the building of the dam. In a somewhat hollow victory, a fraction of the flora was transplanted while the rest was drowned in 1985.

Her Legacy Lived On

Elsie Allen died on the December 31, 1990, at the age of 91. Her daughter, Genevieve Allen Aguilar, maintains the family basket collection, honoring her mother and grandmother's desire to make them available to future generations from all cultures as a testament to Pomo artistry. Allen's grand-niece, Susie Billy, apprenticed with Allen for years to learn the art of Pomo weaving well enough to teach it to others and continue the new tradition of passing the artistry and culture down to future generations. A website chronicling the Allen basketmaking family quoted Billy: "Through basketry, I feel I have made connections with something very ancient within myself and from my people." The work Allen did to maintain her cultural heritage was as important as her own personal artistic contributions, and her dedication was rewarded with the title of "Pomo Sage."

Books

Notable Native Americans, edited by Sharon Malinowski, Gale Research, Inc., 1995.

Worthylake, Mary M., *The Pomo: A New True Book,* Children's Press, 1994.

Online

"Elsie Allen: Pomo basket Family," *Native American Arts,* http://www.kstrom.net/isk/art/basket/elsieall.html (December 28, 2006).

"Pomo Basketmaking: A Supreme Art for the Weaver," *Native American Arts and Crafts Book Reviews,* http://www.kstrom.net/isk/books/art/art2032.html (December 28, 2006). □

Sarah Allen

Missionary Sarah Allen (1764–1849) was one of the most famous and revered church women of her time, beloved for establishing the first recognized charity organization for female parishioners and honored as the African Methodist Episcopal (AME) Church's first female missionary. She also aided runaway slaves through the famous Underground Railroad.

While almost nothing is definitively known about Allen's origins, scholars agree that Sarah Allen was born into slavery in 1764 in Virginia's Isle of Wight with a recorded maiden name of Bass, a detail that has led some historians to speculate about her lineage, without empirical results. Allen was eight years old when she arrived as a slave in Philadelphia, but details about her life before the year 1800 seem to have been lost in the folds of history. It is known that Allen managed to acquire her freedom somehow, because she was a free woman by 1802 when she met and married Richard Allen (1760–1831), who would later become the African Methodist Episcopal (AME) Church's founder and first bishop.

A young Richard Allen became interested in the Methodist faith when he heard an itinerant preacher speak. He was a 17-year-old slave at the time, and found himself so moved that he chose to devote his life to the faith. Richard Allen's master was converted as well, and agreed to allow Richard to buy his freedom. The young man worked hard, freeing himself by the age of 20, and began traveling and spreading the gospel to people of all races. Richard Allen's first wife, Flora, died as the result of a long illness on March 11, 1801.

Sarah Allen is described as a widow when she and Richard met, although nothing is recorded on the subject of her marital status prior to 1802. Richard met Sarah in Philadelphia while on a preaching circuit, and they were married within the year. The Allens had their first child a year after they were married, and three more sons and two daughters followed soon after. Their names, Richard, James, John, Peter, Sara, and Ann were the names of kings, queens and saints. Allen raised all six children, ran a tight household, managed finances, and nurtured the environment her husband required for his spiritual work.

Mrs. Allen

The devout couple made a formidable team from the start, working together to earn enough money to purchase the land and building rights for an abandoned blacksmith shop that was then relocated to Sixth and Lombard Streets in Philadelphia. They bought the old shop for thirty–five dollars, and it was pulled to its new location by a team of horses that the Allens owned. Next they sought the help of the community to convert it into a church. The new sanctuary was dedicated on July 29, 1794, and named Bethel, which means "House of God." The small church quickly grew to

be an integral part of local parishioners' lives, and is affectionately referred to as "Mother Bethel" church to this day.

The modest Bethel church was soon joined by other black churches that sprang to the foreground thanks to the evangelical efforts of the Allens, including Baltimore, Salem, Wilmington, and Attleboro, Pennsylvania. These churches joined together to form the AME Church in 1816, the first independent black church in the United States. The church made Richard its first bishop, placing Sarah Allen in a unique position from which to do good. The blacksmith shop grew too small within 12 years, and it was replaced in 1805 by a roughcast structure, which was then replaced by a brick and stone church ten years after Richard Allen's death.

Do Unto Others

Sarah Allen's distinctive brand of charity made its debut during the AME church's first annual conference. The young church had struggled both financially and emotionally. The preachers had withstood excessive traveling and tireless work without any significant funding, and they returned for that first conference in terrible condition, with their clothes and belongings worn, and in poor physical condition from the difficulties of preaching on the road. Allen's biographical entry in *Profiles of Negro Womanhood* described how the clergy had returned "in a rather 'seedy' condition, whereupon the bishop refused to adjourn their subsequent meeting for the customary dinner at his home . . . After hearing her husband's explanation, [Allen] later saw for herself that the [preachers] had 'ventilators at their knees and ventilators in their elbows and ventilators in the seat of their trousers.' . . . [Allen] and the women of the church . . . [spent] an entire night in productive labor. By morning, the preachers all had new sets of clothes and were thus made presentable in appearance for carrying out their ministerial duties."

Allen's biographical entry in *Notable Black American Women* explained that Richard Allen initially referred to these women as the " 'Dorcas Society,' " a title that "generally refers to a women's auxiliary group that is engaged in clothing and feeding the poor." The same entry also pointed out, however, that Allen's efforts in particular were "directed internally toward preparing good meals, repairing garments, and improving the appearance of AME pastors." This care and support went on before and during each annual conference until 1827, when Allen officially identified the group as the Daughters of Conference. Once formally organized, the group expanded, and began helping the needy outside the clergy. Allen christened this far-reaching group the Women's Missionary Society, which was described in *Notable Black American Women* as one which maintained "a form of children's daycare school during the daytime hours, and helped organize adult classes at night to help educate their church members. They also cooked meals, mended garments, and gathered donated clothes for the needy." This focus on education for the community had served as a foundation for the Bethel church from the beginning, and remains a strong focus to the present day.

In a review in *North Star* of Jualynne Dodson's book *Engendering Church: Women, Power, and the A.M.E.*

Church, Stephen W. Angell called attention to Dodson's assertion that there were three main ways women gained power in the nineteenth-century AME Church: evangelization by word of mouth, church organizations founded and attended by women, and the accumulation of resources. Angell's review also claimed that these methods for acquiring power were "employed with most effect when used quietly and unobtrusively," an apt description of the kind of life-changing work Sarah Allen did best.

Champion of Freedom

Efforts to hide and help runaway slaves made by families like the Allens were later identified as the operation now known as the Underground Railroad. Brave individuals like Richard and Sarah were thought of as "conductors" on this dangerous journey, and Philadelphia was a main stop for slaves fleeing from the south and southeast to the northern states and Canada. Records show that the AME Church was involved in this process from as far back as 1795, when the church building became a haven for 30 runaway Jamaicans.

The Allens used their own home as well as the cellar of the church building to hide people, and earned funds that they then gave to these people to start their new lives in the north. In a Journal of Black Studies review of Allen B. Ballard's book One More Day's Journey (1984), scholar Beth Brown Utada related how Allen "became known for her courage along the Underground Railroad." Allen's obituary, recorded by Bishop Daniel A. Payne in his 1891 History of the A.M.E. Church, related that "the poor, flying slave, trembling and panting in his flight, has lost a friend not easily replaced; her purse now closed in death, kindled with peculiar brightness as she would bid them God speed to the land of liberty, where the slave is free from his master, and the voice of the oppressor is no longer heard." Richard Allen died in 1831, but Sarah Allen continued her good works, thanks in large part to the funds her husband left, which allowed her to focus on her charitable aims without having to hold another job.

Historical Gender Bias

Rosalyn Terborg-Penn, in her bibliographical essay "Teaching the History of Black Women" (published in the February 1980 The History Teacher), called attention to a gulf that has formed between black history and women's history, one which often obscures the details and importance of black women's lives. This intellectual gap, Terborg-Penn argued, has resulted in a severe scarcity of secondary literary sources that deal exclusively with the unique nature of black women's history. Even more specifically, Terborg-Penn revealed that historical records have done an inadequate job of representing the black woman's religious roles, claiming that "the substantial contribution of Afro–American women to religious life certainly merits scholarly study."

Mother Allen

Sarah Allen lived for 85 years, and died on July 16, 1849, at the Philadelphia home of her youngest daughter, Ann Adams. She and her husband were buried side by side in a tomb beneath the Mother Bethel Church, a site that has since been turned into the Richard Allen Museum.

Allen's obituary described her death as the loss of "a bright ornament—a jewel, precious—a relic of her formation when she was first seen to glide from the stormy element of oppression . . . a pillar from the building, a mother in Israel." The AME church's Women's Missionary Society took its founder's name, and the Sarah Allen Women's Missionary Society continues to help on local, state, country and international levels, as a testament to the influence and inspiration of Sarah Allen's life of service.

Books

Black Women in America: An Historical Encyclopedia, edited by Darlene Clark Hine, Carlson Publishing, Inc., 1993.
Notable Black American Women: Book III, Thomson Gale, 2003.
Payne, Bishop Daniel A., History of the A.M.E. Church, Publishing House of the A. M. E. Sunday School Union, 1891.
Profiles of Negro Womanhood: Volume One, 1619–1900, edited by Sylvia G. L. Dannett, Educational Heritage, Inc., 1964.

Periodicals

History Teacher, February 1980.
Journal of Black Studies, June 1986.
North Star, Spring 2002.

Online

"The Richard Allen Museum," Mother Bethel AME Church, http://www.motherbethel.org/museum/exhibit/panel4.html (December 22, 2006).
"Sara Allen," Africans in America, http://www.pbs.org/wgbh/aia/part3/3p246.htm (December 22, 2006). □

Néstor Almendros

Spanish cinematographer Néstor Almendros (1930–1992) won an Academy Award for his work in creating the breathtaking vistas of land and sky meant to depict Texas around 1900 in the movie *Days of Heaven.* But Almendros was equally proud of the work he did for such acclaimed French directors as François Truffaut and Éric Rohmer when they were at the peak of their careers, and also made two documentary films about human rights abuses in Cuba. A three-time political refugee during his lifetime, "Almendros . . . realized that sorrow, pain, and sometimes evil lurk just beneath the surface of the finest, most evenly illuminated compositions," noted the *International Dictionary of Films and Filmmakers.*

Almendros was born in Barcelona, Spain, on October 30, 1930, and was one of three children in his family. His father was a Republican Loyalist and during the Spanish Civil War (1936–39) he fought against the fascist forces of General Francisco Franco (1892–1975). The Republican Loyalists were fighting to preserve the Second Spanish Republic and its progressive liberal ideals, but Franco's side triumphed in the end. It was a brutal and bloody war, and there were repercussions for years to come for the Loyalists; because of this, Almendros's father was forced into exile and fled to Cuba.

Roman Exile

Almendros and his family joined their father in Cuba in 1948. Young Almendros earned a doctorate from the University of Havana, and then fled a Cuban regime headed by General Fulgencio Batista (1901–1973), which began cracking down on University of Havana student protests in 1955 with the use of military force. He settled in Rome, where he enrolled in film school at the Centro Sperimentale di Cinematografia. A friend of his from Havana, a law student and future filmmaker two years his senior named Tomas Gutiérrez Alea (1928–1996), had already graduated from the school. In 1950 the pair made an eight-millimeter film together, *Una confusion contidiana* (A Common Confusion), which was Almendros's first foray into the art form.

Settling in New York City after his stint in Italy, Almendros took classes at the City College of New York, and taught Spanish at nearby Vassar College, a private school in the Hudson River valley town of Poughkeepsie. Enthused by the promise of a socialist revolution back in Cuba that ousted Batista, Almendros returned to Havana and became an early supporter of Fidel Castro (born 1926), who came to power in early 1959. For the next two years Almendros worked for a filmmaking collective co-founded by Alea, making documentary films about the sweeping political changes taking place during this period. Like other progressive-minded young filmmakers at the collective, he was fascinated by fresh ideas coming out of post-World War II Europe, especially French New Wave cinema. Franç Truffaut (1932–1984) was among the pioneers of this movement, which featured realistic portrayals of current social and political issues as well as experimentation on several technical levels, such as lighting, camera angles, and editing.

Almendros was asked to weigh in on a top ten list of the best films of 1959, and included Truffaut's *The 400 Blows,* the tale of a disenchanted Parisian teen that would become an enormous influence on a generation of filmmakers to follow. On his list, Almendros chose this over a release from the Soviet Union, *Ballad of a Soldier,* that Castro preferred. His preference for one of the decadent West's products over a tautly constructed socialist fable was the beginning of the end for Almendros's career in Cuba. Once again he fled, but this time chose France because it was home to the filmmakers of the New Wave. He brought with him a single print of a short film he had made.

Parisian Exile

Almendros struggled to find work, and was hampered by the lack of an official work permit. In what has become a classic documentary film from this era, 1964's *Paris vu Par . . .* (Paris Seen By . . .), his work as the cinematographer for two segments went uncredited. One of these was the "Place de l'Étoile" contribution from Éric Rohmer, and that job began a long and productive working relationship between Almendros and Rohmer (born 1920).

Rohmer hired Almendros as cinematographer for *La Collectionneuse* (The Collector), a 1967 release that became the first feature film credit for Almendros's resume. It was followed by another Rohmer project, *Ma nuit chez Maud* (My Night at Maud's), released two years later and a hit on the international film festival circuit. Almendros was also the cinematographer for Rohmer's *Le Genou de Claire* (Claire's Knee), a 1970 release that scored similarly high marks with critics. At that time, Almendros spoke with Vincent Canby of the *New York Times,* telling the journalist that he preferred working with Rohmer and other visionaries who shared the same views about the art of filmmaking. "When I started, I found that my job consisted principally in de-lighting sets, that is, removing all the fake, conventional movie lighting that had been set up by lighting technicians," he recalled. "They were old-fashioned. They believed in a very glossy kind of photography, that faces should never been in shadow, that there should always be a lot of backlighting, with no shadows in the sets anywhere."

Almendros worked with several other directors of the French New Wave as they progressed to more mainstream, but nonetheless impressive, projects. His cinematography for Truffaut began in 1969 with *L'Enfant sauvage* (The Wild Child), and included *L'Histoire d'Adèle H.* (The Story of Adèle H.), a 1975 period piece that starred Isabelle Adjani, *L'Homme qui aimait les femmes* (The Man Who Loved Women), a 1977 comedy about a womanizer that was later remade in Hollywood, and *Le Dernier Métro,* (The Last Metro), a World War II drama that starred Catherine Deneuve. This movie won a slew of awards at the 1981 Césars, French cinema's equivalent of the Academy Awards, including that of Best Cinematographer for Almendros.

Almendros had already won an Academy Award statuette by this time for *Days of Heaven,* a 1978 drama set in the Texas Panhandle as the nineteenth century turned into the twentieth. Directed by a maverick young filmmaker named Terrence Malick, the movie starred Richard Gere, Brooke Adams, and Sam Shepard in a romantic triangle tied to a real estate scam. Many years later, a *Times* of London contributor asserted that Almendros's "nakedly realistic treatment of the endless vistas of wheatfields, where young immigrants seek a new life after leaving Chicago in the early years of the century, created a vividly realised atmosphere, which more than compensated for the sometimes too-symbolic intentions of the script."

Shot Oscar-Winning Hollywood Projects

Days of Heaven began a productive period in Almendros's career, one which kept him moving around the world working for various directors. His next major job was for director Robert Benton on the multiple Oscar-winning *Kramer vs. Kramer.* The 1979 drama, which starred Dustin Hoffman and Meryl Streep as a divorcing Manhattan couple battling over legal custody of their child, was nominated for nine Academy Awards, including best cinematography, but Almendros missed out that year. The film won the Best Picture award, however, with Canby describing it as "densely packed with ... beautifully observed detail." Canby went on to praise Almendros as "gifted," concluding that "the Manhattan he shows us is familiar enough but we see a lot more than a series of pretty surfaces."

Almendros would work with Benton again on several other films, and also had a productive working relationship with Barbet Schroeder, who served as producer of some of the earliest New Wave movies and went on to a career as director of several major Hollywood films. Other notable projects for Almendros over the years included *Goin' South,* a 1977 Western that starred and was directed by Jack Nicholson; *The Blue Lagoon,* an ill-fated 1980 movie that featured Brooke Shields, a major teen star at the time; and *Sophie's Choice,* the 1982 adaptation of a William Styron novel that won Streep her first Oscar for a lead role.

Almendros recounted these and dozens of other experiences in a book that appeared in English translation in 1984 as *A Man With a Camera.* Part memoir, part textbook, the tome featured Almendros's behind-the-scenes tales of classics and box-office duds alike, and became standard reading for graduate film students for its eloquent writing on technical issues. Reviewing it for the *New York Times,* Gerald Mast commended the author for explaining to readers the reasons behind "the power of the most basic element of the cinema—light—essential for both film making and projection but so often taken for granted."

Chronicled Cuban Crimes

Almendros finally returned to directing his own films in 1984 with *Mauvaise conduite* (Improper Conduct), a documentary about life in Castro's Cuba that was released in the United States as *Improper Conduct.* He served as co-director with Orlando Jimenez-Leal, a Cuban émigré filmmaker, and it would be Almendros's first full-length documentary film as a director. The movie's title is taken from the charges leveled against certain segments of the Cuban population whose personal beliefs put them at odds with the goals of the 1959 revolution. These included gay men and Jehovah's Witnesses, and a critique of the film by John Simon in the *National Review* hinted that Almendros's reason for leaving Cuba back in 1961 may have been linked to more than just the year's top ten films list—Simon described Almendros as "the great cinematographer ... whose concern with homosexuality is not just academic." Giving *Improper Conduct* high marks, Simon wrote approvingly of the way it used "official Cuban footage, especially a long interview in which Castro discourses on the perfect freedom and justice of his state, which would have seemed specious even out of context, but which here becomes a masterpiece of the preposterous and demonstrates the almost physical, aesthetic ugliness of mendacity even beyond its moral canker."

In 1988 Almendros made his second documentary film about Cuba, *Nadie escuchaba* (Nobody Listened). Again, he collaborated with another Cuban exile, this time journalist Jorge Ulla, and the film featured the first-person accounts of dissidents who had managed to flee Cuba after stints in prison where many had survived bestial conditions and even torture. "Making no attempt to give equal time to pro-Castro partisans, the filmmakers allow the sheer weight of testimony here to speak for itself," wrote Janet Maslin in the *New York Times.* " 'Nobody Listened' is an urgent and painful litany, measured in its tone but passionately intent on making its point." Almendros confessed that he had to finance *Nobody Listened* on his own, and nearly went broke doing so. Yet as he explained to another *New York Times* writer, Lawrence Van Gelder, "I've made 47 movies and I've got several awards, and there's a moment when you think you owe something to society. I have access to camera and film, and I know how. The Cuban case is too scandalous not to talk about."

The 1991 film from Robert Benton, *Billy Bathgate,* was Almendros's last job as a cinematographer. He died of lymphoma on March 4, 1992, in New York City.

Books

International Dictionary of Films and Filmmakers, Volume 4: *Writers and Production Artists,* 4th edition, St. James Press, 2000.

Periodicals

National Review, September 7, 1984.
New York Times, September 24, 1969; February 22, 1971; February 28, 1971; December 19, 1979; August 10, 1980; September 30, 1984; December 2, 1988.
Sunday Times (London, England), August 11, 1985.
Times (London, England), May 20, 1976; March 6, 1992. □

Angeles Alvariño

Spanish American fishery research biologist and marine scientist Dr. Angeles Alvariño (1916–2005) became one of the few global authorities on certain types of marine plankton. She discovered 22 new species of ocean animals and made great contributions to the scientific understanding of small marine life forms during the course of her career. Alvariño published over a hundred scientific books, chapters, and articles, and dedicated her later years to studying the historical aspects of early marine science and exploration.

Showed Early Interest in Science

Born to Antonio Alvariño Grimaldos, a doctor, and Maria del Carmen Gonzales Diaz-Saavedra de Alvariño on October 3, 1916, in El Ferrol, Spain, Angeles Alvariño showed an interest in the natural sciences at a young age. Encouraged by her parents, she read her father's books on zoology and hoped to one day become a doctor herself. Her father discouraged this notion, hoping to spare his daughter the unpleasant experiences of working with patients afflicted with incurable conditions. During her youth, Alvariño also studied the piano, but remained true to her hopes of becoming a physician.

Alvariño studied diverse topics including natural sciences, physics, chemistry, mathematics, languages, literature, history, geography, philosophy, psychology, and art history during her time at the Lycee Concepcion Arenel in El Ferrol. She then attended the University of Santiago de Composetla in northwestern Spain, from which she graduated summa cum laude in 1933. As part of her degree, she wrote her dissertations on scientific topics—insects—as well as humanities topics—the women of Spanish literary classic *Don Quixote*. Alvariño later explained her interest in this seemingly odd pairing of subjects by noting that one should "select the profession you love, work hard with enthusiasm, [and] observe and love Mother Nature . . . Creativity and imagination are the basic ingredients for the scientist, as in the arts, because science is an art."

Studied in Madrid

Because her father still discouraged her ambition of becoming a doctor, Alvariño continued her education in the natural sciences at the University of Madrid, though this course of study was interrupted in 1936 by the Spanish Civil War. Alvariño resumed courses at the university upon its reopening in 1939. Decades later, Alvariño's daughter commented in an interview that "It was a time of lying low and hiding. . . . People were being persecuted and killed, and you couldn't go outside because you didn't know whether you would make it back home alive." Alvariño completed her master's degree in natural sciences in 1941. While working on her master's degree (and during the years of enforced hiatus), Alvariño studied French and English, pursued intellectual interests with fellow students, and, in 1940, married Sir Eugenio Leira Manso, a naval captain and Knight of the Royal and Military Order of Saint Hermenegild. After her marriage, Alvariño was sometimes known by her married name, Angeles Alvariño De Leira.

Alvariño and her husband returned to El Ferrol after Alvariño completed her studies at the University of Madrid. In El Ferrol, Alvariño taught biology, zoology, botany, and geology for most of the 1940s. In 1948 Alvariño and her family—which now included a young daughter, Angeles Leira Alvariño—moved back to Madrid so Alvariño could take a position as a fishery research biologist with the Department of Sea Fisheries. Due to a Spanish law dating from the 1700s, women were prohibited aboard Spanish naval vessels; thus, Alvariño could not pursue further research studies at the Spanish Institute of Oceanography in Madrid. However, because of her strong educational credentials Alvariño was admitted to biological, chemical, and physical oceanography courses at the institute as well as being allowed to conduct some research there.

During this time, Alvariño also returned to the University of Madrid to pursue doctoral studies in chemistry. After writing three dissertations—one on personality in experimental psychology, one on phosphates in the ocean for chemistry, and one on the distribution, use, and business of

seaweeds for plant ecology—she received her certificate in 1951. Alvariño had additionally been on staff at the Superior Council of Scientific Research during her doctoral studies, ultimately working there as a histologist (one who studies biological tissues) from 1948–52. In 1952 Alvariño won a position as marine biologist and oceanographer at the Spanish Institute of Oceanography.

Introduced to Zooplankton

In 1953 Alvariño received a British Council Fellowship and traveled to the Marine Biological Laboratory in Plymouth, England, to study zooplankton. At Plymouth Alvariño worked with a respected English marine biologist and expert on zooplankton, beginning her years of study of these creatures. (Zooplankton comprise the small floating animals in the ocean that serve as food for other animals and include jellyfish, coral, and sea anemones.) Until the 1950s, few scientists had investigated these creatures. Alvariño focused primarily on the three general groups of zooplankton: Chaetognatha, Siphonophora, and the medusae. Chaetognaths, also known as arrow worms, are tiny carnivores that feed on other zooplankton. They have individual responses to the sea water in which they live that make them valuable for identifying water type. Siphonophores are invertebrate animals which cluster together to live as a species-specific colony; the best-known example of this type of creature is the Portuguese Man'o'War. Medusae are a form of jellyfish. In addition, Alvariño studied fish larvae, or the immature stages of some fish.

While at the Marine Biological Laboratory, Alvariño studied zooplankton found in the English Channel and in the Bay of Biscay, along the coast of France and Spain. In doing so, she discovered some forms of life which were typically found in other areas, leading scientists to conclude that Atlantic waters had moved northward in an unusual way.

In 1954 Alvariño returned to Spain to continue her studies of plankton. There she designed and made special nets to catch plankton. She then recruited local fishermen as well as naval research vessels to use the nets to collect samples for her. Alvariño used these diverse sample to study forms of life found in the Atlantic near Spain, as well as in the Mediterranean Sea and near Newfoundland.

Moved to the United States

Alvariño won a Fulbright Fellowship in 1956, enabling her to travel to the United States to further her research. She worked with Dr. Mary Sears, a fellow zooplankton researcher and the president of the U.S. Oceanographic Congress, at the Woods Hole Oceanographic Institution on Cape Cod in Massachusetts. Because of the high quality of Alvariño's work, Sears recommended Alvariño to Dr. Roger Revelle, director of the Scripps Institution of Oceanography, part of the University of California at La Jolla. Revelle offered a biologist position to Alvariño, and she continued her research at La Jolla from 1958–69. She primarily studied the small zooplankton found off the coast of California as well as in the Atlantic, Pacific, and Indian Oceans during that time. This research formed the basis of her doctor of science degree, earned summa cum laude and was awarded by the University of Madrid in 1967. In all, Alvariño's research had uncovered 12 new Chaetognatha species, nine new Siphonophora species, and one new medusa species. During this time, Alvariño also produced a model showing the distribution of different species of Chaetognatha and Siphonophora around the world's oceans.

In 1966 Alvariño became a United States citizen. While at Scripps, Alvariño also received grants for study from the U.S. Office of the Navy and from California Cooperative Oceanic Fisheries Investigations. For the majority of the 1960s, Alvariño also received grants from the U.S. National Science Foundation.

In 1970 Alvariño joined the Southwest Fisheries Science Center (SWFSC) as a fishery research biologist. Also located in La Jolla, the SWSFC is a division of the National Marine Fisheries Service, which is part of the National Oceanic and Atmospheric Administration. While at the SWFSC, Alvariño continued her research into Chaetognatha, Siphonophora, and medusae, often looking specifically at the relationships between the predatory behaviors of those organisms and the survival of fish larvae. She examined further the distribution of Chaetognatha and Siphonophora species in the Pacific and Antarctic Oceans. Alvariño also considered the indicators and effects of movement, both natural and artificial, among plankton species. More specifically, Alvariño considered the impact of plankton species that were not native to an area, but had been artificially placed there through pollution or ship movement.

Marine Biology Career

In the later 1970s, Alvariño worked to coordinate oceanic research among Latin American nations. She studied in the Antarctic on research grants between 1979 and 1982. Alvariño also received grants from the Food and Agriculture Organization of the United Nations and from the United National Educational, Scientific, and Cultural Organization (UNESCO).

Alvariño also put her time into educating future marine biologists. She served as a faculty member at the National Autonomous University of Mexico in 1976; at San Diego State University from 1979–82; and later, at the University of San Diego from 1982–85. She also held visiting professorships at the Federal University of Paraná in Brazil in 1982, and at the National Polytechnic Institute of Mexico from 1982–86. During these years Alvariño directed the research of several doctoral candidates and served on thesis committees both in the United States and internationally.

Alvariño officially retired in 1987. However, she continued to conduct research on seagoing vessels hosted by various countries. She was a fellow of the American Institute of Fishery Research Biologists and of the San Diego Society of Natural History, as well as being a member of the Biological Society of Washington and the Hispano-American Association of Researchers on Marine Sciences. In 1993 she received the Great Silver Medal of Galicia from King Carlos I and Queen Sophia of Spain in recognition of her scientific contributions.

Toward the end of her life, Alvariño turned her attention to the history of marine science. She conducted extensive research into the early Spanish explorers and navigators who first mapped the oceans and their currents. Alvariño looked closely at the First Scientific Oceanic Expedition that traveled throughout the western Atlantic Ocean and the Pacific Ocean from 1789–94. In 2000 Alvariño published a full account of this expedition.

Death and Legacy

Alvariño continued to work on a proposed second edition of her historical work, which would have included additional illustrations and updated research, up until her death on May 29, 2005, as the result of lyomiosarcoma, a rare form of cancer that affected soft muscle tissues. Her legacy includes over a hundred scientific publications, including books and journal articles; the 22 news species of sea life she discovered during her career; and her enduring contributions to the research of small life forms in the oceans of the world.

Periodicals

San Diego Union-Tribune, June 10, 2005.

Online

"Angeles Alvariño," *Contemporay Hispanic Biography,* Vol. 4, 1998, reproduced in *Biography Resource Center,* http://www.galenet.galegroup.com/servlet/BioRC (January 6, 2007).
"Angeles Alvariño." *Notable Hispanic American Women,* Book 2, Gale Research, 1998, reproduced in *Biography Resource Center,* http://www.galenet.galegroup.com/servlet/BioRC (January 6, 2007). □

Rudolfo Alfonso Anaya

Chicano author Rudolfo Anaya (born 1937) has been hailed as one of the most renowned, resourceful and productive of Mexican American writers. His work holds an important place in Chicano literary curricula, with his novels appearing as staples on high school and college reading lists.

Rudolfo Alfonso Anaya was born in Pastura, New Mexico, on October 30, 1937. His mother, Rafaelita (Mares), was from a deeply settled, Catholic farming community called Puerto de Luna, while his father, Martin Anaya, was raised by nomadic herders on the New Mexican *llano* or eastern plains country. This dichotomy informed Anaya's sense of self and the rhythm of his writing. One of seven siblings, Anaya was the only male in his family to attend primary school, as his three older brothers served in the military during World War II. Not long after Anaya was born, his family moved from Pastura to Santa Rosa, where he grew up playing Chicano games like *las escondidas* (hide and seek), *la rona* (tag), *adivinanzas* (riddles), and

listening to the *cuentistas,* who were Spanish-speaking oral storytellers. It was as part of a rapt audience listening to the stories of his ancestors that Anaya first experienced the power and vibrance of a well-told tale.

In 1952 jobs started disappearing in and around their small, rural town, and Anaya's family moved to Albuquerque to find work. Anaya found the city both stimulating and intimidating. They lived in the Barelas barrio, and he came into contact with street gangs as well as with the music and culture of his tight-knit community.

Education

Anaya graduated from Albuquerque High School in 1956 and quickly enrolled himself in Albuquerque's Browning Business School from 1956 through 1958, with the intention of becoming a CPA. Unsurprisingly, he found the mechanisms of finance creatively stifling, and left the business school to enter a liberal arts program at the University of New Mexico. Anaya earned a bachelor's degree in literature from that university in 1963, and was working on a master's degree in literature when he met and married Patricia Lawless, a guidance counselor, on July 21, 1966. He finished his literary degree in 1968, but returned for a master's degree in guidance and counseling, which was awarded in 1972.

In an interview with *Contemporary Authors,* Anaya explained how frustrating it was for him to write "without models or mentors . . . I was still imitating a style and mode not indigenous to the people and setting I knew best. I was

desperately seeking my natural voice, but the process by which I formed it was long and arduous . . . [because] the thought was still prevalent in academia that [Chicanos] were better suited as janitors than scholars."

From Student to Teacher

Anaya's desire to sow and cultivate a sense of value in Chicano youth led him to teach in Albuquerque public schools for seven years and serve the local youth as a guidance counselor for three more. He followed his efforts in the public schools by working as an associate professor at his alma mater, the University of New Mexico, for 14 years. He took a position as an English professor there in 1988, then became Professor emeritus in 1993. He remains an integral member of the university staff to this day. In his spare time Anaya lectures, teaches creative writing workshops, and edits.

Celebrated Trilogy

Anaya is most widely known and praised by readers and critics alike for his first three novels. His groundbreaking first book, *Bless Me, Ultima* (1972), explores the relationship between a young Chicano boy and Ultima, a *curandera* or folk healer and spiritual guide. His second book, *Heart of Aztlán* (1976), immerses the reader in the sacrifices and choices a young Chicano boy and his family must make after moving from a small, rural New Mexico town to the hustle and bustle of Albuquerque. The third book, *Tortuga* (1979), follows a paralyzed 16-year-old Chicano boy imprisoned in a full-body cast, as he journeys from ignorance to illumination. Anaya has acknowledged that there is a heavy autobiographical current in these three novels, but insists that they are far from factual. He has simply stated that he wrote what he knew at that time in his life, as any writer would. In *Contemporary Novelists* Anaya explained that the three books do not comprise a traditional trilogy that shares characters and joined plots, but rather that they "offer separate worlds with different characters, [with] suggestions and allusions . . . that loosely connect the three works."

Regardless of what genre, style or form Anaya writes in, the essential elements in his works have remained remarkably firm. The *Oxford Companion to Twentieth-Century Literature in English* explained that his "narrative technique weaves together the historical with the mythical, the imaginative or fantastic, and the ritual aspects of Chicano life to explore the conflict between ethnic and Anglo–American cultures." The *Encyclopedia Latina* identified several features "that are now recognized as Anaya literary hallmarks: an emphasis on tradition, myth and spirituality; the repetition of certain types of characters (shamanic figures and seers both from the real world and from legend); an affinity for dream sequences, archetypal patterns, and mystical motifs; the geographic setting of New Mexico and the U.S. Southwest; symbols related to the natural world and the stress on the need for balance and harmony with the environment."

Critics have often examined Anaya's work with a focus on its incorporated myths and dreams. His writing also has succeeded in bringing the past to light in a vibrant and meaningful way. In an article in *MELUS* on Anaya's multiculturalism, Theresa Kanozaticle pointed out how "historic continuity and spiritual harmony are recurrent strains in much of Anaya's work as he often laments man's weakened connection to the earth, to the past, and to the myths that reveal the proper balance of the cosmos. . . . Rather than condemning or shunning innovation . . . he advocates a measured application of modernization, [insisting that] 'Technology may serve people, but it need not be the new god.' Anaya urges that just as the present can safeguard the past, historical awareness can 'shed light on our contemporary problems.' "

This argument would appear valid when one considers how current Anaya's works remain. Educator Raymond J. Rodrigues, in an *English Journal* review of Anaya's *Bless Me, Ultima,* listed the timeless lessons to be learned from reading the novel: "studying why one picks some peers as friends and rejects others, considering ways in which another culture has influenced one's own, investigating different religious beliefs . . . [and exploring] people of generations older and younger than one's own to determine how their values may differ and why."

Rooted

Anaya has, through his talent and hard work, made himself a significant figure in the landscape of Chicano literature. A versatile writer, he has moved from one genre to another, earning acclaim as a novelist, a poet, a dramatist, an essayist, an anthologist, a playwright, a children's author, a travel writer and an editor. He has also written a series of crime novels as well as many children's stories.

Anaya lives in New Mexico, the same state where he was born, and has said he has no desire to leave. When asked why writers write, he told *Contemporary Authors,* "We write for ourselves and for others. Messages. A sharing. We write to say we exist. The reader reads and also shouts I too exist! We are all together in the structure, which we call creativity. The structure is a house. We all live there. Some write, some do carpentry, plumbing or doctoring. We all live and share what we do. If it wasn't for those guys, I wouldn't have a house to live in. If it weren't for me, they wouldn't have a book of revelation to read. It all works out in the end." While Anaya has been able to make his existence known and his unique voice heard throughout the world, he has said that he still looks forward to a day when Chicano youth will find their own path to such recognition considerably less arduous.

Books

Chicano Writers: First Series, edited by Francisco A. Lomeli and Carl R. Shirley, Gale Research, Inc., 1989.
Contemporary Authors: Volume 124, Thomson Gale, 2004.
Contemporary Novelists: Seventh Edition, edited by Neil Schlager and Josh Lauer, St. James Press, 2001.
Conversations with Rudolfo Anaya, edited by Bruce Dick and Silvio Sirias, University Press of Mississippi, 1998.
Encyclopedia of Folklore and Literature, edited by Mary Ellen Brown and Bruce A. Rosenberg, ABC-CLIO, 1998.
Encyclopedia Latina: History, Culture, and Society in the United States, edited by Ilan Stavans, Grolier Academic Reference, 2005.
Hispanic-American Almanac, edited by Nicolas Kanellos, Gale Research, 1993.
Oxford Companion to American Literature: Sixth Edition, edited by James D. Hart, Oxford University Press, 1995.
Oxford Companion to Twentieth-Century Literature in English, edited by Jenny Stringer, Oxford University Press, 1996.
Twentieth-Century American Western Writers: First Series, edited by Richard H. Cracroft, Gale Group, 1999.

Periodicals

English Journal, January 1976.
MELUS, Summer 1999. □

Anne of Cleves, Queen, consort of Henry VIII, King

The politically motivated fourth bride of Henry VIII, German princess Anne of Cleves (1515–1557) was one of Henry's few wives to survive him. Their marriage was marred by a lack of attraction on the part of both parties, and was annulled after several months. Anne of Cleves lived out her life in England, where she received the honorary title of King's sister.

Upbringing at Cleves

Anne of Cleves was born in Dusseldorf on September 22, 1515, to Johann III and Maria von Geldem. Her father ruled the Duchy of Cleves, a small territory in present day northwestern Germany, until his death in 1538, when Anne's brother, Wilhelm, became Duke. Growing up at the court, Anne was not educated in the manner typical of European royalty at the time. In *Divorced, Beheaded, Survived: A Feminist Reinterpretation of the Wives of Henry VIII,* Karen Lindsey commented that "Anne enjoyed doing needlework, but she was lacking in the range of courtly accomplishments expected of an English noblewoman— playing a musical instrument, singing, dancing, and the ability to converse wittily in at least one or two languages besides English." Anne spoke no languages other than German, which would later prove a difficulty in her marriage to an English monarch. Despite these possible failings, Anne was considered a desirable marriage prospect due to her family's political holdings. Anne became betrothed to the Duke of Lorraine, but the engagement contract was formally cancelled and the couple did not marry. This left Anne's family free to seek other marriage prospects.

A Political Decision

After the death of Henry VIII's third wife, Jane Seymour, in 1537, the king mourned for some time. However, political necessity demanded he seek a new bride in the late

1530s. Despite being married three times, Henry had only one male heir, who was still in delicate infancy; another wife offered Henry the opportunity to produce at least one additional son. Henry and his advisor, Thomas Cromwell, initially considered a marriage alliance with several other European powers, including France and Denmark. These possibilities did not lead to betrothals, and Cromwell urged Henry to consider a German marriage.

By late 1538, tensions between Protestant England and the Catholic powers of Europe had increased. The Duke of Cleves was Protestant, and the family was allied through marriage to a powerful Lutheran ruler, the Elector of Saxony. This made an alliance with Cleves an attractive one, and in March of 1539, Henry sent envoys to Cleves to arrange a marriage with one of the two as-yet unmarried daughters of the ruling family.

Engagement to Henry VIII

Shortly prior to the arrival of the English envoys, Anne's brother, Wilhelm, had taken control of the duchy following the death of his father. Wilhelm was also Protestant, and welcomed Henry's envoys. However, as noted by Alison Weir in *The Six Wives of Henry VIII,* Wilhelm "had strong ideas about feminine modesty, and when his sisters were brought in to be introduced to [the English envoys], they were so well covered with 'a monstrous habit and apparel' that the ambassadors could see very little of their faces, let alone their figures." Cromwell sent renowned portrait painter Hans Holbein from England to paint both Anne and her sister, Amelia. Holbein's depiction of Anne presented her in what was presumably the best possible light; court painters at the time typically painted their subjects in a flattering manner.

Some today argue that Holbein did not overly misrepresent Anne. In *Six Wives: The Queens of Henry VIII,* David Starkey asserted that "[Holbein's] painting . . . highlight[s] the woman's gentle, passive character" rather than effectively altering her appearance. Regardless of the accuracy of Anne's portrait, the piece sufficiently pleased Henry, who appeared to be set on marriage negotiations with Cleves for Anne by that time.

When the envoys from Cleves and Saxony arrived to negotiate on Anne's behalf in mid-September of 1539, Cromwell took charge of the marriage negotiations. The greatest potential problem discussed during these negotiations was Anne's previous marriage contract with the Duke of Lorraine. Such a contract typically forbade other possible marriages, but since both Anne and the Duke had been below the age of consent at the time of the contract's inception, the current Cleves envoys maintained that the Lorraine contract did not carry the force of law. Since the English government hoped to complete the marriage between Anne and Henry, they accepted this explanation. The talks passed quickly, and on October 4, 1539, a marriage treaty between England and Cleves was signed.

"The Flanders Mare"

The marriage negotiations completed, Anne now needed to travel to England herself to meet her soon-to-be groom. Travel arrangements were debated before Anne's route was determined, overland from Cleves to Calais on the northern coast of France, and then across the English Channel to Dover and on to London. Because of Anne's status as a future royal bride, her traveling party was extensive, with 263 attendants and 226 horses. The party's progress was slow, and excited much interest along the way. Having left Cleves in mid-November, Anne did not arrive in Calais until December 11, averaging a little over five miles a day. At Calais, the party was stalled by poor weather. Between her arrival on December 11 and a delayed departure for England on December 27, Anne spent time learning Henry's favorite card games and presumably working on her practically non-existent English.

After crossing the Channel accompanied by 50 royal ships, Anne endured an unpleasant winter journey from Dover. En route to London, Anne was to stop at Canterbury, Sittingbourne, and Rochester. The party arrived at Rochester on New Year's Eve, 1539, with the intent of arriving in London on January 3. Henry, however, had other plans. Having heard so much about his new bride, he determined to surprise her at Rochester.

On New Year's Day in 1540, Henry arrived unannounced and disguised at Anne's room in Rochester. She reportedly paid little attention to him until he left and returned again to reveal his true identify. What followed was by most accounts a somewhat awkward meeting. Henry left disappointed by Anne's appearance, claiming she was considerably less attractive than he had been led to believe by both his envoys' descriptions and the likenesses presented to him. Henry accused his advisors of presenting him with "a great Flanders mare," coining a phrase which has become tied to the enduring memory of Anne of Cleves.

Historians today question whether Anne was, in fact, as unattractive as Henry claimed her to be. It seems likely that Henry had built up an unrealistic vision of Anne in his mind, and the relatively uncultured, provincial princess had little hope of living up to his vision. Because Henry first came upon her unannounced and unexpected, she was not mentally or physically attired for the meeting and probably did not come across in a favorable way. Further, since Henry disguised himself, it seems unlikely Anne would have reacted to him in a favorable manner that might have endeared her to the king. By that time in his life, Henry was aging and overweight—probably not the type of suitor a young princess would have welcomed—at least not without knowledge of his political status. Karen Lindsey noted that Anne "can only have been dismayed by her first sight of this gross old man trying to act like an enthusiastic young swain. In the seconds it took to regain her composure, her horror must have been evident." The damage this horror would have done to the king's ego may be the reason for Anne's reputed ugliness rather than any actual physical cause.

An Unconsummated Marriage

The king hastened back to London, seeking a way to break the engagement with Anne before her still-planned arrival for their formal meeting on January 3. Anne's previous marriage arrangements with the Duke of Lorraine were again discussed, and the representatives of Cleves again maintained that they could readily acquire proof that the marriage pre-contract had been properly and formally canceled. The embassy from Cleves convinced the English government of their honesty, and the decision was made to continue with the plans as already made rather than simply delay the inevitable and cause turmoil between England and Cleves.

Anne and Henry met in a grand ceremony at Blackheath, near London, on January 3. The two rode to Henry's palace at Greenwich together, exchanging formal pleasantries and seemingly on good terms. That evening Henry held a grand banquet in Anne's honor, all the while still trying to find a way out of the marriage. The wedding was planned for January 4, but was delayed while the king sought an escape from the contract. None was found, and the couple married on January 6, 1540. Henry was not resigned to the marriage, despite the political alliances that had driven him to pursue the match originally. The morning after the wedding, Henry informed his advisers that Anne's unattractiveness had left him unable to consummate the marriage. Because Henry still needed male heirs, this inability presented a serious problem to the English crown.

Political Shifts and a Marriage Ended

Changes in Europe's political alliances complicated the king's lack of interest in his new wife. The forces driving the German alliance shifted; Catholic powers began making political overtures to Henry, and his Protestant wife no longer helped him consolidate his position. As weeks passed, the marriage between Henry and Anne remained unconsummated, and Henry continued to ask his council to investigate Anne's previous marriage arrangements with the Duke of Lorraine as possible grounds for annulling the marriage. In April of 1540, Henry began an affair with Katherine Howard, a young English girl and a relative of Henry's previous wife, Anne Boleyn. The marriage between Henry and Anne of Cleves appeared doomed.

By June of 1540, Anne had become aware of Henry's interests in Katherine Howard. Anne had herself admitted that her marriage remained unconsummated, and was presumably unsurprised when the king ordered her to the leave the court for Richmond Palace on June 20. On July 6, Anne was informed of proceedings to annul the marriage; on July 9, those proceedings were completed. Her entire marriage to Henry had lasted barely six months. Anne initially withheld her consent, but Henry offered her an arrangement that would allow her to remain in England under comfortable terms, in exchange for her acceptance of the annulment. Anne had the status of King's sister, use of a number of castles and estates, and a large annual allowance. Anne wrote to her brother, the Duke of Cleves, that she intended to remain in England, and accepted the state of affairs.

Life After Henry

Settling into life after her annulment, Anne of Cleves possessed a degree of freedom remarkable for women of her day. Although Anne was technically free to remarry, as her previous marriage had never existed in the eyes of the church or the court, she did not do so. She became friends with her previous stepdaughter, Princess Mary—later Queen—and lived briefly again at court during Mary's reign. The remainder of Anne's life was a pleasant one; she survived Henry as well as his other five wives, dying in London on July 16, 1557. Anne received a royal funeral and was buried in an inconspicuous spot in Westminster Abbey.

Books

Fraser, Antonia, *The Wives of Henry VIII,* Knopf, 1992.

Lindsey, Karen, *Divorced, Beheaded, Survived: A Feminist Reinterpretation of the Wives of Henry VIII,* Addison-Wesley, 1995.

Starkey, David, *Six Wives: The Queens of Henry VIII,* HarperCollins, 2003.

Weir, Alison, *The Six Wives of Henry VIII,* Grove Weidenfeld, 1991. ☐

Eddie Arcaro

Eddie Arcaro (1916–1997) was one of American thoroughbred racing's legendary figures. A jockey who racked up an impressive string of wins during his peak years in the 1940s and 1950s, the diminutive Italian-American was dubbed "the Master" by sportswriters for the confidence he showed in the heat of the race, as well as for the five Kentucky Derby ribbons he collected. "Like Joe DiMaggio in baseball, Arnold Palmer and Jack Nicklaus in golf and Joe Louis in boxing," noted Joseph Durso of the *New York Times,* Arcaro "symbolized the exploding role of the hero in sports in the middle decades of the century."

Born on February 19, 1916, Arcaro spent his childhood in the Cincinnati metropolitan area, which includes the Kentucky cities of Covington and Newport, just across the Ohio River border between the two states. His parents, Pasquale and Josephine, were Italian immigrants and his father held a number of jobs, including taxi driver and operator of an illegal liquor enterprise during Prohibition. Arcaro was born prematurely, and weighed just three pounds at birth; because of this, he was smaller than his classmates and was rejected when he tried out for a spot on a baseball team. His full height would reach just five-foot, two inches.

Rode First Race Illegally

By the age of 13 Arcaro had found a job as a golf caddy at the local country club, but the bags he carried for members proved nearly as big as he was. Intrigued by a comment one golfer made—that someone of his stature would be ideally suited to jockey racehorses instead—Arcaro headed to nearby Latonia Race Course (later Turfway Park) in

Florence, Kentucky, and was hired as a horse exerciser for 75 cents a day. There was a minimum age requirement for jockeys, however, and he was still too young to obtain a license to ride professionally, but he did run illegally in a race on May 18, 1931, at the Bainbridge Park race track near Cleveland, Ohio. He lost that race, as well as the next 44 events he rode, and decided to head south for the winter racing season in Mexico. His first win came at the Aqua Caliente track in Tijuana, on January 14, 1932, on a horse named Eagle Bird.

Arcaro turned 16 a month later, and could enter the profession legitimately. He landed an apprentice position at the Fair Grounds Racecourse in New Orleans, and did so well that he was hired at the famous Calumet Farm in Lexington, Kentucky. The racehorse breeding and training facility had been founded by a wealthy Chicagoan, William Monroe Wright, who was heir to the Calumet Baking Powder Company fortune. Wright's son, Warren, hired Arcaro and began pairing him with some of the farm's best thoroughbreds. Arcaro racked up a good record at the Washington Park track in Chicago, Jefferson Park in New Orleans, and Narragansett Park in Rhode Island, and soon emerged as one of thoroughbred racing's top new talents. Arcaro, noted Durso, possessed "a street-smart sense that made him a natural in race-riding, a remarkable combination of grace and power on a thousand-pound horse traveling 35 miles an hour for high stakes. He rode with rare technical gifts, but mostly with an uncanny sense of mission that he seemed to share with his horse and a killer's instinct for winning."

Arcaro rose to the pinnacle of his profession during its most rough-and-tumble period. Thoroughbred racing was one of the most popular spectator sports in the pre-television era, and the big-money stakes races were avidly followed during the warm weather months of the season. Competition on and off the track was fierce: jockeys could expect to take home 10 percent of the winnings of that day's prize purse if their horse won, and so they were keen to be paired with the right racer. Illegal moves such as grabbing another horse's saddle silks to scare it, deliberately locking legs with another rider, or even hitting another jockey with the same whip used to urge one's own horse forward were not uncommon. "It's an odd thing about jockeys," Arcaro reminisced toward the end of his career in an interview with *New York Times* journalist Joseph C. Nichols. "They're the only paid athletes who, if you left them alone, would kill one another."

Won 1938 Derby

Arcaro entered his first Kentucky Derby race in 1935, riding a horse named Nellie Flag. The race, held at the Churchill Downs track in Louisville, was one of the three Triple Crown events in U.S. thoroughbred horse racing, along with the Preakness Stakes at Baltimore's Pimlico Race Course and the Belmont Stakes at Belmont Park in Elmont, New York. It took another three years before Arcaro won his first Derby, riding the 1938 winner Lawrin to national acclaim. The press called him "Steady Eddie" for his habit of remaining as still as a statue during the race, but his signature move was switching the whip between his right and left hands as he urged the horse forward.

In 1941 Arcaro rode another horse to victory at Churchill Downs on Derby Day, this one called Whirlaway. "A sensational chestnut thoroughbred colt with a long tail," noted *Sports Illustrated* writer Jim Bolus, Whirlaway had a rather notorious reputation prior to that win for being as temperamental as he was strong. When Arcaro was asked to ride him, he was wary. "I had seen too many good riders that couldn't handle him," he told Bolus. "I didn't know why they thought I could. They were having a lot of trouble with him. He would bolt." Calumet Farms trainer Ben Jones (1882–1961), as famous in his day as Arcaro, noticed that that Whirlaway sometimes strayed off course, and decided to put a blinker over just one eye. Arcaro and Whirlaway won the 1941 Kentucky Derby with a record time of two minutes, one second. That spring, the duo went on to win both the Preakness and the Belmont Stakes, earning them racing's highly coveted and rarely achieved Triple Crown title.

Arcaro and Jones teamed up several times to make Calumet Farm horses stakes winners, and the jockey was courted by other owners and trainers during these peak years of his career. In 1942 his career almost came to an end after trouble at the Aqueduct track in Queens, New York. He and a rival jockey, Vincent Nodarse, had several deliberate and near-deadly encounters during a race, and Arcaro finally managed to knock Nodarse off his horse. When questioned by race officials, he freely admitted, "I was trying to kill the S.O.B.," according to *People*. The incident resulted in an indefinite suspension by racing authorities, but his new patron, Helen Hay Whitney, intervened to have the ban lifted after a year.

Won Triple Crown Title Again

In 1945 Arcaro won his third Kentucky Derby, this time on Hoop Jr. He won again three years later on Citation, another famous horse of the era, and that day in May of 1948 became the first of a long winning streak for the pair: Arcaro rode Citation to 16 consecutive first-place finishes, including the Preakness and the Belmont, which gave him his second Triple Crown title. With that he became the first jockey ever to win the Crown more than once, a feat that has remained his alone well into the twenty-first century. In 1952 Arcaro won his fifth Kentucky Derby race on another Jones-trained mount, Hill Gail. Only one other rider, Bill Hartack (born 1932), has ever won the Kentucky Derby five times or more. Arcaro also won the Preakness Stakes six times, a record for that course, and tied with another jockey for six wins for the Belmont Park Triple Crown contest.

Arcaro was immensely famous at the peak of his career. Thoroughbred racing ranked with baseball and boxing as one of the most widely followed sports in America, in an era when football, basketball, and hockey had yet to find their coast-to-coast fan bases. His 1951 autobiography was titled *I Ride to Win!*, and he continued to achieve that goal for the rest of the decade. He was inducted into the Racing Hall of Fame in 1958, but was thrown from his horse during the Belmont Stakes a year later; knocked unconscious, he nearly drowned in a puddle of water before his rescuers arrived. Though Arcaro was seriously injured, he claimed that the helmet he wore—newly introduced in the sport—had saved his life.

Arcaro's last race came on November 18, 1961, and the following April, at the age of 46, he announced his formal retirement from the sport. Three decades of spills and persistent bursitis in one arm forced him to quit, but he had indeed hesitated, he admitted. "I like being a celebrity. I'm being honest. . . . When I retire I'll be just another little man," Nichols quoted him as saying. Arcaro finished with an impressive career record: he entered 24,092 races, won 4,779 of them, finished second in another 3,807 contests, and racked up 554 victories in the all-important stakes races. For several years during the 1940s and 1950s, he was the highest-paid jockey in U.S. thoroughbred racing. Earnings are calculated on the betting payouts for a horse, and winning riders received a 10 percent cut. His career total was over $30 million, much of which he invested in the oil business, a chain of drive-in restaurants, and even saddlery manufacturers. He retired to Florida, where he played golf and served as a broadcast analyst for Triple Crown races for a number of years. Widowed in 1988 when Ruth, his wife of 51 years, passed away, he remarried and spent the remainder of his years in the Miami area. He died of liver cancer on November 14, 1997, at the age of 81. Survivors included his wife, Vera, and children Robert and Carolyn.

Despite the fiercely competitive atmosphere of thoroughbred racing, Arcaro served as a mentor to a younger generation of jockeys. Earlier, in the 1940s, he was one of the co-founders of the Jockeys Guild, which sought to secure disability assistance for injured riders and guard the profession against abuses such as race fixing. Arcaro was president of the Guild from 1949 until 1961. Years later, he philosophized about the tricky combination of jockey, animal, and oval track in a sport in which many thousands of dollars could be wagered on a single two-minute event. "Race riding is as much physical exertion as you want to put into it," *Investor's Business Daily* journalist Michael Richman quoted him as saying. "You develop strong back and shoulder muscles by pushing with the horse on every stride, by showing him you're the boss and making him keep his mind on the job."

Periodicals

Cincinnati Post (Cincinnati, OH), May 1, 2006.
Investor's Business Daily, February 1, 2002.
Kentucky Post, March 26, 1997.
New York Post, June 9, 1952; September 26, 1958.
New York Times, May 2, 1948; April 4, 1962; November 15, 1997.
People, December 1, 1997.
Sporting News, November 24, 1997.
Sports Illustrated, November 4, 1991; November 24, 1997. □

Martina Arroyo

American soprano Martina Arroyo (born c. 1936) was a pioneer among African-American performers in the operatic field, and in general one of opera's most effective public ambassadors.

"She . . . has a reputation as the wittiest woman in opera," noted Brian Kellow of *Opera News*. Arroyo's down-to-earth sense of humor, coupled with a diva-sized personality, brought opera to new audiences over her three-decade performing career. After her retirement, Arroyo continued to contribute to the opera world as a noted educator. She was a mainstay at New York's Metropolitan Opera in the 1960s and 1970s, frequently portraying the heroines in operas by Giuseppe Verdi, and she made more than 50 recordings.

Grew Up with Opera Broadcasts

Martina Arroyo was born in New York City on February 2, 1936 (or, according to some sources, 1937). Her father, Demetrio Arroyo, was an engineer, born in Puerto Rico, who worked at the Brooklyn Navy Yard; her mother was an African American from Charleston, South Carolina, whose schooling ended after she finished third grade. Both parents encouraged Arroyo to do well in school. The family was middle class, with money for dance lessons for Arroyo, who later took issue with descriptions of her story as a rags-to-riches saga. Arroyo sang in a Baptist church choir, learned to play the piano from her mother, and dreamed of a career in the arts.

Her parents supported her but warned that she should have another career in reserve, since artists of African descent faced barriers to their participation in traditionally all-white performance traditions. The family listened to the Saturday afternoon broadcasts of the Metropolitan Opera (the "Met") on the radio, and Arroyo, who had not studied the French language, learned to sing the "Jewel Song" from Charles Gounod's French opera *Faust* by ear, sounding it out syllable by syllable as she followed along with a record of the opera.

Arroyo's grades were good enough to win her admission to the academically selective Hunter College High School, whose students could attend Hunter College's opera workshop. One day, when Arroyo was 14, she and a group of friends were clowning around in a hallway outside the auditorium, imitating the opera singers who were holding forth inside. The voice teacher, annoyed by the noise, came out and asked Arroyo if she would like to try singing. Perhaps his aim was to punish her, or perhaps he heard the makings of a splendid soprano voice. Whatever the case, she stepped up with the "Jewel Song." Despite Arroyo's mangled French, the teacher was impressed and invited her to begin taking voice courses. As a teenager Arroyo found a mentor, voice teacher Marinka Gurewich, and started learning the role of Madame Butterfly in Giacomo Puccini's opera of the same name.

Nevertheless, she took to heart her parents' advice that she should have a more financially reliable career in reserve. She went on to attend Hunter College, finishing a

degree in Romance languages in three years and receiving a bachelor's degree in 1956. She thought about becoming an academic and enrolled in a graduate program at New York University, beginning a thesis on Italian novelist Ignazio Silone. Arroyo also taught Italian at a New York City public school (P.S. 45 in the Bronx), and was active as a caseworker for the city's welfare department. She continued taking voice lessons with Gurewich, who urged her to devote herself exclusively to opera and even threatened to end their lessons if Arroyo did not get serious. The debut of African-American soprano Leontyne Price at the Met in 1955 was the opera world's equivalent of Jackie Robinson breaking the color barrier in professional baseball, and the pioneering vocalist served as another inspiration to Arroyo. She auditioned at the Met in 1957 and was rejected but encouraged to try again. That year she was part of a joint recital program given at New York's Carnegie Hall; a *New York Times* review of the concert praised her "brilliant, ringing clarity of tone."

Won Broadcast Audition Contest

In 1958 Arroyo entered the Met's Auditions of the Air, a sort of operatic *American Idol* in which young singers competed in a radio concert for admission to the Met's training program. Singing an aria from Verdi's *Aida,* she emerged as one of two winners (the other was Grace Bumbry, another African American who went on to a stellar operatic career). With a $1,000 prize in hand, Arroyo abandoned her various non-operatic careers. She studied drama, German, English diction, and even fencing at the Met's Kathryn Long School. In 1958 she received a break when a storm forced the cancellation of an outdoor performance in upstate New York where she had been scheduled to sing. The opera, Ildebrando Pizzetti's *Assassino nella cattedrale* (Murder in the Cathedral), had been newly composed and was thus moved to Carnegie Hall, vastly increasing Arroyo's visibility.

Once again, Arroyo rose to the moment with a strong performance that gained positive critical notice. The Met began to cast her in small roles, but Arroyo felt that she might be pigeonholed as a bit-part singer, and she wanted more. She began to travel to Europe, spending long stretches of time there and performing in operas, oratorios (sacred unstaged dramatic works), and recital programs. On a 1959 trip to Italy she met violinist Emilio Poggioni, who in 1961 became her first husband. Their marriage, she said, was free of racial tensions but not of musical ones; Poggioni became a stern critic of her performances. Another source of support in Europe was Arroyo's mother, who frequently accompanied her on trips, once breaking out in laughter when her daughter came on stage in a Viking outfit, with blonde braids, in a performance of an opera by German composer Richard Wagner.

Arroyo did encounter racial prejudice. On tour in Macon, Georgia, she was told to keep her black hands off a child whom she had just rescued from falling out of his mother's overloaded arms. "But America is not alone," Arroyo remarked to Thomas Cole of the *New York Times.* "I walked into a Munich [Germany] restaurant once and heard a man remark, 'Here comes a Menschfresser [cannibal].' I shot him a look and said, 'Yeah, but we only use a little pot; you use ovens.' "

Arroyo's career kept building on both sides of the Atlantic. A 1961 *New York Times* review noted that she "has been delighting New York audiences with the beauty of her voice." By 1965 she had been made a permanent member of the Zurich Opera Company in Switzerland, and early that year she received her big break in New York: Met impresario Rudolf Bing called her and asked her to fill in for ailing star Birgit Nilsson in a production of *Aida*. Arroyo first thought the call was a prank on the part of one of her friends, but she was convinced of its veracity in time to make her debut in a lead role at the Met on February 4, 1965. Although Nilsson was one of the biggest names in opera at the time, the tough Met audience cheered Arroyo's performance, and Nilsson quipped that if she got sick again, she would make sure she did it when Arroyo was not in town.

Opened Met Season Twice

In the late 1960s and early 1970s, Arroyo's career epitomized the jet-set lifestyle of the international opera star. She was the featured star in the opening production of the Met's season three times, twice consecutively. Making her debut at London's Covent Garden in 1968 and the Paris Opera in 1973, she was as much in demand in Europe as in the United States. Arroyo was a "lirico-spinto" soprano—one whose voice lay in between the extremes of melodic beauty and dramatic power. Nor were her activities restricted to opera; she sang vocal parts in choral and symphonic works, becoming an especially favored soloist of New York Philharmonic Orchestra conductor Leonard Bernstein, and she had the power for Beethoven's soprano-punishing *Symphony No. 9* and *Missa Solemnis*. The only downside of her hectic career was that her marriage to Poggioni suffered and finally dissolved after the two, deciding independently to take intercontinental flights to surprise each other, crossed paths in midair and ended up on different continents. She later married banker Michel Maurel.

In tandem with her record of musical accomplishment went Arroyo's uncommon gift for communicating the beauty of opera to ordinary people. She became a favorite of *Tonight* show host Johnny Carson and appeared on the program more than 20 times. Arroyo, at the request of actor and opera fan Tony Randall, also made a guest appearance on the television situation comedy *The Odd Couple*. She was a frequent guest on the "Singers' Roundtable" heard during the intermissions of the Met's Saturday radio broadcasts, and it was here that her wit had free rein as she dubbed herself Madama Butterball and bantered with other divas of the day. Her ideal of service to opera also led her to public service, and President Gerald Ford appointed her to a six-year term on the National Council on the Arts, a division of the National Endowment for the Arts.

Arroyo's repertoire grew to include difficult contemporary works such as German composer Karlheinz Stockhausen's *Momente,* in addition to Italian and German standards. Her schedule began to slow down in the late 1970s, and by 1989 she had retired from performing, although she did re-emerge two years later in order to appear in *Blake,* a new opera by Leslie Adams with a story set in the time of slavery. She made the transition easily to a second career as an educator and arts advocate, beginning with a stint at Louisiana State University in Baton Rouge. She also taught at the University of California at Los Angeles and Wilberforce University in Ohio before settling in as distinguished professor of music at Indiana University. In later life she developed a variety of modes of assisting young singers and nurturing their careers in the same way that her own had been carefully encouraged. She established the Martina Arroyo Foundation as a support structure for her new Prelude to Performing program, a 14-week course aimed at helping young singers develop unique and exciting vocal and performance styles of their own. Many of Arroyo's more than 50 recordings were reissued on compact disc, and by the early 2000s she loomed as a major figure in the history of American opera.

Books

Contemporary Black Biography, volume 30, Gale, 2001.
Notable Hispanic American Women, Book 2, Gale, 1998.

Periodicals

New York Times, January 20, 1957; February 18, 1961; April 28, 1968.
Opera News, January 1999, p. 10; October 2006, p. 24.

Online

"Biography," Martina Arroyo Official Website, http://www.martinaarroyo.com (December 17, 2006).
"Martina Arroyo," *All Music Guide,* http://www.allmusic.com (December 17, 2006).
"Martina Arroyo, Distinguished Professor," Indiana University, http://www.indiana.edu/~alldrp/members/arroyo.html (December 17, 2006). □

Red Auerbach

Red Auerbach (1917–2006), one of the most successful sports coaches and executives over a half-century, was the mastermind behind the Boston Celtics' 16 National Basketball Association (NBA) championships, the most in the NBA and third most in professional sports.

The strident Auerbach, among other qualities, was a master strategist, a sharp judge of personnel, and a racial pioneer. "Auerbach was fiercely competitive, sometimes to the point of boorishness," Peter May wrote in the *Boston Globe* after Auerbach died in October of 2006 from a heart attack at age 89. He was the first coach to have won 1,000 games, including playoffs; 14 of his players are in the Hall of Fame and 30 became coaches.

Parents Were Russian Immigrants

Auerbach was raised in the Williamsburg section of Brooklyn, New York. His father, Hyman Auerbach, was an immigrant from Minsk, Russia, who ran a dry-cleaning store. His American-born mother, Marie (Thompson), worked at a deli. Auerbach played basketball at Public School 122 and starred as a 5-foot 9-inch guard at Eastern District High School. "In my area of Brooklyn there was no football, no baseball," Auerbach told Ken Shouler, editor and writer for *Total Basketball: The Ultimate Basketball Encyclopedia,* in an article for the ESPN.com website. "They were too expensive. They didn't have the practice fields. We played basketball and handball and some softball in the street." Hyman Auerbach did not approve of his son playing basketball, but did not intervene.

After attending Seth Low Junior College, a Brooklyn-based division of Columbia University, for one season, Auerbach transferred to George Washington University in Washington, D.C. He lettered for three seasons at GWU and learned a running style of basketball under Coach Bill Reinhart that would serve as a prototype for his Celtics teams.

He earned his bachelor's degree at George Washington, then got a job as basketball director of St. Albans, a prominent prep school in Washington, D.C. "Coaching, not playing, was his future," Shouler wrote. Auerbach married Dorothy Lewis in 1941, got his master's degree from George Washington and worked for Roosevelt High School in Washington. There he taught history, health, and physical education. Auerbach launched his publishing career—he wrote five books on basketball—with an article on indoor obstacle courses for the Journal of Health and Physical Education. He also refereed games for supplemental income. From 1943 through 1946, Auerbach served in the U.S. Navy.

Coached in First NBA Season

After leaving the service, Auerbach began his professional coaching career guiding the Washington Capitols in 1946–47, the initial season of the precursor of the NBA, the Basketball Association of America. In Auerbach's second season there, Washington reached the NBA Finals, losing to the Minneapolis (now Los Angeles) Lakers. Auerbach left Washington amid a contract dispute and, after coaching the Tri-Cities Blackhawks of Iowa in 1949–50, quit when he discovered that owner Ben Kerner had traded a player without consulting him. The Celtics had finished 22–46 that season and owner Walter Brown was seeking a new coach. Brown, deep in debt and on the verge of disposing of the team, accepted the recommendation of advisers and hired Auerbach.

Russell Trade Brought 11 Championships

One noteworthy asset Auerbach had in Boston was flashy guard Bob Cousy. But strangely enough, Auerbach bypassed him at first, drafting a bigger player. Cousy was a three-time All-American at Holy Cross in Worcester, Massachusetts, about 30 miles west of Boston, and would have been seen as a popular choice. Auerbach instead drafted 6-foot 11-inch center Charlie Share and said tersely, according to Shouler: "Am I supposed to win here, or take care of local yokels?" Cousy went elsewhere, but when teams folded, he went into a dispersal draft and Boston drew his name out of the hat. Cousy looked past Auerbach's slight and signed for $9,000 a year. He would become an NBA First Team all-star for ten straight seasons before retiring in 1963.

Still, the Celtics couldn't win because they lacked a big man in the middle. That would all change in 1956, when Auerbach pursued Bill Russell, a 6-foot 9-inch center out who had led the University of San Francisco to back-to-back National Collegiate Athletic Association (NCAA) championships and 55 straight victories, and the United States to an Olympic gold medal. Boston, however, would have to trade up in the college draft to obtain Russell. The Rochester Royals and St. Louis Hawks each selected ahead of the Celtics. While the Royals were inclined to draft center Sihugo Green, Brown offered an extra incentive: He would arrange for Rochester to get the lucrative Ice Capades show. Auerbach recalled to Shouler: "Walter got him the Ice Capades, and [Rochester team manager Les] Harrison said, 'I give you my word that we'll stay away from Russell.'" Auerbach then called St. Louis owner Ben Kerner, and offered 20-points-per-game guard "Easy Ed" Macauley, and Cliff Hagan for the rights to draft Russell.

What Auerbach got from that deal was 11 championships in 13 years, including eight straight from 1959 through 1966. He gave up coaching after 1966 to concentrate on his general manager duties. Russell revolutionized the game with his defense and shot-blocking, which more than compensated for his modest scoring statistics. He would not merely swat balls away, but would do so in a teammate's direction. His rebounds would set into motion the patented Celtics fast break. "The teams of the Celtics era were built on defense and running," May wrote. "Russell dominated the boards and blocked shots. Cousy ran the break. [Bill] Sharman, [Tom] Heinsohn, Frank Ramsay, and Sam Jones delivered at the other end." Russell also knew how to win when absolutely necessary. He won all 21 "winner-take-all" games in college and the NBA.

Auerbach named Russell his successor as coach. The center, who was player-coach for three seasons and won two titles, was the first African-American coach of a professional sports team. Chuck Cooper, also a Celtic, had been the NBA's first black player, in 1950. In the mid-1960s, Boston also fielded the first all-black starting five in the league.

He also selected under-the-radar players that fit into his system—the more intelligent, the better. John Havlicek played second fiddle to Jerry Lucas at Ohio State and tried out for the National Football League's Cleveland Browns, then prospered as Auerbach's initial "sixth man," or first replacement off the bench. Havlicek saved Boston from playoff elimination in 1965 with a famous steal to preserve a seventh-game victory in the Eastern Conference final against the Philadelphia 76ers. Forward Tom "Satch" Sanders, an intellectual social activist who later coached Harvard University, added a cerebral touch. Auerbach also obtained journeymen such as Don Nelson and Bailey Howell who contributed to Celtics championships. "He was a master at handling people—a master psychologist," Howell told Shouler. "Red Auerbach's coaching philosophy was simple: Only one statistic mattered," Lisette Hilton said on the ESPN Classic website. "At the end of the game, he wanted the number next to his team to be greater than that next to his opponent."

Drafted Bird a Year Early

Boston won two more titles in the mid-1970s with center Dave Cowens and guard Jo Jo White as the team's linchpins, then the Celtics fell into decline. Transient ownership aggravated the problem, which hit its nadir in 1979 under the ownership of John Y. Brown—no relation to Walter Brown. Brown meddled in the team's affairs and sarcastically addressed Auerbach as "living legend" during executive meetings. Auerbach was on the verge of taking a general manager's job with the New York Knicks when Brown agreed to sell the team to finance a (successful) run for Kentucky governor. With Brown gone, Auerbach stayed.

Auerbach then made another of his shrewd moves that paid dividends for the Celtics. In 1978 he drafted Larry Bird, then an unknown forward at Indiana State, after Bird's junior year. Bird led the Sycamores to the NCAA title game as a senior, losing to Magic Johnson and Michigan State before joining Boston for the 1979–80 season. Bird led the Celtics to three championships and five Finals appearances from 1981 through 1987. Bird's supporting cast included center Robert Parish and forward Kevin McHale. Veteran backcourt man Dennis Johnson, yet another Auerbach acquisition, contributed to the 1980s title run.

The Celtics' fortunes, however, took a tragic turn in June of 1986. About two weeks after their 16th title, they used their second choice overall in the draft to select forward Len Bias from the University of Maryland. A few days later, Bias died of a cocaine overdose in Washington, D.C. In 1993 star guard Reggie Lewis died of an irregular heartbeat while working out. Boston has yet to win another title.

Known as Extremely Stubborn

The cantankerous Auerbach clashed often with referees and amassed $17,000 worth of fines. He even brawled with Kerner, the Hawks' owner, during the 1958 finals and had other skirmishes with opposing players and fans. His trademark celebration involved the lighting of a victory cigar at the end of games, which critics saw as arrogant. "To the world outside his own huddles and locker room he was ornery and miserable, a boisterous dymano who peered at you through cigar smoke after his troops had impaled yours," Shouler wrote. He was a master at one-upmanship. In the mid-1960s, Auerbach signed Russell to a new contract worth $1 more than Russell's principal rival, Philadelphia 76ers center Wilt Chamberlain.

Auerbach's ways sometimes hurt the team's marketing, some teams maintained. He countered by saying that a winning team sells itself. The Celtics drew lackluster crowds during their championship reign in the 1960s, and even had their games relegated to FM on radio while hockey's Boston Bruins, a last-place team at the time, frequently sold out and were accessible on AM radio.

His acknowledgement of female journalists was grudging. When *Boston Globe* reporter Jackie MacMullan sat next to Auerbach during a college game in 1983, he said to her: "Aren't you the cheerleading coach?" He objected to MacMullan's presence in the locker room, saying: "You don't belong in there."

His Legendary Presence Hovered

Auerbach eventually yielded operational duties and kept the title of team president, living in Washington. His presence, though, still loomed. The club stripped him of the president's title in the late 1990s when Rick Pitino became coach, general manager and president, but Auerbach got it back when Pitino left. In 2002 he approved the hiring of general manager Danny Ainge, a guard from the championship teams of the 1980s.

Auerbach underwent heart surgery, but continued with an active life, playing racquetball and making frequent public appearances. Boston, meanwhile, honored him with a statue at its downtown Quincy Market. His cigar smoking remained legendary. The menu on the Legal Sea Foods restaurant chain read: "No cigar or pipe smoking, except for Red Auerbach."

He died in Washington of a heart attack on October 28, 2006, three days after receiving the Lone Sailor Award from the United States Navy. "Forgive me. Red was so stubborn, I assumed he would live forever. Or maybe I just hoped that was true,'' wrote MacMullan, who recalled a roughly 20-year rapport with Auerbach well beyond their initial testy exchange. ''Our relationship was a work in progress, but over time, I grew to love Red Auerbach. We developed a quirky sort of professional friendship that included spirited debates on women's issues, on the merits of different eras, on the best blacktop playgrounds in the country. He grew to appreciate my love of the game, and became one of my most trusted sources.'' The many extensive tributes to Auerbach included rebroadcasts of famous Boston Celtics victories, run on the NBA Channel and ESPN Classic.

Auerbach's casket was draped, appropriately enough, in Boston Celtics green. He was buried in Falls Church, Virginia, a Washington suburb. ''It was time to say good bye to a truly great American, a man who, had he not channeled his talents into basketball, could have been a Speaker of the House or corporate CEO,'' wrote Bob Ryan, a longtime basketball columnist for the *Boston Globe* and commentator on the ESPN ''Sports Reporters'' show.

The funeral ceremony paralleled Auerbach's bent for simplicity. ''The rabbi said the family had directed that the ceremony be 'brief' and 'punctual,' '' Ryan wrote. ''He read the 23rd Psalm. He read the Kaddish, or prayer of mourning. The casket was lowered. An American flag was placed inside. And that was it. No muss, no fuss, no frills. How positively Auerbachian.''

Periodicals

Associated Press Newswires, August 3, 2005.
Los Angeles Times, January 25, 1986.
New York Times, January 25, 1986.

Online

''Arnold Jacob Auerbach,'' Biography Resource Center, http://www.galenet.galegroup.com/ (December 1, 2006).
''Auerbach, Pride of Celtics, Dies,'' *Boston Globe,* October 29, 2006, http://www.boston.com/sports/basketball/celtics/articles/2006/10/29/auerbach_pride_of_celtics_dies/ (December 17, 2006).
Auerbach profile, Basketball Hall of Fame, http://www.hoophall.com/halloffamers/Auerbach.htm (December 17, 2006).
''Auerbach's Celtics Played as a Team,'' ESPNClassic, http://.www.espn.go.com/classic/biography/s/auerbach_red.html (December 1, 2006).
''Auerbach's Spirit Lives On,'' *Boston Globe,* November 1, 2006, http://www.boston.com/sports/basketball/celtics/articles/2006/11/01/auerbachs_spirit_lives_on/ (December 1, 2006).
''The Consummate Coach,'' ESPN.com, http://www.sports.espn.go.com/nba/feature/featureVideo?page=auerbach (December 1, 2006).
''Tough Man Had a Tender Side,'' *Boston Globe,* October 29, 2006, http://www.boston.com/sports/basketball/celtics/articles/2006/10/29/tough_man_had_a_tender_side/ (December 1, 2006). □

B

Ban Ki-Moon

Ban Ki-moon (born 1944) was sworn in late in 2006 as secretary-general of the United Nations (U.N.). The former South Korean foreign minister took office on January 1, 2007, after predecessor Kofi Annan completed two five-year terms.

Ban, whom the United States backed for the new position, became the first Asian to run the international organization since 1971. His supporters cite his administrative and mediation abilities, while critics call him too bland at a time of geopolitical volatility. Ban's long-time involvement with the U.N. has its roots in the agency's postwar rebuilding of Korea in the early 1950s. "Courtly and deliberate, with an easy smile, Ban, 62, is an unknown at the United Nations, particularly compared with the high-profile globe-trotting diplomat he is succeeding," Warren Hoge wrote in the *International Herald Tribune.*

Raised in Japanese-Occupied Korea

Ban was born in the farming village of Eumseong, when the Japanese occupied Korea before the end of World War II. He grew up the oldest of six children in nearby Cheongu. His father's warehouse business went bankrupt and the family, when Ban was six years old, fled to the mountains during the Korean War, which lasted from 1950 through 1953. "We were safe and in a place where neither the South Korean nor North Korean armies would come, but we were poor and hungry," Ban said in the *International Herald Tribune.* "I could see the fighter jets bombing the towns and cities nearby." Ban said South Koreans view the U.N., which originated in 1948, favorably for its role in

freeing South Korea from the communist North. "We Koreans have quite literally risen from the ashes of war," he said on the British Broadcasting Corporation's website, BBC News.

He studied English fervently amid strict educational standards that included writing English sentences ten times each, to reinforce memory. In 1956 his schoolmates selected Ban to write an appeal to Secretary General Dag Hammarskjold concerning Hungary's uprising against what was then the Soviet Union. "I never found out if they ever sent it," he told Hoge. His diplomatic ambitions intensified when he met U.S. President John F. Kennedy at the White House in 1962, when he visited the United States as part of an American Red Cross program. An all-girls school in his Cheongu hometown sent him off with bamboo strainers, traditional symbols of luck. He would later marry one of the girls, student council president Yoo Soon-taek, in 1971, one year after he passed his diplomat's examination. Ban earned his bachelor of arts degree in international relations from Seoul National University in 1970; he obtained his master's degree in public administration in 1985 from the John F. Kennedy School of Government at Harvard University.

Ban served his country's foreign ministry for about three decades; his postings included India, the United States, and Austria. He began his career with the U.N. in 1975, as a member of its South Korean home office. Ban, while South Korea's ambassador to Austria, was chairman of the preparatory commission for the Comprehensive Nuclear Test Ban Treaty Organization in 1999. According to BBC News, Ban has drawn praise as "a consummate mediator and a world-class administrator." The Reuters news agency added: "Quiet and unassuming, Ban has made few missteps during his long career as a Korean diplomat."

Gaffe Turned into Blessing

One misstep that cost Ban a high-level job in 2001 triggered the events that ultimately led to his top position at the U.N. His aides had accidentally failed to delete praise of the Anti-Ballistic Missile Treaty from a memo, at the same time that the administration of U.S. President George W. Bush had decided to scuttle it. Kim Dae Jung, then the president of South Korea, had to apologize publicly. "I was totally out of work for the first time in my life," he said, according to Hoge.

While awaiting career exile—ambassadorship to some remote country—Ban got an offer from Han Seung Soo, a fellow South Korean and the U.N. General Assembly president that year, to serve as Han's chief of staff. "I had what we call a 'jeon-hwa-we-bok' experience," he told Hoge. "Had I been appointed to an ambassadorship somewhere, I simply wouldn't have had this opportunity to be selected secretary general." Hoge added: "The maxim, well known to Koreans, means that a misfortune has turned into a blessing."

Ban, as South Korea's foreign minister, has been among the leaders in talks among six nations—China, Japan, Russia, the United States, and the two Koreas—that look to curb North Korea's nuclear proliferation. He spent one Chuseok holiday—the Korean Thanksgiving—talking to high-level officials in Washington, Tokyo, Moscow, and Beijing to craft a response to North Korea's intentions to test nuclear weapons. But under his watch, South Korea has also been seen as not forceful enough with its northern neighbor about

human rights; Ban, too, has drawn criticism as overly waffling. He said at one press conference that South Korea's media called him "the slippery eel because I was too charming for them to be able to catch me," according to Elizabeth M. Lederer of the Associated Press. He added that he earned the nickname "because I was very friendly with the media . . . but I promise today that I can be a pretty straight shooter when I need to."

Appointed to Succeed Annan

On October 13, 2006, the U.N.'s 192-member General Assembly in New York appointed Ban its eighth secretary general. He became the first Asian in such a position since U Thant of Burma (now Myanmar). The outgoing Annan praised Ban as "a man with a truly global mind at the helm of the world's only universal organization," the *New York Times* wrote. Annan, the newspaper said, reminded Ban of the advice then-first secretary general, Trygve Lie, told successor Dag Hammarskjold: "You are about to take over the most impossible job on earth."

Speaking to the General Assembly the previous month, Ban, according to the text of his statement printed on South Korea's foreign ministry website, noted the U.N.'s accomplishments over 50 years. He added, "We cannot be sanguine about future trends. If the U.N.'s primary task in the 20th century was to curb inter-state conflict, its core mandate in the new century must be to strengthen states and to preserve the inter-state system in the face of new challenges."

He also declared, "Some assert that the U.N. is poorly equipped to deal with new threats, such as those posed by non-state actors seeking to undermine the international order. . . . Our tools need sharpening. . . . The United Nations remains no more, and no less, than what we make of it."

Inherited Many World Problems

When Annan assumed office, he had to "get used to managing problems beyond the Korean peninsula," Bryan Walsh of *Time* magazine wrote. Recent world conflicts have included the Iraqi war, nuclear buildup in Iran, continuing fighting in Afghanistan, and three years of fighting in the Darfur region of Sudan. In addition, Ban heads an organization that Walsh said "has been dogged for years by mismanagement, inefficiency, and corruption," and by bureaucratic stagnation. Scandal surrounding the $64 million oil-for-food program stained Annan's tenure. The program allowed Iraq, which had been under U.N. sanctions after its 1990 invasion of Kuwait, to sell oil, provided most of the money went toward food, medicine, and other humanitarian causes. But reports largely blamed the U.N. for shoddy oversight.

On December 23, 2006, the 15-member United Nations Security Council imposed sanctions against Iran in a unanimous vote. The resolution ordered all countries to ban the sale of any technology and materials that Iran could use for its nuclear programs. The council warned Iran it would pass further non-military sanctions if the country does not comply. Ban, in a televised interview with ABC News that he taped just before the Security Council vote, urged the Teheran government to revive talks with European nations Great Britain, France, and Germany. Iran, meanwhile, said it would ignore the order and commence work immediately on upgrading its uranium-enrichment capabilities.

Also in late 2006, Ban insisted again that patience was necessary in discussions with North Korea about that country's own nuclear ambitions. But the United States, while supportive of Ban, worries that South Korea's warming relations with communist China and Seoul's policy of engagement with its northern neighbor have hindered the ability of Ban to play hardball with North Korea's leader, Kim Jong Il. "The U.S. is skeptical that Ban, long careful to avoid stepping on toes, would really be willing to challenge the entrenched interests inside the U.N. that are opposed to reform," Walsh wrote.

Ban, according to Walsh, is so determined to resolve the dispute with North Korea that he might visit the Pyongyang capital city himself as secretary general, which his predecessor did not. "I've gained a deeper experience and understanding into this complex issue," he said, as quoted in *Time*. "Having known all the history and background and having known people in both the South and the North, I'm convinced I can do much better than any other person." Ban told Lally Weymouth of *Newsweek*, "North Korea has declared very defiantly that if the Security Council adopts any sanctions, it will regard this as a declaration of war. This is very worrisome and shows total disrespect of the United Nations."

'The Job is Grueling'

By any measure, Ban stepped into a job often considered thankless. "The job is grueling, requiring an extraordinary combination of public advocacy, tough management, and tireless crisis diplomacy," the *New York Times* editorialized. "Mr. Ban got a quick taste of his life to come when the news of his selection was upstaged by North Korea's announcement that it had tested a nuclear weapon."

In his interview with *Newsweek*, Ban said North Korea "should be more realistic." He added: "Considering the economic and political difficulty [North Korea is] facing, they should have taken a wiser path. Why should they take this dangerous and negative action? . . . We need a two-pronged approach. While we take a very strong and stern message and deliver it to North Korea, at the same time we need to leave some room for negotiations so as not to escalate the situation."

China, Japan, and Russia, meanwhile, have urged Ban to limit his role in North Korean talks, according to Bill Varner of the Bloomberg news service. Varner quoted Chinese U.N. ambassador Wang Guangya as saying any involvement "has to be informal, low-key, silent." Ashton Carter, a former U.S. assistant secretary of defense who has worked with Ban, said some nations in the six-party talks may resent Ban's intrusion, but according to Varner he added: "Involvement by Ban would be constructive because the six-party talks have been a failure."

Ban, who has one son and two daughters, also hopes to tackle such issues as HIV/AIDS and other health epidemics,

and the abject poverty that prevails in some parts of the world. "Without the eradication of poverty, you will always see conflicts," he told Weymouth. Reform within the U.N., he added, will help answer critics that say the organization is irrelevant. He called himself a "harmonizer and a bridge-builder," according to the AP's Lederer, and wants to heal the rift between rich and poor nations. "You could say that I'm a man on a mission, and my mission could be dubbed Operation Restore Trust . . . trust in the organization and trust between member states and the secretariat."

Periodicals

New York Times, October 11, 2006; October 14, 2006.
Newsweek, October 23, 2006.
Time, October 16, 2006.

Online

"Ban Ki-Moon Lays Out U.N. Agenda," Associated Press, December 15, 2006, http://www.washingtonpost.com/wp-dyn/content/article/2006/12/15/AR2006121500309.html (December 15, 2006).
"Ban Ki-Moon Sworn in as 8th U.N. Secretary-General," Reuters, December 14, 2006, http://www.en.epochtimes.com/news/6-12-14/49341.html (December 15, 2006).
"Ban Must Limit North Korea Role, Say China, Russia," Bloomberg, December 14, 2006, http://www.bloomberg.com/apps/news?pid=20601080&sid=aqhUjYOsnL.E&refer=asia (December 15, 2006).
"Profile: Ban Ki-moon," BBC News, October 13, 2006, http://www.news.bbc.co.uk/2/hi/asia-pacific/5401856.stm (December 15, 2006).
"Statement by H.E. Mr. Ban Ki-moon," Ministry of Foreign Affairs and Trade of the Republic of Korea, September 21, 2006, http://www.mofat.go.kr/me/me_a002/me_b006/1211055_980.html (December 15, 2006).
"Twist of Fate Led to Top Post at U.N.," *International Herald Tribune*, December 8, 2006, http://www.iht.com/articles/2006/12/08/news/profile.php (December 24, 2006). □

Mary Bancroft

Author and intelligence analyst Mary Bancroft (1903–1997) had a colorful career as a journalist and spy for the United States in Switzerland during World War II. Bancroft was best known for her work with German military intelligence officer Hans Bernd Gisevius, who supplied details regarding a bungled attempt to assassinate Hitler on July 20, 1944.

The Baby in the Basket

Mary Bancroft was the only child of Hugh and Mary Agnes (Cogan) Bancroft, born October 29, 1903, in Cambridge, Massachusetts. Hours after the birth, Bancroft's mother, Mary Agnes, an Irish Catholic housewife, suffered a fatal embolism, leaving her husband both a new father and a widow. Bancroft detailed the hours after her birth in *Autobiography of a Spy* (1983), describing how her paternal grandparents hid her in a laundry basket and whisked her away to their home in Cambridge so that her mother's relatives, whom Bancroft's grandmother referred to derisively as "those Cogans," would not have an opportunity to raise her as an Irish Catholic.

Bancroft's grandmother, Mary (Shaw) Bancroft, was of Irish descent as well, but kept the fact a close secret in a time when there was intense prejudice against Irish immigrants. Nolan, the Bancroft's coachman, referred to by Bancroft's grandmother as "that impossible creature," along with other Bancroft servants who were quietly Irish Catholic themselves, apparently fueled the war over the infant Mary's soul by smuggling her out to her Cogan relatives for a secret Catholic baptism. Despite everyone's efforts, however, Bancroft identified herself later in life as an agnostic.

Bancroft described herself in *Autobiography of a Spy* as a "wildly imaginative and insatiably curious child" and recalled, "When I was nine, I wrote in my journal, 'I am almost an adult.' When I was twelve, I noted, 'I am now an adult, but nobody seems to realize it.'" Her father, a brilliant man who first worked as a lawyer, then a journalist, and finally as a publisher for the *Wall Street Journal*, remarried, moved to Boston, and had three children with his second wife. Bancroft bonded closely with Nolan, whom she described as "my beloved friend and confidante . . . [who] shared my fascination with disasters—earthquakes, hurricanes, typhoons, blizzards, volcanic eruptions—anything that proved the insignificance of man."

Education

Bancroft was a student at the Cambridge School for Girls until age 15, when her Grandfather Bancroft suffered multiple strokes that left him largely incapacitated. She then joined her father and stepmother, transferring to the Winsor School in Brookline, Massachusetts, where she was awarded her high school diploma in 1921. In the summer of 1921 she went to Europe with some girlfriends under the watchful eyes of a group of chaperones. When she returned she enrolled in Smith College in 1922 against the wishes of her family, particularly her father, who put little value on academic achievements despite the fact that he had earned three Harvard degrees by the age of 21. Bancroft was a model student, but found herself increasingly bored by the freshman curriculum and left after the first three-month semester.

Hugh Bancroft's second wife happened to be the stepdaughter of *Wall Street Journal* owner Clarence Barron. Barron recognized Bancroft's intuitive talent for communication early on, and they maintained a lifelong friendship and correspondence that served as a real-life education of sorts for Bancroft and played a large part in her later successes as a journalist and intelligence operative. Bancroft's 1983 autobiography noted that "I learned more on a wide range of subjects [from him] than I ever learned at school."

Married Life

Bancroft married old friend and U.S. figure skating champion Sherwin C. Badger in December of 1923. They followed Badger's job to Cuba, where they lived for a year

before returning to Brookline. Bancroft admitted in her autobiography, "I still felt trapped in the role of a young married woman. And what was a young married woman supposed to do? Have a baby, of course. I got pregnant almost at once—and hated every minute of it. . . . Finally, after a long and difficult labor lasting nearly three days, the baby arrived. . . . I felt genuinely happy and contented. Perhaps life as a young married woman might be worth living after all." The baby developed erysipelas, a fever-inducing skin disease, and died while still an infant.

Bancroft and Badger moved to New York City, where Badger took a job with the *Wall Street Journal*. Bancroft spent her time writing and helping Badger with his articles and stories. They had a son, Sherwin C., in 1928 and a daughter, Mary Jane, in 1930, then divorced amicably in August of 1932. While still married, Bancroft had an affair with, and almost married, Jewish artist and musician Leopold Mannes, and was surprised to meet with virulent anti-Semitism at the prospect. She began a relationship with Swiss banker Jean G. Rufenacht in 1933. That same year Bancroft's father committed suicide by researching and then concocting a poisonous gas that killed him instantly. Bancroft married Rufenacht on October 10, 1935, and spent the next 18 years as a journalist and freelance writer in Zurich, Switzerland. Tiring of what turned out to be an emotionally and physically abusive marriage, Bancroft divorced Rufenacht in October of 1947.

Relationship with Jung

Bancroft, despite appearing to be exceptionally extroverted, suffered silently from asthma and violent sneezing fits that she suspected were psychosomatic and brought on by emotional turmoil. She sought out the celebrated psychologist Carl Jung, who cured her through analysis and became a lifelong friend. Her relationship with Jung was summarized in her *New York Times* obituary: "To Jung . . . her appeal was textbook obvious. In his scheme of things she was an extroverted intuitive, one who had experienced such fierce inter-family battles for her affections as a child that power had become her natural element. She had such an instinctive knack for wielding it, [Jung] told her, that men seeking or holding power would cherish her advice, as indeed they did." The list of Bancroft's male consorts over time included film director Woody Allen, *Time, Inc.* CEO Henry R. Luce, and Allen Dulles, who laid the foundations of what would become known as the Central Intelligence Agency. Bancroft's interactions with Jung fostered a lifelong interest in psychology, and she often lectured on Jung and others in his field when she had the chance. She also became a trustee of the Jung Foundation in New York after his death, and a contributing editor and writer for *Psychological Perspectives,* a Jungian academic journal.

Translation—U.S. Spy

Bancroft, a fluent translator of German and gifted "people person," was recruited by Dulles to serve as an intelligence analyst for the United States Office of Strategic Services (OSS) from 1941 to 1945, while living and working in Zurich, Switzerland. Bancroft's job was described in

Contemporary Authors as "translat[ing] German dispatches and act[ing] as an intermediary between the German resistance and U.S. intelligence." Bancroft proved adept in this field, even identifying an unknown individual named Josip Broz as being worth considerable attention. Broz later adopted the code name "Tito" and rose to power as the leader of the communist party in Yugoslavia. Her most famous contribution to the war effort was the work she did with German military intelligence officer Hans Bernd Gisevius, who revealed details regarding a bungled attempt to assassinate Hitler on July 20, 1944. Bancroft's job was to get to know Gisevius well enough to determine whether or not he was a double agent, and then relay information he revealed to her during conversations regarding the inner workings of the German government.

Back in the U.S.A.

Bancroft's biographical entry in the *Scribner Encyclopedia of American Lives* described how, in an effort to be more involved once the United States joined the World War II effort despite living in Switzerland, Bancroft "joined the American legation's Office of Coordinator of Information in Bern, where she wrote articles and analyzed German news and Nazi speeches and writings." When she returned to the United States she settled in New York City and immersed herself in local politics and her writing. An active Democrat, Bancroft volunteered for Harriman's campaign for governor of New York in 1954, as well as the Adlai Stevenson's campaign for the U.S. presidency in 1956. She served as an executive member of the Lexington Democratic Club from 1958 to 1960 and wrote numerous freelance articles covering specific political issues.

Bancroft published an autobiographical novel, *Upside Down in the Magnolia Tree,* in 1952. The cover depicted Bancroft as a young girl hanging from her knees in a pink-blossomed magnolia tree with Nolan driving a coach in the background. Her next novel, *The Inseparables,* was published in 1958, and her autobiography in 1983. A prolific writer, Bancroft spent a good portion of her life drafting novels, writing articles and keeping detailed diaries, journals, and notes. Her papers were handed over to the Radcliffe College Library by her estate upon her death, with the list of materials alone filling a full 20 pages. More than 20 boxes preserve journals, invitations, diaries, appointment books, clippings, novel drafts and correspondence with individuals like William F. Buckley, Prince Constantine of Liechtenstein, American author Joan Didion, blueblood hostess Muriel Draper, comedian Bob Hope, Dwight D. Eisenhower, John F. and Robert F. Kennedy, Henry Miller, Norman Mailer, Pat Nixon, Harry S. Truman, and Kurt Vonnegut.

Bancroft died on January 10, 1997, of pneumonia at the age of 93, and requested that her ashes be buried in Groton Cemetery in Massachusetts. Her *New York Times* obituary set a tone that many people took when writing about Bancroft. The article used words like "coquettish," "bewitching," "brilliant," "daring," and "restless," and described Bancroft as "a woman with . . . penetrating intelligence, infallible intuition and boundless verve—not to

mention legs that rarely failed to draw a second glance." Whether she was acting as journalist, companion, or spy, Bancroft excelled in her aims and will be remembered for her skills and style as well as for her service.

Books

Bancroft, Mary, *Autobiography of a Spy,* William Morrow and Company, Inc., 1983.
Contemporary Authors: Volume 118, edited by Hal May, Gale Research Company, 1986.
Contemporary Authors: Volume 156, edited by Terrie M. Rooney, Gale Research, 1997.
Scribner Encyclopedia of Amercan Lives: Volume Five, edited by Kenneth T. Jackson, Charles Scribner's Sons, 2002.

Periodicals

New York Times Biographical Service, January 1997.

Online

"Bancroft, Mary—Papers, 1872–1997: A Finding Aid," *Harvard University Library,* http://www.oasis.harvard.edu:10080/oasis/deliver/~sch00042 (January 7, 2007).
"Penwomen of Cambridge Past," *The Cambridge Public Library,* http://www.ci.cambridge.ma.us/cpl/about/penwomen.html (January 7, 2007).
"Upside Down in the Magnolia Tree," *Amazon.com,* http://www.amazon.com/gp/product/customer-images/B0007E72IM/ref=cm_ciu_pdp_images_all/102-9046364-9171314?ie=UTF8&s=books#gallery (January 7, 2007). □

Frederic Baraga

Slovenian-American Bishop Frederic Baraga (1797–1868) spent much of his career as a Roman Catholic priest and missionary to Native American populations in the Upper Midwest and Canada. He baptized thousands of new converts to Christianity, but appreciated the traditions and customs of the Ojibwa and their cousins, the Ottawa Indians, and knew that much of their culture had likely been lost forever after contact with European settlers. Dubbed the "Snowshoe Priest" during his lifetime because he favored the indigenous footwear when traveling the long distances between communities, Baraga was a gifted linguist who compiled the first-ever Ojibway-English dictionary.

The future bishop was born June 29, 1797, as Irenej Friderik Baraga in the town of Dobrnič, Slovenia. At the time, this part of Slovenia—later one of the Yugoslavian federal republics—was known as the Austrian Dukedom of Carniola, and was part of the Austro-Hungarian Empire. Baraga was born at a castle called *Mala vas,* where his father, Johann Nepomuc Baraga, worked as an overseer. Baraga's family was not titled, but they were

daughter of a professor, he entered the seminary in Laibach in 1821. Ordained on September 21, 1823, he served in several parishes in Slovenia for the next seven years, until he heard about a new group in Vienna that was searching for priests willing to venture into the North American wilderness to convert the Native Americans there to Christianity.

The Leopoldine Society, as it was called, raised money to establish parishes in the remoter parts of the United States and Canada, and Baraga became the first missionary it sent over. The journey took two months, and Baraga arrived in Cincinnati, Ohio—the Leopoldine Society headquarters in America—in mid-January of 1831. He began studying the language of the Ottawa, which was called Anishinaabe in their own tongue, in preparation for his first assignment. He was aided by an innate gift for languages, having already become fluent in German, French, Latin, Italian, and English, as well as his own Slovenian.

The Ottawa language that Baraga took up was part of the Algonquian family of Native American tongues. The Ottawa were traders, and related to the larger ethnic group of Ojibwa, who were sometimes called Chippewa. Ottawa communities dotted the shores of Lake Huron in both present-day Michigan and Ontario, but they had also settled further west in the Grand Traverse Bay area on Lake Michigan, and it was here that Baraga was first sent. In May of 1831 he arrived in Arbre Croche, an Ottawa village that much later became part of Harbor Springs, a Michigan resort community. He found about 650 residents there, and had great success in urging them to formally adopt Christianity, reportedly converting 547 of them.

Authored First Ottawa Text

Baraga realized that simple texts with the Roman Catholic catechism—a question-and-answer form of instruction in the beliefs of the faith—and prayer books in their native language would help him better explain the Christian principles to his potential converts, and guide the recently baptized in their new form of religious worship. He authored a combination of the two forms, using the Ottawa terms he had learned, and had it printed in 1832 with the title *Otawa Anamie-Misinaigan*. This became the first book ever published in the Ottawa language.

In 1833 Baraga was sent to start a second mission at Grand River, a community that later grew into the city of Grand Rapids, but encountered problems when he voiced concern about the liquor that fur traders were exchanging with Native Americans, which he felt was ruinous to the health of the community. In the summer of 1835 he moved much further north, this time to La Pointe, an outpost of the American Fur Company in the northernmost part of Wisconsin, on Lake Superior. The settlement included the nearby Apostle Islands, one of which was home to a trading post dating back to 1693. The village was populated by retired traders for the American Fur Company—the immensely successful venture founded by John Jacob Astor in 1808—as well as by the indigenous Ojibwa; there were also many Métis, a mixed-race group that were the product of intermarriage between French-Canadian or British traders and Native American women.

relatively affluent and could afford to send him away to school. His mother, Maria Katharin Josefa Jenčič Baraga, died in 1808, when Baraga was nine years old. That same year he was sent to Slovenia's largest urban center, Llubljana, to live and study at the home of a private tutor. The city was known by its German name, Laibach, at the time.

Became Fluent in Several Languages

Slovenia's strategic position between the Mediterranean and the Alps occasionally stirred geopolitical rivals, and turmoil flared up during Baraga's youth. Lower Carniola was occupied by French troops the year Baraga was born, and again in 1805 and 1806. In 1809 they reverted once more to French control when the area became part of the Illyrian Provinces of France. Because of this, Baraga learned both German and French as well as Slovenian during his youth. He entered Laibach's gymnasium—a school that offered a college preparatory curriculum—in 1809, and went on to the University of Vienna, from which he received his law degree in 1821.

Baraga had been raised in the Roman Catholic faith, and came to know a famous and influential cleric during his years in Vienna, Clemens Maria Hofbauer (1751–1820). Revered posthumously as the patron saint of Vienna, Hofbauer was known for his challenges to the Emperor, who oversaw the Church in Austria, and influenced Baraga's decision to forego a career in law and train for the priesthood instead. Breaking off an engagement to the

Baraga arrived in this area—a vast, frigid land mass that included Michigan's Upper Peninsula, was sparsely populated, heavily forested, and known mainly for the harshness of its long winter—at a time when there were almost no missionaries in the region, nor had there ever been. He set to work learning the Ojibwa language and proselytizing to both indigenous and Métis. The Ojibwa—or Aanishanabe as they called themselves in their own language—were the largest population group of Native Americans after the Cherokee and Navajo in the continental United States. In his eight years at La Pointe, Baraga baptized nearly a thousand Native Americans and whites, and authored his first text in the Ojibwa language, a sermon book tilted *Gagikwe-Masiniagan.*

Achieved Fame as "Snowshoe Priest"

Once Baraga had established a successful mission, he usually left it in the care of another priest and moved on to start another one. In 1843 he arrived in L'Anse, on the shores of Lake Superior at the base of the Keweenaw Peninsula in the Upper Peninsula. The entire region was now a boom town, thanks to newly discovered copper and iron deposits in the Upper Peninsula; new European immigrants with mining backgrounds began flooding in. Baraga found himself the steward of a rapidly growing Roman Catholic population as well as the unofficial one for the Protestant settlers. In 1848 church authorities elevated him to the rank of vicar general; five years later he was consecrated bishop of Amyzonia, which was the original term for the diocese of Upper Michigan, later called the diocese of Marquette. Its seat was originally in Sault Ste. Marie. Furthermore, the bishop of Toronto put Baraga in charge of missions located on the north shore of Lake Superior from Bruce Mines to Thunder Bay, and a few even further north, such as one at Lake Nipigon.

In all, Baraga oversaw an 80,000-square mile territory of land and water, and became increasingly devoted to his vocation as he grew older. He traveled hundreds of miles every year in order to carry out his work, and used the Ojibwa modes of transportation—a canoe in the warmer months, and snowshoes for winter travel. In one letter, he wrote that he planned to visit La Pointe and L'Anse and then go on to Fond du Lac, Wisconsin, a journey of some 690 miles that he would make on foot. "When a person must walk upon such snowshoes all day long and for that many days in succession, especially in those trackless forests, he cannot travel without extreme fatigue and almost total exhaustion," he admitted in the letter, according to an article in the Minneapolis *Star Tribune* by Larry Oakes. He also rose at 3 or 4 a.m. daily in order to devote three hours of his morning to prayer.

Baraga became famous throughout northern Michigan and neighboring areas as the beloved "Snowshoe Priest," and even enjoyed some eminence in Europe, thanks to his writings about his work with the Ojibwa. He was respected by native groups as well as Protestant newcomers to the region, and venerated by his Roman Catholic congregation as an exemplar of Christ's teachings in practice. During the worst months of winter, Baraga remained inside—his permanent home was in L'Anse—and studied the Ojibwa language. He authored two significant works on this Anishinaabe dialect, which was widely spoken in the Upper Peninsula, Wisconsin, and Minnesota. The first, *Theoretical and Practical Grammar of the Otchipwe Language,* was published in Detroit in 1850. His *Dictionary of the Otchipwe Language,* published in Cincinnati in 1853, remained in print for decades to come, and provided an invaluable tool for the priests and other settlers who ventured into the region.

First Bishop of Marquette

In 1865 Baraga moved to Marquette, Michigan, when this city near the shore of Lake Superior was named the new seat of the Upper Michigan diocese. A church commensurate with this status was built, and in 1866 the Cathedral of St. Peter was dedicated by Baraga during a Mass. Later that year, however, Baraga suffered a stroke in Baltimore during an important conference of American bishops; he reportedly begged his aide to help him on the train before his fellow clerics realized his condition and prevented him from returning to what had become his home. Over the next two years, Baraga's health declined further, and he died in Marquette on January 19, 1868. He was buried 11 days later in the Cathedral of St. Peter crypt, a day on which not even a blizzard snowstorm prevented hundreds of mourners from paying their respects.

The Cathedral of St. Peter sits on Baraga Street in Marquette, and there is also a Michigan county—which includes L'Anse, the site of his fourth mission—and village named in his honor. Devoted followers formed a society to honor him, the Bishop Baraga Association. More than a century after his death, the Association presented reams of research and testimony to an official church committee in Marquette in 1972. This hearing was the first step in the process toward Roman Catholic sainthood. Following this, the Vatican officially deemed Baraga a "Servant of God," a designation that is the first step on the path to sainthood. One younger priest, inspired by Baraga's stories of missionary work in America, was Father John Neumann (1811–1860), who later became bishop of Philadelphia and one of the first men and women to be elevated to sainthood for their religious work in America.

Periodicals

Milwaukee Journal, January 30, 1897.
Milwaukee Sentinel, March 27, 1899.
New York Times, September 19, 1972.
Star Tribune (Minneapolis, MN), August 30, 1997.

Online

Baraga, Frederic, *Dictionary of Canadian Biography Online,* http://www.biographi.ca/EN/ShowBio.asp?BioId=38403 (November 26, 2006).
Frederic Baraga, *New Advent Catholic Encyclopedia,* http://www.newadvent.org/cathen/02282b.htm (November 26, 2006). □

Agatha Barbara

Politician Agatha Barbara (1923–2002) achieved several significant firsts for women in her native Malta. During her long career devoted to social and economic reform, Barbara was Malta's first female legislator, cabinet minister, and president. This last post she held from 1982 to 1987, and with that she retired after 40 years in elected office. Known for her fierce commitment to the ideals of the Malta Labour Party (MLP), "Barbara once threw an inkpot at an opponent during a parliamentary debate," reported her *Times* of London obituary. "He ducked, and the pot hit a painting, where the stain remains to this day."

Barbara was born on March 11, 1923, in Żabbar, a town on one of the seven Mediterranean islands that made up Malta and where some exterior walls of houses still bore scars from cannon fire that dated back to Żabbar's uprising against French rule around 1800. The Republic of Malta that Barbara presided over in the 1980s had not yet come into being at the time of her birth: instead it was part of the British Empire and an important naval port for the British Navy since it had passed from French to British rule formally in 1814. This pair of European superpowers would be the last in a long line of foreign rulers over Malta dating back to the Phoenicians, who landed around 1000 BCE and found its aboriginal population mysteriously vanished. The Phoenicians made it an outpost of their Mediterranean sea trade; Roman rule followed that, and Malta's strategic position south of Sicily and near the coast of North Africa made it an attractive property to the Arabs, who held it until 1091. For some 250 years Malta belonged to one of the Roman Catholic militias that had fought in the Crusades—the Sovereign Military Hospitaller Order of Saint John of Jerusalem, of Rhodes and of Malta, known in shorter form as the Knights of Malta—who lost it to forces commanded by Napoleon (1769–1821) in 1798.

Determined to Attend High School

During Barbara's youth, the British military and colonial authorities were the main employers in Malta. Her father was a tug master, a skilled pilot of tugboats used to guide large freighters in and out of harbors or narrow straits, and he worked for the British Navy on the route between Valletta, Malta's capital city, and Alexandria, Egypt. Like many Maltese of his generation and before that, Joseph Barbara had little schooling, and had never learned to read. When he hoped for a promotion that would have brought a meaningful increase in pay, Barbara was 11 years old and recalled that her father brought home a "book of sea regulations and . . . made me read one paragraph after another until he learned the codes off by heart," she told journalist Miriam Dunn in an interview that appeared on the *Malta Today* website. Unfortunately, her father's superiors real-

ized his ruse, and while they gave him the promotion, they kept his pay at the same level.

Barbara's mother, Antonia, struggled to feed the nine children in the family on her husband's wages, and as a teenager Barbara begged her parents to pay the fee for high school, which she desperately wanted to attend. There were no free secondary schools in Malta at the time, and she was able to convince them, but her chance for a college education was cut short when World War II erupted. Malta's strategic position made it attractive to both sides in that conflict; the British had a valuable naval station as well as listening post near to the shipping lanes of the enemy, which in this case was an alliance of Italy and Nazi Germany. Nazi planes bombarded Malta heavily for the first three years of the war, until a large section of Italy fell to Allied forces in 1943. Barbara worked as an air-raid warden during these early years of the war, and also supervised one of the Victory Kitchens, which had been set up by the British military to feed the Maltese. The entire nation of Malta was awarded the George Cross, the highest civilian honor in the British Commonwealth, for their bravery during the war; it was the only instance of the Cross being bestowed on an entire population.

First Woman Elected to Parliament

After the war, Barbara became a teacher at Flores College, but was drawn into the burgeoning political movement for independence from Britain. Colonial authorities granted Malta self-rule after World War II, but as she recalled to Dunn, there was high unemployment and growing social unrest, while those "governing us were not bothered about how these people were going to live. At the time, there was no social justice at all. I wanted to help put things right. I wanted to help people." She joined the *Partit Laburista* (Malta Labour Party, or MLP), a Social Democrat party that was initially a pro-British group, in contrast to the *Partit Nazzjonalista,* or Nationalist Party of Malta. As part of the self-rule scheme, a new constitution was drafted, and it gave Maltese women the right to vote for the first time. Roman Catholic clergy were vociferously opposed to this, but the constitution went into effect in 1947, the same year that legislative elections were held. Barbara ran for one of the 65 seats in the Il-Kamra tar-Rappreżentantion, or Malta's House of Representatives, on the MLP ticket, and was continuously re-elected for the next 34 years.

With that 1947 election, Barbara became the first woman to serve in Malta's unicameral legislature, and in 1955 she became the first cabinet minister as well, when new Prime Minister Dominic "Dom" Mintoff appointed her as his education minister. It was during this three-year period that Barbara achieved what would become her most important legacy in her commitment to improve Malta's standard of living: full-time schooling was made compulsory for all children under the age of 14. Many new schools and trained teachers were needed to meet the expected demand, however, and over the first several months of 1955 Barbara supervised a massive hiring of teachers and the construction of 44 new facilities. By September of 1955 the new education law went into effect, just five months after the decree, thanks to her management of the program. The rest of her stint as education minister was equally busy: she oversaw the establishment of a teachers' training college; transportation services were set up for elementary and secondary students, as well as basic medical care. Barbara also ordered a survey of the developmentally disabled and the vision- and hearing-impaired in the country, and established the first schools for them in Malta. Perhaps most important, she ensured that science classes were open to students of both genders, unlike the high school that she had attended, which was restricted to males.

Barbara supported the MLP shift toward full independence from Britain that came later in the 1950s. The party had initially favored the idea of integration with Britain, which was briefly but seriously considered in a 1955 conference in which the British government agreed to give Malta representation in the House of Commons—the only time a British territory was made such an offer. Mintoff and the rest of the MLP supported the idea, but the Nationalist Party as well as the Catholic church hierarchy were opposed, and the stalemate resulted in a series of political crises and turmoil related to the economic future of Malta. There was, for example, a large deficit that the British government hoped to pass on to the Maltese government, and promises made by the British Ministry of Defence (MoD), the largest employer on the islands, regarding future employment numbers for native Maltese. When the stalemate reached a crisis point, Mintoff resigned and urged the Maltese to fight for independence now, rather than integration. With that, the period of self-rule granted by the British

after the war was revoked to prevent further unrest on April 24, 1958.

Arrested and Jailed

The re-imposition of direct rule prompted outrage and a bitter general strike on Malta. In May of 1958, Barbara and the former health minister were arrested and charged with intimidation because of an event that occurred a few weeks earlier during the general strike. They were charged with obstructing the path of an ambulance, but she and her colleague had urged it to turn back, warning that protesters would probably overturn it. For this, the British authorities sentenced her to 43 days of hard labor, and she served 32 of them, with 11 days credited for time already served. Direct rule lasted until 1962, and Malta was granted independence two years later, though it remained a member of the British Commonwealth. The MLP was the opposition party until 1971, when it took the majority in legislative elections again and Mintoff returned as prime minister. Once again, he named Barbara to serve as minister of education.

Barbara's three-year stint as education minister was once again notable for the reforms she pushed through. Education became compulsory until the age of 16, and new trade and technical schools were established. University fees were abolished, and the government, in line with many Social Democratic European nations, began to offer cost-of-living grants for students from the poorest families. Barbara's portfolio also included responsibilities for culture, and she enacted changes that brought museum treasures and folklore activities to cities outside of Valletta.

In 1974 Malta became the Republic of Malta, with all executive authority resting in the president, who was appointed by the House of Representatives and could also appoint the prime minister. Mintoff, who would serve as prime minister for the next decade, made Barbara his minister for labor, culture, and welfare that same year. Again, she was able to implement several historic reforms, including a law that required employers to pay a woman the same amount they did a man for the same job. Paid maternity leave for women, a work week restricted to 40 hours, retirement pensions, and unemployment benefits were all enacted during her term as labor minister.

Became President of Malta

Barbara had served as deputy prime minister and acting prime minister at various points in her career. On February 16, 1982, she was elected by the House of Representatives to a five-year term as President of Malta, and became the first Maltese woman to achieve that distinction. The position was essentially one of a constitutional head of state, for much of the executive power still rested with the prime minister. During this period, however, Barbara was able to snub the British—the last of whose fleet had left in 1979—in reaction to her 1958 jail sentence. "In 1986 the Government lifted a seven-year ban on British warships to allow a visit by the frigate HMS Brazen to commemorate the 44th anniversary of the arrival of the crucial Allied relief convoy of 1942," noted her *Times* of London obituary. "She, as President, avoided all the official ceremonies."

Barbara stepped down from office in 1987, and retired to Żabbar. She died there on February 4, 2002, at the age of 78. She never married, and once told an interviewer that she had no regrets over her decision to forego a family for a career in politics. "I realised I couldn't have everything, but I also knew that whichever path I took there would be ups and downs," she told Dunn. "I accepted that."

Periodicals

Times (London, England), June 14, 1958; February 6, 2002.

Online

Agatha Barbara, *Malta Today,* http://www.maltatoday.com.mt/
2002/0210/l7a.html (December 18, 2006).
Agatha, The True Socialist, *Malta Today,* http://www.maltatoday
.com.mt/2001/0401/people.html (December 18, 2006).
Miss Agatha Barbara: President of Malta (1982–1987), Department of Information—Government of Malta, http://www.doi
.gov.mt/EN/islands/presidents/barbara_agatha.asp (December 18, 2006). □

Mrs. Barbauld

British author Anna Laetitia Barbauld (1743–1825) was one of just a handful of women writers of her era. Referred to as Mrs. Barbauld in the literature of the time, the largely home-schooled daughter of a schoolmaster came from a prominent liberal family and moved in distinguished circles throughout her life.

Barbauld penned several lengthy poems as well as literary criticism and political commentary, but maybe be best remembered for the early childhood teaching materials she wrote at a time when she and her husband ran their own school in Suffolk. Her 1778 title, *Lessons for Children,* and the subsequent *Hymns in Prose for Children* which appeared three years later, became ubiquitous titles on the bookshelves of English schools and homes for decades to come.

Born Anna Laetitia Aikin on June 20, 1743, Barbauld spent her childhood and early teen years in Kibworth-Harcourt, a village in the county of Leicestershire in central England. Her mother was Jane Jennings Aikin, and her father, John Aikin, was trained as a Presbyterian minister. He was also an educator who became director of a school for boys in the village, and thanks to this Barbauld received a rather solid education for a young woman of her era, including instruction in Greek and Latin. She and her brother, John, four years her junior, remained close throughout their lives.

Raised in Intellectual Atmosphere

Reverend Aikin was a Dissenter, the name given to a loose-knit coalition of ministers and teachers who objected to the strict rules imposed on schools and their curricula. The laws and decrees, imposed by the British monarchy and parliament, were designed to prevent a recurrence of the religious strife that had torn England apart a century earlier during its Restoration and civil war periods. In short, Dissenters, who formed their own schools and even communities in some cases, opposed the king's influence over the Church of England and its requisite religious education course of the era. Several prominent schools came out of this movement, and one of the best known among them was the Warrington Academy in the Cheshire town of the same name.

Barbauld and her family moved to Warrington in 1758 when her father was hired as a teacher at the Academy. She was 15 years old at the time, and would not marry until she was nearly 30. The intervening years were spent immersed in educational pursuits, which were largely self-directed because women were barred from most institutions of higher education such as Oxford and Cambridge universities, and would be until well into the nineteenth century. As a young woman Barbauld also formed close ties with several important Dissenting figures of the era, including Joseph Priestley (1733–1804), a close family friend and chemist known as the co-discoverer of oxygen.

Barbauld's family background led her into political movements of the era. She and others of her generation were particularly enthused by events on the Mediterranean isle of Corsica, considered the first democratic republic of the Enlightenment Age; Corsica's brief period of sovereignty pre-dated the sweeping reforms of the French Revolution but was quashed by invading French forces in 1768. One of her first poems, "Corsica: An Ode," was written a year later in homage to the failed struggle. It appeared in her first volume of poetry, simply titled *Poems,* which was published in 1773. The work was well-received—though published woman poets were still a relative rarity at the time—and helped establish Barbauld's literary reputation in London. She was reportedly encouraged to write by her brother, who had enjoyed some success with his own work; they collaborated on a joint effort, *Miscellaneous Pieces in Prose,* that appeared in August of 1773.

Founded School in Suffolk

On May 26, 1774, Barbauld wed Rochemont Barbauld, a former Warrington Academy student who was by then a Dissenting minister. He was six years her junior, and friends and family were uneasy about the match, because the Barbauld family had a history of mental illness. The union produced no children—they were childless by choice, fearing that the mental illness might pass on to a new generation—but they did adopt one of her brother's sons, Charles, and raised the boy as their own. In the first few years of their marriage, Rochemont found a post as a minister for a parish in Suffolk, while Barbauld continued her literary career. In 1775 *Devotional Pieces, Compiled from the Psalms and the Book of Job* appeared in print.

Barbauld and her husband soon founded their own academy in Suffolk, called the Palgrave School. It proved so successful that she was invited to serve as director of a new women's college planned by noted social reformer Elizabeth Montagu (1718–1800), but Barbauld did not believe that most women were suited for a rigorous education, despite her own talents and abilities, and declined the offer. The Palgrave School thrived until 1785, and it was during this period that Barbauld produced her most important educational materials for the very young. The first was a reading primer, *Lessons for Children,* which appeared in 1778. Its author "urges children to explore the animal, vegetable, and mineral worlds around them," noted Mary Beth Wolicky in an essay for the *Dictionary of Literary Biography.* "As Barbauld was already a respected author and poet when she wrote these pedagogical tracts, her new approach helped to change the direction of children's literature. The *Lessons* were read and alluded to by people of all religious affiliations throughout the nineteenth century."

Barbauld also wrote *Hymns in Prose for Children,* a 1781 title that would likewise endure for several generations to come. It was widely published in North America, too, and even in other languages, and remained in print for more than a hundred years. Her professional life shifted considerably, however, in the mid-1780s. When her husband began to display symptoms of the dreaded mental illness, they sold the Palgrave School, spent a year in France, and settled in London in June of 1786. A year later, Rochemont took a position as pastor of the Rosslyn Hill parish church in north London.

The focus of Barbauld's writings now shifted to political reform. In 1790 she penned *An Address to the Opposers of the Repeal of the Corporation and Test Acts.* Both of these laws had been in place for more than a century and were a form of discrimination against the Dissenters, as well as Roman Catholics in England. According to the Test Act of 1673, for example, public servants were required to be professed members of the Church of England. The Corporation Act, which dated back to 1661, required all elected officials or members of corporations to utter the Oath of Supremacy to the Church of England within one year of taking office. Like many Dissenters and Enlightenment-educated liberals, Barbauld perceived both laws as impositions on civil liberties and a threat to a free society. "Your church is in no danger because we are of a different church," she wrote in her *Address* about the Church of England's control, "but it will be in great danger whenever it has within itself many who have thrown aside its doctrines, or even, who do not embrace them in the simple and obvious sense. All the power and policy of man cannot continue a system long after its truth has ceased to be acknowledged, or an establishment long after its has ceased to contribute to utility."

Barbauld's inflammatory words were published anonymously, but most of her compatriots as well as her foes recognized the tract as her work. In 1791 she issued *The Epistle to William Wilberforce,* a poem paying homage to Britain's leading abolitionist. Like many of Wilberforce's supporters, she and her family boycotted sugar for many years, because it was a product that was imported from British colonies in the Caribbean where slave labor was used to harvest it. She also spoke out against England's renewal of hostilities with France in 1793, writing in *Sins of Government, Sins of the Nation* that "freedom is a good thing, but if a nation is not disposed to accept of it, it is not to be presented to them on the point of a bayonet."

Marriage Ended on Tragic Note

Barbauld continued to work with her brother on various projects. He edited a periodical called *Monthly Magazine* for a number of years, and she was a regular contributor. They also collaborated on *Evenings at Home; or, The Juvenile Budget Opened: Consisting of a Variety of Miscellaneous Pieces for the Instruction and Amusement of Young Persons,* which was published between 1792 and 1795 and sold extremely well at the time; again, it remained a staple in most middle-class English households for several generations. She also edited or wrote introductions and critical essays for several other titles, including a volume of correspondence from the British author Samuel Richardson (1689–1761), one of the first important novelists in the English language.

When John Aikin moved to Stoke Newington, a village outside of London at the time but later incorporated into the borough of Hackney, she and her husband followed him there in 1802. But Rochemont's condition deteriorated, and he grew abusive towards his wife. In January of 1808, he came after her with a knife in hand, and she fled through a window of their house; they separated two months later. "Placed in care in London, he appeared to be improving, but he bribed his attendant for permission to walk alone outside and was discovered dead on November 11, 1808, in the New River," according to Wolicky, who added, "Barbauld was deeply affected by his death and ceased writing for several years."

Barbauld had already agreed, however, to a major project by then, and completed it by the 1810 deadline: she had been invited to choose the novels and write the prefaces for a 50-volume set called *British Novelists* from the publisher Rivington. In January of 1812, one of her most notable poems appeared in print. Titled *Eighteen Hundred and Eleven,* it imagined what a visitor to London might come upon at a future date should England fail to address its abundance of social ills. Her narrator saw the city's most cherished landmark, St. Paul's Cathedral, in ruins, and lamented, "England, the seat of arts, be only known/By the gray ruin and the mouldering stone;/That Time may tear the garland from her brow,/And Europe sit in dust, as Asia now."

The poem was condemned by many for its pessimistic view of England's future, and was attacked in the press. Even a longtime friend of her family, Robert Southey, was revealed to be the author of the most scathing review, and Barbauld published no other works after it. She died on March 9, 1825, in Stoke Newington. Her niece, Lucy Aikin (1781–1864), wrote a memoir of her aunt, but interest in Barbauld and her literary achievements faded considerably after her death. Feminist literary historians in the latter half of the twentieth century rediscovered her poetry and prose, and a long overdue scholarly analysis of her significance to women's literary history began in the last decades of the twentieth century.

Books

Dictionary of Literary Biography, Volume 158: *British Reform Writers, 1789–1832,* edited by Gary Kelly and Edd Applegate, Gale, 1996.

Periodicals

Nation, March 26, 1874.
Review of English Studies, May 1996.

Online

Anna Lætitia Aikin Barbauld (1743–1825), Celebrating Women Writers, http://www.digital.library.upenn.edu/women/barbauld/biography.html (November 20, 2006).
Anna Laetitia Barbauld Website, http://www.usask.ca/english/barbauld/ (November 20, 2006). □

James Barry

British physician James Barry (c. 1795–1865) was a distinguished army surgeon, but achieved that professional rank by disguising herself as a man. She maintained the ruse from 1809, the year she entered medical school in Edinburgh, until the moments following her death, when a maid discovered her true gender. Barry's deception made her the first woman in British history to legitimately practice medicine.

The best guesses of Barry's true identity place her as the daughter of Mary Ann Bulkeley (or Bulkley in other sources), named Alice when she was born around 1795. Her mother was the sister of James Barry (1741–1806), an artist who enjoyed professional acclaim during his lifetime as one of Britain's first Romantic painters. Bulkeley was reportedly abandoned by her husband and left destitute, and her brother took her and her two daughters into his household. Barry's uncle and namesake had an impressive circle of friends that included British feminist writer Mary Wollstonecraft (1759–1797) and David Erskine, the 11th Earl of Buchan (1742–1829). Buchan, a Scottish aristocrat, was a progressive-minded agitator and a notable supporter of women's rights as well. When Barry's uncle died in 1806, Lord Buchan assumed responsibility for the 11-year-old niece.

Entered Medical School

Barry seems to have begun calling herself Miranda Barry, a name borrowed from another renowned family friend, General Francisco de Miranda (1750–1816), a Venezuelan revolutionary and French Revolution fighter. Miranda's home in London had a library rich in hard-to-find medical books, and he reportedly permitted Barry access to it whenever she liked. In 1809 she enrolled at the Edinburgh School of Medicine at the unusually young age of 14. But perhaps even more daring was the decision to mask her gender and dress as a boy. For a young woman of gifted intellect and an interest in science, nearly all professions would have been closed to her in this era, and even universities in Britain did not yet admit women. Medicine, in particular, was deemed far too gory a field, and in the discriminatory attitudes of the era, the male establishment pointed out that a woman physician might faint at a crucial moment when her life-saving skills were needed.

It is known that Barry spent her summer breaks at Buchan's Scottish estate, Dryburgh Abbey, and he probably helped in her ruse. After graduating in 1812, she went on to London for further study and training at St. Thomas's and Guy's hospitals, where one of her instructors was the famed surgeon Sir Astley Paston Cooper (1768–1841), best known for his advances in treating hernias and aneurysms. In 1813, by now firmly committed to presenting herself as a man, Barry made a bold move and joined an institution in which masculinity was firmly entrenched: the British Army. Applying to serve in its military medical corps, Barry likely knew that no extensive physical examination was required for doctor-applicants. It also seems likely that in the course of her long career, a few of her superiors may have known of her true identity, but for whatever reasons decided to protect her identity as well.

After a stint at an army camp in Plymouth, Barry was posted to Cape Town, South Africa, with the rank of Hospital Assistant and was soon promoted to Physician to the Governor's Household. The governor was Lord Charles Somerset (1767–1831), a widower, who was a friend of Buchan's and therefore may have known Barry was a woman. Furthermore, there were persistent rumors in Cape Town that the governor and the physician had an unnaturally close relationship, with the unspoken assumption that they were gay. Barry wore the clothing of a man of her rank and status, adding a red wig and three-inch heels to all footwear to boost her diminutive height of just five feet. She also carried the longest sword available, and quickly developed a reputation for being quick to anger, especially at slights to her masculinity or unnaturally high voice. Such comments usually resulted in an undue amount of trouble for her critic, and she was known to challenge many a fellow to a duel, though probably only participated in one.

Named in Libel Suit

It was not Barry's ruse that earned her trouble in Cape Town, however: it was her protestations against local quack doctors and the ineffective, even toxic, medicines sold by unlicensed pharmacists. Her attempts to have both professions better policed by the colonial government earned her some determined enemies. At one point, a piece of graffiti was written on a wall in which its author claimed to have witnessed an act of "buggery," a British term for sodomy, between Barry and Lord Somerset. A libel lawsuit ensued, which resulted in a great deal of publicity throughout the empire for both parties.

Barry seems to have disappeared for a time. She claimed to have spent time in Mauritius, an Indian Ocean island that was also a British colonial possession, between 1819 and 1820, but there are no official records of James Barry, physician, either there or elsewhere during these months. By November of 1821 she had returned to the Cape, but Somerset had remarried. With the scandal cooled, Barry was promoted again, this time to Colonial Medical Inspector in the Cape Colony. Again, her strong opinions and reformist zeal earned her enemies, for once she began touring the hospitals, prisons, asylums, and leper colonies under her jurisdiction, she was appalled by the conditions. At one hospital, for example, she found animals roaming freely about, including dogs, ducks, and pigeons. Barry proved to be slightly ahead of her time in her belief that proper sanitation and hygiene could prevent deadly infections that patients often picked up during their hospital stays. Diet was also crucial, she believed, and urged that more nutritious fare be served to the recuperating; she herself was a vegetarian who kept a pet goat that provided fresh goat's milk.

In 1826 Barry entered the medical history books for performing one of the first successful caesarean operations—an emergency abdominal incision made to remove a newborn when standard childbirth has stalled or been deemed too dangerous—in which neither mother nor infant died. This took place when she was called to the Cape Town home of a prominent merchant, Thomas Munnik, and the parents named their infant son James Barry Munnik in gratitude. She remained in the Cape Colony for another year or two, and then went on to Mauritius, where records show that she served as an army staff surgeon. From there, she was posted to several British properties in the Caribbean, including Jamaica, Barbados, Antigua, and in Trinidad, where she advanced to the rank of Principal Medical Officer in the colony. But in 1845 she fell ill with yellow fever, a viral disease that was a leading cause of death in many parts of the world well into the twentieth century. Her assistant surgeon apparently discovered her true gender when she was seriously ill, but she managed to elicit a promise from him never to tell anyone before she recovered enough to sail to England for further care.

Toured Crimean War Hospitals

Other posts that Barry held included Malta, the Mediterranean isle that was a key British shipping port at the time, and the Greek island of Corfu, another British outpost where she was promoted to Deputy Inspector General. When British forces allied with the French to help Turkey fight Imperial Russia in the conflict known as the Crimean War (1854–56), Barry traveled to the area—now Ukraine—but did not serve, for her rank was so high that battlefield duty was not required of her. During her stint touring the field hospitals, however, she did manage to make an enemy of Florence Nightingale (1820–1910), the nursing pioneer whose efforts in Crimea were instrumental in establishing the profession as a respectable one for women. The saintly "Lady of the Lamp," as Nightingale was known, received Barry at her station, Scutari Hospital, but described the doctor as "the most hardened creature I ever met throughout the Army," according to Laura Collins in a *Mail on Sunday* article.

Age did not temper Barry's prickly personality or her habit of insubordination with her superiors in asserting her views on medicine. At one point she was forced to return to England under armed guard, but avoided official rebuke and was eventually packed off to Canada in 1857, where she was made Inspector General of Hospitals for Upper and Lower Canada, as the British holdings in present-day Ontario, Quebec, and Newfoundland were then known. There she continued her rather extravagant lifestyle, which had come to include a manservant, footman, and driver for her red sleigh, in which she sat swathed in furs. She also had several white poodles, all named Psyche—perhaps a reference to the mortal figure in Greek mythology of the same name, a woman so beautiful that no man would marry her. The dogs always slept near her, likely to alert her to any nighttime curiosity-seekers.

Sensational Stories of "Lady Doctor"

Barry fell ill in Canada around 1859, and went back to England. She was required to retire at the age of 65, but—not surprisingly—resisted the order vehemently. Her final few years were spent living in rented rooms in London, having cut all ties with her family decades ago and failing to form long-lasting friendships because of her secret. She died in London on July 25, 1865, of dysentery. She left explicit instructions that no post-mortem examination be conducted on her body after death, but a maid who was preparing the body for burial discovered her gender. The woman immediately informed the physician who had cared for Barry in her final hours that "Dr. Barry was a female and that I was a pretty doctor not to know this and that she would not like to be attended by me," according to Brooke Allen in the *New York Times Book Review*.

The story appeared in newspapers and captivated the public for several days, and there seemed to be physical evidence that she once carried a child quite late into term, for there were stretch marks across the abdomen. This may have been the reason behind the mysterious absence for several months between 1820 and 1821. One posthumous account of her life in the *Malta Times* of September 7, 1865, called readers' attention to a former Army doctor on the island and for many years in the Cape Colony, who "was excessively plain, of feeble proportions, and laboured under the imperfection of a ludicrously squeaking voice."

Barry was laid to rest at Kensal Green Cemetery in London, but her intriguing tale has proven the basis for many novels, plays, and films well into the twenty-first century. British actor Rachel Weisz (born 1971) was cast in the role of Barry in a 2007 feature film, *Heaven and Earth*.

Books

Notable Women Scientists, Gale, 2000.

Periodicals

Mail on Sunday (London, England), November 10, 2002.
Malta Times, September 7, 1865.
New York Times, February 2, 2003.
Sun (London, England), January 19, 2006.
Sunday Times (London, England), January 9, 2005. □

Baruj Benacerraf

Venezuelan-born medical researcher Baruj Benacerraf (born 1920) shared the 1980 Nobel Prize in Physiology or Medicine for his investigations into the workings of the human immune system.

Today immunology is one of the hottest topics in medical science, affecting such vital fields as cancer treatment, organ transplantation protocols, and research into autoimmune disease. When Benacerraf entered the field, however, the immune system was much less well understood than it is today. Snell, one of Benacerraf's collaborators on the research that led to their joint Nobel Prize, reputedly said, according to William Borders of the *New York Times,* that the number of people who understood his work at the time could be "counted on his fingers." But Benacerraf's research laid the groundwork for a host of future scientific developments. As a researcher, an educator, and an administrator, Benacerraf has been a highly influential figure in modern medical science.

Had Multicultural Background

Baruj Benacerraf (pronounced Bar-OOK Ben-ah-se-RAHFF) was born into an immigrant Jewish family in Caracas, Venezuela, on October 29, 1920. His father had come to the Americas from Spanish-controlled Morocco in search of improved economic prospects; he started a shoe and textile business in Venezuela and prospered, eventually establishing other enterprises, including an import operation and a bank. Benacerraf's mother came from France, and Benacerraf was educated mostly in the French language. The family moved to Paris when he was five, but in 1939, with the outbreak of World War II, they returned to Venezuela and to the family businesses that had continued to flourish. In 1940 Benacerraf was sent to the United States, where his family felt he could get the best university education.

The hope was that Benacerraf would take over his father's place in those businesses, but Benacerraf showed no inclination to do so. Teachers had inculcated in him strong interests in both science and the arts; he became a competent flutist. Benacerraf, however, strove for a compromise. "The only thing that was considered appropriate, that would lead to a career in the mind of people who are self-made like my father, was the profession of doctor, lawyer, and engineer. Being a doctor was what appealed to me most," he explained to Otile McManus of the *Boston Globe.* In 1940 Benacerraf enrolled at Columbia University's School of General Studies, a branch of the school aimed at nontraditional and foreign students. He blazed through the program in three years, finishing the pre-medical requirements and earning a bachelor of science degree in 1942.

Benacerraf then began applying to medical schools, but found his way blocked. "At that time, it was very hard for Jews to get into medical school," he told McManus. "This country was strongly anti-Semitic in the 1940s. There were quotas. In addition, there was a tendency not to take in foreigners." Benacerraf applied to some 25 schools, including several where he later held top positions, but was turned down by all of them despite his strong accomplishments as an undergraduate. Finally, a friend who worked as an assistant to the president of the Medical College of Virginia smoothed the way for his admission there, and he entered the school in 1943. He was also drafted into the U.S. Army that year but was allowed to finish his schooling with the understanding that he would use his skills in service to the military after receiving his degree.

Also in 1943 Benacerraf married his wife, the former Annette Dreyfus. She too had been raised in France, and the two met in Columbia's French club. She was a descendant of both Alfred Dreyfus, the French Jewish military officer whose wrongful arrest precipitated the "Dreyfus affair" scandal of the 1890s, and of Nobel Prize–winning French biologist Jacques Monod. Annette Benacerraf would often assist her husband in his laboratory work but always refused credit for her contributions. Benacerraf received his medical degree after three years of study, did an internship at Queens General Hospital in New York, and was commissioned as a first lieutenant in the Army Medical Corps in 1946.

Served in France

Pleased to be sent to France, Benacerraf served in Paris and in the city of Nancy before being discharged in 1947. Then, "motivated by intellectual curiosity," he wrote in the autobiographical statement he supplied upon winning the Nobel Prize, he "decided upon a career in medical research at a time when such a choice was not fashionable." Partly because he had suffered from bronchial asthma as a child, he had become curious about allergies and the immune system. He consulted scientists in New York to whom his teachers in Richmond had recommended him, and they steered him toward the laboratory of a pioneering immunologist, Elvin Kabat. Benacerraf began working in Kabat's laboratory in 1948.

"Training with Elvin Kabat was one of the significant experiences in my development as a scientist," Benacerraf wrote in his autobiographical statement. In two years of work with Kabat, Benacerraf obtained a solid grounding in scientific rigor and in the importance of quantifiable results, and he began to gain a deeper understanding of hypersensitivity mechanisms and immune system malfunctions that lead to such phenomena as allergies. Benacerraf's daughter, Beryl, was born in 1949. She grew up to become a radiologist who made major clinical advances in the interpretation of ultrasound fetal images.

Beginning around that time, Benacerraf's career was disrupted, but not derailed, by family problems. His father, by then living in Paris, suffered an incapacitating stroke, and Benacerraf moved there to be closer to him. For six years Benacerraf juggled family business commitments with his own research. He was lucky, at first, to find a job at Paris's Broussais Hospital in the lab of immunology researcher Bernard Halpern, the discoverer of antihistamines. There, working with Italian researcher Guido Biozzi, Benacerraf performed experiments that deepened his understanding of the way phagocytes—cells that eat material extrinsic to the healthy body, such as contaminants—do their work.

Halpern, however, finally informed Benacerraf in no uncertain terms that as a foreigner his chances of establishing a permanent career in France were slim. The truth of Halpern's information was driven home when Benacerraf tried but failed to find a job with another lab in Paris. He returned to the United States in 1956 and was happy to be recruited for the position of assistant professor of pathology at New York University (NYU). The agent responsible for bringing Benacerraf to NYU was Lewis Thomas, the popular physician and essayist who later wrote the book *The Lives of a Cell*. Benacerraf was elevated to associate professor in 1958 and to full professor in 1960.

Investigated Genetic Susceptibility to Disease

The late 1950s and early 1960s were professionally satisfying for Benacerraf as he entered his most productive years as a researcher. "The scientific atmosphere at New York University during that period was particularly favorable to the development of Immunology. Numerous immunologists worked enthusiastically and interacted profitably," he wrote in his Nobel Prize autobiography. Benacerraf worked on various topics as part of several separate teams of researchers. Most far-reaching, however, was the work for which he eventually received the Nobel Prize.

That work was carried out by Benacerraf together with geneticist Snell of the Jackson Laboratory in Bar Harbor, Maine, and Dausset of the University of Paris, France, over a long period in the 1950s and 1960s, and involved major

advances in the understanding of the operation of the immune system. Benacerraf's contribution involved complex work but sprang from a common-sense observation, one related to a phenomenon everyone has experienced: some people tend to be more susceptible to certain diseases than others, even under identical conditions. Benacerraf, working with guinea pigs, noticed that some of the animals produced antibodies to specific antigens (an antigen is any substance that stimulates an immune response, and may be internal or external), while others did not.

As he worked, Benacerraf realized that the sensitivity of the cell surface molecules that initiate an immune response was not random. In fact, it was likely to be controlled by an individual's genetic makeup. Benacerraf demonstrated the existence of a previously unknown gene within the Major Histocompatibility Complex or MHC, the group of genes that controls whether cells within the body coexist or attack each other. This new gene controlled the behavior of cells as they encountered irritants or invaders. In the words (as quoted by the Jewish Virtual Library) of the Royal Swedish Academy of Sciences, the administrators of the Nobel Prize, Benacerraf won the 1980 prize for the "discovery of the Major Histocompatibility Complex genes which encode cell surface molecules important for the immune system's distinction between self and non-self." Nobel Prizes tend to be awarded after several years during which work done by the recipient is shown to be valid and useful; Benacerraf's 1980 prize was given for work done in the 1960s. The new gene Benacerraf discovered is now known as an immune-response gene or Ir gene for short.

Benacerraf's research led him to more prestigious positions within his field. In 1968 he accepted the post of chief of the immunology laboratory at the National Institute of Allergy and Infectious Diseases in Bethesda, Maryland, developing experiments that would further elucidate the operation of the Ir gene. But he missed the academic environment and the opportunity to interact with students. As a result, he moved to Harvard Medical School in 1970, serving as professor and chairperson of a new department of comparative pathology. He remained in that post until his retirement in 1991, settling in Boston after a lifetime of moving around the country and the world. Beryl Benacerraf also established her radiology practice there, and the family remained closely knit, vacationing together in a large summer home in Falmouth, Massachusetts. Benacerraf was closely involved in the training of young scientists, and made that a favorite theme when he addressed professional conferences. In the 1970s he wrote several major immunology texts, including *Textbook of Immunology* (1979).

Still another professional accomplishment lay on Benacerraf's horizon: in 1980 he was named president and chief executive officer of the Dana-Farber Cancer Institute at Harvard. In that post, Benacerraf had the chance to oversee a body of research that depended in many cases upon his own work as one of its pillars. But the work also drew on the other major theme of his life: the experience as a business executive gained from his intermittent management of his family's enterprises. He stabilized the institution's finances and proved an effective fundraiser. The center added two new buildings under Benacerraf's leadership, including a 14-story research tower. Dana-Farber Board of Trustees Vice Chair Vincent O'Reilly told the *Harvard University Gazette* that he had expected to encounter in Benacerraf "an individual of great intellect and scientific acumen. My expectations were met, but what surprised me was how open he was to new ideas from a business perspective and how adept a businessman he was." These ultimate contributions formed a fitting close to a remarkable professional career that Benacerraf summed up in a 1998 autobiography, *From Caracas to Stockholm.*

Books

Benacerraf, Baruj, *From Caracas to Stockholm,* Prometheus, 1998.

Notable Scientists: From 1900 to the Present, Gale, 2001.

World of Anatomy and Physiology, 2 vols., Gale, 2002.

Periodicals

Boston Globe, September 21, 1987.

New York Times, January 22, 1963; October 11, 1980; October 12, 1980.

Online

"Baruj Benacerraf: Autobiography," Nobel Prize Official Site, http://www.nobelprize.org/nobel_prizes/medicine/laureates/1980/benacerraf-autobio.html (December 18, 2006).

"Baruj Benacerraf," Jewish Virtual Library, http://www.jewishvirtuallibrary.org/jsource/biography/benacerraf.html (December 18, 2006).

"Benacerraf Donates Library to Dana-Farber Cancer Institute," *Harvard University Gazette,* http://www.hno.harvard.edu/gazette/1998/04.23/BenacerrafDonat.html (December 18, 2006). □

Elmer Bernstein

During a career that spanned five decades, American film composer Elmer Bernstein (1922–2004) remained at the top of his field. Refusing to be stylistically pigeonholed, his movies ran the gamut from Westerns to epics to comedies to intimate dramas. His innovations included using jazz music in film scores *(The Man With the Golden Arm)* and scoring a comedy as if it were a drama *(Animal House).* In 2002, over fifty years after his first movie, Bernstein received his 14th Academy Award nomination, for *Far From Heaven.* He was 80 years old at the time.

Early Years

Bernstein was born on April 4, 1922, in New York City. He was the only child of Jewish Eastern European immigrant parents, Edward and Selma, and much doted upon. Although his father was a high school English teacher, both parents were extremely interested in the arts, and enjoyed the company of the colorful denizens of that world. As Bernstein fondly recalled for Cynthia Miller of the *Guardian Unlimited,* "They surrounded themselves with Greenwich Village [New York] drunken poets and painters. It was not uncommon for me to find a poet at the foot of my bed reading to me at midnight from the Bible." So it was hardly surprising that the young Bernstein would find himself drawn to the arts, and his parents encouraged his interest.

Bernstein began his artistic explorations with painting and dance classes. He then studied acting at the King Coit Drama School for Children from 1932 until 1935, and appeared on Broadway as Caliban in *The Tempest* when he was just 10 years old. His secondary education was obtained from the Walden School, from which he graduated in 1939. Alongside these pursuits, he had been studying piano, even when the family lived in Paris for a year in 1933, and music soon eclipsed his other artistic pursuits.

At the age of 12, Bernstein received a piano scholarship to study with Henrietta Michelson, who taught at New York's famed Juilliard School of Music. His goal was to become a concert pianist, and he gave his first recital three years later in New York's Steinway Hall. Early in his long association (1934–1949) with Michelson, however, she noticed that he also had an interest in improvisation and composition, and she took him for an evaluation by then-rising star Aaron Copland. Copland encouraged Bernstein to take composition lessons and he did so, through scholarships at the Chatham Square Music School (1936–1940) and in private study with Israel Citkowitz, Roger Sessions, Ivan Langstroth, and Stefan Wolpe. In addition, he studied music education at New York University from 1939 until 1942. Then Bernstein was called for military service in World War II.

First Employment as Composer

Bernstein's time in the U.S. Army Air Corps played to his strengths. He was assigned to special services, where he was charged with arranging folk music and writing scores for Army Air Corps Radio. Bernstein's first experience with the latter was a rush job to fill in for the regular composer who had gone AWOL. He gamely completed a score overnight and then was too nervous to attend the next day's rehearsal. Once it aired though, Bernstein found the immediacy of the process compelling. "It was instant," he told Miller. "You made the music and they played it right away to millions of people. I found it thrilling."

After his discharge from the army, Bernstein tried to find work as a composer, but found no takers, so he returned to giving concerts as a pianist. His luck turned in the late 1940s, when he was asked to write music for a United Nations Radio show called *Sometime Before Morning*. The work was brought to the attention of then-vice president of Columbia Pictures Sidney Buchman, who offered him a job composing music for the movie *Saturday's Hero* (1951). Bernstein thus found himself headed for Hollywood in the autumn of 1950.

Hollywood Transition

Bernstein arrived in Hollywood during its so-called "Golden Age." It was, perhaps, especially convivial for musicians, as studios had their own composers, orchestras, and music departments (the head of which was usually a seasoned composer). There was more time to compose and rehearse, and an autonomy in the creative process that later became largely lost. Commenting on the differences to the *Hollywood Reporter* in 2001, Bernstein said, "There's a tendency, particularly among young directors, to want to dot every "i" and cross every "t" and listen to every note you're writing as you're writing it. Micromanaging is death to creativity. . . . I want to hear what the filmmaker thinks his film is about. . . . But then it's my job to translate all that into musical terms. Tell me about the film, but don't tell me how many trumpets to use."

The Golden Age was not without its dark side, however. The 1950s also encompassed the McCarthy Era, when accusations of Communism could ruin a career almost overnight. After Bernstein completed his first two movies, *Saturday's Hero* (1951) and *Boots Malone* (1952), he found that his progressive political views had placed him in the wasteland of being "gray-listed." That is, although he escaped black-listing (total career banishment) by virtue of not being a card-carrying Communist Party member, his politics were considered sufficiently suspect to relegate him to scoring such second-rate, camp films as 1953's *Robot Monster* and *Cat-Woman of the Moon*. While Bernstein later joked about it, telling the *Hollywood Reporter* that one thing "that

benefited me was that I wasn't important enough for anyone to get very excited about," it was a frightening time. And interestingly, it was one of Hollywood's most rabidly anti-Communist directors, Cecil B. DeMille, who got Bernstein's career back on track.

Genre Master and Innovator

DeMille was directing the biblical epic *The Ten Commandments* (1956) when his regular composer, Victor Young, fell ill. Bernstein had already been recommended to write the film's dance scenes, so DeMille summoned the young composer to see about his taking over the entire score. First, of course, DeMille had to satisfy himself that Bernstein was not a political subversive. He questioned Bernstein directly about his political affiliations, and apparently accepted the reply. He then delivering a short lecture about the perils of Communism. There seems to be little doubt that DeMille's intervention rescued Bernstein's career.

While scoring DeMille's movie, Bernstein was also working on Otto Preminger's *The Man With the Golden Arm* (1955). The story revolved around a man who wanted to be a jazz musician, so Bernstein thought it logical to use jazz music in the score. What he found merely sensible, however, was electrifying in its innovation and impact. Nobody had ever done such a thing before. Critics and audiences alike were enthralled, and the effort earned Bernstein his first nomination for an Academy Award. His once stalled career had kicked into overdrive.

As the years went by, Bernstein proved himself not only a master at conforming to myriad musical genres, but also at making them his own. His score for 1960's *The Magnificent Seven* (also nominated for an Oscar) became the new prototype for Westerns, and its theme became familiar to millions as the signature melody for Marlboro cigarettes. His child's view score for 1962's *To Kill a Mockingbird* (another Oscar nominee) avoided the then-popular large orchestral accompaniment in favor of the simple sounds of piano and flute alone, and was quickly hailed as a film music classic. From epics to dramas to Westerns to comedies, Bernstein spoke the appropriate musical language and imposed his unique stamp.

Among Bernstein's many notable earlier movies were *Sweet Smell of Success* (1957), *God's Little Green Acre* (1958), *Walk on the Wild Side* (1962, title song nominated for an Oscar), and *True Grit* (1969). He also did a great deal of television work, including themes and scores for such diverse programs as *General Electric Theater*, *Gunsmoke*, *Julia*, *The Rookies*, and the famous fanfare for *National Geographic* specials. By 1974 Bernstein had racked up 11 Academy Award nominations and one win, for 1967's *Thoroughly Modern Millie*, but his pioneering spirit was far from resting.

In 1977 Bernstein was contacted by director John Landis, a childhood friend of the composer's son Peter. Landis had an unusual idea for scoring his comedy, *National Lampoon's Animal House* (1978), as if it were a drama, and wanted Bernstein to do the honors. Bernstein finally agreed, and another trend was born. That successful innovation led to a spate of comedies that included *Airplane!* (1980), *The Blues Brothers* (1980), and *Ghostbusters* (1984), and introduced the then-60-something-year-old composer to a new generation of fans. Once again, however, Bernstein resisted being pigeonholed and began to look for another set of challenges.

Remained a Contender

Bernstein came back into the public eye with his scoring of the 1989 drama *My Left Foot.* He then teamed up with eminent movie director Martin Scorsese. To Jeff Bond of the *Hollywood Reporter,* film editor Thelma Schoonmaker recalled Scorsese's response to a colleague who suggested Bernstein might be past his prime: "[Scorsese] said, 'Yes—that probably means he knows something.' " Bernstein subsequently earned his 13th Oscar nomination for Scorsese's *The Age of Innocence* in 1993, at the age of 72.

In his later years, Bernstein spent a fair amount of time composing for traditional concert venues. He wrote a guitar concerto for Christopher Parkening, as well as symphony suites and compositions for viola and piano. Then in 2002, Bernstein defied the odds by winning yet another Oscar nod, over five decades after his start in the business, for Todd Haynes's *Far From Heaven.* At 80, he had once again shown that his work was ageless.

Bernstein's final projects included a performance of his "Fanfare for the Hollywood Bowl," celebrating the inauguration of the Bowl's new stage, in June of 2004 and, fittingly, the score for a documentary on DeMille for Turner Classic Movies. He had long been active in his community, from helping to found such organizations as the Young Musicians Foundation (president, 1960–1970) and the Composers and Lyricists Guild (president, 1970–1979), to presiding over such entities as the Film Music Society (1996–2001) and the Film Music Museum (2002–2004). His multiple accolades, in addition to recognition by the Academy, included one Emmy, two Golden Globes, and several lifetime achievement awards.

When Bernstein died on August 18, 2004, in Ojai, California, the film industry lost one of its most enduring lights. Who else could have written music for such different movies and eras as *The Man With the Golden Arm, The Great Escape, Desire Under the Elms, The Shootist, Meatballs,* and *Far From Heaven*? It could be that Bernstein himself summed it up best to *Time*'s Barbara Isenberg. "I rarely do anything at the same time each day, simply because anything you do routinely cannot possibly be fresh. I think a life with change in it keeps you young." Perhaps that is why Schoonmaker told Bond, "Elmer always seemed like the youngest person in the room to me, full of energy and optimism and a very bouncy personality." Bernstein's infectious enthusiasm for all kinds of music and quick grasp of what was needed to make a movie work would be his lasting legacy.

Periodicals

Back Stage, August 27, 2004.
Billboard, August 28, 2004.
Daily Variety, January 6, 2003.
Entertainment Weekly, March 21, 2003; September 3, 2004.
Hollywood Reporter, December 11, 2001; August 19, 2004; November 16, 2004.
Newsweek, March 10, 2003.
Time, December 2, 2002.
Variety, August 23, 2004.
World and I, December 2004.

Online

"Elmer Bernstein Awards & Nominations," Elmer Bernstein, http://www.elmerbernstein.com/bio/awards.html (November 24, 2006).
"Elmer Bernstein Fact Sheet," Elmer Bernstein, http://www.elmerbernstein.com/bio/facts.html (November 24, 2006).
"Elmer Bernstein (Part 1)," *Guardian Unlimited,* October 6, 2002, http://www.film.guardian.co.uk/interview/interviewpages/0,6737,808687,00.html (November 27, 2006). □

Art Blakey

American jazz percussionist Art Blakey (1919–1990) helped to forge the characteristic sound of hard bop, perhaps the dominant style of modern jazz. His own powerful playing was instantly recognizable among jazz fans, but equally important was his influence— the long list of players who passed through Blakey's band, the Jazz Messengers, formed the nucleus of the jazz scene in the last decades of the twentieth century and into the new millennium.

Grew Up in Foster Care

"I call ours the music of survival," Blakey was quoted as saying by Steve Voce of the London *Independent.* "I'm a Depression baby. I was orphaned in Pittsburgh—I didn't know my dad and my mother died when I was six months old, so I played jazz on account of survival because I didn't like to work in the mines. They had child labour then and I worked in coal mines and steel works." Arthur Blakey, born in Pittsburgh, Pennsylvania, on October 11, 1919, was raised by a woman named Marie Roddericker who was a friend or relative of his mother. He started out musically on piano, playing by ear, and by the time he was a teenager he had skills enough to be able to organize a big band (with as many as 18 musicians) that played in Pittsburgh clubs. He had other bands depending on his income. "When I should have been an adolescent, I was a man," Voce quoted him as saying. "At the age of 14 I had a family and at 15 I was a father. I never had a childhood." Blakey would marry four times and have a reported 12 children, five of them adopted.

His switch to drums came about at the instructions of a gun-toting gangster who owned a nightclub and was present when jazz pianist Erroll Garner happened to sit in as Blakey's group was rehearsing. The owner, impressed by Garner's talent, told Blakey to move over to the drum set. "The pistol gave me no choice," Blakey observed dryly

(according to Voce). Blakey made the best of his new assignment, studying the big percussion sounds of swing drummers like Sid Catlett and Chick Webb, and realizing that the drums could be a lead instrument in jazz in addition to serving as its rhythmic foundation.

Blakey's first break came in 1942, when the always experiment-minded jazz pianist Mary Lou Williams, during a stretch of time she spent in Pittsburgh, asked him to join her band. Blakey moved to New York and used that experience as his calling card to gain percussion jobs with a series of big bands, including those of Fletcher Henderson, Lucky Millinder, and Earl "Fatha" Hines. Tours of the South for black musicians at the time could be dangerous. "We [the Henderson band] drove to Albany, Georgia, and I had some problems down there with the police and got beat up. They put a plate in my head," he recalled to Paul Rubin in a *Jazz Spoken Here* interview reprinted in *Reading Jazz*. Sometimes Blakey turned to drugs to escape hard times early in his career, but in that he had plenty of company among jazz musicians. He fell into an addiction that he conquered only in 1963.

In 1944 Blakey joined a band led by vocalist Billy Eckstine, later renowned as a romantic singer but at this point presiding over one of the most remarkable assemblies of jazz talent in the history of the genre. Blakey spent three years with Eckstine, during which he and his bandmates—saxophonist Charlie Parker, trumpeters Miles Davis and Dizzy Gillespie, and vocalist Sarah Vaughan, among others—elaborated a revolutionary, hard-driving, harmon-

ically ambitious new style of jazz known as bebop. Blakey regarded this period as the central experience of his musical education, and according to the testimony of Gillespie and others, he made immediate contributions to the complex rhythmic vocabulary of bebop. He took away not only musical lessons, but also the realization that the lifeblood of jazz depended on a process in which older musicians participated in shaping the talents of younger ones coming along.

Recorded for Blue Note

By 1947 Blakey was ready to become a leader himself. He formed an octet called the Jazz Messengers, making the first of a long series of recordings for the Blue Note label. In the late 1940s and early 1950s Blakey performed, as leader and sideman, with various groups, expanding the role of percussion in jazz. He experimented with the Messengers' name, heading a large group called the 17 Messengers. With his drug problems worsening, Blakey went to Africa in search of spiritual renewal. He adopted the Islamic faith while he was there, taking the name Abdullah Ibn Buhaina. The "message" referred to in Blakey's group names seemed to allude to drums and their capacity for communication. "[Y]ou can tell a story on the drums," Blakey pointed out (as quoted by the *Boston Globe*'s Derrick Z. Jackson). One Blakey band featured ten percussionists out of 13 players in total.

In 1954 Blakey began performing at the prestigious Birdland club in New York with a quintet that included pianist Horace Silver, saxophonist Lou Donaldson, trumpeter Clifford Brown, and bassist Curly Russell. Blakey and Silver broke off to form their own quintet the following year, reviving the Jazz Messengers name. Blakey kept the name when Silver in turn departed to form a group of his own, and he remained the leader of the Jazz Messengers for the rest of his career. It was in these groups that a refinement of bebop known as hard bop took shape, featuring interactions among intense drumming that could build to peaks of thunderous power, a furiously blowing saxophone, and a pianist adding a field of dense harmonic colors to the music.

As he became a recognized bandleader, Blakey began to apply the other lesson he had learned as a member of Billy Eckstine's band in the 1940s: He surrounded himself with younger musicians and nurtured their careers. "I'm gonna stay with the youngsters," he told an interviewer in 1954 (as quoted by Richard Harrington of the *Washington Post*). "When these get too old, I'm gonna get some younger ones. Keeps the mind active." Blakey, in his mid-30s at the time, stuck to that philosophy all the way up to senior citizen age. The Jazz Messengers had a rotating membership, and a band member might be dismissed with a firm "Hey man, I think it's time for you to go," but at any time from the mid-1950s until Blakey's death, an observer hoping to identify the stars of the next generation of jazz needed only to take a look at the current Jazz Messengers roster. Blakey was eclectic in his choice of players, taking some criticism from black nationalist adherents of jazz as a result; the Jazz Messengers included white and Asian players, and even a Russian trumpeter, Valery Ponomarev.

Toured Japan

The incarnations of the Jazz Messengers in the late 1950s and early 1960s, by which time the group often performed as a sextet, were perhaps the band's best known. Hard bop was hitting its peak among jazz audiences, and Blakey at the time could draw on the talents of two superb saxophonists who were also innovative composers, Benny Golson (who wrote the Jazz Messengers standards "Along Came Betty" and "Blues March") and Wayne Shorter (who composed "Ping Pong"). Blakey argued that jazz was a characteristic product of American culture. "I hear we're sending ballet over to Russia," he said in the 1950s, in reference to U.S. State Department cultural-exchange programs. "They're the masters of ballet, and we're sending them ballet. They don't have jazz. We have jazz. They would go for that." The Jazz Messengers became the first American jazz band to tour Japan and play for Japanese audiences in 1960. Tours of Europe followed later, and Blakey developed a strong base of listeners there.

In the early 1970s, younger jazz players such as Herbie Hancock began to gravitate toward the new "fusion" style, which incorporated electronics and influences from rock music. Blakey rejected suggestions that he modernize his music. "Jazz is an art form, and you have to choose," he was quoted as saying by Jackson. "The record company executives with an eye on trends said to me, 'Well Blakey, if you update your music and change it, put a little rock in there, you'll come along.' I will not prostitute my art for that. It's not worth it. Gain the world and lose your soul? It's no good." Blakey's old associate Miles Davis, who helped create fusion jazz and became its foremost exponent, defended Blakey against the charge that his music was out-of-date. "If Art Blakey is old-fashioned, then I'm white," the African-American trumpeter remarked (according to Jackson).

Blakey's recording pace slackened somewhat during the 1970s, but he continued to bring new talent along in the Jazz Messengers. When the pendulum swung back toward less fusion-oriented jazz in the 1980s, Blakey was ready with the next generation of stars. Chief among these was New Orleans-born trumpeter Wynton Marsalis, who joined the Jazz Messengers as a 17-year-old in 1979 or 1980 as Ponomarev's replacement. Other Jazz Messengers, including Marsalis's brother Branford on saxophone, pianist Mulgrew Miller, and trumpeter Wallace Roney, became stalwarts of the jazz bandstand on their own from the 1980s onward. No player, no matter how talented, stayed with Blakey for long. "If they get comfortable and stay around too long we kick 'em out," Blakey explained (according to the *Toronto Star*). "It is not like the post office." The Jazz Messengers also functioned as a unit, with no one player standing out; Blakey discouraged long, heroic solos, and he was fond of introducing a selection with the quip that the piece would feature no one in particular.

Another player who apprenticed with Blakey was drummer Cindy Blackman, who told Peter Watrous of the *New York Times* that "[h]e adopted me like his daughter. He taught me a lot of things about drummers and music. But

as important, he helped me when I was just starting out and not working too often. He'd ask me to sit in when he was playing, he helped me if I needed money. His influence on all us young musicians is incalculable." Saxophonist Jackie McLean echoed Blackman, telling Watrous that Blakey taught him "[n]ot just how to be a musician, but about being a man and keeping a sense of responsibility." The vigorous renaissance that jazz experienced in the 1980s and 1990s seems at least partly attributable to Blakey's roles as teacher and mentor.

Blakey did not slow his performing schedule as he reached the ages of 60 and then 70, marking the latter milestone with a concert in Leverkusen, Germany, at which several generations of Jazz Messengers performed and honored the man who had been such a crucial developer and maintainer of the tradition in which they worked. Finally silenced by lung cancer, Blakey died in New York City on October 16, 1990. Trumpeter and former Jazz Messenger Freddie Hubbard, who had spoken to Blakey on the phone a few days earlier, told the *Toronto Star* about the drummer's words: "Don't be grieving when I die," Blakey said. "Think about the good moments, what we did together and what you can do later on."

Books

Contemporary Black Biography, Volume 27, Gale Group, 2003.
Gottlieb, Robert, ed., *Reading Jazz: A Gathering of Autobiography, Reportage, and Criticism form 1919 to Now*, Pantheon, 1996.

Periodicals

Boston Globe, October 21, 1990.
Independent (London, England), October 18, 1990.
New York Times, October 17, 1990.
Observer (London, England), October 21, 1990.
Toronto Star, October 17, 1990.
Washington Post, October 21, 1990.

Online

"Art Blakey," *Jazz Review,* http://www.jazzreview.com (September 24, 2006).
"Art Blakey Biography," http://www.artblakey.com (September 24, 2006). □

Charles Blondin

French daredevil acrobat Charles Blondin (1824–1897) gained fame as the first person to walk across Niagara Falls on a tightrope. The amazing feat gained Blondin international recognition and helped make him a wealthy entertainer.

Using the stage name Charles Blondin, Jean-Francois Gravelet rightly earned the reputation as the greatest "funambulist" of his time. Upon first glance that term would seem to imply fun, but in fact it indicates activities involving great personal risk. Literally translated into English, funambulist means tightrope walker, and Gravelet took that popular performance art form to previously unachieved heights.

The future famed tightrope walker and acrobat was born in St. Omer, France, on February 28, 1824. At various times throughout his storied career, Gravelet was billed as "The Great Blondin," "The Daredevil Wire Walker," and "The Prince of Manila," names that are as evocative of a highly specialized skill as they are of an era.

Inspired by Circus Performer

Gravelet became interested in high wire acrobatics at a very early age. In 1829, when he was five years old, a circus troupe performed near his home, and Gravelet became enthralled by the tightrope walker. It was the first time he had ever seen anyone attempting such stunts. He was so impressed that he felt compelled to try and accomplish the same kind of feats. Almost immediately after he returned home from the circus, Gravelet erected a makeshift tightrope in his back yard, using two chairs as supporting structures, and tried to master the skill of rope walking.

Instead of discouraging this rather risky pursuit, which may have been an understandable reaction, Gravelet's father, who was a gymnast, supported his son's ambitions. That same year he enrolled his son in the Ecole de Gymase, a school focused on physical education that was located in Lyon, France. Gravelet proved to be quite adept, and after only six months of training he made his amateur performance debut. Billed as "The Little Wonder," the future Blondin became a popular attraction, as his performances demonstrated surprising skill and originality.

Unfortunately, his early life was marked by tragedy. When Gravelet was only nine years old, his father passed away. Now an orphan, Gravelet was forced to fend for himself. As such, he turned professional to earn a living. Already exhibiting the sensibilities of a true showman with his precociously dramatic style, the resourceful youngster embarked on a career that would bring him great fame and fortune.

Became "Blondin"

In 1851 he was recruited by an agent for William Niblo, the famed theatrical promoter, to perform with the Ravel Troupe of family acrobats in the United States at Niblo's Garden. Gravelet then toured America with the troupe that, at one point, performed in New York City, working for P. T. Barnum as part of the world-famous circus impresario's "Greatest Show on Earth." During this period, Gravelet assumed his stage name, Charles Blondin, which he selected, in part, because of his blond hair.

During his early years in America, Blondin married his first wife, Charlotte, whom he met in New York. The couple had three children, who were all born while the couple were on tour. Their first child, Adele, was born in New York. Son Edward was born in Louisiana, while their second daughter, Isis, was born in Ohio.

Walked Across Niagara Falls

Blondin toured with the Ravel Troupe for several years. In 1858 the itinerary took him to Niagara Falls, located near the United States/Canadian border in upstate New York. Seeing this enormous natural wonder for the first time, he became obsessed with the idea of crossing the gorge on a tightrope. He finally achieved that ambition in 1859, when he became the first person ever to walk a rope across Niagara Falls. It would prove to be the greatest feat of his career, and it garnered him international renown.

At first, official roadblocks thwarted his goal. Blondin originally wanted to string his rope to Goat Island, a small island situated in the middle of Niagara Falls in the Niagara River, but he was denied permission. The surrounding community felt that the stunt would somehow demean the Falls' magnificent splendor and reduce the natural attraction to a stage for lowbrow entertainment. In addition, local officials feared the attempt would result in a horrifying accident. But Blondin was eventually granted permission to string his rope about a mile further downriver from the island, and on June 30, 1859, a crowd of 100,000 people witnessed Blondin's historic feat. For this first attempt, Blondin used a single three-inch hemp cord that was 1,100 feet long and rigged 160 feet above the Falls at one side and 270 feet at the other.

After this first successful crossing, Blondin performed the stunt many times throughout the next year. Each time the crowds grew larger, and he employed different and much more dangerous variations. Once he crossed the Falls while blindfolded. On another occasion, he pushed a wheelbarrow across the rope. On August 17, 1859, he crossed the Falls while carrying his manager, Harry Colcord, on his back. On September 14, 1860, he traversed the tightrope while walking on stilts. During other performances he stopped in mid-crossing to do tricks. Once he carried a small stove on his back, stopped at the middle of the rope and prepared himself an omelet, which he then ate as his amazed audience watched. Another time he balanced a chair on the rope and stood on it. Sometimes he stopped in mid-course to take photographs of the crowd down below. In September of 1860, the Prince of Wales was one of the many witnesses who observed Blondin carrying his assistant, Romain Mouton, on his back. When the Prince was asked if he would like to be carried on Blondin's back for the return journey, he understandably refused. Further, the Prince implored Blondin never to perform such a dangerous stunt again. Blondin, of course, never complied with the request.

When making the crossings, Blondin used ropes that measured either 900 or 1,200 feet in length, depending on where the line was situated. During this period of his career, he became known as "the Prince of Manila," because the rope he used was made of Manila hemp. In all, Blondin walked across Niagara Falls 17 times. In between crossings, Blondin bought a house in the town of Niagara, where he moved with his family.

Achieved Fame and Fortune

Because of his Niagara Falls crossings, Blondin garnered great fame across the world and became known as "The Great Blondin." A true showman with a flair for the dramatic, and described as likeable and charismatic, he remained a popular performer for his entire life and was fondly remembered after his death. Unsurprisingly, he had a large ego, but that quality only endeared him to others.

Because of his feats, he often received personal honors and gifts. His skills also made him a rich man. Following his American high wire triumphs, Blondin became a highly paid attraction and a huge draw. It has been reported that his fee was $500 for a performance, and that during the height of his career he earned nearly half a million dollars a year. Those figures were quite substantial ones for the time.

Toured England and Europe

Not long after his Niagara Falls accomplishments, Blondin retired to Ealing, England, located near London. Now a rich man, he moved his family into a large home that he christened "Niagara Villa." But he did not remain inactive for long. In 1861 Blondin honored the request of the Prince of Wales and performed in London at the famous Crystal Palace, where he recreated his various Niagara Falls stunts (e.g., somersaults, walking on stilts) against a painted backdrop of the North American landmark. Throughout that year and the next, he made numerous noteworthy international appearances as he toured the United Kingdom and Europe. He always drew enormous crowds whenever he appeared.

Notable engagements included his performances in Scotland, where Blondin stretched the limits of his audacity. During a two-performance stint in Edinburgh in September of 1861, held at the Royal Botanic Garden (then known as the Experimental Gardens), more than 5,000 paying customers nervously watched as Blondin was blindfolded and placed in a canvas sack that reached only to his knees, leaving him free to walk across the tightrope. With his characteristic dramatic style, Blondin faked a few slips as he started out across the rope, which produced collective gasps from the audience far below. When he reached the other side, the relieved audience applauded long and loud. In the second performance he carried a man on his back. In Glasgow, Blondin made two outdoor appearances, performing on a tightrope stretched across two 70-foot-high masts that were positioned 300 feet apart. The performances drew crowds estimated at 10,000. The United Kingdom tour was also notable for a Liverpool performance that nearly ended in tragedy. Blondin had strapped a lion into a wheelbarrow and had begun pushing it across the tightrope when a guy rope, a supporting structural device, became ensnared around the wheelbarrow. Fortunately the performer and his four-legged assistant were unharmed.

In 1862 Blondin returned to the Crystal Palace for 12 performances that netted him a total of 1,200 pounds, a huge sum of money at that time. During this extended engagement, he walked on a tightrope rigged across the center transept at a height of 180 feet above the facility's concrete floor. To make the feat even more dramatic, he pushed his five-year-old daughter Adele in a wheelbarrow, as she dropped rose petals down into the large audience. The press and the public reacted in horror at this risk to the child's well being. As a result, Britain's home secretary ordered him to refrain from placing her in such danger. Blondin com-

plied, and during subsequent performances he executed his regular repertoire of feats such as cooking an omelet on the high wire, turning somersaults and walking on stilts, all of which were sufficiently dangerous and breathtaking to satisfy the enormous crowds. His appearances caused famed English writer Charles Dickens to comment, "Half of London is here eager for some dreadful accident."

Later Career

Blondin kept performing into his seventies, and became a living legend on an international scale. Demonstrating that an old performer can indeed learn new tricks, he developed a cycling act on the tightrope. Though he was comfortably settled in his Ealing home, he could still be persuaded to make occasional trips to the United States and Europe. In 1882 he responded to a request to perform in the United States in a series of exhibitions in Staten Island, New York. He made his final appearance in 1896, the year before he died, in Belfast, Ireland.

Despite placing himself at great danger throughout his career, Blondin died peacefully in his bed at his Ealing home on February 19, 1897. He was 75 years old. The cause of death was listed as diabetes. He was buried in Kensal Green Cemetery in London next to his first wife, Charlotte, who died in 1888, and where his second wife, Katherine, who died in 1901, would also be buried.

Honored in Art

Besides the accolades and adulation that he received during his career, Blondin was paid tribute by other artistic efforts both during his life and after his death. In the late nineteenth century, German musician and theater manager Rudolf Bial composed the "The Blondin March" in his honor.

In 1992 a statue of Blondin was erected on the Ladywood Middleway ring road in England, near the Edgbaston Reservoir in Birmingham, where Blondin performed a famous tightrope crossing in 1873. In 1997 the Blondin Community Orchard was planted by the London Borough of Ealing to commemorate the centenary of his death.

In the twentieth century, Peruvian playwright Alonso Alegria wrote "Crossing Niagara," based on Blondin's life. The play was staged in several countries before making its U.S. premiere in New York City at the Folger Theater on February 19, 1981.

Periodicals

New York Times, February 19, 1981.

Online

"Blondin," *Theater History Online,* http://www.peopleplayuk .org.uk/guided_tours/circus_tour/circus_performers/blondin .php (December 5, 2006).

"Charles Blondin in Scotland," http://www.members.fortunecity .com/gillonj/blondin/ (December 5, 2006)

"Stilt History and World Records," *Stiltwalker.com,* http://www .stiltwalker.com/history.htm (December 5, 2006).

"Who is Charles Blondin?," *The Blondin Family,* http://www .simpenguin.com/genealogy/blondin/charlesblondinbio.html (December 5, 2006). □

Kjell Magne Bondevik

Norwegian politician Kjell Magne Bondevik (born 1947) twice served as prime minister of his country. An ordained minister who spent the majority of his career as a legislator, he attracted headlines around the world in 1998 when he took a brief leave of absence during his first term in office. He confessed that the pressures of his job as the leader of a fragile political coalition had brought on a stress-induced depression. Like many Norwegians, Bondevik retreated to his native land's magnificent rural landscape, where long walks near its mountains, lakes, and dramatic fjords quickly restored his equilibrium.

Bondevik was born on September 3, 1947, in Molde, a city on Norway's Romsdal peninsula along the Norwegian Sea. He was the nephew of Kjell Bondevik, who once headed the country's *Kristelig Folkeparti* or Christian People's Party, known by its Norwegian acronym KrF and in English by the letters CPP; the party is also sometimes called the Christian Democratic Party. Like its other political counterparts across Europe, Christian Democrats are social conservatives and believe the government should refrain from interference with economic matters. Its ideological opposite, the Labor Party, has won the majority of parliamentary elections in Norway since the 1920s.

Ordained Lutheran Minister

At the University of Oslo, where Bondevik studied theology, he joined the school's chapter of the Norwegian Young Christian Democrats, and eventually rose to chair the entire student political organization. He was first elected in 1973 to the Storting, as Norway's parliament is called, and rose within the party ranks to become the CPP's vice chair by 1975. During this time he completed his schooling as well, and was ordained a Lutheran minister in 1979. Four years later he was elected CPP chair. In the event the CPP won a majority in parliamentary elections, his position as head of the party would automatically make him prime minister, although Norway's monarch is responsible for officially designating the prime minister after elections.

Norway is a constitutional democracy officially known as the Kingdom of Norway. Its 4.5 million citizens enjoy what usually ranks as the world's highest standard of living. The country is the world's second largest producer of oil after Saudi Arabia, and it is also the leader among European nations in natural gas production. Political, cultural, and economic life is centered in Oslo, where the 165-seat unicameral parliament, the Storting, meets. Norway shares a border with Sweden, with whom it was united for most of the nineteenth century. The royal house, headed by King Harald V (born 1937), was originally of German-Danish heritage, but has served as a symbol of national unity for Norway since the early twentieth century. Norwegian mon-

archs are granted executive powers by the constitution, but they allow the Council of State—the prime minister and his cabinet—to exercise those rights. The country has had a longstanding rivalry with Sweden, and has twice voted in national referendums against joining the European Union (EU). Its border with the Soviet Union, however, prompted it to join the North Atlantic Treaty Organization (NATO) in the years following World War II.

The CPP had not ever won a majority in the Storting, but they did take part in several ruling coalitions during the 1960s and again in the 1980s. During these periods, Bondevik was named to cabinet posts when new governments were formed. He served as minister for foreign affairs after 1989, and as minister for church and education as well as a term as deputy prime minister. Though he had stepped down as CPP chair in 1995, two years later he became prime minister of Norway after a political upheaval involving the Labor Party and pledges it had made. In the October 1997 parliamentary elections, Labor did not do as well as it had hoped, and so prime minister Thorbjørn Jagland fulfilled a promise to step down if his party failed to match its 1993 electoral results.

Oversaw Shaky Coalition

Bondevik and some political allies quickly put together a coalition government made up of the Centre Party (the former farmers' party in the country) and the Liberal Party, Norway's oldest political party and one that still advocates the adoption of a guaranteed minimum income for all citizens, regardless of employment. This unlikely right-center-left coalition still had a slim number of Storting seats compared to Labor legislators. In a country of avid downhill skiers, the new alliance was called the "Slalom Coalition" because of the need for it to zigzag around the various political objectives among the Storting voting blocs.

Bondevik's first government was notable for the high number of women he named as cabinet ministers, which totaled nine in all. But the stress of the Slalom Coalition began to wear on him, and in the late summer of 1998 his office announced that he was taking a brief but indefinite leave of absence. The pressure of his job, the office noted, had brought on what his physician termed a depressive reaction. The leave lasted a few days short of one month, and made Bondevik the first head of state to publicly take a leave of absence for mental health reasons. Though his condition prompted international headlines, Bondevik received an outpouring of support and public sympathy at home, with many Norwegians hailing his courage and honesty.

Bondevik's deputy prime minister, Culture Minister Anne Enger Lahnstein, became acting prime minister. It was believed that while there were several difficult issues facing the government—interest rates were on the rise, and the price of oil on the world market was falling—there was one particular setback that the prime minister had taken to heart: Bondevik had pledged to increase the amount of monthly cash payments to parents. Under this plan, Norwegian parents with a child under the age of two could receive a $388 a month benefit, tax-free, if one parent chose to stay home rather than place the child at a daycare center—which, like much in Norway, is subsidized by the state. Liberals who favored equal treatment for parents of any gender, as well as conservatives who hailed it as a pro-family measure, supported the idea, but the bill failed to make it through the Storting legislative process.

Hoped to End Stigma

When Bondevik returned to work in late September from his coastal vacation, a statement released by his office quoted him as saying that "when I was put on sick leave, the reason was simply that my strength was gone," according to a *Seattle Times* report. "I did not have the energy I needed to meet the challenges." He also stated that it was his hope, by making public his situation, "to demystify something which is fairly common, but which many people have problems talking about openly." After his return, Bondevik enjoyed nearly a year and a half without a major domestic crisis, save for a telecom dispute with Sweden over the merger of their state-owned telephone and wireless communications in 1999.

Bondevik's first stint as prime minister ended in March of 2000, when his government received a no-confidence vote in the Storting after a contentious debate over a proposed natural gas plant. Bondevik suggested waiting to begin construction until various environmental concerns could be fully addressed, but his political opponents wanted the project to begin immediately. When he held his ground, he was forced to resign. His successor was the new chief of the Labor Party, Jens Stoltenberg. Elections were held on September 10, 2001, and though Labor won, it could not gather enough political allies to form a coalition government with another party; instead a center-right coalition made up of the CPP, the Liberal Party, and the Conservative Party formed a government, and Bondevik became prime minister for a second time.

Once again Bondevik named several women to cabinet posts, and with the Norwegian economic still on the upswing, he pledged to increase social welfare spending, particularly in the realm of health care and education. There were several foreign policy issues that came to bear on the country, beginning with the 9/11 attacks just a day after the election. In early 2003, Bondevik was one of several European leaders who spoke out against a U.S.-led invasion of Iraq. Norway, however, like many other nations, pledged humanitarian aid for Iraq. Nearly two years later, with U.S. troops suffering multiple casualties from what appeared to be a complex war of insurgency, Bondevik gave a rare interview to *UPI Perspectives.* When journalist Gareth Harding asked him if he still believed his government's anti-war stance was, in retrospect, the proper strategy, he replied, "I am more and more convinced that this was the right decision. We felt that more should have been done to find a peaceful outcome. . . . But nevertheless this is history and now we have to look to the future. We want to contribute towards stabilizing the situation in Iraq, therefore we've had forces there, we are contributing to humanitarian assistance."

Became United Nations Envoy

Later in 2005, at the four-year mark for elections, Bondevik's CPP came in fifth place. This time, a new "Red-Green" coalition had won a majority of the 169 seats in the Storting; four new seats had been added, thanks to the country's population growth. Red-Green alliances marked a new political shift across Europe, with the staunch leftists (in this case, Stoltenberg's Labor Party) allying with the pro-environment parties. In this case, however, it was a coalition of Labor, the Centre Party, and the Socialist Left Party. The red denoted the traditional shade identified with socialist politics, while the green came from the clover symbol of the Centre Party, which was once the political voice for Norway's farmers as the *Bondepartiet,* or Farmers' Party, the name by which it was known until 1959.

After the results of the September 2005 elections were tallied, Bondevik resigned as prime minister and was succeeded by Stoltenberg; he also appeared to resign from politics altogether. He became president of the Oslo Center for Peace and Human Rights, and in early 2006 United Nations Secretary-General Kofi Annan (born 1938) named Bondevik to serve as the new Special Humanitarian Envoy for the Horn of Africa, an area that includes the troubled regions of Eritrea, Ethiopia, Somalia, and Djibouti.

Bondevik has been married since 1970 to Bjørg Rasmussen, and they have three children. A teetotaler, he is also an avid soccer fan. A few months before he left office in 2005, he made some critical remarks about Swedish housewares giant Ikea in an interview with *Verdens Gang,* an

Oslo newspaper. He found fault with the simple pictorial instructions provided with Ikea's ready-to-assemble furniture because the diagrams always depicted male figures assembling the item. This was done to appeal to a broad base of Ikea customers, and it was thought that images of women putting together bookshelves would offend Ikea's Muslim customers. "It's important to promote attitudes for sexual equality, not least in Muslim nations," Bondevik said, according to a report by the *Guardian's* Jon Henley, but he also admitted that "I myself have great problems with screwing together such furniture."

Books

Worldmark Encyclopedia of the Nations: World Leaders, Gale, 2003.

Periodicals

Economist, August 14, 1999.
Guardian (London, England), March 11, 2005.
International Herald Tribune, September 5, 1998.
New York Times, September 20, 1998; January 9, 2000; December 25, 2003.
Seattle Times, October 28, 1998.
Time International, September 14, 1998.
UPI Perspectives, February 14, 2005. □

Bridget of Sweden

Saint Bridget of Sweden (c. 1303–1373), also known as Birgitta of Sweden, is one of the few Roman Catholic saints of Scandinavia. Sometimes referred to as the "Mystic of the North," Bridget was a wealthy, pious woman who experienced religious visions from her early childhood. After her husband died, she founded a religious order, the Brigittines, and worked to heal a breach in the church that had resulted in the removal of the papacy to Avignon, France. In 1999 Pope John Paul II named her one of the patron saints of Europe, along with St. Therese Benedicta of the Cross and St. Catherine of Siena, two other holy women who devoted their careers to ending religious and political strife in Europe.

Hailed from Prominent Family

B ridget was born into a wealthy, landowning family in the earliest years of the fourteenth century. Her father, Birger Persson, came from the prominent Finsta family, and served as both governor and *lagman* ("law-speaker"), or provincial judge, in the province of Uppland. Situated north of Stockholm on the Baltic Sea coast, Uppland·had a rich history in Swedish lore even in Bridget's day, for its main city of Uppsala was the site of a legendary pagan temple destroyed in some of Sweden's

final pagan-Christian battles in the 1080s. During that century, Swedes had converted from their pagan belief system to Christianity, but Uppland was the final holdout for the Norse god worshippers.

Bridget's mother was Ingeborg Bengtsdotter, who came from a prominent family with links to the house of Bjälbo. Many from this line would serve as the Swedish king's *jarl,* or second in command, during Bridget's lifetime. Another ancestor of hers was Birger Magnusson of Bjälbo, the founder of the city of Stockholm. Both Bridget's parents were devoutly religious, and she adopted their pious ways quite early in her own life. At the age of seven she began to experience mystical revelations; in one vision, she claimed, the Virgin Mary came to her and placed a crown on her head.

Ingeborg Bengstdotter died when Bridget was about 12 years old, and as she entered her teens she hoped to enter a religious order. This was one of two stark choices for well-born women of her time: the first option, marriage, meant a woman would likely spent the next 30 or so years either pregnant or nursing a child—if she survived all the deliveries, that is; for childbirth had an extremely high risk of death before the era of modern medicine. Or a woman could choose to enter a religious order, which necessitated a vow of chastity and cloistering behind the walls of a nunnery for life. But many religious communities in the medieval era were also oases of scholarship, even ones exclusively for women.

Married at 13

But Bridget's father opposed the idea of her entering a convent, and in 1316, when she was 13, she was wed to Ulf Gudmarsson, who was five years her senior and hailed from a similarly well-connected aristocratic family. Gudmarsson was lord of the province of Närke, and came into possession of a castle at Ulvåsa in Östergötland, where Bridget would spend much of her adult life. Fortunately, her new husband was similarly devout in his faith, and it was a solid match that produced eight children. Known as a devoted mother to four sons and four daughters, she refused to use physical discipline on them. Outside the castle, she became known for her works of charity, particularly toward Östergötland's unwed mothers and their children.

Word of Bridget's piety and charitable works spread throughout Sweden, and she befriended prominent theologians and clerics. In this era, Swedes adhered to the same form of Christianity practiced in the rest of Western Europe, before the Reformation caused the split that resulted in separate Roman Catholic and Protestant creeds. Nicolaus Hermanni was one of her close friends; he later became Bishop of Linköping, a famed cathedral city in Sweden. Her confessor, or personal priest, was Peter, also known as Prior of Alvastra, a renowned monastery in Östergötland.

In the early 1340s Bridget and her husband made a pilgrimage to Santiago de Compostela in Spain. This was a lengthy journey by sea and over land, and made by devout Christians with the financial resources that allowed them to leave home for such a long period of time. Located in Galicia in northwest Spain, Santiago de Compostela was a famous medieval pilgrimage destination bearing a name that in translation means "St. James in the Field of the Star." Legend asserted that James, one of Christ's twelve apostles, had preached there. He was known to have died a martyr's death in Jerusalem in 44 CE, but the legend held that his bones were buried in Spain some years later. Nearly 700 years after his death, a star appeared in the sky that showed Spain's Christians the resting place of James's bones, and a church was erected on the spot in 868. It was sacked by the Muslim Moors who ruled over much of Spain a century later, but a more elaborate cathedral was built when religious tensions subsided, and the church became one of Europe's first major pilgrimage sites.

Bridget's husband fell ill on the way home from Galicia, but recovered enough to return to Östergötland. He died soon afterward, in 1344, at the Alvastra monastery. By now in her early 40s, Bridget devoted herself to religious work in earnest. She became a practicing ascetic, a form of religious devotion that entailed voluntary abstinence or hardship such as restricting food intake or wearing uncomfortable garments. Not surprisingly, a drastically curtailed diet could lead to hallucinations, and the mystical visions of her childhood returned. She claimed to have experienced some 600 in all, and wrote down the later ones. They were eventually published by her second confessor, Matthias Magister, who translated them into Latin after Bridget's death. Known as *Revelationes coelestes* ("Celestial revelations"), they circulated in Europe for several generations and were widely read by the small number of men and women who were able to read the official language of the Church.

Founded Religious Order

It was not uncommon for wealthy women to join a religious order when they became widows, but Bridget took this a step further and founded her own order, probably in the year 1346. Originally known as the Order of St. Saviour but later called the Brigittines, the religious community was open to both monks and nuns. She claimed that Christ had told her in a vision that its mission was to plant a "a new vineyard." Its chief monastery was at Vadstena, in Östergötland, which was a gift from King Magnus II of Sweden, at whose court Bridget and her husband had spent time.

A religious order needed official Church approval, however, and so after writing its Rule (bylaws that governed its daily life and spiritual focus), she traveled to Rome in 1349 to seek papal confirmation for it. Pope Urban V (1310–1370) approved the Brigittine Rule in August of 1370. She never returned to Sweden, and she spent some of these years attempting to reconcile the division that had resulted earlier that century when the French city of Avignon was designated the papal residence. She appealed to Urban V to return to Holy See back to Rome, Christianity's historical epicenter. That did not take place until 1377, four years after her death.

Bridget had first traveled to Italy with her daughter, Katarina, and her son, Birger, joined the two of them on a pilgrimage to the Holy Land in 1372. Bridget died in Rome

on July 23, 1373. A year later, her remains arrived at the Vadstena monastery, and several miracles were attributed to their journey north—some who touched her coffin, it was said, had been suddenly healed of their illness or disability. The process toward sainthood was swift in this era, and Pope Boniface IX canonized her as St. Bridget of Sweden on October 7, 1391. She is Sweden's only true saint in the Roman Catholic canon, though others such as the twelfth-century King Erik IX are venerated as holy but were never formally declared saints in the church. Her feast day is July 23.

Katarina, Bridget's daughter, also became one of the few Scandinavian-born saints, known as St. Catherine of Sweden (c. 1332–1381). This daughter returned to the Vadstena monastery and took over the order, which flourished both there and elsewhere in Europe over the next two centuries. Bridget's granddaughter, Ingeborg Knutsdotter, served as the Brigittines' abbess from 1385 to 1403; when she died in 1412 she was the last of Bridget's descendants. The family line ended because so many of her descendants had taken religious vows and never married.

Brigittine Mission Flourished

In the years following Bridget's death, her order established houses across Sweden and Norway and even as far away as Belarus. Before England's Reformation, the Brigittine outpost in Middlesex, called Syon Abbey, had been founded by King Henry V (1387–1422) and grew into a famous center of scholarship over the next century, particularly renowned for one of the most impressive libraries in the British Isles. Syon Abbey was sacked in 1539 during the violence that accompanied the English monarchy's break with Rome.

Many of the Brigittine monasteries in Scandinavia were also destroyed during the Protestant Reformation when it spread there later in the sixteenth century. In Catholic Hapsburg Austria, however, a chapel was built in Vienna to honor St. Bridget in 1651; the surrounding municipal district around this is officially known as Brigittenau. Her religious order died out entirely during the Reformation, but was revived in 1940 by a Swedish woman, Elisabeth Hesselblad, who was a convert to Roman Catholicism. Its center remains in Vadstena, but the order is restricted to women. The contemporary Brigittine convents function as guesthouses, fulfilling a new mission to promote Christianity through hospitality as well as charitable works. In Rome their convent is housed at the Piazza Farnese, also known as the Casa di Santa Brigida. The residence, near Campo de' Fiori, is where Bridget lived during most of her years in Rome. Brigittine sisters also have missions in India, Estonia, the Middle East, and even Darien, Connecticut.

Traditional Roman Catholic iconography of Bridget includes the pen, the ink bottle, and her revelations. She was also portrayed inside Florence's famed Santa Maria Novella church by the artist Andrea da Firenze in a fresco commissioned for its Spanish Chapel by Italian nobles she had befriended. Titled *Via Veritatis,* the fresco depicts her as an older woman alongside her daughter, Katarina, who is young but dressed in the humble clothes of a religious pilgrim. Both are placed near the Pope and Emperor in a painting that commemorates the historic 1368 meeting that restored the Holy See to Rome—a meeting that Bridget had prophesied a few years earlier.

Online

The Life of Saint Birgitta, http://www.birgitta.vadstena.se/ (November 14, 2006).

St. Bridget of Sweden, *Catholic Encyclopedia,* http://www .newadvent.org/cathen/02782a.htm (November 13, 2006). □

Art Buchwald

American journalist Art Buchwald (1925–2007) was one of the most widely read newspaper columnists of the 20th century.

Buchwald's satirical writings, filed first from the Paris offices of the *New York Herald Tribune* and then from Washington, D.C., entertained several generations of readers who faithfully consumed his columns several times a week. Later in life, Buchwald gained attention for autobiographical writings that showed something of the troubled man behind the comic mask. He continued to turn out his columns into the 21st century, and at age 80 he made headlines once again with the remarkable story of his nondeath. Given a death sentence by doctors, he moved into a hospice and put his affairs in order. But predictions of his death proved premature, and after checking out of the hospice he began work on a new book about his experiences.

Never Knew Mother

Arthur Buchwald, born on October 20, 1925, in Mount Vernon, New York, was one of three children born to Eastern European Jewish immigrants Joseph and Helen Buchwald. His father was a curtain installer whose business, never prosperous, floundered during the economic depression of the 1930s. Buchwald's mother, Helen, suffered from paranoid delusions and was institutionalized shortly after he was born; she lived until 1960, but Buchwald never visited her, preferring early on to deal with the pain of her absence by telling acquaintances that his mother had died. Joseph Buchwald, without resources, turned his children over to foster care.

Young Art and his sister, Doris, moved from place to place; both had health problems (Art had rickets as a child) that required specialized care. They lived for several years in a boarding house for sick children run by the Seventh-Day Adventist Church. Joseph Buchwald, although not strongly religious, removed them from that house after hearing them sing the hymn "Jesus Loves Me." "I was five years old and this was the third home from which I had been taken away," Buchwald recalled in his memoir *Leaving Home.* It was not the last—Buchwald moved on to the Hebrew Orphan Asylum in New York and then to the home of a foster family in the borough of Queens.

"I must have been six or seven years old and terribly lonely and confused, when I said something like, 'This stinks. I'm going to become a humorist,' " Buchwald wrote in *Leaving Home.* "From then on, I had one goal in mind and that was to make people laugh. I adopted the role of class clown." At home, he started a newspaper called *The Family Gossip,* and he excelled in English classes at Forest Hills High School, once writing a cowboy poem so accomplished that his teacher accused him of plagiarizing it; she owned up and apologized when it turned out that the poem was indeed Buchwald's own. Buchwald found plenty of time on the side for adventures as he traveled around New York on the subway. He sold magazines, worked as a golf caddy, delivered flowers, lost his virginity to a hotel maid during a summer stint working at a Long Island resort, and as a teenager talked his way into a job in the mail room at the Paramount film studio by spotting the Irish name of O'Connell on a personnel manager's door and claiming that a fictitious Father Murphy had sent him—nearly every Irish New Yorker, Buchwald reasoned, had a treasured Father Murphy somewhere in his background.

This adventurous life was cut short when World War II broke out and Buchwald decided to join the U.S. Marine Corps. He was only 17 at the time, and he was in North Carolina, having gone there to pursue a college student with whom he had enjoyed a summer romance. Needing parental consent because of his age, Buchwald convinced a struggling alcoholic he met on the street to pose as his father and sign the necessary papers, in return for money to buy liquor. Buchwald served in a fighter squadron in the

Marshall Islands, in the Pacific theater; he cleaned guns and planes, did burial duty, and put out a mimeographed comic newsletter for his fellow Marines.

Enrolled at USC

Back in the United States in late 1945, Buchwald enrolled at the University of Southern California. He had never finished high school, as the university soon discovered; he was allowed to remain in school, but was given the status of special or nondegree student. Buchwald enjoyed his job as an editor at the campus humor magazine, the *Wampus,* but by 1948 he was restless once again. Upon hearing from a friend that he could use funding obtained under the G.I. Bill (Servicemen's Readjustment Act) to attend classes in Europe as well as in the United States, he used the money from a New York state veterans' bonus check to buy passage on an ocean liner headed for Le Havre, France. He made vague plans to study the French language at the Alliance Française in Paris, but instead he bribed a clerk to mark him as present on the attendance rolls. Soon he had taken up residence in the Montparnasse district, spending time in cafés and flirting with female American students traveling in France. Although he lived nearly 15 years in that country, Buchwald never learned to speak French well.

Buchwald's first writing job, as a stringer or freelance correspondent for *Variety* magazine, paid nothing but led to big things. He began to attend movie and theater openings and could often wangle invitations to high-powered parties where he ate well from the buffet. As he accumulated a portfolio of articles about Paris nightlife, he set his sights in 1949 on a prime job for American expatriates in Paris: a staff post with the Paris edition of the *New York Herald Tribune* (now the *International Herald Tribune*). Once again, the gift of gab provided Buchwald with his shot. Turned down cold by the first editor he approached, he refined his pitch, referred to the advertising an entertainment column could generate, and was hired by another editor, Geoff Parsons, to write two columns a week, one on movies and one on nightlife, for $25 weekly. Buchwald remained at the *Herald Tribune* until 1961.

As his columns expanded beyond their original focus on entertainment, Buchwald gained readers, and the paper began to syndicate his column in 1952. One of Buchwald's most famous columns was also one of his earliest; in 1953, he wrote what purported to be an explanation of American Thanksgiving Day traditions for French audiences, translating key terms into hilariously fractured French. The column was reprinted in the Thanksgiving editions of American newspapers for decades afterwards. Buchwald evolved into an entertaining restaurant reviewer, using Paris as a home base for trips around Europe and beyond. His romantic fortunes improved dramatically as he hobnobbed with visiting celebrities such as actresses Grace Kelly and Ingrid Bergman, and in 1952 he married Pennsylvania-born fashion designer Ann McGarry. The couple adopted three children, Joel, Conchita, and Jennifer.

Gradually, satire of a political nature began to creep into Buchwald's writing. He recounted his adventures as he and some foreign correspondent friends spoofed the espio-

nage mania of the 1950s by organizing an "International Food Patrol" in Vienna, Austria. "We cannot fight the Russians unless we know how much paprika they are putting in their Hungarian goulash," CBS reporter Alex Kendrick pointed out (as Buchwald recalled in the second volume of his memoirs, *I'll Always Have Paris!*). A 1957 column satirizing the content-free qualities of presidential press briefings raised the ire of President Dwight Eisenhower's press secretary, James Hagerty, who called the column (again as quoted in *I'll Always Have Paris!*) "unadulterated rot." Buchwald rejoined that he actually wrote rot. Eisenhower himself turned out to have been amused by the column, and the controversy boosted Buchwald's popularity.

Moved to Washington

In 1961, leaving what many considered a dream job at the *Herald Tribune,* Buchwald moved to Washington, D.C., and launched a new incarnation of his syndicated column that focused mostly on American politics. The *Herald Tribune* column had run in 85 papers, and Buchwald was not particularly well known in the United States; he was, in effect, barging in at the top floor. With characteristic confidence, Buchwald moved forward and proved the doubters wrong; his new column was a hit from the start, appearing in 550 papers at its peak and staying close to that total for many years.

Inwardly, however, Buchwald was anything but confident. He suffered an attack of major depression in 1963, spending a month in a Washington-area hospital. "I was ready to kill myself," he was quoted as saying in a 1994 article in *People.* "I could not handle the emotional pain." Attributed to stress over his career change, the episode may well have had its roots in the difficulty of Buchwald's lifelong effort to put a facade of humor in front of his childhood feelings of abandonment. Treated with both psychoanalysis and medications at various times, Buchwald suffered another depressive episode in 1987.

Meanwhile, he was maintaining a high level of celebrity. His columns were often noted for their consistency; if he was rarely noted as an especially pungent satirist, he also rarely turned out a column that fell flat. Buchwald was not an ideological satirist, and he made fun of presidents of both political parties. He had little sympathy for the Vietnam War, however, and his toughest barbs were reserved for President Richard M. Nixon. "Just when you think there's nothing to write about, Nixon says, 'I am not a crook,'" he was quoted as saying in the *Chicago Tribune.* Buchwald's columns relied on several formulas that could be varied endlessly for comic effect. One type of Buchwald column resembled the classic satires of English writer Jonathan Swift in the way they presented topsy-turvy versions of reality in order to make a satirical point. Another was the fictitious conversation among powerful government officials; writing in the early 2000s he imagined President George W. Bush vetoing legislation to permit research using human stem cells because he thought the legislation involved cell phones. The imaginary conversation between columnist and a fictitious expert who gives answers with a comic thrust, now a commonplace technique among newspaper columnists great and small, was a Buchwald staple and perhaps his invention.

Buchwald made news in 1988 when he filed suit—successfully, but at great cost—against his old employer Paramount, accusing the studio of having failed to compensate him for his creative contribution to the hit Eddie Murphy film *Coming to America*. His columns were collected in some two dozen books; *While Reagan Slept* won a Pulitzer Prize in 1982. He also wrote two novels (*A Gift from the Boys* in 1958, and the semiautobiographical *Stella in Heaven* in 2000), several children's books, and a play, *Sheep on the Runway* (1970). In 1994 Buchwald was shaken by the loss of his wife to cancer; the pair had separated, but reconciled before Ann Buchwald's death. Buchwald in his eighth decade was still famous enough that his moves—to New York, and then back to Washington—were widely noted media events. He suffered a stroke in 2000 that left him unconscious for two and a half months.

None of the news coverage Buchwald received toward the end of his life approached that which surrounded first the announcement of and then his eluding of terminal illness in 2006. Suffering from kidney failure and forced to undergo a leg amputation due to circulatory problems, Buchwald made plans to die. "After I lost my leg, I was very depressed. I'd taken dialysis about 12 times, and I said, 'I'm not going to do it anymore,'" he told Elaine Shannon of *Time*. He checked into a hospice, visited a funeral home with his son, and took visits from friends who wanted to bid him good-bye. Buchwald embarked on one more unexpected journey, however, when his kidney apparently began functioning on its own. Feeling better, he left the hospice and headed for a family vacation home on the island of Martha's Vineyard, off the Massachusetts coast. In late 2006 he published a new book, *Too Soon to Say Goodbye*—an appropriate farewell, perhaps, for one of America's most durable and beloved writers. Ultimately succumbing to kidney failure, Buchwald died January 17, 2007, in Washington, D.C.

Books

Buchwald, Art, *I'll Always Have Paris: A Memoir,* Putnam, 1996.
———, *Leaving Home: A Memoir,* Putnam, 1993.

Periodicals

Billboard, April 18, 1992.
Chicago Tribune, August 30, 2006.
Columbia Journalism Review, November–December 2001.
People, March 21, 1994; June 12, 2006.
Physical Therapy, October 2002.
Time, June 26, 2006.

Online

Contemporary Authors Online, Gale, 2006. Reproduced in Biography Resource Center. Farmington Hills, Mich.: Thomson Gale. 2006. http://galenet.galegroup.com/servlet/BioRC (September 26, 2006). □

Jack Buck

Jack Buck (1924–2002) maintained a sports broadcasting career that spanned five decades until his death in 2002. He covered eight World Series and 17 Super Bowls, and worked St. Louis Cardinals baseball games from 1954 to 2000. His list of memorable calls is long, and he is a member of the Baseball, Football, and Radio Halls of Fame. "By reputation, Buck put forth irony, a fluent phrase, and a brave front under pressure. Expert at social intercourse, he was always ready with the beguiling gesture and hospitable word," Curt Smith wrote on the website ESPN.com.

Began Broadcasting at Ohio State

Buck was born in Holyoke, Massachusetts, the third of seven children of Kathleen and Earle Buck. He grew up rooting for the Boston Red Sox and listened to such radio broadcasting greats as Red Barber and Mel Allen. He even heard games broadcast from Havana, Cuba, at night. "Our diet was simple," Buck said, according to Smith. "Cereal for breakfast, soup for lunch, bakery leftovers for dinner." When Buck was 15, his family moved to Cleveland, Ohio. As a teen he worked on iron ore boats on the Great Lakes and variously at other odd jobs. He graduated from Lakewood High in January of 1941 and was drafted into the Army during World War II at age 19. While crossing the Remagen Bridge into Germany in March of 1943, Buck suffered arm and leg injuries and received a Purple Heart. Hall of Fame broadcaster Lindsay Nelson, ironically, was also injured in that battle.

Buck returned home in 1946 and enrolled at Ohio State University, commencing his broadcasting career at the campus radio station in Columbus. "When I went on the air to do a sports show at WOSU, I had never done a sports show before," Buck wrote in his autobiography, *That's a Winner*. "When I did a basketball game, it was the first time I ever did play-by-play. The same with football. I didn't know how to do these things. I just did them." A broadcasting teacher at Ohio State actually told Buck to "find something else to do for a living," Smith said.

Buck persisted, however, got minor league assignments, and in 1954 landed a job announcing St. Louis Cardinals games on radio with Harry Caray. Caray himself went on to a Hall of Fame career, as did the man whom Buck beat out for the job—Chick Hearn, who called Los Angeles Lakers basketball games for 42 years. Buck's low-key style blended with that of the boisterous Caray. "The Falstaffian Caray treated reserve like leprosy. By contrast, Buck evoked Casey Stengel telling a player, 'Not too hard, not too easy,'" said Smith.

At his Baseball Hall of Fame inauguration speech in 1987, Buck was self-effacing, even making fun of his profession. "You golf, swim, and shoot pool during the day, go the

park and b.s. a little before the game, do it, and go home. It's real tough," he said, according to Smith.

Passed on Monday Night Football

He left the Cardinals briefly in 1960 to work with ABC when that network carried baseball and the fledgling American Football League. He left that network after a dispute, and did not return the network's phone call when it considered him as play-by-play man for the inaugural year of *Monday Night Football* in 1970, when the AFL merged into the National Football League. Buck instead worked Monday night games—and 17 Super Bowls—on CBS radio from 1978 through 1995 with Hank Stram, who had coached the Kansas City Chiefs to the championship of Super Bowl IV. Buck also worked National Basketball Association and college basketball games, professional bowling, and was host of *At Your Service* shows on KMOX in St. Louis, considered one of the first call-in talk shows in the United States.

He was best known, however, as the voice of the Cardinals. "My dad was the kind of guy who went to bed thinking about the Cardinals, and when he woke up, the first thing he thought about was how the Cardinals played the night before," his son, Fox broadcaster Joe Buck, wrote in *Sports Illustrated* magazine. "The Cardinals set his daily mood. He used to say how they could give him a bad belly no matter how they played." The younger Buck recalled his mother telling him that when he was three or four, he saw his dad on television and thought he was "stuck inside it, somehow jammed into that little box."

Took Over in St. Louis

The Cardinals fired Caray in 1969, and while Caray prospered elsewhere—most notably with the Chicago Cubs—until his death in 1998, Buck emerged as number one in St. Louis. "For 15 years, he was the No. 2 guy in Harry Caray's shadow, but he was able to shine brightly through that shadow," New York Mets broadcaster Gary Cohen said on Major Leaguer Baseball's MLB.com website. "When Harry moved on, Jack took over the town, which sometimes meant speaking to 15 banquets a week," former Chicago White Sox announcer John Rooney told MLB.com. Buck even broadcast a radio show live from the top of the Gateway Arch upon its completion in October of 1965.

"Say Mel Allen, and you recall his boom box of a voice. Howard Cosell changed the parameters of his profession. Curt Gowdy evoked Jack Webb's 'Just the facts, ma'am.' Buck recalls how humor can best life's absurdities, improbabilities, and preposterous cant," ESPN's Smith said. Buck's appeal paralleled that of the team, whose network spanned as many as 124 stations in 14 Midwest states.

Some of the fans who listened to Buck as youngsters later interacted with him as players and broadcasters. "Jack was a big part of my life from the time I was 4 or 5, because my dad was a big Cardinals fan," Kansas City Royals announcer Denny Matthews said, also on MLB.com. "I don't think he ever realized what a big influence he was on my life at an early age. Later, I got to know him and did a few pregame shows with him. He makes you feel so relaxed, so much at ease." Jason Christiansen, an Omaha, Nebraska, native who pitched for four major league teams, including the Cardinals, added: "If you weren't a Royals fan, you were a Cardinals fan, and Jack Buck was one of those reasons."

Long List of Famous Calls

Buck's nearly five decades included several memorable calls. "Go ahead and remember him for a few calling cards," Chuck Finder wrote in the *Pittsburgh Post-Gazette*. "Just don't short-change Jack Buck on his versatility. His ability to broadcast baseball and football. His ability to work in radio and television."

Among Buck's most noteworthy calls and one-liners: His signature conclusion to a Cardinals victory on a local broadcast: *"It's a winner."* The "Ice Bowl," the 1967 NFL championship game between the Dallas Cowboys and Green Bay Packers, played in a wind-chill factor of about 50 degrees below zero in Green Bay, Wisconsin: *"Excuse me while I have a bite of my coffee."* Kirk Gibson's game-winning home run for the Los Angeles Dodgers in Game 1 of the 1988 World Series, while playing on two bad legs: *"Gibson swings, and a fly ball to deep right field. This is gonna be a home run! Unbelievable! A home run for Gibson, and the Dodgers have won the game, 5–4! I don't believe what I just saw. . . . I DON'T BELIEVE what I just saw."* Light-hitting Ozzie Smith's walk-off homer for St. Louis in Game 5 of the 1985 National League Championship Series: *"Smith corks on into right down the line. It may go! Go crazy, folks! Go crazy! It's a home run and the Cardinals have won the game by a score of 3–2 on a home run by the Wizard."* Mark McGwire's 61st home run in

1998, tying Roger Maris's single-season record. "Look at there, look at there! McGwire Flight No. 61 to Planet Maris! Pardon me for a moment while I stand and applaud!"

Stirring Poem after 9/11

When baseball resumed its games one week after the September 11, 2001, terrorist attacks, Buck gave an emotional speech before 32,563 fans at Busch Memorial Stadium in St. Louis before a game against the Milwaukee Brewers. Pregame ceremonies included about 500 police offers and firefighters lining the entire warning track. Buck, who wore a bright red jacket—the Cardinals' color—and a U.S. flag pin on his lapel, approached the microphone. Increasingly ill, and beset with the emotion of the moment, he shook as he read a poem in memory of the victims. His voice cracked and his eyes were watery as he finished the poem. Many fans and rescue personnel were crying. A 21-gun salute and fireworks display followed, then the game began.

'He Battled for His Life'

Buck's health continued to fade late in 2001. A heavy smoker, he underwent surgery for lung cancer that December. A month later he returned to Barnes-Jewish Hospital in St. Louis to have an intestinal blockage removed. Buck underwent five operations in all. He went in and out of a coma for several weeks and died on June 18, 2002. "He made us proud every day," Joe Buck told the Associated Press. "He battled for his life."

Joe Buck called the June 18 game between the Cardinals and Anaheim Angels, realizing it would probably be his father's final day. After the game he rushed to the hospital and embraced his father eight minutes before he died. Jack Buck had worked Cardinals broadcasts while fighting diabetes, Parkinson's disease and vertigo, and while wearing a pacemaker. "It has been an amazing fight that he's put up," Joe Buck told Finder of the *Pittsburgh Post-Gazette.* Throughout his illness, Buck listened to his son's broadcasts—he had ushered in Joe's announcing career by letting him work an inning on his 18th birthday at New York's Shea Stadium. A public memorial service was held at Busch Stadium two days after Buck's death. Buck left his second wife, Carole (Lintzenich). They had two children, Joe and Julie. Buck and his first wife, Alyce (Larson), had six children: Beverly; Jack Jr., Christine, Bonnie, Betsy, and Danny.

Son Carries on Family Tradition

Buck is honored along the St. Louis Walk of Fame, among many other accolades. His son, Joe Buck, has emerged as a top sportscaster in his own right. "I always knew he was something special," the younger Buck wrote about his father in *Sports Illustrated.* "I wasn't the smartest kid, but I didn't have to be to realize people liked having him around. I did, too."

Periodicals

Pittsburgh Post-Gazette, June 24, 2002.
Sports Illustrated, November 1, 2004.

Online

"Buck a St. Louis Institution, Broadcast Legend," ESPN Classic, June 21, 2002, http://www.espn.go.com/classic/obit/s/2002/0618/1396508.html (November 20, 2006).
"Jack Buck Timeline: 1924–2002," *St. Louis Post–Dispatch,* June 19, 2002, http://www.stltoday.com/stltoday/news/special/jackbuck.nsf/Jack + Buck/1BA671B73B96AC1686256BDD0066956C?OpenDocument (November 27, 2006).
"Jack Buck's Tribute to America," ESPN.com, http://www.sports.espn.go.com/espn/espn25/story?page = moments/98 (November 27, 2006). ☐

Mary Bunting-Smith

American educator and scientist Mary Ingraham Bunting-Smith, also known as Polly Bunting (1910–1998), was a pioneering force in the education of women. Her most famous contributions were made in her role as the fifth president of Radcliffe College from 1960 to 1972, where she founded the Radcliffe Institute for Independent Study (later renamed in her honor) and purposefully worked at integrating women into Harvard University. Her ongoing goal was to overcome what she termed the "climate of unexpectation" that existed for females at the time.

Early Years

Bunting-Smith was born to Henry A. and Mary Shotwell Ingraham on July 10, 1910, in Brooklyn, New York. Her father, an attorney, and mother, a community activist who once headed up the Young Women's Christian Association (YWCA), were nurturing and unorthodox parents. Thus, the young Bunting-Smith did not receive any formal education until the eighth grade, instead happily communing with nature at the family's country home on Long Island and cultivating a love of science and learning on her own. This unconventional childhood did not, however, prevent Bunting-Smith from excelling in a more traditional academic environment. Rather, it served her well.

Bunting-Smith began college at her mother's alma mater, Vassar, as a physics major. But it was not long before the nascent field of microbiology attracted her and she changed disciplines. She received her undergraduate degree in 1931 and went on to earn a Ph.D. in bacteriology from the University of Wisconsin at Madison (1934). While there, she met medical student Henry Bunting, who shared her love of science and nature, and the two were married in 1937. For the rest of her life, Bunting-Smith was widely known as Polly Bunting.

Early in her career, Bunting-Smith took on short-term assignments as her husband established himself. Those included stints as an instructor at Bennington College from 1936 to 1937 and at Goucher College from 1937 to 1938. In

the late 1930s the couple settled in Bethany, Connecticut, and started working at Yale University—he as a research pathologist and she as a part-time research assistant. Later in life, Bunting-Smith counted the Bethany years among the happiest of her life. She was professionally fulfilled, as she conducted groundbreaking research in microbial genetics that was published in 1939 and 1940. Her love of nature and family were also satisfied, as she raised goats and bees and brought up her four children. Additionally, she explored her interests in community and education by helping to establish a local high school. From 1946 to 1947 she was a lecturer on botany at Wellesley College, and from 1948 until 1955 she was a lecturer on microbiology at Yale. But Bunting-Smith's life was dramatically altered with the death of her husband in 1954.

Revelation and Douglass College

In keeping with the sexist standards of the times, Yale did not extend a full-time employment offer to the newly widowed Bunting-Smith. Such academic positions for women in the 1950s were nearly unheard of. So the 44-year-old scientist was forced to cast about for another way to support her family. The only opportunity that presented itself was in university administration, when Rutgers University proposed she become dean of its women's school, Douglass College, in 1955. It was a different world from the relatively solitary one of research, but Bunting-Smith drew upon her considerable internal resources and rose to the challenge.

Bunting-Smith had never been particularly interested in the issue of rights for women. Even in her old age, she steadfastly maintained that she had always been able to follow the path she chose and had never felt shunted aside because of her gender. Nonetheless, her new position at a women's college caused her to begin to reevaluate some of her views. And those inklings evolved into full-blown misgivings and, finally, an epiphany that gave Bunting-Smith new purpose.

Bunting-Smith's new direction was crystallized by her service on the Divisional Committee for Scientific Personnel and Education of the National Science Foundation (NSF) in 1958. The committee discovered that 98–99 percent of the top scorers on IQ tests in the United States who did not attend college were female. Even more telling was the blasé reaction of her mostly-male committee colleagues. "Nobody seemed to think it important," Elaine G. Yaffe quoted Bunting-Smith in the *Douglass Alumnae* magazine. "I was deeply puzzled. I felt that I was looking into a great dark cave that had been right beneath my feet all of my life without my knowing it. Beneath their feet too." Upon reflection, she realized that the problem was one of expectations. "Those scientists at the NSF had not valued the scientific potentialities of women. . . . This country didn't expect women to do important things. That was why so few women bothered to go on in the sciences or in many other demanding fields. That explained what inhibited women from developing and using their full intellectual capabilities. There was, I came to see, a climate of unexpectation as to what women were likely to contribute on any intellectual frontier."

That "climate of unexpectation" became Bunting-Smith's "watchphrase" and spurred her into action at Douglass. She secured a grant from the Ford Foundation to assess mathematical talent and interest among New Jersey women and launch the school's program in mathematics. She also recognized the different educational timetables that women often needed because of the demands of marriage and childbearing, and took on college rules against admitting married women and requiring full-time attendance. This resulted in what was eventually called the "Mary I. Bunting Program," a part-time program that allowed older, married women to continue or resume their educations. It was a radical departure from the norm, and the first of its kind in the United States. It was also an unmitigated success, celebrating its 25th anniversary in 1984 and still in full swing in 2007. Yet the innovative and enduring contributions of Bunting-Smith had just begun.

Radcliffe Years

In 1960 Bunting-Smith moved to Cambridge, Massachusetts, to assume the presidency of Radcliffe College. Radcliffe was strictly a women's college then, the sister institution to Harvard. But Bunting-Smith had other ideas. Within her first year she established the Radcliffe Institute for Independent Study (renamed in her honor in 1978). Its purpose was to provide fellowships to enable mature women with family responsibilities to spend a year in study and pick up their once-promising careers again. It was another revolutionary Bunting-Smith project and another resounding success, with alumnae that included poet Anne Sexton, writer Alice Walker, and scientist Sylvia Earle. Indeed, the institute was so original and noteworthy that it landed Bunting-Smith on the cover of *Time* in 1961.

Bunting-Smith also quickly turned her attention toward the integration of Radcliffe into Harvard University. Under her watch, Radcliffe students were first granted Harvard degrees, women gained admission to Harvard's graduate and business schools, and the Radcliffe Graduate School was merged with Harvard's Graduate School of Arts and Sciences. Not incidentally, she also supported co-educational housing, designed a new residential house system for undergraduates, oversaw the building of Hillel Library (which was open to both men and women), and spearheaded a capital-raising campaign that brought in funds for both renovation and financial aid.

By anyone's yardstick or era, Bunting-Smith's myriad accomplishments would have been remarkable. But they are rendered even more so by the period (1960–1972) and environment in which she managed them. The 1960s were a decade of staunch resistance to change among university trustees, administrators, faculty, and alumni reluctant to see tradition tampered with. Conversely, students and university personnel were often caught up in the protests, tensions, and rebellion stemming from the Vietnam War and carrying over to outdated policies and structures of the universities they attended. It was against this tumultuous backdrop that Bunting-Smith efficiently and astutely dealt with conflicting factions and pushed her agendas to fruition. In a meeting of the Harvard Faculty of Arts and Sciences on October 17, 2000, cited in the *Harvard University Gazette,* former colleagues Frederick H. Abernathy, Derek C. Bok, Giles Constable, John T. Dunlop, and Edward L. Keenan posted the following explanation of Bunting-Smith's success included in a memorial to her attributes and endeavors: "Polly Bunting was without the vices of her many virtues. She always had a plan, but never schemed. She was totally dedicated to her goals, but never allowed her deep commitment to distort her judgment. She had grand ambitions for Radcliffe and for women, but was devoid of personal vanity. Possessed of prodigious energy, she was never impatient. She deftly out-maneuvered students, alumnae, faculties, boards, and, on occasion, the undersigned, but made no enemies. She will be remembered as a quiet visionary and thoroughly admirable colleague."

Bunting-Smith left Radcliffe in 1972. That same year, the United States Congress passed the *Title IX Act,* precluding schools from discriminating by gender. There remained work to be done, of course, but Bunting-Smith had left an imprint that few could hope to surpass.

Aftermath

Bunting-Smith's landmark achievements did not go unnoticed. Among the many accolades and honors she received were the Gold Medal of the National Institute of Social Scientists in 1962, service as the first female commissioner of the U.S. Atomic Energy Commission in 1964, and over a dozen honorary degrees. She was also a member of the American Academy of Arts & Sciences, the Committee on the Status of Women during the administration of President John F. Kennedy, and the Task Force on Youth under President Richard M. Nixon.

Nor did Bunting-Smith's life end upon leaving Radcliffe. She became special assistant for co-education at Princeton University in 1972, where she stayed for three years. In 1975 she returned to Cambridge and married Dr. Clement Smith. That marriage lasted until Smith's death in 1988, whereupon Bunting-Smith moved to Hanover, New Hampshire. She passed away there on January 21, 1998, at the age of 87.

In 2004 *Mary Ingraham Bunting: Her Two Lives* was published. Written by Yaffe, it chronicled Bunting-Smith's extraordinary life and legacy. But perhaps the innovator's own prophetic words, as quoted from the *Boston Globe* in the *Fresno Bee,* summed up her formidable foresight and insight in a briefer fashion. "I am convinced the road that lies ahead for women is a dual one of motherhood and career," she said. "It will not only be possible but almost mandatory to do both if you want to do either well." Bunting-Smith did both admirably, and opened the way for other women to do the same.

Periodicals

Boston Herald, January 28, 1998.
Fresno Bee, January 23, 1998.
Women in Higher Education, March 2006.

Online

"Bunting-Smith, Mary, 1910–1998," Harvard University Library, December 1993, http://www.oasis.harvard.edu:10080/oasis/deliver/~rca00011 (November 27, 2006).
"History of Bunting-Cobb," Rutgers University, http://www.eden.rutgers.edu/~wendyi/bc_history.html (November 27, 2006).
"Mary Bunting-Smith Dies at 87," *Harvard University Gazette,* January 29, 1998, http://www.hno.harvard.edu/gazette/1998/01.29/MaryBunting-Smi.html (November 27, 2006).
"Mary Ingraham Bunting," *Harvard Magazine,* March-April 2006, http://www.harvardmagazine.com/print/030638.html (November 27, 2006).
"Memorial Minutes: Mary Ingraham Bunting-Smith: Faculty of Arts and Sciences," *Harvard University Gazette,* January 18, 2001, http://www.hno.harvard.edu/gazette/2001/01.18/22-bunting.html (November 27, 2006).
"Pillar of Radcliffe, Bunting-Smith, Dies," *Harvard Crimson,* January 23, 1998, http://www.thecrimson.com/printerfriendly.aspx?ref=142112 (November 27, 2006).
"Polly Bunting Returns to Radcliffe," *Radcliffe Quarterly,* Winter 2006, http://www.radcliffe.edu/about/news/quarterly/200601/alumae/polly.php (November 27, 2006).
"'The Awakening': Dean Mary I. Bunting's Douglass College Years," *Douglass Alumnae Magazine,* Winter/Spring 2004, http://www.douglass.rutgers.edu/about/bunting.asp?printversion=true (November 27, 2006). □

Olivia Ward Bush-Banks

American writer Olivia Ward Bush-Banks (1869–1944) was a poet and playwright best known for celebrating both her African-American and Montauk

heritages in her works. She founded the Bush-Banks School of Expression in Chicago to foster emerging African-American talents. Some of her plays supported an interracial culture controversial for her day, and were not produced during her lifetime.

The Child of Two Cultures

Olivia Ward Bush Banks had two distinct ethnic identities and strongly identified with both of them. Born at the height of Reconstruction on February 27, 1869, in the Long Island village of Sag Harbor, New York, Olivia Ward was the youngest daughter of Abraham Ward and Eliza Draper. Sag Harbor, located in the eastern portion of Long Island known as the Hamptons, was historically commercially active in fishing, and Abraham probably worked as a fisherman. Both of Ward's parents were of mixed ethnicity, partially African American and partially Montauk Indian. (The Montauk were a tribe of Native Americans who had traditionally lived in the portion of Long Island covering the present-day Hamptons.) These two identities influenced Bush-Banks throughout her life; writing in the introduction to *The Collected Works of Olivia Ward Bush-Banks,* Bernice F. Guilliaume noted that "in sum, [Bush-Banks] represented a living anachronism of assimilation and transculturalism on North America's eastern seaboard."

Bush-Banks's mother died when the child was nine months old, and her father relocated with Bush-Banks and her two elder sisters to Providence, Rhode Island. Her father remarried in 1871, leaving Bush-Banks in the care of her maternal aunt, Maria Draper. Draper greatly influenced Bush-Banks as a child, who attributed her aunt's determination and strength to her Native American heritage and upbringing. Bush-Banks completed her education at Providence High School, where she received training in nursing and developed an interest in drama and literature. Her high school drama instructor, a woman known only as Miss Dodge, recognized Bush-Banks's youthful talent with dramatic interpretation and gave the young girl private drama lessons. Dodge's style was called Behavior Drama; the exact method and style of this technique remains unclear, but seems to have relied on emotional delivery and interpretation of texts. Bush-Banks herself later taught drama using this technique.

First Marriage and Early Writings

A few years after graduating from high school, Bush-Banks married Frank Bush. The couple had two daughters, Rosa Olivia (Rosamund) and Marie. The marriage was not a happy one—Bush-Banks once referred to it as "most extremely unfortunate"—and the two were divorced by 1895. Bush-Banks solely supported herself and her two young children and, after 1890, her now-aged aunt Maria Draper.

After her divorce, Bush-Banks moved frequently back and forth between Providence and nearby Boston in order to find work to support her family. One method she used to

generate income was poetry writing. In 1899 she published her first volume, *Original Poems.* The collection contained ten poems, which *American National Biography* described as "including elegies extolling African-American courage and virtue ('Crispus Attucks,' 'The Hero of San Juan Hill'), imaginative odes to faith and perseverance ('My Dream of the New Year'), and verses celebrating the ecstasies of religion ('Treasured Moments,' 'The Walk to Emmaus')." Preeminent African-American poet Paul Laurence Dunbar praised the volume, and the prominent African-American publication *Voice of the Negro* reprinted several poems from the volume.

Some record of Bush-Banks's time in Boston exists. Sometime around 1900, she because the assistant drama director the Robert Gould Shaw Community House, a Boston settlement house. (Settlement houses, which had become popular in the United States toward the end of the 1800s, were community organizations dedicated to alleviating urban poverty and homelessness through education and self-improvement.) She seems to have worked there as late as 1914. During that era Bush-Banks continued to write and publish works, contributing to *Colored American Magazine* between 1900 and 1904. Bush-Banks was literary editor of Boston's *Citizen* magazine for a time, and participated in the Northeastern Federation of Women's Clubs.

In 1914 Bush-Banks's second poetry collection, *Driftwood,* was published. This work includes 25 poems and two prose pieces, including elegies to figures notable for their importance to the African American community such as Abraham Lincoln, Frederick Douglass, William Lloyd Garrison, Wendell Phillips, and Paul Laurence Dunbar. Bush-Banks's only published play, *Memories of Calvary: An Easter Sketch,* was published around 1917 and was the last of her works to be strongly influenced by religion.

Move to Chicago and a Change in Cultural Identity

Sometimes after 1916 Bush-Banks married Anthony Banks, a porter on the popular Pullman train cars. This marriage took her to Chicago. There she founded the Bush-Banks School of Expression in order to support emerging African-American talents in literature, drama, music, dance, and visual arts. She also taught drama in the Chicago public school system, having become deeply drawn to the medium while teaching at the Robert Shaw Community House in Boston.

While living in Chicago, Bush-Banks wrote a play titled *Indian Trails: or Trail of the Montauk.* This play today survives only in fragments, but seems to have reflected Bush-Banks's identification with her Native American lineage. The work drew upon her familiarity with Montauk language and culture. In 1910 the Montauk tribe had been officially declared extinct following a New York State Supreme Court case, *Wyandank Pharaoh* v. *Jane Benson et al.,* by all accounts much to the surprise and dismay of the 75 members of the tribe standing in the courtroom at the time of the announcement. Bush-Banks's play was presumably written in reaction to this event, and is estimated to date from sometime around 1920. The work reflected the decreasing cultural unity among tribal members, but at the same time promoted future unity when, at its end, later European settlers agreed to return the lands to the native people.

Part of the Harlem Renaissance

Bush-Banks and her daughter Rosa Olivia (Rosamund) had at some time become estranged, probably due to differences in personality and to Bush-Banks's apparent disapproval of her daughter's husband. In 1929, and before the two could reconcile, Rosa Olivia passed away.

Bush-Banks's other daughter, Marie Bush Horton, remained close to her mother. Beginning in 1928 and continuing through the early 1940s, Bush-Banks split her time between Chicago and New York City, where Horton lived. From the 1920s on, Bush-Banks identified more closely with the African-American rather than Native American part of her heritage. Although it remains unclear how much time Bush-Banks spent in New York City and how much in Chicago, it is known that she was active in the intellectual and artistic scene that developed as part of the Harlem Renaissance. The first mainstream flowering of African-American culture, the Harlem Renaissance marked the growth of unique and prominent African-American voices, including Langston Hughes, Paul Robeson, and W.E.B. DuBois. The era is also remembered for its fostering of jazz talents and band leaders in the packed nightclubs of New York City's Harlem neighborhood, long an African-American stronghold.

Bush-Banks's activities in the Great Depression era of the 1930s reflect her association with the Harlem Renaissance. She was part of the Works Progress Administration's Federal Theatre Project in 1936. The Works Progress Administration sought to create jobs for Americans and often supported arts endeavors. She also worked under the Works Progress Administration as a drama instructor at the Abyssinia Community Center in Harlem between 1936 and 1939, during which time she taught using Miss Dodge's Behavior Drama technique. In 1936 Bush-Banks completed an adult teacher education program and at last became a certified teacher. Also in the 1930s, she served as the "Cultural Art" columnist for the *New Rochelle Westchester Record-Courier.*

As the 1930s progressed, Bush-Banks became increasingly disillusioned with the Harlem Renaissance. This is reflected in her works as early as about 1929 in the brief piece "Greenwich Village Highlights," and continued with 1932's "New Year Musings," 1933's "Black Communism," and finally 1935's one-act play "A Shantytown Scandal." All of these works, like most of Bush-Banks's later works, were unpublished. The work that was considered her greatest contribution to the Harlem Renaissance movement is a story cycle known as "Aunt Viney's Sketches." These stories may have been written as a reaction to Paul Laurence Dunbar's short story "Viney's Free Papers." Bush-Banks's Aunt Viney is a fully mature African-American woman who has developed a strong sense of folk wisdom during her years, and the stories themselves comment on both the Great Depression and the world of Harlem. The stories use

vernacular language and identify themselves intensely with African-American culture. Although Bush-Banks began an application for a copyright with the Library of Congress for the stories in 1937, the application was never fully completed and the stories were not published.

Later Life and Legacy

While in New York City, Bush-Banks seems to have been influenced by her daughter Marie Bush Horton and granddaughter Helen on a personal, rather than professional, level. Bush-Banks's religious affiliation shifted during her lifetime. Some speculate her father had been a Mormon and polygamist, with two concurrent wives between 1865 and 1869. *Notable Black American Women* commented that "whatever religious upbringing she received as a child does not seem to have satisfied her when she became an adult." Bush-Banks was interested in the Baha'i faith, a religion that sees all major world religions as differing expressions of one unified God. During the late 1920s and early 1930s, Bush-Banks was a member of New York City's Community Church, run by Minister John Haynes Holmes. Bush Horton and her daughter had become Seventh Day Adventists, and Bush-Banks ultimately converted to this religion.

Bush-Banks died in New York City on April 8, 1944, at the age of 75. Her published works total two books of poetry; one play; two poems published in magazines, "A Picture" (1900) and "On the Long Island Indian" (1916); and three essays also published in magazines, "Undercurrents of Social Life" (1900), "Echoes from the Cabin Song" (1932), and "Essay on John Greene" (1932). Her unpublished works are more numerous and reflect an evolving cultural voice in the first part of the twentieth century. Bush-Banks expressed both the Native American part of her heritage in the early portion of her work, particularly the play *Indian Trails: or Trail of the Montauk,* and the African-American portion of herself in her more mature works. Although Bush-Banks was not as well known as many of her Harlem Renaissance contemporaries, her writings on the era have contributed to our contemporary understanding of the time, and an examination of her overall creative works hav enriched many surveys of early twentieth-century American poetry, drama, and thought.

Books

Guillaume, Bernice F., *The Collected Works of Olivia Ward Bush-Banks,* Oxford University Press, 1991.

Online

"African American Women Writers Biographies," http://www.digital.nypl.org/schomburg/writers_aa19/bio2.html" (January 7, 2007).

"Bush-Banks, Olivia Ward," *American National Biography Online,* http://www.anb.org.ezproxy.libraries.wright.edu (January 7, 2007).

"Olivia Ward Bush-Banks," *Notable Black American Women,* reproduced in *Biography Resource Center,* http://www.galenet.galegroup.com/servlet/BioRC (January 7, 2007). □

C

Paul Cadmus

American artist Paul Cadmus (1904–1999) was a young and unknown painter in 1934, but he became famous overnight when a minor scandal erupted over his painting *The Fleet's In!*

Its depiction of American sailors on shore leave aroused the ire of Navy officials, and it vanished for decades from the public view. That work, as well as Cadmus's subsequent images, usually featured heroically muscled young men, and he later became one of the first contemporary artists to be recognized as a chronicler of gay life. "I wasn't trying to foster gay rights," Cadmus told Howard Feinstein in the *Advocate* about the *Fleet* painting and his other efforts. "I recorded what I saw and thought and knew."

A native of New York City, Cadmus was born on December 17, 1904, and grew up on the Upper West Side, near Amsterdam Avenue and 103rd Street. Both parents were artistically gifted: his father was a commercial lithographer who created advertising images, and his mother had illustrated children's books, but the family, which included Cadmus's younger sister, Fidelma, was quite poor. He told Judd Tully in an interview conducted for the Smithsonian Institution's Archives of American Art that their apartment building was "a horrible tenement. We lived with lots of bedbugs and cockroaches." He also suffered from childhood rickets, a condition brought on by vitamin deficiency.

Went Abroad to Paint

At the age of 14 Cadmus enrolled in art classes at the National Academy of Design, where his parents had met years earlier. Soon afterward he dropped out of his regular high school classes to enroll full-time at the art school, a move his parents encouraged. He became particularly fascinated by the art of the Italian Renaissance, when artists rediscovered some essential principles of human figure drawing that had been lost for more than a millennium. He spent six years at the Academy, winning several student awards and scholarship prize money during his time there, before moving on to classes at the Art Students League of New York City for another two years. By 1930 he had progressed from freelance illustration work for newspapers to a well-paying job with a small advertising agency, but in the autumn of 1931 he quit the job and sailed for Europe with Jared French, a friend from the League classes. Their plan was to live somewhere cheaply and paint full-time.

Cadmus and French discovered Majorca, one of the Balearic Islands off the coast of Spain, and spent nearly two years there before their savings ran out. As Cadmus recalled in the interview with Tully, "I painted very few Majorcan subjects actually. Most of my paintings were things I remembered from America, like the Locker Room and the Sailors Night, the Shore Leave painting. I was working just in oil paints in those days." When he returned to America, the country was deep in an economic recession, and work of any sort was difficult to find. Cadmus applied for and received a spot on the payroll of the Public Works of Art Project (PWAP), a government program that paid him $32 a week to paint. This was later folded into the larger Works Progress Administration (WPA), a federal agency whose aim was to curb widespread unemployment in America by matching job seekers with government-funded assignments. WPA workers built roads, dams, and other major infrastructure projects, but some were hired as artists and writers for various cultural programs.

Within a few months Cadmus had produced two works: *Greenwich Village Cafeteria* and *The Fleet's In!* The latter painting was chosen for a PWAP exhibition planned for the Corcoran Gallery of Art in Washington, D.C. It depicted young sailors on shore leave, chatting with flashily dressed women who were likely prostitutes, with all seeming to be in an exuberant mood that was probably alcohol-induced. There are more than a dozen figures in the painting, but in one section a sailor is depicted accepting a cigarette from a man in a suit. The civilian wears a red tie, one of the quiet sartorial signals that gay men used to identify one another prior to the gay liberation movement of the 1960s; it was a time when nearly all gay men remained "in the closet" for fear of social or professional ostracism.

Career Boosted by Scandal

The Fleet's In! became the center of controversy when the *Washington Evening Star* newspaper ran a photograph of it in a story about the art exhibit the day before it was to open. A retired Navy admiral named Hugh Rodman read the story, and was outraged at the depiction of U.S. Navy personnel carousing while off duty. Rodman managed to get Cadmus's painting removed from the exhibition before it opened to the public, and other newspapers quickly picked up the story. The admiral even asserted that the work should be destroyed, describing it as "an insult to the enlisted men of the American Navy" and "a scene originated in the depraved imagination of someone who has no conception of conditions in our service," according to a story by Eleanor Charles in the *New York Times*. But Cadmus had painted the scene from his own firsthand experiences watching sailors come ashore for the weekend at Riverside Drive around 96th Street, the site of a U.S. Navy pier at the time. "What I actually saw sailors and their girlfriends doing in Riverside Drive Park far exceeded anything that I could have put on canvas," he told Charles.

Cadmus also told the press, as the publicity surrounding his work grew, that Rodman and the other Navy brass who were so irate "must rule an Alice in Wonderland navy in a dream world. They ought to take a walk along the drive some night when the fleet's in," he said, according to Charles. He even received threatening phone calls, and stayed away from his New York City apartment for a time. Most of the debate surrounding *The Fleet's In!* mentioned its depiction of sailors drinking and flirting with women, but the subtle pick-up between two men showed "homoeroticism [at] a time when it was virtually invisible within the public sphere of American painting and all but unspeakable within the official discourses of art criticism," noted Richard Meyer in an *Art Journal* essay. Back in Washington, Rodman had ordered the painting removed from the Corcoran, and it wound up at the Navy Department. Finally Assistant Secretary of the Navy Henry Latrobe Roosevelt took it home with him in order to settle the dispute and end any possibility of it being shown in public. Roosevelt was the cousin of the sitting president, Franklin D. Roosevelt (1882–1945), the man who had launched the WPA project when he took office in 1933.

The scandal generated excellent publicity for the young artist, however, and he would later say that he owed Rodman a debt for the inadvertent career boost. He continued to paint images that displeased a public who hoped to be flattered instead: a 1935 work, *Coney Island,* was included in a show at the Whitney Museum of American Art that year, but residents of the Coney Island neighborhood threatened to sue.

Cadmus also submitted sketches for murals planned for a public library in Port Washington, New York; these murals were common WPA jobs during the late 1930s, but his work was rejected for its satirical look at the leisure habits of the affluent in America. He later completed paintings of *Aspects of Suburban Life: Main Street* and *Aspects of Suburban Life: Golf.* Like most of his work, the paintings quickly wound up in private collections. He signed with the prestigious Midtown Galleries on Madison Avenue and 57th Street, and his 1937 show receive a stunning seven thousand visitors.

Failed to Win Critics' Hearts

Cadmus's artistic fame waned in the years following World War II. His style remained firmly rooted in the social realism he perfected in the 1930s, but by the early 1950s tastes were changing, and abstract painting emerged as a strong new force in American art. Critics sometimes compared Cadmus's images to Normal Rockwell's overly sentimental cover illustrations for the *Saturday Evening Post,* only with a more debauched mood than Rockwell's folksy feel-good Americana. In some instances his work was rejected for museum exhibitions by curators who feared its homoerotic overtones might upset the cadmunity.

Cadmus's career was also hampered by his preferred medium: since the 1940s he had been working exclusively in egg tempera. This was a painstaking method that dated back to the Renaissance era, and it sometimes took him six months to finish a single painting.

Until the late 1980s Cadmus produced one or two paintings a year, working in his later years out of a skylit studio at his home in Connecticut. The house had been a gift from Lincoln Kirstein, who was married to Cadmus's sister, Fidelma. Kirstein was general director of the New York City Ballet, and was one of a roster of eminent friends Cadmus accrued over the years, such as fellow ballet luminary George Balanchine and the writers E. M. Forster, W. H. Auden, and Christopher Isherwood. Interest in Cadmus's work was renewed in the early 1980s when *The Fleet's In!* finally went on public display, first at a Miami museum and then in a retrospective of his work that toured several cities. He was unaware of what had happened to the painting after Admiral Rodman had it removed from the Corcoran. It turned out that when Henry L. Roosevelt died in 1936, he bequeathed the painting to the Alibi Club, a private men's club in Washington, D.C. It hung there for years, unbeknownst to Cadmus, until a graduate student who was writing a dissertation on the work successfully challenged the club to give it up. Philip Eliasoph, later the author of a book on Cadmus, argued that the work had been painted with taxpayer money—Cadmus was receiving his stipend from the Public Works of Art Project at the time—and therefore should be available to the public, not restricted to members of an exclusive private club.

Beginning in the late 1960s Cadmus lived with his partner, Jon Andersson, a former cabaret singer who appeared in many of his later paintings. Cadmus died a few days shy of his 95th birthday on December 12, 1999, in Weston, the Connecticut town where they had lived since 1975. In the lengthy oral history transcribed for Archives of American Art, Cadmus told Tully that after 50 years as a painter, he was happy with the trajectory of his career, though he had never achieved lasting fame or a consensus of critical appreciation. He quoted a line from one of his favorite painters, the French neoclassicist Jean Auguste Dominique Ingres (1780–1867): " 'People say my paintings are not right for the times' or something like that," Cadmus recalled. "But then he says, 'Can I help it if the times are wrong? If I'm the only one that's right, it's all right.' "

Periodicals

Advocate (The National Gay & Lesbian Newsmagazine), August 17, 1999; February 1, 2000.
Art Journal, Fall 1998.
New York Times, March 21, 1982; March 8, 1992; December 15, 1999.

Online

"Interview with Paul Cadmus," Smithsonian Institution, Archives of American Art, http://www.aaa.si.edu/collections/oral histories/transcripts/cadmus88.htm (November 28, 2006). □

Santiago Calatrava

Spanish-born architect Sanitago Calatrava (born 1951) has gained international celebrity for structures that suggest the shapes and the motion of organic entities, even as they rely in their construction on the modernist triad of concrete, glass, and steel.

Calatrava's projects are big; he tends to attract commissions for major civic structures that soon become established as community landmarks. His work is immediately recognizable, and it transcends the common architectural distinction between spare modernist forms and playful postmodernist ones. Their clean, geometrical lines are mellowed as Calatrava shapes them into pleasing forms that for the architect's many ordinary admirers suggest flight or spiritual uplift. As his chief influences Calatrava has named two architects of sharply opposing styles: the Catalonian Spanish maverick Antonio Gaudi (1852–1926), whose irregular buildings evoked organic growth, and the Finnish-American modernist Eero Saarinen (1910–1961), designer of the Gateway Arch in St. Louis and other abstract structures that communicated a peaceful sense of order and of integration with their surroundings. In a way, Calatrava's work combines the best of these diverse predecessors.

Began Art Classes at Eight

Born in Valencia, Spain, on July 28, 1951, Calatrava grew up in an established family involved in the primary industry of that coastal metropolis: agricultural exports. The family's hillside home was imposing, with large rooms that Calatrava later named as an inspiration for his attraction to major projects and big spaces. Though Calatrava's father was oriented toward commercial activities at work, he loved art and took his son to see Spain's greatest museum, the Prado in Madrid. Calatrava started to show an interest in sculpture and drawing, and by the time he was eight he had enrolled in art classes in Valencia.

Calatrava's family had suffered during the political upheavals of the 1930s in Spain, and they saw an international future as their son's best chance. When he was 13, they took advantage of a liberalization of travel restrictions imposed by dictator Francisco Franco in order to send him to Paris under a student exchange program. He later took classes in Switzerland and learned German on his way to eventual fluency in seven languages.

At this point Calatrava still hoped to become an artist. He made plans to attend art school in Paris at the Ecole des Beaux-Arts (School of Fine Arts), but he arrived in mid-1968, with the student protests of that year at their height, and found that his classes had been cancelled. Back in Valencia, he decided to attend the Escuela Técnica Superior de Arquitectura (Technical University of Architecture). He challenged himself with extra work: he and a group of friends wrote two books on the architecture of Valencia and the island of Ibiza while he was enrolled. After he graduated

he returned to Switzerland and entered a civil engineering program at the Eidgenössische Technische Hochschule (ETH) or Federal Technology University in Zurich.

Receiving dual Ph.D. degrees in structural engineering and technical science from that institution in 1979 and 1981, he became one of the few architects fully trained as an engineer. In Zurich, Calatrava met and married his wife, Robertina, a law student and later lawyer who has played an important role in managing his far-flung business enterprises. A glimpse of his growing architectural imagination appeared when he and some other graduate students designed and built a swimming pool in the rotunda of the school's main building—transparent, donut-shaped, and suspended above the floor, it allowed passersby to watch swimmers from below.

Eye-Catching Bridges Gained Attention

Calatrava opened his own architecture firm in Zurich after finishing his degree in 1981. It did not take him long to graduate from small projects to major civic commissions; after he won a contest, his design for Zurich's new train station was built in the early 1980s. The station was situated on a small strip of land that left no room for the spacious interior of a traditional train station. Calatrava responded with a unique design: a series of individual concrete corridors that resembled the ribcage of an animal and in fact was inspired by a dog skeleton a veterinary student in Zurich had given him and which he later mounted on the wall of his office, marveling to interviewers about its mechanical perfection.

In the late 1980s and the 1990s, Calatrava made his reputation as an architect by designing more than 50 bridges, most of them in Europe. Bridges allowed Calatrava to combine his architectural with his engineering expertise. Often made of white concrete and steel, his bridge designs had distinctive profiles. Many were asymmetrical. The Pont de l'Europe (Bridge of Europe) over the Loire River in Orléans, France, featured a seemingly tense arch, leaping out of the water and through the roadway, that some likened to a bowstring. Calatrava's Alamillo Bridge in Seville, Spain, was supported by a single leaning pylon that looked ready to topple over. "Being an engineer frees him to make his architecture daring," noted Doug Stewart in *Smithsonian* magazine. Calatrava's bridges attracted attention in the United States, and a show covering his work was mounted at the Museum of Modern Art in New York in 1993. Commissions for bridge projects in the United States began to come to fruition in the early 2000s. A so-called Sundial Bridge (Turtle Bay Bridge) in a park in Redding, California, had a single spire that served as a sundial, and Calatrava's firm made designs for a series of five massive bridges planned for the Dallas, Texas, area.

Calatrava's first completed U.S. building, however, was an addition to the Milwaukee Art Museum originally designed by Eero Saarinen in 1957. The central feature of his design was a massive two-part sunshade resembling a pair of wings that could open and close in order to change the lighting inside the building. The design was ambitious and difficult; Calatrava at one point was forced to come to Milwaukee and earn state engineering certification in Wisconsin in order to keep the project on track. Parts of the shade were eventually made in Spain and shipped to Milwaukee by plane, and its trademark opening and closing capability was not ready for the structure's unveiling in 2001.

Despite these problems, Calatrava's structure proved a terrific crowd-pleaser. *Architecture* magazine critic Joseph Giovannini, even as he questioned certain aspects of the design, noted that "it is hard to argue with the sheer joy this exuberant museum has stirred in Milwaukee." Attendance at the museum soared, and other cities began to make inquiries about the hot new European architect. The organic forms of Calatrava's buildings appealed to ordinary users put off by the severity of other modern structures, and the ascending, reach-for-the-sky feel of his works often had a spiritual quality that was a perfect fit for American optimism.

Designed Rail Terminal on WTC Site

That spiritual quality helped win Calatrava a major commission in the wake of the September 11, 2001, terrorist attacks at the World Trade Center in New York City. The terminal of the PATH rail system, serving commuters in New York's western suburbs, had been destroyed in the attacks, and in 2003 Calatrava's design was chosen for its replacement. It too was birdlike, with the interior of the building divided into a pair of wings, and the white building seemed to suggest a phoenix rising from the ashes. Slated to open in 2009, the station was delayed several times as Calatrava's design was altered due to security concerns.

Calatrava remained busy in Europe as well, designing an opera house in Tenerife, in the Canary Islands, that evoked a giant ocean wave. His commissions in Europe in the early 2000s included the first modern bridge allowed to be built over the Grand Canal in Venice, Italy's historic city center, and an opera house in his hometown of Valencia, one of a whole complex of museum buildings that he designed there. But Calatrava's most visible European design of the 2000s was the roof of the Olympic Sports Complex in Athens, Greece, viewed by hundreds of millions of people on international television broadcasts. Resembling a double arch shape in distance shots, it proved on closer inspection to consist of a series of curved white spines that suggested the ribcage of an animal.

Little known in the United States even in the late 1990s, Calatrava was something of an architectural star there by the mid-2000s. In 2005 he won the prestigious Gold Medal award from the American Institute of Architects. Cities vied for his services, and he began to attract commissions for top-dollar office and residential projects—somewhat underrepresented in Calatrava's portfolio up to that point even though such projects were central to the work of most architects. With the 80 South Street Tower in New York City, Calatrava continued reshaping the skyline of Lower Manhattan. The structure consisted of a stack of ten cubes, offset from one another and held up by a giant scaffold. Each cube comprised one condominium, with prices starting at $29 million. Calatrava also seemed ready to move into another area with a commission for the new Cathedral of Christ the Light in Oakland, California, a replacement for a cathedral leveled in the 1989 earthquake that shook the San Francisco Bay area. Calatrava's design featured moving vertical planes meant to evoke a pair of praying hands.

The Oakland design, however, was never built. In 2003 Calatrava and the Diocese of Oakland parted ways, with the scope of Calatrava's project reported as one of a group of causes for the break. Calatrava's massive bridges in Dallas also ran into trouble with city government officials in 2006 after the first span, with a cost initially estimated at $57 million, attracted a low bid of a staggering $113 million from the first round of contractors solicited for the job. With massive projects that seemed designed to outdo his previous creations, Calatrava was in danger of pricing himself out of some markets.

Cost issues were of paramount importance as plans for Calatrava's most ambitious project of all took shape in Chicago. In 2005, developer Christopher Carley announced plans for a Calatrava-designed hotel and condominium tower, the Fordham Spire, that would rise 115 stories above a lot near Chicago's lakefront. Each floor of Calatrava's building would make a two-degree turn from the one below, reaching a 270-degree rotation with the narrowest top floor and giving the building a slim, graceful corkscrew shape. If completed, the building would be the tallest in the United States and perhaps in the world.

The building immediately stirred up public interest in Chicago, already home to two of the world's tallest skyscrapers. It also drew criticism from, among others, rival developer Donald Trump, who questioned its feasibility in an era where terrorism fears had hobbled the construction of tall skyscrapers (although construction was underway on his own 92-story Chicago tower). As of 2006 Calatrava's project had acquired a new developer, Ireland's Garrett Kelleher, and a new name, 400 North Lake Shore Drive. Its financing was reported to be on track, despite a ballooning of its estimated cost from $600 million to $1.2 billion. What was certain was that Santiago Calatrava had already reshaped the look of cities around the world with his landmark projects.

Books

Newsmakers, Issue 1, Thomson Gale, 2005.

Periodicals

Architectural Review, February 2001.
Architecture, February 2002; January 2005.
Art in America, March 2001; October 2003.
Chicago Tribune, July 26, 2005.
Smithsonian, November 1996; April 2005.
Time, March 8, 2004; April 18, 2005.

Online

''Bio,'' Santiago Calatrava Official Website, http://www.calatrava.com (September 30, 2006).
''400 North Lake Shore Drive Project Continues to Move Forward,'' New City Skyline, http://www.newcityskyline.com/400NLSD2.html (October 1, 2006). □

Felipe Calderón

Felipe Calderón (born 1962), candidate of the conservative Partido Acción Nacional (National Action Party, known by the acronym PAN), was elected president of Mexico in July of 2006, after a bitter campaign whose almost-deadlocked result was contested and protested for months after the vote took place. At 44, Calderón was one of the youngest presidents in Mexican history.

S upporters of Calderón's chief rival, leftist Mexico City mayor Andrés Manuel López Obrador, painted Calderón as the candidate of Mexico's corporate elites and as a child of privilege out of touch with the aspirations of the country's poor. Calderón responded that the free market economic policies he proposed would be the most effective in alleviating poverty. Whatever the merits of each position in the economic debate, the portrayal of Calderón as a scion of elite power was not entirely accurate. For he was a member of a political family that had helped bring modern democracy itself to Mexico.

Born into Politically Active Family

Felipe de Jesús Calderón Hinojosa was born in Morelia, the capital of the Mexican state of Michoacán, on August 18, 1962. His father, Luis Calderón Vega, was a key backer of the

PAN in the early days after its formation in 1939. "His role was important because he was a student activist, a gentleman, a novelist, a historian, a political crusader, and a devout Christian," wrote historian Donald J. Mabry in his article "Father of a Mexican President: Luis Calderón Vega." He later became the PAN's official historian. At the time of the PAN's founding, and for many years afterward, Mexico was under the virtual one-party rule of the Partido Revolucionario Institucional (Institutional Revolutionary Party, or PRI), descended from some of the groups that had overthrown Mexico's dictatorship in the 1910s and founded the modern Mexican state. The elder Calderón was one of the activists who first began to chip away at the PRI's influence, running hopelessly outgunned candidates in local elections and laying the ideological foundations to attract the next generation of voters. PAN victories were few in the early years, but, party member Luis Meija Guzmán told Jeremy Schwartz of the *Austin American-Statesman,* "Even after they lost, they would continue fighting, until little by little they moved up the ladder." When Calderón was born, his parents were both working on a gubernatorial campaign in Michoacán. The family lived in a modest house and drove used cars.

The political atmosphere rubbed off. Calderón passed out political leaflets and grew up with the sound of campaigns in his ears. His local education occurred in a school run by the Catholic Marist Order, which he attended on a scholarship. When Calderón was 12, a teacher had his class recite their career plans. "We all said normal jobs, but Felipe surprised us all," classmate Alma Delia Álvarez Zamudio told Marc Lacey of the *New York Times.* "He said it like he knew it

was going to happen. He said, 'presidente de la república' "—president of the republic. Calderón was a serious student, not just dreaming of a political career but aiming toward it. Three of his four siblings also entered politics.

The political philosophy into which the young Calderón grew cannot be easily classified according to the modern standards of conservative or liberal. The PAN was, and remains, closely identified with the Catholic Church, whose influence the PRI had historically sought to circumscribe through the maintenance of a strong separation between church and state. Calderón's stances on social issues such as abortion (which is legal in Mexico only in cases of rape or danger to the mother's life) and homosexuality would line up with the PAN's consistently traditionalist and conservative outlook. On economic questions, however, Luis Calderón Vega was influenced by Catholic teachings on social justice, rejecting both Marxism and contemporary capitalist thought. He believed that wealth should be shared across the levels of society, and that, in Mabry's words, "each human existed within a larger social context, never in isolation." In 1981 he left the party he had helped build, believing that it had shifted too far to the right.

Felipe Calderón and his siblings grew up more conservative than their father, emphasizing individualist and entrepreneurial philosophies. In Mabry's words, Calderón "believed that the best public policy was to take care of the rich because wealth trickles down and the government should enforce conservative and reactionary Catholicism." On the campaign trail, however, Calderón affirmed his support for Mexico's traditional separation of church and state. "I'm a bad Catholic," he was quoted as saying by Dudley Althaus of the *Houston Chronicle.* "I appreciate the values my parents instilled in me, but for me religion and politics are completely distinct things. In Mexico there should be a secular government that respects without discrimination all religions."

Earned Law and Economics Degrees

After leaving Morelia, Calderón pursued a rigorous educational course that would equip him either for a career in politics or one at the top of Mexico's corporate world. He received his bachelor's degree in law from the Escuela Libre de Derecho (Free Law School), a private college in Mexico City, and went on for a master's degree in economics from the Instituto Tecnológico Autónomo de México (Autonomous Technology University of Mexico, or ITAM), also located in the capital. He went on to earn a second master's degree, this one in public administration, from Harvard University's Kennedy School of Government in Massachusetts in 1999.

By that time Calderón's political career was already well underway. He entered politics at the age of 26, with a successful run for Mexico City's municipal assembly in 1988. Three years later he won a seat in Mexico's Congress. These campaigns had significance for Calderón on a personal level: he met Congresswoman and fellow PAN activist Margarita Zavala and proposed to her during a 1994 campaign swing. She accepted, and the couple have raised three children in their Mexico City home. In 1995 Calderón returned to Michoacán to run for the state governorship under the PAN banner, but lost.

His loss was no surprise, for at that point the PAN and the leftist Partido de Revolución Democrática (Party of Democratic Revolution, or PRD) had just began to crack the PRI's stranglehold on Mexico's federal and regional offices. For decades PAN organizers (Calderón among them—he took his first party post at 26, as head of its youth wing) had tried to ensure open elections with a level playing field free of the often corrupt influence of the PRI and its huge patronage machine; Calderón himself rounded up neighborhood children to act as poll watchers. In the late 1990s, however, the PRI's hold on power began to crack as several state governorships fell to the PAN. Calderón, meanwhile, was rising through the party ranks, having become its secretary-general in 1993 and party president from 1996 through 1999.

When the PAN's Vicente Fox was elected to the presidency in 2000, becoming the first Mexican president in 71 years who was not a member of the PRI, Calderón ascended to the inner circle of power in Mexican politics. He was rewarded for his long years of work in the political trenches with the post of director of the Banco Nacional de Obras y Servicios Públicos (National Bank of Public Works and Services, known as Banobras), a government-owned bank that financed development projects. In 2002 he became energy secretary in the Fox administration, overseeing the Mexican federal government's vast energy infrastructure. During the 2006 presidential campaign, Calderón's opponents charged that he had used the post to direct contracts toward a company owned by his brother-in-law—a charge that Calderón, who had cultivated a clean-government image, strenuously denied.

Defeated PAN Rival for Nomination

Calderón's own political ambitions were clear, and in 2004 he resigned his post as energy secretary in order to enter the campaign to succeed Fox as president. In order to secure the party's nomination he had to get by Fox's first choice, Santiago Creel. Calderón's deep roots in the PAN organization proved decisive in primaries open to PAN members only, however, and he was nominated to face López Obrador and PRI candidate Roberto Madrazo in the 2006 election.

The race quickly turned into a two-man contest between López Obrador and Calderón, who campaigned on a platform of free trade and a flat tax structure that, he contended, would stimulate investment. For much of the campaign, López Obrador led in the polls. From Calderón's point of view, the problem was what some observers considered his lack of charisma in the new rough-and-tumble world of Mexican campaigning. "Bespectacled, short, and balding, Calderón seems more a bookkeeper than a barnburner," Althaus wrote. Calderón suffered through an awkward public appearance where he was barely visible behind the wheel of a truck used as a campaign prop. His speeches, noted James C. McKinley of the New York Times, "have all the dynamics of a NASCAR race, starting loud and getting louder." López Obrador, by contrast, was a natural orator.

The dynamics of the race shifted when Calderón began running negative advertising that called López Obrador "a

danger to Mexico" (according to the British Broadcasting Corporation) and likened his leftist rival to Venezuelan president Hugo Chávez. Mexico's electoral commission ordered the suspension of the ads, which were widely seen as unfair; López Obrador's fiscal management of the nation's largest city had revealed few grounds for scare attacks. But the ads had their desired effect. Calderón filled out his conservative message with tough anticrime proposals including a unified federal police force to replace Mexico's patchwork of troubled regional authorities. But he also sought to emphasize his moderate credentials. The title of his book El hijo desobediente (The Disobedient Son), issued during the campaign, referred not only to his differences of attitude with his father, but also his independence from Fox, often viewed as having been unable to deliver on his campaign promises.

On July 2, 2006, Calderón took 35.89 percent of the vote to López Obrador's 35.31 percent. The result was immediately challenged, both within Mexico's election certification apparatus and in the streets, where López Obrador's supporters launched a semi-permanent protest encampment in the center of Mexico City. A partial recount did little to change Calderón's margin of victory, and after a hot debate that included a walkout by opposition lawmakers prior to President Fox's annual Informe or state-of-the-union address, Calderón was certified as the winner on September 5, 2006, for a six-year term running until 2012.

Calderón immediately offered an olive branch to his opponents, whose continuing protests threatened Mexico's political stability. Noting that the PAN was still a minority party in Mexico's legislature, he told McKinley that "If you don't have a majority, you have to construct it." He pledged to continue Fox's efforts to oppose the strong immigration restrictions under consideration in the United States, and he expressed a willingness to include members of parties other than the PAN in his cabinet. Beyond specific policy decisions, Mexico's immediate future seemed likely to be influenced by the developing personality of its leader, who embodied some of the country's old and conflicting impulses. "There is an element in his persona that is rigid, belligerent, vertical, almost authoritarian," newspaper editor and Calderón adviser Jorge Zepeda Patterson told Schwartz. "But he has tried to work on those defects."

Periodicals

Austin American-Statesman (Austin, Texas), September 9, 2006.
Dallas Morning News, March 8, 2006.
Financial Times (London, England), June 20, 2006.
Houston Chronicle, February 13, 2006.
New York Times, January 26, 2006; September 6, 2006.
Time, September 11, 2006.

Online

Mabry, Donald J., "Father of a Mexican President: Luis Calderón Vega," http://www.historicaltextarchive.com/sections.pho?op=viewarticle&artid=759 (October 2, 2006).
"Profiles: Mexico presidential candidates," British Broadcasting System, http://www.news.bbc.co.uk/2/hi/americas/5114388.stm (October 2, 2006). □

Bebe Moore Campbell

American writer Bebe Moore Campbell (1950–2006) produced several acclaimed novels before her untimely death in 2006. A journalist who made the successful transition to fiction in the 1990s, "Campbell was part of the first wave of black novelists who made the lives of upwardly mobile black people a routine subject for popular fiction," wrote Margalit Fox in the New York Times. "Straddling the divide between literary and mass-market novels, Ms. Campbell's work explored not only the turbulent dance between blacks and whites but also the equally fraught relationship between men and women."

Born on February 18, 1950, in Philadelphia, Pennsylvania, as Elizabeth Bebe Moore, the future novelist was the only child of Philadelphia native Doris Carter Moore, a social worker, and a college graduate from North Carolina, George Moore. The pair settled in North Carolina, "where my father was the county farm agent," Campbell wrote in an article about her parents that appeared in *Essence*. "There my father learned that he'd married a woman who couldn't cook and had a penchant for correcting his grammar in public. And my mother discovered that the dark eyes that had wooed her had a tendency to stray, that my father drank too much and drove way too fast." This final trait proved George Moore's undoing: ten months after his daughter was born, he was involved in a car crash that left him a paraplegic.

Divided by Parental Loyalties

Campbell's mother, unable to find work in the segregated South that would support them all, returned to Philadelphia with her daughter, found a job, and moved in with her own mother in North Philadelphia. With Campbell's grandmother caring for her while her own mother was at work, she emerged as a diligent, straight-A student at Logan Elementary School and, later, Philadelphia High School for Girls. Summers were spent in North Carolina with her father, whom she idolized, and the less structured, rural Southern way of life marked a distinct contrast to her life back in the city. "I used to write letters to my father and tell him serial stories to keep him writing back quickly," Campbell told one interviewer about her first forays into creative writing, according to the *Philadelphia Daily News*. "He would write back to get the next installment of the story and he would say the story was really good. So I got a lot of praise for it, and that was very important to me."

Campbell graduated summa cum laude from the University of Pittsburgh with a degree in elementary education in 1971, and taught school in Pittsburgh, Atlanta, and Washington, D.C., for the next few years. A marriage to her high school boyfriend ended in divorce not long after the birth of her daughter, Maia, and around this same time she managed to sell a short story to *Essence* magazine. She was elated by seeing her name in print, but became discouraged when subsequent submissions were rejected for publication. Desperate to find out why, she learned that the magazine's editor was scheduled to speak at a conference hosted by Howard University in Washington, where Campbell was living. She brought along her infant daughter and a friend to hold the baby while she followed the editor into the ladies room after her time at the podium ended. Campbell waited until the woman came out of the stall, then introduced herself and explained why she was there. The editor told her, " 'We don't buy that much fiction. If you want to write for us regularly, can you write nonfiction articles?' " Campbell recalled in an interview with Julia M. Klein of the Knight Ridder/Tribune News Service. "And I said 'Yes.' I'd never written one in my life."

Wrote First Book

By 1980 Campbell's byline was appearing regularly in the magazine over articles about single parenthood, travel, and work life, bearing such titles as "Diary of a Corporate Misfit," and she was also writing regularly for *Black Enterprise* as well. She moved to Los Angeles in 1984, and one of her first articles for a national magazine with a gender-, not race-specific readership came in the May 1985 issue of *Savvy* and was titled "Backlash in the Bedroom," about the potential problems that women with careers equal or even surpassing their husbands' sometimes faced. The inspiration for the article had been her own first marriage, but by this point she had married a banker, Ellis Gordon, Jr. The article led to an offer to write a book, and Random House published her debut, *Successful Women, Angry Men: Backlash in the Two-Career Marriage* in late 1986. In an interview with *U.S. News & World Report* a few months later, Campbell explained that "the backlash is men's angry reaction to the feeling that women care more for their jobs than for them," and cited the various forms the hostility might take, such as adultery.

Another magazine article that Campbell penned, this one about Father's Day, became the basis for her second book. *Sweet Summer: Growing Up With and Without My Dad* was published in 1989, and in it she wrote about George Moore's sudden death in 1977, when she was a young wife and mother, from another car accident. She wrote of the North Carolina funeral, and of the many uncles and lifelong friends of her father. "My loss was more than his death, much more. . . . My father took to his grave the short-sleeved, beer-swilling men of summer, big bellies, raucous laughter, pipe smoke and the aroma of cigars," she mourned, in an excerpt that appeared in *Essence*. "My daddy is really gone and his vacant place is my cold, hard border. As always, my life is framed by his absence."

Campbell finally returned to writing fiction when Putnam, her publisher, accepted her novel *Your Blues Ain't Like Mine* for publication. She built the story around a real-life event, however—the 1955 murder of Emmett Till, a 14-year-old Chicago teen whose body was dumped in a river in rural Mississippi after being brutally beaten to death. Till had been visiting family, and reportedly whistled at a white woman whose husband, Roy Bryant, was one of the two men later acquitted of the crime. The crime made national headlines and was said to have influenced public opinion favorably for stronger federal measures needed to combat racism in the South. Campbell's book presented a fictional tale of the two families, the Tills and the Bryants, and what happened to each after the tragedy. A reviewer for *Time* commended Campbell's fiction debut, asserting she "offers a powerful reminder that racism is a crime for which everyone pays."

Second Novel Set in L.A.

Campbell's second novel, *Brothers and Sisters*, appeared two years later and made it onto the bestseller list. Set in contemporary Los Angeles, the story centers around a group of bank employees around the time of the riots that devastated the city in the spring of 1992. The novel is anchored by Esther Johnson, a successful black executive, and the various work-related dramas that played out just before the city erupted in violence and flames after the acquittal of several black police officers charged with beating Rodney King, a black motorist. Campbell herself recalled being outraged at the King verdict in May of 1992. She told Klein, "I was just quaking with anger. I could have thrown a brick."

Another high-earning, ambitious African-American female was the focus of Campbell's next work of fiction, *Singing in the Comeback Choir*, which also spent time on the *New York Times* bestseller list after it appeared in 1998. Los Angeles television producer Maxine McCoy is struggling to save her marriage, but is also worrying about her grandmother, a strong-willed sort who refuses to leave her home even though the neighborhood has fallen into considerable decline. Maxine flies east to visit her, recalling the streets of her childhood, which had always given off an "air of hardscrabble prosperity, as men and women who'd come up from rural Virginia and the Carolinas set off for factories in the morning. The children were left in the care of stern southern grandmothers. . . . As Maxine looked around her now, the same question she'd been asking herself for years rose in her mind: How could we have fallen so far?"

What You Owe Me, Campbell's fourth novel, was published in 2001. Once again, she built a story around race relations and generational passages, this time in the tale of two vastly different women who become unlikely friends in late 1940s Los Angeles. Gilda is a refugee from war-torn Europe and a Holocaust survivor, while Hosanna has also had her share of misfortune. They eventually start a business that grows into a successful cosmetics empire, but Gilda betrays Hosanna, and the anger infects a second generation. "Buried below the story's rhythm and colorful characters are messages from which everyone, at some point in life, should be able to draw lessons," wrote Althia Gamble in *Black Issues Book Review*.

Examined Mental Illness from Child's Viewpoint

Campbell's next work seemed an abrupt shift from her previous efforts. The illustrated children's story *Sometimes My Mommy Gets Angry* provided soothing words for young readers with a family member suffering from bipolar disorder. The story is told through the voice of a young girl, who has a loving grandparent to explain difficult ideas to her and suggest coping strategies. Campbell confessed in some media interviews that bipolar disorder had been an issue in her own family, an admission repeated, albeit in anonymous form, in similar publicity interviews for her next book, *72 Hour Hold,* the story of a mother struggling to help her 18-year-old daughter, a victim of bipolar disorder. The novel won praise from Ariel Swartley in *Los Angeles Magazine*, who commended the author for her "ability to blend ingredients that literature has long considered to be hopelessly at odds: practical information and poetry, stump speech and darn good yarn."

Campbell's second children's book, *Stompin' at the Savoy,* appeared in 2006. Sadly, that work would be the last to appear in her lifetime; diagnosed with brain cancer in early 2006, she died at the age of 56 on November 27, 2006, in Los Angeles. In one of the last interviews she gave, she discussed her family's experiences with mental illness, and the solace she found in support groups. "We don't want to talk about it," she explained to Kenneth Meeks of *Black Enterprise,* of her involvement in the National Alliance for the Mentally Ill, whose Inglewood, California, chapter she co-founded. "I didn't want to talk about it, either. I went into denial. I was ashamed. I was very stigmatized by this illness that had no business in my family."

Books

Singing in the Comeback Choir, Putnam, 1998.
Sweet Summer: Growing Up With and Without My Dad, Putnam, 1989.

Periodicals

Black Enterprise, April 2006.
Black Issues Book Review, July 2001.
Booklist, December 15, 1997.
Essence, June 1989; January 1998; June 2001.
Knight Ridder/Tribune News Service, September 14, 1994.
Los Angeles Magazine, August 2005.
Newsweek, April 29, 1996.
New York Times, November 28, 2006.
Philadelphia Daily News, November 28, 2006.
Time, November 9, 1992; October 17, 1994.
U.S. News & World Report, February 23, 1987. □

June Carter Cash

Born into country music royalty, American singer and songwriter June Carter Cash (1929–2003) enjoyed several claims to fame. The niece of A. P. Carter, she was the daughter of Mother Maybelle, both founders of the seminal folk and country group the Carter Family. Carter Cash was also part of the Carter Sisters, before evolving into a Minnie Pearl style singer-comedienne and the mother of 1990s country hitmaker Carlene Carter. Yet, thanks in no small part to the popular 2005 biopic *Walk the Line,* she is best remembered for aiding the rise and survival of her third husband and frequent duet partner, Johnny Cash.

A Member of the Legendary Carter Family

Born Valerie June Carter on June 23, 1929, in Maces Spring, Virginia, she was raised in the Clinch Mountain area by her father Ezra Carter and mother, the former Maybelle Addington. Father Ezra Carter was the brother of Carter Family founder/songwriter A. P. Carter, while Mother Maybelle was a cousin through marriage to his singing wife, Sara. Maybelle grew up playing banjo, Autoharp, and guitar. In the process, she developed a thumb-pick-based guitar style known as the Carter scratch, which she employed with great success on the Carter Family's recordings, particularly the classic "Wildwood Flower."

While husband Ezra earned his living working for the railroad, Mother Maybelle raised daughters Helen, June, and Anita to sing and play music when she was not busy with her father-in-law's group. Thanks to song publisher/entrepreneur Ralph Peer, the Carter Family had become perennial favorites with their RCA-Victor recordings of "Will the Circle Be Unbroken," "Keep on the Sunnyside," "I'm Thinking Tonight of My Blue Eyes," and dozens of others. The family band broadcast regularly from Del Rio, Texas, over radio station XERA. When Sara Carter, who had divorced A. P. in 1936, left the act to remarry, June and her sisters were drafted into the group to replace her until the band officially disbanded.

By 1943, she was singing regularly as an integral part of the Carter Sisters and Mother Maybelle. With Anita on upright bass, Helen switching off on guitar, accordion, and Autoharp, and June playing guitar and Autoharp, and of course the peerless Mother Maybelle on guitar, they were country music's first self-contained all-female band. Playing the old Carter Family repertoire and country gospel favorites of the era, the group became popular mainstays on such radio programs as the *Old Dominion Barndance* on WVRA, the *Tennessee Barndance* on WNOX, and KWTO's *Ozark Jubilee.*

Carter was not the best singer in her mother's group. That distinction belonged to sister, Anita, whose haunting soprano would grace gospel recordings for many years to come. However, sister June had nerve and wit, and she would play the dumbbell for laughs it that is what it took to get the audience's attention. She was also willing to divert from the Carter Sister's early policy of strictly folk and gospel. Accompanied by her father, in 1949 she went to New York to record with country cutups Homer and Jethro. Together, they did a parody of "Baby, It's Cold Outside," which rose to number nine on the country charts.

With a hit record under her belt, the little group moved to Tennessee and became regulars on the *Grand Ole Opry.* One of the people they brought with them to Music City was none other than Chet Atkins, who played with the act for the next two years while getting his own career established.

(The Carters also helped the Louvin Brothers get their start on record.) The exposure on the Opry led to a couple of hit records on RCA for Anita Carter, most notably "Down the Trail of Achin' Hearts" and a contract for the Carter Sisters with Decca and later Columbia, where they recorded old-timey material well into the 1960s folk revival.

Early Acting Ambition

While not singing with her mother and sisters, June Carter tried her hand at comedy and acting. Early kine-scopes of television appearances on the *Grand Ole Opry* and the *Kate Smith Hour* show her playing a frenetic, boy crazy hick—a more youthful version of Minnie Pearl's classic country character. Her knack for comedic timing, and willingness to do anything for a laugh, helped her punch up the weak material she performed. In sketches, she often uttered the catchphrase, "I am a good ol' girl" as a way of signaling to the audience that her character knew she was plain. As the decade wore on, and it became evident that Carter was indeed a lovely young woman, she dropped some of the hayseed affectations and used more pathos in her comedy routines. Encouraged by famed director Elia Kazan, Carter eventually moved to New York and studied under Lee Strasberg at the famed Actor's Studio.

In 1952, Carter married country singer Carl Smith. Largely forgotten today, the crooner scored 69 Top-40 country hits between 1951 and 1972. Best known for such Columbia smashes as "Let Old Mother Nature Have Her Way," "(When You Feel Like You're in Love) Don't Just Stand There," "Hey Joe," and "Loose Talk," Smith met June when he had employed the Carter Sisters to provide background vocals on one of his gospel sessions. Carter was enamored with the good-looking honky-tonk crooner, but the demands of show business eventually pulled them apart. Their five-year marriage produced one daughter, Rebecca Carlene Smith, better known as Carlene Carter, who grew up to record such early 1990s country hits as "I Fell in Love" and "Every Little Thing."

After divorcing Smith, Carter married a Nashville policeman named Edwin Nix in 1957, and they had one child, Rozanna. Still pursuing an acting career, she was billed as June Carter while performing in sketches on the *Jack Paar Show,* as well as playing supporting roles on *Gunsmoke* and *The Adventures of Jim Bowie.* She also co-starred with country stars Ferlin Husky and Faron Young in the 1958 low-budget film *Country Music Holiday.* By 1961, Carter put her acting career on a back burner to tour with her mother and sisters—now billed as the Carter Family—as they opened shows for Johnny Cash.

Married to Johnny Cash

The Carters had known Johnny Cash since the mid-1950s, although sister June had not heard a single Cash record until another young firebrand named Elvis Presley played one for her on tour one night. (Presley used to tune his guitar to Cash's records.) According to legend, the second he was introduced to her backstage at the *Grand Ole Opry,* Cash blurted out that he would one day marry June Carter. Still married to Carl Smith at the time, Carter laughed

it off, but as their paths continued to cross during the ensuing years, Cash and Carter developed a deep affection for each other. Indeed, that slow burning affection is hinted at in the song Carter co-wrote with Merle Kilgore, "Ring of Fire." Seething with mysticism and delayed gratification, Cash's recording of the tune stayed atop the country charts for seven weeks during mid-1963, and wrested his chart career out of the commercial doldrums.

Appearances from the mid-1960s on the TV show *Shindig* and the 1966 drive-in country music film *The Road to Nashville,* which also feature the Carter Family, show Cash at the height of his addiction to amphetamines. Skinny and twitchy, he performed well, but emitted the look of a junkie. Carter belatedly received a divorce from Edwin Nix in 1966, but before wedding Cash, she insisted that the Man in Black quit drugs and recommit to his faith. Her insistence that he clean up likely saved his life. The duo married in 1968 and gave birth to son John Carter Cash in 1970.

Acting as mother to her own children and stepmother to Cash's daughters from his first marriage, Tara, Kathy, and Rosanne, did not leave Carter much time to pursue a solo career. However, the material she cut with her husband set a benchmark for country duets. Despite her pedigree, recording with his wife could have been risky for Cash; he was an established mainstream star, while Carter was considered more of a personality than a singer. Yet on such efforts as their 1967 duet LP *Carrying on with Johnny Cash and June Carter,* they exhibited the type of sassy interplay typically found on Nancy Sinatra and Lee Hazelwood's pop hits. This is especially true on their Grammy winning remake of "Jackson" and her prickly composition "Long-Legged Guitar Pickin' Man," which boasts twangy guitar licks courtesy of Carl Perkins. Equally fine was their smolderingly romantic version of Tim Hardin's "If I Were a Carpenter," which also won a Grammy in 1970.

A staunch advocate of early country music, Cash would prominently feature his wife and the Carter Family in his live shows into the mid-1980s. June Carter Cash proved a popular feature on both her husband's live concerts and his ABC-TV show, where they would trade dry quips with deadly accuracy, or scream through the ultimate tale of a country wild child "Allegheny." Further, Carter and her sisters can be heard in fine form on the 1969 LP *Johnny Cash at San Quentin,* where June made prisoners laugh heartily when she joked, "Since we're the only girls on the show, I don't know what kind of show you're expecting out of us. Sometimes they do girly type kind of shows. But I've got one type of announcement—I don't want any confusion. This is as sexy as I'm gonna git!"

A Belated Solo Career

Carter Cash also encouraged her husband's pursuit of spiritual matters. During a trip to the Holy Land, she had a dream about her husband high atop a mountain reading about Jesus from the Bible. Subsequently, Cash financed and narrated the 1972 religious film *Gospel Road,* in which he cast his wife as Mary Magdalene. The film, featuring a blonde-haired blue-eyed actor playing Jesus Christ, was a critical failure and commercial flop, although it was later acquired by Reverend Billy Graham and shown to the faithful at fund-raising events.

During her rare slack moments, Carter wrote two volumes of her life story, *Among My Klediments* (1979) and *From the Heart* (1987). As Cash's career began to slowly wane during the 1980s and 1990s, Carter began taking acting roles again. Appearances on such TV programs as *Little House on the Prairie, Dr. Quinn, Medicine Woman,* and in several TV films allowed her to stretch her acting chops.

By the late 1990s, the alternative Country movement had inspired fresh appreciation of the Carter Family sounds, and she was invited by the independent Risk label, where she was the only country act, to record her first solo discs. "I've been on tour with John all these years," she told Robert Wooldridge of *Country Standard Time* in 1999. "I just worked along with him and didn't really think about stopping and recording again. He was always busy thinking about recording, but I was busy helping him get his songs together. I think I put him as my first priority."

Re-cutting such Carter Family staples as "Church in the Wildwood," "Hold Fast to the Right," and the Carter Sister's classic "Kneeling Drunkard's Pleas," she crafted affecting gasps of true warts'n'all old-time country music with a back porch feel. Enthralled, her peers rewarded the 1999 album *Press On* with a Grammy Award. As her husband's health failed, so, too, did Carter's. During heart valve replacement surgery, June Carter Cash died on May 15, 2003. She was honored with two posthumous Grammy Awards for her single "Keep on the Sunny Side" and her album *Wildwood Flower*. Her famous husband died four months after her own death. Their love story was celebrated in the Oscar-winning 2005 film *Walk the Line,* starring Joaquin Phoenix as Cash and Reese Witherspoon as June Carter Cash.

Books

Country Music: The Encyclopedia, edited by Irwin Stambler and Grelun Landon, St. Martin's Griffin, 1997.
Definitive Country: The Ultimate Encyclopedia of Country Music and Its Performers, edited by Barry McCloud, Perigree, 1995.
Miller, Stephen, *Johnny Cash: The Life of an American Icon,* Omnibus Press, 2003.
Newsmakers, Issue 2, Gale Group, 2004.
Zwonitizer, Mark, *Will You Miss Me When I'm Gone: The Carter Family and Their Legacy in American Music,* Simon & Schuster, 2002.

Periodicals

Country Standard Time, May 1999.

Online

"June Carter Cash," *All Music Guide,* http://www.allmusic.com/ (December 13, 2006).
"June Carter Cash," *Internet Movie Database,* http://www.imdb.com/ (December 13, 2006). □

Bonnie Cashin

American fashion designer Bonnie Cashin (1915–2000) was often referred to as one of the "Mothers of American Sportswear." Her productive career spanned over 40 years and ranged from dance halls to Hollywood to Seventh Avenue. Devoted to functional, uncomplicated designs, Cashin's many important innovations included a loose-fitting turtleneck that did not require a zipper to don, jumpsuits, and ponchos. Small wonder that one of her favorite catch phrases was "Chic is where you find it."

California to New York

Cashin was born on September 28, 1915, in Oakland, California. Her father, Carl, was a photographer/inventor (whose customary coveralls later inspired her to design the first woman's jumpsuit) and her mother, Eunice, was a dressmaker and major influence on her life. With her mother's encouragement, Cashin was already drawing sketches of clothing by the time she was eight, and as a mere high school student she got her first job as a designer.

Cashin was a 16-year-old senior at Hollywood High School when she went to audition to be a chorus girl for

Franchon & Marco, a Los Angeles dance troupe. Rather than ending up dancing with the troupe, however, her sketches convinced the manager to hire the teenager as the group's costume designer. He was sufficiently impressed with her work to suggest that Cashin go to New York City to study at the Art Students League. She happily did so, and soon found herself the chief costume designer for the Roxy Theater's "Roxyettes," the theater's answer to Radio City's "Rockettes" in the 1930s. Cashin was only 19 when she landed the job, prompting *Variety* to hail her as "the youngest designer to ever hit Broadway," according to Amy M. Spindler of the *New York Times Magazine.*

While Cashin was designing for the Roxy, *Harper's Bazaar* editor Carmel Snow attended a performance that included a dance number inspired by her magazine. Snow admired the young designer's costumes so much that she arranged for Cashin to become a designer at the prestigious house of Adler & Adler. Cashin worked there from 1937 until 1943. She also, along with such designing luminaries as Claire McCardell and Vera Maxwell, contributed to the war effort during World War II by designing civilian defense uniforms for women workers. The juxtaposition between the utilitarian aspects of the latter and the glamorous showgirls' costumes with which Cashin had started out did much to define what became her signature style.

Hollywood Years

In 1943 Cashin traded the East Coast for the West, and signed on as a designer for 20th Century Fox in Hollywood. She stayed for six years and created clothes for many movies, such as *Claudia* (1943), *Laura* (1944), *A Tree Grows in Brooklyn* (1945), *Anna and the King of Siam* (1946), *I Wonder Who's Kissing Her Now* (1947), *The Snake Pit* (1948), and *Mr. Belvedere Goes to College* (1949). Other films included *The Eve of St. Mark* (1944), *The House on 92nd Street* (1945), *Give My Regards to Broadway* (1948), and *It Happens Every Spring* (1949). Of all these, however, it is likely that *Laura* was the most influential.

Motion pictures of the 1940s tended to showcase their female stars as glamorous ladies of leisure or kittenish young vixens. But Cashin's designs for *Laura's* star, Gene Tierney, were of a different ilk altogether. As Ethel King of the London *Guardian* put it, "Gene Tierney's wardrobe . . . is like no other of the period. She wore, not costumes for an actress's part, but real clothes that could have been owned by a real woman: separates, a witty raincoat and hat. They, more than the script or playing, suggest Laura chooses what she wears: not to advertise nubility or family wealth but to please herself." It was a revolutionary concept and aptly reflected Cashin's real-life views. By 1949, she was headed back to New York to further implement them.

The Bonnie Cashin Look

After Cashin's return to New York, she briefly went back to work for Adler & Adler, winning both the American Designers Coty Award and the Neiman Marcus Award in 1950. But she continued to chafe under the restraints of what she saw as Seventh Avenue's staid and traditional mindset. Indeed, Suzy Menkes of the *International Herald*

Tribune cited one of Cashin's famous quips as, "Much of what is merely dull is called classic." So she set about creating her own style.

In the early 1950s, Cashin opened a studio called "Bonnie Cashin Designs." Her clothes were designed with a comfort, functionality, and practicality that embraced the newly-emerging independent woman and eschewed the ultra-femininity of the time. As design historian and Cashin friend Stephanie Day Iverson told Lisa Schmeiser of *Investor's Business Daily,* "She didn't design for trends or fads. She had a very distinct philosophy in look and dress." That philosophy was clearly displayed by, for instance, the name of her first collection, "We Live as We Please," as well as by the clothes themselves.

As early as 1943, Cashin had demonstrated her innovation and outlook by showing boots worn with tweed suits. Other pioneering designs included canvas raincoats (1952), industrial zippers (1955), and the jumpsuits inspired by her father (1957). Many of her most famous looks stemmed from her search for pragmatic solutions to situations in her own life. Those included the poncho, which came about after she cut a hole into a blanket in order to stay warm while driving her convertible, and clips to hike up a long skirt in the front, which were born from Cashin's effort to carry a cocktail upstairs without mishap. Brass toggles to close handbags and coats, as well as to decorate gloves, were inspired by those that anchored her convertible's top. As she often noted, "Chic is where you find it."

Through the course of being one of the first designers to create and popularize women's sportswear, Cashin introduced other unique designs, later standards in the fashion industry. Among these were a roomy turtleneck that did not need a zipper to get it over one's head, the concepts of layering to deal with temperature changes and the use of such heavyweight materials as leather (she was the first to do a leather dress). Some were utilitarian, such as the now ubiquitous leather tote modeled after a paper shopping bag, and others more whimsical, such as fringed suede dresses; but all were created with the new vibrant, modern woman in mind.

Business Alone

Cashin was uncompromising in her work. She refused to be tied to one label, feeling it would crimp her style. Instead, she collaborated with companies such as Bergdorf Goodman, Liberty of London, American Airlines, Samsonite, and White Stag, that allowed her total creative control. Nor did she ever have a design assistant, preferring to personally monitor each creation from sketch to production. The licensing boom of the 1970s did not tempt her either, although it undoubtedly would have made her an even wealthier woman. Eric Wilson and Janet Ozzard of *WWD* quoted Cashin's comments on this unusual autonomy as, "I didn't want to be boxed in by any one company or any one design problem. I thought I'd let my mind run freely. I wanted to design everything a woman puts on her body. I felt that designing for the entire body was like an artist's composition."

Such independence did not stop Cashin from forming some quite notable alliances, however. Perhaps most prominent among them were those with leather manufacturer Philip Sills and leather goods maker Coach. She worked with the latter as its original designer from the early 1960s until 1974, for example, and revitalized the company's line with such customer-pleasing ideas as sprightly colors and handbags with attached change purses and zip compartments. One of her standouts for the former was her hallmark cream leather jacket with equine clasps. In short, her business requirements may have been unusual, but they appeared to suit both Cashin and her fans just fine.

Life of Beauty and Style

Cashin traveled widely during her life, and took much inspiration from those experiences. As Spindler quoted her, "My interests are people and how they look. I remember the way a fisherman wore his shirt in Portofino—the odd chic of the beige and white starched habit of a little nun in Spain—the straw hat of a man riding a donkey in Rhodes—a man's wedding scarf in India—the elegant drape of a panung in Bangkok." So great was her fascination with other countries and sense of generosity that she was known to return home with a completely different wardrobe from the one she had departed with. That was because she gave away her things to anyone who admired them, and was equally happy to acquire local garments. Naturally, such predilections were often reflected in her designs.

Cashin was also a lover of beauty in her surroundings, and while on the road she adorned her hotel rooms with Thai silks and bouquets of flowers. At home in her apartment overlooking New York's East River, she surrounded herself with color provided by her own clothing designs displayed in open closets and on exposed shelves, as well as with the work of such contemporaries as Charles and Ray Eamse and Isamu Noguchi. In *Victoria*, Iverson described Cashin's home: "Like her fashions, Bonnie's apartment, dazzlingly sunny, informal and intellectual, was autobiographical. . . . It was a kinetic collage of shapes, textures and colors."

In 1972 Cashin was inducted into the Coty American Fashion Critics Hall of Fame. That same year she founded The Knittery, a company devoted to the manufacture of hand-knitted clothing from hand-spun yarns. Along the way, she had also established the Innovative Design Fund, dedicated to funding prototypes of objects for personal or domestic use, as well as served as an advisor to the government of India concerning the development of textiles for export. Clearly, her interests and accomplishments were as diverse as those of the women who wore her clothing.

By 2000 plans for a retrospective on Cashin's work at New York's Museum at the Fashion Institute of Technology and a book by Iverson were in the works. Her designs had been incorporated, adapted, and adopted by so many and become such a part of contemporary styling that they no longer seemed as cutting-edge and avant garde as they once had. And that, of course, was the ultimate testament to their influence. Cashin would likely have understood that perfectly, as evidenced by her words cited by Rosemary Feitelberg of *WWD*. "The moment you think of an idea, it is no longer yours exclusively," she said.

Cashin died on February 3, 2000. A year later, she received a plaque on the Fashion Walk of Fame.

Periodicals

Guardian, (London, England), February 9, 2000.
International Herald Tribune, October 31, 2000.
Investor's Business Daily, December 28, 2004.
New York Times Magazine, January 7, 2001; March 18, 2001.
Record (Bergen County, NJ), October 6, 2000.
Victoria, April 2001.
WWD, February 7, 2000; February 1, 2001; July 25, 2006.

Online

"Bonnie Cashin," http://www.dilpreetbawa.com/historyof fashion/cashin.html (November 29, 2006).
"Bonnie Cashin," IMDb, http://www.imdb.com/name/ nm0143642/ (November 29, 2006).
"Bonnie Cashin," Swank Vintage, http://www.swankvintage .com/cashin.html (November 29, 2006).
"Bonnie Cashin, Who Helped Americans on with Their Sportswear, Dies at 84," *New York Times,* February 5, 2000, http://www.partners.nytimes.com/library/magazine/home/ obit-b-cashin.html (November 29, 2006).
"Cashin, Bonnie," *Britannica,* http://www.britannica.com/eb/ article-9343622/Cashin-Bonnie?source=YNFAF (November 29, 2006).
"1950's and 1960's Influential Fashion Designers and Trends," Rewind the Fifties, http://www.loti.com/fifties_fashion/ 1950s_and_1960s_fashion_designers_and_trends.htm (November 29, 2006). □

Catharine Parr, Queen, consort of Henry VIII, King

Catharine (sometimes spelled Catherine, Katherine or Katharine) Parr (1512–1548) was the sixth and last wife of England's King Henry VIII. Reputedly kind and quite well educated for the time, she apparently enjoyed a fairly harmonious relationship with the king and his three children, Mary, Elizabeth, and Edward. Indeed, many credit her with convincing the king to reinstate Mary and Elizabeth to the line of succession, a decision that eventually led to the Golden Age of Elizabethan England.

Early Life and Marriages

Catharine was born about 1512, the first of the three children of Sir Thomas Parr of Kendal and Maud, daughter of Sir Thomas Green. Her brother, William, and sister, Anne, followed in quick succession. It was just three years into the reign of King Henry VIII. Her father had been knighted at the king's 1509 coronation, and both parents served as courtiers, Thomas as Master of the Household and Maud as a lady-in-waiting to the king's first wife,

Catherine of Aragon. (Some scholars even speculate that Parr was named in honor of the king's first queen.) This happy beginning, however, was rudely cut short when Catharine's father died unexpectedly in 1517.

Although Catharine's deeply religious mother was only 22 years old at the time of her husband's death, she spurned all offers of marriage and dedicated herself to the education and upbringing of her children. They were brought up at the home of their uncle, Sir William Parr (later to become Lord Parr of Horton and Lord Chamberlain of Parr's royal household), in Northamptonshire, and schooled in scripture and languages. In the tradition of the period, Catharine and her sister were also taught the skills necessary for managing a noble household, as well as music and dance. And, also according to the dictates of the era, the mother soon began looking for suitable matrimonial partners for her offspring.

Catharine was just nine years old when her mother instituted negotiations for her betrothal to one Henry Scrope. Those talks fell through, however, and sights were set on Edward Borough of Gainsborough in Lincolnshire. There is, however, some dispute as to who this suitor was. Some sources allege the man was the 2nd Lord Borough, who was in his late fifties or sixties around the year 1526. Others believe he was the eldest son of Thomas, the 3rd Lord Borough, and thus not nearly so old. In any event, an agreement was struck with one of the two, and Catharine was married around 1526, at the approximate age of 14. She was then widowed in 1528 or 1529, while still a teenager.

Shortly after Catharine became a widow for the first time, she also became an orphan upon the death of her mother. With her mother's passing, Catharine inherited a fair-sized fortune. But she was not destined to be on her own for long, as she soon attracted the attentions of John Neville, Lord Latimer. He had been married twice before, once to Dorothy de Vere, mother of his two children, and then to Elizabeth Musgrave, who died soon after they were wed. Nonetheless, the 40-something lord took the much younger Catharine as his third bride early in the 1530s.

As Lady Latimer, Catharine took over the household duties at her husband's immense estate, Snape Hall in Yorkshire. She was adept at her new responsibilities, and was well-liked both at home and at court. A mighty tension came about in 1536 though, as a rebellion called the "Pilgrimage of Grace" against Henry VIII's abolition of papal supremacy (1534) and the ensuing confiscation of monastic properties arose in the North. Latimer, his daughter Margaret, and Catharine were kidnapped and/or held under house arrest by the rebels, but that did not prevent the king from summoning Latimer to London to clarify his loyalties. And although Latimer was found innocent of any complicity in the uprising, the ordeal broke his health and Catharine was soon nursing another ill husband.

Despite the temptations of a young and frivolous court in London, there was never any indication that Catharine was anything less than solicitous and compassionate in the care of her invalid husband. It was undoubtedly helpful to her to have the companionship of her sister, Anne, who had married the grandson of the Earl of Pembroke and was at court as a lady-in-waiting. For all of his wife's tender care, however, Latimer died in the spring of 1543. He left Catharine the care of Margaret and his estates of Nunkmonton and Hamerton. Widowed again at only 31 years old, Catharine had the debatable consolation of being very well off in her own right.

Queen of England

At the time of Latimer's death, King Henry VIII had recently become a widower via the execution of his fifth wife, Catherine Howard. He had divorced his first wife, Catherine of Aragon, along with the Roman Catholic Church, in order to marry his second, Anne Boleyn. After having Boleyn executed, he had married Jane Seymour, who had borne his only legitimate son (Edward) and died soon afterward. Anne of Cleves was the king's fourth bride, but that union had ended in divorce as well. In addition, the years had rendered the king overweight and in poor health. In sum, partly in spite of and partly because of, his royal title, Henry VIII was no longer considered the most desirable bachelor in the land—unquestionably, his attentions had proved to be a definitive liability to many. And that attention was now directed at the Widow Catharine.

As Henry VIII's notice was becoming focused on Catharine, she was enjoying her first flirtation with a contemporary in his prime. The object of her affection was Sir Thomas Seymour, brother of the late Queen Jane and uncle to Prince Edward. However, the king's wishes and Catharine's finely honed sense of duty nipped the bourgeoning romance in the bud, and Seymour was packed off to Brussels on a long-term diplomatic mission. Catharine became the sixth wife of Henry VIII in a ceremony at Hampton Court on July 12, 1543.

Catharine promptly put away whatever misgivings she may have had about her third match and set about making it a success. She chose "To Be Useful in All That I Do" as her motto, and lived up to it admirably. To the king, she was an excellent companion and caring nurse. The two shared a love of music, conversation, and finery that helped bridge the years. To his children she became a champion, overseeing their education, working at reconciliation with their father, and very likely being the moving force behind the new *Act of Succession* of 1544, which placed the Princesses Mary and Elizabeth back into line for the throne. And with the courtiers, she retained the widespread popularity she had enjoyed as Lady Latimer. Indeed, the king was so well pleased with Catharine that he appointed her Regent of England when he went to war with France the year after their marriage.

All were not enamored of Catharine of course. As queen, she continued to exercise her intellectual abilities by becoming proficient in Italian and Latin, and was competent in Greek. She also published her first book, *Prayers and Meditations,* in 1545. But it was her lively interest in the new Protestant faith, about which she liked to engage both the king and courtiers in debate, that nearly brought about her downfall. Theology was a touchy subject in England at the time, as the king had denied papal supremacy and installed himself as head of the Church of England back in 1534. He was, however, equally antagonistic to the teachings of such Protestant reformers as Martin Luther, whose views were seen as heretical. Catharine, nonetheless, found the new faith enticing, much to the hostility of Lord Chancellor Thomas Wriothesley and Bishop Stephen Gardiner, among others. Charges of heresy were drawn up against her in the summer of 1546, but Catharine managed to reconcile with the king in the eleventh hour and avoid arrest.

As 1546 progressed, Henry VIII's health declined steadily. Catharine continued to attentively nurse him and attend to her other duties. By winter the king was gravely ill and on January 28, 1547, he died at the age of 55. Catharine thus became a widow once more at 35; but this time, she also was the dowager queen.

Dowager Queen and New Wife

Prince Edward was crowned King Edward VI on January 31, 1547, and Seymour's older brother, Edward, was named to rule in the young king's name. Catharine chose to retire from court to her house in Chelsea. Her old beau Seymour was back, now resplendent as Baron Seymour of Sudeley Castle, Lord High Admiral for life, and member of the Order of the Garter. He renewed his suit for her hand and, for the first time in her life, Catharine was free to follow her heart. So, with what many considered unseemly haste, Catharine and Seymour were married in the spring of 1547.

Dashing and successful, Seymour was a man of consummate ambition. There were even rumors that he had made advances toward the young Princess Elizabeth that necessitated cutting short her stay in the newlyweds' household at Sudeley Castle. Nonetheless, Catharine apparently loved him and was delighted to find herself pregnant with her first child in November of 1547. That same month and year, she published her second book, *The Lamentations of a Sinner,* which enjoyed widespread acclaim. This idyllic period was unfortunately short-lived. Catharine gave birth to a daughter named Mary on August 30, 1548 and died within the week of puerperal fever. Seymour was executed for treason the following year.

Although it was a sad ending for a woman who had devoted her life to others, Catharine's legacy was more far-reaching than that of a simple kindness of spirit. It was likely that through her efforts the daughters of Henry VIII were restored to the line of succession in 1544. And it was certainly under her guidance that they were highly and broadly educated. While this direction may have produced less than pleasing results in the case of the elder, Princess Mary, its fruits became abundant and obvious when Princess Elizabeth became Queen Elizabeth I in 1558 and ushered in the Golden Age of Elizabethan England.

Periodicals

Coventry Evening Telegraph (England), July 12, 1999.
Guardian (London, England), February 25, 2004.
Times (London, England), September 7, 1996.

Online

"Catherine Parr," About, http://www.womenshistory.about .com/od/tudor/p/Catherine_parr.htm (November 28, 2006).
"Catherine Parr," NNDB, http://www.nndb.com/people/606/ 000096318/ (November 28, 2006).
"Catherine Parr (1512–1548)," *Britannica,* http://www.britannica .com/bios/cparr.html (November 28, 2006).
"Catherine Parr, Queen of England," Tudor Place, http://www .tudorplace.com.ar/aboutCatherineParr.htm (November 28, 2006).
"Elizabethan England," Shakespeare Resource Center, http://www .bardweb.net/england.html (December 14, 2006).
"Katharine Parr," English History, http://www.englishhistory .net/tudor/monarchs/parr.html (November 28, 2006).
"Katherine Parr," *Luminarium,* http://www.luminarium.org/ encyclopedia.katherineparr.htm (November 28, 2006).
"Katherine Parr," Tudor History, http://www.tudorhistory.org/ parr/ (November 28, 2006).
"Pilgrimage of Grace," Infoplease, http://www.print.infoplease .com/ce6/history/A0839039.html (December 13, 2006).
"The Six Wives of Henry VIII," PBS, http://www.pbs.org/wnet/ sixwives/print/cp_handbook.html (November 28, 2006). □

Susie Sumner Revels Cayton

Susie Sumner Revels Cayton (1870–1943) was one of just a handful of black women working in American journalism at the turn of the twentieth century. For several years Cayton served as associate editor of the *Seattle Republican,* the paper her husband founded, that at one time held the number two spot in circulation in the city. They lost much of their

personal wealth, however, when it folded because of racial prejudice and local political turmoil.

C ayton came into the world at an auspicious moment for her family, and for African Americans: she was born in 1870, the same year her father, Hiram Rhodes Revels (1827–1901) became the first black senator in U.S. history. A college-educated native of North Carolina, a second-generation free black, and an African Methodist Episcopal (A.M.E.) minister, Hiram Revels served in a black regiment he helped muster for the Union Army during the U.S. Civil War. He was elected to the state legislature in Mississippi during the postwar period known as Reconstruction, when the white Democratic politicians who had supported the Confederate cause were removed from power and many blacks were allowed to join the political process for the first time. Revels and these other trailblazers did so largely as ardent members of the Republican Party, which had been founded on an anti-slavery platform. In early 1870 he was elected by his legislative colleagues to fill an unexpired term in the U.S. Senate, which prompted immense press coverage and made him nationally famous. At his swearing-in ceremony, however, the other senators declined to follow tradition and usher him to the podium. Only noted abolitionist Charles Sumner (1811–1874) of Massachusetts did so, and to thank him, Revels and his wife named their newborn daughter, Susie Sumner Revels, in his honor.

Spent Childhood on College Campus

Cayton was the fourth of six daughters born to the senator, who served just one year, and Phoebe Bass Revels, a Quaker from Zanesville, Ohio. After the senator's term in Washington ended, he returned to Mississippi with his family, and became the first president of Alcorn Agricultural and Mechanical College (later Alcorn State University). This was the first state-funded institution of higher education for blacks anywhere in the country, and Cayton received an excellent education, thanks to her father's position. As a young woman she taught school while taking courses at State Normal School in Holly Springs (later Rust College), which granted her a degree and then hired her as a teacher.

Cayton had been corresponding with a former Alcorn student named Horace Roscoe Cayton Sr., who had gone West after finishing his education. Horace, about 10 years her senior, had been born into slavery in Mississippi, spent several years at Alcorn, and then made his way to Kansas and Utah before settling in Washington State when it was still Washington Territory. There was a growing influx of blacks to the area, attracted in part by the frontier spirit and an absence of the entrenched racism that existed elsewhere in the United States, and by 1890 Horace had settled in Seattle and was writing for the *Post-Intelligencer* newspaper. For a time, he took over the city's black newspaper, *The Standard,* but in 1894 he founded the *Seattle Republican,* a newspaper aimed at both black and white readers who supported the Republican Party.

Cayton began contributing articles and short stories to the *Seattle Republican* early in 1896, when she was still living in Mississippi. Her first byline appeared above a story she wrote that bore the title "Negroes at the Atlanta Exposition," and for it she had interviewed a West African chief who brought several members of his tribe to the exhibition. That fair, held in September of 1895 and formally known as the Cotton States and International Exposition, was notable for the speech that educator Booker T. Washington (1856–1915) delivered there that became known as the "Atlanta Compromise" for its conciliatory tone on civil right issues.

Moved West

Cayton joined Horace in Seattle in the summer of 1896, and they were married on July 12, 1896. Their union was a mutually beneficial one. She was likely eager to leave the South, where the political, economic, and social achievements of Reconstruction had already faded and had been replaced by discriminatory local ordinances that drastically restricted black life in most of the former Confederate states. For Horace, an ex-slave, marrying a third-generation free black who was also the daughter of a former U.S. senator elevated his standing among Seattle's black elite. They soon began a family that would number five biological children in all: daughters Ruth, Madge, and Lillie, along with sons Horace Roscoe Jr. and Revels; they also raised Emma, the daughter of one of Cayton's sisters, after the mother's death.

Cayton served as associate editor of the *Seattle Republican,* contributing short stories, essays, and feature articles. Her editorials often addressed racial topics, including one about the scarcity of black dolls available for children, and she urged African American mothers to sew their own. In another editorial, dated 1908, she wrote of the importance of education for women, even if they chose to restrict their work to taking care of their home and family. "The mental development of any people is dependent almost solely on the efforts of the woman," she asserted, according to a reprint found on the website of the Seattle Civil Rights and Labor History Project. "It is the hand that rocks the cradle that also directs the destinies of the human family." In her own home, Cayton ensured that every one of her children learned to play a musical instrument, and leisure time activities often featured a performance of the family orchestra.

The *Seattle Republican* had offices in the Burke Building in downtown Seattle, and sold for five cents a copy. An annual subscription cost $2.00. During its two-decade run it attracted a national readership in part because Seattle was a rail hub, and the black passenger train employees known as Pullman porters based in the city took it with them on their routes. The Caytons urged African Americans to come west to escape the racial prejudices of the East, and voiced editorial objections to the growing number of lynchings that began to plague the south in the years before World War I. "May the Lord have mercy on the men's souls who do such for we feel that they are ignorant, semi-barbaric and devoid of either Christian or social influences," one editorial exhorted, according to Mark N. Trahant in the *Seattle Times.*

The Caytons further suggested that such communities might benefit from an influx of Christian missionaries.

Target of Resentment

Cayton and her husband were well known figures in the black community in Seattle, but their fame reached further afield. In 1909, Booker T. Washington came to Seattle for the Alaskan, Yukon and Pacific Exposition, and stayed at their home. Years later, the actor and political activist Paul Robeson (1898–1976) appeared at their home, uninvited but welcomed immediately and offered a room, as well as the poet Langston Hughes (1902–1967). Theirs was the only black household in the affluent Capitol Hill area, home to the city's grandest mansions, and they had a Japanese servant named Nish. Among some members of Seattle's black community, however, the Caytons were resented for what was considered putting on airs by living in a white section of the city and keeping servants. Their neighbors resented their presence, too: in 1909, six years after their purchase of the house, a white real estate agent filed a lawsuit claiming that their presence had reduced property values in the neighborhood. The Caytons mounted a successful legal defense, but had they lost they would have been forced to sell their home.

Cayton played an important part in the running of the newspaper, and was thanked publicly in an article written by her husband that appeared in the July 23, 1909, issue. Titled "Good Woman's Helping Hand," the tribute described her as someone "who not only makes husbands men in the true sense of the word, but who makes the men and women of tomorrow," according to the Seattle Civil Rights and Labor History Project website. Cayton was also active outside of her home and office as a member of numerous charitable and cultural organizations. She also founded the Dorcus Charity Club, which raised funds to help the poorest of Seattle's black community through Christmas toy drives and financial stipends to elderly widows, in an era long before company retirement benefits or Social Security income aided Americans aged 65 or older. In 1907 the Dorcus women played an instrumental role in urging Seattle Children's Hospital to officially adopt an anti-discrimination policy.

The Caytons' newspaper, however, began to lose advertisers, thanks to a Seattle that was becoming increasingly segregated, and Horace's attacks on local elected officials and public figures further damaged its support base. He was arrested twice for libel, and was the defendant in several lawsuits, one after he accused the Seattle's police chief of graft; fortunately, the trial ended with a hung jury, but the skirmish earned the newspaper some influential enemies. Horace had been a well-known figure in local Republican Party politics, and served on the party's state committee, but when racism intensified in the city, many of his political cohorts failed to publicly support him, out of fear of losing their voter base. Finally, the *Seattle Republican* was forced to close due to lack of revenue and mounting debt around the time of World War I. Horace went on to publish *Cayton's Weekly* for several years, but that, too, had folded by 1921.

Impoverished Later Years

Cayton and her husband sold their Capitol Hill home, relocating to Seattle's Italian-American neighborhood, and their financial situation worsened over the years. They had some income from rental properties they owned, and Horace continued to write for other publications, but eventually he was forced to take a position as a janitor, while Cayton worked part-time as a domestic. They were ostracized by some of the black community when their financial status shifted, and their downfall was viewed as a comeuppance for their earlier success.

Except for Ruth, who died young, the Cayton children followed in their parents' footsteps and accrued many professional achievements in their respective careers. Daughter Madge graduated from the University of Washington with a degree in international business, but worked in restaurants for years, unable to find a job in her field. She eventually became a social worker in Chicago. Her sister Lillie overcame alcoholism and was active in the Pacific Northwest organization of Alcoholics Anonymous. The Caytons' son, Revels, became a sailor and then a union organizer, while his brother, Horace Jr., emerged as a prominent sociologist who co-authored a landmark study about blacks in Chicago, *Black Metropolis,* published in 1945. His mother joined him and Madge in that city after the death of Horace Sr. in 1940. She died on July 28, 1943, and her passing was noted in the *New York Times.*

The Cayton family has continued to fascinate scholars of black life in America. In 2002 their saga was chronicled by historian Richard S. Hobbs in *The Cayton Legacy: An African American Family,* published by Washington State University Press.

Books

Notable Black American Women, Book 3, Gale, 2002.

Periodicals

Oregon Historical Quarterly, Summer 2003.
Seattle Republican, February 14, 1908.
Seattle Times, October 8, 1998.

Online

"Susie Revels Cayton: The Part She Played," Seattle Civil Rights and Labor History Project, http://www.depts.washington.edu/civilr/susie_cayton.htm (December 9, 2006). ☐

Jackie Chan

Hong Kong martial arts film star Jackie Chan (born 1954) is one of the most recognizable cinematic personalities in the world. His mixture of literally death-defying stunts and genial, self-deprecating comedy gained a massive following first in Hong Kong, then over much of Asia, and finally, beginning in the late 1990s, in the United States.

C han has been famous for doing his own stunts on film, largely without the aid of special effects, and the closing credits of his more recent releases feature a comic but brutal background montage of stunts gone wrong. The list of body parts Chan has injured while filming includes his head (it has a deep dent into which he will sometimes allow reporters to stick their fingers), eye, mouth, teeth, throat, neck, arm, shoulder, legs, foot, nose, ears, cheekbone, chin, hand, back, chest, pelvis, and knee. Yet the comic side of Chan's film persona has been as important as his action skills, acquired through ten years of rigorous training in Chinese opera. It was comedy that set Chan apart from other kung fu and action stars, including the hard-to-top Bruce Lee. "When Bruce Lee punched someone, he kept going like it didn't hurt," Chan told Gregory Cerio of *People*. "I shake my hand and go, 'Ow!'"

Parents Held Embassy Jobs

Jackie Chan was born Chan Kong-Sang (in Chinese usage the family name, Chan, is written first) in Hong Kong on April 7, 1954. Press accounts and his own website state that his parents were poor but steadily employed Hong Kong residents who worked at the French embassy, his father Charles as a cook and his mother Lily (or Lee-Lee) as a housekeeper. Chan's parents, however, had a colorful past, revealed in the 2003 documentary *Traces of a Dragon*. Chan's father was a spy for China's pre-World War II Nationalist government and later a member of Shanghai's organized crime underworld who was forced to flee to Hong Kong after the Communist takeover of mainland China in

1949. His mother was a stage performer and occasional opium dealer whom Charles Chan arrested as part of his intelligence duties but released and then later married.

Jackie Chan was apparently physically powerful even as an infant; his weight at birth has been reported as anywhere from nine to 12 pounds, and his parents nicknamed him "Shandong Cannon." When he was seven, his parents moved to Australia so that Charles Chan could take a job as head cook at the American embassy there. They decided that Jackie should stay in Hong Kong, and enrolled him at a boarding school there, a strict but world-class institution called the China Drama Academy. Among Chan's classmates at the school were Sammo Hung and Yuen Biao, both of whom went on to careers as major martial arts stars.

At the school, Chan studied traditional Chinese opera, a mix of singing, stagecraft, martial arts, and difficult acrobatics. Chan had to get up in the morning at 5 a.m., often working until midnight. Errors were punished with physical abuse. "I was beaten every day," Chan told Cerio. "I was very angry." Even as a student, however, Chan had small roles in several films, and by the time he graduated at 17, in 1971, he had acquired formidable stunt skills. He found work in Hong Kong's growing film industry, appearing in martial arts films, and even had an uncredited role as an extra in the greatest international action success of them all, Bruce Lee's film *Enter the Dragon* (1973).

For a few years in the early 1970s, the film work petered out and Chan was forced to move in with his parents in Australia. He did construction work, acquiring the nickname "Jackie" (at first it was "Little Jack") from a co-worker named Jack who found his Chinese name hard to pronounce. In 1976 Chan, at the invitation of a talent promoter named Willie Chan (no relation), returned to Hong Kong to give his career another try. He began to bill himself as Sing Lung, which means "to become the dragon," and he became one of a host of young martial artists hoping to fill the shoes of Bruce Lee, who had died in 1973. Several action films, including *Shaolin Chamber of Death* (1976) and *Fist of Death* (1977), met with limited success.

Introduced Comedic Element

Chan's fortunes improved when he began to experiment with comic characterizations. The switch brought a fresh perspective to a genre whose original principles Lee had taken to their limits, and allowed Chan to take advantage of the acting skills he had learned at the opera school. Chan parodied traditional martial arts storylines in such films as *Snake in the Eagle's Shadow* (1977), where instead of modeling his art on the fighting skills of the animals named in the film's title, he emulates his pet cat. In *Half a Loaf of Kung Fu* (1978) he learns martial arts not from a revered master but from a pair of street people.

His breakthrough came in 1978 with *Drunken Master*, a historical tale of a young kung fu student who learns a style in which the fighter appears to be drunk. *Drunken Master* became a hit in Asia and an art house success in the United States, spawning a sequel and eventually a restored American reissue, as Chan's popularity finally crossed the Pacific. Chan's performance was a virtuoso blend of action and perfectly controlled (and often highly comic) false-drunken choreography.

In the early 1980s Chan made his first attempt to break into the American market. His desire to do so was natural enough, but Jeff Rovin and Kathy Tracy, in *The Essential Jackie Chan Sourcebook,* reported that he might also have been motivated by death threats from members of the Chinese underworld who had backed his earlier films. His U.S. experiment failed initially, as Chan took straight action roles in films helmed by directors who failed to appreciate the unique nature of his talents. Two films in which he starred, *The Big Brawl* (1980) and *The Protector* (1985, opposite Danny Aiello), went nowhere, but his face did become implanted in the minds of American audiences as a result of his small role in the hit *Cannonball Run* (1981). Back in Hong Kong, Chan honed his comedic persona in such films as the dizzyingly paced slapstick action comedy *Project A* (1983), in which, borrowing a prop from American silent-film comic Harold Lloyd, he took a headfirst plunge off a giant clock face.

Thanks to the sheer energy of such films, Chan began to acquire a following among American cult film enthusiasts. In Asia, his success had more dramatic financial implications; audiences flocked to see him top himself with newly inventive stunts in each successive release. *Police Story* (1985) contained an especially dangerous pole-sliding stunt that nearly paralyzed Chan after a fall in which he broke two vertebrae in his spine. In *Operation Condor* (1990) he rode a motorcycle off a river dock and jumped off, catching, in midair, a net attached to a nearby crane. His kung fu scenes might use an amazing variety of weapons, including a hat rack and fans of various kinds. Chan's films became slicker as his box office numbers increased—1992's *Twin Dragons* was a flashy comedic take on European action star Jean-Claude van Damme's *Double Impact,* with an awe-inspiring final chase through a Toyota auto-testing facility. But his stunts were always his own, and his everyman comic gift remained endearing. Sometimes Chan's character would be a young man who bumbled through a film's early scenes but had the chance to redeem himself in the end.

Kept Marriage Secret

By the early 1990s Chan was perhaps the top marquee attraction on the Asian continent. He had some success as a singer, later expressing a wish to remake the classic film *The Sound of Music,* and his carefully guarded personal life was the stuff of tabloid headlines. One of his legion of female fans was reportedly driven to suicide by rumors that he was actually involved with another woman, and those rumors turned out to be true; in 1982 Chan married Taiwanese actress Lin Feng-Jiao. He also has a son, Jaycee. Chan revealed the marriage only in his 1998 autobiography, *I Am Jackie Chan.*

Despite his success, Chan's lack of success in the American market still rankled. With strong underground buzz culminating in a 1995 lifetime achievement nod at the MTV Movie Awards, presented by director Quentin Tarantino, Hollywood distributors resolved to give Chan another try. His first new American effort, *Rumble in the Bronx,* was a dubbed version of an earlier Cantonese-language Hong Kong release, but it did well enough to pave the way for subsequent Chan releases stateside. Chan hit paydirt with *Rush Hour* (1998) and *Shanghai Noon* (2000), both genre films featuring American stars (Chris Tucker and Owen Wilson, respectively) with whom Chan could establish comic chemistry. Both films spawned successful sequels, but Chan's original Asian audience was cool to them. *Rush Hour, Shanghai Noon,* and *Rush Hour 2* collectively took in some $50 million in Asian theaters, while two contemporaneous Cantonese-language releases, *Gorgeous* and *The Accidental Spy* earned $90 million or more.

By the mid-2000s, even with the benefits reaped from a lifetime of physical conditioning, Chan faced the problem of where to go next with his career. "I am not so good at healing now," he admitted to *People.* Chan appeared in films beyond the action genre such as the ensemble adventure *Around the World in 80 Days,* a big-budget family film that failed to meet box office expectations. And he gradually expanded his production activities. He starred in and executive-produced the 2005 Hong Kong film *The Myth,* a period adventure in which he portrayed an archaeologist. Chan diversified beyond direct involvement with films, opening a string of restaurants in Southeast Asia (and one in Honolulu, Jackie's Kitchen). He also attached his name to lines of shoes, clothes, golf clubs, skin-care products, and table tennis balls. He considered the idea of opening a school for aspiring stunt specialists.

Chan also began to devote time to humanitarian activities, serving as an ambassador for the UNICEF/UNAIDS children's organization. Still, his energy remained devoted mostly to films. He felt a commitment to continue working in Hong Kong, where film profits had deteriorated under the twin pressures of Communist Chinese oversight of the former British colony and rampant video piracy in Chan's home Asian market. He provided dialogue for an animated television series, *Jackie Chan Adventures,* on the Kids' WB cable network. As of 2006, an American release of Chan's Cantonese-language *New Police Story* was under consideration, and *Rush Hour 3* was in production.

Books

Chan, Jackie, with Jeff Yang, *I Am Jackie Chan: My Life in Action,* Ballantine, 1998.
International Dictionary of Films and Filmmakers, Volume 3: Actors and Actresses, 4th ed., St. James, 2000.
Rovin, Jeff, and Kathy Tracy, *The Essential Jackie Chan Sourcebook,* Pocket Books, 1997.

Periodicals

Entertainment Weekly, February 16, 1996; November 3, 2000.
People, March 11, 1996; June 28, 2004.
Star Tribune (Minneapolis, MN), February 18, 1996.
Time, February 13, 1995; June 5, 2000.
Variety, December 3, 2001; February 4, 2002; February 17, 2003; August 9, 2004; September 26, 2005.

Online

"About Jackie," Jackie Chan Official Website, http://www.jackiechan.com (December 12, 2006). □

Elaine Chao

The first Asian-American woman to serve in the United States cabinet, Elaine Chao (born 1953) was named U.S. Secretary of Labor by President George W. Bush in 2001. After the 2004 presidential election, she was kept on in her cabinet post when Bush moved into his second term.

Sailed on Freighter

Elaine Lan Chao was born in Taipei, Taiwan, on March 26, 1953. She was the oldest of six girls. Her family had come to Taiwan in 1949, fleeing the Communist takeover of the Chinese mainland, and they had connections to two Chinese families who owned shipping companies. In 1958 Chao's father, James, came to the United States, taking a job with one of those companies and enrolling as a student at St. John's University in New York. Three years later the rest of the family came to join him in a one-bedroom apartment in Queens. They booked passage on a freighter that took 30 days to make the trip from Hong Kong to Los Angeles.

Chao arrived in the United States speaking no English. At first she experienced severe culture shock. Her father told her to greet her teacher on her first day of school, and she fulfilled his request by bowing to the teacher in the traditional Chinese manner, provoking peals of laughter from her classmates. Halloween was a special challenge; when children showed up at the door dressed in scary costumes, Chao thought the house was being robbed, and turned over supplies of flour and other staples. Soon, however, her gift for relating to the people around her asserted itself. Within two years Chao had been elected president of her class.

Meanwhile, James Chao's new shipping business, Foremost Maritime Corporation, was prospering. The family moved to a posh area of suburban Westchester County. Elaine Chao was schooled in the value of hard work—and not only in the classroom. Chao and her sisters were given such problem-solving tasks as fixing toilets and resurfacing the family's long circular driveway. Chao was admitted to Mount Holyoke College, an elite all-female institution in South Hadley, Massachusetts. She majored in economics, taking classes in international finance and graduating in 1975.

Chao went on for a master's degree in business administration at the Harvard Business School, working for the Gulf Oil Corporation while she was in school. After receiving her degree, she worked for four years as a lending officer in the international banking division of Citicorp, concentrating on the shipping industry. Chao's first exposure to politics and government came in 1983, when she spent a year as a fellow in the White House Office of Policy Development, working on transportation issues in the administration of President Ronald Reagan.

Gravitated Toward Government Service

After her term at the White House was over, Chao taught briefly at St. John's and then returned to the private sector, spending three years as vice president of BankAmerica's capital markets group. In 1986, however, she reentered public service as deputy maritime administrator in the U.S. Department of Transportation. She was promoted to chairman of the Federal Maritime Commission in 1988, serving as chairman of a group called Asian Americans for Bush/Quayle during that year's presidential campaign. After the inauguration of President George H. W. Bush in 1989, she became deputy secretary of the Transportation Department.

Sometimes serving as an advocate for shipping industry interests in these posts, Chao gained both her first executive position and her first high-profile job when President Bush named her director of the Peace Corps in 1991. There, in the wake of the collapse of Communism in the Soviet Union, she recruited American business students to start new industries that would lay the groundwork for the emergence of Russia's new capitalist economy. She also started the first Peace Corps programs in the newly independent states of the Baltic region. With the defeat of Chao's Republican Party in the 1992 presidential election, she was out of the government sphere once again, but her next job both raised her public profile still higher and tested her managerial skills.

When Chao took over the presidency of the United Way of America, a nonprofit agency responsible for administering more than $3 billion in charitable donations made annually by millions of American workers, the organization was in a state of crisis. Its former president, William Aramony, had resigned after revelations that he spent agency funds on such personal perks as first class airline tickets. Donations were falling, and local United Way branches were reevaluating their relationships with the national agency. Chao moved to reestablish the United Way's credibility. She began with a 50 percent cut in the president's salary, which under Aramony had stood at $390,000, and in subsequent years she refused to accept raises offered to her. She also instituted a new ethics code, along with specific expense accounting controls, and she created a new member services agency to improve communication between the national group and local chapters. Members of the United Way board of directors, satisfied that the group's worst troubles were behind them by the time Chao departed in 1996, pooled personal funds to offer her a going-away bonus of $292,500, but Chao turned that down, too.

By that time Chao had officially become one-half of a Washington power couple, marrying U.S. Sen. Mitch McConnell (R-Ky) in 1993. She assumed the role of stepmother to McConnell's three children from a previous marriage. Working for four years as an editor and senior fellow at the conservative Heritage Foundation think tank, Chao moved to Kentucky with McConnell and became a frequent sight at local sporting events. Asked by *Time* after she became Labor Secretary whether the two discussed policy on their personal time, Chao replied, "No, we're much too busy. We both love what we're doing. When we have time together, we talk about college football, about getting together with friends—the usual kind of stuff—[like] who takes out the garbage. . . . I have to confess, I do." Chao kept a hand in politics as founder of the Independent Women's Forum, a group of conservative women who touted the virtues of individual initiative.

Emerged as Compromise Labor Secretary Pick

After George W. Bush emerged as the winner of the disputed 2000 presidential election, Chao seemed likely at first to be shut out of her ultimate goal of a cabinet seat when fellow Asian American Norman Mineta was chosen as Secretary of Transportation, and former U.S. Treasurer Linda Chavez was nominated as Secretary of Labor. The Chavez nomination, however, collapsed after revelations that Chavez had employed an undocumented alien as a worker in her home, and Bush turned to Chao instead. "She brings to this post the qualities for which she is known and admired—strong executive talent, great compassion, and a commitment to helping people build better lives," Bush said in a statement quoted in the *San Francisco Chronicle*.

At first, although she was a staunch conservative who had dismayed some Asian-American activists with her opposition to affirmative action programs, Chao encountered little resistance. One Republican senator told Anne Kornbluth of the *Boston Globe* that she was a "rock-solid" choice, and even the president's opponents in the labor movement placed no barriers in the way of her confirmation. Chao had worked previously with John Sweeney, president of the AFL-CIO union umbrella organization, who merely said (according to Kornbluth) "I would like to meet with her to discuss the many challenges facing the new secretary of labor."

As she had been in previous posts, Chao was successful as a manager. Devoted to her work, she would sometimes awaken at 2 a.m. for an e-mail session, and then go back to bed. Chao was well liked by her employees, whom she treated to surprise birthday parties and, for her security detail, impromptu frozen yogurt stops. Some of her staff had been with her since the 1980s, as she moved through jobs in a variety of organizations. And Chao's status as the first Asian-American woman cabinet head in American history was not lost on Asian groups, who sent a steady stream of lecture invitations her way. "She gets an Arnold Schwarzenegger [California's popular Austrian-immigrant governor] reaction from Asian Americans," Mitch McConnell told Stephanie Armour of *USA Today*. "They want to meet her, have their picture taken with her."

After several years of Chao's actions in office, however, the bloom was off the relationship between Chao and leaders of some labor groups. Chao and her onetime defender Sweeney clashed over a Chao initiative to strengthen financial reporting rules for labor unions. "She's cut health and safety law enforcement, child-labor regulation, and the minimum wage. She stopped investigations into ergonomic injuries," wrote Mary Conroy of Wisconsin's *Capital Times*. "Although she says there's no money for those items, she can find plenty of money to audit unions." One of Chao's deputies in the Labor Department was a former Heritage Foundation scholar who had written a paper titled "How to Close Down the Labor Department." Chao nevertheless had her defenders, even within the labor movement. Don Carson of the International Union of Operating Engineers told Armour that "she definitely looks out for the welfare of workers. She's been very progressive. She's making a big difference." Chao for her own part told Armour that "all of our initiatives have as their goal to improve the lives of American workers." And she expressed frustration over her interactions with labor leaders, telling David T. Cook of the *Christian Science Monitor* that "we really tried to reach out to organized labor and the leaders of the federation. It is a two-way street. I can't make them work with me if they don't want to."

One of the most sensitive areas under Chao's jurisdiction, in view of several tragic mine disasters that occurred in the mid-2000s, was that of mine worker safety. A *Lexington [Kentucky] Herald-Leader* report in 2006 explored mining industry donations to Mitch McConnell's campaigns, and the overlap between the McConnell and Chao staffs. Specifically, the paper alleged that Chao quashed an investigation into a 2000 coal slurry spill released by Massey Energy Co., a McConnell donor. McConnell rejoined that since both he and Chao were supporters of the Republican agenda, it was no surprise that their positions coincided. "She doesn't need any direction from me," he told John Cheves of the *Herald-Leader*. "In fact, I think that's a little bit insulting. . . . I'm a Republican, and I generally support what the Bush administration is trying to do. She takes her orders from the White House.'' Labor Department officials contended that mine safety citations actually increased in number during Chao's tenure.''

Generally, Chao avoided the controversies that surrounded several other members of the Bush cabinet, and she was asked to stay on for a second term after Bush won reelection in 2004. In 2005 a survey of Republican Party insiders named Chao as the most underrated member of President Bush's cabinet. By the middle of her second term, she had shepherded several major initiatives through the federal bureaucracy. The Labor Department had implemented a new set of white-collar overtime regulations into enforcement of the Fair Labor Standards Act, a plan that had been on the agenda of a succession of Republican and Democratic administrations. And Chao was instrumental in shaping the Pension Reform Act of 2006, which beefed up corporate contributions to a federal pension insurance fund and mandated new pension fund accounting requirements. Chao had also become a tireless advocate for worker retraining programs, many of which were assisted by Labor Department funds. ''I am not pro-business or pro-union,'' she told Cook. ''I'm for the 11 percent [of workers] who are organized and the 89 percent who are not.''

Books

Flanders, Laura, *Bushwomen,* Verso, 2004.
Notable Asian Americans, Gale, 1995.

Periodicals

Boston Globe, January 12, 2001.
Capital Times (Madison, WI), May 19, 2004.
Christian Science Monitor, May 8, 1997; May 29, 2003.
Kentucky Post (Covington, KY), February 22, 2001.
Lexington Herald-Leader (Lexington, KY), October 20, 2006.
New York Times, February 15, 2001.
Orange County Register (Santa Ana, CA), July 11, 2006.
Plain Dealer (Cleveland, OH), February 3, 2006.
Rocky Mountain News (Denver), May 14, 1996.
San Francisco Chronicle, January 12, 2001.
Time, December 19, 2005.
USA Today, August 29, 2003.
Washington Times, June 20, 1996.
Workforce Management, August 1, 2005.

Online

''About Secretary of Labor Elaine L. Chao,'' U.S. Department of Labor, http://www.dol.gov/_sec/aboutsec/chao.htm (December 10, 2006). □

Wendell Chino

Wendell Chino (1923–1998) was a nationally recognized Native American leader. For most of his life he served as the president of the Mescalero Apache Nation. During his tenure he raised his tribe from poverty and helped it become one of the most prosperous in American history.

As an advocate of American Indian rights and tribal sovereignty, Wendell Chino was one of the most innovative and influential Native American leaders. Advancing the philosophy of ''red capitalism,'' he encouraged tribes to regain control of their lands and attain economic freedom. Further, through his example Chino provided tribes with a practical template for self-governance and business management.

Chino, the son of Sam Chino, was born on December 25, 1923, on the Mescalero reservation in New Mexico. The year after his birth, the U.S. Congress granted American citizenship to all Native Americans.

Eleven years before Chino's birth, his parents were freed by the U.S Army after they had been incarcerated as prisoners of war. Upon their release they were afforded two options: They could either move to Oklahoma or to New Mexico, where they could settle on the Mescalero Reservation, located two hundred miles south of Albuquerque. The Chinos chose the New Mexico reservation, an area of land that included 720 square miles nestled in the Sacramento Mountains, in the south central part of the state. The reservation had been established in 1873 and provided a home for approximately 4,000 Apaches.

By the time Chino was born, little had changed on the reservation in terms of the Apaches' lifestyle. Tribal members subsisted on a few farm crops and depended upon supplies from the U.S. government. Further, the reservation housed no form of industry, and job opportunities for the inhabitants were almost non-existent. When he became an adult, Chino would substantially improve the prospects for reservation inhabitants.

Little is known about the early life of the future tribal leader beyond his educational experience. He attended the Santa Fe Indian School in New Mexico and, later, Central College in Pella, Iowa, and the Cook Christian School in Phoenix, Arizona. In 1951 he graduated from Western Theological Seminary in Holland, Michigan. That same year he was ordained as a minister in the Dutch Reformed Church. After ordination he returned to the reservation.

Became Tribal Leader

In 1955, when he was only 28 years old, Chino was elected chairman of the Mescalero tribal governing committee, the reservation's highest elective office. He held that post until 1965, when the tribe changed its constitution and adopted a council form of government that would be headed by a president. Chino easily won the first presidential election and was subsequently re-elected 16 consecutive times, serving in that role until he died in 1998.

In all, he served as president for 43 years. Though he was often described as iron-fisted and autocratic, he proved to be an innovative leader who would successfully develop and diversify his tribe's business pursuits. Intent on securing tribal sovereignty, he helped preserve his people's heritage and at the same time led the tribe into the twentieth century. During his presidency he would advance the notion of "red capitalism," which essentially meant that Native Americans should make their own decisions regarding their tribal lands and business affairs. At once benevolent and brash, charismatic and controversial, he often worked the U.S. legal system to force the government to honor the treaties it had established with Indian nations. Chino launched his arguments with his characteristically loud and commanding voice, and his demeanor and approach gained him both friends and enemies among the highly placed politicians in New Mexico and Washington, D.C.

Helped Develop Reservation Businesses

Chino first advanced his agenda by taking advantage of the expiring contracts with the Bureau of Indian Affairs that covered the reservation's natural resources. Until the mid-1960s (the period when Chino became tribal president), the Bureau managed all resources including mining, timber, water use, and grazing rights. Instead of renewing the contracts, Chino allowed them to lapse. When the contracts ran their course, he was then able to establish lumber production and cattle companies that the tribe could manage. Justifying his actions during a 1977 court case involving control of Mescalero natural resources, Chino stated, "The white man has raped this land and now he wastes six million acres of Indian land use in this state."

Chino often took his fights straight to the federal level. In the process he strongly criticized then-President Jimmy Carter. "If Carter has time enough to worry about human rights in Latin America and poverty in Africa, he should find some time to visit American Indians," he said in 1978.

In working to achieve his vision of "red capitalism," Chino helped provide his people with a level of economic growth never before experienced by any other Native American tribe. Essentially, the reservation became a small business empire. In addition to business enterprises, Chino also helped established schools, a hospital, and a health center.

Established Resort and Casino

At the Mescalero reservation, Chino's most ambitious and profitable project involved the creation of a ski resort, called the Inn of the Mountain Gods, a recreational facility located in the 12,000-foot Sierra Blanca Mountain. The resort, which was built in 1975, not only generated steady income; it also provided employment for reservation dwellers.

The 250-room resort included a championship caliber golf course, the first tribal-owned course in the United States. When Chino first suggested the idea, fellow tribe members were taken aback, as they were completely unfamiliar with the sport. Indeed, even Chino had never played golf. Nevertheless, he went ahead with the project, transforming farmland and picturesque terrain into a 100-acre course within the rocky hillsides, along creeks, and adjacent to Lake Mescalero. The course proved an immediate success. Moreover, it was a pioneering endeavor. Other tribes followed suit. In subsequent years more than 50 tribal-owned golf courses would emerge in 17 states, from the American Southwest to the upper Midwest.

Later the Mescalero resort property housed a casino, even though New Mexico had outlawed gambling. Chino circumvented this legal technicality by claiming tribal sovereignty for the reservation. The casino proved as trend setting as the golf course, and other reservations followed Chino's entrepreneurial and economic lead. About his efforts toward tribal economic self-sufficiency, Chino once reportedly joked that "The Zuni make jewelry, the Navajo make blankets, and the Apache make money."

Because of his leadership abilities and accomplishments, Chino gained national recognition and became a spokesman for Indian issues, even before he established the resort. In 1968 he was a member of the U.S. delegation to the Sixth Inter-American Indian Congress, held at Pátzcuaro, Mexico. That same year he was appointed chairman of the New Mexico Commission of Indian Affairs. He also served as president of the National Congress of American Indians and was appointed by President Lyndon B. Johnson to the National Council on Indian Opportunity, which had been established to foster Native American participation in U.S. government decisions concerning Indian policies.

Generated Controvery

During his career, Chino was sometimes described as a "benevolent dictator." He often generated controversy, as when he strongly opposed the Indian Gaming Regulatory Act of 1988, a revenue-sharing piece of regulation. The Act, Chino believed, restricted his tribe's sovereignty. His argument was that it attempted to regulate an activity that was being carried out on the reservation's domain. When the Act was eventually passed, Chino and other tribal leaders argued against its constitutionality in court. When Chino refused to pay, he alienated other New Mexico tribal leaders.

In a move that was even more controversial, Chino applied to the Department of Energy (DOE) for a grant to study the feasibility of building a Monitored Retrievable Storage (MRS) site to house nuclear waste on the reservation. In October of 1991, the DOE approved a $100,000 grant application to study the possibility of storing spent nuclear fuel rods that were stored on power plant sites. The MRS site on the Mescalero reservation would be a temporary facility, intended to exist for about 40 years until a permanent site could be built elsewhere. Chino predicted that the temporary site would earn the tribe $250 million during the 40-year storage, and that the arrangement would raise his tribe's living standard and increase its economic autonomy. However, he faced opposition from his tribe and the state of New Mexico, as well as from environmentalists. The feasibility study was conducted from 1991 to 1993. Ultimately the federal government withdrew the grant program in 1993 due to the escalating pressure.

But that did not end the controversy. After the withdrawal of the grant, the Mescalero Apache Tribal Council changed its tack and began working directly with 33 nuclear power plant officials. In 1994 the Council signed a nuclear waste storage agreement with Northern States Power, a Minnesota utility, to negotiate the construction of a private nuclear waste storage facility on the reservation. This outraged many tribal members who were not aware that negotiations had taken place. Despite the controversy, and certain that he had the requisite support, Chino put the matter to a vote. In a referendum held in January of 2005, the proposition was defeated by a vote of 490–362. When Chino demanded another vote, the proposition succeeded by a vote of 593–372. However, in April of 1996, negotiations between the tribe and the power plant officials broke down when the parties failed to reach an understanding on several critical issues.

As a result of the whole affair, questions arose regarding Chino's integrity. It was learned that he had accepted gifts from the companies involved in the negotiations. To some, this reeked of bribery. Suspicions were also raised regarding the reliability of the Mescalero voting system. Vote counting was conducted behind closed doors by a tribal election board comprised of members selected by Chino. Other irregularities were perceived, including a lack of financial accounting and favoritism.

Eventually, Chino's critics started to question where the Mescalero business profits went, as they pointed out that many tribal members had not enjoyed any increased prosperity. Chino had a characteristically bold response to these critics. In a 1997 interview with the *Albuquerque Journal,* conducted right before he was elected to his 17th term as tribal president, he said, "Wendell Chino doesn't elect himself. If they didn't like the way I was operating, they would have booted me out a long time ago."

He made a strong point. Also in his favor was the fact that during his presidency, his tribe had risen from poverty to become a viable economic player. Further, the reservation's personal per capita income increased to $16,536

during his tenure. That figure was two to three times that of Native Americans on other reservations that possessed equivalent natural resources.

Suffered Fatal Heart Attack

Later in his life Chino carried himself with stooping shoulders and needed two hearing aids. However, he maintained his gruff and blunt disposition, which was coupled and softened with a sly sense of humor. In this way he remained a vibrant, impressive figure. His sudden death on November 4, 1998, sent out shock waves throughout the Mescalero nation and across the country.

Chino died in Santa Monica, California. According to reports, he suffered a heart attack while exercising on a treadmill at a Pritikin Longevity Center. He was taken to an emergency room at Santa Monica-UCLA Medical Center, where he was revived. However, after he was transferred to the hospital's critical care unit he suffered a second heart attack and died. He was 74 years old.

His body was returned to New Mexico, and the funeral was held at the Mescalero Community Center. He was buried at the Mescalero Cemetery.

After his death he was immediately praised as an inspiration to other Native Americans, due to the leadership that elevated his own tribe from poverty and provided an example for other tribes. Of Chino, Roy Bernal, Chairman of the All Indian Pueblo Council, commented that he was "a Martin Luther King or a Malcolm X of Indian country. He took stances that affected Indians not only on his reservation, but all over the country. He was truly a modern warrior."

Books

The Scribner Encyclopedia of American Lives, Volume 5: 1997–1999, Charles Scribner's Sons, 2002.

Periodicals

Independent (London, England), November 30, 1998.
New Mexico Business Journal, October 1992.
New York Times, March 17, 2006.

Online

"Wendell Chino: Father of Indian Casinos and Apache Leader," *DesertUSA,* http://www.desertusa.com/mag00/jan/papr/chino.html (December 28, 2006).
"Wendell Chino, Mescalero Apache Leader," *First Nations: issues of consequence,* http://www.dickshovel.com/elders.html (December 28, 2006). □

Anne Clifford

Anne Clifford (1590–1676) fought to amend English inheritance laws that prevented her from assuming the aristocratic titles to vast lands in Cumbria, in the north of England, that had been in her family for several centuries. Her legal battle was unsuccessful, but she eventually came into her inheritance merely

by outliving all the males in the family. Her voluminous journals detailed this struggle as well as other aspects of her fascinating life, and the surviving diaries provide a rich glimpse of life in Elizabethan and Jacobean England.

Clifford was born on January 29, 1590, though some sources cite 1591 as the year of her birth. She came from a prominent family that possessed hundreds of acres of land in the north of England, anchored by immense castles, that had been passed down for more than three centuries by the time she was born. These properties included Skipton Castle in North Yorkshire, which had been built around 1100 by Robert de Romillé, a figure of historical importance as part of the French Norman contingent that invaded England in 1066 under the leadership of William the Conqueror (c. 1027–1087). The Cliffords were given that castle and ownership of its adjacent lands in 1310 by decree of King Edward II (1284–1327). By that point they already held Brough Castle in Cumbria, which in its original construction dated back to the 1090s and is thought to be one of the first stone castles in England. There was also another castle in Cumbria, this one called Brougham, which had been built on the site of an old Roman fortification.

Descended from Eminent Forebears

Clifford was born at Skipton Castle to Margaret Russell, daughter of Francis Russell, the 2nd Earl of Bedford. Clifford's maternal grandfather held important diplomatic posts under Elizabeth I (1533–1603) as well as serving as Privy Councillor, one of the monarch's closest advisors. Young Anne was the third child born to Margaret, also known as the Countess of Cumberland, but the first daughter and the first to survive her childhood. The lack of male heirs troubled her father, George Clifford, who was the 3rd Earl of Cumberland and 14th Baron de Clifford of Westmorland. He had inherited Skipton and Brough castles as well as four properties from his father, and this line of Clifford's heritage included some illustrious and even infamous figures in English history. They included John "The Butcher" Clifford, who allegedly beheaded the Duke of York in one notorious battle in 1460 that was a turning point in the War of the Roses, a civil conflict of the mid-fifteenth century that pitted the houses of Lancaster and York against one another in a battle for the throne.

Like his father-in-law, George Clifford was also a well-known figure in the court of Elizabeth. He was the most famous jouster among the queen's highly competitive courtiers, and was made a naval commander during the Anglo-Spanish War (1585–1604). In the first years of that conflict, he nearly captured the island of Puerto Rico for England when he seized the citadel La Fortaleza, but he was forced to flee when his forces were outnumbered. Like most sea captains of the era, George Clifford trod a shifting line between legitimate seizure of enemy ships and outright piracy, and probably earned small fortune from looting Spanish cargo. He was known to have lost money on horse racing

and jousting contests, however, and was forced to sell some of his lands.

Because her father was away at sea or at court for much of her childhood, Clifford was raised in a household dominated by women. She was given a tutor, which was somewhat unusual for a young woman of her time, and hers was the poet Samuel Daniel, (1562–1619), who held the post of poet laureate of England for a time. Daniel was part of Queen Elizabeth's retinue, and in her teen years Clifford spent time at court, like other well-born young men and women whose families were connected to the regime. Daniel penned masques that Clifford and a future queen of England, Anne of Denmark, took part in; these were lavish stage spectacles performed for the queen. The other Anne married James I, who ascended to the English throne following the death of Elizabeth in 1603.

Eyewitness to History

That was a momentous year in English history, and Clifford spent it at court. She chronicled it the earliest of her extant diaries, which is one of the first examples of an English woman's autobiographical writing. In it she wrote of the death of Elizabeth, noting that the "corpse came by night in a barge from Richmond to Whitehall, my Mother and a great company of ladies attending it, where it continued a great while standing in the Drawing Chamber, where it was watched all night by several lords and ladies, my Mother sitting up with it two or three nights, but my lady would not give me leave to watch, by reason that I was held too young."

After James's ascendancy, however, Clifford and her mother found themselves somewhat out of favor, and spent far less time at court. In 1605 George Clifford died, with Anne his sole offspring. His will specified that all titles and properties of his were to pass to his brother, Francis Clifford, and from then on to all other living male heirs. If there were no more Clifford men, only then would his daughter inherit the land and peerages. She was left a sum of 15,000 pounds instead. But Clifford and her mother knew that the original deed from Edward II stated that the baronies would pass to an "heir of the body"—a biological child, that is—with no mention of its gender. Believing that George Clifford's will broke that clause, Anne entered into a long legal battle to take possession of what she believed was rightfully due her as a Clifford.

Clifford's mother encouraged her lawsuit, but those opposed to it were well known and influential figures. They included King James and the Archbishop of Canterbury, who urged her to accept the cash settlement her uncle offered her and to let the matter rest, as well as Richard Sackville, whom she married in 1609, the year she turned 19. Sackville was the third Earl of Dorset, and had inherited his own famous property, Knole House, an immense home in northwest Kent completed in the 1480s. The couple had five children, but only two survived to adulthood: Margaret, born in 1614, and Isabella, born in 1622.

Urged to Abandon Cause

Clifford detailed the most difficult years of her lawsuit, from 1616 to 1619, in a journal that became known as her

Knole Diary. In it she wrote of the late Queen Elizabeth, and had undoubtedly been influenced by the strongwilled monarch during her years at court as an impressionable teenager. Elizabeth had also battled to claim her rightful inheritance—in this case, the throne—against immense and united opposition. Clifford wondered why, if it was possible for an English woman to inherit sovereignty over a nation, was she barred from inheriting the Clifford baronies? In one passage she asserted that "if Queen Elizabeth had lived she intended to prefer me to be of the Privy Chamber, for at that time there was much hope and expectation of me as of any other yong Ladie whatsoever," according to a scholarly article Mihoko Suzuki published in the journal *Clio.*

Richard Sackville died in 1624, and six years later his widow wed Philip Herbert, the 4th Earl of Pembroke and a favorite of King James. Her second husband also served as Lord Chamberlain under King Charles I (1600–1649), as governor of the Isle of Wight, and chancellor of Oxford University; each of these positions meant the two lived apart for much of their marriage. Finally, in 1643 the last of the male Cliffords died, and Clifford inherited at the age of 53 what she had hoped to receive as a teenager. The titles formally passed to her in 1646, but England was enmeshed in a bloody civil war, and she was forced to remain in London for the next few years.

Clifford headed north in the early 1650s when hostilities ceased. She began a series of costly renovations on her castles and the buildings on her land, beginning with the church at Skipton. The small fortune she spent to renovate Skipton Castle helped make it one of best-preserved castles in Britain more than three hundred years later. The other important home, Brough Castle, had not been inhabited since a fire in 1521, and had fallen into a state of disrepair in the intervening 130 years. Clifford fixed much of it and lived there herself for a time, but it was permanently uninhabited after her death and fell again into ruin. Nearby she had a memorial to her mother erected which remained one of the local landmarks three centuries later. Called the Countess Pillar, the 14-foot-high stone column sits at the intersection of the drive from Brough Castle to the main roads, and was the junction where Clifford said good-bye to her mother for the last time before the Countess's death in 1616. Like her mother, Clifford carried on the tradition of charitable giving, or alms, to the poorest of those who lived on the family lands. She established aid centers at Beamsley, near Skipton, and at Dolestone, near Brough, to provide help for impoverished widows in the area. She also established St. Anne's Hospital, a retirement home for the female servants on her estates.

Left Important Historical Record

Even later in her life, Clifford displayed a rebellious streak; she sported a close-cropped head at times, and was known to smoke a pipe. Several images of her, at various stages of her life, are featured in an immense family portrait she commissioned, the *Great Picture of the Clifford Family,* probably painted by Jan van Belcamp around 1647. With it, she sought to affirm her rightful place in the history of her family, as she had done in *The Great Books of the Clifford Family,* a multi-volume chronicle of the line that includes legal documents she and her mother assembled, papers from her own inheritance lawsuit, and biographies of her ancestors that she wrote herself. The last diary entry of her life was written on March 21, 1676, the day before she died at the age of 86 at Brougham Castle, in the same room in which her father had been born.

Clifford's colorful life and determined personality have fascinated subsequent generations. The poet and novelist Vita Sackville-West (1892–1962) was a descendant of Edward Sackville, the brother of Clifford's first husband, and wrote of her own life at Knole House as a young woman; she also served as editor of a 1923 reprint of *The Diary of the Lady Anne Clifford.* The iconoclastic Sackville-West, who was married but bisexual, was also close to the writer Virginia Woolf, who reportedly based some aspects of her 1928 transgender-themed novel *Orlando* on Sackville-West. Scholar Nicky Hallett posited that Woolf modeled the Elizabethan-era character on Clifford herself. The novel was made into a 1992 film that starred Tilda Swinton in the title role.

Books

The Diary of Anne Clifford, edited by Victoria Sackville-West, Doran, 1923.
Dictionary of Literary Biography, Volume 151: *British Prose Writers of the Early Seventeenth Century,* edited by Clayton D. Lein, Gale, 1995.

Periodicals

Clio, Winter 2001.
English Historical Review, February 1999.
Guardian (London, England), May 3, 2003.
History Today, July 1998.
Journal (Newcastle, England), September 5, 2003.
Renaissance Quarterly, Winter 1997.
Times (London, England), August 4, 1924.
Women's History Review, December 1995. ☐

Rosemary Clooney

In 1951 American singer-actor Rosemary Clooney (1928–2002) rose to prominence when Columbia Records issued "Come On-a My House," her first single to sell a million copies. She also starred in one of the most beloved holiday movies, *White Christmas,* with Bing Crosby in 1954. The pressures of fame, however, led to drug addiction and mental breakdown during the 1960s. By the mid-1970s, Clooney had overcome her personal demons and returned to performing, eventually receiving a Lifetime Achievement Grammy Award in 2002.

Emerged From Troubled Childhood

Born on May 23, 1928 in Maysville, Kentucky, Clooney had a turbulent childhood. Her father, Andrew Clooney, was an alcoholic and seldom at home, while her mother, Frances Guilfoyle, often worked away from home. The young Clooneys, Rosemary, Betty, and Nicky, lived with various relatives. "I don't remember all of us living together under the same roof for more than a few weeks at a time," recalled Clooney in her book, *Girl Singer: An Autobiography.* "Sometimes I was with an uncle or an aunt, sometimes at Grandma Guilfoyle's, sometimes with my Clooney grandparents." Because of the turmoil, Clooney learned to fend for herself and look after her younger siblings.

Clooney was surrounded by music from an early age. She sang on stage for the first time at three, performing "When Your Hair Has Turned to Silver (I Will Love You Just the Same)" at the downtown movie house, the Russell Theater. Her Aunt Olivette had led her own band, and Clooney listened to the jazz combos and big band groups on the powerful WLW radio station in Cincinnati. At the age of 17, she and her sister were abandoned once again by their father, and after they ran out of money they gathered and returned pop bottles to collect the deposits. Desperate and unwilling to contact family for help, the Clooney sisters auditioned on the local radio station WLW and were offered a job. "I began singing for a living in April 1945," recalled

Clooney. "I was sixteen; Betty was thirteen. The Clooney sisters were paid $20 a week. Apiece."

During the summer the Clooney sisters performed on two programs, the "Crossroads Café" in the afternoons and "Moon River" at night. In the fall, after returning to school at Our Lady of Mercy, they sang afternoons and evenings. They also sang with a combo at high school dances on Saturday nights, and worked with local bandleader Barney Rapp in Cincinnati. In the summer of 1946 the sisters auditioned for Tony Pastor, another big band leader with a national reputation. Before the Clooney sisters could begin their new career, however, they were faced with an obstacle: both were underage and would require a chaperone. Finally, their uncle George Guilfoyle agreed. "Within a year," wrote Clooney, "we'd gone from schoolgirls in knee socks to big band singers in nylons—with contracts. It was almost too much to take in, an overflow of good luck."

Established Solo Career

For the next three years, Clooney and her sister crisscrossed the United States with Pastor's band, playing one-night stands, traveling in a bus, and sleeping when they could. They performed at nightclubs, fairs, schools, and parks, and each sister received $125 per week, minus hotel and eating expenses (and expenses for Uncle George). The pace was grueling, but fronting a large band trained Rosemary Clooney in diction, delivery, and volume. "Three years is a long time to be on the road," wrote Clooney, "living out of a bus, ironing clothes on hotel room floors, away from people you love."

During this time, the sisters also recorded with Pastor's band on Columbia Records. Critics singled out Clooney's whispery version of "I'm Sorry I Didn't Say I'm Sorry When I Made You Cry Last Night," and eventually she was offered a solo contract with Columbia and the backing of Joe Shribman, an agent in New York City. While she felt conflicted over leaving both Uncle George and her sister behind, her sister had tired of the road and was happy to return home.

Despite her new contract, Clooney was one of many young talents hoping to launch a solo career with hit records. "The competition was tough; I'd landed in the big pond now, and so many people were after the same thing that I couldn't be sure how far I would go." She leased an apartment in New York City and signed with Columbia on her 21st birthday, a contract that paid $50 per recording and paid royalties after the costs of the recording had been covered (about $5,000). In the fall of 1949 Clooney made her television debut on *The Ed Sullivan Show,* singing "Boy Wanted," and she also appeared on the radio program *Camel Caravan.* She had only been in New York City for a year when Frank Sinatra, one of her idols, asked her to sing on "Peachtree Street."

"Come On-A My House" Topped Charts

Clooney's career advanced slowly at first. She recorded "Beautiful Brown Eyes" in January of 1951 and it became her first hit, eventually selling 400,000 copies. Her royalty rate increased, from 3% to 5%, and she was guaranteed

$250,000 over the next five years. She also appeared on the cover of the jazz magazine *Downbeat*. "But one magazine cover and one hit record didn't change my professional life overnight," wrote Clooney.

Clooney's professional life was about to change, however, thanks to a nonsensical song written by William Saroyan and Ross Bagdasarian, the team who had created the Chipmunks. "Come On-a My House" was based on an Armenian folk tune and suggested by arranger Mitch Miller, but Clooney resisted recording what she considered a silly and suggestive song. Even after Miller persuaded her to record it and had 100,000 copies pressed, she still believed the song would flop. "Come On-a My House" had an unusual arrangement featuring harpsichord, further underlining the nonsensical nature of the song. Returning to New York City following a short trip to Havana, Clooney heard "Come On-a My House" pouring out of every record shop along the street. The song, eventually selling over a million copies, established the young singer as an up-and-coming star, and paved the way for other hits including "Batch-a-Me," "Tenderly," "This Ole House," "Hey There," and "Suzy Snowflake."

Soon after, Clooney made her first appearance in Las Vegas, a date that had been booked before her hit. One of her shows was attended by a Hollywood agent, and she soon signed a contract with Paramount. Clooney landed her first role in *The Stars are Singing,* and returned to her home town in Maysville for the film's opening in January of 1953. Her next outing was *Here Come the Girls* with Bob Hope, followed by *Red Garters* (1953), an imaginative Western that mingled songs and satire. On February 23, 1953, Clooney appeared on the cover of *Time.* In the summer of 1953 she teamed with Bing Crosby, Danny Kaye, and Vera-Ellen in *White Christmas* (1954), a movie that has remained a perennial holiday favorite. "Singing together," noted Clooney of singing with Crosby, "came as naturally to each of us as breathing."

Joined Hollywood Jet Set

Clooney moved to Beverly Hills in the early 1950s and married actor Jose Ferrer on July 13, 1953. The couple had their first child, Miguel José Ferrer, on February 7, 1955, and would have four more children by 1960. Clooney's half-sister, Gail, also became part of the household. In Beverly Hills, Clooney immersed herself in the Hollywood lifestyle, associating with noted stars such as Marlene Dietrich and Crosby, and attending lavish parties. She returned to working at the Sans in Las Vegas for $20,000 a week, only six weeks after her first child was born, and shortly thereafter signed a contract for 39 half-hour episodes of *The Rosemary Clooney Show*. During this time, she also recorded duets with her husband, "Man (Uh-Huh)" and "Woman (Uh-Huh)," and with Dietrich, "Dots Nice Donna Fight."

The Rosemary Clooney Show began in May of 1956, and featured Nelson Riddle's Orchestra and the Hi-Los. In 1957 she fronted the *The Lux Show Starring Rosemary Clooney,* and also appeared in the award-winning *The Edsel Show* with Bing Crosby and Frank Sinatra. In 1958 Clooney,

six months pregnant, recorded *Fancy Meeting You Here* with Crosby.

The non-stop activity exacted its toll on the development of Clooney's career. Her film roles came to an abrupt halt in December of 1955 when Paramount released her from her contract due to her current pregnancy. *The Lux Show* was canceled for the same reason. She was also released from Columbia Records, partly due to a conflict between her husband and producer Mitch Miller. "I still thought I could do it all," wrote Clooney. "I would continue to be the perfect wife. . . . I would sign for another television series. I would become pregnant again. I *would* do it all."

Underwent Personal Crisis and Breakdown

For much of the 1960s, Clooney was plagued by relationship, money, and drug problems. She and Ferrer divorced in 1961, remarried the same year, and divorced again for good in 1967. She also had an on-again/off-again relationship with Nelson Riddle. Clooney became interested in politics in 1960 and made appearances for Democratic candidate John F. Kennedy. She continued to record for Coral, MGM, and RCA, but her classic style, like Sinatra's and Crosby's, became less popular following the advent of rock-n-roll. Clooney's personal life was also complicated by her addiction to sleeping pills.

In 1968 Clooney had a nervous breakdown. She had continued to work in Democratic politics, and had befriended Robert F. Kennedy. She worked with his campaign during the Democratic primary during the summer, and was in attendance at the Ambassador Hotel following the California primary. Clooney had also brought two of her children, and they were standing only a few yards from Kennedy when he was shot and killed by Sirhan Sirhan. From that point, her life spiraled quickly into chaos. In Reno for a show, Clooney announced her retirement at an impromptu news conference, then broke down during a show, berating the audience. She later admitted herself to the psychiatric ward at Mt. Sinai Hospital in Los Angeles, and entered therapy.

Re-Established Singing and Recording Career

During the mid-to-late 1970s Clooney returned to performing, slowly rebuilding her career at small venues like Holiday Inns. While far from the glamour of her Reno and Hollywood days, she considered herself lucky to be working at all. Her old friend Merv Griffin invited her to make a number of appearances on his television show. In March of 1976 she joined Bing Crosby during his 50th anniversary tour, including an appearance at the Dorothy Chandler Pavilion in Los Angeles. "Bing's invitation to work with him was a breakthrough both personal and professional, like an apostolic blessing," wrote Clooney.

Clooney recorded her first album for Concord Records in 1977, leading to numerous albums including *Everything's Coming Up Rosie* (1977), *Show Tunes* (1989), and *Do You Miss New York?* (1993). Bob Harrington wrote in *Back Stage,* of a live show in 1992, "What's remarkable is that Clooney, of those singers who are highly musical, sacrifices not a bit of her emotional wallop to achieve her musical feel." In 1995 Clooney received ASCAP's Pied Piper Award, the premier award for performing artists, and an Emmy nomination for a guest appearance on *ER.*

Clooney's sister Betty died of an aneurysm in 1976, eventually leading Rosemary to found the Betty Clooney Center in Long Beach, California. In 1997 Clooney married Dante DiPaolo, a dancer with whom she had been involved during the time of her first marriage in 1953. In 2001 she was diagnosed with lung cancer and underwent surgery at the Mayo Clinic in Rochester, Minnesota. Because of her surgery, Clooney was unable to attend the Grammy ceremony to receive her Lifetime Achievement Award in 2002. Clooney died from complications six months later on June 29, 2002, at the age of 74. "For over 50 years she has brightened our lives with the richness of her personality and her voice," *Daily Variety* quoted Dolores Hope [Bob Hope's spouse]. "Her courage and love have been an inspiration to all who called her friend."

Books

Clooney, Rosemary, *Girl Singer: An Autobiography,* Doubleday, 1999.

Periodicals

Backstage, February, 14, 1992.
Daily Variety, July 1, 2002.
Entertainment Weekly, July 12, 2002.
People, October 15, 1990. □

Jean Michel Cousteau

Jean Michel Cousteau (born 1938), the son of famous oceanographer Jacques Cousteau, has followed in his father's footsteps to become a well-known marine biologist himself. He has taken up the fight to preserve and protect the oceans. He was quoted in Florida's *St. Petersburg Times* as having said, "For years, we have looked at the ocean as a dumping ground. Because it was out of sight and out of mind, we have treated it like a universal sewer." He has fought to bring to the notice of the public the fact that ocean dumping needs to stop if the marine life, and therefore everything on the planet, is going to survive.

Early Interest in Oceanography

Cousteau was born in 1938 in Toulon, France, to well-known oceanographer Jacques-Yves Cousteau and his wife, Simone. The first son of a scientist, Cousteau was brought to the study of marine life at an early age. Cousteau's father was a onetime French naval officer and

the inventor of the famous Aqua Lung, used to help divers stay under water for long periods of time, thereby allowing them to study marine life more extensively. According to Cousteau, his entry into marine biology started when he was only seven years old. Cousteau's father attached a diving tank to his back and thrust him overboard into the Mediterranean Sea somewhere off the coast of the south of France. Instead of being afraid, Cousteau was amazed at the beauty and mystery he saw. He was instantly captivated and from that moment on spent his life exploring the depths of the oceans.

Cousteau's parents had a second son, Philippe. When he was growing up, Cousteau and his younger brother, Philippe, often went with their father on his adventures, traveling across the oceans on the Calypso and Alcyone, their father's research vessels. By the 1960s Cousteau was working with his father on several movies and programs, including the television series *The Undersea World of Jacques Cousteau.* However, despite the fact that it was his eldest son who was helping him with the films, Cousteau's father chose Philippe to be the heir to his oceanography empire. At that time Jean, wanting to continue pursuing his career in a marine field, attended the Paris School of Architecture, graduating with a degree in marine architecture. He went on from there to help with design projects across Europe and beyond.

Started Project Ocean Search

In 1973 Cousteau started the educational field study program Project Ocean Search. He set up the project to organize educational expeditions for groups of interested scientists, divers, and students. That same year he also started an architectural firm called Living Design that dealt with marine architecture. In 1977 he founded the Jean-Michel Cousteau Institute. It was a not-for-profit research foundation focused on oceanographic work. When Philippe died in a seaplane crash in 1979, Cousteau returned to help his father deal with his grief as well as his business issues, taking a more active role in his father's work again. He combined his Institute with his father's Cousteau Society. Cousteau remained as a board member and executive vice president of communications of the Cousteau Society until 1999. He spent all of his time on expeditions, lecturing, or working at the society. He never shared any of the fame of the projects with his father, but it is doubtful that the Cousteau Society could have continued without him.

During his time working with his father, Cousteau was executive producer for the films *Jacques Cousteau: The First 75 Years, Cousteau's Amazon,* and *Cousteau's Mississippi.* He was awarded the prestigious Peabody Award, the Ace Award, and the 7 d'Or, the equivalent in France of an American Emmy for *Cousteau's Amazon.* Besides these, Cousteau produced sixty-one television specials, including the admired *Cousteau's Rediscovery of the World.*

Split From Father

Cousteau's mother died in 1990, and shortly thereafter his father remarried. It has been thought that these events were partly responsible for disagreements between father and son, because the two began to argue extensively. They could not seem to agree on anything. Cousteau and his father had many differences on how to run the company, and in 1993 Cousteau left the Cousteau Society and basically stopped speaking to his father.

In 1995 Cousteau and his father argued again, this time because the younger Cousteau had started his own business: Cousteau's Fiji Island Resort. Cousteau's father did not like his son using his name on the project and began legal proceedings. He dropped them when Cousteau agreed to add "Jean-Michel" to the beginning of the title. Because of the public nature of the legal battle, the estrangement became widely known and much talked of. But there seemed to be a lessening of tensions in 1997, when Cousteau accepted an invitation to attend a black-tie dinner in Orlando, Florida, to honor his father and all his achievements over his lifetime. All eyes were on the pair, but as soon as Cousteau entered the room he went straight to his father, said a few words, and then moments later the two were hugging and toasting each other.

The reconciliation came none too soon. Later that month Cousteau's father fell ill and was hospitalized. Only five months later on June 25, Cousteau's father died of a heart attack in Paris. At the time, the younger Cousteau was in Portland, Oregon, working as part of his Free Willy Foundation, which was working to bring Keiko, a whale, to freedom. Cousteau vowed that he would carry on his father's work, although not through his father's company. Francine, Cousteau's stepmother, was left in charge of the Cousteau Society, and she and Cousteau disagreed com-

pletely over what should be done with the organization. In 1999 the Jean-Michel Cousteau Institute merged with the Free Willy Keiki Foundation to become the nonprofit organization Ocean Futures Society, for which he eventually became president.

Efforts to Bring Attention to Oceans

Besides his diving and movie making, Cousteau started a syndicated column with the *Los Angeles Times,* and his articles have been published in newspapers around the globe. He has also lectured to groups of students and others, taking people on explorations and showing them what the ocean is like and how it can be saved. He firmly believes that if enough young people can be interested in the study of marine life, its survival can be assured. This is the only way, he has said, that the ocean will remain a focus of conservation efforts in the future. He told the Piedmont Triad, North Carolina, *News and Record,* "Experiencing the ocean will help children relate to the role it plays in our lives. . . . They are so open. They are like sponges. Their creativity is unbelievable."

In an interview with Suite101.com website a year after his father's death, Cousteau stated that dumping was one of the real threats to the ocean. According to him, "There are places where it's so bad that aquatic reproduction is affected." He also told the same reporter that it was a shame that humans had mapped the surface of the moon and yet knew very little about the oceans. "We know very little when it comes to depths deeper than conventional divers or submersibles can go. Beyond the continental shelf of 500 feet, we know nothing."

While trying to do his part to map the depths of the ocean, Cousteau has also been involved in the making of several recent films about marine life. These include the IMAX films *Dolphins: At Play in the Wild,* and *Sharks,* shot in 3D. PR Newswire called the film "a stunning immersive diving experience." Cousteau also started a two-day camp on the British Virgin Island of Tortola called "Ambassadors of the Environment."

Cousteau tried many different activities to bring the plight of the ocean to the public's attention. In 2004 he wrote a book about his famous father. According to the London *Independent,* Cousteau "lauds the captain's legacy, condemns his stepmother for failing to keep the flame alive and suggests his father lost the plot after his formidable first wife, Simone (Jean-Michel's mother), died in 1990." In 2006 Cousteau gave a speech at the dedication of a new science building at Fresno State University. While in Fresno he gave a University Lecture Series address about the Great Ocean Adventure at the Satellite Student Union at California State University, Fresno.

Jean-Michel Cousteau: Ocean Adventures

Despite these other activities, however, Cousteau also continued his original love: exploring and filming the oceans. In 2003 Cousteau put together a group of scientists and set off to film the Northwestern Hawaiian Islands for a television special, *Voyage to Kure,* the first film in the series. Cousteau told *USA Today,* "This is just like being back in the old days. We have an all-new team of young men and women who have been training for this mission for about a year.'' When the film was released, the *Orlando Sentinel* wrote, ''Take the plunge offered by *Jean-Michel Cousteau: Ocean Adventures* and you'll luxuriate in rare television. How many programs provide exhilarating adventure, powerful commentary and breathtaking journeys to seldom-seen paradises? . . . This series brings you the world's natural beauty and pushes you, ever so nicely, to appreciate that precious commodity. It's a noble lesson that unfolds as awesome entertainment.''

He aired one of his films about the Northwestern Hawaiian Islands for President George W. and Mrs. Bush, which discussed the need to protect the marine preserve there which is the largest in the world—100 times as big as Yosemite National Park. Only two months after meeting with Cousteau, Bush created the Northwestern Hawaiian Islands Marine National Monument to protect the area and its inhabitants. Apparently Mrs. Bush, upset by what Cousteau had to tell them, urged her husband to all speed. About the project, Cousteau told the *Orlando Sentinel*, ''We're doing justice to the ocean. A lot has to be done, and it's going to take a lot of work. But perhaps with this expedition we can highlight to the world the fact that it's not too late, the fact that it is time to recognize our life-support system has problems and thus so do we.''

After his first release, Cousteau and his team had plans to do films on sharks, whales, and America's underwater treasures. And just as his father did, Cousteau has kept up the family tradition by involving his own children, Celine and Fabien, in the making of the films. Cousteau, who lives in Santa Barbara, has also begun work on treating the Mississippi, which because of pollution dumped into the river has caused a dead zone in the Gulf of Mexico the size of Massachusetts, where no marine life thrives at all. Cousteau is optimistic that changes can be made if the United States government takes the threat seriously. If Cousteau has his way, the governments of the world will work to protect the largest natural resource the planet has.

Books

Newsmakers, Issue Cumulation, Gale Research, 1988.

Periodicals

Atlanta Journal-Constitution, April 23, 2004.
Fresno Bee, March 11, 2005.
Houston Chronicle, July 8, 2003; September 21, 2006.
Independent (London, England), October 10, 2001; April 17, 2004.
News & Record (Piedmont Triad, NC), March 15, 1998.
Orlando Sentinel, April 3, 2006.
PR Newswire, December 10, 2004; March 10, 2005; March 23, 2005; January 5, 2006.
Seattle Post-Intelligencer, September 28, 1998; November 6, 1998.
St Louis Post-Dispatch, April 23, 2002; June 5, 2003.
St. Petersburg Times, March 12, 2000.
Time, June 26, 2006.
USA Today, July 16, 2003.
Washington Times, July 2, 2000.

Online

''An Interview with Jean-Michel Cousteau,'' *Suite 101*, http://www.suite101.com/article.cfm/scuba_diving/14551 (November 27, 2006). □

Paul J. Crutzen

Paul J. Crutzen (born 1933) has led fellow scientists in the attempt to map out the chemicals that affect the ozone layer. He has been instrumental in learning how the ozone layer is formed and destroyed, and in uncovering the role industries play in its destruction. He was awarded the Nobel Prize in Chemistry in 1995 for discovering certain chemical compounds that reduce the ozone layer, and that certain bacteria in the soil can determine its thickness.

Crutzen was born on December 3, 1933, in Holland to Anna Gurk and Jozef Crutzen. He had one sister. Crutzen was raised in a rather cosmopolitan atmosphere filled with international ideas and attitudes. He grew up in a poor family in Nazi-occupied Holland. During his elementary school days World War II was going on, and he and his classmates had to move to a new building after their school was taken over by Nazi troops. Crutzen especially remembered the last winter of the war in 1944–45. He wrote in his autobiography on the Nobel Prize website, ''During the cold 'hongerwinter' (winter of famine) of 1944–45, there was a severe lack of food and heating fuels. Also water for drinking, cooking and washing was available only in limited quantities for a few hours per day, causing poor hygienic conditions. Many died of hunger and disease, including several of my schoolmates.''

Intention to Build Houses

Crutzen was one of the few children who was able to graduate from elementary school on time; the rest were kept back a year. At the time not all children were allowed to attend high school, but Crutzen was selected to do just that after he did very well on the entrance exam. He went to the Hogere Burgerschool, where he focused on natural sciences and learned to speak French, English, and German. He enjoyed playing soccer and bicycling and loved distance ice skating. He was also interested in chess, and at school he was interested in physics and math, not really liking chemistry at all. After graduation he went on to a two-year college, the Middelbare Technische School, because he could not afford to go to a university. He graduated with a degree in civil engineering in 1954. With this degree under his belt he set out to design bridges and houses.

Soon after graduation, while he was vacationing in Switzerland, Crutzen met Tertu Soininen. The couple married two years later and moved to Gavle, Sweden, in 1958, where Crutzen had obtained a job at a building construction

bureau. The Crutzens had a daughter, Ilona, that December. Another girl, Sylvia, was born in March of 1964.

Switched to Atmospheric Chemistry

What Crutzen really wanted professionally, however, was to work for an academic department, not a building bureau, so when the opportunity presented itself he applied for a job as a computer programmer at the Institute of Meteorology at the University of Stockholm. He had no experience in computers, but at the time there were few who did, and he was accepted from a large candidate pool to take on the position. The family moved to Stockholm. He was originally interested in mathematics, but soon lost his passion for it in favor of atmospheric chemistry. While working, Crutzen also earned a doctorate in meteorology at the university.

In 1965 Crutzen went to help a U.S. scientist develop a model of the stratosphere. It was this project that awakened Crutzen's interest in the chemical makeup of the ozone layer. He started reading everything he could on the subject, his interest growing with each new piece of information. It also gave him an idea of the state of research on the ozone layer at that time. He went back to Sweden with a new purpose for his degree research. Crutzen stated in his autobiography on the Nobel Prize website, "Instead of the initially proposed research project, I preferred research on stratospheric chemistry, which was generously accepted."

Researched Ozone Layer

At the time the current research areas at the University of Stockholm were dynamics, the physics of clouds, the carbon cycle, studies of the chemical composition of rainwater, and especially acid rain, which was one of the hottest research topics at that time. However, Crutzen maintained an interest in studying the ozone layer.

Ozone itself is a bluish gas that has a strong scent and is irritating to living organisms. It has three oxygen atoms and forms naturally in the atmosphere through a process called photochemical reaction, having to do with the chemical reaction of light. The ozone layer is located ten miles above the surface of the Earth and is approximately 20 to 30 miles thick. Its purpose is to absorb the ultraviolet radiation that the sun emits. Atmospheric warming occurs when that layer begins to deplete.

In 1970 Crutzen discovered that certain bacteria in the soil gave off a nitrous oxide gas which rose all the way to the stratosphere, where it was changed by a photochemical process into two chemicals, nitric oxide and nitrogen dioxide. He learned that these two gases were part of what caused the ozone to shrink in size. This one realization led scientists across the globe to examine chemicals found on earth to see how they affected the ozone layer's size.

Studied Effects of Smoke and Nuclear War

Crutzen went on from this research to become in 1977 the director of the National Center for Atmospheric Research (NCAR) in Boulder, Colorado. From there he worked on how burning trees and brush in Brazil effected the atmosphere. In Brazil farmers would clear the forests every year by burning them down. It was thought that this burning was releasing carbon monoxide and other carbon compounds into the air that were causing the greenhouse effect, the warming of the atmosphere. When Crutzen collected samples and did his research, however, he found out that the exact opposite was happening. The yearly smoke was actually decreasing the amount of carbon dioxide in the atmosphere. This discovery intrigued Crutzen, and he went on to study the effects of other kinds of smoke on the atmosphere, especially the smoke that would come from a global disaster such as a nuclear war.

Once he made his interest in researching such a topic known, several sponsors came forward. The journal *Ambio* paid Crutzen and his University of Colorado colleague John Birks to study how a nuclear war would effect the planet. The pair put together a model of a worldwide nuclear war. According to the scientists nuclear war would have a fallout of black carbon soot that would result from fires raging across the planet. This soot would absorb up to 99 percent of the sunlight that the Earth needs to survive. This would cause the entire planet to be thrown into a state of perpetual winter so vast that it would destroy every living thing. For proposing this theory Crutzen was named "Scientist of the Year" by *Discover* magazine in 1984 and was awarded the esteemed Tyler Award in 1988.

When these theories and others about the destructive nature of certain chemicals on the ozone layer came to the attention of the general public and to governments around the world, an international treaty was drawn up in 1987. Called the Montreal Protocol, it was negotiated by the United Nations and was eventually signed by 70 countries. The protocol stated that these countries would phase out, no matter how slowly, the production of chlorofluorocarbons and other ozone-depleting chemicals by the year 2000. The United States managed to stop producing things with the harmful chemicals in them by the year 1995, although it still remained the leading producer of carbon emissions in the world. The hole in the ozone layer over the South Pole was still increasing in 2000, but it was thought that it was because of existing products with the harmful chemicals in them that would take a while to deplete. A full reversal of the problem was not expected to take place for hundreds of years.

Crutzen stayed at the NCAR until 1980. At the same time he taught classes at Colorado State University in the department of Atmospheric Sciences. He became director of the Atmospheric Chemistry Department at Germany's Max Planck Institute for Chemistry in 1980 and remained as such until 2000. From 1992 on he taught part-time at Scripps Institution of Oceanography at the University of California and also at Utrecht University's Institute for Marine and Atmospheric Sciences in the Netherlands.

Suggested Interim Solution to Ozone Problems

In 2006 Crutzen was acknowledged to have come up with a solution for helping to stave off the effects of global warming. He suggested that the chemical composition of the Earth's upper atmosphere be altered. Attempts to stave off man-made alterations to the atmosphere had been so meager that according to Crutzen a more drastic approach was necessary. His suggestion was to release some sulphur into the upper atmosphere. The sulphur should reflect sunlight and the heat from it back into space. It was a very controversial solution, but has been receiving some serious consideration because of Crutzen's known track record of excellence in the past. The sulphur could either be scattered by balloons designed for high altitude flight or could be shot into the air by heavy artillery shells. According to the London *Independent*, "Such 'geo-engineering' of the climate has been suggested before, but Professor Crutzen goes much further by drawing up a detailed model of how it can be done, the timescales involved, and the costs."

The idea has raised objections around the globe, most often because such an operation, scientists fear, would be seen as a quick fix and then governments would cease to search for more permanent solutions to the problem. Crutzen has argued that this would be a stopgap measure and that pressures on governments to improve their emissions would remain. In his opinion this would be a way to temporarily reduce global warming issues while countries worked more fervently to change their practices.

His plan was modeled in part on the eruption of the Mount Pinatubo volcano in 1991. Thousands of tons of sulphur were thrown into the air when the volcano erupted causing temperatures around the globe to decrease. Putting the sulphur into the stratosphere rather than lower down, as in the case of the volcano, would create a year or two of lower temperatures rather than just a few weeks. The project would cost about $25 to $50 billion, but it is Crutzen's belief that that cost is nothing to what global warming is doing to all life on Earth. Because of his contributions to modern science, Crutzen was elected in 2006 to become a foreign member of the Royal Society, the United Kingdom's national academy of science and the world's oldest scientific academy in uninterrupted existence. As of 2007 he continued his studies into improving the atmosphere.

Books

Notable Scientists: From 1900 to the Present, Gale Group, 2001.
World of Chemistry, 2 volumes, Gale Group, 1999.
World of Earth Science, Gale, 2003.
World of Scientific Discovery, 2nd edition, Gale Group, 1999.

Periodicals

Environment, April 2004; October 2005.
Independent (London, England), July 31, 2006.
Times (London, England), October 12,1995.
Times of India, August 1, 2006.

Online

"Paul J. Crutzen, *Noble Prize Website,* http://www.nobel.se/chemistry/laureates/1995/crutzen-autobio.html (January 2, 2007). □

D

Thomas De Quincey

English writer Thomas De Quincey (1785–1859) wrote prolifically and in numerous fields, ranging from fiction to biography to economics, and often crossing genre boundaries in unclassifiable works that mixed exposition of others' ideas with autobiography and personal reflections. He remains best known, however, for a single work: *Confessions of an English Opium Eater* (1821). That work, too, was difficult to classify—it mixed autobiographical elements with description and evaluation of the effects of the addictive, analgesic, and psychoactive drug named in its title.

De Quincey was considered one of the greatest prose stylists of the English Romantic era, otherwise best known for poetry, and his imaginative, convoluted prose style, best exemplified in *Confessions of an English Opium Eater* but also on display in a great variety of other works that were widely read in 19th-century England and America, exerted a vast influence on later literary radicals such as American mystery pioneer and experimentalist Edgar Allan Poe and the French poet Charles Baudelaire.

Shaken by Deaths of Siblings

"Among his earliest memories were dreams," wrote De Quincey biographer Grevel Lindop—appropriate for a writer who put a powerful stream of his interior life into everything he penned. De Quincey was born Thomas Quincey in the English city of Manchester on August 15, 1785. The family later adopted the name De Quincey, hypothesizing that they were related to an old Anglo-French family named de Quincis that dated back to the time of the Norman Conquest. De Quincey's father Thomas was a cloth merchant in Manchester, the cradle of English industry, and the family lived in a pleasant country home. De Quincey was the fourth of five children; he was close to his siblings and was deeply affected by the deaths of his sisters Jane and Elizabeth during his childhood. With his brother William he created a rich fantasy life centered on the two imaginary warring kingdoms of Gombroon and Tigrosylvania. De Quincey's father died in 1793, leaving the family with sufficient financial resources for the time being.

De Quincey was educated in private schools and quickly showed a gift for language in general. When he was about eight, he impressed a local bookseller by translating a book of a Latin-language copy of the Bible into English at sight, and by the time he was 15 he could speak, read, and write ancient Greek fluently. One teacher at the Bath Grammar School remarked to a visitor that De Quincey could have given a better oration in front of an ancient Athenian mob than he, the teacher, could have done before an English one.

In 1801 De Quincey began attending the Manchester Grammar School, a prep school-like institution that could have earned him a valuable Oxford University scholarship. He learned some important literary lessons while he was there, reading the early works of William Wordsworth, Samuel Taylor Coleridge, and other English Romantic poets who would greatly influence his own writing in the future. At the time, however, De Quincey was bored. He ran away from the school, defying the wishes of his mother, and wandered around the Wales region, sleeping outdoors in order to stretch his money supply. Finally broke, he went to London to try to borrow money on the strength of his family's good name.

Things went from bad to worse. Lenders refused his applications for loans, and he nearly starved to death. He was apparently befriended by a prostitute named Ann, who at one point revived him after he collapsed on the street by spending her own meager savings on a bottle of port wine and bringing it to him. When De Quincey later returned to London to look for her, she had disappeared, and no record of her other than De Quincey's recollections has ever surfaced. Readers have occasionally wondered whether she might have been a product of De Quincey's imagination, but the details he provides in his descriptions of her are convincing ones.

Began Taking Opium

Eventually De Quincey worked out his problems with his family, and he enrolled in Oxford University's Worcester College in 1803. It was while he was a student there that his opium addiction began. At first he took the drug in the form of laudanum, a liquid tincture (an alcohol-based distillate) that he sought out for toothache relief. De Quincey's career at Oxford was mercurial; he was a brilliant student in English literature and in the Greek, Latin, and German languages. Embarking on his final exams in 1808 he started out strongly but left school before finishing, and he never received his degree.

Instead he plunged more deeply into the literary life. By the time he left Oxford, he had made the acquaintance of several of the leading writers of the day, central figures in what would be known as the Romantic movement. He

donated five hundred pounds anonymously to "Kubla Khan" author and fellow opium user Samuel Taylor Coleridge when Coleridge was in dire financial straits, and he lived for a time with poet William Wordsworth and his wife. Moving frequently from place to place, De Quincey lived in absolute disorder. He accumulated a huge library of books, and his friends began to treat him as something of a mobile lending library. Sometimes he would move out of a house or country cottage when it became too clogged with his papers and unfinished projects—sometimes his landlords had a strong enough belief in his potential that they carefully stored his materials. Despite his often chaotic life, De Quincey was known as a loyal and supportive associate; when his friend John Wilson became a professor and was placed in the position of having to give lectures on subjects with which he was unfamiliar, De Quincey cheerfully ghostwrote the lectures for him.

In 1817 De Quincey married Margaret Simpson, the daughter of a farmer in the Grasmere district of northern England. They eventually had eight children. By the time of the marriage, De Quincey had burned through much of the money he had coming from his family, and his opium usage had ballooned to a massive 340 grains daily—more than 20 grams. Periodically he tried to give up the drug, but he succeeded only in lowering his intake and keeping it at a consistent level.

By the late 1810s, well into his fourth decade of life, De Quincey had written only a few articles and pamphlets despite the brilliance many friends recognized in him. But now, faced with the necessity of supporting his family, he began to contribute prolifically to magazines, submitting everything from popularizations of the theories of pioneer British economist David Ricardo, to literary criticism, to translations of German poetry and drama. His greatest success, however, came when he wrote about himself, in a dizzying style that combined erudition, flights of prose complexity, and bald honesty. His first work in this vein was *Confessions of an English Opium Eater,* which appeared in *London Magazine* in 1821 and was soon reprinted in book form. It remained the best known of all De Quincey's writings.

Described Effects of Drug

The form of *Confessions of an English Opium Eater* was and remains unusual; it is partly memoir and partly an exploration of the effects of a mind-altering substance. In a lengthy section of "Preliminary Confessions," De Quincey recounted the story of his wanderings as a young man, including his encounters with Ann, the London prostitute. But the bulk of the work is given over to personal descriptions of "The Pleasures of Opium" and "The Pains of Opium." At the beginning of the work De Quincey seems to promise a moralistic antidrug stance, observing that "If opium-eating be a sensual pleasure, and if I am bound to confess that I have indulged in it to an excess, not yet recorded of any other man, it is no less true, that I have struggled against this fascinating enthralment with a religious zeal, and have at length accomplished what I never yet heard attributed to any other man—have untwisted, almost to its final links, the accursed chain which fettered me.''

The rest of the document, however, gives equal weight to both the positive and negative aspects of opium usage. ''[T]hou buildest upon the bosom of darkness, out of the fantastic imagery of the brain, cities and temples . . . beyond the splendour of Babylon and Hekatompylos,'' wrote De Quincey, ''and, 'from the anarchy of dreaming sleep,' callest into sunny light the faces of long-buried beauties, and the blessed household countenances, cleansed from the 'dishonours of the grave.' Thou only givest these gifts to man; and thou hast the keys of Paradise, oh just, subtle, and mighty opium!'' He rhapsodized about his heightened perceptions of music while under the drug's influence.

De Quincey was equally eloquent in describing the depressive states that came with drug usage. ''But for misery and suffering, I might, indeed, be said to have existed in a dormant state,'' he recalled. ''I seldom could prevail on myself to write a letter; an answer of a few words, to any that I received, was the utmost that I could accomplish; and often that not until the letter had laid weeks, or even months, on my writing-table. Without the aid of M. [his wife], all records of bills paid, or to be paid, must have perished; and my whole domestic economy . . . must have gone into irretrievable confusion.''

Confessions of an English Opium Eater was a major success and put De Quincey on the literary map. For the next two decades he was in demand as a contributor to England's leading periodicals. He made money off of a translation of a German hoax novel called *Walladmor* that had been promoted as a lost work by Scottish historical fantasy novelist Sir Walter Scott. De Quincey wrote some fiction of his own: the novel *Klosterheim* (1832) and short stories such as ''The Household Wreck'' (1838) had elements of description and fantasy that anticipated the styles and themes of avant-garde writers such as Poe and Franz Kafka. He also penned a widely read series of biographies of writers, with subjects ranging from Roman emperors to the Romantic poets he personally knew. The latter group was as unconventional in form as were his drug memoirs; De Quincey inserted himself into the narratives, producing a unique mix of biography and autobiography.

De Quincey suffered anew from the deaths of family members in the 1830s. One son, Julius, died at age four; another, William, suffered from a brain disorder and died at 18; and De Quincey lost his wife to typhus in 1837. His opium dosages increased sharply. By this time he had moved to Edinburgh, Scotland, in whose environs he spent most of the rest of his life. The aging writer once again was forced to juggle creditors, but things changed for the better when his oldest daughter, Margaret, took charge of the household.

They improved further in the 1840s and 1850s when De Quincey's reputation as one of Britain's greatest writers expanded. He gained readers in the United States, and his collected works were issued in Boston (they ran to 22 volumes) by the Ticknor, Reed and Fields publishing firm. Although it was not required to do so (Britain and the United States had no reciprocal copyright protection at the time),

the firm paid De Quincey royalties. He continued to write in his old age, and to assemble and revise his works for new collected editions. He died in Edinburgh on December 8, 1859. Many critics in the following decades thought of De Quincey as a writer of genius who had never quite reached his full potential, but a new spate of studies and biographies of the author began appearing in the late 20th century—an age sympathetic to outsider figures and to experimenters with psychoactive substances.

Books

Dendurant, Harold O., *Thomas De Quincey: A Reference Guide,* G.K. Hall, 1978.

Lindop, Grevel, *The Opium-Eater: A Life of Thomas De Quincey,* Taplinger, 1981.

Sackville-West, Edward, *Thomas De Quincey: His Life and Work,* Yale University Press, 1936.

Whale, John C., *Thomas De Quincey's Reluctant Autobiography,* Barnes & Noble, 1984.

Online

De Quincey, Thomas, *Confessions of an English Opium Eater,* full text, http://users.lycaeum.org/~sputnik/Ludlow/Texts/Opium/prelim.html (October 3, 2006).

''Thomas De Quincey (1785–1859),'' Books and Writers, http://www.kirjasto.sci.fi/quincey.htm (October 3, 2006). □

John Denver

American singer and songwriter John Denver (1943–1997) gained international popularity in the 1970s with pleasant, well-crafted songs, many of them extolling the beauties and the spiritual gifts of the natural world.

Denver backed up his ideas with activism in later years, devoting his energies to the causes of land conservation and environmental awareness. His death in an aviation accident at age 53 shocked his numerous fans, 1,500 of whom turned out for a memorial service held in Aspen, Colorado, where he had lived for many years. ''We made a fortune, tens and tens of millions of dollars,'' Denver's manager told Peter Castro of *People,* reflecting on Denver's influence. ''If you give Elvis the '50s and the Beatles the '60s, I think you've got to give John Denver the '70s.''

Raised in Military Family

Denver was born Henry John Deutschendorf Jr. on December 31, 1943, in the military town of Roswell, New Mexico. His father, nicknamed ''Dutch,'' was a U.S. Air Force test pilot whose hard-drinking ways were transferred to his son. New Air Force postings took the family to various southern and southwestern states, and temporarily to Japan; Denver often clashed with his conservative father, and he once tried to run away from home. His happiest times came on his grandmother's farm in Oklahoma, where he heard

couple's finances were boosted when "Leaving on a Jet Plane" was recorded by folk superstars Peter, Paul & Mary and became a major pop hit, its depiction of a sweet but slightly ominous separation of two lovers striking a chord at the height of the Vietnam War. Denver was able to fulfill his dream by moving to Aspen, Colorado, in 1970.

He continued to record folk-pop albums for the RCA label, and in 1971 he emerged as a star with "Take Me Home, Country Roads." Denver co-wrote the song with Bill and Taffy Danoff, and over the next decade he would write or co-write most of the material that made him a pop phenomenon. "The songs would just come from him, as if he was a vehicle from God that the songs flowed through," Annie Denver was quoted as saying in the *Denver Post* after Denver's death. "It was a part of him that he wasn't very ego-attached to. The man was driven to write songs. The music came out of a very deep place. And oftentimes, out of that deepness, John felt very alone. If you listen to his songs, there's a lot of loneliness there."

Crossed Genre Boundaries

More hits followed, including "Thank God I'm a Country Boy," "Annie's Song" (dedicated to his wife and reportedly written in ten minutes on a Colorado ski lift), "Sunshine on My Shoulders," and "Some Days Are Diamonds." Perhaps the most memorable, at least for residents of his home state, was the Colorado ode "Rocky Mountain High," which praised "the serenity of a clear blue mountain lake" and wrapped up the back-to-nature philosophies of the 1960s counterculture in a universally appealing package. Colorado governor John Vanderhoof named Denver the state's poet laureate in 1974. Denver's songs were equally popular among pop and country audiences, and Denver took home the Country Music Association's Entertainer of the Year award in 1975. Country traditionalists were dismayed; awards-show host Charlie Rich actually set fire to Denver's award envelope with a cigarette lighter.

The divide between popular taste and the attitudes of music critics was widening in the early 1970s, and Denver was never a critical favorite. British rock writer Dave Laing even referred to "Sunshine on My Shoulders" as "egregious" in Denver's obituary. Denver's image, with his mop-top haircut and wire-rimmed "granny" glasses, was about 15 years out of date at the peak of his fame, harking back to the collegiate-folk stage of his career, and his predominantly optimistic lyrics ("Some Days Are Diamonds" being an exception) were derided as sentimental or over-sweet.

Denver responded mildly to such criticisms, telling *People* that "some of my songs are about very simple things in life. But those simple things are meaningful to me and have obviously meant something to people all over the world, even if it's only in a karaoke bar." His music was defended by country singer Kathy Mattea. "A lot of people write him off as lightweight," she told Alanna Nash of *Entertainment Weekly*. "But he articulated a kind of optimism, and he brought acoustic music to the forefront, bridging folk, pop, and country in a fresh way. . . . People forget how huge he was worldwide."

Indeed, Denver in the mid-1970s was arguably America's most celebrated male entertainer. His 1973 *Greatest*

the classic country music of the era. His other grandmother also shaped his musical education by giving him an antique Gibson guitar. In 1957 the family settled in Fort Worth, Texas; Denver attended Texas Tech University in Lubbock and sang in a folk-music group called the Alpine Trio while pursuing architecture studies.

California's folk and rock music scenes were growing rapidly in the early and middle 1960s, and in 1964 Denver dropped out of Texas Tech and moved to Los Angeles, making up the stage name John Denver to indicate a general attraction to the mountainous West. He began performing at Ledbetter's nightclub and signed on as lead vocalist for a group called the Back Porch Majority. In 1965 he scored a breakthrough when he replaced Chad Mitchell as vocalist, guitarist, and banjoist for the Chad Mitchell Trio, a prime attraction on college campuses and in folk-oriented coffeehouses. Denver bested some 250 other performers who auditioned for the job.

Performing with the group at a college in Minnesota, Denver met sophomore Annie Martell; the two were married the following year and later adopted two children. Denver began to focus on songwriting, and he released a solo album, *Rhymes and Reasons,* in 1968 after the Mitchell Trio disbanded. The album included the "Ballad of Richard Nixon," and another song about Vice President Spiro Agnew; and it also contained "Leaving on a Jet Plane," a song Denver wrote in a single evening after he locked himself in his room, as he later recalled, with a pound of salami and a six-pack of beer. It was originally titled "Babe, I Hate to Go." The young

Hits album remained on *Billboard* magazine's chart of top album sellers for about three years. In 1975 and 1976, Denver won four American Music Awards—honors that measured the sentiments of music buyers rather than industry figures. Of his 24 albums released on the RCA label during his lifetime, 14 were eventually certified gold (for sales of 500,000 copies), and eight of those reached the platinum or million-seller mark.

Formed Foundation

Denver succeeded in extending his run in the spotlight well into the 1980s. He appeared opposite octogenarian comedian George Burns in the film *Oh, God!* (1977), and he served as host for numerous television specials; one of them, 1975's *Rocky Mountain Christmas,* was issued in album form and also won him an Emmy Award. He sang duets with vocalists ranging from opera star Plácido Domingo to musical comedienne Julie Andrews to roots-country revivalist Emmylou Harris (the underrated "Wild Montana Skies"). He founded the Windstar (or Windsong) label, which released the disco hit "Afternoon Delight," recorded by Bill and Taffy Danoff as the Starland Vocal Band. But he also began to look toward a future in which he would work to safeguard the wilderness that had inspired many of his best songs. He founded the nonprofit Windstar Foundation in 1976 and the World Hunger Project in 1977.

The latter enterprise got him appointed to the Commission on World and Domestic Hunger by President Jimmy Carter. Having generally avoided political themes in his music up to that point, Denver devoted much of his energy to political causes in the 1980s and 1990s. In addition to wilderness and wildlife preservation, he was active in support of world anti-hunger initiatives, the United Nations Children's Fund and other projects aimed at improving the lives of children, and of peace groups and organizations opposed to the spread of nuclear weaponry. Although he was critical of Republican presidents Richard Nixon and Ronald Reagan, Denver worked effectively with leaders of both parties, and in 1987 he received the Presidential World Without Hunger Award from Reagan. That was followed by an Albert Schweitzer Music Award for humanitarian activity in 1993, making Denver the first musician from outside the classical sphere to earn the award. (Albert Schweitzer was a world-famous humanitarian, theologian, and classical organist who served as a medical relief worker in Africa.)

When Denver did perform or record during the 1980s and early 1990s his music often served activist ends. He toured the Soviet Union and recorded a song, "Let Us Begin (What Are We Making Weapons For?)," with Russian vocalist Alexandre Gradsky, and in 1992 he became one of the first Western pop artists to tour in modern-day Communist China. Denver also gave a concert in the Soviet Union to benefit survivors of the Chernobyl nuclear-plant disaster, and his 1980 television special *Rocky Mountain Reunion,* dealing with species endangerment, won several awards.

Denver's personal life during his later years was less happy. After what he admitted were multiple episodes of infidelity, Denver's wife, Annie, asked him for a divorce in 1982. A second marriage in 1988 to young Australian actress Cassandra Delaney produced a daughter, Jesse Belle, but also ended in divorce. Denver was also troubled by his inability to get a major label recording contract; his last several albums were issued on his own Windstar label. "There's a thing they call the Dark Night of the Soul," he was quoted as saying by Nash. "I've been through that, and I've survived it." Twice in the early 1990s Denver was arrested on charges of driving drunk.

One bright spot for Denver came from his aviation hobby, which he took up in the mid-1970s. Denver's father taught him to fly, and the experience helped bring about a reconciliation between father and son. He became an experienced pilot, flying his own planes in Colorado, on tour, and in California's Monterey Peninsula area, where he rented a home in Carmel so that he could be near Delaney and Jesse Belle. It was there that he purchased a Long EZ aircraft from a local veterinarian in the summer of 1997. The plane model was classified as experimental, but it was well known among aviation enthusiasts, and Denver experienced no problems during lessons in Santa Maria, California.

On October 12, 1997, Denver played golf with friends and looked forward to an hour of flying his new aircraft over the ocean. Several practice takeoffs and landings went off uneventfully, but apparently drained one of the plane's two fuel tanks. Late in the afternoon, onlookers saw Denver's plane plummet into the ocean after what appeared to be an engine failure. The singer was probably killed instantly. Denver's pilot's license, due to his drunk-driving arrests, was missing the medical endorsement required to make it legal, and toxicology tests were run on his remains, but they came back negative. Denver is thought to have lost control of the plane while fumbling with a lever that shifted the engine's fuel supply from one tank to the other. A strong outpouring of fan emotion followed his tragic death, and a musical featuring his songs, *Almost Heaven,* had its premiere in 2005. The show, noted *Variety* reviewer Mark Blankenship, "pays excellent tribute to an artist who remains great at making people feel good."

Books

Contemporary Musicians, volume 22, Gale, 1998.
Denver, John, *Take Me Home: An Autobiography,* Harmony, 1994.

Periodicals

Denver Post, October 14, 1997.
Entertainment Weekly, October 24, 1997; October 18, 2002.
Guardian (London, England), October 14, 1997.
People, October 27, 1997.
Variety, November 14, 2005. □

Gérard Depardieu

French actor Gérard Depardieu (born 1948) rose from humble beginnings to become a worldwide movie star. The award-winning actor has enjoyed a film career spanning more than four decades, and

has appeared in over 170 films. Many of those films have garnered him critical and commercial successes, both in his native Europe and around the world.

An Impoverished Upbringing

Depardieu was born in Châteauroux, a small provincial community in central France, on December 27, 1948. His taciturn father, René "Dédé" Depardieu, was a barely literate sheet metal worker; his mother, Alice "Lilette" Marillier, came to Châteauroux with her family as refugees during World War II. The couple married in 1944 and had two children—one son and one daughter—before the birth of Gerard. The family lived in cramped quarters and Depardieu's father was not an active parent, so much of the stresses of caring for three small children fell to his mother. Depardieu, who would eventually have five siblings, became the family's charming prankster, earning the nickname of Pétarou, or "Little Firecracker."

When an American Air Force base set up in his hometown, Depardieu became fascinated with Americans and their culture. He and his older brother were regulars both on the base and at social gathering spots popular with the American troops. By the time Depardieu completed his formal schooling in the early 1960s—he completed only grade school, not attending lycée, the French equivalent of

high school—he stood nearly six feet tall and could readily pass for several years older than his true age of 13. Depardieu took to petty crime and wandering, working a series of odd jobs such as printer's apprentice, dishwasher, traveling salesman, and beach club attendant on the Riviera before relocating to Paris at the age of 16.

Introduced to Acting

Depardieu arrived in Paris on a whim, following a friend who was moving to the capital to pursue acting. Depardieu visited the drama school with his friend and immediately showed ability as a performer. Self-doubts about his provincial background and poor education interrupted Depardieu's acting training for a time. However, after being taken into prestigious acting coach Jean-Laurent Cochet's class, Depardieu quickly honed his acting techniques. Depardieu had difficulties speaking fluently, and began working with speech therapist Alfred Tomatis. With Tomatis's help, Depardieu overcame his difficulties not only with language, but with reading comprehension and recall. During his training with Cochet, Depardieu met Elisabeth Guignot, whom he would marry in 1970. The two had their first child, Guillaume, in April of the following year. In 1973 the pair had a daughter, Julie.

By the late 1960s, Depardieu had begun landing roles in theater and television productions around Paris, often playing hulking thugs in keeping with his rough-hewn appearance. Depardieu's film debut came in Roger Leenhardt's *Le Beatnik et le minet,* and his television debut on an episode of the French series *Rendez-vous à Bedenberg.* Depardieu's reputation grew with his strong performance in the theatrical play *Galapagos*; although the production itself was a flop, Depardieu received good reviews. In 1973 Depardieu co-starred in Bertrand Blier's film *Les Valseuses* (known in the United States as *Going Places*). In his biography *Depardieu,* Paul Chutkow noted that "the French critics agreed that the film's three young actors were fresh, unconventional, and outright brilliant." The film's plot placed its protagonists as sexually and otherwise aggressive young people who challenged the accepted standards of conventional society. The controversial film achieved critical and popular acclaim, shepherding in a new era of French filmmaking. In one of the lead roles, Depardieu was transformed from an actor to a star.

Became European Star

After *Les Valseuses,* Depardieu became a film actor in earnest. Throughout the 1970s he appeared in many films, typically playing thugs or deviants. Some of his most noteworthy roles were as a peasant in Italian director Bernardo Bertolucci's epic film *1900,* as a crude chauvinist in the sexually-charged and controversial *La Dernière Femme* (The Last Woman) and, in another film by *Les Valseuses* director Blier, as a husband who seeks to find his sexually stifled wife a new lover in *Preparez vos Mouchoirs* (Get Out Your Handkerchiefs). Even when the films were not critically successful, Depardieu benefited in some way. Bertolucci's *1900* was considered a cinematic flop, but offered Depardieu the opportunity to meet and work with

American actor Robert DeNiro, who served as an inspiration to Depardieu throughout his career. Chutkow commented that both men "were heavyweights, prolific actors who could play anything from light comedy to epic drama, and both had a flair for taking quirky characters and making them poignant and universal."

Depardieu has consistently worked with France's leading film directors—such as Blier—to great success. In 1979 he co-starred with respected French actress Isabelle Huppert in Maurice Pialet's *Loulou*. Playing the title role, Depardieu portrays an unemployed but charming rogue who lures the bourgeois Huppert away from her traditional life and friends by his personal magnetism. In the early 1980s Depardieu began working with respected French director François Truffaut. Their first collaboration, *Le Dernier Métro* (The Last Metro), paired Depardieu with actress Catherine Deneuve. The film tells the story of a Jewish theater owner in Paris during the time of the World War II Nazi occupation. His wife (Deneuve) seeks to protect her husband from the occupying forces. Depardieu plays an actor trying to break into legitimate theater; during the course of the film, he develops a relationship with Deneuve's character. The film was a massive critical success, garnering many prestigious *César* awards at France's Cannes Film Festival, including a Best Actor prize for Depardieu.

Prolific and versatile, Depardieu made nearly every type of film imaginable during the 1980s: drama, romance, comedy, serious film, and lighthearted fare. Depardieu's 1981 comedy *La Chèvre* (The Goat) was Depardieu's biggest box office success and the beginning of a three-film series. The last of these three films was eventually remade in English as *Three Fugitives,* starring Nick Nolte and Martin Short. The following year Depardieu took a turn in the historical film *La Retour de Martin Guerre* (The Return of Martin Guerre). The movie, based on a true story, portrays a man who leaves his small medieval village for a stint in the army, and later returns to reenter the lives of his wife, family, and community. However, there is a question as to whether the man claiming to be Martin Guerre is indeed the real Guerre; Depardieu's delicate handling of the role makes it one of his finest performances.

In the late 1980s Depardieu turned his hand to a different form of expression: writing. After the death of his mother, Depardieu sought to tell people of all kinds what he had never said in life through his book, *Lettres volees* (Stolen Letters). Published in 1988, the book was an intensely personal work displaying another facet of the actor's psyche, and it became a bestseller in France.

Found Success as Cyrano and in the United States

Depardieu continued to find success with his films throughout the remainder of the 1980s. However, a project on which he embarked at the close of the decade would prove to be one of his most career-defining. Based on the life of a real sixteenth-century man named Cyrano de Bergerac, the play *Cyrano de Bergerac* was written in the late 1800s and has remained a staple of French literature since that time. Brought to stage and screen many times previ-

ously, the story returned under the helm of French director Jean-Paul Rappeneau with Depardieu in the title role. Although Depardieu did not initially capture the role, by the time shooting began in earnest his natural ability to weave complex characters had allowed him to immerse himself in the intricacies the part demanded. In the film Depardieu portrays a poet and playwright who falls in love with his beautiful cousin Roxane, but does not believe she will find him attractive because of his large nose. Depardieu won the *César* at Cannes for his performance, and was nominated for an Academy Award for the role.

After the success of *Cyrano de Bergerac,* Depardieu took on a new challenge: playing roles in English rather than his native French. Although his early exposure to English from the American Air Force base in his hometown had given him a rough grasp of the language, Depardieu was by no means an expert speaker. Nevertheless, he paired with American actress Andie MacDowell in the romantic comedy *Green Card.* In the film, the two play a couple who marry for convenience—for Depardieu, the titular immigration green card—but eventually fall in love. A few years later Depardieu appeared in another English-language comedy, *My Father, the Hero,* a remake of his 1991 French film *Mon père ce heros.* In 1996 Depardieu appeared with Whoopi Goldberg and Haley Joel Osment in the film *Bogus.* Again, Depardieu took the title role, this time as the imaginary friend of a young boy struggling to accept the death of his mother. It is noted in the *International Dictionary of Films and Filmmakers* that Depardieu's "charisma allows him to transcend the thinness of the material."

Depardieu appeared in several high-profile projects in the late 1990s, many based on classic literary works. Appearing as the title characters in *The Count of Monte Cristo* and *Balzac,* Depardieu returned to dramas with great success. He also appeared in a small role in Kenneth Branagh's film version of William Shakespeare's classic play *Hamlet,* and in Randall Wallace's English language film *The Man in the Iron Mask* as Porthos, one of the legendary three musketeers.

In the 2000s Depardieu continued to act in diverse films on both sides of the Atlantic. He appeared in the Disney film *102 Dalmatians,* in the gritty drama *City of Ghosts,* and as a gourmet chef in the Queen Latifah vehicle *Last Holiday.* As well as his performances in Hollywood, Depardieu appeared in French films such as *Nathalie,* in which he plays the role of a philandering husband—a role in some ways hearkening back to his first major appearances in the 1970s.

Announced Retirement

Depardieu has many interests outside of acting. A wine enthusiast, he owns a château and winery where he creates his own vintages. In 2005 he announced his retirement from acting with characteristic earthy eloquence, telling the French newspaper *Le Parisien*: "I've got nothing to lose. I did 170 films, and I've got nothing else to prove. I'm not going to keep up like this forever. . . . I retire in style with this film. It's wonderful." However, in December of 2006, *Variety* announced that Depardieu had joined such performers as Joseph Fiennes, Malcolm McDowell, and Jacqueline Bisset in a period biographical film based on the life of composer Antonio Vivaldi. Whether or not Depardieu's career continues at the same frenetic pace which has marked it over the years, Depardieu's reputation as one of France's premiere actors is assured.

Books

Chutkow, Paul, *Depardieu: A Biography,* Knopf, 1994.

International Directory of Films and Filmmakers, Volume 2: Actors and Actresses, 4th ed., St. James Press, 2000.
Newsmakers 1991, Gale Research, 1991.

Online

"Gerard Depardieu Joins the Cast of Vivaldi," http://www.movieweb.com (January 1, 2007).
"Gerard Depardieu Pulls the Curtain on Movie Career," November 16, 2005, http://www.news.yahoo.com (January 1, 2007). □

E

Gerald M. Edelman

American neuroscientist, professor, and author Gerald M. Edelman (born 1929) won the Nobel Prize in Physiology or Medicine in 1972 at the age of 43. He went on to achieve equal prominence for his pioneering theory of mind, referred to as "Neural Darwinism" or "Neuronal Group Selection" (NGS). While his conclusions about the fundamental workings of the human brain were often controversial, they were never dull. Edelman's publications on the subject included *Neural Darwinism: The Theory of Neuronal Group Selection, Bright Air, Brilliant Fire: On the Matter of the Mind,* and *Wider than the Sky: The Phenomenal Gift of Consciousness.* He founded the Neurosciences Institute in New York City in 1981, and moved it to La Jolla, California, in 1993.

Education and Training

Edelman was born on July 1, 1929, in New York City. His father, Edward, was a physician and his mother, Anna, a homemaker. As he was growing up in Ozone Park, Queens, and Long Beach, New York, science was not foremost in his mind. Instead, he trained to be a concert violinist with noted teacher/performer Albert Meiff. Music was to remain a consuming passion of Edelman's over the years, but it was not to become his career.

After attending public schools in New York City through high school, Edelman went to Collegeville, Penn-

sylvania, to study chemistry at Ursinus College. He graduated magna cum laude in 1950 and then headed off to the Medical School of the University of Pennsylvania, from which he received an M.D. in 1954. In 1955 Edelman became a medical house officer at Massachusetts General Hospital. Next up, he joined the U.S. Army Medical Corps as a captain, and practiced general medicine at a military hospital connected with American Hospital in Paris, France, for two years.

Upon his discharge from the army in 1957, Edelman returned to his hometown to pursue a Ph.D. in biochemistry and immunology from the Rockefeller Institute (now Rockefeller University). It was there, under the guidance of Dr. Henry G. Kunkel, that Edelman began the research in immunology that would lead to his Nobel Prize. His thesis explored methods of splitting immunoglobulin molecules, or antibodies, and he received his doctorate in 1960.

Won Nobel Prize

After earning his Ph.D., Edelman stayed on at Rockefeller University as assistant dean of Graduate Studies. In 1963 he became associate dean of Graduate Studies, and in 1966 he became a full professor. He continued his research in his own laboratory, and was soon making some groundbreaking findings.

In the 1950s and 1960s, the understanding of the nature of antibodies was scant. Their role in combating foreign substances, or antigens, in the body was known, but their chemical structure and the way in which they were able to recognize antigens was less clear. English biochemist Rodney R. Porter was investigating the matter, as was Edelman. Throughout the 1960s each scientist came up with independent research, sometimes drawing on one another's research, in order to explain the properties of antibodies

In 1981 Edelman founded the Neurosciences Institute as an independently supported part of Rockefeller University (relocated to La Jolla, California in 1993). Its mandate was to emphasize the scientific "big picture" and investigate creative theories on the workings of the brain, particularly as to higher brain function. Within this organization, Edelman formulated his notable theory of mind.

Neural Darwinism, or Neuronal Group Selection (NGS), was first presented in Edelman's 1987 book *Neural Darwinism: The Theory of Neuronal Group Selection*. The idea is described in his biography on the Cajal Conference website (citation below) as: "the theory that populations of neurons develop individual networks through a Darwinian selection process. [Edelman] thinks that the converse opinion, that neurons are genetically coded to make specific connections, just as transistors are wired in a preset pattern, is untenable given the very limited size of eukaryotic genomes in relation with the explosive number of neuronal connections." Further, Edelman argued against the traditional concept of a fixed human nervous system, suggesting instead that neural systems continuously change. That is, the human brain has variations unique to each individual and modifies itself constantly in response to each new incoming signal.

The forgoing explanation is, necessarily, an extremely simplified and streamlined definition of a multi-faceted and complicated theory. Indeed, some of its controversy stemmed from its very complexity. Edward Rothstein of the *New York Times* quoted the 1988 comment of biologist Gunter Stent on NGS as, "I consider myself not too dumb. I am a professor of molecular biology and chairman of the neurobiology section of the National Academy of Sciences, so I should understand it. But I don't." Other critics found the theory either derivative or based on incorrect interpretations of other models of the mind. But Edelman ignored the naysayers and quietly continued his pioneering work.

more fully. By 1969 Edelman and his team at Rockefeller had succeeded in creating a precise model of an antibody molecule, which was made up of a four-amino-acid-chain (two light and two heavy chains) structure comprised of more than 1,300 amino acids. This enabled the team to identify exact locations of antigenic binding. Edelman's group had just narrowly beaten Porter's in achieving such a goal, and both researchers were awarded the Nobel Prize in Physiology or Medicine in 1972 for their efforts. Their work had many far-reaching effects in medical therapy, including preventing organ rejection in transplant situations. But Edelman, just 43 years old at the time, had even more to offer the world of science.

Neural Darwinism

After winning the Nobel Prize, Edelman changed his focus from immunology to developmental biology and neuroscience. Specifically, he began to investigate how the human body, and especially the brain, operates, by honing in on cellular interactions in early embryonic development and the formation and function of the nervous system. He quickly made innovative inroads into this new area as well, beginning in 1975, when he discovered cell adhesion molecules (CAMs). CAMs bind neurons together to form the brain's fundamental circuitry, thereby guiding the basic processes through which an animal achieves its shape and form and by which nervous systems are constructed. While seminal in its own right, this work also led to the larger theory for which Edelman is likely most famous, that of "Neural Darwinism."

Preeminent Neuroscientist

After his first book on NGS, Edelman went on to write several others elucidating his ideas for both the scientific and lay communities. He started by writing the two volumes that completed his initial trilogy, *Topobiology: An Introduction to Molecular Embryology* (1988) and *The Remembered Present: A Biological Theory of Consciousness* (1989). He followed those up with *Bright Air, Brilliant Fire: On the Matter of the Mind*, published in 1992, *A Universe of Consciousness: How Matter Becomes Imagination* (2000), which presented new data on the neural correlates of conscious experience, and *Wider than the Sky: The Phenomenal Gift of Consciousness* (2005), which included a model of the biology of consciousness. It was in the latter book that Edelman, unenviably, attempted to articulate his ideas for a lay audience. Additionally, he had authored more than 500 research publications by 2006.

By 2005 Edelman had added other responsibilities to his resume besides heading up the Neurosciences Institute. Those included serving as chairman and professor of neurobiology at the Scripps Research Institute, scientific chairman of the Neurosciences Research Program, and president of the Neurosciences Research Foundation. His institute was thriving on its own campus in La Jolla, with 36 research fellows studying nearly every field of neuroscience. Each fellow was fully funded by the institute for up to four years, in order to insulate him or her from the vagaries and distractions of grant writing and laboratory politics, as Edelman felt such independence was necessary for proper original research. And the institute itself was an interesting reflection of its founder: one building devoted to theory, another to experimentation, and a third (a concert hall) to music.

Edelman's unique and significant contributions to science garnered him many accolades, honors, and awards throughout the years. In 1954 he received the Spencer Morris Award from the University of Pennsylvania; in 1965, the Eli Lilly Award in Biological Chemistry of American Chemical Society; and in 1969, the Annual Alumni Award from Ursinus College. He gave the Carter-Wallace Lectures at Princeton University in 1965, the National Institutes of Health Biophysics and Bioorganic Chemistry Lectureship at Cornell University in 1971, and the Darwin Centennial Lectures at Rockefeller University in 1971. He was the first Felton Bequest Visiting Professor at the Walter and Eliza Hall Institute for Medical Research in Melbourne, Australia, in 1972, and became a Vincent Astor Distinguished Professor at Rockefeller University in 1974. Other awards included the Albert Einstein Commemorative Award, the Buchman Memorial Award from the California Institute of Technology, and the Rabbi Shai Schaknai Memorial Prize. And he held memberships in numerous professional and scientific societies. He was one of the few international members of the Academy of Sciences, Institute of France.

Despite the controversy surrounding his theories, and perhaps even because of it, Edelman was indisputably one of the preeminent neuroscientists of his time. His advocates found his ideas breathtaking. His adversaries rarely dismissed him out of hand. And the potential impact of his ideas, whatever one felt about them, was enormous. As Rothstein wrote, ''(Edelman's) vision can also spur discomfort, because it implies that there is no supervising soul or self—nobody is standing behind the curtain. This, for Dr. Edelman, is Darwin's final burden.''

Periodicals

New York Times, March 27, 2004.

Online

"Dr. Gerald M. Edelman," Almaden Institute, http://www .almaden.ibm.com/institute/bio/2006/?edelman (November 29, 2006).
"Edelman," The World Knowledge Dialogue," http://www .wkdnews.org/info/speakers?start=3 (November 28, 2006).
"Edelman, Gerald Maurice," *Britannica,* http://www.britannica .com/nobel/micro/185_88.html (November 28, 2006).
"Gerald Edelman," Cajal Conference, http://www.cajal.unizar .es/eng/part/Edelman.html (November 28, 2006).
"Gerald M. Edelman," *Encarta,* http://www.encarta.msn.com/ text_761582633__O/Edelman_Gerald_M.html (November 28, 2006).
"Gerald M. Edelman," Nobel Foundation, http://www .nobelprize.org/nobel_prizes/medicine/laureates/1972/ Edelman-bio.html (November 28, 2006).

"Gerald M. Edelman," Penguin, http://www.penguin.co.uk/nf/ Author/AuthorPage/0,,1000023730,00.html (November 28, 2006).
"Gerald Maurice Edelman," All Experts, http://www.experts .about.com/e/g/ge/gerald_edelman.htm (November 28, 2006).
"Gerald Maurice Edelman," *Britannica,* http://www.britannica .com/eb/aricle-9031972/Gerald-Maurice-Edelman (November 28, 2006).
"Neural Darwinism," Architecture and the Mind, http://www .architecture-mind.com/neuraldarwin.html (November 29, 2006).
"World of Health Biography," Book Rags, http://www.bookrags .com/printfriendly/?p=bios&u=gerald-m-edelman-woh (November 29, 2006). □

Althea Maria Brown Edmiston

Althea Maria Brown Edmiston (1874–1937) was an African-American missionary who spent more than 30 years serving a Presbyterian mission in the Belgian Congo in Africa in the early part of the twentieth century. Born in Alabama and raised in Mississippi, Brown returned to America several times to give lectures on her work. Despite having no formal linguistic training, she compiled the first grammar and dictionary for the Bakuba tribe, an immense project that took more than a decade to complete.

Althea Maria Brown Edmiston was born near the end of the Civil War, on December 17, 1874, in Russelville, Dekalb County, Alabama. She was the fifth child and second daughter of Robert and Mary ''Molly'' Suggs Brown. In all, her parents had ten children.

When she was two years old, Brown moved with her family to a fertile farming area in the Mississippi delta region. At first the uprooted family lived in a small cabin with three generations of other Brown family members. Later, Robert Brown, who worked as a sharecropper, purchased more than a hundred acres near Rolling Fork, in Mississippi. He and his sons built a cabin, constructing the family home with logs cut from trees growing on the property.

Grew up on a Farm

The Browns turned their substantial acreage into a highly productive farm, growing vegetables, fruits and nuts. To further help support his family, Robert Brown became a trader, traveling to surrounding areas to exchange farm products and animals for salt, sugar, coffee, and other kitchen staples. He was also a community figure of sorts: He helped build a church and a school, and he also taught his neighbors how to preserve their own farm products.

Though Brown's early life was spent in hard surroundings and rough circumstances, she benefited from the positive influence of her caring parents, who raised their children in a loving home filled with strong values. Robert and Mollie Brown had endured the slave era in America's pre-Civil War south, and they fostered in their children a love of independence. Further, though her parents lacked formal education, Brown learned a great deal from them, including how to read and write. Her father helped develop her literacy by making crude instruction boards that he used to illustrate the alphabet. Indeed, Robert Brown placed such a high value on his children's education that seven of the ten Brown siblings were able to go to college. Also, from working with her father on the family farm, Brown learned many agricultural techniques that she would later use as a missionary in Africa.

While growing up, Brown expressed a strong desire to become a teacher, but in her first jobs she worked as a nurse, positions she took when she was still quite young. When she was 10 years old, she became a nurse to the child of a white family. The child's mother recognized Althea's potential and helped her increase her reading and spelling skills. She also helped refine her manner of speech. Brown lived with the family for two years. Later she became a home nurse for a teacher at Oakland College, a black school in Alcorn, Mississippi.

Received College Scholarship

In 1889, when she was 15 years old, Brown began her formal education, along with her siblings, taking a daily one-mile trek to a school for blacks located at Indian Bayou. Later, she completed grammar school in Rolling Fork, walking four miles each day to get to her classroom.

The following year, Brown was fortunate enough to receive a scholarship to attend Fisk University in Nashville, Tennessee. The opportunity meant that she could complete grade school, high school and college at the institution. However, she didn't enter the university until the fall semester of 1892. Brown later recalled that she was frightened at first, and she worried that her unsophisticated, rural appearance would be deemed too unattractive for the campus.

At the university she still harbored ambitions of becoming a teacher. But her motivations were as much self-serving as they were altruistic. By becoming a teacher, she reasoned, she could make a lot of money and live the kind of life she had never before experienced. However, three months after she entered Fisk she became a Christian, a conversion that compelled her to re-evaluate her life purpose. She now felt that she should use her education in service to others.

At the time of her conversion, Brown had only advanced to the seventh grade, and she realized she would need to support herself over the course of her long educational path. As she only received a small allowance from her parents—it was all they could afford—Brown launched several small business ventures. At various times during her nine years at Fisk she made and sold fudge, ran a beauty shop in her dormitory room, and worked as a domestic for faculty members. Later, when she became more educated, she partially realized her earlier dream, working as a substi-

tute teacher in nearby black schools and teaching summer school in rural areas.

Eventually, while she was still attending Fisk, Brown became a teacher for the Lincoln School in Pikeville, Tennessee, where she worked for 19 months. But there were no facilities for black students, so Brown taught in a one-room church, the only teacher for one hundred children of all ages and grade levels.

She graduated with the highest honors from Fisk University in 1901, and earned the distinction as the only female speaker during the commencement ceremony. In a caring and respectful gesture, Brown also delivered her valedictory address to the food services staff that worked in a university cafeteria located in a women's residence hall.

Became a Missionary

After graduation, and continuing with a renewed sense of purpose, Brown applied to the Executive Committee of Foreign Missions of the Presbyterian Church to be a missionary in Africa's Congo Free State. On May 14, 1901, she was commissioned and, after a year of training at the Chicago Training School for City and Foreign Missions, she left for Africa. When Brown boarded a St. Louis steamship on August 20, 1902, her family truly believed they would never see her again, as they felt she was sailing into danger, even certain death, in a continent filled with savage beasts and cruel inhabitants.

After a stop in Southhampton, England, the missionaries landed in Luebo, Africa, where they studied native languages for seven weeks. When the missionaries finally separated to go to their respective locations, Brown headed to Ibanche, which was located deep in the African continent. At this point in her journey no transportation was available, so Brown was transported on a canvas hammock carried by men.

The place where Brown would work, the Ibanche mission station, included a marketplace, park, several buildings, and the Lapsley Memorial Church, a beautiful structure where Dr. William Sheppard, an African American who co-founded the mission, lived with his family. The mission was surrounded by native villages, and the inhabitants came to the mission each day for instruction.

Brown lived in a dwelling built especially for her, which she named "Jubilee Hall," after her residence hall at Fisk University. The modest structure was an adobe-style hut with a thatched roof, with straw matting to cover the dirt floor. To make the structure more homelike, Brown hung pictures on the wall and decorated the hut with draperies and bedspreads that she made herself. Visitors to this humble dwelling would include doctors, judges, agricultural experts, priests and Protestant missionaries.

After she arrived, Brown waited only one day before she set to work. She served as the day school mistress, matron of the Maria Carey Home for Girls, and Sunday school teacher. She also led the women's work and organized the native women into Christian bands.

Survived Tribal Rebellion

Working conditions at Ibanche proved hard. The missionary was understaffed and the climate was harsh, with heavy tropical rains. More important, danger lurked outside the mission perimeter, and the possibility of death was quite palpable, particularly on November 2, 1904, when hostile members of a neighboring tribe engaged in an uprising against the Congo government. The rebels' tribal leader, King Lukenga, ordered all dwellings of white inhabitants to be burned. His warriors went on a destructive march, attacking and burning a Christian village, a trading post and a rubber factory. Further, Lukenga demanded that the hearts of traders and heads of missionaries be delivered to him.

At one point during the day, a runner brought a blood-covered branch to the Ibanche mission, reporting that it was the blood of a murdered Christian. By evening, Ibanche was surrounded, and fierce fighting could be heard just beyond the mission. Understandably, Brown thought she would surely be killed during the seemingly endless night. But she survived. Fighting eased up the next day, only to commence again at night.

After a second terror-filled night, some Congolese soldiers escorted Brown and nearly 500 women and children to Luebo. The retreat was difficult: the soldiers feared an attack and ordered the refugees, many of whom were burdened with heavy loads, to walk at a rapid pace. But Brown made it through the ordeal and, a year later she married Alonzo Edmiston, a man who took part in the march from Ibanche to Luebo.

Married in Africa

Alonzo Edmiston had come to Ibanche to help the understaffed missionaries. Like Brown, Edmiston was an American. He was born in Petersburg, Tennessee, on July 19, 1879. He attended the Stillman Institute in Tuscaloosa, Alabama, and worked his way through school with summer jobs at the Alabama State Hospital. He was skilled in scientific farming, had taken a course in medicine and was schooled in theology. Inspired by the experiences of William Sheppard, he wanted to work as a missionary in Africa. On a business trip to Africa he visited Ibanche, where he met Brown. When asked to remain at the mission, he readily agreed.

Brown and Edmiston worked together for eight months, marrying on July 8, 1905. Brown reportedly made her own wedding garments, as most of her clothes had been burned during the previous year's rebellion. The couple's first son, Sherman Lucius, was born in May of 1906, his delivery accomplished in Luebo by midwives. Alonzo Edmiston later started an industrial school at Ibanche, where young men were taught trades such as carpentry.

One of Althea Edmiston's great accomplishments in Africa, besides her unselfish humanitarian service, was the compilation of a grammar and dictionary of the Bakuba language. The Bakuba people had no written language, and Edmiston began the formidable task of putting their complex and beautiful speech onto paper in 1902. She worked on it intermittently until its completion in 1913. However, the mission didn't have the funds to publish the scholarly work, so Edmiston sought contributions from organizations such as Fisk University and the Women of the Presbyterian Church in the United States. The work was finally published 30 years after its completion, as *Grammar and Dictionary of the Bushonga or Bakuba Language as Spoken by the Bushonga or Bakuba Tribe Who Dwell in the Upper Kasai District, Belgian Congo, Central Africa* (1932). The project was a vast undertaking, but what makes its completion even more noteworthy is the fact that Edmiston never had any formal linguistic training.

While in Africa, Edmiston also translated school books, hymns, parables, lullabies, fairy tales, and folklore for the Bakuba people.

Returned to America Several Times

Five years after she arrived in Africa, Althea Edmiston returned to America with her son for a much needed vacation. Her husband joined them a year later, and the family settled in Tuscaloosa, Alabama. During her stay, Althea Edmiston lectured at churches and schools and at the American Missionary Association of the Congregational Board in the East. The Edmistons also raised money for the Ibanche mission.

When the family returned to Africa, they moved to another mission farther into the Bakuba country, at Bulape. In 1912 they moved to a new missionary outpost established in Mutoto, where the Edmistons' second son, Alonzo Leaucourt, was born in 1913, and where they would work for the rest of their lives.

In all, the Edmistons worked among the Bakuba people for 20 years, but they would revisit America several times. In April of 1920 they visited their two sons, who lived in Selma, Alabama. When the couple returned the following year, Althea Edmiston gave a commencement address at her alma mater, Fisk University, appealing to the university to train more missionaries and encouraging students to live their lives in service to others.

Back at Mutoto, Althea Edmiston served as principal of the day school system and administered aid to the sick. In December of 1924, both Althea and Alonzo fell victim to the "sleeping sickness" epidemic. They returned to America in 1925 for treatment at the Rockefeller Institute in New York. After a year and half, specialists determined that the couple was cured, and the Edmistons later returned to Africa.

Althea Edmiston would visit America only once more, in 1935, when she gave an address before the Missionary Conference of Negro Women in Indianapolis. Two years later she became critically ill with sleeping sickness and pernicious malaria. She suffered for a month, never letting on that she was enduring great pain. She died on June 10, 1937, in Mutoto, where she would be buried. More than 2,000 people attended her funeral, including both American and African friends.

In 1939 Althea Edmiston was honored by the Women's Auxiliary of the Presbyterian Church in the United States, who inaugurated the Althea Brown Edmiston Memorial Fund. The interest went toward a home for girls. In 1947 a biography, *A Life for the Congo: The Story of Althea Brown Edmiston,* written by Julia Lake Kellersberger, was published. Kellersberger wrote that when Althea Edmiston died, both Africa and America played "taps for the soldier of the Jubilee."

Books

A Life for the Congo: The Story of Althea Brown Edmiston, Fleming H. Revell, 1947.
Notable Black American Women, Book 3, Gale Group, 2002.

Online

"Love's Retrospective," *First Scots Sermons,* http://www.first-scots.org/sermons/061008DMLovesRetrospective.pdf (December 8, 2006).
"November 2: Althea Brown Feared for her Life," *Christian History Institute,* http://www.chi.gospelcom.net/DAILYF/2002/11/daily-11-02-2002.shtml (December 8, 2006). □

Roger A. Enrico

American business leader Roger Enrico (born 1944) is best known for his lengthy tenure as chief executive officer (CEO) of PepsiCo Inc. Under Enrico, Pepsi developed a strong image and built profits. Enrico left Pepsi in 2001 and has served as chairman of the board of directors for entertainment company DreamWorks Animation SKG, Inc., since 2004.

Early Life and Education

The son of a maintenance foreman at an iron ore-smelting plant, Enrico was born on November 11, 1944, in the small town of Chisholm, Minnesota. Growing up, Enrico often heard his father comment that it made little sense to him why management at the smelting plant did not listen to the ideas of those who worked in the shop. These words would stay with Enrico later in his career. During high school, he took his first job working at a local soft drink bottling plant. Enrico was never better than an average student, but his hopes of leaving Minnesota were fulfilled when he received a full scholarship to Babson College in Wellesley, Massachusetts.

Enrico did well at Babson, graduating in three years. While there, he edited the college yearbook and headed his fraternity. Because he enjoyed working with people, Enrico decided to enter the field of human resources. After his graduation from Babson, he took a job in the human resources department in the Minnesota office of General Mills. However, Enrico discovered that he did not enjoy the work as much as he had expected, and began considering a career change.

Shortly after returning to Minnesota, Enrico again began dating his high school girlfriend, Rosemary Marge. The two later married and had one son, Aaron.

Found His Strengths

First, Enrico tried to join the Navy. However, he failed a test for colorblindness and was not accepted. Instead, in 1967 he enlisted for service in Vietnam near the height of the conflict. He worked as a supply officer in the northern part of South Vietnam, primarily transporting fuel. There, as noted in the *International Directory of Business Biographies,* Enrico "marveled at his commanding officer's ability to combine resourcefulness and a penchant for not 'going by the book.'" This lesson remained with Enrico throughout his career, helping him build a leadership style that could frustrate co-workers but also fostered innovation.

General Mills rehired Enrico upon his return from Vietnam, this time for their brand management division. Enrico found that he greatly preferred this kind of work to his efforts in human resources, but believed he was not reaching his full potential with General Mills because of his educational background. After a job search, Enrico was offered a position in Dallas with Frito-Lay, a division of PepsiCo, Inc., in 1972. Although initially wary of moving to Dallas, Enrico recognized the value of the opportunity and accepted the position in Frito-Lay's brand management department.

Enrico Took the Pepsi Challenge

Enrico's first job with Frito-Lay was as associate brand manager for Funyuns, an onion-flavored snack food. The position suited Enrico and he quickly established a reputation as a young go-getter. Soon Frito-Lay offered Enrico the position of president of PepsiCo Foods Japan. Enrico accepted the job, and although his time in Japan was challenging and fairly unsuccessful, PepsiCo found a place for him as vice-president of their southern Latin American division. He spent some time in Brazil in the late 1970s before returning to the United States to become senior vice president of sales and marketing of the PepsiCo Bottling Group. While in this position, Enrico impressed PepsiCo's then-president, John Scully, with his marketing prowess. After Scully's departure from PepsiCo in 1983, Enrico rose to the position of president and chief executive officer of beverages.

One of Enrico's primary accomplishments during his years heading the beverage division was the creation of the Pepsi Challenge. This marketing campaign placed Pepsi representative in public places with unmarked cups of both Pepsi and Coca-Cola to recruit passers-by to perform a blind taste test of the product. Most tasters selected Pepsi as their preferred drink, although Coca-Cola at that time had much higher sales. When these tests were shown on a well-known series of television commercials, Pepsi's share of the cola market rose considerably at locations where both beverages were sold. In 1985 Coca-Cola responded to this shift in the market by introducing an unsuccessful reformulation of their flagship beverage, unofficially known as New Coke.

The following year, Enrico, with co-author Jesse Kornbluth, published a book on the phenomenon, *The Other Guy Blinked: How Pepsi Won the Cola Wars.* Unlike many of Enrico's marketing campaigns, his book was not well received; the Jonathan Yardley wrote in *The Washington Post* that "it is a blustery and self-serving book in which Enrico attempts, with little likelihood of success, to make himself into a corporate hero in the Iacocca mode. . . . style rather than substance is Enrico's stock in trade, which makes him the quintessential entrepreneur for the age of advertising." Indeed, much of Pepsi's success in the cola wars can be attributed to strong marketing campaigns such as the Pepsi Challenge and a series of television commercials featuring celebrities such as Michael Jackson.

By 1987 Pepsi had increased its market share significantly and was within a percentage point of traditional leader Coca-Cola, largely due to Enrico's successful marketing. He was promoted to CEO of PepsiCo Worldwide Beverages, a position he held from 1987 to 1991.

Enrico Branched Out from Beverages

Enrico suffered a personal setback in 1990, when he had a heart attack in Turkey during a business trip. In 1991 Enrico left Pepsi's beverage division to become CEO of sister company Frito-Lay and Pepsi Foods International. One of his first actions as CEO was to eliminate 1,800 jobs and streamline domestic operations. He encouraged the creation of healthy snacks, such as baked potato chips. Enrico also implemented several of his signature successful marketing campaigns.

In 1994 Enrico became chairman and CEO of PepsiCo Worldwide Restaurants, the corporate division encompassing chain restaurants Pizza Hut, Taco Bell, and Kentucky Fried Chicken (KFC). The division was struggling financially, and Enrico employed streamlining techniques like those used shortly after his takeover of Frito-Lay and Pepsi

Foods International. After Enrico reduced operational units and costs, the division experienced a 19 percent profit increase. *Business Leader Profiles for Students* noted that "Enrico recognized that [Pizza Hut, Taco Bell, and KFC] were often competing with one another and had become obsessed with growth to the point of losing sight of operations and letting supply outstrip demand." In 1995 Enrico's successes with the restaurant division were much-lauded. Ready for a break, Enrico took a 14-month sabbatical from his duties. He spent much of this time working on a development and mentoring program for promising young PepsiCo executives, implemented at Enrico's personal Cayman Islands residence and his Montana ranch.

Periodicals

BusinessWeek, December 26, 2005.
Washington Post, November 9, 1986.

Online

"Roger Enrico," *Business Leaders Profiles for Students,* Reproduced in *Biography Resource Center,* http://www.galenet.galegroup.com/servlet/BioRC (January 6, 2007).
"Roger Enrico," *International Directory of Business Biographies,* Reproduced in *Biography Resource Center,* http://www.galenet.galegroup.com/servlet/BioRC (January 6, 2007). □

Richard R. Ernst

Swiss Scientist and professor Richard R. Ernst (born 1933) received the 1991 Nobel Prize in Chemistry for his pioneering work in the development of techniques for high-resolution nuclear magnetic resonance spectroscopy. Because of his work, nuclear magnetic resonance techniques became valuable tools in chemistry and also found application in other sciences.

The contributions of Nobel Prize-winning chemist Richard Robert Ernst proved far-ranging, as his work in the area of high-resolution nuclear magnetic resonance (NMR) spectroscopy led to the development of magnetic resonance imaging, which would become one of the most valuable non-invasive diagnostic imaging technologies available to medical professionals.

Ernst was born on August 14, 1933, in Winterthur, Switzerland, to Robert Ernst and Irma Brunner. Ernst later described his hometown as a place of both artistic and industrious activity, and this would influence both his recreational and career pursuits. At an early age, he learned how to play violincello and demonstrated an interest in musical composition. However, he also became fascinated with chemistry. This interest took hold when he was 13 years old. While exploring the family attic, he discovered a case filled with chemicals that had once belonged to his late uncle, who was a metallurgical engineer. Through this discovery, Ernst became intrigued by the possibilities of chemical reac-

practical applications of his research. Ernst had received numerous offers, but he chose Varian because the firm employed well-known scientists such as Weston A. Anderson, Ray Freeman, Jim Hyde, Martin Packard, and Harry Weaver. They were conducting lines of research similar to the ones Ernst had pursued in Zurich. Moreover, they were seeking commercial applications for their research, which attracted Ernst, as he felt it would provide further motivation for his own work.

While at Varian, Ernst worked with Anderson to make NMR spectroscopy more sensitive. They based their work in part on NMR experiments reported in 1945 by Felix Bloch at Stanford University and Edward Mills Purcell at Harvard. Bloch and Purcell had demonstrated that various atomic nuclei could be knocked out of alignment in a strong magnetic field when exposed to a slow sweep of radio frequencies. Further, these nuclei would respond by realigning to resonant frequencies and emit a signature similar to that of a chemical signature. This pioneering research garnered Bloch and Purcell Nobel Prizes.

Purcell foresaw NMR becoming a valuable tool for chemical analysis. However, before that prediction could become true, researchers needed to overcome the limited sensitivity of the early NMR method to the chemical signature of the substance being analyzed. Up to this point, only a few substances (including hyrdrogen, fluorine, and phosphorus) had spectra strong enough for consistent identification.

By 1966 Ernst and Anderson dramatically enhanced NMR spectra by replacing the problematic slow sweep of radio frequencies with short pulses of high intensity. As a result, spectra that was once too weak for identification was now clearly distinguishable. Computer advancements had made this possible. "Of major importance for the success of more advanced experiments and measurement techniques in NMR was the availability of small laboratory computers that could be hooked up directly to the spectrometer," Ernst said in 1991. "During my last years at Varian (1966–68), we developed numerous computer applications in spectroscopy for automated experiments and improved data processing."

Spectra that resulted from exposure to the pulse of radio frequencies were complex. But to evaluate the spectra, Ernst employed the Fourier transformation, which new computer technology could employ to reveal the small fluctuations of brightness in the NMR spectra. Subsequently, Ernst's discovery facilitated analysis of substantially more types of nuclei and smaller amounts of materials.

Advanced NMR Spectroscopy in Switzerland

When Ernst took a job in the United States, one of his goals was to leave the academic setting forever. However, in 1968 he returned to Switzerland and the ETH-Z in order to teach. He became an assistant professor in 1970 and a full professor in 1976.

During this period he developed an even more sophisticated contribution to the field of NMR spectroscopy: a

tions. He soon began cultivating this interest by reading all of the chemistry books that he could get his hands on. Subsequently, he realized that he would rather be a chemist than a musical composer. "I wanted to understand the secrets behind my chemical experiments and behind the processes in nature," he later said in his 1991 Nobel Prize autobiography.

Studied Chemistry in College

Pursuing his fascination with chemistry, Ernst would later enroll at the Swiss Federal Institute of Technology (Eidgenössische Technische Hochschule) in Zurich (ETH-Z). At the same time, he continued his own studies through outside reading. In particular, he cited *Theoretical Chemistry* by S. Glasstone as being very influential, as it revealed to him the fundamentals of quantum mechanics, spectroscopy, statistical mechanics, and statistical thermodynamics. These subjects weren't typically addressed in academic lectures, he would later point out.

At ETH-Z, he received his undergraduate degree in chemical engineering in 1956. He received his Ph.D. in physical chemistry in 1962, working on high-resolution NMR, a field that was then in its infancy.

Moved to America

After Ernst received his Ph.D., he wanted to leave the academic environment and find an industrial job in the United States. He moved to Palo Alto, California, where he took a position as a chemist at Varian Associates and sought technique that enabled a high-resolution, two-dimensional analysis of larger molecules than had previously been accessible to NMR. The technique replaced single pulses of radio frequencies with a sequence of pulses. As a result, scientists could now analyze the three-dimensional structures of organic and inorganic compounds and of proteins and other large biological molecules, or macromolecules. Further, they could study interactions between biological molecules and other substances such as metal ions, water, and drugs, and they were able to identify chemical species and to study the rates of chemical reactions. Ernst's work would provide the basis for the development of magnetic resonance imaging, or MRI, which would become one of the most important diagnostic tools available to medical professionals for diagnoses. It also allowed scientists to gain crucial information about the chemical environment of molecules that they studied.

Won the Nobel Prize

As a result of the impact of his work, Ernst was honored with the Nobel Prize in Chemistry in 1991. That same year he earned the Louisa Gross Horwitz Prize at Columbia University, along with colleague Kurt Wüthrich. The two scientists received the Horwitz prize for their efforts in developing NMR methods that revealed the behavior and structure of complex biological molecules, or macromolecules. Ernst also received the Wolf Prize in Chemistry in 1991. The awards were an illustration of just how widespread the use of his MRI method had become in clinical studies.

In fact, Ernst learned that he had received the 1991 Nobel Prize in Chemistry while he was onboard an airplane flight to receive the Horwitz Prize. In this rather dramatic set of circumstances, the aircraft's pilot called Ernst to the cockpit to give him the news about the Nobel award.

In awarding Ernst the Nobel Prize, the Royal Swedish Academy of Sciences lauded his contribution to NMR spectroscopy. Specifically, the Academy noted Ernst's development of the methodology of high-resolution NMR spectroscopy as the most important instrumental measuring technique within chemistry. "NMR spectroscopy has during the last twenty years developed into perhaps the most important instrumental measuring technique within chemistry," the Academy noted. Underscoring Ernst's impact, the Academy further stated, "This [development] has occurred because of a dramatic increase in both the sensitivity and the resolution of the instruments, two areas in which Ernst has contributed more than anybody else."

Accomplishments and Interests

Before and after receiving the Nobel Prize, Ernst continued his research at ETH-Z. Since 1990 he has been president of the institution's Research Council, and he has served as a professor in the laboratory of physical chemistry. Ernst's research has involved molecular interaction, specifically how molecules interact with each other and how they change their shapes. The work brings into play both chemistry and physics as well as quantum mechanics.

In addition to the Nobel Prize, the Wolf prize and the Horwitz prize, Ernst was awarded for Achievements in Magnetic Resonance EAS in 1992. He is a member of many international institutions, including the American Physical Society, the International Society of Magnetic Resonance, the Deutsche Akademie der Naturforscher, the Royal Society of London and the science academies of India and Korea. He also serves on the editorial boards of several journals dealing with magnetic resonance. The book he published on NMR is considered a classic among the leaders in the field. In addition, Ernst holds several patents for his inventions.

Along with chemistry, Ernst still counts music as one of his major interests, and he remains an enthusiastic musician. He also collects Asian art, an interest he cultivated during a trip through Asia in 1968, and is especially interested in Tibetan scroll paintings.

On October 9, 1963, Ernst married Magdalena Kielholz. The couple had two daughters, Anna Magdalena and Katharina Elisabeth, and a son, Hans-Martin. All three children grew up to become educators. He indicated in his autobiography for the Nobel Foundation Website that his wife was especially supportive throughout their marriage and his career. "I am extremely grateful for the encouragement and for the occasional readjustment of my standards of value by my wife Magdalena who stayed with me so far for more than 28 years despite all the problems of being married to a selfish work-addict with an unpredictable temper," he recalled in 1991. "Magdalena has, without much input from my side, educated our three children."

Ernst attributes his scientific success, in large part, to being in the right place at the right time. "Looking back, I realize that I have been favored extraordinarily by external circumstances, the proper place at the proper time in terms of my Ph.D. thesis, my first employment in the [United States] . . . and in particular having had incredibly brilliant coworkers."

In an interview with *Physics Today,* he expressed surprise about the impact of his work, NMR spectroscopy and MRI. "I did not expect that it would become as useful and practical as it has," he said.

Books

Contemporary Authors Online, Thomson Gale, 2006.
World of Invention, 2nd Edition, Gale Group. 1999.

Online

"The Nobel Prize in Chemistry 1991," *Nobelprize.org,* http://www.nobelprize.org/nobel_prizes/chemistry/laureates/1991/press.html (December 16, 2006).
"Richard R. Ernst," *Britannica Guide to Nobel Prizes,* http://www.britannica.com/nobel/micro/195_62.html (December 16, 2006).
"Richard R. Ernst," *Ten Nobels for the Future,* http://www.hypothesis.it/nobel/eng/bio/ernst.htm (December 16, 2006).
"Richard Robert Ernst," *Famous Chemists,* http://www.emur.org/chemists/richard-robert-ernst.htm (December 16, 2006). □

F

Oriana Fallaci

Italian journalist Oriana Fallaci (1929–2006) became nearly as controversial as the world leaders and dissenting voices she was famous for interrogating during her long and prolific career. Fallaci gained renown in the late 1960s and 1970s for her incisive interviews, during which she fearlessly—and, her critics said, often recklessly—challenged heads of state and revolutionary leaders on their ideologies and tactics. In her later years she became an outspoken opponent of Islam, believing that it posed a threat to peace and stability in Europe.

Born on June 29, 1929, in Florence, Italy, the future journalist was one of three daughters of Edoardo, a cabinetmaker, and Tosca (Cantini) Fallaci. Political activism ran deep on both sides: her mother's father was part of an anarchist movement that flourished in Italy in the years just after World War I, while her father was involved in the anti-fascist resistance against the dictatorship of Benito Mussolini (1883–1945). Fallaci's own political destiny was shaped by World War II, when as a teenager she became active in the underground movement against the Nazi occupation of Italy. The war years also toughened her; at one point her hometown was under heavy aerial bombardment, and after fleeing to an air raid shelter with her family, the 14-year-old began to cry. Her father, seeing her tears, "gave me a powerful slap—he stared me in the eyes and said, 'A girl does not, must not, cry,'" Fallaci recalled in an interview with Margaret Talbot for the *New Yorker*. She claimed those tears were the last she ever shed in her life.

Abandoned Medical-School Studies

Fallaci's parents encouraged their daughters to pursue academic success, and in 1945, with the war over, she entered the University of Florence's medical school. She quickly discovered that science was not her true calling, and decided she wanted to follow in her paternal uncle's footsteps and try journalism. Pressuring editors at *Il Mattino dell'Italia centrale* to give her a job, she began writing for the newspaper in 1946 as a crime beat reporter, but soon progressed to feature stories and interviews. After 1951 her work appeared regularly in a magazine called *Epoca,* and later in another, *Europeo.* In 1958 her first book, *I Sette peccati di Hollywood* (The Seven Sins of Hollywood), was published in Italian; filmmaker Orson Welles (1915–1985) wrote its preface.

During the early part of the 1960s, Fallaci traveled widely for *Europeo* as a special correspondent, and a collection of her articles appeared in 1964 as *The Useless Sex: Voyage Around the Woman.* She also wrote her first novel, *Penelope at War,* in 1962, but soon began to gain attention for her interviews. In 1968 several of these were collected into the volume *The Egotists: Sixteen Surprising Interviews,* in which American writer Norman Mailer (born 1923), film stars Sean Connery (born 1930) and Ingrid Bergman (1915–1982), and the widow of Ernest Hemingway (1899–1961) were among the subjects profiled.

Fallaci's writings and lengthy preambles to her interviews were always tinged with her own left-of-center social and political commentary, but in the latter half of the 1960s she was pulled further into world events and crises by her reporting. She became a war correspondent in Vietnam, covering the Southeast Asian conflict after 1967, and the following year went to Mexico City to report on student unrest there. In the notorious Tlatelolco Massacre, she was

shot three times when government forces fired on demonstrators, an experience she wrote about in her book *Nothing, and So Be It.* Originally published in Italian in 1969, it appeared three years later in English translation. Her dispatches from Vietnam made up the bulk of it, but the account of the Mexico City incident was perhaps more harrowing. Before she was shot, she and the other demonstrators were corralled by authorities. "In war, you've really got a chance sometimes, but here we had none," she wrote, according to Talbot. "The wall they'd put us up against was a place of execution; if you moved the police would execute you, if you didn't move the soldiers would kill you, and for many nights afterward I was to have this nightmare, the nightmare of a scorpion surrounded by fire, unable even to try to jump through the fire because if it did so it would be pierced through."

"A Sinuous, Crafty Intelligence"

Fallaci's reputation as a fearless journalist helped her score some notable interviews with political leaders, and she often pushed her subjects into making controversial statements. In one 1968 interview for the German magazine *Stern,* she met with the vice president of South Vietnam, Nguyen Cao Ky (born 1930). His country was the ostensible ally of the United States, which was providing massive military support to help push back Communist insurgent forces coming out of North Vietnam. Ky's remarks to Fallaci caused a stir, however, for their criticism of American leaders and his frank appraisal of U.S. policy goals. "The Americans are here to defend their interests," Ky said, according

to a *New York Times* report, "and not because they have any particular concern about us."

Over the next several years Fallaci interviewed a slew of controversial world figures. These included Palestine Liberation Organization (PLO) leader Yasser Arafat (1929–2004), the Shah of Iran Mohammad Reza Pahlavi (1919–1980), India's prime minister Indira Gandhi (1917–1984), German chancellor Willy Brandt (1913–1992), and U.S. Secretary of State Henry Kissinger (born 1923). Fallaci's method, explained Talbot, "was deliberately unsettling: she approached each encounter with studied aggressiveness, made frequent nods to European existentialism (she often disarmed her subjects with bald questions about death, God, and pity), and displayed a sinuous, crafty intelligence. It didn't hurt that she was petite and beautiful."

Fallaci's 1972 interview with Kissinger was one of the most memorable of her career; the U.S. foreign-policy architect was famously skilled at handling the press, but when Fallaci challenged him on Vietnam and his powerful role in Richard M. Nixon's (1913–1994) administration, Kissinger likened himself to a cowboy. He explained that he often acted alone and expected others to follow his lead, and said that Americans respected this kind of leadership. Nixon was reportedly angered by the remarks, and the relations between the two cooled because of it. Fallaci also posed the question, "Don't you find, Dr. Kissinger, that it's been a useless war?," according to Talbot, and the first words of his reply were, "On this, I can agree." The statement sent shock waves through foreign policy circles, and served to bolster public opinion against American involvement in Vietnam. Kissinger later said that the Fallaci interview was "the single most disastrous conversation I have ever had with any member of the press," Talbot quoted him as saying.

Charmed Khomeini

The interview with Iranian revolutionary leader Ayatollah Ruhollah Khomeini (1900–1989) was also one of Fallaci's more famous encounters. She journeyed to the holy city of Qum in October of 1979, at the onset of the Iranian Islamic revolution, but had agreed to wear a chador—the head-to-toe garment which all Iranian women were obliged to wear in public under new Islamic law—for the interview, but then challenged Khomeini on it. With audacity she queried the cleric, "How do you swim in a chador?," according to Talbot. Khomeini replied testily, "Our customs are none of your business. If you do not like Islamic dress you are not obliged to wear it," and with that Fallaci removed it, which prompted Khomeini to get up and walk out. She remained in Qum, however, and Khomeini actually agreed to meet with her again if she refrained from mentioning the chador; when Khomeini returned, her first question was on the chador issue. "First he looked at me in astonishment," Fallaci told Talbot. "Then his lips moved in a shadow of a smile. Then the shadow of a smile became a real smile. And finally it became a laugh. . . . And, when the interview was over, [Khomeini's son] whispered to me, 'Believe me, I never saw my father laugh. I think you are the only person in this world who made him laugh.' "

Many of Fallaci's most famous interviews appeared in *Interview with History*, published in English translation in 1976. Over the years, however, political figures became increasingly reticent to sit with her for interviews, knowing her reputation for cornering her prey into making unwise statements. She retreated from public view somewhat, producing the occasional novel, until the events of 9/11 roused her ire and prompted a new nonfiction book, *La Rabbia e l'orgoglio,* (The Rage and the Pride), which became a bestseller in Italy. In it she wrote of Islam's centuries-long desire to conquer Europe, and asserted that the growing Muslim communities in major European cities were becoming a danger to the continent. The democratic ideals which granted such communities the freedom to practice their religion were, she argued, threatening the stability of the West.

Voiced Concern about Islam

Muslims in Europe, Fallaci fumed in *The Rage and the Pride,* "demand, and obtain, the construction of new mosques. They who in their countries don't even let the Christians build a tiny chapel, and who so often slaughter the nuns or the missionaries." Elsewhere in the book she wrote that "the sons of Allah breed like rats," according to the *New York Times,* and she imagined a Europe of the future that was an Islamic colony she dubbed Eurabia. The book caused such a stir that she was even charged under an obscure Italian law prohibiting hate speech against a religion recognized by the state. The controversy continued when she penned a response to her critics, *La Forza della ragione* (Strength of Reason), which appeared in 2004.

Fallaci never married, but for three years was the companion of Alekos Panagoulis (1939–1976), a Greek political activist who died under suspicious circumstances in 1976. Panagoulis fought against Greece's military junta of that era, and she immortalized him in her 1979 novel *Un Uomo: Romanzo* (A Man). During this period in her life she suffered a miscarriage—reportedly after Panagoulis kicked her in the stomach—and wrote of this in another work, *Lettera a un bambino mai nato* (Letter to a Child Never Born). In the 1980s she spent time in Lebanon, which was mired in civil war at the time, and penned a fictional account of the strife in a 1992 work, *Inshallah.*

Diagnosed with cancer in the 1990s, Fallaci divided her time between her native Italy and New York City, where she underwent various treatments for the disease. In one final defiant act, she became one of the first figures outside of the Roman Catholic church leadership to be granted an audience with the new pope, Benedict XVI (born 1927), despite the fact that she described herself as a Christian atheist for much of her life. She died on September 15, 2006, in Florence, at the age of 77. In the preface to one of her most accomplished works, *Interview with History,* she summed up her antagonistic style of journalism, asserting, "I have always looked on disobedience toward the oppressive as the only way to use the miracle of having been born."

Books

Fallaci, Oriana, *The Rage and the Pride,* Rizzoli International, 2002.

Periodicals

Independent (London, England), September 19, 2006.
New Yorker, June 5, 2006.
New York Times, April 1, 1968; September 16, 2006.
Times (London, England), September 16, 2006.
Vanity Fair, December 2006. □

Mimi Farina

American folksinger and activist Mimi Farina (1945–2001) was perhaps best known for her recordings with her late husband, Richard Farina, in the 1960s. After his death in 1966 she recreated herself variously as a dancer, comedienne, and rock musician. But Farina's most enduring work began in 1974, when she founded Bread and Roses, a charitable organization that provided live music to those confined to institutions in the San Francisco Bay Area. Bread and Roses spawned similar groups across the United States and celebrated its 25th anniversary in 2000.

Childhood

Farina was born Margarita Mimi Baez on April 30, 1945, in Palo Alto, California. She was the third daughter of Mexican immigrant Albert Baez and Scottish immigrant Joan Bridge. Her parents ran a boarding house while her father was studying for his doctorate in physics at Stanford University, and the family was a nomadic one as he pursued his career.

After her father earned his Ph.D., the family moved to Redlands, California, so that he could take a job as a teaching assistant. In 1949 he accepted a position as an experimental physicist at Cornell University and the clan headed east to New York. It was about this time that Farina's mother drew upon her childhood education at a Quaker school to introduce her family to the Religious Society of Friends. This Quaker upbringing, especially with its emphasis on nonviolence, made a lasting impression on her daughters and would be often reflected in the choices and stands they made as adults.

One of the family's most unhappy relocations was to Baghdad, Iraq, where Farina's father spent a year teaching and conducting research in 1951. All of them found it a trial on some level, but it was the six-year-old Farina who particularly suffered. She had her first bout with organized education at a convent school there, and the harsh manner of the nuns was an ongoing torment to her. Indeed, she and her father remained convinced later in life that the experience had nipped any untapped love of academics in the bud. The family was tremendously pleased to return to the United States and move back to California.

Throughout their travels, Farina's mother was diligent about exposing her children to the arts, and they were all given music and dance lessons early on. Farina gravitated toward dance as a toddler, and soon joined her older sisters, Pauline and Joan, playing piano and strings as well. The outlet was a godsend to the little girl who felt so out of place in school, as she recalled on the website Richard and Mimi.com. "I was good at the violin and I was a good dancer and I knew it.... Which was such a relief from feeling incompetent. When I danced or played music I could be who I really was." Her sister Joan, who later became the world-famous folk star Joan Baez and was a natural performer even as a child, also had an enormous influence on Farina. The two saw the legendary Pete Seeger perform when Farina was just nine, and both promptly decided that singing would become their careers. They began to make good on those plans after the family relocated, this time to Massachusetts, in 1958.

Richard and Mimi

As Farina's father started a new job at the Massachusetts Institute of Technology, the family settled into the Cambridge suburb of Belmont and Farina enrolled in Belmont High School. Folk music was becoming fashionable in the college coffeehouses, and the younger Baez sisters took up guitar and became immersed in the scene. They often performed as a duo, but it was clear that Joan was the rising star. The London *Times* quoted Farina's recollection of the time as, "It was really Joanie's show. She let me be part of it which was really very nice of her. But I knew she didn't really want anybody else up there." And, in truth, Baez's career took off in short order: By 1959 she was singing at the Newport Folk Festival, and a year later her first album was released by Vanguard. Farina, still in high school, remained on the sidelines.

In 1961 Farina's father accepted a position with UNESCO in Paris, taking his wife and Farina (the only one still at home) with him. At this point, Farina had all but abandoned formal education, continuing instead to focus on dance and music. Then in 1962 she met aspiring novelist and folk singer Richard Farina. He was married at the time, and eight years her senior, much to the disapproval of her parents, but the pair soon became a couple. They secretly married in Paris in 1963, as was disclosed in the liner notes of their first album together, and then had an official ceremony in California later that year with up-and-coming novelist Thomas Pynchon in attendance as best man. Although still a teenager, Farina had discovered the love of her life.

Farina and her new husband set up housekeeping in a small cabin close to Baez's home in California's Carmel Valley. He began work on his first novel, and the two of them composed and played music together. Using guitar and dulcimer, they forged a somewhat unique sound for the time, drawing on a variety of styles and genres likely picked up from their travels. Whatever the different spin, however, their music was still folk music and they made their debut as a duo at the Big Sur Folk Festival in the summer of 1964. The audience liked what it heard, and the couple was in the recording studio for Vanguard by that autumn.

American folk music was a powerful popular force in the early 1960s, and for a time Baez and Bob Dylan were the anointed darlings of the folk world. The Farinas, naturally, were intimately connected with the prince and princess, and that extraordinary period was eventually chronicled by David Hajdu in the book, *Positively Fourth Street: The Lives and Times of Joan Baez, Bob Dylan, Mimi Baez Farina and Richard Farina* (2001). In 1964 the players could hardly have known how great their impact would be, but excitement was surely in the air.

The Farinas released their first album, *Celebrations for a Grey Day,* in April of 1965. The original material included such enduring folk classics as *Pack Up Your Sorrows,* and the album became a big hit. They performed at the Newport Folk Festival that summer, where they won a standing ovation in spite of the torrential rain. In December, *Reflections in a Crystal Wind* was released. On it, Farina debuted her own composition, *Miles,* which was an instrumental tribute to jazz great Miles Davis. The couple may not have been certifiable folk royalty quite yet, but they were most certainly stars.

Life appeared to be looking up even further in the spring of 1966. Farina's husband had just had his first novel, *Been Down So Long It Looks Like Up To Me,* published, and book signings were the order of the day. But the couple's optimism and joy was rudely cut short on April 30, when Richard was killed in a motorcycle accident. It was Farina's 21st birthday.

Explored and Reinvented

Understandably devastated by her loss, Farina moved to San Francisco to attempt to regroup. She took up dancing once again and tried to keep her hand in music. The ever-mercurial music business, however, was then in the process of exchanging the folk phenomenon for that of rock 'n roll. Gamely, she dove into the new waters with an acid-rock band called "The Only Alternative and His Other Possibilities," but it was a short-lived fling. In 1967 she toured Japan with Judy Collins, Bruce Langhorne, and Arlo Guthrie, but as a dancer, not a singer. Later that year, Farina took a turn as a comedienne, joining the San Francisco improvisational group The Committee. Her year with the troupe proved a more productive venture, as she made lifelong friends and honed her stage skills in the process. A compilation of the Farina's work called *Memories* was released in 1968, but Farina had gone through sufficient professional reincarnations by that time to hazard one more on a personal level.

On September 7, 1968, Farina married record producer and radio personality Milan Melvin at the Big Sur Folk Festival. For the next two years, she appeared content to stay close to home, although she did record one song with Baez on the latter's *David's Album.* The second marriage ended in divorce in 1970, however, and Farina headed back into music.

In 1971 Farina teamed up with singer-songwriter Tom Jans to record *Take Heart,* which included one of her most famous songs, *In the Quiet Morning.* The duo toured extensively and made television appearances, but ongoing comparisons to Baez and the commercialism of the music business were getting Farina down. She and Jans split up in

1972, and although she toured as a solo act for a time, Farina began casting about for a new way to make a contribution to the world.

Bread and Roses

Inspiration struck after Farina attended a concert given by eminent bluesman B. B. King at New York's Sing Sing Prison. Joel Selvin of the *San Francisco Chronicle* quoted her recollection of the event as, "It was phenomenal to watch the place go silent, which doesn't happen that much in prison." This experience, coupled with her own appearance at a halfway house, gave rise to the idea of an organization that would provide music, free of charge, to people confined to institutions from convalescent homes to prisons to psychiatric facilities. So in 1974, Farina founded what would prove to be her true life's work and legacy.

Farina called her new creation "Bread and Roses," after a poem for woman laborers and their men by James Oppenheim. First funded by annual benefit concerts, it began to draw upon corporate and private donations by the early 1980s. Still, volunteers were its lifeblood and Farina had no compunction about tapping the talents of such famous friends as Joni Mitchell, Herbie Hancock, Huey Lewis, and Neil Young to help out. Nor, as Steve Uhler of the *Austin American-Stateman* pointed out, could anyone resist her pleas. "Mimi could bewitch anyone from age 7 to age 70 with her wit, beauty and energy, and she always picked up the tab for the post-performance pizza."

In 2000, Bread and Roses celebrated its 25th anniversary and had spawned at least 15 similar organizations across the United States. Its humanitarian mission, as well as its founder, had received myriad accolades and awards. Farina had finally combined her talents to carve a lasting niche for herself on her own terms.

The youngest of the Baez family died on July 18, 2001, of lung cancer, surrounded by the others. Only 56 years old, Farina was yet again ahead of her time. Fittingly, her funeral service was filled with friends and music and tributes. But perhaps most telling of all was the tape Baez played after all the eulogizing was finished. It held the sound of Farina's laughter.

Periodicals

Austin American-Statesman, July 26, 2001.
Billboard, August 4, 2001.
Boston Herald, July 20, 2001.
Daily Telegraph (London, England), August 1, 2001.
Hollywood Reporter, July 20, 2001.
Independent (London, England), May 22, 2001; July 20, 2001.
San Francisco Chronicle, July 19, 2001; July 21, 2001; August 8, 2001; August 17, 2001.
Time, July 30, 2001.
Times (London, England), July 21, 2001.

Online

"Awards and Honors Bestowed to Mimi Farina," Richard and Mimi, http://www.richardandmimi.com/mimi-awards.html (November 24, 2006).
"The Ballad of Mimi Farina," Richard and Mimi, http://www.richardandmimi.com/mimi-bio.html (December 15, 2006).
"Mimi Farina," Marin Women's Hall of Fame, http://www.marinwomen.org/farina_bio.htm (November 24, 2006).
"Mimi Farina," Richard and Mimi, http://www.richardandmimi.com/mimi.html (November 24, 2006). □

Eileen Farrell

American singer Eileen Farrell (1920–2002) had an operatic soprano voice that drew people in and made them cheer. "Note for note, Eileen Farrell's voice is perhaps as close to a flawless soprano instrument as exists in the world today," *Look* magazine raved. And the *New York Post* said that when her voice in one 1967 performance "sounded that first glowing trumpet tone, it was like a fiery angel Gabriel proclaiming the millennium." Such words of praise were common for young Farrell. She reached the heights of popularity only the top echelon of opera performer's reach.

Came to Singing Early

E ileen Farrell was born on February 13, 1920, in Willimantic, Connecticut. Her family moved when she was still quite young to Woonsocket, Rhode Island, which she always called her hometown. She loved her life there and her upbringing in the small New England town, and often returned later in life to visit. But that was all far in the future for the young girl who grew up alongside a brother, John, and a sister, Leona. Her parents were traveling Irish vaudeville singers, so Farrell and her siblings were exposed to the the life of an entertainer from an early age.

When she was still quite young Farrell began taking singing lessons with Merle Alcock. It was evident right from the start that Farrell had an extraordinary voice, and she, with the help of her trainer, tuned her talent like an expensive instrument. She seemed to flourish at everything she tried in singing and it soon became the largest part of her life. She later studied under Eleanor McLellan. In 1940 Farrell made her radio debut at the Columbia Broadcasting Studios. She did so well that shortly afterwards she was given her own radio show.

Toured the United States

While she was training and performing, Farrell also met and married Robert Reagan in 1946. The two remained married until his death in 1986. They had two children: Robert and Kathleen.

In 1947, shortly after her marriage, Farrell toured the United States as a concert singer, taking her tour to South America in 1949. In 1950 she performed in *Wozzeck* as Marie, but it was the recital she gave in October of that year that raised Farrell from a popular singer to one of high critical and popular acclaim. As she was becoming better

Francisco Opera. There she started the company's 1958–59 season in the title role of Luigi Cherubini's *Medea*. Critics called her performance stunning, and it led to her singing with even more famous and exclusive opera companies.

She recorded several operas, including Berg's *Wozzeck* and Donizetti's *Maria Stuarda*. She was known for her recordings of Beethoven and Handel and also sang on compilations of 1940s Radio Hours. Farrell was seen in several films, too, including *Great Performances-A Lincoln Center Special: Beverly! Her Farewell Performance* (1981) and *Interrupted Melody* (1955), and was heard on several soundtracks, including the *1955 Motion Picture Theatre Celebration*, where she performed the popular song "Over the Rainbow." She also recorded the film score for *Interrupted Melody*. Eleanor Parker received an Academy Award nomination for Best Actress in 1955, lip-synching Farrell's singing.

Concert Made Farrell Pop Singer

In 1959 Farrell took part in the Spoleto Festival in Italy. She sang from her classical repertoire, including a performance of Giuseppe Verdi's *Requiem*. When another performer, jazz great Louis Armstrong, became ill, the producers asked Farrell if she could possibly fill in, singing some of the popular ballads and blues of the day accompanied by Armstrong's famous band. She jumped at the chance, and audiences, who had witnessed her classical performances just days before, loved her. She was an instant hit as a pop singer. The song "Sunny Side of the Street," in particular, was such a hit that Farrell became known around the globe for her rendition.

A Columbia Records executive heard her sing and approached her about recording a pop album, and she agreed. She eventually recorded several albums, including *I've Got a Right To Sing the Blues* and *Here I Go Again*. A lot of opera singers crossing over into pop music sounded too operatic for general audiences, but Farrell, with her background of eclectic singing, seemed to possess the feeling necessary to sing pop music well, and her recordings were quite popular.

Sang at the Met

Farrell was married to a police officer and had a family, and she considered her singing to be more of a hobby than a career. She never regretted the time spent with her own family away from the public eye.

Farrell returned to the East Coast, where she was invited to debut at New York's prestigious Metropolitan Opera House in December of 1960 in *Alcestis* by Christoph Willibald Gluck. She stayed with the Met until 1966 with a short break in 1965. In 1962 she opened the Met's season in the role of Maddalena in Umberto Giordano's *Andrea Chenier*, with Robert Merrill. She made her final performance there as Maddalena in March of 1966. During her time at the Met, Farrell was most acclaimed for her portrayals of heroines in *Medea, Ariadne auf Naxos*, and *La Gioconda*.

In 1962 Farrell won a Grammy for Best Classical Performance, Vocal Soloist (With or Without Orchestra) for her recording of Wagner's *Götterdämerung Brunnhilde's Immolation Scene*, which she sang with Leonard Bernstein

known, she was given better known pieces to perform, and this led to her soloing in Beethoven's *Ninth Symphony* with Toscanini and the NBC Symphony Orchestra. It was a coup for any young artist, and one that helped Farrell soar to the heights of fame. With her success she became, in the 1950s and 1960s, the soprano engaged most often by Leonard Bernstein to sing with the New York Philharmonic. She quickly became a favorite soloist of the famous group, and she herself stated that Bernstein was one of her favorite conductors. She also was a recurrent soloist with major orchestras across the country.

Farrell was a popular performer for many reasons, one of which was that she sang pop, jazz, and blues as well as classical music. This versatility gave her singing a range she otherwise would not have had, because she could call on any number of musical styles to color the others. Because of this adaptability she was invited to sing in New York City in 1950 at Carnegie Hall. She sang there for the entire season and her numbers included the U.S. premiere of Milhaud's *Les Choëphores*, among others.

Invited to Sing with Opera Companies

Farrell was best known for singing songs and oratorios rather than full-fledged opera, but she eventually became a soloist with the New York Bach Aria Society in 1953. She made her operatic debut in 1956 as Santuzza in the opera of the same name with the San Carlo Opera Company in Tampa, Florida. In 1957 she joined the Lyric Opera of Chicago as a member. In 1958 she took a position with the San conducting the New York Philharmonic. And as her fame spread, she was invited to appear and sing on several TV series, including *The Carol Burnett Show, Get the Message, The Ed Sullivan Show, The Christophers,* and *The Colgate Comedy Hour.*

After her stint with the Met, Farrell decided to turn her attention to touring. She toured until a knee injury prevented her from keeping up with a heavy touring schedule. In 1971 Farrell decided to try her hand at teaching other young novice singers to follow in her footsteps. She accepted a position with the University School of Music in Bloomington, Indiana, where she was a Distinguished Professor of Music. She moved from there to Maine in 1980 with her husband. There she took a similar position at the University of Maine in Orono in 1983. Her husband died in 1986 and Farrell, upset by his death, said she did not wish to sing anymore.

Returned to Singing

After a short recess, she was prevailed upon to take up her recording career again. "I figured, I still have some voice left," she said.

In 1999 she published her autobiography, *Can't Help Singing: The Life of Eileen Farrell,* co-writing the book with Brian Kellow. She died on March 23, 2002, at a nursing home in Park Ridge, New Jersey. She left an enormous legacy behind. Her recordings included *Eileen Farrell-Opera Arias and Songs; Wagner-Wesendonck-Lieder,* with excerpts from Tristan; *Verdi Duets,* with Richard Tucker; *Carols for Christmas Eve; The Christmas Album;* and *Classics for Children.* These recordings have made it possible for later generations to be introduced to the woman whose voice had been likened to a fiery angel Gabriel.

Periodicals

AP Newswire, March 2002.

Online

"Eileen Farrell," *Fact Monster,* http://www.factmonster.com/ce6/people/A0818295.html (January 2, 2007).

"Eileen Farrell," *Internet Movie Database,* http://www.imdb.com (January 2, 2007).

"Eileen Farrell," *Infoplease,* http://www.infoplease.com/ce6/people/A0818295.html (January 2, 2007).

"Eileen Farrell (Soprano)," *Bach Cantatas,* http://www.bach/cantatas.com/Bio/Farrell/Eileen.htm (January 2, 2007). □

Louise Farrenc

Louise Farrenc (1804–1875) was the only female professor of music to be hired in the nineteenth century at the famous Paris Conservatory. She was a great pianist who was also a composer, mainly of symphonies and chamber pieces. In her day she was greatly admired and her fame is beginning to resurface in the twenty-first century. She was also the co-

editor of a book on early music called *Treasures of Pianists.* She was a great admirer of early music, and its influence can be heard in her own musical compositions.

Early Affection for Piano

Farrenc was born Jeanne Louise Dumont in Paris, France, on May 31, 1804. This also happened to be the year Napoleon was crowned emperor of France, so she was born into a world that was in upheaval. She was born to Jacques-Edme Dumont and his wife. Her brother was Auguste Dumont. She was born into a long line of famous sculptors whose works have been shown in such famous places as the Louvre, Versailles, and Rouen, and in other cities around France. The family of sculptors could be traced back to the beginnings of the seventeenth century. Her family were also painters, and were part of a bohemian set in Paris that was very open to allowing women to explore their artistic abilities. Because of this, Farrenc was allowed the freedom to express her musical passions right from the start. She came to music early and showed great talent for it at a very young age.

Farrenc started her piano studies at a young age. She began studying alongside Senora Soria, a student of the famous musician Clementi. She soon became very proficient, and began taking lessons from great piano masters such as Ignaz Moscheles and Johann Nepomuk Hummel. At the same time she studied the piano she also became interested in composing her own music. When she was only 15 years old her parents decided that she showed so much talent that they enrolled her at the Paris Conservatory, the most illustrious school for music in France. There, while she continued her piano lessons, she also studied the art of music composition under Anton Reicha.

Attended Paris Conservatory

While she was attending the Paris Conservatory she met fellow student Aristide Farrenc. He was ten years older than she and was studying the flute. The two became fast friends. Not long after they met, in 1821, the couple were married, when Farrenc was 17 years old. After they were married, Farrenc left school to travel around France with her husband on a concert tour. Aristide Farrenc was not fond of touring, however, so they soon returned to France. Farrenc's husband decided he wanted to open a publishing house, Editions Farrenc, which became one of the premiere music publishers in France. He was a great proponent of his wife's composition work and he supported her entirely. It is mainly due to him that Farrenc's work is still available to audiences in the twenty-first century, for he published many of her works. The couple had a daughter, Victorine, on February 23, 1826. Victorine also became a talented pianist, but her career was cut short when she died on January 3, 1859.

Farrenc, in the meantime, continued her studies with Reicha at the Paris Conservatory. When she finished she began touring again in the 1830s. She made an entire career of it, becoming quite famous as a piano performer, building quite a reputation for herself over the decade. While she toured, however, she continued composing.

Became Professor at Paris Conservatory

One of her earliest pieces was the Deuxieme Overture, Op 24, 1834. According to the Women of Note website, the famous composer Hector Berlioz, wrote that the piece was "orchestrated with a talent rare among women." Women of Note added, "It has infectious verve and bold harmonic effects, especially in the central development, where the music moves from the home key of E flat to a dramatic climax in D major."

This and other pieces gave a distinction to Farrenc's work, and by 1842 she was appointed to the position of professor of piano at her alma mater. She was the only female professor at the Conservatory, and she held the position for 30 years, becoming one of the best piano professors in Europe and a woman of high professional standing. Although she was well known, she was still paid much less than men in similar positions. She remained in the professorship until 1873.

Among the pieces that Farrenc wrote was the Symphony No 3 in G minor, in 1849. This Symphony was a huge sensation when it premiered at the Société des Concerts du Conservatoire, and it became a critical as well as a popular hit. According to Women of Note, critics wrote about the piece often, still writing of it three years after its premiere. "There is no musician who does not remember Mme Farrenc's Symphony performed at the Conservatory, a strong and spirited work in which the brilliance of the melodies contends with the variety of the harmony."

Premiered Her Famous Nonet

Finally she premiered a piece of music, a nonet played by the well-known violinist Joseph Joachim that was so well received that she was offered equal pay with her male counterparts. Farrenc's famous Nonet in E flat, written in 1850, is a romantic classical piece. Critics and audiences loved the piece because not only did it emphasize the violin with moments of solo work, but it seemed to center on each instrument, highlighting the best of what each instrument had to offer.

Farrenc next wrote Sextet for piano & winds in C minor. Women of Note said of the piece, "The combination of instruments, wind quintet and piano, is used here for the first time, some 90 years before the more famous Poulenc Sextet." It was an immediate hit and garnered Farrenc much praise.

Wrote *Treasures of Pianists*

Besides her performing and training, Farrenc also edited a book about early musical performance styles that was influential and well-received. Farrenc, along with her husband, was a supporter and researcher of early music. The couple were so fascinated by the subject that they put together a 23-volume set of books about piano and harpsichord music, *Le tresor des pianistes* (The Treasures of

Pianists). The music in the book came from the previous 300 years. Farrenc and her husband worked on the anthology together until his death; Farrenc then finished the work on her own.

Farrenc remained popular as a performer, but remained little known as a composer. The famous nineteenth-century music biographer and critic Francois Joseph Fetis explained Farrenc's lack of universal success: "Unfortunately, the genre of large scale instrumental music to which Madame Farrenc, by nature and formation, felt herself called involves performance resources which a composer can acquire for herself or himself only with enormous effort. . . . This is the reason why her oeuvre has fallen into oblivion today, when at any other epoch her works would have brought her great esteem." Audiences of the day reacted better to famous names than they did to lesser known artists such as Farrenc.

Continued to Compose Despite Lack of Fame

Even though she was not gaining popularity as a composer, Farrenc did not give it up. She next wrote the Trio for clarinet, cello & piano in E flat in 1861. This piece was thought by critics to have been inspired by Beethoven in its flowing melodies, but with an added twist that Farrenc brought to her compositions. The Sonata for cello & piano in B flat, written in 1861, was Farrenc's next piece, and is still considered a great duo performance. It is still chosen today by musicians to help cellists and pianists emphasize their skills.

The Trio for flute, cello and piano in E minor was written in 1862. According to Women of Noteb, "Her scherzos always catch fire, this time it's from pace and cross-rhythmic exuberance. She has an ear for haunting sequences of harmonies."

Farrenc wrote several orchestral works such as symphonies and overtures, but she was best known for her chamber music, especially two piano quintets that were popular among critics and those who were knowledgeable in the musical arts. As an acknowledgement of her very fine chamber work, she won the Chartier Prize in both 1861 and 1869, presented by the Academie des Beaux-Arts for her chamber music. Farrenc died on September 15th, 1875, in Paris, but her music is still being played in the twenty-first century.

Books

Evening Standard (London, England), March 27, 2002.
Sunday Telegraph (London, England), May 4, 2003.

Online

"Louise Farrenc," *Voice of Lyrics,* http://www.voiceoflyrics .com/compo/farrenc_e.html (January 2, 2007).
"Louise Farrenc (1804–1875)," *Women of Note,* http://www .ambache.co.uk/wFarrenc.htm (January 2, 2007).
"A Visit with Louise Farrenc (1804–1875)," *Creative Keyboard,* http://www.melbay.com/creativekeyboard/jul03/farrenc .html (January 2, 2007). □

Guy Fawkes

Guy Fawkes (1570–1606), a devout and militant Catholic in an age when the Protestant Church of England had solidified its hold on British religious life, is remembered as the individual who tried to perpetrate what is thought to have been one of history's most notorious terrorist acts. The Gunpowder Plot, also known as the Powder Treason, was a failed conspiracy to blow up Britain's Houses of Parliament on November 5, 1605. Fawkes, lurking in a cellar below the Parliament buildings, was arrested as he prepared to ignite the explosion.

Fawkes was not the originator of the Gunpowder Plot. He was a traveling soldier—mercenary would be the wrong word, for his motivations were primarily religious, not monetary—brought in on the plan because of his munitions experience. Ever since the plot's discovery, however, he has been the figure most associated with it in the public mind. His perceived primacy has been due to a confluence of several factors, first and foremost being that it was he who actually tried to execute the plan, and was tortured afterwards to make him give up the names of his co-conspirators. Fawkes was also a charismatic figure who has seized the imaginations of makers of popular culture, all the way up to the hit film *V for Vendetta* (2006).

Had Mixed Religious Background

The Gunpowder Plot was a chapter in the long history of conflict between Britain's Protestants and Catholics, and the religious dichotomy was present in Guy Fawkes's own family background. Fawkes was born on April 13, 1570, in the town of Stonegate in England's Yorkshire region. He had two sisters, Anne and Elizabeth. His father, Edward Fawkes (sometimes spelled Faux), was a judicial court official. As such, he was required, under the state Church of England religion (now known as Anglicanism, with the Episcopal Church as its American branch), to swear an oath pledging that he was a Protestant, and there was nothing in his own family background to suggest that he was anything else. Fawkes's mother, Edith, was another story. She, like many other Catholics, put up a Protestant facade, but her nephew became a Jesuit priest and some of her relatives were recusants—English Catholics who refused to attend Protestant church services.

Edward Fawkes died when Guy was eight, and his mother showed her true sympathies by marrying another recusant, Denis (or Dionysus) Bainbridge, described by an acquaintance (according to the Gunpowder Plot Society) as "more ornamental than useful." The family moved to a home near the village of Scotton in North Yorkshire. From that point on, Fawkes likely began to come in contact with devout Catholics who were working through official channels and also by underground means to safeguard and advance the rights of Catholics under the country's increasingly entrenched Anglican regime.

He likely received another dose of this underground Catholicism when he attended St. Peter's School in the city of York (which still exists, and notes Fawkes as an alumnus if not as a role model). The school's headmaster, John Pulleine (or Pulleyn), was nominally Protestant, but St. Peter's was likely a hotbed of Catholic resistance; its former headmaster had been imprisoned for 20 years as a convicted recusant, and Pulleine's entire family was sympathetic to the Catholic cause. One local noblewoman, according to Gunpowder Plot historian Antonia Fraser, called the school "Little Rome." Fawkes, according to one source, married Pulleine's daughter Maria and had a son, named Thomas, in 1591. Other early accounts of Fawkes's life make no mention of the marriage, which could suggest that it was very short (perhaps with mother and child dying in childbirth) or that it did not occur at all.

Several contemporary accounts agree, in any event, that Fawkes as a young man had become serious about Catholicism. When he reached adulthood, he took steps to raise cash for an extended period of military service abroad, renting out his family's land near York to one Christopher Lomley under a 21-year lease. For a year or two he worked as a footman to the Catholic nobleman Lord Montague, and he may have met Robert Catesby, the originator of the Gunpowder Plot, through family connections during this period. Around 1593, he left England for Flanders (a Dutch-speaking region now divided among northern Belgium, France, and the Netherlands), which was then under the control of Spain, Western Europe's great Catholic power, and he enlisted in the Spanish army. A military associate (quoted by David Herber) described Fawkes as "a man of great piety, of exemplary temperance, of mild and cheerful demeanor, an enemy of broils and disputes, a faithful friend, and remarkable for his punctual attendance upon religious observance."

Recognized by Superiors

Spain, whose feared Armada had tried unsuccessfully to launch an invasion of England in 1588, had expansionist ambitions, and was also facing resistance to the north from Dutch Protestants. Fawkes saw plenty of military action, serving under the command of the Archduke Albert of Austria, Spain's ally. He fought for the Spaniards in a battle at Calais, in western France, in 1595, and he may have been wounded at the Battle of Nieuport in Flanders in 1600. Among his assignments was one in which he learned to blow up a procession of military wagons. In both these campaigns he came to the attention not only of his Spanish and Austrian commanders but also of a group of English Catholic nobles sympathetic to the Catholic side. He was recognized not only for military valor but also for his virtue and general intelligence.

By 1603 Fawkes was serving in a regiment commanded by one of these English nobles, Sir William Stanley. Styling himself Guido Fawkes, he was an ensign, on his way to the rank of captain. But Stanley and his associates decided that Fawkes's skills might better be put to use in the diplomatic arena. That year he was sent to Spain on a mission to convince the Spanish monarchy that the time was ripe for another invasion of England on behalf of its beleaguered Catholics. At the time, King James I had just acceded to the throne after the death of the childless Queen Elizabeth I. Fawkes, whom Fraser (drawing on contemporary artworks) described as "a tall, powerfully built man, with thick, reddish-brown hair, a flowing moustache in the tradition of the time, and a bushy, reddish-brown beard," presented a powerful case. English citizens, he claimed, were ready to throw off the rule of James, a Scot enmeshed in a variety of political intrigues.

The move, however, had more than a hint of desperation. After the establishment of the Church of England under King Henry VIII and a temporary and gruesome return to Catholicism under Queen Mary ("Bloody Mary"), Protestantism had become well entrenched under Elizabeth, as even the Spaniards recognized. They gave Fawkes a polite reception, but they were moving in the direction of a permanent peace with England, and Fawkes's mission went nowhere. Meanwhile King James, suspicious of the intentions of English Catholics, sharpened his anti-Papist invective and imposed new fines on recusants.

In Brussels after his Spanish mission, Fawkes was introduced by Stanley to Tom Wintour, a Catholic soldier. Wintour or Stanley informed Fawkes of a plot under consideration by English nobleman Robert (or Robin) Catesby, whose father had undergone long imprisonment for his Catholic affiliation, and whose own militancy had deepened as he fell on hard times. Fawkes seemed the perfect foot soldier for the plan's execution. He knew guns and explosives well, and since he had been away from England for many years, his name and face were unknown to Sir Robert Cecil, Earl of Salisbury and the head of the English monarchy's secret police.

Hatched Plot in Pub

In May of 1604, Fawkes, Catesby, Wintour, and two other conspirators met at an inn in London's upscale Strand district and swore an oath to carry out Catesby's plan: to throw England into chaos by killing its king and lawmakers in a massive explosion, to install King James's young daughter, Elizabeth, as Queen and arrange her marriage to a Catholic monarch from elsewhere in Europe, thus restoring a Catholic monarchy. As time passed, other Catholic activists were let in on the plan, which may have contributed to its ultimate undoing. Fawkes assumed the identity of John Johnson, a servant to one of the other plotters, Thomas Percy.

At first the plan was to tunnel under the Parliament buildings, but the plotters benefited from a stroke of good fortune: the empty cellar of an adjoining building extended underneath their target, and they succeeded in renting it. The Westminster district in London's West End was a crowded warren of streets and businesses at the time, and Fawkes/Johnson attracted little notice as he was installed as caretaker. By early 1605 the plotters had begun to fill the cellar with barrels of gunpowder. To disguise it they covered it with iron bars and bundles of kindling, known in British English as faggots. They had to replace the powder as it "decayed" or went stale.

Finally a date for the explosion was set: November 5, 1605, when King James, the House of Lords, and the House of Commons would all be in attendance in the same chamber. The Powder Treason began to unravel on the night of October 26, with the delivery of an anonymous letter to a Catholic nobleman, Lord Monteagle, advising him to concoct an excuse to avoid the opening of the Parliament session on November 5. Monteagle informed Sir Robert Cecil of the letter's contents, and Cecil informed the King. Continuing uncertainty over who wrote the letter, together with signs that pointed to its being a forgery, have given rise over the centuries to theories that the Gunpowder Plot was devised not by Catholic militants but by Cecil himself, with the intention of permanently crippling Britain's Catholics in the ensuing uproar. In this version of events (promoted in recent times by Francis Edwards), Fawkes and Catesby were double agents. The preponderance of historical opinion holds that the Treason was a genuine terrorist plot, but the debate continues.

Whatever the case, the cellars beneath the Parliament buildings were searched on the night of November 4, and Fawkes was discovered, along with the gunpowder. Described as a very tall and desperate fellow, he gave his name as John Johnson. King James, according to Fraser, ordered that "the gentler Tortures are to be first used unto him *et sic per gradus ad ima tenditur* [and so by degrees proceeding to the worst]," although torture was illegal in England at the time, and had been since the signing of the Magna Carta, the 1215 document that restricted the power of the English kings. Fawkes was hung from a wall in manacles and probably placed on the rack, a notorious device that slowly stretched a prisoner's body until he lost the use of his limbs. After two days, Fawkes gave up the names of his co-conspirators, all but one of whom were tracked down and executed or killed. Prior to his execution by hanging in Westminster's Old Palace Yard on January 31, 1606, Fawkes was barely able to sign his own name on a confession. After dying on the scaffold, he was drawn and quartered.

Restrictions harsher than any they had yet experienced were placed on English Catholics by King James, and November 5 became a national holiday in England, known as Firework Night, Bonfire Night, or Guy Fawkes Day. In the colonial United States it was celebrated as Pope Day, featuring a ceremony in which the Pope was burned in effigy, but the holiday was gradually absorbed into the Halloween festivities that occurred a few days earlier. Guy Fawkes Day evolved away from its roots in Britain, where the targets of the fire might include contemporary figures despised by the public. As part of a group of anti-terrorist measures, the cellars of the Houses of Parliament are still searched by guards each year before the legislature opens in November.

Books

Edwards, Francis, *Guy Fawkes: The Real Story of the Gunpowder Plot?*, Hart-Davis, 1969.
Fraser, Antonia, *Faith and Treason: The Story of the Gunpowder Plot*, Doubleday, 1996.

Periodicals

Economist (U.S.), January 11, 2003.
International Herald Tribune, October 14, 2005.
New York Times, November 5, 2005.

Online

"The Gunpowder Plot," Parliament of the United Kingdom, http://www.parliament.uk/faq/gunpowder_plot.cfm#gun7 (October 10, 2006).
"Guy Fawkes," Gunpowder Plot Society, http://www.gunpowder-plot.org.fawkes.asp (October 10, 2006).
Herber, David, "Guy Fawkes," http://www.britannia.com/history/g-fawkes.html (October 10, 2006).
"The Life & Crimes of Guy Fawkes," http://www.guyfawkes.me.uk (October 10, 2006). □

Lawrence Ferlinghetti

American writer Lawrence Ferlinghetti (born 1919) is equally well known for his own works and for his efforts on behalf of other writers. Ferlinghetti's book of poems, *A Coney Island of the Mind*, is among the top-selling volumes in the history of American poetry, with close to a million copies reportedly in print, and his durable San Francisco bookstore, City Lights Books, was the intellectual home of the Beat Generation movement in American literature and culture.

Though not as widely recognized as other writers among the "Beats," such as poet Allen Ginsberg and novelist Jack Kerouac, Ferlinghetti exerted enormous influence. The publishing arm of his bookstore brought the works of the Beats before the public, and it was Ferlinghetti who took up Ginsberg's cause when Ginsberg's classic long poem "Howl" was deemed obscene and seized by San Francisco authorities. Ferlinghetti's own poetry has not only been read, but has been widely imitated. Many a college town coffee house in the 1960s and beyond featured a beret-wearing poet who intoned free verses that were often accompanied, by the rhythms of jazz music, and some of the icons of hipster culture had their origins in his remarkably fertile mind. Ferlinghetti outlived most of his contemporaries by decades, and he continued to write voluminously and advocate vigorously for the free-spirited attitudes he had helped bring to American literature.

Learned French Before English

Ferlinghetti, the youngest of five sons, was born Lawrence Monsanto Ferling in Yonkers, New York, on March 24, 1919. His father, Charles, an auctioneer, real estate agent, and something of an entrepreneur, had shortened his Italian name upon arriving in the United States, and it was not until 1954 that Ferlinghetti discovered the original form of his family name and readopted it. He never knew his father, who died suddenly six months before he was born. The death threw Ferlinghetti's mother, Clemence, into a downward spiral, and she was eventually institutionalized. Ferlinghetti bounced among relatives and orphanages early in his childhood; Emily Monsanto, the wife of his uncle, Ludwig Monsanto, took Ferlinghetti to Strasbourg, France, after separating from her husband, and Ferlinghetti learned French as his first language. He later learned to speak Italian fluently as well.

The family's fortunes fluctuated wildly after the pair returned to New York. For a time they moved back in with Ludwig Monsanto, but funds were short and Ferlinghetti suffered a period of malnutrition that culminated in a diagnosis of rickets. Then Emily Monsanto got a job as a governess with a well-off family named Bisland in Bronxville, New York. Ferlinghetti chose to stay on with the Bislands when Emily later disappeared. His literary education began under the influence of his foster father, Presley Bisland, who had studied the classics of ancient Greek and Latin literature, and it continued at the exclusive Mount Hermon preparatory school in Massachusetts.

Ferlinghetti attended the University of North Carolina from 1937 until his graduation in 1941, initially attracted there by the literary atmosphere that flourished around the circle of novelist Thomas Wolfe. He joined the staff of the *Daily Tar Heel* newspaper while he was there. In the fall of 1941, with German submarines harassing American ships, Ferlinghetti joined the U.S. Navy. He served through most of World War II, commanding a patrol boat during the D-Day invasion of France on June 6, 1944.

The boat was good-sized, and Ferlinghetti took advantage of the chance to requisition reading materials for himself and his shipmates. "We could order anything a battleship could order so we got an entire set of the Modern Library [an inexpensive set of volumes of classic literature]," he recalled to Nicholas Wroe of England's *Guardian* newspaper. "We had all the classics stacked everywhere all over the ship, including the john." After leaving the Navy, Ferlinghetti used his proceeds from the G.I. Bill (Servicemen's Readjustment Act) to further his literary education. He completed a master's degree at Columbia University in New York in 1947 and then enrolled at the Sorbonne, a venerable university in Paris. He received his doctoral degree in 1949, writing his dissertation, about images of cities in modern poetry, in French.

Moved to San Francisco

As a budding writer sitting in Parisian cafés, Ferlinghetti was influenced by two of the giants of modern poetry, the expatriate American writers T.S. Eliot and Ezra Pound. Finally convinced that he was merely imitating them rather than developing his own voice, he banished their works from his home and began looking for new models. He found one in the anarchist-minded critic and essayist Kenneth Rexroth, whom he met in Paris and encountered again in San Francisco. Ferlinghetti landed in that city in 1951 after a cross-country train trip, and found that he loved its European atmosphere. He was soon joined there by his fiancée, Selden Kirby-Smith, known as Kirby, and the two were married. The marriage lasted until 1976 and produced two children, Julie and Lorenzo.

Ferlinghetti and other young writers attended Rexroth's lectures and listened to his programs on Berkeley's KPFA, the first noncommercial radio station in the United States. Ferlinghetti supported himself with teaching and freelance writing jobs while working on translations of the poems of French writer Jacques Prévert. A new literary scene began to grow in San Francisco, with Rexroth as its godfather, containing a political tinge strongly opposed to the dominant conservatism of 1950s America. Ferlinghetti was drawn to the heavily Italian-American North Beach neighborhood, and in 1953 he and a business partner, Peter D. Martin, launched a poetry magazine there, naming it *City Lights* after the 1930 silent film by screen comedian Charlie Chaplin.

To support the magazine, the two soon opened a small bookstore called the City Lights Pocket Bookshop. The name was later shortened to City Lights Books, but the original name was significant: Ferlinghetti's store was said to be the first in the United States dedicated exclusively to the new paperback book medium. City Lights was an immediate hit among San Francisco's resident writers and intellectuals, and it soon became a pilgrimage goal for all kinds of young people who came to the city to experience its wide-open cultural environment. In 1955 Ferlinghetti built on the bookstore's success by launching a publishing operation, City Lights Pocket Poets.

The first volume he issued was a book of his own poems, *Pictures of the Gone World*. But it was another early City Lights product that led to the most famous episode in Ferlinghetti's literary life. In 1955 he heard Allen Ginsberg read his epic poem "Howl," a furious, overwhelming work,

frankly sexual in parts, that exposed a vast dark underside of America's sunny culture. Ferlinghetti sent Ginsberg a telegram (according to Ferlinghetti biographer Barry Silesky) that read, "I greet you at the beginning of a great career," echoing the words of philosopher Ralph Waldo Emerson to poet Walt Whitman a century before. He added a question: "When do I get the manuscript?" Ginsberg's *Howl and Other Poems* sold out quickly, and Ferlinghetti put in an order for a new run with a British printing firm.

The shipment was seized by U.S. Customs on obscenity charges, but then cleared for import. When Ferlinghetti put the book on sale again at City Lights, he was arrested by San Francisco police and charged with printing and selling lewd and indecent material. Ferlinghetti was defended by the American Civil Liberties Union, which put numerous literary figures on the stand to testify in favor of the value of Ginsberg's work, and in October of 1957 he was completely exonerated. Publicity surrounding the trial benefited not only Ginsberg but also Ferlinghetti's entire operation. City Lights Books became firmly ensconced as a center of experimental writing and of the growing counterculture of the San Francisco area.

Published Best-Selling Book of Poems

The "Howl" trial also brought attention to Ferlinghetti's own writing, and in 1958 his poetry collection *A Coney Island of the Mind* was published by New Directions Press in New York. He would go on to write more than 50 other books of poetry and fiction, but *A Coney Island of the Mind* remained his best-known work and one of the most popular volumes of poetry in the American literary canon. Ferlinghetti favored the free, unrhymed verse of his predecessors Eliot and Pound, but in place of the dense web of literary references found in their poems he created an imaginative carnival of images that were often humorous. "Dog" was one of the poems that endeared Ferlinghetti's writings to ordinary poetry readers. The poet traced the wanderings of a dog across San Francisco, noting that "Congressman Doyle" (of the notorious U.S. House Un-American Activities Committee) "is just another / fire hydrant / to him," and he characterized the dog as "a real realist / with a real tale to tell / and a real tail to tell it with."

Ferlinghetti later followed up *A Coney Island of the Mind* with a sequel, *A Far Rockaway of the Heart* (both titles refer to locations in New York City); it was one of numerous books of poetry that covered nearly every conceivable topic, from politics to music, the killing of President John F. Kennedy (in "Assassination Raga"), sex, and personal experience. He also translated the works of European poets, including Italian film director Pier Paolo Pasolini, and spent several years in Italy. He wrote two novels (*Her* and *Love in the Days of Rage*), travel narratives, and several plays. Ferlinghetti rarely adopted the stance of intense alienation that was integral to the approach of most of the Beat poets, and he rejected attempts to classify him with the group, although he applauded their efforts. "In some ways what I really did was mind the store," he told Wroe. "When I arrived in San Francisco in 1951 I was wearing a beret. If anything I was the last of the bohemians rather than the first of the Beats."

Indeed, Ferlinghetti's bookstore continued to prosper as San Francisco became something of a living monument to the American counterculture, and he gradually evolved into an institution in the city. A variety of younger writers, including poet Diane di Prima, had their careers helped along by City Lights Press, and Ferlinghetti's own poetry was collected in *These Are My Rivers: New and Selected Poems, 1955–1993.* In 1998 he was named San Francisco's first poet laureate, and in the early 2000s he wrote a column for the *San Francisco Chronicle* newspaper.

Among the various honors that came his way in later years was the inaugural Literarian Award from the National Book Foundation, recognizing outstanding service to the American literary community, in 2005. By that time Ferlinghetti was entering the last half of his ninth decade, but his pace had not slowed in the least; he published the first volume of a new epic-length poem, *Americus I,* in 2004, and he seemed to revel in his role as a still-active part of American literary history.

Books

Cherkovski, Neeli, *Ferlinghetti: A Biography,* Doubleday, 1979.
Silesky, Barry, *Ferlinghetti: The Artist in His Time,* Warner, 1990.
Smith, Larry, *Lawrence Ferlinghetti: Poet-at-Large,* Southern Illinois University Press, 1983.

Periodicals

Buffalo News, May 9, 1999.
Guardian (London, England), July 1, 2006.
New York Times Magazine, November 6, 2005.
Publishers Weekly, September 28, 1998; March 22, 2004.
San Francisco Chronicle, June 11, 2003.
Seattle Post-Intelligencer, April 10, 2001.

Online

"A Brief History of Lawrence Ferlinghetti," City Lights Books, http://www.citylights.com/CL1f.html (October 14, 2006).
Contemporary Authors Online, Gale, 2006, reproduced in Biography Resource Center, Thomson Gale, 2006, http://www.galenet.galegroup.com/servlet/BioRC (October 14, 2006). □

Anne Finch

Anne Finch, the Countess of Winchilsea (1661–1720), was one of England's first published women poets. Today, some consider her to be England's best female poet prior to the nineteenth century.

As a poet, Finch attained a modest amount of notoriety during her lifetime, which spanned the late seventeenth and early eighteenth centuries. However, her large body of work, written during the Augustan period (approximately 1660–1760), would earn greater attention after her death. While Finch also authored fables and plays, today she is best known for her poetry: lyric poetry, odes, love poetry and prose poetry. Later literary critics recognized the diversity of her poetic output as well as its personal and intimate style.

In her works Finch drew upon her own observations and experiences, demonstrating an insightful awareness of the social mores and political climate of her era. But she also artfully recorded her private thoughts, which could be joyful or despairing, playful or despondent. The poems also revealed her highly developed spiritual side.

Anne Finch was born as Anne Kingsmill in April of 1661, in Sydmonton in Hampshire, located in the southern part of England. Her parents were Sir William Kingsmill and Anne Haslewood. She was the youngest of three children. Her siblings included William and Bridget Kingsmill.

The young Anne never knew her father, as he died only five months after she was born. In his will, he specified that his daughters receive financial support equal to that of their brother for their education. Her mother remarried in 1662, to Sir Thomas Ogle, and later bore Anne Kingsmill's half-sister, Dorothy Ogle. Anne would remain close to Dorothy for most of their lives.

Finch's mother died in 1664. Shortly before her death she wrote a will giving control of her estate to her second husband. The will was successfully challenged in a Court of Chancery by Anne Kingsmill's uncle, William Haslewood. Subsequently, Anne and Bridget Kingsmill lived with their grandmother, Lady Kingsmill, in Charing Cross, London, while their brother lived with his uncle William Haslewood.

In 1670 Lady Kingsmill filed her own Court of Chancery suit, demanding from William Haslewood a share in the educational and support monies for Anne and Bridget. The court split custody and financial support between Haslewood and Lady Kingsmill. When Lady Kingsmill died in 1672, Anne and Bridget rejoined their brother to be raised by Haslewood. The sisters received a comprehensive and progressive education, something that was uncommon for females at the time, and Anne Kingsmill learned about Greek and Roman mythology, the Bible, French and Italian languages, history, poetry, and drama.

Joined the Court of Charles II

The sisters remained in the Haslewood household until their uncle's death in 1682. Twenty-one years old at the time, Anne Kingsmill then went to live at St. James Palace, in the court of Charles II. She became one of six maids of honor to Mary of Modena, who was the wife of James, Duke of York, who would later become King James II.

Apparently Anne's interest in poetry began at the palace, and she started writing her own verse. Her friends included Sarah Churchill and Anne Killigrew, two other maids of honor who also shared poetic interests. However, when Anne Kingsmill witnessed the derision within the court that greeted Killigrew's poetic efforts (poetry was not a pursuit considered suitable for women), she decided to keep her own writing attempts to herself and her close friends. She remained secretive about her poetry until much later in her life, when she was encouraged to publish under her own name.

Married Colonel Finch

While residing at court, Anne Kingsmill also met Colonel Heneage Finch, the man who would become her husband. A courtier as well as a soldier, Colonel Finch had been appointed Groom of the Bedchamber to James, Duke of York, in 1683. His family had strong Royalist connections, as well as a pronounced loyalty to the Stuart dynasty, and his grandmother had become Countess of Winchilsea in 1628. Finch met Kingsmill and fell in love with her, but she at first resisted his romantic overtures. However, Finch proved a persistent suitor and the couple was finally married on May 15, 1684.

Upon her marriage, Anne Finch resigned her court position, but her husband retained his own appointment and would serve in various government positions. As such, the couple remained involved in court life. During the 1685 coronation of James II, Heneage Finch carried the canopy of the Queen, Mary of Modena, who had specifically requested his service.

The couple's marriage proved to be enduring and very happy. Indeed, Anne Finch developed her poetic skills by expressing her joy in marriage. These early works, many written to her husband (such as "A Letter to Dafnis: April 2d 1685"), celebrated their relationship and ardent intimacy. In expressing herself in such a fashion, Anne Finch quietly defied contemporary social conventions. In other early works she aimed a satiric disapproval at prevailing misogynistic attitudes. Still, her husband strongly supported her writing activities.

Despite their court connections, Anne and Heneage Finch led a rather sedate life. At first they lived in Westminster; then, as Heneage Finch became more involved in public affairs, they moved to London. His involvement had increased when James II took the throne in 1685. The couple demonstrated great loyalty to the king in what turned out to be a brief reign.

Refused to take Oath of Allegiance to King William

James II was deposed in 1688 during the "bloodless revolution." During his short reign, James fell under intense criticism for his autocratic manner of rule. Eventually he fled England for exile in Saint-Germain, France. As a result, the British Parliament offered William of Orange the English crown. When the new monarchs, William and Mary, assumed the throne, oaths of allegiance became a requirement for both the public and the clergy. William and Mary were Protestants, and the Finches remained loyal to the Catholic Stuart court, refusing to take the oath. They also viewed their oaths to the previous monarchy as morally binding and constant. But such a stance invited trouble. Heneage Finch lost his government position and retreated from public life. As the loss of his position entailed a loss of income, the Finches were forced to live with friends in London for a period. However, while living in the city the couple faced harassment, fines and potential imprisonment.

In April of 1690 Heneage Finch was arrested and charged with Jacobitism for attempting to join the exiled James II in France. It was a difficult time for Jacobites and Nonjurors (those who had refused to take the oath of allegiance, such as the Finches), as their arrests and punishments were abusive.

Because of his arrest, Heneage and Anne Finch remained separated from April until November of that year. Understandably, the circumstances caused the couple a great deal of emotional turmoil. Living with friends in Kent while her husband prepared his defense in London, Anne Finch often succumbed to bouts of depression, something that afflicted her for most of her adult life. The poems that she wrote during this period, such as "Ardelia to Melancholy," reflected her mental state. Other poems involved political themes. But all of her work was noticeably less playful and joyous than her earlier output.

Moved to Country Estate

After Heneage Finch was released and his case dismissed, his nephew Charles Finch, the fourth Earl of Winchelsea, invited the couple to permanently move into the family's Eastwell Park, Kent, estate. The Finches took up residence in late 1690 and found peace and security on the beautiful estate, where they would live for more than 25 years in the quiet countryside.

For Anne Finch, the estate provided a fertile and supportive environment for her literary efforts. Charles Finch was a patron of the arts and, along with Heneage Finch, he encouraged Anne's writing. Her husband's support was practical. He began collecting a portfolio of her 56 poems, writing them out by hand and making corrective changes. One significant change involved Anne's pen name. Heneage changed it from "Areta" to "Ardelia."

The peace and seclusion at Eastwell fostered the development of Finch's poetry, and the retirement in the country provided her with her most productive writing period. Her work revealed her growing knowledge of contemporary poetic conventions, and the themes she addressed included metaphysics, the beauty of nature (as expressed in "A Nocturnal Reverie"), and the value of friendship (as in "The Petition for an Absolute Retreat").

Returned to Public Life

By the early 1700s the political climate in England had generally improved for the Finches. King William died in 1702, and his death was followed by the succession to the throne of Queen Anne, the daughter of James II, who had died in 1701. With these developments, the Finches felt ready to embrace a more public lifestyle. Heneage Finch ran for a parliamentary seat three times (in 1701, 1705, and 1710), but was never elected. Still, the Finches felt the time was right to leave the seclusion of the country life and move into a house in London.

In London, Anne Finch was encouraged to publish her poetry under her own name. Earlier, in 1691, she had anonymously published some of her poetry. In 1701 she published "The Spleen" anonymously. This well-received reflection on depression would prove to be the most popular of her poems in her lifetime. When the Finches returned to London, Anne acquired some important and influential friends, including renowned writers such as Jonathan Swift and Alexander Pope, who encouraged her to write and publish much more openly.

Still, Anne Finch was reluctant, as she felt the current social and political climate remained oppressive as far as women were concerned. (In her poem "The Introduction," which was privately circulated, she reflected on contemporary attitudes toward female poets.) When she published *Miscellany Poems, on Several Occasions* in 1713, the cover page of the first printing indicated that the collected works (which included 86 poems as well as a play) were "Written by a Lady." However, on subsequent printings, Finch (as Anne, Countess of Winchilsea) received credit as the author.

Became Countess

Anne Finch became Countess of Winchilsea upon the sudden and unexpected death of Charles Finch on August 4, 1712. As Charles Finch had no children, his uncle Heneage Finch became the Earl of Winchilsea, making Anne the Countess. However, the titles came with a cost. The Finches had to assume Charles Finch's financial and legal burdens. The issues were eventually settled in the Finches' favor in 1720, but not before the couple had endured nearly seven years of emotional strain.

During this period, Heneage and Anne Finch faced renewed strains resulting from court politics. When Queen Anne died in 1714, she was succeeded by George I. Subsequently, a Whig government, which was hostile to the Jacobite cause, rose to power. Further, the Jacobite rebellion, which took place in Scotland in 1715, further aggravated the tense political situation. The Finches became greatly concerned about their safety, especially after a friend, Matthew Prior, who shared their political sympathies, was sent to prison.

Suffered Deteriorating Health

All of the worries combined to take a toll on Anne Finch's health, which began to seriously deteriorate. For years she had been vulnerable to depression, and in 1715 she became seriously ill. Her later poems reflected her turmoil. In particular, "A Suplication for the joys of Heaven" and "A Contemplation" expressed her concerns about her life and political and spiritual beliefs.

She died in London on August 5, 1720. Her body was taken back to Eastwell where she was buried, according to her previously stated wishes. Her husband produced an obituary that praised her talents as a writer and her virtues as an individual. A portion of it read, "To draw her Ladyship's just Character, requires a masterly Pen like her own (She being a fine Writer, and an excellent Poet); we shall only presume to say, she was the most faithful Servant to her Royall Mistresse, the best Wife to her Noble Lord, and in every other Relation, publick and private, so illustrious an Example of such extraordinary Endowments, both of Body and Mind, that the Court of England never bred a more accomplished Lady, nor the Church of England a better Christian." Heneage Finch died in 1726.

Poetry Rediscovered

The only major collection of Anne Finch's writings that appeared in her lifetime was *Miscellany Poems, on Several Occasions*. Nearly a century after her death her poetic output had been largely forgotten, until the great English poet William Wordsworth praised her nature poetry in an essay included in his 1815 volume *Lyrical Ballads*.

A major collection titled *The Poems of Anne, Countess of Winchilsea*, edited by Myra Reynolds, was published in 1903. For many years it was considered the definitive collection of her writings. It remains the first and only scholarly collection of Finch's poetry, and includes all of the poems from *Miscellany Poems* and poems retrieved from manuscripts. Further, Reynolds's impressive introduction did as much to re-establish Finch's reputation as Wordsworth's previous praise.

Later, *The Wellesley Manuscript*, which contained 53 unpublished poems, was released. Literary scholars have noted Finch's distinctive voice and her poems' intimacy, sincerity, and spirituality. They also expressed appreciation for her experimentation as well as her assured usage of Augustan diction and forms.

Books

British Writers, Supplement IX, Charles Scribner's Sons, 2004.
Dictionary of Literary Biography, Volume 95: Eighteenth-Century British Poets, First Series, Gale Group, 1990.

Online

"Anne Finch, Countess of Winchilsea (1661–1720)," *A Celebration of Women Writers*, http://www.digital.library.upenn.edu/women/finch/finch-anne.html (December 9, 2006).
"Anne Finch, Countess of Winchilsea (1661–1720)," *The Literary Encyclopedia*, http://www.litencyc.com/php/speople.php?rec=true&UID=1531 (December 9, 2006)
"Biography of Anne Kingsmill Finch," *PoemHunters.com*, http://www.poemhunter.com/anne-kingsmill-finch/biography/ (December 9, 2006). □

Shulamith Firestone

Canadian-born feminist writer Shulamith Firestone (born 1945) was just 25 years old when her first book, *The Dialectic of Sex: A Case for Feminist Revolution*, ignited a minor firestorm of controversy and public debate in 1970. In it, Firestone argued that true gender equality was impossible to achieve until science freed women from their biological role as bearers of children. She envisioned an artificial womb in which fetuses could be grown until they reached the newborn stage, at which point they would be raised for the next several years in a commune-like household of eight to ten adults. *The Dialectic of Sex* was Firestone's sole contribution to the canon of feminist theory, but the book continued

to be required reading in college women's studies programs some thirty years after its appearance.

Firestone was born in Ottawa, the federal capital of Canada, in 1945, into an Orthodox Jewish family that later relocated to St. Louis, Missouri. Her younger sister, Tirzah Firestone, became a well-known rabbi and author of books on female figures in Jewish mysticism and the Kabbalah. As a young woman, Firestone studied at Washington University in St. Louis before moving on to the Art Institute of Chicago, where she earned a fine arts degree in painting in 1967. During her time there, she became interested in new theories about women's roles in society, and was one of the organizers of the Westside Group, which later evolved into the Chicago Women's Liberation Union, the first women's liberation group in the United States.

Founded Trio of Groups

Later in 1967, Firestone headed to New York City, where she continued her involvement in the nascent "women's liberation" movement, as it was termed at the time. She helped found a new group there, New York Radical Women (NYRW), but ideological divisions between the more politically minded members of the group—who were adherents of socialism—and radical feminists like Firestone split the group. The socialist women believed that political reform would bring gender equality, while radicals disagreed with this proposition, contending that leftist-oriented groups still carried over many discriminatory ideas and practices despite their avowed support for the idea of equality on all levels. Many of the political groups that drew feminist women into their fold failed to give women equal status or allowed them to advance to leadership roles, for example, and some even deemed a separate women's movement actually counterrevolutionary to socialist goals.

NYRW disbanded in 1969, and Firestone went on to found another group, called the Redstockings, that same year with Ellen Willis, a writer. The group took its name from the Bluestockings, an informal coalition of women intellectuals in mid-18th century Britain, and used "red" because it was the color of revolution and socialist upheaval. Its founding, noted an essay on Firestone in *Feminist Writers,* had been prompted by their "disgust with the blatant antagonism toward women's liberation shown by leftist men, in this case as directed against a women's protest (during which Firestone gave a speech) scheduled as part of a program of the Counter-Inaugural demonstration organized by the National Mobilization Committee to End the War in Vietnam held in Washington, D.C., in January 1969." Though Firestone's tenure with the group was brief, the Redstockings had a few notable moments: they disrupted the New York State Assembly's debate on abortion-law reform, and staged a sit-in at *Ladies' Home Journal* magazine.

Later in 1969, Firestone left the Redstockings to form a third group, the New York Radical Feminists, with Anne Koedt. Within a year, however, some of its newer members claimed that Firestone and the other leadership were elitist, a charge likely linked to the middle-class backgrounds of women like Firestone and the perceived ease with which they handled the press and publicized the group's cause. "Rather than a matter of jealousy, the concern was over whose version of feminism would become popularized," the *Feminist Writers* essay noted. "The fear was that women with more access to the media would be in a position to become leaders of a movement that officially rejected the idea of leadership."

Book Bought by Mainstream Publisher

Firestone left the New York Radical Feminists in 1970, exhausted by the internal struggles and infighting within the movement over the past few years. Though a painter by training, she drifted into writing almost accidentally by authoring the manifestos of the feminist organizations with which she was involved. She served as editor of a magazine, *Notes from the First Year: Women's Liberation,* published by the NYRW in June of 1968 and on sale for "$ .50 to Women/$1.00 to Men," its masthead read. She also co-edited *Notes from the Second Year: Radical Feminism* with Koedt, in 1970, but was already working on her ground-breaking book, *The Dialectic of Sex: A Case for Feminist Revolution,* by that point.

Published in October of 1970 by William Morrow, *The Dialectic of Sex* drew upon the work of Karl Marx (1818–1883) and Friedrich Engels (1820–1895), the political philosophers whose most important set of theories, known as Marxism, gave rise to the ideology of Communism; the ideas of Austrian psychoanalyst Sigmund Freud (1856–1939) and French feminist writer Simone de Beauvoir (1908–1986) also shaped some of the themes in Firestone's book. Approaching the topic of political theory from a feminist viewpoint, she argued that gender inequality was, in the end, ultimately dictated by biology. Pregnancy, childbirth, and childrearing were a vital part of human existence, but the need to reproduce the species efficiently had made women vulnerable, and a patriarchal system had been imposed on much of the human race as a means of perpetuating the system. Few could dispute the fact, she wrote, "that Women throughout history before the advent of birth control were at the continual mercy of their biology—menstruation, menopause, and 'female ills,' constant painful childbirth, wet-nursing and care of infants, all of which made them dependent on males (whether brother, father, husband, lover, or clan, government, community-at-large) for physical survival."

Firestone's proposed solution borrowed from Marx and Engels: their philosophy maintained that the proletariat workers of the 19th-century Industrial Revolution were the exploited class in a capitalist society, and justice would not come until they seized the means of production, or literally took over the factories and equipment that served to enslave them. Similarly, Firestone argued that women were the oppressed class in modern societies, and that they should seize control over the very thing that exploited them: human reproduction. The process, she theorized, could be turned over to science and privately run laboratories instead. New advances in reproductive technology would lead to an artificial womb, which would forever free women from the burden and dangers of pregnancy and childbirth—the latter which Firestone's text rather infamously likened to expelling a pumpkin, though in far more colorful language. Only by removing the real biological differences between the sexes in this way, she asserted, could genuine equality be achieved.

Provocative Ideas Stirred Debate

The Dialectic of Sex addressed the issue of raising children after their incubation period by imagining a communal living arrangement in which biological parents would not be solely responsible for their offspring; instead a household of eight to ten adults would raise a child. Such units could apply for a license to have a child artificially, Firestone theorized, or a female member could carry the child by natural means but would not be its only parent. Her book also urged unrestricted access to contraception and government-subsidized child care as two more goals that could free women and, she argued, the human race, from what she termed "the tyranny of the biological family. . . . Marx was on to something more profound than he knew when he observed that the family contained within itself in embryo all the antagonisms that later develop on a wide scale within the society and the state. For unless revolution uproots the basic social organisation, the biological family—the vinculum through which the psychology of power can always be smuggled—the tapeworm of exploitation will never be annihilated."

Not surprisingly, Firestone's book caused a stir in the mainstream media. Reviews were largely negative, with a *Times Literary Supplement* critic calling it "atrociously written . . . in language that varies from the most clotted kind of semi-scientific jargon to phrases as ungrammatical as they are ugly." Nevertheless, it became a bestseller as well as required reading in many women's studies programs at the college level. Firestone's ideas about an artificial womb predated the first successful in-vitro fertilization babies by several years, and by the turn of the 21st century, reproductive-biology scientists were seeking to erase the viability line for fetuses, who have a difficult time surviving outside of the womb before the 25th week of pregnancy in the event of premature delivery. Though a true artificial womb had not yet been realized, her ideas about donor-sperm banks and homeschooling via computer did come to fruition a generation later.

Firestone virtually disappeared after the publication of her book. She reportedly suffered from a mental illness, and was hospitalized on several occasions. A later radical feminist, Andrea Dworkin (1946–2005), was interviewed for the British newspaper the *Guardian* in 2000, and told journalist Linda Grant that Firestone was "poor and crazy. She rents a room in a house and fills it with junk, then gets kicked out and moves into another room and fills that with junk." A volume of short stories from Firestone, *Airless Spaces,* appeared in 1998.

Time-Capsule Film *Shulie*

Around that same time, Firestone was the subject of a remake of a short documentary film by an Art Institute of Chicago instructor and filmmaker, Elisabeth Subrin. Subrin had discovered a never-released documentary short featuring Firestone that was made during her final year at the school; Subrin then reshot it in its entirety, with a young woman cast as Firestone instead, and released it in 1997 as *Shulie.* It debuted at the Walker Art Center of Minneapolis, Minnesota, in an exhibit titled *The Shock of the View.* Writing in the exhibition materials, media-arts scholar Bill Horrigan called it a "portrait of an emerging artist, shown in the studio, at her job in the post office, in interviews with the off-screen male filmmakers, and weathering an appalling crit session as her paintings in progress are glared upon by a jury of five male instructors." In the original, Firestone tells the camera, "I just generally identify with minority groups as opposed to, you know, the large masses, the large homogenous mass of people. I just automatically feel a bond with people who aren't exactly in things."

Though her involvement was brief, Firestone is considered one of the key figures in what is called second-wave feminism, the term used for the movement which had begun to challenge long-held ideas about gender roles; first-wave feminists, by contrast, focused on more easily legislated issues such as voting rights and equal pay. Le Tigre, the rock band fronted by Kathleen Hanna, performs a song on their 2001 LP, *Feminist Sweepstakes,* "F.Y.R. (Fifty Years of Ridicule)" whose lyrics were inspired by Firestone's book.

Books

Feminist Writers, St. James Press, 1996.

Periodicals

Guardian (London, England), May 13, 2000.
New York Times, October 29, 1970.
Times Literary Supplement, (London, England), April 23, 1971.

Online

Firestone, Shulamith, *The Dialectic of Sex,* Marxists Internet Archive, http://www.marxists.org/subject/women/authors/firestone-shulamith/dialectic-sex.htm (January 1, 2007).

Firestone, Shulamith, "Women and the Radical Movement," Marxists Internet Archive, http://www.marxists.org/subject/women/authors/firestone-shulamith/radical-movement.htm (January 1, 2007).

Firestone, Shulamith, "The Women's Rights Movement in the U.S.A.: New View," *The CWLU Herstory Website,* http://www.cwluherstory.com/CWLUArchive/womensrights.html (January 1, 2007).

Horrigan, Bill, "Elisabeth Subrin: *Shulie,*" Walker Art Center, *The Shock of the View,* http://www.walkerart.org/archive/6/BE5391BFF2D45424616C.htm (January 2, 2007). □

Myron Floren

A fixture of American television for several decades as the accordionist on the durable *Lawrence Welk Show,* Myron Floren (1919–2005) perhaps achieved wider visibility than any other exponent of his instrument.

Floren shared an upper Midwestern farm background with bandleader Lawrence Welk. "I'm the happiest, the most relaxed when I'm up on stage," he told Michael Kuelker of the *St. Louis Post-Dispatch.* "I tell my audiences that I spent 16 years on a farm in South Dakota, and this is even more fun than farming." Floren played polkas and popular tunes of bygone days in America. His playing was widely admired, and he maintained that the durability of the Welk program, which flourished for 16 years on network television and continued on in independent broadcasts and syndication, was due to musical factors. "Lawrence had the sense to hire fine musicians in every chair," he told Kuelker. "It wasn't the corny band that people sometimes think."

Grew Up on Farm

Myron Floren was born on a farm in Day County, South Dakota, near the town of Roslyn, on November 5, 1919. Floren's birthplace has sometimes been given as the county seat of Webster, but Floren attended Roslyn High School; the family farm was located between the two towns. He was the oldest of seven children of Norwegian immigrant Ole Floren and his wife, Thilde ("Tillie") Louise Lensegrav Floren. People in the area depended on their own resources for entertainment, and when Floren was six he already had the desire to be a music-maker. "All the neighboring families would get together on Saturday nights, roll back the rugs, and do a little dancing," Floren told John Roos of the *Los Angeles Times.* "The thing that intrigued me most was this one neighbor who played a little button-box accordion. He played Scandinavian and German waltzes and polkas, and I just sat there watching him . . . completely fascinated."

The following year Floren's father gave him an accordion, ordered inexpensively from the Sears, Roebuck catalog. Floren was largely self-taught on the instrument, and he once attributed his dexterity (he played both keyboard and button models) to finger strength he had built up milking cows. Wanting to learn to read music, he took piano lessons for a time, bartering eggs to pay for them. Floren attended Augustana College in Sioux Falls, South Dakota, between 1939 and 1941. He hoped to major in music, but was informed by the director of the college orchestra that the services of an accordionist were not needed, and he had no money for the $25-per-semester piano rental fee. Instead, Floren settled for an English major and a music minor, paying his way through school by giving accordion lessons at the Williams Music Company shop and, when he could, performing on the radio.

What would become an illustrious broadcast career for Floren began at Sioux Falls radio station KSOO in 1939, where he played Scandinavian waltzes and polkas to entertain farmers beginning their workdays. He dubbed himself the Melody Man. Floren's show there turned into an ongoing engagement for several years, but as World War II deepened, he tried to enlist in the U.S. Air Force. He was turned down because of heart problems resulting from an episode of rheumatic fever during his childhood, so he decided to make a musical contribution, joining the United

Service Organizations (USO) and entertaining troops at European stops. Floren earned a citation from the U.S. War Department for his efforts.

When Floren returned to the United States in 1945, he married Berdyne Koerner, one of his accordion students. The pair raised five children, all daughters. Floren moved to St. Louis in 1946, joining a country music group called the Buckeye Four that performed on radio station KWK, gaining wider exposure on the Mutual Broadcasting System network and on television station KSD. The accordion was at its high-water mark in country music at the time, due to the efforts of "Tennessee Waltz" creator and Wisconsin native Pee Wee King, and Floren's band flourished. "In those days we were known as hillbillies," he explained to Kuelker. "We'd play things like 'San Antonio Rose' and 'Letter Edged in Black.' We'd always play a tear-jerker." In 1949 and 1950, Floren also taught accordion at the St. Louis College of Music.

Forced Welk to Wave Surrender Flag

On March 7, 1950, Floren took his wife to a floor show at the Casa Loma ballroom in St. Louis for her birthday. The Welk orchestra was featured, and since Welk and Floren knew each other casually from their days performing on the radio in the Dakotas, Floren was invited up on stage. After he wowed the crowd with "Lady of Spain" and a few other pieces, Welk put the accordion parts for a medley of tunes in front of him, "I think to see if I knew how to read music," Floren told Kuelker. After he blazed through the medley he looked around and was surprised that Welk did not seem to be on stage. Then the bandleader emerged from under a piano, waving a white surrender flag. At intermission, Floren was offered a job that would end up lasting until the final new *Lawrence Welk Show* was broadcast in 1982. Welk's manager, according to Dennis McLellan of the *Los Angeles Times,* had counseled the bandleader against hiring Floren, pointing out that Floren as an accordionist was superior to Welk himself. "Sam, that's the only kind of people I hire—the ones that play better than I do," Welk answered.

The affable Floren was given a new nickname, becoming "The Happy Norwegian." He spent a year touring with Welk, playing one-night stands, and then he moved to Los Angeles, where a temporary engagement for the orchestra on radio station KTLA turned into an ongoing engagement. The Saturday night *Lawrence Welk Show* began airing on television in 1953. Two years later the show made the jump to ABC, and Floren became a musician known to millions. His style was distinctive—rhythmically rock-solid but marked by the frequent use of trills and other ornaments.

Floren's role on the Welk program went beyond accordion music, although he could be counted on provide the polkas that remained at the core of the show's repertoire even as it grew to include influences from pop and rock music. "I guess we did one [polka] practically every week," he was quoted as saying on the website of the Polka Hall of Fame after his induction into that body in 1990. "I even remember an instance where we were saluting Duke Ellington and Lawrence added a polka just in case." But the sound of Floren's accordion was integral to that of Welk's entire "Champagne Music" concept, and he was the orchestra's longtime assistant conductor, leading the group when Welk himself picked up his accordion. He also served as the orchestra's manager.

In 1971 longtime Welk fans were dismayed when ABC cancelled the show, in favor of programming for a more youthful audience. The network remained unmoved by an outpouring of protest, but the show made a successful transition to the growing group of television stations unaffiliated with one of the three major networks. At its peak, the program ran on some 250 stations, more than had ever scheduled it during its run on ABC. In the 1970s the Welk orchestra performed at New York's Madison Square Garden for a crowd of 21,000. "You could feel the electricity in the air," Floren told McLellan. "Lawrence and I were looking out at this crowd from the stage, and he leans over to me and says, 'Isn't it wonderful what can happen in this country to a couple of farmers from the Dakotas?'"

Composed Original Polkas

Floren released some two dozen albums over the years, most of them on Welk's Ranwood label. His recordings emphasized polkas and waltzes, some of them original Floren compositions. His 1975 release *The Polka King,* for example, featured Floren pieces such as a Ukrainian-style "Accordion Polka" and the "Happy Norwegian Polka" in addition to standards such as the "Beer Barrel Polka." In later years, on albums such as *First Class Polkas,* Floren teamed with upstate New York polka bandleader Jimmy Sturr and wrote new music with him. Floren's list of compositions includes "Skating Waltz in Swing," "Swingin' in Vienna," "Kavallo's Kapers," "Windy River," "Dakota Polka," "Long Long Ago in Swing," "Minute Waltz in Swing," and "Accordion Man Polka." In 1981 Floren penned an autobiography, *Accordion Man,* with his daughter Randee.

In 1982 the *Lawrence Welk Show* finally came to an end, but reruns of the program had proved nearly as popular as the original shows had been, and the show found a home on the nonprofit Public Broadcasting System (PBS), where as of the early 2000s it was still aired on nearly 300 stations. It became PBS's highest-rated show at one point. The continued television exposure boded well for Floren's solo career, which in the 1980s and 1990s saw him playing about 150 concerts a year and logging a reported 150,000 miles on the road. He toured with other Welk veterans on package tours, and he had a strong presence on the polka circuit as he worked with the Jimmy Sturr Band. Floren also drew diverse audiences to solo shows. "I'm seeing more and more young people showing an interest . . . it's not just old-timers like myself," he told Roos. "Sure, it's a case of nostalgia for the older folks. But we see kids who play in their high school bands coming out as well."

Floren continued playing energetically into his tenth decade, returning to the stage even after a stroke and a colon cancer diagnosis. "It's like when you hear a good talk or sermon, it soaks in and after a while . . . you just feel better," he told Roos, referring to the sound of an accordion.

"I mean, it gets to you. It's like the rush you feel playing golf right after making a hole-in-one." Myron Floren was finally slowed by a variety of health problems, and he died at his home in Rolling Hills Estates, California, on July 23, 2005.

Books

Floren, Myron, with Randee Floren, *Accordion Man,* Stephen Greene, 1981.

Periodicals

Los Angeles Times, December 12, 1997; July 24, 2005.
New York Times, July 25, 2005.
St. Louis Post-Dispatch, July 31, 1997.

Online

"Myron Floren," *All Music Guide,* http://www.allmusic.com (December 19, 2006).
"Myron Floren," International Polka Association, http://www .internationalpolka.com/floren.htm (December 19, 2006).
"Myron Floren," Stars of the Lawrence Welk Show Online, http://www.welkshow.com/floren.html (December 19, 2006). □

Elizabeth Denison Forth

Described by the Lewis and Clark website as "one of the nineteenth century's most remarkable and unlikely philanthropists," Elizabeth Denison Forth (1780s–1866) was the first black landowner in America. She was born as a slave, but after making a trip to Canada she managed to gain her freedom. When she returned to the United States she worked for a good family who gave her hints on how to invest her money by putting it into stocks and real estate. By the end of her life she had accrued a considerable fortune and several pieces of real estate, and she left a portion of her fortune to help build a church for people of all races to attend.

Born a Slave

Nicknamed Lisette, Forth was born Elizabeth Denison in Macomb County in the 1780s or 1790s—the records are unclear. She was born a slave to slave parents Peter and Hannah Denison. She grew up in Macomb County in Michigan, on the Huron River in Saint Clair. Forth's father worked the land and moved produce up and down the river while her mother served in the household. Forth was the second of six children, and as she grew up she played not only with her brothers and sisters, but also with the white and Native American children that also frequented the land. She never learned to read or write, but she was bright and was said to catch on to ideas very quickly and to have learned the Indian languages. She was even able to serve as a translator at times between the Indians and others who could not understand them. When she was old enough, Forth helped her mother around the house with gardening, cooking, and taking care of the silver and fine dishes.

The Denisons' owner, William Tucker, died in March of 1805, and at that time the family thought that they would all be gaining their freedom. However, in his will Tucker granted the Denison parents their freedom only upon Mrs. Tucker's death. And worst of all, he had given the children to his brother to remain as slaves. Even though Congress had already passed the Northwest Ordinance to prohibit slavery in the new territory—that part of the United States that is modern day Michigan, Ohio, Illinois, Indiana, and Wisconsin—the ordinance applied only to new, not existing, slaves. There was no recourse for the Denisons to protest, and so they remained slaves; the parents remained with Mrs. Tucker while all the children were forced to go work for Mr. Tucker's brother.

Ran Away to Canada

After Mrs. Tucker died in 1806 Forth's parents were freed. These two elder Denisons took their first jobs as free citizens of the United States of America, working for the Detroit-based lawyer Elijah Brush. Brush was a good man, and he helped the Denisons sue for custody of their children. When the verdict came back from the Michigan Territorial Supreme Court, however, it was not positive. The court had ruled that all the children would remain slaves for the rest of their lives except for the youngest of the children, who would be freed when he turned 25 because he had been born after the Ordinance took effect. The decision gave the family no option to appeal, but Forth and her siblings refused to give up hope. They felt that with many other similar court cases sweeping the land, one day they would be freed from their forced servitude. In 1807, tired of waiting and being forced to serve others, Forth and her siblings decided to take things into their own hands, and they escaped across the Detroit River into Windsor, Canada.

A short while later all the slaves in Michigan were freed unconditionally. Forth returned to Detroit sometime around 1812 as a free woman. Upon her return, she took a job as a free employee working in the Solomon Sibley household in Detroit. She had a very good relationship with her employers and it is thought that because of them she began investing her money in land and property. She kept a careful record of all her financial transactions, something else that she may have been encouraged to do by her employers. Although she was unable to read, she was very good at numbers and used that skill to aid her financial situation.

Began Amassing Stocks and Real Estate

She soon amassed a great deal of wealth mainly through investments in stock and real estate, and before long she was looking for other ways to invest her money. Finally, after years of investing in stocks and buildings, on April 21, 1825, Forth bought 48.5 acres of land in Pontiac, Michigan. She bought the land from Pontiac's founder, Stephen Mack, who was the head and founder of the Pon-

tiac Company. This one single transaction gave her a spot in history, for it made her the first black property owner in the United States. She purchased the property as an investment, leasing it to one of her brothers. She sold the property in 1837 for $930. Part of what was once Forth's property became the Oak Hill Cemetery and there was still, in the early twenty-first century, a marker stating that the property had been once owned by Forth.

On September 25, 1827, Forth was married to Scipio Forth. Her marriage was rather short-lived, as her husband died sometime around 1830. After her husband's death she began working full-time for the John Biddle family in 1831. She became close to the Biddles and worked for the family for 30 years. She kept saving her money and investing it in whatever caught her fancy. She bought an interest in the steamboat "Michigan," which was a popular dinner cruise boat at the time. She even managed to acquire some shares in Farmers and Mechanics' Bank, one of the most successful banks in the Detroit area in the 1800s. Both investments were profitable. In 1837 Forth decided to buy another plot of land, this time in Detroit.

Moved with Biddle Family to Paris

Records are lacking about where Forth was for the short period between 1849 and 1854. It is thought that she might have moved to Philadelphia along with the Biddle family, but there is no confirmation of this. It is known, however, that as of 1854 Forth was living in downtown Detroit in her own home. She was not there long when the Biddles contacted her and asked if she would go with them to Paris so she could take care of Mrs. Biddle, who was sick and needed constant care.

She gladly took the Biddles up on their offer and ended up moving with them to Paris in the fall of 1854. Forth enjoyed her time in Paris, and her skill with languages proved to be quite helpful, as she was soon proficient in French. She not only took care of Mrs. Biddle, but was also able to explore the great city, a once-in-a lifetime experience for the ex-slave. But despite the glamour of the city she found herself longing to move back home. She returned in 1856. She lived out the last ten years of her life as a free woman living in her own home in Detroit. She died alone at home on August 7, 1866. She was buried at Detroit's Elmwood Cemetery.

Forth Left a Legacy Behind Her

Just before her death, one of the big questions in Forth's later life was who to leave her money and property to, as she had amassed a large number of stocks and other investments over her lifetime. In the end she gave a large amount of money to the Saint James Protestant Episcopal Church and ended up leaving about $1,500 dollars for a chapel to be constructed where blacks and whites, poor and rich, could worship together. The chapel, which was initially funded by Forth, was completed in 1868. In 1958 another building was built with a hallway attaching it to the older chapel. The doors leading into it are dedicated to the memory and benevolence of Elizabeth Denison Forth. The young woman who was born a slave left a grand legacy behind for all to enjoy.

Books

Notable Black American Women, Book 2, Gale Research, 1996.

Online

"Elizabeth Denison Forth Home Site," *Michigan Markers,* http://www.michmarkers.com/pages/L1860.htm (January 2, 2007).

"Historic Sites: Elizabeth Denison Forth," *Wodward Avenue Heritage Sites,* http://www.woodwardavenue.us/heritage/sites/view/?viewType = location&location; = Pontiac&id = 84 (January 2, 2007).

"What Else Happened," *Lewis and Clark,* http://www.lewisandclarkandwhatelse.com/lewis_and_clark_what_else/2005/06/index.html (January 2, 2007). □

Tetsuya Fujita

A master of observation and detective work, Japanese-American meteorologist Tetsuya "Ted" Fujita (1920–1998) invented the F-Scale tornado damage scale and discovered dangerous wind phenomenon called downbursts and microbursts that are blamed for numerous plane crashes. In a career that spanned more than 50 years in Japan and the United States, Fujita is considered one of the best meteorological detectives.

Showed Early Aptitude for Science

Tetsuya Fujita was born on October 23, 1920, in Kitakyushu City on the southern island of Kyushu in Japan. His first name meaning "philosopher," Tetsuya was the eldest child of Tomojiro, a schoolteacher, and Yoshie (Kanesue) Fujita.

Fujita attended Meiji College in Kyushu where he majored in mechanical engineering, and was also interested in geology, volcanoes, and caves. With this love of science, he developed a skill for visualizing weather and drawing three-dimensional topographical projections. Fujita graduated from Meiji College in 1943 with the equivalent of a bachelor's degree in mechanical engineering.

Investigated Rubble at Hiroshima and Nagasaki

About a month after the Americans dropped an atomic bomb on Hiroshima on August 6, 1945 and another one on Nagasaki on August 9, the 24-year-old Fujita traveled to the two cities to investigate the effects of the bombs. He picked through the rubble and analyzed the unique starburst burn patterns perpetrated by the bombs. Working backwards from the starburst patterns, he calculated how high above the ground the bombs were exploded. At Nagasaki, he used scorch marks on bamboo vases to prove that only one bomb had been dropped on that city. Fujita's observations and experience at the bomb sites became the basis of his lifelong scientific research.

Postwar Research in Thunderstorms and Tornadoes

In this postwar environment, Fujita decided to pursue meteorology and in 1946 applied for a Department of Education grant to instruct teachers about meteorology. He took several research trips. On one excursion, he walked up to a mountain observatory during a thunderstorm to record wind velocity, temperature, and pressure. He discovered that downdrafts of air inside the storm made the storm spread out from a dome of high pressure, which he dubbed a "thundernose."

On another trip in 1947, Fujita mapped the motion of a thunderstorm using lightning timings, and found that the storm had three separate subcenters of lightning activity. With his research, Fujita had disproved the smooth path of storms explained in textbooks of the day and began to remake thunderstorm theory.

The first tornado damage that Fujita observed was on September 26, 1948, on Kyushu, which rarely experienced such storms. After he began to give lectures to the Weather Service on his various research findings, he decided he should publish them. He bought an English-language typewriter so he could translate his work into English.

Corresponded with Horace Byers in Chicago

After lecturing on his thundernose concept, his colleagues gave him a meteorological journal they had taken out of the trash from a nearby American radar station. So fascinated was Fujita by the article, "The Nonfrontal Thunderstorm," by meteorologist Dr. Horace Byers of the University of Chicago, that he wrote to Byers. He also sent Byers two of his own research papers that he had translated, one on microanalysis and the other on his thundernose concept.

In Chicago, Byers had been playing a key role in coordinating the scientific program Thunderstorm Project, whose aim was to find the structure of storms. Byers was impressed with the work of the young Japanese meteorologist, especially since Fujita, with just paper, pencil, and a barometer, had proven some of the same fundamentals of storm formation that the Thunderstorm Project discovered after spending millions of dollars.

In 1953, Byers invited Fujita to the University of Chicago to work as a visiting research associate in the meteorology department. A 33-year-old suffering from postwar depression and a stifling lack of intellectual encouragement in Japan, Fujita relished his chance to work in meteorology in the United States. His difficulty with English only strengthened his ability to communicate through his drawings and maps. By 1955 Fujita was appointed to the faculty at the University of Chicago.

Developed Concept of Mesoanalysis

During this time, Fujita published his landmark paper on mesoanalysis. Working with Dr. Morris Tepper of the

Weather Bureau in Washington, D.C., Fujita analyzed barograph traces in connection with tornado formation. Using his meticulous observation and measuring techniques on a 1953 tornado that struck Kansas and Oklahoma, he discovered highs and lows in the barograph traces that he called "mesocyclones." His newly created "mesoscale" plotted individual high pressure centers created by thunderstorms and low pressure areas. The scale could analyze virtually anything between one mile and 600 miles wide.

As a master of observation, Fujita relied mostly on photographs for his deductive techniques. In 1957 a particularly destructive tornado hit Fargo, North Dakota. As the storm moved rather slowly, many people and news agencies took hundreds of photos and film footage. Fujita gathered 150 of these pictures, manipulated them to a single proportional size, then analyzed the movement of the storm and cloud formations in one-minute intervals. He was able to identify the storm's mesocyclone and its wall cloud and tail cloud features, which he described in his paper "A Detailed Analysis of the Fargo Tornado of June 20, 1957."

Created the F-Scale for Tornado Damage

In April 1965, 36 tornadoes struck the Midwest on Palm Sunday. Fujita took extensive aerial surveys of the tornado damage, covering 7,500 miles in the air, and found that mesocyclones explained how one storm path could pick up where another had ended, leaving an apparently seamless track of tornadoes hundreds of miles long. Fujita's experience on this project would later assist in his development of the F-Scale damage chart.

In 1971, Fujita formulated the Fujita Tornado Scale, or F-Scale, the international standard for measuring tornado severity. Earlier, meteorologists recorded only the total number of tornadoes and had no standardized way to measure storm strength or damage. The Beaufort Wind Scale ended at 73 miles per hour, and the low end of the Mach Number started at 738 miles per hour; Fujita decided to bridge the gap with his own storm scale.

Characterizing tornado damage and correlating that damage with various wind speeds, the F-Scale is divided into six linear steps from F0 at less than 73 miles per hour with "light damage," such as chimneys damaged and shallow-rooted trees turned over, up to F5 at 318 miles per hour with "incredible damage," such as trees debarked and houses torn off foundations. Fujita published his results in the Satellite and Mesometeorology Research Project (SMRP) paper, "Proposed Characterization of Tornadoes and Hurricanes by Area and Intensity."

While the F-Scale was accepted and used for 35 years, a thorough engineering analysis of tornado damage had never been conducted for the creation of the F-Scale. A team of meteorologists and wind engineers developed the Enhanced F-Scale, which was implemented in the United States by the National Oceanic and Atmospheric Administration (NOAA) in February 2007.

Discovered Downbursts and Microbursts

After developing the F-Scale, Fujita gained national attention, and he even earned the nickname "Mr. Tornado."

In 1972 he received grants from NOAA and NASA to conduct aerial photographic experiments of thunderstorms to verify data collected by the new weather satellites put into orbit. He studied the tops of thunderstorms, and he helped develop a sensing array of instruments used by tornado chasers on the ground.

In 1974, Fujita discovered a phenomenon he called downbursts. With help from the National Severe Storms Laboratory (NSSL), he studied the 2,584 miles of damage caused by the 148 tornadoes occurring during the Super Tornado Outbreak of April 1974. He had determined that downdrafts from the storms actually had enough strength to reach the ground and cause unique damage patterns, such as the pattern of uprooted trees he had observed at Hiroshima so long ago. Fujita noted in *The Weather Book*, "If something comes down from the sky and hits the ground it will spread out . . . it will produce the same kind of outburst effect that was in the back of my mind from 1945 to 1974."

Although his downburst theory was met with skepticism at first, in 1978 the National Center for Atmospheric Research aided Fujita in his research, which detected 52 downbursts in Chicago in 42 days. As most damage had typically been attributed to tornadoes, Fujita showed it had really been caused by downbursts. He said in *The Weather Book*, "After I pointed out the existence of downbursts, the number of tornadoes [listed] in the United States decreased for a number of years."

Following the Eastern Airlines flight 66 crash at Kennedy Airport on June 24, 1975, Fujita once again was called in to investigate if weather patterns played a part in the crash. With the new Dopplar radar that had been in use for only a few years, Fujita was able to gather incredible amounts of data. He discovered a type of downdraft he called microburst wind shear, which was rapidly descending air near the ground that spread out and could cause 150 mile per hour wind gusts, enough power to interfere with airplanes.

As a direct result of Fujita's research on microbursts, Doppler radar was installed at airports to improve safety. Research meteorologist James Partacz commented in the University of Chicago's *Chicago Chronicle*, "This important discovery helped to prevent microburst accidents that previously had killed more than 500 airline passengers at major U.S. airports." The fact that Fujita's discoveries led to the saving of hundreds of lives filled him with joy. He noted in *The Weather Book*, "When people ask me what my hobby is, I tell them it's my research. I want to spend the rest of my life in air safety and public safety, protecting people against the wind."

Saw His First Tornado

Ironically, "Mr. Tornado," the man who had developed the F-Scale to rate the damage caused by tornadoes, never actually witnessed a live tornado until June 12, 1982. While working on the Joint Airport Wind Shear (JAWS) project in Colorado, Fujita was sitting at a Dopplar radar station, "when I noticed a tornado maybe was coming down. I told all the radars to scan that area. My first sighting of a tornado was one with the best tornado data ever collected,'' he said in *The Weather Book*.

In another quirk of Fujita's research, he distrusted computers and rarely relied on them. The bulk of his observation was with photographs, paper, and pencil. Chicago meteorologist Duane Stiegler who worked with Fujita commented in the *New York Times*,''He used to say that the computer doesn't understand these things.'' Today, computer modeling and automated mapping are the dominant tools of meteorologists.

Left Enduring Legacy

In his later years, Fujita investigated the July 1982 crash of Pan American 727 in New Orleans, the 1985 Delta flight 191 crash at Dallas-Fort Worth, and the hurricanes Alicia in 1983, Hugo in 1989, and Andrew in 1992. He was named director of the Wind Research Laboratory at the University of Chicago in 1988. A year later, the university named him the Charles Merriam Distinguished Service Professor.

After a long illness Fujita died on November 19, 1998, at his home in Chicago at the age of 78. Partacz said in the *New York Times,* ''He did research from his bed until the very end.'' Well respected by his peers, Fujita received an outpouring of honors and accolades after his death. The American Meteorological Society held a memorial symposium and dinner for Fujita at its 80th annual meeting. In 2000, the Department of Geological Sciences at Michigan State University posthumously made Fujita a ''friend of the department.'' That same year, the National Weather Association named their research award the T. Theodore Fujita Research Achievement Award.

Jim Wilson, a senior scientist at the National Center for Atmospheric Research, said of Fujita in the *Chicago Chronicle,* ''There was an insight he had, this gut feeling. He often had ideas way before the rest of us could even imagine them.''

Books

Notable Scientists: From 1900 to the Present, Gale Group, 2001.
Scientists: Their Lives and Works, Vols. 1–7. Online Edition. U*X*L, 2004.
Williams, Jack, *The Weather Book: An Easy to Understand Guide to the USA's Weather,* Vintage Books, 1997.

Periodicals

Chicago Tribune, May 10, 1990.
Discover, May 1983.
National Geographic, April 1972.
New York Times, November 21, 1998.
Weatherwise, May/June 1999.
University of Chicago Chronicle, November 25, 1998.

Online

''A Tribute to Dr. Ted Fujita,'' Storm Track, http://www.storm track.org/library/people/fujita.htm (December 18, 2006).
Fujita, Kazuya, ''Tetsuya 'Ted' Fujita (1920–1998): 'Mr. Tornado,'' Michigan State University, http://www.msu.edu/~fujita/tornado/ttfujita/memorials.html (December 18, 2006).
''Fujita Tornado Damage Scale,'' Storm Prediction Center, National Oceanic and Atmospheric Administration, http://www.spc.noaa.gov/faq/tornado/f-scale.html (December 18, 2006).
''Tetsuya Theodore Fujita,'' The Tornado Project, http://www.tornadoproject.com/fscale/tedfujita.htm (December 18, 2006). □

G

Serge Gainsbourg

Serge Gainsbourg (1928–1991), the greatest French songwriter of the 1960s and 1970s, was as famous for his decadent life and cynical wit as for the songs he sang. He made a career out of writing clever, provocative lyrics, recording many of them himself and giving others to his many famous friends and lovers to sing. His theatrical rudeness and outrageous provocations made him infamous and beloved in France.

The outsider

Gainsbourg was born at the Hôtel Dieu hospital in Paris, along with his twin sister Liliane, on April 2, 1928. His birth name was Lucien Ginsburg. His parents, Joseph and Olia Ginsburg, were Jewish immigrants who had fled the Ukraine around the time of the Russian Revolution. Joseph was a talented pianist in theaters and clubs in Paris, well-versed in both classical music such as Chopin and American pop composers such as Cole Porter and George Gershwin. He taught his son and daughter piano, beginning when they were four years old. Lucien became interested in painting, so his parents sent him to art school in the Montmartre neighborhood of Paris.

World War II began when Gainsbourg was 11 years old, and he spent his early teens in Paris during the German occupation. A 1942 law required Jews to wear yellow stars with the word "Jew" written on them, an experience that hurt and scarred him. "It was like you were a bull, branded with a red-hot iron," he said in an interview quoted in Sylvie Simmons's biography, *Serge Gainsbourg: A Fistful of Gitanes*. The racist shaming magnified his feelings of adolescent alienation. "Even at 13, 14 years old, I had already become an outsider, because the tough guy thing wasn't me." He took refuge in reading books and smoking cheap cigarettes. Soon, an 8 p.m. curfew for Jews made it impossible for Joseph Ginsburg to work in nightclubs, so he sneaked away illegally to Limoges in southern France, where he found work with an orchestra and quietly sent money home. A year and a half later the rest of the family, using false identification, traveled to Limoges to join him. Limoges was in southern France, which was not directly occupied by Germany but controlled by the French government based in Vichy, so it was slightly less dangerous for Jews, though not safe. One day the headmaster of Gainsbourg's school had the young man hide in nearby woods for a night to avoid a military documents check. When Paris was liberated in 1944, the family returned home.

In 1945 Gainsbourg enrolled in the prestigious art school École Supérieure Des Beaux Arts, to pursue painting. Two years later he also enrolled in a music school while continuing his art studies. He started dating Elisabeth Levitsky, secretary to poet Georges Hugnet and a part-time model, and she began supporting him financially. His father, wanting him to provide for himself, paid for him to take lessons from a gypsy guitar player so he could make money performing. While Gainsbourg spent a year in the military (as required of all French men), he developed a drinking habit that stuck with him the rest of his life. In 1951 he and Levitsky married.

The Astonishing Gainsbourg

Joseph Ginsburg began passing some of his piano playing gigs on to his son. As the young Gainsbourg got more work in nightclubs, he gave up painting, frustrated that he

1961 album, "L'Étonnant Serge Gainsbourg" (The Astonishing Serge Gainsbourg), made his literary influences clear; one song, "La Chanson De Prévert," paid tribute to French poet Jacques Prévert.

For a few years, it seemed that Gainsbourg would never attract more than a cult following of jazz intellectuals and bohemians. Several French singers recorded his songs, but French *chanson* fell out of vogue starting around 1962, as French youth embraced American and British rock 'n' roll and French imitations known as yé-yé. Gainsbourg recorded a few songs mocking yé-yé fans and defied the trends by recording the experimental *Gainsbourg Percussions,* influenced by African and Caribbean percussion styles. Later, determined to write a hit song, he began writing material for 16-year-old yé-yé star France Gall, including the hit "Les Sucettes" (Lollipops) and "Poupée de cire, poupée de son" (Wax Doll, Singing Doll), which won the Eurovision Song Contest in 1965. Soon, Gainsbourg's songs were more popular than ever among female French singers, and he spent the next two years focusing on his songwriting.

Gainsbourg married his second wife, Béatrice, whose given name was Françoise-Antoinette Pancrazzi, in early 1964. They soon had a daughter, Natacha. The marriage was doomed from the start, since she was extremely possessive, jealous of his singer friends and his fans. They divorced two years later, reuniting temporarily in 1967 and conceiving another child, Paul, born in 1968. But by then Gainsbourg had left Beatrice permanently. He had fallen in love with one of France's most beautiful and most famous actresses, Brigitte Bardot.

Bardot and Birkin

Gainsbourg was not a conventionally attractive man. In fact, he was often described as ugly; one French fanzine said he resembled a drowsy turtle. Yet one famous sex symbol after another became either his friend or his lover. "He attributed his appeal to women to a charmed sense of vulnerability, as well as his baggy eyes, three-day stubble and perpetual halo of smoke from five daily packs of Gitanes," William Drozdiak wrote in the *Washington Post.* Accordng to Drozdiak, Gainsbourg often said that "ugliness is superior to beauty because it lasts longer."

Bardot, a singer as well as an actress, had already recorded a few of Gainsbourg's songs before they appeared together on a prime time TV show together in late 1967. Bardot's second marriage was in trouble, and she and Gainsbourg discovered a mutual attraction. She invited him to appear on her own TV show, and he began writing new songs for her. Soon they became lovers, meeting discreetly at first, then going out to trendy nightclubs. They sang Gainsbourg's new songs, playful and full of abandon, on her show amid sets wild with pop psychedelia. "Comic Strip" was pop art as song, with Gainsbourg singing lead and Bardot intoning cartoon sound effects: "Shebam! Pow! Blop! Wizz!" To perform "Bonnie and Clyde," they styled themselves as flashy crooks. Next, they recorded "Je T'Aime . . . Moi Non Plus" (I Love You . . . Me Neither), a clever duet punctuated by erotic groans and sighs. According to

was not a genius at it, as he explained decades later. He joined France's songwriters' society in 1954 and registered his first six songs. For his new career, he renamed himself. He had never liked his first name. "He thought it was a loser's name," his longtime girlfriend Jane Birkin said in Simmons's book. "He said it reminded him of hairdressers—they were always called Lucien. Serge, he thought, sounded more Russian. And he chose Gainsbourg because he loved the English painter Gainsborough." Performing in nightclubs, Gainsbourg attracted a lot of female attention, and his womanizing caused Elizabeth to divorce him in 1957.

Gainsbourg began performing at the Milord L'Arsouille nightclub on Paris's Left Bank, he where he gained two important supporters: popular singer Michèle Arnaud, who worked two of Gainsbourg's songs into her act, and Boris Vian, a novelist and composer of songs full of biting humor. Word spread about Gainsbourg's talent. He was signed to the Philips record label and recorded the 1958 album "Du Chant à la une!" (Songs on Page One). A mix of jazz and ballads in the French *chanson* style, the album was filled with lyrics that were cynical and bitter, especially toward women. It did not sell well, but Boris Vian wrote an article praising it, and it won the grand prize of L'Académie Charles Cros, a songwriting award. One song from the album, "Le Poinçonneur des Lilas" (The Ticket-Puncher), about a lonely subway ticket-taker who becomes suicidal, eventually became a classic of French songwriting. The next year, the acclaimed French singer Juliette Gréco released a four-song album of his songs, including one of his first compositions, "Les Amours Perdues" (The Lost Loves). His

Simmons's biography, rumor spread that Gainsbourg and Bardot had been engaged in "heavy petting" while recording it. Enraged, Bardot's husband demanded that the record company cancel the single. Worried he would hurt Bardot's image, Gainsbourg complied, and the Bardot recording was not released until 1986.

Bardot returned to her husband, and Gainsbourg found a new lover, Jane Birkin, a beautiful 22-year-old British actress whose looks evoked the Swinging London fashion scene of the time. They met while acting in the film *Slogan*, and Gainsbourg swept her off her feet with a passionate, all-night trip through the nightclubs of Paris. Gainsbourg re-recorded "Je T'Aime . . . Moi Non Plus" with Birkin and released the new recording as a single. The lyrics were a clever interplay of cynicism and sentiment, but the suggestive vocal effects caught more listeners' attention. The Vatican called the song obscene and the BBC banned it, but it hit the top of the British singles charts anyway, Gainsbourg's only hit outside France. It sold 6 million copies worldwide.

Gainsbourg and Birkin quickly became one of the most famous celebrity couples in Europe. According to some accounts, they secretly married sometime in the 1970s, but other accounts say they never did. Either way, they stayed together for more than a decade. In 1971 Birkin gave birth to their daughter, Charlotte. The same year, Gainsbourg and Birkin released their next musical collaboration, *Histoire de Melody Nelson* (Story of Melody Nelson), a concept album about a middle-aged man in a forbidden romance with a 15-year-old girl. The music included an orchestra and a choir. Some critics considered the 1971 album to be Gainsbourg's masterpiece. "The story is silly," wrote *New York Times* critic Jody Rosen, but "it has real-life emotional resonance and actually holds together like a literary work: Gainsbourg's lyrics are filled with wonderful details and moments of genuine pathos."

Throughout the 1970s Gainsbourg continued writing songs, though a heart attack in 1973 slowed him down for a while. Birkin convinced him to adopt a more casual style, including an unshaven, stubbly look that became his visual trademark. Gainsbourg had enjoyed the scandal around "Je T'Aime . . . Moi Non Plus," and his 1970s output and public appearances seemed increasingly calculated to shock. For instance, his 1975 album *Rock Around the Bunker* was a caustically funny song series about Adolf Hitler and Nazi Germany set to 1950s-style American rock. One song was named after the yellow star the Nazis had forced him to wear as a boy.

Again seeking to innovate and surprise, Gainsbourg traveled to Jamaica and recorded a reggae album in 1978, at a time when reggae was just becoming popular in Western Europe. He booked a session in a Kingston recording studio with accomplished reggae musicians Sly and Robbie. Their meeting was awkward—the musicians were in no mood to record French music—until Sly declared that the only French song he knew was "Je T'Aime . . . Moi Non Plus." Once Gainsbourg told them it was his song, they got along well. Their 1979 album *Aux Armes et cetera* (To Arms, Etc.) included the title track, Gainsbourg's reggae version of the French national anthem, "La Marseillaise." Instead of sing-ing some of the bloodiest lines of the anthem, Gainsbourg sang, "Aux armes, et cetera," and let the lyrics trail off. The radical transformation of the anthem "was, for the French, the equivalent of the Sex Pistols' 'God Save the Queen' and Jimi Hendrix's 'Star-Spangled Banner' rolled into one," Simmons wrote in her biography. The conservative national newspaper *Le Figaro* called it an outrage and declared that Gainsbourg's French citizenship should be revoked. Gainsbourg embarked on a tour of France with the reggae musicians, and the shows sold out, but they were plagued by bomb threats from the extreme right. Before Gainsbourg's show in Strasbourg, a band of paratroopers warned the city's mayor that they would stop the show by force if necessary. Gainsbourg took the stage alone, though several of the paratroopers were in the audience, and sang the national anthem solo, then directed a disrespectful hand gesture at the paratroopers. His defiance made him a hero to much of the younger generation in France.

Gainsbarre

In the 1980s Gainsbourg's life began to turn tragic. Birkin left him in 1980, upset that he had begun drinking more heavily and acting outrageously. They remained friends, however, and Gainsbourg continued to write songs for her albums. A year later, Gainsbourg began a new relationship with the young singer Caroline Von Paulus, better known by her stage name, Bambou. They had a son, Lucien, in 1986.

In his own songs, Gainsbourg began to include references to an alter ego, "Gainsbarre," a character hobbled by alcohol and depression. "His excessive indulgence in booze, tobacco and women seemed to nurture his commercial success, as the French public became more fascinated by him with every outrageous piece of music or behavior," wrote Drozdiak. Once he burned a 500-franc note on live TV to protest high taxes. In 1986, also on live TV, he vulgarly propositioned the American singer Whitney Houston. He did, however, find one taboo the French did not want broken. In 1984 he recorded the song "Lemon Incest" as a duet with his daughter Charlotte, then 13. The video showed them lying near each other on a bed, and the lyrics "come close to extolling carnal relations," as Drozdiak put it. Three years later Gainsbourg directed an entire film, *Charlotte Forever*, as an homage to her. He also continued recording, experimenting with funk and hip-hop, and writing songs for others, including Bambou, Birkin, and the young French singer Vanessa Paradis, mostly known in the United States for later marrying American actor Johnny Depp.

Publicly indulging in too much alcohol and too many cigarettes, Gainsbourg spent 10 years committing suicide, as one friend of his put it. He endured heart problems and a liver operation before dying on March 2, 1991, of a heart attack at his apartment in Paris. Much of France mourned. French President François Mitterand declared that Gainsbourg, "through his love for the language and his musical genius, lifted the song to the level of an art" (as quoted in the *Chicago Tribune*). He was buried in Montparnasse Cemetery in Paris, the final resting place of many of France's greatest writers and artists. Since his death,

Gainsbourg's legend has grown. Many young French, American and British singers acknowledge his influence, and fans still leave huge collections of art and gifts, including packs of Gitanes, outside his old apartment.

Books

Simmons, Sylvie, *Serge Gainsbourg: A Fistful of Gitanes,* Da Capo Press, 2001.

Periodicals

Chicago Tribune, March 5, 1991.
Guardian (London, England), February 2, 2001; April 14, 2006.
New York Times, August 26, 2001.
Washington Post, March 8, 1991.

Online

"Serge Gainsbourg," *Radio France Internationale,* http:www .rfimusique.com (December 31, 2006). □

Martha Gellhorn

American journalist Martha Gellhorn (1908–1998) was one of the first female war correspondents ever and one of the best American war reporters of the twentieth century. Instead of recognizing her for her reporting or for her fiction writing, the public often remembered her as an ex-wife of the legendary American novelist Ernest Hemingway. But Gellhorn, "a cocky, raspy-voiced, chain-smoking maverick," as *New York Times* writer Rick Lyman described her, lived a life at least as exciting, world-spanning, and passionate as her ex-husband's.

Wanderlust

Martha Ellis Gellhorn was born in St. Louis on November 8, 1908. Her father was a doctor and her mother an advocate for women's right to vote. She attended a progressive private school her parents founded in St. Louis, then went to Bryn Mawr College, leaving in 1927 to write for the *New Republic* and take a job in Albany, New York, as a crime reporter. In February of 1930 she traveled to Europe, paying for the boat trip across the ocean by writing a brochure for the Holland American Line. In Paris, while working a series of odd jobs, she met French writer Bertrand de Jouvenel, and they married, or at least presented themselves as husband and wife; it was not clear whether he had successfully divorced his previous wife.

After returning to St. Louis with de Jouvenel in 1931, Gellhorn traveled the American Southwest as a reporter for the *St. Louis Post-Dispatch* and wrote a novel, *What Mad Pursuit,* about a protagonist much like her, a cynical female reporter who has many love affairs. The novel attracted the

attention of Harry Hopkins, a top official in President Franklin D. Roosevelt's administration, and Hopkins hired Gellhorn to travel the country and write about the effects of the Great Depression. Gellhorn fabricated a story about a lynching of a black man in the South and encouraged North Carolina factory workers she was writing about to break the windows of their factory in protest. The window-breaking cost her her job, while the lynching story won her the praise of First Lady Eleanor Roosevelt, who knew Gellhorn's mother from college (and presumably did not know of the fabrication). The line between truth and fiction remained unclear in Gellhorn's book of Depression era writings, *The Trouble I've Seen,* published in 1936.

Hemingway and War

Gellhorn met Ernest Hemingway, whose writing she admired, at Sloppy Joe's Bar in Key West, Florida, around Christmas in 1936. When he told her he was heading to Spain to cover the Spanish Civil War, she decided to go too. She came to Madrid in the spring of 1937 carrying a single knapsack and $50, to cover the war for *Collier's Weekly.* Soon Gellhorn, then 28, and Hemingway, 37, became lovers. Like many writers and artists of her generation, including Hemingway, Gellhorn sympathized passionately with the democratically elected socialist government of Spain in its fight against the fascist generals led by Francisco Franco. Her Spanish dispatches, difficult to find in print today, "revealed a gift for unflinching observation and unforced pathos" and "were much better than Hemingway's," wrote Marc Weingarten in the *Washington Post.*

"In Barcelona, it was perfect bombing weather," Gellhorn wrote, describing Franco's bombers closing in on Republican territory in November of 1938, as quoted by Lyman. "The cafes along the Ramblas were crowded. There was nothing much to drink; a sweet fizzy poison called orangeade and a horrible liquid supposed to be sherry. There was, of course, nothing to eat. Everyone was out enjoying the cold afternoon sunlight. No bombers had come over for at least two hours." When the Spanish fascists won the war in 1939, she was crushed. "Nothing in my life has so affected my thinking as the losing of that war," she wrote in a letter to her friend Hortense Flexner, according to Weingarten. "It is, very banally, like the death of all loved things."

Gellhorn and Hemingway married in November of 1940. Soon after, she took him along to Hong Kong so she could write for *Collier's* about the Chinese Army's retreat from the Japanese invasion. The marriage was difficult. He wanted her to be a deferential wife; she wanted to live life like he did. She was idealistic, tormented by the slave labor conditions she witnessed in Hong Kong; he stoically accepted the world as it was. Both had terrible tempers. "Ernest and I really are afraid of each other, each one knowing that the other is the most violent person either one knows," she wrote to Flexner, as quoted by Weingarten. They broke up 1945 while they were staying at the Dorchester Hotel in London. Afterward, Gellhorn would call Hemingway a bully, while he called her phony and pretentious. In later years, she resented having more fame for being Hemingway's ex-wife than for her own work. "I was a writer before I met him and I have been a writer for 45 years since," she complained, according to the *Chicago Tribune.* "Why should I be a footnote to someone else's life?"

During World War II, Gellhorn often left Hemingway behind to go abroad and report. She covered the 1939 Soviet attack on Finland and the German air attacks on London. In 1944 Hemingway, instead of Gellhorn, was hired by *Collier's* to cover the Allies' D-Day landing in France; she covered the invasion anyway, by stowing away on a hospital ship and going onshore bearing a stretcher. "She brought a fresh approach to war journalism, writing passionately about the dreadful impact of war on the innocent," her *Washington Post* obituary said. Near the end of the war, she witnessed the Allied forces' liberation of Dachau, the infamous concentration camp near Munich. Her article has become one of the most famous accounts of the discovery of the camps. "Behind the barbed wire and the electric fence," she wrote, as quoted by Lyman, "the skeletons sat in the sun and searched themselves for lice. They have no age and no faces; they all look alike and like nothing you will ever see, if you are lucky." The experience forever darkened her outlook on life, so that she was never again able to be as happy as before, she later wrote.

Reporter, Advocate, Novelist

After World War II, Gellhorn left the United States, criticizing it for being a colonial power. She lived in several countries, from France and Italy to Cuba, Mexico, and Kenya, before settling in Great Britain in her later years,

splitting her time between a London apartment and a Welsh cottage. The legacy of the Nazi atrocities continued to occupy her. She covered the trial of German war criminal Adolf Eichmann for the *Atlantic Monthly.* She went to Israel in 1967 to cover the Arab-Israeli War with from an impassioned pro-Israel standpoint, explaining that she saw conflict through the prism of the Holocaust.

In 1966 Gellhorn traveled to Vietnam to write about the war for the London *Guardian.* Her dispatches openly protested the war. "People cannot survive our bombs," she wrote, as quoted by John Pilger of the *New Statesman.* "We are uprooting the people from the lovely land where they have lived for generations; and the uprooted are given not bread but stone. Is this an honorable way for a great nation to fight a war 8,000 miles from its safe homeland?" The South Vietnamese government banned her from returning there, sending her into a long depression.

To her supporters, Gellhorn was heroic to embrace advocacy journalism and, later in life, to criticize most war journalism as too trusting of generals and governments. For Gellhorn and her peers, such as British journalist George Orwell, "the idea was never to just see the show or get the story," wrote Susie Linfield in the *Nation.* They believed, Linfield explained, that "journalism equaled truth, and that truth would inspire people (especially those in the supposedly civilized democracies) to protest, to intervene." A reporter's job, Gellhorn once said, according to the *Chicago Tribune,* was simply to "to limit yourself to what you see or hear and not suppress or invent." But her critics charged she broke her own rules to fit her political convictions. "This essential contradiction—not writing what you knew to be true, in order to uphold a greater good—was something that Martha would avoid confronting all her life," claimed her biographer, Caroline Moorehead, as quoted by Jonathan Yardley of the *Washington Post.*

Gellhorn had hoped for fame as a novelist, and her fiction often attracted good reviews, but did not sell well. The novels included *A Stricken Field,* published in 1939, about refugees in Prague just before the German invasion of Czechoslovakia, and *Liana,* from 1944, about a rich white man and mulatto woman marrying in the French Caribbean. In the 1950s, when she retreated somewhat from the war correspondent's life, seeking mental calm, she wrote the novels *The Honeyed Peace* and *Two by Two.* Critics sometimes suggested that she had a stronger command of novellas, as in the collections *The Weather in Africa* from 1988 and *The Novellas of Martha Gellhorn* in 1993. Her memoir, *Travels With Myself and Another,* was published in 1978.

Though Gellhorn had many lovers over the years, she never found the perfect companion. In 1953 she married her third husband, T.S. Matthews, a managing editor at *Time.* The marriage broke up in 1963, after she discovered that Matthews had carried on a long affair with another woman. In later life Gellhorn became critical of the institution of marriage. She gave birth to one son, George Alexander Gellhorn, whom she raised herself, and she adopted a son, Sandy Matthews.

Gellhorn traveled to El Salvador to cover the brutal war in the 1980s between the U.S.-backed military and Marxist rebels. Later that decade, her failing body slowed her down. In her late seventies a botched cataract operation damaged her sight. She covered the United States' 1989 invasion of Panama but declared herself too old to go to Bosnia after war broke out there in 1993. Her last foreign reporting trip was to Brazil in the mid-1990s, to cover violence against its street people. She wrote a lengthy article about Brazil for the literary magazine *Granta,* but only with great difficulty, since her poor eyesight prevented her from reviewing what she had written.

Stricken with liver and ovarian cancer and various other illnesses, Gellhorn hastened the impending end of her life by taking a fatal dose of medicine. She died on February 15, 1998, at her London home. She was 89.

Periodicals

Chicago Tribune, February 17, 1998.
New Republic, September 11–18, 2006.
New Statesman, March 20, 1998.
New York Times, February 17, 1998.
Washington Post, February 17, 1998; November 9, 2003; August 20, 2006. □

Stan Getz

Of the great instrumental soloists who emerged from the revolution in jazz styles that grew in the years after World War II, tenor saxophonist Stan Getz (1927–1991) was perhaps the greatest sheer melodist, the most avid pursuer of pure beauty and emotion.

Getz in his youth was an admirer of Lester Young, the great saxophonist whose singing melodic lines did much to emancipate the jazz soloist from the procession of chords that underpinned the tune. Coming of age during the evolution of the dense, difficult new music known as bebop, he forged a quieter but no less intense style of his own that commanded the admiration of legions of jazz fans for decades. In the 1960s Getz helped introduce a new Brazilian-inflected variety of jazz that put him in the top reaches of the sales charts, where he remained one of the top musicians in the jazz genre until his death in 1991.

Reproduced Big-Band Sounds on Harmonica

Stanley Getz was born in Philadelphia, Pennsylvania, on February 2, 1927. The birth was a difficult one, during which one of Getz's ears was almost completely torn off by a surgical instrument and had to be reattached. His parents, descended from Jewish immigrants, were never very prosperous; his father, Al, was a low-level printshop employee, and was an alcohol abuser who often drifted from job to job. The family moved to the New York borough of the Bronx when Stan was six. The young Getz had obvious musical talent, but his parents could not afford to buy him an instrument. He got hold of a harmonica and quickly learned to use it to mimic complex jazz arrangements like Benny Goodman's "King Porter Stomp," and he played the bass in classical compositions in a school orchestra. Finally, as a belated 13th birthday present, his parents gave him a battered alto saxophone.

He quickly learned the other saxophones and took lessons on the more difficult bassoon, and his high school teacher recommended him for a scholarship to the educational apex of classical music, the Juilliard School. But Getz was already hooked on the popular big band jazz of the time. Practicing his saxophone for up to eight hours a day, he was encouraged by his parents, who saw his growing skills as a source of extra money for the family. Soon Getz was frequenting jazz band rehearsals, and when he was 15 he seized the chance to fill a chair left absent by a member of trombonist Jack Teagarden's band. He was hired the same day by Teagarden at a salary of $70 a week and told to show up the next morning at Penn Station (a New York railroad terminus) with a tuxedo, toothbrush, and spare shirt.

At first Getz found work because older players were mostly away in the United States Army, but soon his solid skills and quick-study ways got him noticed by bandleaders. In 1944 Getz signed on with the Stan Kenton Orchestra, and one of the veteran musicians in that high profile group talked him into trying heroin on the band's tour bus. Within a few weeks Getz was hooked. But he was young, making good money, and always on the road. Associates noticed that Getz's normally cheerful personality darkened while he was in need of a fix, and saxophonist Zoot Sims, in an interview quoted by Getz biographer Donald L. Maggin, once commented that "Stan's a nice bunch of guys!" But for some years his addiction did not interfere regularly with his playing.

Getz did stints with two more of the best bands in the jazz business, those of Jimmy Dorsey and Benny Goodman, in the mid-1940s. Still in his teens, he listened avidly as saxophonist Charlie Parker, trumpeter Dizzy Gillespie, and a group of other players centered in New York's Minton's nightclub worked out the radical new bebop style in the last years of World War II. Bebop drastically widened the harmonic and rhythmic vocabulary of jazz, challenging players to produce rapid, jagged lines that extended the implications of the underlying chords. Getz, mostly by paying close attention to what avant-garde musicians were doing, mastered the new style in a matter of months.

Influenced by Lester Young

The main influence on Getz, however, was the style of swing tenor saxophonist Lester Young, a performer whose relaxed, lyrical style offered a contrast to those of saxophone players who cultivated the instrument's potential for rough sounds and sharp attacks. Getz worked at updating Young's sound with the speed and harmonic experimentation of bebop, creating a new and highly appealing style—lyrical, elegant, and yielding to no one in sheer dexterity. In 1947 Getz joined the incarnation of Woody Herman's Thundering Herd big band known as the Second Herd, honing his skills as part of the band's formidable "Four Brothers" quartet of saxophones (the others were Sims, Herbie Steward, and Serge Chaloff). The year before he had married jazz singer Beverly Byrne, and the pair, though troubled in their relationship, raised three children.

Getz severed his ties with the Herman band in 1949 and 1950, partly because he was disturbed by the grind of the road, and partly by a specific incident in which a railroad brakeman had been decapitated by a train on which he was riding. He began performing and recording, mostly in New York, with small groups. The timing was perfect, as so-called "cool jazz" began to supplant bebop and audiences flocked to the charismatic young saxophonist whom many called romantic. Getz resisted the identification with cool jazz, saying in a 1950 interview quoted by Maggin that "I'm not trying to shove any style or sound down people's throats. It's fun swingin' and getting 'hot' for a change instead of trying to be cool. I don't want to become stagnant. I can be a real stompin' tenor man." Getz had a major jazz hit with "Early Autumn" in 1949, and in the early 1950s he and trumpeter (and cool jazz pioneer) Miles Davis were arguably the most popular jazz musicians in the United States. Numerous Stan Getz Quintet LPs appeared on a variety of jazz labels and inaugurated a run of more than 130 albums Getz would make over the course of his career.

Getz's heroin addiction caused a major interruption to his jazz career in 1954. After several skirmishes with the law, he tried to ease himself off the drug with the equally dangerous combination of alcohol and barbiturates, but in February he found himself in Seattle, Washington, desper-

ate for heroin and with no ready source of the drug. He entered a drugstore near his hotel and made a clumsy attempt to rob it (no weapon was involved, only a pointed finger under his coat), demanding morphine, a chemical relative of heroin. He was arrested and jailed in southern California, where he had faced earlier charges, for six months. Soon after this episode Getz stopped taking morphine for good, although he began to abuse alcohol.

Immediately after his divorce from Beverly Byrne in 1956, Getz married Swedish-born Monica Silfverskiold; with her he had two more children. Partly to escape Getz's legal problems, the pair lived in Copenhagen, Denmark, in the late 1950s, but wherever he was, Getz recorded prolifically, mostly for the Verve label started in 1956 by the indefatigable jazz promoter Norman Granz. In 1957 alone Getz released six albums, all with star collaborators, and he nurtured the careers of young players in Scandinavia's vigorous jazz scene.

Spearheaded Bossa Nova Craze

By the early 1960s Getz had been on top of the jazz world for more than a decade, and fashions were inevitably changing; the extreme playing of John Coltrane and Ornette Coleman, pushing at the edges of established jazz procedures, attracted the attention of jazz audiences and writers. But Getz found a new and congenial stylistic home for his smooth playing, first with a widely hailed recording with string orchestra called *Focus* in 1962, and then later that year with a then-little-known Brazilian style called bossa nova. Getz teamed with guitarist Charlie Byrd for the *Jazz Samba* album, and "Desafinado" ("Out of Tune") and "Samba de una Nota So" (translated as "One-Note Samba"), both written by Brazilian jazz composer Antonio Carlos Jobim, became major hits. *Jazz Samba* rose to the top spot on *Billboard*'s album sales chart, the first jazz LP to do so.

An international bossa nova craze quickly ignited, and Getz gave it a second wind in 1964 with the *Getz/Gilberto* LP, recorded (as was *Jazz Samba*) for Verve. Getz teamed with Brazilian guitarist João Gilberto and his wife, Astrud, on the hit single "The Girl from Ipanema." The combination of Getz's saxophone and Astrud Gilberto's plain, deadpan voice proved irresistible, and *Getz/Gilberto* outsold *Jazz Samba*. It missed the top spot on the *Billboard* chart only because it appeared simultaneously with the Beatles' *A Hard Day's Night*. Getz remained financially comfortable for the rest of his life as a result of these recordings, and though he eventually tired of playing his big bossa nova hits, he established the Brazilian influence as a permanent part of the jazz vocabulary—one of his most significant accomplishments.

The jazz-rock fusion trends of the 1970s were not really congenial ones for Getz, although he did experiment with the use of electronic instruments from time to time. Recording for the Columbia label he assembled a series of bands that contained the future stars of jazz; one of these was pianist Chick Corea, whose composition "La Fiesta" appeared on Getz's *Captain Marvel* LP of 1975. Getz had a solid core of admirers, many of them in Europe, who continued to support his straight-ahead acoustic jazz concerts and recordings.

Getz's personal life continued to trouble him in the 1980s; a combination of alcohol abuse and depression over the years had left him prone to sprees of rage, and his marriage to Monica dissolved in 1987 in an acrimonious divorce proceeding that eventually reached the U.S. Supreme Court. No matter what demons might beset him, however, Getz was recognized over his entire career for delivering performances of consistently high quality. Getz recorded for the Verve, Concord Jazz, A&M, and Polygram labels, often joining with pianist Kenny Barron and remaining one of the best-selling performers in jazz. His 1987 releases *Serenity* and *Anniversary* were critically acclaimed, and 1989's *Apasionado* returned the saxophonist to a Brazilian zone of influence. In his last years, Getz finally achieved total sobriety.

Looking toward a third marriage and new musical projects near the end of the 1980s, Getz was diagnosed with liver cancer. He kept performing, and the disease remained stable for several years. One of the most beautiful vocal collaborations of his entire career was *You Gotta Pay the Band,* recorded in 1991 with singer Abbey Lincoln. Getz remained active until his death on June 6, 1991. The legacy of musicians he had directly inspired included Arkansas governor Bill Clinton, soon to be elected president of the United States.

Books

Contemporary Musicians, volume 12, Gale 1994.
Maggin, Donald L., *Stan Getz: A Life in Jazz,* Morrow, 1996.

Periodicals

Billboard, June 22, 1991.
Boston Globe, June 8, 1991.
Independent (London, England), June 8, 1991.
New York Times, June 9, 1991.
New York Times Magazine, June 9, 1991.
Washington Post, June 8, 1991.

Online

"Stan Getz," *All Music Guide,* http://www.allmusic.com (October 15, 2006). □

Carlos Ghosn

Brazilian-born executive Carlos Ghosn (born 1954) has become known as one of the automobile industry's great turnaround artists. Dubbed "le cost killer" and "the destroyer" by those on the receiving end of his streamlining, he also had a more positive and more telling nickname: "Mr. Fix-It."

Ghosn's accomplishments were all the more noteworthy because they came at deeply troubled companies—Renault in France and Nissan in

Japan—that analysts had written off as also-rans and even evaluated as approaching bankruptcy. Ghosn did not just rescue these companies; he turned them into market leaders. As the first non-Japanese president of an automaker in notoriously insular Japan, he seemingly broke all the rules of doing business in that country as he planned Nissan's turnaround, but the results he obtained were so persuasive that soon he was not just tolerated but loved by the Japanese public; he even became the subject of a 160-page graphic novel at one point. By 2006, although one major potential deal had fallen through, Ghosn (pronounced with the "gh" as in "ghost," and rhyming with "loan," with a silent "s") was being discussed as a potential savior of yet another troubled auto company, perhaps one in the United States.

Born into Immigrant Family

Carlos Ghosn was born in Porto Velho, Brazil, on March 9, 1954. His father, Jorge, worked for an airline and had a job involving lots of travel, something that would later seem very familiar to Ghosn, who has logged up to 150,000 travel miles in a single year. Ghosn's parents had immigrated from Lebanon, and when Carlos was six he and his mother returned to live there. Ghosn learned to speak four languages fluently, and he later began working on several others, including Japanese. In Lebanon Ghosn attended top-flight schools run by the Jesuit Catholic order, did well, and moved to engineering school in Paris, France. As an adult Ghosn would attribute the ease with which he moved among different cultures to the global upbringing and education he had received. "I've always felt different," he observed to Christine Tierney of the *Detroit News*. "Because you are different, you try to integrate, and that pushes you to try to understand the environment in which you find yourself. That tends to develop one's ability to listen, to observe, to compare—qualities that are very useful in managing."

Ghosn earned two engineering degrees in Paris, the first from the Ecole Polytechnique in 1974 (a school that spawned an unusually large number of innovative European auto engineers) and the second from the Ecole des Mines de Paris in 1978. His career started unremarkably enough, as a management trainee with the French tiremaker Michelin. Soon he was managing a Michelin plant in Le Puy, France. He was promoted rapidly through the Michelin organization, rising to become head of research for the development of industrial tires by the mid-1980s. Then he was asked by Michelin to return to his Brazilian homeland and head the company's problem-ridden operations there as chief operating officer. Just over 30 years old, he was now responsible for a continent-wide manufacturing operation.

He would have had a ready excuse for failure: South American financial markets were chaotic during those years, and Brazil in particular suffered from severe inflation. But Ghosn succeeded brilliantly by overhauling the organizational structure of Michelin's South American operations, using a method that would become something of a trademark. He formed working groups consisting of people from different sections of the organization, and from different countries. French engineers met with Brazilian purchasing managers to plot the development of a new product, resulting in improvements that had been missed when each department had acted in isolation. Within two years Michelin's South American division had turned a profit.

Ghosn repeated this early success after becoming president and chief operating officer (CEO) at Michelin of North America in 1988. Newly married to his wife, Rita, and with a growing family that would eventually include four children, he added the position of chairman in 1990. In the United States, Ghosn engineered a merger with domestic tiremaker Uniroyal Goodrich that doubled the size of his division. He dealt with unionized Uniroyal Goodrich employees not by confronting them, but by convincing union representatives that flexible work rules were in the best interest of employees on the factory floor. But despite his record, there was an unofficial ceiling to Ghosn's advancement at Michelin. The business was family-owned, and its longtime head, François Michelin, had ordained his son Edouard as his eventual successor. In 1996, therefore, he agreed to talk to Louis Schweitzer, CEO of the money-losing French automaker Renault.

Slashed, Then Grew Company

Ghosn described Renault's corporate culture acidly; he was quoted as saying in *Fortune* that the company "put a premium on fine phrases and arcane knowledge," wasted time on "discussions about everything and nothing," and held the noncompetitive collective belief that "you can't always have high productivity and high morale at the same

time." Ghosn pared unproductive fat from Renault, closing a factory in Belgium, idling some 3,300 workers, and acquiring the "cost killer" sobriquet. But he was never exclusively a ruthless economizer. Ghosn's skills lay more in effective management that speeded up new operations and thus increased sales. Renault flourished; it was 80 percent owned by the French government in 1992, but by the mid-2000s the government's share had declined to 16 percent, and Renault was the best-selling brand in Western Europe.

In 1999, realizing that he had a talented young executive as an asset, Schweitzer made a bold move: he injected $7 billion into the Japanese automaker Nissan, acquiring 44.4 percent of its stock, and sent Ghosn to Tokyo as CEO. The task facing Ghosn was daunting. Nissan was saddled with $20 billion in debt, had lost money for seven of the previous eight years, and had hit its production peak ten years before, in 1989. Ghosn himself estimated his chances of success at no better than even money. In his first year, Ghosn had to develop a restructuring plan that took continuing slow sales into account; Nissan's model line was widely viewed as having fallen behind those of rivals Toyota and Honda technologically.

Part of Nissan's problem was excess capacity, brought on by an unofficial contract-for-life arrangement that existed between Japanese auto companies and their employees. Ghosn broke with tradition by closing five factories and cutting some 21,000 jobs. He also took on the close network of relationships between auto companies and their suppliers, relationships denoted by a specific Japanese word, keiretsu. Ghosn slashed Nissan's debt by selling off the company's shares in about half of its roughly 1,100 keiretsu partners. Finally, he infused new engineering blood into the Nissan organization, hiring a top designer from rival Isuzu and bringing Renault personnel in from France. To cope with the variety of languages spoken, he instituted English as the official language for company operations and rewarded managers who learned to speak the language. "Having to speak English is very helpful, as it is not our native tongue; so we have to simplify our thoughts down to core issues," Nissan chief financial officer Thierry Moulonguet told Benjamin Fulford of *Forbes*. Other Westerners had held top executive positions in Japan, but when Ghosn was given the title of president at Nissan in 2000, he was the first foreigner to hold that symbolically significant post in Japan's auto industry.

The day after he was given that post, Ghosn faced a tense meeting of mostly Japanese shareholders, one of whom likened him to the armed forces occupying Japan after World War II. Ghosn was criticized for not having mastered the traditional bow common in Japanese business circles. Ghosn responded unflappably, with a recital of the financial figures and quantifiable business trends that always formed the nucleus of his discussions in meetings. Nearly bankrupt before he came, Nissan would, he said, return to profitability within the year. The company was ahead of schedule in meeting Ghosn's goal of cutting costs by 20 percent, and Nissan had 22 new models, with eye-catching designs, in the pipeline and ready for display at the 2001 Detroit Auto Show.

Touted as Presidential Candidate

In 2003 Ghosn announced a second and equally ambitious three-year plan, known as Nissan 180. His goals were to increase Nissan's worldwide sales by one million vehicles, reduce debt to zero, and achieve an 8 percent level of operating profit. By 2005, again ahead of schedule, the last two goals and been met and the third was well on the way. Ghosn's popularity in Japan skyrocketed after his rocky start. Japanese women named him the country's most desirable husband in one poll (he remained happily married) and a comic book was issued featuring him as its hero. In his troubled second homeland of Lebanon, Ghosn was mentioned as a possible presidential candidate.

Many of Nissan's sales gains came in the United States, where even Ghosn's missteps somehow turned into positive developments. A new Nissan plant, opened in Canton, Mississippi, to manufacture the redesigned Qwest minivan, ran into trouble due to its inexperienced workforce and dropped Nissan toward the bottom of U.S. new car reliability rankings. But Ghosn won plaudits in the automotive press after accepting responsibility for the problems, calling the situation a management error rather than blaming the workers, and sending a task force of 1,000 engineers to Mississippi to address the problems. Other Nissan models, such as a redesigned Altima compact and the luxury Infiniti line, were registering sharp gains at the same time.

The plan had been for Ghosn to take over the CEO position at Renault after Schweitzer's retirement in 2005, but instead he decided to attempt something much more challenging, and indeed virtually unprecedented in the corporate world: he stayed on as co-chairman at Nissan while taking the positions of president and CEO at Renault. *Fortune* noted that "It's as if [professional football coach] Bill Belichick decided to add the [San Francisco] 49ers to his duties as coach of the New England Patriots." Ghosn, shuttling between Paris and Tokyo on his executive jet, with frequent side trips to the United States and other world markets, barely broke his stride. He was not especially known as a technical innovator; indeed, Nissan lagged behind Toyota and Honda in the hot new hybrid engine technology. He was, simply, one of the most efficient managers in the world. "He's just the most disciplined man I've ever worked with," U.S. Nissan marketing chief Steve Wilhite told Dutch Mandel of *Automotive News,* who noted that "Once [Ghosn] has digested a problem, he is like the anaconda that swallowed a goat—everyone else is watching what he has just done, but he is moving on to the next meal. Ghosn has no problem making decisions quickly and decisively."

With the record he had amassed, it was perhaps inevitable that Ghosn would be recruited by General Motors or Ford, the Big Two of the American auto industry and each beset with many of the same problems Ghosn had solved at Renault and Nissan. After rumors that he was being wooed by Ford family patriarch Bill Ford Jr., news emerged in 2006 that General Motors, under pressure from prominent shareholder Kirk Kerkorian, was exploring a series of joint operations with Nissan. Speculation was widespread that Kerkorian hoped to install Ghosn as president of GM, the

world's largest automaker (and world's largest corporation of any kind). After a 90-day review, negotiations between the two firms fell apart in the summer of 2006. Nevertheless, Ghosn refused to rule out a future partnership with an American automaker, and it was still an open question as to where the remarkable career trajectory of Carlos Ghosn would finally take him.

Books

Ghosn, Carlos, *Shift: Inside Nissan's Historic Revival,* Doubleday, 2005.
Magee, David, *Turnaround: How Carlos Ghosn Rescued Nissan,* Collins, 2003.

Periodicals

Automotive News, September 20, 2004; January 31, 2005; July 17, 2006; September 25, 2006.
Economist, February 26, 2005.
Forbes, October 2, 2000; July 22, 2002.
Forbes Global, May 22, 2006.
Fortune, July 21, 2003; March 7, 2005; April 4, 2005; December 11, 2006.
Time, May 19, 2003; March 27, 2006; August 28, 2006.

Online

"Nissan CEO: The Making of a Superstar," *Detroit News,* http://www.detnews.com/2005/autosinsider/0502/27/A01-101491.htm (December 12, 2006). □

Sabiha Gökçen

Turkish aviator Sabiha Gökçen (1913–2001) was the first woman in her country to earn a pilot's license, and is believed to be the world's first female combat pilot. Gökçen was the adopted daughter of Turkey's first president, the eminent reformer Mustafa Kemal Atatürk, and in the 1930s she became the symbol of a recently modernized Turkey and the new horizons offered to its female citizens. "Jetting solo over Turkey and the Balkans in small biplanes," wrote Pelin Turgut in the London *Independent,* "she became the nation's own Amelia Earhart, a celebrity in hat and goggles."

Came of Age in Historic Era

Gökçen was born on March 22, 1913, in Bursa, a city in the northwest of Turkey, and official accounts say she was the daughter of Mustafa İzzet Bey and Hayriye Hanim. Her life intersected with one of twentieth-century Europe's most important leaders in October of 1925, the year she turned 12. Mustafa Kemal Atatürk (1881–1938) had emerged after World War I as the leader of a new nationalist movement in Turkey. The country had been the center of the Ottoman Empire since the year 1299, and unwisely allied with imperial Germany during World War I. Both were defeated when the war ended in 1918, but the vestiges of Ottoman rule soon found themselves battling Atatürk-led forces in a war of independence. Seven hundred years of Ottoman rule ended in 1922, and the Republic of Turkey was proclaimed the following year with Atatürk as its first president.

Gökçen's adoptive father launched a rapid modernization plan for Turkey over the next decade. He replaced the Islamic code of law with a secular one modeled on Switzerland's, and sought to make the nation, which straddled Europe and Asia, a beacon of progress and equality. The ancient Arabic script used in Turkey for centuries was jettisoned in favor of a newly created modern Turkish alphabet, and literacy rates soared, thanks in part to the president's ardent commitment to language reform.

Atatürk spent several years touring the remoter areas of the country, urging villagers to learn the new alphabet, and issued other decrees that reinforced his message that Turkey must move forward. He outlawed the fez, for example, urging Turkish men to abandon this symbol of Islamic identity and solidarity, and did the same with the traditional headscarves worn by women in Islamic societies. On what would prove his last speaking tour of the countryside, he told residents of Akhisar, in western Anatolia, on October 10, 1925, that "the civilized world is far ahead of us," according to Andrew Mango's *Atatürk: The Biography of the Founder of Modern Turkey.* "We have no choice but to catch up. It is time to stop nonsense, such as 'should we or should we not wear hats?' We shall adopt hats along with all other works of Western civilization. Uncivilized people are doomed to be trodden under the feet of civilized people."

Adopted by the President

On that same official trip, Atatürk stopped in Bursa, and newspaper accounts of the day report that a 12-year-old female approached the president and requested assistance with continuing her education at a boarding school. With this bold move Gökçen became one of several children adopted by Atatürk, including two other teenaged girls, Zehra and Rukiye, who preceded her in the household. The others included daughters Afet, Fikriye, Ülkü, Nebile, and a boy named Mustafa. Gökçen arrived in Ankara, Turkey's second largest city and its new capital under Atatürk, and began her education at the Çankara Primary School, which was attached to the presidential residence. She later went on to the Üsküdar Girls College in Istanbul, Turkey's largest city. She reportedly suffered from health problems, however, which curtailed her education.

Gökçen was known simply as Sabiha until Atatürk 's Surname Act of June 21, 1934, went into effect. This required all citizens to take a family name, which had not been part of Turkish society prior to that time. Atatürk had originally been known as Gazi Mustafa Kemal Pasha, with "Pasha," like the "Bey" attached to the name of Gökçen's biological father, serving as an honorific title denoting, respectively, king and chieftain. Atatürk's newly adopted surname meant "Father of All Turks," and he named Sabiha

Gökçen, or "of the sky." It was a prophetic moniker, for she had not yet settled on aviation as her career.

That same year, Atatürk granted Turkish women full political rights, making Turkey one of the first nations in the world to give women the right to vote. In his ongoing modernization plan, aviation ranked high among the national priorities, and in May of 1935 Atatürk presided over the official opening of the Türkkuşsu Flight School. Gökçen was with him that day, and she was reportedly delighted by the skydivers and parachutists who took part in an air show as part of the day's ceremonies. When Atatürk asked her if she would like to do that, too, she reportedly replied she was ready to start training right away. Atatürk informed the director of the Türkkuşsu Flight School that Gökçen was to be enrolled as its first female student.

Trained as Fighter Pilot

Gökçen soon realized she might be better suited to flying aircraft than to jumping out of them, and earned her pilot's license instead. Afterward she was sent to the Soviet Union for advanced training, along with seven other pilots, all of them men. She made her first solo flight in 1936, an achievement excitedly chronicled in the Turkish press as emblematic of the new freedoms available to all Turkish women. Atatürk also permitted her to begin training at Turkey's Military Aviation Academy as a military pilot, but as Mango described, Gökçen recalled in her memoirs that "Atatürk tested her by asking her to press a gun against her head and pull the trigger," and "she did not flinch."

Gökçen trained on bombers and fighter planes at an air base in Eskişehir, a province in the northwest which was also home to the Military Aviation Academy. She flew in standard military flight exercises over the Aegean Sea in 1937, and also took part in her sole combat mission that same year. As Mango noted, because she had not flinched at the firearm test Atatürk allowed her to participate in the bombing of a Kurdish uprising in Dersim, a province later known as Tunceli. "She was given a gun—which was loaded this time—to defend herself if her plane crashed and she fell into rebel hands." Instead she managed to bomb the home of an insurgent leader, killing him and several associates, before returning to base safely.

In 1938 Gökçen made a historic flight around the Balkans that lasted five days until her plane was sidelined by mechanical problems. This was a well-publicized peace mission, and newspapers across Europe chronicled her stops in Greece, Bulgaria, Yugoslavia, and Romania. Atatürk died later that year, on November 11, of cirrhosis of the liver. News reports from the time placed her at his bedside along with his sister and the prime minister. Subsequent news stories mentioned that she began a hunger strike out of grief, but was persuaded to abandon it.

Honored Before Her Death

Gökçen held the post of director of training for the Türkkuşsu Flight School, and the rank of lieutenant in the Turkish Air Force. In 1940 she married Kemal Esiner, an Air Force major, but he died in 1943. She retired in 1955 and officially retired from flying in 1964. Her 1981 memoir, *A*

Life Along the Path of Atatürk, appeared as part of centenary celebrations of his birth. In early 2001 Istanbul's second international airport of Istanbul was named in her honor.

Gökçen died two months after the official opening of the airport, on March 22, 2001, at the Gulhane Military Medical Academy in Ankara, and was one of the last surviving family members of Atatürk's immediate family. In the decades following her adoptive father's death, his firm commitment to the separation of church and state in Turkey was still under attack by more conservative Islamic forces in the country. "There are some unfortunates who are trying to destroy this great individual," she said a year before her death, according to Turgut, the author of her obituary in London's *Independent* newspaper. "I condemn these attacks. May God keep this country on the path which he drew."

Books

Mango, Andrew, *Atatürk: The Biography of the Founder of Modern Turkey,* Overlook Press, 2000.

Periodicals

Economist, March 27, 2004.
Independent (London, England), March 24, 2001.
New York Times, January 22, 1940.
Times (London, England), November 11, 1938.

Online

"Sabiha Gökçen (1913–2001)," Hargrave Pioneers, http://www .ctie.monash.edu.au/hargrave/gokcen.html (November 24, 2006).
"Turkish Heroine's Roots Spark Row," BBC News, http://www .news.bbc.co.uk/2/hi/europe/3519561.stm (November 24, 2006). □

Ernst Hans Josef Gombrich

Austrian-born British writer and educator Ernst Gombrich (1909–2001) penned *The Story of Art* **(1950), a textbook that dominated its field like few others in the twentieth century. Reprinted more than 15 times and translated into 33 languages, including Chinese, by the century's end,** *The Story of Art* **introduced students all over the world to European art history.**

The book was successful partly because it was both accessible and philosophical. Originally written for young people, it featured Gombrich's clear, jargon-free writing. But it also made use of many of its author's fresh, original ideas about the nature of art—ideas upon which he expanded in a large collection of further writings. An individual whose curiosity and interests extended from ancient Greek sculpture to teddy bears, Gombrich was an

influential teacher in both Britain and the United States, and was generally considered one of the most penetrating thinkers of his age.

Mother Turned Pages for Brahms

Ernst Hans Josef Gombrich was born in Vienna, Austria, on March 30, 1909. Gombrich's professional family, of Jewish descent, had adopted a nonsectarian Protestant faith. His father, Karl, was a lawyer and an official with Austria's bar association. His interest in the arts was perhaps inherited from his mother, Leonie, who had studied music with composer Anton Bruckner and had turned the pages of sheet music for an even greater Viennese composer, Johannes Brahms. Gombrich himself became a good cellist. The psychoanalyst Sigmund Freud was a family friend.

World War I disturbed the family's prosperous existence. Allied border controls after the war resulted in widespread famine in Vienna, and Gombrich and his sister were sent, under the auspices of Britain's Save the Children charitable organization, to live for nine months with the family of a Swedish carpenter who built coffins.

Back in Vienna, Gombrich attended a high school called the Theresianum, suffering impatiently in his classes because he found them too easy, but learning a great deal on his own. He was interested in art from the beginning and wrote a long essay on art history while still in high school, but his reading covered diverse subjects. *Scientific American* magazine counted him among its subscribers. At Vienna University, Gombrich studied with one of the most influential founders of modern art history, Julius von Schlosser. He wrote a thesis on the sixteenth-century Italian artist Giulio Romano, a successor to Michelangelo, and he had a gift for explaining art to young people. He believed that the features of artworks resulted from efforts by artists to solve problems specific to their own situations rather than from a vague spirit of the time or timeline of historical development. This approach was to become central to Gombrich's mature writings about art. He apparently enjoyed writing for children; his first book, published in 1936, was called *Weltgeschichte für Kinder* (World History for Children). It was translated into several languages, although never into English. The book's success was fortunate, for anti-Semitism was hampering his search for an academic position.

Fled Austrian Fascism

In 1936 Gombrich married classical pianist Ilse Heller, and the two had a son, Richard, who became a professor of Sanskrit. Gombrich at that time could already see that his parents' conversion to Protestantism would count for nothing with Austria's new fascist government. He left the country, taking a job as a research assistant at the Warburg Institute in London, a private art library that had moved its collections from Germany to England as cultural life in Germany deteriorated under the Nazi regime. In 1938 he was able to help his parents flee Austria as well. That year he began teaching art history classes at London's Courtauld Institute, and he started writing a book about caricature with fellow art historian Ernst Kris. The book was never published, but it was at this time that Gombrich adopted the name E. H. Gombrich for professional purposes—he was irritated by the double "Ernst" that would have resulted on the projected title page.

With the outbreak of World War II in 1939, Gombrich began to serve his new country as a radio monitor with the British Broadcasting Corporation (BBC), translating German broadcasts for intelligence purposes. He stayed in this post until the war's end in 1945, using the work as a way of learning to write English well, and when Adolf Hitler committed suicide, Gombrich personally carried the news to British prime minister Winston Churchill.

After the war Gombrich returned to the Warburg Institute and resumed working on the book that became *The Story of Art*. He had begun writing it in 1937 in response to a commission from the publisher of *Weltgeschichte für Kinder*, and it was originally aimed at young readers. Gombrich's clear, accessible style, however, proved to be ideal for students of all ages. *The Story of Art* was published in 1950 by Phaidon. The book was composed in an unusual way: Gombrich dictated it to a secretary. "There really is no such thing as art," the text famously began. "There are only artists."

What Gombrich meant was that art resulted from the efforts of artists to solve specific problems at specific times. He was not interested in treating art as an eternal pursuit of beauty. "If you try to formulate a principle for beauty in art, somebody can show you a counter-example," he pointed out, as quoted in the *Times* of London. And he never collected art personally. Nor did he see art as the expression of some vague zeitgeist or spirit of its times. He might at times tie art to philosophical ideas, but only in a very specific way. Instead, Gombrich looked at the situations in which specific artworks were created: who commissioned them, where they were to be put, what they were intended to accomplish, and what technical difficulties the artist faced as a result of these factors.

Appointed Oxford Professor

The Story of Art has always had its critics. Gombrich had little sympathy for modern art, with its stress on formal principles and its relentless innovation, and he did not explore art of the non-Western world in any depth. Gombrich's book, however, produced a new generation of students with fresh insights into familiar paintings, and his academic career took off after its publication. Maintaining his association with the Warburg Institute (later part of the University of London) for many years, he became its director in 1959. But he also had stints as an art history professor at Oxford (1950–53) and Cambridge (1961–63) universities, and at Cornell University in New York State (1970–77), and held numerous visiting professorships and lectureships.

In public lectures, such as the prestigious Mellon lecture series he gave in Washington, D.C., in 1956, Gombrich did not simply strive to give entertaining presentations. Instead he treated them as occasions for serious thought, and he took the opportunity to formally develop some of the ideas about art and psychology that lay behind *The Story of Art*. Many of Gombrich's books were reworked versions of lectures he had given. *Art and Illusion* (1960), one of the

most famous, was based on the Mellon lectures of 1956, and it explored how important convention was in the perception of artworks. Artists can never, Gombrich contended, simply draw or paint what they see, but depend on a kind of shorthand based on expectations derived from what audiences have already seen.

In his lectures and writings, Gombrich expanded on his psychological ideas. In later years he enjoyed using the example of the drawings of human beings that were sent out in unmanned probes as they roamed the universe, hoping to communicate something about human beings and their place in the cosmos to any alien beings who might encounter the craft. Any such alien, Gombrich pointed out, would have no frame of reference for interpreting the crude drawings of human beings they would find—unless they happened to have human-like hands they would think, for instance, that the woman whose hand was pictured in profile in one of the drawings actually had a claw. Gombrich applied the same kind of reasoning at a more specific level to famous paintings and to the assumptions that audiences made when they viewed them. He was delighted by new forms of representation that depended on representational assumptions, and he once wrote an essay about teddy bears, pointing out that they were a characteristically modern phenomenon.

Some of Gombrich's later books, such as *The Cartoonist's Armory* (1963) and *Shadows: The Depiction of Cast Shadows in Western Art* (1996) dealt with specific topics within his more general field of ideas about psychology and representation. Other books were collections of essays and speeches on various topics; some of the most widely read included *Meditation on a Hobby Horse, and Other Essays on the Theory of Art* (1963), *The Image and the Eye: Further Studies in the Psychology of Pictorial Representation* (1981), and *Topics of Our Times: Issues in Learning and Art* (1991). Between 1966 and 1988 he also wrote a four-volume series of *Studies in the Art of the Renaissance,* and he maintained a lifelong interest in the art of the ancient world. From 1959 until his retirement in 1976, he held the post of professor of the history of the Classical tradition at London University.

Despite the reliance of his ideas on the specifically modern science of psychology, Gombrich was not noted as a supporter of modern art. One of his most widely read articles appeared in *Atlantic* magazine in 1958; he gave it the title *The Vogue of Abstract Art,* but editors gave it the more provocative title of *The Tyranny of Abstract Art.* He disliked what he saw as a preoccupation with novelty in twentieth-century art, and he devoted a book, *The Ideas of Progress and Their Impact on Art,* to the question of art and its relationship to ideologies spawned by technological change. Gombrich was never categorizable as a strict conservative, however, and he did champion some modern artists, including the semi-abstract British sculptor Henry Moore.

In any event, he lived long enough to see representational modes of art come to the fore once again. Gombrich remained active into his tenth decade, writing and lecturing despite declining health. He died in London on November 3, 2001, with enough finished work on his desk to allow for the publication of a posthumous volume, *The Preference for* the Primitive: Episodes in the History of Western Taste and Art. By that time, an estimated two million copies of The Story of Art had been sold. Gombrich's intellectual legacy was enormous, extending to art history classes in far-flung community colleges where an instructor might point out some kind of distortion of reality in a famous painting and asked the students in attendance why the artist might have done it that way.

Periodicals

Daily Telegraph (London, England), November 6, 2001.
Guardian (London, England), November 5, 2001.
Independent (London, England), November 6, 2001.
GoodBye! The Journal of Contemporary Obituaries, October-December 2001.
New York Times, November 7, 2001.
Times (London, England), November 6, 2001.

Online

Contemporary Authors Online, Gale, 2006, reproduced in Biography Resource Center, Thomson Gale, 2006, http://www.galenet.galegroup.com/servlet/BioRC (December 15, 2006).
☐

Mal Goode

As a network news reporter, Malvin Russell Goode (1908–1995) was the first African American to hold a regular on-air job in the journalism field. He started out in radio news in Pittsburgh before he was hired by ABC television to cover the United Nations in New York City. The move made his career. He stayed in this post for 20 years, inspiring other journalists to follow in his footsteps. He covered civil rights marches and brought civil rights issues to the public eye. He was praised by other journalists as an honest reporter, and he showed a professionalism that impressed everyone he met.

Humble Beginnings in Pennsylvania

Goode was born on February 13, 1908, in White Plains, Virginia, but his family moved to Homestead, Pennsylvania, near Pittsburgh when he was very young. He was the third of four boys and two girls: James, William, Mary, Allan, and Ruth. His grandparents had once been slaves, and their history informed Goode's entire family life, giving them ambition and determination. His mother went to West Virginia State University. A great proponent of education, she stressed its importance to her children. Goode would remember these lessons for the rest of his life as can be seen by his determination and his interest in events that affected the world.

His father had very little education, but was a hard worker and stressed to his children the importance of finding work and being as good as possible at it. Goode's father worked at the Carnegie Steel Company and eventually moved up to the highest position a black man could have at that time in the company—that of first helper in the open hearth. When World War I ended, he opened a fish and poultry business. Along with the lessons Goode learned from his mother, he added to that the lessons his father taught him, those of hard work and industriousness. Goode often credited this beginning with his success throughout his life.

Started Out in a Steel Mill

Goode grew up and attended school in Homestead, Pennsylvania. During high school he got a job working nights at the steel mill where his father worked, and he continued working there throughout his college years at the University of Pittsburgh. He earned a bachelor of arts degree in 1931, but he continued his steel mill job after graduation, staying there until 1936 because jobs were hard to find during the Great Depression. He felt his luck at having such a good job, and spent time putting aside money for the future.

In 1936 Goode managed to get a different job, this time as a probation officer for Pittsburgh's juvenile court. He also worked as a director of boys' works at the Pittsburgh Young Men's Christian Association (YMCA). At that time the YMCA offered many inspirational and popular programs for urban children and for the community at large. Goode worked hard to rid the YMCA of some of its discrimination, which was rampant at the time, and he had some success in his endeavors. Sometime in the 1940s Goode took on the position of manager at the Pittsburgh Housing Authority, where he stayed for six years.

Entered Field of Journalism

It was not until 1948, when Goode was 40 years old, that he began a career in journalism, although it was something he had long considered. He was offered a job at the *Pittsburgh Courier,* Pittsburgh's premiere African-American newspaper. At that time the *Courier* was the most popular and bestselling paper of its type in the United States. Goode then decided to try his hand at some another form of broadcasting, moving over to include radio broadcasts in his working life. He began with a 15-minute news show for the station KQV.

It seemed he had found his calling, for he not only enjoyed the work, he was also good at it. From this one small radio job Goode moved to the station WHOD to do a daily five-minute broadcast, a consistent job that allowed Goode to gain much experience in the world of broadcasting. This was expanded into a full-blown news show that Goode took on with his sister Mary. He became the news director of WHOD radio station in 1952. He had not, however, lost his love of print journalism, and he kept his job at the *Courier,* later becoming the first African-American member of the National Association of Radio and Television News Directors.

First Black Reporter for ABC News

In 1962 ABC News was looking for an African-American reporter. They realized that their base of reporters was all white, and they set out to rectify this problem. Goode was recommended to ABC by one of his friends, baseball player Jackie Robinson, and was chosen from among nearly 40 candidates. He won the position because of his skill and professionalism, and in a history-making event, he was assigned to cover the United Nations in New York City, a job coveted by many reporters. He was the first black reporter hired by ABC.

Only a few months after he took the job with ABC, Goode had to cover the Cuban missile crisis, when it looked like the United States and the Soviet Union might go to war because of the presence of Russian nuclear weapons in Cuba. Goode covered the debates on the topic at the United Nations, taking the difficult and contentious subject and making it accessible to Americans everywhere. He was said to have distinguished himself in the reporting, leading the way for more equality in news coverage across the country. Whereas previously the news had centered around white concerns and issues, there began to be more news about under-represented minorities. This became especially obvious in the 1960s when race riots occurred in Detroit, Los Angeles, and elsewhere. News teams had a hard time covering both sides of the story, and there were few reporters who could do so. Goode was one of the few who was sent in to cover the riots, and he did so with respect and sympathy.

Goode Refused to Be Pigeon-Holed

Goode went on to cover such important issues as the assassination of Malcolm X and the shooting of Martin Lu-

ther King, Jr. But he refused to be pigeonholed into writing only about the subject of race. He covered everything and anything newsworthy that he found to be of interest to him and of importance in the world. He was a huge proponent of journalists helping young people become good future journalists. With that idea in mind, in 1963 Goode took a trip overseas with other black colleagues to help teach journalism in Nigeria, Tanzania, and Ethiopia.

Goode remained working at the United Nations until the 1980s. He then left that post to become a consultant for ABC, although he kept an office at the United Nations Building until he was almost 80 years old and retired from journalism. He also sometimes reported on international affairs for the National Black Network, and was often asked to speak in public about his years as a journalist and about current affairs, as well as civil rights and important events going on at the United Nations.

Goode married Mary Lavelle, with whom he would eventually have six children: Robert, Malvin Jr., Richard, Ronald, Roberta, and Rosalia. He died of a stroke in 1995, at the age of 87, at Margret's Memorial Hospital in Pittsburgh. Those attending his funeral at Pittsburgh's Lincoln Avenue Church of God recalled all the wonderful things he had done as a journalist. *Jet* magazine quoted Peter Jennings, a fellow journalist, as having said that "Mal could have very sharp elbows. If he was on a civil rights story and anyone even appeared to give him any grief because he was black he made it more than clear that this was now a free country. . . . He taught us a lot."

Throughout his lifetime Goode was sought after for public appearances, and he was a member of numerous organizations, including the Association of Radio-TV Analysts, the National Association of Radio and TV News Directors, and the United Nations Correspondents Association, for which he served as president in 1972. Also in 1972 Goode took his place in the President's Plan for Progress Committee alongside other corporate representatives. He was a member of 100 Black Men in New York. He consulted with the National Black Network and was a trustee for the First Baptist Church of Teaneck, New Jersey.

Goode acquired many awards during his career, including the Mary McLeod Bethune Award from Bethune-Cookman College and the Michelle Clark Award from Columbia University School of Journalism. In 1972 he received the Polish Government Award from the United Nations. In 1964 he was named Man of the Year by the Alpha Phi Alpha Fraternity, and was given their Award of Merit. The Pittsburgh *Post-Gazette* wrote, "Goode always remembered friends and family in his hometown of Homestead. He often returned there for homecoming at his boyhood church of Clark Memorial. Goode's creeds of life came from his parents: 'It does not cost you anything to treat people right' and 'You're no better than anyone else, and no one else is any better than you . . . now go out and prove it!'" And it would seem that that was exactly what he did.

Books

Almanac of Famous People, 8th edition, Gale Group, 2003.

Contemporary Black Biography, Volume 13, Gale Research, 1996.

Notable Black American Men, Gale Research, 1998.

Periodicals

New York Times, September 15, 1995.
Time, Sepember 25, 1995.

Online

"Broadcaster Mal Goode remembered hometown roots," *Post-Gazette.com,* http://www.post-gazette.com/magazine/20010214kids9.asp (January 2, 2007).

"Mal Goode," *African American Registry,* http://www.aaregistry.com/african_american_history/2167/Mal_Goode_the_first_Black_network_reporter (January 2, 2007). □

Christine Granville

Polish-born secret agent Krystyna Skarbek (1908–1952) was a heroine of World War II. Using the name Christine Granville, she risked death on multiple occasions in support of Britain's military campaign.

Skarbek, in the words of Murray Davies of London's *Mirror* newspaper, "was the very first Bond girl," serving as the model for Vesper Lynd in the first of novelist Ian Fleming's James Bond books, *Casino Royale.* However, Skarbek's feats, which included scaring off a team of German captors by raising her arms to disclose a live grenade under each one, were real, not fictional. The last chapters of her life, in which a wartime hero floundered during peacetime civilian life, were tragic ones.

Entered Beauty Contest

Krystyna Skarbek was born in or near Warsaw, Poland, on May 1, 1908. Her birth year has been widely reported as 1915, but researcher Ron Nowicki has described Polish and British documents that list the earlier date. She enjoyed an upper-class childhood as the daughter of bank official Jerzy Skarbek, who claimed the noble rank of Count, and his wife, Jewish-born Stephanie Goldfelder. Described as physically stunning from the very start, Skarbek entered the Miss Polonia contest, an early beauty pageant, in 1930 (a date that also supports the earlier birth year) and placed sixth.

After a first marriage to Karol Getlich when she was young, Skarbek married Jerzy Gizycki in Warsaw on November 2, 1938. In Gizycki, she found a husband whose taste for adventure matched her own; he had come to the United States earlier in life and panned for gold in the West. Later he became a diplomat, and after the marriage the couple departed for Addis Ababa, Ethiopia, so that Gizycki could take up the post of Polish consul there. They were in Ethiopia when German forces invaded Poland in September of 1939. Although the battle between Polish troops and the numerically superior Germans was short, underground resistance began along with the official campaign. Skarbek and her husband went to London, where Skarbek volun-teered to work as a spy. She had already prepared a plan: she would go to Budapest, Hungary (initially peaceful because Hungary was allied with Nazi Germany), print propaganda leaflets, and ski into Poland across the Tatra mountain range. An experienced skier, Skarbek had friends in the area who could serve as guides. She would then undertake intelligence missions and assist Polish resistance fighters in escaping from the country.

After some initial skepticism, the British Special Operations Executive (SOE) approved the plan, and Skarbek departed for Budapest on December 21, 1939. In Budapest she met the one-legged Polish war hero Andrzej Kowerski, and the two fell in love. Her marriage to Gizycki ended, but she and Kowerski never married. As their work for the SOE expanded, she was given the name Christine Granville (by which she was generally known in Britain after the war), and he became Andrew Kennedy. Skarbek's initial plan succeeded, as she barely managed, with the help of a member of Poland's Olympic ski team, to cross the mountains into her native country.

In Warsaw Skarbek located her mother, who as an aristocrat with Jewish blood was already in grave danger but refused to give up her work teaching in an underground school. She was later seized by police wearing swastikas, and was taken away, never to be seen again. Skarbek's intelligence activities in Warsaw were successful enough that posters advertising a large reward for her capture were put up in every railroad station in Poland. Working with spies for the Polish resistance, she assembled a dossier with photos of German troops massing on the borders of the Soviet Union, even though the two countries had signed a nonaggression pact.

Feigned Tuberculosis

Pressure on Skarbek and Kowerski increased in Hungary as well, and they were arrested early in 1941 and interrogated by the Gestapo, the German secret police. During her questioning, Skarbek bit her own tongue hard enough to draw blood, coughed hard, and succeeded in convincing a Hungarian doctor that she was suffering from tuberculosis. Kowerski, as a result of her supposed illness, was temporarily released as well. Skarbek was then smuggled out of Hungary in the trunk of a Chrysler car belonging to British ambassador Sir Owen O'Malley, crossing successfully into Yugoslavia. O'Malley, according to Davies, remarked that Skarbek was "the bravest person I ever knew. She could do anything with dynamite—except eat it." Kowerski, who had been working in Hungary under the cover occupation of used car dealer, followed in an Opel he claimed to have sold to someone across the border, and the two made their way through hundreds of miles of Nazi-occupied territory to SOE headquarters in Cairo, Egypt.

At first they were greeted with suspicion, for Syria, through which they had passed, was at the time under the control of the Nazi-collaborationist Vichy government in France, and the British assumed that they could not have made the trip successfully unless they were double agents. After a considerable period of investigation in London, Skarbek was once again in the SOE's good graces, partly because her prediction that Germany would invade the Soviet Union came true on June 22, 1941. British prime minister Winston Churchill, who had heard Soviet leader Josef Stalin dismiss the possibility, dubbed Skarbek his favorite spy.

The British considered sending Skarbek back to Hungary or to Poland itself, missions that were rejected because they were considered too likely to result in her death, although she herself was willing to undertake them. Finally, in July of 1944, she parachuted into southern France. Her mission was to assist French resistance fighters in advance of the American ground invasion of southern France at the end of the summer. The sangfroid of the new agent, code-named Pauline Armand, quickly became legendary among British intelligence agents. One day she was stopped near the Italian border by two German soldiers. Told to put her hands in the air she did so, revealing a grenade under each arm, pin withdrawn. When she threatened to drop them, killing all three of the group, the German soldiers fled. On another occasion she dived into a thicket to evade a German patrol, only to find herself face to face with a large Alsatian hound. She managed to quiet the dog while making noises suggesting to the Germans that they themselves were about to be ambushed, and she took advantage of the confusion to escape another close call.

Skarbek's most celebrated exploit was her rescue of her chief, Resistance leader Francis Cammaerts, who had been imprisoned by the Gestapo along with agent Xan Fielding. Skarbek first located Cammaerts by walking around the prison walls singing the American blues ballad "Frankie and Johnny," which they both knew; after some time, she heard Cammaerts singing along with her quietly. Then she convinced the police holding Cammaerts that she was his wife and managed to make contact with him in the prison. Finally, she identified herself as a British agent and said that she was the niece of a British General Montgomery, who was on his way to participate in the Allied invasion. She threatened Cammaerts's captors with reprisals if he and his agent were harmed, and demanded that she be allowed to negotiate the release of the British agents. Through a Belgian liaison, she secured an agreement that they would be freed in exchange for a ransom of two million francs, dropped by the SOE within 24 hours by parachute. Cammaerts and two other British prisoners were awakened the next morning and herded toward a car, convinced that they were about to be executed. But Skarbek, who could at any point during this process have been taken to a concentration camp like many other SOE agents, was waiting inside the car.

Turned Down for Diplomatic Post

Skarbek was awarded the French Croix de Guerre and the British George Medal, both high military honors, and she was appointed to the Order of the British Empire (OBE). After the war ended and her five months' of severance half-salary from the SOE ran out, however, Skarbek found it difficult to adapt to civilian life. She applied for British citizenship, but because of her murky past the processing of her application was slow. She worked as a hotel housekeeper, switchboard operator, and shopgirl at Harrods department store. She applied for a job at the British United

Nations mission in Geneva, Switzerland, only to be turned down because she was not British.

Well known for her sexual conquests during the time she spent in the field, Skarbek did not slow down after the war even as she remained emotionally faithful to Kowerski. Among the men to whom she was romantically linked was the novelist, former British spy, and future James Bond creator Ian Fleming. The two dated for a year, and Fleming, according to Davies, told a friend that Skarbek "literally shines with all the qualities and splendours of a fictitious character." Fleming gave the name Vesper Lynd to the double-agent "Bond girl" of his first James Bond novel, *Casino Royale* (1953). Vesper had been a nickname given to Skarbek by her father when she was a child.

Fleming finally married another woman, however, and for Skarbek things went from bad to worse. She suffered from depression and from injuries sustained when she was hit by a car. In desperation, she took a job in 1951 as a stewardess on the ocean liner *Rauhine*. The ship's captain ordered the crew to wear their wartime decorations, and Skarbek's splendid George Medal inspired resentment from her English-born crewmates. A bathroom attendant named George Muldowney took her side but misinterpreted Skarbek's gratefulness as a sign of romantic interest. Back in London he became obsessed with her and began to monitor her movements and communications. Skarbek prepared to leave her small hotel room on June 15, 1952, for a trip with Kowerski, their first contact in some years. Muldowney confronted her as she loaded a trunk and demanded to know how long she would be away. When she answered that it would be at least two years, he stabbed her in the chest and killed her. He pleaded guilty, telling an Old Bailey courtroom that to kill was the final possession. Kowerski lived on until 1988, never marrying, and his ashes were buried next to Skarbek's at London's St. Mary's Roman Catholic Cemetery.

Books

Binney, Marcus, *The Women Who Lived for Danger: The Women Agents of SOE in the Second World War,* Hodder and Stoughton, 2002.

Fielding, Xan, *Hide and Seek: The Story of a War-Time Agent,* Secker & Warburg, 1954.

Masson, Madeleine, *Christine: A Search for Christine Granville, G.M., O.B.E., Croix de Guerre,* Virago, 2005.

Periodicals

Daily Mail (London, England), October 26, 2005.
Mirror (London, England), January 13, 2007.
Times (London, England), August 8, 2000.

Online

Christine: A Search for Christine Granville, G.M., O.B.E., Croix de Guerre, Amazon.com, http://www.amazon.com (February 20, 2007).

"The Other Agents—Krystyna Skarbek (Christine Granville)—Biography," 64 Baker Street London W1: Special Operations Executive, http://www.64-baker-street.org/agents/agent_others/christine_granville_01.html (February 20, 2007). □

Zaha Hadid

The designs of Iraqi-born British architect Zaha Hadid (born 1950) are daring and visionary experiments with space and with the relationships of buildings to their urban surroundings.

Often named as the most prominent contemporary female architect, or singled out for notice because of her Iraqi Arab background, Hadid is significant beyond these accidents of birth for her intellectual toughness, her refusal to compromise on her ideas even when very few of them were being realized in concrete and steel. For many years, her designs filled the pages of architecture periodicals but were dismissed as impractical or as too radical, and Hadid even thought about giving up architecture after she suffered a major rejection in her adopted homeland of Britain in 1995. Her star began to rise internationally when her design for Cincinnati, Ohio's new Center for Contemporary Art was selected and built, earning worldwide acclaim. By the mid-2000s Hadid employed nearly 150 people in her London office and was working hard to keep up with new commissions that were coming in, offering her a chance to help reshape the world architectural landscape.

Toured Sumerian Ruins

Born in Baghdad, Iraq, on October 31, 1950, Zaha M. Hadid grew up in a well-educated Islamic family oriented toward Western multiculturalism. Her father was an executive and, for a time, the leader of a liberal Iraqi political party. The drawing ability that would later attract attention in art museums was first absorbed from her mother. Hadid's interest in architecture had roots in a trip her family took to the ancient Sumer region in southern Iraq, the site of one of the world's oldest civilizations, when she was a teenager. "My father took us to see the Sumerian cities," she told Jonathan Glancey of London's *Guardian* newspaper. "Then we went by boat, and then on a smaller one made of reeds, to visit villages in the marshes. The beauty of the landscape—where sand, water, reeds, birds, buildings, and people all somehow flowed together—has never left me. I'm trying to discover—invent, I suppose—an architecture, and forms of urban planning, that do something of the same thing in a contemporary way."

Hadid attended a Catholic school where French was spoken and nuns served as instructors, but which was religiously diverse. As Hadid told *Newsweek*'s Cathleen McGuigan, "the Muslim and Jewish girls could go out to play when the other girls went to chapel." Hadid's family expected her to pursue a professional career, and she studied math at the American University in Beirut, Lebanon. Her family left Iraq after the rise of dictator Saddam Hussein and the outbreak of war with neighboring Iran, but she has retained ties to both Iraq and Lebanon and has at times had difficulty talking to interviewers about the ongoing violence in her home region.

In 1972 Hadid moved to London (later becoming a British citizen) and enrolled at the Architectural Association School of Architecture. She has never married nor had children. "If [architecture] doesn't kill you, then you're no good," she explained to Glancey. "I mean, really—you have to go at it full time. You can't afford to dip in and out." By 1977 Hadid had received her degree, along with a special Diploma Prize, and she began working for a London firm, the Office of Metropolitan Architecture, founded by one of her key teachers, the similarly daring Dutch architect

Rem Koolhaas. One of her student projects was a design for a hotel built atop the span of London's Hungerford Bridge.

Hadid opened an office of her own in 1980, but at first her ideas were more in demand than her actual designs. Hadid taught courses at the Architectural Association and filled notebooks with one-of-a-kind ideas, some of which were published in architecture magazines or exhibited in galleries. Hadid began to enter design competitions, some of them research-oriented and others for buildings intended for construction. Her design for The Peak, a sports club jutting out horizontally from one of the mountain slopes that surround the city of Hong Kong, won the top prize in the institution's competition, but the building was never constructed. Hadid's competition entries in the 1980s and early 1990s were little known to the public at large but stirred up interest among her fellow architects, and even after she became famous, her website continued to list her competition prizes before focusing on her actual building projects.

Designed Fire Station

After several small projects, including one for the interior of the Moonsoon Restaurant in Sapporo, Japan, Hadid's first major building was constructed in 1993 and 1994: it was a small fire station, with numerous irregular angles (Hadid has been widely quoted as saying that since there are 360 degrees, she sees no reason to restrict herself to just one), on the grounds of the Vitra Furniture Company in Weil am Rhein, Germany. In 1994 Hadid seemed to be on the verge of a breakthrough: her design for the new Cardiff Bay Opera House in Britain's Wales region was selected for construction. It was to be an unorthodox building, with sharp angles and interior spaces that ran into and through one another rather than falling neatly into separate areas, but it was also planned to be inviting to the user, with an auditorium surrounded by glassed-in spaces that gave views of nearby Cardiff Bay.

With Hadid an unknown quantity and Britain's Prince Charles in the midst of a widely publicized campaign in favor of neo-traditional architecture in Britain, the design ran into trouble almost immediately. The design competition was reopened, and Hadid's design was once again named the winner, but the project's funder, Britain's National Lottery, eventually withdrew its commitment. Hadid was devastated. "It was such a depressing time," she recalled to Rowan Moore of the London *Evening Standard*. "I didn't look very depressed maybe but it was really dire. I made a conscious decision not to stop, but it could have gone the other way."

At the same time, Hadid began to amass a solid core of admirers among her staff, among architecture experts, and among ordinary observers. At the same time the Cardiff project was going down in flames, Hadid designed a temporary pavilion to house an exhibit for the architecture magazine *Blueprint* at a builders' convention. She had to present the structure, described by Moore as "a thing of flying steel," to a gathering of the magazine's advertisers, most of whom greeted it initially with silence. But an executive from a firm that made portable toilets stood up and said "I think it's bloody marvelous" (according to Moore), and began

applauding. The other advertisers joined in, and Hadid gained a moment in the building-trade spotlight.

As clients became more and more fascinated with Hadid's plans, some of the plans advanced from theory to reality. She designed the unique Bergisel Ski Jump on a mountain near Innsbruck, Austria, and a parking garage and transit station in suburban Strasbourg, France, that later won the Mies van der Rohe Award from the European Union. In 1998 came the biggest commission yet: the Lois and Richard Rosenthal Center for Contemporary Art in Cincinnati, popularly known as the Contemporary Arts Center.

Sidewalk Incorporated into Structure

The new building had to fit the confines of a narrow street corner lot in downtown Cincinnati, but Hadid made a virtue of necessity by linking the museum's internal and external environments: the outdoor sidewalk continued into the building, where it propelled visitors toward a sleek black central staircase that melded dramatically into the structure's back wall. As viewers ascended the staircase they looked into galleries that completely overturned the usual neutral conception of museum display spaces—the galleries had different shapes and sizes, and each one seemed to present something new to those approaching. "Not many people voluntarily walk up six stories anywhere," noted Joseph Giovannini of *Art in America*, "but Hadid's space so intrigues visitors that few think of bypassing the experience by hitching a ride on the elevator: they sense they would miss chapters." A bonus in Hadid's design was its economy: the building used only common materials, and construction costs came in at a reasonable $230 per square foot.

Hadid's creative fulfillment of a plum commission raised her international profile considerably. Where Hadid had sometimes been considered abrasive and difficult to work with, now she was hailed as a pioneer who had stuck to her vision even while facing difficult obstacles. At times, Hadid ascribed the resistance her ideas encountered to her gender and ethnicity. She also conceded that her work and personality were challenging. "I am eccentric, I admit it," she told Moore, "but I am not a nutcase."

Hadid's next major American commission came from Bartlesville, Oklahoma, site of the Price Tower designed by legendary American architect Frank Lloyd Wright. Hadid was hired to design a museum adjoining the Wright building—a choice that made sense, for Hadid was sometimes compared to Wright for her futuristic designs and her visionary rethinking of the relationships between humans and buildings. In 2006 it was one of Wright's most famous structures, the Guggenheim Museum in New York, that played host to a major retrospective of Hadid's work.

Indeed, the links between building and environment, and between building and user, loomed larger in Hadid's thinking as her fame grew and commissions poured into her office. "I started out trying to create buildings that would sparkle like isolated jewels; now I want them to connect, to form a new kind of landscape, to flow together with contemporary cities and the lives of their peoples," she told Glancey. A new factory she designed for German automaker BMW was laid out in such a way that workers and management personnel crossed paths more frequently.

In 2004 Hadid was awarded the Pritzker Architecture Prize, considered the profession's highest honor. She was the first woman to receive the award. In the mid-2000s she finally received a full-scale commission in the British Isles, for a cancer-care building called Maggie's Centre in Fife, Scotland. Highly visible Hadid buildings planned or underway included a bridge in the Persian Gulf state of Abu Dhabi, a movie theater complex in Barcelona, Spain, and several new museums. Greater international exposure seemed assured in a project waiting further down the line: the aquatics building for the 2012 Summer Olympics to be held in London. And she seemed to be outdoing herself with each successive design. "Co-curator Monica Montagut quotes Hadid's statement that 'I still believe in the impossible,' " noted Raymund Ryan in his *Architectural Review* commentary of Hadid's Guggenheim exhibition. "Judging from this display in New York City, there are few limits to what Hadid might do next."

Books

Newsmakers, Issue 3, Thomson Gale, 2005.

Periodicals

Architectural Review, April 2005; July 2006.
Art in America, November 2003.
Evening Standard (London, England), August 25, 2006.
Financial Times, October 17, 2006.
Guardian (London, England), October 9, 2006.
Newsweek, May 19, 2003.
Time, April 5, 1999.

Online

On-line Media Kit, Pritzker Architecture Prize, 2004, http://www.pritzkerprize.com/2004/mediakit.htm (October 20, 2006).
"Profile," Zaha Hadid Architects Official Website, http://www.zaha-hadid.com (October 20, 2006).
"Zaha M. Hadid," archINFORM, http://www.archinform.net (October 20, 2006). ☐

Gunther von Hagens

German anatomist Gunther von Hagens (born 1945) has both inspired wonder and created controversy with his plastination technique of preserving human bodies and his extraordinarily widely viewed *Body Worlds* traveling museum exhibit.

*B*ody Worlds showed dissected and opened-up human corpses, preserved with the plastination process and mounted in lifelike, sometimes humorous poses. The complex workings of the human body were displayed in a comprehensible way, even to visitors with little background in human anatomy. Von Hagens saw himself as an heir to the artists who first made accurate anatomical drawings during the Renaissance era. The object of the

exhibition, he was quoted as saying by BBC News, was "education and enlightenment." The throngs who came to the exhibition seemed for the most part enthusiastic (although guards kept a close lookout for queasy visitors); one museum in Mannheim, Germany, had to remain open for 24 hours a day for a short period in order to accommodate overflow crowds. Some observers, however, were less enthusiastic. British sociologist Tom Shakespeare, writing in *Science,* called von Hagens a "showman who uses the cover of science to reap millions from voyeuristic audiences."

Suffered from Hemophilia

Von Hagens was born Gunther Gerhard Liebchen in Pose (now Poznan) in German-occupied Poland on January 10, 1945. His family moved around eastern Germany in a horse-drawn wagon during the last months of World War II, finally settling in the small city of Greiz in the Thuringia region. As a child, von Hagens liked building cardboard airplanes and was fascinated by the work of a sculptor neighbor. He suffered from hemophilia, a blood disorder that carries a strong risk of dangerous bleeding even after minor injuries, and when he was six he experienced a crisis episode due to internal bleeding in his forehead, and heard doctors say they thought he would die.

Von Hagens survived but was hospitalized for 11 months. He had plenty of time to watch the doctors and nurses who circulated through the children's ward, engaged in a large variety of medical monitoring activities. "I came to the conclusion that the body must be very, very interesting," von Hagens told Russell Working of the *Chicago Tribune*. Despite the risks of working with sharp instruments, von Hagens formed the ambition to pursue a medical career. Soon he was cutting open insects he had found, and at 14 he dissected a calf kept on an uncle's farm. Initially turned down for university study in East Germany's strictly tracked educational system, von Hagens worked as an elevator attendant, mailman, and nurse. The last of these heightened his interest in medicine, and he was finally accepted to the University of Jena Medical School in 1965.

In 1968 von Hagens joined student protesters who demonstrated against the Soviet Union's invasion of Czechoslovakia, and in January of 1969, on the pretext that he was on vacation, he made his way to the Czech border with Austria and attempted twice to cross. On the second try he was arrested and spent 21 months in an East German prison. He was freed in a cash-for-release deal worked out by the West and East German governments, and he enrolled at the University of Lübeck Medical School in West Germany. He did a residency on an island where duty-free liquor was sold, where his work gained him firsthand experience of the effects of alcoholism on the human body—effects that he would later demonstrate graphically in *Body Worlds*. In 1974 he received his medical degree, and the following year he married a classmate, Cornelia von Hagens. Disliking the name Liebchen, which means "little darling," he took her last name. The couple raised three children but later divorced. In 1992 he married Angelina Whalley, a physician who became his business manager.

Bored by his specialty of anesthesiology, von Hagens took a job as a research assistant at the Institute of Pathology and Anatomy at the University of Heidelberg. In 1977 he invented the plastination process (he used the same word in German and English) that would determine the course of the rest of his life. The initial brainstorm came to him at a butcher's shop, and indeed plastination allowed medical students and researchers to use a device like a meat slicer to cut human internal organs into pieces of any desired size. In its essentials, plastination involved the injection of polymers—plastics—into a cadaver that had been frozen and then dehydrated.

Formed Company

Von Hagens devoted his research efforts over the next decade to refining his plastination technique, and he was awarded two German patents for his work. The initial aim of plastination was to guarantee a supply of human organs for medical schools, which have perennially experienced difficulties in obtaining cadavers for instructional purposes. Von Hagens formed a company of his own, Biodur Products, to distribute the materials necessary for plastination, and he organized an International Society for Plastination whose meetings were devoted to applications of the technique. In 1983 the Catholic Church in Rome asked von Hagens to plastinate a preserved heel bone of St. Hildegard of Bingen, a medieval nun, composer, and theologian who experienced mystical visions.

That was among the first indications von Hagens received that anyone aside from medical specialists would be interested in his work. He got another strong hint in 1988, when he worked late one night and noticed a custodian in the building staring in amazement at a group of plastinated body parts. As an experiment, von Hagens organized a small exhibition of plastinated organs in Pforzheim, Germany, and it drew appreciative crowds. Technical advances in the plastination technique went hand in hand with his expanding ambitions, and by 1993 he could plastinate an entire human body, opening it up and displaying it in a variety of ways.

When he suggested the exhibition that became *Body Worlds* to museums and university display spaces, most of them refused, convinced that the public would find the plastinated corpses nothing more than gruesome. Von Hagens persisted, however, and in 1995 he was invited to display his work at Juntendo University in Japan. More than 400,000 visitors came to the exhibition, which benefited from word of mouth over its two months of existence. Indeed, von Hagens pointed to a pattern in which *Body Worlds* opened to sparse crowds but then grew in attendance as early visitors told others about what they had seen. Expanded to a three-year run, *Body Worlds* drew 2.9 million Japanese visitors.

"Everything changed for me after Japan," von Hagens told John Bohannan of *Science*. Von Hagens and Whalley organized a *Body Worlds* exhibit in Mannheim, Germany, in 1997, and there he encountered his first taste of criticism from religious leaders and medical ethicists. Religious figures, however, were split on the merits of *Body Worlds*. "Some like it because they consider it evidence for the existence of God—who could have made the body better?," von Hagens observed to *New Scientist*. "Others don't like it because they say the dignity of the people has been taken away. And it also takes away their monopoly over the body and death." Von Hagens sometimes posed his bodies fancifully, following a tradition established in Renaissance anatomical drawings; one, in a tribute to a Rembrandt artwork, wore a top hat. Any controversies that arose may only have fueled the spectacular success of the Mannheim exhibit.

Differences in National Reactions

To a degree, the reactions to *Body Worlds* varied by country. The sharpest attacks came in Britain, where von Hagens fueled the flames by charging admission to a public autopsy he performed, and in Germany, where Andreas Nechama, chairman of the Jewish Congregation of Berlin, likened von Hagens to Nazi guards who made the skins of Holocaust victims into lampshades. Von Hagens was banned from entering the city of Munich for a time. None of the opposition to *Body Worlds* had much effect in reducing turnout; between June and November of 2002, 550,000 visitors came to London's Atlantis Gallery to see the exhibition. In the more religious United States, although von Hagens was refused a permit to transport some plastinated bodies into the state of Florida in 1998, *Body Worlds* gained a good deal of prestigious sponsorship. Presenting entities for the Great Lakes Science Center showing of *Body Worlds* in Cleveland, Ohio, for instance, included the giant Cleveland Clinic medical center.

The most serious charges leveled against von Hagens had to do with the acquisition of his plastinated cadavers. A Russian court convicted a medical examiner of supplying unclaimed corpses to von Hagens's German-based Institute for Plastination, one of several for-profit or academic enterprises he set up in various countries (others were in China and Kazakhstan). However, a Chinese government investigation of a rumor that *Body Worlds* specimens were the bodies of executed Chinese prisoners found no wrongdoing, and a German court reached the same conclusion. Von Hagens blamed the rumor on a disgruntled employee who hoped to launch a rival exhibition of his own. *Body Worlds* text panels stated that all of the bodies and body parts on display were those of donors who had volunteered for the process, and indeed every showing of the exhibition attracted donors who hoped for a kind of immortality after death. New controversy flared after the German magazine *Der Spiegel* reported that von Hagens's father had been a sergeant in the Nazi SS force during the war and had sent Polish prisoners to concentration camps. Von Hagens asserted that there was no evidence showing his father to have been a war criminal. Von Hagens, in rebutting his various critics, pointed not only to the educational value of the exhibit but also to possible health benefits; one of the most remarked-upon areas of the *Body Worlds* display showed a cigarette smoker's blackened lung, and one independent study of visitors to the exhibit in Germany found large percentages resolving to wean themselves from smoking and other unhealthful behaviors.

Von Hagens welcomed public attention, telling *Forbes* that "a good teacher is a good showman." None of the controversies dented attendance at *Body Worlds,* and the show's website as of early 2007 estimated worldwide attendance at almost 20 million. Von Hagens became wealthy; a *Forbes* magazine study found that he reaped net profits of $40 million from *Body Worlds* between 1999 and 2006, much of which he reinvested in his various research institutes and plastination centers. He had reason to be wary of potential competitors, for companies in the United States and China launched similar touring exhibitions, such as *Our Body: The Universe Within,* showing bodies acquired in China and itself the subject of protests by Chinese Americans. Von Hagens mounted two new exhibitions in response, designated *Body Worlds 2* and *Body Worlds 3,* and his long-range planning included a new Museum of Man to be located in Germany—and plastination of his own body after his death.

Periodicals

Chicago Tribune, August 5, 2005.
Economist, March 23, 2002.
Forbes, January 30, 2006.
New Scientist, March 23, 2002.
Science, August 29, 2003.
Student BMJ, August 2002.

Online

"A Life in Science," *Body Worlds Official Website,* http://www.bodyworlds.com/en/gunther_von_hagens.life.html (January 21, 2007).
"The Plastination Professor," BBC News, http://www.news.bbc.co.uk/1/hi/health/2494643.stm (January 21, 2007). □

Stephen Harper

Stephen Harper (born 1959), an often-underestimated Canadian politician, became his country's first conservative prime minister in 13 years when he led his party to victory in January of 2006. Harper got into politics as part of a conservative revolt against Canada's traditional center-right party, then rethought his movement's strategy and engineered a merger between his upstart right-wing party and the old center-right. As prime minister, he has tried to increase his party's appeal while negotiating with the other three parties in Parliament.

A Young Conservative

The future prime minister was born in Toronto, Ontario, on April 30, 1959. He grew up in a middle class family in the Toronto suburbs. In 1978, after graduating from high school, he moved to Alberta. He worked in the oil industry there, and soon enrolled at the University of Calgary, a bastion of conservative thinking, where he earned bachelor's and master's degrees in economics. Harper and a fellow grad student often debated politics and free market economic ideas outside of class, avidly watched American conservative William F. Buckley's television show *Firing Line,* and followed the careers of Margaret Thatcher and Ronald Reagan, the conservative leaders of Great Britain and the United States.

Not impressed by the center-right politics of then-prime minister Brian Mulroney's Progessive Conservative party, Harper joined the new right-wing Reform Party, which was mostly based in Alberta, a conservative province. The Reform Party made Harper its policy chief in 1987, and he ran for a seat in the Canadian Parliament in 1988 and lost. In 1991 he met Laureen Teskey, a graphic designer, at a Reform Party convention, and they married. They have two children, Benjamin and Rachel.

In 1993 Harper again ran for Parliament, and won. He spent four years in opposition to the center-left Liberal Party, which had won a majority. Harper sharply criticized Liberal rule; he called Canada "a northern European welfare state in the worst sense of the term," meaning that he felt Canada had become too much like socialist-influenced countries such as Sweden. He stepped down from Parliament in 1997 to become vice president of the conservative activist group the National Citizens' Coalition, which argued that the

federal government, with its power base in the eastern provinces of Ontario and Quebec, was not concerned enough about western Canada. He eventually became the coalition's president.

Leaving Parliament was a sign that Harper's political strategy was changing. In a 1998 speech, he revealed that he had decided two years earlier, during a vacation from Parliament after the birth of his son, Benjamin, that the Reform Party could never win a nationwide majority on its own. Reform's principles needed to be combined with the Progressive Conservatives' "penchant for incremental change and strong sense of honorable compromise," he said, according to John Geddes of *Maclean's*. A few years later, Harper made such a merger happen. In 2002 he was elected to Parliament again and successfully ran to replace social conservative Stockwell Day as leader of the former Reform Party, renamed the Canadian Alliance. That made him official leader of the opposition in Parliament. In 2003 a new leader took over the Progressive Conservatives, and Harper negotiated with him to merge the two parties, co-founding the Conservative Party of Canada. Harper became head of the new party in March of 2004.

Harper Took Power

Once Harper became Canada's opposition leader, the governing Liberals did their best to portray him as a right-wing ideologue. They often criticized his public statements from 2000 and 2001, in which he contrasted conservative, free-market-friendly Alberta with the liberal rest of Canada.

In March of 2003, when the Liberal-led Canadian Parliament came out against the United States and Great Britain's invasion of Iraq, Harper rose to dissent, charging that the government had "betrayed Canada's history and values," according to Doug Struck of the *Washington Post*. "The government has for the first time in our history left us outside our British and American allies in their time of need."

When a national election was scheduled in June of 2004, Harper ran as head of the Conservatives. He would have replaced Paul Martin as prime minister if the Conservatives had won. But Martin attacked Harper for supporting the Iraq war, which was unpopular in Canada. Martin also pointed to Harper's pro-American comments to suggest that he was too sympathetic to conservative Republicans in the United States, especially President George W. Bush, who was also unpopular among Canadians. The charge was potent, since Canada's political culture is more liberal than its southern neighbor's, and because Canadians often feel overshadowed by the United States.

Personality was another factor in the race. Harper was still not well known to Canadians, in part because he is unusually private for a politician—"shy to the point of being aloof," observed Clifford Krauss of the *New York Times*. "He is known to have a fiery temper, and he barely disguises his distrust for reporters. His sense of humor on the campaign trail was most revealing in its self-deprecating jokes about his lack of charisma." As a reporter for the *Economist* noted, "when a television reporter asked him to repeat on camera a few sentences 'with feeling,' he shot back, 'I don't do feeling.'" The Liberals won the election, but the election still marked something of a comeback for Conservatives, who increased their bloc in Parliament by 25 seats. That included some wins in Ontario, usually a liberal stronghold.

Two years later, fate gave Harper another chance. The Liberals were tainted by a scandal: a multi-million-dollar government public relations fund in Quebec had been revealed to be a slush fund for Liberal politicians and their supporters. When a new election was scheduled for January of 2006, Harper, learning the lessons of his 2004 defeat, worked to present himself as a moderate who had shifted from his earlier hard-line conservatism. "Over the course of a decade, people's views evolve somewhat and situations change," he told reporters, according to Krauss. "I deal with the situation as I find it." He stressed issues such as anti-corruption reforms in government, a sales tax cut, and longer prison sentences for criminals. He deemphasized foreign policy and divisive social issues. He favored increasing the size of the Canadian military and said he would reexamine Canada's decision not to participate in the U.S. attempt to create a missile defense shield, but he said he would not send troops to Iraq.

Martin again portrayed Harper as a right-winger too close to U.S. conservatives, but this time the strategy did not work. The Conservatives won the election, which took place on January 23, taking 124 seats, the largest bloc in Parliament. Harper was sworn in as prime minister on February 6. Because the vote was split among four parties, however, the Conservatives won only about 36 percent of the popular vote and did not win a majority in Parliament. Instead, Harper became the leader of a minority government, which needs to attract votes from one of the other parties to pass legislation.

Harper Was In Charge

Still a shrewd strategist, Harper immediately reached out to Quebec, hoping to build conservative support there. It was a bold move, since conservatives from Alberta, Harper's base, are usually opposed to addressing mostly-French-speaking Quebec's long list of grievances. But Harper quickly altered the federal budget to give the provinces more control over spending, a popular move in both the west and Quebec. He also gave Quebec a formal role in Canada's delegation to a United Nations' cultural organization. The hope was that Quebec might elect more Conservatives in the next national election, strengthening the party's fragile plurality in Parliament. By November, Harper introduced a bill into Parliament that would declare Quebec a separate nation within a united Canada. He was aiming to pre-empt a similar proposal written by the Bloc Quebecois, the Quebec separatist party in Parliament, that would call Quebec a separate nation, without the "united Canada" language. Harper's bill quickly passed.

In May of 2006, Harper won a significant victory for his pro-American foreign policy, but by the barest of margins. A bill to keep Canada's contingent of 2,300 troops in Afghanistan passed Parliament by a vote of 149 to 145. Ever since the U.S. invasion of Afghanistan in 2001 in response to the September 11 terrorist attacks, Canada had participated in a multi-national force supporting the democratic Afghan government. But the mission had become increasingly unpopular in Canada. "We just cannot sit back and let the Taliban or similar extremist elements return to power in Afghanistan," Harper argued, according to Krauss. The bill approved keeping the troops in Afghanistan until early 2009. But by September, Harper was forced to defend the deployment again. The Canadian troops suffered an increased number of casualties in mid-2006 as they took a wider role in the dangerous province of Kandahar. Four soldiers died in one day in September, and a U.S. plane accidentally killed another Canadian soldier a few days later. "The horrors of the world will not go away if we turn a blind eye to them, no matter how far off they may be," Harper said in a speech commemorating the fifth anniversary of the September 11 attacks, according to Christopher Mason of the *New York Times.*

As a candidate and opposition leader, Harper had spoken out against Canada's 2005 legalization of gay marriage. But his attempt to revisit the issue was rejected by Parliament in December of 2006 by a vote of 175 to 123. The three other parties in Parliament opposed the bill, as did 13 Conservatives.

As 2007 began, political commentators were anticipating that another election would probably take place sometime that year, possibly as early as spring, since minority governments in Canada usually only last a year or two. Harper was assumed to be calculating the best timing to call the election and strategizing how to increase his party's support among voters. As Canadians continued to ponder their leader's strengths and character, Paul Stanway, a columnist for the *Edmonton Sun,* sounded a sympathetic note. Harper's success at "reuniting Canada's fractious conservatives and returning them to government will surely stand as one of the great achievements of Canadian politics," he declared, "particularly if he can produce a majority government in 2007."

Periodicals

Chicago Tribune, November 28, 2006.
Economist, June 12, 2004.
Edmonton Sun, December 31, 2006.
Maclean's, June 14, 2004; May 9, 2005.
New Republic, January 30, 2006.
New York Times, March 21, 2004; January 16, 2006; January 25, 2006; February 11, 2006; May 18, 2006; September 28, 2006; November 23, 2006.
Wall Street Journal, May 15, 2006.
Washington Post, January 25, 2006; December 8, 2006.

Online

"Prime Minister Stephen Harper," *Prime Minister of Canada,* http://www.pm.gc.ca (December 31, 2006). □

Laura S. Haviland

American antislavery activist Laura Smith Haviland (1808–1898) is not as well known as the great writers and orators of the Abolitionist movement, those whose ideas rallied the Northern public to the antislavery cause. Her experiences, however, were representative of what happened to those in the trenches of the fight to abolish slavery, a long and often dangerous struggle that demanded total commitment from its troops.

Haviland was a resident of southeastern Michigan, where she operated a station on the Underground Railroad, the system of safe houses that conveyed fugitive slaves to Canada and freedom in the decades before the U.S. Civil War. Being part of the Underground Railroad was not a simple matter of opening one's home to slaves arriving under cover of night; it involved outwitting armed gangs, violent private investigators, and, after the passage of the Fugitive Slave Act of 1850, law enforcement officers bent on returning slaves to Southern plantations. Much of her autobiography, *A Woman's Life-Work,* reads like an adventure novel. Haviland also established Michigan's first school open to children of all races, and she went undercover in the South before the war to learn firsthand about conditions there. She worked as a nurse during the Civil War and later traveled to various locations, trying to establish new institutions that would put newly freed slaves on a solid financial footing.

Grew Up in Quaker Family

Haviland was born Laura Smith in Kitley Township, Leeds County, in what is now eastern Ontario. At the time of her birth on December 20, 1808, this was part of the British colonial province of Canada West. Her father, Daniel, was a Quaker minister, and her mother, Vermont-born Sene, was an elder in that church, which favored gender equality. When Laura was seven, the family moved to the largely wild Niagara County in New York, near the village of Cambria. The nearest schoolhouse was three miles away, and Laura was educated largely through her own interest in reading, with some help from a neighbor woman who had a daughter the same age as Laura. She had gone to school for four months in Canada, and in New York she borrowed every book she could find.

One of those books was a history of the slave trade by John Woolman, "of the capture and cruel middle passage of negroes," Haviland recalled in *A Woman's Life-Work*, "and of the thousands who died on their voyage and were thrown into the sea to be devoured by sharks, that followed the slave-ship day after day." She read the book until late at night, and even as her parents reassured her that the slave trade had been outlawed, she transferred her sympathies to the few African Americans she knew in her small town, men who often had to endure abuse from local groups of youths.

Another key experience of Haviland's youth came from the contrast she experienced between two of America's frontier religions. Although she was raised as a Quaker, her uncle Ira Smith was a Methodist, and she attended Methodist prayer meetings at her uncle's house. A woman with a powerful religious imagination who was moved by dreams and visions at various points in her life, she found herself drawn to the demonstrative interactions of Methodist worship more than to the more inward meditation of Quaker meetings. Her parents, however, put a stop to her visits. "This Methodist excitement is unprofitable, especially for children," they said, as Haviland recalled in *A Woman's Life-Work*. "They have an overheated zeal, that is not according to knowledge, and we do not think it best for thee to attend; we want our children at a suitable age to be actuated by settled principle, not mere excitement."

At 17 Laura married Quaker farmer Charles Haviland and temporarily set aside her religious quest. Her parents moved in 1826 to Raisin Township in Lenawee County, Michigan, near Adrian, in the first year of the county's existence. Laura and Charles Haviland and their two children joined them three years later, and at first Laura was occupied with the rigors of pioneer life in a 16-by-18-foot log cabin and with the responsibilities of raising a brood of children that eventually numbered eight.

Established Underground Railroad Station

Soon, however, the twinned issues of religion and slavery began to impinge upon her mind once again. Haviland became friends with another pioneer, Michigan abolitionist Elizabeth Margaret Chandler, and joined her in operating the Raisin Anti-Slavery Society, the first in the new state of Michigan. She played a major role in the society's activities after Chandler's death in 1834. The society's meetings were not sedate; two of them were menaced by gunfire from a local gang, which on one occasion hung a blackened doll from a tree outside the building where they were meeting and used it for target practice. The Havilands opened their home to fugitive slaves, making it the first Underground Railroad safe house in Michigan.

After an abortive attempt to start an integrated manual labor school in their home in 1837, Laura and Charles Haviland opened the Raisin Institute in 1839, "considered the first integrated, coeducational school to be opened anywhere in Michigan," according to Charles Lindquist in *The Antislavery–Underground Railroad Movement: Lenawee County, Michigan, 1830–1860*. Laura Haviland noted in *A Woman's Life-Work* examples of white students who arrived at the school and were shocked to find themselves sharing classroom space with African Americans but whose prejudices disappeared as they attended integrated classes.

The slavery question was troublesome for American Protestant churches in the 1830s and 1840s, for slavery had already been outlawed in Britain, and biblical teachings on human equality were plain. The Methodists, however, were more inclined than the Quakers to take the lead in opposing the institution of slavery, partly because Quaker teachings demanded a consensus of all members before undertaking a course of social activism. As a result, Haviland and her husband left the Quaker faith and joined the Wolf Creek Wesleyan Methodist church in 1841.

A turning point in Haviland's life came in 1845, when her entire family contracted erysipelas, a serious skin disease caused by a bacterium of the strep family. Haviland lost her husband, both parents, and one of her children to the disease. She herself contracted it and almost died, but recovered. Facing heavy debts, she was advised by creditors to put her affairs in the hands of a trusted male, but she refused and resolved to carry on with the Raisin Institute. Several creditors later relented on their terms, and, Haviland wrote, "secret praise ascended to Him who melts away the mountain that seems impassable, making a way where there seemed no way."

Reward of $3,000 Promised for Death

After her husband's death, Haviland began to travel more widely in her efforts to aid escaped slaves. A series of ruses she executed at a hotel in Toledo, Ohio, in 1846 succeeded in keeping a family of slaves out of the clutches of slave hunters, who finally overtook Haviland on a train near Sylvania, Ohio, and at gunpoint demanded the return of their property. "Man, I fear neither your weapons nor your threats; they are powerless," Haviland responded, as recalled in *A Woman's Life-Work*. "You are not at home— you are not in Tennessee. And as for your property, I have none of it about me or on my premises. We also know what we are about; we also understand, not only ourselves, but you." A $3,000 bounty was placed on Haviland's head by slave hunters.

It did not discourage Haviland in the least; she responded by broadening the geographic range of her activities. She made several trips to the key slave crossing point of Cincinnati, Ohio, on the border between slave and free states, on one occasion passing as black by joining a light-skinned black woman so that they could sneak onto a Kentucky plantation. She taught classes to ex-slaves in the basement of Zion Baptist Church and also established new schools in Toledo and at the Underground Railroad terminus of Windsor, Ontario. Beginning in 1852 she spent several years teaching school there.

Haviland's most daring trip occurred shortly before the outbreak of the Civil War, when she traveled to Little Rock, Arkansas, in an unsuccessful attempt to rescue the wife of a slave who had succeeded in reaching Michigan. Haviland traveled across the increasingly militant South, making notes on her experiences and answering frequent questions by saying that she was writing letters home. Masquerading as a traveling high-society woman, she struck up an acquaintance with the target family and wangled an invitation to their home. There she witnessed terrible beatings of slaves over minor deviations from procedure, and as she slipped out one night to talk to a few slave contacts she found herself face to face with a trio of bloodhounds. "I fixed my eyes upon the sparkling eyes of the leader, that came within six feet and stopped; soon the growl ceased, the lips dropped over the long tusks, the hair smoothed back, and he quietly walked off with his companions."

When the Civil War broke out, Haviland armed herself with letters of recommendation from Michigan's governor and from a congressional representative, and plunged into work supporting the Union. She nursed wounded soldiers and slaves, and she took up the cause of 3,000 Union soldiers held in hellish conditions on Gulf of Mexico islands, bringing about some improvement in their lot. After the war, Haviland set up schools in Kansas in order to meet the needs of African Americans who fled the rise of militant racism in the South in the 1870s. The towns of Haviland, Kansas, and Haviland, Ohio, were named after her. She worked for a time at the Freedman's Aid Bureau in Washington, D.C., where she became acquainted with the antislavery activist Sojourner Truth. One day the pair rode a streetcar together in defiance of the city's segregation laws, and the conductor attempted to force Truth to exit. Haviland interceded, whereupon the conductor asked whether Truth belonged to Haviland. "No," was Haviland's response, according to recollections of Truth appearing on the Havilands.com website, "she belongs to humanity."

Haviland wrote her autobiography, *A Woman's Life-Work*, in 1881; it is available online at the Project Gutenberg website, as well as on several other sites. She remained active until the end of a life that was unusually long and healthy although lacking in comforts and material resources. In later years she lived with a relative in Grand Rapids, Michigan. Laura Smith Haviland died on or around April 20, 1898. The location of her death has been variously reported as Grand Rapids and Grand Traverse County, Michigan, but the best contemporary report, an *Adrian Daily Telegram* article published on the day of her death, stated that she was living in Grand Rapids. A monument in her honor stands in front of Adrian's city hall.

Books

Danforth, Mildred E., *A Quaker Pioneer: Laura Smith Haviland, Superintendent of the Underground,* Exposition, 1961.
Haviland, Laura S., *A Woman's Life-Work,* Walden & Stowe, 1882.
Lindquist, Charles, *The Antislavery–Underground Railroad Movement in Lenawee County, Michigan, 1830–1860,* Lenawee County Historical Society, 1999.

Online

"Laura Smith Haviland: Wesleyan Pioneer," History's Women: The Unsung Heroines, http://www.historyswomen.com/womenoffaith/LauraSmithHaviland.htm (December 20, 2006).
"Lenawee County Michgian Monument #11: Dedicated to Laura Smith Haviland," http://www.geocities.com/lenaweemi/monu11.html (December 20, 2006).
"Mrs. Laura (Smith) Haviland—Philanthropist/Slavery Abolitionist," Havilands.com, http://www.havilands.org/HavilandsCom/Biographies/LauraSmithHaviland/index.html (February 14, 2007). □

Eliza Haywood

Pioneering English novelist Eliza Haywood (c. 1693–1756) was also a successful playwright and journalist. Though little is known about her early life, and her works were usually published anonymously, Haywood was an important figure in the history of British women's literature.

Her earliest works were immensely popular predecessors of the modern romance novel, but she also wrote satirical plays and novels whose themes foreshadowed a later generation of English literary lionesses, among them Jane Austen and the Brontë sisters. "Haywood's gifts as a storyteller held the attention of her audience," declared Jerry C. Beasley in a profile in the *Dictionary of Literary Biography*, "and some of her books were among the most successful and controversial (if not the most admired) works to be published during the first half of the eighteenth century."

Literary scholars have provided Haywood with a birthdate of 1693, but verifiable details about her background and family history have been lost to time. It was once surmised that she was born Eliza Fowler in London, where her father was a shopkeeper; later scholarship claims she was a product of Shropshire, a West Midlands county. Her surname was once thought to be the result of her marriage to a minister named Valentine Haywood, but subsequent investigations have cast doubt on this. What is known about Haywood, in her pre-literary career, was that she achieved some renown as a stage actor in Dublin, Ireland. The first notice of her name comes in a listing for *The History of Timon of Athens the Man-Hater,* a play staged at the Smock Alley Theatre in 1715.

Acting Led to Playwriting

In 1717 Haywood appeared in London and became a regular performer in plays at Lincoln's Inn Fields. This was a large park where a theater stood for nearly 200 years, and it was known that one of the venue's most famous producers and directors, John Rich (1682–1761), asked Haywood to do a rewrite on a play titled *The Fair Captive.* Two years later, part one of her first novel, *Love in Excess; or The Fatal Enquiry,* appeared, and that segment and the subsequent installments made her famous. The racy tale became one of the earliest examples of the romance novel in the history of printed English literature. Called "amatory fiction," these first bodice-rippers were written primarily for women readers, largely by female authors like Haywood. The two other leading doyennes of the genre, Aphra Behn (1640–1689) and Delarivier Manley (c. 1663–1724), were linked with Haywood's name and deemed "The Fair Triumvirate of Wit" at the height of their fame. Most amatory fiction relied on a formula that involved a naïve young woman deceived by a handsome rogue; genuine romantic love usually brought only misery to the heroine, and adulterous relationships were commonplace plot contrivances.

Love in Excess was a popular work for more than a decade, and was reprinted six times. Its protagonist is the Count D'Elmont, who marries an independent-minded woman named Alovisa; she suspects him of adultery with Melliora, a young woman over whom he serves as guardian. The Count kills his wife by accident, and flees to Italy; Melliora, meanwhile, hides in a convent, ashamed of her unwitting part in the scandal. But the Count pines for her, and through a series of adventures truly reforms himself and is reunited with her. The novel is "energetically written, full of incident, warm with the language of passion, and unmistakably—but never overtly—erotic," noted Beasley.

Haywood wrote several novels in this genre during the 1720s. One of the most intriguing of this period was *Fantomina; or Love in a Maze,* published in 1724. The story revolves around a heroine's repeated seductions of the same man, which she achieves by disguising herself as a servant girl, widow, and other types in order to lure the man called Beauplaisir. "As Fantomina changes character, she modifies her behaviors to align with his expectations," explained Emily Hodgson Anderson in *Eighteenth Century: Theory and Interpretation.* "The result of her actions is that while Beauplaisir seduces the same body night after night, he is convinced that he has conquered four different women."

Penned Opposition Plays

In 1732 Rich, Haywood's former mentor, opened his theater at Covent Garden, which became the first to win the designation "Theatre Royal" from the king. This and Drury Lane, which primarily staged operas at the time, were the "official" theaters, while The Haymarket, which opened in 1720, became their somewhat illegitimate cousin. The novelist Henry Fielding (1707–1754), best known for his novel *Tom Jones,* began staging a series of satires at the Haymarket that became known as opposition plays, and Haywood joined him there. The ribald comedies were highly critical of the government of Robert Walpole (1676–1745), considered Britain's first prime minister.

Haywood's contributions to these political plays included *Frederick, Duke of Brunswick-Lunenburgh,* staged in March of 1729. This German royal, the son of King George II (1683–1760), had become the center of opposition to Walpole's government. By 1733, however, Frederick's mother, Queen Caroline (1683–1737), had helped heal the rift between George II and his father, George I (1660–1727), a dispute related to Walpole's power and influence. When the tensions cooled, Haywood seemed to switch allegiances, and her best-known work for the stage, *The Opera of Operas,* demonstrated this in clear terms. It was a musical adaptation of Fielding's *Tragedy of Tragedies,* but it had a scene that depicted the reconciliation between the two Georges.

The Licensing Act of 1737 virtually stopped all production of new plays in England. The law was enacted at the urging of Walpole, who was irate over the continuing political satires that came from Fielding's pen. The far-reaching censorship law gave the Lord Chamberlain the right of approval over any new dramas, and Haywood quit writing for the stage at this point. She is believed to have run her own bookshop in the area of Covent Garden in the early 1740s, and she found profit by writing a series of manuals on social behavior that were known as conduct books, such as *A Present for a Servant-Maid,* which appeared in 1743. A year later, Haywood started publishing her own magazine, which she called *The Female Spectator,* a reference to the highly successful *Spectator,* which had been launched in 1711. Via four separate pseudonyms, she offered advice on marriage, the running of a household, and education for women. Historians of journalism consider it to be the first magazine for women actually written by a woman, but it folded after three years, as did *The Parrot,* a similar venture she launched in 1746.

Victim of Political Harassment

Later in the 1740s Haywood ran into trouble with the law when a pamphlet titled "A Letter from H—G—g, Esq. . . . To a Particular Friend" was attributed to her. It was a romantic comedy with some political overtones, giving a fictional account of the travels of Charles Edward Stuart (1720–1788), known as "Bonnie Prince Charlie." Stuart, a descendant of the last Jacobite king of England, James II (1633–1701), was a claimant to the British throne and attempted to raise an army in Scotland to seize the throne for himself in 1745. It was this period that "A Letter" chronicled, and the pamphlet was left in a number of London bookshops. The owners all claimed that they had discovered the piles of pamphlets in their shops and did not know who had delivered them, but authorities linked the work to Haywood, and she was arrested and charged with seditious libel. She, in turn, claimed that the pamphlets had been left at her home, and she sent her maid out to distribute them. The prosecutors also believed that William Hatchett, Haywood's common-law husband, was involved, but neither were ever prosecuted.

Hatchett was a pamphleteer, translator, and playwright whom Haywood probably met in the late 1720s. He was involved in the Haymarket Theatre plays, but his best known work was an erotic poem, *The Chinese Tale*. Prior to Hatchett, Haywood was likely involved with Richard Savage (c. 1697–1743), an English poet with whom she had the first of her two children. Savage claimed to be the illegitimate heir of a wealthy and titled family. He murdered a man but evaded a death sentence, was later jailed for debt, and died in prison. He also produced several notable works, including *The Wanderer*, and was a longtime friend of the famous English poet Alexander Pope (1688–1744). Their friendship may have been linked to a notorious attack that Pope unleashed on Haywood in his 1728 work *The Dunciad*. This was an epic poem that honored a goddess Pope called Dulness, and it poked fun at many popular writers of the day. The passage concerning Haywood called her the "phantom poetess"—an illusion to *Fantomina*—and dubbed her a "Juno of majestic size, With cow-like-udders, and with ox-like eyes."

Criticism was not new to Haywood, and she seemed impervious to it and determined to support herself and her two children by her writing, a difficult feat in any century. She once wrote that "it would be impossible to recount the numerous Difficulties a Woman has to struggle through in her Approach to Fame," according to George F. Whicher's *The Life and Romances of Mrs. Eliza Haywood*. "If her Writings are considerable enough to make any Figure in the World, Envy pursues her with unweary'd Diligence; and if, on the contrary, she only writes what is forgot, as soon as read, Contempt is all the Reward."

Betsy Foreshadowed *Emma*

One of Haywood's more enduring works was *The History of Miss Betsy Thoughtless*, published in 1751. Beasley called it "Haywood's longest, most carefully crafted, and most enduringly popular work of fiction. . . . Its cleverly conceived protagonist is effectively portrayed as a type of the good-hearted but naive and careless girl, and the story centers on her often ridiculous and embarrassing experiences as she makes her entrance into society." The heroine of the title consistently repels her overeager seducers but falls in love with man named Trueworth. Circumstances compel them to marry others, however, and Betsy's union is an unhappy one, for her new husband "considered a wife no more than an upper servant, bound to study and obey, in all things, the will of him to whom she had given her hand," the novel reads, according to Anderson's essay. Years later, Betsy flees the marriage and happily reunites with a widowed Trueworth, and their marriage is depicted as one undertaken by two wise, mature partners ideally suited to one another.

In 1753 Haywood's next novel, *Jemmy and Jenny Jessamy*, was published. This was her second attempt at a novel with a dual narrative (the first had been *The Fortunate Foundlings* in 1744), and these novels, along with the aforementioned *Betsy Thoughtless*, foreshadowed the works of a later generation of English women writers. Both Jane Austen (1775–1817) and Charlotte Brontë (1816–1855) wrote novels focusing on the domestic world to which most women

of that generation were restricted. The mid-twentieth century revival of interest in Austen's novels, along with interest in the British women writers who preceded her, led to a rediscovery of Haywood's works, which were largely forgotten after her death on February 25, 1756, in London.

Books

Dictionary of Literary Biography, Volume 39: British Novelists, 1660–1800, edited by Martin C. Battestin, Gale, 1985.
Whicher, George F., *The Life and Romances of Mrs. Eliza Haywood*, Columbia University Press, 1915.

Periodicals

Eighteenth Century: Theory and Interpretation, Spring 2005.
Modern Philology, February 2003.
Notes and Queries, June 1997.
Papers on Language & Literature, Summer 2002. □

Phoebe Apperson Hearst

Phoebe Apperson Hearst (1842–1919) was the mother of newspaper mogul William Randolph Hearst. She was a philanthropist and art collector. Very passionate about education, she was instrumental in making the University of California at Berkeley the illustrious institution it was at the beginning of the twenty-first century.

Born to Farmers in Missouri

Hearst was born Phoebe Apperson on December 3, 1842, in Franklin County, Missouri, to Randolph Walker Apperson and Drucilla (Whitmire) Apperson. They were relatively affluent farmers, and Hearst's childhood was a happy one. Prior to the Civil War, Hearst went to school six months a year and earned her certificate to teach all age groups, becoming a teacher in the Missouri school system.

Married George Hearst

Not long after Hearst began teaching, she met George Hearst. Although George was 41 at the time and she was just 19 years old, the two were married on June 15, 1862. The gap in their ages never bothered them, and they had a long and happy marriage together. The pair honeymooned in Panama. For the young girl from Missouri it was quite an experience, and her love of travel grew.

After their honeymoon Hearst and her husband moved to San Francisco. The next year, in 1863, George and Phoebe Hearst had a son, William Randolph. He was their only child and they doted on him, teaching him a love of everything that was classical and artistic. Hearst made certain her son was educated to the best degree, including traveling to faraway countries. When her son was only ten years, old Hearst took him touring through Europe, visiting many museums, castles, and other cultural sites. They traveled for more than a year, and she showed her son much of what would later inspire him to build and decorate Hearst Castle in California.

In 1887 George Hearst became a United States senator, and the two moved to Washington, D.C., so he could take up his duties. Hearst took to political life and enjoyed entertaining and mingling with the people her husband worked with. Her life in Washington, however, was cut short when George died in 1891. As his widow, Hearst was suddenly thrust into being the head of the family as she took over his estate.

The first thing she did was move back to California. Her son was still there, having built a thriving newspaper empire by that point, and he had begun plans to build a mansion in Pleasanton, California. Now that the elder Hearst was dead, Phoebe Hearst decided to help her son out. To run the project Hearst hired Julia Morgan, who became the architect of the famous Hearst Castle. Hearst focused her abundant energy on the building and designing of Hearst Castle, decorating the place with items she had collected over the years traveling the globe.

Built Up the University of California at Berkeley

Not only did Hearst occupy herself with her son's house, but she also turned her attention back to education. Now that she had the finances to do so, she gave generously to several different organizations. One of her favorite institutions was the University of California at Berkeley, and that was where she gave her first contribution in 1891. The money was in the form of a scholarship to help women attend the university. At that time a college education was not automatic for most women, and Hearst wanted to make it easier for women to better educate themselves. She was, however, not content with simply setting up scholarships. Women in the 1890s were not allowed to enter the social and extracurricular structures that men had available to them. Because of this, in 1900 Hearst created a Women's Student Center in her own home, turning her large pavilion into a place for women to congregate and socialize apart from men.

Hearst often held teas and other social events at her house for the women of the college. She made certain she was kept aware of all new female students so that they could be added to the roster of women invited to her house. She also helped women obtain the necessary funds to continue their education. When she found out that a lot of the women going to school were working for families in the area, she set up Hearst Domestic Industries. Women students who worked for that company sewed for a living, but were only allowed to work a certain number of hours a week, enabling them to find more time for their studies and take advantage of other campus activities. She also hired a part-time doctor, Mary Bennett Ritter, who helped with the women's health matters and instructed them in the use of the gym facilities.

The University of California at Berkeley was still small and not built up yet in the 1890s, so Hearst initiated a building competition to create a plan for the University. The Hearst Memorial Mining Building and Hearst Hall were two

buildings that were constructed to her exact specifications. They ended up being among thirty buildings and six campuses that Hearst helped create. Another building on that list was the Bancroft Library, and Hearst made certain it was stocked with the best educational texts, funding the entire collection herself. As of 2006, Hearst's personal papers were at the Bancroft Library. She served on the board of regents for the University of California and became a voice for females in the male-dominated school. She was the first woman to serve on the board, and she did so until she died.

Built Schools and Libraries Across the Country

Hearst also built several libraries around the United States and filled them with books and other necessities that she purchased. And she continued to support education, especially for women, everywhere she went. She started and funded the National Parent Teachers Association, helped with such organizations as the Young Women's Christian Association, Mills College, and helped fund the women's suffrage movement. She also gave support to kindergartens around the country, setting up a training school for teachers who taught at this level. Eventually she started the first free kindergarten in the country, and set up the Golden Gate Kindergarten Association along with eight other kindergartens. She also gave money to the National Cathedral School for young boys and girls.

Hearst always maintained her interest in other cultures. She helped fund archaeological expeditions, including one to research an ancient site in Florida, and she had a museum built at the university to display the artifacts found during the excavations. She founded the Phoebe Apperson Hearst Museum of Anthropology where, according to the museum's website, "People can learn about the people of the world through artifacts from nearly all geographic regions and cultures across the span of human history. Special exhibitions and public programs draw upon the Hearst's vast collections to highlight aspects of the Americas, Asia, Africa, Oceania, Ancient Egypt, and the Near East."

Improved Mount Vernon Historical Site

Along with Ann Pamela Cunningham and Frances Payne Bolton, Hearst raised money to restore Mount Vernon, George and Martha Washington's home. She served on the board there from 1889 to 1918, and during that time she paid to build a seawall to help stop the erosion of the shoreline that could eventually harm the mansion itself. She helped purchase furniture and art of the historical period to display in the house and give it a more realistic feel.

She belonged to the Bahá'í Faith, and traveled to Akko and Haifa in Israel on pilgrimage, arriving on December 10, 1898. She stayed there for three days and has been said to have named those as the three most memorable days of her life. Hearst continued to travel all over the world with her son until her death in 1919 of Spanish Influenza. After her death an elementary school was named after her in San Francisco, and her son had the Phoebe Apperson Hearst Gym Memorial commissioned in her honor. At the University of California at Berkeley there is a street named after her.

A log cabin in Missouri boasts a sign that says Phoebe Apperson Hearst went to school there. The Phoebe Apperson Hearst Society Museum was built in 1972 with help from the Hearst Foundation. The *St. Louis Dispatch* wrote that the Society considers the museum to be ''a memorial to the modest beginnings of a bright, serious, pioneer girl.''

Books

Dictionary of American Biography, Base Set. American Council of Learned Societies, 1928–1936.

Periodicals

Contra Costa Times (Walnut Creek, CA), October 18, 2005.
San Francisco Chronicle, July 17, 2000; May 10, 2000.
Seattle Times, October 20, 2002.
St. Louis Post-Dispatch, April 12, 1999.

Online

''Ann Pamela Cunningham, Phoebe Apperson Hearst, and Frances Payne Bolton,'' *Mount Vernon,* http://www.mountvernon.org-visit-plan-index.cfm-pid-811- (January 2, 2007).
''Hearst, Phoebe,'' *Learning to Give,* http://www.learningtogive.org-papers-index.asp?bpid = 102 (January 2, 2007).
''Phoebe A. Hearst Elementary,'' *Hearst Elementary,* http://www.hearst.cps.k12.il.us- (January 2, 2007).
''Phoebe A. Hearst Museum of Anthropology,'' *Hearst Museum,* http://hearstmuseum.berkeley.edu- (January 2, 2007).
''Phoebe Apperson Hearst,'' *Find a Grave,* http://www.findagrave.com-cgi-bin-fg.cgi?page = gr&GRid = 2345 (January 2, 2007).
''Phoebe Apperson Hearst (1842–1919),'' *Hearst Castle,* http://www.hearstcastle.org-history-phoebe_hearst.asp (January 2, 2007).
''Phoebe Hearst,'' *Answers.com,* http://www.answers.com-topic-phoebe-hearst (January 2, 2007).
''Phoebe Apperson Hearst Gym Memorial,'' *University of California, Berkeley,* http://sunsite.berkeley.edu-uchistory-archives_exhibits-online_exhibits-romapacifica-partvi.html (January 2, 2007). □

Héloïse

Héloïse (c. 1098–1163) was a French religious figure whose romance with a prominent theologian scandalized twelfth-century Paris. She and Peter Abélard fell passionately in love, but were forced to keep their relationship a secret, and it ended in a shocking act of violence. The torrid declarations in their correspondence with one another, however, provide one of the earliest written examples of romantic love in Western civilization.

Raised by Nuns

Héloïse's exact birth date and family background are details that have been lost to time. Most scholars place the year of her birth around 1098. She may have been the daughter of a woman named Hersint—

surnames were still uncommon in this century—and nothing is known about her father, which leads researchers to surmise that her mother may have been a nun. Some link Hersint to a convent called St. Eloi that was shut down by the Bishop of Paris in 1107 after charges of widespread sexual misconduct among its members had endured for too long. Any children resulting from such liaisons would have been sent off to other convents to be raised by more obedient nuns, and it is known that Héloïse's childhood was spent at the convent of St. Marie in Argenteuil, a Benedictine community near Paris.

Peter Abélard was, by most accounts, at least 15 years older than Héloïse. He came from a wealthy titled family in Brittany, where he was born around 1079. After several years as an itinerant student, he arrived in Paris around 1100 and within a few years had founded his own school. Such academies, often associated with a cathedral or other church body, were the main sources of higher education at the time, for the first universities in Western Europe would not officially come into being until later that century. Abélard was a student of logic, the branch of classical philosophy concerned with the evaluation of arguments, and at a rather young age he emerged as one of the more brilliant masters in the field. Logicians deconstructed declarative statements to discern whether one's opponent was presenting a flawed line of reasoning or a valid one. In an era before the printing press, such battles were verbal, even a form of entertainment for eager audiences of fellow scholars and students, and the combination of Abélard's good looks, arrogance, theatricality, and debating prowess earned him fame as well as a few enemies. He soon moved on to theology, despite his lack of official credentials, and became even more renowned throughout Paris.

Héloïse received an excellent education at Argenteuil, becoming fluent in Latin—the universal language of the Christian church and of all scholarship in Europe and the Western world at the time—as well as Greek and Hebrew, and achieved some renown on her own in the fields of grammar and rhetoric, the two other branches of classical philosophy. She eventually settled into the house of her uncle, Fulbert, who was the canon of Notre Dame Cathedral; a canon held an ecclesiastical position but also an administrative and executive one as well, and cathedral canons were men of influence and power in their parish neighborhood. Héloïse had probably heard of Abélard before they met, for he was already well known by this point and serving as master of the cathedral school attached to Notre Dame.

Her Private Tutor

The ill-fated duo is thought to have met around 1114 or 1115, and by Abélard's account he saw Héloïse and became intent on seducing her. He approached her uncle, whom he knew to be quite proud of his niece's intellectual achievements, and offered to tutor her if he could live in the canon's house, too; he explained that his own lodgings were proving too expensive as well as a drain on his time, and because Abélard even offered to pay rent, Fulbert agreed to the arrangement with enthusiasm. As Abélard later wrote in a memoir, in a short time "more words of love than of our reading passed between us, and more kissing than teaching," according to James Burge's *Héloïse & Abélard: A New Biography.*

As noted, Abélard possessed a mastery of language, both spoken and written, but Héloïse showed early evidence of a literary talent as well. They exchanged many letters during the period of their romance, likely using wax tablets that hinged like a book and were carried from sender to recipient by a servant; after the letter was read, the wax could be smoothed by a candle and used again. Héloïse may have written drafts of some of her letters on parchment, and it is these that survived in fragments over the centuries. The scraps of writing, in Latin, recount an intensely passionate relationship between a pair whose intellect and temperament were well-matched. On his end, Abélard penned love poems to her, and some of these were reportedly copied and passed around among Abélard's already-devoted following of students and other young Parisians. Eventually the rumors of a clandestine romance between Fulbert's niece and her tutor reached the canon, who then confronted Abélard and ordered him to leave.

The timeline of Héloïse and Abélard's story is imprecise, but scholars believe their romance lasted about two years before Fulbert put an end to it; around this same time Héloïse became pregnant, and informed Abélard. He arranged for her to flee Paris and stay at the home of one of his siblings in Brittany, probably a brother named Dagobert; she reportedly wore a nun's habit to disguise herself when he helped her leave the city. They named their son As-tralabe, a distinctly unconventional choice in the era, for it was the name of a scientific instrument used to determine the positions of the sun, moon, stars, and planets.

Astralabe was raised by Abélard's family in Brittany, who were affluent landowners and already rich in offspring. Back in Paris, Abélard approached Fulbert and offered to rectify the scandalous situation by marrying Héloïse. Fulbert consented to this, but Héloïse refused, asserting that it would ruin Abélard's distinguished career as master of the cathedral school, and that in the larger sense, family life was incompatible with the work of a philosopher. At the same time, she noted her own objections to making their union legitimate, writing that marriage struck her as a purely economic arrangement. "The name of wife may seem more sacred or more binding," she ventured in her reply, according to the Burge book, "but sweeter for me will always be the word mistress, or, if you will permit me, that of concubine or whore."

Forced into Marriage

Abélard seemed to have insisted—perhaps fearful of Fulbert's anger—and the two were secretly wed in Paris, with only the uncle and a few friends in attendance. Héloïse returned to live at her uncle's home, and Abélard in his own lodgings; the secrecy of the union seems to have been part of the agreement between Fulbert and Abélard, and was likely kept quiet in the event that either man changed his mind. But rumors spread once again, and Héloïse publicly denied that she was a bride, which angered Fulbert and probably resulted in a household situation that became increasingly untenable for her. After this, Abélard once again helped her escape, again in a nun's habit. The nuns at Argenteuil took her in, and Abélard wrote of at least one assignation that took place in the convent's empty dining hall. Fulbert's fury toward the pair intensified, but in the laws and customs of the time, a wife was essentially the property of her husband once they were wed, and when Abélard took Héloïse from her uncle's home, he was acting within his spousal rights.

Fulbert's reaction was linked to the idea that his family had been dishonored by Abélard, and his eventual decision to take revenge would serve to enshrine the ill-fated couple in history and literature for the next millennium. Abélard wrote, "One night as I slept peacefully in an inner room in my lodgings, they bribed one of the servants to admit them and there took cruel vengeance on me of such an appalling barbarity as to shock the whole world." Associates of Fulbert "cut off the parts of my body whereby I had committed the wrong of which they complained." Historians believe that Abélard was not fully castrated, but only his testicles removed. The method would have been similar to that used on farm animals, using a rope wound around the sac and then a sharp knife to extract the glands. The cord is left tied in order to staunch the bleeding.

By the next morning Parisians had heard of what happened to Abélard, and he wrote in his memoir that a crowd assembled at the home where he was staying—probably that of a well-connected noble family, the de Garlandes. Though most were appalled by what had happened to him, and he won many prominent supporters, he lost his position as master of the cathedral school by decree of the bishop of Paris. To punish Fulbert, the same bishop ordered all his possessions and assets to be seized, and Fulbert lost his position as well—but for less than two years, for his signature began reappearing on official documents related to Notre Dame in April of 1119.

Took Religious Vows

What happened to Héloïse during this period remains unclear. Some historians believe that Abélard may have already grown tired of her and convinced her to take full religious vows, which meant that he was, in effect, divorcing her; upon learning of this, one theory holds, Fulbert's rage took the form that it did in order to avenge his niece's honor. Another hypothesis holds that only after the crime did Abélard convince Héloïse to "take the veil" of a nun, this time in earnest, which she did at Argenteuil.

A life free from sexual temptation was the ideal one for a monk, and Abélard himself entered a monastery, the Abbey of St. Denis, soon after his recovery. There he wrote a treatise on the Holy Trinity, which was condemned as heretical by church authorities, and left St. Denis and settled in the area of Nogent-sur-Seine, in what is now the Aube district in northeast France. Around 1122 he founded his own religious community, which he called the Oratory of the Paraclete. A few years later he was elected abbot of Abbey of St. Gildas in Brittany in 1125, and arranged for Héloïse to take over the Paraclete, for he had learned that she and some of the other women had been evicted from Argenteuil. By that time Héloïse had advanced to the position of prioress, or second in command to the abbess. A local bishop took possession of the Argenteuil property through suspicious means, and the nuns had nowhere to go. Some stayed with their abbess, but a few loyal to Héloïse were homeless and gladly followed her to Nogent-sur-Seine.

Héloïse and Abélard never lived together again, and had no contact for nearly twelve years. Only when Héloïse learned that Abélard had written a lengthy account of their story, *Historia Calamitatum* (Story of My Misfortunes), did she send word. In subsequent letters she professed her still-ardent devotion to him, and confessed that the hours of prayer her religious life demanded were often disrupted by thoughts of the carnal pleasures they had once shared. Their correspondence continued for several more years, until Abelard's death in 1142. Héloïse remained abbess of the Paraclete until her own death on May 19, 1163. Several daughter houses were founded in France during her lifetime, but they were all destroyed in the wave of anti-religious sentiment during the French Revolution. Legend claims the pair were finally laid to rest together at the Nogent-sur-Seine property, but their remains were moved during the Revolution. At the famous Père Lachaise cemetery in Paris there is a monument, but it is unclear whether both, or perhaps just Abélard, rests there. Their son, Astralabe, also entered religious life, and served as abbot of a monastery in what later became Switzerland.

Books

Burge, James, *Héloïse & Abélard: A New Biography,* HarperSanFrancisco, 2003.
Encyclopedia of Women and World Religion, Serinity Young, editor, Macmillan Reference USA, 1999.

Periodicals

Independent on Sunday (London, England), September 10, 2006.
New York Times Book Review, February 13, 2005.
Star Tribune, (Minneapolis, MN), February 12, 2001.

Online

"The Love Letters of Abélard and Heloise," The Internet Sacred Text Archive, http://www.sacred-texts.com/chr/aah/index .htm (December 7, 2006). □

Myra Hess

The concert pianist Myra Hess (1890–1965) started out rather slowly, but eventually hit the heights of musical fame as her skills became more widely recognized. She was famous for playing the works of composers such as Mozart, Beethoven, and Bach, but was especially praised for her renditions of Schumann's works. In World War II, during the Nazi bombing attacks on London, she put together a concert series that continued throughout some of the most desperate days of the war, raising the morale of her fellow citizens and demonstrating that the democratic British spirit would not be crushed. In the early early twenty-first century, Hess's name still stands for British pride and a democratic spirit incapable of being dented.

Early Life in North West London

Hess was born on February 25, 1890, in Hampstead in North West London. She was the youngest of four children. When she was around five years old, Hess began taking piano lessons. At seven she attended the Guildhall School of Music, where she studied under such musical greats as Julian Pascal and Dr. Lando Morgan. She graduated from the Guildhall School when she was 12 years old with the highest honors, and was awarded a scholarship to the Royal Academy of Music.

There she studied piano with Tobias Matthay, often been said to be one of the greatest piano teachers to come out of Britain. It was through work with Matthay that Hess matured as a pianist both mentally and technically, until she was considered good enough to perform as a solo concert pianist. Matthay was aware early on of how talented the young girl was, and so he encouraged her as much as he could. She soon became one of his favorite students. Hess liked Matthay

so well that she worked extraordinarily hard to prove her ability to perform. She wrote about her lessons with him, according to the *Carolina Classical* website: "I had a startling awakening to all the beauties of the music of which I had not even dreamed. . . . Till then, I had just played, now I began to think." She continued with her piano lessons and studied until she passed the junior examinations at Trinity College of Music, again with the highest of honors.

Career Had a Slow Start

After college Hess had a difficult time getting her career going. She had to make all the initial arrangements for her concerts by herself, a challenge she had never faced before. She debuted as a concert pianist on November 14, 1907 when she was only 17 years old.

Her first concert was at Aeolian Hall, where she played Beethoven's Concerto No. 4 in G Major, conducted by the famous Sir Thomas Beecham, one of the best known conductors in England at the time. The concert brought Hess much critical and popular acclaim, and it was thought that her performance would catapult the young pianist to fame and glory. Unfortunately she was overshadowed by other musicians playing at the time, and soon fell back into obscurity.

Tried Teaching and Chamber Music

In between concerts Hess took up teaching. She also worked at becoming a good chamber musician, and ended up playing with such musical greats as violinists Joseph Szigeti and Fritz Kreisler. She also went on to accompany

such well-known musicians of the day as Lotte Lehmann and Nellie Melba. She spent time traveling around and performing in other countries, working to make her name known across Europe. In February of 1912 she performed in Holland. There she played Schumann's Piano Concerto in A minor, with the Concertgebouw Orchestra led by Willem Mengelberg. She was greatly praised for her work and was so well received that she was repeatedly invited back to Holland to perform.

By the end of World War I Hess was starting to regain her earlier popularity in England, and even to surpass it. She also traveled to the United States to perform a concert in New York City, and became a sensation when she debuted there on January 24, 1922. Critics loved the concert, and Hess was praised for her imagination and sensitivity to the music. She went on from New York to perform all over America in some of its largest cities, both in solo recitals and as a guest with different orchestras. The fame she garnered while in America followed her back home to Europe. She had remained close to her mentor, Matthay, during this entire period, and as she traveled across America, Hess referred many promising young pianists to England to be tutored by the great teacher.

Continued Tours Across Europe

In 1936, after her return to England, Hess was made a Companion of the Order of the British Empire by King George V. Five years later she was made a Dame Commander of the Order of the British Empire. She was awarded the Gold Medal of the Royal Philharmonic Society in 1941, an honor awarded only to the very best musicians.

Before World War II began Hess could be found touring all over Europe, including Germany, Austria, France, and Holland. She was most famous for playing Bach, Scarlatti, Beethoven, and Mozart, as well as Schumann and Brahms. She was also known for playing many different types of chamber music. She had a vast repertoire that included contemporary pieces as well as old favorites.

Began Concert Series During World War II

When World War II started all live concert performances stopped in Britain. Hess was in America at the time that war was declared, and she immediately canceled the rest of the tour she had planned in order to return home. Back in London Hess felt the immense need for morale boosting events. With that in mind she initiated lunchtime concerts at the National Gallery, which had been stripped of all its artwork and treasures to preserve them from German air attacks on the city.

The concerts were an instant success. People thronged to the National Gallery to hear the music. The city was suffering from blackouts and it was difficult for Londoners to travel around the city after dark, so Hess planned daytime concerts. As a defiant gesture against the Nazi bombardments, Hess assembled a host of musicians to perform. Much of the music they played was German or Austrian. Hess, who had become famous performing this music, continued to play it. She wanted to show Germans and British alike that it was possible to enjoy and love the art and music of a country while despising the political motivations and actions of its government. As a spiritual and morale boosting project, it worked amazingly well.

Raised Spirits of the British

These concerts not only helped raise spirits in a time of great depression and anxiety, but also introduced classical music to many people who had never heard it before. Over the life of the concerts, Hess and her group played a myriad of songs, but some of the most well-received were performances of the complete series of Mozart Piano Concertos, played by Hess with the famous conductor Alec Sherman and the New London Orchestra.

By the time the war ended, more than 1300 concerts had been given at the National Gallery. The concerts ran throughout the war, even during the bombings of London, and they even brought in a little money for the musicians. When people in Canada and the United States heard of these concerts, they donated money to help keep them going even when very few people could attend.

Continued Touring After War

When the war was over Hess returned to her musical career, and revisited the United States. She wrote an arrangement for piano of the chorale prelude "Jesu, bleibet meine Freude" ("Jesu, Joy of Man's Desiring") from Johann Sebastian Bach's Cantata No. 147. The arrangement was praised internationally and added to her fame.

In the 1960s Hess became ill and could no longer live the strenuous life of a concert pianist. Instead she started teaching again because she did not want to give up the musical world entirely. She died on November 25, 1965, in London, and would be remembered not only as a famous and great pianist but as the person who organized the concerts in London during World War II. She was considered by the British to be a patriotic symbol of the stalwart British spirit that would never falter in the face of adversity.

Books

Almanac of Famous People, 8th edition, Gale Group, 2003.

Online

"Myra Hess," *Arbiter Records,* http://www.arbiterrecords.com/musicresourcecenter/hess.html (January 2, 2007).
"Dame Myra Hess: Concert Pianist," *Carolina Classical,* http://www.carolinaclassical.com/hess/ (January 2, 2007). □

William Hutt

Over a theatrical career lasting more than 50 years, Canadian actor and director William Hutt (born 1920) became virtually the face of the Stratford Festival, an annual live theater extravaganza, lasting from spring to fall, that draws audiences from all over North America. Festival director Richard Mon-

ette told the Canadian Broadcasting Corporation (CBC) that Hutt was "arguably the greatest classical actor in the English-speaking world."

Appeared in Pageant

William Ian DeWitt Hutt, born in Toronto on May 2, 1920, spent his earliest years with an aunt in Hamilton, Ontario; his mother was in poor health. At age four or five he demanded a part in the Christmas pageant at Christ Church, where his aunt was a member. He was cast as a seller in Bethlehem's marketplace, with a single line: "Beads for sale!" When Hutt returned to his parents in Toronto, however, his stage ambitions were discouraged. His father was a journalist and trade publication editor who sold insurance during the economic depression of the early 1930s. "Both my parents," Hutt told the *Toronto Star,* "really thought they were British underneath, all about dignity and reserve. The theatre was a diversion to them, not a career."

Already sensing that he had a talent for making a powerful connection with an audience, Hutt worked on his speaking skills in oratory classes. When he was 12 he won a medal for a speech he gave, written by his father on the theme of the greatness of the British Empire. At two Toronto institutions, the Vaughan Road and North Toronto collegiate or prep schools, Hutt took occasional roles in school operetta productions but did not yet think about acting as a career.

World War II interrupted Hutt's education. As a member of the Canadian army ambulance corps, he was sent to the front in Italy and received a decoration for bravery. On occasional leaves, Hutt made his way to London and took in theatrical productions there. His moment of epiphany concerning his future direction came not during one of the Shakespearean masterpieces for which he later became well known, but during a production of the comedy *Arsenic and Old Lace.* "Instead of enjoying the laugh riot it was supposed to be, I was actually more intrigued with what [the actors] were doing," Hutt told the *Toronto Star.* "I really believed in those people up there. How did they do that? How did they make me feel that they were real? I went away and thought to myself, 'I'd like to do that sometime.' " Forty years later, Hutt would perform, in drag, the role of one of the play's two murderous old ladies.

Returning to Toronto after the war, Hutt was admitted to Trinity College, part of the University of Toronto. He joined a college theatrical group called the Earl Grey Players and won the role of Theseus in Shakespeare's *A Midsummer Night's Dream.* During summer vacations Hutt landed roles with summer stock theatrical companies, and he has credited director Robert Gill at Hart House Theatre, an independent theater based at the university, with honing his skills as a Shakespearean actor.

Appeared During Inaugural Stratford Season

For several years, Hutt crisscrossed Canada with touring theatrical companies, and an ongoing relationship with the Canadian Repertory Theatre in Canada's capital of Ottawa, beginning the late 1940s, gave him a home base. Hutt never married—he was bisexual, having announced his homosexuality at a family dinner during his teenage years when he blurted out (according to biographer Keith Garebian), "I'm another Oscar Wilde!" In 1953 he won the supporting role of Sir Robert Brackenbury in Shakespeare's *Richard III,* playing opposite Alec Guinness in the lead role. It was the first of more than 100 Stratford productions in which Hutt would appear over the next five decades. Hutt was so well received that the following year he received the company's inaugural Tyrone Guthrie Award, named after Stratford's founder, for his performance. He had a variety of supporting roles, most of them in Shakespeare's plays, over the next ten years. He also toured Canada and the United States with the Canadian Players troupe, once playing Shakespeare's King Lear in a production set among the Inuit people of Canada's far north.

During that period, Hutt, along with his directors and fellow players, developed a theatrical style specific to the Stratford Festival, mounted in a picturesque Ontario town that, like its English namesake, was situated on the Avon River. "The key to the company's success was its uniquely Canadian approach," noted *American Theatre,* "a delicate balance between American Method-style realism and the more traditional, artificial, one might say theatrical, British approach." Hutt's presence on stage was formal, but he took care to communicate the emotions in a play directly to the audience. "To this day I'm as confused as anybody by a Shakespeare play the first time I read it," he told the *Toronto Star* in 2005, at age 84. "I'm just like a high school student, reading all the notes, figuring out what it means, then putting it in my mind in language I can understand." He often likened the craft of acting to, as he put it, being private in public.

Audiences responded enthusiastically to the festival's sumptuous yet accessible productions, and by 1962, when Hutt played his first lead role, a summer trip to Stratford had become an annual pilgrimage for hundreds of thousands of theater lovers from Canada and much of the American Northeast and Midwest. Hutt's debut as star was in the role of Prospero in Shakespeare's *The Tempest,* and that role became one of several specialties he cultivated over his years in Stratford. He played King Lear four times in Stratford, and he frequently ranged beyond Shakespeare. He also took the stage four times as James Tyrone, the aging Irish-American actor in Eugene O'Neill's family drama *Long Day's Journey into Night,* and he appeared plays of various types—the classical French comedies of Molière, the incisive social commentaries of Russian dramatist Anton Chekhov, and even, in 1975, the Oscar Wilde comedy *The Importance of Being Earnest,* a favorite of Hutt's fans in which he cross-dressed to play the role of Lady Bracknell.

Having established himself firmly in Canada, Hutt could easily have chosen to seek stardom in American plays and films, a choice that had worked out well for his Stratford contemporaries William Shatner and Christopher Plummer. But Hutt, who strongly preferred the stage to cinema, chose to remain in Canada, eventually moving into a large home in Stratford. "As far as going down to the United States for stage work," he told *American Theatre,* "I don't believe in starving picturesquely in a garret for my art. I think that's soul-destroying. And one thing I was determined not to do was . . . to move to New York and sit in a cold-water flat waiting for the phone to ring." As it happened, Hutt made several critically well-received visits to New York stages, with a Broadway debut in Edward Albee's *Tiny Alice* and a 1968 production of George Bernard Shaw's *St. Joan* at Lincoln Center.

Starred in Miniseries

In Canada, Hutt became well known even beyond the world of theater. In 1974 he starred in *The National Dream,* a miniseries about the early history of the Canadian nation in which he played the country's first prime minister, Sir John A. Macdonald. That role brought him two of Canada's top performing arts awards, an Alliance of Canadian Cinema, Television and Radio Artists (ACTRA) and a Canadian Film Award, the following year. Hutt also appeared in several television productions of Shakespeare's plays. The roster of national honors on his shelf began with his designation as a Companion of the Order of Canada in 1969 and expanded in 1992 when he was given a lifetime achievement award by the country's Governor General.

Despite occasional detours into film and television, the Stratford stage remained Hutt's first love. He played every major lead role in Shakespeare's plays except for Othello. He often took on three major roles in a single season, and he was an instantly recognizable figure no matter what character he played. Hutt was a commanding figure, standing six-feet, two inches tall and weighing over 200 pounds. And his early oratorical training was everywhere in evidence. "Hutt used his deeply sonorous voice to calculated effect," Garebian wrote in a description of a Hutt performance of the lead role in Molière's comedy *Tartuffe.* "It sounded like a grand organ as it quavered sententiously, paused dramatically, and audaciously overemphasized the most sanctimonious phrases." In the grand Shakespearean soliloquies like that of Hamlet, which he named along with James Tyrone as one of his two favorite roles, Hutt was unmatched.

Hutt was appointed associate director of Stratford's touring arm, the Stratford National Company, in the 1970s, and he intermittently directed individual productions at the festival itself. In the 1980s, as the festival drifted through what some saw as an artistically unfocused period, Hutt appeared with other companies, including Canada's rival classical summer repertory event, the Shaw Festival in Niagara Falls, Ontario. Controversy continued after Richard Monette assumed the helm of the Stratford Festival in 1994 and steered the company in what was perceived as a populist direction. But Hutt appeared in several major new Stratford productions and defended Monette, telling *American Theatre* that "he was an actor in the company for a number of years. Then he got an opportunity to direct a couple of productions. Now he heads the joint. I think he's a very exuberant man. And populist? Yes, but I don't think that's a fault. We needed a populist.''

Hutt entered his 70s and then his 80s without slowing down much, remaining in satisfactory health despite a lifelong enthusiasm for both tobacco and alcohol. In 2003 he had a sizable role in the World War II drama *The Statement.* His final *King Lear* in 1996, directed by Monette, inspired Linda Bridges of the *National Review* to call him ''a treasure of the English-speaking theater who seems to gain depth with each passing year.'' Hutt's 2004 appearance at Toronto's Soulpepper Theatre in Samuel Beckett's minimalist-existentialist drama *Waiting for Godot* received wide coverage. ''It's one of those emotional, end-of-the-road things he likes these days,'' former Stratford artistic director Robin Phillips told Ian Brown of Canada's *Globe and Mail* newspaper. But during the production Hutt began to complain of difficulty in remembering his lines. His final Stratford performance came the following year, as Prospero in *The Tempest,* the same role he had first taken as a star more than 40 years earlier. He is retired at his Stratford home. ''Death is fertilizer for the future, that's what I think,'' he told the *Star.* ''We're all annuals, and at the end of our season . . . we go.''

Books

Garebian, Keith, *William Hutt: A Theatre Portrait,* Mosaic, 1988.
Who's Who in the Theatre, 17th ed., Gale, 1981.

Periodicals

American Theatre, November 1998.
Globe and Mail (Toronto, Ontario, Canada), June 19, 2004.
National Review, September 2, 1996.
Toronto Star, April 10, 2005.

Online

''Hutt, William,'' Canadian Theatre Encyclopedia. http://www.canadiantheatre.com (October 21, 2006).
''William Hutt,'' Northern Stars, http://www.northernstars.ca/actorsghi/huttbio.html (October 21, 2006).
''William Hutt takes final bow,'' Canadian Broadcasting Corporation, http://www.cbc.ca/arts/story/2005/10/28/huttretires_051028.html (October 21, 2006). □

Elizabeth Inchbald

British novelist, playwright, and actress Elizabeth Inchbald (1753–1821) was among the first women to find renown as a playwright. Drawing on her experiences on the stage, Inchbald also became the first prominent British female theater critic. In total, she wrote or adapted about 20 plays, as well as publishing two novels later in her career. Her work is primarily remembered for her deft use of comedy and for her expression of contemporary social issues in her works.

Youth and Marriage

Inchbald was born Elizabeth Simpson on October 15, 1753, in a small village called Standingfield near Bury St. Edmunds in Suffolk, located near the eastern coast of England. Inchbald's father, John Simpson, a respected farmer, and her mother, Mary, had seven other children. In 1761 John Simpson died, leaving Mary Simpson to care for their large family. She did so while successfully managing the family farm, maintaining a home that became a center of Suffolk society, and instilling in her children a love of literature by reading to them as well as taking them to see plays in nearby Bury.

As a young person, Inchbald struggled with a speech impediment. However, Annibel Jenkins noted in *I'll Tell You What: The Life of Elizabeth Inchbald* that "no one seemed to mind," and Inchbald, intent from a young age on seeing the world, followed her brother George to London in 1772 to commence a career in acting. Despite being considered a great beauty, Inchbald had a difficult time finding work as an actress due to her speech impediment; not until after her marriage to actor Joseph Inchbald in June 1772 did Inchbald begin working seriously as an actress.

Career as an Actress

Inchbald's first dramatic appearance was on September 4, 1772, as the character Cordelia opposite her husband's King Lear in Shakespeare's *King Lear.* By the end of 1772, the couple—accompanied by Robert, one of Joseph Inchbald's sons from a previous relationship— had traveled to Scotland to join a theatrical company that performed in Glasgow and Edinburgh. There, Inchbald spent much of her time studying parts but little time in playing them; Jenkins commented that Inchbald "was very discouraged about her acting; after all, she had very little experience, but she was then—and always—very impatient." Inchbald continued to struggle with her speech impediment, but made enough progress to appear in several featured roles, such as the eponymous Jane Shore and Desdemona in Shakespeare's *Othello*, during the winter season.

The Inchbalds remained with the Scottish theatrical company until the close of the spring season in 1776. They then left Scotland to travel to France, where they hoped to settle for some time. However, the couple quickly ran out of money and was forced to return to London, arriving there in October of 1776. This stay was also brief, and the Inchbalds again left for the countryside where they could more readily find work. Over the next several months, the Inchbalds passed through Cheshire, Liverpool, Manchester, and Canterbury before taking positions with a theatrical touring company serving York and the surrounding area. They remained there, taking major roles in several productions, until Joseph Inchbald's unexpected death from an apparent heart attack on June 4, 1779.

First Writings

After the death of her husband, Inchbald continued to act—she made her London debut on October 3, 1780, as Bellario in *Philaster*—but increasingly turned her attention to writing. Her first works were short farces titled "A Peep into a Planet," "The Ancient Law," and "Polygamy." The pieces were performed and no manuscript remains, although the *Dictionary of Literary Biography* speculated that the works "were probably in the same broad farcical style as her surviving farces." During the summer of 1781, Inchbald traveled to the country and stayed on a farm with her mother and sister. There she wrote her first comedy.

In 1784 Inchbald had her first work accepted by a theatrical company for production. This play, *A Mogul Tale,* was staged in the summer of that year; Inchbald appeared in the play herself in the role of Selina. The run was successful, and Inchbald received a fair amount of money from the performances. In 1785 another of Inchbald's plays, *I'll Tell You What!,* was staged by the same theatrical company, again with significant success. The money Inchbald earned from her plays made it unnecessary for her to marry again for support; writing in *Ten Fascinating Women,* Elizabeth Jenkins commented that Inchbald "was now impatient of any idea of marriage to which she could not attach some romantic luster of her own peculiar kind." Indeed, Inchbald never remarried.

Also in 1785, another company put on Inchbald's *Appearance is Against Them.* Both the King and Prince saw this play, which became Inchbald's first to appear in print. This work, along with *The Widow's Vow,* are among the few of Inchbald's early works to survive to this day. During the 1780s Inchbald also turned her hand to translation and adaptation. Among these works were a series of plays in a large set called *The British Volume,* and several pieces by the German dramatist Kotzebue. Inchbald's adaptation of one of Kotzebue's plays makes an appearance in Jane Austen's classic novel *Mansfield Park.* Beginning in 1788, Inchbald's plays were presented during the summer theater season at Haymarket.

Succeeded in Drama and Literature

In 1789 Inchbald retired from acting altogether, earning her living exclusively through her writing. She returned to the draft of a novel she had written several years previously. She revised this draft and it was published in February of 1791 as *A Simple Story.* The novel was immediately successful, with its first edition selling out in under a month. Contemporary critics found the story satisfying, and readers continued to buy subsequent editions. *A Simple Story* became the most popular book written by a woman in more than a decade. Over the following two decades, Inchbald revised the novel several times for various editions; today, most scholars prefer to use the first edition of the novel for its provincialisms, colloquialisms, and grammatical oddities.

Despite the success of *A Simple Story,* the dramatic field remained a more lucrative one than that of the novel. Inchbald continued adapting dramatic works, primarily rely-

ing on what the *Dictionary of Literary Biography* called "her basic formula for comedy . . . scenes of comic high life interwoven with a tale of distress, and both plots presided over by one of those moralists so dear to eighteenth-century audiences." Inchbald moved away from these standard concepts with 1792's *The Massacre,* one of her more unusual works. Using events that took place during the then-contemporary French Revolution, Inchbald's play had a tragic ending, although it was not political commentary. She printed *The Massacre* in 1792 and then quickly withdrew it, not wanting to become embroiled in political matters. This year also marked her last with the summer theater at Haymarket.

During the 1790s and early 1800s, Inchbald wrote many of the comedies that defined her as dramatist and remained popular for years to come. Many of these plays were first performed in London's Covent Garden. Typically, these works relied heavily on sentimentalism, exemplifying Inchbald's "basic formula." In the midst of this period of high comedy, Inchbald wrote and published her second novel, *Nature and Art.* This short work was also successful, although less so than *A Simple Story.* Annibel Jenkins commented that *Nature and Art* "was admired, not loved" by contemporary audiences. Elizabeth Jenkins noted that "during the last hundred and fifty years, while *A Simple Story* is remembered, *Nature and Art,* whose brilliant passages are not only painful but short in relation to the whole, has almost disappeared into oblivion."

In 1797 Inchbald published one of her most successful plays, *Wives as They Were and Maids as They Are,* which showed Inchbald at the height of her style. Between her novels and dramatic works, Inchbald made a substantial sum of money. She invested this money wisely and managed to acquire a small income from her investments on which she could rely. This financial security allowed Inchbald to help friends and family, as well as to be active in London society.

Later Career

Beginning in 1805, Inchbald turned her writings in a new direction. Having spent the majority of her life working professionally in the theater as both an actor and writer, Inchbald seemed to her publishers to be an excellent candidate to become a theater critic. They convinced Inchbald to write critical remarks for a series of plays they planned to publish, titled *The British Theatre.* Although Inchbald had no formal training or education as a critic, she took the position because she needed money. The first play in the series, Colman the Younger's *The Mountaineers,* appeared in February of 1806, with subsequent plays released weekly. By the time the collected edition was published in 1808, the plays totaled 125 in 25 volumes. Inchbald's remarks on the plays were considered thoughtful and professional, and were clearly informed by her years of experience working in the theater. The *Dictionary of Literary Biography* summarized Inchbald's commentary by saying: "She knew an abundance of anecdotes about the actors. She had a shrewd knowledge of which plays were vigorous and which [lacked vitality], which scenes and which roles were best. . . . Most enthusiasts of the theater, though they might disagree with her about a scene or a character, approved her remarks." The plays on which Inchbald wrote included both contemporary British drama as well as such classics as *MacBeth*.

Later Years and Legacy

About 1809, Inchbald at last moved permanently to St. George's Row near London's Regent Park. At the time, this area was somewhat removed from the main part of London, and Inchbald soon withdrew from dramatic society, spending much of her time attending church, writing letters, and seeing neighbors. Ten years later, Inchbald moved even farther from the city to Kensington. During the 1810s, her health slowly failed; she consulted physicians for an unidentified condition several times. Finally, Inchbald died in Kensington on August 1, 1821.

Inchbald's works have remained in print and continue to be performed; although she wrote her memoirs, they went unpublished and Inchbald burned them prior to her death. Over the years, interpretations of Inchbald's life and works have varied. Victorians made much of her later piety and generous support of her family and friends. Later feminist critics discussed Inchbald in the context of other eighteenth-century women writers, and typically focused on her novels rather than plays. Today, scholars increasingly have turned to the study of Inchbald's drama, looking for a contemporary understanding of the lives of English men and women in the late eighteenth century.

Books

Jenkins, Annibel, *I'll Tell You What: The Life of Elizabeth Inchbald,* University of Kentucky Press, 2003.

Jenkins, Elizabeth, *Ten Fascinating Women,* MacDonald and Co., 1968.

Manvell, Roger, *Elizabeth Inchbald: A Biographical Study,* University Press of America, 1987.

Online

"Elizabeth Inchbald," *Dictionary of Literary Biography, Volume 89: Restoration and Eighteenth-Century Dramatists, Third Series,* Gale Group, 1989, reproduced in *Gale Literary Databases,* http://www.galenet.galegroup.com (December 30, 2006). □

Steve Irwin

Australian naturalist and television personality Steve Irwin (1962–2006) was best known for his popular wildlife program *Crocodile Hunter*. His unbridled enthusiasm for such unlovely creatures as crocodiles, snakes, and spiders earned him a tremendous following, and his Australia Zoo was a top tourist attraction in his country. An ardent wildlife conservationist, Irwin also invested much of his time and money toward that end. He died in a rare stingray attack while filming off the coast of Australia in 2006.

Born to the Breed

Irwin was born on February 22, 1962 in Essendon, near Melbourne, Australia. His father, Bob, was a plumber and his mother, Lyn, a nurse, but both were naturalists by avocation. They turned their hobby into a business in the early 1970s, when they moved the family to Australia's Sunshine Coast and opened the Beerwah Reptile Park.

Growing up among wild creatures, Irwin soon adopted his parents' affinity for the country's wildlife. He received a python for his sixth birthday, named it "Fred," and never looked back. Before long, he was helping his father rescue crocodiles. "When I was nine, dad took me capturing crocodiles," Irwin told Tessa Cunningham of the London *Mirror*. "We had five in the boat when my flashlight picked out a sixth. 'This one's yours, son,' dad said. He was a whopper—3ft. I got my legs around his neck and he was thrashing about. It was like being tossed around in a washing machine . . . It was an out-of-body experience. I knew then that catching crocs was the only life I wanted."

Emulating his father played a large role in Irwin's ambitions as well. "I totally revered my dad," he told Gary Arnold of the *Washington Times*. "For me, he was the greatest legend on the face of the earth. I just wanted to be him, from the time I was this big. I just watched him, this giant of a man, always larger than life." In addition to his role models and early exposure to animals, Irwin had a natural gift that gave him an extra edge. Paul Farhi of the

Washington Post, cited in the *Seattle Times,* quoted Irwin's explanation of that something extra. "I don't want to seem arrogant or bigheaded, but I have a real instinct with animals," he said. "I've grown up with them . . . It's like I have an uncanny supernatural force rattling around my body. I tell you what, mate, it's magnetism."

Thus, via the combined contributing influences of parents, training, and talent, Irwin made animals his trade. He began by trapping rogue crocodiles and relocating them to the family zoo, which was renamed the Queensland Reptile and Fauna Park in the 1980s. In 1991 his parents gave him the business, which he re-dubbed the Australia Zoo. He then met and married Terri Raines, a fellow nature enthusiast from Eugene, Oregon, whom he met at his zoo. And it was the film footage from their honeymoon that propelled Irwin to fame.

Wildlife Warrior

Irwin and his new bride spent their 1992 honeymoon in Northern Australia, camping and trapping crocodiles for relocation. Through the auspices of old friend and television producer John Stainton, a film of the working vacation became the first episode of *Crocodile Hunter.* The program was picked up by the Discovery Channel and Irwin was soon an international celebrity.

The huge success of *Crocodile Hunter* was, of course, dependent on its star. Irwin, clad in his trademark khaki shorts and shirt, was full of boyish enthusiasm for the scary creatures. Crocodiles, venomous snakes and lizards, scorpions, and spiders were among the less than cuddly wildlife he championed. Sometimes caressing them, and tussling with others, he always met the animals in their own environments. He spoke in a thick Australian accent and peppered his sentences with such catchphrases as "By Crikey!" and "Look at this beauty." It was dangerous work, but Irwin had an abiding respect for his co-stars. As he told the *Houston Chronicle,* "If you see me getting bitten by something, it's my mistake. I knew what I was up against went I went in with that animal, and sometimes my reflexes are a little slow or there's an oversight on my part." Such mishaps, however, were comparatively few.

By 2006, Irwin's program (by then airing on cable television's Animal Planet) was being seen by approximately 500 million people in more than 120 countries. He had branched out onto the silver screen as well, with an appearance in Eddie Murphy's *Doctor Doolittle* and a starring role (with his wife) in *The Crocodile Hunters: Collision Course* (both 2002). Neither was a critical success, but Hollywood was not really Irwin's natural habitat anyway. Commenting on movie studio executives to Richard Deitsch of *Sports Illustrated* in 2002, Irwin said, "These land sharks in Hollywood, you don't know who they are. They're camouflaged in black Armani suits."

Rather, to Irwin, the whole purpose was preserving the animals and their environment. He donated $1 million a year to his charity, Wildlife Warriors, and bought up tracts of land all over Australia to return them to their natural state. He viewed his television programs as ways to get people familiar with and excited about the animals he loved. As he put it to

the *Houston Chronicle* in 2000, "What makes us [Irwin and his wife] tick—our gift to the world—is conservation. We eat, sleep and live for conservation. That's all we're about, that's what we're up to, that's our game. And we will die defending wildlife and wilderness areas. That's our passion."

Controversy

Not everyone was a fan of Irwin's, naturally. His countrymen, for instance, sometimes found his "ultra Aussieism" an embarrassing cliché. Further, some fellow naturalists found his television antics to be those of an irresponsible thrill-seeker who committed the dual sins of exaggerating the dangers of wild animals while minimizing the risks in handling them. Such types of criticism were of slight consequence to Irwin, however.

Irwin ran up against a broader spectrum of critics in 2004. In January he caused an uproar by feeding crocodiles while holding his infant son, Bob. His more vociferous detractors equated the incident with child abuse, but the authorities declined to charge him with an infraction of any kind, and Irwin vehemently denied the child was ever in any danger at all. In June Irwin again came under fire for allegedly filming too close to penguins, whales, and seals in the Antarctic.

Overall though, Irwin was not much of a lightning rod for negative comments. His popularity transcended his isolated lapses in judgment, and his star was only minimally dimmed. Likeability was, after all, the Crocodile Hunter's stock in trade.

Untimely Death

On September 4, 2006, Irwin was filming along Australia's Great Barrier Reef, his boat anchored near Port Douglas in Queensland. He decided to do a segment on a school of stingrays and began snorkeling in relatively shallow waters with his cameraman. Although they possess a barbed tail and a non-life-threatening venom, stingrays are normally extremely docile. On this day, however, chance and bad luck came together in a tragic manner. As Irwin swam over a male ray, it inexplicably struck him in the chest with its tail. His heart was pierced and he died within minutes. Only the third known fatal stingray attack in Australia and the 17th in the entire world, it was a sad and unexpected ending for a man who had made fearsome creatures his life's work. He was 44 years old.

The public outpouring of grief was almost immediate, with tributes coming from everyone from Australian Prime Minister John Howard to actor Russell Crowe to legions of fans all over the world. His father explained that he and his son had long been aware of the dangers in their occupations. He was quoted in *USA Today* as saying, "Both of us over the years have had some very close shaves and we both approached it the same way, we made jokes about it. That's not to say we were careless. But we treated it as part of the job. Nothing to worry about really." Certainly, there was little doubt that Irwin had died doing what he loved to do.

Irwin's legacy was the work and family he doted on. His eight-year-old daughter, Bindi, was already following in his footsteps and had been making a series with him at the time of his death. Environmental organization Planet Ark founder John Dee, a friend of Irwin's, told Jennifer Wulff of *People*, "We've got a fantastic chip off the block ready and raring to go. Hopefully [Bindi will] educate a whole new generation in the way her dad has." That time would, understandably, would be some time off in the future, as his wife and children mourned him.

A lesser known gift Irwin left behind was his discovery of a new snapping turtle. Found on the coast of Queensland, it was called Elseya irwini, in the tradition of naming after the discoverer. But perhaps Irwin's most memorable contribution was his unbridled joy and gusto. "I've never met somebody with such enthusiasm for life," television host Jay Leno told Michaela Boland of *Variety*. His widow and wife of 14 years put it another way in an interview with television personality Barbara Walters, quoted in *People*, when asked what she would miss the most. "He was fun," she said. "He taught me it's okay to play in the rain. And splash in my puddle. And let the kids get dirty. And spill ice cream on your pants. Now I'm going to have to work really hard at having fun again . . . I'm Mrs. Steve Irwin. I've got a lot to live up to."

Periodicals

Daily Post (Liverpool, England), July 29, 2002.
Daily Telegraph (London, England), September 5, 2006.
Daily Variety, September 5, 2006.
Guardian (London, England), September 5, 2006.
Houston Chronicle, November 27, 2000.
Mirror (London, England), February 19, 2000.
People, October 16, 2000; September 18, 2006; October 9, 2006.
Seattle Times, September 5, 2006.
Sports Illustrated, July 15, 2002.
Times (London, England), September 5, 2006.
Variety, September 11, 2006.
Washington Times, July 12, 2002.

Online

"Father: Steve Irwin Wouldn't Have Wanted State Funeral," *USA Today*, September 6, 2006, http://www.usatoday.com/life/people/2006-09-06-irwin-father-comments_x.htm?csp=34 (November 30, 2006).
"Steve Irwin, Crocodile Hunter," About, http://www.goaustralia.about.com/od/knowthepeople/a/steveirwin.htm (November 30, 2006).
"Steve Irwin Dead," ABC News, September 4, 2006, http://www.abc.net.au/news/newsitems/200609/s1732439.htm (November 30, 2006). □

B. K. S. Iyengar

Indian yoga teacher B. K. S. Iyengar (born 1918) has been an instrumental figure in introducing yoga to the Western world.

Yoga, an integrated system of physical and spiritual exercises, had a history that dated back thousands of years in India and was intertwined with the development of the Hindu religion. Yet even there it remained something of a specialized interest when Iyengar began his long career. Iyengar himself could contort his body into seemingly impossible shapes, but he also spread the idea that yoga was something anyone could do, and that it offered numerous benefits for an individual's overall health. Iyengar's 1966 book *Light on Yoga* has appeared in at least 18 languages, and his teachings, writings, and devoted corps of students and followers have spread the practice of his Iyengar yoga over much of the world.

Family Stricken by Influenza Epidemic

Bellur Krishnamachar Sundararaja Iyengar was a native of the southern Indian state of Karnataka, born on December 14, 1918, in the midst of the worldwide influenza epidemic of that year. He was the 11th of 13 children, ten of whom survived. Iyengar spent his early life in a village called Bellur, which has been reported as his birthplace, but he told *Contemporary Authors* that he was born in the larger city of Bangalore in the same region, where the family later moved. Iyengar's family was part of the high-status Brahmin caste, and the name Iyengar is associated with the family's membership in a group of South Indian adherents of a specific philosophical branch of Hinduism. Iyengar's father, Bellur Krishnamachar Iyengar, was a schoolmaster in a nearby village, and the family raised crops on a small plot of land they had inherited.

Iyengar's mother, Seshamma, was stricken with influenza during the pregnancy that culminated in his birth, and Iyengar suffered from health problems that would plague him for much of his childhood. At first he was not expected to survive. He was prone to the diseases endemic to the area and suffered multiple bouts of typhoid, malaria, and tuberculosis. "My poor health was matched, as it often is when one is sick, by my poor mood," Iyengar wrote in his book *Light on Life*. "A deep melancholy overtook me, and at times I asked myself whether life was worth the trouble of living."

Iyengar's situation was worsened by the death of his father from untreated appendicitis when Iyengar was nine. The young boy did poorly in school and he failed a key English-language examination. The exam result brought his schooling to an end, and Iyengar's family began to wonder how the still frail young man might make a living. Iyengar's brother-in-law, Shriman Tirumalai Krishnamacharya, worked as a yoga teacher and scholar in the employ of an Indian noble family in the city of Mysore, and in 1934 Krishnamacharya, who helped create the now widely practiced hatha yoga style, invited Iyengar to move temporarily to Mysore to look after the family while he was away conducting yoga classes in other parts of the region.

Iyengar stayed on in Mysore and took yoga lessons from Krishnamacharya. At first he was, he told Colleen O'Connor of the *Denver Post*, "an anti-advertisement for yoga." Leaning forward, he could barely touch his knees, much less his feet. Krishnamacharya's harsh teaching regime did not endear him to his students, who often sneaked away from their classes, and Iyengar at first was as unenthusiastic as the others. At one point Krishamacharya forced him to do a split-leg exercise for which he was unprepared, and he tore a ligament and was unable to walk for some time. But Iyengar noticed that, for the first time in his life, he was growing stronger, and he persisted in his training. One of Krishnamacharya's top students disappeared just days before the royalty of the area were due in Mysore for an important yoga demonstration, and Iyengar was tapped as a replacement. He did so well that he was able to join his teacher on the road for other classes and demonstrations.

Began Teaching All-Female Class

On one of these tours, a group of women became fascinated with the art of yoga and asked for lessons. Iyengar was chosen to be their teacher because, at 18, he was Krishnamacharya's youngest disciple, and it was thought to be less improper for the women to be taught by a man who had not yet reached full adulthood. Iyengar did well at this assignment and was sent on to a bigger one: Krishnamacharya named him to fill a teaching post at the Deccan Gymkhana Club, an upper class sports club in the city of Pune, in India's Maharashtra state.

Here, once again, Iyengar felt at a disadvantage in many ways. He spoke English badly and the local language, Marathi, not at all (the language of his native Karnataka was Kannada). The yoga students at the Gymkhana were older than Iyengar and in better condition, sometimes more advanced in yoga than he was. Iyengar, fearful of having to return in disgrace to his fearsome teacher in Mysore, embarked on a regime of practice that could last up to ten hours a day. His aim was to become a total yoga expert, fully systematizing the diverse bits of knowledge his teacher had passed on, and getting to know the ultimate potentialities of his own body. Neighbors in Pune, most of them still unfamiliar with yoga, questioned his sanity, but Iyengar's knowledge and strength deepened. It was during this period that the systematic discipline later known as Iyengar Yoga was developed.

As Iyengar's studies began to bear fruit, the Gymkhana extended his original six-month contract to three years. After this term ended, Iyengar launched a career as an independent yoga teacher. At first he had few pupils, and there were days on which he subsisted on little more than rice and tea. Nothing would dissuade him, however, from his hours of daily practice. Iyengar's family, anxious to see him in a more settled existence, arranged his marriage to a 16-year-old girl named Ramamani. At first he refused to do more than meet her briefly, but the relationship flowered into marriage on July 13, 1943. Ramamani became a strong backer of Iyengar's enthusiasm for yoga, and the marriage was a long and happy one that produced six children.

Several facets of Iyengar's yoga teaching set him apart from other gurus. He believed that yoga was not a practice to be restricted to specialists but could benefit anyone, and he began to incorporate aids such as ropes, belts, and blocks into yoga routines for those who needed them. Many elderly people over the years would flock to Iyengar's classes and accomplish feats of which they would not have believed themselves capable. Iyengar was also living testimony to the idea that yoga could aid in the solution of even serious health problems, and tales of miraculous cures began to

accumulate around him. Iyengar began to attract famous Indians as students, including the philosopher J. Krishnamurti and the cardiologist Rustom Jal Vakil.

Taught Yoga to Famed Violinist

It was Vakil's wife who introduced Iyengar to one of his most renowned students, star American classical violinist Yehudi Menuhin. An initial five-minute meeting between the two men in 1952, arranged while Menuhin was on a concert tour in India and expressed an interest in yoga, ballooned into a session lasting several hours. Iyengar and Menuhin became friends, and Menuhin touted the improvement in his violin playing that he said had come about after he began practicing yoga. When Menuhin returned to India in 1954, he suggested that Iyengar return to the West with him and give yoga lessons in Europe and the United States.

The result was a publicity bonanza, for Menuhin's friends and acquaintances were a highly visible group. Iyengar taught Elisabeth, the octogenarian Queen of Belgium, to stand on her head, and he did a yoga demonstration for the Soviet Union's Premier, Nikita Khrushchev. At the invitation of Standard Oil heiress Rebekah Harkness, he came to the United States in 1956. American interest in yoga was growing—indeed, Indian gurus were already active there—but Iyengar was repelled by the country's materialism. "I saw Americans were interested in the three W's—wealth, women, and wine," he told O'Connor. "I was taken aback to see how the way of life here conflicted with my own country. I thought twice about coming back." Iyengar lived for a time in Switzerland and did not return to the United States until the early 1970s.

By that time, however, he had become a well-known author, in America as well as the rest of the world. Frustrated by existing yoga manuals, which he felt cheated the user by giving directions that were inadequate for the realization of the poses depicted in photographs, he wrote *Light on Yoga* in 1966. Iyengar worked closely with a photographer on 4,000 shots of himself in yoga poses or asanas, from which the final images in the book were selected. Four decades later, *Light on Yoga* was considered the preeminent yoga text in the field, with new translations into other languages appearing regularly; it was often referred to as the bible of yoga.

Light on Yoga spawned a large group of Iyengar followers who wanted to disseminate Iyengar's ideas in a systematic way. The popularity of yoga continued to rise in the United States with the debut of the Public Broadcasting System television program *Lilias! Yoga and You* in 1972, and the following year the first Iyengar Yoga studio opened in Ann Arbor, Michigan. Iyengar himself made a return visit to the United States in 1973, and by 1984 the first annual International Iyengar Convention, held in San Francisco, drew a crowd of 800 devotees. Iyengar's followers, who referred to him as Guruji, generally maintained their adherence, despite his habit of physically slapping students who made errors; some complained (according to O'Connor) that his initials, B.K.S., could stand for "beat, kick, slap."

Iyengar divided his time between India and the West over the later decades of his life. In 1975 he established the Ramamani Iyengar Memorial Yoga Institute in Pune, named after his late wife; the institute became a key center for the training of new Iyengar instructors. Working, as he had on *Light on Yoga,* with native speakers of English as co-authors, he wrote seven more books, including *Body the Shrine, Yoga Thy Light* (1978), *The Art of Yoga* (1985), *The Tree of Yoga* (1988), *Yoga: The Path to Holistic Health* (2001), and *Light on Life,* (2005), in which he interwove practical yoga advice, philosophical reflections, and stories from his own life and career.

Gradually retiring from teaching, Iyengar was supplanted as guru by two of his children, daughter Geeta and son Prashant. He continued, however, to practice yoga on a daily basis, and well into his ninth decade he was able to stand on his head and stay in that position for half an hour. In 2005 Iyengar made a tour of the United States in order to promote *Light on Life,* for which he had reportedly received a seven-figure advance. (He plowed the profits from his books back into his institute and into local development projects in Bellur.) By that time, Iyengar counted Hollywood celebrities, including the lithe *Seinfeld* actor Michael Richards and actress Annette Bening, among his followers, and Iyengar Yoga schools were operating in well over 250 cities. "I am leaving everything for posterity, as a guide for generations to come," he told Hilary de Vries of the *New York Times.* "If they read my books, their confidence will grow so that none can shake them."

Books

Iyengar, B.K.S., *Light on Life: The Yoga Journey to Wholeness, Inner Peace, and Ultimate Freedom,* Rodale, 2005.
———, *Light on Yoga,* Schocken, 1979.

Periodicals

Denver Post, October 9, 2005.
Investor's Business Daily, November 30, 2001.
New York Times, October 13, 2005.
Time, April 26, 2004.
Washington Post, October 19, 2005.

Online

"A Biography of BKS Iyengar, Written by Kofia Busia, Yoga Teacher," http://www.kofibusia.com/level_1/BKSIyengar Biography.html (October 24, 2006).
"B.K.S. Iyengar," Newsmakers, Issue 1, Thomson Gale, 2005, reproduced in Biography Resource Center, Thomson Gale, 2006, http://www.galenet.galegroup.com/servlet/BioRC (October 24, 2006).
Contemporary Authors Online, Gale, 2006, reproduced in Biography Resource Center, Thomson Gale, 2006, http://www.galenet.galegroup.com/servlet/BioRC (October 24, 2006). □

J

Jane Jacobs

American-born Canadian writer Jane Jacobs (1916–2006) revolutionized the field of urban planning with her pathbreaking 1961 book *The Death and Life of Great American Cities.*

In the book Jacobs launched a broadside against the concepts of urban renewal that were fashionable at the time. The seeming disorder and unpredictability of cities, she argued, were actually signs of their vitality, and the brave new world of high-rises envisioned by planners would strangle the buzzing street life that fostered community ties and drew newcomers with its energy. Jacobs backed up her ideas with action, leading several community efforts to resist the obliteration of urban neighborhoods by freeway construction. She was always a controversial figure with as many detractors as admirers, and as the central issue in planning evolved from urban renewal to urban sprawl, she took up other topics in her writing. Nevertheless, Jacobs lived long enough to see the vocabulary of city planning become infused with her ideas.

Held Imaginary Conversations

Jacobs was born Jane Butzner in Scranton, Pennsylvania, on May 4, 1916. Both her parents were Jewish, and both, uncommonly enough for the time, were professionals: her father was a doctor and her mother a schoolteacher. Jacobs was an indifferent student who preferred to read a book of her own, concealed under her desk, rather than listen to her teacher. Her real thinking and learning got done when she was sent to run errands by her family. As she walked, she conducted conversations with three imagined companions: U.S. president Thomas Jefferson, inventor Benjamin Franklin, and a Saxon tribal chief named Cerdic who was a character in an English historical novel she read.

Curiously enough, it was Cerdic who stirred her analytical mind. Later, doing housework, she found that "there were only two things in the entire house that were familiar to him, the fire (although he didn't understand the chimney) and the sword [a Civil War collectible]," she said in an interview, later quoted by Douglas Martin in her *New York Times* obituary. "Everything else had to be explained to him." After she finished high school, Jacobs was drawn to the bright lights of New York, which had entranced her on an earlier trip. "In 1928 I went there, with friends, and we came through the Holland Tunnel and right into the middle of the financial district, on a regular working day, and I was just flabbergasted by the number of people on the street and how they were all rushing around," she was quoted as saying in the *Times* of London. Jacobs never obtained a college degree, although she later took courses at Columbia University's adult-oriented School of General Studies.

Her first job was an unpaid newspaper internship in Scranton, but as soon as she could, she headed for New York and moved in with her sister, who was six years older. After she arrived, Jacobs would get on the subway each day, pick a stop at random, and apply for jobs at neighboring businesses. At the Christopher Street stop in Manhattan's Greenwich Village, she found a secretarial job with a candy company and soon an apartment in the colorful neighborhood she came to love. Jacobs and her sister had to scrape together a living in the later years of the Depression, sometimes subsisting on bananas for days at a time, but Jacobs became a confirmed New Yorker. She would live in Lower Manhattan for more than 30 years.

A quick study in almost any new area of knowledge, Jacobs began to write and contribute freelance articles to New York publications. She enjoyed wandering the city and investigating its various neighborhoods and industrial districts, and she wrote about topics ranging from the metals industry—she once penned an article about manhole covers—to sellers of furs in the Garment District. Her financial condition improved, and in April of 1944, while she was working for the federal Office of War Information, she and her two roommates threw a party at which one of the guests was architect Robert Hyde Jacobs Jr. She married him a month later, and the pair raised two sons and one daughter.

Worked as Architecture Editor

In 1952 Jacobs took a job as an editor at the magazine *Architectural Forum.* "I went to *Architectural Forum,* and they said well, you're now our school and hospital expert," Jacobs recalled to Paul Goldberger, writing in *American Scholar.* "That was the first time I got suspicious of experts. I knew nothing, not even how to read plans." With her husband's help, Jacobs mastered the knowledge she needed.

In the optimistic atmosphere of 1950s America, planners believed that urban design had the power to ameliorate poverty and other social problems. Block after block of the older neighborhoods of many cities were leveled and replaced with high-rise towers in parklike settings, some of them with rents subsidized for poorer residents, others quite luxurious. The process went by the name of slum clearance, or, more politely, urban renewal. Jacobs, in her architecture magazine post, had a front row view of the process, which was superintended by an almost exclusively male corps of city government officials. She went on assignment to Philadelphia, where planning director Ed Bacon showed her around a new development.

"First he took me to a street where loads of people were hanging around on the street, on the stoops, having a good time of it, and he said, well, this is the street we're going to get rid of," she recalled to Goldberger. "That was the 'before' street. Then he showed me the 'after' street, all fixed up, and there was just one person on it, a bored little boy kicking a tire in the gutter. It was so grim that I would have been kicking a tire, too. But Mr. Bacon thought it had a beautiful vista." She began to delve more deeply into urban planning, and she contributed an article to a *Fortune* magazine series that was later collected into a book, *The Exploding Metropolis.* Jacobs's husband, along with William H. Whyte, her editor at *Fortune,* urged her to write a book expressing her ideas about what made a city healthy or unhealthy, and, armed with a Rockefeller Foundation grant, she took to the streets of New York, notebook in hand. *The Death and Life of Great American Cities* was published by Random House in 1961.

The book offered a broadside against several generations of received wisdom, and it has often been grouped with other books of the 1960s, written by nonspecialists, that overturned established thinking in their fields—Betty Friedan's *The Feminine Mystique* or Ralph Nader's *Unsafe at Any Speed,* for example. Jacobs took aim at a complex of

ideas she referred to as Radiant Garden City Beautiful, or RGCB. A special target was Swiss architect Le Corbusier (Charles Edouard Jeanneret-Gris), a builder of modernist cubes who advocated a clean separation between residential, commercial, and recreational zones. In Jacobs's view, it was a mixture of these functions, as citizens crossed paths and exchanged goods and news, that gave a neighborhood vitality. She even contended that theaters and music spaces should be integrated into the neighborhoods of the populations they served.

The Death and Life of Great American Cities was not just a polemical attack, however; Jacobs also outlined what she saw as positive features of urban neighborhoods. They were fourfold. First, what would later be called mixed use was beneficial, with residential, retail, civic, and industrial buildings jumbled together and growing organically. Second, city blocks should be compact. Third, buildings should be diverse in age, condition, and size; Jacobs's ideas dovetailed effectively with the growing movement in favor of historic preservation. Finally, population should be dense. For Jacobs, the ideal neighborhood was often represented by her home of Greenwich Village, where she interacted with a wide range of individuals.

Opposed Expressway

In 1962, the year after *The Death and Life of Great American Cities* was published, Jacobs got the chance to move from the realm of theory into activism, when Greenwich Village was threatened by a proposed Lower Manhattan Expressway. The new road would have eliminated much of Washington Square Park and other Manhattan landmarks, and Jacobs soon emerged as a leader of residents opposed to the plan. The effort pitted Jacobs against New York's immensely powerful planning czar, Robert Moses, who did not receive news of the resistance gracefully. "There is nobody against this—NOBODY, NOBODY, NOBODY, but a bunch of . . . a bunch of MOTHERS," Jacobs recalled Moses saying during a meeting (according to Veronica Horwell of the London *Guardian*). Nevertheless, Jacobs and her associates emerged victorious when New York Mayor John Lindsay killed the project in 1969.

Some of the opposition to Jacobs's ideas had a similarly sexist tinge, as when noted architecture writer Lewis Mumford reviewed *The Death and Life of Great American Cities* in the *New Yorker* under the title, "Mother Jacobs' Home Remedy for Urban Cancer." Other criticisms of the book have been more substantive, however. Her observations were centered mostly on the older neighborhoods of the United States Northeast (not only in New York, but also including Boston's North End). "But the problems of the 20th-century were vast and complicated," observed Nicolai Ourosoff in the *New York Times.* Ms. Jacobs had few answers for suburban sprawl or the nation's dependence on cars, which remains critical to the development of American cities." The ideas of Jacobs, a committed liberal and civil rights activist, ironically later found support among conservatives who worked to restrict governmental eminent domain powers. Jacobs was deeply suspicious of eminent domain condemnations of city neighborhoods, telling Bill

Steigerwald of *Reason* that "the courts have never given the kind of overview to this that they should."

In 1968, at her husband's suggestion, Jacobs and her family moved to Toronto, Ontario, Canada, so that the couple's college-age sons could avoid being drafted and sent to serve in the Vietnam War. Jacobs remained in Canada for the rest of her life, later becoming a citizen of that country. Within months of moving to Toronto she had become involved in an ultimately successful effort to stop the building of an expressway that would have sliced through the city's Chinatown, and she found in Toronto a city that exemplified many of the principles she had espoused. She devoted many of her energies to issues facing her adopted country, and in 1980 she penned *The Question of Separatism: Quebec and the Struggle over Sovereignty,* a controversial book that favored the secession of French-speaking Quebec from the rest of Canada. For Jacobs, the issue of Quebec's separatist aspirations was less one of cultural identity than one of local control.

Jacobs continued to write for the rest of her life, and she had two books in progress when she died in Toronto on April 25, 2006, at the age of 89. Her other works are much less well known than *The Death and Life of Great American Cities,* but they often contain fresh perspectives born of Jacobs's common-sense approach and autodidact procedures. Most of her books dealt with cities, but she turned increasingly to the macro dimension of urban existence rather than the micro level explored in her first book. *The Economy of Cities* (1969) disputed the common contention that great cities grew from the roots of productive agriculture; more often, Jacobs noted, innovations in agriculture, since the beginnings of human society, have depended on technology perfected in urban settings. Jacobs's *Cities and the Wealth of Nations* (1984) examined what Jacobs saw as an often intrinsic conflict between the organic development of cities and the ideologically driven constraints of policies implemented at the national level.

The last book published during Jacobs's lifetime was the gloomy *Dark Age Ahead,* issued in 2004; in that book Jacobs contended that the fundamental building blocks of North American society—community and family, higher education, science, taxation, and the influence of well-educated professionals—were eroding. By that time it was commonplace for young people graduating from a college or university to head for one of the North American cities with just the sort of diverse, well-preserved urban neighborhoods Jane Jacobs had championed: New York, Boston, Chicago, New Orleans, or San Francisco, for example. Those young people were Jacobs's intellectual progeny, and the continued existence of many of the neighborhoods themselves was her legacy.

Books

Alexiou, Alice Sparberg, *Jane Jacobs, Urban Visionary,* HarperCollins, 2006.
Jacobs, Jane, *The Death and Life of Great American Cities,* Random House, 1961.
Jacobs, Jane, *The Economy of Cities,* Random House, 1969.

Periodicals

American Scholar, Autumn 2006.
Architecture, June 2006.
Economist (U.S.), May 13, 2006.
Guardian (London, England), April 28, 2006.
Independent (London, England), June 3, 2006.
International Herald Tribune, April 27, 2006.
New York Times, April 26, 2006; April 30, 2006.
Reason, June 2001.
Time Canada, May 24, 2004.
Times (London, England), April 27, 2006.
Winnipeg Free Press, April 29, 2006.

Online

Contemporary Authors Online, Gale, 2006, reproduced in Biography Resource Center, Thomson Gale, 2006, http://www.galenet.galegroup.com/servlet/BioRC (October 31, 2006). □

Victor Jara

Chilean folksinger Victor Jara (1932–1973) was the voice of his country's dispossessed, an internationally admired songwriter, and one of the founders of a new genre of Latin American song. He was killed by Chilean security forces during the coup that deposed the country's elected president, Salvador Allende, in September of 1973.

Grew Up in Rural Poverty

Victor Lidio Jara Martínez was born on September 23, 1932. His parents were farm workers with minimal resources who lived on a plantation near the Chilean town of Lonquen. Jara and his older siblings had to collect firewood, cutting down small trees with an ax, and haul grass back to the house for the pigs the family raised. His mother, Amanda, went out to the neighboring hillsides to gather herbs to sell. Sheer poverty and the alcohol abuse and violence of Jara's father, Manuel, placed the family under great strain, and among Victor's few positive memories of his childhood were the folk songs his mother liked to sing, accompanying herself with a guitar. To earn extra money the family rented a room to a local schoolteacher, who also played the guitar and showed Victor how to produce a few chords.

No matter how difficult things got for the Jara family, Amanda insisted that the children go to school. Jara moved with his mother and siblings to the Chilean capital of Santiago, where his mother found work in a small restaurant. Their neighborhood was chaotic, filled with street gangs and noise, but Victor Jara and his brother Lalo always showed up on time at the local Catholic school. Victor got additional guitar lessons from a neighborhood resident who noticed that he was unusually talented at making up new songs. Jara rarely saw his mother, who worked at one job or another for almost the entire day, and she died when he was 15. He was deeply upset by her death and sought help

Joined Mime Group

His audition was successful, and he appeared on stage in Carl Orff's musico-dramatic work *Carmina Burana,* dressed as a monk. By late 1954 he had made friends among the choir's membership, traveled with them to the north of Chile to learn about the folk music of the region—the one from which Jara had originally come. He joined a mime group consisting of Santiago theater students who were all much better off financially than Jara but accepted him as part of the group. One of them, Fernando Bordeu, gave him cast-off clothes and encouraged him to apply to the theater program at the University of Chile.

The sporadically educated Jara did poorly on the reading portion of the audition but impressed the judges with his stage movements, and he was admitted on a scholarship. Appearing in several plays, he gravitated toward those with social themes, such as Russian playwright Maxim Gorky's *The Lower Depths,* a depiction of the harshness of lower-class life. In the late 1950s Jara met two women who would alter the course of his life. One was an instructor, Joan Turner Bunster, a British-born dancer and dance teacher who was married to a Chilean ballet star. After her marriage broke up, she and Jara slowly moved toward a romantic relationship. They married in 1965 and raised a daughter, Amanda, along with Joan's daughter from her previous marriage, Manuela.

The other major influence on Jara in the late 1950s was Chilean folksinger Violeta Parra, whom he heard and met at Santiago's Café São Paulo in 1957. It was Parra who steered folk music in Chile away from the rote reproduction of rural materials toward modern song composition rooted in traditional forms. Parra tried to incorporate folk music into the everyday life of modern Chileans, establishing musical community centers called peñas. Jara absorbed these lessons and joined a folk group called Cuncumén, with whom he continued his explorations of Chile's traditional music.

Jara maintained his interest in theater, studying stage direction at the university, frequently directing plays in Santiago (with sharper and sharper political content) in the 1960s, and even attending rehearsals of the Royal Shakespeare Company on a trip to Britain. He worked for nine years as a stage director at the Theatre Institute of the University of Chile. But music began to occupy more and more of his energy. He left Cuncumén in 1962 and, inspired by Parra's example, began writing songs of his own. At first his songs were personal and autobiographical, but as he began to perform in the peñas that opened in Chile's cities and university neighborhoods his subject matter became more varied. "As I grew closer to him," Joan Jara wrote, "I realized how profound was Victor's necessity for music and how important his guitar was to him. I could have been jealous of it, because it was almost as though it were another person with whom he conversed. . . . He always seemed to have two or three songs inside him. As he had said to me in one of his letters, 'Something seems to take root in me and then has to find a way of getting out.' "

from a priest, who encouraged him to enter a seminary in the town of San Bernardo, near Santiago. As quoted by his wife, Joan, in her biography *Victor: An Unfinished Song,* Jara said that he hoped "to find a different and more profound love which perhaps would compensate for the lack of human love" in his life.

Jara enjoyed the music he heard and sang at the seminary, but he was not cut out for the requirements of the priesthood, particularly that of celibacy. Students had to whip themselves while taking a cold shower if they experienced sexual desire, and Jara complained (according to his wife) that during the two years he spent at the seminary, "everything healthy, that implied a state of physical well-being, had to be put aside. Your body became a sort of burden that you were forced to bear." In 1952 Jara left the seminary, by mutual agreement with its instructors, and 10 days later he was drafted into the Chilean army.

The future revolutionary singer and poet acquitted himself well in the military, rising to the rank of sergeant first class and earning a glowing final report that praised his leadership qualities and identified him as officer material. But he returned to Santiago after his discharge and lived rather aimlessly for some months, staying with friends and working as a hospital porter. His path toward the artistic activities of his later life began when he tried out for the choir at the University of Chile after seeing a newspaper advertisement for the auditions.

Stirred Up Scandal with Comic Song

Jara released his first album, *Canto a lo humano*, in 1966. Early in his recording career he showed a knack for antagonizing conservative Chileans, releasing a traditional comic song called "La beata" that depicted a religious woman with a crush on the priest to whom she goes for confession. The song was banned on radio stations and removed from record shops, but the controversy only added to Jara's reputation among young and progressive Chileans. More serious in the eyes of the Chilean right wing was Jara's growing identification with the leftist social movement led by socialist politician Salvador Allende. After visits to Cuba and the Soviet Union in the early 1960s, Jara had joined the Communist Party. The personal met the political in Jara's songs about the poverty he had experienced firsthand.

Jara's songs, many of them reflective stories whose music drew on traditional Chilean forms, were given the label of nueva canción or "new song"; the genre developed on parallel courses in the 1960s in various Latin American countries, but Jara was among its most prominent practitioners. Jara's songs spread outside Chile and were known to and performed by American folk artists such as Joan Baez. His popularity was due not only to his songwriting skills but also to his exceptional power as a performer. Jara took a decisive turn toward political confrontation with his song "Preguntas por Puerto Montt" (Questions About Puerto Montt, 1969), which took direct aim at a government official who had ordered police to attack squatters in the town of Puerto Montt. The Chilean political situation deteriorated after the official was assassinated, and right-wing thugs beat up Jara on one occasion.

Jara composed "Venceremos" (We Will Triumph), the theme song of Allende's Unidad Popular (Popular Unity) movement, and he welcomed Allende's election to the Chilean presidency in 1970. Jara and his wife were key participants in a cultural renaissance that swept Chile, organizing cultural events that supported the country's new socialist government. He set poems by Chilean writer Pablo Neruda to music and performed at a ceremony honoring Neruda after the famous writer received the Nobel Prize for literature in 1972. Throughout rumblings of a right-wing coup, Jara held on to his teaching job at Chile's Technical University.

On September 11, 1973, however, Chilean troops under the command of General Augusto Pinochet mounted a coup against the Allende government. Jara was seized and taken to the Estadio Chile, a large sports stadium. There he was held for four days, deprived of food and sleep. He was tortured, and his hands were broken by soldiers who told him to try to keep on playing the guitar with his damaged hands. But Jara continued to sing "Venceremos" and began writing a new song describing the carnage going on in the stadium, as many of those imprisoned were killed; the words of the new song were smuggled out by a prisoner who survived. At some point, probably on September 15, Jara was taken to a deserted area and shot. He was taken to the city morgue in Santiago, where his wife was allowed to retrieve the body and bury it on the condition that she not publicize the event.

Tributes to Jara began with an anonymous Chilean television technician who played an excerpt from Jara's "La plegarí a un Labrador" over a Hollywood film soundtrack the night his death was announced in a one-paragraph newspaper item. For many years, however, Jara's recordings were virtually silenced in Chile. Even after the country's politics began to liberalize in the 1990s, there was the problem of locating the master recordings, which had been given to a group of Swedish television technicians by Joan Jara as she fled the country. (She returned after 10 years and became one of the activists whose efforts eventually led to the restoration of democracy in Chile.) In the early 2000s, however, Jara's recordings were reissued by AOL Time Warner in a handsome box set, and he also became the subject of several rock tribute albums by young Chilean musicians who venerated his courage. "They could kill him," Joan Jara told BBC News, "but they couldn't kill his songs." In 2003 the stadium where Jara spent his last days was renamed the Estadio Victor Jara.

Books

Contemporary Musicians, volume 59, Thomson Gale, 2007.
Jara, Joan, *Victor: An Unfinished Song*, Bloomsbury, 1983 (reprinted 1998).

Periodicals

Austin American-Statesman, May 17, 1998.
Gazette (Montreal, Quebec, Canada), September 10, 2003.
Guardian (London, England), October 22, 1998.
Independent (London, England), September 4, 1998.
New York Times, December 23, 2002.

Online

" 'They Couldn't Kill His Songs,' " BBC News, World: Americas, http://www.news.bbc.co.uk/2/hi/americas/165363.stm (January 16, 2007).
"Victor Jara," *All Music Guide*, http://www.allmusic.com (January 16, 2007). □

Luis Jiménez

The large-scale public sculptures of American artist Luis Jiménez (1940–2006)—mythical, violent, political, garish, sexy, fun, and often profound—reflected their maker's vision of Mexican-American culture and his often critical views of the wider Southwestern and American cultures in which Mexican Americans live.

Jiménez worked in the industrial, unabashedly commercial medium of fiberglass, and he drew on such commonplace art traditions as Mexican wall calendar prints, cowboy imagery, and "lowrider" truck decoration. Yet his work reflected a detailed knowledge of Mexican and European artistic traditions. He made sculptures for public places, intended to be seen and understood by the thousands of ordinary people, in many cases of Latino descent, who would pass by them every day, yet he also had a strong following among sophisticated art collectors. Jiménez's art had many aspects, but perhaps its most distinctive characteristic was the way it was structured to appeal to a variety of audiences. "My working-class roots have a lot to do with it; I want to create a popular art that ordinary people can relate to as well as people who have degrees in art," Jiménez explained to Chiori Santiago of *Smithsonian*. "That doesn't mean it has to be watered down. My philosophy is to create a multilayered piece, like [novelist Ernest] Hemingway's *Old Man and the Sea*. The first time I read it, it was an exciting adventure story about fishing. The last time, I was deeply moved."

Raised by Signmaker and Frustrated Artist

Luis Alfonso Jiménez Jr. was born in El Paso, Texas, on July 30, 1940, and grew up in the city's Segundo Barrio neighborhood. His grandfather had been a glassblower in Mexico, and his undocumented immigrant father, Luis Sr., ran a sign shop and had hoped to become a professional artist himself. He had won a nationwide art competition in the 1930s, but the promised prize money fell victim to Depression-era cutbacks at the sponsoring organization and was never delivered. Instead, he poured his creativity into signs that appeared around El Paso. "Right here was the Fiesta Drive-In," Jiménez told Santiago as he showed her around El Paso. "It had a neon sign that he made of a woman dancing in a flamenco skirt in front of two guys sitting on the ground wearing sombreros. With each flash of light in the circuit, her dress would appear to go higher and higher, until at the end the guys' hats would fly up in the air. That was typical of my dad's signs—lots of action and color."

Jiménez started working in the shop at age six, becoming familiar with industrial materials such as fiberglass and the paints that could be used on them. The family appreciated art where they found it. Sometimes on trips to Mexico they would visit museums or public buildings bearing giant historical paintings by José Orozco or one of the country's other great muralists. Jiménez, however, saw few prospects for himself in El Paso, whose atmosphere for Mexicans he likened to that of apartheid-era South Africa for blacks. He jumped at the chance to attend the University of Texas at Austin in 1960. "College was really a great experience for me, because had I not gone to Austin, I would never have had the kind of exposure to the world that I ended up having," he said in a *Texas Alcalde* interview quoted in the *Austin American-Statesman*. His father was furious when he switched his major from architecture to art, but he persisted and received a fine arts degree in 1964.

After two years spent studying art in Mexico City, Jiménez headed for New York. He felt a new sense of freedom there—in a city with people and artists from all over the world, his Chicano ethnicity did not stand out. As an unknown artist competing against hundreds or thousands of others, however, he faced long odds. He got a job as an assistant to sculptor Seymour Lipton and also worked from 1966 to 1969 for the city of New York as an arts program coordinator. His marriage to his wife, Vicky, which had

begun in 1961 and produced a daughter, Elisa, broke up in 1966. He was married again the following year to Mary Wynn, but that marriage, too, ended in divorce after three years. Jiménez visited numerous galleries, trying to interest them in his work, but he got nowhere.

Finally, in 1969, Jiménez parked his truck in front of the prestigious Leo Castelli Gallery, which he had heard featured works by up-and-coming artists. This time, instead of relying on verbal salesmanship, he dragged three large sculptures through the front door. Gallery director Ivan Karp was outraged at first, but then impressed. He sent Jiménez to the Graham Gallery, which mounted the artist's first solo show. The staff there expressed surprise when Jiménez's sculptures found a ready market among art buyers, and Jiménez's career accelerated when the powerful and notoriously cranky *New York Times* art critic Hilton Kramer praised the Jiménez works displayed in a second Graham Gallery show.

Worked in Fiberglass

By that time, Jiménez had begun to create works with the characteristic cross-cultural imagination that made him famous. "Man on Fire" (1969) was a sculpture of a burning man that suggested both the Buddhist monks who set themselves on fire in protest against the Vietnam War and the story of the Aztec emperor Cuauhtemoc, who underwent fire torture at the hands of Spanish conquistadors. Jiménez's *American Dream* (1967), now housed a the Hirshhorn Museum in Washington, D.C., depicted a sexual coupling between a woman and a Volkswagen Beetle. More controversial was *Barfly* (1969), a portrayal of the Statue of Liberty as an overweight beer drinker. Jiménez worked in fiberglass, which for him carried a more popular touch than marble or bronze.

It was also a material he had been working with since childhood, but at the time it was used by just a handful of artists. Jiménez's art was rooted in those early experiences. "Perhaps because of the experience of working in the sign shop, I realized early on that I wanted to do it all—paint, draw, work with wood, metal, clay," he told Santiago. Although his career was flying high, he felt disconnected from his roots. He returned temporarily to El Paso in the early 1970s, and then in 1972 drove to Roswell, New Mexico, and showed his works to art collector Donald Anderson, who offered Jiménez a job in his private museum. Jiménez moved there, and would live in New Mexico for the rest of his life. He later moved to the rural town of Hondo, living in a converted schoolhouse and hunting small animals in the dry surrounding valleys, always eating his kill. In 1985 Jiménez married Susan Brockman and had one more child, a son.

Jiménez continued to create small sculptures, paintings, and drawings, some of which were purchased by such institutions as the Museum of Modern Art and Metropolitan Museum of Art in New York, and the Art Institute of Chicago. Living in the Southwest, he began to concentrate on Western and Southwestern themes. His *Progress* series of 1974, along with other works, explored the violent reality behind conventional Western stories; *Progress I* showed an Indian hunter piercing a buffalo with an arrow as bloody saliva drips from the animal's mouth. Because of his growing prestige and his new regional focus, Jiménez began to win commissions for large sculptures to be mounted in public spaces in the expanding cities of the Southwest. His first public commission was for a sculpture called *Vaquero,* to be installed in Houston's Tranquility Park, next to the city hall.

Works Stirred Controversy

Public sculptures, with their large audiences, often become lightning rods for controversy, and Jiménez's works, with their rough realism and sharp social agendas, were perhaps more controversial than most. The cowboy shown in *Vaquero* was Mexican, and he was also waving a pistol while riding on horseback. Both images were accurate historically; Jiménez meant the sculpture as a correction to traditional cowboy imagery that generally depicted cowboys as Anglo-American and sanitized the violence inherent in Western life. But city officials balked at installing the sculpture in its original location and instead suggested a location in Moody Park, in a predominantly Latino neighborhood. There, too, the sculpture encountered criticism. Jiménez met with local activists to discuss the work, however, and the result was strong community support for keeping the sculpture. The pattern of official disapproval followed by grassroots support would be repeated several times over the course of Jiménez's career. A cast of *Vaquero* was later installed in front of the Smithsonian Institution's Museum of American Art in Washington, D.C.

Among Jiménez's most famous sculptures was *Southwest Pietà* (1984), which fused Christian and Native American imagery. It showed the mythological lovers Popocatepetl and Ixtacihuatl after whom the two large volcanoes near Mexico City are named; the deceased Ixtacihuatl lies on her lover's lap, in a pose reminiscent of Michelangelo's famous sculpture of the Virgin Mary holding the lifeless body of Jesus. The figures are embedded in the back of a bald eagle. This sculpture too encountered criticism from activists. "Critics, who say it depicts the aftermath of the rape of an Indian maiden by a Spanish conquistador, say it is offensive to those of Spanish heritage," noted an *Albuquerque Journal* article quoted by Santiago. The sculpture was moved to Albuquerque's Martineztown neighborhood.

Some of Jiménez's sculptures addressed Mexican-American experiences directly, such as *Border Crossing* (1989), which showed a man carrying his family on his shoulders as he crossed the Rio Grande (Rí Bravo del Norte) into the United States. But as Jiménez's renown grew, he began to receive commissions in parts of the country with small Hispanic populations. *Sodbuster,* which was mounted for many years in Fargo, North Dakota, showed a muscled farmer behind two massive oxen. A Pittsburgh, Pennsylvania, sculpture called *Hunky—Steel Worker* once again stirred controversy after some objected to the term "Hunky" as an ethnic slur on those of Eastern European descent. Jiménez had his supporters in Pittsburgh as well, but he eventually agreed to grind the word off the sculpture, which was later moved to the University of Massachusetts at Bos-

ton. Jiménez presented a rich look at country music and its culture with *Honky Tonk,* a large, part-plywood rendition of a bar and the interactions among its patrons.

Despite the controversies that attended his sculptures, Jiménez became widely recognized in his later years as one of America's most important sculptors. His various honors included an invitation to dinner at the White House with President George W. Bush, who reportedly admired his work. Jiménez showed up in a pair of red cowboy boots. Personal unhappiness dogged the artist's last years, however; his third marriage was dissolving, and he suffered from health problems. An eye injured in a childhood BB-gun accident had to be replaced with a glass one. Jiménez struggled to finish an enormous fiberglass-and-steel horse sculpture called *Mustang* that had been commissioned in 1992 by the city of Denver for its new airport; it was behind schedule and had been the subject of legal wrangling. On June 14, 2006, the sculpture slipped off a hoist and swung out of control, pinning Jiménez against a beam and severing a major artery. Twenty-eight miles from the nearest hospital, he died in the ambulance from the resultant blood loss. "To know Luis is to know that, for him, work was life," his estranged wife, Susan, told the *Rocky Mountain News.* "Someone said he couldn't have gone out any other way. This was the rearing Mustang; Luis died in battle, the battle of creating."

Books

Contemporary Artists, 5th ed., St. James, 2001.
Sullivan, Edward J., ed, *Latin American Art in the Twentieth Century,* Phaidon, 1996.

Periodicals

Art in America, November 1994; March 1999.
Austin American-Statesman, June 15, 2006.
Houston Chronicle, June 15, 2006.
Pittsburgh Post-Gazette, June 21, 2006.
Rocky Mountain News (Denver, CO), June 24, 2006.
San Francisco Chronicle, June 27, 2006.
Smithsonian, March 1993.

Online

"In Memoriam," Arizona State University Art Museum, http://www.asuartmuseum.asu.edu/jimenez/index.html (December 20, 2006).
"Luis Jimenez: Sodbuster," Plains Art Museum, http://www.plainsart.org/collections/luis.jimenez/shtml (December 20, 2006). □

Antonio Carlos Jobim

Brazilian songwriter and vocalist Antonio Carlos Jobim (1927–1994) was one of the creators of the subtle, whispery, jazz-influenced popular song style known as bossa nova. He has been widely acclaimed as one of Brazil's greatest and most innovative musicians of the twentieth century.

Jobim's place in the annals of popular music was secured by a single hit song, "The Girl from Ipanema" (1964), which he co-wrote with lyricist Vinícius de Moraes. His creative contributions to jazz, however, went much deeper; many of his songs became jazz standards, and, in the words of Richard S. Ginell of the *All Music Guide,* "Every other set" performed in jazz clubs "seems to contain at least one bossa nova." Jobim was sometimes called the George Gershwin of Brazil, not so much because of any musical or lyric similarity—Jobim's songs tended to have oblique, often poetic lyrics quite unlike the clever romantic rhymes of George Gershwin's brother Ira—but because his music became the bedrock for the work of jazz musicians for decades after its creation.

Studied with German Music Teacher

Antonio Carlos Brasileiro de Almeida Jobim, often known by the nickname Tom, was born in Rio de Janeiro on January 25, 1927. He grew up in the seaside southern Rio suburb of Ipanema, later the setting for his most famous song, and many of his compositions reflected Brazil's lush natural world in one way or another. Both of Jobim's parents were educators, and his father, Jorge Jobim, was also active as a diplomat. But Jobim took after an uncle who played classical guitar, and he soon showed unusual talent of his own. Jobim's mother, Nilza, rented a piano for the family home, and when Jobim was 14 he began piano lessons with Hans Joachim Koellrutter, a local music scholar of German background who favored the latest experimental trends in European classical music.

Jobim would later point to the influence exerted by French Impressionist composers Claude Debussy and Maurice Ravel on his own music, but a new set of influences was on its way to Brazil in the form of American jazz. Jobim enrolled in architecture school, lasted less than a year, and worked as an assistant to a local architect in the early 1940s. His real energies were directed toward music, as he gained experience playing piano in small nightclubs known as *inferninhos,* or little infernos. Visits to Rio by the Duke Ellington Orchestra and other American jazz bands shaped Jobim's own attempts at composition (which he buried in a drawer at first) and inspired him to settle on a musical career. In 1949 he married his first wife, Thereza Hermanny; they raised a son, Paulo, and a daughter, Elisabeth.

With his well-rounded musical education, by the early 1950s Jobim was able to graduate from Rio's bars to staff arranging positions with the Continental and Odeon record labels. At this point Jobim was working in the genre of samba, Brazil's national pop song style, and he sometimes performed his own samba compositions. His real breakthrough came about in 1956, as the result of a chance meeting two years earlier with Brazilian playwright Vinícius de Moraes. Moraes was working on a play called *Orfeu da Conceição,* which was later filmed as *Orfeu Negro* (Black Orpheus). The play and film transferred the classic Greek myth of Orpheus and Eurydice to modern-day Rio de Janeiro, and Moraes suggested that Jobim write the music for it.

The film *Orfeu Negro* became an international success, and Jobim's score, featuring guitarist Luiz Bonfá, kicked off a new musical craze that quickly spread beyond Brazil. It was based in samba rhythms, but it featured subtle harmonic shadings drawn from jazz. The new style was given the name bossa nova, meaning "new wave," and the 1958 single "Chega de Saudade" (No More Blues), with music by Jobim, words by Moraes, and guitar by future Brazilian pop star João Gilberto, was the style's first major hit. Both "Chega de Saudade" and the flip side of the original single, Jobim's composition "Desafinado" (Out of Tune), have remained jazz standards.

Performed in New York

Jobim's star rose quickly in Brazil after the release of "Chega de Saudade." He continued to record with Gilberto, began hosting a weekly television show called *O Bom Tom,* and wrote music in which he drew on his classical background for the soundtrack to a film called *Por Toda a Minha Vida* and (with Moraes) *Brasília, Sinfonia da Alvorada,* a four-movement orchestral work with text. By 1962 American jazz musicians had begun to immerse themselves in bossa nova. Jobim sang his "Samba de uma nota só" (One-Note Samba) on an album by Gilberto and jazz flutist Herbie Mann. The bossa nova phenomenon reached the United States as saxophonist Stan Getz and guitarist Charlie Byrd recorded their successful *Jazz Samba* album, and in November of 1962 Jobim and other Brazilian musicians performed a major bossa nova concert at New York's Carnegie Hall. The show was the idea of a Brazilian diplomat who wanted to promote the country's musical accomplishments abroad.

The concert initially seemed to be a flop. The Brazilian players were thrown off their stride by New York's miserable late fall weather, and critics panned the show. Jobim and his compatriots also took criticism from Brazilian observers who felt they were diluting Brazilian music by singing songs in English—Jobim, who spoke several languages, sometimes translated his own songs from Portuguese into English, while others were translated by jazz writer Gene Lees. Nevertheless, the Carnegie Hall concert succeeded in exposing Jobim to American musicians and music industry figures. Jobim recognized the importance of American exposure in broadening the reach of his music, and he quipped that if he had remained in Brazil, he would still just be drinking beer in Rio's corner bars. In 1963 he made his U.S. recording debut on the Verve label with *The Composer of Desafinado Plays.* Jobim followed up that release with several more albums in a smooth jazz vein. He collaborated with one of his most influential American admirers on a successful 1966 release, *Francis Albert Sinatra & Antonio Carlos Jobim,* which was seldom if ever out of print during the next four decades. Jobim sang, played piano, and occasionally strummed a guitar on these recordings, often backed by a small orchestra.

In 1962 Jobim composed a song that was soon to become a worldwide phenomenon, and in the process he added a phrase to the international lexicon. "The Girl from Ipanema" (in Portuguese, "Garota de Ipanema") was written as Jobim and Moraes were sitting at a table in a bar in Jobim's hometown of Ipanema and became infatuated with a passer-by, the "tall and tan and young and lovely" woman described in the song. With a vocal by Gilberto's wife, Astrud, and a verse of English lyrics, the song became a number-two hit in the United States in 1964, eclipsed only by the Beatles' "A Hard Day's Night." Jobim prospered, although he was never canny about the music publishing deals he signed, and he often failed to receive a proper share of the money his songs earned.

Jobim's total output of albums was not large (he recorded ten solo albums, plus nine more with collaborators), but his music remained consistently successful through much of the 1960s. Nothing else became a hit on the scale of "The Girl from Ipanema," but such songs as "Wave," "Insensatez" (How Insensitive), and "Meditation," with vocals by Jobim himself, Astrud Gilberto, or other singers, became part of the record collections of many sophisticates, and were internalized by jazz musicians as quickly as they appeared. Jobim maintained a strong following in Brazil, thanks to duets recorded with female vocalist Elis Regina, and his 1968 album *A Certain Mr. Jobim* reached the top 15 on *Billboard* magazine's jazz sales chart in the United States.

Branched Out Beyond Bossa Nova

Jobim's popularity dipped in the 1970s as bossa nova finally ran out of steam commercially, but he never really slowed down creatively. One of his most widely covered songs of the decade was 1972's "Aguas de Março," which Jobim himself translated into English (with added lyrics) as "Waters of March"; the English version almost completely avoided words with roots in Romance languages (such as Portuguese) in favor of those of Germanic origin. The lyrics consisted of a seemingly disconnected series of images that suggested the impermanence of life. The influential jazz critic Leonard Feather, according to Mark Holston of *Americas*, placed "Waters of March" "among the top ten songs of all time." Jobim recorded with Brazilian-born arranger Eumir Deodato on his *Stone Flower* album of 1970, and he also often worked with German-born arranger Claus Ogerman. Jobim's 1975 album *Urubu* (meaning "The Vulture") reflected his personal fascination with that bird of prey.

In 1976 Jobim met 19-year-old photographer Ana Beatriz Lontra; the pair had a son, João Francisco, in 1979, married in 1986, and had a daughter, Maria Luiza Helena, in 1987. In the late 1970s Jobim was active mostly in film soundtracks, but in 1984 he assembled his Nova Banda or New Band, with his son Paulo on guitar, and began touring once again. His concerts in the United States in the mid-1980s were in venues with the highest profiles: Carnegie Hall and Avery Fisher Hall in New York, and Constitution Hall in Washington. His 1987 release *Passarim* was as well received in the jazz community as any of his 1960s releases had been, and selections from it appeared on several posthumous collections of his work.

Critics by this time recognized Jobim as a living legend, and he received various awards of national and international scope in the last years of his life. These included the Diploma of Honor, the highest arts award given by the Organization of American States, which he received in

1988, and induction into the Songwriters' Hall of Fame in 1991. Jobim never rested on his laurels, and he entered the mid-1990s with a full plate of creative projects. He worked with classical conductor Ettore Stratta in preparing recordings of some of his more classical-oriented works, and he planned to record an album with opera star Kathleen Battle. In 1994 Jobim released a new album, *Antonio Brasileiro*, and rejoined Frank Sinatra for a track on Sinatra's *Duets II* release.

With these career capstones in the works, it came as a shock for Jobim's admirers in both the United States and Brazil when Jobim died suddenly of heart failure at New York's Mount Sinai Hospital on December 8, 1994, shortly after entering the facility for treatment of cardiac disease. Jobim's body was returned to Brazil, where a funeral parade held in his honor in Rio de Janeiro lasted for four hours, and he was buried in a tomb near that of Vinícius de Moraes, who had died in 1980. The pair had created two of the icons of twentieth-century culture, *Black Orpheus* and "The Girl from Ipanema," and the music that came from Jobim's pen lent the music of much of the century's second half a distinct Brazilian tinge.

Books

Castro, Ruy, *Bossa Nova: The Story of the Brazilian Music That Seduced the Word,* A Cappella, 2000.
Contemporary Hispanic Biography, Vol. 3, Gale, 2003.

Periodicals

Americas, March-April 1995.
Billboard, December 24, 1994; July 15, 1995.
New York Times, December 9, 1994.
Times (London, England), December 15, 1994.

Online

"Antonio Carlos Jobim," *All Music Guide,* http://www.allmusic .com (November 3, 2006).
"Chronology," Antonio Carlos Jobim Official Website, http://www.jobim.com.br (November 3, 2006).
"JOBIM—For the Love of . . .," *Jazz Review,* http://www.jazz review.com/articleprint.cfm?ID=439 (November 2, 2006).
□

William Jones

Sir William Jones (1746–1794) was an English philologist, Orientalist, and jurist. While serving as a judge of the high court at Calcutta, he became a student of ancient India and founded the Asiatic Society of Bengal. He is best known for his famous proposition that many languages sprang from a common source. His scholarship helped to generate widespread interest in Eastern history, language and culture, and it led to new directions in linguistic research.

Jones was born in London, England, on September 28, 1746, the son of William and Mary Nix Jones. His father was a mathematician who was a friend of Sir Isaac Newton. The elder William died only three years after his son's birth. He left his widow with modest assets, which she used toward their son's education. As such, Jones was able to attend Harrow School, an exclusive institution regarded as one of the greatest in England. Jones proved a standout student, distinguishing himself in classical scholarship. He also studied Oriental languages, as well as Arabic, Hebrew, French, and Italian.

Even at a very early age, Jones demonstrated his multi-linguistic skills. He would develop into a hyperpolygot, someone possessing fluent understanding of more than six languages. Eventually, Jones would know 28 languages and was self-taught in several.

Attended Oxford

Jones entered University College, Oxford, in 1764. He had already developed a reputation for his impressive scholarship, and college enabled him to increase his knowledge of Middle Eastern studies, philosophy, Oriental literature, and Greek and Hebrew. In addition, he learned Spanish and Portuguese, and also mastered the Chinese language.

He supported himself through college with scholarships and by serving as a tutor to Earl Spencer, the seven-year-old son of Lord Althorp, who was the brother of Georgiana, Duchess of Devonshire.

Jones earned his bachelor of arts degree in 1768. By then he had already become a well-known Orientalist, despite being only 22 years old. That same year, Jones was asked by Christian VII of Denmark to translate a Persian manuscript about the life of Nadir Shah into French. The Danish king had brought the manuscript with him on a visit to England. The task was considerable: the Persian manuscript was a difficult one and, at one point Jones was forced to interrupt his own postgraduate studies for a year to complete the translation. It was eventually published in 1770 as *Histoire de Nader Chah,* and it included an introduction that contained descriptions of Asia and a history of Persia.

Prolific Publishing Output

The publication secured Jones's reputation as a major translator and language scholar, and it would be the first of his numerous works involving the Middle East. In 1771, he published *A Grammar of the Persian Language,* which proved to be one of the best grammar texts ever published in English about a language the Western world considered "exotic." For the project, Jones employed numerous literary quotations in his goal of producing a scholarly work that would be morally uplifting, and that would entertain as well as instruct. The work, which went through several editions and translations, provided a model that later language scholars would follow.

During this period he produced three more books, including the 542-page *Poeseos Asiaticae Commentariorum* (1774), but these had less impact. Still, they demonstrated Jones's brilliance and helped cement his academic reputation, also earning him the nicknames of Persian Jones, Oriental Jones, and Linguist Jones.

During these years in London, Jones also wrote poetry. He spent a great deal of time outlining a prospective epic entitled *Britain Discovered,* which he never completed. However, he did publish *Poems, Consisting Chiefly of Translations from the Asiatick Languages* (1772), which represented an effective and innovative fusion of classical poetic conventions with Middle Eastern themes and imagery.

Jones received his master of arts degree from Oxford on June 18, 1773. He was asked to deliver an oration at the University, but eventually declined when he was pressured to modify his discussion of academic freedom to include favorable comments about Lord North, whose policies toward America he opposed. The unmodified speech was later published as *An Oration Intended to Have Been Spoken in the Theatre at Oxford.*

Meanwhile, his published academic and literary output provided Jones with a high professional rank and important social connections. He became a fellow of the Royal Society, and in 1773 he was elected to Dr. Samuel Johnson's renowned literary group, the Club, which included such well-known figures as James Boswell, Edmund Burke, David Garrick, Thomas Percy, and Adam Smith. Despite his newly elevated status, Jones always maintained a modest and appealing disposition.

Studied Law

For financial reasons Jones also began studying law, entering London's Middle Temple in 1770, but he continued working on translations. He applied his characteristic enthusiasm and thoroughness to his curriculum, studying legal technicalities as well as legal philosophies. He was admitted to the bar in 1774, and made a modest living as a barrister, an attorney, and an Oxford fellow. He also worked with Benjamin Franklin in Paris, trying to help resolves issues involving the American Revolution.

Through his law studies, Jones also became a noted legal scholar. In 1776 he was appointed commissioner in bankruptcy, which led to his famous *Essay on the Law of Bailments* (1781), a lucid study that compared English bailments with other legal systems. The work went through several editions and became a standard for English and American lawyers. Other works included the translation of *The Speeches of Isaeus* (1779), which dealt with the Athenian right of inheritance.

Developed Political Interests

Throughout his legal career, Jones demonstrated a passion for social justice, pro-American sympathies, and a disdain for dictatorial governmental polices. Further, his writings revealed a republican slant. As a result, he was not held in high regard by the reigning British Tory administration. When he ran for a university seat in Parliament in 1780, his political ambitions were frustrated by Tory power figures, who feared his influence.

From 1780 to 1783, Jones wrote four political tracts, the most famous and influential of which was *An Inquiry into the Legal Mode of Suppressing Riots, with a Constitutional Plan of Future Defence* (1780). The others included *A Speech on the Nomination of Candidates to Represent the County of Middlesex* (1780), *A Speech to the Assembled Inhabitants of the Counties of Middlesex and Surry* (1782), and *A Letter to a Patriot Senator* (1783). In 1782, his *The Principles of Government* was published anonymously. When it was deemed libelous by the British government, Jones boldly decided to reprint the pamphlet, this time with his name revealed as its author. The landmark libel case resulted in the Libel Act of 1792, which helped advance the cause of freedom of the press.

Meanwhile, he continued writing poetry and produced four noteworthy political poems including *Julii Melesigoni ad Libertatum Carmen* (1780), which condemned Britain's war against America; "The Muse Recalled" (1781), another defense of America; "An Ode in Imitation of Alcaeus" (1781), regarded as his greatest political poem, as it advanced his ideas on government and morality; and "An Ode in Imitation of Callistratus" (1782), which lauded the emergence of Britain's Whig administration. From these poetic works a rumor arose that Jones would move to America to help write the new nation's constitution.

Moved to India

However, the only transcontinental move Jones would make would be an eventual relocation to Calcutta, where he would assume a Supreme Court Judgeship. In 1778, as he was engaged to marry Anna Maria Shipley, Jones realized that his law practice didn't provide him with adequate financial means. So, when he learned of a well-paying opening on the Supreme Court in the Bengal presidency, he asked his influential friends to help him secure the position. In the meantime, he wrote a translation of seven famous pre-Islamic Arabic odes called *The Moallakát*. His translation, published in 1782, would influence Alfred Lord Tennyson and later important poets. Finally, despite Tory doubts about his suitability for the Indian judgeship, Jones was appointed on March 4, 1783. On March 20 of that year, he was knighted and became Sir William Jones. On April 8, he married Shipley, and he and his wife would live in India from 1783 until 1794, the year Jones died.

The 11 years he spent on the Supreme Court of Calcutta were highly productive ones, and he applied democratic principles to his judicial decisions. The six charges Jones made to the Calcutta Grand Jury during that period helped determine the course of Indian jurisprudence as well as preserve the rights of Indian citizens to trial by jury, as Jones considered Indians to be equal under the law with Europeans.

His most famous accomplishment in India was establishing the Asiatic Society of Bengal, in January of 1784. The founding of the Society grew out of Jones's love for India, its people and its culture, as well as his abhorrence of oppression, nationalism and imperialism. His goal for the Society was to develop a means to foster collaborative international scientific and humanistic projects that would be unhindered by social, ethnic, religious and political barriers. Through the Society, Jones hoped to make Oriental studies much more attractive to people from the West. As a result, Jones exerted a substantial influence on the academic and literary disciplines in Western Europe. He would remain the Society's president until he died.

In addition to establishing the Society, Jones felt compelled to learn Sanskrit so that he could better prepare himself to understand Hindu and Muslim laws. This led to an enormous personal project: the compilation of all such laws. The task was so huge that he was unable to complete it before he died. However, he did publish portions, including *Institutes of Hindu Law, or the Ordinances of Menu, Mohammedan Law of Succession to Property of Intestates* and *Mohammedan Law of Inheritance*. He also published numerous works about India, covering a variety of topics including law, art, music, literature, botany and geography.

The Famous Proposition

While studying Sanskrit, Jones developed the idea of a common source for languages, which proved to be his greatest achievement of all, and the one for which he is best known today. In *The Sanscrit Language*, published in 1786, Jones wrote of how he observed that Sanskrit had a strong resemblance to Greek and Latin, which led him to suggest that the three languages not only had a common root but they were related to the Gothic, Celtic, and Persian languages. The impact of the work was enormous, as it brought about the separation of religion from language and eschewed mythology for a more scientific approach to linguistics. His discovery was regarded as just as important, in its own way, as the scientific discoveries made by men like Galileo, Copernicus and Charles Darwin.

Jones's efforts not only substantially added to the store of human knowledge; his work also generated a renewed interest among the Indian people about their own rich national and literary heritage. In 1789 he completed his translation of *Sakuntala,* a famous drama, and the *Hitopadesa,* a collection of fables. In 1792 he translated the *Ritusamhara* into the original Sanskrit.

Died in Calcutta

Eventually, living in the Indian climate took its toll on Jones and his wife. In November of 1793, Anna Jones was forced to return to England for health reasons. Jones stayed behind, to try and complete his translation of Hindu and Muslim laws so that the Indian people would be able to govern themselves under their own laws. He expected the task to take him two more years. However, on April 27, 1794, Jones died in Calcutta from inflammation of the liver, a condition that he aggravated with overwork. The only portion of the large work that he lived to see published was *Institutes of Hindu Law, or, The Ordinances of Menu, according to the Gloss of Culluca* (1794).

Though this final project was left incomplete, Jones still left behind a rich legacy of scholarship, political tracts and poetry. In particular, his enormous contribution to linguistics is undeniably significant. Further, his translations had the effect of introducing the Western world to the rich heritage of the Middle East. While his artistic efforts are only considered today as minor classics, they proved to have a strong impact on more famous poets and writers. It has been pointed out that his style, which mixed Western and Eastern elements, helped influence poets of England's Romantic movement, especially Samuel Taylor Coleridge and Lord Byron. Later writers that Jones influenced included Matthew Arnold, Rudyard Kipling, Ralph Waldo Emerson, Walt Whitman, Goethe, and T.S. Eliot.

Books

Cannon, Garland, "Sir William Jones," *Dictionary of Literary Biography, Volume 109: Eighteenth-Century British Poets,* Second Series, edited by John Sitter, Gale Group, 1991.

Online

"Biography of Sir William Jones," *Kamat's Potpourri—The History, Mystery and Diversity of India,* http://www.kamat.com/kalranga/people/pioneers/w-jones.htm (December 7, 2006).

"The Restoration and the Eighteenth Century," *The Norton Anthology of English Literature,* http://www2.wwnorton.com/college/english/nael/18century/topic_4/jones.htm (December 7, 2006).

"Sir William Jones," 1911 Encyclopedia, http://www.1911encyclopedia.org/Sir_William_Jones (December 7, 2006). □

Andrea Jung

Andrea Jung (born 1959) went from being a lackluster student to attending the Ivy League's Prince-

ton University, and went on to become the CEO of Avon Products. *Institutional Investor* wrote of Jung, "How many other chief executives embody their companies the way Andrea Jung does? Sleek, stylishly turned out, with signature pearl choker and mane of sable hair, she is confident and assertive, the perfect image for her newly invigorated Avon Products. Jung is the first female CEO at a cosmetics company who wasn't also its founder." Jung took the failing company out of the depths of marketing oblivion into a world of young, hip makeup products.

Born in Toronto

Jung was born in 1959 in Toronto, Ontario, Canada. Her family moved to Wellesley, Massachusetts, when she was only two years old. Jung's mother was born in Shanghai and was a chemical engineer; her father was born in Hong Kong and was an architect. Jung has one younger brother, Mark. When she was young, Jung studied not only the regular subjects offered at a Massachusetts school, but studied the Mandarin language as well. She also began piano lessons, taught by her mother, when she was only five years old. Jung has admitted to being a lackluster student. The only reason she got good grades at first was because her parents would offer her something she wanted in return for earning A's. When she was in fourth grade, for instance, she desperately wanted a set of colored pencils. Her parents told her that if at the end of the grade marking period she earned all A's, they would get it for her. She hunkered down to work, and by the end of the grade period those pencils were hers. It was something she never forgot. She has credited her parents and instances like this one with furthering her resolve and ambition.

In high school Jung used her determination to get involved in extracurricular activities, especially student government. She started out as class secretary before becoming president of the student body, and went on from high school to attend the elite Princeton University. She earned a bachelor of arts degree in English literature in 1979, graduating magna cum laude from Princeton. She intended to continue her studies by going to law school after a short break, but decided on a detour. She had gotten a job at Bloomingdale's as a manager in training, and she saw the position as giving her the edge she would need to make it in the field of law.

Discovered Passion for Marketing

She did so well at Bloomingdale's that she moved to a job at the I. Magnin stores. From there she became the executive vice president in charge of merchandising for women's apparel, cosmetics, and accessories at Neiman Marcus. And with her change of companies came a change of careers. Law vanished into the background as Jung found herself in the midst of a world she liked. She wanted a new challenge, however, and found one when she started working for Avon Products, Inc., as a consultant in 1993. The company that had been around for over a hundred years was ailing, and needed a fresh burst of energy and life to keep it going. The higher-ups at Avon liked what Jung had to bring to the company as a consultant, and they hired her as president of the product marketing group for U.S. operations in 1994. In that position she worked on continuing the company's traditional branding efforts while trying to introduce more modern lines to the mix. She introduced the Avon Apparel line, which proved to be very successful. She also suggested getting rid of a large number of Avon's old fragrances and introducing new ones. She was behind the introduction of such new favorites as Far Away, Millennia, and Natori.

She also worked on coming up with a better marketing pitch for the company. She came up with the slogan "Just Another Avon Lady," which was launched in 1995. With her new slogan, Jung was trying to re-brand the company as younger and hipper, but also as being more sophisticated and quality-filled. This was helped by products such as Anew, which was the first skin cream with alpha hydroxy, made to help hide wrinkles. She also got Olympic athletes Jackie Joyner-Kersee and Becky Dyroen-Lancer to help with the campaign, and Avon became the official fragrance and cosmetics sponsor of the 1996 Olympic Games, held in Atlanta, Georgia. The company put together The Olympic Women exhibition, focusing on women athletes at the games, something that not only promoted female athleticism, but also helped put Avon into the spotlight. Because

of all the things Jung set up in 1996 she was named "Marketer of the Year" for 1996 by *Brandweek.*

Became First Female CEO of Avon

Always looking for bigger and better ways to promote Avon, in 1997 Jung came up with the "Dare to Change Your Mind about Avon" ad campaign, something that showed the company knew about its outdated image, and was about to change it. Also in 1997, the CEO of Avon stepped down. It was thought that Jung might be considered for the job, but instead of promoting someone from inside the company, Avon hired from outside, choosing instead the CEO of Duracell, Charles Perrin. Someone must have felt that Jung was soon to step into power, however, because in 1997 she was named one of the top "25 Women to Watch" by *Advertising Age.* She was also given the National Outstanding Mother Award and the American Advertising Federation's Advertising Hall of Achievement award that year. Perrin, on the other hand, met with problems at the company, and a mere two years later Jung was made the CEO of Avon. She was the first female CEO in Avon's history, and that was quite a long history, as the company was 116 years old at that time. She became chairwoman of Avon in 2001. Prior to that, Jung had been listed at number eight in "Corporate America's 50 Most Powerful Women" in 1998.

Since becoming CEO of Avon, Jung has become known for her professional, businesslike demeanor and for her innovative ideas. Rarely personal in interviews, she once admitted to a reporter that she kept in her desk a letter her father wrote to her. In it he wrote, "Cultivate the absence of arrogance and boastfulness." She was raised in the traditional Asian manner, and her father had worried that as Jung took over as CEO of Avon she might become arrogant and hard, and he wanted to remind his daughter that it was not necessary or advantageous to be that way.

Continued to Raise Avon Out of Obscurity

Two years after taking over the CEO position at Avon, Jung talked to *Harper's Bazaar* about her job. "My job has its pros and its cons. There's the opportunity to be a role model, and then there's a lot of heavy responsibility that can be very difficult. . . . But I'm more comfortable now with my public role as it relates to my personal life than I was two years ago. Statistics show that it's still a story when women reach the very top of the ladder, and we have a responsibility to create paths for women to succeed." Since her rise to CEO, Jung has taken Avon international. It started out as an American company and is still run in a purely American way, with Avon "ladies" selling directly to buyers, but Jung has begun to expand the concept worldwide. By the early twenty-first century Avon was sold in over 143 countries. In 2001 nearly 40 percent of Avon's total profits came from South and Central American alone. In 2003 Jung pushed Avon to start a line of makeup called "Mark," aimed towards teenagers and college-age women. According to *Crains New York Business,* Jung said about the changes: "I want to keep it hip. We have to be able to change in a snap, to have an edge.'' She also has helped raise money for breast cancer, the disease that took her grandmother's life.

Since her acquisition of the CEO position, Jung has learned about personal compromise. She has been married and divorced twice. She has admitted that she has made mistakes as well as sacrifices, but also has said that she feels she is proof that a woman can succeed in business. Jung has two children: Lauren from her first marriage, and James from her second. A lot of public scrutiny has focused on her role as a mother, something she never expected. She has said that she has missed some of her children's events, but never the important ones. And there have been things about the company that have been put on hold so she could be with her children. She has also made an environment at Avon where parents can take time off to attend their children's functions and take care of their family, as long as their work does not suffer for it. She is on the board of General Electric and was nominated to be on the board of the New York Stock Exchange. She is on the boards of such non-profit organizations as the New York Presbyterian Hospital and Catalyst, a company focused on women in business. Jung is one of only two female Fortune 500 CEOs. She has been named one of the 50 Most Powerful Women in U.S. Business by *Fortune* magazine.

Future for Jung and Avon

As for Avon, the company did a turnaround after Jung took over. According to *Fortune* magazine, ''In her first five years as CEO, Andrea Jung gave Avon a badly needed facelift. From 2000 through 2004, revenues rose from $5.3 billion to $7.7 billion, and profits nearly tripled.'' Jung was able to find popular and strong women to advertise the company on television, among them tennis players Venus and Serena Williams. Jung told *Harper's Bazaar,* ''Venus and Serena's story was such a natural fit for us. They have proven to a global audience that women can do anything.'' With so much success, Jung's reign as CEO of Avon was one to continue to watch.

Books

Almanac of Famous People, 8th edition, Gale Group, 2003.
Business Leader Profiles for Students, Volume 2, Gale Group, 2002.
Newsmakers 2000, Issue 2, Gale Group, 2000.

Periodicals

AdAgeGlobal, October 2001.
Crain's New York Business, November 8, 1999; April 28, 2003; August 14, 2006.
Fortune, October 13, 2003; November 14, 2005; March 20, 2006; October 16, 2006.
Harper's Bazaar, September 2001.
Institutional Investor, August 2002.
International Herald Tribune, June 3, 2003.
Newsweek, December 27, 2004.
Times (London, England), September 6, 2003; April 1, 2006.
Xinhua News Agency, March 4, 2006.

Online

''Andrea Jung,'' *Biography Resource Center Online,* http://galenet.galegroup.com/servlet/BioRC (January 2, 2007). □

K

Joseph Kabila

Joseph Kabila (born 1971) became the president of the Congo in 2001 when he was only 29 years old. He was put into the position after his father, Laurent Kabila, president at the time, was assassinated. Striving to end the atrocities that had taken place in his country to that point, Kabila worked to make treaties with Congo's neighbors and fought to remove foreign forces from his lands. In 2006 Kabila won a democratic election to win the presidency.

Mysterious Beginnings

Kabila was born around June 4, 1971, in Ankoro—a small town on the banks of the Congo River—in North Katanga, in the Congo, although his birth year has been given as anywhere from 1968 to 1972, and there has been some debate as to the location. There are also some reports that instead he was born December 4, 1971, at Hewa Bora, Kabila's father's guerrilla headquarters in the Fizi territory of South-Kivu. He was the oldest of 10 children. His father, Laurent Kabila, is said to have been involved in politics early on, although there have been some rumors that he was an ivory and diamond trafficker. Kabila had a twin sister, Jane, and one full blood brother, Saide. His mother was one of Laurent Kabila's three wives, Sifa Maanya. She was a member of the Bangubangu tribe in the Maniema province of eastern Congo, although some have claimed that she was a Tutsi from Rwanda. Whatever the case, Kabila went to school in Tanzania, attending schools based on the British school system where Kabila learned to speak English at a young age. He was also fluent in Swahili, although not in Lingala, which is the language spoken in Congo's capital. While at school he also studied French. After school he trained in the Rwandan military for three years before he went on to continue his education. He went to Makarere University in 1995.

Before he could begin taking classes in 1996, Kabila's father, head at that time of a guerilla force that opposed the government, asked him to join him in a fight to overthrow then-president Mobutu Sese Seko. Kabila's father sent him to China to further his military training, and six months later they led the revolt that overthrew the Congolese government and put Laurent Kabila into the office of president. Kabila's father appointed him to the position of major-general and he was put in charge of the armed forces. When taking over the presidency Kabila's father promised that he would change the corruption and bad politics that had plagued the government for the past 40 years. Unfortunately, his rule was just as corrupt.

Made President of the Congo

In 1998, still in charge of the armed forces, Kabila led a fight against Rwanda and Uganda, both of whom had invaded the Congo and had control over portions of it. The operation was still underway when Kabila returned home. At this time Kabila lived in a military housing unit with his girlfriend, Olive, and their daughter, Josephine, but this life was not to last. Kabila's father was assassinated by one of his own bodyguards, Rashisi Kassereka, in 2001. Kassereka was shot dead on the spot after the murder. After Kabila's father died, Kabila's mother continued to live at the palace, away from the public eye. And Kabila himself became the next president of the Congo at the young age of 29 years old.

After his father was murdered, Kabila met with foreign diplomats and representatives from different Congolese groups from the religious, social, and commercial sectors. It was not really known how Kabila succeeded his father as president, but most believe it was because he was the least controversial choice at the time, not really belonging to any of the factions that were vying for power across the country. Whatever the case, three days after Kimbala took over control of the country troops were sent from Angola, Zimbabwe, and Namibia after their leaders had met together, to help secure Kabila his office and keep the peace around the country. Kabila's father's Parliament unanimously voted Kabila into office on January 27, 2001, only 11 days after Kabila's father was murdered. It made him the youngest leader of any country in the world at that time.

Ascension Caused Suspicions

Nobody knew what kind of leader Kabila would be. In his personal life, Kabila neither drank nor smoked. He did not eat at fancy restaurants or like expensive clothing. He was shy and quiet and apparently down to earth and serious. He was a Christian who often read the Bible. He liked sports and computer games. He was young, so many assumed he would be weak. Many assumed he would be a dictator as his father had been. Some were suspicious of the way he had come to power, and some reports claimed that Kabila had been put into office as a puppet for a hidden regime. Kabila had much to face at the beginning of his tour as president of the Congo.

The whole country watched to see what Kabila would do first as he entered his reign as president. Kabila, however, would have none of it. The important thing, he said, was not what he did, but how the country fared.

Began Touring World as President

Only a week after he was sworn in as president, George Bush invited Kabila to visit Washington. Kabila accepted the invitation and went there to meet with Colin Powell and Paul Kagame, the president of Rwanda. Kabila discussed with the pair the fact that he wanted peace for his country. There had been much fighting between the Congo, Rwanda, and Uganda in the past and Kabila wanted it stopped.

For the next three months of his presidency Kabila reorganized the government. He got rid of anyone too extreme and retired anyone who had been in the parliament so long that Kabila felt that they assumed that their positions were secure and therefore they did not really need to do anything anymore. He wanted only honest, hard-working people in his administration. He made promises to turn Congo's government into a democracy and to improve the economy. According to the AFROL website, Kabila said, ''At the moment the social conditions here are catastrophic. The humanitarian situation is also catastrophic. It's these issues that require our attention and resources.''

Democratic Elections Held in the Congo

In 2003 Kabila ended the war that had started when his father fought with their neighbors Rwanda and Uganda. Since then they had been occupying parts of the eastern Congo. It has been estimated that over four million people were killed in the conflict, but due mainly to Kabila's diplomatic skills and his meetings with officials of the other countries, there was an end to the killing.

On June 16, 2006, Kabila married his girlfriend, Olive Lembe. Later that year elections were held to elect a president in a fair, democratic election. The two main candidates were Kabila and Jean Pierre Bemba, a well-educated millionaire businessman. He had also led one of the militia groups that fought on the border of Uganda, Rwanda, and the Congo during the war that Kabila ended in 2003. His group had been accused of numerous horrible acts such as killing and raping. Because of this Kabila declared that he could not see the country go to Bemba.

One of the problems that Kimbala faced during elections was the fact that he did not speak Lingala, the main language spoken in Kinshasa, the capital of the Congo. For that reason he was seen as an outsider there. The eastern Congo, on the other hand, favored him because he had stopped the war that raged in that part of the country. On the contrary Bemba did speak the language. Kimbala, for this reason, needed help to gain support form western Congo if he was going to win the election. His need for help was so great, in fact, that he went so far as to ask for help campaigning from the son of the dictator, Mobutu Sese Seko, that Kabila's father threw out of office years before. He made a deal with Francois Joseph Mobutu Nzanga for help gain votes from the west where Nzanga is from.

Results Tallied from Election

When the votes were tallied on October 29, 2006, Kabila had won 58.05 per cent of the vote to Bemba's 41.95 per cent. London's *Independent* reported on the election results, quoting Jacqueline Chenard, the UN spokeswoman in Goma, North Kivu. "People are very cheerful. There is a lot of marching and chanting—it is a good atmosphere. People are happy that the Congo now has a president that has been elected by them, the people, for the first time in their lives." As was predicted, a great majority of the people who supported Kabila came from the east where they speak Kabila's native Swahili.

At the beginning of 2007 the Congo had only 300 miles of paved roads, something that needed to be rectified if it was to become a successfully commercial country. There was very little in the way of an infrastructure; there were barely any schools to be had and hospitals were overcrowded, dirty, and under-provisioned. There were also several militia groups still in existence, constantly threatening Congo's peace. If that were not enough, Bemba protested the election results, claiming that Kabila faked votes and miscounted in territories where Bemba was the chosen president. Only two weeks after elections the country was on the brink of war yet again.

Bemba had support from most of Congo's capital city as well as from the Catholic Church. In the Congo church leaders are quite often more successful at influencing their parishioners than politicians are at doing so with their countrymen. The archbishop in Congo urged the people of Congo to reject what he called a fraud. To prevent a civil war, the UN sent members on missions to negotiate an agreement between the two men. One solution suggested Bemba be in charge of the Senate while Kimbala remained president, but Bemba's side refused such a thing. As stated in the *Christian Science Monitor*, " 'This is Africa, it's all or nothing,' says one African observer, working for an African embassy in Kinshasa. 'First place is the presidency. Second place is the grave.' " At the beginning of 2007 it was still not clear what would happen in the Congo or how Kabila would handle it. But many believe he will pull the country out of this problem, too.

Books

Almanac of Famous People, 8th edition, Gale Group, 2003.
Contemporary Black Biography, Volume 30, edited by Ashyia Henderson, Gale Group, 2001.
History Behind the Headlines: The Origins of Conflicts Worldwide, Volume 3, Gale Group, 2001.
Newsmakers, Issue 2, Gale Group, 2003.
Worldmark Encyclopedia of the Nations: World Leaders, Gale, 2003.

Periodicals

African Business, March 2001; October 2006.
Christian Science Monitor, November 16, 2006.
Daily Telegraph (London, England), October 30, 2006; November 16, 2006.
Economist (U.S.), January 27, 2001; November 15, 2003; October 23, 2004; November 18, 2006.
Europe, May 2001.

Financial Times, November 10, 2006.
Guardian (London, England), October 30, 2006; November 16, 2006.
Independent (London, England), August 23, 2006; November 16, 2006.
Jet, February 12, 2001; November 24, 2003.
New York Times, March 5, 2001; August 25, 2006; November 16, 2006.
Times (London, England), October 28, 2006.
Xinhua News Agency, September 10, 2006.

Online

"Interview with President Joseph Kabila," *Afrol News,* http://www.afrol.com/Countries/DRC/backgr_j_kabila_interview.htm (January 2, 2007).
"Joseph Kabila," *Biography Resource Center Online,* http://www.galenet.galegroup.com/servlet/BioRC (January 2, 2007).
"Kabila married Olive Lembe in a civil ceremony," *BBC News,* http://www.news.bbc.co.uk/2/hi/africa/5091284.stm (June 18, 2006). □

Gerome Kamrowski

Though not as widely known as his contemporaries, American artist Gerome Kamrowski (1914–2004) was an important figure in American art's transitional phase into Abstract Expressionism in the 1940s.

Between 1938 and 1946 he lived and worked in New York City, and like a few other up-and-coming young painters was drawn to the ideas of Surrealism, a significant art trend in Europe which failed to catch on across the Atlantic. Kamrowski and his friends, among them Jackson Pollock, borrowed some of Surrealism's tenets and out of these experiments a new, equally important movement that became known as American Abstract Expressionism would emerge. *New York Times* art critic Grace Glueck noted that over the years, Kamrowski's own work "has been variously labeled 'expressionist biomorphic' and 'abstract surrealist,' but whatever it's called, it shares the organic imagery and full-throttle energy of the movement then coming to bloom."

Kamrowski was born on January 29, 1914, in Warren, Minnesota, the son of Felix and Mary (Rizke) Kamrowski and the last of their eleven children. He grew up in St. Cloud, Minnesota, a city on the Mississippi River and where his parents ran a bakery. At the age of 19 he entered the St. Paul School of Art, in the Minneapolis/St. Paul metropolitan area, and spent three years there. In 1937, he settled briefly in Chicago, where he studied under Hungarian painter and photographer László Moholy-Nagy (1895–1946) at the New Bauhaus, the art and architecture school that had just established itself in the city after having been forced to close by authorities in Nazi Germany.

Befriended Jackson Pollock

In 1938, Kamrowski was awarded a Solomon R. Guggenheim Foundation fellowship that enabled him to spend the summer at a school in Provincetown, Massachusetts, run by Hans Hofmann (1880–1966). Hofmann was another who had fled the Nazi threat, and as an émigré teacher would become a serious influence on a generation of future Abstract Expressionists. After his stint in Provincetown, Kamrowski settled in New York City and found steady work as a muralist with the Federal Art Project of the Works Progress Administration (WPA). This government-funded program hired artists to create and execute murals and other embellishments for newly constructed public facilities such as post offices. Through this line of work he met two other young artists, Jackson Pollock (1912–1956) and William Baziotes (1912–1963), who would emerge as leading Abstract Expressionist painters within a decade.

Kamrowski eventually left the job and found a well-heeled art collector baroness, another European émigré, and began painting works that were initially inspired by the Cubist movement. But he and his circle of painter friends were also drawn to Surrealism, a movement that had originated in Europe in the early 1920s and became centered in Paris under the leadership of André Breton (1896–1966). Writing in his Surrealist Manifesto of 1924, Breton defined the movement as "pure psychic automatism, by which one proposes to express, either verbally, in writing, or by any other manner, the real functioning of thought."

The New York artists were particularly intrigued by the concept of "automatism," sought to express, via painting, writing, or music, the true subconscious mind, without self-censorship. With Pollock and Baziotes, Kamrowski began to experiment with the technique both jointly and in their own studios alone. They were guided, in part, by a Chilean-born member of the Surrealist group in Paris, Roberto Matta (1911–2002), who had settled in New York City; Kamrowski, Pollock, Baziotes, and others such as Robert Motherwell (1915–1991) met regularly at Matta's Greenwich Village studio to discuss automatism and other trends.

The Beginnings of Abstract Expressionism

One of the works that Kamrowski, Pollock, and Baziotes completed together was *Collaborative Painting*, from 1941, which was done in Kamrowski's studio. They used a type of commercial paint that dried quickly, and wanted to come up with "a freer way of applying paint to go further with the psychic automatism" suggested by Matta, wrote Phyllis Braff in the *New York Times*. "They tried dripping, pouring and flinging the loosely flowing material. The result is a dark surface bearing bold biomorphic shapes activated by overlapping lines of varying widths. Lines alternately strike a course, then swirl and loop unpredictably, inviting the eye through a maze of visual discovery. Where these energetic strands loop into the canvas's black areas, they eliminate the separation between image and background and suggest the shifting ambiguities that were so important to subsequent phases of abstraction."

The first years of the 1940s were a period of intense creativity and experimentation for Kamrowski. Even more artists fleeing the war in Europe—especially after the German invasion of France in 1940—added to the already rich artistic scene in and around Greenwich Village, and Kamrowski was

eager to learn from them and apply the new ideas of what was becoming known as Abstract Surrealism to his own work. He constructed a series of shadow boxes, reminiscent of the work of American sculptor Joseph Cornell (1903–1972), and exhibited these as well as his paintings regularly at venues that included The Art of This Century Gallery, run by one of Surrealism's most enthusiastic collectors, American heiress Peggy Guggenheim (1898–1979).

Kamrowski's canvases were full of vibrating, other-worldly creatures and landscapes, painted in rich hues and sometimes bisected by dotted lines. "Kamrowski devised fantastic biomorphic forms that refer to animal anatomies and plant parts," wrote *Art in America*'s David Boudon. "His 1945 oil *Script for an Impossible Documentary: The Great Invisibles*, is a majestic portrait of two humanoid plants; a male figure (with broad multibranched torso) and a female creature (with wide pelvis and long wavy hair) have bulbous heads with cyclopean eyes." Another critic, Roberta Smith of the *New York Times*, described it as a work "hovering on the border between period piece and masterpiece."

Returned to Midwest

Kamrowski married Marianna Fargione in 1943, with whom he soon had a son, Felix. They lived in an artists' community in Georgia for a time, but returned to New York City where Fargione died of cancer less than two years after their wedding. Now the single parent of a one-year-old child, Kamrowski decided to take a job that offered a steadier income than the life of an artist, and joined the faculty of the University of Michigan in 1946; it was also a halfway point between New York and his family back in Minnesota. Writing in the *St. Petersburg Times*, Lennie Bennett termed his move "the best thing that could have happened to him artistically. Summers off gave him the opportunity to visit New York haunts and renew associations. But, by being away from New York, he was able to avoid the excesses of many of his peers, such as Jackson Pollock and resist the artistic influences that might have diluted his surrealist vision." Pollock died rather infamously in an alcohol-related car wreck on Long Island in 1956; and Baziotes also died at a relatively young age, still in his early 50s, seven years later.

During this period of his career, Kamrowski's work was singled out by Breton, who included him in a 1947 international Surrealist exhibition in Paris and three years later wrote of him in an essay. The formidable, somewhat autocratic Surrealist master heralded Kamrowski as "the one who has impressed me the most by reason of the quality and sustained character of his research," among the New York City-based American artists Breton had come to know over the previous decade, according to Kamrowski's profile on the website of the Weinstein Gallery. Over the next decade the artist participated in several other notable group exhibitions at the Museum of Modern Art and the Whitney Museum of American Art.

In Michigan, Kamrowski taught several new generations of painters, and continued to work on his own projects as well out of a converted barn studio on the outskirts of Ann Arbor. At one point he created a series of panels for the interiors of a geodesic-dome project designed by visionary architect Buckminster Fuller (1895–1983). He later worked in glass mosaic shards, and was still active well into his eighties, showing regularly at the Joan T. Washburn Gallery in New York City. Art aficionados occasionally rediscovered his work in the infrequent museum surveys of American Surrealism. One of these shows was "Surrealism USA" at the National Academy Museum of New York City in 2005, a year after Kamrowski's death on March 27, 2004, in Ann Arbor. His *Collaborative Painting,* the only surviving work he did with Pollock and Baziotes and on loan from his family, was included, as was the 1945 canvas, *Script for an Impossible Documentary: The Great Invisibles.*

Periodicals

Art in America, December 1996; April 2005.
New York Times, May 2, 1986; April 15, 1990; June 30, 1996; October 4, 1996; March 31, 2005.
St. Petersburg Times (St. Petersburg, FL), September 12, 2002.

Online

"Gerome Kamrowski," Weinstein Gallery, http://www.weinstein .com/kamrowski/about_kamrowski.html (January 3, 2007). □

Florynce Kennedy

American civil rights attorney, political activist, and pioneer in second-wave feminism, Florynce Rae Kennedy (1916–2000) was an outspoken advocate for liberal causes.

In her cowboy hat, pants, and pink sunglasses, Kennedy gained a reputation as a flamboyant activist who stood up to authority and did not care what people said about her. Only the second African-American woman to graduate from Columbia Law School, Kennedy fought for the rights of Black Panther members and African-American singers discriminated against by music companies. Disgusted by the racism in the courts, Kennedy turned her energy to activism, fighting for women's liberation, abortion rights, civil rights, and consumer protection.

Learned that Respect Must Be Earned

Kennedy was born February 11, 1916, in Kansas City, Missouri, the second of five daughters of Wiley and Zella Kennedy. Her father worked as a Pullman porter and waiter, and later owned a taxi business. Florynce got her determined attitude from her father. When Wiley bought a house in a mainly white neighborhood, he had the strength to fend off the Ku Klux Klan. In her autobiography, *Color Me Flo,* Kennedy describes the altercation. "They stood on the sidewalk . . . and said they wanted to see our daddy. When Daddy came out, they told him, 'You have to get out of here by tomorrow.' [Daddy] brought his gun . . . out with him and said, 'Now the first foot that hits that step belongs to the man I shoot. And then after that you can decide who is going to shoot *me.*' They went away and they never came back."

Flo's childhood was stable and uneventful, and the Kennedy girls were often praised. Zella, who was light skinned, was well educated and had attended "normal" schools, as Flo put it. Both parents valued education and instilled the view that authority and respect needed to be earned. Kennedy said in *Color Me Flo,* "We were taught very early in the game that we didn't have to respect the teachers, and if they threatened to hit us, we could act as if they weren't anybody we had to pay any attention to."

Admitted to Columbia Law School

Although Kennedy graduated top of her class from Lincoln High School in Kansas City, in 1934, she delayed going to college immediately afterward. She went into business with her sisters opening a hat shop, and worked at a variety of other jobs, including operating elevators and singing on a radio show. Shortly thereafter, when a local Coca-Cola bottling facility refused to hire black truck drivers, Kennedy organized a boycott—her first foray into social activism.

In 1942, Zella died from cancer. Flo and her sister Grayce moved to New York City, where Flo began attending Columbia University in 1944. Even though she was encouraged to become a teacher, Kennedy graduated four years later with honors and a bachelor's degree in pre-law.

Kennedy applied to Columbia Law School in 1948, but was initially denied admission by the dean. When she confronted him, believing the denial was based on her race and threatening to sue, the dean assured her that race was not the issue, but instead it was her gender. To Kennedy, neither discrimination would stand, and eventually Columbia changed its decision and admitted her. Flo Kennedy was one of eight women in her class, and in 1951 became only the second African-American woman to graduate from Columbia Law School (the first was Elreda Alexander in 1945). After passing the New York Bar in 1952, Kennedy worked as a clerk in a law firm in Manhattan, then opened her own private practice in 1954.

Inconsistent with her independent personality, Kennedy got married in 1957 to Charles Dudley Dye, a Welsh writer ten years younger than her. Feeling constrained by the properties of marriage and intolerant of Dye's alcoholism, Kennedy dissolved the marriage after a few years. They had no children. Dye died shortly thereafter. Kennedy noted, "Anyone who marries a drunk Welshman doesn't deserve sympathy."

Represented High Profile Legal Clients

With her growing desire for civil rights and corporate accountability, Kennedy took on some high profile legal clients, such as civil rights activist H. Rap Brown and a female member of the Black Liberation Front charged with bank robbery. In 1969, she assisted in representing several Black Panther members of the eastern branch of the organization who were charged with conspiracy to blow up stores in New York City. They were acquitted in 1971 after the longest political trial in New York's history.

Taking on discrimination by recording company behemoths, Kennedy represented the estates of jazz legends Billie Holiday and Charlie Parker that were suing to recover withheld royalties and sales. The racism she encountered in the courts and in these cases planted seeds of doubt in her whether practicing law was her calling and if she could bring about social change another way.

"Handling the Holiday and Parker estates taught me more than I was really ready for about government and business delinquency and the hostility and helplessness of the courts . . ." she wrote in *Color Me Flo*. "These . . . marked the beginning of a serious disenchantment . . . with the practice of law. By this time I had learned a good deal about the justice system, and had begun to doubt my ability to work within it to accomplish social change. Not only was I not earning a decent living, there began to be a serious question in my mind whether practicing law could ever be an effective means of changing society, or even of simple resistance to oppression."

Political and Social Activism

In the 1960s, Kennedy broadened her scope to include political involvement and battling oppression in a variety of arenas—racism, sexism, and homosexuality. She led boycotts of large corporations, including picketing the Colgate-Palmolive building in New York, leading protests at CBS headquarters, and participating in anti-Vietnam War and pro-liberation initiatives organized by Youth Against War and Fascism.

In 1966, Kennedy created the Media Workshop, an organization charged with fighting racism and discrimination in the media. The group led boycotts of advertisers who did not feature African Americans in their ads. After picketing in the street in front of an advertiser, Kennedy and the protesters were invited inside to discuss their grievances. Marsha Joyner recalled on the Civil Rights Movement Veterans website that Kennedy then quipped, "Ever since I've been able to say, 'When you want to get to the suites, start in the streets.' "

Kennedy's lecturing career may have started in 1967 after she attended an anti-Vietnam War rally in Montreal. When Black Panther Bobby Seale was not allowed to speak since his topic was going to be racism rather than be focused on the war, Kennedy took the platform and started yelling and protesting. She gained attention and was soon invited to speak in Washington, D.C. Never afraid to speak her mind, she said about herself in *Color Me Flo*, "I'm just a loud-mouthed middle-aged colored lady with a fused spine and three feet of intestines missing and a lot of people think I'm crazy . . . I never stop to wonder why I'm not like other people. The mystery to me is why more people aren't like me."

African-American Women for Women's Liberation

Another of Kennedy's causes was women's liberation, for all women, not just African-American women, and urged the two races to work together. Helen H. King quoted Kennedy in *Ebony* magazine as saying, "It is obvious that many black women are not prepared to work with whites in liberation because of the divide and conquer techniques always employed by an exploitative society. However, in many towns there are movements where black and white women are working one to one (in the movement). . . . It's the same gig wherever you are. Whether you're fighting for women's lib or just black lib, you're fighting the same enemies."

In fighting for women's rights, Kennedy helped found the Women's Political Caucus and the National Black Feminist Organization. She was an original member of the National Organization for Women (NOW) and joined the group Radical Women to protest the 1968 Miss America pageant in Atlantic City, New Jersey. Kennedy also founded the national Feminist Party, which in 1971 nominated Representative Shirley Chisholm (D-NY), the first African-American woman elected to Congress, for president. Kennedy even protested the shortage of female bathrooms at Harvard University by leading a mass urination on the campus grounds.

On the abortion rights front, Kennedy organized feminist lawyers in 1969 to challenge the constitutionality of New York state's antiabortion laws. She collaborated on briefs and cross-examined witnesses in pretrial hearings. The laws were overturned the following year. In 1971, Kennedy co-authored with Diane Schulder a book on the class action suit, *Abortion Rap,* one of the first books on abortion. Kennedy even took on the Roman Catholic Church by filing a tax evasion charge to the Internal Revenue Service, claiming that the church's vocal and financial campaign against abortion breeched its tax-exempt status and violated the federal constitution's call for the separation of church and state.

Ill Health in Later Life

For her 70th birthday in 1985, Kennedy was roasted at Playboy's Empire Club in New York City. Guests who came out to joke with her included comic-activist Dick Gregory, civil rights lawyer William Kunstler, and television talk show host Phil Donahue. On the lighter side of her activities, Kennedy was named director of Voters, Artists, Anti-Nuclear Activists and Consumers for Political Action and Communication Coalition (VACPAC), and director of the Ladies Aid and Trade Crusade, two tongue-in-cheek organizations fighting for consumer rights.

Despite quitting her lecture circuit due to back pains and ill health, Kennedy continued her activism throughout her life and produced a weekly interview show on cable TV. Throughout her career she lectured at more than 200 colleges and universities. She spent much of her later years confined to a wheelchair.

Kennedy died in her Manhattan apartment on December 22, 2000, at the age of 84. Speakers at her memorial at New York's Riverside Church included former New York Mayor David Dinkins, the Reverend Al Sharpton, Father Lawrence Lucas, Judge Emily Goodman, and Ti-Grace Atkinson.

As quoted in her *New York Times* obituary, Dinkins said about Kennedy, "If you found a cause for the downtrodden of somebody being abused someplace, by God, Flo Kennedy would be there." In recognizing Kennedy's tireless advocacy, Justice Goodman of New York State Supreme

Court said, "She showed a whole generation of us the right way to live our lives. . . . Her point was that you have to fight on all the fronts all the time." As someone who was adamant about not wasting her life, Kennedy had said, "Sweetie, if you're not living on the edge, then you're taking up space."

Books

Kennedy, Florynce, *Color Me Flo: My Hard Life and Good Times,* Englewood Cliffs, 1976.
Notable Black American Women, edited by Jesse Carney Smith, Gale Research, 1992.

Periodicals

Ebony, March 1971.
Jet, January 15, 2001.
New York Times, December 23, 2000.

Online

Davis, Sue, "Flo Kennedy: An Irreverent, Outspoken Activist," *Workers World,* http://www.workers.org/ww/2001/flo kennedy0201.php (December 7, 2006).
"Florynce Kennedy," http://www.depts.drew.edu/wmst/core courses/wmst111/timeline_bios/fkennedy.htm (December 7, 2006).
Joyner, Marsha, "Florynce Kennedy," Civil Rights Movement Veterans, http://www.crmvet.org/mem/kennedyf.htm (December 7, 2006).
Moon, Terry, "Recalling Flo Kennedy," *News & Letters—The Journal of Marxist-Humanism,* http://www.newsandletters.org/Issues/2001/Jan-Feb/1.01_flo.htm (December 7, 2006). □

Kirk Kerkorian

American financier Kirk Kerkorian (born 1917) parlayed a charter flight business consisting of a single $5,000 plane into one of the world's great fortunes. In 2007, Kerkorian ranked number 26 on the *Forbes* magazine list of the 400 richest Americans, with assets estimated at $9 billion.

Kerkorian's activities made headlines because, although his personal lifestyle was far from flamboyant, he made deals in high-profile industries: movies, Las Vegas hotels, and most recently automobile manufacturing. Sometimes stereotyped as a purely financial animal who stripped industries of their profits in his quest for ever-greater wealth, Kerkorian was a generous man who by one estimate gave away some 20 percent of his enormous fortune to charity. One of the most noteworthy aspects of Kerkorian's career was its longevity. As he approached his ninetieth year he shunned geriatric activities in favor of a widely publicized bid to increase his influence over General Motors, the world's largest automaker.

English Was Second Language

"When you're a self-made man you start very early in life," Kerkorian told K.J. Evans of the *Las Vegas Review-Journal* in one of his rare interviews (reproduced on the website *The First 100 Persons Who Shaped Southern Nevada*). "In my case it was at nine years old when I started bringing income into the family. You get a drive that's a little different, maybe a little stronger, than somebody who inherited." He was born Kerkor Kerkorian on June 6, 1917, to Ahron and Lily Kerkorian, Armenian immigrants who had settled in California's San Joaquin Valley farming region. The youngest of four children, he spoke Armenian at home, learning English on the streets and during his intermittent schooling.

Ahron Kerkorian, almost illiterate, was a watermelon and raisin farmer who aimed toward higher things; he bought several farms and amassed land holdings of 1,000 acres. But he lost them all during a recession in 1921 when banks foreclosed on his mortgages. The family ran into severe financial difficulties and was forced to move some 20 times, with Kerkorian helping bring in money as a newsboy and as a watermelon dealer in one of the city's produce markets. He spent more time out of school than in it, often getting into minor scrapes as a member of a neighborhood street gang. Kerkorian was sent to a disciplinary school and declared his education over after finishing eighth grade; he was 16 years old.

Applying lessons from learned from street fights, Kerkorian began training as a boxer with his older brother

Nishon. At 20 he won his first fight by decision and went on to a Pacific amateur welterweight championship and a record of 33 wins and 4 losses, earning the nickname "Rifle Right." But Kerkorian soon found another activity that he enjoyed even more than boxing, after a friend with whom he worked installing furnaces took him on a ride in a single-engine airplane. Enthralled but lacking the money for the expensive hobby, he showed up at the Happy Bottom ranch of the celebrity female pilot Florence "Pancho" Barnes and proposed that he take on heavy barn duties, including milking cows and shoveling manure, for payment in flying lessons. The aviatrix agreed, and a flying instructor at the ranch helped Kerkorian get a letter stating, spuriously, that he had completed high school in Los Angeles.

That qualified Kerkorian to enter the military, but instead he spent World War II in a more profitable though no less hazardous position, as a civilian employee of Britain's Royal Air Force, flying Mosquito bombers from Canada, where they were built, to Scotland. The planes were easily destabilized by ice on the wings during their northerly crossing, and often dumped their pilots into the freezing North Atlantic. Kerkorian once ran out of gas just as the clouds parted to reveal his airstrip in Scotland, and glided in. He made 33 bomber deliveries for the R.A.F. and banked most of his generous earnings of $1,000 per run.

Founded Charter Airline

Back in Los Angeles in the summer of 1945, Kerkorian bought a single-engine Cessna plane for $5,000, planning to give flying lessons and operate an occasional charter service. The charter end of the business soon occupied most of his attention as he prospered by offering flights between Los Angeles and fast-growing Las Vegas, Nevada. Kerkorian began spending more and more time in the gambling capital, often gravitating toward the craps tables and gaining a reputation as unflappable even as he won or lost tens of thousands of dollars. He purchased Los Angeles Air Service, a small charter airline, and renamed it Trans International Airlines (TIA) in 1947. In buying and selling used planes he often emerged with healthy profits, and at one point he became the first entrepreneur to offer charter jet service. Married briefly once before, he met his second wife, showgirl Jean Maree Hardy, in Las Vegas. The pair had two daughters, Tracy and Linda, whose names inspired that of Kerkorian's holding company, Tracinda Corporation.

In 1962 Kerkorian made his first million dollars by selling TIA to the automaker Studebaker, investing most of it in an 80-acre plot of land near the growing Las Vegas strip. In 1965 he repurchased TIA and offered stock in the company for sale through a Fresno stockbroker of Armenian ancestry. These two decisions together raised Kerkorian from successful entrepreneur to tycoon. After he made another deal that joined his plot of land to the Strip itself, he leased it to the owners of what became the Caesar's Palace hotel and collected $4 million in rent before selling the land outright for $5 million more. After TIA's stock rose from $9.75 a share to $32, Kerkorian sold the company to the Transamerica Corporation in 1968, netting $85 million in Transamerica stock.

Kerkorian once again plowed his profits back into new enterprises, opening the International Hotel in 1969 and pioneering the idea of Las Vegas as a family vacation destination instead of an illicit adult playground. The hotel had a "youth hostel" kids' activities area and offered family tours to nearby attractions such as Lake Mead. Kerkorian offered stock in the hotel's parent company, International Leisure. He had to sell some of his own stock in order to pay heavy European gambling debts, and he eventually gave up gambling completely. In 1970 he sold the International, as well as the Flamingo Hotel, which he had turned into an unofficial employee training ground for the swank new International, to the Hilton hotel chain.

By that time, Kerkorian had begun what *Money* magazine termed "an epic Hollywood–Wall Street romance": his ongoing relationship with the MGM film studios. Borrowing $42 million from European banks, he wrested control of the company from its existing large stockholders in 1969 with an outlay of about $650 million. He opened the MGM Grand Hotel in Las Vegas in 1973. The MGM studio did not prosper artistically during the period of Kerkorian's leadership, but his financial wizardry was unimpeded. He acquired the United Artists studio for $380 million, formed the conglomerate MGM/UA, and sold the new entity to cable television magnate Ted Turner in 1985 for $1.5 billion. Turner ran into financial problems in the late 1980s, and Kerkorian obligingly repurchased the company for $780 million, selling it once again to controversial Italian financier Giancarlo Parretti for $1.3 billion in 1990. Parretti, under investigation by European financial authorities, submitted in turn to a Kerkorian buyback, whereupon Kerkorian finally cashed out with a $2.9 billion sale to Sony in 2004.

Paid for Own Movie Tickets

Two things were noteworthy about this financial odyssey. The first was that upon Kerkorian's departure, MGM was in much the same financially shaky condition as it was when he acquired it; he did not succeed in creating a global colossus like Turner's CNN. And second, even as he pocketed billions, Kerkorian was legendary for his refusal to accept free passes to MGM-owned movie theaters; he lined up and bought tickets along with other patrons. He acquired a Beverly Hills mansion but lived alone in its small guest house. Kerkorian acquired a reputation as a recluse, but he was regularly seen in Los Angeles and Las Vegas restaurants and bars, wielding a $10,000 bankroll and preferring cash to credit cards. After his second marriage dissolved, he dated several actresses and then married tennis star Lisa Bonder in 1999 after living with her for several years. In 2002 the marriage broke up and spawned a divorce and paternity suit in which Bonder asked for $320,000 a month in alimony and child support. In nonmarital matters he was generous without dispute; he gave hundreds of millions of dollars to charities, particularly in Armenia.

During the last stages of his involvement with MGM, Kerkorian turned to a larger industry still. In 1990 he began buying shares in the Chrysler Corporation, performing a variety of maneuvers designed to increase the value of the company's stock, and in 1994 he and former Chrysler chairman

Lee Iacocca launched a hostile takeover of the company. Their plan was beaten back, but Kerkorian reaped billions in profits from several Chrysler stock buybacks. A $5 billion windfall from Chrysler's incorporation into German automaker Daimler-Benz in 1998 was not enough for Kerkorian, who filed suit (unsuccessfully) against the company for misrepresenting the new DaimlerChrysler entity as a merger of equals; chairman Juergen Schrempp, in comments made in 2000, characterized it instead as a takeover, which would have resulted in additional profits for stockholders.

In 2005 Kerkorian set his sights still higher. He acquired a 9.9 percent stake in General Motors and seated one of his representatives on the company's board, then urged GM to investigate a merger with the already existing partnership of French automaker Renault and Japan's Nissan. Press reports at the time suggested that Kerkorian envisioned high-flying Nissan head Carlos Ghosn as GM's new chairman. These efforts, too, were beaten back by GM's existing management in 2006—with difficulty, for Kerkorian's net worth by this time amounted to more than half of GM's total market valuation of some $16.4 billion. In November of 2006 Kerkorian's Tracinda Corp. sold most of its GM stock.

An inspiration to senior citizens everywhere, Kerkorian made his high finance automotive transactions while he was in his late 80s. He reportedly jogged every morning, and friends reported that his tennis game was improving. Still frugal in his personal habits, he allowed himself the luxury of $150 haircuts for his still-thick mane of gray hair. In an era when finance was increasingly the province of young movers and shakers with advanced degrees, he was a self-made man who outperformed competitors one-third his age.

Books

Newsmakers, issue 2, Gale, 1996.

Periodicals

Automotive News, December 8, 2003; October 9, 2006.
Economist, December 2, 2000.
Forbes, December 15, 1997; October 12, 1998.
Money, May 1, 2002.
Newsweek, July 31, 2006.
People, February 18, 2002.
Time, May 16, 2005.
Variety, April 25, 2005.

Online

"The Quiet Lion," The First 100 Persons Who Shaped Southern Nevada (*Las Vegas Review-Journal*), http://www.1st100.com/part3/kerkorian.html (February 13, 2007).
"#26 Kirk Kerkorian," The 400 Richest Americans (*Forbes*), http://www.forbes.com (February 13, 2007). ☐

Ken Kesey

In 1962 American writer Ken Kesey (1935–2001) rose to prominence when Viking Press published his first novel, *One Flew Over the Cuckoo's Nest*. Kesey

served as a primary link between the Beatniks of the 1950s and the counter-culture movement of the mid-to-late 1960s, and his 1964 cross-country journey with a band of followers known as the Merry Pranksters was immortalized by Tom Wolfe in *The Electric Kool-Aid Acid Test* in 1968. In 1975 a film version of *One Flew Over the Cuckoo's Nest* received five Academy Awards, spreading Kesey's vision to a new generation.

Lived All-American Youth

Over time, Kesey would be seen as one of the primary trendsetters of the counter-culture movement during the 1960s; as a child and young man, however, his dreams and accomplishments were "all-American." He was born Ken Elton Kesey on September 17, 1935, in La Junta, Colorado, the son of Fred A. and Geneve (Smith) Kesey. Beginning in 1941, the family moved several times, eventually settling in Eugene, Oregon, in 1946. Fred Kesey founded Eugene Farmers Cooperative, which marketed Darigold products. Kesey later described his family as "hard shell" Baptists, and he retained great respect for the Bible into adulthood. He and his younger brother Joe (known as Chuck) loved the outdoors, and spent their leisure time fishing for salmon and trout, and hunting for duck and deer. Kesey also enjoyed physical sports like boxing and racing, and was active in both wrestling and football at Springfield (Eugene's adjacent city) high school. His classmates voted him most likely to succeed.

Kesey's accomplishments and interests expanded far beyond the outdoors and physical sports. Kesey decorated sets for assemblies and plays, wrote skits, and won an award for best thespian. He also had a fascination with magic that extended to ventriloquism and hypnotism. Before Kesey enrolled in the University of Oregon's speech and communications program, he spent the summer in Hollywood attempting to find bit parts. He would return the following summer, and though he found little success, he relished the new experience and the people he met.

As with high school, Kesey was an active student at the University of Oregon, participating in the theater, sports, and fraternities. Academically, his major directed his energies toward acting and writing for television and radio. He won a second thespian award at college, and wrote several drama and documentary scripts for a course offered by Dean Starlin. Kesey simultaneously pursued his love of sports, eventually earning a Fred Lowe Scholarship in wrestling. "His friends in Drama could not understand why he was on the wrestling team and associated with athletes," noted Stephen L. Tanner in his book *Ken Kesey*, "and of course his friends among the athletes could not understand why he would involve himself with the theater group." On May 20, 1956, while at the university, Kesey married his childhood sweetheart, Faye Haxby.

Experienced Dramatic Life Change

Kesey earned a bachelor of arts degree in 1957 and returned home to Eugene, where he worked in the dairy business for a year. He had decided to become a writer, though his future remained uncertain: with his teachers' urging he had applied for a Woodrow Wilson Fellowship, which would allow him to continue his education, but there was also the possibility that he would be drafted. Both the answer to the fellowship and draft question arrived in the mail on the same day. Because of a shoulder injury from wrestling, Kesey was classified as 4F, disqualifying him for military service. The Woodrow Wilson Fellowship, on the other hand, was granted, allowing him to sign up for the writing program at Stanford in 1958.

At Stanford, Kesey studied under Wallace Stegner and Malcolm Cowley, and completed his first unpublished novel about college athletics. While Kesey's teachers at Stanford had a significant impact on his writing, he was also greatly influenced by his fellow students and the cultural movements surrounding the community. Kesey befriended Larry McMurty, Robert Stone, and Wendell Berry, and participated in contentious but constructive roundtable discussions with his fellow writers. He formed his closest friendship with Ken Babbs, and the two would become tight-knit co-conspirators in the coming years. Kesey was also attracted to the beat culture. He visited the nearby beat scene of North Beach, and read works by Jack Kerouac, William S. Burroughs, and Clellan Holmes. In a short time, the teetotaling Kesey with a Baptist background was wearing a beard, smoking marijuana,

and working on a second novel titled *Zoo,* about the North Beach beat scene. Although he was unable to find a publisher for the novel, Stanford granted him the $2,000 Saxton Prize for a section of the book.

Kesey lived at Perry Lane while at Stanford, a block-long row of cottages on the outskirts of a golf course within Menlo Park. Perry Lane had a long, bohemian tradition, and Kesey and his friends quickly became a part of that tradition. "In the Lane he was introduced to wine drinking, marijuana smoking, wife swapping, and a variety of new attitudes and practices," wrote Tanner. His most radical transformation, however, came after he enlisted in a number of experiments at the Veterans' Hospital in Menlo Park at the suggestion of a friend, Vic Lovell. There, Kesey was paid to ingest a number of psychedelic substances including LSD, an experience that led to his own experimentation with hallucinogenics in order to heighten consciousness. Later, he was hired as an aide at the hospital where he worked third shift.

One Flew Over the Cuckoo's Nest

Kesey's next novel was based on his work at the Veterans' Hospital and influenced by his ongoing use of psychedelics, and served to make him a notable literary figure. Narrated by the character Chief Bromden, *One Flew Over the Cuckoo's Nest* tells the story of Randle Patrick McMurphy, an exuberant, vivacious outsider who avoids a correction facility sentence by pleading insanity. He is sent to a mental hospital where his vitality and willingness to stand up to the oppressive Big Nurse Ratched re-energizes a number of inmates whom he befriends. Kesey, reportedly, even received a clandestine treatment of shock therapy to aide his descriptions of the hospital experience. *One Flew Over the Cuckoo's Nest's* metaphor, which centered on the relationships between authority figures and the oppressed, posed a larger social question for the so-called silent generation, born and reared in America's middle class suburbs: Are the people in charge (the government, the corporations) less sane than the people following orders (citizens, workers)? Kesey finished the book in the summer of 1961, and with the help of Cowley, *One Flew Over the Cuckoo's Nest* was published by Viking in February of 1962. The book became an immediate critical and popular success.

Kesey returned to Eugene briefly in the summer of 1961 and worked at the creamery with his brother Chuck. He started gathering material for his next book, *Sometimes a Great Notion,* and continued working on the manuscript when he returned to Perry Lane in the fall. Unlike *One Flew Over the Cuckoo's Nest,* which took ten months to write, the new book would take two years. As he worked on the project, *One Few Over the Cuckoo's Nest* continued to gain attention. In 1963–64, a Broadway version, adapted by Dale Wasserman, starred Kirk Douglas and ran for 82 performances. The book also sold well, allowing Kesey the money necessary to buy land in La Honda, California, an isolated locality in the Santa Cruz Mountains.

Kesey finished *Sometimes a Great Notion* in La Honda, and Viking published it in 1964. While the book never achieved the critical and popular success of *One Flew Over the Cuckoo's Nest,* many critics prefer it. "In terms of structure, point of view, and theme," wrote Barry H. Leeds in his book *Ken Kesey*, "it is more ambitious, more experimental, and ultimately more successful."

Initiated Mythic Bus Trip

After Kesey finished *Sometimes a Great Notion*, he bought a 1939 International Harvester School Bus (called Furthur) and planned a cross-country trip to New York City that coincided with the book's publication in July of 1964. The trip, however, would be unlike any that Americans had ever witnessed, with Kesey serving as the unofficial leader of a small group of friends who had gathered at La Honda. Together, they prepared the International Harvester for the trip, installing tape players and loud speakers, painting it psychedelic colors, and stocking various psychedelics (LSD was legal at the time), and the crew left La Honda on June 14, 1964. Kesey and the "Merry Pranksters" embarked upon an expedition that served as a signpost to a rising generation, introducing the hippy prototype to American towns and cities from coast-to-coast. "It became a metaphor for the carefree (and, at times, careless), hedonistic, authority-challenging, back-to-nature, alternative-seeking qualities of the 1960s," wrote Paul Berry in the book *On the Bus*.

By the end of August of 1964, Kesey and the Pranksters had returned to La Honda. Kesey busied himself editing 45 hours of home movies taken during the trip, though he was unable to shape the footage into a theatrical release. As the unorthodox community around Kesey grew, it attracted more attention from both neighbors and law enforcement. On April 23, 1965, the police arrested Kesey and he was charged with possession of marijuana. During this time, Kesey and the Pranksters also conducted a series of "Acid-Tests," festival-like events held at various venues where LSD was introduced to a wider audience. Following a second drug arrest at the beginning of 1966, Kesey left the United States for Mexico to avoid prosecution. He remained in Mexico for the next nine months, where he, his family, and followers continued living a lifestyle similar to the one they had established in La Honda. When Kesey returned to the United States, he eventually received two light sentences totaling nine months and a $1500 fine.

Settled on Oregon Farm

Following his release, Kesey moved his family and members of the Merry Pranksters to a farm in Pleasant Hill, Oregon, which remained his residence for the rest of his life. In 1969 he decided to forego a trip with the Pranksters to the Woodstock Festival, and made it clear that they were unwelcome at his farm upon their return. Kesey remained relatively isolated until 1973 when he published *Kesey's Garage Sale*, a collection of commentaries and plays. In 1986 he published a second collection, *Demon Box*, followed by the children's book, *Little Tricker the Squirrel Meets Big Double the Bear*, in 1990.

Kesey released *Sailor Song* in 1992, his first novel since *Sometimes a Great Notion* 28 years earlier. Set in an Alaskan fishing village of Kunjak, *Sailor Song* takes place in the near future, following a number of ecological disasters. Critical reaction to the book was mixed. "If Kesey himself weren't a cult figure of sorts," suggested Gene Lyons in *Entertainment Weekly*, "*Sailor Song* would probably not have been published." *Publisher's Weekly*, however, noted that the book found Kesey's "baroque humor in top form."

The influence of Kesey's life and work, especially during the 1960s, has had a broad impact on American culture. Kesey and the Merry Pranksters' mythic bus trip and counter-culture lifestyle was immortalized in Tom Wolfe's highly popular nonfiction book, *The Electric Kool-Aid Acid Test*, in 1968. Wolfe was one of the first commentators to identify Kesey as the essential link between the beatnik culture of the 1950s and the hippy culture of the mid-to-late 1960s. In the 1990s, even the Smithsonian Institute recognized Kesey's cultural impact, and attempted (unsuccessfully) to purchase the "Furthur" bus. By the mid-1970s, when *One Flew Over the Cuckoo's Nest* had been turned into an Academy Award film, the book itself had sold over four million copies and been adapted to countless college courses. In 2006 *One Flew Over the Cuckoo's Nest* was transformed once again, this time into a musical.

Kesey suffered a mild stroke in 1997. Four years later, on November 10, 2001, Kesey died of liver cancer in Eugene, Oregon, at the age of 66. "All his life," wrote novelist Robert Stone in the *New Yorker*, "he was searching for the philosopher's stone that could return the world to the pure story from which it was made."

Books

Babbs, Ken, and Paul Perry, *On the Bus: The Complete Gude to the Legendary Trip of Ken Kesey and the Merry Pranksters and the Birth of the Counterculture,* Thunder's Mouth Press, 1990.
Leeds, Barry H., *Ken Kesey,* Frederick Ungar, 1981.
Tanner, Stephen L., *Ken Kesey,* Twayne, 1983.

Periodicals

Entertainment Weekly, August 28, 1992.
New Yorker, June 14, 2004.
Publishers Weekly, June 22, 1992. □

A. Q. Khan

Through a process that began with the theft of designs and documents from a Dutch centrifuge manufacturing facility, Pakistani metallurgist A. Q. Khan (born 1936) became the father of his country's nuclear weapons program—and then a rogue scientist of historic significance who is thought to have marketed atomic bomb designs to states around the world, without oversight from his government or anyone else.

Khan aided North Korea's nuclear program, which apparently culminated in the test of a small weapon in October of 2006. He has shared information with Iran, but the nature and extent of the help he gave to that country's nuclear program has been unclear, and remains

an issue of vital importance in ongoing debates over Iran's intentions with regard to nuclear weaponry. Khan was finally reined in by the Pakistani government in 2004, forced to make a televised confession of illicit activities leading to nuclear proliferation, and placed under house arrest. The activities of the worldwide underground supplier network he established, however, have remained the focus of intense international investigation.

Influence Predicted by Fortune-Teller

Abdul Qadeer Khan was born in 1936 in Bhopal, India. Although he was not strongly religious during young adulthood, he grew up in a devoutly Muslim household in an urban atmosphere marked by Hindu-Muslim tensions. His father, a schoolteacher, was a member of the local Muslim League. But Khan as a child devoted himself mostly to his studies. His mother took him to a fortune teller who predicted, according to a Pakistani biography of Khan quoted by William Langewiesche in the *Atlantic,* that "he is going to do very important and useful work for his nation and will earn immense respect."

Great Britain's 1947 partition of the Indian subcontinent into the new nations of majority-Hindu India and majority-Muslim Pakistan brought upheaval to Khan's life, as it did for millions of others. Several of his siblings left India for Pakistan, and Khan, at age 16, followed them there in 1952. The trip was a difficult one, during which some of Khan's traveling companions suffered robberies and beatings at the hands of Indian railroad police. At the end, Khan

is said to have walked barefoot across a five-mile stretch of desert, carrying only schoolbooks and a few possessions, to reach Pakistan.

These experiences left Khan with a lifelong distrust of India, but he still took some interest in politics. He enrolled at the D. J. Science College of Karachi, Pakistan, and continued to excel as a student. After graduating in 1960 he got a job as a Pakistani government inspector, but he wanted to pursue further education, and in 1961 he managed to put together funding to enroll in a metallurgical engineering program in Germany. He moved to The Hague in the Netherlands the following year because he had met a Dutch woman named Henny, who soon became his wife. Khan attended Delft Technological University for four years, learning to speak both Dutch and German so well that at one point he was asked to translate a sensitive document from one language to the other. He was also fluent in English, Urdu, and Hindi, and spoke some French and Persian.

Khan and his wife moved on to Catholic University in Leuven, Belgium, where they had two daughters and where Khan pursued a doctorate in metallurgical engineering. He wrote and published papers in his field, made friends easily, and seemed to enjoy life in Europe and the prospect of a well-paid engineering career to come. He received his doctorate in 1972 and began looking for a job, finding one with a Dutch consulting firm called FDO that specialized in the design of centrifuges—giant spinning drums used for a variety of industrial processes including, as it happened, the enrichment of uranium for nuclear weapons. It was at this point that Khan's career began to intersect with the unfolding of world events.

Volunteered Services to Pakistani Government

In 1971 eastern Pakistan, separated from the rest of the country by the northern part of India, launched a war of independence. At first the rebellion was crushed, but after India entered the war on East Pakistan's side, the newly independent nation of Bangladesh was formed. Pakistanis, who had already fought several wars against India over the disputed Kashmir region, suffered national humiliation at the loss of substantial parts of its territory and population. When Pakistani leader Zulfikar Ali Bhutto learned that India had launched a nuclear research program he formed one of his own, vowing at one point that Pakistanis would "eat grass"—make any conceivable sacrifice—in order to obtain the nuclear weapons that would, from their point of view, protect them from Indian domination. After India detonated an underground nuclear explosion in 1974, Khan wrote to Bhutto, outlining his credentials and offering his help in building a bomb based on enriched uranium. This was a better plan, Khan argued, than the plutonium-based bomb Pakistan had been pursuing. After some time, his offer was accepted.

Khan's company, FDO, provided consulting services to a Dutch-German uranium enrichment facility called URENCO that supplied fuel for peaceful nuclear energy uses (although the double edge of nuclear energy technology is its frequent applicability to weaponry). He realized that the company's centrifuge designs could potentially be used to enrich uranium to bomb-level concentrations, and, having been given a security clearance by the Dutch government (which at the time had no reason to suspect him of anything), he simply walked through the URENCO facility taking notes, in Urdu. When questioned, which he rarely was, he said that he was writing letters home to Pakistan. Later he became acquainted with a Dutch co-worker, the machinist and photographer Frits Veerman, from whom he obtained additional information about, and photos of, the URENCO centrifuge designs.

Veerman eventually realized that Khan was a Pakistani spy. He tried to alert his superiors, but was told to keep quiet lest he make trouble for his company lab. Finally the suspicions of the Dutch government were raised by Khan's persistent questioning of a variety of individuals on technological subjects. In late 1975 Dutch intelligence agents instructed FDO to move Khan to a less sensitive position, but by now it was too late. At the end of that year Khan returned to Pakistan with a good grasp of the most sophisticated uranium-enrichment technology known to the Western world. He assumed leadership of one branch of Pakistan's nuclear weapons program, the one concerned with the effort to make a bomb from highly enriched uranium.

Various legal proceedings launched against Khan in the Netherlands came to nothing, and he twice eluded arrest by Dutch intelligence agents when the United States Central Intelligence Agency (CIA) told them to hold off so that additional information could be gathered about Khan's contacts. The CIA, however, was unaware of the full extent of Khan's knowledge and network of contacts. "We knew a lot," an American nuclear intelligence official told William J. Broad and David E. Sanger of the *New York Times,* but we didn't realize the size of his universe."

Obtained Dual-Use Technology from Europe

In 1976 Khan created the Engineering Research Laboratories in Kahuta, Pakistan, a small town southeast of Islamabad. Uranium from Pakistani mines was sent to the facility, and Khan made steady progress with its enrichment to the high concentrations necessary for a nuclear bomb. He and his staff claimed that the lab was doing only work relevant to the peaceful uses of nuclear technology, but engineers under Khan's charge also worked on rocketry and weapons delivery systems. Precision parts were imported from a Khan-developed network of suppliers, many of them in Europe, who may have believed that the materials they were sending would be used for nuclear power rather than nuclear weaponry. In 1981 Bhutto's successor, Zia ul Haq, renamed Khan's lab the Khan Research Laboratories.

Pakistan conducted a nuclear test for the first time only in 1998, after a comparable test by India, but Khan had probably produced several nuclear warheads by the late 1980s, and Pakistan may have threatened to use them during a period of tension with India. At around this time, Khan apparently began offering his expertise to other countries. Iraq, whose initial efforts were disrupted by the Gulf War of 1991, and Iran, which may have received an inferior version of his designs, may have been among his first clients.

Khan's motivations were complex. Partly they were financial; already a renowned figure in Pakistan, he became extremely wealthy and powerful, able to operate partly beyond the reach of Pakistani government control. "Every schoolchild knows his name and recognizes his face," a Western diplomat in Pakistan told Edward Luce of the *Financial Times* in 2004. "A.Q. Khan enjoys almost legendary status across Pakistan." Khan also resented the Western monopoly on nuclear weaponry, and specifically Israel's often-rumored possession of an arsenal of atomic bombs. "All Western countries," he was quoted as saying by Sanger and Broad in the *New York Times,* "are not only the enemies of Pakistan but in fact of Islam."

Khan's activities were closely followed by Western intelligence agencies, with an American nonproliferation official telling Langewiesche that "our interest in this man is so intense that you can assume if he takes a toilet break and goes to the john, we know about it." However, the obstacles to combating Khan's operations were often political rather than logistical. Pakistan was an ally of the United States and became a much closer one after the terrorist attacks of September 11, 2001; pressing the Pakistani government and military, layers of which were closely involved with Khan's activities, for a crackdown on the rogue scientist was a delicate operation. Khan traveled freely among Asian, Middle Eastern, and African capitals, and his assistants openly advertised his expertise at conferences and trade shows.

The list of Khan clients grew during the 1990s, but its ultimate membership remains unknown. Khan, by his own testimony in a 2004 confession, shared information with Iran, Libya, and North Korea. He had contacts in many other countries, but whether they were customers or suppliers remained the focus of intense investigation. It was Libya that proved Khan's undoing; after the 2003 interception of a ship loaded with centrifuge parts, linked to a Khan associate and headed for Libya, Libyan leader Muammar Quaddafi decided to suspend his nuclear weapons program and cooperate with Western investigators. The documents Libya released showed a reliance on the URENCO centrifuge designs mastered by Khan, and some of them contained details pointing toward an origin in Khan's lab, perhaps with Khan himself.

Pakistani President Pervez Musharraf was finally forced to act. He launched an investigation that resulted in Khan's nationally televised confession of February 4, 2004, a carefully worded speech in which Khan admitted to "alleged proliferation activities" (as quoted by Langewiesche) without going into many specifics. Khan was placed under house arrest at his mansion near Rawalpindi. Since then, investigators from the United States and from the International Atomic Energy Commission have tried to locate parts of the far-flung network that Khan put in place, but U.S. officials have not been allowed to question him. Reportedly suffering from prostate cancer, he could only watch from the sidelines as the potentially terrifying processes he had set in motion began to unfold.

Periodicals

Atlantic Monthly, November 2005, January-February 2006.
Bulletin of the Atomic Scientists, September 1993.

Financial Times, February 3, 2004.
New York Times, January 4, 2004; December 26, 2004; March 21, 2005.
Time, February 14, 2005.

Online

"Pakistan's nuclear hero, world's No. 1 nuclear suspect," *Christian Science Monitor,* http://www.csmonitor.com/2004/0202/p25s01-wose.htm (December 23, 2006). □

Dong Kingman

Artist Dong Kingman's (1911–2000) name became synonymous with artwork that depicted a variety of urban cityscapes. In an article following Kingman's death, the *San Francisco Chronicle* declared, "Mr. Kingman's watercolors of San Francisco's cable cars and Golden Gate Bridge were nearly as popular as the landmarks themselves." Kingham worked mainly in watercolors, and his paintings are exhibited in museums across the country, including the Museum of Modern Art, the Art Institute of Chicago, and the Metropolitan Museum of Art.

Moved from California to Hong Kong

Kingman was born Dong Moy Shu Kingman on March 31, 1911, in Oakland, California. He was the second of eight children born to immigrants from Hong Kong. His father was a laundryman who also owned and ran a dry goods store, and his mother was a housewife. It was not long after he was born that World War I started in Europe. At that time the draft was in effect, and there was no end in sight for the war, so the Kingman family moved back to Hong Kong because the parents did not want to risk the father being called to fight in the war. After they arrived in Hong Kong, Kingman's father took up what he had done in the United States, and he ran a successful department store in Hong Kong.

While he was living in Hong Kong, Kingman came to discover art at a relatively young age. He seemed to have a skill for it right from the start, and his mother encouraged his interest, pushing him to practice his drawing and painting. He was sent to the Lingnan Branch School when he was a teenager to study painting with the instructor Szetsu Wei, who was a well-known and highly respected Chinese painter. While he was there he studied not only traditional Chinese art, but also Western artists who had become masters in their respective fields. He especially studied the French Impressionists like Pierre-Auguste Renoir and Claude Monet, who were of particular interest to Kingman for their use of light in their paintings.

Moved Back to United States

In 1929, when Kingman was 18, he moved to the United States, where his family thought he would have a better chance to make something of his art. He moved to San Francisco, California, where he took on jobs such as working in a factory that his brother owned, or working in a restaurant, as well as working in several households for San Francisco families, doing odd jobs. No matter what he did to earn money, however, he kept in mind his reason for being there, and continued to pursue his art.

After a short time living like this, Kingman began submitting his work to group art shows, and it was while his work was being displayed in such a show that he came to public notice, and in 1936 he was hired as an artist by the federal government for the Works Progress Administration, a Great Depression program established by the New Deal. That same year Kingman held his first solo art show at the San Francisco Art Center. The show was well-received and garnered good reviews, and Kingman's name began to be known throughout the art world. He was so well thought of that he was offered a job teaching art at the Academy of Advertising Art in San Francisco.

Work Bought by Metropolitan Museum

Kingman worked primarily in watercolors, which was the medium of choice for artists at that time, and his work became increasingly popular. One day a rich art collector saw Kingman's work and purchased several pieces for his collection. It was quite a coup for the young artist. The collector later donated his Kingman collection to museums around the country, displaying Kingman's work to the many people who had never had the opportunity to see his work.

In 1940 one of the highest compliments in the art world was paid to Kingman: the Metropolitan Museum of Art in New York City, New York purchased one of his works to display in their collection. It was the first piece of Asian-American art to be displayed there. It was perhaps because of this introduction that in 1941 Kingman was given a two-year fellowship from the famous Guggenheim Museum, which focused on modern art. The fellowship paid for Kingman to travel extensively around America, offering the artist a chance to paint myriad views of landscapes he saw on the trip. During this tour Kingman got to see America the way almost no one ever does: in its eclectic entirety. But of all the sights he beheld and painted, his favorite was New York City, and Kingman decided that one day he would move there.

Drafted Into Military During World War II

In 1942 Kingman held a solo art exhibit at the Midtown Gallery in New York City. Critics from papers around New York wrote favorably of the show, and it seemed that Kingman's name in the art world was set. But in 1943, before he could pursue his art any further, Kingman was drafted into the military. It was World War II, and Pearl Harbor had just been attacked by the Japanese. Luckily, however, Kingman was not sent into battle; his art skills were considered too important, and he was sent to Washington, D.C., where he worked as an illustrator for the OSS, the precursor to the CIA. While there he spent his free time completing a series of paintings of the sights around the capital. After the war was over he returned to New York City, where he held an exhibition of these paintings. Kingman's wish came true, and in 1945 he was able to settle in New York City.

During the 1940s and 1950s Kingman kept painting and showing his work. He also taught painting at Columbia University, Hunter College, and at the Famous Artists School in Westport, Connecticut. He became a full-time teacher at Hunter College in 1948. In 1951 the Midtown Gallery held a show of the artist's work from the early days until 1950, commemorating the fact that it had been 10 years since they had last shown the artist's work.

Toured Asia with His Artwork

In 1953 the U.S. State Department's education exchange program invited Kingman to tour Asia to show off his work. Kingman's work was very popular in Asia, and wherever he stopped to exhibit his work, large crowds came see it and to listen to the lectures he gave. On this tour Kingman traveled to Hong Kong, Singapore, Malaya, Bangkok, New Delhi, and Istanbul. On his way home Kingman stopped in Europe, visiting Vienna, Copenhagen, Oslo, London, and Reykjavik, Iceland. He spent his trip giving lectures and showing his work, but also painting the different scenes he saw on his travels. After his return the paintings were sent on tour throughout the United States, funded by the State Department. The *New York Times* said of Kingman's work: "His urban scenes have a cheery, gently humorous flavor, best sampled in a 40-foot rice-paper scroll that he created in 1954 while on a cultural exchange program sponsored by the State Department. The scroll was published in *Life.*"

Kingman was also invited to paint sets for Hollywood films that needed a special Asian flavor. Movies he painted for included *The World of Suzie Wong* (1960), the musical *Flower Drum Song* (1961), and *55 Days at Peking* (1963). As his fame spread, Kingman also showed his artwork in such prestigious galleries as the Wildenstein and the Hammer in New York. But it was when he began illustrating movie posters, magazine articles, and magazine covers, including covers for *Time, Life* and the *Saturday Review,* that he became a household name. Kingman's work was also used in many other areas, such as posters for airlines, textile designs for sheets and towels, and illustrations for children's books.

Taught and Wrote About Art

In 1957 Kingman began teaching annual painting workshops in many different countries in Europe, Asia, and Latin America. While doing so he continued his painting, continuing to show his work, especially his favorite scenes of urban New York. The Ministry of Culture of the People's Republic of China put together a showing of Kingman's work in 1981 so that the Chinese might be exposed to his work, which they deemed worthy. In 1994 an exhibit called "40 Years of Watercolors by Dong Kingman" was put together in Taiwan by the Taipei Fine Arts Museum. An exhibit looking at the entire body of Kingman's work was also shown at the Taichung Provincial Museum in Taiwan in 1999. In 2000–2001 just such a show of Kingman's works toured across the United States.

Kingman wrote his autobiography later in life. In *Dong Kingman's Watercolors,* he looked back on his career as an artist: "Over the years, I've had some difficult times. But whenever I felt discouraged, I would stop and think of how something had always come along which enabled me to continue learning. I would tell myself to have faith and that with time and perseverance I could overcome anything. And I did." Kingman died of pancreatic cancer on May 12, 2000, at his home in New York City, when he was 89 years old.

Legacy Lived On

In his personal life, Kingman married twice. His first marriage to Janice Wong was cut short when she died in 1954. He then married Helena, who died just before him in 1999. He had two sons: Dong Jr. and Eddie, and four grandchildren.

As of the beginning of 2007 Kingman's works continue to be exhibited in some of the major museums in America, including the Metropolitan Museum, the Museum of Modern Art in New York, the Whitney Museum of American Art, the Brooklyn Museum of Art and the Museum of Fine Arts, Boston. Several private collectors also number Kingman's works among their collections.

Books

Almanac of Famous People, 8th edition, Gale Group, 2003.
Contemporary Authors Online, Gale, 2002.
Notable Asian Americans, Gale Research, 1995.

Periodicals

Art in America, October 2000.
New York Times, May 16, 2000.
San Francisco Chronicle, May 16, 2000. □

Athanasius Kircher

The German-born Jesuit scholar Athanasius Kircher (c. 1601–1680) was, in the words of an article reprinted on the website of the Museum of Jurassic Technology, an "inventor, composer, geographer, geologist, Egyptologist, historian, adventurer, philosopher, proprietor of one of the first public museums, physicist, mathematician, naturalist, astronomer, archaeologist, [and] author of more than 40 published works." It might be easiest to call him, as did Paula Findlen, the editor of a book of articles about Kircher, "the last man who knew everything."

Kircher's erudition was vast, but it was dwarfed by his curiosity. He investigated volcanoes (by having himself lowered into one while it was erupting), hieroglyphics, infectious organisms, magnetism, the relationships between languages, astronomy, and biblical scholarship. He

was likely the first scientist to propose the germ theory of disease, and he invented the magic lantern or refined it from previous models. In addition to his formal publications, Kircher corresponded voluminously with learned individuals and religious figures around the world. Perhaps his posthumous reputation is the most surprising part of Kircher's saga: despite all his accomplishments, Kircher fell into obscurity after his death and was mostly forgotten until the last decades of the twentieth century.

Suffered Accidents in Youth

Kircher, named after the saint whose feast day marked Kircher's birthday, was born on May 2, 1601 or 1602, in the village of Geisa, near Fulda in what is now central Germany. His father was a teacher and lecturer who had studied religion and philosophy. Kircher experienced the first of several brushes with death when he was accidentally run through part of a mill apparatus. He attended Jesuit schools, and in 1618 he made plans to study at the Society of Jesus in the city of Paderborn, a religious institution with an educational component. Kircher injured one of his legs in an ice-skating accident prior to his admission, and it turned gangrenous. He was examined when he arrived at the school, and doctors told him his condition was incurable. Kircher, however, retired to a chapel containing a statue of Mary that was reputed to have curative powers. The next morning, his leg was once again whole.

The chaos of the Thirty Years' War, which tore Germany apart along religious lines, left its mark on the rest of Kircher's education. Forced to flee Paderborn along with his teachers, Kircher was stranded on an ice floe while trying to cross the frozen Rhine River. He swam to shore and eventually made his way to a Catholic university in Cologne, where he continued his studies of philosophy, science, and classical languages. He learned to speak Hebrew and Syriac on his way to mastery of some ten languages, possibly including Chinese. Kircher was sent to teach mathematics and languages at Jesuit schools in the cities of Heiligenstadt and Koblenz, encountering new hazards as he crossed Protestant-held territory. Captured and nearly hanged at one point, he was spared by a soldier who was struck by his calmness in the face of death.

Kircher's first influential patron was the Elector of Mainz, who brought him to that city after hearing reports of Kircher's skill in mounting a fireworks display. At the Elector's court Kircher wrote a book, *Ars magnesia,* about magnetism. After the Elector's death Kircher began studying for the priesthood, making astronomical observations on the side; he was one of the first astronomers to view sunspots through a telescope. Kircher was ordained as a Catholic priest in 1628. He embarked on a period of study and reflection at a Jesuit college in Speyer, finding a book of ancient Egyptian hieroglyphics in the college's library and applying himself to the age-old problem of deciphering them. His guesses at the meaning of the hieroglyphics were wrong but wildly original—he thought they constituted a set of religious symbols rather than a writing system.

Kircher began teaching mathematics, ethics, and ancient languages at the University of Würzburg. In 1630 he was fascinated by reports of the eruption of the Mount Vesuvius volcano in Italy. Apparently wanting to explore the world, he petitioned his superior to be allowed to travel to China as a missionary, but his application was refused. Kircher was forced to flee the outbreak of war once again in 1631 as Swedish Protestant troops invaded the Würzburg region, and this time he had to leave Germany for good. Arriving in the eastern French city of Avignon, a center of Catholic learning in France, he began teaching and attracted the attention of an influential patron, the French nobleman Sicolas Peiresc. Peiresc had a large collection of Egyptian artifacts and had heard of Kircher's investigations into their meaning.

Shipwreck Led to Residence in Rome

In Avignon Kircher penned another wide-ranging study covering the hieroglyphics as well as astronomy and geography. His growing renown had reached Vienna, Austria, and in 1633 he was summoned there to replace Johannes Kepler as court mathematician to the Hapsburg dynasty. Peiresc, distressed by this turn of events, wrote a letter to Pope Urban VIII asking that the summons be revoked, but Kircher was already en route. This time he traveled by sea in order to avoid German war zones, but he was once again plagued by near-fatal bad luck: his ship foundered in high winds, and he was forced to take refuge in the small Italian seaport of Città Vecchia, near Rome. Making his way into the eternal city, his luck improved. Peiresc's letter had reached the Vatican, and he was appointed to teach and to continue his research at the Jesuits' Roman College (now the Pontifical Gregorian University). He learned the Coptic language of ancient African Christianity and identified it as a relative of ancient Egyptian.

In 1637 Kircher made another unsuccessful attempt to be posted to China. Instead he began to travel through southern Italy, studying the volcanoes of the region and, in 1638, he climbed Mount Vesuvius near Naples and had himself lowered into its fiery maw. "The whole area was lit up by the fires," he wrote, as quoted in a *Chronicle of Higher Education* article, "and the glowing sulphur and bitumen [coal] produced an intolerable vapor. It was just like hell, only lacking the demons to complete the picture." Kircher eventually synthesized his investigations of geology into a book called *Mundus subterraneus,* (The Subterranean World, 1665).

As a result of his growing reputation, Kircher was allowed to stop teaching and devote all his time to pure research. During the 1650s and 1660s he wrote most of his books and made his most noteworthy and unusual discoveries. They covered an enormous variety of subjects. In 1646 his *Ars magna lucis et umbrae* (The Great Art of Light and Shadows) described the magic lantern, a forerunner of the slide projector, in detail. The idea of projecting drawings on glass onto a wall existed before Kircher, but he was the first to treat the phenomenon rationally. Kircher experimented with clocks and constructed new musical instruments. He teamed with the sculptor and designer Gian Lorenzo Bernini in installing the Egyptian obelisk that still stands at the center of the Piazza Navona in Rome.

He owned a microscope and used it, when plague ravaged Rome in 1656, to examine the bodily fluids of some of the many plague sufferers under his care. He saw small organisms in the blood that he thought caused the disease—an unheard-of idea at the time, but one that evolved into the modern germ theory of infection (it is not clear exactly what he saw). Kircher was an early advocate of such measures as quarantine in combating the plague. He immersed himself in biblical history and devoted one book (in 1675) to a massive attempt to understand Noah's Ark and the question of how all the species of animals in the world could have fit on one boat, however large. His treatise, festooned with diagrams, involved ingenious speculations as to how some animals, such as insects, might have arisen spontaneously in the epochs since biblical times.

Indeed, Kircher's varied researches might be seen as part of a wider effort to understand the entire history of the world according to a literal biblical viewpoint. However, Kircher may have worked to subvert that viewpoint as well. His research into the ancient world likely suggested to him that the biblical account of creation was not literally true; at one point he wrote out a list of Egyptian kings indicating, as Sarah Boxer noted in the *New York Times,* "that Egypt existed long before the world was even supposed to have been created." Yet Kircher was careful not to go too far in questioning religious orthodoxy. Although he likely realized the truth of the discovery by Nicolas Copernicus and Galileo Galilei that the earth revolved around the sun, he did not publicly back the idea.

Ideas Challenged by Rationalist Thinkers

That restraint formed part of the reason Kircher's work eventually fell out of favor. In his day he was an internationally famous figure, his books in demand all over the Christian world, even in the Western Hemisphere. The self-taught and erudite Mexican nun and writer Sor Juana Inés de la Cruz was one of his admirers. Kircher's lavishly illustrated volumes, Paula Findlen told Boxer, were "the first great coffee-table books," prized by educated readers everywhere. But by the end of his lifetime new intellectual trends were taking hold, as the foundation of the individual modern arts and sciences appeared to make Kircher's "Renaissance man" approach obsolete. Rationalist figures such as the French philosopher René Descartes questioned Kircher's ideas.

In his later years Kircher continued to write and to break new ground. In an age when maps often bore little resemblance to terrestrial reality, he created a map of China whose shape came close to the actual boundaries of Chinese dominions. In one book he attempted to create a universal language. Yet he also seemed to deploy his vast knowledge in playful ways. In the 1670s he opened the Museum Kircherianum, one of the first public museums, in which he displayed many of the fruits of his inventiveness. He made robot-like models, equipping them with speaking tubes so that an automaton would seem to greet visitors from another room. He built a box of mirrors that would create a cascade of optical illusions and hopelessly confuse an unfortunate cat that he would place inside the container.

Kircher died in Rome on November 27, 1680. His heart was buried separately from the rest of his body. For most of the next three centuries he was almost unknown except to specialists and Jesuit historians, but the late twentieth century saw a sharp revival of his reputation. To use Boxer's words, "His subversiveness, his celebrity, his technomania, and his bizarre eclecticism" all echoed traits of contemporary culture. The Museum of Jurassic Culture in Culver City, California, devoted a large permanent exhibit to Kircher, and a variety of new books and scholarly conferences have investigated his remarkable legacy.

Books

Findlen, Paula, ed., *Athanasius Kircher: The Last Man Who Knew Everything,* Routledge, 2004.
Godwin, Joscelyn, *Athanasius Kircher: A Renaissance Man and the Quest for Lost Knowledge,* Thames and Hudson, 1979.

Periodicals

Chronicle of Higher Education, May 28, 2002.
International Herald Tribune, March 17, 2001.
New York Times, July 4, 1999; May 25, 2002.

Online

"Athanasius Kircher," *Catholic Encyclopedia,* http://www.newadvent.org/cathen/08661a.htm (January 22, 2007).
"Athanasius Kircher, S.J.," Contributions from the Museum of Jurassic Technology: Collections and Exhibitions, http://www.mjt.org/exhibits/kircher.html (January 22, 2007). □

Klaus von Klitzing

The Von Klitzing constant, which looks like this: $R_K = h / e^2 = 25812.807449(86)\Omega$, was named in honor of Klaus Von Klitzing's (born 1943) discovery of the Quantum Hall Effect. The constant has been listed on the National Institute of Standards and Technology Reference on Constants, Units, and Uncertainty. In his constant, Von Klitzing gave the inverse value of one quantum of electrical conductance. It was an important step in the development of the science of physics, for it opened the door to allow a more precise measurement of the ohm, the standard unit of electrical resistance.

Early Study of Physics

Von Klitzing was born on June 28, 1943, in Schroda, Germany, near the Polish border. He was born to Bogislav von Klitzing and Anny Ulbrich. Because of World War II, which was in full force at the time of his birth, von Klitzing's family was relocated several times when he was very young. As the tide of the war changed from Germany's side to that of the the Allies, the von Klitzings were forced to move again in order to stay ahead of the Soviet army, which was advancing across Germany to claim victory for the Allied Nations.

The von Klitzings ended up in the town of Lutten for a short while. In 1948 they moved again, this time to the town of Oldenburg. Their last move was in 1951, when they moved to Essen in the north. Von Klitzing attended high school at the Artland Gymnasium in Quakenbruck in Lower Saxony, near Essen.

In 1962, after he had finished his high school studies, von Klitzing decided to go on to university, so he enrolled at the Technical University at Braunschweig. He had always been good at science, especially physics, so it was his intention to get a degree in that field. He graduated with a bachelor's degree in 1969, having written his graduate paper on the "Lifetime Measurements on InSb," which concentrated on the electrical properties of indium antimonide. The substance was a compound of two semi-conducting elements: indium and antimony.

Worked and Researched at University of Wurzburg

After graduation von Klitzing was accepted to the University of Wurzburg, where he studied under Dr. G. Landwehr. While he was there he also took a job teaching physics to premedical undergraduate students. He knew he wanted to continue his work on semi-conductors, so he took classes and discussed the issue with his mentor, Landwehr. In his research he became enthralled by the effects of strong magnetic fields on semi-conductors. It was a field of study that had always held a fascination for him.

His first paper on the subject was published in 1971. It was about "Resonance Structure in the High Field Magnetoresistance of Tellurium," and was co-written with Landwehr. He earned a Ph.D. in 1972, having done his research and work on the "Galvanomagnetic Properties of Tellurium in Strong Magnetic Fields."

Von Klitzing went on to do post-graduate work at the university. His research, however, began to require stronger and stronger magnetic fields, which could only be created with large and very expensive equipment: something not all research facilities could afford to provide. For this reason he had to leave the university to pursue his studies. He did some research work at the Clarendon Laboratory at Oxford University from 1975–76. He went to Oxford University for the powerful superconducting magnets that were being made there. After he was finished with his work at Oxford he returned to Wurzburg. There he continued any work he could do at the university, and in 1978 he worked on and completed his "habilitation," a type of certification needed to gain a professorship in Germany.

Studied the Hall Effect

He had continued his research in Wurzburg, but now needed an even stronger magnetic field in which to do his work. He went to the High Magnetic Field Laboratory at the Institute Max von Laue-Paul Langevin in Grenoble, France, from 1979–80. While there he discovered the quantum values in the Hall effect, and found the Von Klitzing constant, $R_K = h / e^2 = 25812.807449(86)\Omega$. A group of scientists from Japan, Tsuneya Ando, Yukio Matsumoto, and Yasutada Uemura, had theorized the quantum effect as early as 1975, but the first person to get experimental research results proving it was von Klitzing. The three Japanese men did not, however, guess at how precise the constant would be.

When he came up with his constant von Klitzing was working on a discovery that physicist Edwin Hall made more than a century before von Klitzing did his work. Hall had discovered that a transverse volt is created across a conducting or semi-conducting material when a magnetic field is applied to that material at a right angle and an electrical current is flowing through it. It was named the Hall effect. The Hall effect is done on three-dimensional objects and involves passing an electrical current one way through a material that can conduct electricity while a magnetic field has been applied to the current at a right angle. The Hall effect, according to the Dictionary.com website, "is a phenomenon that occurs when an electric current moving through a conductor is exposed to an external magnetic field applied at a right angle, in which an electric potential develops in the conductor at a right angle to both the direction of current and the magnetic field."

Von Klitzing was doing his research and discovered that as the magnetic field grew stronger, the Hall resistance also grew stronger for a while and then evened out. After its leveling stage no increase in magnetism had any effect on the Hall resistance for a time, then it would increase again, then level off, then increase, and so on. When it was graphed, the measurements looked like a flight of stairs, ever increasing upwards. This was not what the Hall effect had said would happen. Normally the Hall resistance was a continual line, with no steps of leveling off or stagnation. Von Klitzing set out to discover why this leveling off had occurred.

Discovered the von Klitzing Constant

First he set up his experiment to conform to extremely precise ingredients. He used an extremely thin sheet of silicon to make the test two dimensional rather than the usual three. Then he made the temperature extremely cold, almost to absolute zero. Only then did he apply the magnetic field. He got the same results again, only this time he discovered something else. What he discovered was that the steps in the graph were all of a certain, never-changing value. The constant was 25,813 ohms. It was an important number because it happened to be exactly the ratio of the electron's electrical charge squared compared to Planck's constant.

Von Klitzing tried the test again, taking the Hall effect to extremes, focusing on two-dimensional objects that were kept at a temperature near absolute zero. Again, when these were exposed to extraordinarily strong magnets he discovered that the Hall effect was not continual, but only occurred in discrete steps with a finely tuned precision. It was an important discovery in the study of electrical currents. The von Klitzing constant soon became the standard unit used to describe electrical resistance. The constant has since been listed on the National Institute of Standards and Technology Reference on Constants, Units, and Uncertainty, which is where all the universally excepted theories and formulas are written. Von Klitzing in his constant gave the inverse value of one quantum of electrical conductance. According to the Royal Swedish Academy of Sciences his discovery opened up a new research area that has become very significant and important since its discovery. *Research and Development* magazine said, "By making it possible to probe the conductivity of electronic components very precisely, the discovery has allowed physicists to make standardized specifications for a wide variety of materials."

His discovery was also very important in the field of physics. It is one of the only times that quantum effects, usually guessed at on very small scales such as that of electrons and atoms, were seen in a laboratory. It also meant that it was possible that one day a more precise value for the ohm, the standard unit of electrical resistance, could be found.

Won the Nobel Prize

In 1980 von Klitzing left the University of Wurzburg to take a position as professor with the Technical University in Munich, Germany. While he was there he garnered many awards for his research on the Hall effect. He was awarded the Walter-Schottley Prize of the German Physical Society in 1981, and the Hewlett Packard Prize of the European Physical Society in 1982. He stayed at the University of Munich until December of 1984. In 1985 he went on to become the director of the Max Planck Institute for Solid State Research in Stuttgart. The change in job titles was advantageous and allowed him unfettered access to the sorts of equipment he needed to continue his experiments with magnetic fields.

In 1982 some researchers at Bell Labs in New York discovered that the von Klitzing constant worked not only for integers, which is what he tested, but also for fractions of the quantum Hall effect. These were equally important discoveries, but could not have been found had it not been for von Klitzing's original research. This research brought von Klitzing back into the public eye, and so for his earlier discovery von Klitzing was awarded the Nobel Prize in 1985. It was a rather late but welcome acknowledgement of von Klitzing's work.

On a personal note, Von Klitzing married Renate Falkenberg in 1971. The couple had two sons and one daughter. As of the beginning of 2007 von Klitzing was still director of the Max Planck Institute for Solid State Research in Stuttgart. He has continued his work on low dimensional electronic systems that are kept at low temperatures and afflicted with high magnetic fields.

Books

Almanac of Famous People, 8th edition, Gale Group, 2003.
Notable Scientists: From 1900 to the Present, Gale Group, 2001.
World of Biology, 2 volumes, Gale Group, 1999.
World of Physics, 2 volumes, Gale Group, 2001.
World of Scientific Discovery, 2nd edition, Gale Group, 1999.

Periodicals

Research & Development, December 1985.
Times (London, England),October 17, 1985.

Online

''Klaus von Klitzing,'' *Almaz,* http://www.almaz.com/nobel/physics/1985a.html (January 2, 2007).

''Klaus von Klitzing,'' *Magnet Lab,* http://www.education.magnet.fsu.edu-education-tutorials-pioneers-klitzing.html (January 2, 2007).

''Klaus von Klitzing,'' *NNDB,* http://www.nndb.com-people-808-000099511- (January 2, 2007).

''Klaus von Klitzing,'' *Nobel of Physics,* http://www.nobel.se/physics/laureates/1985/index.html (January 2, 2007).

''Klaus von Klitzing,'' *Nobel Prize,* http://www.nobelprize.org-nobel_prizes-physics-laureates-1985-klitzing-cv.html (January 2, 2007).

''Klaus von Klitzing,'' *Nobel Winners,* http://www.nobel-winners.com-Physics-klaus_von_klitzing.html (January 2, 2007).

''Welcome to von Klitzing's department,'' *FKF,* http://www.fkf.mpg.de-klitzing- (January 2, 2007). □

Walter Kohn

Theoretical physicist Walter Kohn (born 1923) received the 1998 Nobel Prize in Chemistry for developing the density functional theory. The revolutionary theory, which became widely applied in the field of chemistry, physics, and materials science, substantially changed how scientists viewed the electronic structure of atoms, molecules, and solid materials. Kohn also made significant contributions to the physics of semiconductors, superconductivity, surface physics and catalysis.

The early life of the theoretical physicist was as dramatic as his later scientific contributions. Kohn personally experienced major events during the bloodiest period in modern history. His parents were victims of the Nazi Holocaust, and he observed the devastation that World War II wrought in his European homeland. He later moved to the United States at a time when the country unveiled a horrifying new weapon, the atomic bomb. As a result, he became an outspoken pacifist, and he would later seek to find less destructive applications for quantum physics, a field that he would help revolutionize.

He was born as Walter Samuel Gerst Kohn on March 9, 1923, in Vienna, Austria, to Salomon and Gittel Kohn. He was raised in a middle class Jewish family. Kohn described his mother as a highly educated woman, well versed in German, Latin, Polish and French and possessing some knowledge of Greek, Hebrew, and English. His father ran a printing business. According to Kohn, the main products of this business were high quality, artistic postcards, with designs most often based on paintings by contemporary artists commissioned by the firm. The business flourished in the early part of the twentieth century, but in the 1920s and

1930s it fell on hard times, primarily due to a worldwide economic depression.

Kohn's early education focused on Latin and Greek. His favorite subject was Latin and, ironically enough, he had little interest in mathematics. However, he did demonstrate an interest in physics at an early age. Still, his parents anticipated that he would take over the family business, a prospect that Kohn looked forward to with little enthusiasm. However, world affairs substantially changed the direction of his life.

Parents Died at Auschwitz

In 1938, when Kohn was 15 years old, Austria was annexed by Nazi Germany. As his family was Jewish, Kohn was expelled from public school by Austrian officials and was transferred to an all-Jewish school, where he studied for two years. His experience at the school would influence his educational direction, as he was inspired by one of his teachers, Emil Nohel, who had worked with famed scientist Albert Einstein. Nohel exposed Kohn to his analysis of Einstein's groundbreaking theories.

In 1939 Kohn's parent sent him and his sister to England, where Kohn lived with one of his father's business associates. In this way, the brother and sister were spared the horrors of the Holocaust. However, Kohn's parents weren't as fortunate. Salomon and Gittel Kohn were both later murdered at the German concentration camp at Auschwitz.

In England Kohn worked on a farm until he suffered a physically debilitating bout of meningitis. In 1940, during the German Blitzkreig, British authorities sent Kohn to an internment camp on the Isle of Man because he had a German passport. Only 17 years old, Kohn suffered harsh conditions and food shortages. He was then transferred to Quebec, Canada, where he spent the next year and a half in different camps. But the move proved fortunate: conditions were less harsh at the Canadian camps, and Kohn met a family whose sponsorship later enabled him to attend the University of Toronto.

Despite his incarceration, Kohn now considered himself a Canadian. He felt the country treated him well, and he harbored a strong bitterness toward Austria. When he was released from Canadian internment camps in 1943, he voluntarily enlisted in the Canadian Infantry Corps. That same year he enrolled at the University of Toronto. Even though he had never completed high school, Kohn earned bachelor's degrees in mathematics and physics.

Moved to America

In 1946 Kohn earned a master's degree in applied mathematics at the University of Toronto. He even published his first research paper, on applied mathematics, before completing his undergraduate work. His master's degree led to a fellowship at Harvard University in the United States. Originally, following the completion of the fellowship, Kohn had planned to return to Canada. However, he could not find a position in that country, so he remained in the United States, where he studied nuclear physics at Harvard with future Nobel laureate Julian Schwinger. He earned his doctorate in only two years. Except for two years he later spent at the Niels Bohr Institute in Copenhagen, Denmark, Kohn would remain in the United States.

After acquiring his physics Ph.D in 1948, Kohn served as an instructor at Harvard for two years. In 1950 he became a professor at Carnegie-Mellon University in Pittsburgh, Pennsylvania, where he taught for 10 years. On June 19, 1955, he married Mara Schiff. The couple would have three children: Sharon Ruth, Martin Steven, and Thomas David. In 1957, Kohn became a naturalized citizen of the United States.

At Carnegie-Mellon, in addition to teaching, Kohn sought to find ways of applying the quantum theory to semiconductors, a new technology at the time. In 1960 he moved to San Diego, California, where he served as a professor at the University of California and sought even broader applications of the theory. His work in this area would later culminate in a Nobel Prize in chemistry in 1998.

Developed Density-Functional Theory

After the first major paper on quantum mechanics was published in 1926, it became possible, on a theoretical level, to comprehend how subatomic particles interacted to form molecules. Before the structure of a molecule and its interactions could be known, scientists needed to know the geometrical arrangements of its atoms and how its components united to exchange energy. They believed they were able to determine how each electron of each atom would perform during interactions, but practical applications of

these laws resulted in equations that were, as indicated by Paul Dirac, the co-founder of quantum physics, "too complex to be solved."

Kohn's research would help simplify the issues, as he would show that it wasn't necessary to track the motions of each individual electron. In 1964 Kohn, collaborating with colleague Pierre Hohenberg, demonstrated what would come to be known as the "density-functional theory," which suggested that it is only necessary to know the average number of electrons located at any given point in space (electron density) to make the appropriate calculations that determine a molecule's properties. Kohn and Hohenberg proved the existence of a universal, constant relationship (called the "density functional") between the structure of a molecular system and the arrangement of its electrons. Physicists sought ways to define this "density functional." Kohn himself, working with L. J. Sham in 1965, came up with a set of equations that served as an approximation. Still, these equations required refinement over the course of three decades before they could be of any practical use to chemists. British scientist John A. Pople from Northwestern University in Evanston, Illinois, would provide the most important breakthrough.

Received Nobel Prize in Chemistry

In 1970 Pople, later the co-recipient of the 1998 Nobel Prize in chemistry with Kohn, designed the GAUSSIAN computer program to model and test structures of small molecules. In 1992 he integrated the "density functional" into his program. This made the program faster and more accurate in analyzing larger molecules and complex interactions. In turn, it made the principles of quantum physics applicable to chemistry.

The combined work of Kohn and Pople had a dramatic impact on various fields of research. It made it possible to construct, according to the laws of quantum chemistry, computer models of molecules that could not be replicated in a laboratory setting.

In 1998 the Royal Swedish Academy of Sciences awarded the Nobel Prize in Chemistry to both Kohn and Pople, lauding the two scientists' pioneering contributions in developing methods that could be used for theoretical studies of the properties of molecules and the chemical processes in which they are involved.

Headed New Institute

Kohn stayed at the University of California at San Diego until 1979, when he became the first director of the National Science Foundation's new Institute of Theoretical Physics, located at the University of California in Santa Barbara. Kohn's leadership helped the Institute become one of the world's foremost research facilities, as it brought together international scientists to work on the most complex issues in theoretical physics and related areas. The Institute, under Kohn's leadership, was instrumental in developing new applications for quantum theory. He served as director from 1979 to 1984, and he served as a professor at the university from 1984 to 1991, when he was named professor emeritus and research professor.

Retired in California

Since retiring from teaching in 1991, Kohn has dedicated himself full time to research. He lives in Santa Barbara with his wife, Mara. In his spare time he pursues hobbies and interests that include classical music, reading (especially French literature), and cooking. He remains physically active by taking walks alone or with his wife and by roller blading once a week. He also enjoys spending time with his family, as all three of his daughters and his three grandchildren live in California.

In addition to receiving the Nobel Prize, Kohn was awarded the National Medal of Science in 1988. He was named to the American Academy of Arts and Sciences in 1963 and the National Academy of Sciences in 1969. He is also a member of the American Association for the United Nations. He served as president in 1962–63 and has been a member of its board of directors since 1963. He is a member of numerous other professional, scientific, and social organizations, and has authored numerous books and more than 200 articles and reviews that have been published in scientific journals and popular periodicals.

During his teaching career he was a visiting scholar at many universities in the United States and in Europe, including the University of Pennsylvania, the University of Michigan, the University of Paris, the University of Jerusalem, and Imperial College in London. He also served on many advisory boards and committees.

Promoter of Humanitarian Causes

Though he was born in Austria and became an American citizen, Kohn considers himself a citizen of the world. His scientific work coupled with his life experiences helped break down, in his own mind, the barriers of national borders and geographic boundaries. Still, he has a great affection for Canada, Denmark, England, France and Israel, as he lived and worked in these countries throughout his life. However, because of his early life experiences and the death of his parents, he still has some bitterness toward Austria, his homeland. And perhaps because of his harsh memories, Kohn has retained a strong sense of Jewish identity. Throughout his life he has remained committed to applying quantum mechanics toward peaceful purposes and has also worked to promote pacifist and environmentalist causes. He served on the advisory board of the Statewide Institute of Global Conflict and Cooperation from 1982 to 1992, and actively lobbied to stop nuclear physics projects at places such as Los Alamos. In 1992 Kohn joined 1,700 other leading scientists in signing the "Warning to Humanity," a statement that sounded an alarm about international environmental issues such as global warming.

Periodicals

Daily Nexus, January 17, 2001.

Online

"Walter Kohn," *Biography Resource Center Online,* http://www.galenet.galegroup.com/servlet/BioRC (December 8, 2006).

"Walter Kohn: Nobel Prize in Chemistry in 1998," *Indian Academy of Sciences,* http://www.ias.ac.in/currsci/jun10/articles18.htm (December 8, 2006).

"Walter Kohn: Nobel Prize in Chemistry, 1998," *NobelPrize.org,* http://www.nobelprize.org/nobel_prizes/chemistry/laureates/1998/kohn-autobio.html (December 8, 2006).

"Walter Kohn," *Notable Scientists: From 1900 to the Present,* http://www.galenet.galegroup.com/servlet/BioRC (December 8, 2006).

"Walter Kohn," *Walter Kohn Website,* http://www.physics.ucsb.edu/~kohn/ (December 8, 2006).

"Walter S(amuel) G(erst) Kohn," *Contemporay Authors Online,* http://www.galenet.galegroup.com/servlet/BioRC (December 8, 2006). □

Harold Walter Kroto

British chemist Sir Harold Walter Kroto (born 1939) received the 1996 Nobel Prize for Chemistry, along with Robert F. Curl Jr., and Richard E. Smalley. The scientists were honored for the discovery of fullerenes, a new form of carbon called Carbon 60. The discovery opened the way for new branches in chemistry and helped to advance the area of nanoscience and nanotechnology. Kroto was knighted in 1996.

Kroto was born on October 7, 1939, in Wisbech, Cambridgeshire, England, to Heinz and Edith Krotoschiner (his father changed the family name to Kroto in 1955). His parents were born in Berlin, Germany, and were compelled to flee to England in 1937 after the rise of the Nazi Party.

In 1940, during World War II, the British government sent Kroto's father to an internment camp on the Isle of Man, as he was considered an enemy alien. Kroto then moved with his mother to Bolton, in Lanchashire, where he was raised.

Later, Kroto would affectionately describe his parents as "eccentric," but, on a much more serious note, he expressed great compassion for their plight. "I always felt that my parents had a really raw deal, as did almost everyone born in Europe at the turn of the Century," he recalled when he received his Nobel Prize in 1996. "The First World War took place while they were teenagers, then the Depression struck and Hitler came to power while they were young adults. They had to leave their home country and then the Second World War broke out and they had to leave their home again. When my father was 45 he had to find a new profession, when he was 55 he set up his business again."

Kroto indicated that his father had early ambitions to become a dress designer but ended up operating a graphics business that printed images on balloons. Kroto's parents' ordeal no doubt influenced the values and philosophies that he adopted as an adult. A self-described humanist and "devout atheist," he had difficulty accepting the concept of a "humanitarian" God.

Kroto would also come to reject the notion that the "good" of the community must override individual rights.

That notion, he believed, only justified the oppression of individuals by the state. As such, he would later become a supporter of Amnesty International.

Studied Chemistry in College

As a boy, Kroto demonstrated an interest in physics, math, and especially chemistry. He also played sports, concentrating on gymnastics and tennis. As his interest in chemistry grew, he was encouraged by a grade school teacher to enroll at the University of Sheffield, the British educational institution that reputably had the best chemistry department in the United Kingdom.

In 1961 Kroto graduated from Sheffield with a degree in chemistry. In 1963 he married Margaret Henrietta Hunter, and the couple had two sons. The following year Kroto earned his Ph.D. at the University of Sussex, where his post-graduate work involved high-resolution electronic spectra of free radicals produced by flash photolysis—chemical decomposition by the action of radiant energy. At Sussex, while still keenly interested in chemistry, Kroto became fascinated by quantum mechanics when he was introduced to spectroscopy. "It was fascinating to see spectroscopic band patterns which showed that molecules could count," he recalled in 1996.

In 1964, after receiving his Ph.D., Kroto received several job offers. After conferring with his wife, he accepted a postdoctoral position at the National Research Council (NRC) in Ottawa, Canada, as both he and his wife wanted to experience life abroad. Kroto described the NRC as "a mecca of spectroscopy" and the only international research facility at the time that was deemed successful.

In 1966 Kroto received an offer for another postdoctoral position, this time at the University of Sussex in the United Kingdom. However, Kroto and his wife wanted to live in the United States, so he accepted another position at Bell Laboratories in Murray Hill, New Jersey, where he conducted research in quantum chemistry, specifically on liquid phase interactions by laser Raman spectroscopy. After a year Kroto accepted the position at Sussex, and began teaching and conducting research at the university in 1967. He became a full professor in 1985 and a Royal Research Professor in 1991.

Became Involved in Carbon Chain Research

During the 1970s Kroto was engaged in a research program that he initiated at Sussex, designed to detect carbon chains existing in interstellar atmospheres and interstellar gas clouds. He collaborated with scientists from the NRC to find such molecules, and during research conducted between 1975 and 1978, they indeed found several carbon chains. In carrying out this research, Kroto employed microwave spectroscopy, a science that can be used to analyze gas in space. This led to his discovery of carbon chains residing in the atmospheres of carbon-rich giant stars and gas clouds. Kroto hypothesized that the chains had been formed in stellar atmospheres and not in gas clouds, but he did not know exactly how the chains were formed. His search for an answer would result in the discovery of the Carbon-60, or C_{60}, molecule.

In 1984 Kroto traveled to Rice University in Houston, Texas, to further investigate the formation of carbon chains. Specifically, he wanted to study the vaporization of carbon to determine how the chains formed. He chose the University because he became aware of the studies being conducted by researchers Richard Smalley and Robert Curl in laser spectroscopy. At Rice, Smalley had developed the laser-supersonic cluster beam apparatus, an instrument that could vaporize just about any known material, and the device was then used to analyze the clusters of atoms or molecules resulting from the vaporization. Kroto felt that he could use the technology to replicate the temperatures in space necessary to form the carbon chains. Previously, Smalley and Curl, who would later receive the 1996 Nobel Prize in Chemistry with Kroto, had been using laser spectroscopy to examine semiconductors such as silicon and germanium, but they had not looked at simple carbon.

However, in a series of experiments conducted in September of 1985, Kroto, Smalley and Curl directed the laser at graphite. They vaporized the graphite in an atmosphere of helium, in the process generating clusters of carbon atoms and discovering a molecule that had 60 carbon atoms. The discovery surprised them, as carbon had been known to have only two molecular forms, diamond and graphite. The new form of carbon had a complex, highly symmetrical arrangement that resembled a soccer ball or, more precisely, the geodesic dome, a structure that had been popularized by inventor and architect R. Buckminster Fuller. Because of its resemblance to the dome, the scientists named the new carbon structure buckminsterfullerene, which they later shortened to fullerene. They also called it the "buckyball" (Fuller's nickname was "Bucky."). The discovery would lead to a new branch of chemistry developed to manipulate the fullerene structure.

The discovery compelled Kroto to suspend his dream of building a studio to do scientific graphic design. He had a long term interest in graphic design and had been doing it semi-professionally for about a year, and he perceived how recent advances in computer technology had substantially advanced the artistic potential of graphic design. However, he now deemed it much more important to explore the consequences of the C_{60} discovery.

Kroto then proceeded forward at full throttle into research. In 1991 he was awarded a Royal Society Research Professorship, which freed him from teaching and enabled him to fully concentrate on his experiments.

Received Nobel Prize

Kroto, Smalley and Curl became the first scientists to completely identify and then stabilize Carbon-60, and the Royal Swedish Academy of Sciences awarded them the 1996 Nobel Prize in Chemistry. In addition, as a result of his important discovery and the subsequent Nobel Prize, Kroto was knighted. There was a bit of irony attached to the British honor and the Nobel award. Only two hours before it was announced that Kroto had won the Nobel Prize, the British government had turned down his request for research funding. The research would have involved the same work that earned him the Nobel Prize in the first place.

That may be one of the reasons why Kroto was some-what ambivalent about winning the Nobel Prize. Another reason, which he stated in 1996, was that he felt the work of the graduate students involved in the 1985 research, J.R. Heath and S.C. O'Brien, did not receive adequate recognition. Likewise, he felt that the accomplishments (extracting C_{60}) of Wolfgang Krätschmer and Don Huffman and their students Kostas Fostiropoulos and Lowell Lamb were not sufficiently recognized. Moreover, Kroto never felt he needed awards to justify or validate his work or to provide him with a sense of satisfaction.

Nevertheless, his discovery was a remarkable achievement with substantial impact. The Royal Swedish Academy of Sciences recognized its implications for the natural sciences. "The discovery of fullerenes has expanded our knowledge and changed our thinking in chemistry and physics," the Academy stated, when it honored Kroto and his colleagues. "It has given us new hypotheses on the occurrence of carbon in the universe. It has also led us to discover small quantities of fullerenes in geological formations. Fullerenes are probably present in much larger amounts on earth than previously believed."

Further, the Academy noted, "From a theoretical viewpoint, the discovery of the fullerenes has influenced our conception of such widely separated scientific problems as the galactic carbon cycle and classical aromaticity, a keystone of theoretical chemistry."

Moved Back to America

Following his Nobel Prize, Kroto continued conducting fundamental research on the fullerene, examining its basic chemistry and how it has changed the way the scientific world perceives carbon-based materials. On July 14, 2004, Kroto received the Royal Society of London's Copley Medal "in recognition of his seminal contributions to understanding the fundamental dynamics of carbon chain molecules, leading to the detection of these species (polyynes) in the interstellar medium by radioastronomy, and thence to the genesis of a new era in carbon science." The medal is the highest award the Society presents.

Later that year, he left Sussex University to join the faculty of Florida State University in Tallahassee, Florida. Kroto left Britain because it would have been difficult to raise funds for his work after he reached retirement age in October of 2004. By joining Florida State, he was guaranteed funding for his research.

On April 25, 2006, Kroto was elected a member of the U.S. National Academy of Sciences, one of the highest honors that a scientist could receive.

Books

Notable Scientists: From 1900 to the Present, Gale Group, 2001.
World of Scientific Discovery, 2nd Edition. Gale Group, 1999.

Online

"The Nobel Prize in Chemistry 1996—Press Release," *Nobelprize .org,* http://www.nobelprize.org/nobel_prizes/chemistry/ laureates/1996/press.html (December 20, 2006).

"Sir Harold Kroto, the Nobel Prize in Chemistry 1996— Autobiography," *Nobelprize.org,* http://www.nobelprize .org/nobel_prizes/chemistry/laureates/1996/kroto-autobio .html (December 20, 2006).

"Sir Harold Walter Kroto," *Encyclopedia Britannica,* http://www .search.eb.com/nobelprize/article-9003029 (December 20, 2006). □

John Agyekum Kufuor

John Agyekum Kufuor (born 1938) was one of the prime movers bringing democracy back to Ghana after the country had been subjected to a long line of coups and military dictators. In 2000 he became president of Ghana, defeating Jerry Rawlings, who had been in office for 20 years. It was a peaceful transfer of power, perhaps signifying that peace and democracy had at long last triumphed in Ghana. Kufuor has proven to be a good diplomat, and the West African nation has seen a period of peace since his election. Ghana has managed to improve its economy as well, and much of the improvement seems due to Kufuor's policies, which have been applauded by many leaders around the world.

Descended from Oyoko Royalty

John Agyekum Kufuor was born on December 8, 1938 in Kumasi, Ghana, the country's second largest city and the Asante capital. He was born the seventh of ten children to Nana Kwadwo Agyekum, head of the Oyoko royal family, and Nana Ama Dapaah, a Queen mother. The family had royal Asante lineage. Kufuor was raised by his mother. At the time the ruler, Kwame Nkrumah, had a vision of a unified Ghana that had chords of socialism and dictatorship about it. Kufuor's mother was completely against such a thing, and before long Kufuor's home became the center for people who were opposed to Nkrumah's plans for Ghana. The group called themselves the Asante Movement, although they later renamed themselves the National Liberation Movement. The group originated in Kufuor's home, so he was introduced at an early age to many leaders of the liberal movement.

At school Kufuor was good at both academics and sports. He liked school and so after graduation went on to attend and graduate from Prempeh College in Kumasi in 1959. At his graduation he was awarded five of the six awards given to the best students. He went on to study law at Lincoln's Inn in London, England. He passed his bar exam in 1961 and went on to Exeter College at Oxford University to pursue legal studies. After only one year of studying law, however, Kufuor realized that his passion lay not in the law but in politics. He switched degrees and started studying philosophy, politics, and economics. He graduated a mere two years later.

Entered Politics in Ghana

While he was studying at Oxford, Kufuor met and fell in love with a woman named Theresa Mensah, who was also from Ghana and had gone to England to study nursing. The two married in 1962, and had five children together. In 1965 Kufuor's mother convinced him to bring his family—at the time his wife and two young children—back to Ghana. He agreed and took up law there until 1969 as a way to make a living. He became the chief legal officer and the city manager of Kumasi in 1967, posts he held until 1969. Both of these posts allowed Kufuor a view of politics from the inside that he had never had before, and they inspired him on his future path.

He left the law in 1969 to take up his first ministerial appointment in the Progress Party government, as a deputy foreign minister under Victor Owusu, one of the men who used to visit his home when he was a boy. In 1972 the government was overthrown by the military, and many officials were thrown into jail, including Kufuor. After his release he took up a career in business. He became chairman of the board of the Ashanti Brick and Construction Company.

Elected President of Ghana

Kufuor spent a long time in business before he returned to politics. It was not until 1992 that he ran for the office of chairman for the New Patriotic Party, which had just been formed. He was not elected to the post until 1996, but was then re-elected in 1998. He faced a lot of competition each time he ran, but refused to give up, and eventually succeeded in being elected. He next turned his sights towards becoming Ghana's president. He was confident of being elected president, and in fact predicted it to U.S. President Bill Clinton when he visited in 1998.

Kufuor was indeed elected president in 2000, defeating longtime president Jerry Rawlings. It was considered by many to be a turning point in Ghana's future. In 1957 Ghana was the first country in sub-Saharan Africa to claim independence from colonists. The country was then basically handed from one man to another through a system of personal and political loyalties, and without the benefit of democratic elections. There are two distinct groups in Ghana: the Nkrumah, who are anti-imperialistic, pan-Africa, socialist, and believe in government involvement in the economy; and the Danquah-Busia, who believe in democracy, the sovereignty of the individual, private enterprise, and free markets. Kufuor belonged to the latter.

Turnover of Power Went Smoothly

After such an extended period of rule by one person, many were nervous about how the turnover of power would go, but the change went smoothly. Kufuor managed to win the election with the platform of "zero tolerance for corruption." The country had been rife with it before, and so the idea was appealing to many. The country was also doing poorly economically, mostly because of such corruption, and people were ready for a change. Kufuor was nicknamed the "gentle giant" because he was tall—at six feet, three inches—and quiet, and yet he seemed to instill confidence in those he was to lead.

In 2001 Kufuor made his first trip to the United States as president of Ghana. He went there to take part in the United Nations General Assembly special session on HIV/AIDS. He attended a luncheon set up to establish links between Ghana and black American business leaders, with the goal of forging links that would help his country in the future.

Set up Truth and Reconciliation Committee

Although he was called the "gentle giant," Kufuor meant business. In 2002 he set up a Truth and Reconciliation Committee to examine abuses of power occurring under the five governments that had ruled Ghana since 1966. Some felt these measures were undertaken in order to discredit anyone opposing Kufuor's government. But whatever the opposition Kufuor faced, he was reelected in 2004. This time his campaign message was "So far, so good," showing that there had been progress in Ghana in his first term.

More than 80 percent of the population turned out to vote in the 2004 elections; it was the largest turnout in west African history. After Kufuor won his second term in office the PR Newswire said, "Domestic and international election observers agreed that the contest was free, fair, and transparent. Ghana, many observers noted, is one of the few countries in Africa to have held four consecutive multiparty elections since 1992."

Traveled After 2004 Re-election

By August of 2005 Kufuor had visited over 63 countries as president of Ghana, and Kufuor had great support from the international community. He helped Liberia achieve peace, was the first ruler to submit his country to review by the New Partnership for Africa's Development, and was a spokesperson for the six leaders from Africa who attended the G8 summit in 2004. He has been seen as one of a handful of leaders of an African Renaissance, helping to bring stability and success to Africa.

Kufuor has been called a "boring" leader by some in his own country, but that is something that does not upset the ruler. He has said that if boredom has brought with it the peace and stability his country needs, then he thinks there should be more boredom in the world. *African Business* said of Kufuor, "True, he does not go for fiery, clenched-fist speeches that seem to characterize some of Africa's more 'charismatic' leaders, but he has unmistakable gravitas, a disarming sense of humor and most important, people listen when he speaks and then go home and think about what they have heard. He treats ordinary people as sane, reasonable human beings who will respond to sane, reasonable propositions rather than as a mass who can be manipulated through demagoguery." Ghana, however, was not out of trouble completely. In 2004 the country had a poverty level of 40 percent, and it was Kufuor's goal to reduce the number significantly.

Fought Poverty and Lack of Amenities

In 2005 Kufuor worked to update the country's railway system, establishing the Ghana Railway Development Authority. In 2006 he declared a Year of Action in Ghana. He met with his Investment Advisory Council and declared, according to *African Business,* that "talking was past and that this would be the year of 'implementation, implementation and implementation.'" Kufuor's goal was to turn Ghana into a middle income country by the year 2015. Although the rate of growth has been about 5.8 percent in recent years, that rate was not high enough to fulfill Kufuor's goal, and much more was needed.

With this goal in mind and the realization of how difficult it would be, Kufuor looked internationally for aid. In 2006 he appealed to South Korea for support in attracting private investments. He also met with U.S. President George W. Bush to discuss receiving aid from the Millennium Challenge Account. The world was watching Kufuor at the beginning of 2007, and much was expected of the determined ruler.

Books

Contemporary Black Biography, Volume 54, Thomson Gale, 2006.

Newsmakers, Issue 4, Thomson Gale, 2005.

Worldmark Encyclopedia of the Nations: World Leaders, Gale, 2003.

Periodicals

African Business, February 2001; January 2005; April 2005; May 2006.

Economist (U.S.), December 14, 1996; April 28, 2001; May 26, 2001.

PR Newswire, December 17, 2004.

Xinhua News Agency, October 5, 2006; November 8, 2006. □

Aleksander Kwaśniewski

Polish politician Aleksander Kwaśniewski (born 1954) served two terms as president of his country between 1995 and 2005, disproving critics who claimed that the former Communist would lead Poland back to the bleak days of one-party, authoritarian rule. Instead of cronyism and restrictions on democratic freedoms, Kwaśniewski's decade in office was notable for the several milestones achieved, including Poland's entry into the European Union.

When Kwaśniewski first won the presidency in November of 1995, he admitted that he was "irritated" by reports in the foreign media that consistently identified him as a member of what had been the only political party permitted to exist in Poland from 1948 to 1989, as he told *New York Times* correspondent Jane Perlez. "Not because I wasn't a member of the party. I was, of course. But first, from an ideological point of view, I was never a Communist. In Poland I've seen very few Communists, especially since the 1970's. I met a lot of technocrats, opportunists, reformers, liberals."

Witnessed U.S. Bicentennial

Kwaśniewski was born on November 15, 1954, in Białogard, Poland, a small town located in the western part of Poland, a region once known as Pomerania and part of Germany, though its native citizens were Poles. His father was a physician, and his mother a nurse, and their son was born nine years after the end of World War II. This six-year conflict was yet another chapter in Poland's long struggle as a nation with no natural borders but rich in natural resources and caught between two immensely powerful neighbors and rivals, Russia and Germany. Occupied by Nazi Germany in 1939 in the move that launched World War II, Poland became a battlefield as the Soviet Army moved west to defeat German forces. When the war ended, Soviet troops remained in Poland to restore order, and the psychological and economic devastation of the war—which included the deaths of six million Jews, many of them killed in camps located on Polish soil—enabled the Soviets to install a puppet regime in Warsaw, as they did in several more Eastern European capitals.

Kwaśniewski was able to travel abroad during his young adult years, at a time when obtaining a visa to visit the West was no easy feat. He worked in Sweden, visited London, and in 1976 criss-crossed the United States when he took a job delivering cars for an automotive company. For the July 4, 1976, U.S. Bicentennial celebrations, Kwaśniewski was in New York City for the event, and recalled that the diversity of

the opposition movement had its roots in the massive Lenin Shipyards in Gdańsk in the summer of 1980. Workers there, led by an electrician named Lech Wałęsa (born 1943), formed a renegade trade union that became the first independent organization for workers anywhere in the Communist Eastern bloc.

Solidarity was outlawed when martial law was declared, and a PZPR loyalty review process began in all workplaces and institutions. When the publishing ban was finally lifted, Kwaśniewski wrote editorials that were remarkable for their ambiguous take on current events. Outlets like *ITD* were expected to follow procedure and praise the PZPR's actions and voice support for decisions made by Jaruzelski and the other leaders, but instead Kwaśniewski wrote in one editorial that "It seems important right now for Poles to reject emotions and myths and concentrate on genuine social and state interests," according to another of Perlez's reports. Andrzej Nierychlo, a colleague from that era, recalled the major battles in the office at press time with party censors, telling the *New York Times* correspondent that Kwaśniewski "was simply ideal for these kinds of talks. He could sit there for hours, squabble over commas and in the end win a major argument."

In early 1984, several months after martial law formally ended, Kwaśniewski became editor-in-chief of *Sztandar Młodych* (Youth Banner), a daily newspaper also published by the PZPR, and a year later co-founded *Bajtek,* the first magazine for personal computer enthusiasts in Poland. Soon afterward he joined the government as Minister for Youth Affairs and Sport, and after 1987 served as chair of the Polish Olympic Committee. He held these posts until the very end of the PZPR reign in Poland, and was involved in the relatively peaceful transition as a PZPR leader who urged hardliners in the government to cooperate with Solidarity. He was still in his early thirties at this point, and became somewhat of a minor celebrity as the handsome, athletic rebel communist who wore fashionable suits and appeared to be a fan of the tanning beds that were becoming newly popular in Western Europe.

Formed New Political Party

In early 1989 Kwaśniewski participated in a momentous event in Poland's postwar history, the two-month-long talks that resulted in the Round Table Agreement in April of that year. Initiated by the PZPR, the meetings brought together leaders of Solidarity and other opposition movements in an effort to defuse growing social unrest, and Kwaśniewski served on the task group that negotiated trade-union pluralism, or the recognition of new labor groups not allied with the PZPR. The Agreement also ended with a decision to divide political power between the Communist government and opposition parties—a historic moment, not just for Poland but across the Eastern bloc. Previous, tentative steps toward democracy in Poland, Hungary, and Czechoslovakia had nearly always been met with a swift, military-force response from Moscow, but by now the Soviet Union was undergoing its own wave of political, social, and economic reform.

the city stunned him. "To see blacks, whites, Indians, Orthodox Jews—it was unbelievable—people working together and having tolerance for each other," he told Perlez.

Some of Kwaśniewski's travels occurred during his summer breaks from the University of Gdańsk, which he entered in 1973. He studied transport economics and foreign trade for four years, but failed to earn a degree. Because membership in official Communist organizations was obligatory for any Pole who hoped for professional advancement during this era, Kwaśniewski became a member of the Socialist Union of Polish Students, the government-sanctioned group for university students. He held local leadership posts as well as serving on its national leadership council, and was a member of its governing board from 1977, his last year at college, until 1982.

Challenged Government Censors

With the job on the governing board, Kwaśniewski moved to Warsaw and formally joined Poland's Communist Party, known more formally as the Polish United Workers' Party (PZPR). In November of 1981 he took over as editor-in-chief of a student newspaper, *ITD,* a weekly published under PZPR auspices. A month later, its publication was suspended, along with most other news media, when the PZPR First Secretary, General Wojciech Jaruzelski (born 1923), declared martial law. The crackdown was in response to growing dissent across Poland that was reaching into all aspects of life and undermining the control the PZPR had enjoyed for decades. Known as *Solidarność* (Solidarity),

Elections were held in June of 1989, and the now formally established political party called Solidarity won several seats in the Sejm, or lower house of Polish parliament. Early the next year, the PZPR was dissolved in favor of a new leftist political group, Social Democracy of the Polish Republic, which Kwaśniewski had co-founded. He was the overwhelming choice to chair it, elected by more than two-thirds of the 1,500 delegates at its founding convention. Later in 1990, in the first direct presidential elections in Polish history, Wałęsa became the country's president.

Kwaśniewski still headed the Social Democracy Party, and was instrumental in the formation of the Democratic Left Alliance (SLD) in 1991, a coalition of leftist parties. Later that year he became an SLD candidate in parliamentary elections, representing the district of Warsaw, and polled the highest number of votes of any candidate. The SLD also did well in the 1993 Sejm elections, and after his re-election that year Kwaśniewski advanced to one of the most important posts in the National Assembly, as the combined Sejm and Senate are known: he was voted chair of the constitutional committee, a select group chosen to draft the country's first post-communist constitution.

Wałęsa and Solidarity experienced a number of difficult issues during this first part of the decade, much of it related to Poland's painful transition from a planned to a free market economy. As his term neared the end of its five-year mark and new presidential elections loomed, Kwaśniewski emerged as the best candidate to beat the incumbent. During the campaign he pledged to improve Poland's troubled economic situation, while Wałęsa played up the fact that his opponent had once been a Communist Party member.

Scored Television Debate Victory

In those 1995 presidential elections, Kwaśniewski ran as the SLD candidate and finished with a 2 percent lead over Wałęsa. A runoff election was scheduled, and the tanned, athletic Kwaśniewski scored a dramatic media victory over the Nobel Peace Prize-winning former electrician in a televised debate. "The portly and greying Mr. Wałęsa," noted a report in the *Economist* about the event, "with his convoluted speech and working-class manners, appeared by comparison to be a relic of a bygone era."

Kwaśniewski won the runoff election, and scored the most impressive achievement of his first term in 1997 with the adoption of Poland's constitution. He also became an ardent supporter of Poland's bid to join the European Union, and when the country became one of three new member nations of NATO (the North Atlantic Treaty Organization, created in 1949 to address the threat of a Soviet takeover of the rest of Europe), he termed it "the most important moment in our history," according to a *New York Times* report by Steven Erlanger.

In October of 2000 Kwaśniewski faced Wałęsa once again in the presidential elections, along with a crowded field of ten other challengers. This time, Kwaśniewski received a resounding majority of votes—taking 53.9 percent over that of the second-place finisher at 17.3 percent, with Wałęsa finishing seventh. The most significant milestone of Kwaśniewski's second term in office came on May 2, 2004, when Poland became one of 10 new member nations of the European Union. Inside Poland, he maintained the relative political stability of his first term, overseeing alliances and smoothing over the ideological differences that had made the first years of Poland's democracy so contentious when Wałęsa was president. In late 2004, Kwaśniewski was tapped to lead talks to resolve the crisis in neighboring Ukraine, when a democratically elected presidential candidate, Viktor Yushchenko (born 1954), was prevented from taking office. Overall, Kwaśniewski won high marks in his decade as president for his impartiality and commitment to moving Poland forward in the global community.

The Polish constitution limits the president to two terms, and Kwaśniewski stepped down gracefully after the December 2005 elections. His successor was Lech Kaczyński (born 1949) of the conservative *Prawo i Sprawiedliwość* (Law and Justice) Party. Kwaśniewski has been married since 1979 to a lawyer, the former Jolanta Konty, who proved so popular as First Lady that some in Poland asserted she should run for office herself. They have a grown daughter, psychologist Aleksandra Kwaśniewska, born the same year that martial law went into effect in Poland. In 2006 she was a finalist on *Taniec z Gwiazdami,* the Polish version of *Dancing with the Stars.* Her father, meanwhile, had returned to the United States once again, this time as a visiting foreign policy scholar at Georgetown University.

Periodicals

Economist, November 25, 1995; January 9, 1999.
New York Times, November 12, 1995; November 21, 1995; November 29, 1995; March 12, 1999.
Time, December 4, 1995.
Times (London, England), January 30, 1990; July 11, 2001; November 10, 2005. □

L

Ricardo Lagos

In 2000 Ricardo Lagos (born 1938) became the first Socialist president in Chile since the downfall of an earlier government run by Salvador Allende and the reign of the dictator General Augusto Pinochet. He managed to turn the country around and began the righting of many wrongs that had happened in the years before his turn in office. By the time he stepped down as president he had become one of Chile's favorite rulers and had done much to improve the country internally, while forging international ties with countries around the world.

Early Interest in Law and Politics

Lagos was born Ricardo Lagos Escobar on March 2, 1938, in Santiago, Chile, to Don Froilan Lagos, a landowner, and Emma Escobar, a piano teacher. Lagos's father died when he was only eight years old. When he was 16, Lagos went to the University of Chile. There he studied law and was first interested in politics, becoming active in student politics around the university. While he was at university he joined the Radical Party. He also wrote his graduation thesis on economic theories that were radical for Chile at the time. This brought him to the attention of the public and even got him interviewed for *Time* magazine. He went from there to Duke University where he earned a Ph.D. in economics in 1966. He married Carmen Weber in the early 1960s and the couple had two children, Ricardo and Ximena. The marriage ended in divorce in 1967 when he returned to Chile.

Back in Chile Lagos took the position of director at the University of Chile's School of Political and Administrative Sciences. He also taught economics and in 1970 was given the position of Secretary-General of the university by Salvador Allende. Allende was the president of Chile at the time, having been elected in 1970. He represented a socialist platform for the country, and did many things to improve life for the poor of his country that made powerful people nervous. This included nationalizing the banking and copper industries, something that scared the middle class and upset international leaders such as Richard M. Nixon, the president of the United States at that time. During his time at the university, Lagos met his second wife, Luisa Duran de La Fuente, whom he married in 1971. Fuente brought two children to the marriage, and she and Lagos had one more together: a daughter, Francisca.

Fled the Country with Family

In the meantime, the Chilean people who did not like Allende's socialist ways finally decided to do something about it. On September 11, 1973, after there had been a week of strikes across the nation, Allende's home was fired upon and the army stormed in to put him under arrest, overthrowing his government. It was said officially that Allende committed suicide, for he was dead after the conflict with the army ended; however, many believed that Allende had been assassinated. Shortly thereafter, one of the leaders of the coup, General Augusto Pinochet Ugarte, named himself president and took over rule of the country. Pinochet was the worst kind of dictator. He disallowed any sort of political opposition, and prevented the press from being able to publish freely.

After this happened many people left the country, including Lagos and his family. Lagos went to Argentina.

There he became Secretary-General of the Latin American Faculty of Social Sciences in Buenos Aires. He later returned to the United States, where he became a visiting professor of Latin American studies at the University of North Carolina at Chapel Hill. Lagos and his family returned to Chile in 1978 to find that Pinochet had been very busy stomping out freedoms and squashing out any remnants of a more radical, left-wing politics. It was not a happy picture, but Lagos and his family wanted to be home. Lagos got a job as a consultant and economist for the United Nations' regional development agency.

Stood up to Pinochet

In September of 1986 an attempt was made to assassinate Pinochet, and immediately almost 50 people known to be politically liberal were arrested, including Lagos. Lagos was held for almost three weeks, even though he had nothing to do with the attempt to kill the president. He came out of the situation angry and ready to do whatever he could to return democracy to Chile.

In 1987 Lagos founded the Party for Democracy. That and more brought pressure on Pinochet, until finally in 1988 he agreed to hold a vote to see whether or not he should remain in office. Even though it was dangerous at the time to be seen disagreeing with Pinochet, Lagos took part in a television interview in which he urged Chileans to vote Pinochet out of office. People around Chile were impressed and awed by Lagos's bravery, and an unprecedented number of people turned up to vote Pinochet out of office.

Elected President of Chile

In December of 1989 elections were held and Lagos ran for a seat in the Senate, although he lost. In 1990 a new president, Patricio Aylwin Azocar, took office. He asked Lagos to serve as minister of education. During his time in this position, Lagos instituted many changes, including allowing female students to continue their educations even if they were pregnant, something that had been absolutely forbidden before. Lagos tried for president in 1993 but lost in the primary race.

In 1999 Lagos ran for president again. This time he ran as a Socialist Party candidate. He did very well in the primary, but when it came time to go against Joaquin Lavin, a Pinochet supporter, he did not do quite as well. He won more votes, but did not win the 51 percent majority necessary for a decided win. A runoff election was held in January of 2000 and this time Lagos won, with 51.3 percent of the vote. While waiting to hear the election results, Lagos gave a speech in which he honored Allende's widow, who was in the crowd of more than 20,000 people gathered at Santiago's Plaza de la Constitucion. He became the first Socialist president elected since Allende.

Looked to Right Past Wrongs

Later that evening Lagos appeared on a balcony with Lavin, his contender, and embraced him. This had never been done before in Chile and won Lagos much favor among the people. Lagos promised that he would bring the right and left sides of the government together during his term, and Lavin during his concession speech promised to help Lagos in his efforts. In March of 2000 Lagos was inaugurated and became the president of Chile.

One of the first things Lagos did, at the call of the people, was put Pinochet in the hands of the judicial system. It was important to Lagos that the human rights issues of Chile were resolved and improved upon, and therefore much of what happened during Pinochet's reign was brought to light and examined. Santiago archbishop emeritus Sergio Valech was put in charge of the commission looking into the crimes. They discovered thousands of victims of torture, and Lagos promised that such horrible infringements on human rights would never happen again in Chile. It was thought by Valech and his commission that those who had been tortured should receive life pensions, and Lagos approved the idea, giving about half the average monthly wage in Chile to each harmed person each month.

Realized Need to Improve Economics

One of the biggest problems Lagos had to face was the huge division in his country between rich and poor. He entered office during Chile's first economic recession in a long time, and he had much to do to improve things. He soon acquired free trade agreements with the United States and the European Union, among others, and he met with President Bush in 2004 to discuss just how the agreement was working. He also gave money to social institutions for better health care, housing, and education.

On the heels of these agreements, Chilean exports to the United States rose by 80 percent, and United States imports went up by 90 percent, helping both economies. Although there were disagreements between the countries concerning the war in Iraq, the two remained allies. According to the *New York Times,* Secretary of State Condoleezza Rice told reporters, "We have had an outstanding relationship with President Lagos. I think he has been not just a great president for Chile, but he's been really a wise and strong force for democracy and for free economies throughout the region."

On June 26, 2000, Lagos and Allende's widow unveiled a statue to the late president, trying to make up for the horrors done to the man decades before. Presidents have six-year terms in Chile, and Lagos set to work right away. He made great headway in his term and changed many laws and situations that no one had considered changing before. In the beginning he set out to improve conditions in the small Andean mining towns. Mining there had slowed down and the people there now needed help. In May of 2004 he signed a bill that stated that divorce was no longer illegal. He also opened his home, the Palacio de La Moneda, the seat of the president, to the public for the first time in a long while, and he rescinded the ban on censorship in movies.

Stepped Down as President

While he was in office, Lagos became known as a deep thinker. He never acted on impulse and he applied reason to everything he did, which was quite opposite to those who came before him. He was a favorite of the people. He enjoyed gardening and rock climbing, reading, classical music, tennis and the theater.

In 2006 Lagos stepped down as president with an approval rating of nearly 75 percent. Lagos left office more popular than when he entered it, something uncommon in Latin America. He was still not popular with either the far right, who found him too radical, or the far left, who found him too timid, but for the majority of his country, Lagos was seen as an effective leader. Chile's economy, in a recession when he took over, was growing faster than that of any other country in South America.

A definite sign of approval for Lagos was the fact that the person taking his place, new president Michelle Bachelet, was also a socialist. Just six years before, people had been suspicious of the party and in 2006 they endorsed it wholeheartedly. "We have had many differences with him, but in retrospect, during the Lagos administration Chile has made the most impressive progress on human rights issues as well as justice reform and freedom of expression," said Jose Miguel Vivanco, a Chilean lawyer who is director of Human Rights Watch Americas, according to the *New York Times.* Lagos did not leave politics after he stepped down as president, but instead became the government spokesperson for the new president, continuing in his quest to make Chile a country to be reckoned with.

Books

Contemporary Hispanic Biography, Volume 4, Gale, 2003.

Newsmakers, Issue 3, Thomson Gale, 2005.
Worldmark Encyclopedia of the Nations: World Leaders, Gale, 2003.

Periodicals

Banker, November 1, 2004.
Commonweal, April 7, 2000.
Economist (US), August 22, 1998; January 22, 2000; March 11, 2000; March 8, 2003.
Financial Times, January 17, 2006.
Institutional Investor, March 2001.
NACLA Report on the Americas, July-August 2003.
New York Times, March 11, 2006.
PR Newswire, January 13, 2004; July 19, 2004.
Xinhua News Agency, July 15, 2006.

Online

"Ricardo Lagos," *Biography Resource Center Online,* http://www.galenet.galegroup.com/servlet/BioRC (January 2, 2007). □

Hedy Lamarr

Austrian-born American actress Hedy Lamarr (1913–2000) was among the leading screen sirens of Hollywood in the 1940s. Her life was an eventful one that involved six marriages, a groundbreaking electronic invention, and several cinematic milestones.

Born to Bank Director and Pianist

Lamarr was born Hedwig Kiesler in Vienna, Austria, on November 9, 1913. Her family was Jewish and well off; her father was a Bank of Vienna director and her mother a concert pianist. Lamarr attended schools in Vienna and was sent to a finishing school in Switzerland as a teenager. By that time she was already unusually beautiful, attracting the attention of both prospective lovers and film producers. After an unsuccessful audition with famed stage director, Max Reinhardt, from whom she had taken acting lessons, Lamarr moved into films. Her screen career began in 1930 with a pair of Austrian films, *Money on the Street* and *Storm in a Waterglass.*

She had several other small roles in German-language films, but it took controversy to put Lamarr on the cinematic map. In 1932 she made a film called *Extase* (or *Ecstasy*) in Czechoslovakia; it was released the following year. The film told the simple story of a young woman whose husband is impotent, causing her to seek out the companionship of a younger man. Two scenes were responsible for the film's notoriety and quick banning by Austrian censors: one in which Lamarr runs nude through a sunlit forest, the other a sex scene in which she seems to experience orgasm (her intense facial expressions actually resulted from the application of a safety pin to her buttock by director Gustav Machaty). Lamarr later said that she had been a naive young woman pressured into doing these scenes, but cameraman

Jan Stallich told Jan Christopher Horak of *CineAction* that "as the star of the picture, she knew she would have to appear naked in some scenes. She never made any fuss about it during the production."

Controversy and condemnation from Pope Pius XI temporarily halted Lamarr's film career, but *Extase* did attract the attention of millionaire Austrian arms dealer Fritz Mandl, whom Lamarr met in December of 1933 and then married. Mandl had converted from Judaism to Catholicism in order to be able to do business with Germany's fascist regime (he was nevertheless exiled to Argentina after Austria came under German control in 1938), and Lamarr also made her religious conversion in 1933. An often-repeated story holds that Mandl tried to buy and destroy every outstanding copy of *Extase,* but this is thought to be legend rather than fact. Whether out of revulsion toward her husband's politics or from sheer restlessness, Lamarr packed a single suitcase with jewelry, drugged her maid, and fled to Paris and then London in 1937. That September she sailed for New York.

On board, she began negotiating with producer Louis B. Mayer of the Metro-Goldwyn-Mayer (M-G-M) studio, who had signed Swedish actress Greta Garbo several years earlier and was on the lookout for exotic European talent. Lamarr had refused Mayer's contract offer in London, but by the time the ship docked in New York she had a $500-a-week contract and the new name of Hedy Lamarr—up to that point she had used Hedi Kiesler. Mayer devised the name, inspired by that of silent film actress Barbara La Marr.

Starred Opposite Charles Boyer

Lamarr's first film in the United States was *Algiers* (1938), in which she played opposite French actor Charles Boyer as a woman who, though engaged to another man, has an affair with an escaped thief (Boyer). The film was a successful launch for Lamarr's American career, but it was followed by two flops, *Lady of the Tropics* (1939) and *I Take This Woman* (1940), the latter co-starring Spencer Tracy and dubbed *I Re-Take This Woman* after Mayer demanded numerous changes in the script. The actress's fortunes turned around later in 1940 with *Boom Town,* with Clark Gable in the lead role, and *Comrade X,* a sort of anti-Communist romance in which Lamarr played a Soviet streetcar driver who falls in love with an American reporter (Clark Gable).

Throughout World War II, Lamarr was a fixture on American movie screens with such films as *Come Live with Me* (1941), *Ziegfeld Girl* (1941), and the steamy *White Cargo* (1943), in which Lamarr played a mixed-race prostitute on an African rubber plantation (although censors demanded that references to her character's ethnicity be removed from the script). With such films as 1943's *The Heavenly Body* (the title ostensibly referred to astronomy), Lamarr emerged in the first rank of screen sex symbols. A poll of Columbia University male undergraduates ranked Lamarr as the actress they would most like to be marooned with on an island, and in 1942 Lamarr participated in the World War II mobilization effort by offering to kiss any man who would purchase $25,000 in War Bonds. She raised $17 million with 680 kisses. In 1943, Lamarr was rumored to have been in the running for (or to have turned down) the role that eventually went to Swedish actress Ingrid Bergman in *Casablanca.*

Lamarr had plenty of space in celebrity gossip columns to go with her screen stardom. She dated silent comedian Charlie Chaplin in 1941, and had flings with Burgess Meredith and several other actors. Lamarr married producer Gene Markey in 1939, divorcing him the following year. For four years she was married to English actor John Loder and had two children by him. Later in life Lamarr was married three more times, to bandleader Teddy Stauffer, Texas oil magnate Howard Lee, and lawyer Lewis Boles. All her marriages ended in divorce. Another man with whom Lamarr may have been romantically involved was composer George Antheil.

Antheil played an important role in Lamarr's life in another way as well—as a collaborator on an important electronics innovation. Lamarr was slightly dismissive of her glamorous image, saying (according to her *U.S. News & World Report* obituary), "Any girl can be glamorous. All you have to do is stand still and look stupid." Lamar, by contrast, had been astute enough to pick up a good deal of practical knowledge pertaining to munitions engineering during her marriage to Mandl. In 1940 she had the idea for a solution to the problem of controlling a radio-guided torpedo. At that time, electronic data broadcast on a specific frequency could easily be jammed by enemy transmitters. Lamarr suggested rapid changes in the broadcast frequency, and Antheil, who had experimented with electronic musical instruments, devised a punch-card-like device, similar to a player-piano roll, that could synchronize a transmitter and receiver. The system Lamarr and Antheil invented relied on using 88 frequencies, equivalent to the number of keys on a piano.

Realized No Money from Invention

The pair were jointly awarded a patent for their discovery, but Antheil later credited the original idea entirely to Lamarr. Credit did not matter, however, for the idea, later given the name of frequency hopping, was never applied by the military during World War II. It was later rediscovered independently and used in ships sent to Cuba during the missile crisis of 1962. The real payoff of frequency hopping came only decades later, when it became integral to the operation of cellular telephones and Bluetooth systems that enabled computers to communicate with peripheral devices. By that time, Lamarr and Antheil's patent had long since expired.

Experiment Perilous (1944), directed by Jacques Tourneur, was considered one of Lamarr's best films, but her career gradually declined after World War II. The most visible outing from this phase of her career was the Cecil B. DeMille-produced *Samson and Delilah* (1949), with Victor Mature and Lamarr in the title roles. The film, in Horak's words, "marries an Old Testament-style, evangelical Christian moralism with the theatrical exploitation of unadulterated sex." For David Thomson of London's *Independent on Sunday,* the film had "many moments where [Lamarr's] foreign voice, her basilisk gaze, and her sinful body combine to magnificent effect."

Lamarr made several films in the 1950s, mostly operating outside of the Hollywood system. In the 1954 Italian-made feature *The Loves of Three Queens* she played Helen of Troy, and she took on another historical role as Joan of Arc in *The Story of Mankind* (1958). Her heyday was past, however, and she stayed away from Hollywood for much of the time. In 1950 she sold off all of her possessions in an auction and announced that she was moving to Mexico. A marriage brought her back to the United States and to Texas in 1955, and in retirement she moved to Florida. Occasionally she appeared on television. In 1967 she published an autobiography, *Ecstasy and Me: My Life as a Woman,* but sued the ghostwriters she had employed, claiming (according to Thomson), that the book was "fictional, false, vulgar, scandalous, libelous, and obscene."

That was one of several episodes that saw Lamarr entering courtrooms in her later years. Lamarr was arrested in 1966 for shoplifting at Macy's department store, but was acquitted. She complained to a columnist that she had once had a $7 million income but by the late 1960s was subsisting on a $48-a-week pension. Another round of litigation came after the release of director Mel Brooks's Western film parody *Blazing Saddles* in 1974; the actress objected to the fanciful "Hedley Lamarr" name of one of the movie's characters.

Lamarr lived mostly in isolation in a small house in Orlando in the last years of her life, reportedly staying out of the spotlight partly because of unsuccessful plastic surgery.

She antagonized the organizers of a film festival with unreasonable demands for a makeup retinue. In 1990, however, she had a cameo role in the satire *Instant Karma,* and she lived long enough to see a modest renewal of interest in the sexually independent persona she had often projected on film. The story of her radio transmission invention also became widely publicized in the 1990s, and she received an Electronic Frontier Foundation Pioneer Award in 1997, although she never received any monetary award for her ingenuity. On January 19, 2000, Hedy Lamarr died at her home in Orlando.

Books

Lamarr, Hedy, *Ecstasy and Me: My Life as a Woman,* Fawcett, 1967.
World of Invention, 2nd ed., Gale, 1999.
Young, Christopher, *The Films of Hedy Lamarr,* Citadel, 1978.

Periodicals

CineAction, Spring 2001.
Economist, June 21, 2003.
Entertainment Weekly, February 4, 2000.
Forbes, May 14, 1990.
Independent on Sunday (London, England), January 30, 2005.
People, February 7, 2000.
U.S. News & World Report, January 31, 2000.

Online

"Hedy Lamarr," *All Movie Guide,* http://www.allmovie.com (January 20, 2007). □

Dick Lane

Defensive back Dick "Night Train" Lane (1928–2002) overcame a rough-and-tumble upbringing to make the Pro Football Hall of Fame. As a rookie in 1952, Lane set the National Football League (NFL) record for interceptions in a season, with 14. Though the NFL later expanded its schedule to 16 games from 12, the record still stood as of 2006. Over a 14-year career, Lane played in seven Pro Bowl all-star games. "I've played with him and against him, and he was the best I've ever seen," Pat Summerall, a former placekicker and broadcaster for Fox Sports, told the *Austin American-Statesman* newspaper.

Overcame Hardscrabble Upbringing

Lane was born in 1928. His mother was a prostitute who abandoned him when he was three months old; his father was a pimp that people called Texas Slim. Ella Lane, a woman living on East 9th Street in Austin, Texas, heard a crying baby in a dumpster, and first thought it was a cat. To her astonishment, it was a child swathed in old

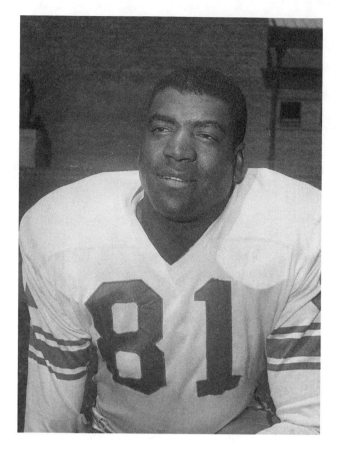

newspapers. Lane adopted the infant. "I never made any attempt to meet my dad. I figured if he didn't want me around, I didn't want to meet him, either," Lane said in Mike Burns's book about him, *Night Train Lane—Life of Hall of Famer Richard 'Night Train' Lane,* as quoted in the *Statesman.*

Lane's rough upbringing extended into adolescence. He earned the nickname "Cue Ball" after an incident in which a teenaged Lane won a pool match and the vanquished opponent tried to renege on a ten-cent bet. Lane threw a cue ball at the youth, hitting him on the back of the head. "It was a curve ball," a smiling Lane told Rick Cantu of the *Statesman* in 2001. "I'd never seen a cue ball thrown like a curve."

Ella Lane tried to keep her adoptive son on the straight and narrow. She assigned him such household chores as cleaning the chicken coops, washing clothes, and emptying washtubs. She once beat him with a leather belt for ripping his clothes while playing football in the neighborhood. "He became familiar with that leather strap many times," Cantu wrote. Lane said, according to Cantu: "I'm screaming and yelling so hard, some people yelled over the back fence, 'Ella, what are you doin' to that boy?' I'm sure they thought I was being murdered."

Lane sharpened his football skills in the streets of Austin, even in the wilting summer humidity and despite Ella's urgings to pursue other activities. He was a three-sport athlete at L.C. Anderson High School in Austin. Although he enjoyed basketball the most, he was best in football. He

helped Anderson, who played in an all-black conference, win the state championship in 1944. Head Coach W.E. Pigford was a big influence on Lane, even in later years.

Not anticipating a pro football career, Lane joined the Army at age 19, following one season at Scottsbluff Junior College in Nebraska. He served as a lieutenant colonel in World War II and then in the Korean War, while he continued to play football recreationally. When he left the military, he worked at an aircraft plant, lifting sheets of oil-covered metal into bins.

Rams Gave Him a Chance

In 1952 Lane walked into the office of the defending NFL champion Los Angeles Rams, armed with clippings of his high school and junior college achievements, and asked for a tryout. He wanted to be a wide receiver, but the Rams were well-stocked at that position with the likes of Tom Fears, Elroy "Crazylegs" Hirsch, and Bob Boyd. Head Coach Joe Stydahar put him on defense, at cornerback, a position that involved pass coverage. Not having played at a four-year college, Lane struggled with such concepts as pass patterns and defensive schemes. Fears tutored him on the game's finer points during training camp. "Lane went to Fears' dorm room so many times, it became a running joke," Cantu wrote.

Lane got more than tutoring from those visits—he got a permanent nickname. "Fears liked to play records, and his favorite was 'Night Train,'" Lane recalled of the Buddy Morrow tune, as quoted in the *New York Times.* "Every day I'd be going in his room and he'd be playing it. He roomed with a guy named Ben Sheets, and whenever I'd walk into the room, Sheets would say, 'Here comes Night Train.' He started calling me that, and it stuck."

Playing for only $4,500 as a rookie, Lane picked up 14 passes in the 12-game season. He gave short shrift to his accomplishment. "I probably dropped 10 passes the year I caught 14," he recalled to Cantu. "But I kept getting hit in the head with the ball." Still, Lane combined speed, reflexes and work ethic to play regularly on a Rams team that won nine of 12 games, then lost a National Division tiebreaker playoff to the Detroit Lions, 31–21 at the Los Angeles Memorial Coliseum. Lane proved adept at tackling as well as pass coverage.

Lane played two more seasons for the Rams before they traded him to the Chicago Cardinals in 1954. He spent six years in Chicago and six more years with the Detroit Lions, with whom he had his best years. He was an all-pro in 1960 through 1962, inclusive; in all, he made seven Pro Bowls in his 14 seasons. Overall, he picked off 68 passes, five for touchdowns, with 1,207 return yards. He retired after the 1965 season, and entered the Hall of Fame in 1974.

Remembered as All-Time Great

Lane, despite playing mostly on losing teams, helped revolutionize defensive secondary play. "He's one of the guys who transformed the cornerback position: a physical cornerback who could also make plays on the ball," said Aeneas Williams, a frequent all-pro at that position during his NFL career from 1991 through 2006. "He'll always be remembered as one of the great cornerbacks who played this game," Williams said, according to William C. Rhoden of the *New York Times*.

His peers on both sides of the ball highly praised Lane. "Lane was an icon for the cornerback position," former Lions defensive back Lem Barney said in the *Chicago Tribune*. Barney replaced Lane at left cornerback in 1965. "Guys like Herb Adderley, Mel Blount, Mel Renfro, Willie Brown and myself [all of whom played in the 1960s and 1970s] called him the 'Godfather of the Cornerbacks.'... Train was a prototype."

Known for his physical play, Lane frequently tackled players with a maneuver known as the "Night Train Necktie," a clothesline-style tackle, often involving a blow to the neck or head—that the league since has banned. "At 6 feet 3 inches and 185 chiseled pounds, Lane was often taller and faster than his opponents. He tackled players by wrapping his long arms around their necks and taking them to the ground like a rodeo calf," Cantu wrote. "I told him once, 'Night Train, you need to tackle a little lower—for my health,'" Hall of Fame wide receiver Tommy McDonald told the *Chicago Tribune*. Dave Robinson, a linebacker on three Green Bay Packers' championship teams from 1963 through 1972, said many players feared Lane, and cited one play when the defensive back hammered Robinson's teammate, fullback Jim Taylor. "I remember a streak of blue," Robinson told Cantu. "It was Night Train blowing by us, jumping over the guard, crushing our guy. It might be the last thing Jim Taylor remembered."

Lane, who had originally objected to his nickname, finally took to liking it, especially when he saw a headline in 1954 after his Chicago Cardinals dominated the Washington Redskins, 38–16. He was particularly adept that day against Redskins running back Charlie "Choo Choo" Justice. A Chicago newspaper sported a headline the next day: "Night Train Derails Choo Choo."

He retired in 1965. His accomplishments included intercepting passes in six consecutive games. He wanted to coach in the NFL, but the Lions did little to help him. Owner William Clay Ford instead hired him as special staff assistant, a position he held from 1966 to 1972. "The Detroit Lions, and by extension the NFL, never did right by Lane," Rhoden said. "Like so many great players, he was allowed to fade away. Players come and go, and few are kept around as treasures. The league too often treats the past like a worn pair of shoulder pads."

Experienced Personal Tragedy

Lane married and divorced three times. His best-known marriage was his second one, to singer Dinah Washington, often called the "Queen of the Blues." Basketball standout Wilt Chamberlain was best man at that wedding. The marriage, however, lasted less than one year. Broken marriages and struggles with alcohol and hard drugs burdened Washington for much of her life, and shortly before Christmas in 1963, Lane found her unconscious with an empty bottle of pills nearby. She died at age 39.

Lane, meanwhile, remained active with football after his playing days. He coached at Southern University in

Baton Rouge, Louisiana, and at Central State University in Wilberforce, Ohio. Then, Detroit Mayor Coleman Young named him the first director of the Police Athletic League, which provided a sports outlet and adult guidance for underprivileged youngsters. Memories of his rough adolescence motivated Lane to make the program a success. He also served briefly as a road manager for entertainer Redd Foxx, although that arrangement dissipated after a year.

In his later years, Lane developed diabetes and high blood pressure. His pension from the NFL was a mere $200 a month, at a time when modern athletes make millions. The pension and Social Security paid his rent in Austin. Lane's highest annual salary was $25,000. But, "I have no regrets; absolutely no regrets," he told Cantu. He had two sons but saw them infrequently.

Lane died of a heart attack on January 29, 2002, in Austin. He had listened to jazz music that evening. "I just helped him to bed," his personal care worker, Terry Yates, said in the *Chicago Tribune*. "When he lay down he took a big gasp of air. He was having difficulty breathing. It wasn't 20 minutes before he was gone."

Players and non-players alike remembered him for his toughness on and off the field and for his loyalty as a friend. "Train had great size and speed," said Hall of Fame middle linebacker Joe Schmidt, a teammate of Lane's in Detroit, also in the *Chicago Tribune*. "I have never seen anyone with the type of closing speed on a receiver that he had. Train took pride in getting to the receiver and making the tackle."

People paid respects to Lane at his funeral in Greater Mount Zion Baptist Church in Austin. "He was like a magnet," his niece, Dorothy Yancy, told the *Austin American–Statesman*. "You would fall in love with him the moment you met him. If you didn't, something was wrong with you. He had a twinkle in his eye and a smile that lit up the place."

Pastor Gaylon Clark noted Lane's survival instincts. "You don't go from being the son of a prostitute and reach the NFL Hall of Fame without fighting," he said, according to Cantu. He raised his voice to emphasize the message.

Periodicals

Austin American–Statesman, January 19, 2001; February 3, 2002.
Chicago Tribune, January 30, 2002.
Jet, February 25, 2002.
New York Times, January 31, 2002; February 1, 2002.

Online

Dick (Night Train) Lane Official Website, http://www.cmgworld wide.com/football/lane/index.php (December 5, 2006).
"Dick (Night Train) Lane," Pro Football Hall of Fame, http://www .profootballhof.com/hof/member.jsp?player_id=120 (December 5, 2006). □

Alicia de Larrocha

Pianist Alicia de Larrocha (born 1923) has been much admired in the music world practically since her birth. She is known for her interpretations of Spanish music, and "for the elegance of her playing, for the fine details and for the distinctive colors that emerge particularly in the repertoire of her native country," according to the *Seattle Times*.

D e Larrocha has an exuberant style while playing the piano and yet has a masterful technique that is polished and mature enough to play the most difficult of pieces by a variety of classical composers. The *Rocky Mountain News* said of the pianist, "For seven decades, Alicia de Larrocha has stood tall as the voice of Spanish keyboard music. Don't let her diminutive size fool you. At 4-foot-6, the pianist is a giant in the concert world."

Developed an Early Interest in Music

De Larrocha was born Alicia de Larrocha y de la Calle on May 23, 1923, in Barcelona, Spain. She came to the piano young and was so accomplished that she was soon studying with such famous teachers as Frank Marshall and theorist Ricardo Lamote de Grignon. As a young child de Larrocha worked especially with Marshall, a pianist who had been a student of the famous Spanish pianist and composer Enrique Granados, who would later prove to be one of de Larrocha's favorite composers to play. But it was Joaquin Turina who, when the young pianist was a mere five years old, discovered the young talent and helped her make her performing debut at a young age.

She met the famous child soprano Victoria de los Angeles when they were both still quite young, and the two remained friends for the rest of their lives. For a number of years the two performed duo recitals in Spanish around Barcelona, and eventually played across the country. They were both instant successes, and de Larrocha was invited to play at the Palau de la Musica in Barcelona when she was only six. When she was 11 years old she was already a soloist with the Orquesta Sinfonica in Madrid.

Became International Sensation

De Larrocha continued to practice and improve her talents as she grew older. Unlike some child stars, de Larrocha proved to have a style and skill that transcended her age and continued to improve. In 1940, when she was 17 years old and therefore through with her school studies, she began to focus even more seriously on her career as a concert pianist, and she was invited to play for sold out audiences all over Spain. It was a cosmopolitan life that thrilled the young girl. In 1947 she started making major tours throughout Europe, playing all of the major musical arenas that the continent had to offer.

In 1955 de Larrocha made her first trip to the United States to perform. It was this trip that helped her gain worldwide acclaim, and from this trip onward she was a

sought-after pianist at venues all over the world. She performed regularly for the interpreters series at Lincoln Center in New York and was often seen as part of the Mostly Mozart Festival, for which she played over 80 times during her lifetime.

Like many musicians, de Larrocha was too busy playing and practicing to plan her own travels around the globe. She hired Herbert Breslin to be her manager, and he arranged for her hectic and expansive touring career. Breslin was also the agent of Luciano Pavarotti. With his help de Larrocha toured around the world, becoming more and more famous to musical audiences everywhere. In 1959 de Larrocha was invited to take on the position of director of the Marshall Academy of Barcelona, which she accepted.

Opposed Video Recording and Comparisons

Over the years de Larrocha made her views on being recorded on video very clear. It was something she disliked greatly as she felt that music should be listened to, not watched. Despite that, however, many videos of her performances were much admired by critics and audiences alike. *Notes* magazine found the video *Nights in the Gardens of Spain* to be ". . . outstanding. Not only do we hear a terrific performance by the wonderful Alicia de Larrocha, but the camera moves smoothly between the concert hall and absolutely gorgeous footage filmed in the Spanish gardens themselves."

Brought Spanish Composers to Audiences Everywhere

Throughout her touring and recording careers, de Larrocha played the works of an enormous number of composers, including Mozart, Beethoven, Schumann, and others. She was especially well known, however, for her interpretations of the Spanish composers Granados and Albeniz, and has been credited for introducing them to many who had not heard their works before. She also introduced lesser-known Spanish composers to the world, such as Joaquin Turina, Carlos Surinach, Oscar Espla, Antonio Soler, and Xavier Montsalvatge. Most pianists at the time did not play these composers, and it gave de Larrocha's an exotic flavor that others could not offer.

De Larrocha participated in collaborations with a number of other famous performers during her career, including her friend Victoria de los Angeles, Montserrat Caballe, and the Guarneri and Tokyo Quartets. The Newark, New Jersey, *Star Ledger* commented on her playing with the latter group: "The four men in front of her seemed to be playing too, but it was the Spaniard who dominated the performance with her magnetic attachment to the music of Mozart. Her grace notes were immediately recognizable-decorative flourishes as light as lace. She played the familiar melodies as both seasoned performer and old friend." She also performed the Concerto for two pianos by Francis Poulenc with the composer himself, playing the second piano part in the duet. De Larrocha was also an intimate friend of the composer Federico Mompou, who composed several works for her.

Won Several Awards for Recording Career

She recorded copiously, and was given many awards for her popular records. These awards included the French Grand Prix du Disque of the Académie Charles Cros in Paris, the Dutch Edison Prize in Amsterdam, and a number of Grammy Awards in 1974, 1975, and 1978 for Isaac Albeniz's *Iberia* and Granados's *Goyescas,* as well as two piano concertos by Maurice Ravel. Other awards that Larrocha garnered over her long and prosperous career were the German critics' Schallplatten Preis in 1976, the Cervantes Prize of the Jacinto and Inocencio Guerrero Foundation in 1991, the Franz Liszt Prize of Budapest, and the Principe d'Astoria Prize in 1994. She was also Musician of the Year for Musical America. She was popular around the world, but she was always a special favorite in her own country. Because of this the Spanish King Juan Carlos gave her a gold medal for fine arts.

De Larrocha was involved in many organizations over her lifetime. Among others, she became a member of the Spanish Academia de Bellas Artes. She was given the rank of Commandeur dans l'Ordre des Arts et des Lettres in Paris, France. She received the Paderewski Memorial Medal and the Principe de Asturias prize.

Gave Grand Tour for Retirement

In 2003, at the age of 80, de Larrocha decided it was time to retire. At the time of her retirement she had been playing for over 75 years. To celebrate her retirement, de Larrocha made a tour of her usual haunts, performing farewell concerts all around the world. She played one last time for the Mostly Mozart Festival, and later played again with the New York Philharmonic. The *Financial Times* commented on her farewell performance in Britain: "De Larrocha never was a dazzling technician and certainly cannot be one now. It hardly matters. Her dynamic forte remains piano. She always specialized in understatement, and her powers of persuasion have increased over the decades. There was nothing fussy, nothing mannered about her playing here. Scoring her points gently, she kept the scale intimate, the expressive impulses propulsive. It worked beautifully on her terms." As always de Larrocha played it her way, and her way drew audiences in.

At another stop on her farewell tour, the *National Review* said that de Larrocha "is, as always, stately and dignified as she makes her way-a little slowly now-to the piano . . . Her playing? It remains de Larrochian, only more so: that is, her mannerisms have become more pronounced, as tends to happen to every musician. De Larrocha has a big, robust, 'fat' sound. Her playing is generally detached-not legato or limpid-and it can be percussive, even harsh; but it is always in balance (as one note relates to another), and it always makes musical sense. In Spanish music, rhythm (along with color) is everything, and de Larrocha-in whatever she plays, Spanish or no-has fabulously good rhythm." Musical audiences lost a truly unique performer when de Larrocha retired, but luckily her recordings and videos are still available for listening.

Books

Almanac of Famous People, 8th edition, Gale Group, 2003.

Periodicals

Arizona Daily Star, October 27, 2000.
Daily Telegraph (London, England), July 22, 2006.
Financial Times, August 19, 2003.
Grand Rapids Press (Michigan), October 17, 2004.
Mail on Sunday (London, England), June 29, 2003.
Milwaukee Journal Sentinel, October 8, 1999.
National Review, December 17, 2001.
New York Times, November 23, 1995; November 27, 2002.
Notes, March 1994.
Rocky Mountain News, October 26, 2001.
San Francisco Chronicle, November 4, 2002; November 8, 2002.
Scotsman (Edinburgh, Scotland), August 19, 1998.
Seattle Post-Intelligencer, April 10, 1996.
Seattle Times, April 9, 1996; October 20, 2000.
Star-Ledger (Newark, NJ), November 23, 2002.
Star Tribune (Minneapolis, MN), July 20, 1996; March 29, 1997.

Online

"Alicia de Larrocha," *Christa Phelps Artist Managmenet,* http://www.rundetaarn.dk/engelsk/cgf01/larrochauk.htm (January 2, 2007).
"Alicia de Larrocha," *Como Piano Academy,* http://www.comopianoacademy.com/courses/Alicia%20de%20Larrocha/ (January 2, 2007).
"Alicia de Larrocha," *Copenhagen Guitar Festival '01,* http://www.freespace.virgin.net/christa.phelps/larrocha.htm (January 2, 2007). □

Shelly Lazarus

As chairman and CEO of advertising giant Ogilvy & Mather, American businesswoman Shelly Lazarus (born 1947) has been described as one of the most powerful executives in advertising.

One of a handful of women to graduate from Columbia University with an MBA in the early 1970s, Lazarus propelled herself through the corporate world to become chairman and CEO of the billion dollar advertising agency Ogilvy & Mather in 1997. Encouraged by legendary founder David Ogilvy, Lazarus became an evangelist for the power of brands and created an integrated multimedia advertising giant with clients worldwide. A role model for businesswomen, Lazarus has stressed the need for balance between work and family life, and has advocated that people love the work they do.

Attended Smith College and Columbia University

Rochelle "Shelly" Braff was born in Oceanside, New York, on September 1, 1947, the daughter of Lewis Braff, a certified public accountant, and Sylvia Braff. Shelly attended Smith College, an all-women's school in

Northampton, Massachusetts. During her senior year she was inspired by a conference presented by the Advertising Women of New York that led her to consider a career in advertising. In 1968 she graduated from Smith with a bachelor's degree and went on to Columbia University. One of four women in her class, she earned an MBA from Columbia in 1970. That same year she married George Lazarus, a pediatrician, with whom she had three children.

Shelly Lazarus steadily worked her way through the corporate world, beginning at Clairol where she became assistant product manager in 1970, but soon moving to Ogilvy & Mather in 1971. She served as an account executive until 1974, when she followed her husband to Dayton, Ohio, while he served in the Air Force. Lazarus spent two years as a department store buyer. In 1976, the family returned to New York, and Lazarus returned to Ogilvy & Mather, the company where she would spend the next thirty plus years.

Ogilvy & Mather

At Ogilvy, Lazarus resumed as an account supervisor for Avon, Campbell Soup, and Ralston Purina. After serving as management supervisor from 1976 to 1987, she shot up the corporate ladder, becoming Ogilvy & Mather Direct general manager in 1987, Ogilvy & Mather Direct U.S. president in 1981, then Ogilvy & Mather New York president in 1991.

In the 1990s, Lazarus attracted American Express as a client and convinced IBM to consolidate its scattered advertising operations into one account at Ogilvy. She gained experience in every product category in both general advertising and direct marketing, eventually running Ogilvy & Mather Advertising and the North American direct marketing arm, Ogilvy & Mather Direct, which is now known as Ogilvy One.

Woman Broke the Glass Ceiling

A slight woman, Lazarus began at Ogilvy as the only woman in an industry in which 90 percent of the consumers were female. She remarked in *Across the Board,* "I had this enormous power because there would inevitably come this moment in a meeting. It would be me and fourteen men, and we would be talking about something—like tampons, which was the case once—and they would all turn to me and go, 'Well, Shelly, what do women think?' And I would be talking on behalf of all women everywhere in the world."

In a meteoric rise, she was named president of North American operations in 1994, president and chief operating officer in 1995, chief executive officer in 1996, chairman of Ogilvy & Mather Worldwide in 1997, and finally to the highest office where she remains today, chairman and CEO of Ogilvy & Mather Worldwide in 1997.

As a sign of the slow but progressive change in attitude toward the glass ceiling, Lazarus replaced Ogilvy's first woman CEO, Charlotte Beers, in 1996, making Ogilvy & Mather the first firm in the industry to have one female CEO succeed another. Beers helped pave the way for women in leadership roles, and both women have said that the Ogilvy succession was an important signal to the corporate world that women were equally competent in top agency posi-

tions. Nevertheless, today women comprise only 12 percent of corporate officers in the *Fortune* 500 list of biggest companies in America, and there are only six female CEOs in those companies.

Under Lazarus' stewardship, Ogilvy secured an impressive list of large and very profitable American and international clients, such as American Express, British Petroleum, Coca-Cola, DuPont, Ford, IBM, Kodak, Morgan Stanley, Motorola, and Unilever. In a daring move, Ogilvy's choice to reject stereotypes of pencil-thin models and instead use medium-sized women in its Dove soap campaign garnered immense attention and even awards. Ogilvy also gained prominence when it captured Johnson & Johnson's 2008 Olympic campaign.

Influenced by David Ogilvy

At the time Lazarus was working at Ogilvy & Mather, legendary founder David Ogilvy was working a semiretired schedule of a few months a year, yet he made a lasting impression on her. One basic idea that stuck with Lazarus was that advancement came through merit regardless of gender. Although David was not directly Lazarus' mentor, she said in *Lessons from the Top,* "I did get to know David because he's very democratic in the sense that he had no idea what titles or positions anyone every had in the agency. . . . I always talk about this place as a meritocracy and that's because of the way David ran it. Not only did he not care that I was a woman and pregnant, he actually liked it, because it was like a challenge to what everyone else believed. At General Foods, at that time, as soon as you wore maternity clothes you had to leave the building. To David, this was another way of challenging the status quo."

David Ogilvy also gave Lazarus advice that she would remember during her long tenure at the agency. In *Harvard Business Review,* Lazarus said that when she knew she would be named CEO, David gave her the best advice she ever received. "No matter how much time you spend thinking about, worrying about, focusing on, questioning the value of, and evaluating people, it won't be enough. . . . People are the only thing that matters, and the only thing you should think about, because when that part is right, everything else works." Lazarus said that his advice drives not only how she thinks about and mentors people but also how she forms business strategies and makes critical decisions.

Promoted 360-Degree Branding

David Ogilvy also preached the driving need to build brand awareness, a message that got through to Lazarus like a religious edict. Lazarus promotes the concept of 360-degree branding, which involves making a significant impression on a consumer at every point of contact between that consumer and the brand. From the packaging to the advertisements, the brochure, the sales materials, the order forms, every message about the product should reinforce the other messages in the consumer's mind. In today's world, that includes electronic contact, such as the Internet, e-mail, and interactive experiences.

In one 360-degree turn of advertising strategy, Lazarus confronted Ford Motor Company, which bristled at a woman trying to explain how to run an automotive company. She said in *Lessons from the Top,* "One of the first things I said to them was, I'm relatively new to the car category, but here's something I don't understand. If a Ford is different from a Jaguar, is different from a Mazda, is different from a Buick and a Volkswagen, why do all the showrooms look the same?" Lazarus's point hit its mark as Ford executives then realized that this is where 360-degree branding at every point of contact was needed.

In the late 1990s and early 2000s, Ogilvy & Mather was now getting more than half its revenue from nonadvertising business, a testament to its 360-degree branding.

"Love What You're Doing"

When young professional women ask Lazarus for advice, she quickly has one emphatic response: "You have to love what you're doing." She said in *Lessons from the Top,* "If you ever want to find balance, you have to love your work, because you're going to love your children, that's almost a given. When things get out of balance, and where women become miserable, is when they actually don't like what they're doing professionally. They then resent every minute that they're away from the things they love and, therefore, the job gets worse and worse, because more resentment fills their lives."

In *Business 2.0,* Lazarus offers more advice on how business should not supersede happiness. "The truth is that balance is achieved through a host of individual dance steps, from being willing to suffer a little domestic chaos to insisting that performance be measured by results, not just time spent in the office." She added that company employees who have found this balance are more creative and productive and build more successful business environments that tend to prevent employees from leaving.

Named One of the Most Powerful Women

It was Lazarus' powerful vision and success that earned her top awards and recognition in her field, not the novelty of being a woman at the helm. In 1999, *Forbes* magazine named her the fourth most powerful woman in America. She consistently appeared in the magazine's 100 Most Powerful Women in the World list, appearing at number 93 in 2004, at number 78 in 2005, and at number 87 in 2006. She gained the attention of *Fortune* magazine as well, returning several times to its list of the 50 Most Powerful Women in Business, reaching number 11 in 2001, number 14 in 2002, and number 30 in 2006.

Among her numerous business awards and women achievement awards, she was the first woman to receive the Distinguished Leadership in Business Award in 2003 by the Columbia University Business School. She was also named Advertising Woman of the Year in 1994, Business Woman of the Year in 1996, and Woman of the Year in 2002 by the Direct Marketing Association.

But Lazarus takes the accolades in stride. She commented in *Adweek,* "In a way, I'm thrilled that there are 50 women in such prominent positions, and the list is a nice

acknowledgment of pioneers." She continued, "But at the same time I think we're coming to the day when noting the gender of a powerful person in business will be a thing of the past."

In addition to her position at Ogilvy & Mather, Lazarus is currently serving or has served on numerous prestigious boards in industry, business, and academia, including American Museum of Natural History, Ann Taylor Stores, Columbia University's Board of Overseers, General Electric, Merck, New York-Presbyterian Hospital, and the World Wildlife Fund. She was one of only two women to serve as chairman of the American Association of Advertising Agencies, and is an adviser at venture capital firm RRE Ventures. At her alma mater she served a five-year term as chairman of the Board of Trustees.

Role Model

Lazarus even finds time for a lecture circuit, speaking at industry and leadership forums, and especially at her alma maters. She was keynote speaker at the 2006 conference of the Marketing Association of Columbia at Columbia University. In May 2005, she provided the commencement address at Smith College describing how in the 1960s, the high point of a woman's life was getting engaged, but that women could break from expectations and create their own plan for their lives.

At Smith she said, "I never dreamed that I would some day be standing on this platform getting an honorary degree, and giving this speech. . . . You know, we are all such products of our own expectations. When the world portrays us in a certain way, we tend to see ourselves as pictured. Accept it and expect it. . . . I never set out to be a role model, to get to the corner office, or to have a big career. . . . After Smith, the only reason I went on to get an MBA from Columbia was because I needed a job and I heard that if a woman had an MBA they probably wouldn't make her type."

Books

Neff, Thomas J., and James Citrin, *Lessons from the Top: The Search for America's Best Business Leaders,* Random House, 1999.

Periodicals

Across the Board, September/October 2005.
Advertising Age, November 20, 2006.
Adweek (Western Edition), October 7, 2002.
Business 2.0, December 2005.
Harvard Business Review, January 2005.
Times (United Kingdom), March 13, 2002.

Online

"Shelly Lazarus '70," Marketing Association of Columbia, http://www0.gsb.columbia.edu/students/organizations/mac/conferencewebsite2006/bios.htm (December 7, 2006).
"Smith Tradition," Smith College Commencement Address 2005, www.smith.edu/collegerelations/com2005.php (December 7, 2006).
"Who, Where, How Much?: Board Members, Shelly Lazarus," *Corporate Watch,* www.corporatewatch.org.uk/?lid-388 (December 7, 2006). □

Tanaquil LeClercq

Dancer Tanaquil LeClercq (1929–2000) was affectionately called Tanny by all who knew her. Jerome Robbins, the choreographer who cast her in his "Afternoon of a Faun," told the New York Times the ballerina "could do anything." She won instant success as a dancer right from the start and became a solo premiere performer for the New York City Ballet Company at its inception. Her career was cut short when she was diagnosed with polio while on tour. LeClercq, however, did not let the illness stop her and she remained in the dancing world, teaching other young dancers to perform.

Led an International Childhood

L eClercq was born on October 2, 1929, in Paris, France. Her parents were Jacques LeClerq, a French poet and writer, and Edith Whittemore, an American. She was given the name of Tanaquil, after the Etruscan Queen Tanaquil, who was known to be a wise reader of omens. When LeClercq was three years old her family moved to New York City where she was raised, although she often visited Europe with her parents.

LeClercq took up ballet at a very young age and studied with the ballet great Mikhail Mordkin until 1941. At that time she auditioned for the School of American Ballet. She was only 12 years old at the time, but the famous choreographer George Balanchine saw her at auditions and was so impressed by what he saw that he immediately offered her a scholarship to the school. After attending the school for several years she won a fellowship, and was able to continue her education under Balanchine.

Three years later Balanchine, still actively watching LeClercq's progress as a dancer, found himself was even more impressed by the young ballerina's skill. When she was 15, Balanchine asked her to perform with him in a ballet he choreographed for a polio charity benefit. In the ballet Balanchine danced the part of a character named Polio and LeClercq danced the part of a victim whom he paralyzed.

Premiere Dancer of New York City Ballet

After graduating from the School of American Ballet at age 17, LeClercq was invited to take part in a new ballet company, the Ballet Society, which was started by Balanchine and Lincoln Kirstein. It would later be renamed the New York City Ballet, one of the most famous dance companies in the world. Balanchine started out doing all the choreography for the new ballet company. He was enthusiastic about LeClercq, who was a lead dancer in the group. She was the first ballerina Balanchine had worked with and choreographed for who had been taught by him. In fact, LeClercq came to be known as the epitome of a Balanchine

dancer, with her long legs and fluid, graceful lines. She was so limber, in fact, that there was a famous story told by another girl who danced with her. Apparently this other dancer came to class one day to find LeClercq with a bandage on her nose. When asked what had happened to her, LeClercq replied that she had kicked her leg too high and accidentally kicked herself in the nose. She seemed the perfect choice to dance Balanchine's ballets, and the pair became very close.

In her first year with the Ballet Society, Balanchine gave LeClercq a solo spot as Choleric in his famous ballet *The Four Temperaments.* Just a short while later she was given a role in *Divertimento,* also choreographed by Balanchine. As her career progressed, LeClercq also danced in the premieres of works by other great choreographers, such as John Taras and William Dollar, as well as in *The Seasons* by Merce Cunningham and John Cage. She was also seen as the Princess in *The Spellbound Child.* Every dance she performed in seemed to be made for her, and she amazed audiences and critics alike.

Choreographers Made Ballets For Her

Just four years later, Balanchine was choreographing all of his ballets for her, the first one being *La Valse.* By 1948, after the Ballet Society had become the New York City Ballet, LeClercq was one of its principal dancers and she remained so throughout her dancing career. She made ballet popular and brought some of the more famous ballets to television. Balanchine wrote his first ballet for television for her as *Cinderella,* dancing to Tchaikovsky's music.

But despite her closeness and relationship to Balanchine, LeClercq also worked with other choreographers. She worked closely with Jerome Robbins and it was she who inspired him to create and choreograph his version of *Afternoon of the Faun.* She premiered many ballets choreographed by others, including *The Minotaur* by Taras, 1947; *Highland Fling* by Dollar, 1947; *The Seasons* by Cunningham, 1947; *Ondine* by Dollar in 1949; *Illuminations* by Ashton, 1950; and *Cakewalk* by Ruthanna Boris, 1951.

One of the reasons people liked to choreograph dances for her was because she was known for her great professionalism as well as her grace and skill. One story about LeClercq described an accident on stage: one of the dancers in *The Nutcracker* dropped a large wooden hoop in the middle of the stage. Audience and dancers alike were distracted by it, with some dancers trying without success to kick it off the stage. LeClercq, according to *Dance* magazine, took care of the problem. "Tanny looked unconcerned. During one of her solos, when she was hovering close by, she kicked the hoop cleanly off stage with precise musical aim, not missing a beat in the choreography, and she brought the house down. A small, inscrutable smile beamed on her face for a second or two while she continued her work."

Married Balanchine Before Polio Struck

In 1952, on Christmas day, Balanchine and LeClercq became engaged. They were married just a week later. She was Balanchine's fourth wife. In 1956, when she was 27,

LeClercq toured Europe as part of the New York City Ballet Company. While she was in Copenhagen she started feeling ill. She went to the hospital, where it was discovered that she had somehow contracted the disease of polio. She soon became paralyzed from the waste down. She was moved to a Danish hospital that specialized in polio treatments, and while she was there she was visited by many, including the Queen of Denmark. No one could quite believe the tragedy that had struck down the woman who had been a muse and inspiration to Balanchine and Robbins, among many others.

LeClercq had danced for only ten years professionally, but she premiered an unprecedented number of ballets, many of which were choreographed especially for her. It was an immensely tragic way for a woman's career to end who had danced in such ballets as Balanchine's *Haieff Divertimento,* 1947; *Symphonie Concertante,* 1947; *The Triumph of Bacchus and Ariadne,* 1948; *Symphony in C,* 1948; *Elegie,* 1948; *Orpheus,* 1948; *Bourrée Fantasque,* 1949; *Caracole,* 1952; *Metamorphoses,* 1952; *Concertino,* 1952; *Valse Fantaisie,* 1953; and *Divertimento No. 15,* 1956. She had also been seen in premieres choreographed by Robbins, including *Age of Anxiety,* 1950; *The Pied Piper,* 1951; *Ballade,* 1952; and *The Concert,* 1956. Robbins and Balanchine got together to choreograph *Jones Beach* in 1950. Tragically, however, LeClercq's dancing career was now at an end.

Life After Dance

LeClercq returned to the United States, and Balanchine took a year off to take care of his ailing wife. LeClercq had a hard time dealing with her illness at first, but she slowly became accustomed to her life and began taking on new ventures. She frequently stayed at her country home in Weston, Connecticut, becoming increasingly interested in reading and writing. She became a benefactor of the local library and wrote several books of her own. Her first book was a cookbook filled with recipes she gathered from dancers along with beautiful pictures of those dancers doing ballet. It was called *The Ballet Cookbook.* Her second book was a children's book about a cat that was trained to dance ballet by Balanchine himself because he attended rehearsals of the New York City Ballet. This one was titled *Mourka: The Autobiography of a Cat.* She developed a great interest in photography and also in crossword puzzles. She not only did the puzzles, but she created them, and some were published as part of the famous New York Times crossword puzzle series.

She maintained a position in the world of dance by teaching at the Dance Theater of Harlem, demonstrating moves with her hands from her wheelchair. She also trained dancers at the New York City Ballet Company who were taking on roles that she had once danced herself.

Left a Tremendous Legacy

In 1969 Balanchine fell in love with his next young dancing muse, Suzanne Farrell, and he and LeClercq were divorced. The pair remained close throughout their lives, however, and LeClercq visited him daily when he was on his deathbed.

LeClercq died in Manhattan of pneumonia on December 31, 2000. She was 71 years old. The dance world mourned her death but honored her spirit. The *Dance Insider* website wrote, "In a brief but moving sermon, the Reverend Stephen S. Garney, vicar of Calvary Church, noted that 'When she saw she could no longer dance, Tanny soon revealed that she had other gifts up her sleeve,' teaching younger dancers, and writing books."

LeClercq left an amazing legacy behind her. She inspired Balanchine, Robbins, and others to create a total of 32 roles just for her. The poem *Ode to Tanaquil LeClercq* was written about her by Frank O'Hara. She was an inspiration to everyone who knew her long after she stopped dancing. Even after her death her great influence could be felt, when fashion designer Alberta Ferretti made a collection for the spring/summer of 2004 inspired by pictures of LeClercq from the 1950s.

Periodicals

Back Stage, January 5, 2001; June 8, 2001.
Dance Magazine, April 2001.
Harper's Bazaar, January 2004.
Independent (London, England), January 6, 2001.
Milwaukee Journal Sentinel, January 2, 2001.
Newsweek, January 15, 2001.
Newsweek International, January 15, 2001.
New York Times, January 1, 2001; January 5, 2001; May 22, 2001.
Time, January 15, 2001.
Time Inernational, January 15, 2001.
Times (London, England), February 15, 2001.

Online

"Flash Report 2, 1–7: LeClercq Laid to Rest, Ballet World Bids a Ballerina Adieu," *Dance Insider,* http://www.danceinsider.com-f2001-f107_2.html (January 2, 2007).
"Tanaquil LeClercq," *Ballet Encyclopedia,* http://www.the-ballet.com-leclercq.php (January 2, 2007).
"Tanaquil LeClercq," *Carnegie Mellon University,* http://www.cmi.univ-mrs.fr-~esouche-danse-LeClercq.html (January 2, 2007). □

Lee Jong-Wook

Dr. Lee Jong-Wook (1945–2006) was the sixth general-director of the World Health Organization (WHO), the international health agency of the United Nations (U.N.). When elected to the post, Lee became the first South Korean to head a U.N. agency. Trained as a physician, he became an expert on the treatment of leprosy. Later, as head of WHO, he focused on immunization and disease prevention. During his 23 years with the agency he demonstrated strong leadership and exerted a substantial impact on health concerns on a global scale. In 2004 *Time* magazine named him as one of the world's one hundred most influential people.

Lee was born on April 12, 1945, in Seoul, South Korea. He was the son of a civil servant, and his family endured great hardships during the Korean War (1950–53). During the conflict, Lee, along with his two brothers and his mother, traveled on foot from his home in Seoul to Taegu to find his father, who had been exiled to a remote post. The grueling trip encompassed 400 miles and took nearly three months. During the punishing trek, Lee developed an appreciation of the sufferings of refugees.

After the 1953 cease fire, Lee's father and brothers became politicians. But Lee, at the urging of his mother, decided to become a doctor. He earned his medical degree at Seoul National University's College of Medicine. After Lee graduated, his mother further encouraged him to become a plastic surgeon, as it would be a more lucrative medical direction. But Lee had become deeply interested in the disease of leprosy, as he perceived the profound social and emotional impact the disease wrought, and he started his medical career serving a leper colony in South Korea.

While working at the colony Lee met his wife, Reiko, a Japanese woman who worked with a Catholic organization to help care for leprosy sufferers. The couple had one son, Tadahiro. Also during this early stage in his career, Lee decided to change his focus from private practice to public health, as he thought he would be able to help more people.

Began Long Association with WHO

Eventually Lee and his small family left South Korea, so that he could continue his education in the United States. In 1981 he earned his master's degree in epidemiology and public health from the University of Hawaii's School of Public Health, where he specialized in tropical diseases. In 1983 Lee began his long association with the World Health Organization (WHO) by accepting a position as a leprosy consultant at the agency's regional office in Fiji. A year later, WHO appointed him as a team leader for leprosy control in the South Pacific region. Lee never intended to remain with WHO for a long time, but he ended up spending most of the rest of his career with the organization.

In 1986 Lee transferred to WHO's Western Pacific Regional Office, located in Manila in the Philippines. At first he was involved in the Regional Leprosy Control Program. Later he became Regional Adviser on Chronic Diseases. Over the course of Lee's early involvement with WHO, officials at the organization's headquarters, located in Geneva, Switzerland, took favorable note of his work. In 1994 Lee was selected to serve as head of WHO's Global Program on Vaccines and Immunizations (GVP). In accepting the position, he moved to Geneva to work in WHO's home office.

At the time, Lee also served as executive secretary of the Children's Vaccine Initiative, a global campaign designed to foster development of new and more effective vaccines. Lee's specific goals were to increase access to vaccinations for all children, thereby ridding the world of poliomyelitis (polio) and other childhood diseases that were preventable through vaccines. He proved a strong leader and developed an innovative approach to working with the drug manufacturing industry, initiating discussions with companies to determine how they could develop vaccines to specifically treat diseases that primarily affected developing nations.

Lee's other strategic initiatives included a review of the immediate and long-term mission of GPV, and an increase in funding from $15 million to nearly $70 million between 1994 and 1998. He also introduced management reforms that would ensure the highest technical competence of staff as well as increase the number of women in professional posts. Lee's leadership had a substantial impact on polio eradication in the western Pacific region. The number of reported polio cases decreased from 5963 in 1990 to 700 in 1994 to nearly none by 2004. Because of Lee's successful efforts, *Scientific American* magazine called him the "Vaccine Czar" in 1997.

Assumed Leadership of Tuberculosis Program

In 1998, when Norwegian physician Go Brundtland became head of WHO, she chose Lee to be a senior policy advisor and to serve as her special representative. He held these positions until 2000, when Brundtland selected Lee to head WHO's Stop TB program. His mission, as the program's name indicates, was to stem the worldwide spread of tuberculosis.

In assuming the post, Lee took over a program that lacked a comprehensive global strategy and was beset with organizational problems. To address the problems, Lee placed WHO at the center of the program and helped install proven treatments. He drew on his previous managerial experience with the GVP to develop a complex global partnership called the Global Drug Facility (GDF), an initiative designed to increase access to tuberculosis drugs. The partnership included more than 250 international members, including WHO member countries, donors, non-governmental organizations, pharmaceutical industry representatives, and foundations. This coalition came to be recognized as one of the most successful health related public-private partnerships. The *Boston Globe* credited Lee with having provided superior leadership and political skills in order to build a consensus and "spur former antagonists to work together." The GDF would serve as a model for other initiatives seeking to increase access to drugs for other so-called diseases of poverty such as HIV/AIDS and malaria.

Elected to Lead WHO

On January 28, 2003, Lee was nominated by WHO's executive board to head the organization. Bruntland's term was ending in July of that year, and she decided not to seek a second term. On May 21, an executive committee of the United Nations elected Lee to the post of director-general for a five-year term. Lee became WHO's sixth director-general and the first South Korean to head a U.N. agency. He began his term on July 21, 2003.

Lee's election came as a surprise. He was considered the long shot in a field of five candidates for the post, as he was the only candidate who lacked experience as a minister in a governmental department or as head of a U.N. agency. Further, it was felt that he lacked sufficient political strength to work with heads of state to promote a global agenda. However, Lee disproved that belief by convincing 53 members of the U.S. Congress to write letters of support for his bid to Colin Powell and Tommy Thompson, who were then cabinet members in the George W. Bush administration. As a result of this personal campaign, Lee won the election by a narrow margin.

Established Influential WHO Agenda

At the beginning of his term, Lee established a set of clearly defined goals. First, he wanted to improve international monitoring of infectious diseases to help control outbreaks of afflictions such as severe acute respiratory syndrome (SARS). To meet this goal, he sought increased funding from some countries to enhance disease monitoring via increased staff and training. Second, he sought to develop a better plan for fighting HIV/AIDS, malaria, and tuberculosis in underprivileged countries saddled with poor health care systems. To do this, he created a team focused on improving the agency's role in the battle against these diseases, particularly in Africa. Indeed, Lee's WHO leadership tenure was marked by his strong focus on healthcare problems in poor countries, as he firmly believed that disease risk was directly linked to a nation's poverty level.

Despite his well-defined agenda, Lee was compelled to shift his focus due to developing international healthcare concerns such as the widely publicized outbreak of the avian flu throughout Africa, Asia, and Europe, as well natural catastrophes such as the 2004 Asian tsunami and the earthquake in Pakistan. Still, he remained mindful of his priorities, which also included reducing the world's nic-

otine dependence. He hoped to accomplish this by increasing the number of smoke-free areas in the world and by advocating for an anti-tobacco treaty that would increase taxes on tobacco products, which would, in turn, encourage more people to refrain from smoking.

He also kept sight of the Millennium Development Goals established in the year 2000 by the U.N. These included reduction of global childhood malnutrition by 50 percent as well as a decrease in the percentage of the world's population forced to subsist on a one-dollar-per day existence. Specifically, he hoped to see the number reduced to 15 percent by 2015.

In addition, his plans included increasing the agency's global relevance, something he hoped to achieve by directing 75 percent of WHO's resources toward regional and national application. To do this, he implemented several new programs including one called the Epidemic Intelligence Service, where epidemiologists were trained to fight localized disease outbreaks and help developing countries battle the AIDS and Ebola viruses. He based the program on one established by the U.S. Government's Centers for Disease Control and Prevention.

During his tenure, Lee released several landmark publications, including the annual World Health Reports, which were intended to generate strong response to the major health challenges facing the world. These challenges included the AIDS treatment gap, the burden of suffering and death faced by pregnant women and children, the healthcare workforce crisis present in poor countries, and healthcare as it related to issues of peace and human security.

Overall, Lee assumed a forward-thinking approach with a vision that addressed potential, and even inevitable, problems. In the absence of such a futuristic approach, he believed, the world would face an eventual "day of reckoning." He firmly believed that concrete steps could be taken to ensure the welfare of new generations. One of these steps involved universal access to treatment.

Died Suddenly After Suffering a Stroke

Lee had a worldview that was compassionate and empathetic, but unfortunately he did not see his efforts come to fruition. He died suddenly and unexpectedly on May 22, 2006, in Geneva, at the U.N.'s European headquarters. His death occurred during the first day of the World Health Assembly, the annual conference for WHO members. Two days earlier he had suffered a stroke while attending an assembly function. He died after undergoing surgery for a blood clot in the brain. He was 61 years old and had served three years of his five-year term as WHO's director-general.

During the assembly's opening session, attendees observed a two-minute silence while flags flew at half mast. His funeral was held May 24 in Geneva. More than a thousand people attended. Eulogies were given by his son, Tadahiro, by his top aide, William Kean, and by Rhyu Simin, minister of health of Lee's native Korea.

Friends and colleagues recalled Lee as a friendly man who possessed an endearing, self-deprecating wit and a quirky sense of humor that often put people at ease, a characteristic that had often proved useful in diffusing tense situations. He reportedly he had a wide range of intellectual interests and a voracious appetite for knowledge. A multi-linguist, he spoke Korean, English, French, and Japanese. He enjoyed classical music, the theater, Shakespeare's plays, and other examples of great literature.

Lee was survived by his wife and son, and by two brothers and one sister.

Periodicals

Honolulu Advertiser, May 25, 2006.
Newsletter of the Pan American Health Organization, August 2006.
Newsmakers, Issue 1, Thomson Gale, 2005.
The Scotsman, May 24, 2006.
Time, April 26, 2004.

Online

"Dr. Lee Jong-wook: Biography," *World Health Organization,* http://www.who.int/dg/lee/biography/en/index.html (December 21, 2006).
"A tribute to Dr Lee Jong-wook, Director-General of WHO," *World Health Organization,* http://www.who.int/dg/lee/tribute/en/index.html (December 21, 2006). □

Stanislaw Lem

With the possible exception of France's Jules Verne, Polish author Stanislaw Lem (1921–2006) has been the best-known science fiction writer to work in a language other than English. His books have been translated into more than 40 languages, with total sales estimated at some 27 million copies by 2006.

L em's highly philosophical novels were quite different in style and content from the largely adventure-oriented science fiction popular in the West, most of which he mercilessly disparaged; the Science Fiction Writers' Association in the United States revoked his honorary membership in a celebrated 1976 incident. His writing, often grim but leavened by dry humor, was shaped by influences specific to the time and place in which he lived. Yet Lem's popularity was truly international. At the height of the Cold War he commanded a large readership in both the United States and the Soviet Union, and his single best-known work, the 1961 novel *Solaris,* was filmed by both countries. His work was generally readable and entertaining, and he told Peter Swirski, in an interview published in *A Stanislaw Lem Reader,* "I am a staunch adherent to the maxim that literature, much as philosophy, should never bore its readers to death."

Father Escaped Execution

Stanislaw Lem was born in the Polish city of Lvov (now Lviv, Ukraine) on September 12, 1921. His family was of Jewish background, although Lem himself was never religiously observant. One theme that marked his writing was

that of the arbitrariness of life. Lem himself wrote in his memoir *Highcastle* that "I really don't know when it was that I first experienced the surprise that I existed, surprise accompanied by a touch of fear that I could just as easily have not existed, or been a stick, or a dandelion, or a goat's leg, or a snail." Perhaps that attitude was rooted in Lem's own experiences and those of his family as they lived through the terrible upheavals of Europe in the twentieth century. Before Lem was born, his father was nearly executed by a firing squad (he was saved by the last-minute intervention of a friend), and Lem himself had brushes with death during World War II.

After things settled down in newly independent Poland, however, the Lem family prospered. Lem's father was an otolaryngologist, and his son was fascinated by the drawings in his medical books. "Each volume [of a German otolaryngology handbook] had no fewer than a thousand glossy pages," Lem wrote in *Highcastle.* "There I could look at heads cut open in various ways, innumerable ways, the whole machinery drawn and colored with the utmost precision." Lem developed a knack for detailed scientific description and combined it with a rich fantasy life—he was not an especially happy child, and he wrote that "as a young boy I certainly terrorized those around me." He enjoyed reading, and early in life he encountered the writings of science fiction pioneers H.G. Wells and Jules Verne.

In 1939 Lem graduated from secondary school in Lvov and enrolled at the Lvov Medical Institute just as Soviet troops overran the city in the early days of World War II. The city soon fell to the German army, placing Lem and his family in grave danger. They pulled strings and obtained forged documents that did not identify them as Jewish, enabling them to remain in the city. His medical education put on hold, Lem worked as an auto mechanic; he soon learned, as he was quoted as saying in the *Times* of London, "to damage German vehicles in such a way that it wouldn't immediately be discovered." He later worked as a welder in a German-owned scrap yard. Lem was active in Poland's Jewish anti-Nazi resistance, smuggling arms into the Krakow ghetto from which he eventually saw most of his Jewish friends deported to their deaths. In 1944, after the Soviets displaced the Germans from Lvov, he resumed his medical classes.

In 1946, with Lvov having been absorbed into the Soviet Union, he moved to Krakow, Poland, which remained his home for much of the rest of his life. Lem worked slowly toward a medical degree at the Jagiellonian University in Krakow, but his family had lost all of its property during the war, and he was essentially penniless. To make ends meet he began to write pulp fiction for magazines and poetry for a Catholic weekly newspaper. Among his friends was Karol Wojtyla, later Pope John Paul II. Lem finished his studies in 1948 but intentionally flunked his final exams because he realized that he would likely be conscripted as a military doctor if he passed. He was also dismayed by the ideological control over the sciences that the Soviet Union was beginning to exert in Poland.

Worked in Socialist Realist Genre

That decision left writing as Lem's most promising career option. At first he tried to adapt himself to the tenets of Socialist Realism, the officially improved style of the Communist world, with realistic, optimistic plots in which science and industry ultimately work for the good of the people. He repeatedly rewrote his novel *Szpital Przemieniena* (Hospital of the Transfiguration) in an attempt to please Polish censors. In 1951, almost by accident, Lem turned to science fiction. After a casual discussion with a publishing official about the lack of science fiction in Polish, he received a book contract in the mail, with a blank space for the title. He filled in the blank with "Astronauci" ("Astronauts") and quickly delivered the promised manuscript. With his fortunes on the rise, Lem married Barbara Leszniak, a radiologist, in 1953. In 1968 the two had a son, Tomasz, who later became curator of a website devoted to Lem's works.

In later life Lem spoke negatively about *Astronauts* and his other early novels like *Oblok Magellana* (The Magellan Nebula, 1955), but these books gained him a wide readership in Poland. *Czas nieutracony* (Time Not Lost) dealt with life in Nazi-occupied Poland. Lem found that literary authorities considered science fiction a trivial genre and exercised less oversight when it came to his works in that genre. After the Soviet Union repressed a revolt by Hungarian reformers in 1956, Lem began to write science fiction prolifically. He never explicitly positioned himself as a dissident with respect to Poland's Communist regime, but

some of his works had a satirical streak that might have caused him trouble in any genre other than science fiction.

Iskry (Eden, 1959) was one of Lem's first fully characteristic novels, built on the science fiction convention of a spaceship crew discovering a remote and mysterious planet, but emerging in the end as skeptical about the possibility of human communication with cultures whose technology might differ fundamentally from that found on earth. Two years later Lem published *Solaris,* which remains his best-known work. *Solaris,* again, was outwardly a science fiction adventure: the inhabitants of a space station encounter a mostly water-covered planet whose ocean seems to have intelligent properties. As the crew tries to communicate with this radically different life form and then attacks it in frustration, a bewildering disaster occurs: the ocean creates physical manifestations of their deepest fears. *Solaris* was filmed by Soviet director Andrei Tarkovsky in 1972, and an American version directed by Steven Soderbergh was filmed in 2002, with actor George Clooney in the lead role.

Other Lem novels and stories also featured space explorers as protagonists, although Lem often introduced a note of satire and a psychological edge that left the reader quite distant from triumphant *Star Trek* territory in the end. His writings featured two recurring characters. The adventures of astronaut Ijon Tichy (who appeared in *Dzienniki Gwiazdowe* (Star Diaries and Memoirs of a Space Traveler, 1971) commented either directly or indirectly on the militarism and bureaucracy of Earth's own societies. Nathan M. Powers wrote on the Modern Word website that "Tichy lives in a universe teeming with life, where humanity jostles shoulders with creatures bizarre and grotesque, yet somehow always familiar, for this is a world where humanity's flaws and virtues are writ large across the stars. These stories may be read as sharp social satire, depicting the bizarre customs of other places to drive home surprising points about our own; they have been aptly compared to the philosophical fictions of Swift and Voltaire."

Pirx the Pilot, who appeared in a series of Lem's short stories, was an ordinary man living in a world that science had made bizarre. Lem in the Pirx stories, unlike other science fiction authors, accurately described the dullness as well as the psychological challenges that would face an interplanetary traveler, and his writings generally extrapolated from firm groundings in scientific fact. One of the Ijon Tichy novels, *Pokoj na ziemi* (Peace on Earth, 1987) fused satirical themes with up-to-the minute science: Earth has temporarily rid itself of war by setting machines loose on the Moon to fight battles in which no humans are hurt, but soon the Earth is threatened with invasion from its own now-malevolent lunar machines. Tichy is sent to the moon to investigate, but he is subjected to a procedure in which the right hemisphere of his brain is disconnected from the left, leaving him unable to speak.

Wrote Experimental Works

Many of Lem's writings pushed the imagination of the reader to its limits in the worlds they conjured, and he wrote some works that fell into the experimental category even as they retained a strain of humor. *Cyberiada* (The Cyberiad,

1965) features traveling robots as its central characters; humans are present only as minor characters who are disliked by the robots for their mushy consistency. *Bezsennosc* (1971, translated as *The Futurological Congress*) depicts an Earth transformed by the introduction of mind-altering drugs into the atmosphere; the hero, Tichy, cannot separate reality from a texture of interlocking mass hallucinations.

Some of Lem's books abandoned science fiction altogether; *Doskonala proznia* (1971, translated as *A Perfect Vacuum*) consisted of a set of reviews of nonexistent books written at some point in the future. (In several books Lem seemed to anticipate the "information overload" that would become a feature of the Internet age.) He also wrote nonfiction science commentaries such as *Summa technologiae* (1964), a play, literary essays, and magazine articles. Lem remained prolific for several decades; some two dozen of his books were translated into English (mostly by American writer Michael Kandel directly from Polish, but some from German or French editions of Lem's work), but many others remain available only in Polish or other languages.

Lem moved briefly to Austria after the Polish government cracked down on the Solidarity labor union in the early 1980s, but he soon returned to Krakow. He did not write fiction for some years after the dissolution of Communist rule in Eastern Europe in 1989, but remained in good health and continued to lead an active literary life. Although he had never used his pen to attack one-party rule directly, it seemed that the experience of living under totalitarianism had inspired his work at some level. Both before and after the fall of Communism, however, Lem was paraded by the Polish State as a kind of national culture hero, and he was given the Polish State Prize for Literature in 1976. Lem's writings of the 1990s remain mostly untranslated. He died in Krakow on March 27, 2006.

Books

Davis, J. Madison, *Stanislaw Lem,* Starmont, 1990.
Lem, Stanislaw, *Highcastle: A Remembrance,* Harcourt Brace, 1995.
St. James Guide to Science Fiction Writers, 4th ed., St. James, 1996.
Swirsky, Peter, *A Stanislaw Lem Reader,* Northwestern University Press, 1997.

Periodicals

Daily Telegraph (London, England), March 30, 2006.
Independent (London, England), March 31, 2006.
New York Times, March 28, 2006.
Time, September 17, 1984.
Times (London, England), March 28, 2006.
Weekly Standard, April 10, 2006.

Online

Contemporary Authors Online, Gale, 2006, reproduced in Biography Resource Center, Farmington Hills, Mich.: Thomson Gale, 2006. http://www.galenet.galegroup.com/servlet/BioRC (November 6, 2006), 2006.
"Lem About Himself," Official Stanislaw Lem Website, http://www.lem.pl (November 6, 2006).
"Stanislaw Lem," http://www.kirjasto.sci.fi/slem.htm (November 6, 2006).
"The Time of Cruel Miracles," The Modern Word, http://www.themodernword.com/scriptorium/lem.html (November 6, 2006). □

William Arthur Lewis

Sir William Arthur Lewis (1915–1991), born on the Caribbean island of St. Lucia, virtually founded the entire discipline of development economics.

Entering the field of economics when blacks were normally barred from that academic profession, Lewis broke one barrier after another by dint of sheer brilliance. He was the first black professor in Britain's university system, and later the first one at Princeton University in the United States. The Nobel Prize he received in 1979 was the first given to a person of African descent in a field other than literature or peace. Lewis added the voice of a colonial subject to British government policy in his early years, and later in his life he tried to apply his ideas about economic development with on-the-ground consulting posts in Africa. He helped to build the modern university that united the newly independent countries of the Caribbean, and from his socialist youth to his moderate old age he remained a believer in the ideals of Western democracy.

Homeschooling Accelerated Education

The child of two schoolteachers and the fourth of five sons, William Arthur Lewis was born on January 23, 1915, in the small city of Castries, St. Lucia, then part of the British West Indies. (He used the name W. Arthur Lewis professionally.) His parents had emigrated to St. Lucia from Antigua, partly because they believed that their children could get a better education in the British-dominated schools of their new home. When he was seven, Lewis contracted an illness that required him to stay home from school for several weeks. His father took over his education during his convalescence, and when the boy returned to school, he had learned as much in three months as his fellow students were scheduled to cover over the next two years. Lewis was promoted two grades forward and grew up a bookish child with a sense of physical inferiority.

He was also obviously talented academically, as were his siblings—one became a psychiatrist, and two others were top government officials in St. Lucia. Lewis finished school at 14 but had to work in a government office for two years because he was too young to compete for a scholarship to attend a British university. In 1932, when he finally did enter the competition, he won, and set sail the following year to attend the London School of Economics. His aim at the time was to study business administration (management) and prepare himself for a position in private industry or in St. Lucia's colonial government.

Blacks were rare in London at the time. Lewis wrote little about his experiences there, but other Caribbean writers who arrived in England in the 1930s have described strong racial prejudice. Lewis made a trip to Denmark and wrote, according to Robert L. Tignor in *W. Arthur Lewis and the Birth of Development Economics,* that in place "of the supercilious stare which you got in London, Cardiff, or any of the seaport towns of Britain, you get a smile of welcome." Lewis, studious by nature and nurture, immersed himself in his classes and found himself drawn to the study of economics in particular. He recalled in a lecture given when he received the Nobel Prize that "I had no idea in 1933 what economics was," but he found himself fascinated by such questions as why some countries were rich and others poor, and why steel was expensive but coffee cheap.

Lewis joined the League of Coloured Peoples, a group of black intelligentsia, and began to write articles for its publication, *The Keys.* He was socialist in orientation and believed that the progress of civilization offered the hope of racial equality. Even early in his career, Lewis was mistrustful of radical viewpoints, particularly those of the Soviet Union, which at the time was held up as a model society by both black and white thinkers of Britain's far left. Lewis graduated from the London School of Economics in 1937 with first class honors and continued on for a Ph.D. in industrial economics. He received that degree in 1940 and worked as a lecturer at the school, and then was given a four-year teaching contract, staying out of World War II due to physical problems.

Refused to Accept Racial Slight

Lewis received glowing recommendations from his mentors, but his application to join the faculty of the University of Liverpool was turned down on what appeared to be racial grounds. He was invited to make several visits so that he could make the acquaintance of people in Liverpool's university and business communities, but declined, writing (according to Tignor) that he did not relish visiting "so that the public may be able to look at me and decide whether they can stand my appearance." Instead, he was hired at the University of Manchester in 1948, becoming Britain's first black university professor. He had married a Grenadian woman, Gladys Jacobs, the year before. The couple raised two daughters and remained together despite what would soon turn into a globetrotting career on Lewis's part.

Lewis's first area of specialty (other than industrial economics, which he abandoned upon joining Manchester's faculty) was the history of the world economy, which he began to study while he was still at the London School of Economics. The school's acting economics department chairman, Frederick Hayek, suggested that Lewis teach a course on the economics of the period between World War I and World War II. "I replied to Hayek that I did not know what happened between the wars; to which he replied that the best way of learning a subject was to teach it," Lewis recalled in his Nobel Prize speech. The result was the first in an influential series of 12 books by Lewis; *Economic Survey, 1919–38* was published in London in 1949.

At the time, although he had begun to read widely in economic history, Lewis had no special expertise in the economics of the developing world. The topic was not a part of formal economics curricula at the time, for what was called the developing world had until the post–World War

II years been largely under European colonial control. But Lewis was motivated by demographic changes in British education to try to investigate the economic lives of people in the former colonies. "It was the throng of Asian and African students at Manchester that set me lecturing systematically on development economics from about 1950, following Hayek's rule that the way to learn is to teach," he said in his Nobel Prize autobiography.

Lewis believed that several conditions were necessary in order for industrial development to come to an agrarian society. But one, which he called unlimited supplies of labor, was key. The Industrial Revolution in England, he reasoned, had depended upon the existence of a large class of unemployed farm laborers, themselves the product of changes and new efficiencies in British agriculture. Developing economies, Lewis reasoned, worked the same way; the profits of industrial companies rose while wages remained depressed. Lewis's model explained persistent poverty in the developing world, and he also investigated trade between wealthy and poor countries, using the model of trade involving coffee and steel that had fascinated him when he began to study economics.

Pioneered Field of Development Economics

Lewis summarized his ideas in 1954 in a short article, "Economic Development with Unlimited Supplies of Labour," which was published in a journal called *Manchester School.* He expanded on his thesis in a book, *The Theory of Economic Growth,* which appeared the following year. The original article, noted Tignor, was "short, well written, easy to understand, original, and self-evident, at least to nonspecialists." For economists it was even more: it broke new ground in a field that had been little studied, and it provided hypotheses that could be modeled and tested. Lewis had supporters and detractors in the years after the article appeared, but no one doubted its influence. It was for his 1954 article that Lewis received the Nobel Prize in 1979.

Remaining at Manchester until 1958, Lewis also worked with several governments in the developing world in an attempt to put his ideas into practice. His most prominent post was as an adviser to Ghana's prime minister, Kwame Nkrumah, for a two-year stint shortly after Ghana gained its independence in 1957. Lewis found his prudent plans overruled as factional conflicts began to come to the fore in Ghana, and he finally resigned, writing to a friend (as quoted by Tignor) that "I have taken nearly as much as I can stand. In the first place, the Prime Minister has messed up the Development Plan by insisting on spending lavishly on unnecessary projects, mostly in Accra [Ghana's capital], and by pushing up the total to an unrealistic level." Lewis then moved back to the Caribbean to become principal (president) of University College at the University of the West Indies in Jamaica in 1959. In 1962 and 1963 he also served as vice chancellor of the university.

The University of the West Indies, a cooperative project among several of the Caribbean's small island nations, grew during Lewis's tenure there, with enrollment increasing from about 700 to over 2,000 students. He established a new engineering school and obtained funding for it from international agencies. Once again, however, Lewis was frustrated by bureaucratic infighting, this time among the university's national sponsors. Suffering from stomach ulcers, he wrote (according to Tignor) to Princess Alice, the university's chancellor, that his condition was caused by "excessive stress and strain on this job for which I am ill-fitted by temperament. I take things too seriously, worry too much, and cannot stand the strain. I must therefore resign."

Knighted by Queen Elizabeth II in 1963, Lewis took a post that year teaching at Princeton University in New Jersey. He remained there for the rest of his life, writing several more books about development and the world economy. In the late 1960s Lewis served as mentor to younger black scholars but was critical of the movement toward African-American militancy. He opposed the creation of black studies departments, but backed the inclusion of African-centered materials in the university curriculum. The black student, he wrote (as quoted by Tignor), should study "engineering, medicine, chemistry, economics, law, agriculture, and other subjects, which are going to be of value to him and his people. And let the clever whites go to college to read black novels, to read Swahili, and to record the exploits of Negro heroes of the past. They are the ones to whom this will come as an eye-opener." From 1971 to 1973 Lewis took a leave from Princeton to serve as the first president of the Caribbean Development Bank.

An anthology of Lewis's works, *Selected Economic Writings of W. Arthur Lewis*, appeared in 1983. In 1985 he made a visit to St. Lucia, where the Morne Educational Complex was renamed the Sir Arthur Lewis Community College. Lewis retired to a home in Barbados, where he died on June 15, 1991. His body was flown back to St. Lucia and buried there.

Books

Tignor, Robert L. *W. Arthur Lewis and the Birth of Development Economics,* Princeton University Press, 2006.

Periodicals

Jet, November 20, 2000.
Times (London, England), June 17, 1991.

Online

Contemporary Authors Online, Gale, 2007, reproduced in *Biography Resource Center,* Thomson Gale, 2007, http://www.galenet.galegroup.com/servlet/BioRC (January 24, 2007).
"Sir Arthur Lewis: Autobiography," Nobel Prize Committee, http://nobelprize.org (January 24, 2007).
"Sir Arthur Lewis, 1915–1991," http:www.stlucianobellaureates.org/arthur_lewis.htm (January 24, 2007). □

Alan Lomax

No individual has done as much to catalog and preserve traditional American music as American folklorist Alan Lomax (1915–2002). A folklorist, pub-

lisher, author, and part-time musician, Lomax was a driving force in the folk and blues boom of the 1950s and 1960s, and helped the world discover such artists as Leadbelly, Pete Seeger, and Muddy Waters.

If ever a man was born into the field of folklore and musicology, it was Lomax. Born January 31, 1915, in Austin, Texas, he was the son of John Avery Lomax, a onetime banker who became the preeminent collector of cowboy songs and Southwestern American folklore. Growing up in Texas, the younger Lomax listened to his father's many findings and became a confirmed advocate of America's true music. Along with his brother John, Jr., and sisters Bess and Elizabeth, young Alan often acted as an assistant, and learned his trade firsthand on many expeditions with his father. In a 1960 article for *HiFi/Stereo Review,* reproduced in Rounder's 1997 edition of *The Alan Lomax Sampler Collection,* Lomax wrote about his first major Library of Congress trip with his father. "In the summer of 1933, Thomas A. Edison's widow gave my father an old-fashioned Edison cylinder machine so that he might record Negro tunes for a forthcoming book of American ballads," he wrote. "For us, this instrument was a way of taking down tunes quickly and accurately; but to the singers themselves, the squeaky, scratchy voice that emerged from the speaking tube meant that they had made communicative contact with a bigger world than their own."

Eventually, the Library of Congress supplied the Lomaxes with a state-of-the-art disc-cutting recorder that was mounted in the back of his father's Model T-Ford. Armed with camping gear, cots, and cooking utensils, father and son covered 16,000 miles of a southeastern section of the United States in four months. The result of this hardscrabble music archaeology was the songs they gathered for the 1934 book *American Ballads and Folk Songs.* Subsequently, the Lomax family moved to Washington, D.C., so John Lomax could work full-time for the Library of Congress. Meanwhile, Alan attended one year of college at Harvard before transferring to the University of Texas where he earned his degree in philosophy in 1936. Upon graduation, he was appointed to head the Archive of American Folk Song, which he and his father helped establish at the Library of Congress, before he and his wife left on their honeymoon to do field research in Haiti. Later that year, he joined his father—now the honorary curator for the Library of Congress—as the first federally funded employee of that government office.

Working ceaselessly, the Lomaxes put out more song collections in the ensuing years, including the revised edition of *Cowboy Songs and Other Frontier Ballads* (1938), *Negro Folk Songs as Sung by Leadbelly* (1936), *Our Singing Country* (1941), and *Folk Song: U.S.A.* (1947). Together, the father-son duo changed the popular perception of folk music from archival nostalgia to a living expression of the common man and contemporary culture. In the process, they unearthed musical artists who would change the sonic landscape of the nation.

Aided Leadbelly, Woody Guthrie, and Pete Seeger

Alan Lomax was with his father when he discovered legendary blues singer and guitarist Huddie Ledbetter, better known as Leadbelly, at Angola Prison in Texas. Ledbetter, who was serving time for murder, had always claimed he killed in self-defense, and the Lomaxes championed his cause. Among the seven songs they recorded by the fabled black artist upon their first meeting was an early rendition of a song that would eventually become an American standard, "Goodnight Irene." John Lomax was instrumental in securing the singer's release from prison and the whole family knew the singer well. Indeed, Leadbelly even taught young Alan, with whom he developed a genuine rapport, licks on his trademark 12-string guitar. Acting as co-managers, the Lomaxes introduced Leadbelly to other folk scholars, enthusiastic college audiences, and the mainstream music world, creating an interest in the performer and his songs that continues to this day. Moreover, their book about the singer's life and music, *Negro Folk Songs as Sung by Leadbelly,* was the first published biography specifically about a folk performer.

When the elder Lomax decided he could no longer tolerate the volatile singer's antics, he severed their association with Leadbelly. However, much to his father's dismay, Alan Lomax continued a friendly relationship with the seminal folk star, and continued recording the singer on his trusty disc-cutting machine for the Library of Congress. He also temporarily dropped out of the Columbia graduate program to raise bond money when the troubled star was arrested on

assault charges, and arranged for him to be signed by independent MusicCraft label, and acted in an advisory capacity until the singer's death.

Lomax was important to other emerging performers as well, including jazz pianist Jelly Roll Morton, bluesman Josh White, and the granddaddy of American folksingers Pete Seeger. Through Lomax, Seeger also met Woody Guthrie, with whom he played under many different circumstances. Yet, it was Lomax who figured strongly in the revival of Guthrie's flagging career. Besides encouraging the hardluck performer to recommit to writing and getting him to record his works for the Library of Congress, Lomax featured him on a primetime CBS radio program he produced, *Back Where I Come From.* Years later, Lomax observed that the best years of his life were spent working with Guthrie and Leadbelly.

Whether serving as producer, writer, or singing host, radio proved an important educational tool for Lomax. Some projects, such as CBS's *School of the Air,* where he attempted to have folk music orchestrated and played like a symphony, simply did not work. Others like *American Folk Songs, Wellsprings of Music,* and the live *Midnight Special* broadcasts from Town Hall were successful in communicating what was special about folk and blues music to mass audiences. These shows also provided valuable exposure for such artists as Guthrie, Seeger, Leadbelly, White, the Golden Gate Quartet, and up-and-coming folk revivalist Burl Ives. However, such high profile projects did not quell his compulsive need to go out into the field and seek new recordings.

Traveling with Fisk University musicologist John Work, Lomax made a famous trek into the Deep South in 1941 and 1942, where he documented the music and stories of the fife and drum bluesmen, and conducted the first recordings and interviews with McKinley Morganfield, better known as Muddy Waters. In his 1993 book *The Land Where Blues Began,* Lomax described the sessions that would kick-start the singer's highly influential career. "I remember thinking how low-key Morganfield was, grave even to the point of shyness," he wrote. "But I was bowled over by his artistry. There was nothing uncertain about his performances. He sang and played with such finesse, with such a mercurial and sensitive bond between voice and guitar, and he expressed so much tenderness in the way he handled his lyrics, that he went right beyond all his predecessors—Blind Lemon, Charley Patton, Robert Johnson, Son House, and Willie Brown." Although he was responsible for first fixing national attention on the bluesman, Lomax did not see Muddy Waters again for another ten years. When they met the former cotton chopper was driving a Cadillac, while Lomax was still driving an old Ford.

Innovated and Educated

When the Library of Congress decided they could no longer fund Lomax's expeditions, which were mostly done on a shoestring budget, he left them in 1943. Joining the army, he served in the Office of War Information and with the Army's Special Services until the end of World War II. As a civilian, he picked up where he left off, exploring the origins of the blues with Sonny Boy Williamson, Memphis Slim, and Big Bill Broonzey, and later hosting a folk music series *On Top of Old Smokey* for the Mutual Network in 1948. More importantly, he fed the fires of the burgeoning folk music revival by signing on as the director of folk music at Decca Records. From 1951 to 1957, he served as the editor for the Columbia Records World Library of Folk and Primitive Music. Yet, he spent most of the 1950s in Great Britain, where he began his hunt for the folk music of the British Isles, eventually releasing his findings on the ten-disc set *Folksongs of Great Britain* (1961).

When he returned to the United states, Lomax revisited the Deep South where he continued documenting African-American culture. Along the way, he also rediscovered bluesman Mississippi Fred McDowell, who quickly became the darling of emerging rockers around the world. Like his father before him, Lomax was in demand as a lecturer and visiting scholar, but he also received occasional offers to record as an artist in his own right. However, the albums that featured his voice and guitar for Tradition (1958) and Kapp Records (1963) received mixed reviews at best.

Funded by numerous grants Lomax continued to travel the world, documenting music in Spain, Africa, France, the Caribbean, the West Indies, and various prisons around the world. The results of these trips have been steadily released by the Rounder label in what may be a series of 100 plus albums. In 1966, he began dabbling in film and accumulated enough footage to fill several documentary films, including the 1990 PBS series *America Patchwork*. Always innovative and forward thinking, he proposed the idea for the Global Jukebox, an interconnected database of music and dance cultures from all over world, so that people may more easily study them. Unfortunately, the idea, which is being carried on by the Association for Cultural Equity, was nearly stopped cold when Lomax suffered two strokes at the age of 80. Yet, working with his daughter Anna, he was somehow able to continue his many works until his 2002 death. In 2004, PBS told the story of some of his extensive travels with their documentary *Lomax the Song Hunter*.

Despite the many accolades and awards Lomax received during his lengthy career, he had his detractors as well. Respected rock writer Dave Marsh is among the critics of Lomax's methods. Responding to the glowing New York Times postmortem tribute by Jon Pareles, Marsh, wrote in *Counterpunch*, "As a veteran blues observer wrote me, 'Don't get too caught up in grieving for Alan Lomax. For every fine musical contribution that he made, there was an evil venal manipulation of copyright, publishing, and ownership of the collected material.' "

Like many publishers, promoters, agents, and even disc jockeys of his time, Lomax did impose his publishing imprint on a great many public domain songs. However, when a published song made money, Lomax proudly tracked down the writer in question and paid the royalties— something few of his contemporaries did. Further, the thousands of performers he captured on recordings would have never gotten a chance to share their culture and songs if he had not sought them out.

In a 1991 interview with Charles Kuralt, an audio snippet of which appeared on the 1997 Rounder release *The Alan Lomax Collection Sampler*, Lomax spoke of his work and how it changed the lives of the many artists he recorded. "The incredible thing was, when you could play this material back to the people, it changed everything for them. They realized that their stuff and they were just as good as anybody else. Then I found out that what I was really doing—and what my father was really doing—was giving an avenue for these people to express themselves and their side of the story."

Books

Axelrod, Alan and Harry Oster, with Winton Rawls, *The Penguin Dictionary of American Folklore,* Penguin Reference, 2000.

Lomax, Alan, *The Land Where the Blues Began,* Pantheon Books, 1993.

Stambler, Irwin and Lyndon Stambler, *Folk and Blues: The Encyclopedia,* 3rd ed., St. Martin's Press, 2001.

Wolfe, Charles and Kip Lornell, *The Life and Legend of Leadbelly,* DaCapo Press, 1999.

Online

"Alan Lomax," *All Movie Guide,* http://www.allmovie.com/ (January 1, 2007).

"Alan Lomax," *All Music Guide,* http://www.allmusic.com/ (January 1, 2007).

"Alan Lomax," *American Folklife Center,* http://www.loc.gov/folklife/lomax.html (January 1, 2007).

"Alan Lomax," *Association for Cultural Equity,* http://www.culturalequity.org/alanlomax/bio.html (January 1, 2007).

"Alan Lomax," *Contemporary Authors Online,* http://galenet.galegroup.com/servlet/BioRC (January 1, 2007).

"An Interview with Pete Seeger by David Kupfer," *Whole Earth,* http://www.wholeearthmag.com/ArticleBin/406.html (January 1, 2007).

Marsh, Dave, "Mr. Big Stuff—Alan Lomax: Great White Hunter or Thief, Plagiarist and Bigot?" *Counterpunch,* http://www.counterpunch.org/marsh0721.html (January 1, 2007).

Other

The Alan Lomax Collection Sampler, Rounder, 1997. □

Luiz Inácio Lula da Silva

Luiz Inácio Lula da Silva (born 1945), known as Lula, steered a middle course between helping his country's poor and stabilizing the country economically after his election as Brazil's president in 2002.

L ula came to the presidency from a labor union background, and he won the presidency partly through populist appeals. Yet the first part of his presidency was not marked by the turn to the political left undertaken by his Venezuelan counterpart, Hugo Chávez. Lula expanded government antipoverty programs while maintaining stability in Brazil's financial relationships with the rest of the world. He

was seen as a new breed of Latin American leader who worked around the intense polarization between left and right that had characterized the region's politics. But Brazil, under Lula, still faced major economic challenges.

Shined Shoes

Lula was born Luiz Inácio da Silva on October 27, 1945, in Garanhuns, in the state of Pernambuco in Brazil's historically poverty-ridden northeast. Lula was a nickname that he legally incorporated into his full name after political followers began to use the nickname. He was the seventh of eight children in a very poor family that moved around looking for work and often separated. His father, Aristedes, worked for several years at the port of Santos on the Atlantic coast, and Lula did not meet him for the first time until he was five. In 1952 the family moved to Guarujá, on the coast of the state of São Paulo, traveling for 13 days in the back of a truck. Contributing to the family income by shining shoes and selling peanuts on the streets, Lula had a spotty education and did not learn to read until he was 10.

A year after that, Lula's parents divorced, and he moved with his mother to the metropolis of São Paulo. By 12 he had a job at a dry cleaning shop, and by 14 he was working in a warehouse. He did factory work throughout his teens, losing the little finger of his left hand in an industrial accident. He later moved to the Marte Screw Factory and was able to enroll in a three-year government metalworking course that qualified him for the skilled jobs of mechanic and lathe operator. With Brazil under the military dictator-

ship of General Humberto Castelo Branco, Lula joined the Metalworkers' Union but had little interest in politics.

Lula's path to political power started in Brazil's trade union movement. In 1969, in mourning over the death of his first wife, Maria, during childbirth, he was urged by his union-activist brother to run for a low-level post in the local group of the Metalworkers' Union. He won, and immediately showed a talent for organizing and for negotiating with factory owners. Reelected in 1972 to the local post, by 1975 he became the president of a union organization of more than 100,000 workers. Lula fathered a child in 1972 and then married Marisa Leticia Casa in 1974. Bringing one child each to the marriage, they raised five children in all.

By the late 1970s Lula was still not a member of any political party, but he began to enter the sphere of national events as he sought to influence government labor policies. Labor unions under Brazil's dictatorship had been mostly government-sponsored organizations, but Lula was one of a group of leaders who led them toward greater advocacy for workers' rights and welfare. Police actions against a 1979 metalworkers' strike hardened his resolve and made him consider the creation of a labor-oriented political party. Government repression of independent political activities was slowly being lifted, and on March 10, 1980, Lula, along with a group of union activists, intellectuals, and social reformers, announced the formation of the Partido dos Trabalhadores, or Workers' Party. By 1982 the party had some 400,000 members, and Lula ran for the governorship of the state of São Paulo. He was unsuccessful, but the party won seats in Brazil's Chamber of Deputies. In 1986, Lula won the election to the Chamber of Deputies with the largest vote total in all of Brazil, and he emerged as a figure of national significance.

Party Moderated Stands

In the beginning, the Workers' Party had a far-left orientation that included Communist elements, but it gradually grew more moderate as Lula and its other leaders attempted to forge national coalitions with stands that approximated those of European social democratic parties. Until Lula's election, however, his anti-American stands were pronounced. In 1989 Lula ran as the presidential candidate of the Workers' Party in the first direct presidential election held in Brazil since 1960. He lost narrowly in a runoff, but Workers' Party representation increased sharply in the elections for the Chamber of Deputies the following year.

In the 1990s Lula ran twice more for president, losing by substantial margins in 1994 and 1998 to Fernando Henrique Cardoso of the centrist Brazilian Democratic Movement Party. But the decade was no electoral wasteland for the Workers' Party, which increased its representation in the Chamber of Deputies in every election between 1982 and 2002. Lula devoted himself to the building of a viable national party organization, working tirelessly to elect candidates at all levels, from the Brazilian Senate all the way down to local mayoral offices. "The left can never dispense with popular organization," he observed to Paulo de Mesquita Neto of the North American Congress on Latin America. "It is the most important thing for a party of the left. The PT neglected it for some time and now we have to make up for lost time.'' From 1980 to 1995 he was the national president of the Workers' Party, relinquishing that position to head a liberal think tank called the Instituto Cidadania, or Citizenship Institute, that had among its goals the enfranchisement and full participation of all Brazilians in the political process.

In 2002 Lula ran for the Brazilian presidency once again, with Cardoso's hand-picked successor, José Serra, as his main opponent. Capitalizing on widespread disenchantment with Cardoso's free-market policies, which had brought prosperity to Brazil's business sector but failed to dent the country's substantial social problems, Lula ran a shrewd campaign in which he called for increased government spending while also cultivating allies in the business community. The centerpiece of his effort was a pledge to end hunger in Brazil during his first term. Defeating Serra by a margin of 61 to 39 percent in an October runoff, Lula led the Workers' Party to its best showing ever; it became the single largest bloc in the Chamber of Deputies. Upon taking office he said that if he could make it possible for all Brazilians to eat breakfast, lunch, and dinner, he would have fulfilled his life's mission.

Keen international attention was focused on the first months of Lula's term, as governments and foreign investors tried to determine whether he would follow the leftist course of Venezuelan president Hugo Chávez or steer in a centrist direction. The results they observed were mixed, and were signaled by twin trips at the beginning of his terms to the World Economic Forum in Davos, Switzerland, and to the antiglobalization World Social Forum meeting in Brazil. Aided by growing markets for Brazilian exports, notably in China, Lula registered trade surpluses, a favorable sign from the point of view of the International Monetary Fund. Domestic budgets remained under control, and Brazil's notoriously high inflation rate dropped from 12.5 percent in 2002 to 4 percent by 2006. The commercial sector was pleased by a reduction in Brazil's small business taxes. Lula stepped onto the international stage with a program aimed at relief for African AIDS sufferers, and he even earned praise for his efforts from his ideological polar opposite, U.S. President George W. Bush.

Expanded Family Stipend

Domestically, Lula pursued some of the activist antipoverty programs he had promised. The centerpiece of his domestic agenda was the Bolsa Familia, or Family Fund, a program begun by Cardoso but vastly expanded by Lula. The Bolsa Familia was a monthly stipend of between $6 and $60, eventually paid to about 11 million poor families, for which the only requirements were that children attend school (85 percent of the time) and receive government-required vaccinations. The result was a dramatic 19 percent reduction in Brazil's poverty rate, long one of the most severe in Latin America. Lula also raised Brazil's minimum wage in the last year of his first term and dispatched federal troops to halt gang wars in Brazil's slums.

These measures materially improved the situation of numerous ordinary Brazilians and gave Lula a cushion of

support he would need as problems began to mount later in his term. Annual growth in Brazil's gross domestic product was an anemic 2.6 percent, lower than that of neighboring countries, to say nothing of emerging economic titans like China and India that Brazil had long considered its main competitors. Environmentalists pointed out that despite the establishment of new protected areas, enforcement of laws safeguarding the fragile and ecologically critical Amazon rainforest remained underfunded and lax.

Lula faced opposition from both the left and the right. An organization composed of landless rural peasants mounted demonstrations protesting the slow pace of rural land reform. The most serious problems for Lula during his first term came from scandals connected with Workers' Party officials, who were charged with bribing lawmakers to cast certain votes, with soliciting illegal contributions during the 2002 campaign, and with a variety of dirty tricks aimed at the party's political rivals. Lula was never personally connected to any of the allegations, but his centrist opponents made an issue of government corruption as the 2006 elections approached. Economic conservatives in Brazil blamed the country's high rate of government spending for slow growth.

With candidates from two small leftist parties gaining 9 percent of the vote in the election's first round on October 1, 2006, Lula was in a weakened position, gaining only 49 percent of the vote. But he fired back at his centrist opponent, São Paulo state governor Geraldo Alckmin, with charges that his opponent wanted to privatize Brazil's state industries. The strategy proved successful as Lula reversed Alckmin's lead in the vote-rich São Paulo region and rolled up large majorities in his native Northeast. On October 29 he was elected to a second term with 61 percent of the vote. In December he announced a second hike in Brazil's minimum wage, raising it by 8.5 percent to $177 per month.

The scandal-plagued Workers' Party lost seats in the Chamber of Deputies for the first time since Lula had established it, but Lula forged ahead with a second term agenda that included economic development, education (he proposed new university scholarships for poor Brazilians), and antipoverty initiatives. Notably absent from his plans was any effort to expel foreign companies in an effort like that undertaken by Hugo Chávez in Venezuela. ''Lula's heart may beat to the left, but his head tells him foreign investment is essential for Brazil to grow,'' noted Steve Kingstone of the BBC. Having experienced Brazilian poverty firsthand, Lula promised to continue to work to ameliorate it. ''The foundation is in place,'' he told crowds in São Paulo after the election (according to the BBC), and now we have to get to work.''

Books

Worldmark Encyclopedia of the Nations: World Leaders, Gale, 2003.

Periodicals

Boston Globe, October 25, 2006.
E, September-October 2005.
Economist, January 6, 2007.
Newsweek International, October 2, 2006.

NotiSur, November 3, 2006.

Online

''Brazil Stands Poised to Reelect Lula,'' *Business Week Online,* http://www.businessweek.com/globalbiz/content/sep2006/gb20060928_127091.htm (February 7, 2007).

''Luiz Inácio Lula da Silva.'' Biography Resource Center Online, Gale, 2003, reproduced in Biography Resource Center, Thomson Gale, 2007, http://www.galenet.galegroup.com/servlet/BioRC (February 7, 2007.

''Luiz Inácio Lula da Silva: Union Activist and Presidential Candidate, Brazil'' (interview), North American Congress on Latin America, http://www.nacla.org/art_display/php?art = 1849 (February 7, 2007).

''Lula Bounces Back from the Ropes,'' BBC News, http://www.news.bbc.co.uk/2/hi/americas/6100928.stm (February 7, 2007).

''Profile: Luiz Inácio Lula da Silva,'' BBC News, http://www.news.bbc.co.uk/2/hi/americas/5346744.stm (February 7, 2007). □

M

Peter Maas

American writer Peter Maas (1929–2001) gained fame as an investigative journalist and novelist. He became best known for his non-fiction works that explored organized crime and political and police corruption. Many of his books were made into movies, and almost all of them became bestsellers. His most famous works included *The Valachi Papers* and *Serpico.*

Maas emerged as one of the writing "stars" of the so-called New Journalism style of reporting that came into vogue in the 1960s and 1970s. Typically, the proponents cut their professional teeth in the newspaper industry and later graduated into magazine writing, producing articles for magazines such as *Esquire, Life,* and *Look.* Later their names became fixtures on bestseller book lists.

Typically, the new journalists were more "literary" than traditional journalists: They either introduced a subjective perspective when writing about contemporary issues, or they applied a novelistic approach to their investigative reporting. In the process, many of them became as famous as the subjects they covered. Some marquee names in the new journalism included Norman Mailer, Tom Wolfe, Hunter S. Thompson, and Gay Talese. Maas joined this pantheon by producing a string of highly successful works that addressed his signature themes and subjects: organized crime, political and personal corruption, police corruption, and the lone whistle-blower who, at great personal sacrifice, takes a moral stand against large, powerful organizations.

Maas was born in New York City on June 27, 1929, the son of Carl and Madeleine (Fellheimer) Maas. He grew up in the Hamilton Heights area of New York City's Upper West Side, a multi-cultural neighborhood that included German, Jewish, Italian, and Irish families. His own ethnic heritage included Dutch and Irish bloodlines.

Maas's journalistic ambitions unfolded when he attended Duke University in Durham, North Carolina, in the late 1940s. A political science major, Maas worked for the university newspaper, the *Duke Chronicle,* receiving assignments from editor Clay Felker, who would later gain fame in New York City as the editor of such influential and trend-setting publications as *The Village Voice* and *New York* magazine. Felker heard that Walter Reuther, the then-president of the United Auto Workers Union, was recuperating in the Duke University Hospital from nothing less than an assassination attempt. With such a significant story so close at hand, he dispatched a reporter, Maas, to get an interview. Maas proved more than up to the task, and he accomplished the kind of journalistic coup that jumpstarts a career.

Early Career

However, the trajectory to the top was not straightforward. Following graduation from Duke where he received a bachelor of arts degree in 1949, he moved to Paris in 1950, where he studied at the Sorbonne and cut some more journalistic teeth filing stories as a reporter for *The New York Herald Tribune.* This was followed by a military detour: during the Korean War he voluntarily enlisted in the U.S. Navy and served from 1952 to 1954. Eventually he found his way back to New York City, where he worked as an entertainment writer for *Collier's* magazine (1955–56). When the magazine folded, Maas was forced to find work and income as a crew member on a lobster boat.

He resumed his journalism career in 1959, when he became senior editor at *Look* magazine. In that position, he garnered national recognition for his story about a black inmate in Angola, Louisiana, who had been on death row longer than anyone else in the United States (14 years). Maas later served as a special consultant for the NBC television program "David Brinkley's Journal" (1961–62) and then became a senior writer for the *Saturday Evening Post* in New York City (1963–66).

Wrote *The Valachi Papers*

While working for the *Saturday Evening Post* he secured a major "scoop," and a big break, when he learned about Joe Valachi, a Mafia "hit man" who was turning informer for the U.S. Government. Maas came across the story quite by accident, while he was researching an article about famous New York lawyer Roy Cohn, who had worked with Senator Joe McCarthy in the 1950s. While visiting the New York office of U.S. attorney Robert Morgenthau, Maas conducted a lunch interview with U.S. Attorney General Robert Kennedy, who had also worked with McCarthy during the same period as Cohn. During the lunch, Kennedy let it slip out that Valachi was testifying before a Senate committee. During the committee hearings, Valachi provided organizational information about the Cosa Nostra and revealed the identities of its major figures. Maas seized upon the accidental tip and broke the story in a three-article series for the *Saturday Evening Post,* which he later followed with the book *The Valachi Papers,* which was eventually published in 1969.

But the path to publication was fraught with controversy and legal barriers. The U.S. Justice Department had encouraged Valachi to write his memoirs, hoping that the information he would provide would benefit law enforcement. The former racketeer produced a rambling 1,180-page manuscript titled *The Real Thing.* Maas was retained as the book's editor, and Justice Department officials permitted Maas to interview Valachi in his Washington, D.C., jail cell.

When word of this project leaked to the press in 1966, the county's Italian-American community expressed anger and indignation, believing that the work would further foster the negative impression that all Italians were connected to organized crime. Prominent Italian-Americans, including Congressman Peter Rodino, protested the book to then-Attorney General Nicholas Katzenbach. This intervention seemingly killed the project. However, Maas, complaining that the Justice Department was influenced by political pressure, stood by his contract and indicated that he would complete the book.

Maas's adamant posture prompted the Department to file suit in federal district court for an injunction against publication of Valachi's memoirs. The Department brief claimed that publication would be "detrimental to law enforcement" and cause the United States "immediate and irreparable harm." The Department also claimed that Maas had violated the terms of the original agreement when he applied for a copyright and revealed book portions to a literary agent without Department permission.

In response, Maas and his attorneys took a free speech stance, claiming the Justice Department's actions amounted to censorship. Maas also pointed out that he could not have breached a contract when he applied for a copyright, as a completed manuscript did not exist and could not be submitted to the Justice Department for its final approval.

The court rendered its decision in 1968. It upheld a government regulation that prohibits a prisoner from writing and publishing a book about his or her criminal activities. At the same time, the court said Maas could not be stopped from writing a book based on information he gathered from personal interviews, tape recordings, and other sources. In other words, it was a "go," and Maas proceeded at work on the manuscript that would become *The Valachi Papers.*

Despite the favorable court decision, Maas's troubles were not over. He still had to find a publisher, and that would prove difficult. In all, 20 publishers rejected his manuscript. At the time, the conventional wisdom in the publishing world said the Mafia "does not sell" (this was in the pre-"Godfather" era, before Mario Puzo's book and the film adaptation became a cultural phenomenon). Finally, in 1969, Putnam decided to publish *The Valachi Papers,* and Maas's efforts were vindicated by the book's sales. In its first hardcover publication, the book sold out only a few days after its release. It was subsequently released in paperback to a first-run printing of 1.75 million copies, and paperback sales would eventually reach 2.5 million copies. In 1972 *The Valachi Papers* was made into a movie, produced by famous film mogul Dino De Laurentiis and starring Charles Bronson as Valachi. The film adaptation grossed $20 million.

Succeeded with *Serpico*

After working as a writer for nearly 20 years, Maas became an overnight sensation with *The Valachi Papers*. His next work, *Serpico,* would bring him even greater success.

Serpico, published in 1973, told the true story of an honest police officer, Frank Serpico, who encounters rampant corruption within the New York City Police Department. In the early 1970s, frustrated that top NYPD officers did nothing about his allegations of the insidious corruption, Serpico took his case to the press, providing the *New York Times* with documented evidence. In February of 1971, during a narcotics raid, Serpico was shot in the face by a drug dealer. Many believed that Serpico had been set up by fellow police officers in retaliation for his whistle-blowing activities.

In the fall of 1971, Serpico agreed to work with Maas on a book about his career as a police officer. Maas's project entailed six months of interviews with Serpico, followed by six months spent corroborating Serpico's story. His research included examining confidential police files and inter-office memos, and followup interviews with hundreds of witnesses. Maas even visited various crime scenes. At the end of this voluminous research, Maas could only conclude that Serpico was completely truthful.

Actually writing the book took Maas nine months. Surprisingly, Putnam Publishing Co., which had published *The Valachi Papers,* rejected his manuscript. This time, Maas was told that books about cops would not sell. Putnam no doubt rued its decision. Viking published the book in 1973, and *Serpico* became a bestseller, eventually selling more than three million copies. Producer De Laurentiis bought the rights for $400,000, and the film version, starring Al Pacino (who earned an Academy Award nomination playing Frank Serpico), was a critical and commercial smash. It later spawned a short-running television series. Maas gave half of the $400,000 he earned from De Laurentiis to Frank Serpico.

Tragedy Struck

Two years after the publication of *Serpico,* Maas's life was marked by tragedy. On July 2, 1975, his wife, Audrey Gellen, was killed in an automobile accident. Maas had married Gellen, who was a producer and writer (she co-produced director Martin Scorsese's *Alice Doesn't Live Here Anymore* in 1974), on April 4, 1962. They had one son, John Michael, who was born in 1968. This personal catastrophe resulted not only in obvious emotional turmoil; it produced substantial legal problems. The couple had no will, and Maas spent a fortune settling the financial entanglements.

Maas managed to gain back some of the incurred financial losses with his next book, *King of the Gypsies,* yet another successful non-fiction venture. Published in 1975, the book related a struggle for power within the "royal" gypsy family. It was made into a movie in 1978, starring Sterling Hayden, Shelley Winters, Eric Roberts, and Judd Hirsch. Maas sold the film rights for $350,000.

Wrote First Novel

Maas followed *King of the Gypsies* with a work of fiction titled *Made in America* (1979). Maas's friends, including novelist E.L. Doctorow, had encouraged Maas to try his hand at fiction writing. The plot concerns Richie Flynn, an ex-pro football player turned beer salesman, who devises a get-rich-quick scheme and funds his dream with money obtained from a loan shark. With the story, Maas attempted to depict the human condition and, more specifically, how an ordinary man's essentially decent spirit can be corrupted.

In 1983 it was back to non-fiction for Maas. *Marie: A True Story* related how a lone woman, Marie Ragghianti, stood up against the Tennessee government and a corrupt governor who was selling clemency for cash. In telling the story, Maas conducted extensive research. He reviewed nearly 3,000 pages of trial transcripts and legal depositions and produced 4,200 pages of transcriptions from interviews with Ragghianti and 76 witnesses. In 1985 the book was made into a movie, *Marie,* starring Sissy Spacek.

Later Works

In 1986 Maas wrote another hard-hitting exposé, *Manhunt,* which told the story of Edwin Wilson, the ex-CIA agent who engaged in illegal weapons trafficking with Libya's Colonel Muammar el-Qaddafi. Three years later he released his second novel, *Father and Son,* a tragic tale whose title characters included Michael McGuire, a widower and New York City advertising executive, and his son, Jamie, whose support for the Irish Republican Army leads him to becoming a pawn for the terrorist organization.

Maas then wrote a true-crime book, *In a Child's Name,* released in 1990, about a dentist named Kenneth Taylor who murdered his wife, Teresa Taylor. The focus of the book was the couple's orphaned infant son, who was caught in the middle of a bitter custody batter involving Kenneth Taylor's parents and his wife's relatives. The novel was made into a television mini-series.

This was followed four years later by Maas's third novel, *China White.* The title referred to the purest form of heroin, and the plot concerned the efforts of a lawyer and an FBI agent to stop the flow of the drug into the United States. Their efforts take them into the shadowy underworld of Chinese crime organizations.

Maas's next book was the non-fiction work *Killer Spy: The Inside Story of the FBI's Pursuit and Capture of Aldrich Amos, America's Deadliest Spy,* released in 1995. The book detailed how FBI agents tracked down Amos, a CIA operative who became a KGB spy. Amos's mercenary activities had led to the death of at least 12 U.S. agents.

Maas returned to the world of organized crime in 1997 with *Underboss: Sammy the Bull Gravano's Story of Life in the Mafia.* Like Valachi, Gravano turned government informant. His testimony led to the conviction of Mafia leader John Gotti.

Died in New York City

Maas's last book was *The Terrible Hours,* released in 1999, the story of a successful U.S. submarine rescue that took place right before World War II. The book was adapted into a television movie titled *Submerged*. Like nearly all of Maas's works, *The Terrible Hours* was a bestseller.

Mass died in on August 23, 2001, in New York City, from complications following surgery for an ulcer. He was 72. Before his death, he lived in a Manhattan apartment and regularly wrote articles for publications such as *Parade*, *George* (the magazine published by the late John Kennedy Jr.), and *Gourmet* magazine.

After the death of his first wife, Maas married two more times. On September 14, 1976, he married real estate broker Laura Parkins. They separated in 1979 and subsequently divorced. On February 1, 1986, he married Suzanne Jones.

During his career, Maas had became a "star" writer, and his name was frequently placed above the title on the book covers. However, late in his life he decried the celebrity attitude that infected the writing profession. New writers, he felt, were more focused on personal ambition and achievement instead of the story and the work it took to bring that story to print.

Periodicals

New York Times, August 24, 2001.
Independent (London, England), August 27, 2001.
St. Petersburg Times, October 31, 2000.

Online

"Peter Maas," *Contemporary Authors Online*, http://www.gale net.galegroup.com/servlet/BioRC (December 2, 2006). ☐

Elizabeth Maconchy

Born and educated during an era that rarely encouraged women to practice the art of musical composition, Elizabeth Maconchy (1907–1994)—British but of Irish descent and upbringing—became, in the words of Martin Anderson of London's *Independent* newspaper, "one of the most substantial composers these islands have yet produced." Her accomplishment was magnified by the fact that her style was largely original, not adhering to any of the schools and "isms" that defined musical compositions in the classical field for much of the twentieth century.

Composed Music Despite Lack of Exposure

Maconchy, known by the nickname of Betty, was born in the town of Broxbourne in eastern England's Hertfordshire region on March 19, 1907. Her father was an Irish-born lawyer. Unlike many creative figures in music, she had very little exposure to the art form growing up; the family had neither a radio nor a record player, and she heard a symphony orchestra for the first time only when she was in her mid-teens. Maconchy's creative drive, however, came from within, and she made her own music; she started playing the piano and writing pieces of her own when she was six, and it did not take her long to announce that composing music was to be her life's work.

Maconchy's family moved to Ireland around the end of World War I so that her father could take a job in Dublin. After her father's death in 1922, Maconchy applied to the Royal College of Music in London and was accepted, impressing professors of piano (Arthur Alexander) and composition (Charles Wood). She suffered a setback when RCM director Sir Hugh Allen refused to allow her to be named as recipient of the school's prestigious Mendelssohn Scholarship, saying, according to the *Times* of London, "If we give you the scholarship you will only get married and never write another note." More sympathetic to her ambitions was Ralph Vaughan Williams, a member of the school's composition faculty and arguably England's greatest composer of the era. He steered Maconchy toward devoting herself to composition full time. According to Anderson, when she graduated, Williams wrote in her final evaluation that he was "very sorry to lose her—but I can teach her no more—she will work for her own salvation and will go far."

Maconchy as a composer was only slightly influenced by Vaughan Williams; the evocations of the English countryside contained in his so-called pastoralist style held little appeal for the culturally Irish Maconchy. However, Williams did steer Maconchy toward works by other twentieth-century composers who would exert greater impact on her. He suggested that after leaving the RCM she go not to Vienna, dominated by composers in the heavily systematic 12-tone style, but instead to Prague, Czechoslovakia. There Maconchy studied with Czech composer Karel Jírak and expanded her knowledge of the music of the most innovative Central European modernist of the time, Hungary's Béla Bartók. It was not Bartók's experiments with Eastern European folk music that interested Maconchy, however, but his way of using counterpoint—the combination of independent lines of music, often in different instruments—to develop a unique structure for each composition. Bartók emerged as the single most important influence on Maconchy's style. As she rounded out her education, Maconchy and Welsh-born composition student Grace Williams visited Vienna and enjoyed smoking cigars in the city's fabled cafés.

The year 1930 was eventful for Maconchy. She married medical historian William LeFanu that year. And two of Maconchy's works received premieres from major ensembles: a concerto (or concertino) for piano and orchestra was conducted by her teacher Jírak, leading the Prague Philharmonic Orchestra, with Czech pianist Erwin Schulhoff (who later died in a concentration camp) as soloist, and her orchestral suite *The Land*, which she had sent on an impulse to conductor Henry Wood, was included in the summer programming of London's popular Promenade Concerts, known as the Proms, and had a positive reception from audiences. The *Daily Telegraph* newspaper (according to the website of Ireland's Contemporary Music Centre) introduced its review of the concert with the headline "Girl Composer's Triumph."

Suffered from Tuberculosis

This promising beginning to Maconchy's compositional career was cut short by health problems: in 1932 she contracted tuberculosis, which was untreatable at the time and often fatal. The disease killed both Maconchy's father and her younger sister. Doctors recommended that she go to a sanitarium in Switzerland, but Maconchy replied that she wanted to die in Ireland or England if it came to that. Maconchy went to live alone on England's southeast coast and eventually recovered completely. She dropped out of the musical world at what could have been a critical time, but she made good use of her convalescence by thinking about how to develop her individual musical style.

Maconchy's *Times* of London obituary suggested that she turned to chamber music—music for small groups of instruments—because of continuing physical weakness after her illness, but an alternative explanation would refer to Bartók's string quartets of the 1920s, dense yet highly expressive works, each with an original structure. Maconchy favored the string quartet form throughout her career, feeling that it combined intellectual accomplishment with the representation of strong dialogue among individuals. "Music should be passionately intellectual and intellectually passionate," Maconchy said (according to the MusicWeb International website). "Just intellectual would make the music dry and driven by an emotional force; whereas passion without a mind behind it is no good at all."

In 1933 Maconchy's String Quartet No. 1 was performed at London's Macnaghten Concert Series, a prominent venue for new music, and another chamber work, her Oboe Quintet, won the *Daily Telegraph* newspaper's chamber music prize. Maconchy's works were performed at festivals of the International Society for Contemporary Music in Prague (1935) and Paris (1937), but her critical success at home in England was inconsistent, perhaps because of lingering prejudice against female composers. Some called her music colorless. In 1939 Maconchy's first child was born: a daughter name Anna. During World War II she and her family fled London for Herefordshire in England's West Midlands.

Maconchy's second daughter, Nicola LeFanu, was born in 1947. She would become a noted composer and professor of music at King's College in London. Maconchy sometimes talked to friends about the problems of squeezing composition in among childcare activities, and during the postwar years she added music administration jobs to her responsibilities, working for the Macnaghten concerts that had supported her career in the 1930s, becoming chairwoman of the Composers' Guild of Great Britain, and taking over from Benjamin Britten as president of the Society for the Promotion of New Music. Maconchy never divorced, but she lived separately from her husband at times. One of Maconchy's major works from the postwar years was a symphony that was given its premiere by one of England's legendary conductors, Sir Adrian Boult.

Pushed Boundaries of Tonal System

Maconchy's style was difficult to classify with reference to those of other composers. Influences upon her, beyond that of Bartók, included Czech composer Leos Janacek and Austria's Alban Berg. She moved to the edges of but did not abandon the system of keys and conventional harmonies in music, and though complex, her music remained accessible to audiences. "Her music is often fiercely dissonant but never gratuitously so, always as a result of motivic argument," Anderson wrote. "Her acute sense of rhythm can produce an electrifying tingle in the nape of the neck. Her use of instrumental color is piquant, tart, fresh. And her structures are never static: they bowl along with a long-legged vigor that is inordinately exciting."

In the late 1940s and 1950s Maconchy reached the high point of her popular and critical appeal. Her String Quartet No. 5 of 1948 was among the most widely performed of her set of 14 quartets, which Anderson called "alongside the 15 of Robert Simpson, the most important quartet cycle by any British composer, and an achievement no other woman composer has come near." The String Quartet No. 9 (1969) had a tragic slow movement alluding to the Soviet Union's invasion of Maconchy's beloved Prague the year before it was written. There are only 13 numbered quartets, for Maconchy, fearing the unlucky associations of the number 13, left one work without a number. Maconchy began to expand into larger forms, writing a Symphony for Double String Orchestra in 1952 and 1953, and the shorter orchestral overture *Proud Thames* (1953), which won a prize from the London County Council. Top British conductors, including Boult, Sir Malcolm Sargent, Sir Arthur Bliss, and Sir Thomas Beecham continued to program new orchestral works by Maconchy in concerts.

In the late 1950s and 1960s Maconchy turned to vocal works, producing three one-act operas, *The Sofa* (1957, with a libretto by Ursula Vaughan Williams, the widow of Maconchy's one-time teacher), *The Departure* (1961), and *The Three Strangers* (1967). She read widely among the classics and contemporary manifestations of British poetry in search of texts to inspire her, resulting in a series of distinctive choral works that included *And Death Shall Have No Dominion* for choir and brass (1969) and *Prayer Before Birth* (1971). Her solo vocal works included the large cantata *Héloise and Abélard* for soprano, tenor, baritone, chorus, and orchestra, but she never wrote a full-scale opera.

A noteworthy aspect of Maconchy's career was her consistent output that lasted into great old age. Her *Music for Strings* had its premiere at the 1983 Proms concerts, and one three-year period while she was in her seventies saw the composition of four choral pieces, a Clarinet Concertino, a string orchestra work, a solo bassoon piece, and a group of songs. Maconchy traveled to Australia for performances of her works when she was 77, and a 1984 documentary sponsored by the Arts Council of Great Britain provided an overview of her career. The list of honors Maconchy received in later life was topped by her designation as Dame Commander of the British Empire in 1987.

At the time of her death in Norwich, England, on November 11, 1994, Maconchy's music was in temporary eclipse on British concert programs. With the inclusion of her Oboe Quintet and Theme and Variations for Strings on the touring programs of the prominent British chamber ensemble The Ambache in the early 2000s, however, Maconchy's reputation would begin to outlast her lifetime. A 1989 recording of her complete string quartets, originally released on the Unicorn label, was reissued on the Regis imprint, and the centenary of her birth in 2007 promised additional performances and recordings.

Periodicals

Independent (London, England), April 13, 2001.
Times (London, England), November 12, 1994.

Online

"Elizabeth Maconchy," Chester Novello, http://www.chester novello.com (February 11, 2007).
"Elizabeth Maconchy: Intense but Disciplined," Contemporary Music Centre, http://www.cmc.ie/articles/article-maconchy .html (February 11, 2007).
"Elizabeth Maconchy," MusicWeb International, http://www .musicweb-international.com/maconchy/index.htm (February 11, 2007). □

Mako

Japanese-American actor Mako (1933–2006), who used only that single name professionally, almost single-handedly established a tradition of Asian-American theater in the United States, providing inspiration in the process to several generations of film and television performers. Mako himself had a high-visibility Hollywood career, beginning with an Academy Award–nominated performance in the film *The Sand Pebbles* (1966).

"In 1965," noted David Henry Hwang in the *Los Angeles Times*, "there were no Asians in America. At least according to Hollywood, there were only Orientals, Japanese and Korean enemies, mysterious foreigners crammed into exotic Chinatowns, geisha girls beguiling American servicemen abroad, Charlie Chans, Fu Manchus, and the cook on 'Bonanza.' . . . Yet in 1965, a young actor named Mako believed Asians did exist in this country, and he spent his life proving it." As a result of Mako's efforts, audiences flocked to plays by Hwang himself, such as *M. Butterfly* and other works by Asian American authors.

Raised by Grandparents in Japan

Mako was born Makoto Iwamatsu in Kobe, Japan, on December 10, 1933. When Mako was five, his parents moved to New York City to study art, but with relations between the United States and Japan deteriorating, Mako was left with his grandparents in Japan. Unlike the majority of Japanese in the United States, Mako's parents, because of

their New York City location, escaped imprisonment in the internment camps set up in the Western states during World War II, and they worked for the U.S. government Office of War Information. They were later granted U.S. residency, and Mako came to New York to join them in 1949. Moving from devastated postwar Japan to New York, he was amazed and disoriented by the contrasts between wealth and poverty in America. At first he aimed toward the former, giving up his Japanese ways. But his father scolded him. "You don't know the assets and legacy you were born with," his father said, as Mako recalled to Patrick Pacheco of the *Los Angeles Times*. "You're a fool if you let them erode."

Mako enrolled at New York's Pratt Institute to study architecture, but he found his true vocation when a friend asked him for help designing a set for a children's play. Mako began spending time around actors and theater students. "That's when the trouble began," he was quoted as saying by Jocelyn B. Stewart in the *Los Angeles Times*. "I was out of class so much that I lost my deferment." Drafted into the U.S. Army, he served for two years in Korea, visiting Japan on leaves and reestablishing his connections with his native culture.

When he was discharged, Mako settled in Los Angeles, California, where his parents had moved in the meantime. Using funds he was paid under the Servicemen's Readjustment Act, known as the G.I. Bill, he enrolled in theater classes at the Pasadena Community Playhouse, an important theater education institution in the Los Angeles area. He married dancer, choreographer, and actress Shizuko Hoshi, and the pair raised two daughters, Sala and Mimosa. With little acting experience and few role models to follow, Mako lacked confidence in his skills. But the classes at the Pasadena Playhouse were competitive, with students being cut from the program after each quarter-year term. As Mako continued to make the cut, he became more confident and more committed to the idea of an acting career. He became a naturalized U.S. citizen in 1956.

After he completed the program in Pasadena, Mako went to New York for two years and took classes in so-called "Method" acting, the technique of having an actor immerse himself or herself in the emotions being portrayed. His teacher was Nola Chilton, whom he credited in a 1986 interview with Janice Arkatov of the *Los Angeles Times* as "the foundation I have now as an actor and director." He paid his way during this training by working as a cab driver and produce market assistant, telling Arkatov that "all the things I did in those days gave me a 'file' on the various characters I had to work on." Finally he returned to Los Angeles and tried to break into the acting profession in Hollywood. He faced long odds, for many serious Asian roles at the time were still played by Western-born actors. The few roles open to Mako were written in a stilted, stereotyped dialect that hardly resembled the actual speech of Asian Americans.

Landed Series of *McHale's Navy* Roles

Starting out in his career, however, Mako took what roles he could get. His first television role came in an episode of *McHale's Navy* in 1962, and he appeared in seven episodes of the show, in various roles, over the next three seasons. For decades, to his dismay, he remained identified with those roles. "I go into a young film director's office these days and he says, 'Hey man, I know who you are. I grew up watching *McHale's Navy,*'" Mako told Pacheco. "And I think, 'Oh boy, here we go again.'" Mako also had roles in such popular series as *I Dream of Jeannie, I Spy,* and *Burke's Law.*

Frustrated with these roles and with the lack of serious acting opportunities for Asian Americans generally, Mako and a group of like-minded friends founded the East West Players in 1965. It was the first Asian-American theatrical organization in existence. *Star Trek* actor George Takei lent the group financial support during its financially precarious early years, which saw its inaugural production, *Rashomon,* mounted in a church basement in 1966. David Henry Hwang's mother served as piano accompanist during the company's early years. Later the organization prospered, moving to a storefront on Santa Monica Boulevard and then to a 240-seat theater in Los Angeles's Union Center for the Arts.

Mako invited Hollywood director Robert Wise to attend that first production, and the director agreed. That led to Mako's casting as Po-han in Wise's epic film *The Sand Pebbles,* set in China in 1926. The role was still a typically subservient one (and portrayed a Chinese, rather than Japanese, character), although Mako's character did win a boxing match against an American sailor at one point. More important, Mako virtually remade the role with his performance, which added multiple dimensions to the character and made him a sympathetic figure integrally involved in the action. Mako was nominated for an Academy Award as Best Supporting Actor, and he won a Golden Globe for his performance. Takei, as quoted by Stewart, pointed to the performance as a turning point in the depiction of Asian Americans on film. Other actors, Takei said, "did what they were told to do: giggle here, shuffle over there, bow, and go out. [Mako] was one of the early truly trained actors who was able to take stock roles, roles seen many times before, and make an individual a live and vibrant character."

Mako continued as a linchpin of the East West Players until his departure from the company over artistic disagreements in 1989. He acted in plays, directed them, and even wrote several, including *There's No Place Like a Tired Ghost* (1972) and *Christmas in Camp* (written with Dom Magwili in 1981). The company moved beyond contemporary Asian-American plays, mounting productions of works by Shakespeare, Anton Chekhov, Bertolt Brecht, Henrik Ibsen, Federico Garcia Lorca, and other Western playwrights from whose productions Asian Americans had long been excluded. "Ninety-nine percent of us are born and raised here," he told Arkatov, referring to the company of actors at East West, "so sometimes we feel a lot closer to Western than Eastern culture. We do those plays to show that we, too, can accommodate the work, give audiences a chance to see us in untraditional roles."

Appeared on Broadway

Publicity from *The Sand Pebbles* also propelled Mako to a new variety of film and television roles. He appeared in several episodes of the hit Korean war comedy-drama *M*A*S*H* in the 1970s, and in other successful series such as *Love, American Style, Hawaii, Five-O,* and *The Incredible Hulk.* His film roles included Walt Disney Studios' *The Ugly Dachshund,* and *Fools* (1970), in which he played a psychiatrist. Mako's biggest role in the 1970s, however, was in a field in which he had no training at all: the Broadway musical. In 1976 he was signed to play the Reciter in Stephen Sondheim's musical *Pacific Overtures,* which featured an all-Japanese cast.

The role was a difficult one, with Mako's Reciter character both commenting on and taking part in the action. He had to sing rapid rhymes reminiscent of the operettas of Gilbert and Sullivan, such as "The man has come with letters from Her Majesty Victoria, as well as little gifts from Britain's various emporia." At one point, struggling with the tough opening number, "The Advantages of Floating in the Middle of the Sea," Mako offered to turn the role over to another actor, but the offer was refused. Mako's performance became one of the musical's strongest drawing cards, and he won a Tony nomination for his performance.

Among general moviegoers, Mako was perhaps best known for his major role as Akiro the Wizard in *Conan the Barbarian* (1982), starring Arnold Schwarzenegger, and its sequel *Conan the Destroyer* (1984). But he worked consistently in films in the 1980s and 1990s, keeping up his theatrical activities on the side. Mako made one film, *Chinmoku* (Silence), in Japan in 1972 but never returned. He returned to Broadway in 1992 in the play *Shimada,* which took as its theme the then-front-burner issue of Japanese domination of world business. Between 1980 and 2000 he generally made one or more series television appearances each year. After the break from East West he returned to the company in 2001 to direct the Frank Chin play *The Year of the Dragon.*

In 1994 Mako received a star on the Hollywood Walk of Fame, but the depth of his contributions to American dramatic arts remained underappreciated, and toward the end of his life he felt that, despite the fact that Asian roles in films had progressed from subservient characters to gangsters and the like, stereotyping was still flourishing. Suffering from cancer of the esophagus, he continued to work. He had a small role in the epic *Memoirs of a Geisha* (2005). Mako provided a voice in several animated films, and at the time of his death he had completed a vocal track for the animated *Teenage Mutant Ninja Turtles,* slated for release in 2007. He died on July 21, 2006, in Somis, California, outside of Los Angeles. "Mako's life," wrote Hwang, "touched that of every Asian American theater artist, whether he or she knew him or not; when he passed away on July 21, we all lost a colleague, a friend, and an ardently supportive father."

Books

Notable Asian Americans, Gale, 1995.

Periodicals

Independent (Los Angeles, California), July 25, 2006.
Los Angeles Times, April 3, 1986; April 19, 1992; September 27, 1992; July 23, 2006; July 29, 2006.

New York Times, July 25, 2006.
Star-Ledger (Newark, New Jersey), July 23, 2006.
Times (London, England), July 25, 2006.
Variety, July 24, 2006; July 31, 2006.

Online

"Mako," *All Movie Guide,* http://www.allmovie.com (December 21, 2006). □

Alice Marriott

American restaurant executive Alice Sheets Marriott (1907–2000) helped her husband build a chain of successful eateries and hotels that became Marriott International. When she died at the age of 92, the company was still in family hands and posted sales that neared the $10-billion mark.

"Almost from the start, my parents—especially my father—launched the process of figuring out how to do something right and then writing it down," Marriott's son J. W. Jr. wrote in his autobiography, *The Spirit to Serve: Marriott's Way,* according to *New York Times* writer Alex Berenson. "From washing windows to burnishing silverware to arranging buffet tables and processing customers' checks, no aspect of the workplace went untouched."

Born on October 19, 1907, in Salt Lake City, Utah, Marriott was the daughter of an attorney, Edwin Spencer Sheets, who died when she was 12 years old during the 1918–19 Spanish flu epidemic. She was named after her mother, Alice Taylor Sheets, who encouraged her daughter to do well in school and follow the tenets of their faith, the Church of Jesus Christ of Latter-Day Saints, also known as the Mormon Church. Marriott entered college at the age of 16, studying Spanish at the University of Utah, and met John Willard "Bill" Marriott there during her junior year. Her future husband came from a farm near Ogden, Utah, and was seven years her senior. Bill Marriott also had a proven success record with entrepreneurial ventures all the way back to his early teens, when his father let him plant some lettuce on an unused patch of their land and the 13-year-old turned over $2,000 in profit at the end of the season. He later took the family's sheep to San Francisco, California, and Omaha, Nebraska, and handled the sales on the livestock markets in each city.

Married and Moved East

Bill Marriott was also a Mormon, and completed the two years of missionary service that the church asked its young men to give. One of his fellow proselytizers in New England was Hugh Colton. After their missionary stint ended, they went into business together with a stock of woolen goods they sold at lumber camps in the Pacific Northwest. Bill entered the University of Utah to complete an education already started at a junior college. When he began dating honor student Alice Sheets—known as "Allie"—they liked to spend time together drinking root beer floats at the A&W soda fountain near campus. The soft drink brand had been founded in 1919 by Roy Allen (died 1968) in Lodi, California, and opened its first restaurants three years later. In 1924 Allen began franchising the concept.

Marriott's husband graduated from the University of Utah a year ahead of her, in 1926, and traveled to Washington, D.C., to visit Colton, then a law student at Georgetown University. The climate was a mild one, with sweltering summers, and he thought an A&W eatery might do well there with its ice cream float specialty. He returned to Utah, contacted Roy Allen with his idea, and won the franchise for A&W in the District of Columbia, along with the cities of Baltimore, Maryland, and Richmond, Virginia. He and Colton opened their first venture, at 3128 14th Street N.W., on May 20, 1927. Then Bill returned to Salt Lake City and married Allie on June 9, 1927, two days after her graduation ceremony.

The couple headed to Washington in a Model T Ford, a drive that took several days and was made on simple two-lane roads in an era before the U.S. interstate highway system existed. Bill and Colton opened a second stand, and though Marriott had not planned on joining the enterprise, she found herself the bookkeeper at the end of the day. Because the floats sold for a nickel each, that denomination was the bulk of the cash receipts. "We joked around that Mom had the sticky-nickel job," her son J. W. Jr. told Richard Papiernik in *Nation's Restaurant News* decades later. "That syrup would somehow always wind up on the coins. And there she would be, with $50 in nickels sticking together, trying to clean them up to get to the bank."

Introduced Mexican Cuisine

Marriott also possessed a gift for sensing new business opportunities. When sales dropped as the cooler weather arrived, she used her fluent Spanish to ask the chef of the nearby Mexican Embassy about traditional Mexican cuisine. He provided her with recipes for chili con carne and tamales, and she tried them out at home, perfecting the dishes over a two-day period. The A&W stands put the items on the menu, which proved such a hit that they renamed their business "The Hot Shoppe" once the franchise agreement ended. In 1928 the Marriotts opened the first drive-in restaurant east of the Mississippi River. As their company expanded rapidly over the next few years, Marriott would often sit with her husband for hours in a parked car, counting the passing cars to ensure the piece of land they were thinking of buying could bring in enough customers.

By 1932 there were seven Hot Shoppes, and Marriott often went along with her husband on his daily rounds. "I used to go with him, sit in the car at night, and wait for him. I would be out on the walk and would watch the curb service to see what they were doing," she recalled, according to the Marriott Company website. That same year, their first son, John Willard "J. W." Jr., was born, followed seven years later by a second, Richard Edwin. By then there were 65 Hot Shoppes across several states. At this point, Marriott began devoting more time to her family and home, and less to helping her husband in the business on a daily basis, but she remained an influential voice as the company continued to expand.

In the late 1930s the Marriotts began providing meals to airline passengers, thanks to an arrangement with the company that later became Eastern Airlines; her husband, who had noticed that travelers were picking up box lunches at his Hot Shoppe near the Washington, D.C., airport at the time, called Hoover Field—later the site on which the U.S. Department of Defense headquarters known as the Pentagon was built—and struck a deal with Eastern for pre-prepared inflight meals. Over the next several decades, that venture would grow into Caterair International, a flight kitchen division that was the largest of its kind when it was sold off in 1989. During World War II the company entered the food service management sector with contracts to run cafeterias and lunch wagons for U.S. government office workers.

Hung First Hotel's Art

The Marriott company became a publicly traded firm in 1953, and four years later entered the hotel business when it opened the 365-room Twin Bridges Motor Hotel in Arlington, Virginia. Marriott reportedly spent the final 48 hours of preparation hanging all of the art work in the rooms. Over the next decade, urged by their son J. W. Jr., the hotel division expanded to meet the demand for lodging spurred by the new interstate highway system. The family continued to build their restaurant division, opening or acquiring several chains, among them Roy Rogers, Sirloin and Saddles,

the Kona Kai Hawaiian-themed restaurants, and Bob's Big Boy. The Marriott empire grew to include a lucrative airport concession stand division, and Fairfield Inns, its lower-priced hotel chain.

Marriott served as a vice president and director of the Marriott Corporation, as the family business became known. She and her husband were active in Republican Party politics, and she served as vice chair of the 1969 presidential inaugural committee for newly elected Richard M. Nixon (1913–1994). She held the same title on the Republican National Committee, and was treasurer of the Republican National Conventions of 1964, 1968, and 1972. She was also active in Mormon groups in the Washington area, joined cultural activities such as the Washington Ballet Guild, and served for two decades on the board of the John F. Kennedy Center for Performing Arts. Her generosity to her and her husband's alma mater took the form of the Alice Sheets Marriott Center for Dance at the University of Utah, dedicated in 1989. She was also active in the National Commission on Child Abuse and sat on the advisory council of the National Institutes of Health Arthritis and Musculoskeletal and Skin Diseases agency. Widowed in 1985, she died at the age of 92 in Washington on April 17, 2000. Her legacy, aside from the crucial early work she provided to her husband in the early years of his venture, also included eight grandchildren and 23 great-grandchildren.

Books

Scribner Encyclopedia of American Lives, Volume 1: 1981–1985, Charles Scribner's Sons, 1998.

Periodicals

Hotel & Motel Management, May 15, 2000.
Nation's Restaurant News, February 1996; May 1, 2000.
New York Times, April 20, 2000.

Online

"Alice Sheets Marriott," Marriott Culture/Company Heritage, http://www.marriott.com/corporateinfo/culture/heritageAliceS Marriott.mi (December 11, 2006). □

Marianne Martinez

Marianne Martinez (1744–1812) was an Austrian composer active and widely esteemed during the age of Haydn and Mozart. She was the author of the only symphony composed by a woman during the Classical period in music (c. 1750–1790), and she also wrote a number of other ambitious vocal and instrumental works.

A member of the Viennese court aristocracy who never held a formal post as composer, Martinez and her music fell out of favor as the new concept of the composer as independent genius came into vogue. Musical accounts written in her own time testify to her high level of activity and to the quality of her compositions, but after her death she was almost completely forgotten. However, a new wave of musical scholarship in the 1980s and 1990s aimed at uncovering the often-undervalued contributions of women to musical life through history has led to an upward reappraisal of her importance.

Descended from Spanish Soldier

Martinez was born Anna Katharina Martinez on May 4, 1744, in Vienna. She had four brothers and one sister. Her Hispanic surname came from her paternal grandfather, a Spanish soldier who came to Naples, Italy, in the late seventeenth century. Her father, Nicolo Martinez, also served Neapolitan rulers as a military officer. He also pursued a wider education and struck up a friendship with an Italian poet, Antonio Trapassi, who called himself Metastasio and over the course of the eighteenth century became the most prolific and most honored Italian opera librettist (text-writer) of his time. Many of his libretti were set by multiple composers, and his fame lasted for most of the century. In the early or middle 1720s Martinez took a job at the nuncio or papal ambassador's office at the Habsburg court in Vienna, Austria, and he was reunited with Metastasio when the latter became the court's poet laureate. Martinez's mother, Maria Theresia, was Austrian.

The name Anna Katharina Martinez underwent several evolutions in German-speaking Vienna. Germans tended to pronounce it "Martinetz," and the English music historian and traveling critic Charles Burney spelled her name that way. In order to correct the mispronunciation, she began to spell her surname Martines, apparently changing her first name to Marianna out of personal preference. Sometimes that name too was spelled in the German manner, Marianne, and as a descendant of her father, who had noble rank, she was also entitled to use the "von" prefix for her last name. However, she normally signed her letters "Marianna Martines."

She showed musical gifts early on, and her father's friendship with Metastasio resulted in opportunities for her to develop them. Initially inclined toward singing, she was steered by Metastasio toward Nicola Porpora, an Italian transplant to Vienna who composed some of the most technically spectacular operatic vocal parts of the middle of the eighteenth century. Taking voice lessons with Porpora, Martinez was sometimes accompanied on the harpsichord by a penniless young musician from the Hungarian countryside who rented a room on the top floor of the handsome Vienna townhouse where her family lived—Franz Joseph Haydn. Metastasio took the responsibility for Martinez's education, which was impressive for the time even by the standards of Vienna's upper nobility. Although she apparently never left Vienna, she mastered French in addition to German and Italian, and she spoke English to Burney when he visited the court in 1772.

Trained as a singer, Martinez was said (the story may have been embellished after the fact) to have won the favor of the Empress Maria Theresa and even to have induced her son, the future emperor Joseph II to turn the pages of her music for her when she gave concerts as a teenager. By that time she had also shown skills as a composer, and her education in music theory was entrusted to Maria Theresa's court composer, Giuseppe Bonno. She may also have studied with a leading operatic composer, Johann Adolf Hasse.

Composed Masses at Age 16

Many of the manuscripts of Martinez's compositions were destroyed in a fire in 1927, so there is no way to know exactly when she began (or ceased) to be active as a composer. But the year 1760 saw three dated compositions by the 16-year-old Martinez: two settings of the Catholic mass and one motet (during this period, a religious work with an original text, for solo voice and orchestra or other accompaniment). One of them, the Mass No. 1 in D major, includes a passage that resembles the parallel music in a mass by the young Wolfgang Amadeus Mozart and may have influenced it. Some of these early works were performed at Vienna's Michaelerkirche (St. Michael's Church, which served as the chapel of the emperor's court) and resulted in a growing appreciation for Martinez's talents as a composer as well as a singer and keyboard player. Indeed, these performances may have showcased her skills in various capacities; she may have played the harpsichord in the small orchestra that accompanied the masses, and the vocal parts of many of her works contained technical difficulties that reflected her own training as a singer.

In the 1760s Martinez's reputation spread beyond Vienna. Metastasio sent some of her compositions to the most celebrated composition teacher of the day, Padre Giovanni Battista Martini (among whose students was Mozart). He responded with praise, and Martinez's compositional reach expanded. Her third mass, written in 1761, runs to more than 150 pages in manuscript score and contains parts for soloists, chorus, and a large orchestra with trumpets, oboes, flutes, strings and organ. After Joseph II assumed the throne in 1765 he mandated a simpler style of church music, and Martinez from then on wrote large religious compositions only for special occasions. She continued to compose smaller motets and cantatas for solo voice with accompaniment, often with texts by her mentor Metastasio, and many of these were apparently made for her own enjoyment and use.

Indeed, the economically noteworthy aspect of Martinez's compositional activity was that it was unconnected with any formal employment. Composers in the late eighteenth century were still mostly employees of churches or of Europe's noble families. A few—Mozart, and eventually the young Beethoven—looked toward the future as independent creative figures, making an income by giving concerts and selling their works to music publishers. But it would have been inconceivable for Martinez, as a woman, to compete for top ecclesiastical jobs or for a music director post in a noble household. Nor was she in a position to barnstorm around Europe like the young Mozart, giving concerts and composing music for patrons in new cities. Instead, Martinez remained in Vienna and wrote music for associates and for court and religious events. As an adult woman she held salons—parties devoted to music and art—in her home.

Martinez never married, which was unusual for a woman of her time and social status. She had a wide circle of acquaintances, and portraits show her to have been attractive. No evidence pertaining to this situation has come down to the present time; one nineteenth-century historian, F.J. Fétis, speculated that she might have been the aging Metastasio's mistress, but later writers refuted the suggestion. Possibly her single status resulted simply from a combination of financial independence and satisfying professional activity. Martinez and her sister cared for Metastasio in his old age, and after his death in 1782 were handsomely rewarded in his will with annual incomes sufficient to lead a more than comfortable existence in Vienna. And Martinez found plenty of outlets for her music. Early cataloguers listed some 150 Martinez compositions, of which about 65 are extant today.

Inducted into Italian Academy

In 1773 Martinez won an important honor when she was admitted to the Accademia Filarmonica (Philharmonic Academy) of Bologna, a society of composers and musical connoisseurs. For the academy she composed a grand motet, *Dixit Dominus,* for chorus, soloists, and orchestra. Although Irving Godt noted in the *Journal of Musicology* that it "may well be her masterpiece," it apparently fell victim to internal academy politics and was never performed. Martinez was the first woman composer inscribed in the Accademia's membership rolls, and her induction marked her emergence as one of Vienna's prominent composers, suitable for commissions for major events. Some of those were religious. Before his death, Metastasio furnished Martinez with texts for two oratorios (dramatic but unstaged religious works for soloists, chorus, and orchestra), *Santa Elena al Calvario* (St. Helen at Calvary, 1781) and *Isacco figura del Redentore* (Isaac, Symbol of the Redeemer, 1782). The orchestra for *Isacco* was as elaborate as that in any work by Haydn or Mozart at the time, including paired trumpets, horns, oboes, flutes, and bassoons; timpani; and strings. The work was mounted at Vienna's Tonkünstler-Soziätaet with a choir of some 200 singers.

In everyday life at court, however, it was Martinez's instrumental works and performances that attracted attention. She played the harpsichord, perhaps the more intimate clavichord, and perhaps the piano, which was just coming into wide use in the 1770s. Burney, visiting Vienna in 1772, wrote (as quoted on the Women of Note website): "Her performance indeed surpassed all that I had been made to expect. She [sang two arias] of her own composition, to words of Metastasio, which she accompanied on the harpsichord . . . and in playing the ritornels [instrumental refrains], I could discover a very brilliant finger. . . . After these two songs she played a very difficult lesson of her own composition, on the harpsichord, with great rapidity and precision."

Martinez and Mozart were apparently well acquainted and frequently performed together; Mozart may have written his Piano Concerto No. 5 for Martinez to perform. On her own, Martinez composed various keyboard sonatas and concertos for piano and orchestra, in C major and A major. Of the first movement of the latter work, Diana Ambache wrote in Women of Note that "the sudden plunge into a harmonically unexpected world dispels any expectation of

polite, early classical decorum. Her keyboard writing is reminiscent of Haydn in athletic mode." In 1770 she also composed a Symphony in C major, the only Classical period symphony by a woman.

The last surviving composition by Martinez was a chamber (small-group) cantata for solo voice, dated 1786. It is difficult, owing to the destruction of many of her manuscripts, to know whether her compositional activity ceased at that time, and information from her later years is sparse. A 1796 musical yearbook reported that she was giving weekly academies, probably vocal lessons. Martinez may have been in attendance in 1808 at a giant performance of Haydn's oratorio *The Creation,* mounted to honor the aged composer. She died of tuberculosis on December 13, 1812. Her sister Antonia, with whom she had lived during her last years, died two days later.

Although Martinez's music had energy and originality, it was essentially conservative in style. During the nineteenth century, when musical innovation was at a premium, her reputation was eclipsed; it was initially sent on a downward trajectory by a negative evaluation in the memoirs of a female Viennese novelist, Caroline Pichler. Martinez was little more than a footnote in history books until the 1990s, when feminist scholarship stimulated a spate of new research, performance, and recording activities.

Books

Pendle, Karin, *Women & Music: A History,* Indiana University Press, 1991.

Periodicals

Journal of Musicology, Autumn 1995; Winter 1998.

Online

"Marianne Martinez," Women of Note: Celebrating Two Hundred and Fifty Years of Music by Women," http://www .ambache.co.uk/wMartinez.htm (February 12, 2007). □

Deepa Mehta

With her epic trilogy of films named after the elemental forces of *Fire, Earth,* and *Water,* Indian-Canadian director Deepa Mehta (born 1950) vaulted to the first rank of artists concerned with the status of women, as traditional roles collided with the forces of the contemporary world.

Exploring the experiences of women in her native India has placed Mehta in the midst of intense controversy. She has been burned in effigy, seen the stars of her films threatened with violence, and struggled to see her films completed and shown. Nevertheless, she has persisted in the face of daunting obstacles. "I see myself as a very emotional filmmaker rather than a radical," Mehta told Diane Taylor of London's *Guardian* newspaper (referring to

Fire). "I made [*Fire*] because I want to understand myself." Early in her career she told Pamela Cuthbert of *Take One*, "The point is: if you want to make films, you'll find ways of making them." Her career has borne out that confident assertion.

Grew Up in Film Industry Family

Mehta was born in Amritsar in northwestern India in 1950, but she moved with her parents to the capital of New Delhi when she was a child. Her family spoke English at home. The marriages of Mehta's mother, and of several of her aunts, were arranged by their parents. She grew up with India's vigorous film industry in her blood, for her father worked as a film distributor. The family's fortunes rose or fell according to the success of his latest releases. "I grew up with cinema, with Friday-night openings and Monday-morning grosses," she told Carrie Rickey of the *Philadelphia Inquirer*. It was a favorite family maxim that there are two things one never knows: when one is going to die, and how a film will do at the box office. At first, she herself showed little interest in a film career, majoring in Hindu philosophy at the University of New Delhi.

After finishing her studies, Mehta made a few short documentaries for an Indian studio. A marriage to a filmmaker both solidified her return to cinema and precipitated her departure from India; she met Canadian documentarian Paul Saltzman when he was in India making a film, married him, and moved with him to Toronto in 1973. Raising a daughter, Devyani Saltzman, she worked as a scriptwriter

for children's films. She also made several documentaries of her own; *At 99: A Portrait of Louise Tandy Murch* (1975) depicted an almost-centenarian who remained an active and vital yoga practitioner. Mehta became a Canadian citizen but retained strong ties to India.

In 1983 Mehta and Paul Saltzman divorced, a wrenching process that saw Devyani forced to choose which parent she wanted to live with. She stayed with her father, and mother and daughter were estranged for some years. After the divorce Mehta returned to filmmaking with renewed energy. She made several more documentaries, including one about her brother, photojournalist Dilip Mehta, and in 1988 and 1989 she directed episodes of the Canadian television series *The Twin* and *Danger Bay*. With two other women she made a feature-length film, *Martha, Ruth & Edie* (1988), consisting of three separate vignettes about three women who meet at a self-help conference.

The experience gained on that film gave Mehta traction in getting financing for a feature of her own. *Sam & Me*, released in 1991, told an intergenerational story about an elderly Jewish man living in Toronto and a young Indian Muslim immigrant who works as his caretaker. The film won the prestigious Camera d'Or award for the best work by a first-time filmmaker at the Cannes Film Festival, and Mehta's career was launched. Although she remained less well known in the United States than in Canada and much of Europe, the film won influential U.S. admirers. These included *Star Wars* director George Lucas, who hired Mehta to direct several episodes of his *Young Indiana Jones Chronicles* television series in the early 1990s. She also served as executive producer for the Canadian lesbian-themed drama *Skin Deep*.

Directed Jessica Tandy

In her first big budget feature, Mehta had the opportunity to direct the 84-year-old British theatrical actress Jessica Tandy in one of her last roles (and in a brief nude scene). *Camilla* was a story of friendship that crossed generational lines, dealing with two women, an elderly concert violinist and a young composer (Bridget Fonda) whose ambitions are frustrated by her husband. Mehta, as a first-time major director, was not given final control over the shape of the film, which earned mixed reviews, and she was dissatisfied with the results, telling William Arnold of the *Seattle Post-Intelligencer* that "I don't want to talk about that one—it's terrible."

Mehta had more success when she returned to familiar terrain. She planned *Fire*, which appeared in 1996, and then conceived the idea of a trilogy of films, all set in India and all dealing with forces that had shaped Indian culture either in the present day or over the last few generations. And it was *Fire* that first introduced Mehta to the pressure of dealing with large-scale controversy, the result of the film's unprecedented-for-India depiction of a lesbian relationship. The film was mostly in English, but at one point a character says that in Hindi there is not even a word for lesbianism. The creative process that led to the film began as Mehta was looking at a colorless, frozen Canadian lake in winter, and pictured orange, white, and green—the colors of the Indian flag. From there, she began to devise a story of unhappy women in arranged marriages. She has said that she did not set out to make a film about lesbianism per se, but about emotional connection and honesty.

In *Fire,* for which Mehta directed her own screenplay and also served as co-producer, she depicted two sisters-in-law; one, Sita, has found that her husband is more attracted to his Chinese mistress, while the other, Radha, is frustrated because her spouse has taken a vow of celibacy on the advice of a local spiritual leader. The two women become emotionally close and then physically involved. As with most Indian films, the on-screen depiction of sexuality was tame by Western standards, but the reaction from Hindu fundamentalists after the film's release in India was swift and immediate.

Mobs, with the tacit and even stated support of Hindu extremists in India's ruling BJP party, attacked and looted theaters in New Delhi, Bombay, and other cities that had booked the film. Mehta, on her way to India for the opening in late 1998, was met by a phalanx of 40 armed guards assigned to protect her. A major battle over the film erupted in the Indian press, and the country's legislature divided into pro- and anti-Mehta camps. The threat of violence hung in the air. "I did have supporters, but they, too, were intimidated and threatened," Mehta told Arnold. "A group of doctors and lawyers in Bombay decided to put up posters around the city defending me. But no one in Bombay—a city of 11 million—would print the poster. They finally had to go all the way to Madras to find a printer who would take the job. It was that scary."

Made Film About India-Pakistan Partition

The controversy simmered down after a few months, not coincidentally after fundamentalist Hindus suffered a setback in their efforts to control the BJP. Indian censors approved the film, which had won 14 film festival awards around the world, and it opened largely without incident. By that time Mehta had already completed the second film in the trilogy, *Earth.* That film was set in Lahore, in what is now Pakistan. When it had been home to Mehta's parents, however, India and Pakistan were both part of the same British-ruled colonial territory. As India achieved its independence from Britain in 1947, however, majority-Hindu India and mostly Muslim Pakistan were split into two different countries, with large, violence-ridden migrations occurring as adherents of each religion streamed toward the new borders. Hundreds of thousands of people were killed. Mehta's film, plotted through the eyes of an eight-year-old girl, took place against the backdrop of these events and showed the dissolution of friendships and romantic relationships under the pressure of religious hatreds.

Earth (1999), based on a novel by Bapsi Sidwa, drew calls for a ban from Hindu extremists who believed that it showed Hindus in a bad light. Mehta's portrayal of the violence of India's partition, however, was nonsectarian. "Not only did it seem imperative to show what the Partition did to innocent people," she told Bridget Kulla of *Off Our Backs,* "but somehow, in doing so, we hoped to understand why war is waged and why friends turn enemies, and why

battles are inevitably fought on women's bodies." Protests associated with *Earth* were nonviolent, and the film played successfully across India.

Protests flared again after Mehta began filming *Water* in the Hindu holy city of Varanasi (formerly Benares), in northeastern India's Uttar Pradesh state, in January of 2000, and this time they were aimed at shutting the film down before it could be made. Protesters burned Mehta in effigy, and although she tried to raise the cast's spirits by asking what the effigy had been wearing, the situation soon became intolerable after thugs set fire to sets and threatened the film's female stars with rape. Hindu fundamentalists objected not only to the film's story, but to the title as well, which referred to the sacred Ganges river simply as water.

The film dealt with the historical plight of widows in India, centering on a widowed child bride who is sent to an ashram or sanctuary in Varanasi after her husband's death. There she meets a variety of women, some of whom try to escape from the grim conditions in which they find themselves. Michael Buening of the *All Movie Guide* called the film "a Dickensian exposé on the poverty and societal oppression associated with widows' ashrams." (The fundamentalists' view was that the widows were living in an exalted state.) Mehta tried to calm the protests by agreeing to cut certain lines from the film, and once again she had backers as well as detractors: an organization of Indian prostitutes staged a march in support of Mehta. But renewed attempts at filming were once again met with violence, and the actors and crew were trapped in a hotel at one point. "We have done everything according to law," star Shabana Azmi told Sudip Mazumdar of *Newsweek International.* "Yet we're being punished, and lawbreakers are moving about freely." Once again, it seemed that officials were ignoring the intimidation of Mehta and her crew. Finally Mehta suspended filming and returned to Canada. A budding renewal of her ties to her daughter Devyani, who had signed on as an assistant camera operator, was interrupted as well.

Despite offers (questionable in terms of security) from other Indian states to let Mehta film there, *Water* languished for several years. Mehta's troubles mounted when Indian novelist Sunil Gangopadhyay accused her of plagiarizing the film's plot from his book *Those Days,* an accusation Mehta answered with denials and a lawsuit that was eventually settled out of court. Azmi, who had shaved off her hair for the film, became the subject of a fatwa from Islamic clerics. Mehta lightened the mood of her filmmaking with a romantic film made in Canada. *Bollywood/Hollywood* (2002) was a lighthearted take on India's film musicals. She also directed *The Republic of Love* (2003), a romantic drama.

Finally, after filming in secret in the island nation of Sri Lanka off of India's southern coast in 2004, Mehta completed *Water.* The filming also reunited her with her daughter, who chronicled their experiences in a memoir, *Shooting Water.* The film was screened at the Toronto Film Festival, where U.S. director Stephen Spielberg told Mehta that it was the best film he had seen in the past five years. The film did strong business in Canada and Europe, was shown widely in the United States, and was slated for distribution in India at the end of 2006. Looking back on the violence she had faced, Mehta told Bob Longino of the *Atlanta Journal-Constitution* that "It was a horrific time, but later I could put it in perspective. I thought about the relationship between politics and art and freedom of expression and what that means and what drives extremists. I realized it really wasn't about me." In 2006 she was signed to make a new film, *Exclusion,* a historical drama about a group of Indians on a ship who were refused entry to Canada. Filming in India for part of the film was planned.

Books

Saltzman, Devyani, *Shooting Water,* Penguin, 2006.
Women Filmmakers and Their Films, St. James, 1998.

Periodicals

Atlanta Journal-Constitution, May 19, 2006.
Guardian (London, England), November 13, 1998; April 21, 2000.
New Internationalist, September 2000.
Newsweek International, February 28, 2000.
Off Our Backs, March 2002.
Philadelphia Inquirer, April 27, 2006.
Seattle Post-Intelligencer, September 27, 1999.
Star Tribune (Minneapolis, MN), May 7, 2006.
Take One, December–February 1996.
Time Canada, September 12, 2005.
Times of India, September 6, 2006.

Online

"Deepa Mehta," *All Movie Guide,* http://www.allmovie.com (December 16, 2006). □

Georges Méliès

French filmmaker Georges Méliès (1861–1938) was in the words of Jim Gilchrist of the *Scotsman,* "one of the great pioneers of the cinema." The special effects and onscreen magic of movies made more than a century after his heyday still reflect the impact of his innovations and his imagination.

Beginning with the mere raw materials of a new medium, which had done little more than record scenes of everyday life, Méliès began to use film to tell stories, and then, drawing on his background as a stage musician, to enchant. Largely by accident he began exploring the uses of stop-action photography. He made the first science fiction film, was the first to use the split-screen technique, and experimented with slow motion, fadeouts, and double exposure. Yet as fascinating as his technical innovations was the sheer profusion of fantasy Méliès brought to the screen. In the surviving films of Méliès (many have been lost), cut-off heads are thrown into the air and land on telegraph wires, strumming them to the tune of "God Save the King." A

spaceship, launched by chorus line of waving showgirls, lands in the eye of the man in the moon. An ancient Egyptian rejoices as his deceased wife is brought back to life by a magician, only to recoil in horror as she turns into a skeleton in his arms. Subsequent generations improved on the special effects capabilities of Méliès, but the visual surprises of his films have lost little of their impact.

Constructed Marionette Shows

The son of a prosperous French shoe manufacturer and his Dutch-born wife, who also had a background in the shoe business, Méliès was born in Paris, France, on December 8, 1861. Attending school at the Lycée Impérial in suburban Vanves, he got into trouble with teachers by filling his notebooks with caricatures of them. Another of his passions was marionettes, and he built his own sets for small marionette shows he mounted beginning at age 10. At about that age he received another push in the direction of a stage career: taken to the theater for the first time, he saw a performance by Jean Eugène Robert-Houdin, one of the great magicians of the age and one whose influence was memorialized in the stage name of American magician Harry Houdini.

At first Méliès had the ambition to become a painter, but his father insisted that he enter the family shoe business. Serving in the French military as a teenager, Méliès had the good luck to be assigned to a garrison near Robert-Houdin's estate; he likely picked up some instruction from the magician during this period. After finishing his military service, Méliès went to London; his father wanted to open a new branch there, and the plan was for the young Méliès to learn to speak English well. Working in a clothing store and uncomfortable in his new environment, Méliès sought out evening entertainment that did not depend on language. He attended performances by Maskelyne and Cooke, the so-called Royal Illusionists. Their shows both diverted audiences and debunked the claims of spiritualists and seers who claimed to call ghosts forth into the tangible world.

The mobile skeletons and other illusions of Maskelyne and Cooke's shows had a powerful effect on Méliès, and in 1888 he got the opportunity to put his theatrical ideas into action. His father retired, leaving the family business to Méliès and his brothers, whereupon Méliès sold his share and used the profits to buy the theater where his first inspiration had worked his magic—the Théâtre Robert-Houdin. Reopening in 1888 with Méliès as owner-manager, the theater presented a variety of live acts. But it was projections—large slide shows of exotic scenes projected onto a wall or screen—that proved most popular.

In 1895 Méliès paid the one-franc admission fee and attended a demonstration by Antoine Lumière, one of the true inventors of cinema. He watched as a photograph of a street scene suddenly began to move, with a horse and cart moving toward the audience. "We sat with our mouths open, without speaking, filled with amazement," he recalled, according to the Missing Link website. Méliès immediately realized the importance of the invention and offered to buy one of the Lumière projectors. He was turned down but soon bought a rival camera offered by British inventor Robert William Paul and acquired several other movie cameras as well. He imported short films made in America by Thomas Edison to show in his theatre. Even the plain shots of factory workers leaving for home were fascinating to audiences at the time. Beginning in the spring of 1896, Méliès started making films of his own.

At first these films consisted of a single short reel, but Méliès advanced quickly. He made 80 films in the year 1896 alone, broadening his reach from single takes lasting about a minute to, by the end of the year, a three-reel, nine-minute extravaganza. From the start he had a wider palette of subjects than those of his early competitors; these early efforts included little dramas, comedies, newsreels, product advertisements, and even what would later be called pornography. Méliès almost always served as star, director, writer, producer, and even set-builder and costumer of his films, a development that fascinated later chroniclers of film as an art form but eventually damaged Méliès's financial fortunes. He built a studio (probably the first in cinema history) so that bad weather would not slow down filming, using glass walls to admit natural light. And at the end of 1896 he formed a new company, Star Film.

Early movie camera equipment was notoriously unreliable, and while Méliès was filming an ordinary street scene for one 1896 film he discovered that the film had jammed inside the machine. As he examined the film, he noticed that the resultant gap had created a curious illusion: a carriage moving along the street appeared to have been replaced suddenly by a hearse. An earlier filmmaker had experimented with what would be called stop-action cine-

matography, but once again it was Méliès who saw that the device had tremendous potential in extending theatrical realms of fantasy and imagination. Méliès began to introduce special effects into his films of 1897, one of the best of which, still extant, was *L'auberge ensorcelé* (The Bewitched Inn), in which a traveler bedding down for the night is dismayed to find his clothes moving around his room under their own power. That year Méliès also released a film called *Le chirugien américain* that featured what may be the earliest example on film of the mad scientist character type. Although its title meant "The American Surgeon," that film was released with the English title *A Twentieth-Century Surgeon*. Films by Méliès soon became popular in England and America, where they sometimes appeared under slightly altered titles.

In the late 1890s and early 1900s Méliès expanded his range, both technically and in the realm of fantasy. He probably hit upon the stop-action idea independently of other early filmmakers who experimented with it, and he is thought to have filmed the first double exposure (in *La caverne maudite*, 1898), the first split-screen shot (*Un homme de tête*, 1898), and the first dissolve effect (*Cendrillon*, or Cinderella, 1899). *Un homme de tête* was the first Méliès film to feature a special-effects decapitation, treating the viewer to severed heads that float around a room. Méliès appeared as the Devil in several films.

Méliès turned to more exotic settings for some of his films. In *La chrysalide et le papillon* (released as *The Brahmin and the Butterfly*, 1901), the filmmaker dressed as an Indian man observing a caterpillar that changes into an alluring butterfly woman. Unlike other early filmmakers, Méliès employed professional actors—often chorus girls from nearby theaters for the female roles—to make his films as entertaining as possible. Yet at times he made serious works with no fantasy element. *L'affaire Dreyfus,* his longest film before 1900, was a multipart nonfiction treatment, essentially a documentary, about the controversial espionage trial of Jewish army officer Alfred Dreyfus. The film stirred street violence and was banned, becoming among the first films subjected to political censorship.

Filmed Space Shot

The year 1902 saw the release of several Méliès films that survived the later mass destruction of his work and became icons of the early silent film era. In *L'homme à la tê de caoutchouc* (released as *The Man with a Rubber Head*), a man's head (as usual, that of Méliès) seems to inflate as his assistants squeezes bellows. The illusion was created by putting Méliès on a little wagon on a miniature track and then moving the track toward the camera. Similar tricks (later with the camera instead of the subject moving—Méliès never hit upon the ideas of close-ups and long shots) lay behind special effects using a "dolly" for decades afterward. More ambitious financially was *Le voyage dans la lune* (The Trip to the Moon), filmed in May of 1902. The film cost Méliès 10,000 francs to make, and in a way it was cinema's first big-budget spectacular. The film featured lunar inhabitants called Selenites, played by a large cast of music-hall actors and acrobats whom Méliès attracted by offering higher salaries than they could make in live theater. The film's most famous image, frequently reproduced later, showed an earth spaceship landing in the eye of the man in the moon.

Le voyage dans la lune marked the beginning of another long-term cinematic trend—it was widely pirated and circulated in unauthorized copies. Méliès tried to keep control over the distribution of his films, opening offices in Barcelona, Berlin, London, and New York by 1903. But the new studio model of filmmaking, pioneered in France by the Pathé Frères corporation, was beginning to make inroads on Méliès's do-it-yourself operations. Méliès continued to make successful films, including *Sorcellerie culinaire* (released as *The Cook in Trouble*), in which a man is himself cooked in the stew he has been preparing, and several other adventure stories, including a 1907 parody of Jules Verne's *20,000 Leagues Under the Sea,* in which a fisherman is attacked by a giant octopus. In 1908 he made a film of Shakespeare's *Hamlet.*

By 1911 Méliès was in financial trouble and had to form a distribution deal with the Pathé studio in order to survive. He made a few more films, including *A la conquête du Pole* (The Conquest of the Pole, 1912), which featured a giant Bigfoot-like marionette. But he devoted most of his energy toward his Robert-Houdin Theatre, which was in turn financially hurt by the outbreak of World War I. Méliès converted part of his studio building into a small theater called Variétés artistiques, where he and his family made up most of the performing forces. He limped along until 1923. When the Robert-Houdin Theatre was torn down as part of a road-building project, Méliès had to remove a lifetime's worth of materials from the building, and much of it, including many of his precious film negatives (he made some 500 films in all), was discarded or sold as scrap. Many of the Méliès films that survive today are copies originally made by distributors or pirates.

Coming full circle in the 1920s, Méliès scratched out a living by doing magic shows at French casinos. His first wife died, and in 1925 he married one of his former actresses, Charlotte Stéphanie Faëes, and the two operated a small toy kiosk at the Montparnasse train station in Paris. His fall from prominence was interrupted when French film journalist Léon Druhot spotted Méliès working in the toy shop and wrote about him. A retrospective of Méliès films, with several new prints, was organized in 1929 by theater owner and experimental film advocate Jean-Paul Mauclair, and Méliès was given a rent-free apartment in a housing development devoted to cinema pioneers. He appeared in two advertising films in the mid-1930s and was inducted into the French Legion of Honor. Méliès died in Paris on January 21, 1938. Painters of the Surrealist movement have cited Méliès as an influence, and his style is plainly reflected in the work of contemporary Canadian filmmaker Guy Maddin.

Books

Ezra, Elizabeth, *Georges Méliès: The Birth of the Auteur,* Manchester University Press, 2000.
Robinson, David, *Georges Méliès: Father of Film Fantasy,* Museum of the Moving Image, 1993.

Periodicals

New York Times, March 3, 2002.
Scotsman (Edinburgh, Scotland) January 3, 2002.

Online

"Georges Méliès," Senses of Cinema, http://www.sensesofcinema.com/contents/directors/04/melies.html (February 16, 2007).
"Marie Georges Jean Méliès," Adventures in Cybersound, http://www.acmi.net.au/AIC/MELIES_BIO.html (February 16, 2007).
"Méliès: Inspirations & Illusions," The Missing Link, http://www.mshepley.btinternet.co.uk/melies.htm (February 16, 2007).
□

Adam Mickiewicz

A poet and Polish nationalist, Adam Bernard Mickiewicz (1798–1855) occupies a central position in the literature of his country. Polish students study and memorize his epic poem *Pan Tadeusz* (Master Thaddeus), and his writings have effectively connected the cause of Polish nationhood to the imaginative themes of the rising Romantic movement in literature.

Referred to Lithuanian Homeland in Poems

Ironically, this Polish national hero never set foot in the Polish capital of Warsaw or in most other parts of the modern-day country of Poland. Mickiewicz (pronounced "Mits-KYEV-itch") was born in or near the town of Nowogrodek, now Navahrudak, Belarus, on December 24, 1798. The area was then part of the Polish-Lithuanian Commonwealth, ruled by Russia; it was multicultural and multilinguistic, but Mickiewicz was culturally Polish and wrote mostly in that language (sometimes in French, but never in Lithuanian). Some of his poems, including the famous opening lines of *Pan Tadeusz,* make patriotic references to Lithuania, but these should be understood in a regional rather than a national sense. Mickiewicz's father was a lawyer and a minor Polish nobleman; the family was never rich and fell into difficult financial straits after the father's death.

Mickiewicz's childhood was quiet, but his life began to intersect with world events when Napoleon Bonaparte's troops marched east toward Moscow in 1812, passing through Lithuania. He saw the defeated French army marching back westward after their brutal winter in a hostile country stripped of supplies, and his school was turned into a field hospital. In 1815 Mickiewicz began attending the University of Vilnius, studying physics and mathematics but also attending literature and other humanities lectures. He applied to a teachers' college there and was given a scholarship that granted him tuition-free education in return for a promise to teach in the area after he graduated.

While a student at the university, Mickiewicz joined a literary group called the Philomats' Society that also had a strong interest in liberal reformist politics and discussed such forbidden ideas as self-determination for the peoples of the western part of the Russian empire. Mickiewicz eventually began a thorough study of classical literature (he was able to work later in life as a professor of Latin classics) and of history and language. His first poem, "Zima Miejska" (City Winter) was published in 1818. Mickiewicz graduated in 1819 and was sent, according to the terms of his scholarship, to teach at a school in the then majority Polish town of Kowno (now Kaunas, Lithuania). Cut off from his friends in the city, he launched a hopeless romantic pursuit of a local nobleman's daughter and plunged into reading the poetic works of German and English Romantic poets: Friedrich Schiller, Johann Wolfgang Goethe, and George Gordon, known as Lord Byron. Mickiewicz read English well and later translated some of Byron's works into Polish.

In 1822 Mickiewicz published a volume of poetry, *Baladi i romanse* (Ballads and Romances) that included love poems inspired by his recent romantic debacle. A second book, simply called *Poezje II* (or Poems II), included more extended poetic works. *Grazyna* was a long historical narrative poem set in medieval times, about a woman warrior who puts on her sleeping husband's armor and leads Lithuanian fighters into battle against a Teutonic tribe. The poem was among Mickiewicz's first in a strong nationalist vein. The book also included parts two and four of a fantastic and massive four-part poetic drama, *Dziady* (Forefathers' Eve), that Mickiewicz worked on for 10 years, finishing only the last three parts. The individual parts, only loosely connected, fit into a framework provided by the old Belorussian folk ritual named in the title, a ritual comparable to the Western Days of the Dead, in which ancestral ghosts are summoned. Part Two featured such characters as a the ghost of a heartless landlord, surrounded by predatory birds (the ghosts of his tenants) who quickly snatch away food before he can eat it.

Arrested and Exiled

In 1823, after an investigation of Lithuanian student groups by the czar's secret police, Mickiewicz was seized, charged with unlawful Polish nationalist activities, and put under house arrest for six months in a monastery. This was not a disaster; the punishment meted out by Russian courts was simply that Mickiewicz would no longer be permitted to live in the politically volatile western region of Russia's dominions. He was allowed to move freely to St. Petersburg, Russia, in the fall of 1824 and soon moved southward to Odessa (now in Ukraine) and then farther south still to the Crimea region, on the coast of the Black Sea. He published a new volume of poetry, *Sonety krymskie* (Sonnets from the Crimea, 1825), which used Turkish words and depicted the customs of the region's Tatar and Turkic peoples. His situation in Russia was eased by the musician Karolina Sobanska, a Polish noblewoman with whom he had an affair. She was also an agent of the Russian secret police, and apparently sent word to Moscow that Mickiewicz was not a political threat.

In fact, Mickiewicz did have friends who were participants in the Decembrist conspiracy of 1825, an attempted coup that sought to overthrow the Czar and bring democracy to Russia. After the coup's failure, however, Mickiewicz settled uneventfully in Moscow and gained admirers among the city's intellectuals and literati. He was gifted at improvising poetry—not in Russian but in French, widely spoken and understood by educated Russians. "What a genius!" exclaimed Russia's greatest poet, Alexander Pushkin, on hearing Mickiewicz's recitations (according to the Books and Writers website). "What sacred fire! What am I compared to him?" The friendship of the two poets cooled after Mickiewicz became more involved with Polish resistance to Russia, but they retained a deep mutual respect.

Mickiewicz's Polish nationalism took shape in his writing. In 1828 in St. Petersburg he published *Konrad Wallenrod*, one of his most famous long narrative poems. *Konrad Wallenrod* told the story of a Lithuanian pagan raised and Christianized by a German tribe in which he becomes a commander. But one day he hears a performance by an old Lithuanian minstrel singing in his native tongue. He then intentionally leads the Teutons into a military disaster. Prefaced by a motto from Italian political theorist Machiavelli to the effect that it is necessary to be a fox and a lion at the same time, the poem was widely read by Poles as an allegorical call to arms against Russia. Russian censors, however, were fooled by the remote setting and permitted the work to appear.

In 1829 Mickiewicz was granted a Russian passport and decided to travel to Western Europe. Before he left he wrote "Faris," a poem about a Bedouin horseman that he modeled on Arabic literary forms (he read Arabic poems in translation). In Weimar, Germany, he visited Goethe, one of the few other writers to experiment with Arab literature. Moving on through Switzerland to Rome, Italy, he met the American writer James Fenimore Cooper, a sympathizer with the Polish cause; the two enjoyed riding in the hills around the city. Mickiewicz for his part admired the young American republic; one of his early poems, "Kartofla" (The Potato), prophesied that America would "kindle new fires in Europe from the spark of Freedom."

In late 1830 Polish military officers launched the November Uprising, an attempt to throw off Russian control of Poland. The rebellion lasted for several months, but by the time Mickiewicz could return north the Russians were back in control. Rather than attempting to cross a Russian-guarded border in Prussia, he joined a flood of Polish refugees in Dresden. There he wrote the third part of *Dziady*, a work both revolutionary and mystical that likened the suffering of Poland to Christ's Passion and featured references to a future savior, known by the mysterious name of "44." Perhaps troubled by guilt that he been on the sidelines during the struggle in Poland, Mickiewicz wrote several political tracts and edited a journal, the *Polish Pilgrim*. In 1832 he moved to Paris.

Composed Unconventional Epic

Mickiewicz's greatest work, however, had little to do with political struggles; he wrote *Pan Tadeusz*, he said, partly as an escape from the European continent's tumult. *Pan Tadeusz,* published in 1834, was a vast panorama of the vanished Lithuanian society of the poet's youth, composed entirely of 13-syllable Alexandrine couplets. Its 12 books run to about 260 pages in a new English translation published in 2006 by HarrowGate Press (available online). Centered on a feud between two noble families, the poem had comic elements and numerous remarkable passages of pure description of social institutions, rarely matched even in the vast nineteenth-century novels that the poem in some ways resembled. In other sections the poem had fairytale-like elements. *Pan Tadeusz,* wrote Czeslaw Milosz in *The History of Polish Literature,* "gradually won recognition as the highest achievement in all Polish literature for having transformed into poetry what seemed by its very nature to resist any such attempt. In it, Mickiewicz's whole literary training culminates in an effortless conciseness where every word finds its proper place as if predestined throughout the many centuries of the history of the Polish language."

Mickiewicz's later years were troubled. He married Celina Szymanowska in 1834, and the pair had six children between 1835 and 1850. Celina, however, was afflicted by mental illness, and Mickiewicz, who had no fixed source of income, made ends meet by teaching courses in classics and Slavic literature at the Lausanne Academy and the Collège de France. During this period he read the transcendentalist essays of American philosopher Ralph Waldo Emerson, gave lectures about them, and translated some of them into French for the first time. He came under the spell of a Lithuanian-born mystic, Andrzej Towianski, who believed, among other things, that Napoleon Bonaparte was an intermediary figure between the human and divine worlds. Such mystical cults were not uncommon in Paris at the time, but using such ideas as the stuff of university lectures was unacceptable, as was Mickiewicz's growing sympathy with radical political movements in France. These factors caused Mickiewicz the loss of his university posts.

In 1848 revolutions broke out across Europe, as progressive forces attempted to overthrow the old monarchical regimes. Finally given the chance to put his patriotic ideals into direct action, Mickiewicz went to Italy and organized a legion of Polish fighters supporting northern Italy's independence from the Austro-Hungarian empire. His hope was that the empire would dissolve and propel Slavic peoples to freedom, but the rebellions fizzled. Discouraged, Mickiewicz returned to Paris and founded a journal called *La tribune des peuples* (The Tribune of the People), but it was soon shut down by the authorities. He took a job as an archivist at the Arsenal Library in 1852.

Mickiewicz never gave up his belief that a new order would emerge in Europe, and he sometimes espoused the idea that the Poles, the French, and the Jews would become a group of modern chosen people. In 1855 Western powers confronted Russia in the Crimean War, and Mickiewicz once again took up arms, organizing a battalion of Polish Jews and traveling to Constantinople (modern-day Istanbul, Turkey). While there he contracted cholera and died suddenly on November 26, 1855. His status as a Polish national hero survived the Communist period and persisted into the

new capitalist era; Polish filmmaker Andrzej Wajda made a film of *Pan Tadeusz* in 1999 that was seen by large segments of Poland's population, and schoolchildren still learn to memorize its elegant phrases.

Books

Krzyzanowki, Julian, *A History of Polish Literature,* Polish Scientific Publishers, 1978.
Milosz, Czeslaw, *The History of Polish Literature,* Macmillan, 1969.

Online

"Adam Mickiewicz," Books and Writers, http://www.kirjasto.sci.fi (February 16, 2007).
"Adam Mickiewicz," Polish Culture, http://www.culture.pl/en/culture/artkuly/os_mickiewicz_adam (February 16, 2007).
"Adam Mickiewicz," Virtual Library of Polish Literature, http://www.univ.gda.pl/~literat/autors/mick.html (February 16, 2007). □

Muhammad Ali Pasha

Often referred to as the founder of modern Egypt, Muhammad Ali Pasha (c. 1769–1849) was an Ottoman Turkish military leader who ruled Egypt for much of his adult life, amassing such military power that he was able to threaten the rule of the Ottoman Sultan himself.

The reforms undertaken by Muhammad Ali as he centralized his power brought the foundations of modern statehood to Egypt. He put in place a vast military and economic apparatus financed by efficient tax collections, and his armies of drafted conscripts vanquished and then permanently replaced the feuding warlord groups that had ruled much of the Middle East. Muhammad Ali modernized education, ordering the translation of European books on a large scale, vaccinated children against smallpox and offered them medical care, conducted censuses, and undertook huge public works projects that established cotton as a key Egyptian cash crop, which it remains today. Early in his career he curbed the spread of the fundamentalist Wahhabi Islam from the Arabian Peninsula.

Worked as Tobacco Dealer

Muhammad Ali was born around 1769 in Kavala, a seaport town in the Macedonian region and now part of Greece; the surname Pasha, a designation of high noble rank in the Ottoman Turkish empire, was given to him after he assumed Egyptian rule. After this point he would have been referred to as the Pasha; the Turkish form of his name, used by Ottoman ruling elites, was Mehmet Ali Pasa. He was probably an ethnic Albanian; his father, Ibrahim Agha, was a local Ottoman military commander. After his father's death, Muhammad Ali was raised by the local governor and married to one of the governor's relatives, the mother of the first five of what were said to be an eventual total of 95 children he sired. As a young man he worked as a tobacco dealer, a factor that may have influenced his later focus on agricultural trade.

It was military service that put Muhammad Ali on the path to his political career, and it was Napoleon Bonaparte's invasion of Egypt in 1798 that initially set that career in motion. Napoleon's forces easily defeated those of the ruling Mamluks, a hereditary military caste originally composed of slave converts to Islam. At the time, Egypt was a partly autonomous province of the Ottoman Empire, with ultimate control residing with the Ottoman Sultan in Constantinople (modern-day Istanbul). Napoleon's troops in turn were driven out of Egypt by British forces in 1801, but the result was a power vacuum, with the Mamluks, the Sultan's forces, a contingent of feared Albanian troops under Muhammad Ali's command, and various local powers all contending for control. Muhammad Ali managed to align himself with local merchants and Islamic clerics, and in 1805 the Sultan Selim III named him *wali,* or viceroy, of Egypt.

He faced a series of obstacles in consolidating his power in such a chaotic situation. In the words of Khaled Fahmy, writing in *The Cambridge History of Egypt,* "Egypt's history in the first half of the 19th century was considerably shaped by [Muhammad Ali's] attempt to make his tenure more secure and permanent." He was threatened by the Mamluks, the expansionist British, village leaders and warlords from other parts of Egypt (he essentially controlled only Cairo at this point), and not least by the Sultan himself, who was leery of giving any of his subjects too much power. The first challenge came when the Sultan ordered the *wali* of Salonika to go to Cairo and change places with Muhammad Ali, but that ruler backed off from the plan in the face of Muhammad Ali's strong local support.

The British at the time supported the Mamluks as a counterweight to the power of the Ottoman Sultan, and they had interests of their own in opening up secure transportation routes to their colonies in India. In 1807 the British attacked Alexandria and Rosetta, but were repelled by the Pasha's force of 5,000 crack Albanian troops even as earlier fighters from the Islamic world had quickly capitulated to European forces. The most brutal chapter in Muhammad Ali's consolidation of power came in 1811, when he invited a large contingent of Mamluk fighters to participate in a large military parade. Bringing up the rear, the Mamluks entered a narrow passage leading out onto the large Roumaliya Square, whose entrances were controlled by gates. As the Mamluks bunched up in the passage, the Pasha's forces closed the gate in front of them and opened fire from the walls above. The result was a massacre that put an end to the period of Mamluk influence in Egypt.

Checked Wahhabi Expansion

The parade to which the Mamluks had been invited celebrated the dispatch of the Pasha's troops, under his son Tusun Pasha, to recapture the Hijaz, the region of the Arabian peninsula that contains the spiritually important cities of Mecca and Medina, from forces loyal to the philosophy of eighteenth-century Islamic leader Ibn Abd al-Wahhab, the founder of the Wahhabi sect whose ideas still determine

many aspects of life in Saudi Arabia today. The Pasha's campaign was inconclusive, but Mecca and Medina were captured and brought once again under the rule of the new Sultan, Mahmud II. The Pasha dispatched an emissary to the Sultan bearing the keys to both cities, but the Sultan's response was to urge the emissary, Latif Agha, to mount a coup against the Pasha. Mohammed Ali learned of the plot and had his deputy, Muhammad Lazughlu, seize Latif Agha and have him beheaded.

Influenced by the military drills and clear chain of command he had witnessed among European forces, the Pasha set about training his Albanian troops in accordance with a *nizam al-jadid,* or new order. This effort resulted in an assassination attempt, which the Pasha foiled. Gradually, however, Muhammad Ali regularized Egypt's army and began to enlarge it by drafting peasants from Egypt's outlying districts. He employed a French officer, a Colonel Sève, to train the new recruits, giving him the Ottoman name of Suleyman Pasha. The initial result of Muhammad Ali's growing military power was that Sultan Mahmud II attempted to blunt it by sending forces commanded by the Pasha's son Ibrahim Pasha to battle fighters struggling for Greece's independence from the Ottoman Empire. As the Pasha himself had foreseen, the campaign was unsuccessful, and the modern nation of Greece was the result. The Pasha increasingly began to regard the Ottoman central government with suspicion.

The chief aim of the Pasha's modernization schemes was always to finance his growing military (by the 1830s it numbered some 130,000 troops) by increasing tax revenues, for which he devised an efficient collection bureaucracy. Whatever their aim, his infrastructure projects were ambitious and far-reaching, if brutal. His most impressive accomplishment was the rebuilding of an ancient canal that linked Alexandria with the Nile River, an effort that reportedly cost the lives of some 100,000 of the Egyptian peasants who were ordered to do the digging. Under the Pasha's reign, the total length of Egypt's irrigation channels more than doubled, and the amount of land under cultivation between 1813 and 1830 increased by about 18 percent. Also costly in human terms was a military campaign in Sudan in the early 1820s, intended to swell the ranks of Egyptian slaves; only 3,000 of 20,000 Sudanese survived a forced march from their homeland to the Egyptian city of Aswan.

One effect of these developments was an increase in Egyptian cotton exports to Europe's hungry markets, with the Pasha and his relatives, whom he installed in key administrative posts, profiting at each checkpoint. Another form of foreign exchange was tourism, with members of the European nobility flocking to Egypt to experience its rich heritage of treasures from the ancient world. The Pasha replaced Egypt's patchwork of village, tribal, and religious governments with a modern set of administrative divisions modeled on those of European countries. And, anxious to ensure a steady supply of new military draftees, he established new hospitals and took the advice of European doctors regarding the efficacy of the new smallpox vaccine, invented by Edward Jenner in Britain in 1796.

Invaded Syria

The 1830s marked the apex of Muhammad Ali's expansionist ambitions. After initial consideration of a thrust westward toward Tripoli, he launched an invasion of Syria in 1831, using the excuse that he was only trying to arrest a group of 6,000 Egyptian draft dodgers. A force of 30,000 fighters under his son Ibrahim Pasha captured the city of Acre (now in northern Israel) after a siege lasting six months, overran the rest of Syria, and then moved forward into the Anatolia region of present-day Turkey in 1832. In a battle on the Anatolian plains north of Konya, Turkey, the Pasha's forces defeated Ottoman troops under Grand Vizier Muhammad Rashid Pasha, leaving them with an open road to Constantinople and the imperial palaces.

Although Ibrahim Pasha urged his father to declare Egypt's independence from the empire, Muhammad Ali, who was culturally, linguistically, and administratively Ottoman, hesitated. The Turkish Sultan took advantage of this window of opportunity to ask for help from the European powers; turned down by British foreign minister Lord Palmerston, he persuaded a Russian navy to come to his aid. The result was 1833's Peace of Kutahia, which recognized Muhammad Ali's legitimacy as *wali* of Egypt, the Hijaz, and Crete, and granted Ibrahim Pasha the same status in several Syrian territories. The Pasha's tax-collecting prerogatives were also expanded.

That did not prevent a decline in Egypt's financial fortunes in the 1830s, however, as the Pasha's enormous administrative and military reach showed signs of overextension. The Pasha proposed a giant Nile River flood control project, to be built of stones from the Pyramids; it was initially abandoned but was later completed in 1861. Disaffection rose in Egypt due to high taxes and punishing military conscription rates among the young, but a second glorious campaign once again showed Ibrahim Pasha's military skills, as Egyptian forces defeated those of the ailing Mahmud II at the Battle of Nezib, near Urfa in southeast Turkey, in 1839. Once again the Pasha seemed on the brink of regional rule, and once again he hesitated. This time it was British intervention that saved the new 16-year-old Sultan, Abid-ul-Mejid, and allowed him to maintain control over the Ottoman Empire.

According to the Treaty of London that was then negotiated, Muhammad Ali agreed to limit his army to 18,000 troops and to relinquish his Syrian conquests. In return, he was declared ruler of Egypt for life, and his rule was extended to his heirs, giving them a unique status within the Ottoman realm. During the 1840s Muhammad Ali consolidated many of his innovations before beginning to show signs of age-related cognitive deterioration. He was removed as *wali* in 1848, died in Alexandria on August 2, 1849, and was buried in the magnificent Muhammad Ali mosque that remains a Cairo landmark today.

Books

Fahmy, Khaled, *All the Pasha's Men: Mehmed Ali, His Army and the Making of Modern Egypt,* American University in Cairo Press, 1997.

Fahmy, Khaled, "The Era of Muhammad Ali Pasha, 1805–1848," *The Cambridge History of Egypt,* Cambridge University Press, 1998.

Hourani, Albert, *A History of the Arab Peoples,* Faber and Faber, 2002.

Sowell, Kirk H., *The Arab World: An Illustrated History,* Hippocrene, 2004.

Online

"Muhammad Ali and Alexandria," Tour Egypt!, http://www.touregypt.net/featurestories/alialexandria.htm (February 16, 2007).

"Muhammad Ali Pasha," Tour Egypt!, http://www.touregypt.net/featurestories/muhammadali.htm (February 7, 2007). □

Anne Murray

Canadian singer Anne Murray (born 1945) was the first Canadian female singer to reach the top spot on the American music charts as well as being the first to earn a gold record, for 1970's "Snowbird." During her long career she has sold over 50 million albums. Her alto voice has garnered her fans and accolades from many different genres, including pop, country, and adult contemporary as well as winning her dozens of music awards.

A Childhood of Song

Born Morna Anne Murray on June 20, 1945, singer Anne Murray is the only daughter of James Carson Murray, a doctor, and Marion (Burke) Murray, a registered nurse and homemaker. The Murray family lived in Springhill, Nova Scotia, a town of only a few thousand people centered around the coal mining industry. One of six children, Murray grew up with five active brothers. On her website Murray noted that "I often think that perhaps the reason I became a successful singer was that, as a kid, I could never do anything as well as my brothers. I wanted to do something better than they did." With that inspiration coupled with her love of music, Murray first studied piano and then, from the age of 15, voice. One of Murray's earliest performances was of the religious song "Ave Maria" at her high school graduation in 1962.

Murray studied at Mount Saint Vincent University in Halifax briefly, then transferred to the University of New Brunswick at Fredericton to study physical education. She completed her degree in 1966. However, she did not forget her love of music during those studies. She unsuccessfully auditioned for a Canadian network television series, *Singalong Jubilee,* in 1964; in 1966, she again auditioned for the same series, and this time was cast. She worked on the show during the summer following her graduation from the University of New Brunswick before turning to a more stable career as a physical education instructor at a high school on Prince Edward Island.

Became a "Snowbird"

Her career as a teacher never progressed beyond that first year. Murray returned to *Singalong Jubilee* as a featured soloist during the summer of 1967 and also accepted a spot on another television show, *Let's Go,* aimed at teenagers. After appearing on the cast recording for *Singalong Jubilee,* Murray received an offer from the show's musical director, Brian Ahern, to record a solo album. In 1968 Murray released her first album, *What About Me.* She made her major label debut the following fall with the Capitol Records release *This Way Is My Way.* Not a songwriter herself, Murray performed and interpreted the songs of others, including a track called "Snowbird" penned by novice Canadian songwriter Gene MacLellan.

Although not selected as a single from *This Way Is My Way,* "Snowbird" appeared on the b-side of the album's second single, "Biding My Time." Radio stations began playing the song and it quickly became a hit. The song was one of the most played selections in North America in 1970 and garnered Murray an American gold record (meaning that the single had sold over 500,000 copies), a first for a Canadian female solo artist. Murray's song became both a pop and country standard. Speaking to an interviewer for Canada's *Globe and Mail* in 2006, Murray recalled, "I definitely fought against being labeled country at a very early stage in my career because I wanted to do everything. I didn't want to be labeled. I love all the music and was influenced by so many different kinds of music that I should be able to do any of it if I chose to." Murray's fans included

even John Lennon, who told Murray at the 1974 Grammy Awards that her version of "You Won't Tell Me" was his favorite Beatles' cover. At that same awards ceremony, Murray received her first Grammy for Best Country Vocal Performance, for her hit "Love Song." However, this was not Murray's first major award—her first was the Juno award (the Canadian equivalent of the Grammy) for Best Female Vocalist in 1971.

With the success of "Snowbird" and other songs, Murray began appearing regularly on *The Glen Campbell Goodtime Hour* and other popular variety shows of the time, including such major programs as *American Bandstand, The Muppet Show,* and *Saturday Night Live.* Both Murray's professional and personal lives blossomed during the 1970s. In 1975 Murray married Bill Langstroth, and the following year the couple had their first child, William. In 1979 Murray gave birth to a daughter, Dawn. For a few years after her marriage, Murray essentially dropped out of the music world to focus on her family.

Murray returned to record more diverse material in the late 1970s, including a children's album called *There's a Hippo in My Tub* in 1977. This album won the Juno for Best Children's Album in 1979; that same year, Murray again received the Juno for Best Female Vocalist. In 1978 she scored a major country and pop hit with the song "You Needed Me." This track earned Murray her second Grammy Award.

A Prolific Artist

Murray continued to record and perform extensively during the 1980s, releasing at least one album every year except 1985. In 1980 Murray received her third Grammy Award in the Best Country Vocal Performance category for the song "Could I Have This Dance." That same year, she was honored with a star on Hollywood's Walk of Fame. In 1983 Murray's song "A Little Good News" garnered her a fourth Grammy, again for Best Country Vocal Performance.

In July of 1989 Murray opened the Anne Murray Centre in her hometown of Springhill, Nova Scotia. The community's coal mining industry unexpectedly shut down in the 1958 after a series of mining accidents, and Murray wanted to promote a new industry for the struggling area. The Anne Murray Centre displays artifacts from Murray's career and aims to promote music appreciation in the Nova Scotia region. Shortly after the opening of the center, *Maclean's* magazine noted that Murray "herself is coming to terms with the idea that she is a Canadian institution."

In 1984 Murray became a Companion of the Order of Canada, Canada's highest civilian honor. From the mid-1980s on, Murray's commercial appeal declined somewhat. In the late 1980s country music listeners' tastes shifted considerably from softer, more adult contemporary-influenced sounds to harder, more traditional rock-country bands. Despite this shift, Murray's albums continued to be commercially and critically acclaimed.

A Long and Celebrated Career

In 1993 Murray was inducted into the Canadian Music Hall of Fame. After the death of her longtime friend and manager, she signed with a new manager and her career took a different turn. During this transitional phase Murray did not release any material; the period between 1993 and 1996 remains her longest musical hiatus. In 1997 Murray released her first live album, and two years later she again explored a new style with an album of inspirational songs, *What a Wonderful World*. This album went platinum in both the United States and Canada, showing Murray's continued commercial appeal. The following year, Murray became one of the charter inductees on the Canadian Walk of Fame.

Murray entered another new genre in 2001 with the release of her album *What a Wonderful Christmas*. Achieving gold status in Canada—an unusual feat for a seasonal album—*What a Wonderful Christmas* became one of the more successful Christmas albums of all time. In 2002 Murray released an album of classic country songs entitled *Country Croonin'*. The album went platinum in Canada and Murray embarked on a tour to support it. Three years later Murray released her 33rd studio album, *All of Me*, to critical praise. Writing in *People* magazine, Ralph Novak commented that "All in all, this excellent album makes for an ideal companion piece to Murray's 2002 collection of country standards, *Country Croonin'*."

In a rare crossover between Murray's personal and professional life, she and her daughter Dawn set out in the late 1990s to promote awareness of the eating disorder anorexia nervosa. Dawn suffered from the disease for several years before seeking treatment, and mother and daughter appeared on television talk shows in the hopes of preventing other young women from experiencing the same problem.

During her career, Murray has sought to put her talents to use for many good causes. After a tsunami devastated southeast Asia in late 2005, Murray joined a contingent of Canadian performers to appear in the massive benefit Canada for Asia, sponsored by the CBC (Canadian Broadcasting Corporation). In 2006 Murray received a Legacy Award from the Canadian Songwriters' Hall of Fame, acknowledging her long career as a premiere interpreter of songs. During her career, Murray has performed more than 80 songs written by Canadian songwriters, showing her dedication to the arts of her native country. Unlike many successful Canadian performers, Murray has lived in Canada her entire life, mostly in the Toronto area.

To date, Murray has sold over 50 million albums. In addition to her four Grammy awards, she has received nearly 25 Juno awards, three American Music awards, three Country Music Association awards, and three Canadian Country Music Association awards. In addition to these wins, she has been nominated for many other awards. With a career spanning 40 years, Murray's storied alto seems guaranteed to please fans for years to come.

Periodicals

Globe and Mail (Toronto, Canada), February 3, 2006.
MacLean's, December 25, 1989; January 18, 1999.
People, February 28, 2005.
Toronto Star, January 14, 2005.
Toronto Sun, February 6, 2006.

Online

"The Anne Murray Centre," AnneMurray.com, http://www .annemurray.com/amc/ (January 2, 2007).
"Anne Murray," CMT.com, http://www.cmt.com (January 2, 2007)
"Anne Murray's Story So Far," AnneMurray.com, http://www .annemurray.com (January 1, 2007).
"Every Show, every winner...," TheEnvelope.com, http://the envelope.latimes.com (January 2, 2007)
"Grammy Award Winners," Grammy.com, http://www.grammy .com (January 2, 2007).
"Juno Awards Artist Summary," Juno Awards, http://www.juno awards.ca (January 2, 2007) □

Arthur Murray

American entrepreneur Arthur Murray (1895–1991) became a household name with the chain of dance schools he founded early in the twentieth century.

Once a shy, uneasy teenager, Murray believed that social dancing was the key to an improved self-image, and his business strategy often targeted those in need of a little encouragement. His schools, staffed by well-trained instructors, also featured easy-to-learn methods for a wide array of touch-dancing—the term for two-person dance floor couplings such as the waltz and the polka—at a time when dancing was a obligatory part of nearly all social interaction for teens and adults. By the time he formally retired in 1969, the Arthur Murray International Dance Schools had grown into a lucrative worldwide franchise and had earned their founder millions.

Arthur Murray Teichman was born on April 4, 1895, in New York City, to Jewish immigrant parents who had come from Austria a year earlier. The family lived on the Lower East Side of Manhattan, home to many poor émigrés who had also fled anti-Semitism in Europe, and Murray's father, Abraham, found work selling bread from a street vendor's cart. Within a few years, he and his wife, Sara, opened a bakery in East Harlem, far to the north of the city, but the family still struggled financially to provide for Arthur and the four children who followed him. Murray was a sickly child, and grew into a shy teenager who was embarrassed by his family's lack of financial security. Realizing that being a good dancer could easily boost his popularity with young women from any social milieu, he asked a female friend to teach him how, and quickly realized he had a gift for it. For extra practice he sometimes crashed weddings, where he found non-stop music and an abundance of female guests looking for a dance floor partner.

Trained at Castle House

Murray dropped out of Morris High School in the Bronx, one of the city's top public high schools at the time, and took a job with an architect, planning to become one himself. He also took drafting courses at Cooper Union, a private college in the city that offered adult education

programs for students from low-income backgrounds. The dance floor still lured, however, and he quit both job and college when he won a waltz contest in 1912. He found work instead as a dance instructor with the G. Hepburn Wilson Dance Studios, which was busy capitalizing on a raft of new dance crazes that young urbanites picked up and then just as quickly abandoned for new ones. The dances went by memorable names such as the bunny hug, grizzly bear, kangaroo dip, and turkey trot, and required some instructional how-to, which businesses like the Wilson Dance Studio offered cheaply.

In addition to his regular job, Murray also spent several more hours of each day training at a school for dance instructors run by husband-and-wife team Vernon and Irene Castle. Vernon (1887–1918) and Irene (1893–1969) had lived in Paris, where they first gained fame and ignited a craze for American ragtime music and the dances that went with it, and they went on to appearances on vaudeville and in Hollywood films. Both were major celebrities by the time that Murray enrolled at Castle House, their school on Long Island. There he met Baroness de Kuttleson, a well-known dance instructor in her time, and went with her to Asheville, North Carolina, a popular resort for the wealthy. Around this time, he heeded de Kuttleson's advice to drop his German-sounding "Teichman" surname, because World War I was underway and a wave of anti-German sentiment had swept across much of America.

The partnership between Murray and the Baroness was short-lived, ending when he learned that she charged one

tycoon's wife $50 for each lesson Murray gave the woman, but paid him only $5. He headed to Atlanta, where he enrolled once again in college but this time pursued a business management degree. To pay his tuition and living expenses, he found a job as a dance teacher at one of the city's most elegant hotels, the Georgian Terrace. His classes for children and teenagers proved so successful that he soon had nearly a thousand pupils, and was featured in a *Forbes* magazine article titled "This College Student Earns $15,000 a Year."

Sold Mail Order Course

Murray's first dance studio of his own was located in Atlanta, and local radio broadcasts of his dance instruction boosted his business prospects. Hoping to keep up with the demand, he tried selling a mail order package that included dance instruction along with a kinetoscope, which was a small motion picture exhibition device. He lost money when the kinetoscopes proved too fragile for the mail, and then their manufacturer went out of business. A second idea proved to be the winning one, however: recalling his architecture classes and the precise drawings he made in his drafting job, he sketched out diagrams for the footsteps of various dances, with the feet in silhouette and lines and arrows illustrating the correct movements. He named his business the Arthur Murray Correspondence School of Dancing, and solicited customers by running ads in pulp magazines and the Hollywood gossip weeklies. The venture proved so profitable that he had moved back to New York City by 1923, opened an office, and hired a staff to keep up with the demand.

Murray also opened a dance studio in the city, and began franchising his more professionally geared instructional materials to hotels across the United States. Again, he showed a knack for writing advertising copy, and his school ads began to feature faux first-person testimonials under headlines such as "They Gave Me the Ha-Ha When I Stepped Out Onto the Dance Floor," "Thirty Days Ago They Laughed at Me," and "How I Became Popular Overnight." Murray's business thrived over the next decade, but he shut down the mail order division when demand fell off during the Great Depression. By this time he had married Kathryn Kohnfelder, a schoolteacher from New Jersey, and the escalating success of his empire enabled them to move to Mount Vernon, an affluent Westchester County suburb of New York City. Years later, he and his wife revealed that during the early years of their marriage Kathryn had suffered from post-partum depression following the birth of twin daughters, and once even attempted suicide.

Because of Kathryn's fragile state, the Murrays divided their time between residences in New York and California for much of the 1930s, but by 1938 had settled back in the New York area permanently. That same year Murray launched another franchise business, this one also using his name, for freestanding dance studios across the United States. Like the instructors at his New York studio, Murray personally screened his instructor franchisees, looking for those who could project a certain grace and warmth, which he believed would best appeal to potential students and keep them committed to the courses. The first such studio opened in Minneapolis, Minnesota, and by 1946, when he formally incorporated the franchise school business, there were 72 studios in operation that produced total revenues of $20 million annually.

Showed Genius for Publicity

Murray's talent for promotion helped make him a household name as far back as 1927, when he delivered a dance lesson to a student in London via the first transatlantic telephone lines for a sum of $425. He courted the famous to boost publicity, personally instructing First Lady Eleanor Roosevelt (1884–1962), the Duke of Windsor (1894–1972), and scions of American fortunes such as John D. Rockefeller Jr. (1874–1960) and heiress Barbara Hutton (1912–1979). With the advent of television, he shifted his radio promotion efforts to the new medium, and Kathryn began hosting a 15-minute series on the CBS network titled *The Arthur Murray Party* in 1950. The show proved enormously popular over the next decade, expanding to a half-hour showcase of dancing instruction, dance contests, and comedy skits that featured a few stars long before they were famous, such as Johnny Carson (1925–2005). The highly rated broadcast also served to lure new franchisees, and there were 450 schools bearing Murray's name in 1960, the year that he and his business became the subject of a highly publicized consumer fraud investigation.

The U.S. Federal Trade Commission (FTC) inquiry was launched after local Better Business Bureau offices filed complaints that the Murray Studios' advertising materials featured ridiculously simple riddles. Callers dialed a telephone number to give the correct answer, and were offered a cut-rate instruction package for answering correctly; even those who gave a wrong answer were offered a consolation prize of classes at a reduced rate. Murray's company was served with a cease-and-desist order for this, but in May of 1964 he found himself the target of some dreadfully unexpected publicity when law enforcement authorities appeared at his Fifth Avenue apartment in Manhattan to take him into custody. The arrest came because he had ignored a subpoena to appear before a grand jury in Minnesota on a related fraud charge, but the arrest warrant was cancelled when he agreed to testify. A few months later, he resigned as president of Arthur Murray Dance Studios.

A year later Murray sold his controlling stake in the company to a group of investors, but remained on board as a consultant. He formally retired in 1969, settling in Honolulu, Hawaii, and enjoyed a lucrative second career as a financial adviser for a coterie of affluent friends in his social circle. He traded stocks and invested in companies from a corner of the living room of his penthouse apartment, telling *New York Times* writer Robert Trumbull that his "telephone bill runs between $2,000 and $3,000 a month," according to a 1980 article about his investment savvy.

Despite the changing times, Murray's dance studios continued to thrive in the 1960s and 1970s. They offered classes when disco dancing became one of the most unexpected trends of the 1970s, and maintained a steady stream of clients by appealing to couples who were planning their weddings and realized they had little experience with touch dancing. The company even began opening studios in Asia and the Middle East in the 1990s, which pushed revenues from $38 million in 1994 to $55 million six years later.

Murray had passed away by then. Inactive after a 1983 tennis injury, he died of pneumonia on March 3, 1991, in Honolulu. Kathryn Murray died eight years later. One of their twin daughters, Jane, married the doctor who invented the Heimlich maneuver to prevent choking deaths.

Periodicals

Investor's Business Daily, June 29, 2004.
Miami Herald, July 8, 2001.
New York Times, July 2, 1939; May 9, 1960; September 21, 1980; December 4, 1981; March 4, 1991.

Online

"History of Arthur Murray International, Inc.," Arthur Murray Greater Cincinnati Studios, http://www.arthurmurraytristate.com/history_of_am.html (December 1, 2006). □

N

Oodgeroo Noonuccal

Author and political activist Oodgeroo Noonuccal (1920–1993) is most commonly lauded as the first Aboriginal poet to publish a collection of verse. Her writing, informed by the oral traditions of her ancestors and guided by her desire to capture that unique, Aboriginal inflection using the English language, strove to share the nuances of the author's beloved culture with a wide audience.

Oodgeroo Noonuccal (pronounced UJ–uh–roo nu–NUH–kl) was born Kathleen Jean Mary Ruska on November 3, 1920, in Minjerriba, also known as North Stradbroke Island. Stradbroke, unlike other Aboriginal areas, managed to maintain an unusually high level of tribal culture. Oodgeroo's father, Edward, was of the Noonuccal tribe (sometimes spelled *Noonuckle, Nunukul,* or *Nunuccal*) and her mother, Lucy, was from inland. Unlike so many of their Aboriginal neighbors, the couple was not made to relocate, and Oodgeroo vividly recalled how her father taught his children about Aboriginal ethics and hunting skills. They hunted small game and fished only to feed themselves and others in their tribe, never for the sake of killing. She was taught to be resourceful, and took pride in her family's ability to circumvent many of the difficulties of Government–instituted poverty by making what they needed from whatever was around, particularly the things left in the white man's garbage dumps.

Early Life

Oodgeroo began life left-handed, which was never an issue until she entered school and was punished for using her left hand to do writing and needlework. She attended the Dulwich Primary School, where she frequently received blows to the back of her left hand and was made to use her right hand instead. Not surprisingly, her formal education stopped at the primary level. She left school in 1933, during the thick of the Depression, and started working in people's homes as a domestic servant at the age of 13. In Roberta Sykes's *Murawina: Australian Women of High Achievement* (1993), Oodgeroo is recorded as saying that an Aborigine could not hope for better than a domestic job, even with schooling. At the age of 16, Oodgeroo wanted to pursue a career in nursing, but found herself turned away by racist regulations that barred Aborigines from joining the program. She spent most of World War II serving as a switchboard operator for the Australian Women's Army Service from 1941 to 1944.

Kath Walker: Writer and Activist

In December of 1942 Oodgeroo became Kath Walker when she married Bruce Walker, a dockside welder and champion bantam-weight boxer. They had two sons, Denis and Vivian, but divorced 12 years later in 1954. Oodgeroo chose to become a member of the Australian Communist Party in the early 1960s when faced with the inadequacy of the established political parties, in particular their failure to address Aboriginal issues and rights. In 1961 she took a position as secretary of the Queensland State Council for the Advancement of Aboriginals and Torres Strait Islanders, and served in that post until 1970. The goal of this group, according to the *Encyclopedia of Women Social Reformers,* was to work "toward the integration rather than the assimilation of Aboriginals and [toward] improvements to their civil and political status."

1964 marked Oodgeroo's first publication, *We Are Going,* and her commitment to using her writing as a weapon wielded on behalf of her people. *We Are Going* was initially popular with white Australian readers, and grew to be an extremely successful verse publication that still sells a formidable number of copies annually. The title poem was described by the *Cambridge Guide to Literature in English* as "a moving elegy on the dispossession of the Aboriginal people." Noonuccal, quoted in *The Oxford Companion to Australian Literature,* described it as "a warning to the white people: we can go out of existence, or with proper help we could also go on and live in this world in peace and harmony . . . the Aboriginal will not go out of existence; the whites will." Shirley Walker's summary of the Australian literary tradition in *The Bloomsbury Guide to Women's Literature* explained, "Aboriginal women writers in English, such as Oodgeroo Noonuccal . . . while maintaining their separate identity and the authenticity of their cultural voice, are now taking their rightful place in the Australian literary tradition. . . . The distinctive feature of women's writing in Australia is its energy, its resilience, and its determination to tell the truth. . . . [providing] the voice of the 'other', a voice from the periphery sometimes harmonizing with, but more often challenging the insistent, optimistic, centralist version of Australian life."

Oodgeroo continued to challenge the minds and hearts of her readers with *The Dawn is at Hand,* published in 1966. Aboriginal suffrage was finally officially realized in 1967, thanks to amendments to the Australian Constitution introduced and championed by individuals like Oodgeroo Noonuccal. She published *My People: A Kath Walker Collection* in 1970, which gathered *We Are Going* and *The Dawn is at Hand* together under one cover, along with new poetry and prose. The year 1970 was an influential one for Oodgeroo, who was awarded the Mary Gilmore Medal and made a Member of the Order of the British Empire (MBE). That same year, she returned to Stradbroke and purchased some property on which she built a cultural center and school she named Moongalba. Thousands of people came there to learn about the Aborigines through Oodgeroo Noonuccal's storytelling and boundless energy.

Oodgeroo continued to write, publishing *Stradbroke Dreamtime* in 1972. This was a divided collection, the first half autobiographical sketches from her childhood and the second half stories told in the traditional manner. In 1975 she was presented with the Jessie Litchfield Award for *The Dawn is at Hand* (1966), and awarded the Fellowship of Australian Writers Patricia Weickhardt Award in 1977 as well. From 1978 to 1979 Oodgeroo traveled to the United States on a Fulbright Scholarship, lecturing on Aboriginal rights. She won the Black Makers Award in San Francisco, California, (1977) for her part in the film *Shadow Sister,* then wrote and illustrated the children's story *Father Sky and Mother Earth* in 1981.

Oodgeroo continued to publish a steady stream of material, including a collection of her artwork edited by Ulli Beier in 1985 titled *Quandamooka: The Art of Kath Walker,* a children's story called *Little Fella* (1986), *Kath Walker in China* (1988), described in the *Oxford Companion to Twentieth-Century Literature in English* as a collection of verse that affirmed the author's "belief in the power of people to effect positive change." Other works included the children's story *The Rainbow Serpent* (1988) as a collaboration with one of her sons, *The Spirit of Australia* (1989), *Towards a Global Village in the Southern Hemisphere* (1989), *Australian Legends and Landscapes* (1990), and *Australia's Unwritten History: Some Legends of Our Land* (1992). One common theme in this body of work was her attempts to make the Aboriginal perspective approachable.

She also took her activism beyond the written word, working on many committees dedicated to Aboriginal interests, like the Aboriginal Arts Board. Australian composer Malcolm Williamson even paired a selection of her poetry to music, calling it *The Dawn is at Hand.* She taught, spoke and mentored at many schools such as the University of the South Pacific, and received honorary doctorates from multiple institutions.

The Birth of Oodgeroo Noonuccal

In 1988 Oodgeroo Noonuccal returned the MBE she had been awarded 18 years earlier to Queen Elizabeth II, protesting the two-century anniversary of European settlement. Her obituary in the *New York Times* quoted her opinion that the revelry applauded "200 years of humiliation and brutality to the aboriginal people," and she was recorded in *Stradbroke Dreamtime* as insisting on returning the honor until "all Aboriginal tribes in Australia were given unconditional land rights in their country." She explained that she had accepted it initially because she and other Aboriginals hoped it would open doors, but she explained in the *Australian Women's Archives Project,* "Since 1970 I have lived in the hope that the parliaments of England and Australia would confer and attempt to rectify the terrible damage done to the Australian Aborigines. The forbidding us our tribal language, the murders, the poisoning, the scalping, the denial of land custodianship, especially our spiritual sacred sites, the destruction of our sacred places especially our Bora Grounds . . . all these terrible things that the Aboriginal tribes of Australia have suffered without any recognition even of admitted guilt from the parliaments of England . . . From the Aboriginal point of view, what is there to celebrate?."

Kath Walker also changed her name in 1988 as a way of stripping the label given to her by invading forces, and adopted a traditional name. Oodgeroo means paperbark, and Noonuccal is her tribe's name—hence Oodgeroo of the Noonuccal tribe.

Gone, but not Forgotten

Oodgeroo died on September 9, 1993, at the age of 72 in Brisbane, Australia, of cancer, leaving behind her two sons. A national celebration of black Australian writers had been planned for September 30th of that year at Moongalba, and her family assured the participants that she would have wanted it to take place despite her absence. A trust was established in February of 1994 with the goal of continuing

Oodgeroo's work toward an understanding between Aboriginal and non-Aboriginal Australians. Oodgeroo Noonuccal has been described by those who knew her as "direct," "impassioned," "deeply committed," "charismatic," and "controversial." She spoke and wrote bluntly about the mistreatment of her people, so much so that she frequently ruffled the feathers of her many readers while trying to open their eyes. In *Stradbroke Dreamtime* (1972), she described her girlhood home as a place "stocked with natural beauty . . . [with] ferns and flowers growing in abundance [and] white miles of sand stretching as far as the eye could see." In the same piece, she lamented the fact that "Stradbroke is dying. The birds and animals are going. The trees and flowers are being pushed aside and left to die," and assured the reader that "greedy, thoughtless, stupid, ignorant man . . . will suffer. His ruthless bulldozers are digging his own grave." Mudrooroo, an Aboriginal intellectual, coined the term *poetemics* to describe Noonuccal, whom he identified more as a polemicist than a poet.

In July of 2002 *The Australian Workers Heritage Centre* opened with the exhibition "A Lot on Her Hands," which focused on Australia's working women. Oodgeroo Noonuccal's life is featured as one of the exhibitions. The *Oxford Companion to Twentieth–Century Literature in English* wrote, "Overall her work, and life, was a passionate and articulate expression of wrongs inflicted upon Australian Aboriginal people and of the Aboriginal's indomitable will not only to survive but to flourish." Oodgeroo's seemingly timeless popularity is a testament to both her survival and her prosperity.

Books

Articles on Women Writers: Volume Two, 1976–1984, edited by Narda Lacey Schwartz, ABC-Clio, Inc., 1986.
The Bloomsbury Guide to Women's Literature, edited by Claire Buck, Bloomsbury Publishing, Ltd., 1992.
The Cambridge Guide to Literature in English: Third Edition, edited by Dominic Head, Cambridge University Press, 2006.
The Encyclopedia of Women Social Reformers, edited by Helen Rappaport, ABC-Clio, Inc., 2001.
Encyclopedia of World Literature in the 20th Century: Volume 3: L-R, St. James Press, 1999.
The Feminist Companion to Literature in English: Women Writers from the Middle Ages to the Present, edited by Virginia Blain, Patricia Clements and Isobel Grundy, Yale University Press, 1990.
Noonuccal, Oodgeroo, *Stradbroke Dreamtime: Aboriginal Stories,* Lothrop, Lee and Shepard Books, 1994.
The Oxford Companion to Australian Literature, edited by William H. Wilde, Joy Hooton and Barry Andrews, Oxford University Press, 1994.
The Oxford Companion to Twentieth-Century Literature in English, edited by Jenny Stringer, Oxford University Press, 1996.
The Oxford Companion to Twentieth-Century Poetry in English, edited by Ian Hamilton, Oxford University Press, 1994.
Twentieth-Century Poetry in English, edited by Ian Hamilton, Oxford University Press, 1994.

Periodicals

New York Times Biographical Service: Volume 24 Number 9, September 17, 1993.

Online

"Kath Walker: Poet and Activist," *Equality Media,* http://www.equalitymedia.com.au/equality/video/ev021.htm (December 18, 2006).
"Oodgeroo," *Australian Works Heritage Centre,* http://www.australianworkersheritagecentre.com.au/10_pdf/oodgeroo.pdf (December 18, 2006).
"Oodgeroo Noonuccal," *Australian Women Exhibition,* http://www.womenaustralia.info/biogs/IMP0082b.htm (December 18, 2006).
"Women in Australia's Working History," *Australian Women Exhibition,* http://www.womenaustralia.info/biogs/AWE2155b.htm (December 18, 2006). □

Indra K. Nooyi

In 2006 Indian-born executive Indra K. Nooyi (born 1955) was named chief executive officer of PepsiCo, parent company of the ubiquitous Pepsi-Cola, the giant multinational drink and snack-food maker. With her elevation to the post, PepsiCo became the second-largest company in the United States with a female CEO—the largest if a ranking of companies by total stock value was used.

Nooyi was also one of the few foreign-born executives of either gender in top U.S. corporate ranks. "Being a woman, an immigrant, and a person of color made it thrice difficult" for her to succeed, she said in an interview quoted in England's *Guardian* newspaper. PepsiCo, with its products sold all over the world, had taken strides to diversify its workforce by gender and ethnicity, aiming to staff itself with personnel who would understand the markets in which the company operated. Yet there was general agreement in business publications that Nooyi's fast-track ascent up the corporate ladder was due not to diversity initiatives but to her brilliant moves as a strategic planner. Thanks to initiatives she had spearheaded, some of them risky ones, PepsiCo eclipsed its longtime rival, Coke, in many measures of performance in the early 2000s.

Solved Political Problems as Game

Nooyi was born Indra Krishnamurthy in Madras (now called Chennai), in southern India, on October 28, 1955. Her family was part of India's middle class; her father was a bank official, and a grandfather, whom she later credited as an inspiration, was a district judge. Nooyi's mother also stretched her children's minds, making up improvised games for Nooyi and her sister, Chandrika, based on world problems. Nooyi had to place herself, for example, in the position of prime minister of India. She loved to read and to watch Tamil-language film comedies. She also had a younger brother, Narayanan, who followed her to Yale and to the American corporate world. Nooyi broke the mold in India's society, which was still defined by strong gender roles. She played cricket and was a member of an all-girl rock band. Even as a corporate executive she remained an enthusiastic

singer and electric guitarist. "I was a wild one," she told Sarah Murray of the *Financial Times*.

Nooyi, a devout Hindu, attended Madras Christian College, majoring in chemistry and graduating with a bachelor's degree in 1976. She got her first experience in business managing advertising for a campus newspaper. Nooyi went on to earn a master's degree in business administration, majoring in finance and marketing, at the Indian Institute of Management in Calcutta (now Kolkata), one of just two business schools in India at the time, finishing in 1978. Her first job after getting her degree was as a product manager with a textile maker, Mettur Beardsell, but she soon moved on to a similar position with Johnson & Johnson, an American-based multinational maker of personal care products.

The job posed severe challenges for the young business graduate, for she was given the task of managing the introduction of Stayfree sanitary napkins to India, where advertising for the product was banned. Nooyi got around the restrictions by marketing Stayfree pads to young women directly, at schools and colleges. Then, while leafing through a magazine in her new home of Bombay (now Mumbai), she read an article about the Yale University School of Management, then only two years old. Friends in the United States convinced her that she should apply for admission, and Nooyi mailed her application off without really thinking it would be successful. She was not only admitted but was also offered financial aid. Despite societal pressures, Nooyi's parents got on board with her plans. "It

was unheard of for a good, conservative, south Indian Brahmin girl to do this," she told Murray. "It would make her an absolutely unmarriageable commodity after that."

Even that prophecy turned out to be inaccurate, as she later married Raj Nooyi, a management consultant, and raised two daughters. Nooyi adjusted easily to life in the United States, but at first she lived on the edge financially, working an overnight shift at a reception desk and wearing saris to her summer jobs because she could not afford a Western suit. (She was still seen wearing them occasionally in the halls at PepsiCo, however.) The program at Yale, however, proved a perfect fit for Nooyi. She jumped enthusiastically into novel American management ideas like team-building exercises, going out with a group on an Arctic survival expedition at one point. A Yale course on communication was unlike any she had taken before. "That was invaluable for someone who came from a culture where communication wasn't perhaps the most important aspect of business, at least in my time," she told Murray. She learned to analyze problems in detail and to work with a team on typical American corporate planning projects.

Followed Strategic Planning Career Track

After receiving the degree of master of public and private management from Yale in 1980, Nooyi went to work as a director of international corporate strategy projects for the Boston Consulting Group. She moved from there to the automotive division development team at electronics maker Motorola in 1986, and in 1988 she was promoted to vice president and director of corporate strategy and planning there. In 1990 she accepted the post of senior vice president and director of corporate strategy and strategic marketing at Asea Brown Boveri (ABB), a diverse collection of American businesses, associated with power plant construction and industrial equipment fabrication, that had been acquired by a Swiss-Swedish conglomerate. She told Laurie Kretchmar of *Fortune* that it was like a "$6 billion startup," for it was left to Nooyi to forge a group of some 15 separate businesses into a cohesive operation. In her first year at ABB, she assembled a group of managers across corporate division lines to develop a program that assisted electric utilities in complying with Clean Air Act regulations.

By 1994 Nooyi, regarded as a rising star in management, was being aggressively courted by corporate headhunters. Nooyi studied video recordings of Chicago Bulls basketball games, not only to become familiar with the pro sports world but also to glean insights about teamwork. "She was on every packaged-goods company's list in terms of CEO jobs," consultant Kenneth A. Harris Jr. told Claudia Deutsch of the *New York Times*. PepsiCo thought enough of her to bring in former CEO Christopher Sinclair, who had grown up in India as the son of an Exxon Mobil executive, to her interview to try to help sell her on the organization. She joined PepsiCo in 1994 as senior vice president of corporate strategy and development.

Working closely with PepsiCo CEO Roger Enrico, Nooyi remapped the company's future. "I wake up in the middle of the night and write different versions of PepsiCo on a sheet of paper," she told Melanie Wells of *Fortune*.

At the time, the company owned the KFC, Pizza Hut, and Taco Bell restaurant chains, which were part of a single division. Nooyi, over the objections of her new boss Enrico, pushed the company to spin the restaurants off. "Indra is like a dog with a bone," Enrico told Wells after being brought around to Nooyi's position. The restaurants were divested in 1997.

At that point, the outlines of Nooyi's grand strategy were coming into view. She believed that PepsiCo's core products, its soft drinks and Frito-Lay salty fried snacks, faced flat or declining sales in the future owing to consumers' desires for healthier lifestyles, and that the company needed to diversify into new products within the field of packaged foods. Nooyi steered PepsiCo toward the acquisition of the Tropicana juice producer in 1998, a $3.3 billion outlay that was questioned by many PepsiCo executives. Nooyi, who personally liked Tropicana orange juice, was vindicated when PepsiCo posted four consecutive quarters of growth in revenues, profits, and return on investment in 2000. She was promoted to chief financial officer of the company that year.

Supervised Quaker Oats Merger

When Enrico retired due to ill health, Nooyi found herself with a new boss, CEO Steve Reinemund. The two implemented an even bigger deal, a joining of Pepsi with the venerable Quaker Oats Company that was variously described as a takeover and a merger. The details of the negotiations were mostly handled by Nooyi. The fusion of the two companies was a difficult process, but once again Nooyi's instincts were vindicated, as PepsiCo posted strong growth in the early 2000s, even as Coke sales were stagnant. The deal gave PepsiCo ownership of Gatorade, the top-selling American sports drink.

Reinemund and Nooyi were portrayed in business circles as something of a corporate odd couple. Reinemund, a former U.S. Marine, was the classic buttoned-down executive, but Nooyi was less conventional in her saris or long scarves. Sometimes she went barefoot at the office. Nooyi, whose aunt was a noted Indian vocalist, said that she had music running through her head constantly, and she sometimes hummed during tense business meetings. "She has a sort of guileless, unencumbered quality," Lincoln Center for the Performing Arts president Gordon J. Davis told *Business Week*. "She'll say something almost naïve, very personal and romantic in a sense, but totally truthful." Spontaneous and often humorous, Nooyi had a brush with controversy after a Columbia University commencement speech in which she likened the five continents and their economic functions to the thumb and four fingers of the hand, with North America as the middle finger (she denied any unpatriotic intent, contending that her remarks had been taken out of context and misconstrued).

Sometimes there were rumors of tension between Nooyi and Reinemund, but they maintained that constructive tension was essential to the functioning of a healthy organization, and PepsiCo's strong balance sheets seemed to support the contention. Between 2001 and 2006, PepsiCo's annual revenue increased from $24 billion to $33 billion, and in 2006 its total market capitalization (the value of a company's outstanding stock shares) passed that of longtime market leader Coca-Cola. Part of that growth came from international operations, which were placed under their own PepsiCo International umbrella in 2003. Some of the credit went to Nooyi. "Steve and I have worked closely for the past five years on everything related to PepsiCo," she told Deutsch, "from long-term strategy to day-to-day business. We complete each other's sentences." Despite their contrasting styles, the combination of Nooyi's planning expertise and Reinemund's operational focus was a powerful one.

So it was no surprise when Nooyi was named PepsiCo's new chief executive on August 14, 2006, after Reinemund announced his retirement. There had been speculation that she would be given the leadership of a PepsiCo division to add to her experience in the field of day-to-day operations management, the one gap in her resumé, but she was the clear choice as Reinemund's replacement, especially in view of a crisis facing PepsiCo in her native India, where both Pepsi and Coke soft drinks had been banned in several Indian states after an activist group charged that they showed high levels of pesticide contamination. More broadly, PepsiCo was a company in need of constant reinvention as consumer preferences shifted. At the end of 2006, having topped *Fortune* magazine's list of the 50 most powerful women in U.S. business, she was, it seemed, the right woman for the job.

Books

International Directory of Business Biographies, 4 vols., St. James, 2005.

Periodicals

Business Week, January 29, 2001.
Chicago Tribune, August 15, 2006.
Economic Times (India), September 23, 2006; September 28, 2006.
Economist, August 19, 2006.
Financial Times, January 26, 2004; August 15, 2006; August 17, 2006.
Forbes, January 20, 2003.
Fortune, May 6, 1991; October 16, 2006.
New York Times, August 15, 2006.
San Jose Mercury News, August 15, 2006.
Times (London, England), August 15, 2006.
Times of India, May 20, 2005.
World and I, May 2001.

Online

"Indra Nooyi: New CEO of Pepsico Inc.," Overseas Indian, http://www.overseasindian.in/2006/aug/news/18newsmaker.shtml (December 23, 2006).
"The Rise & Rise of Indra Nooyi," *Economic Times* (India), http://www.economictimes.indiatimes.com/articleshow/1896315.cms (December 23, 2006).
"A Woman with Fizz and Bottle," *Guardian Unlimited* (London, England), http://www.observer.guardian.co.uk/business/story/0,,1853951,00.html (December 23, 2006). □

O

Michael Babatunde Olatunji

Nigerian drummer Michael Babatunde Olatunji (1927–2003), though less well known than other African musicians who have exported their traditions to the West, deserves recognition as a pioneer among them. His *Drums of Passion* album (1959) paved the way not only for a host of other releases of African music, but in many ways for the entire category of world music.

*D*rums of Passion, in the words of Olatunji's autobiography collaborator Robert Atkinson, "introduced hundreds of thousands and perhaps millions of Americans to African drumming." And Olatunji's influence extended into other realms as well. His African drum ensembles were important adjuncts to the meetings and public events that shaped the civil rights and Black Power movements of the 1960s. The long period of experimentation with African traditions on the part of jazz musicians can be traced back in many cases to their exposure to Olatunji's music. And the modern popularity of hand drumming and drum circles in the United States grew from Olatunji's educational activities.

Groomed for Chieftancy

Babatunde Olatunji grew up in a traditional Yoruba cultural setting in what was then British-ruled colonial Nigeria. He believed that he was born in 1927, in the coastal village of Ajido. His father was a successful fisherman who was about to ascend to the rank of village chief, and after his father's sudden death the family began to raise Olatunji with the idea that he would replace his father in that role. But Olatunji gravitated toward the music he heard every day in Yorubaland. "I heard the drum while I was in my mother's womb," he wrote in *The Beat of My Drum.* "I woke up every day to the beat of the drum. I grew up hearing the drummers heralding the dawn of each day in front of the chief's compound, serenading shoppers in the marketplace, playing at name-giving ceremonies."

Even when he was very young he would tag along with the area's master drummers and beg for lessons. "In my village there was always music and everyone would grab something to play," Olatunji wrote. "But I went beyond that. . . . The master drummers would all say, 'Are you here again?' And I would say, 'Yeah.' Those of us who became drummers were the ones who went beyond that common exposure and learned the craft." First the master drummers gave him a cowbell, whose simple rhythmic pattern forms the basis for Yoruba traditional percussion, and then he was allowed to handle some of the huge variety of Yoruba drums, each connected with a specific religious or social purpose, or with a deity in the Yoruba pantheon.

Olatunji came to realize that he did not want to be Ajido's chief. He wrote that, when he was 12 or 13, "I was saying to myself, 'I really don't want this kind of power, or to be the center of attention where I cannot express myself truly.' " Instead, Olatunji was sent to live with an uncle and aunt in the capital city of Lagos, and went to school there. He learned to speak English, and a new layer was added to his religious education by his uncle, a member of the African Methodist church and a devout individual whose observation of the Sabbath even prohibited cooking.

Lagos brought the musical sounds of the world to Olatunji's ears. He owned a shortwave radio on which he could pick up British Broadcasting Corporation programs featuring American big-band jazz and classical music. And he became fascinated with the idea of coming to America, a desire that intensified as he continued his education at the American-sponsored Baptist Academy in Lagos. Olatunji worked for two years in the port city of Sapele as a "vacancy officer," a government human resources administrator. But when he and a cousin heard about scholarships offered for college study in the United States by the Rotary Education Foundation, they decided to apply. They were accepted for study at historically black Morehouse College in Atlanta, and on April 27, 1950, a cargo ship on which they had booked passage docked in New Orleans.

Introduced Black Students to African Culture

Arriving in Georgia, Olatunji began a full experience of Southern segregation when he was told to take a black-only taxi. The idea of black consciousness was still mostly in the future as he began to interact with his classmates at Morehouse, who included Martin Luther King Jr. and future Atlanta mayor Maynard Jackson. "Don't you ever tell me I'm of African descent," Jackson told Olatunji, as the latter recalled in his autobiography. "I am a Negro. I am born in America." Some Morehouse students believed Africa was a place inhabited by beings like the fictional character Tarzan. Olatunji was planning to become a diplomat, but he added a second aim to his outlook. "I have a job to tell these people about the rich cultural heritage of Africa," he remembered deciding. "I better get on with this mission now."

Olatunji began giving lecture demonstrations at both black and white Atlanta churches, playing a small hand drum he had brought from Lagos and interspersing biblical quotations among his musical explanations. At Morehouse he organized a small group to play African music at school social gatherings, and as the pioneering studies of the African roots of black American culture began to filter through the African-American academic world, he began to find more receptive audiences. Elected president of Morehouse's student body, Olatunji graduated in 1954 and enrolled at New York University in a graduate program in public administration.

Trying to earn money on the side in order to make tuition payments, Olatunji organized a small African drum ensemble. He married Amy Bush, and the pair had two sons and two daughters. Olatunji eventually had to withdraw from his graduate program due to lack of funds, but music was steadily taking its place in his life. He began giving concerts, and his group played at civil rights rallies led by King and others. In 1958 he returned to Africa to attend the All African People's Conference organized by Ghanaian independence leader Kwame Nkrumah, who urged him to give up his ambitions to become a diplomat and instead devote himself to spreading African culture. That year Olatunji found a job playing drums in a Radio City Music Hall dance production called "African Fantasy." There he was spotted by Columbia label talent administrator John Hammond, who also discovered such performers as Billie Holiday and Bruce Springsteen.

Signed to Columbia, Olatunji released *Drums of Passion* in 1959. At first he used the name Michael Olatunji (he had previously used Michael Babatunde Olatunji as a Christianized form of his name), but later printings restored the name Babatunde Olatunji. The impact of the album, in Atkinson's words, "can hardly be overstated, yet much about it needs to be qualified." *Drums of Passion* was the first album of African drumming recorded in a modern studio. Previously, most recordings of African music had been made by scholars. The music on the album was not a pure representation of Olatunji's Yoruba traditions, although it did feature Nigerian rhythms. Instead it offered a hybrid music containing Ghanaian, Afro-Caribbean, and African-American elements. The musicians, except for Olatunji, were not African. Critics later accused Olatunji of presenting a watered-down version of African music, but Anthony C. Davis, writing in the *Black Issues Book Review*, argued that Olatunji succeeded in blending various traditions into "something new that represented the spread of African culture throughout the Diaspora."

Influenced Jazz and Rock Musicians

Olatunji recorded five albums for Columbia between 1959 and 1966, as jazz musicians flocked to his shows and began to incorporate African drumming into their own albums. He appeared on a 1960 album that marked a high point of the confluence between jazz and the civil rights movement: drummer Max Roach and playwright Oscar Brown Jr.'s *We Insist: Freedom Now Suite*. In 1961 he performed at the prestigious Village Gate club with jazz saxophonist John Coltrane and drummer Art Blakey. Another fan was rock musician Carlos Santana, who covered Olatunji's "Jin-Go-Lo-Ba" (from *Drums of Passion*) in 1969, retitling it "Jingo." The piece was also remade in 2004 by English dance musician Fatboy Slim, this time under its original title.

In 1964 Olatunji performed at the African Pavilion of the New York World's Fair. He established the Olatunji Center for African Culture in New York's Harlem neighborhood, and wrote a children's book, *Musical Instruments of Africa*. The center served as an important site in New York's black culture; the last performance given by Coltrane before his death in 1967 was held there, and Olatunji used it as a home base for school-based educational programs. One young person who had attended an Olatunji school workshop was future Grateful Dead drummer Mickey Hart. However, Olatunji had signed away his rights to the considerable profits reaped by *Drums of Passion* and its successors, and he faced persistent financial problems as his Harlem center attracted little institutional support. It closed in the early 1980s. For a short time he returned to Nigeria and considered entering politics in that country.

The revival of Olatunji's career coincided with a new wave of American interest in African music in the 1980s, now manifest as much among white as among black audiences. After Olatunji met Mickey Hart once again, he was invited to open for the Grateful Dead at a 1985 New Year's Eve concert in Oakland, California. Some of early albums were reissued on compact disc by the Rykodisc label. In 1991 Olatunji appeared on Hart's Grammy-winning global percussion compilation *Planet Drum.* By this time, hand drumming and drum circle meetings had become popular in communities oriented toward New Age spirituality; one 1992 drum circle organized by Hart in Marin County, California, drew 2,000 participants. Though such drummers reproduced few of the complexities of African percussion, they looked toward Olatunji as a spiritual forefather.

Never wealthy, and troubled by diabetes symptoms in his later years, Olatunji made a living by touring and by teaching at spiritual retreats such as upstate New York's Omega Institute and (as artist-in-residence) the Esalen Institute in California's Big Sur area, where he resided toward the end of his life. Occasionally he received guest academic posts in Europe and Africa. Olatunji recorded new albums, including *Drums of Passion: The Beat* (1986), *Drums of Passion: The Invocation* (1988), and *Love Drum Talk* (1997). He also made an instructional video, *African Drumming.* In 1997 he performed at the Million Woman March in Washington, D.C. Babatunde Olatunji died in Big Sur, California, on April 6, 2003.

Books

Contemporary Black Biography, volume 36, Gale, 2002.
Olatunji, Babatunde, with Robert Atkinson, *The Beat of My Drum: An Autobiography,* Temple University Press, 2005.

Periodicals

Black Issues Book Review, May-June 2005.
Independent (London, England), April 11, 2003.
New York Times, April 9, 2003.
San Francisco Chronicle, April 10, 2003.
Times (London, England), April 12, 2003. □

Mark Oliphant

Mark Oliphant (1901–2000) was considered a great leader in the sciences, one who inspired his students by his own show of zeal for his research and his positive view of life in general. He was a physicist who helped develop the atom bomb, although he later protested its use and became an ardent humanitarian. In Oliphant's obituary, the *New York Times* wrote, "He pressed for the peaceful use of atomic energy and spoke out against all weapons capable of mass destruction. Starting in 1945 he insisted that the world must 'get rid of war or die,' and that the use of nuclear arms would be a 'moral crime.' Using nuclear weapons, he said, was 'a dirty, rotten way to kill people' that could not be justified 'in any circumstances,' even in retaliation."

Born and Raised in Australia

Oliphant was born Markus Laurence Elwin Oliphant on October 8, 1901, in Adelaide, Australia. He was the oldest of five sons. Oliphant's father was a very religious man and he wanted his oldest son to be a priest, but Oliphant had always been more interested in gadgets and science than in religion. Oliphant was quoted on the Australia Biography website as saying, "I was always fooling about in the shed at the back of the garden with bits of wire and bits of wood, making what my brothers called my 'raggedy, baggedy engines.' " Still he was highly influenced by religion as a young man, and he always held a healthy respect for it. As he grew up he also held an appreciation for education, partly instilled by his mother, who was a schoolteacher. He graduated from high school with good grades before he went on to attend the University of Adelaide. He was originally interested in dentistry or medicine, but a teacher of his, Dr. Roy Burdon, saw an aptitude for physics in the young man and persuaded him to switch his major. After a short while Oliphant agreed, and he graduated with a degree in physics. To pay for his education he took any odd job he could find, working his way through university.

After graduation he got a job cleaning floors for a jewelry manufacturer. He married Rosa Wilbraham, who was also from Adelaide, in 1925, and the two had one daughter. It was while he was working at the jewelers in 1925 that Oliphant attended a lecture given by New Zealand physicist Ernest Rutherford. He was so impressed by what Rutherford had to say that he immediately decided that if he could possibly bring it about, he would work for Rutherford one day. Rutherford worked at the Cavendish Laboratory in Cambridge, England, one of the most advanced research facilities in nuclear power at that time. In 1927 Oliphant won an exhibition prize at Adelaide University, and then was accepted to Cambridge University. He took a job as exhibition scholar at the Cavendish Laboratory, fulfilling his wish. He worked there under Rutherford with a team of scientists whose task was to find a way to split an atom.

Team First to Split the Atom

Oliphant and the team he worked with managed to split the first atom in 1932. It was an amazing accomplishment, but did not take up all of Oliphant's time. Besides his work on splitting the atom, Oliphant concentrated on artificially disintegrating the nucleus and positive ions of the atom as well as designing a particle accelerator. While doing these things, Oliphant himself discovered helium 3 and tritium, and also figured out that the nuclei of heavy hydrogen could be forced to react with one another and to fuse together. It was this discovery of fusion that led the way to the hydrogen bomb, although Oliphant never wanted nor intended the knowledge to be used in such a way. It was American scientist Edward Teller who used Oliphant's knowledge to build the atom bomb.

In 1937 Oliphant took a position with the University of Birmingham, where he became a professor of physics.

While at the university, along with John Randall and Harry Boot, he continued his research, and in 1939 he received a grant to help develop a short wavelength radar. It was this radar that helped the fight against the German U-boats and bomber offensives during World War II. Former wavelengths had been around 150 centimeters, very widely spread out; but these new ones were only 10 centimeters, which meant that the radar waves could be focused in narrow beams on one specific point to find ships, submarines, and aircraft, as well as cities. It was a world-changing discovery. That was the same year that Oliphant took a trip to visit Berkeley, California. He there met Ernest Lawrence, who taught Oliphant how to build a 60-inch cyclotron. Because of the advent of World War II he was unable to finish the project until 1950.

World War II Brought About Atom Bomb

In 1940 two men, Otto Frisch and Rudolf Peierls, who also worked at the University of Birmingham, theorized that uranium-235 could be used to create an atom bomb. Oliphant was charged with taking their ideas to a committee, which had the code name of Maud. Maud in turn sent the theory to the United States and its Uranium Committee in March of 1941, but the United States seemed to be uninterested in the idea, as they made no reply to the report. Britain, however, entrenched in war with Germany, thought the bomb was necessary and important to their efforts. Oliphant was sent to America, where he arranged to meet with the Uranium Committee. He stressed the importance of the project and urged that the committee begin implementing a plan to develop an atomic weapon.

After speaking to the committee he went to visit his friends and fellow scientists Ernest Lawrence, James Conant, and Enrico Fermi. He stressed to them the importance of the project, looking to them to back him up. Because of his efforts, the United States established the Office of Scientific Research and Development. This office took on the Uranium Committee as one of its projects, and in December of 1941, after Pearl Harbor was attacked by the Japanese, they set up the Manhattan Engineering District to house what would soon be called the Manhattan Project, to research the building of a uranium atom bomb.

Oliphant Appalled by Bomb's Power

Oliphant moved to America in November of 1943 to work on the Manhattan Project, sent as a British delegate. After the use of the bomb in 1945 on Hiroshima and Nagasaki, Japan, however, he was appalled by the devastation, and argued against its ever being used again. He especially argued against an American monopoly on nuclear technology. *Time International* wrote, "Oliphant made key contributions to the understanding of nuclear disintegration and the design of particle accelerators. 'We had no idea,' he later said, 'that this would one day be applied to make hydrogen bombs.'" Although he had been sent to press America to build a bomb, no one at the time knew how devastating such a bomb would be, and Oliphant has said he would not have pressed for its creation if he had known. He did little work on the actual bomb, however, because the idea of it made him

anxious. Instead he spent most of his time at Berkeley with Lawrence trying to refine Uranium 235. It was an important project, if less militarily focused. For his work with this he was awarded the Hughes Medal in 1943.

In April of 1945 Oliphant returned to England. After VE-Day he returned to the University of Birmingham to continue on as professor of physics. It was while he was there that he first heard how the atom bomb was used and exactly how powerful it was. He felt justifiably divided about the report. On the one hand he felt a scientist's excitement that an idea he had helped create had worked, but on the other hand, the stronger side, he had a humane abhorrence at what the bomb had cost in human lives. Like so many of the scientists who had worked on the project, Oliphant had never expected that the bomb's effects would be so devastating. From this point on, Oliphant became an extreme critic of nuclear weapons. He joined the Pugwash Conferences on Science and World Affairs to discuss with people all over the world the idea that no one should ever use such a weapon again. The *Economist* wrote, "Like many of the scientists who helped to make the atomic bomb, Mark Oliphant expressed dismay when it was used to destroy Hiroshima and Nagasaki. During the cold war years he was labeled a 'peacenik,' the contemptuous term used to describe those who questioned the morality of using nuclear weapons."

Returned to Australia and Knighted

Because of his anti-nuclear weapons stance, Oliphant was often left out of scientific experiments involving nuclear power. The U.S. government refused to give Oliphant a visa in 1951 when he wanted to attend a nuclear physics conference in Chicago. The British neglected to ask Oliphant for help when they tested 12 nuclear weapons from 1952 to 1957, even though he was exceptionally qualified to assess the safety of the tests to make certain no one was hurt by them. But Oliphant never again changed his opinion on the weapons. Because of the work he did during the war, Oliphant was given a Congressional Medal of Freedom with Gold Palm, but the Australian government vetoed the honor.

Oliphant returned to Australia in 1950. There he became the first director of the Research School of Physical Sciences at the new Australian National University in Canberra. While there, he helped design and build the world's largest homopolar generator, which was used to give power to a large scientific railgun instrument. He also set up the Australian Academy of Science in 1954 and became its first president in 1956. In 1959 Oliphant was knighted.

Became State Governor of South Australia

He retired from the Australian National University in 1967. He was then invited to become the state governor of South Australia. He accepted the honor and held office from 1971 to 1976. As governor he used his position to oppose France's nuclear testing in the Pacific. He went so far, in fact, that he said he would join anyone putting together an expedition to try to stop them. In 1977 he was made a Companion in the Order of Australia.

Oliphant's wife, Rosa, died in 1987. After witnessing her suffering prior to her death, he became a strong proponent for voluntary euthanasia for debilitating and incurable diseases. Oliphant died in Canberra on July 14, 2000, at the age of 98. Oliphant will not soon be forgotten, however. Many locations have been named after the great scientist, including the Mark Oliphant Conservation Park, the Oliphant building at Australian National University, the Oliphant wing of the Physics Building at the University of Adelaide and the Mark Oliphant Building in Bedford Park, South Australia. A South Australian High School science competition was also named in his honor. He will be remembered as the scientist who unwillingly helped to build the atomic bomb, but who stuck by his principles in trying to stop the further development and use of nuclear weapons.

Periodicals

Economist, July 22, 2000.
New York Times, July 18, 2000.
Time International, October 25, 1999; July 31, 2000.

Online

"Oliphant, Markus Laurence Elwin (1901–2000)," *Bright Sparcs,* http://www.asap.unimelb.edu.au-bsparcs-biogs-P000683b.htm (January 2, 2007).
"Sir Markus Oliphant," *Australian Biography,* http://www.australianbiography.gov.au-oliphant-bio.html (January 2, 2007). □

Buck O'Neil

John Jordan "Buck" O'Neil (1911–2006) loved baseball, and immersed himself in the game from age 12 to 94. A standout Negro League player and two-time batting champion, O'Neil went on to become the first black manager of a major league team.

As a scout, O'Neil was responsible for recruiting such Hall of Fame players as Lou Brock and Ernie Banks, and a tireless spokesman for the history of Negro League baseball. For all his efforts, O'Neil came to be considered an "architect" of the game, as Brock described him in the *Columbia Daily Tribune.* "He helped shape the game. But even greater, he shaped the character of young black men. He touched the heart of everyone who loved the game." He was "perhaps the greatest ambassador baseball has ever known," in the words of Jane Forbes Clark, chairperson of the Baseball Hall of Fame, as quoted in *Sporting News.*

Discovered Baseball at Early Age

John Jordan O'Neil was born on November 13, 1911, in Carrabelle, Florida. He was the second of three children born to John Sr., a sawmill worker, and Luella, a restaurant manager. The family moved to Sarasota in 1923. It was there

that O'Neil received his first taste of professional baseball. As a 12-year-old, O'Neil began his semi-professional career as a member of the Sarasota Tigers and traveled throughout Florida. He took his nickname from Miami Giants semi-pro team co-owner Buck O'Neal. To support himself, he shined shoes and worked as a box boy. O'Neil related a pivotal moment in his life to Steve Wulf of *Sports Illustrated,* "I was considered a good box boy because, while most of the box boys could only carry two crates at a time, I was big and strong enough to carry four. I did that for about three years, at $1.25 a day. One day I was having lunch by myself next to a big stack of boxes, and it was so hot, I said out loud, 'Damn, there has got to be something better than this.'" That "something," O'Neil decided, was baseball.

Following completion of the eighth grade, O'Neil wanted to continue his education. Because of his skin color, however, he was not admitted to the high school in Sarasota. O'Neil was eventually able to obtain his high school diploma and earned a baseball and football scholarship to Edward Waters College in Jacksonville. He completed two years of college before leaving school to play baseball in 1934.

Played, Managed, Scouted in the Negro League

From 1934 to 1938 O'Neil played on various teams, including the Miami Giants, New York Tigers, and the Shreveport Acme Giants. In 1937 he signed with the Memphis Red Sox, earning $100 per month. That same year, he played for one month with the Zulu Cannibal Giants, a barnstorming team. The Giants, owned by Harlem Globetrotters founder Abe Saperstein, wore straw skirts instead of uniforms, but the team paid well and the players didn't have to wear war paint as some "African-themed" teams did. In 1938, after four years of moving from team to team, O'Neil earned a spot as the first baseman for the Kansas City Monarchs, one of the elite teams of the Negro Leagues.

From 1939 to 1942, Kansas City won four consecutive Negro American League pennants. O'Neil told *Sports Illustrated* about the glory years of the Monarchs: "We were like the New York Yankees. We had that winning tradition, and we were proud. We had a strict dress code—coat and tie, no baseball jackets. We stayed in the best hotels in the world. They just happened to be owned by black people. We ate in the best restaurants in the world. They just happened to be run by blacks. And when we were in Kansas City, well, 18th and Vine was the center of the universe. We'd come to breakfast at Street's Hotel, and there might be Count Basie or Joe Louis or Billie Holiday or Lionel Hampton."

In 1942, O'Neil led the Monarchs to a four-game sweep of the Homestead Grays in the Negro World Series, hitting .353. He won batting titles in 1940 and 1946, hitting .345 and .350 respectively. O'Neil was also named to the West team of the East-West All-Star Classic in 1942, 1943, and 1949 and was a member of Satchel Paige's All Stars. Paige's team, made up of Negro League stars, played a team of white major league players known as Bob Feller's All Stars in a 14-game barnstorming series in 1946. O'Neil remembered that the players who performed in those exhibitions had a mutual respect for the abilities of their opponents. The Negro League All Stars won the majority of the games played.

In 1944, with the United States deeply involved in World War II, O'Neil enlisted for a two-year stint with the U.S. Navy. He was stationed at Subic Bay in the Philippines and worked as a bosun loading and unloading ships. Although he was proud to serve his country, O'Neil regretted the fact that he was not a member of the Monarchs in 1945. That was the year that Jackie Robinson played in Kansas City before signing with the Brooklyn Dodgers.

Following the end of World War II, O'Neil returned to the Monarchs in 1946. He won the batting title that year and also married Memphis schoolteacher Ora Lee Owen. In 1948, O'Neil was named player-manager of the Monarchs. He led Kansas City to league pennants in 1948, 1950, 1951, and 1953 and two Negro World Series titles. Alfred "Slick" Surratt, who played outfield for O'Neil, told Mark Goodman of *People Weekly* about O'Neil's managerial style: "He knew what it took to win a ball game, and he gave you confidence in yourself. After every game, when we got on the bus, he'd go over the game with us, whether we'd won or lost."

O'Neil left the Monarchs in 1956 to become a scout for the Chicago Cubs. He traveled throughout the South searching for talented African American baseball players. He is credited with bringing formidable talents such as Ernie Banks, Lou Brock, Oscar Gamble, Lee Smith, and Joe Carter to the Cubs. In 1962, O'Neil made history by becoming the first African-American coach in the major leagues. Although he had broken through an important barrier, O'Neil eventually realized that the Cubs were not interested in making him a big-league manager and returned to scouting. He remained with the Cubs until 1988, capping a 33-year career with the organization. He returned to Kansas City the following year and joined the Kansas City Royals as a scout, which he would do until his death.

Championed Negro League History

In 1990, O'Neil began raising money for a museum to preserve and celebrate the history of the Negro Leagues. O'Neil was adamant about the need to preserve memories of the Negro Leagues: "It's very important that we know our history. We have to do that . . . this is not a sad story. It's a celebration!" he said, according to the *Pittsburgh Post-Gazette*. His efforts led to the opening of the Negro League Baseball Museum in Kansas City, Missouri. As a co-founder of the museum and one of the most articulate and engaging spokesman for the Negro Leagues, O'Neil began to appear regularly on radio and television programs. In 1994, he was featured prominently on Ken Burns's PBS documentary "Baseball." O'Neil was a key contributor to the segment entitled "Shadow Ball," which chronicled the greatness of the Negro Leagues, but also the pain of discrimination and exclusion from the major leagues. Burns, who won international acclaim for his 1990 documentary about the Civil War, told People Weekly's Goodman about O'Neil's contribution to the nine-part series: "He's the conscience of the program. Because of his dignity, his lack of bitterness and his sense of humor, Buck makes a wonderful ambassador

for the game." Although the "Baseball" series was not as well-received as Burns's Civil War documentary, O'Neil's appearance made him a media celebrity.

In 1996, O'Neil published his autobiography *I Was Right on Time: My Journey From the Negro Leagues to the Majors* with *Sports Illustrated* editor Steve Wulf and David Conrads. In the late 1990s O'Neil remained active in the Royals organization, served as the chairman of the Negro Leagues Baseball Museum Board of the Directors, and was a member of the Veterans' Committee of the National Baseball Hall of Fame in Cooperstown, New York. He worked as a spokesman to secure pensions for surviving Negro League players and to preserve the history of the Negro Leagues. He told Dave Kindred of *The Sporting News* that Negro League baseball was not the clowning, barnstorming jumble commonly portrayed in movies such as *The Bingo Long Traveling All-Stars and Motor Kings*. "Negro League baseball wasn't anything like that. It was like the white major leagues, serious baseball, well organized. There were 16 Negro League ball clubs, each with at least 15 players—the Monarchs had 18 players. There were all those people putting on the games, booking agents, traveling secretaries, trainers. Baseball was black entertainment and was important to black communities."

In February 2006, O'Neil was among the nominees to be inducted into the Baseball Hall of Fame, but he fell one vote short. His fans rallied and promised to make amends for what they perceived to be an error in judgment. Yet O'Neil took the news in stride. "Shed no tears for Buck," O'Neil announced to his fans after hearing the news, according to the *Pittsburgh Post-Gazette*. He pointed to past sorrows caused by racial discrimination that kept him from gaining the education he wanted, admitting "That hurt." From his perspective, he explained "not going into the Hall of Fame, that ain't going to hurt me that much, no." O'Neil bore no grudge. He hosted the induction ceremony in Cooperstown with characteristic charm and grace. He then spent the summer continuing his promotion of baseball, traveling to functions in several states. In July, at age 94, O'Neil became the oldest man to play professional baseball when he stepped up to bat twice at the Northern League All-Star game. Shortly thereafter, O'Neil succumbed to fatigue, spending periods in the hospital. He never regained his strength; he died in Kansas City, Missouri, on October 6, 2006. Buck O'Neil will be remembered as one of the finest players in the Negro Leagues and a legend in the game of baseball. Through his willingness to share his memories of the Negro Leagues, fans everywhere have a greater understanding and deeper appreciation for a significant period in baseball history. To honor his legacy, the Negro Leagues Baseball Museum began raising money to open the John "Buck" O'Neil Education and Research Center in Kansas City. He may yet be honored by the Hall of Fame, which had begun to reconsider O'Neil's exclusion from its halls after his death. Despite any posthumous honors, O'Neil's contributions to the game had already made him, as *Major League Baseball* columnist Mike Bauman called him: "a baseball immortal."

Books

Wheelock, Sean D. *Buck O'Neil: Baseball Legend*, Amereon, 1997.

Periodicals

Chicago Tribune, October 8, 2006.
Columbia Daily Tribune, October 15, 2006.
New York Times, October 8, 2006.
People Weekly, September 26, 1994.
Pittsburgh Post-Gazette, October 7, 2006.
Sports Illustrated, September 19, 1994.
Sporting News, September 5, 1994; October 27, 2006.

Online

Missouri Sports Hall of Fame, www.mosportshalloffame.com/boneil.htm (January 11, 2007).
"O'Neil Bigger than Game Itself," *Major League Baseball*, http://kansascity.royals.mlb.com/NASApp/mlb/news/article_perspectives.jsp?ymd=20060929&content_id=1689281&vkey=perspectives&fext=.jsp (November 6, 2006).

Other

Burns, Ken, *Baseball* (television documentary), PBS, 1994. ☐

Donny and Marie Osmond

Performing together, separately, and as part of a larger family vocal group, American vocalists Donny (born 1957) and Marie (born 1959) Osmond remained icons of popular culture even as their careers passed through phases of varying success. With their distinctively wholesome public images—which did not foreclose private turmoil—the pair were both recognizable figures who embarked on a variety of performance activities and were never out of the spotlight for long.

Raised in Mormon Household

Donald Clark Osmond was born December 9, 1957, in Ogden, Utah, and his sister Olive Marie Osmond followed on October 13, 1959, in the same location. They were the fifth and eighth of George and Olive Osmond's nine children. They were devout members of the Church of Latter-day Saints (known as Mormons); Marie was the only daughter. Donny Osmond's four older brothers began performing at Mormon church services, adding Donny to form a quintet when he was four years old, and their letter-perfect harmonies and precise coordination won the hearts of churchgoers. They began to perform beyond their home church and were eventually invited to Mormon churches around the western United States. As their fame grew, they added barbershop-style secular singing to their repertoire. Beginning in 1966, Marie was part of

the family group called the Osmonds. They were, in the words of *Good Housekeeping*'s Kate Coyne, "America's von Trapp family: a squeaky-clean lineup of eight Mormon brothers and their little sister, Marie."

The Osmonds, managed by their father, were spotted and hired to perform by an executive at the Disneyland amusement park while the family was on vacation there, and with Donny increasingly often filling the role of lead vocalist as his voice grew, they landed spots on the television variety shows of Jerry Lewis and Andy Williams. The group, at first consisting only of the five oldest Osmond brothers for recording purposes, was signed to the MGM label and became the Osmond Brothers, beginning to move from gospel and barbershop harmonies to pop styles but resolutely maintaining a wholesome image. Despite the numerous changes in popular culture fashions over the next four decades, the Osmonds never abandoned that basic orientation.

The breakthrough for the Osmond Brothers came after the Jackson 5, an African-American quintet with a similar age composition, scored a series of hits beginning in 1969. The Osmonds' "One Bad Apple" roosted atop U.S. pop charts for five weeks in 1971 and launched a series of Osmond Brothers hits that spawned an animated children's television series with the brothers contributing their own voices. Donny Osmond also had several solo hits, the biggest of which was "Go Away Little Girl." As the group tried to maintain its momentum in the fast-moving "bubblegum" teen pop scene, they added another brother, Jimmy, and finally Marie Osmond in a series of concert appearances.

Not a hint of strain appeared in the group's well-choreographed concerts and television appearances, but the young Marie Osmond was suffering internally. In her book *Behind the Smile: My Journey Out of Postpartum Depression,* she revealed that she had been sexually abused as a child, although she did not name the abuser. "When I look back," she wrote, according to *Good Housekeeping,* "I see myself as a little girl with no time for childhood. . . . While other kids played, we worked—memorizing scripts, learning to sing a song in Swedish or Japanese for a foreign tour, spending long days dancing, playing instruments, and singing." As a child she was "scared, overwhelmed, and demoralized," and as a teenager "scrutinized, criticized, and sexualized."

Marie Osmond Scored Country Hits

Her recording career, however, got off to a strong start as she took a country-flavored remake of the Anita Bryant hit "Paper Roses" to top chart positions in both the pop and country fields in 1973. The song reached number one on *Billboard* magazine's country singles chart, making Marie one of the youngest singers ever to accomplish that feat. With Donny Osmond's solo recordings, including another cover, "The Twelfth of Never" (formerly recorded by Johnny Mathis), reaching top chart levels that year, Donny and Marie were consistently outstripping the chart performance of the larger Osmonds group. As a result, Donny & Marie Osmond took shape as a performing entity in 1974.

They continued to mine the mixture of country and pop styles that Marie Osmond had exploited successfully, and with adult groups such as the Eagles riding high in the mid-1970s, the new duo was immediately successful. They had major pop hits in 1974 with "Morning Side of the Mountain" and "I'm Leaving It All Up to You." They scored several more pop hits, still specializing in family-safe covers of songs originally rendered more passionately by other artists. These included "Deep Purple" (originally by Nino Tempo and April Stevens) and "Ain't Nothing Like the Real Thing" (by the Motown-label duo of Marvin Gaye and Tammy Terrell). Seven Donny & Marie Osmond albums were released on the MGM and Polydor labels in the 1970s.

In 1975 they co-hosted television's daytime talkshow *Mike Douglas Show* for a week and were spotted by ABC television executive Fred Silverman as potential headliners on their own. They were given an ABC variety special in November of 1975 and were signed on for a weekly slot after positive viewer reaction. *Donny & Marie* made its debut in January of 1976. The fast-paced show exploited the duo's multiple talents as performers. A figure-skating routine, starring Donny and Marie themselves with backing from a group called the Ice Vanities, opened each show for the first two seasons. The still-teenaged Marie Osmond sandwiched high-school-level private tutoring among the rigorous tasks of an 18-hour workday.

Donny & Marie relied heavily on performances of the duo's own hits and those by other artists, with an emphasis on the emerging "oldies" radio format. In a recurring num-ber, Marie proclaimed that she was "a little bit country," while Donny rejoined that he was "a little bit rock 'n' roll." There were also comedy skits and appearances by guest stars including other members of the Osmond family, Andy Williams, Andy Gibb (of the Bee Gees), *Charlie's Angels* series star Cheryl Ladd, *Hollywood Squares* quipmeister Paul Lynde, singer Kris Kristofferson, and even veteran African-American comedian Redd Foxx. The show was created by producers Sid and Marty Krofft, who had previously worked in children's television, but creative tension between the Osmonds and ABC executives became a factor in the show's development, and in 1979 production facilities for the show were moved to a new Osmond Studios complex in Orem, Utah. The duo branched out into film, with limited success, releasing *Going Coconuts* in 1978.

Changing Fashions Spelled Show's Demise

Donny & Marie did not fare well when musical fashions changed in the direction of the urban-oriented disco style in the late 1970s, even though the duo attempted to ride the trend with the release of a dance instruction paperback book, *Disco with Donny and Marie.* The show's look, epitomized by the purple socks worn by Donny, became the butt of jokes and satire on other television programs. Fashion designers retooled *Donny & Marie* for its third season, and in 1979, its fourth season, *Donny & Marie* was retitled *The Osmond Family Hour,* with regular appearances by all the performing Osmond siblings. The tinkering was to no avail, as the show was cancelled in 1979. "In many ways," noted an essayist on the Memory Lab website, the show "represented the end of an era for the televised variety show. Just the same, it managed to close this era with a bang. The costumes and sets were always dazzling and colorful, the leads were unfailingly charming and multi-talented, and everything moved at a consistently lightning-fast pace."

Donny and Marie Osmond maintained their identity as a duo even after the show's demise. A children's book, *Donny and Marie: The Top Secret Project,* was one of several spinoffs that carried their name forward in time. Marie launched a line of sewing patterns and had a short-lived solo television variety show in 1981. For much of the 1980s, however, it was Marie Osmond who took the lion's share of the family spotlight. She scored several country hits that reached top chart levels, including "There's No Stopping Your Heart" (1986) and the duets "Meet Me in Montana" (1985, with Dan Seals) and "You're Still New to Me" (1986, with Paul Davis), and made television and film appearances.

In 1989 it was Donny Osmond's turn to experience a career revival as he released the album *Donny Osmond,* which spawned the number-two dance hit "Soldier of Love" along with other successful singles. In the 1990s both Donny and Marie Osmond embarked on touring careers in stage musicals, with Donny appearing in *Joseph and the Amazing Technicolor Dreamcoat* and Marie taking on a variety of roles that included Maria in *The Sound of Music.* Donny's theatrical career continued to flourish with an appearance (as villain Gaston) in the hit 2006 stage version of *Beauty and the Beast.* He had some success, particularly in Britain, with his 2005 album *What I Meant to Say.*

The *Donny & Marie* show was revived in 1998, again emerging as an alternative to less wholesome fare presented on rival shows. The new *Donny & Marie* lasted until 2000. Marie Osmond received attention in the early 2000s for her memoir about postpartum depression and for her divorce from and subsequent reconciliation with her second husband, Brian Blosil; the Mormon Church frowns on divorce. She regularly appeared on the QVC television shopping channel in the mid-2000s. Both Donny and Marie Osmond have raised large families; Donny has five children and Marie seven. ''We [Mormons] don't drink or smoke, so we've got to do something,'' Donny observed to Joel Stein of *Time.* Through the mid-2000s both Osmonds kept up a steady performing schedule, sometimes appearing together.

Books

Contemporary Musicians, vol. 3, Gale, 1990.

Osmond, Donny, with Patricia Romanowski, *Life Is Just What You Make It: My Life So Far,* Hyperion, 1999.
Osmond, Marie, with Marcia Wilkie, *Behind the Smile: My Journey Out of Postpartum Depression,* Warner, 2001.
Slonimsky, Nicolas, ed. emeritus, *Baker's Biographical Dictionary of Musicians,* Schirmer, 2001.

Periodicals

Billboard, January 22, 2005.
Good Housekeeping, May 2001; March 2005.
Time, July 5, 1999.

Online

''Marie Osmond,'' Contemporary Authors Online, Gale, 2007, reproduced in Biography Resource Center, Thomson Gale, 2007, http://www.galenet.galegroup.com/servlet/BioRC (February 11, 2007).
''TV Show—Donny and Marie,'' The Memory Lab, http://www.memorylab.deanlabs.com/TVDetails.aspx?ID = 1115 (February 11, 2007). □

P

John Peel

As a longtime program host on Britain's BBC Radio 1 station network, British disc jockey John Peel (1939–2004) anticipated the appeal of popular musical innovators from the skiffle ensembles of the early 1960s to punk bands in the 1970s, world musicians in the 1980s, and roots-rock and electronic performers in the 1990s. "He had the best ears on the radio," wrote Allan Laing and Cameron Simpson in Scotland's *Herald* newspaper after Peel's death.

Even more important than the specific musicians Peel championed over the years, however, were the curiosity and free spirit he brought to broadcasting and to the exploration of new music. Some 90 percent of the music he played was new to radio broadcasts, whether those of the BBC or anyone else. Peel never claimed to be a tastemaker, and his manner was modest and generous toward musicians. "You get a lot of credit for putting these bands on the radio, but the fact is that it's like being the editor of a newspaper—you don't claim credit for the news," he was quoted as saying in the *New York Times.*

First Saw Father at Age Six

Peel was born John Robert Parker Ravenscroft in Heswell, near Liverpool in northwest England, on August 30, 1939. His father, a cotton broker, fought in Africa for much of World War II, and Peel did not meet him for the first time until he was six. He was not much closer to his mother, who, as he was quoted as saying in London's *Daily Telegraph,* "was frightened of me from the moment I was born,"

and "told me that she was never sure what I was for." It was as a child, listening to recorded music programs on U.S. Armed Forces Radio and Radio Luxembourg, that Peel thought he might like to become a radio presenter, and his encounter with the rock and roll music of Elvis Presley in the mid-1950s deepened his interest in popular music.

At the time, he was attending the Shrewsbury School (a "public school" in British terms, but what Americans would call a private boarding school open to the public). He did poorly there in classes and on exams but was a star soccer player. School authorities, he was quoted as saying in the *Daily Telegraph,* "practically had to wake [me] up during the night in order to administer the required number of sound beatings." After finishing school Peel worked briefly in the cotton industry. "My father shrewdly got me a job for one of his competitors," Peel recalled dryly, according to Spencer Leig of the London *Independent.* From 1957 to 1959 he served as a radar operator in the Royal Artillery of the British army.

Following his discharge, Peel headed for Dallas, Texas, telling his family that he could learn more about the cotton business there. But he soon became more engrossed in his musical interests. After meeting a disc jockey named Russ Knight, known as "The Weird Beard," Peel landed a small slot (called "Kats Karavan") playing rhythm and blues records on Dallas radio station WRR. For several years he made ends meet by selling storm insurance to Texas farmers, and in 1963, claiming that he was a correspondent for a Liverpool newspaper, he talked his way into the press conference, which turned out to be the one at which John F. Kennedy assassin Lee Harvey Oswald was shot by Jack Ruby.

Peel's English accent was a professional asset in the United States from the start, and the mania for the Beatles

Corporation (BBC) for its new Radio 1 popular music service. By the early 2000s he would be the only member of the original staff still active.

Peel championed the early recordings of the unclassifiable psychedelic band T. Rex (originally Tyrannosaurus Rex) and did much to introduce the music of experimentalists such as Jimi Hendrix and Captain Beefheart to British audiences on his "Night Ride" (later "The John Peel Show") and "Top Gear" programs. He was the only presenter on the BBC who was allowed to play music beyond the hits of the day, and at several points in his career his standing at the network was tenuous, especially due to the open, confessional tone of some of his shows. His path through the BBC bureaucracy was often smoothed by his longtime producer, John Walters, and he described their relationship (according to the *Daily Telegraph*) as being like that of "the organ-grinder and the monkey. With each one believing the other to be the monkey." Peel's influence extended beyond radio; the Dandelion label, which he operated between 1968 and 1972, was a financial wash, but many LPs issued on the label are prized collectors' items.

A unique feature of Peel's shows sprang from necessity: a BBC regulation left over from the era of classical orchestras and big bands mandated that certain percentages of programming had to be devoted to live music. Peel hosted thousands of bands on what became known as the Peel Sessions after he began issuing them on his own Strange Fruit label in the mid-1980s. As Peel's popularity grew, an appearance on his show became an eagerly sought-after career boost for young bands. Peel was generous with his time, trying to listen to all of the numerous demonstration tapes sent his way, and he sometimes fronted money to promising musicians for equipment and even transportation. He began a long association with the Glastonbury Festival, a large outdoor rock event, in 1971. In 1974 Peel married Sheila Gilhooly, and the two raised two sons and two daughters.

Peel neither tried to create novelty for its own sake nor sought to influence the direction of British musical taste. He played what he liked, and he gained a reputation for integrity. Sometimes he said that he selected music for his shows that did not fit into any category he had heard before, and his enthusiasm ranged from the enormously popular Rod Stewart and the Faces, and later on the dance duo the Pet Shop Boys, to experimental German noise ensembles, to reggae and hip-hop, to (well in advance of other radio programmers) music from around the world. In terms of sheer influence his high-water mark was probably his championing of punk rock beginning in 1976, when bands such as the Sex Pistols, the Ramones, and the Undertones (whose "Teenage Kicks" was Peel's favorite song) had very few footholds in the music scene beyond the small clubs where they played. The few musical scenesters who did not get along with Peel questioned the commitment of the middle-aged, conventionally dressed, private-school-educated disc jockey to the angry new music. Yet Peel's liking for punk and new wave rock continued into the 1980s through several generations of the music; such bands as the Fall, XTC,

that swept the country beginning in 1964 accelerated his radio career. A few hints that he might be acquainted with Beatle George Harrison earned Peel a legion of teenage female admirers, one of whom, 15-year-old Shirley Anne Milburn, he married in 1965. Peel landed a full-time job at Dallas station KLIF and also worked for stations in Oklahoma City, Oklahoma (KOMA), and San Bernardino, California (KMEN, where his free-spirited broadcast style began to take shape), before returning to England with his young wife in 1967. The marriage quickly broke up, dissolving officially in 1971.

Worked for Pirate Station

Peel's first radio slot in Britain was on a pirate station called Wonderful Radio London, broadcasting from a converted minesweeper in the North Sea (and actually established by a Texas salesman, Don Pierson). He adopted the name John Peel, which came from an English folksong (in California he had shortened his birth name to John Ravencroft), and the playlists on his program "The Perfumed Garden" tended toward West Coast American rock and the psychedelic side of early British folk rock. Peel aired an experimental American band with folk roots, the Grateful Dead. He also liked mainstream English folk-rock such as the music of Fairport Convention. Despite the hippie-oriented atmosphere of the time and the outlaw nature of the radio station itself, Peel was never known to use illicit drugs. Wonderful Radio London was shut down after several months of operation (although later intermittently revived), and Peel was hired by the British Broadcasting the Smiths, and the political punk-folk pioneer Billy Bragg all found homes on his program and owed their success to him at least in part.

Stayed Ahead of Trends

In the 1990s and early 2000s Peel completed his long transition from rebel pirate broadcaster to British national institution. A confirmed "Liverpudlian," he was renowned for his devotion to the Liverpool FC soccer team. He won several awards, including a Godlike Genius award in 1994 from the music magazine *Melody Maker,* which had often named him DJ of the Year, and he received the Order of the British Empire in 1998. Even as he approached senior citizen status, however, Peel kept his ability to identify promising musical developments. One of his Peel Session guests in the mid-1990s was American rock duo the White Stripes, early in its career; another was the alternative-country vocalist Neko Case. Peel also branched out beyond his usual shows, hosting a variety of BBC documentaries in the 1990s. In 1998 he started a new series on the BBC 4 network called *Home Truths,* a family interview program that bore little resemblance in atmosphere to his punk-rock programming but nevertheless found a large audience even in an undesirable time slot. His quietly conversational on-air style, much imitated, proved transferable to new kinds of programs.

Peel was riding high in 2004 with a 1.5-million pound advance on his autobiography in the bank, a new grandchild, and a continuing commitment to his BBC 1 show even after passing the age of 65. The John Peel Show remained fresh and personal, including in later years a feature called "Pig's Big 78," showcasing a 78 rpm record selected by Peel's affectionately nicknamed wife, Sheila. Peel was heard around the world on broadcasts by the BBC's International Service, increasingly marketed to local broadcasters in other countries as well as to low fidelity shortwave radio. Peel lived with his family in the Suffolk region, in a country house he called Peel Acres, complete with a flock of chickens. Peel and his wife headed for Cuzco, Peru, on what was described as a working vacation. He had already been suffering with problems related to diabetes, and while in Peru he died from a sudden heart attack on October 25, 2004.

The news, in the words of Ian Inglis of *Popular Music and Society,* caused "an outpouring of national grief not seen in the world of popular music since the deaths of John Lennon, Freddie Mercury, or George Harrison." Peel's death was the lead story in newspapers across Britain and on the evening news programs of both the BBC and ITV television networks. Around the world some 300 tribute concerts and club performances were dedicated to Peel's memory. Biographies of Peel that were quickly rushed onto the market in the following weeks were criticized by the disc jockey's brother, but Peel's own autobiography, *Margrave of the Marshes,* covering his life up to his experiences in Texas, was completed with the aid of recollections from his family. The book, with a foreword by White Stripes leader Jack White, was slated for publication in the United States in 2007.

Books

Contemporary Musicians, volume 43, Gale, 2004.
Peel, John, and Sheila Ravenscroft, *Margrave of the Marshes,* Chicago Review Press, 2007.

Periodicals

Daily Telegraph (London, England), October 27, 2004.
Economist, November 6, 2004.
Herald (Glasgow, Scotland), October 27, 2004; November 13, 2004.
Independent (London, England), October 27, 2004.
Independent on Sunday (London, England), October 31, 2004.
Liverpool Echo, December 16, 2004; December 17, 2004.
New York Times, October 27, 2004.
Popular Music and Society, July 2005.
Variety, November 1, 2004.

Online

"Keeping It Peel," British Broadcasting Corporation, http://www .bbc.co.uk/radio1/johnpeel (December 31, 2006). □

Grigory Perelman

The reclusive Russian mathematician Grigory Perelman (born 1949), in a series of short articles posted on the Internet beginning in late 2002, solved the Poincaré conjecture, one of the most fundamental problems in the entire field of mathematics.

Almost as distinctive as the quality of Perelman's achievement were the eccentricities of his interactions with the outside world. Perelman worked alone, living a spartan life in his birthplace of St. Petersburg, and during the period in which he must have made his key discoveries he apparently told no one what he was working on. In 2006, when awarded the Fields Medal, the most prestigious prize in mathematics, he turned it down. And instead of seeking the public eye, he was almost reclusive, living with his mother in St. Petersburg and seemingly retired from mathematical research.

Solved Math Puzzles as Child

Born in Leningrad in the Soviet Union (now St. Petersburg, Russia) on June 13, 1966, Perelman was the son of an electrical engineer father who liked to challenge him with brain teasers. "He gave me logical and other math problems to think about," Perelman told Sylvia Nasar and David Gruber of the *New Yorker.* "He got a lot of books for me to read. He taught me how to play chess. He was proud of me." Perelman's mother was a math teacher. The family was Jewish, and Perelman had a younger sister, Elena, who also became a mathematician.

At the age of 14 Perelman was noted as the top achiever in his St. Petersburg mathematics club, and Sergey Rukshin, head of the St Petersburg Mathematical Center for Gifted Students, began to nurture his abilities. Two years later he won a gold medal with a perfect score at the International Mathematical Olympiad in Budapest, Hungary. Perelman was something of a loner but was never perceived as hostile or unfriendly by classmates and coworkers. His interests extended beyond math to Italian opera, and he spent his small amounts of pocket money on recordings.

Perelman entered Leningrad State University at age 16 and quickly was placed in advanced geometry courses. He impressed one of his teachers, Yuri Burago, who told Nasar and Gruber, "There are a lot of students of high ability who speak before thinking. Grisha was different. He thought deeply. His answers were always correct. He always checked very, very carefully. He was not fast. Speed means nothing. Math doesn't depend on speed. It is about *deep*." For relaxation, Perelman played table tennis and sometimes played the violin, which was also his mother's instrument.

Perelman continued straight through the programs at Leningrad State, earning the equivalent of a Ph.D. in the late 1980s after writing a dissertation on Euclidean geometry. He worked in the early 1990s at the Steklov Institute of Mathematics, part of the USSR Academy of Sciences. Publishing several papers on topics in geometry, he gained a reputation as a promising young scholar. In 1992 he was invited to spend a year in the United States as a guest scholar at New York University and then the State University of New York at Stony Brook. The timing was lucky, for the Russian economy was contracting rapidly in the aftermath of the fall of Communism and the breakup of the Soviet Union.

Grew Fingernails Long

Finding the environment in America stimulating, Perelman was well liked even if some found him a bit eccentric. He lived on bread (Russian black bread when he could get it), cheese, and milk, and he let his fingernails grow to a length of several inches. "He looked like Rasputin, with long hair and fingernails," University of California at Los Angeles mathematician Robert Greene later told Dennis Overbye of the *New York Times*. A hobby from back in Russia that Perelman described to friends was hunting mushrooms on hikes in the woods. A central focus of Perelman's intellectual life was a weekly lecture series at the Institute for Advanced Study at Princeton University in New Jersey, which he and Chinese colleague Gang Tian, later a key explicator of his work, attended in order to interact with the top mathematical minds in the country and the world.

At Princeton Perelman encountered mathematician William Thurston, who had developed a set of generalizations abstracted from the Poincaré conjecture and expounded upon them in lectures. Perelman also met Cornell University mathematician Richard Hamilton, and, realizing the importance of his work, approached him after one talk. "I really wanted to ask him something," he recalled to Nasar and Gruber. "He was smiling, and he was quite patient. He actually told me a couple of things that he published a few years later. He did not hesitate to tell me. Hamilton's openness and generosity—it really attracted me. I can't say that most mathematicians act like that."

The Poincaré conjecture was described this way by Overbye: "It asserts that if any loop in a certain kind of three-dimensional space can be shrunk to a point without ripping or tearing either the loop or the space, the space is equivalent to a sphere." The problem of proving the conjecture had implications for, among other things, the study of the shape of the universe. Numerous proofs had been suggested and quickly discarded over the years since 1904, when French mathematician Henri Poincaré first proposed the conjecture. But Thurston's "geometrization conjecture," creating a typology of three-dimensional "manifolds" or abstract surfaces derived from geometrical shapes, was regarded as a promising development. Perelman was granted a two-year fellowship to work at the University of California at Berkeley beginning in 1993, and during one lecture he gave on campus he indicated that he had joined the hunt for a proof of Poincaré's conjecture.

Perelman published several well-regarded papers while at Berkeley and was invited to give a lecture at the International Mathematical Union conference in Zurich, Switzerland, in 1994. Top universities in the United States and Israel then began to court the hot young scholar, but at this point something new—prickliness or perhaps just singlemindedness—began to manifest itself in his personality. He refused to submit a CV (an academic resumé) for a position at Stanford University, arguing that if the committee was familiar with his work, they should not need the document summarizing it. Using similar reasoning, he turned down a prize offered by a European group when he did not feel they were qualified to judge his work.

Returned to Russia

Perelman was offered several jobs but turned those down as well, opting instead to return in 1995 to St. Petersburg and his old post at the Steklov Institute of Mathematics. He had, he told friends, enough money saved from a few years in America to provide for himself for the rest of his life in Russia. He moved in with his mother—there was space in her small apartment because Perelman's father had departed for Israel. Perelman wrote a letter to Hamilton, proposing that they collaborate, but Hamilton did not reply. So Perelman forged on alone; he had little contact with his colleagues for several years. Though he was isolated from other mathematical thinkers, the rapidly growing Internet medium allowed him to keep abreast of developments in the field.

Then virtually out of the blue, Perelman posted an article on the Internet on November 11, 2002. It appeared on the website arXiv.org, a site devoted to "preprints" or articles ready to be published in mathematical journals. Perelman's article was called "The Entropy Formula for the Ricci Flow and Its Geometric Applications." He did not refer directly to the Poincaré conjecture but rather to Hamilton's concept of the Ricci flow, demonstrating its applicability to the larger Poincaré conjecture. Perelman's article was terse and telegraphic, with large gaps in his reasoning, but after he sent e-mails to a few of his former colleagues they sensed the importance of his discovery.

Perelman seemed uninterested in the prestige or glory his discovery might have brought. His work would have been worthy of a book or a series of articles in top mathematical journals, but he offered nothing other than his three Internet postings. After a series of lectures at American universities in 2003, Perelman essentially withdrew from public communication, although he was friendly enough to reporters intrepid enough to track him down in the labyrinthine streets of his central St. Petersburg neighborhood. "He placed the papers on the web archive and basically said 'that's it,' " Oxford University mathematics professor Nigel Hitchin told James Randerson of the London *Guardian.*

As other researchers filled in the gaps in Perelman's proof (one explication by two researchers at the University of Michigan ran to 473 pages), Perelman's isolation deepened. He may have been unhappy when a group of Chinese researchers published a set of parallel findings that referred to Perelman's work (and Hamilton's), apparently without fully crediting Perelman for his discoveries. Lingering doubts about Perelman's work may have contributed to his departure from the Steklov Institute in 2006, but those doubts were gradually settled. "I think for many months or even years now people have been saying they were convinced by the argument," Hitchin told the *Guardian.* "I think it's a done deal."

The International Mathematical Union apparently agreed, for the group prepared to award its prestigious Fields Medal to Perelman in 2006. But Perelman refused to accept the prize or to attend the IMU's 2006 congress in Madrid, despite a personal visit to St. Petersburg from IMU president Sir John M. Ball. His reasons, he told Nasar and Gruber, were simple. "It was completely irrelevant for me. Everybody understood that if the proof is correct then no other recognition is needed." Perelman also seemed set to turn down a million-dollar prize offered by the Clay Mathematics Institute in Boston after he solved one of seven "Millennium Problems" of mathematics—the Poincaré conjecture was one. In order to claim the prize, he would have had to publish his proofs in a refereed mathematical journal, and he had shown no signs of doing so. As of late 2006, he was reported to have given up mathematical work. His reputation, however, seemed to be outliving his activity. In Russia Perelman became the subject of popular speculation, jokes, and cartoons. And his solution of the Poincaré problem was, in Overbye's words, "a landmark not just of mathematics, but of human thought."

Periodicals

Daily Telegraph (London, England), August 17, 2006.
Economist, August 26, 2006.
Guardian (London, England), August 16, 2006; August 26, 2006.
International Herald Tribune, August 31, 2006.
New Scientist, August 26, 2006.
New York Times, August 15, 2006.
New Yorker, August 28, 2006.

Online

"Grigory Perelman: Jewish genius of Russian math," RIA Novosti, http://www.en.rian.ru/analysis/20060823/53055987/html (January 6, 2007). □

Molly Picon

Jewish-American actress Molly Picon (1898–1992) was known as the great comedienne of Yiddish theater over a career that lasted for nearly 90 years. In later life her appearances in English-language films and plays drew substantial audiences as well.

At the height of Picon's fame, Murray Schumach of the *New York Times* noted that "[s]he was idolized in Jewish neighborhoods, where children and clubs were named after her during her heyday in the 1920s." Picon had various talents. She sang, danced, wrote songs, and excelled in the conventional English-language roles she took on from time to time. But at the center of her art lay Yiddish plays, in which she usually performed one of a set of variations on a basic character: a young woman who dresses or acts like a boy, making her way in the world with a combination of nerve and presence of mind.

Father Often Absent

Picon (accented on the second syllable, pronounced as in "con") was born in New York City on June 1, 1898, to immigrant garment workers who lived in Manhattan's teeming Lower East Side. Her Polish-born father, Louis Picon, held work only intermittently, and the family bounced around when Picon was very young, living in New Jersey and in Chicago before moving to Philadelphia. Three generations, including nine of Picon's cousins, shared an apartment there. "As for Papa—well, Papa was disdainful of life in general and, I think, of me in particular," Picon recalled, as quoted on the website of the Jewish Women's Archive. "He never worked. He was just too 'educated' to do menial labor. Basically, he was just 'anti': anti-capitalist, anti-religion, anti-labor, and anti-girls. . . . He just faded out of our lives."

If there was a bright side to this situation, it was that Picon became exposed to the stage after her mother found work sewing costumes at a Yiddish-language theater in Philadelphia. Picon was a born performer who began her career at age five in a talent show—and picked up a few dollars in tips by trying out her act on trolley car riders on the way to the show. Soon she had graduated to song-and-dance routines at local theaters, and she had a role in a Yiddish-language dramatization of *Uncle Tom's Cabin.* Picon dropped out of William Penn High School at 16 to take a role in a traveling vaudeville show called *The Four Seasons.*

When the troupe arrived in Boston at the height of the 1918 influenza epidemic, it fell apart owing to the lack of available work; all the theaters except one in the city were closed. The only one that remained active was a Yiddish-language group that held performances at the Boston Grand Opera House. Picon auditioned and was hired by producer Jacob "Yonkel" Kalich. The two married in 1919. "I always said influenza was our matchmaker," Picon was quoted as saying on the Jewish Women's Archive website. The couple

suffered a setback when a daughter was stillborn in 1920 and Picon emerged from the ordeal unable to bear any more children.

Picon, who had tried to become Americanized, had performed in both English and Yiddish, but spoke a colloquial variety of Philadelphia street Yiddish that was difficult even for New York audiences to understand. Kalich, on the other hand, was a Polish immigrant devoted to the idea of Yiddish theater. In 1920 the two toured Europe. Picon refined her Yiddish, and the two went to see Yiddish plays and devised new material that they performed to large crowds. The American-born Picon actually became a star in Europe first, stirring up interest in the United States as European Jews wrote to their American relatives about the appealing young comedienne they had seen.

Played Featured Stock Characters

Back in the United States in 1923, Picon and Kalich began building a small theatrical empire among New York's growing immigrant audiences. With Picon as star and Kalich as writer, they turned out numerous short comic plays. The music was often provided by composer Joseph Rumshinsky, but Picon also wrote nearly one hundred songs herself. Kalich's output seems prodigious, but the plays were not conceived from scratch each time; instead they featured recurring characters such as Yonkele, a Peter Pan–like figure whom Picon saw as a reflection of herself, and Schmendrick, an amiable dunce. Some of Picon's characters were ambiguous in gender, either tomboy-like or actu-

ally calling for Picon to dress as a boy. Among Picon's hits were *Yonkele* (1923), *Gypsy Girl* (1925–26), and *The Radio Girl* (1929). The shows were primarily in Yiddish, but Picon, attuned to the aspirations of her immigrant audiences, kept up on the latest Broadway dance routines and sprinkled her act with English dialogue.

Picon also began a film career, making several silent features in Austria. The first, *Das Judenmadel* (The Jewish Girl, 1921), has been lost, but *Ost und West* (East and West, 1923), a satirical look at the differences between Americanized and Old World Jewish families, survives and is considered by historians to be the earliest Yiddish film (although silent, it would have had text panels with dialogue and narration). Picon remained well known in Europe, and in the 1930s she traveled to Poland to film two productions that became among the best-known examples of Yiddish cinema. *Yiddle Mitn Fiddle* (Yiddle with the Fiddle, 1937) fit Picon's personality, with its story of a girl who dresses as a boy so she can work as a klezmer musician. In *Mamale* (1938) the 40-year-old Picon played a 12-year-old girl. It was the last Yiddish film made in Poland before the Holocaust, and both films are priceless documentaries of the lives of the Eastern European village Jews who were killed by the Nazi regime in Germany.

By the time she made those films, Picon was a star whose popularity in the United States extended beyond Jewish audiences. She and Kalich lost money in the stock market crash of 1929 but bounced back quickly, opening a Molly Picon Theatre at Second Avenue and 12th Street in Manhattan. In 1934 Picon began performing in a long-running radio program that gained sponsorship from the makers of Jell-O desserts, and for the film *Yiddle Mitn Fiddle* she was paid the then-unheard-of sum of $10,000. Cast in the English-language drama *Morningstar* (1939), she had the makings of a career independent from Kalich. Their marriage suffered but survived.

The upheavals of World War II helped to bring the couple together. They adopted a teenaged Belgian Jewish orphan in 1941 and later adopted two more children. Picon performed on the USO (United Service Organizations) circuit, entertaining American troops during World War II. Picon toured the world during the war years, reportedly becoming a favorite with a Zulu audience in South Africa for her imitations of film comedian Charlie Chaplin. After the war's end her activities continued to be motivated by public service, as she gave performances for displaced European Jews. One young mother, according to Schumach, approached Picon and Kalich and said, "My child is two years old and she has never heard the sound of laughter," to which Kalich answered, "Molly, that's our job. Make them laugh!" Picon was also a supporter of the new state of Israel, traveling there in 1954 and wading into the debate over whether Hebrew or Yiddish was to be the language of the new country—she performed in Yiddish.

Co-Starred with Sinatra

Picon and Kalich attempted to maintain the traditions of Yiddish theater with new shows, including *Abi Gezunt* and *Sadie Was a Lady* (both 1949) and *Mazel Tov, Molly*

(1950). She wrote new songs for a 1959 Yiddish show, *The Kosher Widow,* which allowed the audience to select from alternate endings by applauding and having their noisemaking metered. The use of Yiddish was declining in the United States, however, as second-generation American Jews overwhelmingly began to favor English. So Picon, entering her sixth decade of performing, branched out once again and attempted, with considerable success, to move beyond the niche of ethnic actress in which she had been placed. She appeared in the London production and in many regional American productions of the long-running romantic comedy *A Majority of One,* and in 1962 she had a starring role in the Frank Sinatra comedy *Come Blow Your Horn,* playing opposite Lee J. Cobb as the (Italian-American, not Jewish) mother of Sinatra's on-screen co-star and romantic rival, Tony Bill. The role brought Picon an Academy Award nomination as Best Actress in a Musical or Comedy. In the 1960s Picon made guest appearances on *Gomer Pyle* and other television series, and she was a frequent guest on *The Merv Griffin Show* and other television talk programs.

Having already appeared on stage in 1957 in *The World of Sholom Aleichem,* a tribute to the great Russian Jewish Yiddish-language writer, Picon was a natural pick for casting when the stage musical *Fiddler on the Roof,* based on Aleichem's stories about the milkman Tevye, was made into a film in 1971. Picon played Yente, a village matchmaker, and she and Kalich, who had already done so much in the 1930s to document the shtetls or Jewish villages of Eastern Europe on film, helped to re-create the vanished world for the new production.

Picon took several years off from performing when Kalich fell ill in the early 1970s, caring for him until his death in 1975. After that, the nearly 80-year-old Picon resumed touring, traveling around the United States, Canada, and Israel. Picon mounted a one-woman show, *Hello Molly,* in 1979, dancing the can-can and doing deep knee bends on stage. In 1980 Picon published her autobiography, *Molly!.* She had a small part in the Burt Reynolds slapstick comedy *The Cannonball Run* (1981), and its 1984 sequel, *Cannonball Run 2.* That year Picon made her final film appearance in *Grandma Didn't Wave Back,* a drama about a child forced to come to terms with his grandmother's mental decline.

Performing well into her eighties, Picon received several major awards toward the end of her life. In 1981 she became the first actress with a background on the Yiddish stage elected to the Theatre Hall of Fame, and among her various awards from Jewish organizations was a "Goldie" from the Congress of Jewish Culture in 1985. Picon accepted that award clad in a tuxedo. She died in her sleep at the home of her sister in Lancaster, Pennsylvania, on April 6, 1992, aged 94. In 2005 a new Yiddish-language biographical musical, *Picon Pie: A Slice of Life of Molly Picon,* celebrated her accomplishments. The show's creator, Rose Leiman Goldemberg, told the *New York Times* that Picon "had this idea that she could just get in there and do something. There was no question of could she do this, should she do this. She just did it, she followed her heart."

Books

Contemporary Theatre, Film, and Television, volume 12, Gale, 1994.
Picon, Molly, with Eth Clifford Rosenberg, *So Laugh a Little,* Messner, 1962.
Picon, Molly, with Jean Bergantini Grillo, *Molly!,* Simon & Schuster, 1980.

Periodicals

New York Times, April 7, 1992; September 18, 2005.
Times (London, England), April 16, 1992; April 24, 1992.

Online

Contemporary Authors Online, Gale, 2007, reproduced in Biography Resource Center, Thomson Gale, 2007, http://www.galenet.galegroup.com/servlet/BioRC (January 19, 2007).
"Molly Picon, All-American Maydl," American Jewish Historical Society, http://www.ajhs.org/publications/chapters/chapter.cfm?documentID=291 (January 19, 2007).
"Molly Picon," Jewish Virtual Library, http://www.jewishvirtuallibrary.org/jsource/biography/picon.html (January 19, 2007).
"Molly Picon," Jewish Women's Archive, http://www.jwa.org/exhibits/wov/picon (January 19, 2007). □

Anna Politkovskaya

Russian journalist Anna Politkovskaya (1958–2006) joined a long list of dissidents who died because of their outspoken criticism of their country's regime. A war reporter who chronicled Russian attempts to subdue extremists in the breakaway republic of Chechnya, she remained objective in describing the ghastly atrocities committed by both sides. Politkovskaya further warned that Russia seemed to be reverting to a Soviet-style climate of fear under the leadership of President Vladimir Putin, a former spy. "I have no hope left in my soul," she told Andrew Osborn in Britain's *Independent* newspaper. "Only a change of leadership would allow me to have hope but it's a political winter." Less than two years later, she became the victim of what appeared to be an assassination.

Politkovskaya was the daughter of two diplomats of Ukrainian heritage whose loyalty to Soviet Russia and the Communist Party was deemed secure enough to give them a highly coveted foreign mission in the West. In the strict, one-party authoritarian rule back in the Soviet era, only party members who did not appear to be candidates for defection were granted permission to travel or live in the West. Politkovskaya's parents were posted to the United Nations headquarters in New York City, where she was born on August 30, 1958. Her privileged background was a vastly different one from that of the man who would become her greatest foe, Russian president Vladimir Putin

(born 1952). Putin's autobiography recounted a St. Petersburg childhood in a vermin-infested communal apartment before he rose through the ranks of the KGB, the Soviet Union's secret police and intelligence agency. Politkovskaya, by contrast, "was part of the elite," noted the *Guardian*'s David Hearst. "For her family, Vladimir Putin is not a distant object of fear and veneration, but a former KGB staffer rather too lowly for them to have come across socially."

Worked for Aeroflot

Politkovskaya studied journalism at Moscow State University, and went to work for the national daily newspaper *Izvestia* when she graduated in 1980. She later worked for Aeroflot, the state-owned airline of the Soviet Union, and her position with its company newspaper came with an all-access airline pass, good for free domestic travel anywhere Aeroflot touched down. Politkovskaya put it to good use, and the experience transformed her from a member of the privileged class familiar with only the main urban centers and summer resort areas of the Soviet sphere to a well-informed journalist. "Thanks to this I saw the whole of our huge country," she said in an interview with the *Guardian*'s James Meek. "I was a girl from a diplomatic family, a reader, a bit of a swot [nerd]; I didn't know life at all."

Energized by the era of reform ushered in after 1985 by new Soviet leader Mikhail Gorbachev (born 1931), Politkovskaya eagerly returned to daily journalism once press censorship began to abate, taking a job with a pro-democracy newspaper *Obshchaya gazeta.* Founded in Au-

gust of 1991—the same month that the Soviet communist regime finally crumbled—the weekly newspaper was an ideal forum for Politkovskaya, and she made her name as a journalist in the late 1990s when she began reporting from Chechnya. This mountainous region in the North Caucasus had a long history of enmity with its Russian overlords dating back to the early nineteenth century. In the early years of post-Soviet Russia, there had been a small war for independence that pitted Chechen rebels against Russian federal troops. But public pressure on Russian president Boris Yeltsin (born 1931), fueled by the new press freedoms available to media outlets like *Obshchaya gazeta,* resulted in a withdrawal of Russia's troops and a 1997 peace agreement that recognized Chechnya as an independent republic. Succeeding Yeltsin in late 1999, Putin ordered the deployment of more troops to quell internal disorder within Chechnya between the government and Islamic extremists; there had also been a series of Moscow bombings in 1999 that were blamed on Chechen terrorists, but journalists like Politkovskaya began to suspect that the tragedy had been instigated by hardline Russian conservatives as an excuse to subdue Chechnya for good. This renewal of hostilities came to be known as the Second Chechen War.

By then Politkovskaya was a columnist for *Novaya gazeta,* another liberal newspaper, and continued her reporting from Chechnya. Her stories were critical of human rights excesses on both sides, including one gripping tale about the mystery surrounding a mass grave discovered near a Russian military base; the bodies were possibly civilian casualties, and land mines had been planted to prevent their retrieval. Politkovskaya already had made some prominent enemies because of her journalistic exposés, but for this one she was taken into custody and accused of spying on behalf of Shamil Basayev, the Chechen warlord. For three days in February of 2001 she was kept in a pit with no food or water. Later that year she was forced to flee Russia for a time when rumors reached her that one police captain, accused of human rights abuses in her stories, wanted her dead. Her aptly titled first book, *A Dirty War: A Russian Reporter in Chechnya,* appeared in English translation that same year.

Trusted Negotiator at Moscow Hostage Scene

In October of 2002 Politkovskaya became a participant in a news story herself, when a group of heavily armed Chechen rebels stormed a Moscow theater and took 850 hostages. They demanded a pullout of Russian troops from Chechnya. Politkovskaya asked to meet with the hostage-takers, hoping to secure food and water for the actors, musicians, and theatergoers being held. As she wrote in a report filed for *Novaya gazeta,* she waited long minutes before being allowed to meet with a senior commando, and feared for her life. "Masks come and go, the time fading away grips the heart with foreboding, and the senior still doesn't come. Maybe they'll just shoot us now?" Finally, she met with a leader of the group, who apologized to her for the semi-automatic weapon he was carrying. "Even without these explanations, I can see it all already—he's from the generation of Chechens that has been fighting for its entire life," she wrote. She was given permission to bring in juice and water, but as the standoff neared the three-day mark, a special forces unit of the Russian Army stormed the building with the help of a powerful gas that was probably a nerve agent; all 42 hostage-takers died, along with 129 civilians.

Worse incidents ensued after the Moscow theater siege. In September of 2004 another group of Chechen rebels took an elementary school hostage in the southern Russian town of Beslan. The children had been assembled for a ceremony in the schoolyard, marking the first day of class for the year, when 32 masked men arrived and began herding the teachers, parents, and children into the gymnasium. On the third day, a battle erupted between Russian military forces and the hostage-takers, and more than 300 of the 1,200 hostages died. Upon hearing of the crisis, Politkovskaya immediately boarded a flight to Beslan in order to help negotiate a safer outcome, but became violently ill after drinking a cup of tea en route. She believed she was poisoned.

By 2005 *Novaya gazeta*—one of whose owners was Gorbachev—remained among the few independent media outlets that had not been forced out of business by Putin's government. Politkovskaya's third book, *Putin's Russia: Life in a Failing Democracy,* had not even been published in Russia in 2004, though it was appreciatively reviewed when it appeared in English translation in 2006. In it, she chronicled Putin's rise to national political power, and analyzed his strategy for courting Western powers—he counted British Prime Minister Tony Blair and U.S. President George W. Bush among his allies—while cracking down on hard-won civil liberties at home in the name of fighting terrorism at home and abroad. Much of the text reiterated what she had already written in articles about him, asserted Osborn. "Politkovskaya does what few other Russian commentators dare and steps over an invisible line, mocking Mr. Putin in an intensely personal way; comparing him to Soviet leader Josef Stalin . . . and to a bland, over-promoted spy who should never have been elevated to the dizzy Kremlin heights."

Death Prompted Outrage

On October 5, 2006, Politkovskaya gave a radio interview in which she discussed an upcoming story for *Novaya gazeta,* an exposé on torture practices linked to a militia unit controlled by Chechnya's Putin-friendly prime minister, Ramzan Kadyrov. She planned to file the story on Saturday, October 7, but was found shot to death in her apartment building in central Moscow just before 5 p.m. A Makarov pistol, which in Russia is often used for contract killings, and four shell casings were found near her body; the four bullets to her head also pointed to evidence that it had been an assassination rather than a random act of violence. Police seized her computer, and though a fragment of her story was published several days later that included stills from a grainy video depicting Kadyrovite militia personnel torturing suspects, other important photographs were lost.

News of Politkovskaya's death prompted consternation on an international level. Heads of state from Europe, as well as Blair and Bush, issued official statements questioning her untimely death. Her supporters, as well as human-

rights activists around the world, called it a political assassination. Even the *New York Times* editorial page weighed in, remarking that she was one of a long line of recent suspicious deaths of Putin's foes, and the newspaper ventured that "it would be hard to imagine that Mr. Putin's Kremlin, swollen with oil riches and power, could not find those who ordered her murder or so many others."

Putin did promise a full investigation of her death, but commented also that she was a figure of "minor" importance. The number of mourners who turned out for her funeral on October 10 seemed to contradict that claim. Nearly a thousand paid their respects on a rainy Tuesday, among them Western diplomats, fellow journalists, and ordinary Muscovites. One of those in attendance was *Time International*'s Moscow correspondent Yuri Zarakhovich, who explained in his report that funerals were one expression of dissidence in the repressive Soviet era. "Moscow had not, until last week, seen a mass dissident demonstration for years," wrote Zarakhovich. "Nor had cities like St. Petersburg, or Yekaterinburg in the Urals, where rallies all paid homage to Politkovskaya." The *Time* journalist also commented that that few mourners at Politkovskaya's burial "would have expected that, 15 years after the collapse of the Soviet Union, they would have occasion to once again feel like dissidents in the face of a too-powerful state."

Linked to Litvinenko

Politkovskaya left two adult children, the product of a marriage that had ended because of her frequent travels to Chechnya and the danger it posed to her. U.S. Secretary of State Condoleezza Rice (born 1954) met with her son 10 days later on visit to Moscow, and also met with the editor of *Novaya gazeta,* Dmitry Muratov. Several weeks later, with her death still under investigation, a former KGB agent and critic of Putin gave a statement from his London hospital bed. Near death, Alexander Litvinenko (1962–2006) blamed Putin for the mysterious illness that had caused him to become deathly ill within a matter of days. Politkovskaya had met with Litvinenko in London not long after her own suspicious illness in 2004, and Litvinenko had reportedly been investigating whether or not she had been poisoned. Shortly before he fell ill, Litvinenko told a Chechen website that he had come into possession of documents that linked officers of the Federal Security Service of the Russian Federation (FSB), the successor to the KGB, to Politkovskaya's murder.

Periodicals

Guardian (London, England), March 16, 2002; October 15, 2004; March 1, 2006; October 23, 2006.
Independent (London, England), October 15, 2004.
New York Times, October 10, 2006.
Sunday Telegraph (London, England), October 15, 2006.
Time International (Europe Edition), October 23, 2006.
Times (London, England), October 13, 2006; November 21, 2006.

Online

"My Hours Inside the Moscow Theatre," Institute for War & Peace Reporting, http://www.iwpr.net/?p=crs&s=f&o=159401&apc_state=henfcrs159398 (December 1, 2006). □

Martín Porres

Saint Martín de Porres (1579–1639) spent his entire life in Lima, Peru. A Dominican monk known as a healer and an indefatigable worker in charitable service to the poor, Martín was canonized in 1962 by Pope John Paul XXIII, who designated him the patron saint of universal brotherhood.

Always a famous figure within Latin American Catholicism, Martín began to receive renewed attention in the later years of the twentieth century. Partly this was due to his mixed-race background; he was one of a comparatively small number of Catholic saints who could be classified as black, and he ministered without distinction to Spanish nobles and to slaves recently brought from Africa. Another fascinating aspect of Martín's life and legacy has emerged from the fund of miraculous legends that surround his memory. Such legends are not unique to Martín, but he was clearly a religious leader with a perennial appeal to the popular imagination. Finally, Martín's sometimes defiant attachment to the ideal of social justice achieved deep resonance in a church attempting to carry forward that ideal in today's modern world.

Born to Freed Panamanian-Born Slave

Martín de Porres was born in Lima, Peru, on December 9, 1579. His father was a Spanish conquistador named Don Juan de Porres and his mother was a freed slave from Panama, of African or possibly part Native American descent, named Ana Velázquez. Seeing that the child had African rather than European features, Don Juan de Porres refused to acknowledge his paternity. Martín was baptized the day he was born, with notation on the baptismal certificate reading "father unknown" (it is quoted in full by J.C. Kearns in *The Life of Blessed Martín de Porres*). He was raised by his mother in extreme poverty, on the very lowest rungs of early Spanish colonial society; in the eyes of the nobility, a mark of illegitimacy was exceeded in shamefulness only by a child's racially mixed heritage.

Stories of Martín's remarkable generosity apparently began to surround him even in childhood; sent to the local market by his mother, he would often give away the contents of his basket to homeless persons before reaching home. By the time he was 10 he was spending several hours of each day in prayer, a practice he maintained for the rest of his life. He once asked his landlady for the stumps of some candles she had discarded, and she later saw him using their meager light to behold a crucifix before which he knelt, weeping. Perhaps as a result of the boy's spiritual accomplishments, Don Juan de Porres acknowledged when Martín was eight years old that he was Martín's father, a remarkable admission at the time. (He finally abandoned Ana Velázquez for good after the birth of another daughter.) Ana recognized in her son the signs of an intense spiritual quality, and she tried to obtain for him an education beyond mere subsistence level. When Martín was 12, he was apprenticed to a barber—a profession that in sixteenth-century society involved much more than cutting hair. Young Martín learned the rudiments of surgery: administering herbal remedies, dressing wounds, and drawing blood—something that was thought to be curative at the time.

At 15, Martín decided to devote himself to the religious life. He applied to join the Convent of the Rosary in Lima, a Dominican monastery. Racial restrictions dictated that he be given the position of "tertiary" or lay helper, which he enthusiastically accepted. The bishop at the monastery, according to an early biography quoted by Alex García-Rivera in *St Martín de Porres*, said that "there are laws that we must respect. These indicate that the Indians, blacks, and their descendants, cannot make profession in any religious order, seeing that they are races that have little formation as of yet." Martín was able to exercise his medical skills after being put in charge of the monastery infirmary, and he was often given the monastery's basic chores such as cleaning, cooking, and doing laundry.

Both before and after joining the monastery, Martín suffered incidents of harassment that may well have been racially motivated. The monks for whom he was cooking would hide the kitchen's potholders, and one of the early stories surrounding the young holy man was that he could then pick up the pots with his bare hands and not be burned. Another story concerned Martín's tendency toward self-denial—or, read another way, his determination to identify himself with the lives of Peru's indigenous poor. Told by his superior to retire to bed, Martín responded (according to Kearns), "What! Do you command me, who at home would never have enjoyed the luxuries of life, to betake myself to a soft bed! Father, I beseech you, do not force me to enjoy such an unmerited gratification." Cleaning a toilet one day, he was asked by a monk whether he might not prefer life at the splendid offices of the Archbishop of Mexico. Martín responded, according to Kearns, by quoting the biblical Psalm 83: "I have chosen to be an abject in the house of my God rather than to dwell in the tabernacles of sinners." He qualified this remark by saying that he was not referring to the Archbishop as a sinner, but rather simply that he himself preferred menial tasks. He wore robes until they fell apart, refusing the luxury of new ones.

Religious Devotion Celebrated in Stories

When Martín was 24, in 1603, he gave the profession of faith that allowed him to become a Dominican brother. He is said to have several times refused this elevation in status, which may have come about due to his father's intervention, and he never became a priest. As with any other famous holy man, Martín's life is surrounded by stories, and those stories constitute the primary means of remembering him at a distance of four centuries. The stories surrounding Martín are of two kinds. Some consist of testimony about his character and accomplishments by church officials who knew him, while others seem to be of a more popular character, arising among Lima's impoverished populace, and coming down to the present time partly via oral tradition.

Many stories attest to Martín's exceptional piety. He was said sometimes to be surrounded by a bright light when he prayed, and to be levitated off the floor of a chapel by sheer religious ecstasy. He subsisted for days on bread and water and would do penance for sins by whipping himself with chains. Martín was said to be capable of bilocation (being in two places at once), and individuals from both Africa and Mexico swore that they had encountered him in their home villages even though he was never known to have left Lima. Patients under his care spoke on several occasions of his having walked through locked doors in order to render medical help.

Other tales of the miracles and wonders worked by Martín, however, were more specific to his time and place. He was said to have a supernatural rapport with the natural world. The most famous single story connected with Martín had to do with a group of mice (or rats) that infested the monastery's collection of fine linen robes. Martín resisted the plans of the other monks to lay poison out for the mice. One day he caught a mouse and said (in the rendering of Angela M. Orsini of San Francisco's Martín de Porres House of Hospitality, one of many institutions and schools in the United States named after the Peruvian healer), "Little brothers, why are you and your companions doing so much harm to the things belonging to the sick? Look; I shall not kill you, but you are to assemble all your friends and lead them to the far end of the garden. Everyday I will bring you food if you leave the wardrobe alone"—whereupon Martín lead a Pied Piper-like mouse parade toward a small new den. Both the mice and Martín kept their word, and the closet infestation was solved for good. Martín loved animals of all kinds and seemed to have unusual skills in communicating with them. He would apply his medical skills to the treatment of a wounded dog found wandering the streets with the same energy he would devote to a sick human. Paintings of Martín often depicted him with a mouse, dog, or cat—or sometimes with a broom, symbolizing his devotion to everyday tasks.

Ministered to the Poor and Sick

Many other stories of Martín's goodness pertained to his unwavering efforts to help Lima's poor and ill, often against the wishes of his superiors at the monastery. A sick, aged street person, almost naked and covered with open sores, was taken by Martín to his own bed at the monastery. A fellow monk was horrified, but Martín responded (according to the Lives of the Saints reported on the website of Canada's Monastery of the Magnificat), "Compassion, my dear Brother, is preferable to cleanliness. Reflect that with a little soap I can easily clean my bed covers, but even with a torrent of tears I would never wash from my soul the stain that my harshness toward the unfortunate would create."

He treated victims of bubonic plague without regard to whether they were white, black, or Native American. During one plague outbreak he brought a wounded Native American man into the monastery for treatment even though the Superior administrator of the province had forbidden the admission of the sick owing to fears of contagion. Given a reprimand for disobedience, Martín replied (according to the Monastery of the Magnificat site), "Forgive my error, and please instruct me, for I did not know that the precept of obedience took precedence over that of charity." Martín's

skills as a physician spread his name far and wide, and even the Archbishop of Mexico came to Lima to seek his services at one point. He was said to have a miraculous ability to know whether or not a patient would recover. Sometimes he sent sick people (or animals) to the home of his sister Juana when the monastery's facilities were overwhelmed.

Martín was, in the words of Richard Cardinal Cushing (writing in *St. Martín de Porres*), "a precursor of modern social science," and the Convent of the Rosary while he was there "became the forerunner of the modern medical clinic." To finance all these activities, Martín also became an early specialist in the art of nonprofit fundraising. Spanish nobles gave him large donations so that he could continue his work, and one estimate placed his weekly disbursements of funds at the level of $2,000, an astonishing sum for the period. Martín did not devote these funds exclusively to those in misery, but also tried to level class distinctions. For example, he sometimes provided money for a poor young woman's dowry so that she could marry. When the monastery's finances suffered as a result of his activities, Martín responded (according to *American Catholic*'s Saint of the Day website), "I am only a poor mulatto. Sell me. I am the property of the order. Sell me."

Martín died of a fever in Lima on November 3, 1639, at the age of nearly 60. Despite his renown throughout Latin America, recognition from the Catholic church was slow to come. In 1837 he was beatified, and his feast day is celebrated on November 3. He was canonized as a saint by Pope John XXIII on May 6, 1962, with a contingent of 350 African-American Catholics in attendance. Both Kearns and Cushing called Martín "a pioneer social worker," and when canonized he was designated the patron saint of universal brotherhood. On a more earthly plane, he was also the patron saint of interracial relations, social justice, public education, Peruvian television and public health, trade unions in Spain, mixed-race individuals, and barbers and hair stylists in Italy.

Books

Cushing, Richard Cardinal, *St. Martin de Porres,* St. Paul Editions, 1962.

García-Rivera, Alex, *St. Martín de Porres: The "Little Stories" and the Semiotics of Culture,* Orbis, 1995.

Kearns, J.C., O.P., *The Life of Blessed Martín de Porres: Saintly American Negro and Patron of Social Justice,* P.J. Kenedy & Sons, 1937.

Periodicals

Manila Bulletin (Philippines), November 3, 2006.

Online

"About St. Martín de Porres," Martin de Porres House of Hospitality, http://www.martindeporres.org (January 21, 2007).

"Saint Martin de Porres," Lives of the Saints, Monastery of the Magnificat, Mont-Tremblant, Quebec, Canada, http://www.magnificat.ca/cal/engl/11-03.htm (January 21, 2007).

"St. Martin de Porres: A Brief Biography," St. Martin de Porres School, Oakland, CA, http://www.stmdp.org/SmdPBioPage.html (January 21, 2007).

"St. Martín de Porres," *American Catholic:* Saint of the Day, http://www.americancatholic.org (January 21, 2007).

"St. Martin de Porres," St. Patrick's Catholic Church, Washington, DC, http://www.saintpatrickdc.org/ss/1103.htm#mart (January 21, 2007). □

Jacques Prévert

With the publication of his book *Paroles* in 1945, Jacques Prévert (1900–1977) became France's most popular poet of the twentieth century. He was also an innovative screenwriter who helped create some of the most influential French films of the 1930s and 1940s, including the beloved *Les Enfants du paradis* (The Children of Paradise). His satirical attacks on rigid French education and the Catholic Church and other institutions of authority expressed France's post-war disillusionment and defiant spirit.

Prévert the Young Rebel

Prévert was born on Feburary 4, 1900, in Neuilly-sur-Seine, France, near Paris. He grew up in a middle class family, the middle of three sons, and enjoyed a mostly happy childhood. His autobiographical prose poem, "Enfance" (Childhood), is filled with pleasant memories of street life in his hometown, including street performers such as singers and clowns. His father worked for the Office Central des Pauvres de Paris (Central Office for the Poor of Paris) and often took his son with him when his work took him to poorer sections of the city. Those experiences gave Prévert a lifelong sympathy with the poor and working class. His father also reviewed plays for local newspapers, and he often took his sons to the theater or the movie house, stimulating their imaginations. Prévert found school rigid and stifling, and he dropped out at 14. He was proud to say that the streets gave him his education.

In 1920 Prévert began his military service, required of all French men. While stationed at Lunéville in eastern France he befriended Yves Tanguy, who would later become a Surrealist painter. In 1921, while stationed in Constantinople (now Istanbul, Turkey), he met another friend, Marcel Duhamel. All three were eager to throw off the discipline of the military. Once their service was done, they moved to Paris and threw themselves into a rebellious, bohemian life. They moved to Rue du Château, a street in the artistic Montparnasse neighborhood of Paris. Duhamel got a job managing a hotel and supported himself, Prévert, Tanguy, and their girlfriends as they hung out in cafés, went to movies and threw parties full of games of charades.

In 1925 Prévert married a longtime friend, Simone Dienne, and he, Tanguy, and Duhamel were introduced to the young leaders of the Surrealism movement, including the writer Andre Bréton. The Surrealists also found a home and a meeting place on Rue du Château. "The most absolute non-conformity, total irreverence and thorough good humor reigned there," Bréton recalled in his book of interviews, *Entretiens,* according to Claire Blakeway in her book *Jacques Prévert: Popular French Theatre and Cinema.* "In a corner plastered with cinema posters—of vamps' eyes and pointed pistols – there was a little built-in bar which was always well-stocked." Though Prévert did not become a leading thinker among the Surrealists as his friend Tanguy did, he was an inspiration for his fellow artists. "With his anarchic sense of humor and his lively, nonconformist nature, he imparted great vitality into the movement," Blakeway wrote.

The alliance with the Surrealists lasted until around 1928, when Prévert, Tanguy, and Duhamel had a falling-out with Bréton over his heavy-handed leadership of the movement and moved out of Rue du Château. Prévert began working for an ad agency and writing poetry. His first poems, full of surrealist cleverness, were published in the early 1930s, including his influential and popular "Tentative de description d'un dîner de têtes à Paris-France" (Attempt to Describe a Dinner of Heads in Paris-France), published in *Commerce* in 1931.

Prévert's left wing politics led him in 1932 to join the workers' theater company Groupe Octobre, which was affiliated with the Communist Party. He wrote plays for the troupe that mixed Surrealist freedom and wordplay with strong political themes. The troupe appeared in the Surrealist film *L'Affaire est dans le sac* (The Affair Is In the Bag), which Prévert wrote with his brother, Pierre, in 1932. Prévert traveled to Moscow with the Groupe Octobre in 1933 to the International Workers' Theater Olympiad, to premier Prévert's play *La Bataille de Fontenoy* (The Battle of Fontenoy). He also began writing songs for singers such as Marianne Oswald.

Prévert and Carné

By the mid-1930s, Prévert began developing into a major screenwriter and dialogue writer. He collaborated with Jean Renoir, one of France's leading filmmakers of the 1930s, and the two co-wrote the 1935 film *Le Crime de Monsieur Lange.* He also began working with filmmaker Marcel Carné on the film *Jenny.* During this time he broke up with his wife, Simone, and soon fell in love with Jacqueline Laurent. In 1936 the Groupe Octobre broke up, unsure of how to react to changes in French and European left-wing politics, and Prévert's major poem "La Crosse en l'air" (The Cross in the Air) was published.

Carné and Prévert became frequent collaborators. Their startling, groundbreaking films of the late 1930s, *Drôle de drame* (aka Bizarre, Bizarre), *Quai des brumes* (Port of Shadows), and *Le Jour se lève* (The Day Dawns) established the French film genre of poetic realism, which would heavily influence American film noir. The films shared signature preoccupations of Prévert's, including "a somewhat doom-laden sensibility and a free-flowing romanticism regarding youthful love, especially when contrasting such love with the corruption and cynicism of the world at large," wrote Bruce Eder of allmovie.com.

After Nazi Germany invaded France in 1940, Prévert moved to Saint-Paul-de-Vence in the south of France. He made another film with his brother, *Adieu, Leonard,* in 1942 and *Lumière d'été* (Light of Summer) with Jean Grémillon in

1943. Meanwhile, he continued to work with Carné, first on 1942's *Les Visiteurs du soir* (Evening Visitors). Aware that historical dramas stood a better chance of avoiding the censorship of the German occupying authorities and the Vichy government of southern France, they based their film on a fifteenth-century French legend. Its scenes in which two lovers defy their imprisonment in a castle by imagining themselves elsewhere struck a chord with the French during the Occupation.

Between 1943 and 1945, Carné and Prévert produced their masterpiece, *Les Enfants du paradis* (The Children of Paradise). The film was extremely difficult to make, since it involved assembling large crowds for several scenes and since much of it was made during the Occupation. The film, which depicts several street performers in nineteenth-century Paris, is centered on four men in love with the same woman. It was inspired by the nineteenth-century story of a famous mime who killed a man that insulted his girlfriend. Thanks to its evocative depiction of historic Paris, its romantic themes, and the populist, anti-authoritarian themes that surprisingly made it past the censors, it became one of France's most popular and celebrated films of all time.

Prévert the Poet

The peak of Prévert's career came immediately after World War II. In 1945, the same year that *Les Enfants du paradis* was released, he published his collected poems, *Paroles*. The book sold more than 500,000 copies, almost unheard of for a book of poems in France. "Prévert spoke particularly to the French youth immediately after the War, especially to those who grew up during the Occupation and felt totally estranged from Church and State," wrote Lawrence Ferlinghetti in the introduction to the 1990 edition of *Paroles*, which he translated into English in 1958. Looking back in 1960, prominent French critic Gaëton Picon called Prévert "the only genuine poet who, at present, has succeeded in reaching beyond the bounds of a more or less specialized public," according to Blakeway's book. The verses in *Paroles* became even more popular when Joseph Kosma, a Hungarian composer who worked with Carné on his films, set some of them to music. Perhaps the most famous was "Les Feuilles Morts" (Autumn Leaves), which was recorded by Yves Montand and Juliette Gréco, two famed French singers of the post-war era. Montand's version appeared in the 1946 film *Les Portes de la nuit* (The Doors of the Night), the last collaboration between Carné and Prévert. He also published *Contes pour enfants pas sages* (Stories for Children Who Aren't Very Well-Behaved) in 1947.

Prévert's career suffered twin setbacks in 1948. His partnership with Carné fell apart when the film *La Fleur de l'âge* was cancelled during production. Also, while at the office of Radiodiffusion Nationale in Paris, he fell and was severely injured, spending weeks in a coma. Once he recovered, he moved with his family—his second wife, Janine Loris, was an alumna of the Groupe Octobre—back to Saint-Paul-de-Vence.

In 1951 Prévert published *Spectacle*, a collection of poetry and dramatic works, followed by *La Pluie et le beau temps* (Rain and Good Weather) in 1955. He also worked on films and books for children, such as *Bim, le petit âne* (Bim the Little Donkey). In 1955 he moved back to Paris. He had become so popular that strangers approached him on the street and quoted lines of his poems to greet him.

American poet Eve Merriam went to visit Prévert in 1959 and spent hours with him talking about poetry and art. Writing in the *New Republic,* she recalled him as "a short, white-haired man with blue eyes, blunt expressive fingers, cigarette dangling from his lips like a corny Apache dancer. Wearing a blue sweater the color of his eyes, dapper gray flannels, and black leather moccasins newly polished, he looked like a sportive dandy." In 1961, when Serge Gainsbourg, soon to become France's most revered songwriter, wrote the tribute song "La Chanson De Prévert," he went to Prévert's house to seek his blessing and ended up spending a morning drinking champagne with him.

Prévert produced several art collages during the late 1950s and early 1960s. "They were surreal, comic and beautiful, scathingly anti-church, anti-corporation, anti-hypocrisy," Merriam wrote in the *New Republic*. They were exhibited in Paris in 1957 and in Antibes in southern France in 1963. He continued to publish books, including *Histoires et d'autres histoires* (Stories and Other Stories) in 1963 and *Choses et autres* (Things and Other Things) in 1972.

After a long illness, Prévert died on April 11, 1977, at his home in Omonville-La-Petite, in Normandy, France. That day, Carné (as quoted in the *New York Times*) called him "the one and only poet of French cinema," whose "humor and poetry succeeded in raising the banal to the summit of art" and whose style reflected "the soul of the people." Prévert wanted to be remembered as a people's poet. A few years before his death, in an interview quoted in Harriet Zinnes's introduction to her book *Blood and Feathers*, Prévert said, "I was popular even before being fashionable. That's how it was. What gave me pleasure was having readers. . . . They are the greatest literary critics. . . . These are the people who know the best literature, those who love it, not the connoisseurs."

Books

Baker, William, *Jacques Prévert*, Twayne Publishers, 1967.
Blakeway, Claire, *Jacques Prévert: Popular French Theatre and Cinema*, Associated University Presses, 1990.
Prévert, Jacques, *Blood and Feathers: Selected Poems of Jacques Prévert*, (translated by Harriet Zinnes), Schocken Books, 1988.
Prévert, Jacques, *Paroles* (translated by Lawrence Ferlinghetti), City Lights Books, 1990.
Simmons, Sylvie, *Serge Gainsbourg: A Fistful of Gitanes*, Da Capo Press, 2001.

Periodicals

New Republic, July 9 & 16, 1977.
New York Times, April 12, 1977.

Online

"Biography of Jacques Prévert," *Hommage à Jacques Prévert,* http://www.xtream.online.fr/Prévert (December 20, 2006).
"Jacques Prévert," *Encyclopedia Britannica,* http://www.search.eb.com (December 20, 2006).
"Jacques Prévert: Overview," *allmovie.com,* http://www.allmovie.com (January 1, 2007). □

Q

Mae Questel

Movie lovers might remember American singer and actor Mae Questel (1908–1998) best as the dotty old woman who wrapped the family cat as a gift in *National Lampoon's Christmas Vacation*, or as Woody Allen's omnipresent nagging mother in "Oedipus Wrecks" included in the 1989 film *New York Stories*. However, she achieved lasting pop culture fame as the voice of animated cartoon characters Betty Boop and Olive Oyl.

Questel, a singer, comedienne, and character actress, paved the way for such modern day voice actors as June Foray, Tress MacNeill, and Nancy Cartwright. Never exactly a household name, the diminutive actress consistently made a solid living in vaudeville, on network radio, television, playing memorable character parts in films, and on the Broadway stage. Moreover, she provided voices for literally hundreds of cartoons that are still seen and heard around the world today.

Born Mae Kwestel September 13, 1908, in New York City, she was raised in the Bronx by parents Simon Kwestel and Frieda Glauberman, where she honed her abilities as a mimic and dialect comic at local charitable functions. Although her parents demanded she quit her dramatic studies and latch on to a steady career in teaching, the youngster's love of performance determined her fate. By the time she graduated high school at age 17, young Mae was already working in vaudeville, doing her spot-on singing impersonations of such contemporary stars as Fanny Brice, Eddie Cantor, Marlene Dietrich, Ruth Etting, and Maurice Cheva-

lier. When her impersonation of singer Helen Kane—the Madonna of the flapper era—helped her win a talent contest at the RKO Fordham Theater in 1925, her career kicked into a higher gear. Now billed as "Mae Questel, Personality Singer of Personality Songs," she began performing regularly on radio and took steady work with the RKO vaudeville circuit, culminating in a much-prized gig at the prestigious Palace Theater in New York in 1930.

The Voice of Betty Boop

Cartoon filmmaker Max Fleischer saw Questel's impersonation of Helen Kane in 1931 and asked her to use it for his cartoon creation Betty Boop. The character, which began life as a cartoon dog with Kane-like affectations, had already been voiced by various actresses, most notably Margie Hines, Little Ann Little, Bonnie Poe, and Kate Wright. Each of these actresses utilized Kane's flirty, babydoll voice and catchphrase "boop-oop-a-doop," but it was Questel who made Betty Boop a media phenomenon. A better singer and improviser than her predecessors, she also modeled for Fleischer's animators who based many of the character's emerging physical quirks on Questel's own mannerisms. Indeed, Questel told Leslie Cabarga, author of *The Fleischer Story,* "I actually lived the part of Betty Boop; walked, talked, everything! It took me a long time to sort of lower my voice and get away from the character."

During that era, cartoons were part of a movie package shown to as many adults as children. As a result, the early on-screen antics of Betty Boop were considered somewhat risque for the times. Pre-1935 cartoon gags show the character losing her dress, revealing a nude silhouette, and dancing suggestively to hot Cab Calloway jazz. (Later the character's skirts were lengthened, and her dialogue was written with less suggestive overtones.) The saucy cartoons,

299

Kane. To quote Andrew J. Lederer of *Animation World Magazine,* "However, Mae had to have known that Betty was based on Helen. Her entire career was based on her original impersonation of Helen Kane. On the night of the fateful contest, Kane had autographed a photo to Mae that said, 'To another Helen Kane.'"

Questel, who voiced Betty Boop until the cartoon ceased production in 1939, was always grateful to the Fleischer Brothers and never publicly admitted that she copied Kane for the cartoons. Ironically, when she sang the 1920s knockoff "Chameleon Days" in Woody Allen's 1983 faux documentary *Zelig,* a close-up of the mock 78 rpm record reveals that the song is falsely credited to Helen Kane.

The Voice of Olive Oyl, Caspar, Little Lulu, and Little Audrey

When she wasn't providing Betty Boop's voice, Questel was also supplying the voice for Olive Oyl in Fleischer's *Popeye the Sailor* cartoons. Olive Oyl's voice was based on the fluttering utterances of 1930s and 1940s film comedienne Zasu Pitts, but Questel added her own little touches. "The character of Olive Oyl . . . I saw the storyboard and Max Fleischer showed it to me," she recalled in a 1986 interview at the Sons of the Desert Convention. "I said, 'There is an actress that sort of reminds me of a scrawny old lady that's always using her hands.' . . . And I thought, 'That should sound like Olive Oyl' and it was a crackly kind of voice, *Yoo-hoo, here I ah-am! It's Olive Oyl!'* And, of course Max seemed to like the voice and he used it."

Popeye was originally voiced by William Costello, better known as Red Pepper Sam, who also worked with Questel on her *Betty Boop's Frolics* radio show as Gus Gorilla. He was later replaced by former animator Jack Mercer, who would supply the spinach-eating sailor's voice for the next three decades. Mercer also voiced Wimpy, Poopdeck Pappy, and Popeye's four nephews. In addition to Olive Oyl, Questel voiced the infant Swee'pea, the Sea Hag, and when Mercer was in the service during World War II, she even stepped in and did Popeye's voice.

Many Popeye aficionados prefer the early to mid-1930s run because of its mix of well-planned slapstick and verbal spontaneity. Working with director and gagman Dave Fleischer, Questel and Mercer were allowed to improvise reactions and snappy patter whether the animated characters were speaking or not. Often this somewhat surreal technique provided the illusion that Popeye and Olive were humorously complaining under their breath.

The Fleischers moved their operation to Florida in 1939, and Questel chose not to go with them, although she did provide voices for their ill-fated feature-length cartoon *Mr. Bug Goes to Town* in 1941. When Paramount foreclosed on Fleischer's loan for the Miami studio in 1942, the Popeye cartoons began being produced by their own company Famous Studios, and Questel returned to voice acting full time. Working with Seymour Kneitel, who had directed many of the Fleischer cartoons, Questel began voicing the role of popular *Saturday Evening Post* cartoon Little Lulu in 1944. The quintessential curious little girl, Lulu

many of which featured a song from Questel, made a major splash with moviegoers. Soon, the Betty Boop character was part of a hot commercial trend that encompassed everything from candy, toys, clothes, and beauty products to network radio programs and newspaper comic strips. Further, Questel herself recorded a version of "The Good Ship Lollipop" in her Betty Boop voice that sold over two million records for Decca in 1934. She also appeared as the character in a live action short subject film titled *Hollywood on Parade No. A-8.* The Fleischer Brothers and their parent company, Paramount Pictures, were presumably raking in the profits. However, the person upon whom the character was based, Helen Kane, did not benefit.

Kane's career reached its height during the late 1920s when her cutie-pie renditions of "Button Up Your Overcoat" and "I Wanna Be Loved By You," replete with her signature "boop-oop-a-doop" interjections, made her the toast of Broadway. She had made a few singing short subject films at the beginning of the sound era, but her career was clearly in decline by 1934 when she filed a $250,000 suit against the Fleischer Brothers. Kane claimed that the cartoons had subverted her popularity by appropriating her singing style and especially her catchphrase "boop-oop-a-doop."

Fleischer testified that Betty Boop came from his own imagination and had five women who had voiced the character, including Questel, take the stand and testify they did not base their performances on Kane. Nevertheless, it is generally held that Questel's characterization was based on was an immediate hit with moviegoers, but Paramount, hoping to avoid paying royalties to the character's creator Marge, ceased production on the cartoon in 1948. The following year, they had Questel providing the voice for their Little Lulu knockoff Little Audrey, another bright, curious little girl who often got into comedic trouble. Equally successful was her uncredited role as the voice of Caspar, the Friendly Ghost, which also enjoyed a successful run in movie theaters.

The Consummate Character Actress

Although married (first to Leo Balkin, later Jack Shelby), the mother of two, and grandmother of three, Questel worked constantly and found no reason to ever leave New York. Besides appearing in a series of short subject pictures during the 1930s and 1940s, she played character roles and provided animal sound effects for various network radio programs, including *The Green Hornet* and *Perry Mason.* When not starring in radio incarnations of *Betty Boop* (1933) and *Popeye* (1935–1938), she was a regular performer on Jack Pearl's (also known as Baron Munchausen) many radio shows, and the comic book spin-off *Land of the Lost.* Frequently recording as Olive Oyl, Betty Boop, and Little Audrey for Decca until 1940, she achieved a true novelty classic with the effusive skittering contained on "The Broken Record," which still receives airplay on YouTube and Dr. Demento's wacky radio show.

Staying in New York also allowed Questel to tackle roles in Broadway plays such as *Dr. Social* (1948) and Carl Reiner's autobiographical *Enter Laughing* (1963). During the early years of network television, she was a regular on the popular game show *Stop Me If You've Heard This One* (1948–1949). The consummate character actress also appeared in the daytime drama *Somerset* (1970) and in dozens of television commercials, in which she is best remembered as Aunt Bluebell for the Scott Paper Company.

A major figure in early television animation, Questel provided the voice of the starring character on the first interactive television show for children *Winky Dink and You* (1953, 1957), which sold kits that allowed viewers to draw on washable clear plastic draped over the screen whenever host Jack Barry prompted them. Questel also wrote and supplied voices for ABC's Saturday morning cartoon show *Matty's Funday Funnies* (1959–1961), where she reprised her roles as Little Audrey and Caspar, the Friendly Ghost.

During the 1950s and early 1960s, when Popeye cartoons became a staple of local children's television pro-

gramming, Questel found herself in demand as Olive Oyl once again. Besides re-teaming with Jack Mercer for 200 Popeye cartoons for syndicated television (1959–1963), she did voice-overs for the CBS Saturday morning series *The All New Popeye Hour* (1978–1983). When the nostalgia boom hit, she even voiced Betty Boop again for a series of commercials during the 1970s, an ill-fated TV pilot, and the 1988 film *Who Framed Roger Rabbit,* wherein she demonstrated her trademark flirty zest.

After decades of turning down offers, Questel finally deigned to work in Hollywood in 1961. Typed as the wacky aunt, mother, or even grandmother, the actress provided much needed spunk to Jerry Lewis' film *It's Only Money* (1961), Barbara Streisand's debut *Funny Girl* (1968), and the Elliot Gould vehicle *Move* (1970). Her final two film roles proved particularly memorable. She demonstrated comedic perfection as the Jewish mother who disappears in a magician's act and then celestially reappears to relentlessly nag her son in Woody Allen's segment of *New York Stories* titled "Oedipus Wrecks." She also garnered big laughs as the forgetful Aunt Bethany, who, when asked to say grace recited the Pledge of Allegiance, in the John Hughes-directed *National Lampoon's Christmas Vacation* (1989).

However, Questel's final screen appearance proved close to the truth. Diagnosed with Alzheimer's disease, she soon retired from the screen. She died on January 4, 1998.

Books

Cabarga, Leslie, *The Fleischer Story,* rev. ed., DaCapo Press, 1988.

Fleischer, Richard, *Out of the Inkwell: Max Fleischer and the Animation Revolution,* University Press of Kentucky, 2005.

McNeil, Alex, *Total Television: The Comprehensive Guide to Programming from 1948 to the Present,* 4th ed., Penguin Books, 1996.

Online

Lederer, Andrew J., "Mae Questel: A Reminiscence, History, and Perspective," *Animation World Magazine,* http://www.awn.com/mag/issue2.12/2.12pages/2.12ledererquestel.html (December 17, 2006).

"Mae Questel Interview from 1986 Sons of the Desert Convention," *Cartoon Brew.com,* http://www.cartoonbrew.com/archives/2006_01.html#001570 (December 17, 2006).

"Mae Questel," *Internet Movie Database,* http://www.imdb.com (November 9, 2006).

"Mae Questel," *The Scribner Encyclopedia of American Lives,* Charles Scribner's Sons, 2002. Reproduced in *Biography Resource Center,* http://www.galenet.galegroup.com.servlet/BioRC (November 17, 2006). □

R

Ranavalona I, Queen of Madagascar

Ranavalona I, Queen of Madagascar (c. 1788–1861) ruled that large Indian Ocean island with dictatorial ruthlessness from 1828 until her death. Yet she is noted as one of the few African leaders who succeeded in keeping foreign powers at bay during a period when colonial expansion put much of Africa under European rule.

The true story of Ranavalona's reign has been difficult to establish. She was illiterate, and accounts of her activities have been told throughout history from people who either mistrusted her or were her outright enemies—Christian missionaries whom she persecuted and exiled, the few Europeans whom she allowed to remain on the island as she consolidated her power, and travelers and traders who viewed her as bloodthirsty and at various times plotted to destabilize her regime. Yet there is general agreement that she was responsible for the deaths of thousands of people whom she suspected of opposing her, and her level of paranoia increased as she grew older.

Adopted into Royal Family

Little is known of Ranavalona's origins; she is thought to have been born on Madagascar in 1788, and may have been named Ramavo. Her ancestry, like that of many other members of the island's dominant Merina ethnic group, was probably mostly Indonesian; Madagascar's language and culture, denoted by the adjective Malagasy, are more closely con-

nected to Southeast Asia, from whence prehistoric colonizers had come, than to the African mainland. She was a commoner, not part of any hereditary noble family by birth. Instead, her ascent to the monarchy began with an accident of fate—her father happened to learn of a murder plot against future Merina king Andrianampoinimerina, and informed his master of what was afoot.

The plot was foiled, and when Andrianampoinimerina later became king, he rewarded the informer by adopting Ranavalona as his own daughter. As an additional reward, Ranavalona was given in marriage to the king's son, Radama. Later on Radama became King Radama I, and Ranavalona was the first of his 12 wives. The marriage was apparently not a particularly close one, and Ranavalona had no children. This meant that the question of who would succeed Radama at his death was very much an unsettled one.

Matters came to a head when Radama, laid low by the effects of what may have been syphilis or cirrhosis of the liver, died in the summer of 1828; by some accounts he was suffering so horribly that he cut his own throat. Ranavalona's position was perilous. Prince Rakotobe, the son of the king's oldest sister, was the rightful heir to the throne, but in the Malagasy belief system, any child she might bear, even after Radama's death, would be considered his own offspring, and would thus become a threat to the ruling monarch. It thus would have made sense for Rakotobe to eliminate the threat by having Ranavalona killed.

She acted swiftly. Radama had been open to Western influence, allowing Christian missionaries to set up schools on Madagascar and even sending two of his children to England for an education. Ranavalona, however, had allied herself with religious figures and lawgivers in the traditional Merina belief system. Over a few evenings, while news of the king's death was still making its way around Merina lands, she quickly mobilized a group of military men from her home village and occupied the palace. Defenders of the traditional succession who showed up at the gates were given a choice—accept Ranavalona as queen or suffer the consequences. As the ranks of men who depended on the coup's success increased, her grip on power tightened.

Adopted French Dress

On August 1, 1828, she was proclaimed Queen of Madagascar, and the following June she underwent a secret accession ceremony in which her body was anointed with the blood of a freshly killed bull. Her giant coronation, however, had more of a European flavor as she dressed in the garb of a French monarch. By that time she had ruthlessly eliminated her potential rivals; Rakotobe was speared to death, and Rakotobe's mother, so as not to break a taboo by shedding royal female blood, was starved. Most of Rakotobe's relatives met similarly gruesome deaths. "Never say," Ranavalona demanded of the crowd at her coronation (according to biographer Keith Laidler), "she is only a feeble and ignorant woman, how can she rule such a vast empire? I *will* rule here, to the good fortune of my people and the glory of my name! I will worship no gods but those of my ancestors. The ocean shall be the boundary of my realm, and I will not cede the thickness of one hair of my realm!"

The fact that she was a woman ruler was not so remarkable in itself, for Merina culture had a strong matrilineal element, partly overlaid by male-dominant gender roles that had come to Madagascar from the Arab world. But the speed with which Ranavalona moved to consolidate her rule was remarkable. She rapidly undid most of Radama's reforms and terminated trade agreements with English and French representatives, repelling a resultant attack by a French naval force, thanks partly to a fortuitous attack of malaria that struck the invaders. Merina society was restored to its traditional structure, and those who were suspected of resistance were given an age-old loyalty test called *tangena*. The *tangena* was a poisonous nut that caused the eater to vomit; suspects were forced to eat three pieces of chicken skin, and had to vomit all three of them up to show their innocence. More serious accusations were met with torture by progressive amputation.

One unfortunate person mandated to undergo the *tangena* was a high-ranking military official and former lover of Ranavalona named Andrianamihaja. He may have been the father of a son born to Ranavalona in the early years of her reign—it is unclear exactly when—but she turned against him after he was linked romantically with another woman. Andrianamihaja refused the test, and was speared in the throat as he coolly directed his executioner as to where the spear should enter his body. Tribes other than the Merina, living in different parts of Madagascar, suffered under her rule as her troops were given free rein to make annual pillaging trips to their defeated villages.

Christian missionaries from Europe also felt Ranavalona's power in the form of a series of restrictions on their activities. At first, however, Ranavalona was wary of confrontation with the missionaries. She could not hope to prevail in a direct conflict with European powers, and she needed the income that their cottage industries generated. Christianity, today practiced by about half of Madagascar's inhabitants, continued to grow in influence as the missionaries set up European schools and compiled a Malagasy-English dictionary.

That situation changed after Ranavalona made a shrewd decision to allow a European into her inner circle—a young French fortune hunter named Jean Laborde who had swum ashore after a shipwreck in 1831. Laborde and Ranavalona may have had a romantic as well as a political relationship; he has also been proposed as the father of her son, Rakoto, the future King Radama II. More important was Laborde's breadth of practical knowledge. An ingenious man with a broad grasp of metallurgy, munitions, and engineering, he directed the construction of a new factory town called Mantasao, some miles from the capital of Antananarivo. There he supervised the manufacture not only of guns and gunpowder for Ranavalona's army, but also of soap, silks, ceramics, and other items for which the kingdom previously had to trade. He also directed construction of an elaborate palace for Ranavalona on a hill above Antananarivo, which was destroyed by fire in 1995.

Christianity Suppressed

Ranavalona was now prosperous as well as powerful, and French forces, distracted by political upheaval at home in the 1830s, had completely given up their attempts to establish a foothold in the country. She was regarded by the Malagasy people as a ruler favored by powerful gods, and now she turned her attention to the last vestige of European influence: the Christian church. The teaching of Christianity in mission schools was restricted, then banned, and missionaries began to leave the island or go underground. In the mid-1830s, a series of what Laidler called judicial murders of Christians began with an especially notorious incident—the 1836 martyrdom of 14 Christians who had resisted orders to give up their religion.

Despite her attempts to resist Western influence, Ranavalona had a curiously ambivalent attitude toward the West. It was French life that fascinated her; she had courtiers dressed in French clothing, often mixing the styles of a variety of eras, and she kept a battered piano on hand, sometimes inviting visitors to play it. When it came to economic and political matters, however, Ranavalona was the West's implacable foe. A combined French and English attack on Madagascar in 1849 failed miserably as European sailors were surprised by a false-fronted native fort that concealed a much more substantial structure. A struggle between French and English troops over a temporarily captured Malagasy flag also contributed to Ranavalona's victory. A set of 21 European skulls was mounted on poles and placed along the shoreline to discourage future invasions.

This event forever cemented Ranavalona's belief in her own divinely ordained power and in the later years of her reign, her actions apparently became more and more capricious and violent. In 1845 she ordered a buffalo hunt, requiring attendance from all of the nobles at her court. Each courtier had to bring along a full retinue of underlings and slaves, and the expedition grew to an unwieldy crowd of some 50,000 people. Ranavalona commanded that a road be built, as the group proceeded, in order to smooth her progress. The expedition devolved into disaster as it went on, for it had departed with little advance planning; there were no food supplies for the workers other than what they could extract from villages along the way, and even noblemen were forced to pay exorbitant prices for rice. As road builders fell ill and died, they were replaced by fresh recruits. "The royal road was littered with corpses, most of which were not even buried, but simply thrown into some convenient ditch or under a nearby bush," wrote Laidler. "In total, 10,000 men, women, and children are said to have perished during the 16 weeks of the queen's 'hunt.' In all this time, there is no record of a single buffalo being shot."

Eventually even Ranavalona's son, Rakoto, and her confidant, Laborde, turned against her and conspired with a French shipping merchant, Joseph Lambert, to drive her from power. The plot, launched in 1857, was well documented by an Austrian world traveler, Ida Pfeiffer, who was visiting Madagascar at the time and unwittingly became entangled in the intrigue. Ranavalona, probably with the help of spies, foiled the plan and toyed with the conspirators. Rakoto survived the resulting purges and pleaded for the lives of his European friends, and Ranavalona seemingly agreed.

Her actual plan, however, was to send them on a forced march through malaria-ridden swamps. Many of the conspirators died, but Laborde survived. He later returned to Madagascar as an adviser to Radama II after Ranavalona's death on August 16, 1861. The intrigues suppressed by the queen's brutal rule returned with a vengeance after she died, and Radama II was assassinated after only two years on the throne. A series of increasingly weakened rules opened the country to European exploitation, and in 1896 Madagascar became a French colony. Today the island is unusually rich in traditional arts—probably because it remained free of European influence for much of the nineteenth century.

Books

African Biography, U*X*L, 1999.

Laidler, Keith, *Female Caligula: Ranavalona, the Mad Queen of Madagascar,* Wiley, 2005.

Stratton, Arthur, *The Great Red Island,* Scribner's, 1964.

Sweetman, David, *Women Leaders in African History,* Heinemann, 1984.

Periodicals

Journal of African History, August 1987.

Online

"History of Madagascar," Historyworld, http://www.historyworld.com (December 11, 2006). □

Shloyme Zanul Rappoport

The Russian Jewish writer S. Ansky (1863–1920) is renowned as the creator of *The Dybbuk,* a beloved Yiddish-language play that has been translated into many languages and performed all over the world.

Ansky wrote more than just that single play, however. His works, in Yiddish and Russian, included plays, fiction, folklore monographs, personal memoirs, and a harrowing account of his experiences traveling among Jewish communities in Eastern Europe during World War I. Ansky's life intersected with major intellectual currents of his time, including noncommunist leftist thought in Russia in the pre-Soviet period, and the awakening of Jewish consciousness. The publication in the 1990s and early 2000s of some of Ansky's writings beyond *The Dybbuk* pointed toward a fascinating figure who had witnessed long-obscured events and cultures.

Began Jewish Education

Ansky was born Shloyme Zanvel ben-Aaron Hacohen Rappaport (Rapaport, Rapoport) on November 8, 1863. The Yiddish form of his name was Solomon Seinwill Rappaport. Ansky (a pen name he later derived from the first name of his mother, Anna) came from Vitebsk, then part of Russia's Belorussia region, and now Vitsyebsk, Belarus. The city was part of the Pale of Settlement, a zone of western Russia originally established by Catherine the Great, in which Jews were permitted to live. The city was a center of several major schools of Jewish thought, and Ansky, whose family adhered to Orthodox Judaism, likely grew up with firsthand knowledge of traditional rabbinical figures like the one he depicted in *The Dybbuk.* He was enrolled in a Hasidic Jewish school.

As a teenager, however, Ansky abandoned the religious life of his forefathers. He became interested in the Haskalah or Enlightenment movement, which advocated an accommodation to Western ideas, and he threw himself into a more general attraction to socialism. As a 17-year-old, Ansky even started a commune near Vitebsk for other boys who had rejected religious education, and he went undercover in a heavily religious shtetl or village, attempting to convert the people who lived there to his progressive ideas. For several years he scratched out a living as a tutor, traveling from village to village while deepening his engagement with political ideas. He joined a Russian political party called the Narodnicki that promoted the interests of peasants and laborers.

When Ansky was 24 he moved to Yekaterinoslav, outside the Pale in southern Russia, and began working as a miner. He was well liked by his fellow workers, who called him Semyon Akimovich Rappaport, a Russian version of his name. Three years in the mines left him mostly toothless as a result of a bout with scurvy, and plagued with a variety of other chronic health problems. The experience also convinced him of the validity of socialist ideals. Ansky moved to St. Petersburg, Russia. He began to speak and write in Russian exclusively, referring to his life under Jewish traditions, his earlier use of the Yiddish language, and even the great figures of Yiddish literature, such as Sholem Aleichem, as decadent. And he began to write, contributing articles to local political publications. In addition to political essays, Ansky penned accounts of rural Russian life, work, and folklore. Like many young people to come, Ansky idealized the life of the working classes.

Ansky's political activities raised the suspicions of the Russian czar's secret police, however, and in 1892 he was exiled. He went to Paris, working as a secretary for the left-wing Russian philosopher Piotr Lavrov and spending time with artists, writers, and members of what would later be termed a counterculture. He became involved romantically with several women. He lived for a time in Switzerland, where he and a group of like-minded friends founded the Russian Social Revolutionary Party in 1901. Ansky was allowed to return to Russia in the early 1900s. He continued to write, and he helped form a labor union, the Jewish Labor Bund.

Returned to Writing in Yiddish

In 1905 Ansky returned to St. Petersburg and came under the influence of the Yiddish and Hebrew writer Y.L. Peretz. Peretz convinced Ansky that Yiddish could be used as a modern written language like any other in Europe, and soon Ansky had turned his attention to the village Jewish life and folklore of the Pale in his own writing. He became involved in the intellectual life of Jewish St. Petersburg, writing plays, editing a literary magazine called *Evrenski Mir,* and joining a society devoted to Jewish music. He began to speak Yiddish and promote its use, and he was soon in demand as a lecturer. At first his Yiddish, which he had not used since childhood, was of a rather stilted type, sticking close German- and Russian-influenced syntax and making little use of the rich vocabulary of old Hebrew and Aramaic words that gave the language much of its zest. As he re-immersed himself in Jewish life, however, his knowledge of the language deepened.

In 1911 Ansky began to do what would now be called anthropological fieldwork in the areas in which he had grown up, investigating and recording the traditional culture of Jewish villages in the Pale of Settlement. He worked under the auspices of a Jewish Ethnographic Society financed by a nobleman, Baron Vladimir Ginsbourg. Even at that point, the culture Ansky remembered was under pressure from a variety of sources—pogroms or massacres carried out by Christian terrorists and rioters, forced and voluntary emigration (many Eastern European Jews fled the anti-Semitism of their home countries for America during these years), and the incursion of modern life. But things were soon to become dramatically worse for Eastern European Jewry.

The outbreak of World War I had devastating effects on the Pale of Settlement, as Russian, Austro-Hungarian, and German armies contending for control of territory displaced whole populations and felt free to unleash long held anti-Semitic prejudices under the cover of wartime chaos. Between 100,000 and 200,000 Jewish civilians lost their lives, and many more became refugees. Ansky, who had both Jewish and non-Jewish friends in influential Russian circles (the latter group included the ill-fated future prime minister Alexander Kerensky), made several trips to the Pale to try to mitigate conditions there. Working under the auspices of the Russian army and of established Russian relief organizations, he tried to bring food and medical help to displaced Jews and to work on their behalf with military authorities.

He became a combination of a fundraiser and a Schindler-like figure who helped individuals when he could, and scrupulously wrote down the names of ordinary people whom he might never meet again.

Ansky wrote of his World War I experiences in a book called (in Yiddish) *The Destruction of Galicia,* later translated into English as *The Enemy at His Pleasure: A Journey Through the Jewish Pale of Settlement During World War I.* The book's translator, Joachim Neugroschel, called it "an extraordinary catalogue of barbarism: commonplace rape and looting; expulsions of whole villages and towns; scorched-earth withdrawals; humiliations, lynchings, kidnappings, torture, massacres." Ansky matter-of-factly depicted the indifference to Jewish suffering, especially among Russian soldiers. "Military circles, from the highest to the lowest," he wrote, "were cruel and cold-blooded when talking about the most horrible violence perpetrated on Jews. . . . And a large part was also played by the savaging and systematic deadening of the most elementary human feelings—a process I witnessed day after day."

Villagers Reacted Merrily to Corpse

At one point, Ansky helped to arrange for the burial of an old Jewish man who had died on a refugee train. "The Jewish burial society hurried over and carried away the body," he wrote. "The weeping and shouting Jews, the terrified members of the burial society, who were dashing along with the corpse—the soldiers and the Gentiles lingering on the platform found it all strange and funny. A few wanted to roar with laughter. But they restrained themselves; the mystique of death won out." When the Czar was overthrown in 1917 and Ansky's friend Kerensky was installed as prime minister, Ansky was elected to the Russian Duma or parliament as a member of his Social Revolutionary party. He was forced to leave St. Petersburg once again, however, after Communists deposed Kerensky and seized control of the government in November of 1917.

He moved to Vilna, now in Lithuania, and continued to do humanitarian work there as the new Soviet Union erupted into civil war, but soon he began to devote himself to writing. It was during this period that he completed *The Destruction of Galicia,* which was not published until 1925. He also founded a new historical and ethnographic society in Vilna and wrote fictional and dramatic works. One play from the end of his life, *The Dybbuk (Der Dybbuk* in Yiddish), became his most famous single piece of writing and, in the words of *Denver Post* critic Jeff Bradley, "by far, the most popular drama in Yiddish theater."

The play was drenched in the small-town Jewish folklore that Ansky had studied for so long. Its story deals with a young man and woman who love each other and are engaged to be married. The girl's father, however, hopes for a richer suitor and calls off the marriage, whereupon the young man commits suicide. The young woman becomes possessed by his soul—a dybbuk, and a well-known rabbi, who sees into the deeper currents of the situation, is called in to set things right.

Ansky's other works ran to 15 volumes in a collected edition published in Vilna after his death, but most of them remain unexamined by Western scholars (among whom knowledge of Yiddish is increasingly rare). His investigations of Eastern European Jewish and Russian folklife would seem to merit further investigation. Ansky also wrote works that drew on the tensions between Judaism and assimilation in his own life; a satirical story called *Ashmedai* depicted a Jewish-born demon queen who tries to return to Judaism but is rejected by both Jews and demons. His story "Behind a Mask" drew on his experiences as a troublemaking teacher during his youth. A collection of Ansky's writings was issued in English in 1992 by editor David Roskies, including *The Dybbuk* and several other Yiddish plays, *Father and Son, The Grandfather,* and the posthumously completed *Day and Night.*

In the last months of his life, Ansky fled violence in Vilna and moved to Warsaw, in the part of Poland that had been annexed to Germany at the end of the war. He contracted pneumonia and died there of the disease on his birthday, November 8, 1920. *The Dybbuk* was never staged during his lifetime, but a theatrical troupe in Vilna mounted it in his memory shortly after he died. The work's reputation continued to rise as it spread through Jewish communities around the world. American composer George Gershwin was commissioned to turn it into an opera in 1930, seven years before he wrote his operatic masterpiece *Porgy and Bess,* but he never completed the commission. In 1938 a sumptuous Yiddish-language film version of the play was made in Poland, shortly before Adolf Hitler launched a campaign to wipe out every trace of the culture Ansky had captured in his writings.

Books

Ansky, S., *The Enemy at His Pleasure: A Journey Through the Jewish Pale of Settlement During World War I,* ed. and trans. Joachim Neugroschel, Metropolitan Books/Henry Holt, 2002.

International Dictionary of Theatre, Volume 2: Playwrights, St. James, 1993.

Periodicals

Commentary, December 1992.
Denver Post, January 19, 1996.

Online

Contemporary Authors Online, Gale, 2006, reproduced in Biography Resource Center, Thomson Gale, 2006, http://www .galenet.galegroup.com/servlet/BioRC (December 3, 2006).

"S. Ansky," Jewish Heritage Online Magazine, http://www.jhom .com/personalities/ansky/index.htm (December 3, 2006). □

Anders Fogh Rasmussen

Danish politician Anders Fogh Rasmussen (born 1953) served as his country's prime minister during the early and middle 2000s. He found himself confronted after his election in 2001 with some of the hot-button international issues of his time: relations

between the West and the Islamic world, immigration, and war in the Middle East.

A charismatic figure who led his center-right party to its first victory over Denmark's left-leaning Social Democrats in many years, Rasmussen was emblematic of a new breed of conservatives coming to power in Western Europe. He hoped to slash the size of Denmark's large social welfare bureaucracy without eliminating the basic protections it offered, and he implemented restrictions on immigration while offering as few concessions as possible to far-right nationalist groups.

Raised on Farm

Rasmussen (ROS-muess-en) was born on January 26, 1953, in Northern Djursland, in Aarhus County in the rural eastern part of Denmark's Jutland Peninsula mainland. He grew up on the family farm with his parents, Knud and Martha Rasmussen, but he showed an instinct for political life from the start: according to an article in the *Financial Times,* he and his brothers often played a game they called "politics" and he would invariably choose the role of prime minister. In 1969 he enrolled at the centuries-old Viborg Cathedral School, taking courses in languages and social studies.

While he was there, he organized a chapter of a Danish national organization called Young Liberals. The term "liberal" has a connotation in Denmark (and many other countries) opposite to its meaning in the United States but close to the classical sense of the term, indicating a philosophy or political party devoted to minimizing governmental interference in the affairs of private industry. What motivated Rasmussen to become involved was the outbreak of student demonstrations around Europe in May of 1968, many of which were oriented toward Marxist or Communist ideas. "That was my reaction to the events of May 1968," he told the *Economist.* Rasmussen remained involved with Denmark's Liberal Party after he entered the University of Aarhus in 1972, and by 1974 he had become chairman of the party's national youth wing. He joined its national central committee in 1976.

In 1976, while still a university student, Rasmussen began doing consulting work for the Danish Federation of Crafts and Small Industries, and he continued to do that work until 1987. Finishing a master's degree in economics at Aarhus in 1978, Rasmussen was immediately elected to Denmark's Folketing, or parliament, from the Viborg district. He married, and he and his wife, Anne-Mette, raised three children. In the early 1980s Rasmussen served as vicechairman of the Folketing's housing committee.

In the 1980s and 1990s, Rasmussen worked his way up through the Liberal Party hierarchy, moving in and out of the top echelons of government as the party's fortunes fluctuated. In 1984 he was named to the Liberals' parliamentary management committee, and he became vice-chairman of the national party the following year. From 1987 to 1992 he was Minister for Taxation in the Danish cabinet, adding the title of Minister for Economic Affairs to his portfolio in 1990.

For much of the 1990s he was out of the Folketing, but he worked as the Liberal Party's national spokesman from 1992 to 1998. In 1998 he became the party's national chairman, after his predecessor, who had been expected to win that year's election, failed to come out on top. Rasmussen held several other administrative posts in the 1990s.

Authored Economic Studies

Denmark enjoyed one of the highest per-capita income figures in the world, but it had correspondingly high tax rates, second only to Sweden in personal income tax rates, by one calculation. Rasmussen's Liberals believed that the country's cradle-to-grave social welfare system had become bloated and could be pared, and a series of books authored by Rasmussen himself provided ammunition for the arguments of party members. Those books included *Showdown with the Tax System* (1979), *The Struggle for Housing,* and *From Social State to Minimal State* (1993).

As party chairman, Rasmussen led the Liberals into Denmark's 2001 national elections against the ruling Social Democratic party and its leader, Poul Nyrup Rasmussen (not a relative). In Denmark's parliamentary system, the leader of the party that wins the most seats in the parliament is given the chance to form a government. Rasmussen's platform was toned down from the conservative economic policies he advocated in his books; in place of the "minimal state" of his free-market 1993 broadside he merely advocated a system in which some of the services of Denmark's welfare state would be opened up to participation by private industry. Rasmussen's telegenic appearance also played a positive role in the campaign when placed in contrast with that of his bearded, lumbering opponent. The *Economist* called him "a professional politician to his fingertips." He also campaigned on promises to freeze taxes, reduce crime, reduce growing hospital waiting lists in the country's government-run health system, and introduce measures that would help Denmark's large elderly population.

The results of the election displaced the Social Democrats from power for the first time since the 1920s, with the Liberals taking 31 percent of the vote to the Social Democrats' 29 percent. The result was ambiguous, however, for Rasmussen was forced to seek the support of several more conservative parties in order to form a government. These included the Conservative People's Party (Konservative Folkeparti) and Danish People's Party (Dansk Folkeparti), the latter a nationalist group that called for new immigration restrictions and specifically deplored the influence of immigrant Muslims on Denmark's ethnically homogeneous society (with an immigrant population of just over 5 percent, the country was less diverse than most of the rest of Western Europe).

Anti-immigrant sentiment was rising in Denmark in the wake of the U.S. terrorist attacks of September 11, 2001. The Danish People's Party, which had received just over 7 percent of the vote in the elections, was still seen as extreme, but Rasmussen finessed the issue by lining up the party's support in parliamentary votes but excluding it from his cabinet. He became Danish prime minister on November 27, 2001.

Eliminated Government Boards and Committees

Rasmussen's working majority held together early in his term, and he was able to implement major sections of his agenda. By June of 2002 the governing Liberals had shaved almost $830 million of spending from Denmark's $53 billion budget. They had taken steps to benefit Danish business interests, and Rasmussen took the seemingly noncontroversial step of closing down 103 government boards, councils, and committees, a step that was projected to save $35.5 million. "We wish to tidy up the intermediate layer [of government], which drains our resources and removes attention from the essential matters," Rasmussen explained in his New Year's speech of 2002, according to Maria Bernborn of *Europe.*

One of those panels eliminated, however, was the Board for Ethnic Equality, whose disappearance drew widespread criticism. The controversy arose because the move was viewed as a concession on Rasmussen's part to the Danish People's Party. Rasmussen cut legal immigration levels, and he put new curbs on foreigners who claimed refugee status when trying to enter Denmark; refugees had to prove that they had actually been victimized by religious, political, or ethnic persecution. The number of refugees seeking asylum dropped from 12,000 in 2001 to 3,000 in 2004. Many refugees headed for other European countries, particularly Sweden, which criticized the actions of its Scandinavian neighbor.

The economic specialist Rasmussen was quickly faced with issues that had international implications. In 2003 he backed the U.S. invasion of Iraq, making Denmark one of just a few continental European countries to line up behind the U.S. and Britain, and he sent 500 Danish troops to Iraq in support of the war effort. Danish public opinion first backed the move but later turned decisively against it. A Continental economic slowdown toward the middle of Rasmussen's first term in office dented his popularity, and a massive train bombing in Madrid, Spain, on March 11, 2004, affecting one of the war's other European supporters, raised speculation that Rasmussen could be headed for defeat in the next election.

Rasmussen's Liberals bounced back after he called an election for February 8, 2005, however. Rasmussen campaigned once again on economic issues, claiming that an assortment of tax cuts had added an average of $3,000 to annual Danish family incomes. Teenagers were denied certain welfare benefits, but, noted the *Economist,* such moves were seen by the Danish electorate as "necessary tweaks, not a conservative revolution." And the new immigration restrictions won support across a wide spectrum of Danish public opinion, excluding only the leftmost segments of the political spectrum. In the February elections, both Rasmussen's Liberals and the Social Democrats actually lost seats, while parties farther to the left and right made gains. Rasmussen's majority in the new Danish parliament was unchanged, standing at 94 of the Folketing's 179 seats.

The major challenge in the first part of Rasmussen's second term came in early 2006, when Islamic anger exploded worldwide after a series of cartoons were published in Denmark's *Jyllands-Posten* (Jutland Post) newspaper late the previous year. The cartoons depicted the Prophet Muhammad in a disparaging way, with one of them showing him with a bomb-shaped turban. Protests flared in Copenhagen and in many Islamic capitals, and Danish consumer goods were removed from shelves in Islamic markets.

Rasmussen referred in his 2006 New Year's message, quoted in the *Economist,* to "unacceptably offensive instances" of attempts "to demonize groups of people on the basis of their religion or ethnic background," but he maintained that owing to the principle of freedom of the press in Denmark, the government had no control over what Danish newspapers printed. A group of 11 ambassadors from predominantly Islamic countries asked to meet with Rasmussen. He initially refused, drawing strong condemnation from a group of Danish foreign service officers, but later met with several of the Islamic ambassadors. The controversy simmered down slowly, and the threat of terrorist attacks in Denmark reportedly remained high through 2006 as Rasmussen turned to other aspects of his foreign agenda that included support for the European Union and North Atlantic Treaty Organization (NATO). Early in 2007, Rasmussen unveiled a plan to cut Denmark's dependence on imported energy, aiming to provide 30 percent of Denmark's energy needs from wind power, hydrogen, and biofuels by 2025.

Books

Worldmark Encyclopedia of the Nations: World Leaders, Gale, 2003.

Periodicals

Economist, November 24, 2001; March 20, 2004; December 18, 2004; February 5, 2005; January 7, 2006.
Europe, June 2002.
Financial Times, November 22, 2001.
New York Times, November 22, 2001.

Online

"Denmark unveils plan to reduce fossil fuels, double use of renewable energy," *International Herald Tribune,* http://www.iht.com/articles/ap/2007/01/19/europe/EU-GEN-Denmark-Cleaner-Energy.php (January 23, 2007).
"Prime Minister of Denmark: Anders Fogh Rasmussen," Prime Minister's Office of Denmark, http://www.stm.dk (January 23, 2007).
"Rasmussen, Anders Fogh," Parliament (Folketing) of Denmark, http://www.folketinget.dk (January 23, 2007). □

James Earl Ray

American criminal James Earl Ray (1928–1998) pled guilty to assassinating civil rights activist Martin Luther King Jr. and was sentenced to 99 years in prison on March 10, 1969. Three days later he recanted his plea. He then spent almost 30 years vainly attempting to win the right to the trial he had forsworn. He

eventually gained such unlikely allies as members of the King family and the Reverend Jesse Jackson in his protestations of innocence and quest for a trial. Ray's death on April 23, 1998, did little to quell the unanswered questions and conspiracy theories that abounded, but a 2000 probe led by then-U.S. Attorney General Janet Reno found no credible evidence to reopen the investigation. Nonetheless, there were some who remained unconvinced.

Unhappy Childhood

Ray was born into poverty on March 10, 1928, in Alton, Illinois. He was the eldest child of Lucille and George Ellis Ray, who briefly moved the family to Bowling Green, Missouri, when Ray was two. In 1935 the family relocated again, this time to a bleak and arid 60-acre farm in Ewing, Missouri, that was bought while Ray's father was out on bond for a forgery conviction. The family's dismal prospects did not improve with the move.

Ewing was located in Lewis County, a poor white region across the Mississippi River from Quincy, Illinois. The Ku Klux Klan thrived there in the 1920s and 1930s, and the Rays reportedly embraced the group's racist beliefs. The family's life was undeniably difficult, whatever its members' unsavory views. Grinding deprivation, the death of an eight-year-old daughter, and another of a 19-year-old son were just a few of their hardships over the years. Ray himself was troubled early in life, suffering from such problems as recurring nightmares, stuttering, and bed-wetting. He attended school only sporadically, and because of his ragged clothes and antisocial behavior, was unpopular when he did make an appearance. One teacher, according to Harold Jackson of the *Guardian,* went so far as to note in her report on him that Ray was "repulsive" in appearance. It could not have been an easy beginning to his life.

Unsurprisingly, crime and alcohol were integral parts of the family dynamic, and the young Ray was soon following suit by brawling in saloons and engaging in petty theft. At 14, he was running errands for the proprietress of a local brothel when he was caught stealing a customer's pair of pants. That same year, he had his first official run-in with the police when he stole some newspapers and attempted to sell them. He was released with a warning and went on to a brief reprieve of regular employment at a shoe company near St. Louis, Missouri, but lost the job in 1945 at the end of World War II. Ray's next, and last, best hope lay with the U.S. Army.

Career Criminal

Unfortunately, military service was too late to change Ray's future. He signed on with the U.S. Army shortly after World War II was over, but it proved an unhappy alliance. Ray was posted to Germany, where his pro-Nazi sympathies and black marketeering activities quickly absorbed him. Characteristically, however, it was not such major infractions that were his downfall. Instead, he was court-martialled for drunkenness and received a general discharge for being inept. Thus, in December of 1948, Ray found himself back in the United States no further ahead than he had been before.

Once again, crime became Ray's mainstay. He attempted the straight and narrow path via a job at a rubber company in Chicago, Illinois, but was serving a three-month sentence for burglary in California by December of 1949. In 1952, he was handed a two-year sentence for armed robbery in Chicago, and 1955 saw his graduation to the federal system with a four-year stint at Leavenworth, Kansas, for a post office robbery. He was back in St. Louis in 1959, and back in prison in 1960. That intended incarceration of 20 years, for armed robbery, at the Missouri State Penitentiary in Jefferson City, lasted until Ray's escape in 1967.

Assassination of Martin Luther King Jr.

In April of 1967 Ray escaped from prison by hiding inside a bakery van. Little is known about his activities in the following year, but it appears he spent much of his time in Canada. What is clear is that he had made his way to Memphis, Tennessee, by April of 1968.

Dr. Martin Luther King Jr. was in Memphis that April to lend his support to striking city sanitation workers. At the time, King was the most prominent leader of the American civil rights movement. On April 4, he was standing on the balcony of the city's Lorraine Motel when he was shot at 6:01 PM. King died within the hour, sparking riots across the country and dimming hopes for the nonviolent means he had espoused.

That same day, Ray had checked in to a boarding house across the street from King's motel. He then allegedly shot King with a Remington 30.06 from the bathroom window of the motel, abandoned the rifle, which bore his fingerprints, and escaped to Atlanta in a rented Ford Mustang. From there, he led authorities on a chase as he fled from Atlanta to Canada to England to Portugal and back to England. They finally caught up with him at London's Heathrow Airport on June 8, 1968.

Ray eventually waived extradition and was returned to the United States. He pled guilty to King's murder on March 10, 1969, and was sentenced to 99 years in prison. Three days later he recanted his plea and claimed innocence of the crime. That refrain, along with the attendant pursuit of the trial he had given up, would consume the remainder of Ray's life.

Conspiracy Theories

Claiming he was coerced into giving his guilty plea, Ray delivered various versions of King's assassination over the years. One version was a theory of conspiracy, generally in the form of a shadowy gunrunner named "Raoul," who Ray maintained was part of a Federal Bureau of Investigation (FBI) plot to frame him. Raoul was never located, but the story led to a spate of conspiracy theories. Favorite suspects included the Mafia, racists, the Central Intelligence Agency (CIA), and the FBI. Of the latter, its director, J. Edgar Hoover, was certainly no fan of King's. Over time, those proclaiming Ray's innocence, or at least the theory that he did not act alone, included such unlikely Ray supporters as members of King's family and the Reverend Jesse Jackson.

Supporters of Ray's claims, or of the idea that he had not acted alone, pointed to the unlikely scenario. How did a comparatively ineffective petty criminal plan and fund such a crime? How did an unschooled and not particularly bright misfit elude law enforcement authorities for over two months in four countries? Few argued Ray's probable motivation as a bigot, although some even denied the rather overwhelming evidence of his racism, focusing instead on his lack of resources. In short, was it truly plausible that a prison escapee of limited financial means and decidedly unremarkable intellect could pull off such a horrendous crime and efficient escape without assistance?

Law enforcement officials and historians generally dismissed such lingering questions and remained convinced that the right man had been convicted. As Memphis lead state prosecutor William Gibbons succinctly told the *Houston Chronicle* after Ray's death, "I believe the history books will accurately record that James Earl Ray was the killer of Dr. King." Others, such as Evan Thomas of *Newsweek,* saw the conspiracy faction as a natural, if inaccurate, reaction to the murder of an illustrious man. "Attraction to the larger theories about the fallen leader's death is not hard to fathom. A federal conspiracy seems more commensurate with the genuine greatness of the target than the sad truth that a hater lucked into the shot of a lifetime," he wrote. Still, the rumors persisted.

Penitentiary Years

Ray's time in jail was turbulent. He escaped and was recaptured twice from Tennessee's Brushy Mountain State Prison (1977 and 1979). On October 13, 1978, he married courtroom artist Anna Sandhu. He was repeatedly stabbed by black inmates in 1981 and transferred to the Tennessee State Penitentiary for his safety soon afterward. The year 1991 saw the release of his book *Who Killed Martin Luther King? The True Story of a Convicted Assassin,* and 1993 brought the dissolution of his marriage. Along the way, likely from blood transfusions after the stabbing, he contracted hepatitis-C, which eventually led to the kidney and liver disease that killed him. But through it all, Ray tirelessly campaigned for a new trial. It was not to be.

During Ray's incarceration, a total of eight Tennessee and federal courts refused to grant him the trial he had passed up in 1969. Four separate investigations, the latest of which was conducted by then-U.S. Attorney General Janet Reno in 2000, found no credible evidence of conspiracy or basis upon which to reopen the case. Toward the end of his life, Ray set his sights on obtaining official government records regarding the assassination opened in hopes of proving his innocence, but those files were to remain sealed until the year 2027. Even such powerful new allies as King's widow, Coretta Scott King, and the Rev. Jesse Jackson could not budge the prevailing view that justice had already been served in the case.

In 1996 Ray's health began to fail markedly. He was hospitalized more than 15 times between December of that year and April of 1998, thrice lapsing into nearly fatal comas. He was refused permission to travel to Pittsburgh, Pennsylvania, for a liver transplant and denied clemency to spend his final days at his brother's home or a veterans' hospital. On April 23, 1998, Ray died of kidney failure and complications from liver disease.

Reactions to the death of one of the United States' most notorious criminals aptly delineated the opposing views on his guilt. Arthur Brice and Jack Warner of the *Atlanta Journal-Constitution* quoted King's widow's statement as, "America will never have the benefit of Mr. Ray's trial, which would have produced new revelations about the assassination of Martin Luther King Jr. as well as establish the facts concerning Mr. Ray's innocence. It is regrettable that Mr. Ray was denied his day in court, but the American people have a right to the truth about this tragedy, and we intend to do everything we can to bring it to light." Memphis Assistant District Attorney John Campbell, on the other hand, told Brice and Warner, "James Earl Ray killed Martin Luther King. It's a shame he never would spell out the circumstances of the crime—why he did it. He had the power to do that. Now his legacy will be all these wild conspiracy theories that will be spun out." Whichever side one came down on, Ray was gone; and whatever secrets he may or may not have had were gone with him.

Periodicals

Atlanta Journal-Constitution, April 24, 1998.
Guardian (London, England), April 24, 1998.
Houston Chronicle, April 24, 1998.
Independent (London, England), April 25, 1998.
Jet, June 26, 2000.
Newsweek, May 4, 1998.
People, May 11, 1998.
San Francisco Chronicle, April 24, 1998.
St. Louis Post-Dispatch, April 24, 1998.
U.S. News & World Report, May 4, 1998; December 20, 1999.

Online

"James Earl Ray," http://www.maxautographs.com/james_earl_ray.htm (November 29, 2006).
"James Earl Ray," NNDB, http://www.nndb.com/people/682/000034580/ (November 29, 2006).
"James Earl Ray," Who2?, http://www.who2.com/ask/jamesearlray.html (November 29, 2006).
"James Earl Ray Biography," Biography Base, http://www.biographybase.com/biography/Ray_James_Earl.html (November 29, 2006).
"James Earl Ray: Timeline," CBS News, April 23, 1998, http://www.cbsnews.com/stories/1998/04/23/national/printable7878.shtml (November 29, 2006). □

Dennis Ritchie

Dennis MacAlistair Ritchie (born 1941) is best known for his work on computer languages and operating systems ALTRAN, B, BCPL, C, Multics, and especially Unix. For a man who did not start out in the computer industry, he has had a profound influence on the entire computer programming world. He told

Investor's Business Daily, **"It's not the actual programming that's interesting. But it's what you can accomplish with the end results that are important." And if that is the case, then Ritchie has had an important effect on most, if not all, computer users today.**

Early Fascination with Harvard's Univac I

Ritchie was born on September 9, 1941, in Bronxville, New York. He was born to Alistair Ritchie, a switching systems engineer for Bell Laboratories, and Jean McGee Ritchie, a homemaker. Ritchie grew up in New Jersey, and after a childhood in which he did very well academically, he went on to attend Harvard University. There he studied science and graduated with a bachelor's degree in physics. While he was still going to school, Ritchie happened to go to a lecture about how Harvard's computer system, a Univac I, worked. He was fascinated by what he heard and wanted to find out more. Outside of his Harvard studies, Ritchie began to explore computers more thoroughly, and was especially interested in how they were programmed.

While still at Harvard, Ritchie got a job working at the Massachusetts Institute of Technology (MIT). At that time computer programming was not a degree, and computer labs were looking for anyone with potential to help on their computers. Ritchie, with his unflagging curiosity, seemed perfect for the job. Ritchie worked at MIT for many years helping develop, alongside other scientists, more advanced computer systems and software.

Began Work on Operating Systems

He also began work on developing an operating system for more portable computers. Most computers at the time took up entire rooms and had limited dial-in access, but smaller desktop computers were being developed, and these did not have easy to use operating systems. Ritchie decided that one was needed. MIT, Honeywell, and General Electric agreed, and administered his project. Other scientists from colleges and private companies came to help build the system, one that was able to handle up to a thousand users at once and could be run 24 hours a day. Ritchie never saw programming as a problem but rather as a puzzle to be solved.

After the project was finished, just about the time that he graduated, Ritchie determined that computers, rather than physics, would be his career. He got a job at Bell Labs, where his father had worked for years. At the time, in 1967, it was the nation's primary phone provider, and it had one of the best labs in the world, one that was responsible for developing a multiplicity of technical advances, from new switching devices to transistors, as well as new computer advances. Ritchie told *Investor's Business Daily,* "Instead of focusing on specific projects, I wanted to be around people with a lot of experience and ideas. So I started working on various projects to learn my way around the profession."

Built Unix to Fulfill Computer Needs

Ritchie began working with Kenneth Thompson, who had joined Bell Labs in 1966. Both men had been watching how the minicomputer was becoming more and more popular in the early 1970s. What was needed, they thought, was a simpler and more feasable interaction between various computers. It took them months to come up with a solution, but when they were finished they had written the Unix operating system. An operating system is necessary for a user to copy, delete, edit, and print data files. It allows a person to move data around from disk to screen to printer and back to disk for storage. Without an operating system computers would not be accessible to anyone but an expert few. Before the creation of Unix, operating systems had been complex and expensive. Unix was comparatively cheap and simple, and it could be used on just about any machine, which meant buyers were not stuck with the cumbersome software that came with their computers. They could buy and install a variety of software systems, because Unix was compatible with all of them. This had not been possible before.

Ritchie and his team released Unix to the public at a symposium on Operating Systems Principles that was hosted by IBM, and it was an immediate success. Ritchie and Thompson then set out to improve the system.

Development of C Programming Language

Unix was written in machine language, which had a small vocabulary and did not deal well with multiple computers and their memories. So Ritchie combined some aspects of the older systems with aspects of the new one, and came up with the "C" programming language. In the early twenty-first century, "C" is still the dominant language of computer programming. It was such a simple, concise language that almost every single computer maker at the time switched to it.

"C" uses very little syntax and few instructions, but it is extremely structured and modular. Because of this it was easy to use in different computers. There were large blocks of "C" functions that were already written that programmers could copy whole into their own programs without having to start from scratch, making it faster and easier to implement. These blocks were easily accessible, available in libraries so programmers could access them. By the middle of the 1980s "C" had become one of the most popular programming languages in the world. Because of the speed with which "C" could be used to write programs and run them, companies began using "C" to develop their own software.

Continued Drive to Improve Computer Functionality

By 1973 Ritchie and Thompson had re-written the Unix operating system, using "C" instead of machine language, and had done massive testing on it. It was so simple to use

that programmers all over were switching to smaller machines to do their programming, giving up the larger computers they thought they would never want to leave. Bell Labs became Lucent Technologies Inc., and began to sell Unix to developers, creating a whole new division for the company. Ritchie has credited his success in part to the fact that he did not have a computer background and therefore had an open mind to possibilities that others might not have thought existed.

Ritchie became the leader of the Computing Techniques Research Department at Lucent Technologies in 1990. In that role he wrote applications and managed the growth of already released operating systems. Over the years Ritchie has received numerous awards, including the ACM award for the outstanding paper of 1974 in systems and languages, the IEEE Emmanuel Piore Award in 1982, a Bell Laboratories Fellow in 1983, an Association for Computing Machinery Turing Award in 1983, an ACM Software Systems Award in 1983, and an IEEE Hamming Medal in 1990. He was also elected to the United States National Academy of Engineering in 1988. In April of 1999 he was the recipient of the United States National Medal of Technology. All of the awards Ritchie received were in conjunction with Thompson. Ritchie is now the head of Lucent Technologies' Systems Software Research Department, and is still striving to make computers work better and more easily for users.

Personal Life Mirrored Professional

Asked what he liked to do in his personal life, Ritchie admitted that his personal and professional lives are mixed together. He said in an interview on the Old Unix website, "I've done a reasonable amount of traveling, which I enjoyed, but not for too long at a time. I'm a home-body and get fatigued by it fairly soon, but enjoy thinking back on experiences when I've returned and then often wish I'd arranged a longer stay in the somewhat exotic place."

Books

Almanac of Famous People, 8th edition, Gale Group, 2003.
Newsmakers 2000, Issue 1, Gale Group, 2000.
Notable Scientists: From 1900 to the Present, Gale Group, 2001.
World of Computer Science, 2 volumes, Gale Group, 2002.

Periodicals

Economist, June 12, 2004.
Investor's Business Daily, January 27, 2003.

Online

"Dennis M. Ritchie," *Bell Laboratories,* http://cm.bell-labs.com-who-dmr- (January 2, 2007).
"Dennis M. Ritchie," *Bell Laboratories,* http://cm.bell-labs.com-cm-cs-who-dmr-bigbio1st.html (January 2, 2007).
"Interview-Dennis Ritchie," *Unix,* http://old.unix.se-article-articleview-950-1-24 (January 2, 2007). □

S

Edward W. Said

The American writer and academic Edward Said (1935–2003) has been ranked among the most influential thinkers of the twentieth century, with much of the field of postcolonial studies springing directly or indirectly from his ideas. He was also an intellectual in action, devoting much of his energy to advocacy for the Palestinian people and their aspirations.

Controversial in his work, Said had both admirers and detractors. Few statements beyond the bare facts of his life would meet with universal agreement from observers, and even those bare facts were sometimes in dispute. But divergent views of Said were, in a way, inevitable, for Said was a man of many contradictions. He was an academic, and yet he spent much of his time addressing the public, often having to cancel classes he taught at Columbia University because he was booked for television appearances. He was a Christian Arab who both defended the Islamic world and, by his own testimony, felt close to Jews for much of his life. He spent many years working toward the goal of Palestinian nationhood but renounced that goal in the last decade of his life. He was attacked by Israelis as a terrorist, and by Palestinians as too accommodating to Israel. Said's scholarly works indicted Western cultural traditions as complicit in colonialism, but he played and wrote about European classical music extensively and enthusiastically.

Grew Up in Cairo

Said (sah-EED) was born in Jerusalem on November 1, 1935, when the city was part of British-occupied Palestine.

His father was an American citizen who had fought for the United States in World War I, and Said himself was named after Britain's King Edward VIII. Said's father, Wadie, who preferred the name of Bill, operated a profitable stationery business, and Said was discouraged from speaking Arabic while growing up; the household language was English. He was a member of the Anglican church. Later in his life Said occasionally spoke of himself as a refugee displaced by the formation of the country of Israel in 1948, but he actually spent much of his childhood in Cairo, Egypt, sometimes traveling to Jerusalem to spend time with relatives, or to Beirut, Lebanon.

The family moved permanently to Cairo in 1947, and for a time Said attended Victoria College, an upscale British preparatory school there. Among his classmates were actor Omar Sharif and Jordan's future King Hussein. At 15, Said came to the United States to attend Mount Hermon School, an elite boarding institution in Massachusetts. Said, who had already traveled through many countries but never really called any of them home, felt out of place at Mount Hermon and frequently circulated among a group of Jewish friends. He did take to American classroom teaching, which encouraged more independent thinking than had the British instructors he had experienced previously.

Said, a charismatic figure who favored tailored suits, found a natural place in academic life. He spoke English, French, and Arabic fluently, and he could read Spanish, German, Italian, and Latin. He attended Princeton University, graduating in 1957, and earned master's and Ph.D. degrees at Harvard, receiving his doctorate in 1964. Hired at Columbia University in New York as an instructor in 1963, Said spent the rest of his working life there, becoming assistant professor in 1965, associate professor in 1968, and professor of English and comparative literature in 1970;

this thesis was perhaps the book's most original component, as he showed how such stereotypes found their way into scholarly writings, literary and popular fiction, and journalistic writing in an interconnected web.

Some reviewers felt that the book painted the works of Western writers with too broad a brush, but Said's elegant style (his writing was free of academic jargon) quickly made the book a favorite. Said's work opened up numerous new avenues for investigation of Western representations of other cultures—and of indigenous responses to such representations in so-called post-colonial literature. Three decades after it was written, *Orientalism* has remained a solid part of reading lists in college and graduate-level English courses in the United States and beyond. The book's tone, sharp and provocative yet with arguments buttressed by an obvious depth of knowledge, have made it ideal for educational uses. The ideas of postcolonial studies and of the relationships between language and power became fodder for academic studies and graduate school papers over the next few decades, and these ideas were traceable to Said's innovations.

Said expanded and generalized on the ideas in *Orientalism* in *Culture and Imperialism* (1992). He was also a prolific writer of both academic and general articles, and bits and pieces of his ideas on Western culture emerged in such writings as his introduction to a new edition of Rudyard Kipling's *Kim,* and in several collections of writings by others that he edited. In the 1980s, however, Said became equally well known for purely political writings and public appearances, in which he argued for recognition of the fundamental rights of the Palestinian people. According to the *New York Times,* Said describe himself as "a man who lived two quite separate lives," although one could equally well describe him as an intellectual in action. Indeed, Said's book *The World, the Text, and the Critic* (1983) dealt with how literary critics could come to terms with their own cultural assumptions.

In 1977 Said became a member of the Palestinian National Council, a provisional parliament established with the goal of pursuing eventual Palestinian nationhood; he was an independent, not a member of Palestinian leader Yasser Arafat's Palestine Liberation Organization or any other group. Said wrote his first book on the Middle East situation, *The Question of Palestine,* in 1979. He rejected the use of violence (although in some statements he argued that it was understandable) and accepted the existence of Israel, saying in an interview quoted in the London *Guardian,* "I don't deny [Israel's] claims" to land in the Palestine region, "but their claim always entails Palestinian dispossession." In the 1980s Said favored a two-state solution, with Israel and a Palestinian state existing side by side. In 1988 he was sent by Arafat to negotiate on the Palestinians' behalf with U.S. Secretary of State George Shultz.

Became Disillusioned with Peace Process

Said's attitudes changed during the negotiations leading to the so-called Oslo Accords of 1993 (the Declaration of Principles on Interim Self-Government Arrangements), which called for Israeli withdrawal from parts of the territories it had occupied in the Gaza Strip and West Bank areas,

later his title of professor was attached to several endowed chairs at Columbia. He was married twice; with his second wife, the former Mariam Cortas (a Quaker), he raised a son and a daughter.

Said's first book, *Joseph Conrad and the Fiction of Autobiography,* published by Harvard University Press in 1966, dealt with an author to whom he felt a kinship (Conrad, Polish by birth, traveled the world and learned English later in life). The following year, Israel defeated the combined forces of several Arab countries in the Six-Day War, an event that began to awaken Said's political consciousness. He wrote a book called *Beginnings: Intention and Method* (1975) about literary creativity, but he was at work on a larger project that broke new ground in literary studies.

Examined Language of Western Enlightenment

That book, *Orientalism,* was published by Pantheon (a mainstream, not an academic publisher) in 1978. It remains Said's best-known and most influential work. The book took issue with Western depictions of the Middle East, and the methods of analysis Said employed were quickly applied to the West's relations to other cultures of the developing world by other scholars. Indeed, Said observed that the "East," as opposed to the "West," was an invention partly designed as an ideological underpinning for Western colonialism. Said's central thesis was that Western views of Middle Eastern cultures were rife with stereotypes of irrationality, degeneracy, and violence. His demonstration of as well as for the establishment of the Palestinian Authority as a governing body, and for continued negotiations on remaining issues such as the status of the city of Jerusalem. Said became a critic of the Palestinian leadership, which he felt was giving up too much in the negotiations, and he resigned from the Palestinian National Council in 1991.

Specifically, Said objected to the lack of provision in the PLO's position for the so-called right of return, the right of Palestinians to inhabit lands from which they had been expelled when the Israeli state was established. In the 1990s he began to advocate the peaceful coexistence of Palestinians and Israelis in a single democratic country—a solution viewed by many Israelis as tantamount to the destruction of their country as it had existed. "I see no other way than to begin now to speak about sharing the land that has thrust us together, and sharing it in a truly democratic way, with equal rights for each citizen," Said wrote in the *New York Times*.

Said outlined his case for Palestinian aspirations in *The Politics of Dispossession: The Struggle for Palestinian Self-Determination* (1994) and *End of the Peace Process: Oslo and After* (2000), as well as in numerous shorter writings and in U.S. television appearances. But he had many interests other than those of politics and scholarship. A pianist of near concert-level skill, he wrote extensively on classical music, penning a column for the *Nation* magazine. In the early 1990s he was diagnosed with leukemia but was able to continue his public activities after treatment. One of several books published after Said's death (he wrote voluminously during his final years) was *On Late Style* (2006), an examination of works produced by literary and musical artists toward the ends of their lives. Beginning in 1999, he and conductor Daniel Barenboim co-founded the East West Divan Orchestra, a joint Israeli-Palestinian youth ensemble that continued to win acclaim after Said's death. In 2002 Barenboim and Said published a joint book of their collected conversations, *Parallels and Paradoxes: Explorations in Music and Society*.

Controversy continued to envelop the ailing Said, with the magazine *Commentary* referring to him (according to the *Guardian*) as a "professor of terror." He was photographed throwing a stone at an Israeli guardhouse, but maintained that his gesture was symbolic and that he had not aimed the stone toward any individual; Columbia, despite calls for his censure, found in his favor and took no action. Said participated vigorously in the give-and-take of debate, carrying on long disputes in print with Princeton scholar Bernard Lewis and other conservative thinkers. In 1999 an article in *Commentary* by an Israeli scholar charged that Said had deliberately falsified the details of his childhood in order to heighten the impression that his family had been refugees displaced from their Jerusalem home in the 1940s. The article pointed to such statements by Said as one that appeared in the *London Review of Books*: "I was born in Jerusalem and spent most of my formative years there and, after 1948, when my entire family became refugees, in Egypt." But Said's memoir *Out of Place*, which appeared that same year, went into detail about his Cairo childhood. "I don't think it's that important, in any case,"

Said told the *New York Times*. "I have never represented my case as the issue to be treated. I've represented the case of my people, which is something quite different.

Said's medical condition worsened in 2002, and he worked against the clock to finish several new books, including *On Late Style, From Oslo to Iraq and the Road Map*, and *Humanism and Democratic Criticism*. All were published after his death from leukemia on September 25, 2003, in New York. Among the literary awards he received in his last years was one for lifetime achievement, bestowed by the Lannan Foundation in 2001.

Books

Said, Edward, *Out of Place: A Memoir*, Knopf, 1999.
Sprinker, Michael, ed., *Edward Said: A Critical Reader*, Blackwell, 1993.

Periodicals

Commentary, September 1999.
Daily Telegraph (London, England), September 26, 2003.
Economist (U.S.), October 4, 2003.
Financial Times, September 26, 2003.
Guardian (London, England), September 26, 2003
Irish Times, September 27, 2003.
New Statesman, March 29, 2004; June 14, 2004; May 29, 2006.
New York Times, September 26, 2003.

Online

Contemporary Authors Online, Gale, 2007, http://www.galenet.galegroup.com/servlet/BioRC (January 7, 2007). □

Joseph Boulogne, Chevalier de Saint-George

Joseph Boulogne, Chevalier de Saint-George (1745–1799), a musician, athlete, and soldier, was among the most fascinating figures during the years at the end of France's old regime and during its age of revolution at the end of the eighteenth century.

Saint-George is known today as one of the major early contributors of African descent in the tradition of European classical music. He gained fame as a violinist, conductor, and composer; some of Europe's top composers created violin works with Saint-George in mind as the soloist, and he led the premieres of some of Franz Joseph Haydn's greatest symphonies. The music of Saint-George himself, long forgotten, has been successfully revived. In his own time, however, Saint-George was known for much more than music. A champion fencer as a young man, he was the object of often veiled and sometimes overt racial controversy. He survived two assassination attempts. In his later years he abandoned the aristocratic world of his upbringing to fight for revolutionary ideals, and he was an early supporter of racial equality in France and England.

Product of Extramarital Liaison

Saint-George was born on the French-ruled Caribbean island of Guadeloupe on December 25, 1745. His last name has sometimes been spelled "Saint-Georges," but his father generally dropped the final "s," and a street named after the younger Saint-George in Paris also omits it. Saint-George's father, George de Bologne Saint-George, was a plantation owner and slaveholder on Guadeloupe who while still in France had been part of the inner circle of King Louis XV. He was married and had a legitimate daughter, but he also had a slave mistress, likely born in Senegal, named Nanon and said to be exceptionally beautiful. It was unorthodox for George de Bologne Saint-George to acknowledge this interracial infidelity, and more unusual still when he took not only his wife but his mistress and illegitimate son with him to France in 1748, fleeing a court conviction for killing a man in a duel. Joseph Boulogne, as a man who was half black, was barred from French noble status but did enjoy his father's support and patronage.

Saint-George received the tutoring appropriate for a young member of the French nobility, attending a boarding school run by a famous swordsman named La Boëssière. Besides fencing and swordsmanship, his studies included literature, the sciences, and horseback riding. The teacher became the first of several observers to write admiringly of Saint-George's prowess with the sword. Saint-George was tall, handsome, and gracious, and he quickly found his way into the halls of the French aristocracy. In 1765 a fencer named Picard insulted Saint-George and challenged him to a duel. Saint-George at first refused, but his father promised him a new carriage if he fought and won. At the duel in the city of Rouen, Saint-George quickly emerged the victor. He suffered his first defeat the following year at the hands of the famed Italian fencer Giuseppe Gianfaldoni, who praised Saint-George and said that he would soon be the best fencer on the European continent.

In music, too, Saint-George was a standout student. Several of France's leading composers had benefited from the elder Saint-George's patronage in the past, and young Saint-George benefited from their musical attentions. He is thought to have studied the violin with one of the great French virtuosi, Jean-Marie Leclair the Elder, and he mastered the harpsichord (an ancestor of the piano) as well. By the late 1760s he had become the recipient of a dedication from François-Joseph Gossec, the composer at the center of Parisian concert life. In 1769 Saint-George joined an orchestra called Le Concert des Amateurs, directed by Gossec, as first violinist, and in 1773, when Gossec moved on to a different conducting post, Saint-George became the group's director.

Even as he notched these successes, Saint-George's status in French society was an ambivalent one. Religious leaders were agitating for the end of slavery, and King Louis XVI himself was opposed to the practice. But interracial marriages were forbidden (Saint-George was never able to marry), and belief in the genetic inferiority of Africans was widespread. As word of his athletic and musical exploits spread, Saint-George became famous. Word even reached America of how he could swim across the Seine River using

only one arm or shoot at and hit a coin thrown into the air, and he was something of a fashion trendsetter as well. But there was always an undercurrent of racial controversy surrounding his reputation. Saint-George had powerful backers who appreciated his talents, including Queen Marie Antoinette (to whom he was unusually close). But when he was considered for the prestigious post of director of the Paris Opéra in 1775, two of the company's leading sopranos objected and petitioned the Queen (according to a biography of Saint-George appearing on the Artaria publishing company website), asserting that "their honor and the delicacy of their conscience made it impossible for them to be subjected to the orders of a mulatto."

Premiered Haydn Works

Nevertheless, Saint-George was a major star in Paris in the 1770s. By 1772 he had written several violin concertos (works for violin and orchestra) for his own use as a performer; lyrical pieces of ambitious dimensions, they reentered the classical concert repertoire at the end of the twentieth century. The concertos are not flashy showpieces but bespeak a performer with a smooth, velvety tone even at the highest reaches of the violin's range. Saint-George also played chamber music (music for small ensembles), enthusiastically submerging his own talents in a group sound, and he and Gossec were among the first French composers to write music in an important new genre of Austrian origin—the string quartet.

Saint-George, though not prolific, wrote a modest body of music that showed an awareness of current trends generally, and was widely heard. Mozart based a passage in his ballet score Les petits riens (The Little Nothings) on one of Saint-George's melodies. Saint-George wrote a concerto for harp and orchestra, several symphonies and operas, and several works in characteristically French genres: the symphonie concertante (for a small group of instruments with orchestra) and quartet concertante (for a mixed group of small instruments). He also composed several symphonies and operas, some of which have been lost. The music publisher Bailleux signed a six-year agreement with Saint-George giving him publication rights to the composer's future violin concertos.

One of the most celebrated individuals in the French capital, Saint-George had various nicknames. One was "Le Mozart Noir," or the Black Mozart; on concert posters advertising both Mozart's music and that of Saint-George, the two often received equal billing. Another was Le Don Juan Noir, the Black Don Juan, but it is unclear whether this part of Saint-George's reputation was exaggerated. What was clear was that he aroused resentment in some quarters. In 1779 Saint-George and a friend were attacked by six men while walking. The still agile Saint-George fought them off successfully, but an investigation into the attack was mysteriously squashed, with rumors circulating that the attackers were secret police from the court in Versailles, and that the reason for the attack was Saint-George's closeness to Marie Antoinette, with whom he often played music.

After the disbanding of the Concert des Amateurs, Saint-George founded a new group called the Concert de la Loge

Olympique in 1781. Working with an aristocratic patron, he arranged for the composition of and conducted the first performances in 1787 of the six "Paris Symphonies" of Franz Joseph Haydn, widely considered the greatest composer in Europe at the time (Mozart was better known to connoisseurs than to the general public). He was still flying high as a composer, writing the successful opera *La fille-garçon* (The Girl-Boy) and also an opera for children, *Aline et Dupré ou le Marchand des marrons* (Aline and Dupré or The Chestnut Seller). The extent of his fame was shown when he gave a fencing exhibition in England in 1787 against an opponent believed to be a woman, the Chevalière d'Éon (actually a male French diplomat dressed as a woman): the event was depicted in paintings that circulated all over Europe.

Joined Anti-Slavery Activist Group

In England, Saint-George became involved with the country's growing anti-slavery movement, and he founded a similar French group called the Société des amis des noirs (Society of the Friends of Black People). Apparently these activities were irritating to British slave dealers; Saint-George was attacked once again by a group of five men armed with pistols in London, but once again escaped serious injury, using his stick as an impromptu sword. Although he had broken an Achilles tendon when he was 40, he was still a formidable swordsman. Saint-George became France's first black Freemason, rising to 33rd-degree rank.

Much of the last decade of Saint-George's life was shaped by the French Revolution and its aftermath. He sympathized with the revolution's democratic aims, and, living in the city of Lille, he became a captain in the National Guard. With his strong connections to the deposed French court, however, he was also the object of suspicion among revolutionary leaders; in the 1790s he truncated his aristocratic name to Monsieur de Saint-George and later to simply George. As war broke out between France and the Austrian monarchy, Saint-George joined a group of black Frenchmen who hoped to form a new corps that would volunteer for the fighting. Saint-George became a colonel in the new force, and another measure of its fame was that it was popularly known as the Saint-George Legion, although its official name was different.

Saint-George and his regiment saw heavy action, and Saint-George claimed credit for victory over the Austrians at Lille. He also played a key role in foiling the so-called Treason of Dumouriez, a plot by a renegade French officer, General Dumouriez, to seize the city; Saint-George fooled the officer's agent, a General Miaczinski, into thinking he would offer no resistance, but then had him arrested. Dumouriez was forced to flee the country. Saint-George was hailed as a hero, but the power struggles that engulfed the Revolutionary government soon affected him as well. One of the deputies in Saint-George's black regiment, Alexandre Dumas (father of the famous French novelist of the same name), was an ally of the revolutionary leader Robespierre and his Reign of Terror. He denounced Saint-George, charging him with corruption and financial mismanagement. Saint-George was imprisoned in 1793 but released a year later after Robespierre's fall.

The last years of Saint-George's life were not happy ones. He returned to the Caribbean for several years in the 1790s and was deeply disillusioned by the black-on-black warfare he witnessed on the island of Santo Domingo (now Haiti and the Dominican Republic), as slave rebellions broke out and the French government sent troops, many of them former members of the Saint-George Legion, to quash them. Back in France he became the director of a new orchestra called Le Cercle de l'Harmonie (The Circle of Harmony), which performed at the Palais Royale, the former home of the Duke of Orléans. His fame was still such that the orchestra attracted large crowds that admired its precision and energy. Living alone, Saint-George contracted a bladder infection and died on June 10, 1799. Several commemorative editions of his music appeared. But soon new restrictions on blacks appeared across France's empire; slavery, which had been abolished in 1794, was reimposed by Napoleon Bonaparte, and fighting deepened in the Caribbean between slave rebels and French troops. Saint-George and his music were removed from orchestra repertoires and essentially from the history books, not to be rediscovered for nearly 200 years.

Books

Banat, Gabriel, *The Chevalier de Saint-Georges: Virtuoso of the Sword and the Bow,* Pendragon, 2006.

Guédé, Alain, *Monsieur de Saint-George: Virtuoso, Swordsman, Revolutionary, a Legendary Life Rediscovered,* trans. Gilda M. Roberts, Picador, 2003.

Smidak, Emil F., *Joseph Boulogne called Chevalier de Saint-Georges,* Avenira, 1996.

Periodicals

Investor's Business Daily, January 19, 2006.

Virginian Pilot (Norfolk, VA), August 5, 2004.

Online

"Le Chevalier de Saint-George," AfriClassical.com, http://www.chevalierdesaintgeorges.homestead.com.Page1.html (January 28, 2007).

"The Historical Biography of Joseph Boulogne (Le Chevalier de Saint-George): The Remarkable Life of a Superman Revisited," http://www.chevalierdesaintgeorge.com/bio_fulltext.html (January 28, 2007).

"Joseph Boulogne Chevalier de Saint-Georges," *All Music Guide,* http://www.allmusic.com (January 28, 2007).

"Saint-Georges, Joseph Boulogne de," Artaria Editions, http://www.artaria.com/SystemLink_ComposerFM_23 (January 28, 2007). □

Samoset

An ambassador and interpreter, Samoset (c. 1590–c. 1653) of the Abenaki people was the first Native American to greet the English Pilgrims at Plymouth and to introduce them to the Wampanoag chief Massasoit.

The Abenaki chief Samoset from what is today Maine learned to speak English from fishermen who visited his coastal territory. So it was a surprise to the Pilgrims of Plymouth Plantation when he entered their settlement and announced, "Welcome, Englishmen!" The first Indian to greet the Pilgrims, Samoset fostered goodwill and trade with the Europeans. He introduced the white men to Squanto, an emissary of the great Wampanoag chief, Massasoit, who facilitated the long-term peace between the Pilgrims and Massasoit. In later years, Samoset signed the first land sale transaction to the colonists.

Sagamore of the Abenaki

Samoset, whose name means "He Who Walks over Much," was born circa 1590 in what is today the state of Maine in the New England region of the United States. From Pemaquid Point on the southeast coastline of the state, Samoset was a member of the Abenaki people, which means "People of the Eastern Dawn." Like most of the tribes in New England, the Abenaki spoke the Algonquian language and could easily communicate with the native Nauset and Wampanoag people of the region. Samoset was a sagamore, or lesser chief, of his tribe.

Near Pemaquid Point, between the Kennebec and the Penobscot rivers, colonial Englishmen and Frenchmen vied for fishing and fur rights. Samoset would have had frequent contact with these fishermen, and was able to pick up a moderate understanding of the English language. It is assumed Samoset had the opportunity to ship with Captain Dermer from Monhegan Island to Cape Cod around the time of the English Pilgrims' arrival at Plymouth in what is today Massachusetts and what was then the Patuxet region.

Pilgrims Settled in Plymouth

The English Pilgrims arrived in Plymouth, Massachusetts, in 1620, after fleeing religious persecution in England and Europe. After roughly half of the Pilgrims fell victim to disease and harsh conditions and died during the first winter, the survivors were too weak and in short number to defend themselves against any large planned attack by Indians.

As the remaining Pilgrims were establishing plans for a militia to defend their settlement, men on patrol had noticed two Indians on a hill about half a mile away and sounded an alarm. The colonists had complained that some of their tools that they had left on the ground had been stolen, presumably by the roving Indians. William Bradford wrote in *Of Plymouth Plantation*, "All this while the Indians came skulking about them, and would sometimes show themselves aloof off, but when any approached near them, they would run away; and once they stole away [the Pilgrim's] tools where they had been at work and were gone to dinner."

Myles Standish and Stephen Hopkins were chosen to confront the Indians. They armed themselves and approached the area, but the Indians fled before they could make contact. A militia was a necessity as the Pilgrims were unwilling to let the Indians see how few and weakened they were and what easy prey they would be in case of attack.

Announced, "Welcome! Welcome, Englishmen!"

As the colonists decided to conclude their plans for a defense, they were interrupted the day of March 16, 1621, by an Indian walking directly into their encampment—it was Samoset. Alexander Young, who collected the historical documents recording the lives of the Pilgrims and events at Plymouth Plantation, reprinted in *Chronicles of the Pilgrim Fathers of the Colony of Plymouth*, "He very boldly came all alone, and along the houses, straight to the rendezvous; where we intercepted him, not suffering him to go in, as undoubtedly he would out of his boldness."

Samoset walked toward the white men, saluted them, and announced, "Welcome! Welcome, Englishmen!" in English. The startled colonists described him as a tall and straight man with long black hair down his back and short hair in the front, and without a beard. In a pragmatic gesture of caution but also a gesture of peace, Samoset carried with him his bow and an empty quiver. In his hand he held two arrows, one tipped and ready for battle, the other untipped.

To the Puritan Pilgrims, Samoset was considered virtually naked, as he wore only a fringed loincloth around his waist and moccasins on his feet. The day was mild but windy, and they offered him a horseman's coat to cover his body. In *Chronicles of the Pilgrim Fathers*, documents describe how the Pilgrims gave Samoset food, "He asked some beer, but we gave him strong water, and biscuit, and butter, and cheese, and pudding, and a piece of mallard; all which he liked well."

As Samoset was the first native that the Pilgrims encountered up close and were actually able to converse with, they questioned him considerably to learn everything they could about him and the area. Although Samoset spoke in broken English, the Pilgrims admired his ability to communicate with them, reporting in *Mourt's Relation*, that "he was a man free in speech, so far as he could express his mind, and of a seemly carriage."

Learned English from Fishermen

Samoset explained that he was originally from Monhegan Island, which was five days' journey by land but one day by ship, and he was a sagamore, a lesser chief or lord, there. He had been in the Patuxet region for the past eight months visiting the Wampanoag tribe, but that he was intending to return to his people shortly.

He had learned English from contact with the English fishermen and traders who visited the Monhegan region. In fact, he even became acquainted with some of the ship captains and commanders and knew them by name. Historians speculate that when Samoset greeted the Pilgrims, he had mistaken the Mayflower in Plymouth harbor as just another fishing vessel.

Told the Pilgrims about Squanto and Massasoit

In their conversations, Samoset provided much beneficial information to the Pilgrims, describing the land, the people, places, and distances. In *Chronicles of the Pilgrim*

Fathers, documents record, "He discoursed of the whole country, and of every province, and of their sagamores, and their number of men and strength."

Samoset explained that the region the Pilgrims had settled in originally belonged to the Patuxet, who, along with some neighboring tribes, fell victim to a terrible plague four years earlier that ravaged the region, leaving no one alive. To a degree, the Pilgrims accepted the fate of the Patuxet as divine providence that they should take over the territory. *Chronicles of the Pilgrim Fathers,* records "There is neither man, woman, nor child remaining, as indeed we have found none; so as there is none to hinder our possession, or to lay claim unto it."

Samoset had mentioned that one of the few Patuxet left, who was not present during the plague, was an Indian by the name of Squanto, who had a better command of English. Samoset said that he would arrange a meeting between Squanto and the Pilgrims. Samoset also talked about Massasoit, the great chief of the Wampanoag tribe, who was currently in the area with the 300-strong Nemasket people.

Samoset described the Pilgrim's other neighbors, the Nauset, who were angry with the white men for killing numerous Indians and taking others as slaves. In "The Pilgrims & Plymouth Colony: 1620" on Rootsweb, it is reported that Edward Winslow wrote that the Nausets were, "ill-affected towards English, by reason of one [man named] Hunt, a master of a ship, who deceived the people, and got them under colour of trucking [trading] with them, twenty out of this place where we inhabit [Plymouth] and seven men from Nausites, and carried them away, and sold them for slaves, like a wretched man (for 20 pound a man) that cares not what he does for his profit."

Stayed with the Pilgrims

Samoset stayed much of the afternoon and evening talking with the Pilgrims, who suspected that their guest was not intending to leave. When they realized they needed to put him up for the night, the Pilgrims first planned to have him sleep on the Mayflower, where it would be easy to watch him and where he would be unlikely to commit any treachery. However, the water in the harbor was too low and the wind too strong for the shallop, or shallow boat, to reach the Mayflower. So Stephen Hopkins allowed Samoset to lodge at his house where he set a guard upon the Indian.

That next Saturday morning, Samoset left the Pilgrims after they gave him a knife, a bracelet, and a ring. He promised to return shortly with more men and goods to trade, such as beaver and deerskins.

Samoset returned the next day with five Indian men. They wore fur leggings and carried bows and arrows, along with deerskins and wildcat-skins. They even returned some of the Pilgrims' tools that had been lost or stolen from the fields. The Pilgrims refused to engage in commerce with the Indians, however, since it was Sunday, and asked that they bring their goods another time.

Nevertheless, the Pilgrims entertained their guests and offered food. The Indians in turn were friendly and amiable, singing and dancing, and introducing the white men to a cornmeal biscuit the Indians carried with them on long journeys. When the Indians left, Samoset was either actually sick or pretended to be sick in order to remain with the colonists for several more days. When he finally left that Wednesday, they gave him a hat, a pair of stockings and shoes, a shirt, and some cloth to tie around his waist.

Introduced Squanto

On the next day, Thursday, March 22, 1621, Samoset returned to the colonists with a special companion, Squanto. Also known as Tisquantum and considered the last surviving member of the Patuxet, he had been kidnapped by Europeans and brought to Spain and to England, where he learned to speak English quite well. He had been returned to America before the Pilgrims arrived in Plymouth.

Samoset and Squanto conducted some business with the Pilgrims, offering dried herring. But the real reason for Squanto's visit was to inform the colonists that the great sachem, or king, of the Wampanoag named Massasoit was waiting nearby with the Nemasket and wanted to meet with the Pilgrims.

Later that day, Massasoit did appear, with his brother Quadequina and 60 of his men, at the top of the hill overlooking the colonists. Although there was some initial reluctance on the part of both parties to send emissaries, they eventually met and exchanged gifts and entertainment. The meeting was the beginning of Massasoit's long-term friendship and defense pact with the Pilgrims.

Returned in 1624 and Sold Land

Samoset appears again in historical accounts in 1624 in his home region of Maine when he made deals with the English trader Christopher Levett. Calling Levett his "cousin," Samoset decreed that only the Englishman could buy the fur his tribe had to sell. This monopoly angered competing traders so much so that one company attacked Samoset. Trade relations quickly degraded into beatings and corruption that led to retaliation by the Indians, and eventually progressed into full-scale wars in the latter part of the century.

Nevertheless, Samoset continued to live in peace with the white men. An accomplished diplomat for more than 30 years, Samoset recognized the need for mutually beneficial alliances and treaties with the European colonists that would help his people survive the wars, plagues, and slave traders. On July 15, 1625, Samoset signed the first land sale transaction between the eastern coastal Indians and the colonists. He deeded 12,000 acres of Pemaquid Point to John Brown, thus establishing that the true owners of the land in the new world were the Indians, not the English Crown. After Samoset signed another deed of land in 1653, he disappeared from historical records and is believed to have died soon after in what is today Bristol, Maine.

Books

Bonfanti, Leo, *Biographies and Legends of the New England Indians,* Pride Publications Inc., 1968.

Bradford, William, *Of Plymouth Plantation 1620–1647,* Alfred A. Knopf, New Edition, 1984.

Deetz, James, and Patricia Scott Deetz, *The Times of Their Lives: Life, Love, and Death in Plymouth Colony,* W. H. Freeman and Co., 2000.

Encyclopedia of North American Indians, Marshall Cavendish, 1997.

Mourt's Relation: A Journal of the Pilgrims at Plymouth, edited by Dwight B. Heath, Applewood Books, 1986.

Notable Native Americans, Gale Research, 1995.

Young, Alexander, *Chronicles of the Pilgrim Fathers of the Colony of Plymouth, from 1602 to 1625,* Charles C. Little and James Brown, 1841. Reprinted DaCapo Press, 1971.

Periodicals

Cobblestone, September 2001.

Online

Cline, Duane A., "The Pilgrims & Plymouth Colony: 1620," www.rootsweb.com/~mosmd/index.htm (December 18, 2006). □

Artur Schnabel

Austrian-born pianist Artur Schnabel (1882–1951) was the first artist to record all of Beethoven's piano sonatas. Only modestly gifted technically, he was renowned for the depth of his interpretations.

A short man with a large moustache, Schnabel had little charisma. Indeed, he mistrusted the cult of personality that surrounded the world of classical piano, and according to his biographer, Cesar Saerchinger, he felt that the great traditions of piano playing amounted to little more than "a collection of bad habits." For Schnabel, by contrast, the intentions of the composer were paramount, and it was Beethoven who challenged him above all other composers. Audiences in turn venerated Schnabel as the supreme Beethoven interpreter. Harold C. Schonberg, in *The Great Pianists,* noted that "to many of the last generation, there was but one Beethoven pianist and his name was Artur Schnabel."

Schnabel was born on April 17, 1882, into a Jewish family in Lipnik, Austria. The village, now part of Poland, was described by Schnabel in *My Life and Music* as "tiny and rather poor"—a kind of suburb to a small town." His father, Isidor, was a salesman with a small textile company, and the family often traveled between their small home town and the Austrian capital of Vienna, gaining an awareness of its musical riches. Schnabel's piano career began at age six, when his sister's piano teacher noticed that he instantly mastered, without teaching, the lessons his sister had to practice. Schnabel quickly started lessons himself, with a teacher who would disappear through a door and return smelling of liquor. A year later he was sent to Vienna to study with the best teachers Austria had to offer. Anonymous well-off donors paid most of his bills; he boarded partly with his own family and partly in rented rooms. His first desire, later partially realized, was to become a com-

poser, but his family and teachers believed that he had the skill to become renowned as a piano prodigy.

One of Schnabel's instructors, the virtuoso and famed teacher Teodor Leschetizky, realized the unique nature of his talent. "He said to me repeatedly throughout the years, and in the presence of many other people: 'You will never be a pianist. You are a musician,' " Schnabel recalled in *My Life and Music.* Leschetizky's statement has been taken to indicate that Schnabel's gifts lay in his ability to understand music rather than in his technical brilliance. Schnabel studied music theory as well as piano in Vienna; his teacher, Eusebius Mandyczewski, was a friend of the composer Johannes Brahms, and Schnabel met Brahms once on a nature outing. As a pianist, he would often tackle Brahms's dense piano works.

Schnabel made his public debut at age 11. By 1898 he was still studying piano in Vienna but was good enough to take on piano students himself; financially independent, if barely so, he headed for Berlin, Germany. In that city, as musically rich as Vienna, Schnabel managed to make a slender living. He had a bohemian lifestyle, often playing pool late into the night and not getting up until noon. Sometimes his diet consisted of bread rolls with mustard, which he could get free of charge at a bar after buying a beer. During this period Schnabel fathered an illegitimate daughter, learning about it only some years later.

Schnabel's career was slow to build, but after he gave a Berlin debut concert featuring the music of Franz Schubert, he acquired an agent and began to find intermittent concert engagements. One of those took him in the middle of winter to the small Prussian town of Rastenburg, where he was to accompany a singer named Therese Behr. Seeing a pair of large snow boots in the hall outside of her hotel room, Schnabel joked about them to a companion. The next morning at breakfast, Behr said to Schnabel (as he recalled in *My Life and Music*), "I heard you talking about my big feet." Within a year the two were engaged, and in 1905 they married. (She was six feet tall, Schnabel just five feet four.) They raised two sons, one of whom, Karl Ulrich Schnabel, became a concert pianist.

Toured Europe

After a series of performances as soloist with the renowned Berlin Philharmonic Orchestra, Schnabel became a recognized name in German musical life. In the years prior to World War I he toured most of the major European countries, including Russia. Monolingual up to that point, he began to learn foreign languages and mastered English in two months, after going on walks with a tutor who would correct him whenever he made a mistake. Schnabel kept his career going during the war with performances in neutral countries such as Sweden and Switzerland, where he later bought a summer home on Lake Como.

In 1921 Schnabel set sail for the United States, the last major classical music market he had not yet conquered. His first trip to the United States was a disagreeable experience, not helped along by Schnabel's own tart sense of humor—he wrote a letter (according to Saerchinger) saying that he was slated to play an afternoon concert for "the ladies who don't happen to be playing bridge." Turnouts for his concerts were moderate, although the cognoscenti who did attend realized his brilliance. His promoter, the legendary agent Sol Hurok, urged him to play a repertoire of a more popular type, but he refused. Schnabel returned to the United States in 1922 for another tour, with similar results.

Schnabel's refusal to meet his audiences halfway was characteristic. His repertoire ran straight up the middle of the intellectual Germanic tradition, seldom straying from that path. He favored music that seemed to hold profundities that would forever be just beyond his grasp, once saying, according to Saerchinger, "Now I am attracted only to music which I consider to be better than it can be performed." He loved the comparatively simple sonatas of Wolfgang Amadeus Mozart, pointing out that "children are given Mozart because of the small *quantity* of the notes; grown-ups avoid Mozart because of the great *quality* of the notes."

The most important of the serious composers for Schnabel was Ludwig van Beethoven, especially the 32 piano sonatas that spanned most of his career. Schnabel edited a new edition of the sonatas in sheet music form in the late 1920s, and then, although he had thus far refused to make any recordings at all, he recorded all 32 sonatas between 1931 and 1935 for the His Master's Voice label. Many other pianists in the future would record the complete cycle, but Schnabel's was the first. The recordings were made on 78 rpm discs lasting slightly over three minutes each, meaning that the pianist had to stop every few minutes

and then pick up from where he had left off. Sound quality was poor, but in spite of these technical limitations the Schnabel Beethoven sonata recordings have rarely been out of print since their release. New versions recorded on compact discs were issued in the late 1990s, with digital processes applied in order to reduce distortion and background noise.

Unconcerned by Errors

Schnabel's recordings were prized by collectors in spite of the fact that in Beethoven's more difficult pieces (such as the Piano Sonata No. 29 in B flat major) his technique was clearly not up to the job. Schnabel considered errors incidental flaws in a performance, rather than major difficulties to be agonized over. Schonberg related a famous Schnabel story wherein the pianist suffered a memory lapse in the middle of a performance with the New York Philharmonic Orchestra—severe enough to cause the music to grind to a halt. Any other pianist would have been mortified, but Schnabel, Schonberg wrote, "merely grinned, shrugged his shoulders, got up from the piano, and walked over to the podium" to confer with the conductor, after which he began the music again. For Schnabel, what mattered was the communication of the meaning of the music to the audience, not a display of technical perfection.

For several years he avoided performing in the United States, but returned in 1930 as a soloist with the Boston Symphony. In 1936, performing his live cycle of the Beethoven sonatas at Carnegie Hall, he drew a crowd of 18,000 total listeners, and this softened his attitude toward what would become his adopted country. He felt more relaxed partly because he booked his own performances, rather than leaving his promotion in the hands of professional agents. He left Germany in 1933; after the Nazi takeover of the country, his concerts had been abruptly canceled, and he had quit his teaching job at the State Academy of Music as he noticed a hardening in the attitudes of his non-Jewish colleagues. For several years he and his family lived mostly at their villa in Switzerland. Schnabel visited his mother in Vienna in 1937 and never saw her again; she was arrested after Germany's annexation of Austria in 1938 and disappeared.

Schnabel was performing in a small town in Texas when he received word of the annexation. "It is a singular experience for a grown man to learn from the daily paper that he has lost his fatherland," he wrote to his wife, as quoted by Saerchinger. With a strong premonition of the anti-Semitic horrors to come, Schnabel decided that the United States was the best place for himself and his family. He took up residence in a New York City apartment hotel in 1939 and became a naturalized citizen during World War II. He lived for part of the year on a New Mexico ranch that he found congenial for composing, and he taught at the University of Michigan and other institutions. In 1945 he gave a series of autobiographical lectures that was posthumously published as *My Life and Music*. Schnabel wrote two other books, *Reflections on Music* (1933) and *Music and the Line of Most Resistance* (1942).

During his own lifetime, Schnabel's own music remained much less well known than his piano performances.

In contrast to the conservative nature of his piano repertoire, which rarely, if ever, encompassed contemporary music, Schnabel as a composer was something of a radical, writing three massive symphonies that employed dissonant modern harmonies and, wrote Mark L. Lehman in the *American Record Guide,* "make grueling demands on performers and audiences." Schnabel also wrote chamber music (music for small ensembles) and a sonata for solo violin that lasted for nearly an hour. "Chances are that Schnabel's music has disappeared for good," Schonberg opined in the 1960s, but a series of new recordings of Schnabel's compositions beginning in the late 1990s cast doubt on that assessment.

Schnabel continued to live in the United States after World War II ended, but he often made return trips to Europe to perform and to spend time at his Swiss second home, where sympathetic neighbors had kept his possessions in good order during the many years he had been absent. His last concert was given in New York in January of 1951, by which time he was already suffering from heart problems. Schnabel died in Axelstein, Switzerland, on August 15, 1951. His playing, wrote Samuel Lipman in *Commentary,* had "the palpable aura of greatness."

Books

American Decades, Gale, 1998.
Saerchinger, Cesar, *Artur Schnabel: A Biography,* Dodd, Mead, 1957.
Schnabel, Artur, *My Life and Music,* St. Martin's, 1963.
Schonberg, Harold C., *The Great Pianists,* rev. ed., Fireside, 1987.

Periodicals

American Record Guide, September–October 1996; November–December 1996.
Atlantic, October 1986.
Commentary, April 1994.

Online

"Artur Schnabel," *All Music Guide,* http://www.allmusic.com (January 2, 2007). □

Mary Seacole

British war nurse Mary Seacole (1805–1881) cared for the wounded and maimed during the Crimean War of the 1850s, but her fame was eclipsed by that of fellow army nurse Florence Nightingale. A Jamaican by birth who was a staunch British patriot, Seacole enjoyed a rather adventurous and well-traveled life for a woman of part African heritage during that era. She operated several successful businesses in the Caribbean and Latin America, but was best known for her talents as an herbal medicine specialist. Her service during the Crimean conflict endeared her to hundreds of British soldiers she treated. "I do not pray to God that I may never see its like again, for I wish to be useful all my life," she wrote of the horrors of that war in her autobiography.

Seacole was born Mary Jane Grant in Kingston, Jamaica, in 1805. Her mother was creole, or a person of mixed race, and Seacole's father was white and a native of Scotland. He was an officer in the British Army and probably stationed there as part of a military contingent whose duty it was to secure the island against the Spanish, from whom Britain had seized it originally back in 1655. At the time of Seacole's birth, Jamaica was emerging as the world's leading exporter of sugar, which was shipped out of the bustling port city of Kingston to the rest of the vast British Empire and its assorted trading partners. Blacks were not native to Jamaica, but brought in by the British from Africa to serve as free labor on sugar plantations. In 1800, just five years before she was born, the island's 300,000 slaves outnumbered the white population 10 to 1.

Learned Craft from Her Mother

Seacole belonged to a small number of free blacks and creoles on the island, estimated at ten thousand or so. Her mother ran a boarding house that catered to both military personnel and civilians who fell ill in the tropical climate. Yellow fever, a vicious viral disease that was prevalent in the Caribbean at the time, was a leading killer, and Seacole's mother probably learned the herbal remedies she used to treat that and other sicknesses through slave women whose medical expertise had been passed on from their African ancestors. Seacole was eager to inherit the career, as she wrote in her 1857 bestselling autobiography, *The Wonderful Adventures of Mrs. Seacole in Many Lands.* "I saw so much of her," she wrote of her mother, "and of her patients, that the ambition to become a doctress early took firm root in my mind."

In her autobiography, Seacole makes almost no mention of political events that shaped Jamaica, including numerous slave uprisings and the eventual abolition of slavery in 1834. Fiercely committed to the notion of Empire, and proud to be a British subject, she had longed to visit London since her girlhood, and finally made her first trip there around 1821. As a single woman, she had to have a male accompany her, and wrote in her autobiography that her companion's skin was darker than hers and they were sometimes taunted by children on the street, for blacks were still a rarity anywhere in Europe. She made another trip to London about a year later, this time bringing with her a large cache of West Indian spices and her own homemade jams to sell, and stayed until around 1825. In her autobiography, Seacole was vague about many details of her life and exact whereabouts, and therefore how she may have earned a living at times has been the subject of conjecture. She did visit the Bahamas, Haiti, and Cuba, probably selling her jams and spices, and helped her mother at the boarding house back in Kingston.

Moved to Panama

In 1836 Seacole married Edwin Horatio Seacole, a man described in various historical sources as English, a merchant in Jamaica, and the godson of famed British naval hero Lord Nelson (1758–1805). He was in poor health, however, and died eight years later. It was one of a series of tragic events that befell Seacole around this time: her mother died, and in August of 1843 both her Kingston home and boarding house were destroyed in a fire that nearly killed her. She resurrected her mother's enterprise, called Blundell Hall, and returned it to profitability within a few years.

In 1850 Seacole joined her half-brother in Panama, which was receiving a steady influx of travelers on their way to the California gold rush. On the Panamanian isthmus she had a provisions business that sold supplies to the travelers, but continued to run a boarding house and serve clients as a doctress, as female herbal medicinists were called at the time. Her reputation grew after she treated many cholera victims during one outbreak with a remedy that involved giving the patient large amounts of water in which cinnamon had been boiled. Cholera was a bacterial disease most commonly caused by drinking contaminated water, and cinnamon's essential oil has antimicrobial properties. She also became particularly adept at treating victims of violence in the rough-and-tumble Spanish garrison towns of the isthmus, where fights and knife wounds were common. By 1852 she had returned to Jamaica, where she established a makeshift military hospital for British soldiers sickened by another yellow fever epidemic on the island.

Seacole returned to Panama and set up another clinic near a mining camp. When she learned about Britain's involvement in a faraway conflict known as the Crimean War (1853–56), and the need for nurses to tend the wounded, she decided to volunteer her services. Most of the battles took place on the Crimean peninsula, which later became part of Ukraine. There, British troops had joined their French counterparts to help Turkey push back Russian forces for control of the area, and when reports reached England about how terribly the invalid soldiers had suffered during the first winter, a wealthy British woman who had already made nursing her career began a public awareness campaign to recruit and train women to serve as army nurses. That woman was Florence Nightingale (1820–1910), and her services during the Crimean War made her one of the most famous women in the world.

Earned Fame as War Nurse

Nightingale was already in Turkey by the time Seacole arrived in London to offer her services. The doctress, well-known in the Caribbean world, brought with her several letters of reference from British officers in Kingston attesting to her medical skills, compassion, and selflessness, but Nightingale's recruiter was the wife of a cabinet minister who informed her that all nursing positions had already been filled. "I read in her face the fact that had there been a vacancy I should not have been chosen to fill it," Seacole wrote, according to a *Times* of London report published on the centenary of the war in the same newspaper. She and her business partner, Thomas Day—the superintendent of the Panama mining camp—decided to go anyway, using their own funds. They arrived in Constantinople, Turkey's main city, where

Seacole located Nightingale, who again turned down her request to join the official army nurses' corps.

Seacole and Day built their own establishment from salvaged materials in the port city of Balaclava. Called the "British Hotel," it served as a hospital and rest center for officers, but required payment for services, because the enterprise had been funded on a negligible budget. Seacole also ventured out to the battlefield when she could to tend to the wounded. Both there and back in Constantinople she encountered many British military personnel who knew her from their own stints in Jamaica, and were pleased to see her. She was even commended in dispatches sent by the *Times* of London war correspondent, William Howard Russell, who wrote that "a more tender and skilful hand about a wound or broken limb could not be found amongst our best surgeons," he wrote, according to the newspaper's commemorative article a century later. "I saw her at the fall of Sebastopol . . . laden not with plunder, good old soul, but with wine, bandages, and food for the wounded or prisoners."

It was the wine that earned Seacole a few notable enemies in her line of work, chief among them Nightingale. Serving alcohol to troops was contrary to conventions of the day, and the idea that a woman of color was providing it to soldiers prompted some moral outrage among prim-minded Victorians. Nevertheless, Seacole was greatly beloved by the troops, especially one Christmas when she found enough ingredients to make several plum puddings, the traditional English holiday dish, for the soldiers and officers. Many wrote lovingly of her care in letters back home, calling her "Aunty" or "Mother Seacole."

Rescued from Poverty by Officers

After the war ended, Seacole returned to London, where a business venture with Day seemed to have gone badly under Day's mismanagement, and she was forced to declare bankruptcy. Notice of the bankruptcy hearing appeared in the *Times* in November of 1856, and this elicited a groundswell of sympathy for her from the officers and soldiers she had tended. Her plight came to the attention of Lord Rokeby, a division commander from the war, who urged that a fund be set up to help her. The magazine *Punch* joined in, printing a poem titled "A Stir for Seacole" and providing an address for donations. The efforts culminated in the Grand Military Festival, held in Seacole's honor, at the Royal Surrey Gardens in July of 1857. The benefit was the work of Rokeby and another lord, George Paget (1818–1880), who had also been impressed by Seacole's dedication to his troops. The four-day event featured a thousand performers and some 80,000 attendees, but its finances were allegedly mismanaged, and Seacole received little from it. It did help publicize her recently printed autobiography, *The Wonderful Adventures of Mrs. Seacole in Many Lands*, however, for which the *Times*'s war correspondent had written the introduction.

Seacole's memoir, the first autobiography written by a black woman published in Britain, became a bestseller, but she returned to Jamaica in 1859, somewhat dejected for failing to have won an audience with Her Majesty, Queen Victoria (1819–1901). Race did not seem to be a factor, for the queen had been known to meet with and even financially assist subjects of the Empire who were of African or Asian heritage. Seacole's biographers speculate that Florence Nightingale—who became close to the monarch in the years following her Crimean War fame—had spread rumors that Seacole ran a brothel, and seemed to have known that Seacole had given birth to a daughter out of wedlock, whom she brought to Crimea but never mentioned in her autobiography.

Returning to London around 1870 as a new conflict, the Franco-Prussian War, raged in Europe, Seacole contacted a member of parliament who was heading British relief services for it—an agency that was the forerunner of the Red Cross—and offered her help, but the politician was Nightingale's brother-in-law, and once again her generosity was spurned. For a time she served as masseuse to Alexandra, the Princess of Wales, who suffered from painful rheumatism. On May 14, 1881, Seacole died at her home in Paddington, London, with the cause of death listed as apoplexy, or a stroke. Her uniquely adventurous and service-oriented life was largely forgotten for decades, until her name advanced to the top of the list in a 2004 national online poll for the Greatest Black Briton. In January of 2005, a previously unknown portrait of Seacole was permanently installed at the National Portrait Gallery of Britain.

Books

The Wonderful Adventures of Mrs. Seacole in Many Lands, Bristol, England, 1857.

Periodicals

African American Review, Winter 1992.
Guardian (London, England), February 14, 2004; January 11, 2005.
History Today, February 2005.
New Statesman, January 17, 2005.
Times (London, England), November 7, 1856; November 29, 1856; December 24, 1954.
Women in Higher Education, February 2006. □

William Joseph Seymour

William Joseph Seymour (1870–1922) was a prominent African-American religious leader in the early twentieth century. An ordained minister and the son of freed slaves, he is regarded as one of the founders of modern Pentecostalism.

S eymour was one of the most influential African-American religious leaders of his time, and his impact can be felt even today. Seymour was largely responsible for the establishment of the modern Pentecostal movement. Moreover, many aspects of his message resonate with the concerns of today's religious and social leaders. He advocated for racial integration, as it would lead to unity with Christ, and he also had no objections to women taking leadership roles in the church.

Seymour was born on May 2, 1870, in Centerville, Louisiana, within the St. Mary Parish. His parents, both recently freed slaves, were Simon Seymour and Phyllis Salabarr. During Seymour's infancy and childhood, his family had affiliations with the Baptist and Catholic churches. On September 4, 1870, he was baptized in a Catholic ceremony at the Church of the Assumption in Franklin, Louisiana.

Not much else is known about his early life, except that he was raised in poverty, received little formal education, and claimed to have visions of God. During his years as a young man, he traveled a great deal. In 1895, when he was 25 years old, Seymour moved to Indianapolis, Indiana. While working as a waiter in upscale restaurants and hotels, he joined the Simpson Chapel Methodist Episcopal Church, which was an African-American congregation of the predominately white Methodist Episcopal Church.

In 1900 he moved to Cincinnati, Ohio, where he joined the Church of God Restoration Movement, which was also called The Evening Light Saints. The group was part of the growing Holiness movement that embraced a radical doctrine that included faith healing and a belief in the imminent return of Christ, an event that would be indicated by the integration of races in worship—a conciliation that Seymour tried to bring about, often with great success, throughout his career. The group also believed in the doctrine of sanctification, a concept dating back to nineteenth-century Protestantism. However, the group believed in an immediate, and not gradual, conversion and sanctification following the acceptance of Christ and a baptism of the Holy Spirit.

Became Ordained Minister

While living in Cincinnati, Seymour suffered a bout of smallpox. The attack caused him to lose his left eye (later in life he used a glass eye). His recovery from the potentially fatal illness compelled him to become a preacher, and in 1902 he was ordained as a minister in the Church of God.

For the next three years, he traveled as an evangelist, stopping in Chicago as well as in Georgia, Mississippi, Louisiana, and Texas. In 1905 he settled in Houston, where his family had moved. That summer he served as the temporary replacement pastor for Lucy Farrow, a Holiness minister and niece of black abolitionist Frederick Douglass. Through Farrow, Seymour would meet the man who would have a strong impact on his spiritual direction and career.

Met Charles Fox Parham

Farrow encouraged Seymour to contact Charles Fox Parham, a white evangelist who ran a Texas Bible school, as Seymour was interested in the concept of "speaking in tongues," or glossolalia. Farrow had once worked in Topeka, Kansas, as a servant for Parham, who had founded the first Pentecostal Bible school in that city and who taught that speaking in tongues was a sign of the working of the Holy Spirit. Parham had moved to Texas, and, in December of 1905 he opened the Bible Training School in Houston.

Seymour asked Parham if he could join the Bible school. Parham agreed, but because of his segregationist tendencies he would not provide Seymour with a seat in the class. Instead, Parham would only allow Seymour to listen to lessons through an open door or window. Seymour's attendance did not last very long (according to different sources, it only lasted from a few days to a few weeks), and he was offended by Parham's racism, as he believed that racial integration in worship was a sign of Christ's return. But through Parham, Seymour appeared to have learned more about speaking in tongues, and his exposure to Parham's teachings, particularly concerning glossolalia, would soon have an enormous impact on the development of Pentecostalism in the United States and even the world.

Moved to Los Angeles

While living in Houston, Seymour also met Neeley Terry, a woman who had moved from Los Angeles and who was part of the Holiness movement. What happened next is hard to verify: Seymour was either led to Los Angeles by Terry, or he traveled there on his own, intrigued by Terry's descriptions of what was happening in the city's religious community. Also, he may or may have not been aided in his trip by financial backing from Parham. Whatever the exact details, Seymour wasted no time making his presence felt.

On February 22, 1906, Seymour preached in a church established in Los Angeles by Julia M. Hutchins, who had been expelled from the Second Baptist Church in that city because of her Holiness views. Seymour's sermons extolled the importance of an interracial religious community and of speaking in tongues as a sign of the Holy Spirit. However, Hutchins was upset that he included glossolalia in the Holiness doctrine, and she subsequently and literally locked Seymour out of her church.

Following his lockout, Seymour was invited by the more spiritually sympathetic Mr. and Mrs. Richard Asberry to hold services at their home on North Bonnie Brae Avenue. It was at the Asberry home where Seymour finally experienced speaking in tongues for himself. Events leading up to his own glossolalia began on April 9, 1906, when his enthusiastic preaching caused several members of his congregation to start speaking in tongues. The religious fervency continued for three nights, and on April 12 Seymour began speaking in tongues as well.

Started the Azusa Street Revival

As excitement increased about the events taking place at North Bonnie Brae, more and more people came to witness the meetings, and the Asberry home quickly became too small to accommodate the services. Seymour moved the congregation into an unused church on Azusa Street.

The building, located at 312 Azusa Street and situated in the business district, measured 40 by 60 feet. It had once housed the African Methodist Episcopal Church, but it was now being used as a warehouse and livery stable. Seymour's integrated congregation cleaned out the building and then filled the interior with makeshift church furnishings. The pulpit was made of two boxes nailed together and pews were made from planks nailed to empty barrels. Seymour made his home on the floor above the church and began holding services three times a day, seven days a week. A diverse volunteer staff, including blacks and whites and men and women, assisted Seymour in holding the services.

The dilapidated building would quickly gain national attention as the Azusa Street Revival, but its prominence lasted for only a short time, from 1906 to 1909. Still, it was a huge catalyst for the expansion of the Pentecostal movement, which in subsequent years, grew to include 20 million U.S. members and more than 200 million international members.

Soon after it opened, the church became overwhelmed by great numbers of people—including both the faithful and the curious—due to word of mouth, an important newspaper story about the church, and a force of nature: the San Francisco earthquake.

The newspaper story, which ran in the April 18, 1906, edition of the *Los Angeles Times,* provided extensive coverage of the church's activities. As fate would have it, the article ran on the very same day of the San Francisco earthquake, and the two occurrences became connected in many people's minds. A rumor had even started that the earthquake had been predicted at the Azusa mission. Soon after, more than 100,000 pamphlets were printed up that tied together the emergence of the church, the earthquake, and the impending end of the world. In this way, the San Francisco earthquake is sometimes regarded as a significant factor in the growth of Pentecostalism on a national scale.

By May, the Azusa Street Revival was always filled beyond capacity, as it attracted more than a thousand people a day. It had also gained a reputation as a setting for "wild scenes," as participants reportedly spoke in tongues and engaged in exuberant, physically active prayer. The church garnered a great deal of local press coverage that in turn attracted reporters from newspapers throughout the country. However, published stories were sensationalistic and often not favorable.

However, the press coverage only generated more interest in the revival, and Seymour's congregation continued to grow. In the ensuing months he ordained ministers for his church, established other congregations, and began publishing the church newspaper *The Apostolic Faith.* Introduced in September of 1906, the publication eventually garnered a national and international circulation of 20,000 readers. In 1907 Seymour incorporated the Azusa mission as the Pacific Apostolic Faith Mission, Los Angeles.

Throughout 1909 the Revival continued holding three services a day and conducting prayer meetings 24 hours a day. Services communicated elements of Holiness teachings, but Seymour had begun to downplay the importance of speaking in tongues.

During its brief three-year peak, the church managed to exert a profound influence, as Seymour's message was disseminated across the country. People seemed impressed that Seymour had realized his vision of a completely integrated religious community, and many religious leaders who visited the church took the Pentecostal teachings back to their own congregations, and soon more Pentecostal churches were being established across the United States. Its impact was even felt overseas.

Mission Experienced Rapid Decline

But even as Pentecostalism went on to flourish across the country, the Azusa mission's importance diminished. After 1909 the Revival no longer attracted large crowds. Problems within the organization alienated the faithful and factors from without decreased its influence. Some of Seymour's followers were put off by the "throne" he had built for himself. Also, as happens with other movements that forecast the soon-to-come end of the world, followers' interest in and expectancy of the supposedly imminent "Last Days" began to dwindle. Moreover, Seymour's vision for racial integration suffered. Starting in 1908, white Pentecostals were separating from the black. White members were forming their own groups, while in areas such as the South, black members were encouraged to form separate denominations. Even in Los Angeles, white members were moving toward segregated Pentecostal churches.

The church's hugely successful newspaper, *The Apostolic Faith,* also faced substantial problems. After Seymour married Jennie Evans Moore on May 13, 1908, the paper's administrative assistant, Clara Lum, moved to Portland, Oregon, where she became the paper's editor. She took with her the paper's large subscription list, and after the paper failed under her leadership, Seymour was never able to recover the valuable list.

Problems continued to mount. In 1911, while Seymour was traveling, William H. Durham, a white preacher, attempted a takeover of the mission. The coup was unsuccessful, but when Durham was forced to leave, he took about 600 members with him. By 1913 there were only about 20 members left in Seymour's congregation.

Suffered Fatal Heart Attack

Seymour spent the final years of his life traveling across the country, speaking mostly to black audiences. In 1915 he published a handbook, *The Doctrines and Discipline of the Azusa Street Apostolic Faith Mission of Los Angeles,* but his influence as a religious figure was waning.

On September 28, 1922, Seymour died of a sudden heart attack in Los Angeles. He was buried at Evergreen Cemetery in East Los Angeles. After his death, Jennie became pastor of the church and continued her husband's work until she died, even after she lost the Azusa mission in 1931. She died in 1936.

William Seymour died before he could accomplish many of his goals. He had planned to establish schools and rescue missions and form other congregations, but these dreams were never fulfilled. Still, despite the rapid decline in his influence, Seymour had tremendous impact on the Pentecostal movement, which grew to include more than half a billion believers throughout the world. Indeed, the Azusa Street Revival is often cited as one of the roots of modern-day Pentecostalism.

Books

American Decades, Gale Research, 1998.
Notable Black American Men, Gale Research, 1998.
Religious Leaders of America, 2nd Edition, Gale Group, 1999.

Online

"Bishop William J. Seymour," *312 Azusa Street,* http://www.azusastreet.org/WilliamJSeymour.htm (December 11, 2006).
"William Joseph Seymour," *Famous Christians in History,* http://www.mhmin.org/FC/fc-0696WilliamS.htm (December 11, 2006).
"William Joseph Seymour (1870 - 1922)," *Spirit of Life Ministries,* http://www.holytrinitynewrochelle.org/yourti84643.html (December 11, 2006). □

William Sheppard

William Henry Sheppard (1865–1927), dubbed the "Black Livingstone" after the famed Scottish explorer of Central Africa, was among the first African-American missionaries sent to Africa. He gained national and international fame after he exposed the violent practices of Belgian rubber companies as they manipulated the political relationships among Congolese tribes in order to profit from slave labor.

Raised in Blue Ridge Mountain Town

William Henry Sheppard was born on March 8, 1865, in Waynesboro, Virginia, in the state's southwestern corner. Although Waynesboro was still part of the Confederacy (Robert E. Lee's surrender at Appomattox coming just over a month later), Sheppard was never a slave; his mother was a free woman of mixed-race background. His father was a barber and also the sexton at a predominantly white Presbyterian church. As a child he enjoyed playing with a detailed toy model of Noah's Ark. The town, with its comparatively small black population, had somewhat more harmonious race relations after the Civil War than did parts of Virginia with large slave plantations, and Sheppard was enrolled at the town's new "colored" school. He later recalled, according to William E. Phipps in *William Sheppard: Congo's African American Livingstone,* that a white woman once told him, " 'William, I pray for you, and hope some day you may go to Africa as a missionary.' I had never heard of Africa, and those words made a lasting impression."

In his early teens Sheppard worked as a servant for a S. H. Henkel, a Presbyterian dentist in Staunton, Virginia, cleaning horse stables and improving his reading skills by picking up books discarded by the Henkel family. In 1880 he enrolled at the Hampton Institute, the pioneering institute of black higher education in Hampton, Virginia; among his teachers there was Booker T. Washington. He was fascinated by the "Curiosity Room," an anthropological collection maintained by the school's white founder, General Samuel Armstrong. Graduating from Hampton in 1883, Sheppard moved on to the historically black Tuscaloosa Theological Institute (now Stillman College), a Presbyterian institution in Alabama. Finishing his studies there in 1886, he was ordained as a Presbyterian minister two years later. In Tuscaloosa the nearly penniless Sheppard met Lucy Gantt, a teacher in a one-room schoolhouse, and the two became engaged.

Sheppard assumed the pastorate at Zion Presbyterian Church in Atlanta, but immediately found himself restless and made several applications to be sent to Africa as a missionary. The request was controversial within the white Presbyterian hierarchy. Some argued that blacks might function with special effectiveness as missionaries in African countries, but the Presbyterian Church's foreign missions committee refused to send Sheppard to Africa without white supervision. Sheppard got his chance in 1890 after a young white minister, Samuel Lapsley, volunteered to go to the Congo to set up Presbyterian missions there, and to take on Sheppard as his partner.

There was little supervision involved. "The arc of the relationship between Lapsley and Sheppard fascinated me," Sheppard biographer Pagan Kennedy told *National Geographic*. "It started out almost as servant and master, but very quickly when they got to Africa the tables turned because Sheppard was so much more capable." Arriving on Africa's Atlantic coast at the mouth of the Congo River in what is now the Democratic Republic of the Congo, the two made their way inland to the lands of the Kuba (now often known as Bakuba) people and, in 1891, founded a mission at a village called Luebo. Polish-English novelist Joseph Conrad was traveling up the Congo River at the same time, and he and Lapsley later met in the town of Kinshasa.

Experienced African Adventures

Sheppard's adventures began with a close call crossing the Congo in an African-style canoe. "Being ignorant of its great drawing power . . . we were drawn in as a floating stick," he wrote, according to Phipps. "We spun round and round like a top, the boat all the time at an angle of about forty degrees, till we were dizzy. . . . We thought of our watery graves and all of our past life flashed before us." Africans asked them whether they were rubber traders, but Sheppard and Lapsley said that they were there to teach about God. "They laughed and thought that was a strange business," Sheppard wrote. The pair's first night in their new home was a frightening one, as Africans from a nearby village showed up to gawk, armed with bows, arrows, and spears, "but we put on our broadest and best smiles. . . . Mr. Lapsley on his couch was sobbing audibly and so was I." The driver ants of central Africa caused Sheppard grief. "There were millions," he wrote. "They were in my head, my eyes, my nose, and pulling at my toes. When I found it was not a dream, I didn't tarry long. . . . In an incredible short space of time they can kill any goat, chicken, duck, hog, or dog on the place." In the eyes of the Africans he met, Sheppard had an ambiguous position: he was black but a stranger. They called him "black white man" or "black man with clothes."

Soon, however, Sheppard relaxed and became a keen observer of the culture into which he had transplanted himself. He recorded his observations of Kuba crops, textiles, and music. He wrote long descriptions of the ancestor worship of the Kuba without judging the people according to Christian

standards, although he was disturbed by trials in which a villager showing insufficient grief at a funeral might be accused of witchcraft and forced to drink a poisonous liquid. He began to hunt, and was photographed at one point with a giant snake he had killed, surrounded by a crowd of admiring Africans. Killing a hippopotamus with his rifle in order to feed a group of starving villagers, Sheppard later shot other hippos and dried their meat so that he could make trades and keep the mission well provisioned. He adapted to life in Africa better than Lapsley, who died of a fever in 1892.

Sheppard also learned to speak the Kuba language, and this helped him discover parts of the Congo region that no American or European had ever visited. Traveling cross-country and offering to buy eggs in each village he came to, he would then be given a local guide who would show him the way to the next village market so that he could buy more. According to John G. Turner in his article "A 'Black-White' Missionary on the Imperial Stage," Sheppard recalled, "For three months we did nothing but buy and eat eggs." He preached the gospel at each stop. Finally he neared the village of the king, Luckenga, who had threatened to kill anyone who helped Western strangers find his capital city. Sheppard's fluency in the language, however, persuaded the king's retinue that he was a reincarnation of one of the king's deceased relatives. Sheppard also discovered a nearby lake.

In 1893 Sheppard left Africa temporarily. He traveled to London, where he met Queen Victoria and was inducted into England's Royal Geographic Society. Back in the United States he found himself in demand as a lecturer, and experienced some financial success. He married Lucy Gantt and the two started a family that eventually included two offspring, Wilhelmina and Max, who survived childhood. Sheppard and his wife returned to Africa in 1894, expanding the Luebo mission and starting a second settlement, with American-style street names, in a place called Ibaanc (or Ibanj). Two children succumbed to childhood diseases, and in 1898 Lucy took their third baby, a daughter, back to the United States.

Documented Belgian Atrocities

In 1899 Sheppard encountered new challenges. Belgium's King Leopold II, the Congo's colonial ruler, had faced international criticism for his exploitation of the region's peoples and natural resources, all of it carried out under a banner of claimed humanitarianism. The colonial government of the Congo Free State used Africans as slaves to harvest rubber and build railroads, setting one African tribe against another in order to find traders with whom they could deal in the traffic of human lives. The Presbyterian church in the United States, which took a role in opposing these activities, dispatched a new white missionary, William Morrison, to replace Lapsley and bring the story of Belgian plunder to the world.

At first reluctant to bring controversy to his mission and to confront white Europeans, Sheppard showed great courage when he applied his familiarity with Africa to the task at hand. The Belgians' African allies came from a tribe called the Zappo-Zaps, whom they had armed with rifles and given the task of punishing uncooperative peoples. These included the Kuba, and Sheppard was dismayed to find some of the villages he had visited seven or eight years before reduced to destitution. Sheppard located a village where Zappo-Zap warriors had demanded payment in rubber, slaves, and food from a group of Kuba, a ransom the Kuba could not produce. They were slaughtered and left to rot in a courtyard in the steaming tropical air.

Sheppard made an exact count of severed hands in the courtyard, noting 81 of them in a report that was later presented to colonial authorities, initially with little result. Back in the United States once more, Sheppard began to publicize his findings and wrote an article about them for a Presbyterian magazine. His allegations gained international attention, and by the later part of the twentieth century's first decade, Sheppard had become well known around the United States and Europe as a human rights activist. In 1908 he and Morrison were sued for libel by Belgium's state-controlled rubber company and were put on trial in the colonial capital of Leopoldville. Publicity surrounding the trial, which was heavily covered in American newspapers, only exposed other corrupt practices in the Belgian Congo, and the charges were dropped.

In 1910 Sheppard returned to the United States for good, and not entirely by choice. In closed-door meetings with Presbyterian Church officials he confirmed rumors that he had committed adultery with African women, beginning after his wife's return to the United States in 1898. He had three additional adulterous affairs between 1896 and 1910, and at least one of them produced an illegitimate son, named Shepete. The allegations were kept quiet by church officials, for Sheppard's name was still an important part of their long-term campaign to reduce the sufferings of the native population in Belgian-controlled Africa. Sheppard was allowed to resign his mission posts quietly.

Sheppard and his family moved to Louisville, Kentucky, where Sheppard spent the rest of his life as pastor at Grace Presbyterian Church during the most virulent years of racial segregation in the American South. He still gave lectures, but had to depart before eating when talking in hotels to white groups, and he had to read in a Louisville newspaper article (quoted by Turner) of the writer's surprise that "a little pickaninny" had become a fellow of the Royal Geographical Society. Felled by a stroke in 1926, Sheppard died on November 25, 1927, in Louisville. Large interracial memorial services were held in both Louisville and Waynesboro, and a park and housing project in Louisville's Smoketown neighborhood were named after him.

Books

Kennedy, Pagan, *Black Livingstone: A True Tale of Adventure in the Nineteenth-Century Congo,* Viking, 2002.

Phipps, William E., *Congo's African American Livingstone,* Geneva, 2002.

Periodicals

New York Times, January 8, 2002.

North Star, Fall 2002.

St. Louis Post-Dispatch, February 6, 2002.

Online

" 'Black Livingstone' Blazed Trail in Dark Congo of 1800s," *National Geographic News,* http://www.news.national geographic.com/news/2002/02/0228_0301_livingstone .html (January 27, 2007).

"A 'Black-White' Missionary on the Imperial Stage: William H. Sheppard and Middle-Class Black Manhood," *Journal of Southern Religion,* http://www.jrs.fsu.edu/volume9/Turner .htm (January 27, 2007).

"Jewel in the Kingdom: William Sheppard," Urbana.org, http://www.urbana.org/_articles.cfm?RecordId=252 (January 27, 2007). □

Edward Soriano

Army Lt. Gen. Edward Soriano (born 1946) was one of the highest-ranking Filipino Americans in the history of the American military. He was involved in some of the most difficult offensives in the Gulf War and after September 11, 2001. He joined the Army as a second lieutenant of infantry and retired as a three-star lieutenant general.

Born in Philippines to Army Father

Soriano was born on November 12, 1946, in Alcala, Pangasinan, Philippines, to natives of Ilocos Sur. Alcala is a small city some hundred miles north of Manila. Soriano was born to Federico Soriano, a military officer, and Encarnacion, a homemaker who raised Soriano and his sister Blez. He spent his youth struggling through one illness after another and even had to have an operation when he was five years old to have kidney stones removed. At one point his mother recalled that he was so sick he almost died, but somehow the young Soriano managed to fight his way out of his childhood illnesses to become a strong and healthy adult. When he was still quite young the Soriano family moved to Guam for his father's career. It was one of many moves that the children would go through over their lifetimes. Both Soriano and his sister enjoyed their youth as children of a military man because they lived in interesting locales and met many different people. Soriano told *Starweek,* "I thought what my father was doing was good. He was a great example for me. He was probably the reason I joined the military."

When Soriano was only seven years old, his father, a corporal in the 57th Infantry Regiment of the Philippine Scouts, was captured during the Korean War when the Japanese attacked Corregidor. Along with all the other men captured in battle, Soriano's father was forced to march to a camp for prisoners of war in Tarlac. Many men, including Federico's brother, died on the march to the camp, known as a death march, but Soriano's father survived and was forced to stay at the internment camp for three years. When her husband was captured, Soriano's mother packed her family up and moved them back to the Philippines to keep them all safe. The family stayed there until Federico was released.

Moved to the United States

In the 1960s, not long after Soriano's father was reunited with his family, the Sorianos moved to Salinas, California. After they became citizens of the United States Soriano's father joined the United States Army as a corporal. When he retired he was a major. As the children were getting used to their new home, Soriano's parents took care to make certain that their children learned English quickly after their move so that they could quickly become integrated into their new world.

Soriano graduated from the Salinas High School. While he was in high school he participated in sports, and also joined a Filipino dance troupe with his sister. Dance classes taught Soriano, among other things, how to do the tinikling, which is a Filipino folk dance done with poles. Soriano's family, while wishing their children become easily integrated into their new society, also wanted to make certain that they kept a connection with their home heritage, and this was one great way to do that. Both children were raised to be independent, free-thinking individuals, but were also instilled with a dose of the Filipino view of family values and respect for elders. His upbringing would serve Soriano well in his future endeavors.

Joined Army as Second Lieutenant

After high school Soriano went on to attend San Jose State University. He graduated in 1969 with a degree in management. He went on to get a master's degree at the same school. When it was time for Soriano to choose a career, he asked his father about a career in the military, and his father responded positively. The military opened a range of opportunities for young Soriano that other careers simply could not offer him. He told the Asian Week website, "I was interested in that way of life, which can be personally and professionally rewarding."

Soriano joined the Army, and in 1970 was commissioned through the San Jose State University's ROTC program as a second lieutenant of infantry. At the time he entered the military it was already a very diverse organization, and Soriano has said that he suffered none of the racism that had afflicted minorities earlier. He told *Starweek* magazine, "I never really thought about [racism] much. If I did I don't remember." It was actually the diversity of the military that had encouraged Soriano to join-he has always believed that diversity gave the military much of its strength.

Gulf War and Other Assignments

Throughout his career Soriano attended several military schools. In 1989 he graduated from the Army War College. He believed that skills learned in the military could be taken successfully into any profession. Rather than racial difficulties, Soriano faced the regular challenges of progression in the military: working alongside thousands of others for an increasingly smaller number of positions as he moved up. He told *Starweek*, "The challenge is always seeking those opportunities that allow you to progress, that allow you to get better. And that's what I did, that's how I rose through the ranks, how I got all the right jobs, the right

positions. I worked as hard as I could, tried to be the best that I could possibly be."

After his initial training, in 1973 Soriano commanded Company C, 3d Battalion, 47th Infantry of the 3d Brigade of the U.S. 9th Infantry Division. He held that position until 1975. Soriano was next given the position of assistant commander of the 1st Infantry Division of American peacekeeping forces in Bosnia. He also served in the Gulf War, becoming the chief of a liaison team to the 1st Marine Expeditionary Force sent to Saudi Arabia. In 1992 he was sent to be the Army Section chief of the Secretary of Defense Gulf War Report team for operations Desert Shield and Desert Storm.

Part of Homeland Security After September 11th

Because of his good performance record, Soriano became the director for operations, readiness, and mobilization at the Office of the Deputy Chief of Staff for Operations and Plans. In that position he made certain that Army units were prepared to be instantly deployed on missions around the world. He was specifically in charge of troops in Haiti, Bosnia, Somalia, and other areas of tension around the world. Of all his positions Soriano told the Asian Week website, "It's a significant responsibility. You're entrusted with the lives of the soldiers and their families. It takes dedication and hard work to succeed." And these were things that Soriano was more and more proving that he had.

After September 11, 2001, when the World Tade Center buildings were destroyed by terrorists, the U.S. government set up a homeland security department under the Joint Forces Command. This department ran separately from the its civilian counterpart. Soriano was given the office of the second director of homeland security in the military in November of 2001. He held the position for ten months before he was made, in 2002, a commanding general of I Corps and Fort Lewis in Washington, a position he held for the rest of his career.

Retired and Visited Philippines

When he retired in 2004 Soriano was a three-star lieutenant general. The day he attained that position he became the highest-ranking Filipino-American in the United States armed forces, and only the second general ever to have Filipino roots. Soriano attended an event at the White House when President Arroyo of the Philippines and his wife visited the United States.

Soriano married Vivian Guillermo, whose parents were from Laoag in the Philippines. She was born in California. The two had two children, Melissa and Keith. In 2004 Soriano and his family went back to the Philippines to visit relatives. It was Soriano's first return to the country of his birth. Soriano told *Starweek* that it was possible to achieve success in one's chosen field "if a person establishes the goals and objectives, works very hard at what he does, and if that person doesn't give up too easily and commits himself, dedicates himself to what he wants to do."

Soriano has been given many awards over the lifetime of his careers, including the Distinguished Service Medal, two awards of the Defense Superior Service Medal, four awards of the Legion of Merit, the Bronze Star, the Defense Meritorious Service Medal, three awards of the Meritorious Service Medal, and several Army Commendation and Achievement Medals. He has also received many badges over his career, including the expert infantryman's badge and has been ranger and airborne qualified.

Periodicals

Starweek, October 1, 2004.

Online

"Edward Soriano: Encyclopedia," *Experts.com,* http://experts .about.com-e-e-ed-edward_soriano.htm (January 2, 2007).

"Major General," *Asian Week,* http://www.asianweek.com-082297-newsmaker.html (January 2, 2007).

"President Bush Welcomes President Arroyo in State Arrival Ceremony," *The White House,* http://www.whitehouse.gov-news-releases-2003-05-20030519-1.html (January 2, 2007). □

Walter Spies

German-born artist Walter Spies (1895–1942), who spent much of his life in what is now Indonesia, was noted for a unique style that combined Western and Eastern elements, exploring spiritual motifs drawn from the artist's adopted culture while applying techniques of contemporary European art.

Spies was an energetic and influential traveler among multiple cultures whose talents extended far beyond painting. He performed both Western and Indonesian musical styles, co-wrote a pioneering study of dance on the island of Bali, and stimulated new developments in Balinese art. Scholars had studied Indonesian expressive culture before Spies arrived in the archipelago, but Spies spread the word about its beauties as he entertained celebrities such as Charlie Chaplin at his home on Bali. The ongoing Western fascination with Indonesian arts was partly the result of Spies's efforts.

Raised in Diplomatic Household

Walter Spies (VAHL-ter SCHPEEZ) was born in Moscow, Russia, on September 15, 1895. His father was a German diplomat. The Spies family was wealthy and well connected in their foreign home, and they were interested in the arts as well as in political affairs. Spies met the Russian composers Sergei Rachmaninoff and Alexander Scriabin as a child, and he began composing in contemporary styles when he was quite young. He also had a strong affinity for the natural world, collecting reptiles and amphibians that he would sometimes release at the family dinner table. When he was 15, Spies was sent to school in Dresden, Germany,

but he returned to Russia on summer vacations, and he was there when World War I broke out in 1914.

Spies's father was arrested immediately, and when Spies reached military age in 1915 he too was arrested by Russian soldiers and sent to an internment camp at Sterliamak in the remote Ural Mountains. This experience was much less severe than might be assumed, however. Though unable to leave the remote village, Spies was not restricted to a prison; he worked for local farmers and lumbermen and learned their folktales and songs. "The significance of those years cannot be emphasized enough," wrote Spies's biographers, Hans Rhodius and John Darling. "Here, among the simple country folk of the Urals, Spies discovered his own identity." Spies was able to paint, and he turned away from the fashionably advanced styles he had seen in Dresden and toward simpler, down-to-earth themes.

As Russia became immersed in political change in 1917 and withdrew from the war, Spies was able to return to Moscow. Disguised as a peasant he rode trains as a hobo toward Germany and then sneaked across the battlefront, arriving once again in Dresden. There he worked for sculptor Hedwig Jaenischen Woermann in her studio and became acquainted with top German Expressionist artists Oskar Kokoschka and Otto Dix. The major influence on his style as an artist, however, was French: painter Henri Rousseau's large, stylized paintings of tropical wildlife and flora formed the point of departure for Spies's own work.

Spies mounted his first exhibition of paintings in 1919, making a living on the side as a ballroom dance teacher (he was an expert practitioner of the tango, a sensational new dance imported from Argentina). In 1920 he moved to Grunewald near Berlin in order to work for silent film director F. W. Murnau. In Berlin, Spies was exposed to new trends in German contemporary music and wrote more music of his own. Sometimes he escaped to the North Sea Island of Sylt for relaxation. Spies lived intermittently with a couple in the Netherlands, exhibiting his works at the Dutch Painters' Circle. Another decisive event in his career was a visit to the Koloniaal Institute, now the Tropenmuseum (Tropical Museum) in Amsterdam, where he saw artworks imported from the Netherlands' Indonesian colonies and connected them in his own mind with the natural themes and slightly surrealist constructions he had been cultivating ever since his internment in the Ural Mountains.

Made Living with Music

Obtaining passage to Indonesia by signing on with a freighter crew, Spies arrived in Bandung on the island of Java in October of 1923 and quickly got a job accompanying silent Chinese films on the piano. Moving on to the old Javanese capital city of Yogyakarta he entertained guests at the residence of the Dutch colonial administrator but was immediately fascinated by the magnificent gamelan, or traditional Indonesian orchestra of metallophones and gongs, at the *kraton,* or palace of the Sultan of Yogyakarta. His enthusiasm for the court music attracted the attention of the Sultan himself, who hired Spies as conductor of a small European orchestra he also maintained. Spies quickly mastered both the Javanese language and Malay, which served as a common language for Indonesia's thousands of islands and became the basis for the modern Indonesian language.

Spies learned to play all the gamelan instruments, and he began to experiment with fusions of Indonesian and European music. At one point he tuned two pianos in the Javanese tuning system and arranged a performance in which two Indonesian singers would perform first to the accompaniment of a gamelan, then to that of his two pianos, and then finally with the gamelan once again. The singers finished the performance without missing a beat. But Spies was still beset with doubts about the accuracy of his work in representing Javanese gamelan music, and he refused to allow his hybrid pieces to be published. They were lost for good after Spies's death when Japanese armies occupied Java.

Resuming his painting career, Spies exhibited some of his new works in 1925 at a group show in the eastern Javanese city of Surabaya. His complex new works showed the influence of his new surroundings and of Asian art more generally. *Heimkehrende Javaner* (Javanese Returning Home, 1924) showed a group of farmers returning home with their implements in the foreground of a many-layered mountain landscape. Determined to devote full time to his art and to penetrate deeper into the essence of Indonesian culture, Spies moved from Yogyakarta to the island of Bali in 1927. Among Indonesia's large islands, Bali had been the least affected by Dutch colonization and retained much of its traditional culture. Artistic activities were central to that culture although they were not designated with that name, since art and music for the Balinese were not special realms of life but rather activities that most people engaged in during moments of relaxation.

Building a Balinese-style house and studio (today a hotel) in the heavily traditional village of Ubud in 1928, Spies flourished. His paintings deepened, and some of them began to reflect the spiritual outlooks of the Balinese themselves. His *Sawahlandschaft mit Gunung Agung* (Rice Paddy Landscape with Gunung Mountain) incorporated the image of a volcano that plays a central role in the Balinese Hindu religion into a rich landscape of irrigated rice fields and jungle vegetation. The paintings from the period of Spies's residence in Bali are those on which his international reputation rests, and they helped forge an enduring impression of Bali as a tropical paradise. "In creating the image of Balinese idyll," noted Kadek Krishna Adidharma in the *Jakarta Post,* "the influence of German painter, photographer, and musician Walter Spies . . . is still visible and tangible today."

Founded Arts Society

With local Balinese nobleman Tjokorda Agung Sukawati, Spies founded the Pita Maha Arts Society (Pita Maha means "Great Forbears"), a group that aimed to encourage the efforts of local Balinese painters. The result was an explosion of creativity that was strong even by Balinese standards. Each Saturday, a four-person jury selected winners from among a group of about 150 submitted works. The winners were sold to international buyers, and the proceeds were plowed back into the collective. Spies's legacy lived

on in a vigorous Balinese arts scene for several decades after his death; he also introduced European art to the Balinese, who experimented with such details as playful treatment of perspective and created hybrid forms of their own.

Spies did not neglect his interests in music, cinema, and dance. With dancer and photographer Beryl de Zoete he published *Dance and Drama in Bali,* for many years a standard work covering Bali's traditional large-scale theatrical presentations. One of the iconic images of Balinese culture in the eyes of many Western students is the ketjak dance, often known as the Ramayana Monkey Chant. The spectacular dance, often performed for tourists, involves a crowd of 100 or more dancers, emulating monkeys verbally and kinetically as they enact a battle scene from the Hindu *Ramayana* epic. Though based on traditional materials, the dance owed its modern form to Spies; working with Indonesian dancer Wayan Limbak (who died in 2003), he choreographed the monkey chant for the 1932 German film *Island of Demons.* Spies served as art director for the film, which exposed many Westerners to Balinese culture, although some scholars have criticized Spies for oversimplification of the Balinese legends involved in the story.

Campuan, Spies's Balinese home, became an established stop on the circuit of well-informed international travelers, and such well-known figures as Chaplin, anthropologist Margaret Mead, and Mexican artist and caricaturist Miguel Covarrubias passed through as guests. In the words of Rhodius and Darling, "Hundreds of Balinese artists called at 'the house of the meeting of the waters,' either just to pass the time of day, or to report on coming events such as dances or ceremonies in remote villages, to display the work of their hands or discuss the better tuning of an instrument." Spies also often served as a go-between who tried to insure smooth relationships between the local Balinese and Dutch colonial administrators.

His own relationships with those administrators, however, were troubled for various reasons, one of which may have been their jealousy over Spies's ability to get along with the Balinese. The most serious issue was what they saw as a libertine atmosphere in the Spies circle; Spies was gay, and that fact, combined with his German citizenship, helped to seal his doom as Germany menaced the rest of Europe in the late 1930s. The cultural atmosphere in Indonesia tightened, and Spies was arrested on charges of indecent behavior in December of 1938, serving a prison term that lasted until September of 1939. During this initial period of imprisonment he was visited by sympathetic Dutch authorities and allowed to paint and play music; some of his greatest final works, such as *Palmendurchblick* (View Through the Palms, 1938), showing a magnificent palace glimpsed from a great distance by a solitary figure carrying water, were painted while he was in prison.

When Germany invaded Holland soon after the outbreak of World War II, the few German citizens in the Dutch East Indies were arrested. Spies was held for 20 months in internment camps on Java and Sumatra. Even there he could occasionally paint and study musical scores sent to him by relatives. But early in 1942 he was put on a transport ship bound for Ceylon. A day after it left Sumatra, on January 19, 1942, the ship was hit off Nias Island by a Japanese bomb, and the Dutch crew abandoned ship without setting its German prisoners free. Spies drowned with the rest of the prisoners. Never prolific, he left a modest body of paintings that sometimes yielded prices of more than $1,000,000 in art auctions by the early 2000s.

Books

Rhodius, Hans, and John Darling, ed. John Stowell, *Walter Spies and Balinese Art,* Tropical Museum, 1980.

Periodicals

Atlantic Monthly, August 1999.
Jakarta Post, July 2, 2006.
New Straits Times (Singapore), March 22, 2001.

Online

"Walter Spies," Network Indonesia, http://www.users.skynet.be/network.indonesia/bart003.htm (January 25, 2007). □

Rudolf Steiner

Austrian philosopher and educational reformer Rudolf Steiner (1861–1925) remains perhaps best known for the educational methods he pioneered in his Waldorf schools, which have spread slowly but steadily around the world since his death.

The philosophy underlying those schools grew out of a lifetime of innovative thinking that encompassed fields as diverse as traditional philosophy, spiritualism, color theory, art, agriculture, medicine, music, and architecture. A trained philosopher and at the same time a mystic, Steiner believed that spiritual insights could be gained through systematic thought. He founded the spiritual belief system called Anthroposophy, an offshoot of Theosophy, and disseminated his ideas through an energetic campaign that included years of lectures and a group of writings that ran to some 350 volumes when collected. Influential in the worlds of education, occult studies, organic farming, and even interior design (he was fascinated by color and its relationship to personality), Steiner remains an imperfectly understood and often controversial figure.

Moved Often During Childhood

Rudolf Steiner was born February 27, 1861, in Donji Kraljevec (Lower Kraljevec), a town that was then part of the Austro-Hungarian Empire (it is now in northern Croatia). His father was a telegraph operator who worked for the Southern Austria railway. Steiner's childhood, noted Gary Lachman of the *Fortean Times,* "had an equal measure of both natural beauty and modern technology"—the Kraljevec area boasted gorgeous Alpine scenery, and the railroad and the telegraph were both new technologies in the 1860s. Steiner's railroad company family moved several times, however, and he spent time in Neudörfl in southern

Austria and then attended high school in Wiener-Neustadt near Vienna. An introverted youngster, Steiner enjoyed mathematics and later spoke of several episodes in which he seemed to display unusual psychic abilities.

Steiner's family was not wealthy, and as he continued his schooling he often made ends meet as a private tutor (sometimes to his own classmates) of mathematics and science. In 1879 Steiner enrolled at the Technische Hochschule (Technical University) of Vienna, taking math and science classes but also immersing himself in German philosophy and literature. The writings of Johann Wolfgang von Goethe (1749–1832) made an immediate and lifelong impression on Steiner when he was an undergraduate student. Goethe, though best known outside German-speaking countries for his play *Faust,* was a prolific writer on science and metaphysics who attempted to construct an overarching, holistic philosophy of human perception and belief. Another influence on the young Steiner was a man named Felix Koguzki who gathered and sold herbs for a living but also had a rich life of spiritual and mystical experiences.

One of Steiner's professors noted his enthusiasm for Goethe and his systematic mind, and recommended him for a position as editor of a series of Goethe's scientific writings for a scholarly *Deutsche National Literatur* (German National Literature) publication project. He began work even before his graduation in 1883. For much of the first part of his life, Steiner made a living as an editor and archivist, working on a complete edition of Goethe's writings in the

1880s and moving to Weimar in eastern Germany in 1890 to take a position at the Schiller-Goethe Archives there. On the side, Steiner took more classes and received a Ph.D. in philosophy from the University of Rostock in 1891. His dissertation was published as a book, *Wahrheit und Wissenschaft* (Truth and Science).

During this part of his life Steiner was primarily a philosopher, and one who espoused the concept of idealism—the belief that experience is located in the mind—rather than materialism, which holds that the world, including mental processes, is ultimately reducible to matter and its interactions. *Philosophie der Freiheit* (Philosophy of Freedom, 1894) was his most important work of these years. Steiner studied the tradition of nineteenth-century German philosophy going back to Hegel and to the radical idealism of Johann Fichte. He continued to make a living as an editor of several different magazines, moving to the German capital of Berlin in 1897. In one article in the *Magazine for Literature,* Steiner rejected anti-semitic ideas. His positions on the relationship of Germanic peoples to those of other cultures would later prove controversial, however. Steiner married Anna Eunike in 1899, but the marriage later ended in divorce.

Taught at Workers' School

Gradually, Steiner's interests broadened beyond philosophy (and if they had not, his name would likely be little known today). He began teaching two evenings a week at the Arbeiterbildungsschule (School for the Education of Workers) in Berlin, a progressive institution where he could discuss ideas of universal education and freedom as they related to the working class. Steiner also joined the Berlin Theosophic Society, a branch of the international theosophy movement. Theosophists held that existing religions were paths, often equally valid, to a higher spiritual truth. By 1902 Steiner had given numerous lectures on theosophy and became the German Theosophic Society's general secretary. To describe his system of "spiritual science," he began to use the word "anthroposophy," derived from Greek roots meaning human wisdom. Among the many books Steiner devoted to Anthroposophy were *Outline of Occult Science* (1909) and *Outline of Esoteric Science* (1910).

It was clear that Steiner had found his calling. He became what would now be called a full-time motivational speaker for the last quarter-century of his life, giving some 6,000 lectures that ranged over numerous topics related to the nature of human spiritual life. Steiner lectured on Christian themes, on history, drama, science, agriculture, and virtually any other area of human endeavor that he saw as related to the spiritual quest. He saw the human being as consisting of body, soul, and an eternal spirit that manifested itself anew—he believed in reincarnation. Among the spiritual beings who oversaw human development were the Archangel Michael and a negative Antichrist-like figure he called Ahriman, who sought to prevent human spiritual evolution. One of his favorite themes was that of the Threefold Social Order (or Social Threefolding—the German term is *Soziale Dreigliederung*: he advocated the separation in human soci-

ety of the cultural (including educational), political, and economic realms. After his first marriage dissolved, he met anthroposophy devotee Marie von Sivers, an actress from the Baltic region, and the two were married in 1914.

It was around that time that Steiner's relationship with Theosophy dissolved. It had been under strain for some time due to religious disagreements. Steiner remained a Christian, but avoided affiliation with either Catholicism or Protestantism and instead forged his own mystical version of the Christian religion, shaped partly by the beliefs of the Rosicrucian Order. In the early 1910s English-born Theosophy society head Annie Besant, who lived in India, had contended that Jiddu Krishnamurti, a spiritually gifted boy she encountered on a beach, was the Second Coming of Christ. Steiner rejected the idea and led 55 of 65 German chapters of the theosophical movement in a breakaway plan to form a new Anthroposophical Society. The new group grew rapidly under Steiner's charismatic leadership, and Steiner began work on designing a temple-like headquarters building called the Goetheanum in Dornach, Switzerland. Even during World War I, workers from around Europe, including citizens of warring countries, cooperated without incident in its construction.

Steiner argued that World War I showed the need for a new social order that entailed peaceful methods of conflict resolution. In 1919 he explored these themes in a lecture he gave to workers at the Waldorf-Astoria cigarette factory in Stuttgart, Germany. After Steiner's speech, factory owner Emil Molt suggested that he set up a school for children of the factory workers, modeled on the ideas he had expressed. Steiner agreed, and the result was the first Waldorf school, named for the factory itself. He stipulated that the school should be run cooperatively by its teachers, and Waldorf schools since that time have all featured cooperative management schemes. Despite his considerable fame, Steiner shunned personal adulation and once remarked that if he could have changed the name of Anthroposophy to something new every day, he would have done so in order to emphasize the need for his followers to think for themselves.

Favored Natural Farming Methods

The Waldorf schools were not Steiner's only forward-looking innovation. He also anticipated the growth of organic farming in his opposition to chemical fertilizers. In Steiner's view, a farm should be a self-contained ecological entity. He devised a unique compost recipe that included a stag's bladder; a cow's gut; the head of a cow, goat, sheep, or pig, filled with oak bark; stinging nettles wrapped in peat moss; a cow's intestine filled with chamomile flowers; and crushed valerian flowers. As with others among Steiner's ideas, his followers have discarded some of the more exotic specifics in his writings while maintaining the general ideas. Most controversial among his writings were his racial theories, which assigned specific traits to individual races. In Germany especially, Steiner's devotees came under attack as a result of this aspect of his philosophy.

In the early 1920s Steiner began to encounter heavy criticism. Some of it came from members of the Nazi party angered because Steiner backed independence for the contested German province of Upper Silesia (now part of Poland). But Steiner was also attacked by the Catholic and Protestant churches, Marxists, and rival spiritual leaders. On December 31, 1922, the Goetheanum burned to the ground shortly after its completion. The Nazis were generally blamed for the fire, although its cause remained uncertain. Steiner announced plans for a second Goetheanum, built of concrete; it still stands in Switzerland, and both buildings are considered architectural landmarks of the twentieth century.

The attacks, including one in an article by Adolf Hitler himself, took their toll on Steiner, who redoubled his lecture schedule even as he fell into poor health. Toward the end of his life he emphasized his natural farming methods and a new anthroposophic system of medicine that he developed, and in which he began to train physicians. In the fall of 1924 he had to give up his speaking activities due to illness. Steiner suffered from an unknown stomach ailment, and some rumors spread among his followers that he had been poisoned. Steiner, however, discouraged such speculation before his death in Dornach on March 30, 1925.

The Waldorf concept grew slowly as Anthroposophy devotees set up new institutions. By 1939 there were schools in Switzerland, England, Hungary, Norway, and the United States, in addition to seven in Germany. The German schools were shuttered by the National Socialist government but reopened after World War II, at which time Waldorf education began a steady spread around the world. By the year 2000 more than 700 Waldorf schools worldwide featured classrooms painted in the colors Steiner had specified as appropriate for each stage of human development, and focused on learning through direct experience of materials (reading was often delayed until the third or fourth grade), engaging in the structured system of exercise and dance Steiner called Eurythmy, and reciting Steiner's poems about the natural world. Public schools in the United States and Britain were impressed by data showing Waldorf education's ability to reach students who had previously proven disruptive in conventional classroom settings. A large network of educational institutions around the world devoted itself to training Waldorf teachers and to the study of other aspects of Anthroposophy and of Steiner's thought.

Books

Encyclopedia of Occultism and Parapsychology, 5th ed., Gale Group, 2001.

Hemleben, Johannes, and Leo Twyman, *Rudolf Steiner: An Illustrated Biography,* Rudolf Steiner Press, 2001.

McDermott, Robert, *The Essential Steiner,* Harper Press, 1984.

Religious Leaders of America, 2nd ed., Gale Group, 1999.

Tummer, Lia, and Horacio Lato, *Rudolf Steiner and Anthroposophy for Beginners,* Writers & Readers Publishing, 2001.

Periodicals

Atlantic Monthly, September 1999.

Independent (London, England), November 1, 1997; January 24, 2007.

Instructor, November 1999.

Online

"Rudolf Steiner: Chronological Biography," http://www.sab.org/br/steiner/biogr-eng.htm (February 3, 2007).

"Rudolf Steiner: Dweller on the Threshold," *Fortean Times,* http://www.forteantimes.com/articles/205_steiner1.html (February 3, 2007).

"Rudolf Steiner (1861–1925)," Skylark Books, http://www.skylarkbooks.co.uk/Rudolf_Steiner_Biography.htm (February 3, 2007).

Steiner, Rudolf, *The Story of My Life,* Rudolf Steiner Archive, http://www.wn.rsarchive.org/Books/GA028/TsoML/GA028_index.html (January 3, 2007). □

John Summerson

British art historian John Summerson (1904–1992) enjoyed a long and eminent career as an expert on London architecture of the eighteenth and nineteenth centuries. His 1945 work *Georgian London* has been termed "a masterpiece of British art history" by Simon Jenkins in a London *Sunday Times* review of the book's 1988 edition. Jenkins called the work "a great shout of clarity amid a postwar babble of destruction and stylistic confusion. See beauty and worth in the London all around us . . . before trying to improve on it."

Summerson was born on November 25, 1904, in Darlington, England. This town in northeast England had been known for nearly a century by then as the birthplace of the English railroad, and John's grandfather Thomas Summerson served as director of the local steel foundry that played a leading role in making the first locomotives for public transport. But Summerson's father died in 1907, and he and his mother, Dorothea, moved frequently for the next few years around Europe. Many years later he would write of coming upon an abandoned garden near the Rhine River in Germany as a lonely child, and how from that point forward "the 'wilderness with a broken swing' has been a recurrent theme in my life," according to an article by Alan Powers in *Building Design*. It was then, Summerson continued, that he first understood "that mysterious sense of inspiration in the presence of forgotten, deserted, broken things: derelict houses, forlorn castles, overgrown gardens, neglected graves, blitz ruins."

Joined "Old Harrovian" Ranks

Between 1915 and 1918 Summerson attended school in Derbyshire, a county in the East Midlands region of England. That school was located at Riber Castle, a monstrosity from 1862 that was the work of a local tycoon who had declined to hire a professional architect for the job. In his teens Summerson attended the Harrow School, a prestigious private academy for boys in northwest London that opened in 1572, and graduated as a talented organist. Rejecting the pursuit of a musical education or career, he enrolled at the University College of London's Bartlett School of Architecture in 1922, and after graduating he practiced as an architect for a few years. In 1929 he headed north to Scotland, taking a teaching job at the Edinburgh College of Art School of Architecture for a year. He then spent some time traveling throughout Europe and the Soviet Union. Hired by the Modern Architectural Research Group (MARS), a think tank founded by a group of modernist architects, he settled back in London, moving on to a job as an assistant editor for the magazine *Architect and Building News* in 1934.

In 1932 Summerson had come upon some drawings by architect John Nash (1752–1835) in a print shop. Nash had been responsible for London's famous Regent Street, a graceful thoroughfare designed as the ceremonial route from St. James Palace to Regent's Park for the Prince Regent; after it was laid out in 1811 it became one of the city's most elegant shopping streets, and remained so well into the twenty-first century. Nash also designed Trafalgar Square and many other London landmarks for the prince, who later became King George IV (1762–1830). Summerson believed that it was time for a renewed appraisal of Nash's important contributions to what became known as Regency London, and his 1935 book *John Nash, Architect to George IV* was the result.

The king's interest in architecture spawned the term "Regency," which denotes the period from 1810, when his father, George III (1738–1820), became too ill to rule, and he was designated "Prince Regent" until formally assuming the throne in 1820. Regency architecture followed many of the same tenets as the previously dominant style, Georgian, so named for the quartet of King Georges who reigned from 1714 to 1830, though the term is usually used in British architecture to refer to the years between 1720 and 1840. Georgian architecture was neo-classical, or a revival of the signature elements of Greek and Roman antiquity. In the parts of London laid out during these periods, entire façades of homes or businesses on a street were planned in such a way as to give off a harmonious, symmetrical appearance. There was also an emphasis on balance, with mathematical ratios used to set exact proportions for roofs, windows, and other elements of a building's interior and exterior.

London In Flux

When Summerson began his career as an architectural historian, some of the most famous Regency properties in London were in danger of extinction. The original 99-year leases on the parcels were ending, and a British aristocracy suddenly impoverished by World War I and the Great Depression could no longer afford to keep some of the century-old Regency villas built in the western part of the city. Summerson hoped to draw public attention to the beauty of this style and help preserve London for future generations. His mission brought him to the National Buildings Record in 1941, a professional, largely voluntary organization dedicated to photographing London landmarks before they were destroyed by bombs during World War II, when German aircraft inflicted heavy damage on the city. Summerson served as the deputy director of the organization, and

roamed the streets with a camera photographing many of the landmarks himself.

In 1944 Summerson was appointed a member of the Listed Buildings Committee, a government agency that designated certain public or private properties as protected because of their architectural, historical, or cultural importance. He served on the committee for the next 22 years, chairing it once in the early 1960s, and held similar posts as a member of the Royal Fine Art Commission, the Royal Commission on Historical Monuments, and the Historic Buildings Council. At Oxford and Cambridge universities, he held the Slade Professorships for one academic year at each, beginning in 1958 and 1966, respectively, and also lectured for many years on the history of architecture at the Architectural Association and then at Birkbeck College, part of the University of London system. As his *Times* of London obituary noted years later, Summerson "was a first-rate lecturer in spite of a somewhat aloof, and seemingly haughty style, which was much in vogue among certain art historians at the time. He was also an effective broadcaster and was heard regularly on the [British Broadcasting Corporation's] *Third Programme*. Both as a writer and as a speaker he was remarkable for his polished elegance and fluency, peppered by a dry wit."

Summerson's best known work, *Georgian London,* appeared in 1945, delayed in its publication due to World War II. In it, he chronicles this period of the city's architecture in detail, describes its most important figures and their contributions, and explains the influence of commercial real estate developers on urban planning over the years. He termed London "the least authoritarian city in Europe. It is remarkable for the freedom with which it developed," he noted, according to a *Times Literary Supplement* review from Charles Vince that appeared in March of 1946. Vince gave the work high marks, noting that "Summerson's judgements on both buildings and men are brief, firm and clear." *Georgian London* quickly became the classic text of the period for historians of art and architecture, and remained in print for decades. More than 40 years later, a new edition of the work, updated by Summerson, was critiqued in the *Sunday Times* by Jenkins, who commended the author for his "analysis not just of the major buildings, but of the integrated nature of the 18th and early-19th century townscape. To him, Georgian London was an interplay of taste and wealth, producing a distinctive pattern of street and square, terrace and church, market and shopping arcade."

Knighted by Queen

In 1945 Summerson became curator of Sir John Soane's House and Museum at Lincoln's Inn Fields. Soane (1753–1837) was an important architect of the Georgian era who designed several notable buildings, and left his equally noteworthy home and collection of art and artifacts to the British public. Summerson served as curator for the museum until his retirement in 1984, and the job allowed him time to pursue his scholarly work. He published several more volumes, including *Heavenly Mansions, and Other Essays on Architecture,* a 1949 collection of his essays that became a staple for first-year architecture students for decades to come. The survey *Architecture in Britain, 1530–1830* appeared in 1953, followed by *Sir Christopher Wren,* a biography of the architect of St. Paul's Cathedral.

Made Commander of the Order of the British Empire in 1952 and knighted in 1958 for his professional achievements, Summerson was a well-known expert in his day. He wrote regularly on preservation issues, such as the bid to save Euston Station in north London. In a article that appeared in the June 11, 1960, issue of the *Times* of London, he deemed it "perhaps . . . the greatest railway curiosity in the world" and "the first of Europe's metropolitan terminals" when it was built in the 1830s. His contribution to the rescue effort helped make it successful, and Euston remains both a "tube" stop for the London Underground subway system and the terminus for rail lines that carry passengers to and from London and the cities of England's northwest and Midlands. Several years later Summerson penned another essay for the newspaper, in which he wrote about the coming European Architectural Heritage Year of 1975. "The preservation of historic buildings is not (as, say, tree-planting is) something which can be activated as a gesture of celebration in a designated year," he asserted. "The essence of both conservation and of preservation is in long-term policy, watchfulness, technical research and, above all, the intelligent analysis of problems, whether structural or financial, before they actually arrive on the doorstep."

When Summerson retired from the Soane Museum in 1984, he had been there since the year World War II ended. As his *Times* of London obituary noted, the architectural historian "preferred the past. While others might have been tempted to modernise both the organisation and presentation of the collections, Summerson worked on an antique typewriter, amazing callers by answering most of the calls himself on the museum's only telephone." His final published work, *The Unromantic Castle,* appeared in 1990. This anthology collected some of his best writings about the rich history of England's architecture. He died in London of Parkinson's disease on November 10, 1992. His wife, a dancer he married in 1938 named Elizabeth Alison Hepworth, preceded him in death. They lived in the Chalk Farm section of London, where they raised triplet sons.

Summerson left an unfinished autobiography, but his legacy remains unmatched. An essay on him in the online source *Dictionary of Art Historians* praised him for his stewardship of the Soane Museum, during which he "transformed the quaint though stodgy institution into a specialty museum of international stature. As an architectural historian," the profile continued, Summerson "changed British architectural history from the hobby of architects to an academic discipline."

Periodicals

Building Design, November 2, 2001; June 18, 2004.
Sunday Times (London, England), August 28, 1988.
Times (London, England), October 11, 1951; June 11, 1960; July 12, 1974; November 12, 1992.
Times Literary Supplement, August 31, 1940; March 30, 1946; January 13, 1950; January 22, 1954; January 5, 1967; August 17, 1990.

Online

"John (Newenham) Summerson," *Contemporary Authors Online,* http://www.galenet.galegroup.com (December 5, 2006).
"Summerson, John (Newenham)," Dictionary of Art Historians, http://www.dictionaryofarthistorians.org/summersonj.htm (December 6, 2006). □

T

Louise Juliette Talma

American composer Louise Talma (1906–1996) wrote in a distinctive, often neo-Classical style. She wrote many vocal pieces, including song cycles and the first American opera by a woman to be staged at a major European opera house. In all, Talma composed more than 40 significant works in her lifetime. Additionally, she became the first American to teach at the prestigious Fontainebleau School, and was a faculty member at New York City's Hunter College for over a half-century.

Early Life and Education

The daughter of two American professional musicians, Talma was born on October 31, 1906, in Arcachon, France, a resort town near Bordeaux. Talma's father died while she was still a child; Talma's mother, a singer, moved with her daughter to New York City in the summer of 1914. There, Talma studied chemistry at Columbia University while pursuing piano and composition studies at the Institute of Musical Art, the institution that later became the prestigious Juilliard School of Music. Talma attended courses at the institute from 1922 until 1930, winning the Seligman Prize for composition there in 1927, 1928, and 1929. She earned her bachelor of music degree from New York University in 1931, and two years later a master of arts degree from Columbia.

During summers from 1926 to 1939, Talma traveled to Fontainebleau, France, to study at the American Conserva-

tory. She first studied piano under Isidor Philipp, one of France's most renowned piano instructors. From 1928 to 1939 she studied composition under Nadia Boulanger. Boulanger was one of the twentieth century's most influential instructors of composition and also of conducting, and she trained Talma intensely. By this time, Talma was a teacher as well as a student. She was an instructor in music theory and ear training at the Manhattan School of Music from 1926 to 1928, leaving to become a faculty member at Hunter College, a large public institution now part of the City University of New York. Talma taught at Hunter College for over 50 years, finally leaving the institution in 1979. Additionally, she became the first American to teach at the Fontainebleau School, where she herself had studied under Philipp and Boulanger.

During the late 1920s Talma was recognized for her skills in piano playing and in composition by the Institute of Musical Art, the Fontainebleau School of Music, and the National Federation of Music Clubs.

Neo-Classical Compositions

By 1935 Boulanger had convinced Talma to focus exclusively on composition, and Talma's career truly took shape. In a later article, Talma told the *New York Times*: "It took some time before I knew I was a composer. . . . I thought all composers were dead. Composers were people you found in a book, who had written all this wonderful music that you heard at concerts. I knew from a very early age that I wanted to compose, but the idea that there were actually people out there now, in the flesh, actively writing music, did not occur to me for quite some time." While studying in New York City and Paris, Talma composed in a spare, neo-Classical style that became her signature; Grove Music noted that Talma's "whole output is marked by clarity of line, gesture and proportion." This style came from Talma's studies with Boulanger, particularly centering on the works of Stravinsky.

Talma's earliest compositions included *Song of the Songless* (1928); *Three Madrigals* (1928), a piece for voice and string quartet, foreshadowing the vocal settings that characterized much of Talma's later work; *Two Dances* (1934); and a sacred work titled *In principio erat verbum* (1939). This composition won the Stovall Prize at the Fontainebleau School in both 1938 and 1939.

Beginning in the early 1940s Talma visited the MacDowell Colony, an artists' retreat in Peterborough, New Hampshire. There she met and was greatly influenced by composers of the Boston school, including Lukas Foss, Irving Fine, Harold Shapero, Claudio Spies, Arthur Berger, and Alexie Haieff. Talma composed most of her pieces while staying at the MacDowell Colony. In 1943 Talma won the North American Prize for her Piano Sonata No. 1. She composed several other pieces in the mid-1940s, including *Toccata for Orchestra,* which later won the Juilliard Publication Award and became one of Talma's best-known compositions. These works show the range of Talma's style, incorporating distinctly American sounds such as jazz into her compositions.

In 1946 and 1947 Talma was awarded two Guggenheim fellowships, making her the first woman to receive that honor. These fellowships were created to allow outstanding individuals the ability to focus on their work without financial hardships; receiving these fellowships signified the respect others had for Talma's growing body of work. She composed the *Venetian Folly: Overture and Barcarolle, The Devine Flame,* and parts of *Two Sonnets* during these years.

Shifts in Style

In 1951 Talma was recognized by the French government with the Prix d'Excellence de Composition (Prize for Excellence in Composition). The following year she became a full professor at Hunter College. From the early 1950s on, Talma began experimenting with a form of tonality known as twelve-tone, which rejected the traditional major/minor settings of most music. Her first work to draw on the twelve-tone style was *Six Etudes for Piano* (1953–54). This was a fruitful period for Talma. She composed many works, progressively exhibiting a more mature, fuller style incorporating the twelve-tone style with her clear, often linear style.

Among the pieces she composed in the 1950s was an opera, *The Alcestiad.* Written partially with the proceeds from a Senior Fulbright Research Grant which the composer used to work in Rome, the opera featured a libretto written by respected playwright and novelist Thornton Wilder; the story of the opera was adapted from his play *Life in the Sun.* Talma had met Wider at the MacDowell Colony in 1952, and he later asked her to compose a score with his play in mind. The *AllMusic.com* website commented that "the opera contains widely contrasting moods attained mainly through harmonic coloration." This opera became the first by an American woman to be performed in a major European opera house; it was presented in Frankfurt in 1962 where it received a 20-minute standing ovation. Speaking in an interview in 1995,

Talma recalled that "it took [Wilder] over a year to persuade me . . . because I was not at all the kind of person who went for opera or thought that I had anything that I could do with operatic libretto." In 1960 Talma received the Marjorie Peabody Waite Award from the National Institute of Arts and Letters honoring *The Alcestiad.* However, it has not been performed in the United States.

Throughout the 1960s Talma further developed the style she had moved into during the preceding decade. With *A Time to Remember* (1966–67), a piece for choir and orchestra incorporating the speeches of recently assassinated President John F. Kennedy, she moved away from the repetitive serialism typically associated with twelve-tone tonality, creating a unique tonal voice. She continued to receive numerous awards for her composition skills, including three in 1963 alone: a National Federation of Music Clubs Award, a National Association for American Composers and Conductors Award, and the Sibelius Medal for Composition at the Harriet Cohen International Awards in London.

Talma's career included not only composition but pedagogy. She published two textbooks, drawing on her experiences both as a composer and as a teacher: in 1966, *Harmony for the College Student,* and in 1970, with James S. Harrison and Robert Levin, *Functional Harmony.* (The term "functional harmony" is typically used to describe the twelve-tone system Talma embraced in her mature compositions.)

Later Career

In the early 1970s, Talma again returned to Fontainebleau during her summers to study. This era of study gave rise to a work entitled *Summer Sounds for Clarinet and String Quartet,* written between 1969 and 1973. Talma became the first female composer elected to the American Institute of Arts and Letters in 1974. The following year, she held the position of Clark lecturer at Scripps College in Claremont, California. Talma continued to teach at Hunter College until mandatory retirement in 1976, and then remained as a professor emerita until 1979. During the summer of 1978 Talma returned to the Fontainebleau School as an instructor. There, she taught solfege—a way of reading the musical scale—analysis, and harmony, becoming the first American woman to serve as an instructor at the school. She returned to teach during the summers of 1981 and 1982.

Talma composed several works in the 1970s, including several inspired by nature. In addition to *Summer Sounds,* a chamber piece, she wrote *Rain Song* and *Thirteen Ways of Looking at a Blackbird.* Talma also was known for her pieces reflecting Biblical themes, such as the 1978 work *Psalm 84.* She returned to the theme of nature in the chamber piece *Ambient Air,* written between 1980 and 1983. In the 1980s and 1990s Talma wrote many Biblical and devotional pieces, including *A Wreath of Blessings* (1985) and *Ave Atque Vale* (1989), a setting of the text of *Psalm 115* (1992).

Throughout her life Talma was active in professional outreach. She served on the boards of trustees of the Edwin MacDowell Association, the League of Composers, the International Society for Contemporary Music, the American

Music Center, and the Fontainebleau Fine Arts and Music Association. Talma was also a charter member of the American School of University Composers and a fellow of the American Guild of Organists.

Death and Legacy

Talma died on August 13, 1996, at the Yaddo artists' colony near Saratoga Springs, New York. At the time of her death, she was working on a song cycle. She is buried in Hawthorne, New York, at the Gate of Heaven Cemetery.

Talma never married and left no surviving relatives. However, her compositions have made her one of the United States' foremost composers of the twentieth century. She is particularly remembered for her contributions to the neoclassical style and her innovative work with the twelve-tone structure during the majority of her career; Talma is also noted for her piano pieces, her vocal settings of sacred and secular texts, and her influence as an educator and music professional.

Periodicals

New York Times, October 19, 1986; August 15, 1996.

Online

"Louise Talma: a Biography," http://www.omnidisc.com (January 2, 2007).
"Louise Talma," *AllMusic.com,* http://www.allmusic.com (January 2, 2007).
"Louise Talma." *Grove Music Online,* http://www.grovemusic .com (January 2, 2007).
The Scribner Encyclopedia of American Lives, Vol. 4, reproduced in *Biography Resource Center,* http://www.galenet .galegroup.com/servlet/BioRC (January 2, 2007). □

Emma Thompson

British actor Emma Thompson (born 1959) has accrued a long and impressive list of film credits to her name, many of them literary adaptations. Early in her career she appeared in Shakespearean classics along with her then-husband, actor-director Kenneth Branagh, and won her first Academy Award for her lead in the film adaptation of an E. M. Forster story from 1910, *Howards End.* In 1995 she achieved an unusual distinction in Academy Award history when she won her second Oscar, in this case for the screenplay to *Sense and Sensibility*; with that win Thompson became the only person ever to have won Academy Awards in both the performing and writing categories.

Thompson was born into a family of actors on April 15, 1959, in London. Her father, Eric Thompson (1929–1982), was a television and stage actor, and during Thompson's childhood served as the narrator for a

much-loved children's television series, an animated French import called *The Magic Roundabout.* Her mother, Phyllida Law (born 1932), was a native of Glasgow, and the family—which soon included a younger sister, Sophie— spent their summer vacations in Scotland.

Joined Cambridge Theater Group

As a teen, Thompson attended the Camden School for Girls near her north London home. In the mid-1970s she visited the United States for the first time when her father took a stage directing job in Los Angeles, a city she later described as "the strangest, most alien place I'd ever been to. My sister and I went down to [the] supermarket one time and came back with sliced bacon and ice cream and makeup," she told Robbie Coltrane for *Interview* magazine. "I couldn't believe you could get them all in the same place."

Though her sister, Sophie, was determined to follow her parents onto the stage from an early age, Thompson had little interest in the performing arts. Instead she majored in English literature at Cambridge University, where her quick wit prompted friends to persuade her to audition for Cambridge Footlights, the school's renowned amateur theater club. The annual Footlights Revue had become a noted showcase for up-and-coming comedians, and had previously helped launch the careers of members of Monty Python. Thompson's stint during the late 1970s and early 1980s was another notable era for the troupe, which included future talents Stephen Fry (born 1957) and Hugh Laurie (born 1959). In the summer of 1981, Thompson and the group took their revue to the Edinburgh Fringe Festival, where it won a festival prize and was offered a London theater run.

In 1983, her degree finished, Thompson became part of a short-lived television comedy sketch series with Fry and Laurie called *Alfresco.* Over the next few years her career progressed steadily, and she won rave reviews for a 15-month stage run as the lead in a revival of the 1930s musical *Me and My Girl* alongside Fry. Following that, she was cast in the lead in a 1987 BBC television miniseries, *Fortunes of War,* as one-half of a pair of British newlyweds who find themselves stranded in Romania at the start of World War II. Her co-star was Kenneth Branagh (born 1960), a native of Northern Ireland who was being hailed as Britain's next great Shakespearean actor. The pair became romantically involved and married in 1989.

Earned First Oscar

Over the next few years, Thompson's union with Branagh resulted in several film projects and an immense amount of press coverage. They were described as the modern-day successors to other notable husband-and-wife teams such as Alfred Lunt (1892–1977) and Lynne Fontanne (1887–1983) and even Richard Burton (1925–1984) and Elizabeth Taylor (born 1932). Their work included an impressive *Henry V* in 1989, a Hollywood thriller from 1991 called *Dead Again* in which they played dual roles, and *Peter's Friends,* about a reunion of English university friends whose re-enactments of their days in a comedy troupe rang quite credibly on screen, for the cast included Fry, Laurie, and several other onetime Footlights members.

Thompson turned in a brilliant comedy bit in a 1992 episode of *Cheers,* in which she played Frasier Crane's former wife, a children's folk singer named Nanny Gee, the same year that a relatively unknown actor named Sharon Stone became famous for her lead in *Basic Instinct,* a role that Thompson had turned down. She also declined *The Piano,* the melodrama that earned Holly Hunter an Academy Award. Instead, Thompson had chosen to work with Ismail Merchant (born 1936) and James Ivory (born 1928), the acclaimed filmmakers who cast her in *Howards End.* This 1992 period drama, chronicling three separate English families whose lives intersect, paired her with Anthony Hopkins and won her an Academy Award for Best Actress. Reviewing it in the *New York Times,* Vincent Canby mentioned her previous films with Branagh but noted that in this one she "comes into her own as the wise, patient Margaret Schlegel. Hers is the film's guiding performance. Ms. Thompson even manages to be beautiful while convincingly acting the role of a woman who is not supposed to be beautiful, being all teeth and solemn expressions."

A year later Thompson appeared in another Merchant-Ivory project alongside Hopkins, *The Remains of the Day,* and with her husband in *Much Ado About Nothing.* Despite their respective career successes, the couple were often the target of jibes in the British media, mocked for their dedication to their art and for Thompson's habitual appearances in anything that her husband directed for the screen. Though her career was well on its way by the time she met Branagh,

she was often accused of riding on her spouse's coattails to stardom. One well-told comedy skit mocking the pair had Thompson returning home, at which Branagh called out, "I'm in the kitchen," to which her reply was, "Oh, can I be in it too?." Both were sometimes derided as "luvvies," a pejorative British slang term for actors who project an uncomfortable amount of flair while not performing. At some point, Thompson stopped doing press in Britain altogether, but she did display a sense of humor when *Entertainment Weekly* 's Lisa Schwarzbaum asked her about the ribbing, remarking that "it would perhaps be a little unhealthy if one weren't satirized and lambasted regularly."

Endured Highly Publicized Divorce

When Thompson's marriage began to falter amidst rumors of infidelity on both sides, the press coverage was brutal. Thompson had been slated to take a role in *Frankenstein,* which Branagh would direct and star in, but the part went to Helena Bonham Carter (born 1966), who played Thompson's sister in *Howards End.* On the set of *Sense and Sensibility,* meanwhile, Thompson became involved with actor Greg Wise, who played the handsome rogue John Willoughby in the Jane Austen story that Thompson had adapted for the screen—her first writing project since an ill-fated British sketch-comedy series back in 1988. Her work won her a second Academy Award, which made her the first person ever to win an Oscar statuette for both performance and writing.

Thompson's career slowed down for a few years, partly as a result of her plan to become a mother, which took somewhat longer than she would have liked and was finally done with the help of in-vitro fertilization (IVF). She and Wise became parents in 1999 to a daughter they named Gaia Romilly Wise. During these years she worked on several writing projects, including a telefilm adaptation of a stage play, *Wit,* that won acclaim when it ran on HBO in 2001 with Thompson in the lead as a cancer-stricken scholar. She made another appearance in another one of the cable channel's much-admired projects, the 2003 miniseries *Angels in America.* Both of these were directed by Mike Nichols, who knew Thompson from working with her on the 1998 political comedy *Primary Colors,* in which she played the beleaguered spouse of a randy U.S. presidential candidate.

Nichols was just one among a long list of Thompson's well-connected professional colleagues on both sides of the Atlantic, whose devotion to her as a friend and respect for her as an actor would result in a rich range of parts. Another was the actor Alan Rickman (born 1946), who made his directorial debut with the 1997 drama *The Winter Guest* starring Thompson and her mother, Phyllida Law; Rickman later played her cold-hearted husband in the 2003 ensemble romantic comedy, *Love Actually*; in 2004 she joined him as one of the staff at Hogwarts School in the third Harry Potter film, *Harry Potter and the Prisoner of Azkaban,* in which she played Professor Sybil Trelawney. A co-star from *Love Actually,* Colin Firth, was the other lead opposite Thompson in 2005's *Nanny McPhee,* in which she took the title role as the new caregiver to a brood of monstrous children. Thompson had written the screenplay from a children's book series called *Nurse Matilda.*

Took on Diverse Projects

A year later Thompson appeared in a Will Farrell comedy, *Stranger than Fiction,* as the unlikable, tormented novelist whose most popular character turns out to have a real-life counterpart in Farrell's lead. In 2007 she appeared in *Harry Potter and the Order of the Phoenix,* the fifth movie of the series and one that teamed her with another old friend, Scottish actor Robbie Coltrane (born 1950). Two other long-term projects were a reworking of a story about the Black Death epidemic in London in the 1660s, tentatively called *Harrow Alley,* and another about a Chilean dissident folk singer who died in the 1970s. Political causes have long interested Thompson. In 1983, fresh out of Cambridge, she was one of the comedy writers for *An Evening for Nicaragua,* a benefit for leftist groups in the Central American nation; in 1991, she joined in the London street protests against the first Gulf War; and a 2003 film she appeared in alongside Antonio Banderas, *Imagining Argentina,* earned a mixed reaction when it premiered at the Venice Film Festival for its mix of torture scenes and magic realism in a tale of missing political dissidents.

Thompson and Wise wed in 2003, and make their home on the same North London street as her mother and sister, and where she had previously lived at two other addresses. Unafraid to take on distinctly non-glamorous parts, such as the gruesome Nanny McPhee, Thompson has avoided the pitfalls that have reduced many female stars to supporting roles as mothers-in-law or the ingenue's boss as they enter their 40s. As far back as 1994, the year she turned 35, Thompson was already appreciative of the fact that her screen career might only last so long, which is why she returned to her original plan to write for a living. "Actresses have a short shelf life," she told *New York Times* journalist Brenda Maddox. "It stops at about 40, apart from those at the very top, like Anjelica Huston or Glenn Close. An actress has to find a future for herself." She was somewhat surprised a dozen years later, to realize that she was offered "better roles now than when I was younger," she told *Entertainment Weekly* writer Christine Spines in 2006. "It used to be that if I got a script that said, 'A fabulously beautiful woman walks into the room,' I'd stop reading."

Periodicals

Entertainment Weekly, June 25, 1993; November 24, 2006.
Herald (Glasgow, Scotland), October 8, 2005.
Interview, May 1993.
New York Times, March 13, 1992; November 20, 1994.
Observer (London, England), March 24, 1996.
Sunday Times (London, England), February 8, 2004.
WWD, March 16, 2001. □

Elizabeth Tilberis

British journalist Liz Tilberis (1947–1999) had an impressive career as editor-in-chief of British *Vogue*

before arriving at *Harper's Bazaar* in 1992 to oversee a much-lauded redesign of the venerable American fashion magazine. Her career was tragically cut short by ovarian cancer, first diagnosed in 1993 but beaten back by aggressive chemotherapy that Tilberis detailed in her 1998 memoir *No Time to Die.*

Tilberis was born Elizabeth Jane Kelly on September 7, 1947, in Alderley Edge in Cheshire, England, near the city of Manchester. She was the first of three children in the family of Janet Stome Kelly, a cartographer, and Thomas Stuart-Black Kelly, an ophthalmologist. The family also lived in the Bristol and Hereford areas of England during Tilberis's childhood before settling in the city of Bath around 1959. The first-born and her siblings enjoyed a quintessential English upbringing, complete with horseback riding, piano lessons, and ballet school, but Tilberis loved art, design, and fashion. During her teen years at the Worcestershire boarding school Malvern Girls' College, she proved not particularly adept at academics, and did poorly on the national examinations required for college entrance in Britain. Reluctantly, her parents agreed to let her enroll in art school.

Kicked Out of College

Tilberis had somewhat of a rebellious streak as a teenager, and even refused the sacrament of confirmation, asserting she was an atheist. Just before she entered the art and design course at Leicester Polytechnic College, she discovered she was pregnant; she went to London for an abortion, and was horrified to realize the doctor with whom she had made the appointment knew her father professionally. As she wrote in her autobiography, *No Time to Die,* the doctor immediately informed her parents by telephone, "and to his everlasting credit Daddy gave his permission for the abortion and came to pick me up. It sent shock waves through my genteel family, but it was never spoken of again."

Tilberis's wild streak continued at Leicester Polytechnic, where she was expelled within weeks when her boyfriend was caught in her dormitory room—a transgression that, at the time, was deemed quite serious. Undaunted, she transferred to Jacob Kramer Art College in Leeds, and promptly began dating her tutor, Andrew Tilberis, whom she would marry in 1971. She spent the remainder of the 1960s immersed in her studies and pursuing tentative career options, even serving for a time as the fashion writer for the *Bath Evening Chronicle.* In 1969, a year before she earned her degree, she submitted an entry to a British *Vogue* essay competition in which the first prize was an internship at the magazine. She earned second place, but when the first-place winner decided not to interrupt her studies for the three-month internship, Tilberis won the chance to work at *Vogue.*

Tilberis's future husband was the son of a Greek immigrant family in London who ran a restaurant, and she and Andrew moved in with her future in-laws when she started at *Vogue.* At the time, the magazine "was like a finishing school, liberally populated with daughters of the aristocracy," she wrote in her autobiography. "They were dining in glamorous restaurants while I went home each night to Andrew's parents' in North London." *Vogue* was at the media epicenter of swinging London, where daring new ideas in fashion, art, and music were converging, and the jet-set lifestyles of some of the senior staff members were not that distant from those of the tastemakers and idle rich who were chronicled on the magazine's pages. It was a formidable atmosphere for a young woman with no real industry contacts or even genuine professional credentials, but "I succeeded by knowing the right answers but [also] when to keep my mouth shut, when to smile and how to do really good ironing," Tilberis recalled, according to the London *Independent.* She succeeded well enough to be offered a job as an assistant to Grace Coddington, a former model and *Vogue*'s fashion editor at the time.

Advanced Up Masthead Ranks

One of Tilberis's first regular assignments at *Vogue* was compiling the "More Dash than Cash" pages, which gave readers tips on how to adapt the designer looks shown in the lavish editorial spreads to a lesser budget. She eventually advanced to Coddington's job, fashion director, and in 1986 was bypassed for the top job, editor-in-chief, when a fellow Brit named Anna Wintour (born 1949) returned from working at *New York* magazine to take the post. In early 1987 Tilberis decided to take a job with American designer Ralph Lauren (born 1939) in New York. She put her house up for sale, and began preparations to move her family, which by then included two young boys adopted after Tilberis tried, for several years, to conceive a child on her

own. Two days after she informed her bosses at Condé Nast, the magazine publishing giant that owned the British, U.S., and several foreign editions of *Vogue,* they offered her Wintour's job, for the latter had decided to return to New York and take over American *Vogue.*

As editor-in-chief, Tilberis was finally able to give her creative ideas free reign at British *Vogue.* One of her first covers showed a teenaged Naomi Campbell (born 1970) wearing Chanel couture against a desert backdrop in what became the supermodel's first of dozens of *Vogue* covers. Over the next four years Tilberis steered the magazine into fresh discoveries in fashion and the arts, and scored a major coup with a cover featuring the woman who was the world's biggest celebrity at the time, Diana, Princess of Wales (1961–1997). It was the first magazine cover the British royal had ever sat for, and Tilberis and Diana became friends over the next few years.

In early 1992 Tilberis found herself the target of intense media scrutiny when she jumped ship to Hearst Magazines—the archrival of Condé Nast—to revitalize its flagship fashion magazine *Harper's Bazaar.* As the newest editor-in-chief, she moved her family to New York in earnest this time, but had a difficult first few months on the job; she was once seated by herself in the first row of the Paris couture shows, and the press speculated on the supposedly astronomical salary she had been offered to revitalize the flagging title, which had always lagged behind the U.S. edition of *Vogue* in sales, advertising pages, and fashion-industry influence. The first redesigned issue under Tilberis hit newsstands just before September of 1992, and its new typeface, uncluttered layout, and retro-styled cover model Linda Evangelista dressed in black under the headline "Enter the Era of Elegance" was hailed as a great success. Tilberis was credited with re-establishing the magazine's former reputation as an avant-garde image maker, and newsstand sales posted an impressive spike from the previous year's September issue and continued to jump over the next several months.

Press Fueled Rumors of Rivalry

Tilberis worked hard over the next year to keep the ad pages—the sign of a magazine's financial health—up, though they never neared the figures that *Vogue* posted. The New York fashion and advertising media liked to claim that Tilberis and her former boss, Wintour, were archrivals who poached photographers and models from one another for their respective titles. But the feud seemed to be largely a manufactured one; those who knew them claimed they had professional respect for one another, and each recognized that juicy media gossip about a supposed enmity only boosted their magazines' profiles and bottom line in the end. Certainly their obvious differences made both easy targets: Tilberis wore a size 14, refused to color her silver bob, and was much-loved by her staff; the rail-thin Wintour was almost always seen in trademark dark glasses, and was such a feared boss that years later she inspired a thinly disguised fictional account by her former assistant that became a bestseller and then a Hollywood movie, *The Devil Wears Prada.* Indeed, Tilberis was shocked to find herself the object of any media scrutiny at all when she came to New York. "Editing British *Vogue* was a bit like being a princess, sitting apart," she told Colin McDowell in an interview for the London *Sunday Times*. "Nobody outside the magazine cared a damn about you."

Harper's Bazaar won two National Magazine Awards for photography and design, thanks to Tilberis's revamping, and she herself won the Editor of the Year honor for 1993 from *Advertising Age*. As she wrote in her autobiography, she had reached the pinnacle of professional and personal success, and was about to host a major gala in her New York City brownstone for 250 guests in December of 1993 to celebrate the magazine's latest round of industry awards, when she learned she had ovarian cancer. Her doctor had wanted to admit her for surgery immediately, but Tilberis hosted the party anyway, telling no one but her husband and longtime friend Grace Coddington, and checked herself in for surgery the next day to remove her uterus, part of her colon, and one ovary. That was followed by a debilitating round of chemotherapy, but Tilberis continued to oversee the magazine by working out of her home and having her staff bring the layouts to her there for editorial meetings.

Tilberis believed that her cancer was the result of the nine fertility treatments she had undergone back in the late 1970s and early 1980s, when she was given hormone-stimulating drugs to boost her chances of in vitro fertilization. She was not informed of any risks to her future health, and it was only a year before her own diagnosis that a research study found that women who underwent such procedures and failed to conceive were 27 more times likely to contract ovarian cancer. Her illness was briefly mentioned by the press as a past event, but in 1995 there was a recurrence, and she underwent more chemotherapy and then a bone marrow transplant that nearly killed her.

Cheered By Diana's Words

She wrote in her memoir that she was so sick she could not even swallow her own saliva at one point, and found herself "reduced to an almost animal level of survival . . . all privacy and dignity gone, trying to hold on to something that represented the routine of life I'd taken for granted." She also wrote in her book—published just a few months after Diana was killed in a Paris automobile crash—that one day the Princess of Wales telephoned her in the hospital, where her platelet count—vital to the blood's ability to clot itself—was still too low for her to be discharged; Tilberis was so cheered to hear Diana's voice that her platelet numbers surged enough for doctors to let her go home.

Tilberis's cancer returned twice more, in December of 1996 and again in July of 1997. She became an ardent spokesperson for the disease, and added a second job as president of the Ovarian Cancer Research Fund to her *Harper's Bazaar* duties. She hosted the charity's first major fundraiser in December of 1997 in New York City, a black-tie event that drew the biggest names in fashion and raised $750,000 in one evening alone. She died on April 21, 1999, at Mount Sinai Medical Center in New York City at the age of 51, working until the very last week of her life when, from her hospital bed, she went over layouts for the June issue with her staff.

Periodicals

Daily Mail (London, England), March 11, 1998.
Good Housekeeping, April 1998.
Harper's Bazaar, July 1999.
Independent (London, England), April 23, 1999.
Newsweek, April 6, 1998; May 3, 1999.
New York Times, August 23, 1992.
New York Times Book Review, April 12, 1998.
People, December 7, 1992; May 18, 1998.
Sunday Times (London, England), July 21, 1996; May 10, 1998.
□

Pramoedya Ananta Toer

Arguably Indonesia's best-known writer, Pramoedya Ananta Toer, also known as Pramoedya or Pram (1925–2006), was the author of novels that chronicled much of that Southeast Asian country's turbulent history. His writing had special force because he lived that history, doing much of his best work while imprisoned as a result of his dissident activities.

First it was Indonesia's Dutch colonizers who put Pramoedya in prison, then the independent country's first two rulers. For a 10-year period beginning in 1969 he was held in a notorious prison camp on the island of Buru, writing four novels while he was imprisoned, or narrating them orally when he had no access to writing materials. He later documented his experiences in a memoir, *Nyanyi sunyi seorang bisu* (The Mute's Soliloquy, 1995, translated 1999). Pramoedya has often been compared with Russian author Alexander Solzhenitsyn and other dissident writers around the world.

Father Was Independence Activist

Pramoedya Ananta Toer (Prah-MOU-dia ah-NAHN-ta Tour) was born in Blora, in central Java, on February 6, 1925, when Indonesia was still a colony of the Netherlands. He was one of nine children. Pramoedya's father was an educator and a member of a pro-independence group called Budi Otomo. In *The Mute's Soliloquy*, Pramoedya described his father as "a Javanese who had a near-mystical feeling about words" and explained that the name Pramoedya was constructed from the syllables of a revolutionary slogan, "Yang Pertama di Medan," or "First on the Battlefield." The phrase was not in Pramoedya's native language of Javanese but in Indonesian, the language used to unify the numerous ethnic and linguistic groups of the huge Indonesian archipelago. Pramoedya wrote his books in the Indonesian language. His father was a charismatic independence campaigner, "a lion at the rostrum," Pramoedya wrote, but he also suffered from a gambling addiction. In order to attend a broadcasting vocational school in the

larger city of Surabaya, Pramoedya had to save money by working with his mother as a rice trader.

Pramoedya graduated from the school in 1941, just as World War II broke out. Japanese naval forces quickly defeated the combined "ABCD" (American, British, Chinese, Dutch) forces in Southeast Asian waters and occupied Indonesia. Pramoedya, like many other Indonesians, initially welcomed the Japanese as liberators from Dutch colonial occupation, and he worked during the war for Japan's Domei news agency. Later in the war, however, many Indonesians were conscripted by the Japanese into forced labor brigades. In the power vacuum that followed Japan's surrender in 1945, Indonesia, led by the country's first president, Sukarno (many Javanese Indonesians use only one name), declared independence. The Netherlands launched a four-year war to recover its colony, and Pramoedya fought for a time in a guerrilla group.

He later moved to Jakarta, Indonesia's largest city, and edited a pro-independence journal. For these activities he was imprisoned by Dutch authorities between the summer of 1947 and the end of 1949, when the Dutch, under international pressure, ceased hostilities. While he was in prison, guards gave Pramoedya a copy of John Steinbeck's epic novel *Of Mice and Men,* which Pramoedya used as a way to learn the English language. He also began to combat the despair of prison life by writing, a practice he would likewise follow during later stretches in prison, and he completed his first novel, *Perburuan* (The Fugitive, translated into English in 1990). Published in 1950, it was set during

the last days of Japan's occupation of Indonesia in World War II. The book earned Pramoedya widespread recognition and confirmed his gift for weaving historical events into compelling narratives of characters with complex personal motivations.

Pramoedya was fond of saying that he became a writer because he had no other marketable skill, and his reception of the young country's Balai Putaska literary prize helped stabilize his financial situation. He married for the first time, eventually fathering eight children during two marriages. Pramoedya wrote several novels, including *Keluarga Gerilya* (The Gerilya Family), set during the war of Indonesian independence. He also penned short stories that were collected into several books; one of these, *Cerita dari Blora* (Stories from Blora, 1952), featured settings from his home region. The novel *Korupsi* (Corruption, 1954), written after Pramoedya spent a year in the Netherlands on a cultural exchange program, was aimed at corruption in Indonesian society. Pramoedya also traveled to China in 1956, and over the course of the 1950s he gradually moved leftward politically. Many of his writings of the late 1950s were nonfiction essays on themes of social criticism.

Championed Cause of Ethnic Chinese

Pramoedya began to speak out about the conditions facing ethnic Chinese in Indonesia, a prosperous but often persecuted minority in the country. This earned him the enmity of Sukarno, whom Pramoedya generally admired, and in 1960 he spent another nine months in prison. Between 1962 and 1965 he edited the cultural section of the leftist-oriented *Bintang Timur* (Eastern Star) newspaper. In 1965, however, chaos broke out in Indonesia. A group of army officers was assassinated under murky circumstances, and Indonesia's Communist Party was blamed.

An Indonesian general, Suharto, seized power from Sukarno and ruled Indonesia as strongman of the country's "New Order" government until 1998. The country's military launched a brutal program of repression against members of Communist organizations, resulting in hundreds of thousands of deaths. Pramoedya, whose works had already begun to appear in foreign language editions, was not killed, but he was arrested in October of 1965 and again imprisoned. A beating he received from soldiers left him partially deaf for the rest of his life, and his entire library was destroyed. "For the first few months," he wrote in *The Mute's Soliloquy*, "torture was the prisoners' constant diet." In 1969 he was sent to a prison camp on the island of Buru, where new horrors awaited him.

Working rice fields on a penal farm, Pramoedya and his fellow prisoners suffered from extreme malnutrition. Pramoedya began to eat rats and lizards, and worse. "In 1949 I wrote a story about a refugee who tried to keep her children alive by feeding them stray animals, cats included," he wrote in *The Mute's Soliloquy*. "Now I found myself doing the same thing. Eating snakes was common. Some of the men ate wood worms, too, disposing of the head first and then eating the fatty lower part of the body, sometimes raw. Dogs, too, found their way into our stomachs. . . . The humiliation, the beatings, the forced labor: these things made the situation more worrisome.''

Grim as the situation was, Pramoedya managed to recount some episodes with a dry detachment. The government sent Islamic clerics to the island to minister to the prisoners. "I have no doubt that this year, just as in previous years, at the beginning of the fasting month my mates and I will be treated to a lecture by a religious official specially brought in from the free world, on the importance of fasting and controlling one's hunger and desires. Imagine the humor of that!'' To hold himself together mentally, Pramoedya turned once again to writing. At first he was not allowed to have pencils and paper, and he formed his stories by telling them aloud to the other inmates. Later, prison regulations were relaxed slightly, and Pramoedya's fellow prisoners worked to provide him with writing implements.

Penned Quartet of Books

In 1979 Pramoedya was released from prison, partly as a result of intercession by the administration of U.S. President Jimmy Carter, and placed under house arrest in Jakarta. Although his writings were mostly banned, he was allowed to write, and he turned his prison stories into a linked series of four novels, known as the Buru Quartet. The four books were *Bumi Manusia* (translated as *The Earth of Mankind,* 1991), *Anak Semua Bangsa* (*Child of All Nations,* 1993), *Jejak Langkah* (*Footsteps,* 1993), and *Rumah Kaca* (*House of Glass*). These books, especially the first one, were hailed internationally as masterpieces and were translated into some 20 languages. Set in Indonesia in the early twentieth century, they traced the mechanisms of colonial repression through the interlocking tales of an Indonesian and a Dutch family. The central character, an Indonesian named Minke who narrates several of the books, was based on an actual figure, a journalist named Tito Adi Surya who was influential in early Indonesian nationalism.

Despite the acclaim Pramoedya was receiving, his books, including the Buru Quartet, remained banned in Indonesia through the 1990s. Asked by *Michigan Today* why the Quartet books were banned even though they dealt with Dutch colonial power in Indonesia, Pramoedya replied, "Well, apparently Suharto identified with the target!'' Indeed, Pramoedya became an international symbol of creative freedom, and he was given the prestigious Freedom-to-Write Award by the international PEN writers' organization in 1988. With the rise of Internet technology, scanned copies of Pramoedya's books began to find their way into Indonesia and to circulate clandestinely. Although the ban on his works was never formally listed, copies of the Buru Quartet were available in some Jakarta bookstores by the early 2000s.

The Suharto dictatorship was faced with rising dissent in Indonesia in the 1990s, especially after the country faced hardships resulting from the Asian economic crisis of 1997. Pramoedya penned a series of newspaper essays supporting the efforts of dissidents. His works of the 1990s, in addition to the memoir *The Mute's Soliloquy,* included the historical novel *Arus Balik* (*Turn of the Tide,* 1995). It was the publication of *The Fugitive* in 1990 that drew attention to Pramoedya in the United States. He also translated a variety of Russian and American novels into Indonesian, and many of his earlier short stories were translated and issued in collections in the West. Pramoedya signed a multi-book publishing deal with the large Morrow publishing house, which promoted his works in the United States.

After Suharto's fall in 1998, Pramoedya was officially liberated and allowed to travel freely. He visited the United States in 1999 and received an honorary doctoral degree from the University of Michigan. Although Indonesian politics were liberalized in the early 2000s, leading to the inception of free presidential elections, Pramoedya viewed such developments skeptically, pointing to the continuing influence of the country's military. He was likewise skeptical of the infusion of Western capital into the developing country, telling Matthew Rothschild of *The Progressive* that "now is the absolute victory of the multinationals. Now, in reality, the whole of the Third World hopes for the aid of capital. . . . There is an alternative. That's what Sukarno taught. Do not invite capitalism, but if you want to develop, it's OK to borrow money. I'm against capitalism but not capital.''

Pramoedya continued to write and to develop innovative ways of incorporating Indonesian history into his work. His 2001 book *Perawan Remaja dalam Cengkraman Militer* (Young Virgins in the Grip of the Military) dealt with the sex slavery imposed during the Japanese occupation of Java; although documentary in nature, it was written in the form of a novel. Discussions about filming the Buru Quartet story stalled, Pramoedya told *Michigan Today,* after "an American filmmaker told my editor in this country the movie would have to be based on Minke's fair-skinned first wife Annelise rather than Minke. Otherwise, he said, there would be too many little brown people running around for an American audience!'' Pramoedya was often mentioned as a candidate for the Nobel Prize for Literature, but never won. He suffered from health problems, brought on partly by a lifetime of smoking Indonesian clove cigarettes, and he died in Jakarta on April 30, 2006.

Books

Toer, Pramoedya Ananta, *The Mute's Soliloquy: A Memoir,* trans. Willem Samuels, Hyperion, 1999.

Periodicals

Catholic New Times, June 20, 1999.
Financial Times, May 1, 2006.
Guardian (London, England), May 3, 2006.
Independent (London, England), May 2, 2006.
Nation, February 3, 1992.
Progressive, October 1999.
Publishers Weekly, February 9, 1990.
World Literature Today, Summer 2000.

Online

"Ananta Toer, Pramoedya," *Contemporary Authors Online,* Gale, 2007, http://www.galenet.galegroup.com/servlet/BioRC (January 13, 2007).
"Biographical Data: Pramoedya Ananta Toer," http://www.radix .net/~bardsley/biodata.html (January 13, 2007).

"A Chat with Pramoedya Ananta Toer," *Michigan Today,*
  http://www.umich.edu/~newsinfo/MT/99/Sum99/mt9j99.html
  (January 13, 2007).
"Pramoedya Ananta Toer," Books and Writers, http://www
  .kirjasto.sci.fi/pram.htm (January 13, 2007). □

Tokyo Rose

Iva Toguri, more commonly known as Tokyo Rose, (1916–2006) was the first woman in the United States to be tried and convicted for treason. American prosecutors accused her of being "Tokyo Rose," an infamous Japanese-American radio personality who broadcast Japanese propaganda intended to demoralize American troops stationed in the Pacific during World War II.

Although Toguri did indeed work for Radio Tokyo during the war, her profession was by circumstance rather than by choice, and her later prosecution has come to be viewed as persecution. Charged with eight counts of treason, she was convicted in 1949 on only one count and was sentenced to ten years in prison. She was found guilty despite the fact that no written or recorded evidence existed to prove her guilt. Throughout her highly publicized trial, and in subsequent years, she adamantly proclaimed her innocence as well as her loyalty to the United States. She eventually received a presidential pardon.

Ironically enough, accused traitor Iva Toguri was born on the fourth of July, specifically on July 4, 1916. Born in Los Angeles, California, she was the second of four children of Jun and Fumi Toguri, Japanese immigrants who operated a small import business.

Though she was a nisei, a Japanese term that indicates the first generation born to parents who have left Japan, Toguri's childhood reflected the typical middle-American experience. She was popular in school, attended church, became a Girl Scout, played on the high school tennis team, took piano lessons, and enjoyed hiking. She liked to listen to swing music and popular radio programs such as "The Shadow" and "Little Orphan Annie."

Her father wanted his family to become as Americanized as possible. He discouraged his children from learning to speak or write Japanese. Intent on having his family assimilate into the American culture, he even forbade his offspring to use chopsticks. The Toguri children were raised as Methodists and grew up in a predominantly white neighborhood, enjoying a comfortable middle income lifestyle. Iva Toguri flourished under her father's influence. A caring child, she took care of her mother, who was disabled by diabetes. She was also responsible and mature. After high school Toguri attended Compton Junior College and then entered the University of California at Los Angeles (UCLA), graduating in 1941 with a bachelor's degree in zoology and ambitions of practicing medicine.

Became Stranded in Japan

Toguri's trajectory toward negative notoriety began in 1941. That year her family learned that a relative in Japan, her Aunt Shizu, was seriously ill. As Toguri's mother was too sick to travel, Toguri was sent by her family to visit her aunt. Toguri did not have a passport, but the U.S. State Department gave her a certificate of identification that allowed her to travel. She left the United States for Japan on July 5, 1941, the day after her 25th birthday.

When she arrived, she immediately had trouble adjusting to the Japanese society. She could not speak the language, found people to be rude, and disliked the food (especially rice). In a letter home she wrote, "I have finally gotten around to eating rice three times a day. It's killing me, but what can I do?"

Toguri's aunt soon recovered, but Toguri had unwittingly placed herself in a precarious situation. The world's Allied powers were coming up against the Axis powers. Tensions were running high between the United States and Japan, and in Europe, Hitler's army was on the march. As Toguri could not read Japanese, she was not able to keep abreast of world affairs as reported in local papers. However, by November of 1941, she had become fully aware of the mounting international crisis and had decided to go home. She was to sail on December 2, but passport problems forced her to miss her ship.

Only five days later, on December 7, 1941, "Day of Infamy," Japan attacked Pearl Harbor and the United States officially entered World War II. Toguri now found herself stranded in Tokyo with nearly 10,000 fellow Japanese-Americans. Japanese officials considered her an enemy alien, and they demanded that she renounce her U.S. citizenship. She adamantly refused and asked to be interned with other foreign nationals, a request that the government denied because of Toguri's gender and her Japanese heritage. The government also denied her a food ration card, which later led to her near starvation. In addition, because of her enemy status Koguri endured constant surveillance and even harassment by the Kempeitai, Japan's military police.

Her troubles compounded when her aunt and uncle turned Toguri out of their home because of her pro-American sentiments. Essentially all alone in a hostile environment, Toguri had to struggle to survive. She scrambled to find work, and eventually found positions as a piano teacher and later as a typist at the Domei News Agency, where she transcribed English-language news broadcasts. Through her Agency work, she learned that her family had been placed in a Japanese-American internment camp in the United States. Later, she would learn that her mother died during relocation.

While working at the Agency, Toguri found a sympathetic friend in Felipe d'Aquino, a Portuguese national with a Japanese heritage who also became trapped in Japan during the war. After she became ill from malnutrition, he loaned her money to cover her hospital expenses. To repay d'Aquino, Toguri took on a second job with Radio Tokyo, typing English-language scripts written by Japanese officials for broadcast to Allied troops. Through this job she made another friend: Major Charles Cousens, who had been a famous radio personality in Australia before the war. Cousens had been captured by the Japanese in the Philippines and was forced to produce a radio propaganda show, "Zero Hour," intended to harm the morale of Allied soldiers.

When Radio Tokyo officials wanted to add a woman's voice to the "Zero Hour" show, Cousens recommended Toguri. She joined the broadcasting lineup in November of 1943, calling herself "Orphan Ann," a broadcast name that subtly suggested her status as an American refugee. During her broadcasts, which lasted 20 minutes each day, Toguri played popular records and spoke to the Allied soldiers, whom she also considered "orphans." As Toguri's approach suggests, the intent was to subtly and playfully undermine Radio Tokyo's propagandistic message. The nuanced delivery and double entendres went over the heads of the Japanese officials, who felt Toguri was an effective broadcaster.

The Myth of "Tokyo Rose"

In 1945, while still working for Radio Tokyo, Toguri married d'Aquino and moved in with his family. That same year World War II ended, but Japan's defeat would provide Toguri with little cause for celebration. Subsequent events in her life would lead to personal tragedy and a travesty of justice.

After the war, a myth circulated about the existence of a so-called "Tokyo Rose," supposedly a treasonous, English-speaking female broadcaster in Japan who taunted American soldiers stationed in the Pacific. Reporters searched the

defeated country, hoping to secure an exclusive interview with this shadowy, notorious broadcaster. However, they discovered that several women worked as on-air personalities for Radio Tokyo, although none called themselves "Tokyo Rose." Indeed, a "Tokyo Rose" never existed. In his introduction to Masayo Duus's 1979 book, "Tokyo Rose: Orphan of the Pacific," Edwin O. Reischauer, the American Ambassador to Japan from 1961 to 1966 and a scholar at Harvard specializing in East Asian affairs, wrote, "A mere wartime myth, Tokyo Rose was to become a disgrace to American justice." Even before the war had ended, the U.S. Office of War Information concluded that the name "Tokyo Rose" was only a G.I. invention. Moreover, the Office reported that U.S. counterintelligence monitors who listened to Far East radio broadcasts 24 hours a day never heard the name even mentioned. But at the time, ambitious reporters were unwilling to accept the apparent truth. The myth had become too big and they did not want to loose a potential "scoop."

Reporters then offered a reward to anyone who could help them track down "Tokyo Rose." Subsequently, a Radio Tokyo employee named Kenkiichi Oki, who had married one of the other English-speaking Japanese broadcasters, indicated that Toguri was "Tokyo Rose." Of course, Toguri denied that she was "Tokyo Rose," as no such person existed. However, two reporters, Clark Lee of International News Service and Harry Brundidge of *Cosmopolitan* magazine, offered her $2,000 if she would admit that she was "Tokyo Rose" and sit down for an exclusive interview. Toguri accepted the offer, after her husband convinced her that an exclusive interview might force other reporters to leave her alone.

Arrested in Japan

On September 1, 1945, Toguri did the interview. To receive payment, she needed to sign a statement that said she was "Tokyo Rose." She complied, somewhat blithely, but at the time she didn't realize that the subtly coerced gesture would later lead to treason charges, or that the reporters would characterize the interview as her "confession." U.S. Army officials took notice, and on October 17, 1945, they arrested Toguri and placed her in a six-by-nine-foot cell in Sugamo Prison, where her treatment was abusive. She was only allowed to wash every three days (and curious civilian visitors were allowed to watch her emerge from a shower naked); guards kept her cell light on until she agreed to sign autographs, and she was only allowed one 20-minute visit a month with her husband (she was incarcerated for a year). While in prison, she learned that her mother had died.

Soon, the press had characterized this confinement as the "capture" of the infamous "Tokyo Rose." However, six months after Toguri was imprisoned, the U.S. Army reported that no evidence indicated she had committed treason during her broadcasts—that is, she didn't identify names and locations of Allied units, warn of attacks, broadcast any military secrets, or engage in any similar activities that could have been officially designated as treasonous. As such, no charges were brought against her. Still, Toguri remained in prison, as the military feared a public and political backlash if they set her free. She was finally released on October 25, 1946.

The following year, she became pregnant. Wanting her child to be born in the United States, Toguri applied for a passport, but her request was hindered because she lacked proper documentation. The male child was born in Japan but died shortly after birth, in January of 1948. Soon after, the U.S. State Department enabled her to obtain a passport.

Tried for Treason

News of Toguri's imminent return created an uproar of protest in the United States. The American Legion was outspoken in its outrage. Walter Winchell, an influential newspaper columnist and radio broadcaster with strong right wing leanings, used his powerful position to call for Toguri's prosecution.

The sensationalistic publicity compelled the U.S. Justice Department to reopen the case. On August 28, 1948, Toguri was again arrested and then brought to America to stand trial, even though Assistant Attorney General L. Caudle had previously confirmed Toguri's innocence. Her on-air activity, he reported, "consisted of nothing more than the announcing of music selections." Toguri was taken to San Francisco, where she was held in a county jail for a year. Her trial began on July 5, 1949, only one day after her birthday (she was now thirty-three). She was charged with eight counts of treason.

During the three-month trial, U.S. prosecutors focused on the testimony of Kenkichi Oki and George Mitsushio, who had worked with Toguri at Radio Tokyo. Also, Toguri's signed statement, given to reporters and claiming that she was "Tokyo Rose," came back to haunt her. Still, the government's case was not very strong. Nine out of ten reporters covering the trial even predicted that Toguri would be acquitted.

Even the jury was not totally convinced that Toguri should be convicted. After they reported that they were deadlocked on a decision, the judge presiding over the case, Michael J. Roche, pressured them to reach a verdict. Finally, on September 29, 1949, they returned a guilty verdict on one of the eight counts, a decision that came as a surprise to observers. Years later, one juror who wanted to vote for acquittal, John Mann, told the *Washington Post* and the CBS news program *60 Minutes* that he felt pressured by Roche to return a guilty verdict and he said that he wished he had "had a little more guts to stick with my vote for acquittal." Roche later admitted his own bias in the case, revealing that he had believed that Toguri was guilty from the beginning of the trial. Also, in a 1976 interview with the *Chicago Tribune,* Oki said about his testimony, "We had no choice. . . . The FBI and U.S. Occupation police told us we would have to testify against [Toguri] or else they said Uncle Sam might arrange a trial for us, too."

Later in her life, during a 1976 interview with *60 Minutes,* Toguri said, "I supposed they found someone and got the job done, they were all satisfied. It was eeny, meeny, miney and I was 'moe.' "

On October 6, Roche sentenced Toguri to 10 years in prison and a $10,000 fine. Further, he stripped her of her U.S. citizenship. She was sent to the Federal Reformatory for Women in Alderson, West Virginia, where she served six years and two months of her sentence before being released on good behavior. She was set free on January 28, 1956.

Received Presidential Pardon

After her release, Toguri settled in Chicago, Illinois, where she led a relatively quiet life, helping to operate a small import business that her father had started. But a great deal of activity went on behind this seemingly quiet facade. In the two years following her release from prison, Toguri successfully battled the U.S. government's attempts to have her deported. As early as 1954, when Toguri was still imprisoned, sympathetic parties filed petitions on Toguri's behalf for a presidential pardon. Nothing came of these efforts until 1976, after news reports and the pivotal *60 Minutes* segment revealed the essentially false nature of the prosecution's trial testimony. Finally, on January 19, 1977, President Gerald Ford, in one of his last acts before leaving office, pardoned Toguri and restored her U.S. citizenship. Ford's action was supported by a unanimous vote of the California State Legislature. Toguri viewed the pardon as, in her words, "an act of of vindication." Further, she expressed a desire to simply get back to work and get on with her life. She took over her father's business after he died in 1972.

Still, she continued enduring consequences from the "Tokyo Rose" myth and its promulgation: She was never able to see her husband again, as d'Aquino had been forbidden from re-entering the United States after he testified at her trial. The couple reluctantly and legally separated, finally divorcing in 1980.

In her later years she reportedly developed a tough exterior—no other emotional response could make any sense after she was geographically separated from her mother's death during her family's unjust internment; was imprisoned in a foreign land that during another time might have recognized her as one of its own; lost a child during her enforced exile; found herself unwillingly divorced from her husband; and, most significantly, suffered persecution from a nation (the United States) whose values both she and her father had enthusiastically embraced. At the same time, the friends she had made in her later life described her as an elegant, literate, and engaging woman. Following her imprisonment and release, she reportedly enjoyed the low-key pleasures of quilting (a craft she actively engaged in) and music (she appreciated concerts presented at the Chicago Lyric Opera). Until her death she remained a productive member of her community. She died on September 26, 2006, at the Advocate Illinois Masonic Medical Center in Chicago, reportedly from natural causes. She was 90 years old. As a final injustice, in her printed obituaries the press continued identifying her as the notorious "Tokyo Rose," a convicted traitor.

Periodicals

American History, October 2002.
Chicago Sun-Times, September 28, 2006.

New York Daily News, July 3, 2006.
New York Times, September 27, 2006.
Washington Post, September 28, 2006.

Online

''Death ends the myth of Tokyo Rose,'' *BBC News,* http://www
    .news.bbc.co.uk/2/hi/americas/5389722.stm (December 1,
    2006).
''Famous Cases: Iva Toguri d'Aquino and ''Tokyo Rose,'' *FBI.gov,*
    http://www.fbi.gov/libref/historic/famcases/rose/rose.htm
    (December 1, 2006).
''The Myth of Tokyo Rose,'' *History News Network,* http://www
    .hnn.us/articles/461.html (December 1, 2006). □

P. L. Travers

British author P. L. Travers (1899–1996), although the author of many writings for children and adults, was best known for her 1934 book *Mary Poppins* and its sequels. This fantasy, about a nanny with magical powers, became one of the great publishing successes of the twentieth century, enjoying new bursts of popularity after the book's adaptation to film in 1964 and to a stage musical in the early 2000s.

Imagined Self as Hen

Travers was born Helen Lyndon Goff on August 9, 1899, in Maryborough, in the Australian province of Queensland. She later took the surname Travers from the first name of her father, Travers Goff, a bank employee and an alcohol abuser who fell on hard times during her childhood; Pamela, a fashionable name in the years after World War I, was her own invention. As a writer she used only her first and middle initials, a common device in British letters especially among women who wanted their work to be appreciated on its own merits. Her father was of Irish descent and sometimes waxed maudlin about his ancestral home; her mother was fond of raising her daughter with the aid of maxims and sayings, some of which found their way verbatim into the Mary Poppins books. Often as a child, Travers imagined herself as a bird, specifically as a hen. '' 'She can't come in, she's laying,' her family and friends would say,'' according to *Mary Poppins, She Wrote,* Valerie Lawson's biography of Travers. She loved animals and had a rich fantasy life, often arranging corners of her family's backyard into miniature parks. She also loved to read fairy tales.

Travers's father died when she was seven. The family moved to the resort town of Bowral in New South Wales, where her great-aunt (the model for the title character in Travers's 1941 book *Aunt Sass*) owned a sugar plantation. Travers attended Normanhurst Private Girls School but was bored with her classes and demanded to be allowed to read on her own, whereupon she began the weighty history *The Decline and Fall of the Roman Empire.* Even as a teenager, Travers was writing poems that appeared in Australian periodicals. (The editor who published her first poem was the father of future media magnate Rupert Murdoch.) She also took a music class, which led her into theater. When she was 17, she headed for Sydney, Australia, and embarked on an acting career. It was during this period that she adopted the name Pamela Lyndon Travers.

Although she had moderate success on the stage, appearing in Shakespeare's plays and touring New South Wales with a repertory company in 1921, Travers had to make ends meet by working as a journalist. She penned a column for a Sydney newspaper for two years. She became fairly widely published as a poet in Australia, publishing a number of pieces in a literary magazine called *The Bulletin* in 1923. Some were on Irish themes; many were surprisingly erotic in nature. But she was frustrated with life among conservative Australians, who, she wrote (according to Lawson), ''took their fun very seriously'' and ''were incapable of undressing delight delicately, garment by mysterious joyous garment.'' The Australian sense of humor, she felt, was ''stodgy, mutton fed.'' She had a strong desire to see more of the world, and she felt that England was the literary center of the English language. So in 1924, she sailed for London.

Travers often told a story that she arrived in England with just ten pounds in her pocket, and promptly lost five of them. Actually, she had succeeded in turning the voyage into several travel articles that she sold to Australian publications, and she hit the ground running as a writer in London, sending articles about the arts back to Australia and

New Zealand, with a number of them appearing in New Zealand's *Christchurch Herald.* Soon she was finding publishers for her writing in the British Isles as well, and one would turn into her primary influence: in 1925 she sent some poems to the *Irish Statesman,* and its editor encouraged her. The editor was the poet, Irish nationalist leader, and mystic theosophist George William Russell, who used the pen name AE.

Became Immersed in Irish Mythology

Travers and Russell began a friendship that lasted until Russell's death in 1935. "Pamela Travers would spend much of her life in an attempt to live out George Russell's ideas," noted Lawson. "She did not just love Russell. She felt as if he was her sun." The relationship was platonic, however, and Travers never married, although she later adopted a son named Camillus Travers. Russell introduced Travers to Irish poet William Butler Yeats and to other Irish literary figures who drew on Ireland's mythical past in their works. Travers, already a writer given to fantasy and imagination, soaked up more of Ireland's rich history of storytelling and poetry. She also delved into mystical thought and studied for a time with the celebrated Armenian-born spiritual teacher George Gurdjieff. She visited the United States and also the Soviet Union; a chronicle of the latter journey, *Moscow Excursion,* became her first published book.

In 1934 Travers suffered from pleurisy, a lung illness, and took time off from writing to recuperate in an old cottage in England's Sussex region, where she lived with a roommate. AE had suggested that she write a story about a witch. One day she had to entertain two visiting children, and concocted a story for them about a nanny who carried her belongings in a carpetbag and had an umbrella with a parrot's head on the handle. This governess, Mary Poppins, came to Number 17 Cherry Tree Lane to care for the Banks children: Jane, Michael, and twins John and Barbara. Mary Poppins had magical powers, such as the ability to throw a tea party that would be held on the ceiling of a room. The story grew into the book *Mary Poppins,* illustrated by Mary Shepard (the daughter of the original illustrator of *Winnie the Pooh*) and published in 1934.

The book was successful from the start, and Travers soon followed it with a sequel, *Mary Poppins Comes Back* (1935). The reasons for the success of the Mary Poppins books have been the subject of numerous literary studies, but among those reasons is certainly the books' seamless mixture of fantasy and everyday elements. The books also had deeper patterns of fantasy drawn from Travers's studies of myth and legend, and Travers never thought of them as being exclusively for children. They also incorporated aspects of her own life (the father in the books, George Banks, was a bank manager like Travers Goff), and, when asked by interviewers later what had given her the idea for Mary Poppins, she sometimes said it seemed the character had always been with her. The *New York Times* quoted her as saying that "the ideas I had [as a child] move about in me now," and that "sorrow lies like a heartbeat behind everything I have written." Travers returned to Mary Poppins several times throughout her long and productive career,

issuing *Mary Poppins Opens the Door* in 1944, *Mary Poppins in the Park* in 1952, *Mary Poppins from A to Z* in 1962, *Mary Poppins in Cherry Tree Lane* in 1982, and *Mary Poppins and the House Next Door* in 1989. All were illustrated by Shepard, and all maintained the world of the original book, frozen in time.

Travers also issued various Mary Poppins compilations, along with related projects such as *Mary Poppins in the Kitchen: A Cookery Book with a Story* (1975). But she also wrote other books, and pursued many interests beyond the imagined feats of her most famous creation. In 1939, after the outbreak of World War II, Travers began working for Britain's Ministry of Information. She was sent to the United States, and wrote a young adult novel, *I Go by Sea, I Go by Land* in 1941, cast as the diary of an 11-year-old girl evacuated from England during the war. Travers used part of her time in the United States to further her interest in mysticism, spending the summer of 1944 living in a boarding house in Window Rock, Arizona, on a Navajo reservation. She earned the trust of some of the Navajos and was given an Indian name, obeying their injunction that it be kept secret.

Wooed by Disney

American film executive Walt Disney realized within a few years of the release of the original *Mary Poppins* that the series could be made successfully into a film, and first made an offer to Travers in 1945. She was skeptical about the idea and resisted it for many years, demanding, among other things, that any film be live action, not animated. She finally agreed to sell the rights to Mary Poppins in 1959, with the stipulation that she would serve as consultant on the script of the film. Even so, she was dissatisfied with the final product, which she felt was too saccharine.

The film took several years to finish, partly due to disagreements between Travers and Disney scriptwriters, and the straightforward if charming musical that eventually resulted had a very different flavor from that of Travers's stories. However, *Mary Poppins* (1964) left Travers a wealthy woman for the rest of her life. With the young British actress Julie Andrews cast in the lead role, the film grossed more than $75 million, included several songs (by Robert and Richard Sherman) that became popular standards, and introduced the term "supercalifragilisticexpialidocious" to English vocabulary. Its plot included elements from several Mary Poppins books but was mostly based on the first one. The film was adapted into a stage musical that had its premiere in London in 2004. The 1934 *Mary Poppins* had already been turned into a stage play around 1940, but Travers refused to give permission for a musical extravaganza by *Cats* creator Andrew Lloyd Webber.

Though well over 60 years old when the film appeared, Travers was not content to rest on her laurels. She served as writer-in-residence at Smith College in Massachusetts in 1966. She had continued to deepen her interest in mysticism and the occult, contributing articles to the world mythology magazine *Parabola,* and many of her later books reflected this interest. A lecture series she gave at Scripps College in California was turned into a book, *In Search of the Hero: The Continuing Relevance of Myth and Fairy Tale*

(1970), and she penned the full-length study *What the Bee Knows: Reflections on Myth, Symbol and Story* in 1989, at the age of 90. Travers also wrote a biography of Gurdjieff, and her 1971 children's book *Friend Monkey* also reflected her study of world mythological literature; it was based on the Indian epic *The Ramayana*.

Travers remained active until the end of her life. She planned a *Goodbye, Mary Poppins* book in which she would terminate her character, but publishers and letters from upset children dissuaded her. She was given the Order of the British Empire in 1977. Although she was friendly to the parade of interviewers who came to her home in London's Chelsea district, she was usually reticent about the details of her own life, many of which emerged only with the publication of Lawson's biography in 1999. Travers died in London on April 23, 1996, at age 96.

Books

Lawson, Valerie, *Mary Poppins, She Wrote*, Simon & Schuster, 1999.
Major Authors and Illustrators for Children and Young Adults, 2nd ed., Gale, 2002.

Periodicals

Daily Mail (London, England), April 25, 1996.
Guardian (London, England), April 25, 1996.
Horn Book Magazine, September–October 1996.
New York Times, April 25, 1996.
Times (London, England), April 24, 1996.

Online

"P(amela) L(yndon) Travers," *Contemporary Authors Online*, Gale, 2006, http://www.galenet.galegroup.com/servlet/BioRC (January 12, 2007). □

Michel Tremblay

The French Canadian writer Michel Tremblay (born 1942), in the words of the Canadian Theatre Encyclopedia website, "is probably the most-produced playwright" in Canada "and arguably the most important playwright in the history of the country."

Tremblay's writing was motivated at first by his status as a closet homosexual, and some of his plays and prose works have addressed gay themes. But he first became well known for his portrayals of a larger outsider group: the working class residents of the province of Quebec itself. Until Tremblay began to gain attention with his writings in the late 1960s, Quebec had little in the way of independent theater; French-language dramas were mostly imported from France. Tremblay's life and work have also been closely bound up with the efforts of Quebec nationalists to bring about the province's separation from Canada and its emergence as an independent nation. For all their appeal to these specific constituencies, however, Tremblay's plays have demonstrated a universal appeal

with their vividly drawn characters and impressive stagecraft. They have been widely produced in English and in other languages all over the world.

Father Worked as Printer

Tremblay was born on June 25, 1942, and grew up on Montreal's French-speaking, working class east side. He recalled his upbringing in a memoir, *Un ange cornu avec des ailes de tôle* (Horned Angel with Metal Wings). Tremblay's family was poor, and his childhood, though troubled by poverty, was colorful and culturally rich. His father, a heavy drinker, worked as a printer and claimed to have formulated the ink mixture used on Campbell's soup cans. Tremblay's mother, born in Providence, Rhode Island, was part Cree. His maternal grandmother, though largely uneducated, was a voracious reader who introduced him to books of all kinds, including the French-language *Tintin* adventure comics, mass-market novels, and a story called *L'auberge de l'ange-gardien* (The Inn of the Guardian Angel), which fascinated the young Tremblay because it had sections in dramatic dialogue like a play.

Tremblay came early to a realization of his homosexuality, which in heavily Catholic Quebec in the 1950s was cause for severe discrimination. But it also inspired him to experiment with writing on his own. "When you're 12 and you sit and write something, it's often about something you have to hide from the rest of society," he observed to Matthew Hays of the *Gay & Lesbian Review Worldwide*. "I don't know if you have this expression in English, but in French we say that we have to confide to the white sheet." He felt alienated as well by his linguistic heritage; as he learned more about literature he realized how few writers had emerged from predominantly French-speaking Quebec as compared with the rest of Canada, or with other countries.

Tremblay attended a Catholic high school, the Ecole de Saint-Stanislas, in Montreal. A talented student, he earned a prep school scholarship but after a short time decided to follow his father into the printing profession instead. He enrolled at the Institute for Graphic Arts in 1959 and worked until 1966 as a linotype operator. "I saw that if I stayed on at that school and then went to university, I would have to reject my roots, my background—to forget where I came from," he explained to Harry Eyres of the London *Times*. "After that I became a sort of auto-didact."

While still a teenager, he began writing short stories in which gay themes were disguised by fantasy elements. These stories were published in 1966 by the pioneering Quebec house Les Editions du Jour as *Contes pour buveurs attardés* (Stories for Late-Night Drinkers). Tremblay also entered a play, *Le train,* in a Radio Canada contest for young writers. It won, and was performed twice, earning Tremblay a grant from the Canada Council. A one-act play called *Cinq* (Five), later reworked as *En pièces détachées* (In Detached Pieces), appeared in 1966 and provided an early example of Tremblay's ability to make compelling drama out of his own Montreal east-end background.

Featured Trading Stamps in Play

In 1968 Tremblay scored his first major triumph with the play *Les belles-soeurs* (The Sisters-in-Law), which he had written in 1965. The play was given a public reading at Montreal's Center for Dramatic Authors; picked up by the commercial Théâtre du Rideau Vert, it became a hit. *Les belles-soeurs* was unlike anything else that had been presented on Quebec stages up to that time. It was written in the working-class Quebec dialect of French known as *joual,* previously considered unsuitable for literary expression. (Tremblay demolished that supposition with a lyrical speech about bingo.) The play treated previously taboo topics such as sex and abortion, and the characters employed profanity in a realistic way. And most unusual of all was its dark comic plot, which centered on trading stamps: a group of Montreal housewives gather for a stamp-pasting party and fall into a nasty morass of competition and recrimination.

Les belles-soeurs was at once a play that was specific to Quebec and one that dovetailed with new trends in world theater; Tremblay's Quebec housewives were counterparts of British playwright Harold Pinter's terse but poetic British working-class characters. The play soon made Tremblay famous. It was presented in Paris in 1973 and won an award for best foreign play of the year. *Les belles-soeurs* was also translated into English, and even at one point into Scots dialect, but Tremblay refused to allow it to be performed in English until the separatist Parti Québécois won elections in the province in 1976. He was a staunch supporter of independence for Quebec, and his works helped to define a

cultural sphere in Quebec that helped nurture separatist sentiment. But he avoided openly political themes.

Instead, Tremblay embarked on a cycle of 11 plays, set mostly in the Montreal east end locale of *Les belles-soeurs,* in which individuals try to escape from the despair of their environments by advancing toward new sexual or social realms. *Damnée Manon, Sacrée Sandra* (1977) depicted two women, one of whom tries to lose herself in sexual experiences while the other turns toward mysticism. Several characters appeared in more than one play. Two of Tremblay's plays, *La duchesse de Langeais* (1970) and *Hosanna* (1973) featured gay characters, a new development in serious theater at the time. But Tremblay was living in the midst of a profound transformation in Quebec society. After coming out as a homosexual during a 1975 television interview, he reported that he had faced very few instances of overt hostility or discrimination. "Maybe it's because we [Quebeckers] were so closed, like a press, for so long, that when we opened, we opened up wide," he mused to Hays. "What saved us in Quebec is that we have a big monster living to the south, but we have our own language. We don't get the pressure the rest of Canada does constantly from the American culture."

Tremblay began to work in the medium of film in the 1970s, often working with a friend, director André Brassard. *Françoise Durocher, Waitress* (1972) won three Genie awards at the Toronto Film Festival. Tremblay and Broussard joined forces once again for *Il était une fois dans l'est* (Once Upon a Time in the East, 1974) and *Le soleil se Lè en retard* (The Sun Rises Late, 1977). Tremblay also translated and adapted various English-language plays for the Quebec market, including the ancient Greek comedy *Lysistrata* by Aristophanes, Edward Albee's *Who's Afraid of Virginia Woolf?,* and various works by Tennessee Williams, whose oblique treatments of homosexuality and working class life, as well the dramatic gift that drew general audiences to his works, showed affinities with Tremblay's own works.

Penned Fiction Tetralogy

Although he continued to write drama, Tremblay's most characteristic mode of production from the late 1970s onward was the novel. He has written 14 novels, among the most famous of which was a tetralogy (a linked set of four) published between 1978 and 1984 under the title *Chroniques du plateau Mont-Royal* (Chronicles of the Mount Royal Plateau). The title referred to Tremblay's own childhood neighborhood east of Mount Royal in downtown Montreal, and the novels had strong autobiographical aspects. The four novels in the tetralogy were *La grosse femme d'a côté est enceinte* (The Fat Woman Next Door Is Pregnant), *Thérèse et Pierrette a l'école des Saints-Anges* (Therese and Pierrette and the Little Hanging Angel), *La duchesse et le roturier* (The Duchess and the Commoner), and *Des nouvelles d'Edouard* (News of Edward).

Tremblay was less prolific as a playwright in the 1980s and 1990s, but he produced some of his best-known works during this period. These included *Le vrai monde?* (The Real World?, 1987), in which Tremblay looked back on and questioned his own artistic uses of the milieu in which he had grown up, and *La maison suspendue* (The Suspended House, 1990), a multigenerational saga that, unlike the vast majority of Tremblay's Montreal-based works, was set in rural Quebec. Tremblay's *For the Pleasure of Seeing Her Again* paid tribute to the influence the playwright's mother had on his artistic personality. It was mounted in the United States in a 2002 production starring Olympia Dukakis in the role of Tremblay's mother. Tremblay himself named *Albertine en cinq temps* (Albertine in Five Times, 1984) as his personal favorite among his plays; it depicted five stages in the life of an old woman, with dialogue among the figures representing the phases of her life. The play was one of several that transcended the specific themes of Tremblay's earlier work.

In the early 2000s Tremblay branched out into the television field with scripts for a series called *Le coeur découvert* (The Open Heart), the first on Quebec television to explore on ongoing gay relationship. By that time his plays had been translated into more than 20 languages, including Spanish, Yiddish, and Polish, and had been staged at Canada's Stratford Festival among other prestigious international venues. Tremblay stirred up controversy in 2006 when he seemed to waver on the issue of Quebec separatism, criticizing the sovereignty movement for its focus on economic issues to the exclusion of cultural ones. He had already raised separatist eyebrows by accepting Canada's Governor General's Award in 1999, but he continued to express his devotion in general to the ideal of Quebec independence. Given his continued high rate of literary production and the growing international popularity of his plays, Tremblay's reputation as one of Quebec's—and Canada's—greatest cultural figures appeared secure.

Books

Dictionary of Literary Biography, volume 60, second series, Gale 1987.

Usmiani, Renate, *Michel Tremblay: A Critical Study*, Douglas & McIntyre, 1981.

Periodicals

American Theatre, July-August 2002.
Americas, September-October 1995.
Economist, April 22, 2006.
Gay & Lesbian Review Worldwide, May-June 2005.
Time International, December 16, 2002.
Times (London, England), February 12, 1990.

Online

"Michel Tremblay," Contemporary Authors Online, Gale, 2007, reproduced in Biography Resource Center, Thomson Gale, 2007, http://www.galenet.galegroup.com/servlet/BioRC (February 4, 2007).

"Michel Tremblay," Great Names of the French Canadian Community, http://www.franco.ca/edimages.grandspersonages/en/carte_j06.html (February 4, 2007).

"Tremblay, Michel," Canadian Theatre Encyclopedia, http://www.canadiantheatre.com (February 4, 2007).

"Tremblay, Michel," GLBTQ, http://www.glbtq.com/literature/tremblay_m.html (February 4, 2007). □

Sarah Trimmer

Sarah Trimmer (1741–1810) was one of the founders of the Christian Sunday school, as well as an apologist, a person who argues in defense or justification of something, such as a doctrine, policy, or institution. In the case of Trimmer, she wrote about Christianity. In the nineteenth century she became one of the most influential people involved in education and literature for children. She had so much influence on the style and content of children's books that she has been likened to such notable critics as John Locke, Jean-Jacques Rousseau, and John Newbury. Her books were so well circulated that she became one of the best selling authors of her time.

Early Love of Education and Books

Trimmer was born Sarah Kirby on January 6, 1741, in Ipswich, England, to Sarah Bull and John Joshua Kirby, a landscape artist. She had one brother. She attended a local private boarding school as a child, although she went as a day student. At the school she was taught all the subjects considered fitting for a woman in the 1740s. It was at home, from her father, that she learned theological and biblical studies, the foundation of her later works. John Kirby was famous for his knowledge of theological matters and although he had never been ordained, he was invited to join a local clerical club. In her education Trimmer was most fond of English and French literature and she studied both throughout her youth.

Trimmer also worked hard on translating literature from several different languages into English, and she enjoyed reading out loud, something she practiced quite often to improve her delivery. As there was no television or radio in the 1700s, reading aloud was a favorite form of entertainment. Besides these pursuits Trimmer also concentrated on improving the quality of her writing. She became so accomplished at all of these practices that when her brother went away to boarding school he often asked her to write English compositions, which he would then translate into Latin. Through these correspondences with her brother Trimmer improved her writing even more, and her parents began to suspect that she would make the writing arts her field.

Thrust Into Literary Circles

Trimmer moved to London with her parents in 1755 when her father was asked to tutor Prince George, the future King George III. The move proved to be helpful to young Trimmer because in London she was thrown into a social circle that included artists and writers such as Samuel Johnson, Sir Joshua Reynolds, William Hogarth, Dr. Gregory Sharpe, and Thomas Gainsborough. She became friends with Johnson in particular one day at a literary gathering.

Trimmer often attended literary meetings, but at this particular one the group was discussing John Milton's famous poem *Paradise Lost,* and Trimmer joined in. Impressed by her erudition, Johnson invited her to visit him the next day. She agreed immediately, and the next day the young woman went to visit the famous writer. At some point during their meeting Johnson gave her a copy of his own work, *Rambler,* a book of essays that he had written in the form of a journal. The work inspired Trimmer so much that she decided to create her own journal in its likeness. She kept her journal for 25 years.

Met and Married James Trimmer

In 1759, when Prince George no longer needed a tutor, Trimmer's father was appointed to be clerk of works at the palace. Trimmer moved with her family to Kew, where the appointment was located. It was there that Trimmer met James Trimmer. They were married in 1762, after which Trimmer moved to her new husband's estate at Old Brentford, near London. There she would raise her family of 12 children.

She became intensely interested in children's education early on in her marriage, and studied the developments of Dr. Andrew Bell in order to gain some advice on teaching her own children. All of her daughters were taught solely at home, while her sons started out there but went outside the home for their classical studies.

Began the Guardian of Education

She read all the books intended for her children; each child was different, so each was given a different set of books to read. She began to feel that the children's books of her time were sorely in need of improvement, so she created the *The Guardian of Education* in 1802. *The Guardian of Education* was a monthly magazine containing reviews of popular children's literature of the age, focusing mainly on those with religious content that were suitable for young impressionable readers. The magazine became an instant hit with parents everywhere.

Trimmer believed in *The Guardian* for several reasons. She felt that children were the ones who could bring about social change, so she wanted to educate them to do the best they could for the future, and watching what they were exposed to was one way to ensure that their minds were formed correctly. It was in the eighteenth century that children began to be seen as a national resource, and Trimmer believed that hope for the country rested on the shoulders of the young. For this reason Trimmer wanted to ensure that poor children received a good education just as the rich ones did. She helped by writing blurbs about the books with the intention of directing children into lives filled with morality, education, and piety.

Wrote Article for *Edinburgh Review*

Trimmer continued to use Dr. Bell's methods of instruction, and wrote an article that was published in the *Edinburgh Review,* discussing how Bell's ideas could be used to help the Anglican Church spread its doctrines. This article led to the creation of the National Society for Promoting the Education of the Poor in the Principles of the Established Church. And the article led her to write educational texts specifically for children. Her first book, published in 1780, was *Easy Introduction to the Knowledge of Nature.*

Next she revised and published *The Ladder to Learning: A collection of fables; arranged progressively in words of one, two, and three syllables; with original morals.* It was written by someone else, but Trimmer took on the task of revising the work. One of the biggest changes she made was to organize the text into sections according to reading difficulty. She determined the level of difficulty by the number of syllables in the words in the text. It took a lot of work for Trimmer to redo the text, but she felt it was worthwhile as a tool for teaching young children how to read. She chose this work to revise because each story had a moral lesson that her children could try out in the nursery.

Continued to Write for Children's Edification

Trimmer had earlier complained about Edward Baldwin when he attempted to improve on the morals to be found in Aesop's fables. In *The Guardian of Education* she had written how these stories now seemed forced and overly preachy. When she went about updating *The Ladder to Learning* she kept this in mind, making changes that simplified the texts and clarified the stories.

She also wrote *Easy Lessons for Young Children, The Charity School Spelling Book,* and *Fabulous Histories: Designed for the Instruction of Children, respecting their Treatment of Animals.* The last one is her most lasting book. It was later renamed *The History of the Robins,* and is still being published in the early twenty-first century. The book has stories about the robins Pecksy, Flapsy, Robin, and Dick, and also a story about a learned pig. According to the Bartleby's website, "Even though the story is unflinchingly didactic, it has everywhere naturalness and charm. Its earnestness is so simple, and the author's own interest in the narrative so clear, that age has not destroyed its individuality." Because she wrote for rather than about children, she held a power during her lifetime that other children's writers did not possess. Trimmer died on December 15, 1810.

Books

Dictionary of Literary Biography, Volume 158: British Reform Writers, 1789–1832, Gary Kelly, editor, Gale Group, 1996.

Online

"Children's Books: Sarah Trimmer," *Bartleby's,* http://www .bartleby.com-221-1613.html (January 2, 2007).

"Sarah Trimmer," *Ask.com,* http://www.spartacus.schoolnet.co .uk-EDtrimmer.htm (January 2, 2007).

"Sarah Trimmer," *CTS,* http://www.cts.dmu.ac.uk-AnaServer ?hockliffe+478+hoccview.anv (January 2, 2007). □

V

Suzanne Valadon

French artist Suzanne Valadon (1865–1938) was an artist's model before becoming a respected painter herself. Part of a circle of artists living and working in Paris's Montmartre neighborhood at the turn of the twentieth century, Valadon was one of the most notable female artists of the period. Valadon is also remembered for her many love affairs and as the mother of prominent French painter Maurice Utrillo.

Worked During Childhood

Valadon was born Marie Clémentine Valadon on September 23, 1865, in the small town of Bessines, located in northeastern France. (Later in life, Valadon claimed her date of birth was July 23, 1867, although this date is not supported by records.) Her mother, Madeleine Valadon, worked as a sewing maid; the identity of her father was not known. At the age of five, Valadon relocated to Paris with her mother. She attended a convent school for a few years before taking a job in a milliner's workshop at age 11. Valadon also worked as a funeral wreath maker, a vegetable seller, and a waitress while still a child.

When Valadon was a teenager, she befriended some artists living in the Montmartre neighborhood of Paris, a bustling artist's community. These artists helped Valadon get a job as an acrobat at the Mollier circus. Here, artist Berthe Morisot painted the young Valadon as a tightrope walker. In March of 1880, Valadon fell from a trapeze while practicing her act and injured her back. After several weeks she essentially recovered, but remained unable to perform in a circus for the remainder of her life due to the injury. However, her brief stint with the circus remained one of her fondest memories.

Was Artists' Model and Lover

After Valadon recovered from her back injury in 1880, she caught the eye of painter Pierre Puvis de Chavannes. This began Valadon's career as an artist's model. For the next seven years, Valadon posed for several of Puvis's paintings and was presumed to have been sexually involved with him. Writing in *Suzanne Valadon: Mistress of Montmartre*, June Rose noted that "her employers assumed the right to make love to their girls," and the career of model was at that time a somewhat scandalous one. Valadon also sat for other major Impressionist painters, including Auguste Renoir and Henri de Toulouse-Lautrec. Some of the more notable paintings featuring Valadon include Puvis's 1884–1886 piece *Sacred Wood* and Toulouse-Lautrec's 1889 *The Hangover*.

As an artists' model, Valadon became an active member of the artistic community of Montmartre. She shortened her name to "Maria" and became a regular at the famed tavern Lapin-Agile as well as the early cabaret *Le Chat Noir*. During this time in her life, Valadon made a name for herself as a feisty, vivacious girl, known for stunts such as sliding down the banister at a popular club while wearing only a mask. In 1881 Valadon began a relationship with Spaniard Miguel Utrillo. On December 26, 1883, Valadon gave birth on to an illegitimate son, Maurice Utrillo, who later became a renowned painter in his own right. Valadon herself seemed uncertain as to who the father of her child was; Utrillo formally acknowledged the boy as his own in 1891, but several other possible fathers have been suggested, including Puvis, Renoir, and another young Paris artist named

Boissy. Valadon gave her young son to her mother to raise, returning to work as a model.

From Model to Painter

Valadon's first known works, a pastel called *Self-Portrait* and a drawing of her mother called *The Grandmother,* date from 1883. During the mid- to late-1880s, Valadon produced many drawings and pastels of people and of street scenes. Her artistic endeavors were assisted by Toulouse-Lautrec, for whom she often modeled and with whom she had a lengthy affair. Valadon worked to hone her skills by observing the techniques of the artists who painted her, becoming a fully self-taught artist over the years. In 1890 she became friends with painter Edgar Degas. After seeing some of Valadon's work, Degas encouraged her efforts to become an artist, buying some of her pieces and helping her get her career started. Due to encouragement from Degas, in 1894 Valadon became the first woman to show at the Société Nationale des Beaux-Arts, a major French artistic accomplishment.

All of Valadon's early works were drawings executed in pencil or pastel. In the early 1890s she commenced working in oils, producing her first paintings. One of these first oils, dating from 1893, was of composer Erik Satie. Valadon and Satie had an intense though short-lived romantic involvement. Satie proposed to Valadon, but she turned him down; Rose noted that "at that stage in her life, her love affairs seemed to pass over her like sunshine." After the affair with Satie ended, Valadon's involvement with Montmartre stockbroker Paul Mousis intensified, and the pair married in 1896. This marriage provided Valadon with financial stability, enabling her to quit modeling and dedicate herself to drawing and painting full-time.

Artistic Growth and Personal Turmoil

Valadon's unique style became more apparent once she had the freedom to practice her craft unfettered by financial concerns. Because Valadon was untrained, she approached art with a different perspective than the other artists of her day. Foremost among Valadon's subjects were portraits of all types and female nudes. In the former genre, she captured an intensity of feeling and depth in her subjects with bold, heavy strokes. In *Great Women Masters of Art*, Jordi Vigué noted of Valadon's treatment of the female nude that "she reinvented [it] to a certain degree, rendering it with notable sincerity, frankness, and energy."

Following her marriage to Mousis, Valadon left the city for a home in the country. Here, she tried to balance her new duties as conventional wife with those of a working artist. In the late 1890s Valadon produced less work of artistic value, and made only a few sales, primarily to fellow artists. However, two of her engravings appeared at a large London show put on by the International Society of Painters, Sculptors, and Engravers in 1898, probably due to the influence of Degas.

Valadon's son, Maurice, did not adjust well to country life. He completed primary school outside of Paris, but as a teenager attended school in Montmartre. He did well with his studies, but began to develop a problem with alcohol.

Valadon turned her attention to her son's wellbeing, neglecting her fledgling artistic career; however, Maurice became progressively more unstable. In the early 1900s, Valadon began encouraging Maurice to paint as a means of therapy. Maurice exhibited artistic talent, but his mental problems did not cease. In 1904 Maurice was committed to a mental hospital for treatment of alcoholism and other problems. Valadon continued his art lessons after his release a few months later.

A New Lover

Valadon's relationship with husband Mousis was marred by problems nearly from the start. In 1906 Valadon met a friend of her son's, Andre Utter, who was himself a young painter. Utter was intrigued by Valadon, and three years later the two began an affair. Valadon was by then 44 to Utter's 23. Prodded by Utter, Valadon returned more seriously to her art, producing a significant number of paintings for the first time in years. Among these works were the definitive *Summer, After the Bath,* and *Adam and Eve.* This last painting, modeled on Valadon and her young lover, was the first piece executed by a female artist to show a nude man and woman together. As the relationship between Valadon and Utter intensified, she at first tried to hide it from her husband. However, she became careless and Mousis found out, breaking off the marriage. He officially divorced Valadon in March of 1910.

After the dissolution of her marriage, Valadon continued to paint in earnest, as well as producing a lesser number of drawings and engravings. In 1910 she painted her first landscape and her first nude self-portrait. Despite these advances, Valadon was beginning to be overshadowed by her tumultuous artist son and his contemporaries, including Picasso. Over the next few years, Valadon, her lover, and her son lived together in the Montmartre on the proceeds of their artwork. When World War I erupted in 1914, Utter volunteered for military service. He and Valadon married so that she could receive an allowance from the military as a soldier's wife.

World War I and Beyond

In 1915 Valadon's mother died at the age of 84. Valadon's son was called up and subsequently rejected for military service, and was again committed to a mental institution at the end of that year. Caught up in these matters, Valadon painted little; however, among the works she produced was a somewhat more traditional portrait of Mauricia Coquiot, wife of an art critic and aspiring dealer. Valadon's first one-woman exhibit also occurred in 1915, although the show produced practically no sales. The following year Valadon commenced a series of paintings using a young model with whom she tried to arrange a marriage for her son. Although the marriage did not occur, Valadon produced many drawings using the young model. In 1917 Utter received a bullet wound and Valadon traveled to the country to be closer to him. She remained outside of Paris for some time, painting landscapes. After the war ended in 1918, both Utter and Valadon returned to the city. Utter marketed his works, as well as those of Valadon and Maurice Utrillo, most successfully those of the latter.

However, Valadon had reached her peak as an artist. She produced paintings and drawings at a rapid pace, and in 1920 was elected to the Salon d'Automne. That December, Valadon exhibited alone at a Paris gallery to good critical reception. For the remainder of her career, Valadon would show frequently to critical acclaim but only moderate sales. Her increasingly unstable son's artworks consistently overshadowed those of his mother commercially.

Later Life and Legacy

In 1924 Valadon signed a contract with the art gallery Bernheim-Jeune, enabling her to again live in financial comfort. She purchased a country estate called Saint-Bernard and spent much of her time there. However, tensions among Valadon, Utter, and Utrillo continued, fueled somewhat by Utrillo's continuing dominance professionally. By the end of the 1920s, Utter had taken up drinking and womanizing. Valadon continued to produce works, showing at a major retrospective in 1929. Many works from this period depict her beloved pets, much as her early drawings had shown her mother and son. Another major retrospective of Valadon's work was held in 1932.

Through the 1930s Valadon's health slowly declined. In 1935 she entered the hospital for complications of diabetes and kidney dysfunction. That same year, her son married and left his mother's home. Utter had also moved out, although he and Valadon never divorced. Valadon's life continued to be filled with friends, visitors, and art despite the exodus of her family. In 1937 the prestigious Musée du Luxembourg purchased three of Valadon's major paintings as well as many of her drawings. Rose noted in her book that Valadon craved "recognition as an artist . . . not personal fame."

On April 7, 1938, Valadon was painting at her easel when she unexpectedly suffered a stroke. She died at the hospital just hours later, at the age of 72. A complete survey of her work totals over 475 paintings, nearly 275 drawings, and 31 etchings; this does not include many works destroyed or lost over the years. For years after her death, Valadon's reputation remained closely linked to her son's; however, in the latter part of the twentieth century, increasing interest in the works of women artists such as Valadon led to an increased appreciation of her life, art, and contributions.

Books

Rose, June, *Suzanne Valadon: Mistress of Montmartre,* St. Martin's, 1999.
Vigue, Jordi, *Great Women Masters of Art,* Watson-Guptill, 2002.
Warnod, Jeanine, *Suzanne Valadon,* Crown, 1981. □

Wang Guangmei

Former Chinese first lady Wang Guangmei (1921–2006) lived through many of the most turbulent events of twentieth-century Chinese history.

Born into Well-Off Family

Wang Guangmei (in Chinese names, the family name is given first) was born in Beijing on September 26, 1921. Her family was old and distinguished, and her father, Wang Huaiqing, was a business executive who served as a senior official in the government of the Republic of China. Her mother was a teacher. Wang became a fluent speaker of English, French, and Russian. After studies at an American missionary school, she attended Fu Jen Catholic University in Beijing, gaining a master's degree in physics by 1945. She was one of the first people in China to do advanced study in the field of atomic physics. After the upheaval of the Cultural Revolution in the 1960s and 1970s, Wang's brother, Guangying, returned to the business world as an executive at Hong Kong's Everbright electronics firm.

As an educated and idealistic young person in the 1940s, Wang supported the revolutionary Communist forces of future Chinese leader Mao Tse-tung, which waged guerrilla warfare against the Chinese government. Wang accompanied Mao to the Communist Party headquarters in remote Yan'an, where she served as an interpreter in unsuccessful peace talks, mediated by U.S. Gen. George Marshall, between Mao and Chinese leader Chiang Kai-shek. While there she met Liu Shaoqi, a close associate of Mao

who had been with the Red Army on its Long March retreat of 1934 and 1935. Liu was nearly twice Wang's age and had already been married four (or five) times. He asked her to come and talk to him at his hideout in a cave, suggesting that she become his secretary. Soon after that the two were married in a ceremony that consisted of the sharing of a wedding cake among Liu, Wang, Mao, and future Chinese premier Zhou En-lai.

In 1949 the Communists seized power from Chiang Kai-shek's government. Mao, as chairman of the Chinese Communist Party, was supreme leader, and the right-hand men from his long military campaign were installed in top positions in the government, with Liu becoming president in 1959 and frequently undertaking diplomatic missions to foreign governments. Wang, often described as sophisticated and glamorous, took naturally to her new role as first lady. She accompanied Liu on trips to Pakistan, Afghanistan, Burma, and Indonesia.

The last of these trips caused controversy in China, instigated partly by Mao's wife, Jiang Qing, who was said to be jealous of Wang's sophisticated ways. Wang resisted the drab military-style clothing favored in Communist China, and sometimes wore strings of pearls despite a specific request not to do so from Jiang Qing. On her trip to Indonesia she wore a tight-fitting dress to a banquet hosted by the Indonesian leader Sukarno, well-known as a womanizer, and on Sukarno's return visit to Beijing she was seen lighting his cigarette.

Embroiled in Power Struggle

The implications of incidents such as these went far beyond mere celebrity gossip, for China in the early 1960s was turning into a power struggle between Liu's moderate faction and the radicals, led by Mao but temporarily suffering in prestige due to the catastrophic failure of Mao's Great Leap Forward program of collectivization and the famine that resulted, killing some 28 million Chinese. At Liu's urging, Wang became involved in political activities. She was part of a work team that investigated corruption in the Chinese countryside, and in the early days of the Cultural Revolution of 1966, when Mao left the reins of government in Liu's hands during an absence from Beijing, Liu deputized Wang to head a team attempting to restore order at Quinghua University.

The move was disastrous, for it soon transpired that Mao was using the Cultural Revolution movement to eliminate his political rivals. When Mao returned to Beijing, he let it be known that student gangs would face no punishment if they attacked Wang's team. Wang was denounced as a counterrevolutionary, and there were also accusations that she was an American spy. At a rally in June of 1966, 300,000 students gathered in the university's main square for a "struggle session" aimed at Wang. She was seized and draped with a necklace of table-tennis balls that mocked her fondness for pearls. Wang kept her dignity, telling her persecutors that it was the wrong time of year for summer clothes. The event was remembered as one of the defining visual images of the Cultural Revolution.

At that point Wang was seen as a surrogate for her husband, who was still untouchable to the students. But soon Liu was removed from the Chinese presidency and denounced as the "No. 1 Capitalist Roader" and as a "lackey of imperialism." Wang was placed under house arrest in the Forbidden City. In 1967 both Liu and Wang were arrested, becoming among the first victims of the repeated purges of professionals that marked the Cultural Revolution years. They were paraded before crowds in Tiananmen Square, forced into humiliating, submissive positions, and beaten in front of their four young children. Taken to separate interrogation rooms and then to separate prisons, they never saw each other again. Liu died, probably from untreated pneumonia, in an unheated prison cell in 1969.

In 1971 Wang's children (who had themselves been imprisoned) asked Mao directly whether they could see their parents. They were told that their father was dead, but that they could see their mother. They found her in a weakened state, barely able to stand, wearing an old army jacket and staring blankly in front of her. It was only then that she learned of her husband's death. Reportedly Wang herself had been marked for execution but was spared by Chou En-lai, who had shared her wedding cake 30 years before. After Mao's death in 1976, Jiang Qing and her radical "Gang of Four" were deposed, but it was not until 1978 that Wang was released and allowed to retrieve her husband's ashes and bury them. At his request, she scattered them at sea—like those, he had said, of Friedrich Engels, one of the founders of Communist thought.

Received Compensation from Chinese Government

In 1980, although deceased, Liu was officially rehabilitated by the Chinese government, and Wang received monetary compensation for her years of imprisonment. She witnessed the trials of Jiang Qing and the rest of the Gang of Four, attributing her problems, at least in interviews, to Jian Qing rather than to Mao himself. Meeting Mao's daughters later in life, she was gracious to them. Wang returned to China's newly revived academic sector, becoming the director of the Chinese Academy of Social Sciences. She also reentered political life as a member of the Standing Committee of the National Committee of the Chinese People's Political Consultative Conference, or Politburo.

Much of the last part of Wang's life was devoted to charitable good works. In 1996 she sold off a collection of antiques that had belonged to her own mother in order to help poverty-stricken mothers in China. The collection had been seized from Wang during her imprisonment but was never destroyed and had been returned to her after she was freed. Some of the antiques were rare historical specimens; one ivory brush-holder dated back to the Song Dynasty (960–1279). "I would be reluctant to part with what my mother left me without a reason," Wang explained, according to the *International Herald Tribune,* but "my heart aches even more when I see impoverished mothers. It shouldn't be like this. The country led by our Communist Party cannot let families be this destitute."

The auction resulted in a new children's charity called Project Happiness, founded by Wang with proceeds from the auction of more than 500,000 Chinese yuan (about $62,500). By 2006 the charity had disbursed about $387,500 on a total of 389 projects that involved 154,000 families. As chairperson of the charity's executive board, Wang remained immersed in her work until the end of her life. She also made contributions as an artist, donating a calligraphic scroll called "Present Love by Spreading Morals and Conducting Good Deeds" that sold for $25,000 at auction. In 2006, a month before her death, she was nominated for a China Poverty Eradication Award.

Wang died in Beijing on October 13, 2006, at the age of 85. Her funeral was attended by Jia Qinglin, the fourth most important figure in the Chinese Communist hierarchy, but the excesses of the Cultural Revolution were still a sensitive topic in China, and her death was not widely publicized by the government. Wang's son, Liu Yuan, had by that time become political commissar of China's Academy of Military Sciences, a post roughly corresponding to a cabinet ministry in the United States. Her daughter, Ting Liu, attended the Harvard Business School and became president of the corporate finance consultant Asia Link Group.

Books

Salisbury, Harrison, *The New Emperors: China in the Era of Mao and Deng,* Little, Brown, 1992.

Periodicals

Guardian (London, England), October 20, 2006.
International Herald Tribune, October 16, 2006.
New York Times, October 17, 2006.
Seattle Times, October 22, 2006.
Times (London, England), October 17, 2006.
Washington Post, October 18, 2006.
Xinhua News Agency, July 5, 2006. □

Dorothy West

During a long writing career that began when she was a teenager, Dorothy West (1907–1998) wrote two novels and numerous short stories, and worked as a magazine editor and newspaper journalist. She is best remembered for her first novel *The Living is Easy* (1948), as well as for being a member of the Harlem Renaissance, a movement comprised of African-American artists and intellectuals that emerged in the early part of the twentieth century.

D orothy West was born on June 2, 1907, in Boston, Massachusetts, to Isaac and Rachel Benson West. Though she was the couple's only child, West grew up among the numerous relatives from her mother's side of the family. Her mother, who was born in South Carolina, was one of 22 children.

West's life and career would be greatly influenced by her parents. Rachel West was a beautiful woman with a sharp sense of humor, a quality that would later inform West's novels, short stories and essays. In addition, Rachel West raised her daughter to be proud and self-confident. Isaac West, a former Virginia slave who was freed when he was seven years old, was an extremely ambitious man. He became a thriving produce merchant in Boston and also ran a restaurant. Like her father, West demonstrated a strong will to succeed. "The gifts he had given me were endurance and strength of will," West later wrote in an essay that was included in *The Richer, The Poorer: Stories, Sketches and Reminiscences,* a collection of West's writings released in 1998.

Enjoyed Advantages of Affluence

Because of Isaac's success, the Wests became one of Boston's richest African-American families, easily commingling with the city's upper middle class black society. Moreover, the family developed strong connections within the African-American social and artistic elite. Acquaintances included composer Harry T. Burleigh and writer James Weldon Johnson. Dorothy West herself developed a close relationship with her cousin, Helene Johnson, who would later become a famous black poet.

Affluence afforded West a privileged childhood. She spent her summers at the family's vacation house on Martha's Vineyard, an island located off Massachusetts where many rich people had summer homes. Her parents also provided her with the best education. She received private tutoring at home, starting when she was two years old. One of her tutors was Bessie Trotter, who was the sister of Monroe Nathan Trotter, the editor of the *Boston Guardian.* She received most of her elementary education at the Martin School, located in Boston's Mission Hill District. Later she attended the exclusive, prestigious Girls' Latin School, where she was an excellent student. Following her graduation in 1923, she attended Boston University.

Began Writing at an Early Age

Such advantages were enhanced by West's own precociousness. She entered the second grade at the Farragut School in Boston when she was four years old. She was only 10 when she entered the Girls' Latin School. Her precocity extended to her writing. She wrote her first story when she was seven years old. By the time she was a teenager she had won several writing competitions sponsored by local newspapers. In particular, when West was 14 years old her short story "Promise and Fulfillment" won the weekly fiction writing contest held by the *Boston Post.*

In 1926 her story "The Typewriter" placed second in a contest held by *Opportunity* magazine, a New York City-based periodical published by the National Urban League. In addition, the magazine published the story, which helped start West's professional writing career. West went to New York to receive the second-place award, and the trip turned out to be a life-altering occasion.

West was so enchanted by the New York environment that she decided to make the city her home. With her cousin, Helene Johnson, who accompanied West on the trip, she moved into the Harlem YMCA. Once settled, West enrolled in Columbia University, where she studied philosophy and journalism. She also met and became friends with African-American writer Zora Neale Huston, who encouraged West.

Became Part of the Harlem Renaissance

Through Huston, West met other talented black artists, including painters, musicians and writers, who were living in New York City's Harlem section. Among the notables in this circle was poet Langston Hughes. Other members of the artistic community included writers Arna Bontemps, Countee Cullen, Alain Locke, Claude McKay and Wallace Thurman. All of the artists formed what would come to be known as the Harlem Renaissance. West was the emerging movement's youngest member, and for that reason, Hughes nicknamed her "The Kid."

West also developed alliances with influential white writers such as H. L. Mencken, Carl Van Vechten, and Fannie Hurst. Both Van Vechten and Hurst became West's mentors. Despite these strong connections, West had trouble publishing her works. At the time, her stories, which dealt with black themes, had only a limited appeal for contemporary white readers. Also, few publications geared toward black audiences existed. But she did manage to publish two stories in the 1920s ("An Unimportant Man" [1928] and "Prologue to a Life" [1929]), which appeared in the black periodical *The Saturday Evening Quill.*

Became Involved in Acting and Film

Starting in 1927, to supplement her writing income, West became involved in acting. That year she found work as an extra in the original stage production of George Gershwin's opera *Porgy and Bess.* She stayed with the cast for several years, performing on Broadway and then in London.

By 1932, nearly broke and discouraged by publishers' repeated rejections, West joined a group of 20 other black artists and intellectuals, which included Hughes, who traveled to Russia to make a film about racism in the United States. The film was to be titled *Black and White.* However, when the group reached Russia, the members learned that the production had been canceled. No reason was ever provided. Compounding the problem, group members were accused of being Communist sympathizers. Despite the disappointment and accusations, West liked Russia and stayed there for more than a year. Hughes remained with her. Eventually, West asked Hughes to marry her, but he declined. She finally left Russia to return home in 1933 when she learned that her father had died.

Launched Literary Magazines

Times were hard for West when she arrived back in the United States. The country was in the midst of the Great Depression, her father's death had followed the failure of his business, and she was broke. Further, she was depressed about the apparent failure of her writing career. However, rather then succumb to despair, she summoned her inner strength. In New York City in 1934, seeking to make a new start for herself, West used her meager savings of $40 to found a literary magazine called *Challenge,* to showcase black writing talent. Serving as the magazine's editor, West sought to recapture some of the excitement of the Harlem Renaissance, which had fallen apart during the Depression. She used the magazine as a vehicle to present the works of older black writers as well as to introduce young, emerging black writers such as Richard Wright, who would later gain fame with his highly acclaimed novels *Native Son* and *Black Boy.*

The first two issues included works by established writers like Bontemps, Cullen, Hughes, Hurston, Johnson, and McKay. But West would be disappointed in her effort to introduce new talent. While she received many submissions from young black writers, she felt that most lacked sufficient literary quality to merit publication. As a result, she and her magazine were criticized for a seemingly tame approach to new black writing. West persevered with the magazine for four years, producing six issues, before the publication folded in April of 1937.

Undaunted, she began another publishing venture that same year, teaming up with Wright to create a periodical called *New Challenge.* But it only lasted for one issue, which was published in 1937. This sole publication was notable for its inclusion of an essay by Wright ("Blueprint for Negro Writing"), as well as the first published work of Ralph Ellison, who would later write the groundbreaking novel *Invisible Man.*

Following the failure of her magazines, West sought regular employment, and for a time she served as a welfare relief worker in Harlem. It was an eye-opening experience for West, as she was horrified by the living conditions that many black families had to endure. She distilled her work experience into a short story titled "Mammy," which was published in *Opportunity.* In 1940 West took a job with the Works Projects Administration Writer's Project. While working with the agency, she wrote many more stories, but none of them were published. However, that same year she began a long association with the *New York Daily News,* and for the next two decades she contributed more than 24 short stories to the newspaper.

Returned to Martha's Vineyard

In 1947 West went back to her family's vacation home on Martha's Vineyard, where she would live for the rest of her life. Once she settled in, she started work on her first novel, *The Living is Easy,* which was published in 1948. A partly autobiographical work, the novel involved upwardly mobile African Americans and the problems they had assimilating. The work garnered praise from prominent literary critics such as Seymour Krim of the *New York Times,* and it was a modest financial success. West had hoped to earn more money from the book through its planned serialization in the *Ladies' Home Journal.* However, the magazine called off the project due to the negative reaction of white readers. "I was going to get what at that time was a lot of money. But weeks went by before my agent called again," West recalled in a 1995 interview for *Publishers Weekly.* "The Journal had decided to drop the book because a survey indicated that they would lose many subscribers in the South."

Financially, the cancellation was a hard blow for West. In need of a job, she found work with the local newspaper, the *Martha's Vineyard Gazette.* Amazingly enough, West, a writer of substantial stature, was hired to be a billing clerk. But her literary talent proved too hard to contain, and she would later become one of the paper's most popular writers.

Wrote Second Novel

During this period, West turned back to a book manuscript that she had started in the 1920s. She had been revising it over the course of several decades, both in her head and on paper, but she did not entertain any great ambitions of trying to have it published. Indeed, the book would have most likely remained unfinished if it had not been for the encouragement of Jacqueline Kennedy Onassis, who had a summer home on Martha's Vineyard and knew of West through her work with the *Gazette.*

At the time, Onassis was working with Doubleday, a major publishing house, as a book editor. When one of West's friends told Onassis about the novel in progress, Onassis met with West and told her that she wanted to have Doubleday publish the work. Encouraged by the interest, West began working on the novel again, this time with greater determination. The novel, titled *The Wedding,* was eventually published in 1995. West dedicated it to Onassis. Unfortunately, Onassis died in 1994 before it was released.

Set on Martha's Vineyard, *The Wedding* related the multigenerational tale of a well-to-do African-American family. As with a lot of West's writings, the book provided a somewhat satirical look at affluent blacks and related social and racial issues. The book proved popular and, for the most part, received good critical notices. As a result, it renewed the public's interest in West, and that same year Doubleday published *The Richer, The Poorer: Stories, Sketches and Reminiscences,* a collection of West's previously unpublished short stories and essays. As with her novels, pieces in the collection addressed class- and color-consciousness among upper-middle-class blacks.

In 1997, two years after the novel's release, in celebration of West's ninetieth birthday, a party was held on Martha's Vineyard to honor West's life and career accomplishments. The event attracted many celebrities, including then-First Lady Hillary Rodham Clinton. In 1998 Oprah Winfrey, the well-known television personality and noted book enthusiast, adapted *The Wedding* as a two-part television miniseries. Aired on ABC in February of that year, the adaptation starred Halle Berry, Lynn Whitfield, and Michael Warren.

Died in Boston

West died later that year, on August 16, in a Boston Hospital. She was 91 years old. She had never married or had children. At the time, it was noted that she was the last surviving member of the Harlem Renaissance.

Following her death, collections of her works were released, including *The Dorothy West Martha's Vineyard* (2001), which included some of her newspaper columns written for the *Martha's Vineyard Gazette,* and *Where the Wild Grape Grows: Selected Writings, 1930–1950* (2005). Most of West's papers have been archived at the Mugar Memorial Library at Boston University. Others are included in the James Weldon Johnson Collection at Yale University.

In a posthumous appreciation of West, written for *Poets & Writers* ("Dorothy West 1907–1998: A Tribute to the Long Legacy of 'The Kid' " [1998: volume 26 issue 6]), poet E. Ethelbert Miller commented that West's "essays and fiction attest to the fact that she was a writer who traveled the distance, exploring with dignity, insight, and elegance the important issues of race, color, and class within the African-American community."

Books

Contemporary Black Biography, Volume 54, Thomson Gale, 2006.
Notable Black American Women, Book 1, Gale Research, 1992.

Periodicals

Poets & Writers, volume 26, issue 6, 1998.
Publishers Weekly, July 3, 1995.

Online

"Dorothy West," *20th Century American Women Writers,* http://www.faculty.ccc.edu/wr-womenauthors/pinkver/west.htm (February 1, 2007).
"Dorothy West Biography (1907–1998)," *Biography.com,* http://www.biography.com/search/article.do?id = 205632 (February 1, 2007).
"Oak Bluffs Writer Dorothy West Dies-August 16, 1998," *Mass Moments,* http://www.massmoments.org/moment.cfm?mid = 238 (February 2, 2007).
"West, Dorothy," *American National Biography Online,* http://www.anb.org/articles/16/16-03513.html (February 2, 2007). □

Opal Whiteley

The life of American author Opal Whiteley (1897–1992) was a tragic one, shrouded in mystery. About the reputation of her best-known work, however, there is no mystery at all: her nature diaries, titled *The Story of Opal,* reached bestseller lists when they were published in 1920, and found appreciative new audiences when they were rediscovered toward the twentieth century's end.

Everything about the literary genesis of *The Story of Opal* was strange. The manuscript consisted of many thousands of tiny, torn-up pieces when Whiteley first brought them to a magazine editor in a hat box. The writing itself was unusual. Seemingly without literary models, Whiteley had written beautiful observations of nature that seemed to imbue plants and animals with individual souls—and she had purportedly done it at age six. Stranger still was the personal story Whiteley told: she was not, she claimed, Opal Whiteley, the daughter of a Pacific Northwest lumber worker, but the offspring of a member of the French royal family. Sustained efforts by several investigators have failed to produce definitive accounts of Whiteley's life. In the historical saga of Opal Whiteley, truth and fiction have combined to exert a lasting fascination over readers.

Raised in Lumber Community

According to most accounts, Opal Whiteley was born in Colton, Washington, on December 11, 1897. She was raised as the first of five children of Ed and Lizzie Whiteley, who soon moved to Cottage Grove, Oregon, in search of work in the area's growing lumbering industry. Whiteley's parents said that she had been born at home, and no birth certificate for her was ever recorded, one piece of what later became a complex puzzle. Another was Opal's dark skin and black hair, which gave her a somewhat Mediterranean appearance, but pictures of Lizzie Whiteley's ancestors reveal some with the same traits. As a child, Whiteley wandered freely in what was still a heavily forested area, and by all evidence she was a child who had an unusual rapport with wild animals and a deep love for the natural world.

She was also precocious, reading and reportedly reciting Bible passages by age three. According to Steve McQuiddy, writing in "The Fantastic Tale of Opal Whiteley," Opal's maternal grandmother described her as "always a queer girl. When she wasn't chattering or asking questions, or reading or writing, she would be looking at nothing with big eyes, in what some people call a 'brown study,' but what I call inattention and absentmindedness." She was a dreamer, but there was a scientific streak to her mind as well; she collected thousands of specimens of insects, plans, and rocks.

By the time she was a teenager, Opal had become something of a local celebrity. She joined a group called Junior Christian Endeavor, and under its auspices began to give lectures. In some of them, she connected natural processes to the biblical story of Christ's resurrection. She shared her vast knowledge of the area's natural resources, and parents who brought their children to see her came away impressed themselves. Sometimes she would take children to a park and have them pledge friendship to a tree. She became the Oregon state superintendent of Junior Christian Endeavor in 1915, and she was profiled in the Cottage Grove *Sentinel* by editor Elbert Bede, one of the many writers who later tried to unravel the mysteries of her life. He wrote, according to McQuiddy, that "she is a product of the Oregon outdoors who knows that outdoors almost as well as the One who made it."

In 1916 Opal visited the University of Oregon in Eugene. Although she had not finished high school, she was admitted to the university after faculty members with whom she met were stunned by her knowledge of the natural sciences. Opal was remembered well by students who went to college with her. She was what would later be called a flower child, wearing her hair in long braids and speaking of the necessity of universal love. "She was New Age before New Age ever came along," said Opal investigator and editor Benjamin Hoff, according to McQuiddy. She attended a lecture by paranormal speaker Jean Morris Ellis and afterwards wrote in her notebook, "Our imagination is the instrument of reality."

Publicized Lectures with Posters

Library officials at the university marveled at Whiteley's rapid reading pace, but her academic career was checkered. She had a habit of accumulating large lists of unreturned library books all over Oregon, and after the deaths of her mother and maternal grandfather on successive days in 1917, she became withdrawn and her schoolwork became more erratic. She drifted away from classes and began giving nature lectures with a ten-cent admission charge, living in a small apartment in Eugene. She publicized these lectures with a poster that showed her in a white dress, with butterflies resting on her shoulders and on her long hair.

She posed for other pictures as well, one of them showing her as a Native American girl in a fringed skin, holding a fishing pole and two large fish. That picture was part of a publicity portfolio intended to launch the next phase of Whiteley's career: she headed for Los Angeles, fearlessly walking into the offices of directors and casting agents. This attempt to break into the movies came to nothing, however, and Whiteley returned to giving nature lectures. A woman of strong personal charm, she made friends among wealthy Southern Californians and among creative figures as she traveled in the Southwest.

The years of 1918 and 1919 remain a critical gap in Whiteley's biography. What is known is that she wrote a nature book for children called *The Fairyland Around Us,* and sold it in an old-fashioned way, by subscription, which would now be called advance order, to admirers and people who attended her lectures. In this way she raised $9,400 in funds, an amount that was sufficient to begin printing of the book but not to finish it. Whitely worked on the remaining copies by hand, pasting in and captioning thousands of illustrations, and she withdrew from contact with her family.

In 1919 she appeared in Boston, Massachusetts, at the offices of the venerable *Atlantic Monthly.* Her initial stated aim was to find a publisher for *The Fairlyland Around Us.* The magazine's editor, Ellery Sedgwick, told the story that he coaxed out of Whiteley the information that she had kept a diary as a girl, but Whiteley biographer Kathrine Beck presented a sequence of events in which Sedgwick was aware of a diary before the two ever met. In any event, Whiteley said that when she was seven she had written about her life in Oregon in a diary, often stored in a hollow log, that her sister had later torn up. She produced box of scraps, some of them containing only a single block capital letter written in crayon, and she spent eight months living at the home of Sedgwick's mother-in-law, assembling them like a jigsaw puzzle.

Book Became Bestseller

Whiteley's diary was serialized in the *Atlantic* and then published as a book in August of 1920 by the Atlantic Monthly Press. It was both compelling and unusual, and it was immediately successful. She named the animals in her life after figures from European literature and art; an example of her charming sense of humor was the pig Peter Paul Rubens, named for the Belgian artist who loved to paint figures of ample frame. Whiteley vividly communicated the emotion of her interactions with the world around her. "When I feel sad, I talk things over with my tree," she wrote. "I call him Michael Raphael. It is such a comfort to nestle up to Michael Raphael. He is a grand tree. He has an understanding soul." Not so understanding was the mother depicted in the diary, who sometimes beat Opal for minor transgressions. In some passages the book's syntax was odd but arresting, seeming as if it had originated in a language other than English.

The Story of Opal: The Journal of an Understanding Heart was a bestseller, by some accounts ranking behind only Sinclair Lewis's *Main Street* in sales for the year 1920. Almost as soon as the book appeared, however, charges began to appear that no child could have written it. Extensive investigations were launched by Bede, who thought that his small-town newspaper had a major scoop on how a major East Coast magazine had been duped, and also by Sedgwick, anxious to prove that it had not. The two men cooperated but also worked at cross purposes, and Oregonians who had known Whiteley earlier in her life soon tired of the questioning. The remaining members of Whiteley's family left Oregon and hid their identities, and a Harvard University student newspaper spoofed the entire controversy in a story about a Whiteley-like figure named Isette Likely.

More widely questioned even than the diary's authenticity were Whiteley's claims, expressed in the book's introduction and cryptically in the diary itself, that she had been adopted by the Whiteley family and that her true father was Henri d'Orléans, a naturalist and a relative of France's royal family. She had, she maintained, been born not in Washington, but in Rome, Italy. Her parents, whom she called her Angel Father and Angel Mother, had died (Henri d'Orléans died in India in 1901), and guardians had placed her with the Whiteley family. The first lines of a passage in the diary spelled out the name Henri d'Orléans. Many of the details in Whiteley's story seemed to accord with known facts, and Lizzie Whiteley had apparently occasionally indicated that Opal was adopted. However, University of Oregon psychology professor E. S. Conklin pointed to the frequent appearance of such a "foster-child fantasy" among individuals with difficult family backgrounds.

Whiteley lived for a time in New York and attempted to interest Sedgwick in more of her writings. She published a book of poems, *The Flower of Stars,* in 1923, and she had lost none of her ability to charm the financially well-off. With help from friends she traveled to England, where a fresh round of publicity and then controversy awaited her after her diary was published there. Members of the d'Orléans family and other European aristocrats at first accepted the story of her noble birth but later doubted it.

Gradually Whiteley fell out of the spotlight, and the story of her later years was a grim one. In the 1930s she turned up in India, in the Udaipur region where Henri d'Orléans had died, and lived as a houseguest of an Indian noble. British colonial authorities, however, forced her to leave the country after she and an Indian guru reportedly committed sexual indiscretions. The next sightings of Whiteley proved more disturbing; in 1948 she was living in London, in a small apartment crammed with books that she had snatched from the rubble of bombed buildings during World War II. Unable to afford basic nutrition, she had difficulty caring for herself. She insisted that her name was Françoise d'Orléans. Committed to Napsbury Hospital in suburban St. Albans, an institution for the mentally ill, she received visitors pleasantly and even poetically but objected vehemently to the use of the name Opal Whiteley. She died on February 16, 1992. During her lifetime she had been diagnosed as schizophrenic; Asperger's Syndrome has also been proposed as a possible cause for many of her behaviors.

Controversies over Whiteley's authorship of her diaries and over her background continued to rage during the later part of her life, and after it ended. Among her detractors was Bede, who summarized his findings in the 1954 book *The Fabulous Opal Whiteley.* He contended that Whiteley had written the diary shortly before approaching the *Atlantic Monthly,* and that the book, along with the story of her French parentage, was nothing more than an elaborate hoax. The most detailed investigations into Whiteley's work have been carried out by Benjamin Hoff, also author of *The Tao of Pooh.* He published Whiteley's diary, along with biography and commentary, as *The Singing Creek Where the Willows Grow: The Mystical Nature Diary of Opal Whiteley* in 1986. Hoff, arguing that Whiteley could not have forged the hundreds of thousands of diary scraps in the short time available to her before her trip to Boston, argued that it was genuine but that the story of Whiteley's background was a fantasy. Biographer Kathrine Beck, in *Opal: A Life of Enchantment, Mystery, and Madness* (2003), presented evidence on both sides of the controversy. As the dispute continues, *The Story of Opal* remains one of the most beloved children's books in American libraries. Her story has been made into a musical, *Opal* (1995), and the diaries were a basis for a cycle of songs recorded by vocalist Anne Hills.

Books

Beck, Kathrine, *Opal: A Life of Enchantment, Mystery, and Madness,* Viking, 2003.
Hoff, Benjamin, *The Singing Creek Where the Willows Grow: The Rediscovered Diary of Opal Whiteley,* Penguin, 1995.

Periodicals

Morning Call (Allentown, PA), June 9, 2006.
Publishers Weekly, January 17, 1994.
Seattle Times, March 3, 1996.

Online

Contemporary Authors Online, Gale, 2007, reproduced in Biography Resource Center, Thomson Gale, 2007, http://www.galenet.galegroup.com/servlet/BioRC (February 19, 2007)
"The Fantastic Tale of Opal Whiteley," http://www.intangible.org/Features/Opal/OpalHome.html (February 19, 2007).
The Opal Whiteley Memorial, http://www.efn.org/~opal/ (February 19, 2007). □

Narcissa Whitman

In 1836, American missionary Narcissa Whitman (1808–1847) became the first woman of European heritage to cross the Rocky Mountains into the western United States. She and her husband were on an

arduous journey westward, hoping to bring Christianity to Native American tribes in the Columbia Plateau region in what is present-day Washington state. They built one of the first permanent settlements in the area, but 11 years later their mission was attacked after long-simmering tensions with the Cayuse erupted into violence, and both were killed.

The daughter of a carpenter, Whitman was born Narcissa Prentiss on March 14, 1808, in Prattsburgh, New York, and was one of nine children in her family. The Prentisses were Presbyterians, but at the age of 11 Whitman converted to the Congregationalist faith, the Protestant group whose earliest American adherents were the Puritans of Massachusetts Bay Colony in the 1630s. The conversion had come as a result of her contact with religious groups that were part of the Second Great Awakening, a renewal of evangelical fervor that swept through New England in the first decades of the nineteenth century.

Arranged Own Marriage

Whitman was schooled at the Franklin Academy in Prattsburgh, and later went on to train as a teacher at the Female Academy in Troy, New York. She was active in various church groups, and in the Amity, New York, area, to which her family had moved around 1834. There she attended a lecture by a minister in which he urged young people to become missionaries out West. There was a

widely repeated story of the time, which circulated in Protestant groups, that in 1831 a mixed-blood Wyandot Indian who had converted to the Methodist faith had come to St. Louis, looking for a copy of the Bible to bring back to his Native American community. The largely apocryphal tale seemed to be aimed at arousing sympathy and raising money for Christian missionary groups who were focused on converting the vast communities of indigenous Americans who were living somewhat unbothered in the wide-open lands of the Western United States.

Whitman decided to join that missionary brigade. She applied to the American Board of Commissioners for Foreign Missions (ABCFM), the first American Christian foreign mission agency. At the time, the lands west of the Mississippi River were technically called "foreign," because they were populated by Spanish settlers, indigenous peoples, and sparse communities of fur traders. The ABCFM would not allow single men or women to serve as missionaries, however, and the same quandary was faced by a physician from Wheeler, New York, named Marcus Whitman. When he heard of her attempt, he contacted her by letter, and they began corresponding with one another; he proposed marriage, she accepted, and they were wed on February 18, 1836, in Angelica, New York.

By that time, Dr. Whitman had already made one scouting trip out West with another missionary, reaching the Nez Percé in Montana and Idaho. Shortly after the wedding, he and his new bride set off again on a trip that was notable for being the first large contingent of European Americans to head west by wagon train. They traveled with a pair of other newlywed missionaries, Henry and Eliza Spalding. The trip took more than five months, with the first major leg of it undertaken on the Ohio, Mississippi, and Missouri rivers. From Kansas they traveled by horse with fur traders who already knew the route, camping at night and feasting on fresh buffalo. For some of the Native American communities they encountered, Whitman and Eliza Spalding were the first white women they had ever seen. The journey was a long one, covering 15 miles or so in a good day, but as Whitman wrote to her sisters back in New York, "I never was so contented and happy before; neither have I enjoyed such health for years," she enthused, according to the PBS.org website *New Perspectives on the West*.

First White Woman Across Rockies

Whitman's party was the first major party to use the Oregon Trail, which followed river valleys westward from Kansas City, Missouri, to present-day Oregon. It avoided areas known for communities hostile to European encroachment—such as South Dakota's Blackfoot tribe—and stretched more than 2,100 miles through Nebraska, Wyoming, Idaho, and Oregon; U.S. Highway 26 was later constructed over much of the same path. The Trail's most daunting obstacle was the Continental Divide, the immense mountain range that bisected the continent and proved notoriously difficult for large wagons to cross. Earlier traders, however, had discovered the Rocky Mountains' South Pass, a broad valley in southwestern Wyoming. When Whitman's party went through this, she and Eliza Spalding became the first white women to cross the Continental Divide.

The Whitmans and their party arrived at Walla Walla Fort, near present-day Walla Walla, Washington, on September 1, 1836. This was an outpost of the Hudson's Bay Company, the major fur trading enterprise in the region, and soon she and her husband had settled on a site some six miles away. It was called Waiilatpu, or "place of the rye grass" in Cayuse, the language of the Plateau Indians who initially greeted the new arrivals with enthusiasm. Both the Cayuse and the Nez Percé were the majority population in the area, and lived a nomadic lifestyle dictated by the availability of seasonal food resources such as bison and salmon.

Over the next several months the two families built a small house and various outbuildings for their mission, and set to work converting the Native Americans, urging them to adopt a more settled, farming-centered lifestyle. Whitman taught bible study classes at the mission, but neither she nor her husband ever learned the native languages, which hampered their efforts considerably. They also found some of the indigenous customs distasteful or ridiculous, such as the practice of elaborate gift-giving, which they considered a form of extortion foisted on the recipient.

Cultural Differences Caused Tension

In letters home to her family, Whitman wrote of the lack of privacy at the mission after four other missionary couples arrived in 1838. She was also uneasy with the Cayuse and Nez Percé at their mission, who held different beliefs about the sanctity of a home as exclusively for the use of a single family; the tribes saw less of a distinction between host and guest, and furthermore considered a home the optimum setting for spiritual worship in their own religious practices. To them, a separate church building seemed superfluous, and they ignored the Whitmans' suggestions to build their own church. "They are so filthy they make a great deal of cleaning wherever they go, and this wears out a woman very fast," Whitman complained in one letter to her mother about the locals using her home as their favorite gathering place, according to the book American Eras.

The early promise of Whitman's life on the frontier was diminished by hardship and tragedy. She was pregnant when they had arrived in Oregon, and on March 14, 1837, her twenty-ninth birthday, a daughter was born to her and her husband, whom they named Alice Clarissa after their own mothers. The girl was the first white American child born in Oregon Country, but she drowned in the Walla Walla River at the age of two. Whitman sank into a depression, and spent hours writing in her journal and chronicling her difficulties in letters to her family back East. Her husband built a larger house in 1840, but their banishment of the Cayuse from its more delineated family quarters intensified the dislike the locals felt toward them and especially Whitman, whom they considered haughty.

An influx of nearly a thousand new settlers in 1843, brought back by Whitman's husband, served to increase hostilities between the missionaries and their Cayuse and Nez Percé neighbors. The natives felt that the white settlers received preferential treatment at the mission, and struggled to feed their families as the once-plentiful game in the area they hunted grew scarce, along with their traditional grazing lands for livestock, as the newcomers settled in. Some in the tribe began to hint that they had not been paid for the use of the land, and Whitman voiced her displeasure in another letter to her family. "They are an exceedingly proud, haughty and insolent people, and keep us constantly upon the stretch after patience and forbearance. We feed them far more than any of our associates do their people, yet they will not be satisfied." Nevertheless, she continued to maintain her optimistic attitude about their missionary goals. "Notwithstanding all this, there are many redeeming qualities in them, else we should have been discouraged long ago. We are more and more encouraged the longer we stay among them."

Adopted Several Children

Whitman seemed to have come out of her grief over the death of their toddler when she began taking in other children. She and her husband informally adopted a Nez Percé girl named Helen Mar Meek, who had been abandoned by her mother, in 1840, followed by an Indian/Spanish boy they named David. In 1844, seven children of the Sager family appeared at the mission after having lost both parents on the Oregon Trail, and Whitman and her husband took them in. In letters to her family back in New York, she still extolled the virtues of life in Oregon. "This is a fine, healthy climate," she wrote in a letter to her brother, Edward, dated April 13, 1846. "I wish you were here to enjoy it with me, and pa and ma, too. We have as happy a family as the world affords. I do not wish to be in a better situation than this."

The following winter, of 1846–47, was an unusually cold one, and the Native Americans suffered the brunt of it, losing large numbers of their cattle. Later that year a measles epidemic swept through the mission, and the Cayuse and Nez Percé, who had no natural immunities to the disease, were also hardest hit by this. They suspected a deliberate plot to kill off their people and take their land, and accused Dr. Whitman of aiding the whites who were sick instead of their own stricken. The strained relationship turned to violence on November 29, 1847: several Cayuse were in the outer room of the Whitman house, and saw Narcissa getting some milk; they demanded it, but she told them it was for one of the children and firmly shut the door on them. One began pounding on it, asking for medicine, and when Dr. Whitman came into the outer room, he was struck from behind by a tomahawk blow. More Cayuse arrived, and in the melee 13 settlers were slain, including three of the Sager boys. Fifty whites were taken hostage, and after a discussion, a decision was made to avoid any further bloodshed—except for Narcissa Whitman, who was taken outside and hacked to death.

The siege at the mission lasted a month, and the hostages were eventually released for a ransom. Harsh reprisals against the Cayuse and Nez Percé followed, and finally the local chief, Tiloukaikt, turned himself in to authorities as a last resort, hoping to save his tribe from being killed off one by one. He was one of five Cayuse sentenced to death, and said, according to the New Perspectives on the West website, "Did not your missionaries teach us that Christ died to save his people? So we die to save our people." The event was a turning point for Oregon Country, with white settlers so fearful of further uprisings that federal troops began to be permanently deployed in the area.

Books

American Eras, Edition 1, 1997.

Periodicals

American Indian Quarterly, Summer 1993.
Christian History, May 2000.
Historian, Autumn 1992.
New York Times, May 31, 1993.
Seattle Times, November 16, 1997.

Online

"Biography of Narcissa Whitman," Whitman Mission NHS— History & Culture, http://www.nps.gov/archive/whmi/ history/narcbio.htm (December 23, 2006).
"The Letters and Journals of Narcissa Whitman 1836–1847," *New Perspectives on the West,* PBS.org, http://www.pbs.org/weta/ thewest/resources/archives/two/whitman1.htm (December 30, 2006).
"Marcus Whitman (1802–1847), Narcissa Whitman (1808– 1847)," *New Perspectives on the West,* PBS.org, http://www .pbs.org/weta/thewest/people/s_z/whitman.htm (December 30, 2006). □

Benjamin Lee Whorf

American linguist Benjamin Lee Whorf (1897–1941) is remembered for a group of speculative ideas about thought and language that remain controversial but have exerted strong influence on popular scientific thinking.

The most famous of these ideas is the so-called Sapir-Whorf Hypothesis, derived largely from Whorf's research among Native American tribes and the writings that resulted (indeed, it is sometimes simply called the Whorfian hypothesis). Simply stated, the hypothesis (never laid out as such by its supposed authors) proposed that language is not only a part of culture, influenced by the groups of human beings who construct it, but also an influence on culture and thought. Human beings, Whorf believed, see the world in the ways they do because of the structure of the languages they speak. The Sapir-Whorf Hypothesis might be considered part of a larger group of ideas classified as examples of linguistic relativism, or the belief that languages are different at a fundamental level. That belief has come under attack in recent decades, but Whorf's ideas have given birth to a rich literature of popular writing about language. His ideas, for the most part, became well known only after his death.

Loved Codes as Child

Whorf was born on April 24, 1897, in Winthrop, Massachusetts, near Boston. His father, Harry Whorf, was a commercial artist with varied interests: he dabbled in art, playwriting, acting, and theatrical production. Benjamin Whorf, even as a child, soon began to show an even wider curiosity. He read books on almost any subject he encountered, and he had special enthusiasm for codes and puzzles. Whorf was religious (his family was Methodist), and he later came under the influence of the French mystical writer and linguist Antoine Fabre d'Olivet (1767–1825), whose metaphysical thinking was linked to his belief that the texts of the Bible and other sacred volumes contained hidden meanings.

Parallel with his rich intellectual life, however, Whorf pursued a more conventional career. He attended the Massachusetts Institute of Technology (MIT), majoring in chemical engineering and receiving a bachelor of science degree in 1918. He moved from MIT into a position with the Hartford Fire Insurance Company (now the Hartford Financial Services Group) as a fire prevention engineering trainee. His interest in languages intensified, but business trips gave him the chance to read academic journals and keep up with new developments in linguistics. In 1920 he married Celia Inez Peckham, and the pair raised three children. For the rest of his life, Whorf made the Hartford, Connecticut, area his home.

Whorf shared insurance as a profession with several other thinkers of his time who were among the most original figures in their fields—the poet Wallace Stevens actually worked at the Hartford during the same years as Whorf, although they are not thought to have known each other, and composer Charles Ives, a fellow Connecticut resident, commuted to an insurance office in New York City and wrote music on the side. Whorf, who was recognized as an authority on industrial fire prevention, never complained that his vocation took time away from his research and writing, and in fact later in life he refused offers of teaching jobs, preferring to remain independent of the academic world.

Under the influence of Fabre d'Olivet, Whorf spent time in the early 1920s learning to read biblical Hebrew. The perceived conflict between science and religion was a major issue at the time, and Whorf looked to language as a way of resolving the conflict. Fascinated by the seemingly powerful significance of the letters of the Hebrew alphabet, he began to search for similar phenomena in other languages. He became interested in Native American languages and familiarized himself with the long effort to reconstruct the languages of the ancient Mayan and Aztec societies.

Wrote Letters to Professional Linguists

In the late 1920s Whorf took the first steps toward communicating his ideas to the wider intellectual community: he wrote letters to specialists in linguistics, archaeology, and anthropology. A skillful writer with a gift for couching his highly unorthodox ideas in conventional academic language, he stirred up interest among established scholars with this correspondence. They suggested that he apply for grants to do linguistic fieldwork, and Whorf took their advice, winning funding from the Social Science Research Council for a trip to Mexico in 1930. Traveling among Native tribes in that country, he made significant contributions to ongoing research on the Aztec or Nahuatl language. In 1931 top linguist Edward Sapir took a job teaching at Yale University, and Whorf enrolled there as a part-time, nondegree graduate student.

The result was something of a meeting of the minds. Sapir was an expert on Native American languages, which differ in striking ways from those of Europe and Asia. (Navajo, for example, classifies objects according to their physical characteristics; a verb applying to a flexible object would be different from one applying to something stiff.) Sapir urged Whorf to study the Hopi language, and Whorf learned to speak it, probably better than the other languages about which he wrote. He traveled to the Hopi reservation in New Mexico and also took lessons from a Hopi individual living in New York City, learning the language well enough to compile a Hopi-English dictionary that was found among his papers at his death.

Whorf was a quick study, under both Sapir and his Native teachers, and he soon began to write articles that were accepted for publication in linguistics and anthropology journals. Whorf issued several dozen articles in the 1930s, many of which were collected posthumously in the book *Language, Thought, and Reality* (1956). Some of his writing was quite technical, but he was also an effective communicator with general audiences, contributing several essays on linguistics to MIT's nonspecialist-oriented *Technology Review*.

For his writing, Whorf took examples from various Native American languages, but it was Hopi that formed the basis for many of his most original ideas. "I find it gratuitous to assume," Whorf wrote (all quotations are taken from *Language, Thought, and Reality*), "that a Hopi who knows only the Hopi language and the cultural ideas of his own society has the same notions . . . of time and space that we have, and that are generally assumed to be universal." Instead, Whorf contended, a Hopi individual "has no general notion or intuition of time as a smooth flowing continuum in which everything in the universe proceeds at an equal rate, out of a future, through a present, into a past; or in which, to reverse the picture, the observer is being carried in the stream of duration continuously away from a past and into a future."

Traced Hopi Concepts to Language

According to Whorf, then, the Hopi did not think in terms recognizable in English as past, present, and future. Instead they divided the world into what he called the manifested and manifesting, with the former comprising the physical universe and the latter involving not only the future but also the world of processes, desires, power, thought, intelligence, and life forces. But this distinctive Hopi philosophy was not located just in the realm of ideas, it proceeded from the structure of the Hopi language itself. Hopi (like other Native American languages) has relatively few nouns, tending to express as verbs concepts that would be nouns in English. A "wave" in English (actually a rather awkward

simplification of a complex phenomenon), would be expressed in Hopi in words corresponding to "plural waving occurs," and all-verb sentences in Hopi are possible.

Part of Whorf's argument was originally laid out in an article titled "An American Indian Model of the Universe." After his ideas were published in *Language, Thought, and Reality,* they were expanded upon by many other writers, popular and scientific, who saw them as supportive of philosophies that viewed the universe as composed of processes rather than of the subdivided atoms of modern science. More generally, the idea of strong connections between language and culture has exerted a strong influence on contemporary thinking about the relativity of cultures. One idea attributed to Whorf has become almost a commonplace of journalism and conversation—the idea that the Inuit have 20 (or some similar number) different words for "snow." In fact, however, Whorf probably misunderstood the process by which compound words are formed in Inuit; there is a single root meaning "snow," just as in any other language.

Whorf lived life at a furious pace, discharging the responsibilities of his insurance job while writing voluminously. He held a formal teaching position only once, as a lecturer at Yale in the 1937–38 academic year, for which he took a leave of absence from the Hartford. It was mostly Whorf's linguistic ideas that gained professional attention, but posthumous examination of his materials revealed a mystical mind that had educated itself on an astonishing variety of subjects. He wrote about gravity, the philosophical idea of being, the perception of color, the structure of trees and plants, the theory of evolution (which he rejected), and dreams. He made a unique translation of the biblical Book of Genesis, casting the story as a set of abstract philosophical concepts. At his death he left an outline for a magnum opus covering the mysteries of science and religion. Whorf's papers are kept at the Yale University Library.

When he published three papers in MIT's *Technology Review* in 1940 and 1941, Whorf became for the first time a name known to the general public. He had no time to build on his growing renown, however, for he succumbed to cancer at the age of 44 on July 26, 1941, at his home in Wethersfield, Connecticut. By the mid-1950s a *New York Times* reviewer could refer to Whorf's ideas as accepted and generally valid, writing that "As Benjamin Whorf's work . . . has now made the reading public aware, all languages are loaded with implicit and often conflicting philosophies." The growth of the linguistic ideas of Noam Chomsky, however, dented Whorf's reputation, as linguists discovered common mental structures and learning processes that underlay all languages and their acquisition.

Toward the end of the twentieth century, Whorf's ideas experienced a resurgence (documented in a 1992 article in *Scientific American* magazine entitled *New Whoof in Whorf: An Old Language Theory Regains Its Authority*). The widely read books of linguist George Lakoff, showing the preconceptions embedded in a culture's use of metaphor, owe something to Whorf conceptually. And the rapid disappearance of many of the world's languages as the new millennium began was of great concern to linguists for reasons Whorf himself might have articulated: when a language is lost, a way of looking at the world, unique and interrelated and irreplaceable, is lost with it, and lost forever.

Books

Whorf, Benjamin, *Language, Thought, and Reality,* ed. John B. Carroll, MIT Press, 1956.

Periodicals

Scientific American, February 1992.

Online

"Benjamin Lee Whorf: Biography," The Benjamin Lee Whorf World Wide Website, http://www.mtsu32.mtsu.edu:11072/whorf/

"The Mind of Benjamin Whorf," http://www.mtsu32.mtsu.edu:11072/Whorf/mindblw.htm (December 24, 2006). □

Bert Williams

Bahamian-born African-American comedian and singer Bert Williams (1874–1922) was a phenomenally popular figure in the field of American theatrical entertainment during his heyday in the first two decades of the twentieth century.

Williams, who wore blackface makeup over his own black face to conform to the racist theatrical stereotypes of the era, was in many ways a tragic figure. He worked in the genre of the blackface minstrel show, which was one of the key components of a longstanding attempt by white Americans to degrade Americans of African descent. Yet Williams made comedy out of the sadness he felt behind the mask, creating hard-luck stage characters and songs that appealed to a wide cross-section of audiences. In terms of the development of African-American opportunities in American show business, Williams was widely recognized as a pioneer. Williams was described by film comedian W. C. Fields (quoted by Ann Charters in *Nobody: The Story of Bert Williams*) as "the funniest man I ever saw, and the saddest man I ever knew."

Raised in Bahamas

Egbert Austin Williams was born in Nassau, in the Bahamas, on November 12, 1874. His background was mixed: his mother was from Antigua, and among his ancestors on his father's side was a Danish diplomat. When Williams was born, his father was working as a waiter at Nassau's Royal Victoria Hotel. The family thought of immigrating to the United States and made a temporary trip to New York when Williams was two, but then returned to the Bahamas, Williams's home until he was 11. His natural accent was lightly Caribbean, and the stylized black dialect of the American minstrel show, he was quoted as saying by Charters, "to me was just as much a foreign dialect as that of the Italian."

In 1885 the Williams family came to the United States for good, following a Bahamian migration to Florida and then moving on to southern California and its growing fruit farms. Williams attended Riverside Boys High School, treating classes with indifference but singing enthusiastically in the choir. Once, when he was called on to recite from a book the class had been reading, he entertained his classmates with jokes he had been absorbing from a second book concealed on his lap. "I was always doing something funny, and my teachers didn't know what to do with me," he recalled in an interview quoted by Eric Ledell Smith in *Bert Williams: A Biography of the Pioneer Black Comedian.* "They couldn't spank me for being funny, and I wasn't a mischievous boy."

Tall like both his parents, agile, and obviously talented, Williams ran away from home at age 16 to join a medicine show but then returned home to his family. He thought of attending Stanford University but could not afford the tuition. In order to earn the money, he joined a minstrel show that traveled among the lumber camps of northern California. Things went from bad to worse when the company floundered and Williams arrived in San Francisco, as he recalled in an interview quoted by biographer Smith, "without a stitch of clothing, literally without a stitch, as the few rags I wore to spare the hostility of the police had to be burned for reasons that everyone will understand who has read of the experiences of the soldiers in the trenches." But he bounced back with another job with a Hawaiian troupe (impersonating a Pacific islander) and then, in 1893, signed on with Martin and Selig's Minstrels.

In that company he met George Walker, a fellow aspiring comedian who would be his stage partner for the next 16 years. The pair sang and performed comic routines, often with Walker in the role of a sharp-dressed straight man and Williams as his down-at-the-heels counterpart, bumbling but quick-witted. The two made their way across the country, performing minstrel shows and billing themselves as The Two Real Coons. The trip was a difficult one; in Colorado they were robbed of their clothes by a white gang who thought they were too well-dressed and forced them to wear burlap bags. They were not the first African Americans associated with minstrel shows, which for many decades after the Civil War represented the only performing opportunities of any kind open to blacks.

Used Burnt Cork Makeup

Williams and Walker downplayed the minstrel show's racist aspects and turned its humor to their own ends. At an 1895 Detroit performance, Williams adopted the minstrel show's strongest visual symbol—he put on burnt cork makeup to darken his face and went on stage to perform a song of his own composition, called "Oh, I Don't Know, You're Not So Warm." "Nobody was more surprised than I was when it went like a house on fire," he said (as quoted by Charters). "Then I began to find myself. It was not until I was able to see myself as another person that my sense of humor developed." The financially precarious Williams and Walker barnstorming tour arrived in New York in 1896, where the two landed roles in the Victor Herbert operetta *The Gold Bug.*

That and the duo's other initial forays into New York theater were unsuccessful, partly because classically trained New York pit musicians could not handle the ragtime rhythms of the songs they interpolated into vaudeville programs. But ragtime in the late 1890s was rapidly on the rise, and Williams and Walker were in the right place at the right time. They landed an engagement at Koster and Bial's, one of the city's top music halls, and the craze for the cakewalk dance—a comic black imitation of white society dances that in turn became popular among white audiences—fit their comic style perfectly. They gained publicity by visiting the mansion of tycoon William Vanderbilt, who had been seen doing the cakewalk at a dance, and leaving a letter (quoted by Charters) with his butler, suggesting a cakewalk contest: "We, the undersigned world-renowned cakewalkers, believing that the attention of the public has been distracted from us on account of the tremendous hit which you have made, hereby challenge you to compete with us in a cake-walking match, which will decide which of us shall deserve the title of champion cake-walker of the world." In 1900 Williams married Charlotte (Lottie) Thompson.

The career of Williams and Walker gained some momentum, and they were able to put their resources behind a nascent attempt to mount shows with all-black casts. In 1902 they performed in a musical by composer Will Marion Cook, with texts by poet Paul Lawrence Dunbar, with an African theme, called *In Dahomey.* Although still dealing in racial comedy to an extent that would make modern audiences uncomfortable, *In Dahomey* was a landmark in African-American theater history. Williams and Walker toured widely with the show, which reached England in 1903 and brought the duo to the chambers of King Edward VII for a private performance. The king reportedly struck up a friendship with Williams, who attempted to teach him the cakewalk, the game of craps, and a few of his dialect comedy routines.

In Dahomey spawned all-black musical successors including *Abyssinia* (1906) and *Bandanna Land* (1908); these shows, like those mounted by white performers in New York's theaters and music halls, spawned hit songs and new dance steps that spread around the country. Williams became a star, but his life was never free of the tragic sting of racism. In an essay later published in *The American Magazine* (quoted by Steven C. Tracy in *MELUS*), he related how some white actors treated him as an equal associate but that their "brainless and envious" rivals took the opportunity to use racial restrictions to humiliate him. Williams often responded to discrimination with the mild but firm observation (quoted by Charters) that "in truth, I have never been able to discover that there was anything disgraceful in being a colored man. But I have often found it inconvenient—in America."

Developed Solo Act

Walker's ill health and his death in 1911 put an end to his partnership with Williams, but by that time Williams had taken on a new stage persona that did not reject minstrel comedy but transcended it. He premiered several new songs that established him as a hard-luck figure who was funny, to be sure, but who had a deep undercurrent of melancholy. Among these were "I'm a Jonah Man," written by frequent Williams collaborator Alex Rogers, and the most famous Williams number of all: "Nobody," with words by Rogers and music by Williams himself. The song was first introduced in *Abyssinia.* For many years afterward, Williams was obliged to sing "Nobody" in personal appearances even as he introduced other satirical material like "Woodman Spare That Tree (It's the Only One My Wife Can't Climb)" and "I Want to Know Where Tosti Went (When He Said 'Goodbye Forever')," the latter parodying a prominent Italian-American song of the day.

"Nobody" lay at the heart of the Williams image. Its individual sections began with semi-spoken verses in which Williams lamented his lonely state: "When life seems full of clouds and rain / And I am full of nothin' but pain, / Who soothes my thumpin', bumpin', brain? / Nobody!" Then its slow ragtime chorus continued: "I ain't never done nothin' to nobody, / I ain't never got nothin' from nobody, no time." Increasingly the musical revues in which Williams appeared drew white as well as black audiences (often segregated, depending on where in the country they were presented). One of his admirers was the pioneer African-American educator Booker T. Washington, who wrote a tribute to Williams that appeared in *American Magazine* in 1910. Washington, as quoted by Smith, declared that Williams "puts into this form [vaudeville] some of the quality and philosophy of the Negro race." In 1910, despite resistance from some of the company's white performers, Williams joined the cast of the Ziegfeld Follies and become the first black star of a leading white Broadway revue.

Appearing in the Follies between 1910 and 1912 and intermittently thereafter, Williams became a major national star. At one point his annual salary reportedly exceeded that of the President of the United States, but money could not buy him freedom from segregation restrictions. After having to ride the freight elevator of a hotel to reach his room, he remarked to singer Eddie Cantor (according to an interview quoted by Tracy), "It wouldn't be so bad, Eddie, if I didn't still hear the applause ringing in my ears." Williams made a series of popular 78 rpm recordings for the Columbia label in the 1910s, featuring comic routines and songs; one of the most popular, "Darktown Poker Club," anticipated hip-hop themes in its mixture of violence, rapid spoken text, and atmosphere of illicit gambling. Williams's comic sketches, such as the ghost story "You Cant' Do Nothin' Till Martin Gets Here," drew on African-American southern folklore.

Williams became a naturalized American citizen in 1918, and he appeared with Cantor in the 1920 show *Broadway Brevities.* He lived to see younger black performers benefit from the opportunities he had done so much to create. Eugene O'Neill's *The Emperor Jones* became the first major drama by a white playwright to feature a black lead character, and the Noble Sissle/Eubie Blake revue *Shuffle Along* spawned a new generation of African-American stars. Williams mounted a new production of his own called *Under the Bamboo Tree,* but he fell ill during a performance in Detroit while the show toured nationally. Suffering from pneumonia brought on by heart problems, he died in New York on March 4, 1922. Tributes that flowed in from both black and white performers were collected in Mabel Rowland's 1923 biography *Bert Williams: Son of Laughter,* but after that Williams's star dimmed for many years, largely due to the decline of racial stereotyping in American performing arts. Toward the end of the twentieth century, however, interest in Williams reawakened with the publication of two biographies and the reissue on the Archeophone label of many of his recordings in compact disc form. The play *Nobody: The Bert Williams Story* by Frank Jenkins, and the novel *Dancing in the Dark* by Caryl Phillips were both fictionalized treatments of Williams's tragicomic life.

Books

Charters, Ann, *Nobody: The Story of Bert Williams,* Da Capo, 1983.
Contemporary Black Biography, volume 18, Gale, 1998.
Notable Black American Men, Gale, 1998.
Riis, Thomas, *Just Before Jazz,* Smithsonian, 1989.
Rowland, Mabel, *Bert Williams: Son of Laughter,* English Crafters, 1923 (repr. Negro Universities Press, 1969).
Smith, Eric Ledell, *Bert Williams: A Biography of the Pioneer Black Comedian,* McFarland, 1992.

Periodicals

Buffalo News, December 4, 2005.
Houston Chronicle, September 25, 2005.
MELUS, Summer 2004.
Sarasota Herald Tribune, March 17, 2006.

Online

"Bert Williams (1876–1922)," DuBois Learning Center, http://www.duboislc.org/ShadesOfBlack/BertWms.html (February 8, 2007).
"Bert Williams," Songwriters Hall of Fame, http://www.songwritershalloffame.org/artist_bio.asp?artistId=73 (February 8, 2007). □

Henry Clay Work

Little heralded even in histories of music that focus on popular song, American songwriter Henry Clay Work (1832–1884) nevertheless left a legacy that lived on in the memories of audiences and musicians.

In the early 1950s, musicologist Richard S. Hill could point to a list of songs by Work "that would be instantly recognized by most Americans today—certainly more songs than by any other mid-nineteenth century writer with the possible exception of George F. Root." Several decades of youth-oriented popular music have displaced some of those songs from memory, but Work still ranks as perhaps the preeminent composer of one of American music's crucial genres, the Civil War song. And Work's serio-comic "Grandfather's Clock" remains a standard in the repertoire of bluegrass musicians and others who cultivate a crop of older songs.

Background Marked by Abolitionism

Henry Clay Work was born in Middletown, Connecticut, on October 1, 1832. Of Scottish descent, he took his family name from that of Auld Wark Castle in Scotland. Work moved with his family to Quincy, Illinois, when he was three. His father, Alanson Work, was a noted anti-slavery activist whose Illinois home served as a way station on the Underground Railroad. The elder Work was arrested and imprisoned for these activities, and after his release the family returned penniless to Connecticut in 1845. There Work received an ordinary high school education and became a printer's apprentice after refusing an apprenticeship with a tailor.

Work had a strong inclination toward music from the start, but financially stable music careers were rare in nineteenth-century America. Like other composers of popular song at the time, he spent parts of his life on the financial margins of society. Working in the print shop of one Elihu Greer in Hartford, Connecticut, he taught himself to read and write music during off-hours. His limited keyboard capabilities came from practice on a melodeon. Work began writing songs of his own to sing to friends, and when he was 21 he experienced his first taste of success: his "We Are Coming, Sister Mary" was purchased by E. P. Christy, leader of the nationally popular singing group Christy's Minstrels. Christy published the song under his own name, but Work nevertheless realized a modest profit.

"We Are Coming, Sister Mary" was a minstrel song, or a song, generally by a white composer, that depicted African-American life and was often performed in blackface makeup. Such songs are now often avoided because of the racist attitudes they contain, but in Work's time they embodied a wide range of attitudes toward African Americans. "We Are Coming, Sister Mary" was not a comic minstrel song but a depiction of a group of people who sing to a departed soul as they prepare for a funeral. Work moved to Chicago in 1854 or 1855, finding work as a printer, and he began to think about how to combine songwriting with the abolitionist sympathies he inherited from his father.

With the outbreak of the Civil War, those abolitionist sympathies turned to wholehearted devotion to the Union cause. After several more small successes, Work showed some of his songs to George F. Root, a partner in the firm of Root & Cady. Root took special interest in one of Work's songs, "Kingdom Coming," and said that if he had more like it, he could retire from the printing business. Work thus not only found a publisher for the Civil War songs that had begun to flow from his pen; he was also hired as editor of Root & Cady's in-house music magazine, *The Song Messenger of the Northwest.* A legendary story about Work held that he could combine his expertise in music and printing, composing songs directly by setting movable musical type without writing them down in notation or playing them on a piano. The story, however, would seem to contradict the recollections of Root in his autobiography (quoted on the Public Domain Music website) that "Mr. Work was a slow, pains-taking writer, being from one to three weeks upon a song." Root did note that "when the work was done it was like a piece of fine mosaic, especially in the fitting of words to music."

Song Heard Among Slaves

"Kingdom Coming," though written in the ersatz black dialect of minstrelsy, was an explicitly pro-Northern song that depicted slaves chortling as their masters fled the approaching Northern troops. The Root & Cady firm was the largest music publisher in what was then the Western United States, and it mounted perhaps the first music advertising campaign in American history, beginning with plain posters and advertisements that read simply "Kingdom Coming" and then progressed to more detailed publicity supporting sales of the sheet music. The results were spectacularly successful, as the song became known all over North America. It was later collected among traditional singers in the Canadian province of Nova Scotia, and Union soldiers heard slaves themselves singing it in Louisiana. Work could, of course, have based the song on a preexisting slave melody, but observations of it among African Americans corresponded closely to the period when it was popular among whites as well. The song was still familiar in the era of radio entertainment as the theme for the Sunday-evening program of ventriloquist Edgar Bergen and his dummy Charlie McCarthy.

"Kingdom Coming" and another Civil War-era Work hit, "Wake Nicodemus," referred to slaves' anticipation of the Jubilee, a biblical concept denoting a year of celebration that was frequently identified among slaves with emancipation. "Wake Nicodemus" maintained its popularity well into the era of early country music in the twentieth century with its depiction of a slave "of African birth" who "was sold for a bag full of gold." At his death, he makes a final request to the children of his masters: " 'Wake me up,' was his charge, 'at the first break of day; wake me up for the great Jubilee!' The song was published after President Abraham Lincoln's Emancipation Proclamation in 1863, marked by the refrain's exclamation that "the good times a-comin' is almost here; it was long, long, long on the way."

The most famous of Work's Civil War songs, however, did not have an African-American theme. "Marching Through Georgia" (1865), based on a rousing march beat, depicted the devastating campaign of General William Tecumseh Sherman in the later stages of the war, as he laid waste to the city of Atlanta and then cut a swath of destruction as his troops marched toward Savannah and the Atlantic. The song, noted historian Sigmund Spaeth, "deliberately rubbed Yankee salt into one of the sorest wounds of the Civil War," and it aroused bitterness among Southerners for some years after his composition. Its "Hurrah! Hurrah!" refrain, however, was irresistible enough to evolve, with modified lyrics, into the fight song of the Princeton University football team.

Work also scored a hit with the comic song "Grafted into the Army," and he was sometimes dubbed the War Poet. But another Work hit of the Civil War era was not connected to the war at all. "Come Home, Father" (1864) was an early example of the temperance song, its theme of a child pleading for an alcoholic father to return home from

the barroom serving as a pattern for several similar later compositions. Once again Work's gift for linking words to music (he wrote almost all of his own lyrics) insured the song's success; its melody emphasizes the successive hour strikes of a clock—one, two, three—in the song's verses. The overall maudlin atmosphere of the song inspired parodies in later years, but parodies themselves attest to the familiarity of the originals on which they are based.

Lost Money in Land Investment

By the end of the war, Work was one of the most popular musicians in the United States, and his songs, along with those of Root and minstrel balladeer Stephen Foster, had set a prevailing pattern: that of verse and chorus, with the chorus centered around a memorable detail that would later be called a "hook" in American popular songs, a pattern that would last well into the twentieth century. Life turned sour, however, for Work in the late 1860s. He lost money investing in a New Jersey fruit farm and was once again reduced to bare essentials—the concept of copyright was unknown at the time, and such money he had earned from Root & Cady came in the form of flat fees. In 1871 he left Chicago, after his office burned to the ground in the great fire of that year. Work settled in Philadelphia and resumed his former occupation of print shop employee. He wrote songs occasionally, but his output tailed off sharply between 1865 and the early 1870s. His few successes included "The Ship That Never Returned" (1865), which lived on in the melody of the early country hit "The Wreck of the Old 97." In 1868 Work published a long comic poem called "The Upshot Family."

Nor was Work's family life happy. His wife suffered from mental illness and had to be institutionalized. Of Work's four children, two died in childhood and another, a son named Waldo, contracted tuberculosis and died after he and Work had embarked on a long outdoor tour of the California mountains. Work rented rooms in Philadelphia from a family named Mitchell, and he centered his frustrated romantic attentions on the daughter of the family, named Susie. No relationship resulted, and it was partly to escape the dead-end situation that Work undertook his California trip.

He kept up a voluminous correspondence with Susie Mitchell, however, and his link to her seemed to result in a revival of his creativity. Temporarily returning to Chicago in 1875, he had one more major hit with "Grandfather's Clock," a song about a clock that accompanies a man through life: it was "bought on the morn of the day that he was born, and was always his treasure and pride. But it stopped short, never to go again, when the old man died." Sheet music for the song was reported to have sold 800,000 copies and to have brought Work $4,000 in profits. "Grandfather's Clock" was still going strong in the early twenty-first century, performed by brass bands in England and by Japanese vocalists and jazz artists. In 2004 the song appeared in a cover version by R&B vocal group Boyz II Men.

Moving to the small town of Bath, New York, in 1882, Work composed several songs that were not widely distributed but that historians regard as among his best; these include "The Silver Horn" and "Drop the Pink Curtains." He died suddenly from a coronary episode in Hartford, Connecticut, on June 8, 1884.

Books

Epstein, Dena J., *Music Publishing in Chicago Before 1871: The Firm of Root & Cady,* Information Coordinators, 1969.

Hitchcock, H. Wiley, and Stanley Sadie, eds., *The New Grove Dictionary of American Music,* Macmillan, 1986.

Howard, John Tasker, *Our American Music,* 4th ed., Crowell, 1965.

Spaeth, Sigmund, *A History of Popular Music in America,* Random House, 1948.

Periodicals

Music Library Association Notes, March 1953.

Online

"Henry C. Work," Songwriters Hall of Fame, http://www.song writershalloffame.org (January 31, 2007).

"The Music of Henry Clay Work," Public Domain Music, http://www.pdmusic.org/work.html (January 31, 2007). □

Tammy Wynette

One of country music's most compelling rags-to-riches figures, American singer and songwriter Tammy Wynette (1942–1998) rose from dire poverty to become the first female performer to sell a million albums in her genre. Dubbed the "First Lady of Country Music," she racked up 57 Top 40 country hits between 1967 and 1988 and won dozens of awards from her industry peers. Despite worldwide acclaim and riches, the singer-songwriter did not enjoy a particularly happy life and her 1998 death remains a controversial subject.

First Sang in Church

Born Virginia Wynette Pugh, May 5, 1942, in Itawamba County, Mississippi, she was the daughter of a local musician William Hollice Pugh, who recorded briefly in 1939 and 1940. When Wynette was only eight months old, her father died of a brain tumor. Subsequently her mother, Mildred, left her with grandparents while she took a wartime factory job in Birmingham, Alabama. Chopping cotton and baling hay on her grandfather's farm for spending money, the youngster discovered her musical inclinations at age nine when she began picking out little melodies on her father's old instruments. She first sang publicly in church and liked it so well that she began attending two different churches so she could sing even more. Teaming with high school friend Linda Cayson, she sang

gospel tunes at church events, on local radio, and even attempted a little Everly Brothers style rock'n'roll on local television.

As she listened to such stars on the radio as George Jones, Webb Pierce, Kitty Wells, Jim Reeves, and Patsy Cline, Wynette dreamed of stardom. However, at age 17, she married Euple Byrd, an itinerant carpenter, and the routine of a housewife and mother temporarily buried her career ambitions. By all accounts, the marriage was a rocky one, heavy on financial burdens and light on luxuries, and it ended five years later in a nasty divorce and an even nastier child custody battle. Supporting children on her salary as a beautician proved tough, especially when her third child developed spinal meningitis. Hoping to raise money to pay doctor bills, she began to sing locally again. A stint on WBRC-TV's *Country Boy Eddie Show* in Birmingham, Alabama, and a 10-day tour with Porter Wagoner built her confidence sufficiently so she could pack up her kids and move to Nashville.

Discovered by Billy Sherrill

After suffering rejections from United Artists, Hickory, and Kapp, producer Billy Sherrill took pity on the desperate singer-songwriter and signed her to Epic Records. Sherrill is best known today as the architect of the "Countrypolitan" sound, a country music hybrid that employs large dollops of adult contemporary strings and vocal chorus. Sherrill, who had previously recorded hits with pop singer Bobby Vinton and country crooner David Houston, was a gifted songwriter as well as commercial music visionary. The Alabama-born producer and songwriter knew how to pick songs that fit his artist's style and often helped writers hone their material to make it catchier and more direct. He would eventually write or co-write many of Wynette's biggest hits while grooming her to be a fine songwriter in her own right. Moreover, he knew how to craft a singer's image on record and off. Sherrill's first step in that process with Wynette came when he observed that the bottle blonde's ponytail made her look like a Tammy, so he re-christened the singer Tammy Wynette.

Under Sherrill's guidance Wynette made her recording debut with a cover version of Bobby Austin's regional hit "Apartment #9." It so successful that Wynette received hundreds of sympathy letters from fans who thought the song was her true story. The follow-up, "Your Good Girl's Gonna Go Bad," was shrill sass on the order of Loretta Lynn, but it became Wynette's first of 20 number one records.

Few artists sang about domestic discord as convincingly as Wynette; her confidential vocal tone and the little catch in her voice combined to create the illusion of a woman who's trying hard not to frighten you to death while she's telling you something horrible. This schism gave her work undeniable power and personal credibility. Wynette's great early hits—"I Don't Wanna Play House," "D-I-V-O-R-C-E," and "Kids Say the Darndest Things"—resonated with American women, who felt she was singing about their lives. As a result, in a matter of a few months, she became one of the top singing stars in America.

The singer's most enduring classic, "Stand by Your Man," was written at the tail end of a session when Sherrill and Wynette realized they needed one more song. The resulting recording vaulted to the number one spot for three weeks in the fall of 1968, and it angered members of the feminist movement along the way. Sherrill was quoted in *The Billboard Book of Number One Country Hits* as saying that critics of the song can "like it or lump it," before clarifying, " 'Stand by Your Man' is just another way of saying 'I love you—without reservations.' " Wynette herself has famously quipped, "I spent 15 minutes writing ['Stand by Your Man'], and a lifetime defending it." As late as 1992, President Clinton's spouse Hillary Rodham Clinton caused a rift with her husband's southern base when she declared on TV's *60 Minutes* that she wasn't "like some little woman standing by my man like Tammy Wynette." (Mrs. Clinton later apologized.)

Married to George Jones

More out of convenience than love, Wynette married Don Chapel in 1967. Best known for writing the hit "When the Grass Grows Over Me" for George Jones, the singer-songwriter tried to cash in on his wife's newfound fame by making himself a prominent addition to her stage show. When a dispute with David Houston's manager left her without an on-stage partner for their hit duet "My Elusive Dreams," Wynette first sang with her childhood hero George Jones. Jones, who had been a highly regarded country hit-maker since the mid-1950s, was instantly smitten. Their infatuation grew as Wynette's marriage to Chapel began disintegrating. When Wynette divorced Chapel in 1968, the two stars married in 1969. Two years later they welcomed their only child, Tamala Georgette Jones.

Jones paid the Musicor label $300,000 to terminate his contract with them so he could sign with Epic in 1971. Taking the place of his former singing partner Melba Montgomery, Wynette recorded an immensely popular string of duet hits with her new husband including, "We're Gonna Hold On," "Golden Ring," and "We're Not the Jet Set." Dubbed Mr. & Mrs. Country Music, their harmony was spirited yet tender, and together they presented the perfect sonic image of a couple who sang their way through life's troubles.

As a solo artist, such singles like "There Are So Many Ways to Love a Man," "My Man," and "Singing My Song" perpetuated Wynette's mythology as a woman triumphing over adversity because, presumably, she was well loved. In truth, her marriage to Jones began falling apart almost from the start due to his lengthy, drunken absences and abusive behavior. In the book he wrote with Tom Carter, *I Lived to Tell It All,* Jones disputed many of his ex-wife's claims, adding, "A lot of folks think that if it hadn't been for my drinking Tammy and I would have had a storybook marriage. But that isn't true. We argued about other things than the bottle."

When they finally divorced in 1974, the media laid the blame on Wynette, crowing that the woman who wrote "Stand by Your Man" was getting a "D-I-V-O-R-C-E." Meanwhile, her personal life seemed to be in free fall. Her

third marriage, to real estate broker Michael Tomlin, lasted only 44 days. A much publicized relationship with actor Burt Reynolds fizzled. More sinister, a botched kidnapping, a series of vindictive burglaries, and mysterious assaults were seen by a cynical press, and some friends, as a cry for attention. Her 1977 hit "Til I Can Make It on My Own" became her personal anthem of survival. She sought to deflect the unflattering media attention with her 1979 autobiography *Stand by Your Man,* but the book only seemed to exacerbate the bad press she was getting. (The book was later made into a 1981 TV movie starring Annette O'Toole as Wynette and Tim McIntyre as Jones.)

Despite the acrimony that led up to it, Jones and Wynette enjoyed a reasonably happy aftermath to their divorce; Wynette wrote the hit "These Days I Barely Get By" for her ex-husband, and Jones gave her his touring band. In 1982 they reunited to record Wynette's "Two-Story House," which reached number one on the charts. To the delight of their legions of fans, they made well-publicized appearances together both on and off record into the mid-1980s.

Plagued By Poor Health

However, the eventual departure of the overbooked Billy Sherrill from her creative team and changing trends in country music resulted in Wynette's hits tapering off during the late 1980s. But there were bright spots. Her 1978 marriage to songwriter and producer George Richey (also known as George Richardson), turned out to be the lasting one. She even tried her hand at acting in a recurring role as a singing waitress on the daytime drama *Capitol* in 1986. In 1987, her LP *Higher Ground* was critically acclaimed. And just when everyone figured her days as a chart presence were over, she teamed up with British synth-pop group KLF and recorded the 1992 international disco smash "Justified & Ancient."

Wynette, Loretta Lynn, and Dolly Parton teamed up for 1993's *Honky Tonk Angels,* which achieved instant gold record status. As Wynette was enjoying her commercial resurgence, a bile duct infection nearly took her life; the national media, which had previously treated her with scorn, provided vigilant coverage of her condition. Eventually Wynette recovered and went on tour to more favorable publicity than she had enjoyed in decades.

That was not the first time the singer had been hospitalized. Starting in 1972, she had endured 30 surgical procedures to correct various medical problems and subsequently found herself increasingly relying on higher doses of medication to manage her pain. Still, no one was prepared for her 1998 death, least of all her daughters, who were suspicious about the events surrounding Wynette's demise. They sued their stepfather, a Nashville pharmacy, and the singer's doctor for wrongful death. (Richey was eventually dropped from the suit.) Daughter Jackie Daly wrote about the controversy in great detail in her book with Tom Carter, *Tammy Wynette: A Daughter Recalls Her Mother's Tragic Life and Death.*

Although her life was a soap opera right up to the end, none of the lurid accusations or personal controversies could ever dampen Wynette's achievements. She won two Grammy Awards, three Country Music Association awards, eight Billboard awards, and 16 BMI songwriter awards. Wynette was posthumously inducted into Country Music Association Hall of Fame in 1998.

Books

The Billboard Book of Number One Country Hits, edited by Tom Roland, Billboard, 1991.

Country Music: The Encyclopedia, edited by Irwin Stambler and Grelun Landon, St. Martin's Griffin, 1997.

Daly, Jackie with Tom Carter, *Tammy Wynette: A Daughter Recalls Her Mother's Tragic Life and Death,* G.P. Putnam's Sons, 2000.

Definitive Country: The Ultimate Encyclopedia of Country Music and Its Performer, edited by Barry McCloud, Perigree, 1995.

Jones, George with Tom Carter, *I Lived to Tell It All,* Villard, 1996.

MusicHound Country: The Essential Album Guide, edited by Brian Mansfield and Gary Graff, Visible Ink, 1997.

Online

''Tammy Wynette,'' *All Music Guide,* http://www.allmusic.com (December 13, 2006).

''Tammy Wynette,'' http://www.tammywynette.com./ (December 13, 2006).

''Tammy Wynette,'' *Internet Movie Database,* http://imdb.com/ (December 13, 2006). □

Y

Susilo Bambang Yudhoyono

Susilo Bambang Yudhoyono (born 1949) won election as president of the Republic of Indonesia in October of 2004, thus becoming his country's first directly elected president.

An officer in the Indonesian army, but one regarded as a moderate with few links to the military's history of violent excesses, Yudhoyono found himself at the center of some of the world's biggest news stories of the mid-2000s. He faced the challenge of responding to an unprecedented series of natural disasters, including the devastating tsunami of 2004. As Indonesia, the world's most populous predominantly Islamic country, suffered the effects of terrorist attacks by Islamic extremists, it was Yudhoyono who had to bring the perpetrators to justice without alienating the country's Islamic clergy. Educated partly in the United States, Yudhoyono was one of that country's few defenders in the Islamic world in the years after the launch of the Iraq war. And he encountered problems common to leaders of developing countries: reducing institutional corruption, improving infrastructure, and attracting foreign investment. A deliberate man sometimes dubbed "the thinking general," Yudhoyono maintained strong popularity among ordinary Indonesians who used a different nickname: his initials, SBY.

Born into Military Family

Susilo Bambang Yudhoyono was born in the small town of Pacitan, in eastern Java (Indonesia's largest and most populous island), on September 9, 1949. He would later speak out in favor of the preservation of the local language, Javanese, in the face of the increasing influence of Indonesian, the national lingua franca. Yudhoyono's father was a retired lieutenant in the Indonesian army, and Yudhoyono, out of high school and newly married, entered the country's national military academy. He and his wife, Ani, raised two sons.

Yudhoyono graduated in 1973 at the top of his class. He served several tours of duty in the volatile East Timor region, where a separatist movement battled the Indonesian government for two decades until finally winning independence in 1999. In between deployments, Yudhoyono came to the United States for further study. He earned a master's degree in management from Webster University in St. Louis in 1981 and also completed military training programs at Fort Benning, Georgia (1976 and 1982), and the Command and General Staff College at Fort Leavenworth, Kansas (in 1991). Yudhoyono is a fluent English speaker, and, in an interview quoted by the Al Jazeera television network, he said, "I love the United States, with all its faults. I consider it my second country."

As he completed these programs, Yudhoyono was promoted through the ranks of the Indonesian army. By 1995 he had a reputation for integrity and respect for human rights that led to his appointment as chief military observer with the United Nations peacekeeping force in Bosnia, and as head of a contingent of Indonesian soldiers there. Back in Indonesia he became an army territorial commander for a region covering Java and the southern part of the island of Sumatra.

Yudhoyono's increasing responsibilities coincided with a period of instability in Indonesia. In the late 1990s the reign of the country's longtime strongman Suharto (many Indonesians use only one name) was coming to an end under popular pressure. Mobs with connections to the

375

military attacked the offices of an opposition party in the Indonesian capital of Jakarta in 1996 while Yudhoyono was in command, but he was never charged with involvement in the incident. He also escaped charges connected with war crimes committed in the final stages of the East Timor independence struggle even though his direct supervisor, Wiranto, was indicted by a special Timorese tribunal. From 1997 to 2000, as Indonesia endured fallout from the Asian economic crisis of 1997 and the end of Suharto's reign a year later, Yudhoyono served as chief of the army's social and political affairs staff.

Joined Indonesian Government

Yudhoyono's defenders pointed out that he was never part of the Indonesian military's inner circles of power. Nominally a four-star general, he received that rank only as an honorary title after joining the government of President Abdurrahman Wahid in 2000, at which time he retired from active military service. His first position was that of minister of mines, but he was soon installed as minister of security and political affairs. In 2001 he was fired by Wahid, who was facing impeachment proceedings and wanted Yudhoyono to declare a state of emergency. Yudhoyono refused, laying the foundation for his later national reputation as a figure not beholden to the country's power structure.

Yudhoyono was rehired the following year by the country's new president, Megawati Sukarnoputri, and was given the grim task of investigating the terrorist hotel bombings that rocked the resort areas of the island of Bali in 2002

and 2003. Yudhoyono won plaudits for the quick arrest and prosecution of a large group of conspirators, although the identity of the ultimate ringleaders of the plots remained a matter of international debate. He approved a military crackdown on separatist rebels fighting in the Aceh region. In 2004 he resigned his post once again after a disagreement with Sukarnoputri, said to be over access to consultation with her.

The disagreement could have been a manufactured one, for Sukarnoputri's popularity was dropping as Indonesia remained mired in economic problems, and leaving her government was a smart political move for Yudhoyono. "Even though SBY was a senior member of a deeply unpopular government, he has come to be seen as a victim of that government rather than part of it," Indonesian political analyst Denny Ja told Rachel Harvey of the British Broadcasting Corporation. With the approach of Indonesia's first direct presidential elections in 2004, Yudhoyono entered the race.

Yudhoyono had no prior political experience, but on the stump he displayed what Simon Elegant of *Time International* called "a Bill Clinton-like ability to communicate with ordinary Indonesians." Facing Sukarnoputri and Wiranto, another retired general, in the election's first round, Yudhoyono presented himself as a strong leader who nevertheless respected human rights and Indonesia's fledgling democratic traditions. Negative campaigning designed to link him with the U.S. Central Intelligence Agency failed to stick. He placed first in the opening round and then, in a runoff held on September 20, 2004, he defeated Sukarnoputri with nearly 61 percent of the vote. In the midst of the campaign he managed to complete a Ph.D. degree in agricultural economics at Bogor Agricultural University, with one of his dissertation defenses coming just two days before the election. Yudhoyono, whose personal library contains some 13,000 books, told reporters that televised political debates had been good practice for defending his doctoral dissertation.

Was Visible During Tsunami Response

Before he had the chance to implement any of the plans he had discussed during his campaign, Yudhoyono had to deal with the effects of a natural disaster of unprecedented magnitude—the Indian ocean tsunami of December 26, 2004, which killed more than 200,000 people, 100,000 of them in Sumatra alone. He earned high marks from international observers for his performance during the crisis. "The tsunami was Yudhoyono's first big test," Ray Jovanovich of Hong Kong's Credit Agricole Asset Management told Assif Shameen of *Business Week*. "He has shown leadership, poise, and grace under extreme pressure." Before long, Yudhoyono's ambitious program was back on track. He took steps long demanded by international investors, such as increasing the independence of Indonesia's judiciary and cracking down on corruption in the country's local government structures, making headway even though his Democratic party controlled only 10 percent of the seats in the country's parliament.

Yudhoyono's open communication style continued to win him the affection of Indonesians accustomed to top-down decision making. During one appearance he broadcast what he said was his personal cell phone number, inviting listeners to send text messages describing problems they were having with Indonesian bureaucracy. The system set up to receive the messages was soon overwhelmed but still logged over 5,000 of them. Yudhoyono added to Indonesia's prestige by attempting to play a role on the world stage, offering his services as mediator in the Israeli-Palestinian conflict and in the growing showdown between the United States (with other Western countries) and Iran over the latter's nuclear program. His efforts met with little success, but Indonesia's sometimes fractious relationship with the United States improved. Yudhoyono played host to U.S. president George W. Bush in 2006. His diplomatic skills yielded another major accomplishment:

In courting favor in the United States, Yudhoyono was treading a fine line, for large majorities in Indonesian opinion polls expressed disapproval of American policies. Yudhoyono also had to make other difficult decisions during his first two years in office. The most politically dangerous was the slashing of an $11 billion government subsidy that kept fuel prices artificially low in Indonesia but amounted, all by itself, to 5 percent of the country's gross domestic product. Previous attempts to cut the subsidy had contributed to the downfall of the Sukarno government and had damaged Sukarnoputri's popularity. The first phases of a 90 percent price rise touched off protests but generally went smoothly after Yudhoyono introduced a compensation scheme for poorer households and promised to invest part of the savings in government health and education programs.

Likewise controversial was a proposal to let the giant American oil company ExxonMobil implement a plan to tap major oil reserves believed to lie off the East Javanese coast. In promoting the plan, Yudhoyono sidestepped the state oil monopoly, Pertamina, and risked a backlash of nationalist feeling. Yet the offshore oil platforms held enormous potential; Indonesia, despite its proven oil reserves, had become a net importer of oil by the mid-2000s, and in general the country and its 250 million people, lagging behind those of the other rapidly growing economies of Asia, were viewed as something of a sleeping giant economically. Yudhoyono's programs in general—cutting budget deficits, improving transportation facilities and other infrastructure, and strengthening legal protections—were aimed at stabilizing the country and attracting international investment. He succeeded in cutting the average time for approval of new business enterprises from 150 to 60 days, telling *Newsweek International* that he would "do my best to bring it down to one month." Difficult reforms were carried out early in his term so that by 2009, when Yudhoyono would likely face election again, growth would accelerate.

Perhaps the most difficult issue of all early in Yudhoyono's term was that of radical Islamic terrorism. The island of Bali was hit with another wave of suicide bombings, killing 22 people, on October 1, 2005, and Yudhoyono, visiting the site, grimly told Joe Cochrane of *Newsweek International* that "It is obvious that we need to take more effective action to anticipate suicide bombings. His government, however, was slow to officially acknowledge the existence of the Jemaah Islamiah organization, a southeast Asian Islamic group with ties to the international terrorist network al-Qaida, that was thought to have orchestrated both Bali attacks. The effects of a 2006 earthquake that killed 6,200 people on Java were, like those of the 2004 tsunami, swiftly addressed by Yudhoyono's government, but he seemed to be in a race against time to bring material benefits to his disaster-weary people.

Periodicals

Asiamoney, October 2004.
Business Week, January 24, 2005; July 4, 2005.
Capper's, July 19, 2005.
Chronicle of Higher Education, October 15, 2004.
Economist, October 23, 2004; October 1, 2005; May 20, 2006; June 3, 2006.
ICIS Chemical Business Weekly, July 17, 2006.
Newsweek International, June 21, 2004; October 17, 2005; March 6, 2006; March 17, 2006.
Time International, June 28, 2004; October 4, 2004.

Online

"Biography of President Susilo Bambang Yudhoyono," Office of the President of the Republic of Indonesia, http://www.presidensby.info/index.php/eng/profile/index.html (January 6, 2007.
"Javanese Language," Indonesia Matters, http://www.indonesiamatters.com/686/javanese-language (January 6, 2007).
"Profile: Susilo Bambang Yudhoyono," Al Jazeera English, http://www.english.aljazeera.net/news/archive/archive?ArchiveId=4965 (January 6, 2007).
"Profile: Susilo Bambang Yudhoyono," British Broadcasting Corporation, http://www.news.bbc.co.uk/1/hi/world/asia-pacific/3725301/stm (January 6, 2007). □

Z

Abu Mussab al-Zarqawi

Jordanian-born terrorist Abu Mussab al-Zarqawi (1966–2006) was killed in a United States air strike in central Iraq on June 8, 2006. The chaos he had helped set in motion in that country, however, only deepened after his death.

Zarqawi had been cast by the administration of U.S. president George W. Bush as the Iraq-based leader of the international al-Qaida terrorist organization. But his ties with that group were uncertain, tense and volatile, as were many of the other alliances he formed over the course of his short life. Ultimately Zarqawi's allegiances lay only with his particular brand of extremist Sunni Islam, a belief system in which Muslims who subscribed to other ideas were hated as much as, or even more than, the Western presence in the Middle East. Of the various horrific terrorist acts Zarqawi and his henchmen planned and executed, perhaps the most destructive—the simultaneous suicide bombing of three hotels in Amman, Jordan, in November of 2005—was aimed at an Arab target, not a Western one.

Used Cemetery for Playground

Zarqawi was born Ahmed Fadeel al-Khalayleh on October 20, 1966, in Zarqa, Jordan, a large, economically depressed city north of the Jordanian capital of Amman. The name "al-Zarqawi" he adopted later simply indicated that he was from Zarqa. One of ten children, he was raised in a poor family with roots in one of the Bedouin Arab tribes of the region's deserts. Zarqawi was remembered as a disruptive and untalented student, and he had little to do outside of school. Sometimes he had to use a local cemetery as a

playground, but his family life provided a bright spot. Zarqawi "was the apple of our father's eye," one of his sisters told Loretta Napoleoni of *Foreign Policy.* He briefly worked as a clerk in a video store.

Already in trouble with the law—at 15 he had been involved with a home invasion during which one of his relatives was killed—the teenaged Zarqawi was thrown into a downward spiral by the death of his father in 1984. He left school and began to abuse alcohol and drugs, joining a local street gang and gaining a reputation as a thug and a trafficker in illicit materials of various kinds. Jordanian police also accused him of sexual assault, and he may have been active as a pimp. In all, he was charged with 37 separate crimes. He served a brief prison term, and it was in prison that he first encountered strict forms of Islam. After his release he married (in 1988 or 1989), and began attending a mosque oriented toward radical Islamic ideas.

Recruiters for the Islamic jihad or holy war against the government of Afghanistan, which was allied with the officially atheist Soviet Union, found Zarqawi an easy mark. He left for Afghanistan to join the fighting in 1989 and saw action with Islamic mujahedeen fighters in several battles that eventually led to the takeover of Afghanistan by the repressive Taliban militia. "He was an ordinary guy, an ordinary fighter, and didn't really distinguish himself," one militiaman recalled to Mary Anne Weaver of the *Atlantic Monthly.* "He was a quiet guy who didn't talk much. But he was brave. Zarqawi doesn't know the meaning of fear." Wounded several times, Zarqawi seemed "to place himself in the middle of the most dangerous situations."

Zarqawi's commitment to Islamist thought also deepened as he came under the influence of Sheikh Abu Muhammad al-Maqdisi, a radical Sunni cleric and fellow native of Zarqa whom Zarqawi met in Afghanistan. Soon he would come to share al-Maqdisi's hatred of Shiite Muslims. Back in Jordan in 1993, the two planned to blow up a movie theater that was showing X-rated films. The plot was botched, and another plan went awry when Zarqawi was caught by police carrying seven hand grenades. Sentenced to 15 years in prison, "he would flourish there," in the words of the *Atlantic*'s Weaver.

Became "Emir" of Prison

In prison, Zarqawi apparently became a combination of Islamic scholar and gang leader. He spent long hours memorizing the Koran, but he also wore the outfit of an Afghan militiaman and made an impression on his fellow prisoners. "He decided who would cook, who would do the laundry, who would lead the readings of the Koran," journalist Abdullah Abu Rumman, a journalist who served time with Zarqawi, told Weaver. "He was extremely protective of his followers, and extremely tough with prisoners outside his group." Released after a stretch in solitary confinement following a brawl, Abu Rumman recalled, he returned to the ward with a phalanx of bodyguards. "By that time Zarqawi was already called the 'emir,' or 'prince,'" Abu Rumman said. "He had an uncanny ability to control, almost to hypnotize; he could order his followers to do things just by moving his eyes." Like so many other prisoners, he acquired an intimidating group of tattoos.

While still in prison the barely literate Zarqawi, with help from Maqdisi, began to write militant Islamic tracts that were smuggled out by sympathizers and posted on the Internet. The legend of Zarqawi among disaffected Arab youth with few prospects in life began to spread, and one of his Internet postings found its way to al-Qaida leader Osama bin Laden. When Jordan's King Abdullah II declared an amnesty in 1999, Zarqawi was released, but the Jordanian government suspected him of involvement in plans for the bombing of a series of hotels and Christian sites, to be executed on New Year's Eve, 1999. The plan was foiled, and Zarqawi left the country, hoping to join separatist Islamic rebels in the Russian province of Chechnya. Instead he was arrested in Pakistan for having an expired visa. Forced to leave the country, he entered Afghanistan. Equipped with a letter of introduction from a Jordanian cleric, he was taken to the city of Kandahar to meet bin Laden.

By some accounts, the meeting between the two men was tense, with bin Laden, whose mother was a Shiite Muslim, finding himself disturbed by the young Zarqawi's violent sectarianism. Zarqawi, for his part, refused to swear *bayat*, or allegiance, to al-Qaida. Finally he was given seed money by bin Laden allies in Afghanistan's radical Islamic government to set up a militia training camp in the desert near Herat, in western Afghanistan. Once again Zarqawi emerged as a natural leader; his band of followers grew from a few dozen to some 3,000 men between early 2000 and the American invasion of Afghanistan in late 2001.

As Zarqawi's influence grew, money and guns flowed his way. He was summoned to bin Laden's headquarters in Kandahar five times to swear allegiance to al-Qaida, but refused each time. "He never followed the orders of others," a former fighter in the Herat camp told Napoleoni. "I never heard him praise anyone apart from the Prophet

[Muhammad], this was Abu Mussab's character. He never followed anyone."

After the Americans attacked Afghanistan in the wake of bin Laden's terrorist bombings of September 11, 2001, Zarqawi and his men joined with the Afghan government to fight the invasion. Zarqawi was wounded in the chest when a building that was bombed by American planes collapsed on top of him. In December of 2001 he and a group of about 300 followers slipped out of Afghanistan and crossed into Iran.

Built Sunni Resistance Organization in Iraq

Over the next months, Zarqawi shuttled among Iran, Syria, Lebanon, Jordan, the autonomous northern Iraq region of Kurdistan, and southern Iraq's "Sunni triangle" region, collecting fighters and money. His motivations were diverse. For some time, his primary aim was to form an Islamic force that would eventually overthrow Jordan's moderate government. In October of 2002 American diplomat Laurence Foley was killed in Amman, Jordan, reportedly on Zarqawi's orders. But he also anticipated the disorder that would follow a threatened American invasion of Iraq. Working with a separatist northern Iraqi militia, Ansar-al-Islam, he worked to expand his power in that country, and he found new followers among Iraq's Sunni minority.

In a speech at the United Nations in February of 2003, laying out the case for invading Iraq, U.S. Secretary of State Colin Powell named Zarqawi as a key al-Qaida operative in Iraq, an assertion that probably surprised Zarqawi greatly, inasmuch as his ties with that organization were tenuous at best. Powell also said that Zarqawi was Palestinian, and that he had lost a leg in the Afghanistan bombing, both false statements. After the American-led invasion deposed Iraqi dictator Saddam Hussein, insurgent Sunni Muslims flocked to Zarqawi's side as he came to southern Iraq and likely lived in the violence-riddled city of Fallujah.

Zarqawi's attention was still concentrated on his homeland of Jordan. He organized a massive plot in 2004 to blow up the buildings that housed Jordan's intelligence service. This included a convoy of truck bombs containing lethal chemicals that could have killed 80,000 people. The plan was disrupted, and in May of 2004 Zarqawi became known to the American public at large when his group released a video showing the beheading of American contractor Nicholas Berg. Zarqawi himself may have been the hooded figure wielding the knife in the video. Numerous less-publicized attacks by Zarqawi's bands of Sunni insurgents increased in intensity, eventually killing an estimated 6,000 Iraqis. Late in 2004, Zarqawi finally pledged allegiance to al-Qaida; by the middle of 2005, the $25 million bounty placed on his head by the American government equaled that offered for the capture of bin Laden himself.

Even at that point, Zarqawi still hoped to create chaos in Jordan, and on November 9, 2005, he succeeded, when suicide bombers hit the Radisson SAS, Grand Hyatt, and Days Inn Hotels in Amman. Zarqawi claimed credit for the attacks, which killed over 55 people, including a group of Palestinians attending a wedding. Even al-Qaida's leadership had reportedly reprimanded Zarqawi for the bad publicity generated by his grisly tactics, and now street opinion in the region began to turn against him. Large demonstrations in Amman demanded his death, and tips on his whereabouts began to cross the paths of Jordanian and American spies. Several times he eluded capture as American troops closed in on his hideout.

In April of 2006, Sunni insurgent fighter Huthaifa Azzam told Weaver Zarqawi had been placed in a purely military role within the organization—perhaps a demotion, perhaps a recognition of the fact that his talents lay in the area of recruitment. Seemingly in response, Zarqawi posted a 35-minute video on the Internet, showing him firing an automatic weapon and discussing strategy in a desert training camp. The tape attacked Iraq's elected government for its alliance with the United States and promised mayhem to come. The American intelligence net was closing around him, however, and on June 8, 2006, an American F-16 fighter jet dropped a 500-pound bomb on a safe house in Hibhib, Iraq, north of Baghdad, where Zarqawi was talking with an Islamic advisor; he was carried out the building alive, "muttering prayers," according to *Newsweek,* but he died soon afterward. *Newsweek* speculated that "Zarqawi's demise may turn out to be a turning point in the long, frustrating war on terror," but instead, violence between Sunni and Shiite Muslims in Iraq continued to intensify in the coming months.

Periodicals

Atlantic Monthly, July–August 2006.
Foreign Policy, November–December 2005.
New Yorker, June 19, 2006.
Newsweek, June 19, 2006.
Time, December 19, 2005; June 19, 2006.

Online

"Abu Musab al-Zarqawi," Biography Resource Center Online, Gale, 2004, reproduced in Biography Resource Center, Thomson Gale, 2006, http://www.galenet.galegroup.com/servlet/BioRC (December 6, 2006). □

Dieter Zetsche

German automotive executive Dieter Zetsche (born 1953) was credited with a sharp improvement of the fortunes of the United States-based Chrysler division of the DaimlerChrysler auto firm in the early 2000s. Zetsche's feats as a corporate turnaround artist, which went back to his days at the helm of the truck manufacturer Freightliner in the early 1990s, propelled him to the leadership of DaimlerChrysler in 2006.

Enjoyed Difficult Equestrian Sport

Dieter Zetsche (TSET–shuh) was born in Istanbul, Turkey, on May 5, 1953. His parents were German; his father was in Turkey to work in the field of bridge construction. When Zetsche was two, his family returned to Germany and settled in the Frankfurt area. He attended school in a Frankfurt suburb, and his penchant for attempting difficult balancing acts showed in his choice of sport as a teenager: he practiced the difficult activity of equestrian vaulting, which might be defined as doing gymnastics while mounted on the back of a moving horse. To earn extra money he drove a beverage delivery truck. Zetsche passed the German Abitur, or university entrance exam, in 1971 and entered the engineering program at the University of Karlsruhe.

When he received his degree in electrical engineering in 1976, it was roughly the equivalent of a master's degree in the United States. He went to work as an engineer in the research division of Germany's oldest automaker, Daimler-Benz, the makers of Mercedes-Benz automobiles as well as other automotive products, while doing work on a Ph.D. in mechanical engineering at the Technical University of Paderborn. He was granted the degree in 1982. Zetsche's first car was a 1971 Volkswagen Beetle. Shortly after finishing his education, Zetsche married his wife, Gisela; the pair raised three children.

By that time Zetsche had already advanced to the position of assistant to the chief engineer of Daimler-Benz's commercial vehicle division. His promotion in 1981 was the first in a rapid series of advances that would, within a decade, see him emerge as a leader in national and then international operations. Part of his career was spent on the truck manufacturing side of Daimler-Benz. He became coordinator for commercial vehicle development activities in 1984, and senior manager and chief engineer of the company's cross-country vehicle unit in 1986.

The following year, Zetsche moved to South America to head the engineering and product development departments of Mercedes-Benz of Brazil. His skill with foreign languages proved an asset to his career in the increasingly international auto business; he speaks six languages—German, English, French, Portuguese, Spanish, and Latin. In 1989 Zetsche was named president of Mercedes-Benz Argentina. He was credited with engineering a turnaround in Daimler-Benz's troubled operations there.

Headed Freightliner

In 1991 Zetsche came to the United States for the first time, as president of the Freightliner truck firm, owned by Daimler-Benz and headquartered in Portland, Oregon. His open, informal management style meshed well with American corporate culture, and he would later express the opinion that stereotypical differences between American and German corporate styles were often overstated. The results he achieved at Freightliner were rapid, involving the layoffs of some 3,800 workers. Over 14 months the company increased its market share and surged past rivals such as Volvo and Navistar.

Clearly now being groomed for the higher corporate ranks at Daimler-Benz, Zetsche returned to Germany in 1992. He became chief engineer of the development division for Mercedes-Benz, joining several of the company's sales management boards. He was seen as a protégé of Daimler-Benz chairman Jürgen Schrempp. The challenges the pair faced with the Mercedes-Benz auto line were substantial; once unchallenged as Europe's premier luxury auto nameplate, the company had suffered under competition from German automaker BMW and from Japanese upstarts Lexus and Acura, and had failed to introduce new models that caught the public imagination.

Much of the task of reviving Mercedes-Benz fell to Zetsche—and not only on the engineering side. Zetsche brought an informal new management style to the more than one hundred-year-old company, derived partly from his experiences in America but equally from his own relaxed personality. "My style is my style. It is who I am and how I am. I won't change that," he told Mark Landler of the *International Herald Tribune.* Zetsche took steps to bring senior managers closer to the day-to-day processes of product design, eliminating the Daimler-Benz executive dining room and moving managers' offices physically closer to those of other employees.

Under Zetsche's initiatives, the pace of new model introduction at Mercedes-Benz accelerated markedly. When Daimler-Benz merged with the Chrysler corporation in the United States to form DaimlerChrysler, a fusion billed at the time as a merger of equals but later widely viewed as a corporate takeover, Zetsche seemed to be a logical candidate to become chief executive of the new Chrysler group. He claimed to have no inkling that he was under consideration for the Chrysler top spot, but when Chrysler profits plummeted in the year 2000, Zetsche was tapped. "The

company sees him as a highly respected turnaround guy who's handled problems before," auto analyst Jim Mateyka told Jeffrey McCracken of the *Detroit Free Press.*

Downsized Chrysler

Zetsche negotiated a path through the minefields that awaited him early in his tenure at Chrysler, including mistrust from longtime Chrysler managers wary of a strong new German presence in the company's Auburn Hills, Michigan, headquarters. Robyn Meredith of *Forbes* called Zetsche and chief operating officer Wolfgang Bernhard "two of the most hated men in Detroit" shortly after Zetsche's appointment. But Zetsche brought just a few senior German managers with him to the United States. Having suffered through losses of $3 billion in the five quarters leading up to Zetsche's appointment as CEO in the fall of 2000, the company was ripe for restructuring. Zetsche oversaw a difficult contraction that involved the elimination of about 40,000 jobs over several years, many through early-retirement packages offered to workers. Several Chrysler plants were closed. White-collar jobs were also cut, but the corps of engineers responsible for developing new product, a key group in any Zetsche turnaround strategy, were spared the worst of the cutbacks. And Zetsche won high marks for the way the layoffs were handled. "While Zetsche's decisions . . . were not popular," Landler noted, "no one could complain that they did not understand why they were happening."

By April of 2002, Zetsche's restructuring had begun to yield financial dividends, as Chrysler posted a profit of $111 million in the first quarter of that year, the strongest result within the entire DaimlerChrysler organization. During a period when the market share of American automakers was dropping sharply, Chrysler's rose from 12.6 percent in the last three months of 2001 to 13.6 percent in the first quarter of 2002. First-quarter profits rose to $366 million in 2003, receding only slightly to $327 million in the first quarter of 2004, by which time the company was considered to be out of the woods financially. Part of the credit went to the company's aggressively styled new Chrysler 300 luxury sedan.

Though a private and reserved individual, Zetsche proved to be a strong motivator of his American workforce. He parked in the employee parking lot at Chrysler headquarters and ate lunches in the company cafeteria, generally creating the impression of a leader focused on results. "The least productive thing you can do is to point fingers, always longing for the good old days," he observed in a speech quoted by Sarah A. Webster of the *Detroit Free Press.* Zetsche and his wife became closely involved in a number of Detroit-area community institutions and charitable organizations, directing millions of dollars in Chrysler contributions to the Detroit Institute of Arts and appearing in a commercial for the United Way.

By 2005 Zetsche had such a positive image in Detroit that there were rumors he might be poached for a top position by crosstown rival Ford. Clouds appeared on the horizon as increasing gasoline prices caused large unsold inventories of large Dodge and Jeep trucks and sport utility vehicles to build up on dealer lots. Chrysler responded with an advertising campaign featuring Zetsche himself as a comical "Dr. Z" character who touted the German engineering in Chrysler vehicles and dealt good-naturedly with joshing from callers concerning his large, instantly recognizable white handlebar moustache. The campaign failed to improve the situation much, but by that time DaimlerChrysler was facing more serious problems. The company's flagship Mercedes-Benz line was once again flagging. The company was barely breaking even, with a much-touted small car for the European market, called the Smart, losing money. Most ominously, quality problems began to surface in Mercedes cars, which had long had a reputation for reliability.

Zetsche, the company's turnaround specialist, was brought home to Germany to deal with the problems—displacing in the process his longtime mentor Schrempp, who retired. On January 1, 2006, Zetsche assumed the positions of chairman of the board of management of DaimlerChrysler and head of the Mercedes Car Group. Financial markets reacted positively to the appointment, with DaimlerChrysler stock rising more than 30 percent in the months after he took the reins. Zetsche began to apply some of the all-for-one, one-for-all symbolism that had worked well in Michigan, moving much of the DaimlerChrysler executive corps out of its plush Stuttgart headquarters and into a factory building.

In a situation far from the initial American fears of a complete German takeover of DaimlerChrysler, Zetsche installed several key North American managers in positions in Germany (since the 1998 merger, company business had been conducted in English). By late 2006 he had implemented a new, more centralized administrative structure at DaimlerChrysler that resulted in savings of an estimated $950 billion annually, and he laid the groundwork for the introduction of the Smart car into the crucial American market. More generally, he shook up the company's well-entrenched office politics. "Dieter is making an enormous contribution to the company culture by putting an end to the Stuttgart mentality of self-interest," one former Daimler-Chrysler employee told the *Economist*. The process of reinvigorating the DaimlerChrysler organization as a whole was expected to involve several years of work, but it was in the hands of a longtime "car guy" who seemed very little motivated by self-interest. In 2006 *Time* magazine named him one of 100 "People Who Shape Our World."

Books

International Dictionary of Business Biographies, 4 vols., St. James, 2005.

Periodicals

Automotive News, November 22, 2004; August 11, 2005; January 30, 2006; September 25, 2006.
Detroit Free Press, November 16, 2000; June 10, 2005; July 30, 2005.
Economist (U.S.), September 23, 2006.
Forbes, March 5, 2001.
Indianapolis Star, April 26, 2002.
International Herald Tribune, November 5, 2005.
Newsweek, December 5, 2005.
New York Times, July 18, 2006.

Online

"Dieter Zetsche," Ask Dr. Z, http://www.askdrz.com (January 2, 2007).
"Dr. Dieter Zetsche," DaimlerChrysler, http://www.daimlerchrysler.com (January 2, 2007).
"Resume: Dieter Zetsche," *Business Week Online,* http://www.businessweek.com/magazine/content/01_38/b3749005.htm (January 2, 2007).
"Time 100: The People Who Shape Our World, Dieter Zetsche," *Time,* http://www.time.com/time/magazine/article/0,9171,1187492,00.html (January 2, 2007). □

Zhang Yimou

Perhaps the most critically acclaimed filmmaker to emerge from mainland China in modern times, Zhang Yimou (born 1950) came to critical attention in the 1990s for his tense films that seemed indirectly to subvert the centralized power of China's Communist government.

Several of Zhang's early films were banned in his homeland but gained strong viewership in the West as a result. Zhang grew cannier about dealing with Chinese censors as he grew older, and to some critics, both within and outside China, his later films seemed to have less of an edge. His technical prowess only grew, however, and the film through which many international moviegoers encountered his work was the visually stunning historical martial arts epic *Hero* (2002).

Suffered from Suspect Family Background

Zhang Yimou (who has always used the traditional Chinese ordering that places the family name first, then the given name) was born in Xi'an, in China's Shaanxi province, on November 14, 1950, shortly after the defeat of China's Nationalist government by the Communist armies of Mao Tse-tung. Zhang's father was a dermatologist who served as an officer in the Nationalist Kuomintang army, and one of his brothers fled mainland China for the Nationalist-ruled island of Taiwan. These facts made life difficult for Zhang from the start, and things became worse during the repressive Cultural Revolution of the 1960s and 1970s. After finishing high school, he was sent to work in farm fields with Chinese peasants. Later he was transferred to Textile Factory No. 8 in the city of Xianyang.

Fascinated by film and visual imagery even in the government propaganda films that were the sole approved source of entertainment, Zhang managed to acquire a camera by selling his own blood. The restrictions of the Cultural Revolution lessened after Mao's death in 1976, and Zhang applied to the Beijing Film Academy. At 27, he was over the regulation age for admission, but he was able to persuade officials to make an exception after showing them some of his photographs. At the academy, Zhang became part of the

so-called Fifth Generation of the school's trainees; his class-mates included several other young directors who had lived through the Cultural Revolution and were skeptical of the unchecked power of China's totalitarian state. He graduated from the academy in 1982.

Zhang began his career as a cinematographer. Among other films, he worked on Chen Kaige's *Yellow Earth* (1984), the film that introduced contemporary Chinese cinema to Western audiences. For much of his career Zhang's films would be hailed above all for their visual appearance, often based on a specific color scheme that pervaded the entire work. As a director he would tour countryside locations tirelessly, searching for the backdrop he wanted for a specific scene.

Zhang served as both cinematographer and actor on the 1987 film *Old Well*, a rural tale that returned him to his hometown of Xi'an. In one of his rare interviews (often, when asked about a film's prospects, he would quietly respond that it was the audience's decision), Zhang told James Harding of the *Financial Times* that "basically, I'm a northerner—a little wild and unconstrained. I like things that are strong and rich, like . . . lamb with wheatcakes. I'm not keen on things that are light and delicate. Like films, images, stories, they've got to have something rich and powerful about them."

Onto this provincial background, however, Zhang transferred wide cinematic education. He was familiar with American film traditions such as the Western, and he sometimes used non-Chinese personnel, such Chinese-speaking Australian cinematographer Chris Doyle, on his films. Zhang was a voracious reader. "I do read, to get cultivated," he told Harding. "I can't read during the daytime, but I have to read for hours in the evening."

Directed First Film

In the late 1980s Zhang discovered actress Gong Li when she was a 21-year-old drama student, and he elevated her to national and international stardom. She appeared in the first film he directed, 1987's *Red Sorghum,* and for much of the first part of his career he would shape his films around her talents. In *Red Sorghum* she played a young woman sold into marriage, and she was often cast by Zhang as a woman oppressed by the rules of the feudal societies in which most of Zhang's historical dramas were set. In *Ju Dou* (1990) she once again played a woman forced into marriage by poverty, this time beginning an affair with tragic consequences, and in *Raise the Red Lantern* (1991) she portrayed a new concubine introduced into the household of an aristocrat in the traditional Chinese society of the 1920s. The lighter but still edgy *The Story of Qiu Ju* featured Gong Li as a peasant woman whose husband is insulted, and who climbs the ladder of authority in demanding justice for him.

Among Zhang's early films, only *To Live* (1994) dealt directly with contemporary China. Authorities, however, were quick to grasp the anti-authoritarian overtones of Zhang's feminist themes, and *Raise the Red Lantern, The Story of Qiu Ju,* and *To Live* were all banned in China. (*Red Sorghum* was restricted to certain locales as well.) The combination of implied dissent and cinematic skill—the dark interiors of *Raise the Red Lantern* were perhaps particularly notable for their overwhelming feeling of claustrophobia—was irresistible to Western film connoisseurs; the Golden Bear Award that *Red Sorghum* received at the 1987 Berlin Film Festival in Germany was the first in a long sequence of awards and nominations honoring Zhang at international events.

During the filming of Zhang's next movie, the gangster-themed drama *Shanghai Triad,* Gong Li reportedly dissolved her relationship with the director; she later married a Singaporean business executive. The pace of Zhang's career slowed for several years, although he participated in 1996 in a unique operatic experiment: the transfer of the Giacomo Puccini opera *Turandot* to its actual Chinese setting for a massive outdoor performance. After the little-seen 1997 comedy *Keep Cool,* Zhang returned to international screens in 1999 with *Not One Less,* the story of a young schoolteacher in a rural Chinese village who pursues one of her students when he runs away to a large city. In contrast to the star-driven vehicles of his earlier career, Zhang cast nonprofessional actors as the villagers in the film.

The runaway child's hunger as he tries to make his way in the city is vividly shown, but the deeper horrors that might have awaited him in real life are avoided. *Not One Less* clearly addressed the divide between China's growing cities and the still-medieval living conditions of much of its countryside, but this time Zhang opted for a happy ending. "You always have to take censors into account in China," he explained to Howard Feinstein of the London *Guardian.*

"I wouldn't have been able to make a story in which the child wasn't found." *Not One Less* won the Golden Lion Award at the 1999 Venice Film Festival, and his romance *The Road Home* (2000) and comedy *Happy Times* (2001) cemented his position as a major director in China. *The Road Home* also introduced actress Zhang Ziyi, who would later achieve stardom in the martial arts extravaganza *Crouching Tiger, Hidden Dragon,* directed by Taiwanese-American filmmaker Ang Lee.

Filmed Martial Arts Epic

In 2002 Zhang made a martial arts epic of his own; Zhang Ziyi appeared along with Jet Li and a host of other internationally known Hong Kong film stars in *Hero,* set in China's early Qin dynasty. The film deployed martial arts in a sumptuous pageant drawn from Chinese history. Riding a wave of popularity for martial arts films set in motion by *Crouching Tiger, Hidden Dragon* and other more popularly oriented action films, *Hero* became the highest-grossing film in Chinese history and handsomely recouped its original $30 million cost. The film was successful in the United States even though its release was delayed for nearly two years by its American distributor, Miramax, and it earned an Academy Award nomination for Best Foreign Film. Some critics, however, argued that the film, in contrast to Zhang's earlier films, had a message that legitimized China's authoritarian government.

Zhang had several opportunities to direct films outside of China but turned them down, preferring not to leave his home country for long. He became involved with several small projects that involved Chinese national pride, directing a small video that was part of China's successful application to host the Summer Olympic games in 2008. He also created a live performance for tourists in the Chinese resort of Guilin, in which, according to the Xinhua News Agency, "hundreds of bamboo-made boats float on the clear water, candle light sparkles with the moon and stars, [and] thousands of people dressed in Chinese minority ethnic costumes hum a folk song." Zhang also returned to opera, serving as producer of *The First Emperor,* slated for presentation at New York's Metropolitan Opera in 2007 with music by Chinese American composer Tan Dun.

By that time Zhang had released several more films. *House of Flying Daggers* (2004) was another martial arts historical epic, while *Riding Alone for Thousands of Miles,* from the following year, featured Japanese actor Ken Takakura as the father of an ailing documentary filmmaker. The two are alienated, but the father travels throughout rural China, trying to finish a documentary about Chinese opera that his son has begun. Zhang was back in blockbuster territory in 2006 with *Curse of the Golden Flower,* which Steven Rea of the *Philadelphia Inquirer* called "a dazzling costume epic, a spectacle for the eyes and for the soul," although the *Washington Times* warned that "the director occasionally gets dazed by the beauty of his own work." That film reunited Zhang with Gong Li for the first time in more than a decade, and it helped cement Zhang's reputation as China's most ambitious filmmaker.

Books

International Directory of Films and Filmmakers, Volume 2: Directors, 4th ed., St. James, 2000.

Periodicals

Economist, February 11, 1989.
Financial Times, January 31, 1998.
Entertainment Weekly, December 17, 2004.
Guardian (London, England), June 16, 2000; August 1, 2002.
Newsweek, October 9, 1995.
New York Times, February 6, 2000.
Opera News, January 2007.
Philadelphia Inquirer, December 28, 2006.
St. Louis Post-Dispatch, February 8, 2002.
Time, March 18, 1991.
Time International (Asia edition), August 9, 2004.
Time International (South Pacific edition), November 15, 2004.
Variety, November 20, 2006.
Washington Times, December 26, 2006.
Xinhua News Agency, August 18, 2005; February 22, 2006; December 20, 2006.

Online

"Zhang Yimou," *All Movie Guide,* http://www.allmovie.com (January 6, 2007). □

Zinédine Zidane

Zinédine Zidane (born 1972) was the toast of France after leading that country to its only World Cup soccer championship in 1998. The midfielder, nicknamed "Zizou," scored twice in the championship match that year as the French, playing at home, defeated Brazil.

Amid the soccer euphoria, Zidane, a devout Muslim born to Algerian immigrants, was also embraced as an ethnic unifier. But Zidane left the game in disgrace in 2006. With France back in the World Cup final, Zidane, in what he said would be his final game, was ejected from the title match for a head butt during overtime. The French, without Zidane for the shootout, lost to Italy. "Zinédine Zidane has written glorious chapters in football's recent history—how sad that he should save the most shameful episode for the final page of his story," Phil McNulty wrote on the British Broadcasting Corporation's website, BBC Sport.

Early Years

Zidane was the fifth child of Smail and Malika Zidane. His parents arrived in France from the Kabylie region of northern Algeria in 1953. Zidane grew up in La Castellane, a crime-ridden housing development in Marseille, a port city in the south of France. Unemployment and suicide rates are alarmingly high in La Castellane. His father had steady work as an overnight department store watchman, though the

family had to live in tight quarters—not all seven could sit down together and eat.

As a youth, Zidane played soccer games in Place Tartane, the public square in La Castellane. At age 14 he was a ballboy during a France-Portugal European Cup playoff game at Stade Vélodrome in Marseille. At age 13, Zidane signed with the Cannes club team at the junior level. He made the elite squad at 17; at age 19, Zidane scored his first goal at that level and the club president fulfilled his promise to him—he gave Zidane a car, a red Clio.

In the early 1990s Zidane signed with Bordeaux and his play there caught the attention of the elite Italian team Juventus of Turin. With Zidane in the fold, Juventus won five championships—including international events—in three years. In Turin, Zidane played for Marcello Lippi, who would later coach Italy to victory in the 2006 World Cup title match against Zidane's France. Back home, however, Zidane had trouble pleasing the French media, which called him *le chat noir* (the black cat). They accused him of playing poorly in consequential games, such as the Champions League, which features the top club teams throughout Europe.

Zidane, though, remained popular in Marseille, where he would return during his breaks from soccer. "He knows everyone at La Castellane," Philippe Jerome wrote in the London *Guardian*. "When he comes, we sit on a bench and talk about everything. He has remained very unassuming," longtime friend Richard Mendi told Jerome. His status also "gave a strong sense of pride to many North

Africans in France [known as Maghrebs]," Jasey Dasey said on ESPNStar.com.

Cup Victory Captivated France

In his first international game, Zidane entered as a substitute and scored both goals as the French tied the Czech Republic, 2–2. "It was soon clear that Zidane, wityh his immaculate dribbling and passing skills, was the midfield general that France [was] looking for to fill the boots of the long-retired Michel Platini," Dasey said. France missed the World Cup final round in 1994, but was building for 1998, when it would host the quadrennial event for the first time in 60 years.

France breezed through the first round, defeating South Africa, Saudi Arabia, and Denmark. Zidane, however, was suspended for two games for scraping his cleats against the back of Saudi captain Fuad Amin. He missed his country's one-goal victories over Denmark and Paraguay but returned to score a penalty kick during a shootout in which France outlasted Italy to reach the semifinals. The French edged Croatia 2–1 in the semis to reach their first-ever title match, against defending champion Brazil.

Zidane, normally a playmaker, became scorer in the final. He connected in the 27th and 46th minutes, both on picturesque headers. Emmanuel Petit fed him from the left corner on the first goal, and Youri Djorkaeff set him up from the right side on the second. Petit scored a breakaway goal near the end of the game to finish off Brazil. The victory on July 12—two days before Bastille Day, the national holiday—set off bedlam in the Stade de France and the celebration spilled into the streets of Paris and other communities.

Seen as Ethnic Unifier

While France celebrated the World Cup victory, many observers took note of the multi-ethnic nature of the team at a time of racial strife. "I had never seen French people so happy with each other," Nick Fraser wrote in London's *Guardian*. "As I walked around the crowds, however, I noticed something else. There were many Arabs and blacks in the crowd, and many of them were carrying tricolor flags."

During the mid–1990s, Jean-Marie Le Pen, the far right president of the National Front party, known for his staunch anti-immigration stance, railed at the French squad for its inability to sing the national anthem, the Marseillaise. The team was snidely called "noir, blanc et bleu" (black, white and blue)," because many players were not strictly French. Zidane, with Algerian parents, was from a dilapidated section of Marseille; other top players such as Patrick Thierry, Marcel Desailly, and Berbard Diomede were black. Fraser said Le Pen and other political leaders had "indiscriminately fanned the flames of disgruntlement." Le Pen, however, as did French President Jacques Chirac, joined in the celebration and spoke of national unity immediately after the World Cup triumph.

As the World Cup celebration and the national holiday blended into one, the Arab presence was noteworthy on the streets of Paris. Soccer fan Rabah Khedache, whose parents emigrated from Algeria's Kabylie region, thanked Zidane "for everything he has done for out [Kabylie] people," according to Lara Marlowe in the *Irish Times.* "It is stunning to hear blond, blue-eyed French school children telling reporters that the shy, balding, darker-skinned Zidane is the most handsome man in France, that they would like to have him as their father," Marlowe wrote. At a garden party in the Elysée palace, in the presence of Chirac, crowds chanted "Zizou president."

Named Top Player Three Times

Zidane earned player of the year honors in 1998 from Fédération Internationale de Football Association, or FIFA, the governing body of world soccer. He earned the same honor in 2000 and 2003. France won the Euro 2000 tournament, defeating Italy in the final. In 2001 Zidane signed a four-year contract with the Real Madrid team of Spain. The transfer fee of €66 million ($86 million) was the highest ever at the time. Zidane in 2002 scored the winning goal, as Real Madrid beat Bayer Leverkusen of Germany in the title match of the Champions League, a tournament involving the top club teams in Europe. He announced his retirement in 2004, but returned to international soccer a year later.

One month before the 2006 World Cup in Germany, Zidane said the tournament would be his last and that he would stay retired. Zidane "has tended to do things his own way," Dasey wrote. "He's always unique and often surprising."

Career Ended in Disgrace

France advanced past group play in the 2006 World Cup with a victory and two draws. Zidane scored the insurance goal as the French, after falling behind early, defeated Spain 3–1 in the round of 16. His perfectly placed free kick set up Thierry Henry's goal in the 57th minute as *Les Bleus* defeated Brazil in the quarterfinals, 1–0. Some observers had pegged Brazil as the pre-tournament favorite. Zidane's first-half penalty kick was enough for a 1–0 triumph over Portugal in the semifinals and the French were back in the title match, paired against three-time champion Italy on Sunday, July 9, 2006, at Berlin's Olympic Stadium.

In the seventh minute of play, Zidane put France up 1–0, chipping a penalty kick off the crossbar and into the net behind Italian goalkeeper Gianluigi Buffon. Twelve minutes later, Marco Materazzi evened the score, heading a shot past French goalie Fabien Barthez. The teams remained even, and went into overtime.

At the 110th minute, or the 20th minute of overtime, Zidane lost his composure in "a moment of madness which cost him a second World Cup title," Jonathan Stevenson wrote on BBC Sport. Angry after an exchange with Materazzi—Matt Hughes of the *Times Online* reported that Materazzi had called Zidane "the son of a terrorist whore"—Zidane headbutted the Italian defender in the chest. Referee Horacio Marcelo Elizondo of Argentina ejected Zidane after the assistant referee informed him of the incident. The French played the rest of overtime without Zidane, but more important, their star was unavailable for the penalty kick shootout necessary to determine the winner. Italy won the shootout 5–3.

"It was a calamity on all levels for Zidane and France," McNulty wrote. "And whatever words or actions of provocation Materazzi may have offered Zidane, his reaction was simply inexcusable. . . . France lost a talisman, a leader and a man who may have won them the World Cup—and they even lost their most reliable penalty [kick] taker in the shootout." He added, "It was not meant to end like this for one of the game's legendary figures—sent from the world's biggest stage in shame and into retirement."

Won Golden Ball, Anyway

In another odd twist to the bizarre denouement in Berlin, Zidane the following day received the Golden Ball as best player in the tournament, edging Italian defender Fabio in the balloting. Most journalists covering the match had cast their votes by halftime. Ironically, Zidane did not win the award in 1998, when he led France to its World Cup victory—Ronaldo of runner-up Brazil took the prize. "The vast majority of those votes were cast by journalists before the final was over and I'm sure that is why Zidane has come out [on] top," BBC correspondent Gordon Fahrquar told BBC Radio Live Five, according to the British news agency's website. But it's going to be a bit embarrassing for FIFA. . . . If you'd asked the 2,012 journalists—who voted for him—after the game whether they wanted to change their vote, they probably would have."

French Coach Raymond Domenech defended Zidane, saying Italy and other opponents engaged in rough play against him. "When one has to put up with what Zidane had to and the referee doesn't do anything, one understands. You can't excuse it, but you can understand it," he said, according to BBC Sport. The incident surprised Franz Beckenbauer, who led West Germany to the 1974 World Cup championships and is president of the prominent German club team Bayern Munich. "Something must have been said to Zidane. He is actually a reserved and inoffensive person," Beckenbauer said in BBC Sport.

Zidane's wife, Véronique, a former model, is a Frenchwoman of Spanish descent. They have four children: Enzo, Luca, Theo, and Elyas. Zidane became Christian Dior's first male model ever. Zidane, who has promoted ethnic tolerance in his visits throughout Europe, visited Algeria late in 2006. In his first visit to the former French colony since 1986, Zidane spent nearly a week in Aguemoun, the village where his parents grew up.

Periodicals

Guardian (London, England), July 15, 1998.
Irish Times, July 15, 1998.

Online

"France 1998," FIFA World Cup Germany 2006, http://www.fifa worldcup.yahoo.com/06/en/p/pwc/1998.html (December 7, 2006).
"From A to Z: The Zeal of Zizou," ESPNStar.com, http://www .espnstar.com/studio/studio_coldetail_1676927.html (December 13, 2006).
"Italy 1, France 1 (aet)," BBCSport, July 9, 2006, http://www.news .bbc.co.uk/sport2/hi/football/world_cup_2006/4991652.stm (December 1, 2006).

"Reaction to Zidane's Sending Off," BBCSport, July 10, 2006, http://www.news.bbc.co.uk/sport2/hi/football/world_cup_2006/teams/france/5152728.stm (December 1, 2006).

"Read My Lips: The Taunt That Made Zidane Snap," *Times Online,* July 11, 2006, http://www.timesonline.co.uk/article/0,,30249-2263995,00.html (December 14, 2006).

"Sent-Off Zidane Named Best Player," BBCSport, July 10, 2006, http://www.news.bbc.co.uk/sport2/hi/football/world_cup_2006/5154248.stm (December 1, 2006).

"Vive la France," World Cup 1998 (France)," *CNNSI.com,* December 1, 1998, http://www.sportsillustrated.cnn.com/soccer/world/events/1998/worldcup/ (December 14, 2006).

"World Cup 1998 (France)," 2002 FIFA World Cup Korea–Japan, http://www.worldcup.espnsoccernet.com/story?id=203643 (December 7, 2006).

"Zidane's Red Mist," BBCSport, July 9, 2006, http://www.news.bbc.co.uk/sport2/hi/football/world_cup_2006/5163528.stm (December 1, 2006).

"Zinédine Zidane," Biography Resource Center, http://www.galenet.galegroup.com (December 1, 2006). □

Slavoj Zizek

Slovenian philosopher Slavoj Zizek (born 1949) is an academic star, the "Elvis of Cultural Studies," according to one often-quoted journalistic formulation. His lectures, dealing in ideas that are often dense to the point of impenetrability, draw crowds numbering in the hundreds, with their mix of philosophical theory and topical political ideas, both often illustrated by examples drawn from American popular culture.

Zizek talks as fast as he thinks, and writes nearly as fast as he can talk (he has published as many as three books in the course of a single year), often making things even more difficult for the reader with a style of argument in which he often seems to contradict himself. James Harkin, writing in the London *Guardian,* called him "a one-man heavy industry of cultural criticism." Yet Zizek's fame rests on more than sheer mental agility. Consistent with his origins in Communist-era Yugoslavia, Zizek has espoused Marxist-Leninist ideas, which have remained current in academic circles even as they have lost ground in the wider political sphere. Zizek has reinvigorated Marxist-Leninist thought with an approach that brings together philosophy, psychology, film studies, humor, and engaging prose. His writing encompasses both political philosopher Karl Marx and film comedian Groucho Marx. Documentary filmmaker Astra Taylor, who made a film about Zizek, told Reyhan Harmaci of the *San Francisco Chronicle* that Zizek seems "to make intellectualism exciting and fun and vital in a climate of anti-intellectualism." In Zizek's own biography on the website of the European Graduate School, where he is a faculty member, he indicated that he "uses popular culture to explain the theory of [French philosopher] Jacques Lacan and the theory of Jacques Lacan to explain politics and popular culture."

Grew Up Under Communism

A native and lifelong resident of Ljubljana, Slovenia, Slavoj Zizek (SLAH-voy ZHEE-zhek) was born on March 21, 1949, when the small Alpine capital was part of Communist Yugoslavia. An only child, he grew up in the household of professional parents. Like many other young people in the former satellite states of the Soviet Union, he consumed Western popular culture avidly in preference to officially approved domestic television, books, and films. Much of his encyclopedic knowledge of Hollywood cinema was acquired during his teenage years, when he spent long hours at an auditorium that specialized in showing foreign films. The "Prague spring" reform movement of 1968 in Czechoslovakia during which Czechs agitated for greater freedom but were repressed by the Soviet Union, had an important effect on Zizek, even though he was not one of the demonstrators agitating in favor of greater freedom.

Zizek was in the Czech capital when Soviet troops invaded, and he observed the collision of totalitarian power with the aspirations of ordinary people. "I found there, on the central square, a café that miraculously worked through this emergency," he told Rebecca Mead of the *New Yorker.* "I remember they had wonderful strawberry cakes, and I was sitting there eating strawberry cakes and watching Russian tanks against demonstrators. It was perfect."

Not that Zizek was a supporter of Communist orthodoxy. As an undergraduate at the University of Ljubljana he read widely, not sticking to approved course lists. He spoke six languages, and immersed himself in the works of Lacan,

Jacques Derrida, and other philosophers, mostly French, whose writings had found little favor in socialist circles. In the case of Lacan, that philosopher's work relied on psychology—a suspect science from a collectivist point of view because of its preoccupation with the self and the individual mind. Zizek would, in time, set out to reconcile that seeming dichotomy.

Zizek earned a bachelor's degree in philosophy and sociology in 1971, and then pursued a master's degree, also at the University of Ljubljana, writing his master's thesis on the French philosophers whose ideas he had been studying. The brilliance of his thesis stirred up interest among the university's philosophy faculty, but its ideologically suspect qualities were more troublesome. Finally, after being forced to add an appendix in which he outlined the divergences of his ideas from approved Marxist theory, Zizek was awarded a master's degree in philosophy in 1975. The taint on his reputation kept him from finding a teaching position. For several years Zizek depended on his work as a translator to pay his bills, but in 1977 he gave in to pressure and joined the Communist Party. This opened up government speechwriting jobs, as well as the chance to take a job as a researcher at the Institute of Sociology and Philosophy at the University of Ljubljana in 1979. He retained that position for the next several decades, even after gaining international renown.

Worked as Speechwriter

In 1981 Zizek headed to Paris, where he studied with Lacan's son-in-law and was psychoanalyzed by him. He finished a dissertation and received his doctoral degree from the university that year. By that time Zizek had emerged as something of an expert on Lacan, and as the leader of a group of so-called Ljubljana Lacanians, contributing to a level of familiarity with Lacan in Slovenia that perhaps exceeded even that in France itself.

Zizek's playful side began to emerge during this period, when he wrote, under a pen name, a negative review of one of his own books. Sometimes during his career Zizek would seem to adopt one position and then switch to the exact opposite, but this tendency had roots in the dialectical tradition of philosophy in which his thought was rooted—the conviction that truth is ultimately obtained through the resolution of a series of opposites or conflicts. Zizek's first book published in the West was *The Sublime Object of Ideology* (1989), which focused on the greatest of all the dialectical philosophers, Georg Wilhelm Friedrich Hegel (1770–1831), through the prism of Lacan's thought. It was a daring combination; Zizek drew new links between philosophy and psychology by considering how these thinkers treated the idea of the Other—anything that is not part of the Self.

Zizek also cultivated his more public persona during the 1980s, a period during which Yugoslavia's Communist central government gradually began to lose control over the country's cultural life. He penned a popular newspaper column, and in 1990, when Slovenia was on the brink of independence from Yugoslavia (achieving it after a ten-day war in 1991), he entered the race to become part of the group of four leaders who would hold the country's joint

presidency. Of the five candidates, he finished fifth, and was thus not elected. It was at this time that the impressive spurt in Zizek's productivity began. He was living alone; a marriage from the early 1970s, which produced a son, had ended, and his second and third marriages (the second produced another son) were still in the future. Zizek had few responsibilities other than to think and write. His post was that of researcher, and he rarely if ever taught classes.

Partly this kind of financial freedom for an academic was a holdover from the Communist system, in which intellectuals were considered an important part of the theoretical underpinning of the state, and were thus financially supported if they were seen to be making useful contributions. Zizek cherished this freedom. As his fame grew, he was frequently offered teaching positions in the United States, where he garnered a strong following in university cultural studies departments. He turned them all down, although he cheerfully accepted visiting scholar appointments and often spent much of the year traveling from one academic center to another. "When people ask me why I don't teach permanently in the United States," Zizek was quoted as saying in the *Philadelphia Inquirer*, "I tell them that it is because American universities have this very strange, eccentric idea that you must work for your salary. I prefer to do the opposite and not work for my salary."

Used Film to Illustrate Ideas

In any event, Zizek repaid his university's investment by bringing international intellectual attention to tiny Slovenia. He turned out books quickly, and they were translated into some 20 languages; in the United States many were published by Verso in New York, which profited from its association with Zizek, for the books sold well. Zizek communicated and expanded upon Lacan's difficult ideas about perception, desire, and aggression by illustrating them with examples drawn from decades of popular films that students and general readers knew well. Zizek's own books, such as *Looking Awry; An Introduction to Jacques Lacan Through Popular Culture* (1991) and *Enjoy Your Symptom!: Jacques Lacan in Hollywood and Out* (1992), were joined on bookstore shelves by collections of articles he edited, including *Everything You Always Wanted to Know About Lacan (But Were Afraid to Ask Hitchcock)* (1992).

Zizek's international fame grew after a 1997 essay written by the influential British literary critic Terry Eagleton was published in the *London Review of Books*. The essay reviewed several of Zizek's books and concluded, as quoted in *Contemporary Authors*, that they "have an enviable knack of making [Continental philosophers] Kant or Kierkegaard sound riotously exciting; his writing bristles with difficulties but never serves up a turgid sentence." It was around this time that Zizek's lectures began to attract large crowds of young intellectuals. Police had to be called to a Zizek appearance at a Lower Manhattan art gallery after the shutout portion of an overflow crowd began banging on the building's windows, demanding admission. Nor was his fame confined to America and Europe; a documentary film, *Zizek!,* followed the philosopher to Buenos Aires, Argentina, where similar crowds awaited him.

Zizek's popularity was due partly to the dizzying virtuosity of his speeches, which were free form traversals of the history of philosophy, mixed with observations on anything from the *Matrix* film series to surfing, to world events, to theology (although an atheist, Zizek was fascinated by the figure of Saint Paul, seeing in him an analogue to early Soviet Communist leader Vladimir Lenin in terms of building an organization motivated by ideas). One audience member at a Zizek talk told Scott McLemee, author of the "Zizek Watch," a column published in the *Chronicle of Higher Education,* "I have no idea where we just went, but that was one wild trip." Another explanation of Zizek's success came from McLemee, who noted the theorist's continuing enthusiasm for American films. "One source of Slavoj Zizek's lasting appeal as a cultural theorist is that he provides a really good excuse to go to the video store," McLemee wrote.

Zizek also showed a knack for keeping himself in the headlines, at least those of intellectual journals. He broadened the focus of his writing to include current events, and he even contributed an essay to the staid U.S. journal *Foreign Policy* that examined the psychological motivations behind the failed U.S. search for weapons of mass destruction during the Iraq war. *The Art of the Ridiculous Sublime: On David Lynch's Lost Highway* (2000) was one of several Zizek tomes on contemporary entertainment. With *Welcome to the Desert of the Real!: Five Essays on 11 September and Related Dates,* Zizek showed an uncharacteristic tendency to edit himself, recalling the book several times for revisions as it went through subsequent printings. Zizek's *Iraq: The Borrowed Kettle* (2004) critiqued not only the rationale for war but also explored psychological factors involved in the restrictions placed on American civil liberties after the September 11 attacks.

Academic fashions come and go, but as of the mid-2000s the bearded Zizek had spent nearly a decade as what Carlin Romano of the *Philadelphia Inquirer* called "the ultimate hottie in recent years on the global intellectual circuit." In April of 2005 he married a 27-year-old Argentine model. He joined the faculty of the European Graduate School, an international institute of communications theory with locations in several countries, and he worked for an unusually long time on *The Parallax View,* a lengthy philosophical tract that attempted to redefine the dialectical idea itself, leaving room, as ever, for discussions of films, the war on terror, and hot topics such as neuroscience. By the time it was published, Zizek had moved on to a new book, *In Defense of Lost Causes,* in which he discussed the Christian legacy, class struggle, and problems in the world of theory itself. The book was slated for publication in the summer of 2007.

Periodicals

Artforum International, March 1993.

Chronicle of Higher Education, February 6, 2004; April 2, 2004; June 4, 2004.

Guardian (London, England), October 8, 2005.

New Yorker, May 5, 2003.

Philadelphia Inquirer, December 7, 2005.

Tikkun, January–February 2005.

World Literature Today, Spring 2002.

Online

Contemporary Authors Online, Gale, 2006, reproduced in *Biography Resource Center,* Thomson Gale, 2006, http://gale net/galegroup.com/servlet/BioRC (December 31, 2006).

"Slavoj Zizek: Biography," The European Graduate School, http://www.egs.edu/faculty/zizek.html (December 31, 2006).

☐

HOW TO USE THE *SUPPLEMENT* INDEX

The *Encyclopedia of World Biography Supplement (EWB)* Index is designed to serve several purposes. First, it is a cumulative listing of biographies included in the entire second edition of *EWB* and its supplements (volumes 1–27). Second, it locates information on specific topics mentioned in volume 27 of the encyclopedia—persons, places, events, organizations, institutions, ideas, titles of works, inventions, as well as artistic schools, styles, and movements. Third, it classifies the subjects of *Supplement* articles according to shared characteristics. Vocational categories are the most numerous—for example, artists, authors, military leaders, philosophers, scientists, statesmen. Other groupings bring together disparate people who share a common characteristic.

The structure of the *Supplement* Index is quite simple. The biographical entries are cumulative and often provide enough information to meet immediate reference needs. Thus, people mentioned in the *Supplement* Index are identified and their life dates, when known, are given. Because this is an index to a *biographical* encyclopedia, every reference includes the *name* of the article to which the reader is directed as well as the volume and page numbers. Below are a few points that will make the *Supplement* Index easy to use.

Typography. All main entries are set in boldface type. Entries that are also the titles of articles in *EWB* are set entirely in capitals; other main entries are set in initial capitals and lowercase letters. Where a main entry is followed by a great many references, these are organized by subentries in alphabetical sequence. In certain cases—for example, the names of countries for which there are many references—a special class of subentries, set in small capitals and preceded by boldface dots, is used to mark significant divisions.

Alphabetization. The Index is alphabetized word by word. For example, all entries beginning with *New* as a separate word (*New Jersey, New York*) come before *Newark*. Commas in inverted entries are treated as full stops (*Berlin; Berlin, Congress of; Berlin, University of; Berlin Academy of Sciences*). Other commas are ignored in filing. When words are identical, persons come first and subsequent entries are alphabetized by their parenthetical qualifiers (such as *book, city, painting*).

Titled persons may be alphabetized by family name or by title. The more familiar form is used—for example, *Disraeli, Benjamin* rather than *Beaconsfield, Earl of*. Cross-references are provided from alternative forms and spellings of names. Identical names of the same nationality are filed chronologically.

Titles of books, plays, poems, paintings, and other works of art beginning with an article are filed on the following word (*Bard, The*). Titles beginning with a preposition are filed on the preposition (*In Autumn*). In subentries, however, prepositions are ignored; thus *influenced by* would precede the subentry *in* literature.

Literary characters are filed on the last name. Acronyms, such as UNESCO, are treated as single words. Abbreviations, such as *Mr., Mrs.,* and *St.,* are alphabetized as though they were spelled out.

Occupational categories are alphabetical by national qualifier. Thus, *Authors, Scottish* comes before *Authors, Spanish,* and the reader interested in Spanish poets will find the subentry *poets* under *Authors, Spanish.*

Cross-references. The term *see* is used in references throughout the *Supplement* Index. The *see* references appear both as main entries and as subentries. They most often direct the reader from an alternative name spelling or form to the main entry listing.

This introduction to the *Supplement* Index is necessarily brief. The reader will soon find, however, that the *Supplement* Index provides ready reference to both highly specific subjects and broad areas of information contained in volume 27 and a cumulative listing of those included in the entire set.

INDEX

393

AKIBA BEN JOSEPH (circa 50-circa 135), Palestinian founder of rabbinic Judaism **1** 97-98

AKIHITO (born 1933), 125th emperor of Japan **1** 98-99

AKIYOSHI, TOSHIKO (born 1929), Japanese musician **24** 10-12

AKUTAGAWA, RYUNOSUKE (Ryunosuke Niihara; 1892-1927), Japanese author **22** 13-14

AL-ABDULLAH, RANIA (Rania al-Yasin; born 1970), Queen Rania of Jordan **25** 8-10

ALAMÁN, LUCAS (1792-1853), Mexican statesman **1** 99-100

ALARCÓN, PEDRO ANTONIO DE (1833-1891), Spanish writer and politician **1** 100-101

ALARCÓN Y MENDOZA, JUAN RUIZ DE (1581?-1639), Spanish playwright **1** 101

ALARIC (circa 370-410), Visigothic leader **1** 101-102

ALA-UD-DIN (died 1316), Khalji sultan of Delhi **1** 102-103

ALAUNGPAYA (1715-1760), king of Burma 1752-1760 **1** 103

AL AQQAD, ABBAS MAHMOUD (Abbas Mahmud al Aqqad; 1889-1964), Egyptian author **24** 25-27

ALBA, DUKE OF (Fernando Álvarez de Toledo; 1507-1582), Spanish general and statesman **1** 103-104

AL-BANNA, HASSAN (1906-1949), Egyptian religious leader and founder of the Muslim Brotherhood **1** 104-106

AL-BATTANI (Abu abdallah Muhammad ibn Jabir ibn Sinan al-Raqqi al Harrani al-Sabi al-Battani; c. 858-929), Arab astronomer and mathematician **25** 10-12

ALBEE, EDWARD FRANKLIN, III (born 1928), American playwright **1** 106-108

ALBÉNIZ, ISAAC (1860-1909), Spanish composer and pianist **1** 108-109

ALBERDI, JUAN BAUTISTA (1810-1884), Argentine political theorist **1** 109-110

ALBERS, JOSEPH (1888-1976), American artist and art and design teacher **1** 110

ALBERT (1819-1861), Prince Consort of Great Britain **1** 110-112

ALBERT I (1875-1934), king of the Belgians 1909-1934 **1** 112

ALBERT II (born 1934), sixth king of the Belgians **1** 112-113

ALBERTI, LEON BATTISTA (1404-1472), Italian writer, humanist, and architect **1** 113-115

ALBERTI, RAFAEL (born 1902), Spanish poet and painter **18** 13-15

ALBERTUS MAGNUS, ST. (circa 1193-1280), German philosopher and theologian **1** 115-116

ALBRIGHT, MADELEINE KORBEL (born 1937), United States secretary of state **1** 116-118

ALBRIGHT, TENLEY EMMA (born 1935), American figure skater **23** 3-6

ALBRIGHT, WILLIAM (1891-1971), American archaeologist **21** 1-3

ALBUQUERQUE, AFONSO DE (circa 1460-1515), Portuguese viceroy to India **1** 118-119

ALCIBIADES (circa 450-404 B.C.), Athenian general and politician **1** 119-120

ALCORN, JAMES LUSK (1816-1894), American lawyer and politician **1** 120-121

ALCOTT, AMOS BRONSON (1799-1888), American educator **1** 121

ALCOTT, LOUISA MAY (1832-1888), American author and reformer **1** 122

ALCUIN OF YORK (730?-804), English educator, statesman, and liturgist **1** 122-123

ALDRICH, NELSON WILMARTH (1841-1915), American statesman and financier **1** 123-124

ALDRIN, EDWIN EUGENE, JR. (Buzz Aldrin; born 1930), American astronaut **18** 15-17

ALDUS MANUTIUS (Teobaldo Manuzio; 1450?-1515), Italian scholar and printer **21** 3-5

ALEICHEM, SHOLOM (Sholom Rabinowitz; 1859-1916), writer of literature relating to Russian Jews **1** 124-125

ALEIJADINHO, O (Antônio Francisco Lisbôa; 1738-1814), Brazilian architect and sculptor **1** 125-126

ALEMÁN, MATEO (1547-after 1615), Spanish novelist **1** 126

ALEMÁN VALDÉS, MIGUEL (1902-1983), Mexican statesman, president 1946-1952 **1** 126-127

ALEMBERT, JEAN LE ROND D' (1717-1783), French mathematician and physicist **1** 127-128

ALESSANDRI PALMA, ARTURO (1868-1950), Chilean statesman, president 1920-1925 and 1932-1938 **1** 128-129

ALESSANDRI RODRIGUEZ, JORGE (born 1896), Chilean statesman, president 1958-1964 **1** 129-130

ALEXANDER I (1777-1825), czar of Russia 1801-1825 **1** 130-132

ALEXANDER II (1818-1881), czar of Russia 1855-1881 **1** 132-133

ALEXANDER III (1845-1894), emperor of Russia 1881-1894 **1** 133-134

ALEXANDER III (Orlando Bandinelli; c. 1100-1181), Italian pope 1159-1181 **24** 12-14

ALEXANDER VI (Rodrigo Borgia; 1431-1503), pope 1492-1503 **1** 134-135

ALEXANDER VII (Fabio Chigi; 1599-1667), Roman Catholic pope **25** 12-13

ALEXANDER, JANE (nee Jane Quigley; born 1939), American actress **26** 9-12

ALEXANDER, SADIE TANNER MOSSELL (1898-1989), African American lawyer **25** 13-15

ALEXANDER, SAMUEL (1859-1938), British philosopher **1** 141

ALEXANDER OF TUNIS, 1ST EARL (Harold Rupert Leofric George Alexander; born 1891), British field marshal **1** 135-136

ALEXANDER OF YUGOSLAVIA (1888-1934), king of the Serbs, Croats, and Slovenes 1921-1929 and of Yugoslavia, 1929-1934 **1** 136-137

ALEXANDER THE GREAT (356-323 B.C.), king of Macedon **1** 137-141

ALEXIE, SHERMAN (born 1966), Native American writer, poet, and translator **1** 141-142

ALEXIS MIKHAILOVICH ROMANOV (1629-1676), czar of Russia 1645-1676 **1** 142-143

ALEXIUS I (circa 1048-1118), Byzantine emperor 1081-1118 **1** 143-144

ALFARO, JOSÉ ELOY (1842-1912), Ecuadorian revolutionary, president 1895-1901 and 1906-1911 **1** 144-145

ALFIERI, CONTE VITTORIA (1749-1803), Italian playwright **1** 145-146

ALFONSÍN, RAUL RICARDO (born 1927), politician and president of Argentina (1983-) **1** 146-148

ALFONSO I (Henriques; 1109?-1185), king of Portugal 1139-1185 **1** 148

ALFONSO III (1210-1279), king of Portugal 1248-1279 **1** 148-149

ALFONSO VI (1040-1109), king of León, 1065-1109, and of Castile, 1072-1109 **1** 149

ALFONSO X (1221-1284), king of Castile and León 1252-1284 **1** 150-151

ALFONSO XIII (1886-1941), king of Spain 1886-1931 **1** 151

ALFRED (849-899), Anglo-Saxon king of Wessex 871-899 **1** 151-153

ALGER, HORATIO (1832-1899), American author **1** 153-154

ALGREN, NELSON (Abraham; 1909-1981), American author **1** 154-155

ALI (circa 600-661), fourth caliph of the Islamic Empire **1** 155-156

ALI, AHMED (1908-1998), Pakistani scholar, poet, author, and diplomat **22** 16-18

ALI, MUHAMMAD (Cassius Clay; born 1942), American boxer **1** 156-158

ALI, SUNNI (died 1492), king of Gao, founder of the Songhay empire **1** 158-159

ALIA, RAMIZ (born 1925), president of Albania (1985-) **1** 159

ALINSKY, SAUL DAVID (1909-1972), U.S. organizer of neighborhood citizen reform groups **1** 161-162

AL-KASHI (Ghiyath al-Din Jamshid Mas'ud Al-Kashi; 1380-1429), Iranian mathematician and astronomer **26** 12-13

ALLAL AL-FASSI, MOHAMED (1910-1974), Moroccan nationalist leader **1** 162

ALLAWI, IYAD (born 1945), Iraqi prime minister **25** 15-17

ALLEN, ELSIE (Elsie Comanche Allen; 1899-1990), Native American weaver and educator **27** 10-11

ALLEN, ETHAN (1738-1789), American Revolutionary War soldier **1** 163-164

ALLEN, FLORENCE ELLINWOOD (1884-1966), American lawyer, judge, and women's rights activist **1** 164-165

ALLEN, GRACIE (1906-1964), American actress and comedian **22** 18-20

ALLEN, PAUL (Paul Gardner Allen; born 1953), American entrepreneur and philanthropist **25** 17-19

ALLEN, PAULA GUNN (born 1939), Native American writer, poet, literary critic; women's rights, environmental, and antiwar activist **1** 165-167

ALLEN, RICHARD (1760-1831), African American bishop **1** 168
Allen, Sarah **27** 12-13

ALLEN, SARAH (Sarah Bass Allen; 1764-1849), African American missionary **27** 12-13

ALLEN, STEVE (1921-2000), American comedian, author, and composer **22** 20-22

ALLEN, WOODY (born Allen Stewart Konigsberg; b. 1935), American actor, director, filmmaker, author, comedian **1** 169-171

ALLENBY, EDMUND HENRY HYNMAN (1861-1936), English field marshal **1** 171-172

ALLENDE, ISABEL (born 1942), Chilean novelist, journalist, dramatist **1** 172-174

ALLENDE GOSSENS, SALVADOR (1908-1973), socialist president of Chile (1970-1973) **1** 174-176
Jara, Victor **27** 183-185

ALLSTON, WASHINGTON (1779-1843), American painter **1** 176-177

ALMAGRO, DIEGO DE (circa 1474-1538), Spanish conquistador and explorer **1** 177-178

ALMENDROS, NÉSTOR (Nestor Almendros Cuyas; 1930-1992), Hispanic American cinematographer **27** 13-15

ALMODOVAR, PEDRO (Calmodovar, Caballero, Pedro; born 1949), Spanish film director and screenwriter **23** 6-9

ALONSO, ALICIA (Alicia Ernestina de la Caridad dei Cobre Martinez Hoya; born 1921), Cuban ballerina **24** 14-17

ALP ARSLAN (1026/32-1072), Seljuk sultan of Persia and Iraq **1** 178-179

AL-SHUKAIRY, AHMAD (1908-1980), Lebanese diplomat and Arab nationalist **25** 20-21

ALTAMIRA Y CREVEA, RAFAEL (1866-1951), Spanish critic, historian, and jurist **1** 179

ALTDORFER, ALBRECHT (circa 1480-1538), German painter, printmaker, and architect **1** 179-180

ALTERMAN, NATAN (1910-1970), Israeli poet and journalist **24** 17-18

ALTGELD, JOHN PETER (1847-1902), American jurist and politician **1** 180-182

ALTHUSSER, LOUIS (1918-1990), French Communist philosopher **1** 182-183

ALTIZER, THOMAS J. J. (born 1927), American theologian **1** 183-184

ALTMAN, ROBERT (1925-2006), American filmmaker **20** 12-14

ALTMAN, SIDNEY (born 1939), Canadian American molecular biologist **23** 9-11

ALUPI, CALIN (Calinic Alupi; 1906-1988), Romanian artist **24** 18-19

ALVARADO, LINDA (Linda Martinez; born 1951), American businesswoman **25** 21-23

ÁLVAREZ, JUAN (1780-1867), Mexican soldier and statesman, president 1855 **1** 184-185

ALVAREZ, JULIA (born 1950), Hispanic American novelist, poet **1** 185-187

ALVAREZ, LUIS W. (1911-1988), American physicist **1** 187-189

ALVARIÑO, ANGELES (Angeles Alvariño Leira; 1916-2005), Spanish American marine scientist **27** 15-17

AMADO, JORGE (born 1912), Brazilian novelist **1** 189-190

AMBEDKAR, BHIMRAO RAMJI (1891-1956), Indian social reformer and politician **1** 190-191

AMBLER, ERIC (born 1909), English novelist **1** 191-192

AMBROSE, ST. (339-397), Italian bishop **1** 192-193

AMENEMHET I (ruled 1991-1962 B.C.), pharaoh of Egypt **1** 193-194

AMENHOTEP III (ruled 1417-1379 B.C.), pharaoh of Egypt **1** 194-195

American art
  basket weaving
    Allen, Elsie **27** 10-11
  homosexual themes
    Cadmus, Paul **27** 64-66
  Mexican-American themes
    Jiménez, Luis, Jr. **27** 185-187
  Native American
    Allen, Elsie **27** 10-11
  sculpture (20th century)
    Jiménez, Luis, Jr. **27** 185-187
  social realism
    Cadmus, Paul **27** 64-66
  surrealism
    Kamrowski, Gerome **27** 197-199
  watercolors
    Kingman, Dong **27** 208-209

American Broadcasting Company (United States)
  Goode, Mal **27** 151-153

AMERICAN HORSE (aka Iron Shield; 1840?-1876), Sioux leader **1** 195-198

American literature
  about music
    Lomax, Alan **27** 242-244
  African American fiction and drama
    Bush-Banks, Olivia Ward **27** 61-63
    West, Dorothy **27** 359-361
  African American poetry
    Bush-Banks, Olivia Ward **27** 61-63

ANGELL, JAMES ROWLAND (1869-1949), psychologist and leader in higher education **1** 236-237

ANGELOU, MAYA (Marguerite Johnson; born 1928), American author, poet, playwright, stage and screen performer, and director **1** 238-239

ANGUISSOLA, SOFONISBA (Sofonisba Anguisciola; c. 1535-1625), Italian artist **22** 22-24

ANNA IVANOVNA (1693-1740), empress of Russia 1730-1740 **1** 240-241

ANNAN, KOFI (born 1938), Ghanaian secretary-general of the United Nations **18** 19-21

ANNE (1665-1714), queen of England 1702-1714 and of Great Britain 1707-1714 **1** 241-242

ANNE OF CLEVES (1515-1557), German princess and fourth wife of Henry VIII **27** 19-21

ANNENBERG, WALTER HUBERT (1908-2002), American publisher and philanthropist **26** 16-18

ANNING, MARY (1799-1847), British fossil collector **20** 14-16

ANOKYE, OKOMFO (Kwame Frimpon Anokye; flourished late 17th century), Ashanti priest and statesman **1** 242-243

ANOUILH, JEAN (1910-1987), French playwright **1** 243-244

ANSELM OF CANTERBURY, ST. (1033-1109), Italian archbishop and theologian **1** 244-245

ANTHONY, ST. (circa 250-356), Egyptian hermit and monastic founder **1** 246-248

ANTHONY, SUSAN BROWNELL (1820-1906), American leader of suffrage movement **1** 246-248

ANTHONY OF PADUA, SAINT (Fernando de Boullion; 1195-1231), Portuguese theologian and priest **21** 7-9

Anthropological linguistics
see Linguistics

Anthroposophy
Steiner, Rudolf **27** 331-333

ANTIGONUS I (382-301 B.C.), king of Macedon 306-301 B.C. **1** 248-249

ANTIOCHUS III (241-187 B.C.), king of Syria 223-187 B.C. **1** 249-250

ANTIOCHUS IV (circa 215-163 B.C.), king of Syria 175-163 B.C. **1** 250

ANTISTHENES (circa 450-360 B.C.), Greek philosopher **1** 250-251

ANTONELLO DA MESSINA (circa 1430-1479), Italian painter **1** 251-252

ANTONIONI, MICHELANGELO (born 1912), Italian film director **1** 252-253

ANTONY, MARK (circa 82-30 B.C.), Roman politician and general **1** 253-254

ANZA, JUAN BAUTISTA DE (1735-1788), Spanish explorer **1** 254-255

AOUN, MICHEL (born 1935), Christian Lebanese military leader and prime minister **1** 255-257

Apache Indians (North America)
Chino, Wendell **27** 86-88

APELLES (flourished after 350 B.C.), Greek painter **1** 257

APESS, WILLIAM (1798-1839), Native American religious leader, author, and activist **20** 16-18

APGAR, VIRGINIA (1909-1974), American medical educator, researcher **1** 257-259

APITHY, SOUROU MIGAN (1913-1989), Dahomean political leader **1** 259-260

APOLLINAIRE, GUILLAUME (1880-1918), French lyric poet **1** 260

APOLLODORUS (flourished circa 408 B.C.), Greek painter **1** 261

APOLLONIUS OF PERGA (flourished 210 B.C.), Greek mathematician **1** 261-262

APPELFELD, AHARON (born 1932), Israeli who wrote about anti-Semitism and the Holocaust **1** 262-263

APPERT, NICOLAS (1749-1941), French chef and inventor of canning of foods **20** 18-19

APPIA, ADOLPHE (1862-1928), Swiss stage director **1** 263-264

APPLEBEE, CONSTANCE (1873-1981), American field hockey coach **24** 24-25

APPLEGATE, JESSE (1811-1888), American surveyor, pioneer, and rancher **1** 264-265

APPLETON, SIR EDWARD VICTOR (1892-1965), British pioneer in radio physics **1** 265-266

APPLETON, NATHAN (1779-1861), American merchant and manufacturer **1** 266-267

APULEIUS, LUCIUS (c. 124-170), Roman author, philosopher, and orator **20** 19-21

AQUINO, BENIGNO ("Nino"; 1933-1983), Filipino activist murdered upon his return from exile **1** 267-268

AQUINO, CORAZON COJOANGCO (born 1933), first woman president of the Republic of the Philippines **1** 268-270

ARAFAT, YASSER (also spelled Yasir; 1929-2004), chairman of the Palestinian Liberation Organization **1** 270-271
Abbas, Mahmoud **27** 1-3

ARAGON, LOUIS (1897-1982), French surrealist author **1** 271-272

ARANHA, OSVALDO (1894-1960), Brazilian political leader **1** 272-273

ARATUS (271-213 B.C.), Greek statesman and general **1** 273-274

ARBENZ GUZMÁN, JACOBO (1913-1971), president of Guatemala (1951-1954) **1** 274-276

ARBUS, DIANE NEMEROV (1923-1971), American photographer **1** 276-277

ARCARO, EDDIE (George Edward Arcaro; 1916-1997), American jockey **27** 21-23

ARCHIMEDES (circa 287-212 B.C.), Greek mathematician **1** 277-280

ARCHIPENKO, ALEXANDER (1887-1964), Russian-American sculptor and teacher **1** 280-281

Architecture
Calatrava, Santiago **27** 66-68
Hadid, Zaha **27** 155-157

ARCINIEGAS, GERMAN (1900-1999), Colombian historian, educator, and journalist **24** 27-29

ARDEN, ELIZABETH (Florence Nightingale Graham; 1878?-1966), American businesswoman **1** 281-282

ARENDT, HANNAH (1906-1975), Jewish philosopher **1** 282-284

ARENS, MOSHE (born 1925), aeronautical engineer who became a leading Israeli statesman **1** 284-285

ARETE OF CYRENE (c. 400 B.C.-c. 340 B.C.), Grecian philosopher **26** 18-20

ARÉVALO, JUAN JOSÉ (1904-1951), Guatemalan statesman, president 1944-1951 **1** 285-286

ARIAS, ARNULFO (1901-1988), thrice elected president of Panama **1** 286-287

ARIAS SANCHEZ, OSCAR (born 1941), Costa Rican politician, social activist, president, and Nobel Peace Laureate (1987) **1** 287-289

AZHARI, SAYYID ISMAIL AL- (1898-1969), Sudanese president 1965-1968 **1** 399-401

AZIKIWE, NNAMDI (born 1904), Nigerian nationalist, president 1963-1966 **1** 401-402

AZUELA, MARIANO (1873-1952), Mexican novelist **1** 402

B

BÂ, MARIAMA (1929-1981), Senegalese novelist **26** 25-27

BA MAW (1893-1977), Burmese statesman **1** 480-481

BAADER and MEINHOF (1967-1976), founders of the West German "Red Army Faction" **1** 403-404

BAAL SHEM TOV (circa 1700-circa 1760), founder of modern Hasidism **1** 404-405

BABA, MEHER (Merwan Sheriar Irani; 1894-1969), Indian mystic **24** 35-38

BABAR THE CONQUEROR (aka Zahir-ud-din Muhammad Babur; 1483-1530), Mogul emperor of India 1526-1530 **1** 405-407

BABBAGE, CHARLES (1791-1871), English inventor and mathematician **1** 407-408

BABBITT, BRUCE EDWARD (born 1938), governor of Arizona (1978-1987) and United States secretary of the interior **1** 408-410

BABBITT, IRVING (1865-1933), American critic and educator **22** 36-37

BABBITT, MILTON (born 1916), American composer **1** 410

BABCOCK, STEPHEN MOULTON (1843-1931), American agricultural chemist **1** 410-411

BABEL, ISAAC EMMANUELOVICH (1894-1941), Russian writer **1** 411-412

BABEUF, FRANÇOIS NOEL ("Caius Gracchus"; 1760-1797), French revolutionist and writer **1** 412

BACA-BARRAGÁN, POLLY (born 1943), Hispanic American politician **1** 412-414

BACH, CARL PHILIPP EMANUEL (1714-1788), German composer **1** 414-415

BACH, JOHANN CHRISTIAN (1735-1782), German composer **1** 415-416

BACH, JOHANN SEBASTIAN (1685-1750), German composer and organist **1** 416-419

BACHARACH, BURT (born 1928), American composer **22** 38-39

BACHE, ALEXANDER DALLAS (1806-1867), American educator and scientist **1** 420

BACKUS, ISAAC (1724-1806), American Baptist leader **1** 420-421

BACON, SIR FRANCIS (1561-1626), English philosopher, statesman, and author **1** 422-424

BACON, FRANCIS (1909-1992), English artist **1** 421-422

BACON, NATHANIEL (1647-1676), American colonial leader **1** 424-425

BACON, PEGGY (Margaret Francis Bacon; 1895-1987), American artist and author **25** 29-31

BACON, ROGER (circa 1214-1294), English philosopher **1** 425-427

BAD HEART BULL, AMOS (1869-1913), Oglala Lakota Sioux tribal historian and artist **1** 427-428

BADEN-POWELL, ROBERT (1857-1941), English military officer and founder of the Boy Scout Association **21** 16-18

BADINGS, HENK (Hendrik Herman Badings; 1907-1987), Dutch composer **23** 26-28

BADOGLIO, PIETRO (1871-1956), Italian general and statesman **1** 428-429

BAECK, LEO (1873-1956), rabbi, teacher, hero of the concentration camps, and Jewish leader **1** 429-430

BAEKELAND, LEO HENDRIK (1863-1944), American chemist **1** 430-431

BAER, GEORGE FREDERICK (1842-1914), American businessman **22** 39-41

BAER, KARL ERNST VON (1792-1876), Estonian anatomist and embryologist **1** 431-432

BAEZ, BUENAVENTURA (1812-1884), Dominican statesman, five time president **1** 432-433

BAEZ, JOAN (born 1941), American folk singer and human rights activist **1** 433-435
Farina, Mimi **27** 117-119

BAFFIN, WILLIAM (circa 1584-1622), English navigator and explorer **1** 435-436

BAGEHOT, WALTER (1826-1877), English economist **1** 436-437

BAGLEY, WILLIAM CHANDLER (1874-1946), educator and theorist of educational "essentialism" **1** 437-438

BAHR, EGON (born 1922), West German politician **1** 438-440

BAIKIE, WILLIAM BALFOUR (1825-1864), Scottish explorer and scientist **1** 440

BAILEY, F. LEE (born 1933), American defense attorney and author **1** 441-443

BAILEY, FLORENCE MERRIAM (1863-1948), American ornithologist and author **1** 443-444

BAILEY, GAMALIEL (1807-1859), American editor and politician **1** 444-445

BAILEY, MILDRED (Mildred Rinker, 1907-1951), American jazz singer **23** 28-30

BAILLIE, D(ONALD) M(ACPHERSON) (1887-1954), Scottish theologian **1** 445

BAILLIE, ISOBEL (Isabella Baillie; 1895-1983), British singer **26** 27-29

BAILLIE, JOHN (1886-1960), Scottish theologian and ecumenical churchman **1** 445-447

BAKER, ELLA JOSEPHINE (1903-1986), African American human and civil rights activist **18** 26-28

BAKER, HOWARD HENRY, JR. (born 1925), U.S. senator and White House chief of staff **18** 28-30

BAKER, JAMES ADDISON III (born 1930), Republican party campaign leader **1** 447-448

BAKER, JOSEPHINE (1906-1975) Parisian dancer and singer from America **1** 448-451

BAKER, NEWTON DIEHL (1871-1937), American statesman **1** 451

BAKER, RAY STANNARD (1870-1946), American author **1** 451-452

BAKER, RUSSELL (born 1925), American writer of personal-political essays **1** 452-454

BAKER, SIR SAMUEL WHITE (1821-1893), English explorer and administrator **1** 454-455

BAKER, SARA JOSEPHINE (1873-1945), American physician **1** 455-456

BAKHTIN, MIKHAIL MIKHAILOVICH (1895-1975), Russian philosopher and literary critic **1** 456-458

Bakuba (African tribe)
Edmiston, Althea Maria **27** 108-111

BAKUNIN, MIKHAIL ALEKSANDROVICH (1814-1876), Russian anarchist **1** 458-460

BAYNTON, BARBARA (1857-1929), Australian author **22** 46-48

Baziotes, William (born 1912), American painter
Kamrowski, Gerome **27** 197-199

BBC
see British Broadcasting Corporation

BEA, AUGUSTINUS (1881-1968), German cardinal **2** 79

BEACH, AMY (born Amy Marcy Cheney; 1867-1944), American musician **23** 30-32

BEACH, MOSES YALE (1800-1868), American inventor and newspaperman **2** 79-80

BEADLE, GEORGE WELLS (1903-1989), American scientist, educator, and administrator **2** 80-81

BEALE, DOROTHEA (1831-1906), British educator **2** 81-83

BEAN, ALAN (born 1932), American astronaut and artist **22** 48-50

BEAN, LEON LEONWOOD (L.L. Bean; 1872-1967), American businessman **19** 14-16

BEARD, CHARLES AUSTIN (1874-1948), American historian **2** 84

BEARD, MARY RITTER (1876-1958), American author and activist **2** 85-86

BEARDEN, ROMARE HOWARD (1914-1988), African American painter-collagist **2** 86-88

BEARDSLEY, AUBREY VINCENT (1872-1898), English illustrator **2** 88-89

Beat Generation (American literature)
Ferlinghetti, lawrence **27** 125-127
Kesey, Ken Elton **27** 203-205

BEATLES, THE (1957-1971), British rock and roll band **2** 89-92

BEATRIX, WILHELMINA VON AMSBERG, QUEEN (born 1938), queen of Netherlands (1980-) **2** 92-93

BEAUCHAMPS, PIERRE (1636-1705), French dancer and choreographer **21** 27-29

BEAUFORT, MARGARET (1443-1509), queen dowager of England **20** 29-31

BEAUJOYEULX, BALTHASAR DE (Balthasar de Beaujoyeux; Baldassare de Belgiojoso; 1535-1587), Italian choreographer and composer **21** 29-30

BEAUMARCHAIS, PIERRE AUGUST CARON DE (1732-1799), French playwright **2** 93-94

BEAUMONT, FRANCIS (1584/1585-1616), English playwright **2** 95

BEAUMONT, WILLIAM (1785-1853), American surgeon **2** 95-96

BEAUREGARD, PIERRE GUSTAVE TOUTANT (1818-1893), Confederate general **2** 96-97

BECARRIA, MARCHESE DI (1738-1794), Italian jurist and economist **2** 97-98

BECHET, SIDNEY (1897-1959), American jazz musician **22** 50-52

BECHTEL, STEPHEN DAVISON (1900-1989), American construction engineer and business executive **2** 98-99

BECK, LUDWIG AUGUST THEODOR (1880-1944), German general **2** 99-100

BECKER, CARL LOTUS (1873-1945), American historian **2** 100-101

BECKET, ST. THOMAS (1128?-1170), English prelate **2** 101-102

BECKETT, SAMUEL (1906-1989), Irish novelist, playwright, and poet **2** 102-104

BECKHAM, DAVID (David Robert Joseph Beckham; born 1975), British soccer player **26** 36-38

BECKMANN, MAX (1884-1950), German painter **2** 104-105

BECKNELL, WILLIAM (circa 1797-1865), American soldier and politician **2** 105-106

BECKWOURTH, JIM (James P. Beckwourth; c. 1800-1866), African American fur trapper and explorer **2** 106-107

BÉCQUER, GUSTAVO ADOLFO DOMINGUEZ (1836-1870), Spanish lyric poet **2** 107-108

BECQUEREL, ANTOINE HENRI (1852-1908), French physicist **2** 108-109

BEDE, ST. (672/673-735), English theologian **2** 109-110

BEDELL SMITH, WALTER (1895-1961), U.S. Army general, ambassador, and CIA director **18** 30-33

BEEBE, WILLIAM (1877-1962), American naturalist, oceanographer, and ornithologist **22** 52-54

BEECHAM, THOMAS (1879-1961), English conductor **24** 46-48

BEECHER, CATHARINE (1800-1878), American author and educator **2** 110-112

BEECHER, HENRY WARD (1813-1887), American Congregationalist clergyman **2** 112-113

BEECHER, LYMAN (1775-1863), Presbyterian clergyman **2** 113

BEERBOHM, MAX (Henry Maximilian Beerbohm; 1872-1956), English author and critic **19** 16-18

BEETHOVEN, LUDWIG VAN (1770-1827), German composer **2** 114-117
influence of
Schnabel, Artur **27** 319-321

BEGAY, HARRISON (born 1917), Native American artist **2** 117-118

BEGIN, MENACHEM (1913-1992), Israel's first non-Socialist prime minister (1977-1983) **2** 118-120

BEHAIM, MARTIN (Martinus de Bohemia; 1459?-1507), German cartographer **21** 30-32

BEHN, APHRA (1640?-1689), British author **18** 33-34

BEHRENS, HILDEGARD (born 1937), German soprano **2** 120-121

BEHRENS, PETER (1868-1940), German architect, painter, and designer **2** 121-122

BEHRING, EMIL ADOLPH VON (1854-1917), German hygienist and physician **2** 122-123

BEHZAD (died circa 1530), Persian painter **2** 123

BEISSEL, JOHANN CONRAD (1690-1768), German-American pietist **2** 123-124

BELAFONTE, HARRY (Harold George Belafonte, Jr.; born 1927), African American singer and actor **20** 31-32

BELASCO, DAVID (1853-1931), American playwright and director-producer **2** 124-125

BELAÚNDE TERRY, FERNANDO (1912-2002), president of Peru (1963-1968, 1980-1985) **2** 125-126

BELGRANO, MANUEL (1770-1820), Argentine general and politician **2** 126-127

BELINSKY, GRIGORIEVICH (1811-1848), Russian literary critic **2** 128

BELISARIUS (circa 506-565), Byzantine general **2** 128-129

BELL, ALEXANDER GRAHAM (1847-1922), Scottish-born American inventor **2** 129-131

BELL, ANDREW (1753-1832), Scottish educator **2** 131-132

BELL, DANIEL (Bolotsky; born 1919), American sociologist **2** 132-133

BELL, GERTRUDE (1868-1926), British archaeologist, traveler, and advisor on the Middle East **22** 54-55

BELL BURNELL, SUSAN JOCELYN (born 1943), English radio astronomer **2** 133-134

BELL, VANESSA (Vanessa Stephen; 1879-1961), British painter **25** 36-38

BELLAMY, CAROL (born 1942), American activist and political servant **25** 38-40

BELLAMY, EDWARD (1850-1898), American novelist, propagandist, and reformer **2** 134-135

BELLARMINE, ST. ROBERT (1542-1621), Italian theologian and cardinal **2** 135-136

BELLECOURT, CLYDE (born 1939), Native American activist **2** 136-137

BELLI, GIACONDA (born 1948), Nicaraguan author and activist **24** 48-50

BELLINI, GIOVANNI (circa 1435-1516), Itlaian painter **2** 137-138

BELLINI, VINCENZO (1801-1835), Italian composer **2** 138-139

BELLMAN, CARL MICHAEL (1740-1794), Swedish poet and musician **25** 40-42

BELLO, ALHAJI SIR AHMADU (1909-1966), Nigerian politician **2** 139-140

BELLO Y LÓPEZ, ANDRÉS (1781-1865), Venezuelan humanist **2** 140-141

BELLOC, JOSEPH HILAIRE PIERRE (1870-1953), French-born English author and historian **2** 141

BELLOW, SAUL (1915-2005), American novelist and Nobel Prize winner **2** 141-143

BELLOWS, GEORGE WESLEY (1882-1925), American painter **2** 143

BELLOWS, HENRY WHITNEY (1814-1882), American Unitarian minister **2** 143-144

BELMONT, AUGUST (1816-1890), German-American banker, diplomat, and horse racer **22** 56-57

BELO, CARLOS FELIPE XIMENES (born 1948), East Timorese activist **25** 42-44

BEMBERG, MARIA LUISA (1922-1995), Argentine filmmaker **25** 44-46

BEMBO, PIETRO (1470-1547), Italian humanist, poet, and historian **2** 144-145

BEMIS, POLLY (Lalu Nathoy; 1853-1933), Chinese American pioneer and businesswoman **25** 46-47

BENACERRAF, BARUJ (born 1920), American medical researcher **27** 42-44

BEN AND JERRY ice cream company founders **18** 35-37

BEN BADIS, ABD AL-HAMID (1889-1940), leader of the Islamic Reform Movement in Algeria between the two world wars **2** 147-148

BEN BELLA, AHMED (born 1918), first president of the Algerian Republic **2** 148-149

BENDIX, VINCENT (1881-1945), American inventor, engineer, and industrialist **19** 18-20

BEN-GURION, DAVID (born 1886), Russian-born Israeli statesman **2** 160-161

BEN-HAIM, PAUL (Frankenburger; 1897-1984), Israeli composer **2** 161-162

BEN YEHUDA, ELIEZER (1858-1922), Hebrew lexicographer and editor **2** 181-182

BENALCÁZAR, SEBASTIÁN DE (died 1551), Spanish conquistador **2** 145-146

BENAVENTE Y MARTINEZ, JACINTO (1866-1954), Spanish dramatist **2** 146-147

BENCHLEY, ROBERT (1889-1945), American humorist **2** 150-151

BENDA, JULIEN (1867-1956), French cultural critic and novelist **2** 151-152

BENEDICT XIV (Prospero Lorenzo Lambertini; 1675-1758), Italian pope **23** 32-35

BENEDICT XV (Giacomo della Chiesa; 1854-1922), pope, 1914-1922 **2** 153-154

BENEDICT XVI (Joseph Alois Ratzinger; born 1927), Roman Catholic pope (2005-) **26** 295-297

BENEDICT, RUTH FULTON (1887-1948), American cultural anthropologist **2** 154-155

BENEDICT, ST. (circa 480-547), Italian founder of the Benedictines **2** 154-155

BENEŠ, EDWARD (1884-1948), Czechoslovak president 1935-1938 and 1940-1948 **2** 155-157

BENÉT, STEPHEN VINCENT (1898-1943), American poet and novelist **2** 157-158

BENETTON, Italian family (Luciano, Giuliana, Gilberto, Carlo and Mauro) who organized a world-wide chain of colorful knitwear stores **2** 158-159

BENEZET, ANTHONY (1713-1784), American philanthropist and educator **2** 159-160

BENJAMIN, ASHER (1773-1845), American architect **2** 162-163

BENJAMIN, JUDAH PHILIP (1811-1884), American statesman **2** 163-164

BENJAMIN, WALTER (1892-1940), German philosopher and literary critic **20** 32-34

BENN, GOTTFRIED (1886-1956), German author **2** 164

BENN, TONY (Anthony Neil Wedgewood Benn; born 1925), British Labour party politician **2** 164-166

BENNETT, ALAN (born 1934), British playwright **2** 166-167

BENNETT, ENOCH ARNOLD (1867-1931), English novelist and dramatist **2** 167-168

BENNETT, JAMES GORDON (1795-1872), Scottish-born American journalist and publisher **2** 168-169

BENNETT, JAMES GORDON, JR. (1841-1918), American newspaper owner and editor **2** 169-170

BENNETT, JOHN COLEMAN (1902-1995), American theologian **2** 170-171

BENNETT, RICHARD BEDFORD (1870-1947), Canadian statesman, prime minister 1930-1935 **2** 171-172

BENNETT, RICHARD RODNEY (born 1936), English composer **2** 172

BENNETT, ROBERT RUSSELL (1894-1981), American arranger, composer, and conductor **21** 32-34

BENNETT, WILLIAM JOHN (born 1943), American teacher and scholar and secretary of the Department of Education (1985-1988) **2** 172-174

BENNY, JACK (Benjamin Kubelsky; 1894-1974), American comedian and a star of radio, television, and stage **2** 174-176

BENTHAM, JEREMY (1748-1832), English philosopher, political theorist, and jurist **2** 176-178

BENTLEY, ARTHUR F. (1870-1957), American philosopher and political scientist **2** 178

BENTON, SEN. THOMAS HART (1782-1858), American statesman **2** 178-179

BENTON, THOMAS HART (1889-1975), American regionalist painter **2** 178-179

BENTSEN, LLOYD MILLARD (1921-2006), senior United States senator from Texas and Democratic vice-presidential candidate in 1988 **2** 180-181

BENZ, CARL (1844-1929), German inventor **2** 182-183

BERCHTOLD, COUNT LEOPOLD VON (1863-1942), Austro-Hungarian statesman **2** 183-184

BERDYAEV, NICHOLAS ALEXANDROVICH (1874-1948), Russian philosopher **2** 184-185

BERELSON, BERNARD (1912-1979), American behavioral scientist **2** 185-186

BERENSON, BERNARD (1865-1959), American art critic and historian **20** 34-35

BERG, ALBAN (1885-1935), Austrian composer **2** 186-187

BERG, PAUL (born 1926), American chemist **2** 187-189

BERGER, VICTOR LOUIS (1860-1929), American politician **2** 189-190

BERGMAN, (ERNST) INGMAR (born 1918); Swedish film and stage director **2** 190-191

BERGMAN, INGRID (1917-1982), Swedish actress **20** 35-37

BERGSON, HENRI (1859-1941), French philosopher **2** 191-192

BERIA, LAVRENTY PAVLOVICH (1899-1953), Soviet secret-police chief and politician **2** 192-193

BERING, VITUS (1681-1741), Danish navigator in Russian employ **2** 193-194

BERIO, LUCIANO (1925-2003), Italian composer **2** 194-195

BERISHA, SALI (born 1944), president of the Republic of Albania (1992-) **2** 195-197

BERKELEY, BUSBY (William Berkeley Enos; 1895-1976), American filmmaker **20** 38-39

BERKELEY, GEORGE (1685-1753), Anglo-Irish philosopher and Anglican bishop **2** 197-198

BERKELEY, SIR WILLIAM (1606-1677), English royal governor of Virginia **2** 198-199

BERLE, ADOLF AUGUSTUS, JR. (1895-1971), American educator **2** 199-200

BERLE, MILTON (1908-2002), American entertainer and actor **18** 37-39

BERLIN, IRVING (1888-1989), American composer **2** 200-201

BERLIN, ISAIAH (1909-1997), British philosopher **2** 201-203

BERLINER, ÉMILE (1851-1929), American inventor **20** 39-41

BERLIOZ, LOUIS HECTOR (1803-1869), French composer, conductor, and critic **2** 203-205

BERLUSCONI, SILVIO (born 1936), Italian businessman and politician **25** 48-50

BERMEJO, BARTOLOMÉ (Bartolomé de Cárdenas; flourished 1474-1498), Spanish painter **2** 205

BERNADETTE OF LOURDES, SAINT (Marie Bernarde Soubirous; 1844-1879), French nun and Roman Catholic saint **21** 34-36

BERNANOS, GEORGES (1888-1948), French novelist and essayist **2** 206-207

BERNARD, CLAUDE (1813-1878), French physiologist **2** 208-210

BERNARD OF CLAIRVAUX, ST. (1090-1153), French theologian, Doctor of the Church **2** 207-208

BERNARDIN, CARDINAL JOSEPH (1928-1996), Roman Catholic Cardinal and American activist **2** 210-211

BERNAYS, EDWARD L. (1891-1995), American public relations consultant **2** 211-212

BERNBACH, WILLIAM (1911-1982), American advertising executive **19** 20-22

BERNERS-LEE, TIM (born 1955), English computer scientist and creator of the World Wide Web **20** 41-43

BERNHARDT, SARAH (Henriette-Rosine Bernard; 1844-1923), French actress **2** 212-214

BERNIER, JOSEPH E. (Joseph-Elzéan Bernier; 1852-1934), Canadian explorer **23** 35-37

BERNINI, GIAN LORENZO (1598-1680), Italian artist **2** 214-216

BERNOULLI, DANIEL (1700-1782), Swiss mathematician and physicist **2** 216

BERNOULLI, JAKOB (Jacques or James Bernoulli; 1654-1705), Swiss mathematician **23** 37-39

BERNSTEIN, DOROTHY LEWIS (born 1914), American mathematician **2** 217

BERNSTEIN, EDUARD (1850-1932), German socialist **2** 218

BERNSTEIN, ELMER (1922-2004), American composer **27** 44-46

BERNSTEIN, LEONARD (1918-1990), American composer, conductor, and pianist **2** 218-219
Farrell, Eileen **27** 119-121

BERRI, NABIH (born 1939), leader of the Shi'ite Muslims in Lebanon **2** 220-222

BERRIGAN, DANIEL J. (born 1921), activist American Catholic priest **2** 222-223

BERRUGUETE, ALONSO (1486/90-1561), Spanish sculptor **2** 223-224

BERRY, CHUCK (born 1926), African American performer **2** 224-226

BERRY, MARY FRANCES (born 1938), African American human/civil rights activist and official **2** 226-229

BERRYMAN, JOHN (John Allyn Smith, Jr.; 1914-1972), American poet and biographer **19** 22-25

BERTHIER, LOUIS ALEXANDRE (1753-1815), French soldier and cartographer **20** 43-44

BERTHOLLET, CLAUDE LOUIS (1748-1822), French chemist **2** 229-230

BERTILLON, ALPHONSE (1853-1914), French criminologist **2** 230-231

BERTOLUCCI, BERNARDO (born 1940), Italian film director **18** 39-41

BERZELIUS, JÖNS JACOB (1779-1848), Swedish chemist **2** 231-233

BESANT, ANNIE WOOD (1847-1933), British social reformer and theosophist **2** 233-234

BESSEL, FRIEDRICH WILHELM (1784-1846), German astronomer **2** 234-235

BESSEMER, SIR HENRY (1813-1898), English inventor **2** 235-236

BEST, CHARLES HERBERT (1899-1978), Canadian physiologist **2** 236-237

BETANCOURT, RÓMULO (1908-1990), Venezuelan statesman **2** 237-238

BETHE, HANS ALBRECHT (1906-2005), Alsatian-American physicist **2** 238-239

BETHMANN HOLLWEG, THEOBALD VON (1856-1921), German statesman **2** 239-240

BETHUNE, HENRY NORMAN (1890-1939), Canadian humanitarian physician **2** 240-241

BETHUNE, MARY MCLEOD (1875-1955), African American educator **2** 241-242

BETI, MONGO (Alexandre Biyidi; born 1932), Cameroonian novelist **2** 242-243

BITZER, BILLY (George William Bitzer; 1872-1944), American cinematographer **21** 36-38

BIYA, PAUL (born 1933), president of Cameroon **18** 41-43

BIZET, GEORGES (1838-1875), French composer **2** 296-297

BJELKE-PETERSEN, JOHANNES ("Joh;" born 1911), Australian politician **2** 297-299

BJERKNES, VILHELM (1862-1951), Norwegian meteorologist **20** 48-50

BJØRNSON, BJØRNSTJERNE (1832-1910), Norwegian author **2** 299-300

BLACK, CONRAD MOFFAT (born 1944), Canadian-born international press baron **2** 300-301

BLACK, HUGO LAFAYETTE (1886-1971), American jurist **2** 301-303

BLACK, JOSEPH (1728-1799), British chemist **2** 303

BLACK, SHIRLEY TEMPLE (born 1928), American actress and public servant **2** 303-305

BLACK ELK, NICHOLAS (1863-1950), Oglala Sioux medicine man **2** 305-306

BLACK HAWK (1767-1838), Native American war chief **2** 308

Black Panther Party (United States; established 1966) Kennedy, Florynce Rae **27** 199-201

BLACKBEARD (Edward Teach; 1680-1718), English pirate **21** 38-41

BLACKBURN, ELIZABETH HELEN (born 1948), Australian biologist **18** 43-45

BLACKETT, PATRICK M.S. (1897-1974), British physicist **2** 306-307

BLACKMUN, HARRY (1908-1999), United States Supreme Court justice **2** 309-310

Blacks see African American history (United States); Africa

BLACKSTONE, SIR WILLIAM (1723-1780), English jurist **2** 310-311

BLACKWELL, ANTOINETTE BROWN (1825-1921), American minister and suffragette **21** 41-43

BLACKWELL, ELIZABETH (1821-1910), American physician **2** 311-312

BLACKWELL, EMILY (1826-1910), American physician and educator **19** 27-29

BLAGA, LUCIAN (1895-1961), Romanian poet and philosopher **24** 52-54

BLAINE, JAMES GILLESPIE (1830-1893), American statesman **2** 312-313

BLAIR, BONNIE (born 1964), American athlete **23** 42-44

BLAIR, FRANCIS PRESTON (1791-1876), American journalist and politician **2** 313-315

BLAIR, JAMES (1655-1743), British educator and Anglican missionary **2** 315-316

BLAIR, TONY (born 1953), British prime minister **18** 45-47

BLAKE, EUBIE (James Hubert Blake; 1883-1983), African American composer and pianist **25** 50-53

BLAKE, WILLIAM (1757-1827), English poet, engraver, and painter **2** 316-318

BLAKELOCK, RALPH ALBERT (1847-1919), American painter **2** 318

BLAKEY, ART (Arthur Blakey; Abdullah Ibn Buhaina; 1919-1990), African American jazz musician **27** 46-48

BLANC, LOUIS (1811-1882), French journalist, historian, and politician **2** 318-319

BLANC, MEL (1908-1989), American creator of and voice of cartoon characters **2** 319-320

BLANCHARD, FELIX ("Doc" Blanchard; born 1924), American football player and military pilot **21** 43-45

BLANCHE OF CASTILE (1188-1252), French queen **21** 45-47

BLANCO, ANTONIO GUZMÁN (1829-1899), Venezuelan politician, three-times president **2** 320-321

BLANDIANA, ANA (born Otilia-Valeria Coman, 1942), Romanian poet **2** 321-322

BLANDING, SARAH GIBSON (1898-1985), American educator **2** 322-323

BLANKERS-KOEN, FANNY (Francina Elsja Blankers-Koen; born 1918), Dutch track and field athlete **20** 50-52

BLANQUI, LOUIS AUGUSTE (1805-1881), French revolutionary **2** 323-324

BLAVATSKY, HELENA PETROVNA (Helena Hahn; 1831-1891), Russian theosophist **22** 67-69

BLEDSOE, ALBERT TAYLOR (1809-1877), American lawyer, educator, and Confederate apologist **2** 324-325

Bless Me, Ultima (book) Anaya, Rudolfo Alfonso **27** 17-19

BLEULER, EUGEN (1857-1939), Swiss psychiatrist **2** 325

BLEY, CARLA (nee Carla Borg; born 1938), American composer and pianist **26** 40-42

BLIGH, WILLIAM (1754-1817), English naval officer and colonial governor **2** 325-326

BLOCH, ERNEST (1880-1959), Swiss-born American composer and teacher **2** 326-327

BLOCH, ERNST (1885-1977), German humanistic interpreter of Marxist thought **2** 327-328

BLOCH, FELIX (1905-1983), Swiss/American physicist **2** 328-330

BLOCH, KONRAD (born 1912), American biochemist **2** 330-332

BLOCH, MARC (1886-1944), French historian **2** 332-333

BLOCK, HERBERT (Herblock; 1909-2001), American newspaper cartoonist **2** 333-334

BLODGETT, KATHARINE BURR (1898-1979), American physicist **24** 54-56

BLOK, ALEKSANDR ALEKSANDROVICH (1880-1921), Russian poet **2** 335

Blondin, Charles see Blondin, Jean Francois Gravelet

BLONDIN, JEAN FRANCOIS GRAVELET (Charles Blondin; 1824-1897), French tightrope walker and acrobat **27** 48-50

BLOOM, ALLAN DAVID (1930-1992), American political philosopher, professor, and author **2** 335-337

BLOOMER, AMELIA JENKS (1818-1894), American reformer and suffrage advocate **2** 337

BLOOMFIELD, LEONARD (1887-1949), American linguist **2** 338

BLOOR, ELLA REEVE ("Mother Bloor"; 1862-1951), American labor organizer and social activist **2** 338-340

BLÜCHER, GEBHARD LEBERECHT VON (Prince of Wahlstatt; 1742-1819), Prussian field marshal **2** 340-341

Blues Brothers, The (film) Bernstein, Elmer **27** 44-46

BLUFORD, GUION STEWART, JR. (born 1942), African American aerospace engineer, pilot, and astronaut **2** 341-343

BLUM, LÉON (1872-1950), French statesman **2** 343-344

BLUME, JUDY (born Judy Sussman; b. 1938), American fiction author **2** 344-345

BLUMENTHAL, WERNER MICHAEL (born 1926), American businessman and treasury secretary **2** 345-346

BLY, NELLIE (born Elizabeth Cochrane Seaman; 1864-1922), American journalist and reformer **2** 346-348

BLYDEN, EDWARD WILMOT (1832-1912), Liberian statesman **2** 348-349

BOAS, FRANZ (1858-1942), German-born American anthropologist **2** 349-351

BOCCACCIO, GIOVANNI (1313-1375), Italian author **2** 351-353

BOCCIONI, UMBERTO (1882-1916), Italian artist **2** 353-354

BÖCKLIN, ARNOLD (1827-1901), Swiss painter **2** 354-355

BODE, BOYD HENRY (1873-1953), American philosopher and educator **2** 355-356

BODIN, JEAN (1529/30-1596), French political philosopher **2** 356-357

Body Worlds (museum exhibition) Hagens, Gunther von **27** 157-159

BOEHME, JACOB (1575-1624), German mystic **2** 357

BOEING, WILLIAM EDWARD (1881-1956), American businessman **2** 357-358

BOERHAAVE, HERMANN (1668-1738), Dutch physician and chemist **2** 358-359

BOESAK, ALLAN AUBREY (born 1945), opponent of apartheid in South Africa and founder of the United Democratic Front **2** 359-360

BOETHIUS, ANICIUS MANLIUS SEVERINUS (480?-524/525), Roman logician and theologian **2** 360-361

BOFF, LEONARDO (Leonardo Genezio Darci Boff; born 1938), Brazilian priest **22** 69-71

BOFFRAND, GABRIEL GERMAIN (1667-1754), French architect and decorator **2** 361

BOFILL, RICARDO (born 1939), postmodern Spanish architect **2** 362-363

BOGART, HUMPHREY (1899-1957), American stage and screen actor **2** 363-364

BOHEMUND I (of Tarantò; circa 1055-1111), Norman Crusader **2** 364

BOHLEN, CHARLES (CHIP) EUSTIS (1904-1973), United States ambassador to the Soviet Union, interpreter, and presidential adviser **2** 364-366

BÖHM-BAWERK, EUGEN VON (1851-1914), Austrian economist **2** 366

BOHR, AAGE NIELS (born 1922), Danish physicist **25** 53-55

BOHR, NIELS HENRIK DAVID (1885-1962), Danish physicist **2** 366-368

BOIARDO, MATTEO MARIA (Conte di Scandiano; 1440/41-1494), Italian poet **2** 369

BOILEAU-DESPRÉAUX, NICHOLAS (1636?-1711), French critic and writer **2** 369-371

BOIVIN, MARIE GILLAIN (née Marie Anne Victorine Gillain; 1773-1841), French midwife and author **25** 55-56

BOK, DEREK CURTIS (born 1930), dean of the Harvard Law School and president of Harvard University **2** 371-372

BOK, EDWARD WILLIAM (1863-1930), American editor and publisher **22** 71-73

BOK, SISSELA ANN (born 1934), American moral philosopher **2** 372-374

BOLEYN, ANNE (1504?-1536), second wife of Henry VIII **18** 47-49

BOLINGBROKE, VISCOUNT (Henry St. John; 1678-1751), English statesman **2** 374-375

BOLÍVAR, SIMÓN (1783-1830), South American general and statesman **2** 375-377

BOLKIAH, HASSANAL (Muda Hassanal Bolkiah Mu'izzaddin Waddaulah; born 1946), Sultan of Brunei **18** 49-51

BÖLL, HEINRICH (1917-1985), German writer and translator **2** 377-378

BOLTWOOD, BERTRAM BORDEN (1870-1927), American radiochemist **2** 378-379

BOLTZMANN, LUDWIG (1844-1906), Austrian physicist **2** 379-380

BOMBAL, MARÍA LUISA (1910-1980), Chilean novelist and story writer **2** 380-381

BONAPARTE, JOSEPH (1768-1844), French statesman, king of Naples 1806-1808 and of Spain 1808-1813 **2** 381-382

BONAPARTE, LOUIS (1778-1846), French statesman, king of Holland 1806-1810 **2** 382-383

BONAVENTURE, ST. (1217-1274), Italian theologian and philosopher **2** 383-384

BOND, HORACE MANN (1904-1972), African American educator **2** 384-386

BOND, JULIAN (born 1940), civil rights leader elected to the Georgia House of Representatives **2** 386-387

BONDEVIK, KJELL MAGNE (born 1947), Norwegian politician **27** 51-53

BONDFIELD, MARGARET GRACE (1873-1953), British union official and political leader **2** 388-389

BONDI, HERMANN (1919-2005), English mathematician and cosmologist **18** 51-52

BONHAM CARTER, HELEN VIOLET (nee Helen Violet Asquith; 1887-1969), English author and orator **26** 42-44

BONHOEFFER, DIETRICH (1906-1945), German theologian **2** 389-391

BONHEUR, ROSA (Marie Rosalie Bonheur; 1822-1899), French artist **19** 29-31

BONIFACE, ST. (circa 672-754), English monk **2** 391

BONIFACE VIII (Benedetto Caetani; 1235?-1303), pope 1294-1303 **2** 392-393

BONIFACIO, ANDRES (1863-1897), Filipino revolutionary hero **2** 393-394

BONINGTON, RICHARD PARKES (1802-1828), English painter **2** 394-395

BONNARD, PIERRE (1867-1947), French painter **2** 395-396

BONNIN, GERTRUDE SIMMONS (Zitkala-Sa; Red Bird; 1876-1938), Native American author and activist **18** 52-54

BONNY, ANNE (Anne Bonn; Anne Burleigh; 1700-1782), Irish American pirate **25** 56-58

BONO (Paul Hewson; born 1960), Irish musician and activist **24** 56-59

BONO, SONNY (Salvatore Bono; 1935-1998), American entertainer and U.S. Congressman **18** 54-56

BONTEMPS, ARNA (Arnaud Wendell Bontemps; 1902-1973), American author and educator **21** 47-50

BONVALOT, PIERRE GABRIEL ÉDOUARD (1853-1933), French explorer and author **2** 396

BOOLE, GEORGE (1815-1864), English mathematician **2** 396-397

BOONE, DANIEL (1734-1820), American frontiersman and explorer **2** 397-398

BOORSTIN, DANIEL J. (born 1914), American historian **2** 398-400

BOOTH, CHARLES (1840-1916), English social scientist **2** 400-401

BOOTH, EDWIN (1833-1893), American actor **2** 401-402

BOOTH, EVANGELINE CORY (1865-1950), British/American humanist **2** 402-403

BOOTH, HUBERT CECIL (1871-1955), English inventor of the vacuum cleaner **21** 50-52

BOOTH, JOHN WILKES (1838-1865), American actor **2** 404

BOOTH, JOSEPH (1851-1932), English missionary in Africa **2** 404-405

BOOTH, WILLIAM (1829-1912), English evangelist, Salvation Army founder **2** 405-406

BOOTHROYD, BETTY (born 1929), first woman speaker in Great Britain's House of Commons **2** 406-407

BORAH, WILLIAM EDGAR (1865-1940), American statesman **2** 408

BORDEN, GAIL (1801-1874), American pioneer and inventor of food-processing techniques **2** 409

BORDEN, SIR ROBERT LAIRD (1854-1937), Canadian prime minister, 1911-1920 **2** 409-411

BORGES, JORGE LUIS (1899-1986), Argentine author and critic **2** 411-412

BORGIA, CESARE (1475-1507), Italian cardinal, general, and administrator **2** 412-413

BORGIA, LUCREZIA (1480-1519), Italian duchess of Ferrara **2** 413-416

BORGLUM, JOHN GUTZON DE LA MOTHE (1867-1941), American sculptor and engineer **2** 416-417

BORI, LUCREZIA (Lucrezia Gonzá de Riancho; 1887-1960), Spanish American opera singer **23** 44-45

BORJA CEVALLOS, RODRIGO (born 1935), a founder of Ecuador's Democratic Left (Izquierda Democratica) party and president of Ecuador (1988-) **2** 417-418

BORLAUG, NORMAN ERNEST (born 1914), American biochemist who developed high yield cereal grains **2** 418-420

BORN, MAX (1882-1970), German physicist **2** 420-421

Borneo (island)
see Indonesia

BOROCHOV, DOV BER (1881-1917), early Zionist thinker who reconciled Judaism and Marxism **2** 421-422

BORODIN, ALEKSANDR PROFIREVICH (1833-1887), Russian composer **2** 422-423

BORROMEO, ST. CHARLES (1538-1584), Italian cardinal and reformer **2** 423-424

BORROMINI, FRANCESCO (1599-1667), Italian architect **2** 424-425

BOSANQUET, BERNARD (1848-1923), English philosopher **2** 425-426

BOSCH, HIERONYMUS (1453-1516), Netherlandish painter **2** 426-428

BOSCH, JUAN (born 1909), Dominican writer, president, 1963 **2** 428-429

BOSE, SATYENDRANATH (1894-1974), Indian physicist **20** 52-54

BOSE, SIR JAGADIS CHANDRA (1858-1937), Indian physicist and plant physiologist **2** 430-431

BOSE, SUBHAS CHANDRA (1897-1945), Indian nationalist **2** 430-431

BOSOMWORTH, MARY MUSGROVE (Cousaponokeesa;1700-1765), Native American/American interpreter, diplomat, and businessperson **20** 54-56

Bossa nova (music)
Getz, Stan **27** 143-145
Jobim, Antonio Carlos **27** 187-189

BOSSUET, JACQUES BÉNIGNE (1627-1704), French bishop and author **2** 431-432

Boston Celtics (basketball team)
Auerbach, Red **27** 25-28

BOSWELL, JAMES (1740-1795), Scottish biographer and diarist **2** 432-434

BOTERO, FERNANDO (born 1932), Colombian artist **24** 59-61

BOTHA, LOUIS (1862-1919), South African soldier and statesman **2** 434-436

BOTHA, PIETER WILLEM (1916-2006), prime minister (1978-1984) and first executive state president of the Republic of South Africa **2** 436-438

BOTHE, WALTHER (1891-1957), German physicist **2** 438-439

BOTTICELLI, SANDRO (1444-1510), Italian painter **2** 439-440

BOUCHER, FRANÇOIS (1703-1770), French painter **2** 440-442

BOUCICAULT, DION (1820-1890), Irish-American playwright and actor **2** 442-443

BOUDICCA (Boadicea; died 61 A.D.), Iceni queen **18** 56-58

BOUDINOT, ELIAS (Buck Watie; Galagina; 1803-1839), Cherokee leader and author **21** 52-54

BOUGAINVILLE, LOUIS ANTOINE DE (1729-1811), French soldier and explorer **2** 443-444

BOULANGER, NADIA (1887-1979), French pianist and music teacher **20** 56-58

BOULEZ, PIERRE (born 1925), French composer, conductor, and teacher **2** 444-445

BOULT, ADRIAN CEDRIC (1889-1983), English conductor **24** 61-64

BOUMEDIENE, HOUARI (born 1932), Algerian revolutionary, military leader, and president **2** 445-446

BOURASSA, JOSEPH-HENRI-NAPOLEON (1868-1952), French-Canadian nationalist and editor **2** 446-447

BOURASSA, ROBERT (born 1933), premier of the province of Quebec (1970-1976 and 1985-) **2** 447-449

BOURDELLE, EMILE-ANTOINE (1861-1929), French sculptor **2** 449-450

BOURGEOIS, LÉON (1851-1925), French premier 1895-1896 **2** 450-451

BOURGEOIS, LOUISE (born 1911), American sculptor **2** 451-452

BOURGEOIS, LOUYSE (Louise Bourgeois; c. 1563-1636), French midwife **25** 58-60

BOURGEOYS, BLESSED MARGUERITE (1620-1700), French educator and religious founder **2** 452-453

BOURGUIBA, HABIB (1903-2000), Tunisian statesman **2** 453-455

BOURKE-WHITE, MARGARET (1904-1971), American photographer and photojournalist **2** 455-456

BOURNE, RANDOLPH SILLIMAN (1886-1918), American pacifist and cultural critic **2** 456-457

BOUTROS-GHALI, BOUTROS (born 1922), Egyptian diplomat and sixth secretary-general of the United Nations (1991-) **2** 457-458

BOUTS, DIRK (1415/20-1475), Dutch painter **2** 458-459

BOVERI, THEODOR HEINRICH (1862-1915), German biologist **25** 60-62

BOWDITCH, HENRY INGERSOLL (1808-1892), American physician **2** 459-460

BROWN, TINA (Christina Hambly Brown; born 1953), British editor who transformed the English magazine *Tatler*, then the United States magazines *Vanity Fair* and the *New Yorker* 3 47-48

BROWN, TONY (William Anthony Brown; born 1933), African American radio personality **24** 68-70

BROWN, WILLIAM WELLS (1815/16-1884), African American author and abolitionist 3 48-49

BROWNE, SIR THOMAS (1605-1682), English author 3 49-50

BROWNE, THOMAS ALEXANDER (Rolf Bolderwood; 1826-1915), Australian author **22** 85-87

BROWNER, CAROL M. (born 1955), U.S. Environmental Protection Agency administrator 3 50-52

BROWNING, ELIZABETH BARRETT (1806-1861), English poet 3 52-53

BROWNING, ROBERT (1812-1889), English poet 3 53-55

BROWNLOW, WILLIAM GANNAWAY (1805-1877), American journalist and politician 3 55-56

BROWNMILLER, SUSAN (born 1935), American activist, journalist, and novelist 3 56-57

BROWNSON, ORESTES AUGUSTUS (1803-1876), American clergyman and transcendentalist 3 57-58

BRUBACHER, JOHN SEILER (1898-1988), American historian and educator 3 58-59

BRUBECK, DAVE (born 1920), American pianist, composer, and bandleader 3 59-61

BRUCE, BLANCHE KELSO (1841-1898), African American politician 3 62-63

BRUCE, DAVID (1855-1931), Australian parasitologist 3 63

BRUCE, JAMES (1730-1794), Scottish explorer 3 63-64

BRUCE, LENNY (Leonard Alfred Schneider; 1925-1966), American comedian **19** 39-41

BRUCE OF MELBOURNE, 1ST VISCOUNT (Stanley Melbourne Bruce; 1883-1967), Australian statesman 3 61-62

BRUCKNER, JOSEPH ANTON (1824-1896), Austrian composer 3 64-65

BRUEGEL, PIETER, THE ELDER (1525/30-1569), Netherlandish painter 3 65-67

BRÛLÉ, ÉTIENNE (circa 1592-1633), French explorer in North America 3 67-68

BRUNDTLAND, GRO HARLEM (1939-1989), Norwegian prime minister and chair of the United Nations World Commission for Environment and Development 3 68-69

BRUNEL, ISAMBARD KINGDOM (1806-1859), English civil engineer 3 69-70

BRUNELLESCHI, FILIPPO (1377-1446), Italian architect and sculptor 3 70-72

BRUNER, JEROME SEYMOUR (born 1915), American psychologist 3 72-73

BRUNHOFF, JEAN de (1899-1937), French author and illustrator **19** 41-42

BRUNNER, ALOIS (born 1912), Nazi German officer who helped engineer the destruction of European Jews 3 73-74

BRUNNER, EMIL (1889-1966), Swiss Reformed theologian 3 74-75

BRUNO, GIORDANO (1548-1600), Italian philosopher and poet 3 75-76

BRUTON, JOHN GERARD (born 1947), prime minister of Ireland 3 76-77

BRUTUS, DENNIS (born 1924), exiled South African poet and political activist opposed to apartheid 3 77-78

BRUTUS, MARCUS JUNIUS (circa 85-42 B.C.), Roman statesman 3 79-80

BRYAN, WILLIAM JENNINGS (1860-1925), American lawyer and politician 3 80-82

BRYANT, PAUL ("Bear;" 1919-1983), American college football coach 3 82-83

BRYANT, WILLIAM CULLEN (1794-1878), American poet and editor 3 83-85

BRYCE, JAMES (1838-1922), British historian, jurist, and statesman 3 85

BRZEZINSKI, ZBIGNIEW (1928-1980), assistant to President Carter for national security affairs (1977-1980) 3 85-87

BUBER, MARTIN (1878-1965), Austrian-born Jewish theologian and philosopher 3 87-89

BUCHALTER, LEPKE (Louis Bachalter; 1897-1944), American gangster **19** 42-44

BUCHANAN, JAMES (1791-1868), American statesman, president 1857-1861 3 89-90

BUCHANAN, PATRICK JOSEPH (born 1938), commentator, journalist, and presidential candidate 3 90-91

BUCHWALD, ART (Arthur Buchwald; 1925-2007), American journalist **27** 55-57

BUCK, JACK (John Francis Buck; 1924-2002), American sportscaster **27** 57-59

BUCK, PEARL SYDENSTRICKER (1892-1973), American novelist 3 91-93

BUCKINGHAM, 1ST DUKE OF (George Villiers; 1592-1628), English courtier and military leader 3 93-94

BUCKINGHAM, 2D DUKE OF (George Villiers; 1628-1687), English statesman 3 94-95

BUCKLE, HENRY THOMAS (1821-1862), English historian 3 95-96

BUCKLEY, WILLIAM F., JR. (born 1925), conservative American author, editor, and political activist 3 96-97

BUDDHA (circa 560-480 B.C.), Indian founder of Buddhism 3 97-101

BUDDHADĀSA BHIKKHU (Nguam Phanich; born 1906), founder of Wat Suan Mokkhabalārama in southern Thailand and interpreter of Theravāda Buddhism 3 101-102

BUDÉ, GUILLAUME (1467-1540), French humanist 3 102-103

BUDGE, DON (J. Donald Budge; born 1915), American tennis player **21** 57-59

BUECHNER, FREDERICK (born 1926), American novelist and theologian 3 103-105

BUEL, JESSE (1778-1839), American agriculturalist and journalist 3 105

BUFFALO BILL (William Frederick Cody; 1846-1917), American scout and publicist 3 105-106

BUFFETT, WARREN (born 1930), American investment salesman 3 106-109

BUFFON, COMTE DE (Georges Louis Leclerc; 1707-1788), French naturalist 3 109-111

BUGEAUD DE LA PICONNERIE, THOMAS ROBERT (1784-1849), Duke of Isly and marshal of France 3 111

BUICK, DAVID (1854-1929), American inventor and businessman **19** 44-45

BUKHARI, MUHAMMAD IBN ISMAIL AL- (810-870), Arab scholar and Moslem saint 3 111-112

CHAPMAN, JOHN (Johnny Appleseed; c. 1775-1847), American horticulturist and missionary **21** 77-78

CHAPMAN, SYDNEY (1888-1970), English geophysicist **3** 441

CHARCOT, JEAN MARTIN (1825-1893), French psychiatrist **3** 442

CHARDIN, JEAN BAPTISTE SIMÉON (1699-1779), French painter **3** 442-443

CHARGAFF, ERWIN (1905-2002), American biochemist who worked with DNA **3** 444-445

CHARLEMAGNE (742-814), king of the Franks, 768-814, and emperor of the West, 800-814 **3** 445-447

CHARLES (born 1948), Prince of Wales and heir apparent to the British throne **3** 448-450

CHARLES I (1600-1649), king of England 1625-1649 **3** 450-452

CHARLES II (1630-1685), king of England, Scotland, and Ireland 1660-1685 **3** 452-454

CHARLES II (1661-1700), king of Spain 1665-1700 **3** 454

CHARLES III (1716-1788), king of Spain 1759-1788 **3** 454-455

CHARLES IV (1316-1378), Holy Roman emperor 1346-1378 **3** 455-456

CHARLES IV (1748-1819), king of Spain 1788-1808 **3** 456-457

CHARLES V (1337-1380), king of France 1364-1380 **3** 459-460

CHARLES V (1500-1558), Holy Roman emperor 1519-1556 **3** 457-459

CHARLES VI (1368-1422), king of France 1380-1422 **3** 460-461

CHARLES VII (1403-1461), king of France 1422-1461 **3** 461-462

CHARLES VIII (1470-1498), king of France 1483-1498 **3** 462-463

CHARLES X (1757-1836), king of France 1824-1830 **3** 463-464

CHARLES XII (1682-1718), king of Sweden 1697-1718 **3** 464-466

CHARLES XIV JOHN (1763-1844), king of Sweden 1818-1844 **2** 205-206

CHARLES, RAY (Robinson; born 1932), American jazz musician—singer, pianist, and composer **3** 469-470

CHARLES ALBERT (1798-1849), king of Sardinia 1831-1849 **3** 466

CHARLES EDWARD LOUIS PHILIP CASIMIR STUART (1720-1788),

Scottish claimant to English and Scottish thrones **3** 466-467

CHARLES THE BOLD (1433-1477), duke of Burgundy 1467-1477 **3** 467-469

CHARNISAY, CHARLES DE MENOU (Seigneur d'Aulnay; circa 1604-1650), French governor of Acadia **3** 470-471

CHARONTON, ENGUERRAND (circa 1410/15-after 1466), French painter **3** 471

CHARPENTIER, MARC ANTOINE (1634-1704), French composer **3** 471-472

CHARRON, PIERRE (1541-1603), French philosopher and theologian **3** 472

CHASE, MARY AGNES (1869-1963), American botanist **24** 79-81

CHASE, PHILANDER (1775-1852), American Episcopalian bishop and missionary **3** 472-473

CHASE, SALMON PORTLAND (1808-1873), American statesman and jurist **3** 473-475

CHASE, SAMUEL (1741-1811), American politician and jurist **3** 475-476

CHASE, WILLIAM MERRITT (1849-1916), American painter **3** 476-477

CHATEAUBRIAND, VICOMTE DE (1768-1848), French author **3** 477-479

CHATELET, GABRIELLE-EMILIE (1706-1749), French physicist and chemist **22** 102-103

CHATICHAI CHOONHAVAN (1922-1998), prime minister of Thailand (1988-1990) **3** 479-480

CHATTERJI, BANKIMCHANDRA (1838-1894), Bengali novelist **3** 480-481

CHATTERTON, THOMAS (1752-1770), English poet **3** 481-482

CHAUCER, GEOFFREY (circa 1345-1400), English poet **3** 482-485

CHAUNCY, CHARLES (1705-1787), American Calvinist clergyman and theologian **3** 485-486

CHÁVEZ, CARLOS (1899-1978), Mexican conductor and composer **3** 486

CHAVEZ, CESAR (1927-1993), American labor leader **3** 486-487

CHÁVEZ, DENNIS (1888-1962), Hispanic American politician **3** 488-489

CHÁVEZ, HUGO (Hugo Rafael Chávez Frí; born 1954), Venezuelan political and military leader **26** 64-66

CHAVEZ, LINDA (born 1947), Hispanic American civil rights activists **3** 489-491

CHAVEZ-THOMPSON, LINDA (born 1944), Mexican American businesswoman and labor activist **24** 81-83

CHAVIS, BENJAMIN (born 1948), African American religious leader, civil rights activist, labor organizer, and author **3** 491-493

CHEEVER, JOHN (1912-1982), American short-story writer **3** 493-494

CHEKHOV, ANTON PAVLOVICH (1860-1904), Russian author **3** 494-497

CHELMSFORD, 1st VISCOUNT (Frederic John Napier Thesigner Chelmsford; 1868-1933), English statesman **3** 497

Chemistry (science)
chemical structure
Kroto, Harold Walter **27** 216-218
gas studies
Crutzen, Paul J. **27** 95-97

CH'EN TU-HSIU (1879-1942), Chinese statesman and editor **3** 501-502

CHENEY, RICHARD B(RUCE) (born 1941), U.S. secretary of defense under George Bush **3** 497-499

CHENG HO (1371-circa 1433), Chinese admiral **3** 500

CHÉNIER, ANDRÉ MARIE (1762-1794), French poet **3** 500-501

CHERENKOV, PAVEL ALEKSEEVICH (1904-1990), Russian physicist **3** 502-503

CHERNENKO, KONSTANTIN USTINOVICH (1911-1985), the Soviet Union general secretary from February 1984 to March 1985 **3** 503-504

CHERNYSHEVSKY, NIKOLAI GAVRILOVICH (1828-1889), Russian journalist, critic, and social theorist **3** 504-505

CHERUBINI, LUIGI CARLO ZANOBI SALVATORE MARIA (1760-1842), Italian-born French composer **3** 505-506

CHESNUT, MARY BOYKIN (1823-1886), Civil War diarist **3** 506-508

CHESNUTT, CHARLES WADDELL (1858-1932), African American author and lawyer **20** 78-82

CHESTERTON, GILBERT KEITH (1874-1936), English author and artist **3** 508-509

CHEUNG, KATHERINE (Katherine Sui Fun Cheung; 1904-2003), Chinese American aviator **25** 88-90

CHEVALIER, MAURICE (1888-1972), French singer and actor 26 66-68

Chevalier de Saint-Goerge, Joseph Boulogne
see Saint-George, Joseph Boulogne, Chevalier de

CHEVROLET, LOUIS (1878-1941), auto racer and entrepreneur 20 82-84

CH'I PAI-SHIH (1863-1957), Chinese painter and poet 3 526-527

CHIA SSU-TAO (1213-1275), Chinese statesman 3 514-515

CHIANG CHING-KUO (1910-1988), chairman of the Nationalist party and president of the Republic of China in Taiwan (1978-1988) 3 509-510

CHIANG KAI-SHEK (1887-1975), Chinese nationalist leader and president 3 510-513

CHIARI, ROBERTO (born 1905), president of Panama (1960-1964) 3 513-514

CHICAGO, JUDY (Judith Cohen; born 1939), American artist and activist 3 515-516

Chicano literature
Anaya, Rudolfo Alfonso 27 17-19

CHICHERIN, GEORGI VASILYEVICH (1872-1936), Russian statesman 3 516-517

CHICHESTER, FRANCIS (1901-1972), British yachter 24 83-85

CHIEN-LUNG (Hung-li; 1711-1799), Chinese emperor (1735-1799) 21 78-79

CHIEPE, GAOSITWE KEAGAKWA TIBE (born 1926), intellectual, educator, diplomat, politician, and cabinet minister of external affairs of Botswana 3 517

CHIFLEY, JOSEPH BENEDICT (1885-1951), Australian statesman 3 518

CHIH-I (Chih-k'ai, 538-597), Chinese Buddhist monk 3 518-519

CHIKAMATSU, MONZAEMON (1653-1725), Japanese playwright 23 70-72

CHILD, JULIA McWILLIAMS (1912-2004), chef, author, and television personality 3 519-520

CHILD, LYDIA MARIA FRANCIS (1802-1880), American author and abolitionist 3 520-521

CHILDE, VERE GORDON (1892-1957), Australian prehistorian and archeologist 3 521-522

Children's literature
see Literature for children

CHILDRESS, ALICE (1920-1994), African American dramatist, author, and poet 3 522-524

Chile, Republic of (nation, South America)
cultural renaissance (1970s)
Jara, Victor 27 183-185
presidents
Lagos, Ricardo 27 223-225

Chilean literature
Jara, Victor 27 183-185

Chilean music
Jara, Victor 27 183-185

CH'IN KUEI (1090-1155), Chinese official 3 524-525

CHINN, MAY EDWARD (1896-1980), African American physician 3 525-526

CHINO, WENDELL (1923-1998), Native American tribal leader and activist 27 86-88

CHIPPENDALE, THOMAS (1718-1779), English cabinetmaker 4 1-2

CHIRAC, JACQUES (born 1932), French prime minister 4 2-3

CHIRICO, GIORGIO DE (1888-1978), Italian painter 4 4

CHISHOLM, CAROLINE (1808-1877), British author and philantropist 4 4-7

CHISHOLM, SHIRLEY ANITA ST. HILL (1924-2005), first African American woman to serve in the United States Congress 4 7-9

CHISSANO, JOAQUIM ALBERTO (born 1939), a leader of Mozambique's war for independence and later president of Mozambique (1986-) 4 9-11

CHISUM, JOHN SIMPSON (1824-1884), American rancher 4 11

CH'I-YING (circa 1786-1858), Chinese statesman and diplomat 4 12

CHMIELNICKI, BOGDAN (1595-1657), Cossack leader of Ukrainian revolt 4 12-13

CHOATE, JOSEPH HODGES (1832-1917), American lawyer and diplomat 22 103-106

CHOATE, RUFUS (1799-1859), American lawyer and statesman 22 106-107

CH'OE CH'UNG-HON (1149-1219), Korean general 4 13

CHOMSKY, NOAM AVRAM (born 1928), American linguist and philosopher 4 13-15

CHONG CHUNG-BU (1106-1179), Korean general 4 15

CHONGJO (1752-1800), king of Korea 4 15-16

CHOPIN, FRÉDÉRIC FRANÇOIS (1810-1849), Polish-French composer and pianist 4 16-18

CHOPIN, KATHERINE ("Kate"; born Katherine O'Flaherty; 1851-1904), American writer, poet, and essayist 4 18-20

CHOPRA, DEEPAK (born 1946), Indian physician, author, and educator 20 84-86

CHOU EN-LAI (1898-1976), Chinese Communist premier 4 20-22

CHOU KUNG (flourished circa 1116 B.C.), Chinese statesman 4 22-23

CHRESTIEN DE TROYES (flourished 12th century), French poet 4 23-24

CHRÉTIEN, JOSEPH-JACQUES-JEAN "JEAN" (born 1934), French Canadian politician and Canada's 20th prime minister 4 24-25

CHRISTIAN IV (1577-1648), king of Denmark and Norway 1588-1648 20 86-89

CHRISTIE, AGATHA (Agatha Mary Clarissa Miller; 1890-1976), best selling mystery author 4 25-26

CHRISTINA OF SWEDEN (1626-1689), queen of Sweden 1632-1654 4 26-29

CHRISTINE DE PISAN (1364/65-circa 1430), French author 4 29-30

CHRISTO (Christo Vladimiroff Javacheff; born 1935), Bulgarian-born sculptor noted for large-scale environmental artworks 4 30-31

CHRISTOPHE, HENRI (1767-1820), Haitian patriot and king 4 32

CHRISTOPHER, WARREN MINOR (born 1925), United States secretary of state 4 32-33

CHRISTUS, PETRUS (circa 1410-1472/73), Flemish painter 4 33-34

CHRISTY, EDWIN P. (1815-1862), American minstrel 4 34-35

CHRYSIPPUS (circa 280-circa 206 B.C.), Greek Stoic philosopher 4 35-36

CHRYSLER, WALTER PERCY (1875-1940), American manufacturer 4 36-37

Chrysler Corp. (automobile firm)
Zetsche, Dieter 27 380-382

CHU YUAN-CHANG (Hongwu; T'ai Tsu; Kao-ti; 1328-1398), Chinese emperor (1368-1398) 21 79-81

CHU, PAUL CHING-WU (born 1941), Chinese-American experimentalist in solid-state physics 4 37-39

CLEMENT I (died c. 100 A.D.), Bishop of Rome, pope **23** 78-81

CLEMENT V (1264-1314), pope 1304-1314 **4** 101-102

CLEMENT VII (Giulia de Medici; 1478-1534), pope (1523-1534) **21** 81-83

CLEMENT XI (Giovanni Francesco Albani; 1649-1721), Italian pope 1700-1721 **24** 90-92

CLEMENT OF ALEXANDRIA (circa 150-circa 215), Christian theologian **4** 102-103

CLEMENTE, ROBERTO (1934-1972), Hispanic American baseball player **19** 70-72

CLEOMENES I (flourished circa 520-490 B.C.), Spartan king **4** 103

CLEOMENES III (circa 260-219 B.C.), king of Sparta 235-219 **4** 103-104

CLEON (circa 475-422 B.C.), Athenian political leader **4** 104-105

CLEOPATRA (69-30 B.C.), queen of Egypt **4** 105-106

CLEVELAND, JAMES (1932-1991), African American singer, songwriter, and pianist **4** 106-108

CLEVELAND, STEPHEN GROVER (1837-1908), American statesman, twice president **4** 108-110

CLIFFORD, ANNE (1590-1676), English author and philanthropist **27** 88-90

CLINE, PATSY (born Virginia Patterson Hensley; 1932-1963), American singer **4** 110-112

CLINTON, DeWITT (1769-1828), American lawyer and statesman **4** 112-113

CLINTON, GEORGE (1739-1812), American patriot and statesman **4** 113-114

CLINTON, SIR HENRY (1738?-1795), British commander in chief during the American Revolution **4** 114-115

CLINTON, HILLARY RODHAM (born 1947), American politician and first lady **4** 115-117

CLINTON, WILLIAM JEFFERSON ("Bill" Clinton; born 1946), 42nd president of the United States **4** 117-119

CLIVE, ROBERT (Baron Clive of Plassey; 1725-1774), English soldier and statesman **4** 119-120

CLODION (1738-1814), French sculptor **4** 121

CLODIUS PULCHER, PUBLIUS (died 52 B.C.), Roman politician **4** 121-122

CLOONEY, ROSEMARY (1928-2002), American singer and actress **27** 90-93

CLOUET, FRANÇOIS (circa 1516-circa 1572), French portrait painter **4** 122-123

CLOUET, JEAN (circa 1485-circa 1541), French portrait painter **4** 122-123

CLOUGH, ARTHUR HUGH (1819-1861), English poet **4** 123-124

CLOVIS I (465-511), Frankish king **4** 124

COACHMAN, ALICE (Alice Coachman Davis; born 1923), African American athlete **26** 71-73

COBB, JEWEL PLUMMER (born 1924), African American scientist and activist **22** 112-114

COBB, TYRUS RAYMOND (1886-1961), baseball player **4** 124-126

COBBETT, WILLIAM (1763-1835), English journalist and politician **4** 126-127

COBDEN, RICHARD (1804-1865), English politician **4** 127-128

COCHISE (circa 1825-1874), American Chiricahua Apache Indian chief **4** 128

COCHRAN, JACQUELINE (Jackie Cochran; 1910-1980), American aviator and businesswoman **18** 94-96

COCHRAN, JOHNNIE (1937-2005), African American lawyer **4** 128-131

COCHRANE, THOMAS (Earl of Dundonald; 1775-1860), British naval officer **20** 91-93

COCKCROFT, JOHN DOUGLAS (1897-1967), English physicist **4** 131-132

COCTEAU, JEAN (1889-1963), French writer **4** 132-133

COE, SEBASTIAN (born 1956), English track athlete **20** 93-95

COEN, JAN PIETERSZOON (circa 1586-1629), Dutch governor general of Batavia **4** 133

COETZEE, J(OHN) M. (born 1940), white South African novelist **4** 133-135

COFFIN, LEVI (1789-1877), American antislavery reformer **4** 135

COFFIN, WILLIAM SLOANE, JR. (1924-2006), Yale University chaplain who spoke out against the Vietnam War **4** 135-137

COHAN, GEORGE MICHAEL (1878-1942), American actor and playwright **4** 137-138

COHEN, HERMANN (1842-1918), Jewish-German philosopher **4** 138-139

COHEN, MORRIS RAPHAEL (1880-1947), American philosopher and teacher **4** 139-140

COHEN, WILLIAM S. (born 1940), American secretary of defense **18** 96-98

COHN, FERDINAND (1829-1898), German botanist **20** 95-97

COHN-BENDIT, DANIEL (born 1946), led "new left" student protests in France in 1968 **4** 140-141

COKE, SIR EDWARD (1552-1634), English jurist and parliamentarian **4** 141-142

COLBERT, JEAN BAPTISTE (1619-1683), French statesman **4** 142-143

COLBY, WILLIAM E. (1920-1996), American director of the Central Intelligence Agency (CIA) **4** 143-145

COLDEN, CADWALLADER (1688-1776), American botanist and politician **4** 145-146

COLE, GEORGE DOUGLAS HOWARD (1889-1959), English historian and economist **4** 146-147

COLE, JOHNNETTA (born 1936), African American scholar and educator **4** 147-149

COLE, NAT (a.k.a. Nat "King" Cole, born Nathaniel Adams Coles; 1919-1965), American jazz musician **4** 149-151

COLE, THOMAS (1801-1848), American painter **4** 151-152

COLEMAN, BESSIE (1892-1926), first African American to earn an international pilot's license **4** 152-154

COLERIDGE, SAMUEL TAYLOR (1772-1834), English poet and critic **4** 154-156

COLES, ROBERT MARTIN (born 1929), American social psychiatrist, social critic, and humanist **4** 156-157

COLET, JOHN (circa 1446-1519), English theologian **4** 157-158

COLETTE, SIDONIE GABRIELLE (1873-1954), French author **4** 158-159

COLIGNY, GASPARD DE (1519-1572), French admiral and statesman **4** 159-160

COLLETT, CAMILLA (nee Camilla Wergeland; 1813-1895), Norwegian author **26** 73-75

COLLIER, JOHN (1884-1968), American proponent of Native American culture **4** 160-162

COOKE, JAY (1821-1905), American merchant banker **4** 215-216

COOLEY, CHARLES HORTON (1864-1929), American social psychologist, sociologist, and educator **4** 216-217

COOLEY, THOMAS MCINTYRE (1824-1898), American jurist and public servant **22** 116-119

COOLIDGE, JOHN CALVIN (1872-1933), president of the United States 1923-1929 **4** 217-219

COOMBS, HERBERT COLE (Nugget; born 1906), Australian economist **4** 219-220

COONEY, JOAN GANZ (born 1929), American television program producer and publicist **19** 74-76

COOPER, ANNIE (Anna Julia Cooper; 1858-1964), African American educator, author, and activist **22** 119-121

COOPER, GARY (Frank James Cooper; 1901-1961), American motion picture actor **21** 85-87

COOPER, JAMES FENIMORE (1789-1851), American novelist and social critic **4** 220-223

COOPER, PETER (1791-1883), American inventor and manufacturer **4** 223-224

COOPER, THOMAS (1759-1839), English-born American scientist and educator **4** 224

COORS, ADOLPH (Adolph Herrman Kohrs; 1847-1929), American brewer and businessman **19** 76-78

COPEAU, JACQUES (1879-1949), French dramatic theorist, director, and actor who established the Vieux Colombier **4** 225

COPERNICUS, NICOLAUS (1473-1543), Polish astronomer **4** 226-227

COPLAND, AARON (1900-1990), American composer **4** 227-228

COPLEY, JOHN SINGLETON (1738-1815), American portrait painter **4** 228-230

COPPOLA, FRANCIS FORD (born 1939), American filmmaker and author **18** 102-104

CORDOBA, GONZALO FERNANDEZ DE (1453-1515), Spanish military leader **20** 99-100

CORELLI, ARCANGELO (1653-1713), Italian composer and violinist **4** 230-231

CORI, GERTY T. (born Gerty Theresa Radnitz; 1896-1957), American biochemist **4** 231-234

CORINTH, LOVIS (1838-1925), German artist **4** 234

CORMAN, ROGER (born 1926), American film director and producer **21** 87-89

CORNEILLE, PIERRE (1606-1684), French playwright **4** 234-236

CORNELL, EZRA (1807-1874), American financier and philanthropist **4** 236-237

CORNELL, JOSEPH (1903-1972), American artist **4** 237-238

CORNFORTH, JOHN WARCUP (born 1917), Australian chemist **24** 92-94

CORNING, ERASTUS (1794-1872), American merchant and financier **4** 238-239

CORNPLANTER (c. 1732-1836), Seneca village leader **4** 239-241

CORNWALLIS, CHARLES (1st Marquess Cornwallis; 1738-1805), British soldier and statesman **4** 241-243

CORONA, BERT (born 1918), Hispanic American union organizer **4** 243-247

CORONADO, FRANCISCO VÁSQUEZ DE (1510-1554), Spanish explorer and colonial official **4** 247

COROT, JEAN BAPTISTE CAMILLE (1796-1875), French painter **4** 247-249

CORREGGIO (circa 1494-1534), Italian painter **4** 249-251

CORRIGAN, MICHAEL AUGUSTINE (1839-1902), American Catholic archbishop **4** 253

CORRIGAN and WILLIAMS founders of the women's peace movement in Northern Ireland **4** 251-253

CORT, HENRY (1740-1800), English ironmaster **4** 254

CORTE REÁL, GASPAR AND MIGUEL, Portuguese explorers **4** 254-255

CORTÉS, HERNÁN (1485?-1547), Spanish conquistador **4** 255-256

CORTONA, PIETRO DA (1596-1669), Italian painter and architect **4** 256

COSBY, WILLIAM HENRY, JR. ("Bill" Cosby; born 1937), American entertainer **4** 257-258

COSELL, HOWARD (Howard William Cohen; 1920-1995), American sportscaster **24** 94-97

COSGRAVE, LIAM (born 1920), Irish foreign minister and prime minister (1973-1977) **4** 258-260

COSIO VILLEGAS, DANIEL (1898-1976), Mexican teacher, civil servant, and

author of studies of Mexican history **4** 260-261

Cosmetic industry
Jung, Andrea **27** 192-194

COTTEN, ELIZABETH ("Libba"; born Elizabeth Nevills; 1892-1987), African American musician **4** 261-263

COTTON, JOHN (1584-1652), American Congregationalist clergyman **4** 263-265

COUBERTIN, PIERRE DE (Pierre Fredy, Baron de Coubertin; 1863-1937), French organizer of the modern Olympic Games **21** 89-92

COUGHLIN, CHARLES EDWARD (1891-1979), Canadian-American priest and politician **4** 265-266

COULOMB, CHARLES AUGUSTIN DE (1736-1806), French physicist **4** 266-267

COULTON, GEORGE GORDON (1858-1947), English historian **4** 267

Council of Elders
see French Revolution—Council of Elders

Countess Pillar (England)
Clifford, Anne **27** 88-90

Country Music Hall of Fame
Wynette, Tammy **27** 372-374

COUNTS, GEORGE S(YLVESTER) (1889-1974), American educator and educational sociologist **4** 267-269

COUPER, ARCHIBALD SCOTT (1831-1892), British chemist **4** 269-270

COUPER, JAMES HAMILTON (1794-1866), American agriculturist **4** 270

COUPERIN, FRANÇOIS (1668-1733), French composer, organist, and harpsichordist **4** 270-271

COURBET, JEAN DESIRÉ GUSTAVE (1819-1877), French painter **4** 271-273

COURLANDER, HAROLD (1908-1996), American folklorist and author **19** 78-80

COURNOT, ANTOINE AUGUSTIN (1801-1877), French mathematician, philosopher, and economist **4** 273

COUSIN, VICTOR (1792-1867), French educator and philosopher **4** 273-274

COUSINS, NORMAN (1912-1990), editor-in-chief of the *Saturday Review* and advocate for world peace **4** 274-276

COUSTEAU, JACQUES-YVES (1910-1997), undersea explorer, photographer, inventor, writer, television producer, and filmmaker **4** 276-277
Cousteau, Jean-Michel **27** 93-95

COUSTEAU, JEAN-MICHEL (born 1938), French oceanographer **27** 93-95

COUSY, BOB (Robert Joseph Cousy; born 1928), American basketball player and coach **21** 92-94

COUZENS, JAMES (James Joseph Couzins, Jr.; 1872-1936), American industrialist, politician, and philanthropist **22** 121-125

COVERDALE, MILES (1488-1568), English Puritan **4** 278

COVILHÃO, PEDRO DE (circa 1455-circa 1530), Portuguese explorer and diplomat **4** 278-279

COWARD, NOEL (1899-1973), English playwright, actor, and composer **4** 279-280

COWELL, HENRY DIXON (1897-1965), American composer and pianist **4** 280-281

COWLEY, ABRAHAM (1618-1667), English writer **4** 281-282

COWPER, WILLIAM (1731-1800), English poet **4** 282

COX, ARCHIBALD (born 1912), American lawyer, educator, author, labor arbitrator, and public servant **4** 283-284

COX, HARVEY (born 1929), American theologian and author **4** 284-285

COXE, TENCH (1755-1824), American political economist and businessman **4** 285-286

COXEY, JACOB SECHLER (1854-1951), American reformer and businessman **4** 286-287

COYSEVOX, ANTOINE (1640-1720), French sculptor **4** 287-288

CRABBE, GEORGE (1754-1832), English poet **4** 288

CRAFT, ELLEN (ca. 1826-1897), African American activist **22** 125-127

CRAIG, EDWARD GORDON (1872-1966), European actor, designer, director, and theoretician **4** 288-289

CRANACH, LUCAS, THE ELDER (1472-1553), German painter, engraver, and designer of woodcuts **4** 289-290

CRANDALL, PRUDENCE (1803-1890), American educator **4** 291

CRANE, HART (1899-1932), American poet **4** 291-293

CRANE, STEPHEN (1871-1900), American writer and poet **4** 293-295

CRANMER, THOMAS (1489-1556), English reformer, archbishop of Canterbury **4** 295-296

CRASHAW, RICHARD (1612/1613-49), English poet **4** 296

CRASSUS DIVES, MARCUS LICINIUS (circa 115-53 B.C.), Roman financier and politician **4** 296-297

CRAVEIRINHA, JOSÉ (born 1922), Mozambican journalist and lyric poet **4** 297-299

CRAWFORD, JOAN (Lucille Fay LeSueur; 1906-1977), American actress **19** 80-82

CRAWFORD, WILLIAM HARRIS (1772-1834), American politician **4** 299-300

CRAXI, BETTINO (1934-2000), statesman and prime minister of the Italian republic (1983-1987) **4** 300-301

CRAY, SEYMOUR (1925-1996), American computer engineer **4** 301-303

CRAZY HORSE (circa 1842-1877), American Indian, Oglala Sioux war chief **4** 303-304

CREEL, GEORGE (1876-1953), American writer and journalist **4** 304-305

CRÉMAZIE, OCTAVE (1827-1879), Canadian poet **4** 305-306

CRERAR, THOMAS ALEXANDER (1876-1975), Canadian political leader **4** 306

CRESSON, EDITH (born 1934), first woman prime minister of France **4** 306-307

CRÈVECOEUR, ST. JOHN DE (1735-1813), French-American farmer and writer **4** 307-308

CRICHTON, (JOHN) MICHAEL (a.k.a. Michael Douglas, Jeffrey Hudson, and John Lange; born 1942), American novelist, screenwriter, and director **4** 308-310

CRICK, FRANCIS HARRY COMPTON (1916-2004), English molecular biologist **4** 310

Crimean War (1853-1856)
medicine and journalism
Barry, James **27** 40-41
Seacole, Mary **27** 321-323

Criminals, American
Ray, James Earl **27** 308-310

CRISPI, FRANCESCO (1819-1901), Italian statesman **4** 310-311

CRISTIANI, ALFREDO ("Fredy" Cristiani; born 1947), president of El Salvador (1989-) **4** 311-313

CRISTOFORI, BARTOLOMEO (1655-1731), Italian musician and inventor of the piano **21** 94-96

CROCE, BENEDETTO (1866-1952), Italian philosopher, critic and educator **4** 313-314

CROCKETT, DAVID (1786-1836), American frontiersman **4** 314-316

Crocodile Hunter (television program)
Irwin, Steve **27** 176-178

CROGHAN, GEORGE (ca. 1720-1782), American Indian agent and trader **22** 127-129

CROLY, HERBERT DAVID (1869-1930), American editor and author **4** 316-317

CROLY, JANE (Jennie June; 1829-1901), American journalist **21** 96-96

CROMER, 1ST EARL OF (Evelyn Baring; 1841-1907), English statesman **4** 317

CROMWELL, OLIVER (1599-1658), English statesman and general **4** 317-320

CROMWELL, THOMAS (Earl of Essex; circa 1485-1540), English statesman 1532-1540 **4** 320-321

CRONIN, JAMES WATSON (born 1931), American physicist **24** 97-99

CRONKITE, WALTER LELAND, JR. (born 1916), American journalist and radio and television news broadcaster **4** 321-322

CROOK, GEORGE (1828-1890), American general and frontiersman **4** 322-323

CROOKES, SIR WILLIAM (1832-1919), English chemist and physicist **4** 323-324

CROSBY, HARRY LILLIS (Bing; 1903-1977), American singer and radio and television personality **4** 324-326
Clooney, Rosemary **27** 90-93

CROWLEY, ALEISTER (1875-1947), English author and magician **18** 107-109

CROWTHER, SAMUEL ADJAI (circa 1806-1891), Nigerian Anglican bishop **4** 326

CRUMB, GEORGE (born 1929), American composer and teacher **4** 326-328

CRUTZEN, PAUL J. (born 1933), Dutch chemist **27** 95-97

CRUZ, CELIA (1925-2003), Cuban American singer **24** 99-101

DALY, MARCUS (1841-1900), American miner and politician **4** 379-380

DALY, MARY (born 1928), American feminist theoretician and philosopher **4** 380-381

DALZEL, ARCHIBALD (or Dalziel; 1740-1811), Scottish slave trader **4** 381-382

DAM, CARL PETER HENRIK (1895-1976), Danish biochemist **4** 382-383

DAMIEN, FATHER (1840-1889), Belgian missionary **4** 383

DAMPIER, WILLIAM (1652-1715), English privateer, author, and explorer **4** 384

DANA, CHARLES ANDERSON (1819-1897), American journalist **4** 384-385

DANA, RICHARD HENRY, JR. (1815-1882), American author and lawyer **4** 385-386

DANDOLO, ENRICO (circa 1107-1205), Venetian doge 1192-1205 **4** 386-387

DANDRIDGE, DOROTHY (1922-1965), African American actress and singer **18** 112-114

DANIELS, JOSEPHUS (1862-1948), American journalist and statesman **4** 387

Danish literature and culture
see Denmark—culture

D'ANNUNZIO, GABRIELE (1863-1938), Italian poet and patriot **4** 388

DANQUAH, JOSEPH B. (1895-1965), Ghanaian nationalist and politician **4** 388-389

DANTE ALIGHIERI (1265-1321), Italian poet **4** 389-391

DANTON, GEORGES JACQUES (1759-1794), French revolutionary leader **4** 391-393

DANTZIG, GEORGE BERNARD (1914-2005), American mathematician **26** 81-83

DARBY, ABRAHAM (1677-1717), English iron manufacturer **20** 106-107

DARÍO, RUBÉN (1867-1916), Nicaraguan poet **4** 393-394

DARIUS I (the Great; ruled 522-486 B.C.), king of Persia **4** 394-395

DARROW, CLARENCE SEWARD (1857-1938), American lawyer **4** 396-397

DARWIN, CHARLES ROBERT (1809-1882), English naturalist **4** 397-399

DARWIN, ERASMUS (1731-1802), English physician, author, botanist and inventor **18** 114-116

DARWISH, MAHMUD (born 1942), Palestinian poet **4** 399-401

DAS, CHITTA RANJAN (1870-1925), Indian lawyer, poet, and nationalist **4** 401-402

DATSOLALEE (Dabuda; Wide Hips; 1835-1925), Native American weaver **22** 130-131

DAUBIGNY, CHARLES FRANÇOIS (1817-1878), French painter and etcher **4** 402

DAUDET, ALPHONSE (1840-1897), French novelist and dramatist **4** 402-403

DAUMIER, HONORÉ VICTORIN (1808-1879), French lithographer, painter, and sculptor **4** 403-405

DAVENPORT, JOHN (1597-1670), English Puritan clergyman **4** 405-406

DAVID (ruled circa 1010-circa 970 B.C.), Israelite king **4** 406-407

DAVID, JACQUES LOUIS (1748-1825), French painter **4** 407-409

DAVID, SAINT (Dewi; 520-601), Welsh monk and evangelist **23** 83-85

DAVID I (1084-1153), king of Scotland **4** 407

DAVIES, ARTHUR BOWEN (1862-1928), American painter **4** 409-410

DAVIES, RUPERT (1917-1976), British actor **18** 116-117

DAVIES, WILLIAM ROBERTSON (1913-1995), Canadian author **18** 117-119

DAVIGNON, VISCOUNT (ETIENNE) (born 1932), an architect of European integration and unity through the Commission of the European Communities **4** 410-411

DAVIS, ALEXANDER JACKSON (1803-1892), American architect **4** 411

DAVIS, ANGELA (Angela Yvonne Davis; born 1944), African American scholar and activist **4** 412-413

DAVIS, ARTHUR VINING (1867-1962), general manager of the Aluminum Company of America (ALCOA) **4** 413-414

DAVIS, BENJAMIN O., SR. (1877-1970), first African American general in the regular United States Armed Services **4** 414-415

DAVIS, BETTE (1908-1989), American actress **18** 119-121

DAVIS, COLIN REX (born 1927), British conductor **22** 131-133

DAVIS, ELMER HOLMES (1890-1958), American journalist and radio commentator **22** 133-136

DAVIS, GLENN (1925-2005), American football player **21** 101-103

DAVIS, HENRY WINTER (1817-1865), American lawyer and politician **4** 415-416

DAVIS, JEFFERSON (1808-1889), American statesman, president of the Confederacy 1862-1865 **4** 416-418

DAVIS, JOHN (circa 1550-1605), English navigator **4** 419

DAVIS, MILES (1926-1991), jazz trumpeter, composer, and small-band leader **4** 419-421

DAVIS, OSSIE (1917-2005), African American playwright, actor, and director **4** 421-422

DAVIS, RICHARD HARDING (1864-1916), American journalist, novelist, and dramatist **4** 422-423

DAVIS, SAMMY, JR. (1925-1990), African American singer, dancer, and actor **4** 423-424

DAVIS, STUART (1894-1964), American cubist painter **4** 424-425

DAVIS, WILLIAM MORRIS (1850-1934), American geographer and geologist **4** 425-426

DAVY, SIR HUMPHRY (1778-1829), English chemist and natural philosopher **4** 426-427

DAWES, HENRY LAURENS (1816-1903), American politician **4** 427

DAWSON, WILLIAM LEVI (1899-1990), African American composer, performer, and music educator **4** 427-428

DAY, DOROTHY (1897-1980), a founder of the Catholic Worker Movement **4** 428-429

DAYAN, MOSHE (1915-1981), Israeli general and statesman **4** 429-431

DAYANANDA SARASWATI (1824-1883), Indian religious leader **4** 431

Days of Heaven (film)
Almendros, Néstor **27** 13-15

DE ANDRADE, MARIO (Mario Coelho Pinto Andrade; born 1928), Angolan poet, critic, and political activist **4** 434-435

DE BEAUVOIR, SIMONE (1908-1986), French writer and leader of the modern feminist movement **4** 440-441

DONNER, GEORG RAPHAEL (1693-1741), Austrian sculptor **5** 63

DONOSO, JOSÉ (1924-1996), Chilean writer **5** 63-65

DONOVAN, WILLIAM JOSEPH (1883-1959), American lawyer and public servant **22** 147-149

DOOLITTLE, HILDA (1886-1961), American poet and novelist **5** 65-66

DOOLITTLE, JAMES HAROLD (1896-1993), American transcontinental pilot **5** 66-68

DORIA, ANDREA (1466-1560), Italian admiral and politician **18** 123-125

DORR, RHETA CHILDE (1868-1948), American journalist **5** 68-69

DORSEY, JIMMY (James Dorsey; 1904-1957), American musician and bandleader **19** 93-95

DORSEY, THOMAS ANDREW (1900-1993), African American gospel singer and composer **22** 149-151

DOS PASSOS, RODERIGO (1896-1970), American novelist **5** 69-71

DOS SANTOS, JOSÉ EDUARDO (born 1942), leader of the Popular Movement for the Liberation of Angola and president of Angola **5** 71-72

DOS SANTOS, MARCELINO (born 1929), Mozambican nationalist insurgent, statesman, and intellectual **5** 72-74

DOSTOEVSKY, FYODOR (1821-1881), Russian novelist **5** 74-77

DOUGLAS, DONALD WILLS (1892-1981), American aeronautical engineer **5** 77

DOUGLAS, GAVIN (circa 1475-1522), Scottish poet, prelate, and courtier **5** 77-78

DOUGLAS, SIR JAMES (1286?-1330), Scottish patriot **5** 80-82

DOUGLAS, MARY TEW (born 1921), British anthropologist and social thinker **5** 79-80

DOUGLAS, STEPHEN ARNOLD (1813-1861), American politician **5** 80-82

DOUGLAS, THOMAS CLEMENT (1904-1986), Canadian clergyman and politician, premier of Saskatchewan (1944-1961), and member of Parliament (1962-1979) **5** 82-83

DOUGLAS, WILLIAM ORVILLE (1898-1980), American jurist **5** 83-85

DOUGLAS-HOME, ALEC (Alexander Frederick Home; 1903-1995), Scottish politician **20** 117-119

DOUGLASS, FREDERICK (circa 1817-1895), African American leader and abolitionist **5** 85-86

DOUHET, GIULIO (1869-1930), Italian military leader **22** 151-152

DOVE, ARTHUR GARFIELD (1880-1946), American painter **5** 86-87

DOVE, RITA FRANCES (born 1952), United States poet laureate **5** 87-89

DOVZHENKO, ALEXANDER (Oleksandr Dovzhenko; 1894-1956), Ukrainian film director and screenwriter **25** 120-122

DOW, CHARLES (1851-1902), American journalist **19** 95-97

DOW, NEAL (1804-1897), American temperance reformer **5** 89-90

DOWLAND, JOHN (1562-1626), British composer and lutenist **5** 90

DOWNING, ANDREW JACKSON (1815-1852), American horticulturist and landscape architect **5** 90-91

DOYLE, SIR ARTHUR CONAN (1859-1930), British author **5** 91-92

DRAGO, LUIS MARÍA (1859-1921), Argentine international jurist and diplomat **5** 92-93

DRAKE, DANIEL (1785-1852), American physician **5** 93-94

DRAKE, EDWIN (1819-1880), American oil well driller and speculator **21** 108-110

DRAKE, SIR FRANCIS (circa 1541-1596), English navigator **5** 94-96

DRAPER, JOHN WILLIAM (1811-1882), Anglo-American scientist and historian **5** 96-97

DRAYTON, MICHAEL (1563-1631), English poet **5** 97-98

DREISER, (HERMAN) THEODORE (1871-1945), American novelist **5** 98-100

DREW, CHARLES RICHARD (1904-1950), African American surgeon **5** 100-101

DREW, DANIEL (1797-1879), American stock manipulator **5** 101-102

DREXEL, KATHERINE (1858-1955), founded a Catholic order, the Sisters of the Blessed Sacrament **5** 102-103

DREXLER, KIM ERIC (born 1955), American scientist and author **20** 119-121

DREYER, CARL THEODOR (1889-1968), Danish film director **22** 152-155

DREYFUS, ALFRED (1859-1935), French army officer **5** 103-105

DRIESCH, HANS ADOLF EDUARD (1867-1941), German biologist and philosopher **5** 105

DRUCKER, PETER (1909-2005), American author and business consultant **21** 110-112

Drums (musical instrument) Olatunji, Michael Babatunde **27** 277-279

DRUSUS, MARCUS LIVIUS (circa 124-91 B.C.), Roman statesman **5** 105-106

DRYDEN, JOHN (1631-1700), English poet, critic, and dramatist **5** 106-107

DRYSDALE, SIR GEORGE RUSSELL (1912-1981), Australian painter **5** 107-109

DUANE, WILLIAM (1760-1835), American journalist **5** 109

DUARTE, JOSÉ NAPOLEÓN (1926-1990), civilian reformer elected president of El Salvador in 1984 **5** 109-111

DUBČEK, ALEXANDER (1921-1992), Czechoslovak politician **5** 112-113

DUBE, JOHN LANGALIBALELE (1870-1949), South African writer and Zulu propagandist **5** 113

DU BELLAY, JOACHIM (circa 1522-1560), French poet **5** 113-114

DUBINSKY, DAVID (1892-1982), American trade union official **5** 114-115

DUBNOV, SIMON (1860-1941), Jewish historian, journalist, and political activist **5** 115-116

DU BOIS, WILLIAM EDWARD BURGHARDT (1868-1963), African American educator, pan-Africanist, and protest leader **5** 116-118

DU BOIS-REYMOND, EMIL (1818-1896), German physiologist **5** 118-119

DUBOS, RENÉ JULES (1901-1982), French-born American microbiologist **5** 119

DUBUFFET, JEAN PHILLIPE ARTHUR (born 1901), French painter **5** 119-120

DUCCIO DI BUONINSEGNA (1255/60-1318/19), Italian painter **5** 121-122

DUCHAMP, MARCEL (1887-1968), French painter **5** 122-123

DUCHAMP-VILLON, RAYMOND (1876-1918), French sculptor **5** 123

DUDLEY, BARBARA (born 1947), American director of Greenpeace **5** 123-124

EVARTS, WILLIAM MAXWELL (1818-1901), American lawyer and statesman **5** 340-341

EVATT, HERBERT VERE (1894-1965), Australian statesman and jurist **5** 341-343

EVELYN, JOHN (1620-1706), English author **5** 343-344

EVERETT, EDWARD (1794-1865), American statesman and orator **5** 344

EVERGOOD, PHILIP (1901-1973), American painter **5** 345

EVERS, MEDGAR (1925-1963), African American civil rights leader **5** 345-348

EVERS-WILLIAMS, MYRLIE (born Myrlie Louise Beasley; born 1933), civil rights leader, lecturer, and writer **5** 348-350

EWING, WILLIAM MAURICE (1906-1974), American oceanographer **5** 350-351

EWONWU, BENEDICT CHUKA (born 1921), Nigerian sculptor and painter **5** 351-352

EYCK, HUBERT VAN (died 1426), Flemish painter **5** 352-354

EYCK, JAN VAN (circa 1390-1441), Flemish painter **5** 352-354

EYRE, EDWARD JOHN (1815-1901), English explorer of Australia **5** 354

EZANA (flourished 4th century), Ethiopian king **5** 354-355

EZEKIEL (flourished 6th century B.C.), Hebrew priest and prophet **5** 355-356

EZRA (flourished 5th century B.C.), Hebrew priest, scribe, and reformer **5** 356-357

F

FABERGÉ, CARL (Peter Carl Fabergé; Karl Gustavovich Fabergé; 1846-1920), Russian jeweler and goldsmith **21** 125-127

FABIUS, LAURENT (born 1946), prime minister of France in the 1980s **5** 358-359

FACKENHEIM, EMIL LUDWIG (born 1916), liberal post-World War II Jewish theologian **5** 359-361

FADIL AL-JAMALI, MUHAMMAD (born 1903), Iraqi educator, writer, diplomat, and politician **5** 361-362

FADLALLAH, SAYYID MUHAMMAD HUSAYN (born 1935), Shi'i Muslim cleric and Lebanese political leader **5** 362-364

FAHD IBN ABDUL AZIZ AL-SAUD (1920-2005), son of the founder of modern Saudi Arabia and king **5** 364-366

FAHRENHEIT, GABRIEL DANIEL (1686-1736), German physicist **5** 366

FAIDHERBE, LOUIS LÉON CÉSAR (1818-1889), French colonial governor **5** 366-367

Fair, A. A.
see Gardner, Erle Stanley

FAIR, JAMES RUTHERFORD, JR. (born 1920), American chemical engineer and educator **20** 131-131

FAIRBANKS, DOUGLAS (Douglas Elton Ulman; 1883-1939), American actor and producer **19** 107-108

FAIRCLOUGH, ELLEN LOUKS (1905-2004), Canadian Cabinet minister **5** 367-368

FAIRUZ (née Nuhad Haddad; born 1933), Arabic singer **5** 368-369

FAISAL I (1883-1933), king of Iraq 1921-33 **5** 370-371

FAISAL II (1935-1958), king of Iraq, 1953-1958 **20** 132-132

FAISAL IBN ABD AL AZIZ IBN SAUD (1904-1975), Saudi Arabian king and prominent Arab leader **5** 371-372

FALCONET, ÉTIENNE MAURICE (1716-1791), French sculptor **5** 372

FALLA, MANUEL DE (1876-1946), Spanish composer **5** 372-373

FALLACI, ORIANA (1929-2006), Italian journalist **27** 115-117

FALLETTA, JOANN (born 1954), American conductor **5** 373-375

FALWELL, JERRY (born 1933), fundamentalist religious leader who also promoted right-wing political causes **5** 375-376

FAN CHUNG-YEN (989-1052), Chinese statesman **5** 376-377

FANEUIL, PETER (1700-1743), American colonial merchant and philanthropist **5** 377

FANFANI, AMINTORE (1908-1999), Italian prime minister **5** 378-379

FANON, FRANTZ (1925-1961), Algerian political theorist and psychiatrist **5** 379-380

FARABI, AL- (Abou Nasr Mohammed ibn Tarkaw; 870-950), Turkish scholar and philosopher **22** 14-16

FARADAY, MICHAEL (1791-1867), English physicist and chemist **5** 380

FARGO, WILLIAM GEORGE (1818-1881), American businessman **5** 380-381

FARINA, MIMI (Margarita Mimi Baez Farina; 1945-2001), American singer and activist **27** 117-119

FARLEY, JAMES A. (1888-1976), Democratic Party organizer and political strategist **5** 381-383

FARMER, FANNIE MERRITT (1857-1915), American authority on cookery **5** 383

FARMER, JAMES (1920-1999), American civil rights activist who helped organize the 1960s "freedom rides" **5** 383-385

FARMER, MOSES GERRISH (1820-1893), American inventor and manufacturer **5** 385

FARNESE, ALESSANDRO (Duke of Parma; 1545-1592), Italian general and diplomat **20** 132-135

FARNSWORTH, PHILO T. (1906-1971), American inventor of the television **5** 386-387

FAROUK I (1920-1965), king of Egypt 1937-1952 **5** 387 388

FARRAGUT, DAVID GLASGOW (1801-1870), American naval officer **5** 388-389

FARRAKHAN, LOUIS (Louis Eugene Walcott, born 1933), a leader of one branch of the Nation of Islam popularly known as Black Muslims and militant spokesman for Black Nationalism **5** 389-390

FARRAR, GERALDINE (1882-1967), American opera singer **23** 106-108

FARRELL, EILEEN (1920-2002), American singer **27** 119-121

FARRELL, JAMES THOMAS (1904-1979), American novelist and social and literary critic **5** 390-391

FARRELL, SUZANNE (née Roberta Sue Ficker; born 1945), American classical ballerina **5** 391-393

FARRENC, LOUISE (Jeanne Louise Dumont; 1804-1875), French pianist **27** 121-122

FASSBINDER, RAINER WERNER (1946-1982), German filmmaker **26** 101-103

"Father of. . ."
see Nicknames

Fathers of the Church
see Religious leaders, Christian—Fathers

FAUCHARD, PIERRE (1678-1761), French dentist **26** 103-105

FIGUEIREDO, JOÃO BATISTA DE OLIVEIRA (born 1918), Brazilian army general and president (1979-1985) **5** 445-446

FILLMORE, MILLARD (1800-1874), American statesman, president 1850-1853 **5** 447-448

FILMER, SIR ROBERT (died 1653), English political theorist **5** 448

FINCH, ANNE (Anne Kingsmill Finch; 1661-1720), English poet **27** 127-129

FINK, ALBERT (1827-1897), American railroad engineer and economist **21** 133-135

FINKELSTEIN, RABBI LOUIS (born 1895), American scholar and leader of Conservative Judaism **5** 448-450

FINLAY, CARLOS JUAN (1833-1915), Cuban biologist and physician **5** 450

FINNEY, CHARLES GRANDISON (1792-1875), American theologian and educator **5** 450-451

FIORINA, CARLY (Cara Carleton Sneed; born 1954), American businesswoman **25** 131-133

FIRDAUSI (934-1020), Persian poet **5** 451-452

Fire (film)
Mehta, Deepa **27** 258-261

FIRESTONE, HARVEY SAMUEL (1868-1938), American industrialist **5** 452-453

FIRESTONE, SHULAMITH (born 1945), Canadian feminist **27** 129-131

FIRST, RUTH (1925-1982), South African socialist, anti-apartheid activist, and scholar **5** 453-454

First Ladies
Wang Guangmei **27** 357-358

FISCHER, BOBBY (born 1943), American chess player **5** 454-456

FISCHER, EMIL (1852-1919), German organic chemist **5** 456-457

FISCHER, HANS (1881-1945), German organic chemist **5** 457-459

FISCHER VON ERLACH, JOHANN BERNHARD (1656-1723), Austrian architect **5** 459-461

FISH, HAMILTON (1808-1893), American statesman **5** 461-462

FISHER, ANDREW (1862-1928), Australian statesman and labor leader **5** 462

FISHER, IRVING (1867-1947), American economist **5** 462-463

FISHER, JOHN ARBUTHNOT (Baron Fisher of Kilverstone; 1841-1920), British admiral **22** 171-173

FISHER, SIR RONALD AYLMER (1890-1962), English statistician **5** 463-464

FISK, JAMES (1834-1872), American financial speculator **5** 464-465

FISKE, JOHN (1842-1901), American philosopher and historian **5** 465-466

FISKE, MINNIE MADDERN (Mary Augusta Davey; 1865-1932), American "realistic" actress who portrayed Ibsen heroines **5** 466-467

FITCH, JOHN (1743-1798), American mechanic and inventor **5** 467-468

FITCH, VAL LOGSDON (born 1923), American physicist **24** 135-138

FITZGERALD, ELLA (1918-1996), American jazz singer **5** 468-469

FITZGERALD, FRANCES (born 1940), American author **5** 469-470

FITZGERALD, FRANCIS SCOTT KEY (1896-1940), American author **5** 470-472

FITZGERALD, GARRET (born 1926), Irish prime minister (1981-1987) **5** 472-474

FITZHUGH, GEORGE (1806-1881), American polemicist and sociologist **5** 474

FITZPATRICK, THOMAS (1799-1854), American trapper, guide, and Indian agent **5** 474-475

FIZEAU, HIPPOLYTE ARMAND LOUIS (1819-1896), French physicist **5** 475

FLAGLER, HENRY (1830-1913), American industrialist **21** 135-137

FLAGSTAD, KIRSTEN MALFRID (1895-1962), Norwegian opera singer **25** 133-135

FLAHERTY, ROBERT (1884-1951), American documentary filmmaker **5** 476-477

FLAMININUS, TITUS QUINCTIUS (circa 228-174 B.C.), Roman general and diplomat **5** 477

FLAMSTEED, JOHN (1646-1719), English astronomer **5** 477-478

FLANAGAN, HALLIE (1890-1969), American director, playwright, and educator **5** 478-479

FLANNAGAN, JOHN BERNARD (1895-1942), American sculptor **5** 480

FLAUBERT, GUSTAVE (1821-1880), French novelist **5** 480-482

FLEISCHER, MAX (1883-1972), American animator, cartoonist, and inventor **22** 173-175
Questel, Mae **27** 299-301

FLEISCHMANN, GISI (1894-1944), Czechoslovakian leader who rescued many Jews from the Nazi Holocaust **5** 482-483

FLEMING, PEGGY GALE (born 1948), American figure skater and sportscaster **24** 138-140

FLEMING, SIR ALEXANDER (1881-1955), Scottish bacteriologist **5** 485-486

FLEMING, SIR JOHN AMBROSE (1849-1945), British engineer and scientist **25** 135-138

FLEMING, SIR SANDFORD (1827-1915), Scottish-born Canadian railway engineer **5** 485-486

FLEMING, WILLIAMINA (1857-1911), American astronomer **22** 175-176

FLETCHER, ALICE CUNNINGHAM (1838-1923), American anthropologist **5** 486-487

FLETCHER, JOHN (1579-1625), English playwright **5** 487

FLETCHER, JOSEPH FRANCIS (1905-1991), American philosopher who was the father of modern biomedical ethics **5** 488-489

FLEXNER, ABRAHAM (1866-1959), American educational reformer **5** 489-490

FLINDERS, MATTHEW (1774-1814), English naval captain and hydrographer **5** 490

FLOREN, MYRON (Myron Howard Floren; 1919-2005), American musician **27** 131-133

FLORES, CARLOS ROBERTO (Carlos Roberto Flores Facussé;born 1950), Honduran politician **18** 138-140

FLORES, JUAN JOSÉ (1801-1864), South American general, president of Ecuador **5** 491

FLORES, PATRICK FERNANDEZ (born 1929), American archbishop **26** 109-112

FLOREY, HOWARD WALTER (Baron Florey of Adelaide; 1898-1968), Australian pathologist **5** 491-492

FLORY, PAUL (1910-1985), American chemist and educator **5** 492-494

FLOYD, CARLISLE (born 1926), American composer of operas **5** 494-496

FOSTER, WILLIAM ZEBULON (1881-1961), American Communist party leader **6** 27-28

FOUCAULT, JEAN BERNARD LÉON (1819-1868), French physicist **6** 28-29

FOUCAULT, MICHEL (1926-1984), French philosopher, critic, and historian **6** 29-30

FOUCHÉ, JOSEPH (1759-1820), French statesman **6** 30-31

FOUQUET, JEAN (ca. 1420- ca. 1480), French painter **6** 31

FOURIER, FRANÇOIS CHARLES MARIE (1772-1837), French socialist writer **6** 31-32

FOURIER, BARON JEAN BAPTISTE JOSEPH (1768-1830), French mathematical physicist **6** 32-33

FOWLES, JOHN (1926-2005), English novelist **6** 33-35

FOX, CHARLES JAMES (1749-1806), English parliamentarian **6** 35-37

FOX, GEORGE (1624-1691), English spiritual reformer **6** 37-38

FOX, VICENTE (born 1942), Mexican president **21** 142-143

FOX, WILLIAM (1879-1952), American film producer **21** 143-144

FOYT, A.J. (born 1935), American race care driver **24** 145-147

FRACASTORO, GIROLAMO (Hieronymus Fracastorius; c. 1478-1553), Italian physician, poet, astronomer, and logician **21** 144-147

FRAENKEL, ABRAHAM ADOLF (Abraham halevi Fraenkel; 1891-1965), Israeli mathematician **23** 109-111

FRAGONARD, JEAN HONORÉ (1732-1806), French painter **6** 38-39

FRANCE, ANATOLE (1844-1924), French novelist **6** 39-40

FRANCIS I (1494-1547), king of France 1515-1547 **6** 40-43

FRANCIS II (1768-1835), Holy Roman emperor 1792-1806 and emperor of Austria 1804-1835 **6** 43-44

FRANCIS FERDINAND (1863-1914), archduke of Austria **6** 44

FRANCIS JOSEPH (1830-1916), emperor of Austria 1868-1916 and king of Hungary 1867-1916 **6** 45-46

FRANCIS OF ASSISI, SAINT (1182-1226), Italian mystic and religious founder **6** 46-47

FRANCIS OF SALES, SAINT (1567-1622), French bishop **6** 47

FRANCIS XAVIER, SAINT (1506-1552), Spanish Jesuit missionary **6** 48

FRANCK, CÉSAR (1822-1890), French composer **6** 48-49

FRANCK, JAMES (1882-1964), German physicist **6** 49-52

FRANCO BAHAMONDE, FRANCISCO (1892-1975), Spanish general and dictator **6** 52-54

FRANCO OF COLOGNE (Franco of Paris; flourished circa 1250-1260), French music theorist **6** 52

FRANK, ANNE (1929-1945), 16-year-old holocaust victim who kept a famous diary **6** 54-56

FRANKENHEIMER, JOHN (1930-2002), American filmmaker **22** 182-185

FRANKENTHALER, HELEN (born 1928), American painter **6** 56-57

FRANKFURTER, FELIX (1882-1965), American jurist **6** 57

FRANKLIN, ARETHA (born 1942), African American singer and songwriter **6** 58-60

FRANKLIN, BENJAMIN (1706-1790), American statesman, diplomat, and inventor **6** 60-64

FRANKLIN, SIR JOHN (1786-1847), English explorer **6** 68-69

FRANKLIN, JOHN HOPE (born 1915), pioneer African American historian **6** 65-67

FRANKLIN, MILES (1879-1954), Australian novelist **6** 68-69

FRANKLIN, ROSALIND ELSIE (1920-1958), British physical chemist and molecular biologist **6** 67-68

FRANKLIN, WILLIAM (circa 1731-1813), American colonial administrator **6** 69-70

FRANKS, TOMMY RAY (born 1945), American military leader **25** 142-144

FRASER (PINTER), LADY ANTONIA (born 1932), popular British biographer, historian, and mystery novelist **6** 70-71

FRASER, MALCOLM (born 1930), prime minister of Australia (1975-1983) **6** 71-73

FRASER, PETER (1884-1950), New Zealand prime minister 1940-49 **6** 73-74

FRASER, SIMON (1776-1862), Canadian explorer and fur trader **6** 74-75

FRASER-REID, BERT (born 1934), Jamaican chemist **20** 145-146

FRAUNHOFER, JOSEPH VON (1787-1826), German physicist **6** 75-76

FRAZER, SIR JAMES GEORGE (1854-1941), Scottish classicist and anthropologist **6** 76

FRAZIER, EDWARD FRANKLIN (1894-1962), African American sociologist **6** 77

FRÉCHETTE, LOUIS-HONORÉ (1839-1908), French-Canadian poet **6** 77-78

FREDEGUND (Fredegunda, Fredegond; c. 550-597), Frankish queen **20** 146-149

FREDERICK I (1123-1190), Holy Roman emperor 1152-1190 **6** 78-79

FREDERICK II (1194-1250), Holy Roman emperor 1215-1250 **6** 79

FREDERICK II (1712-1786), king of Prussia 1740-1786 **6** 81-84

FREDERICK III (1415-1493), Holy Roman emperor and German king 1440-1493 **6** 84-85

FREDERICK WILLIAM (1620-1688), elector of Brandenburg 1640-1688 **6** 85-86

FREDERICK WILLIAM I (1688-1740), king of Prussia 1713-1740 **6** 86-87

FREDERICK WILLIAM III (1770-1840), king of Prussia 1797-1840 **6** 87

FREDERICK WILLIAM IV (1795-1861), king of Prussia 1840-1861 **6** 87-88

FREDHOLM, ERIK IVAR (1866-1927), Swedish mathematician **24** 147-149

FREED, JAMES INGO (1930-2005), American architect **6** 88-90

FREEH, LOUIS J. (born 1950), director of the Federal Bureau of Investigation (FBI) **6** 90-91

FREEMAN, DOUGLAS SOUTHALL (1886-1953), American journalist **6** 91-92

FREEMAN, ROLAND L. (born 1936), American photographer of rural and urban African Americans **6** 92-93

FREGE, GOTTLOB (1848-1925), German mathematician and philosopher **6** 93-94

FREI MONTALVA, EDUARDO (born 1911), Chilean statesman **6** 94-95

FREIRE, PAULO (born 1921), Brazilian philosopher and educator **6** 95-96

FRELINGHUYSEN, THEODORUS JACOBUS (1691-circa 1748), Dutch Reformed clergyman and revivalist **6** 96-97

GILSON, ÉTIENNE HENRY (1884-1978), French Catholic philosopher **6** 327-328

GINASTERA, ALBERTO EVARISTO (1916-1983), Argentine composer **6** 328-329

GINGRICH, NEWT (born 1943), Republican congressman from Georgia **6** 329-332

GINSBERG, ALLEN (1926-1997), American poet **6** 332-333
Ferlinghetti, Lawrence **27** 125-127

GINSBURG, RUTH BADER (born 1933), second woman appointed to the United States Supreme Court **6** 333-336

GINZBERG, ASHER (Ahad Ha-Am; means "one of the people;" 1856-1927), Jewish intellectual leader **6** 336-337

GINZBERG, LOUIS (1873-1953), Lithuanian-American Talmudic scholar **6** 337-338

GINZBURG, NATALIA LEVI (1916-1991), Italian novelist, essayist, playwright, and translator **6** 338-339

GIOLITTI, GIOVANNI (1842-1928), Italian statesman **6** 339-340

GIORGIONE (1477-1510), Italian painter **6** 340-341

GIOTTO (circa 1267-1337), Italian painter, architect, and sculptor **6** 342-345

GIOVANNI, YOLANDE CORNELIA, JR. (born 1943), African American poet **6** 346-347

GIOVANNI DA BOLOGNA (1529-1608), Italian sculptor **6** 345-346

GIPP, GEORGE (1895-1920), American football player **19** 124-126

GIRARD, STEPHEN (1750-1831), American merchant and philanthropist **6** 347-348

GIRARDON, FRANÇOIS (1628-1715), French sculptor **6** 348-349

GIRAUDOUX, JEAN (1882-1944), French novelist, playwright, and diplomat **6** 349-350

Girl from Ipanema, The (song)
Getz, Stan **27** 143-145
Jobim, Antonio Carlos **27** 187-189

GIRTY, SIMON (1741-1818), American frontiersman **6** 350

GISCARD D'ESTAING, VALÉRY (born 1926), third president of the French Fifth Republic **6** 350-352

GISH, LILLIAN (1896-1993), American actress **20** 155-158

GIST, CHRISTOPHER (circa 1706-1759), American frontiersman **6** 352-353

GIULIANI, RUDOLPH WILLIAM (born 1944), mayor of New York City **6** 353-355

GIULIANI, MAURO (Mauro Giuseppe Sergio Pantaleo Giuliani; 1781-1829), Italian guitarist and composer **25** 156-157

GJELLERUP, KARL ADOLPH (1857-1919), Danish author **25** 157-159

GLACKENS, WILLIAM (1870-1938), American painter **6** 355-356

GLADDEN, WASHINGTON (1836-1918), American clergyman **6** 356-357

GLADSTONE, WILLIAM EWART (1809-1898), English statesman **6** 357-360

GLASGOW, ELLEN (1873-1945), American novelist **6** 360-361

GLASHOW, SHELDON LEE (born 1932), American Nobel Prize winner in physics **6** 361-362

GLASS, PHILIP (born 1937), American composer of minimalist music **6** 362-364

GLASSE, HANNAH (Hannah Allgood; 1708-1770), English cookbook author **21** 166-167

GLEDITSCH, ELLEN (1879-1968), Norwegian chemist **23** 124-126

GLENDOWER, OWEN (1359?-1415?), Welsh national leader **6** 364-365

GLENN, JOHN HERSCHEL, JR. (born 1921), military test pilot, astronaut, businessman, and United States senator from Ohio **6** 365-367

GLIDDEN, JOSEPH (1813-1906), American businessman and inventor **21** 167-170

GLIGOROV, KIRO (born 1917), first president of the Republic of Macedonia **6** 367-369

GLINKA, MIKHAIL IVANOVICH (1804-1857), Russian composer **6** 369-370

GLOUCESTER, DUKE OF (1391-1447), English statesman **6** 370-371

GLUBB, SIR JOHN BAGOT (1897-1986), British commander of the Arab Legion 1939-56 **6** 371-372

GLUCK, CHRISTOPH WILLIBALD (1714-1787), Austrian composer and opera reformer **6** 372-374

GLUCKMAN, MAX (1911-1975), British anthropologist **6** 374-375

GLYN, ELINOR (born Elinor Sutherland; 1864-1943), British author and filmmaker **23** 126-128

GM
see General Motors Corporation

GOBINEAU, COMTE DE (Joseph Arthur Gobineau; 1816-1882), French diplomat **6** 375-376

GODARD, JEAN-LUC (born 1930), French actor, film director, and screenwriter **19** 126-128

GODDARD, ROBERT HUTCHINGS (1882-1945), American pioneer in rocketry **6** 376-377

GÖDEL, KURT (1906-1978), Austrian-American mathematician **6** 377-379

GODKIN, EDWIN LAWRENCE (1831-1902), British-born American journalist **6** 380

GODOLPHIN, SIDNEY (1st Earl of Godolphin; 1645-1712), English statesman **6** 380-381

GODOY Y ÁLVAREZ DE FARIA, MANUEL DE (1767-1851), Spanish statesman **6** 381-382

GODUNOV, BORIS FEODOROVICH (circa 1551-1605), czar of Russia 1598-1605 **6** 382-383

GODWIN, WILLIAM (1756-1836), English political theorist and writer **6** 383-384

GOEBBELS, JOSEPH PAUL (1897-1945), German politician and Nazi propagandist **6** 384-385

GOEPPERT-MAYER, MARIA (1906-1972), American physicist **6** 385-387

GOETHALS, GEORGE WASHINGTON (1858-1928), American Army officer and engineer **6** 387-388

GOETHE, JOHANN WOLFGANG VON (1749-1832), German poet **6** 388-391

GOGOL, NIKOLAI (1809-1852), Russian author **6** 391-393

GOH CHOK TONG (born 1941), leader of the People's Action Party and Singapore's prime minister **6** 393-395

Going Places (film)
Depardieu, Gerard **27** 102-105

GOIZUETA, ROBERTO (1931-1997), Cuban American businessman and philanthropist **18** 160-162

GÖKALP, MEHMET ZIYA (1875/76-1924), Turkish publicist and sociologist **6** 395-396

GÖKÇEN, SABIHA (Sabiha Geuckchen; 1913-2001), Turkish aviator **27** 147-149

GOSHIRAKAWA (1127-1192), Japanese emperor **6** 460-461

GOSHO, HEINOSUKE (1902-1981), Japanese filmmaker **22** 199-200

GOTTFRIED VON STRASSBURG (circa 1165-circa 1215), German poet and romancer **6** 461-462

GOTTLIEB, ADOLPH (1903-1974), American Abstract Expressionist painter **6** 462-463

GOTTSCHALK, LOUIS MOREAU (1829-1869), American composer **6** 463-464

GOTTWALD, KLEMENT (1896-1953), first Communist president of Czechoslovakia (1948-1953) **6** 464-466

GOUDIMEL, CLAUDE (circa 1514-1572), French composer **6** 466

GOUJON, JEAN (circa 1510-1568), French sculptor **6** 466-467

GOULART, JOÃO (1918-1976), Brazilian statesman **6** 467-469

GOULD, GLENN (1932-1982), Canadian musician **6** 469-470

GOULD, JAY (1836-1892), American financier and railroad builder **6** 470-472

GOULD, STEPHEN JAY (1941-2002), American paleontologist **6** 472-473

GOUNOD, CHARLES FRANÇOIS (1818-1893), French composer **6** 473-474

GOURLAY, ROBERT (1778-1863), British reformer in Canada **6** 474

GOURMONT, REMY DE (1858-1915), French author, critic, and essayist **6** 475

GOWER, JOHN (circa 1330-1408), English poet **6** 475-476

GOYA Y LUCIENTES, FRANCISCO DE PAULA JOSÉ DE (1746-1828), Spanish painter and printmaker **6** 476-478

GOYEN, JAN VAN (1596-1656), Dutch painter **6** 478-479

GRACCHUS, GAIUS SEMPRONIUS (ca. 154-121 B.C.) member of a Roman plebeian family referred to as the Gracchi; flourished 3rd-2nd century B.C. **6** 479-480

GRACCHUS, TIBERIUS SEMPRONIUS (ca. 163-133 B.C.) member of a Roman plebeian family referred to as the Gracchi; flourished 3rd-2nd century B.C. **6** 479-480

GRACE, WILLIAM RUSSELL (1832-1904), Irish-born American entrepreneur and politician **6** 480-481

GRACIÁN Y MORALES, BALTASAR JERÓNIMO (1601-1658), Spanish writer **6** 481-482

GRADY, HENRY WOODFIN (1850-1889), American editor and orator **6** 482-483

GRAETZ, HEINRICH HIRSCH (1817-1891), German historian and biblical exegete **6** 483

GRAHAM, KATHARINE MEYER (1917-2001), publisher who managed *The Washington Post* **6** 483-485

GRAHAM, MARTHA (1894-1991), American dancer and choreographer **6** 485-486

GRAHAM, OTTO (born 1921), American football player and coach **21** 174-176

GRAHAM, SYLVESTER (1794-1851), American reformer and temperance minister **6** 486-487

GRAHAM, WILLIAM FRANKLIN, JR. ("Billy"; born 1918), American evangelist **6** 487-488

GRAINGER, PERCY (Percy Aldridge Grainger; George Percy Grainger; 1882-1961), Australian American musician **25** 160-161

GRAMSCI, ANTONIO (1891-1937), Italian writer and Communist leader **6** 488-489

GRANADOS, ENRIQUE (1867-1916), Spanish composer and pianist **6** 489-490

GRANGE, RED (Harold Edward Grange; 1903-1991), American football player **19** 128-130

GRANT, CARY (born Archibald Alexander Leach; 1904-1986), English actor **6** 490-492

GRANT, ULYSSES SIMPSON (1822-1885), American general, president 1869-1877 **6** 492-494

GRANVILLE, CHRISTINE (Krystyna Skarbek; c. 1915-1952), Polish secret agent **27** 153-154

GRANVILLE, EVELYN BOYD (born 1924), African American mathematician **6** 494-496

GRASS, GÜNTER (born 1927), German novelist, playwright, and poet **6** 496-497

GRASSELLI, CAESAR AUGUSTIN (1850-1927), third generation to head the Grasselli Chemical Company **6** 497-498

GRATIAN (died circa 1155), Italian scholar, father of canon law **6** 498-499

GRATTAN, HENRY (1746-1820), Irish statesman and orator **6** 499

GRAU SAN MARTIN, RAMÓN (1887-1969), Cuban statesman and physician **6** 499-500

GRAUNT, JOHN (1620-1674), English merchant and civil servant **21** 176-178

GRAVES, EARL GILBERT, JR. (born 1935), African American publisher **23** 130-132

GRAVES, MICHAEL (born 1934), American Post-Modernist architect **6** 500-502

GRAVES, NANCY STEVENSON (1940-1995), American sculptor **6** 502-504

GRAVES, ROBERT RANKE (1895-1985), English author **6** 504-506

GRAY, ASA (1810-1888), American botanist **6** 506-507

GRAY, HANNAH HOLBORN (born 1930), university administrator **6** 507-508

GRAY, ROBERT (1755-1806), American explorer **6** 508-509

GRAY, THOMAS (1716-1771), English poet **6** 509-510

GRAY, WILLIAM H., III (born 1941), first African American to be elected House Whip for the U.S. House of Representatives **6** 510-511

Great Proletarian Cultural Revolution
see Cultural Revolution (China)

Greater New York
see New York City (New York State)

GRECO, EL (1541-1614), Greek-born Spanish painter **6** 511-514

GREELEY, ANDREW M. (born 1928), American Catholic priest, sociologist, and author **6** 514-515

GREELEY, HORACE (1811-1872), American editor and reformer **6** 515-517

GREELY, ADOLPHUS WASHINGTON (1844-1935), American soldier, explorer, and writer **6** 517-518

GREEN, CONSTANCE MCLAUGHLIN (1897-1975), American author and historian **6** 518-519

GREEN, EDITH STARRETT (1910-1987), United States congresswoman from Oregon (1954-1974) **6** 519-520

GREEN, THOMAS HILL (1836-1882), British philosopher **6** 520-521

GREEN, WILLIAM R. (1872-1952), American labor union leader **6** 521

HESS, MYRA (1890-1965), British pianist **27** 169-171

HESS, VICTOR FRANCIS (1883-1964), Austrian-American physicist **7** 362-363

HESS, WALTER RICHARD RUDOLF (1894-1987), deputy reichsführer for Adolf Hitler (1933-1941) **7** 363-365

HESS, WALTER RUDOLF (1881-1973), Swiss neurophysiologist **7** 365

HESSE, EVA (1936-1970), American sculptor **7** 365-367

HESSE, HERMANN (1877-1962), German novelist **7** 367-369

HESSE, MARY B. (born 1924), British philosopher **7** 369-371

HEVESY, GEORGE CHARLES DE (1885-1966), Hungarian chemist **7** 371

HEWITT, ABRAM STEVENS (1822-1903), American politician and manufacturer **7** 371-372

HEYDRICH, REINHARD (1904-1942), German architect of the Holocaust **20** 176-178

HEYERDAHL, THOR (born 1914), Norwegian explorer, anthropologist and author **18** 194-196

HEYSE, PAUL JOHANN LUDWIG (1830-1914), German author **7** 372-373

HEYWOOD, THOMAS (1573/1574-1641), English playwright **7** 373-374

HIAWATHA (c. 1450), Native American Leader **23** 143-145

HICKOK, JAMES BUTLER ("Wild Bill"; 1837-1876), American gunfighter, scout, and spy **7** 374-375

HICKS, EDWARD (1780-1849), American folk painter **7** 375

HIDALGO Y COSTILLA, MIGUEL (1753-1811), Mexican revolutionary priest **7** 375-377

HIDAYAT, SADIQ (1903-1951), Persian author **7** 377-378

HIGGINS, MARGUERITE (1920-1966), American journalist **7** 378-380

HIGGINSON, THOMAS WENTWORTH (1823-1911), American reformer and editor **7** 380

HIGHTOWER, ROSELLA (born 1920), Native American dancer **26** 154-156

HILDEBRANDT, JOHANN LUCAS VON (1663-1745), Austrian architect **7** 380-381

HILDRETH, RICHARD (1807-1865), American historian and political theorist **7** 382

HILFIGER, TOMMY (born 1952), American fashion designer **19** 144-146

HILL, ANITA (born 1956), African American lawyer and professor **7** 382-385

HILL, ARCHIBALD VIVIAN (1886-1977), English physiologist **7** 385-386

HILL, BENJAMIN HARVEY (1823-1882), American politician **7** 386-387

HILL, HERBERT (1924-2004), American scholar and civil rights activist **7** 387-388

HILL, JAMES JEROME (1838-1916), American railroad builder **7** 388-389

HILL, ROWLAND (1795-1879), British educator, postal reformer, and administrator **21** 202-204

HILLARY, EDMUND (born 1919), New Zealander explorer and mountaineer **7** 389-390

HILLEL I (circa 60 B.C. -circa 10 A.D.), Jewish scholar and teacher **7** 390-391

HILLEMAN, MAURICE RALPH (1919-2005), American microbiologist **26** 156-158

HILLIARD, NICHOLAS (circa 1547-1619), English painter **7** 391-392

HILLMAN, SIDNEY (1887-1946), Lithuanian-born American labor leader **7** 392-393

HILLQUIT, MORRIS (1869-1933), Russian-born American lawyer and author **7** 393-394

HILLS, CARLA ANDERSON (born 1934), Republican who served three presidents as lawyer, cabinet member, and U.S. trade representative **7** 394-396

HILTON, BARRON (William Barron Hilton; born 1927), American businessman **19** 146-148

HILTON, CONRAD (1887-1979), American hotelier **20** 178-180

HIMES, CHESTER BOMAR (1909-1984), American author **22** 242-244

HIMMELFARB, GERTRUDE (born 1922), American professor, writer, and scholar **7** 396-398

HIMMLER, HEINRICH (1900-1945), German Nazi leader **7** 398-399

HINDEMITH, PAUL (1895-1963), German composer **7** 399-400

HINDENBURG, PAUL LUDWIG HANS VON BENECKENDORFF UND VON (1847-1934), German field marshal, president 1925-1934 **7** 400-401

HINES, GREGORY OLIVER (born 1946), American dancer and actor **7** 401-403

HINOJOSA, ROLANDO (born 1929), Hispanic-American author **7** 403-405

HINSHELWOOD, SIR CYRIL NORMAN (1897-1967), English chemist **7** 405-406

HINTON, SUSAN ELOISE (born 1950), American novelist and screenwriter **7** 406-407

HIPPARCHUS (flourished 162-126 B.C.), Greek astronomer **7** 407-408

HIPPOCRATES (circa 460-circa 377 B.C.), Greek physician **7** 408-410

HIROHITO (1901-1989), emperor of Japan **7** 410-412

HIROSHIGE, ANDO (1797-1858), Japanese painter and printmaker **7** 412-413

HIRSCHFELD, AL (Albert Hirschfeld; 1903-2003), American caricaturist **25** 197-199

HISS, ALGER (1904-1996), U.S. State Department official convicted of having provided classified documents to an admitted Communist **7** 413-415

Historical linguistics
see Linguistics

Historical preservation
Summerson, John **27** 333-335

History of Miss Betsy Thoughtless, The (book)
Haywood, Eliza **27** 163-165

HITCHCOCK, ALFRED (1899-1980), English-born film director **7** 415-416

HITCHCOCK, GILBERT MONELL (1859-1934), American publisher and politician **7** 416-417

HITLER, ADOLF (1889-1945), German dictator, chancellor-president 1933-1945 **7** 417-420

HO, DAVID DA-I (born 1952), American AIDS researcher **23** 145-148

HO CHI MINH (1890-1969), Vietnamese revolutionary and statesman **7** 426-428

HOBART, JOHN HENRY (1775-1830), American Episcopal bishop **7** 420-421

HOBBES, THOMAS (1588-1679), English philosopher and political theorist **7** 421-423

HOBBY, OVETA CULP (1905-1995), American government official and businesswoman **7** 423-425

HOBHOUSE, LEONARD TRELAWNY (1864-1929), English sociologist and philosopher **7** 425-426

HUERTA, DOLORES (born 1930), Hispanic American labor activist **18** 204-207

HUERTA, VICTORIANO (1854-1916), Mexican general and politician **8** 13-14

HUGGINS, SIR WILLIAM (1824-1910), English astronomer **8** 14-15

HUGHES, CHARLES EVANS (1862-1948), American jurist and statesman **8** 15-16

HUGHES, HOWARD ROBARD (1905-1976), flamboyant American entrepreneur **8** 16-17

HUGHES, JOHN JOSEPH (1797-1864), Irish-American Catholic archbishop **8** 17-18

HUGHES, LANGSTON (1902-1967), African American author **8** 18-19

HUGHES, RICHARD (1900-1976), English author **19** 158-160

HUGHES, TED (1930-1998), English poet laureate **8** 19-21

HUGHES, WILLIAM MORRIS (1864-1952), Australian prime minister 1915-1923 **8** 21-22

HUGO, VICOMTE VICTOR MARIE (1802-1885), French author **8** 22-25

HUI-TSUNG (1082-1135), Chinese emperor and artist **8** 25

HUI-YÜAN (334-416), Chinese Buddhist monk **8** 25-26

HUIZINGA, JOHAN (1872-1945), Dutch historian **8** 26-27

HULAGU KHAN (Hüle'ü; circa 1216-1265), Mongol ruler in Persia **8** 27-28

HULL, BOBBY (Robert Marvin Hull; born 1939), Canadian hockey player **20** 181-183

HULL, CLARK LEONARD (1884-1952), American psychologist **8** 28

HULL, CORDELL (1871-1955), American statesman **8** 28-29

HULL, WILLIAM (1753-1825), American military commander **8** 29-30

Human figure
preservation of bodies
Hagens, Gunther von **27** 157-159

Humanitarians
Rappoport, Shloyme Zanul **27** 304-306

HUMAYUN (1508-1556), Mogul emperor 1530-1556 **20** 183-185

HUMBOLDT, BARON FRIEDRICH HEINRICH ALEXANDER VON (1769-1859), German naturalist and explorer **8** 30-31

HUMBOLDT, BARON WILHELM VON (1767-1835), German statesman and philologist **8** 31

HUME, BASIL CARDINAL (George Haliburton Hume; 1923-1999), English clergyman and theologian **22** 249-250

HUME, DAVID (1711-1776), Scottish philosopher **8** 31-34

HUMMEL, JOHANN NEPOMUK (1778-1837), Austrian pianist and composer **25** 204-206

HUMPHREY, DORIS (Doris Batcheller Humphrey; 1895-1959), American dancer and choreographer **23** 157-159

HUMPHREY, HUBERT HORATIO, JR. (1911-1978), mayor of Minneapolis, U.S. senator from Minnesota, and vice-president of the U.S. **8** 34-36

HUN SEN (born 1951), Cambodian prime minister **8** 39-42

HUNDERTWASSER, FRIEDENSREICH (Friedrich Stowasser; 1928-2000), Austrian-born visionary painter and spiritualist **8** 36-37

HUNG HSIU-CH'ÜAN (1814-1864), Chinese religious leader, founder of Taiping sect **8** 37-38

HUNG-WU (1328-1398), Chinese Ming emperor 1368-98 **8** 38-39

HUNT, H. L. (1889-1974), American entrepreneur **8** 42-44

HUNT, RICHARD MORRIS (1827-1895), American architect **8** 44

HUNT, WALTER (1796-1859), American inventor **21** 210-212

HUNT, WILLIAM HOLMAN (1827-1910), English painter **8** 44-45

Hunter College
Talma, Louise Juliette **27** 336-338

HUNTER, ALBERTA (1895-1984), African American blues singer **23** 160-162

HUNTER, FLOYD (born 1912), American social worker and administrator, community worker, professor, and author **8** 45-46

HUNTER, MADELINE CHEEK (1916-1994), American educator **8** 47-48

HUNTER, WILLIAM (1718-1783), Scottish anatomist **8** 48-49

HUNTINGTON, ANNA HYATT (Anna Vaughn Hyatt; 1876-1973), American sculptor and philanthropist **23** 162-164

HUNTINGTON, COLLIS POTTER (1821-1900), American railroad builder **8** 49

HUNTLEY AND BRINKLEY (1956-1970), American journalists and radio and television news team **8** 49-51

HUNYADI, JOHN (1385-1456), Hungarian military leader, regent 1446-1452 **8** 51-52

HURD, DOUGLAS (born 1930), English Conservative Party politician and foreign secretary **8** 52-55

HURSTON, ZORA NEALE (1903-1960), African American folklorist and novelist **8** 55-56

HUS, JAN (a.k.a. John Hus; ca.1369-1415), Bohemian religious reformer **8** 56-59

HUSÁK, GUSTÁV (born 1913), president of the Czechoslovak Socialist Republic (1975-1987) **8** 59-61

HUSAYN, TAHA (1889-1973), Egyptian author, educator, and statesman **8** 61-62

HUSAYNI, AL-HAJJ AMIN AL- (1895-1974), Moslem scholar/leader and mufti of Jerusalem (1922-1948) **8** 62-63

HUSEIN IBN ALI (circa 1854-1931), Arab nationalist, king of Hejaz 1916-1924 **8** 63

HUSSEIN IBN TALAL (1935-1999), king of the Hashemite Kingdom of Jordan (1953-80s) **8** 65-67

HUSSEIN, SADDAM (1937-2006), socialist president of the Iraqi Republic and strongman of the ruling Ba'th regime **13** 415-416

HUSSEINI, FAISAL (1940-2001), Palestinian political leader **19** 160-162

HUSSERL, EDMUND (1859-1938), German philosopher **8** 67-68

HUSTON, JOHN MARCELLUS (1906-1987), American film director, scriptwriter, and actor **22** 250-252

HUTCHINS, ROBERT MAYNARD (1899-1977), American educator **8** 68-69

HUTCHINSON, ANNE MARBURY (1591-1643), English-born American religious leader **8** 69-71

HUTCHINSON, THOMAS (1711-1780), American colonial governor **8** 71-72

HUTT, WILLIAM (William Ian DeWitt Hutt; born 1920), Canadian actor and director **27** 171-173

HUTTEN, ULRICH VON (1488-1523), German humanist **8** 72-73

HUTTON, JAMES (1726-1797), Scottish geologist **8** 73-74

HUXLEY, ALDOUS LEONARD (1894-1963), English novelist and essayist **8** 74-75

I

JACKSON, SHIRLEY ANN (born 1946), African American physicist 8 183-184

JACKSON, THOMAS JONATHAN ("Stonewall"; 1824-1863), American Confederate general 8 184-185

JACOB, JOHN EDWARD (born 1934), African American activist and president of the National Urban League 8 185-188

JACOBI, ABRAHAM (1830-1919), American physician 8 188-189

JACOBI, DEREK (born 1938), British actor 19 168-170

JACOBI, FRIEDRICH HEINRICH (1743-1819), German philosopher 8 189-190

JACOBI, MARY PUTNAM (1834-1906), American physician 8 188-189

JACOBS, ALETTA HENRIETTE (1854-1929), Dutch physician and social reformer 26 171-173

JACOBS, HARRIET A. (1813-1897), runaway slave and abolitionist 8 190-193

JACOBS, JANE (Jane Butzner; 1916-2006), Canadian author and urban planning activist 27 181-183

JACOBSEN, JENS PETER (1847-1885), Danish author 8 193-194

JACOBSON, DAN (born 1929), South African author 22 266-268

JACOPONE DA TODI (circa 1236-1306), Italian poet and mystic 8 194

JACQUARD, JOSEPH MARIE (1752-1834), French inventor 21 216-218

JAELL, MARIE TRAUTMANN (1846-1925), French pianist and composer 24 189-191

JAGGER, MICHAEL PHILIP ("Mick"; born 1944), lead singer for the Rolling Stones 8 194-196

JAHAN, NUR (Mihrunnissa; Nur Mahal; 1577-1646), Indian queen 24 191-193

JAHANGIR (1569-1627), fourth Mughal emperor of India 8 196-199

JAHN, HELMUT (born 1940), German-American architect 8 199-201

JAMES I (1394-1437), king of Scotland 1406-1437 8 206-207

JAMES I (James VI of Scotland; 1566-1625), king of England 1603-1625 8 204-206

JAMES II (1633-1701), king of England, Scotland, and Ireland 1685-1688 8 207-208

JAMES III (1451-1488), king of Scotland 1460-1488 8 208-209

JAMES, DANIEL, JR. ("Chappie"; 1920-1978), first African American man in the U.S. to become a four star general 8 209-211

JAMES, ETTA (Jamesetta Hawkins; born 1938), African American singer 25 213-215

JAMES, HENRY (1843-1916), American novelist 8 211-212

JAMES, JESSE WOODSON (1847-1882), American outlaw 8 212-213

JAMES, P. D. (born 1920), British crime novelist 8 213-215

JAMES, WILLIAM (1842-1910), American philosopher and psychologist 8 215-217

JAMESON, SIR LEANDER STARR (1853-1917), British colonial administrator 8 218

JAMI (Maulana Nur al-Din Abd al-Rahman; 1414-1492), Persian poet 8 218-219

JAMISON, JUDITH (born 1944), American dancer and choreographer 26 173-175

JANÁČEK, LEOŠ (1854-1928), Czech composer 8 219

JANCSO, MIKLOS (born 1921), Hungarian filmmaker 25 215-217

JANET, PIERRE MARIE FÉLIX (1859-1947), French psychologist 8 220

JANSEN, CORNELIS (1585-1638), Dutch Roman Catholic theologian 8 220-221

JAQUES-DALCROZE, EMILE (1865-1950), Swiss teacher and composer who developed eurhythmics 8 221-222

JARA, VICTOR (Victor Lidio Jara Martinez; 1932-1973), Chilean singer and songwriter 27 183-185

JARREAU, AL (Alwin Lopez Jarreau; born 1940), African American musician 26 175-177

JARRELL, RANDALL (1914-1965), American poet and critic 8 222-223

JARUZELSKI, WOJCIECH WITOLD (born 1923), career soldier who became Poland's head of state (1981-1990) 8 223-225

JARVIK, ROBERT KOFFLER (born 1946), American physician and inventor 25 217-220

JASPERS, KARL (1883-1969), German philosopher 8 225-226

JAURÈS, JEAN (1859-1914), French Socialist and politician 8 226-227

Java (island)
see Indonesia

JAWARA, SIR DAUDA KAIRABA (born 1924), Gambian statesman 8 227-228

JAWLENSKY, ALEXEJ VON (1864-1941), Russian Expressionist painter 8 228-229

JAWORSKI, LEON (1905-1982), American lawyer and independent prosecutor of Watergate 8 229-230

JAY, JOHN (1745-1829), American diplomat and jurist 8 230-232

JAY, WILLIAM (1789-1858), American reformer 8 232-233

JAYEWARDENE, JUNIUS RICHARD (JR; 1906-1996), leader of the nationalist movement in Ceylon and president of Sri Lanka 8 233-234

Jazz (music)
Blakey, Art 27 46-48
Getz, Stan 27 143-145
Jobim, Antonio Carlos 27 187-189
Olatunji, Michael Babatunde 27 277-279

Jazz Messengers (musical group)
Blakey, Art 27 46-48

JEAN DE MEUN (circa 1240-1305), French author 8 234-235

JEANS, SIR JAMES HOPWOOD (1877-1946), English mathematician, physicist, and astronomer 8 235-236

JEFFERS, JOHN ROBINSON (1887-1962), American poet 8 236-237

JEFFERSON, JOSEPH (1829-1905), American actor 8 237

JEFFERSON, THOMAS (1743-1826), American philosopher and statesman, president 1801-1809 8 238-241

JEFFREYS, SIR HAROLD (1891-1989), English mathematician, astronomer, and philosopher 8 241-242

JELLICOE, JOHN RUSHWORTH (1859-1935), English admiral 8 242-243

JEMISON, MAE C. (born 1956), African American physician and astronaut 8 243-244

JENKINS, ROY HARRIS (born 1920), British Labour politician and author 8 244-245

JENNER, BRUCE (born 1949), American track and field athlete and motivational speaker 21 218-221

JENNER, EDWARD (1749-1823), English physician 8 245-246

JENNEY, WILLIAM LE BARON (1832-1907), American architect and engineer 21 221-223

KALAKAUA, DAVID (1836-1891), king of Hawaiian Islands 1874-1891 **8** 413-414

KALIDASA (flourished 4th-5th century), Indian poet and dramatist **8** 414-415

KALMAN, RUDOLF EMIL (born 1930), Hungarian scientist **24** 199-201

KALMUS, NATALIE (Natalie Mabelle Dunfee; 1883?-1965), American inventor and cinematographer **21** 233-235

KAMARAJ, KUMARASWAMI (1903-1975), Indian political leader **8** 415

KAMEHAMEHA I (circa 1758-1819), king of the Hawaiian Islands 1795-1819 **8** 416

KAMEHAMEHA III (circa 1814-1854), king of the Hawaiian Islands 1825-1854 **8** 416-417

KAMENEV, LEV BORISOVICH (1883-1936), Russian politician **8** 417-418

KAMERLINGH ONNES, HEIKE (1853-1926), Dutch physicist **8** 418-420

KAMMU (737-806), Japanese emperor 781-806 **8** 420

KAMROWSKI, GEROME (1914-2004), American artist **27** 197-199

KANDER, JOHN (born 1927), American composer and lyricist **21** 235-237

KANDINSKY, WASSILY (1866-1944), Russian painter **8** 420-422

KANE, JOHN (1860-1934), Scottish-born American primitive painter **8** 422

KANE, PAUL (1810-1871), Canadian painter and writer **8** 422-423

K'ANG YU-WEI (1858-1927), Chinese scholar and philosopher **8** 426-428

K'ANG-HSI (1654-1722), Chinese emperor 1661-1722 **8** 423-426

KANISHKA (ca. 78- ca. 103), Kashan ruler **8** 428-429

KANT, IMMANUEL (1724-1804), German philosopher **8** 430-432

KAO-TSUNG (1107-1187), Chinese emperor **8** 433

KAPITSA, PYOTR LEONIDOVICH (born 1894), Soviet physicist **8** 433-435

KAPLAN, MORDECAI MENAHEM (1881-1983), American Jewish theologian and educator **8** 435-436

KAPP, WOLFGANG (1858-1922), German nationalist politician **8** 436

KAPTEYN, JACOBUS CORNELIS (1851-1922), Dutch astronomer **8** 436-437

KARADZIC, RADOVAN (born 1945), leader of the Serbian Republic **8** 437-440

KARAJAN, HERBERT VON (1908-1989), Austrian conductor **26** 190-192

KARAMANLIS, CONSTANTINE (1907-1998), Greek member of parliament, prime minister (1955-1963; 1974-1980), and president (1980-1985) **8** 440-441

KARAMZIN, NIKOLAI MIKHAILOVICH (1766-1826), Russian historian and author **8** 441-442

KARAN, DONNA (born 1948), American fashion designer and businesswoman **8** 442-444

KARENGA, MAULANA (born Ronald McKinley Everett; born 1941), African American author, educator, and proponent of black culturalism **8** 444-447

KARIM KHAN ZAND (died 1779), Iranian ruler, founder of Zand dynasty **8** 447

KARLE, ISABELLA (born 1921), American chemist and physicist **8** 447-449

KARLOFF, BORIS (William Henry Pratt; 1887-1969), English actor **26** 192-194

KARLSTADT, ANDREAS BODENHEIM VON (circa 1480-1541), German Protestant reformer **8** 449

KARMAL, BABRAK (born 1929), Afghan Marxist and Soviet puppet ruler of the Democratic Republic of Afghanistan (1979-1986) **8** 449-451

KÁRMÁN, THEODORE VON (1881-1963), Hungarian-born American physicist **8** 451-452

KARSH, YOUSUF (1908-2002), Canadian photographer **23** 184-187

KARTINI, RADEN AJENG (1879-1904), Indonesian activist **24** 201-203

KARUME, SHEIKH ABEID AMANI (1905-1972), Tanzanian political leader **8** 452-453

KASAVUBU, JOSEPH (circa 1913-1969), Congolese statesman **8** 453-455

KASSEBAUM, NANCY (born 1932), Republican senator from Kansas **8** 455-457

KASTRIOTI-SKANDERBEG, GJERGJ (1405-1468), Albanian military leader **23** 187-189

Katanga secession
see Congo, Democratic Republic of—Katanga secession

KATAYAMA, SEN (1860-1933), Japanese labor and Socialist leader **8** 457

KAUFFMAN, ANGELICA (Maria Anna Angelica Catherina Kauffman; 1741-1807), Swedish artist **25** 229-231

KAUFMAN, GEORGE S. (1889-1961), American playwright **8** 457-458

KAUFMAN, GERALD BERNARD (born 1930), foreign policy spokesman of the British Labour Party **8** 458-460

KAUFMANN, EZEKIEL (1889-1963), Jewish philosopher and scholar **8** 460

KAUNDA, KENNETH DAVID (born 1924), Zambian statesman **8** 460-461

KAUTILYA (4th century B.C.), Indian statesman and author **8** 462

KAUTSKY, KARL JOHANN (1854-1938), German Austrian Socialist **8** 462-463

KAWABATA, YASUNARI (1899-1972), Japanese novelist **8** 463-464

KAWAWA, RASHIDI MFAUME (born 1929), Tanzanian political leader **8** 464-465

KAYE, DANNY (David Daniel Kaminsky; 1913-1987), American film and stage actor **25** 231-234

KAZAN, ELIA (born 1909), American film and stage director **8** 465-466

KAZANTZAKIS, NIKOS (1883-1957), Greek author, journalist, and statesman **8** 466-468

KEAN, EDMUND (1789-1833), English actor **21** 237-239

KEARNEY, DENIS (1847-1907), Irish-born American labor agitator **8** 468

KEARNY, STEPHEN WATTS (1794-1848), American general **8** 468-469

KEATING, PAUL JOHN (born 1944), federal treasurer of Australia (1983-1991) **8** 469-470

KEATON, BUSTER (Joseph Frank Keaton; 1895-1966), American comedian **20** 199-201

KEATS, JOHN (1795-1821), English poet **8** 470-472

KEFAUVER, CAREY ESTES (1903-1963), U.S. senator and influential Tennessee Democrat **8** 472-474

KEILLOR, GARRISON (Gary Edward Keillor, born 1942), American humorist, radio host, and author **22** 271-273

KEITA, MODIBO (1915-1977), Malian statesman **8** 474-475

KEITEL, WILHELM (1882-1946), German general **18** 224-226

KHACHATURIAN, ARAM ILICH (or Khachaturov; 1903-1978), Russian composer **8** 530-531

KHALID BIN ABDUL AZIZ AL-SAUD (1912-1982), Saudi king and prime minister **23** 194-196

KHALIL, SAYYID ABDULLAH (1892-1970), Sudanese general, prime minister 1956-1958 **8** 531-532

KHAMA, SIR SERETSE M. (born 1921), Botswana political leader **8** 532-533

KHAMENEI, AYATOLLAH SAYYID ALI (born 1939), supreme spiritual and political leader of the Islamic Republic of Iran **8** 533-535

KHAN, ALI AKBAR (born 1922), Indian musician **24** 203-206

KHAN, A. Q. (Abdul Quadeer Khan; born 1936), Pakistani metallurgical engineer **27** 205-208

KHOMEINI, AYATOLLAH RUHOLLAH MUSAVI (born 1902), founder and supreme leader of the Islamic Republic of Iran **8** 535-537

KHORANA, HAR GOBIND (born 1922), Indian organic chemist **8** 537-538

KHOSROW I (died 579), Sassanid king of Persia 531-576 **8** 538-539

KHRUSHCHEV, NIKITA SERGEEVICH (1894-1971), Soviet political leader **8** 539-540

KHUFU (ruled 2590-2568 B.C.), Egyptian king **8** 540-541

KHWARIZMI, MUHAMMAD IBN MUSA AL- (died circa 850), Arab mathematician, astronomer, and geographer **8** 541

KIBAKI, MWAI (born 1931), Kenyan presidnet **25** 240-242

KIDD, WILLIAM (c. 1645-1701), Scottish pirate **21** 242-244

KIDDER, ALFRED VINCENT (1885-1963), American archeologist **8** 541-542

KIDMAN, SIDNEY (1857-1935), "The Cattle King" of Australia **8** 542-544

KIEFER, ANSELM (born 1945), German artist **8** 544-546

KIENHOLZ, EDWARD (born 1927), American Pop artist **8** 546-547

KIERKEGAARD, SØREN AABYE (1813-1855), Danish philosopher **8** 547-549

KIESLOWSKI, KRZYSZTOF (1941-1946), Polish film director **25** 242-244

KILBY, JACK ST. CLAIR (1923-2005), American electrical engineer and inventor **25** 244-246

KILPATRICK, WILLIAM H. (1871-1965), American educator, college president, and philosopher of education **9** 1-3

KIM DAE-JUNG (born 1925), worked for the restoration of democracy and human rights in South Korea after 1971 **9** 3-4

KIM IL-SUNG (born 1912), North Korean political leader **9** 4-6

KIM JONG IL (born 1941), heir-apparent of Kim Il-sung, the founder and leader of the Democratic People's Republic of Korea **9** 6-7

KIM OK-KYUN (1851-1894), Korean politician **9** 7-8

KIM PUSIK (1075-1151), Korean statesman, historian, and general **9** 8-9

KIM YOUNG SAM (born 1927), South Korean statesman **9** 9-10

KINCAID, JAMAICA (Elaine Potter Richardson; born 1949), African American author **23** 196-199

KINDI, ABU-YUSUF YAQUB IBN-ISHAQ AL- (died 873), Arab philosopher **9** 10-11

KING, B. B. (born Riley B. King; born 1925), African American blues musician, singer, and songwriter **9** 11-14

KING, BILLIE JEAN (born 1943), international tennis star **9** 14-15

KING, CLARENCE (1842-1901), American geologist and mining engineer **9** 15-16

KING, CORETTA SCOTT (1927-2005), American advocate of civil rights, nonviolence, international peace, full employment, and equal rights for women **9** 16-17

KING, ERNEST JOSEPH (1878-1956), American admiral **9** 17-18

KING, FREDERIC TRUBY (1858-1938), New Zealand doctor and founder of the Plunket Society **9** 18-19

KING, MARTIN LUTHER, JR. (1929-1968), African American minister and civil rights leader **9** 20-22
assassanation of
Ray, James Earl **27** 308-310

KING, MARY-CLAIRE (born 1946), American geneticist **19** 182-183

KING, RUFUS (1755-1827), American statesman and diplomat **9** 22-23

KING, STEPHEN (a.k.a. Richard Bachman and John Swithen; born 1947), American horror novelist **9** 23-25

KING, WILLIAM LYON MACKENZIE (1874-1950), Canadian statesman **9** 25-26

KINGMAN, DONG (Dong Moy She Kingman; 1911-2000), Chinese American artist **27** 208-209

KINGSFORD SMITH, SIR CHARLES ("Smithy"; 1897-1935), Australian long-distance aviator **9** 26-28

KINGSLEY, CHARLES (1819-1875), English author and Anglican clergyman **9** 28

KINGSLEY, HENRY (1830-1867), British author **22** 278-280

KINGSLEY, MARY (1862-1900), English explorer and author **20** 201-204

KINGSTON, MAXINE HONG (Maxine Ting Ting Hong; born 1940), Asian-American feminist author **18** 231-232

KINNOCK, NEIL (born 1942), British Labour Party politician **9** 29-30

KINO, EUSEBIO FRANCISCO (1645-1711), Spanish missionary, explorer, and cartographer **9** 30-31

KINOSHITA, KEISUKE (1912-1998), Japanese screenwriter and film director/producer **24** 206-208

KINSEY, ALFRED C. (1894-1956), American zoologist **9** 31-32

KINUGASA, TEINOSUKE (Teinosuke Kogame; 1896-1982), Japanese screenwriter and film director **24** 208-209

KIPLING, JOSEPH RUDYARD (1865-1936), British poet and short-story writer **9** 32-33

KIPNIS, ALEXANDER (1891-1978), Ukrainian American musician **24** 209-211

KIRCH, MARIA WINCKELMANN (1670-1720), German astronomer **20** 204-205

KIRCHER, ATHANASIUS (1601-1602-1680, German polymath **27** 209-211

KIRCHHOFF, GUSTAV ROBERT (1824-1887), German physicist **9** 33-34

KIRCHNER, ERNST LUDWIG (1880-1938), German expressionist painter **9** 34-35

KIRKLAND, JOSEPH LANE (1922-1999), American labor union movement leader **9** 35-37

KIRKLAND, SAMUEL (1741-1808), American Congregationalist missionary **9** 37

KIRKPATRICK, JEANE J. (1926-2006), professor and first woman U.S.

ambassador to the United Nations **9** 37-39

KIRSTEIN, LINCOLN (1906-1996), a founder and director of the New York City Ballet **9** 39-41

KISHI, NOBUSUKE (1896-1987), Japanese politician **9** 41-43

KISSINGER, HENRY ALFRED (born 1923), U.S. secretary of state and co-winner of the Nobel Peace prize **9** 43-45

KITCHENER, HORATIO HERBERT (1850-1916), British field marshal and statesman **9** 45-46

KITT, EARTHA (nee Eartha Mae Kitt-Fields; born 1927), African American actress and singer **26** 194-197

KIVI, ALEKSIS (Aleksis Stenvall; 1834-1872), Finnish author **25** 246-247

KIWANUKA, BENEDICTO KAGIMA MUGUMBA (1922-1972), Ugandan politician **9** 46-47

KLEE, PAUL (1879-1940), Swiss painter and graphic artist **9** 47-49

KLEIN, A. M. (1909-1972), Canadian journalist, lawyer, novelist, and poet **9** 49-50

KLEIN, CALVIN (born 1942), American fashion designer **9** 50-52

KLEIN, MELANIE (1882-1960), Austrian psychotherapist **9** 52

KLEIST, HEINRICH VON (1777-1811), German author **9** 52-53

KLEMPERER, OTTO (1885-1973), German conductor **20** 205-207

KLIMA, VIKTOR (born 1947), Austrian chancellor **18** 232-234

KLIMT, GUSTAV (1862-1918), controversial Austrian painter **9** 53-55

KLINE, FRANZ (1910-1962), American painter **9** 55

KLITZING, KLAUS VON (born 1943), German physicist **27** 212-214

KLOPSTOCK, FRIEDRICH GOTTLIEB (1724-1803), German poet **9** 55-56

KLUCKHOHN, CLYDE (1905-1960), American anthropologist **9** 56-57

KLYUCHEVSKY, VASILY OSIPOVICH (1841-1911), Russian historian **9** 57-58

KNAPP, SEAMAN ASAHEL (1833-1911), American educator and agricultural pioneer **9** 58

KNIGHT, FRANK HYNEMAN (1885-1972), American economist **9** 58-59

KNIGHT, PHIL (born 1938), American businessman **19** 183-186

KNIPLING, EDWARD FRED (1909-2000), American entomologist **9** 59-60

KNOPF, ALFRED A. (1892-1984), American publisher **9** 60-61

KNOPF, BLANCHE WOLF (1894-1966), American publisher **9** 61-62

KNOWLES, MALCOLM SHEPHERD (1913-1997), American adult education theorist and planner **9** 62-64

KNOX, HENRY (1750-1806), American Revolutionary War general **9** 64

KNOX, JOHN (circa 1505-1572), Scottish religious reformer **9** 65-66

KNOX, PHILANDER CHASE (1853-1921), American statesman **9** 66-67

KNUDSEN, WILLIAM S. (1879-1948), American auto industry leader **9** 67-68

KOBAYASHI, MASAKI (1916-1996), Japanese film director **23** 199-201

KOCH, EDWARD I. (born 1924), New York City mayor **9** 68-69

KOCH, MARITA (Marita Meier-Koch; born 1957), German athlete **26** 197-199

KOCH, ROBERT HEINRICH HERMANN (1843-1910), German physician and bacteriologist **9** 69-70

KODÁLY, ZOLTÁN (1882-1967), Hungarian composer **9** 71

KOESTLER, ARTHUR (1905-1983), author of political novels **9** 71-73

KOGAWA, JOY NOZOMI (née Na Kayama; born 1935), Japanese Canadian author and activist **25** 247-250

Koguryo
see Korea—50-668 (Koguryo)

KOHL, HELMUT (born 1930), chancellor of West Germany (1982-1990) and first chancellor of a united Germany since World War II **9** 73-74

KOHN, WALTER (born 1923), German-American physicist **27** 214-216

KOIZUMI, JUNICHIRO (born 1942), Japanese prime minister **25** 250-252

KOJONG (1852-1919), Korean king **9** 74-75

KOKOSCHKA, OSKAR (1886-1980), Austrian painter, graphic artist, and author **9** 75-76

KOLAKOWSKI, LESZEK (born 1927), philosopher who wrote on broad themes of ethics, metaphysics, and religion **9** 76-77

KOLCHAK, ALEKSANDR VASILIEVICH (1873-1920), Russian admiral **9** 77-78

KOLLONTAI, ALEKSANDRA MIKHAILOVNA (1872-1952), Soviet diplomat **9** 79

KOLLWITZ, KÄTHE (1867-1945), German expressionist graphic artist and sculptor **9** 79-81

KONEV, IVAN STEFANOVICH (1897-1973), Soviet marshal **9** 81-82

KONOE, PRINCE FUMIMARO (or Konoye; 1891-1945), Japanese premier 1937-1939 and 1940-1941 **9** 82-83

KOONS, JEFF (born 1955), American artist **9** 83-84

KOOP, C. EVERETT (born 1916), American surgeon general **18** 235-237

KÖPRÜLÜ, AHMED (Köprülüzade Fazil Ahmed Pasha; 1635-1676), Turkish statesman and general **9** 84-85

KORBUT, OLGA (born 1955), Belarusian gymnast **24** 211-213

Korea (nation; eastern Asia)
• SINCE 1948 (TWO REPUBLICS) South Korea (Republic of Korea) Ban Ki-Moon **27** 29-31

KORNBERG, ARTHUR (born 1918), Americna biochemist **9** 85-87

KORNILOV, LAVR GEORGIEVICH (1870-1918), Russian general **9** 87-88

Koryo
see Korea—918-1392

KOSCIUSZKO, TADEUSZ ANDRZEJ BONAWENTURA (1746-1817), Polish patriot, hero in the American Revolution **9** 88

KOSINSKI, JERZY (Jerzy Nikodem Lewinkopf; 1933-1991), Polish-American author **26** 199-201

KOSSUTH, LOUIS (1802-1894), Hungarian statesman **9** 88-90

KOSYGIN, ALEKSEI NIKOLAEVICH (1904-1980), chairman of the U.S.S.R. Council of Ministers and head of the Soviet government (1964-1980) **9** 90-91

KOTZEBUE, OTTO VON (1787-1846), Russian explorer **9** 91-92

KOUFAX, SANDY (Sanford Braun; born 1945), American baseball player **20** 208-210

KOUSSEVITZKY, SERGE (Sergey Aleksandrovich Kusevitsky;1874-1951), Russian-born American conductor **24** 213-215

KOVACS, ERNIE (1919-1962), American comedian **19** 186-188

L

LA FONTAINE, JEAN DE (1621-1695), French poet **9** 156-157

LA GUARDIA, FIORELLO HENRY (1882-1947), American politician, New York City mayor **9** 166-167

LA METTRIE, JULIEN OFFRAY DE (1709-1751), French physician and philosopher **9** 179-180

LA ROCHEFOUCAULD, FRANÇOIS, DUC DE (1613-1680), French moralist **9** 208-209

LA SALLE, SIEUR DE (René Robert Cavelier; 1643-1687), French explorer and colonizer **9** 210-211

LA TOUR, GEORGE DE (1593-1652), French painter **9** 222

LA VERENDRYE, SIEUR DE (Pierre Gaultier de Varennes; 1685-1749), French-Canadian soldier, explorer, and fur trader **9** 239-240

LABROUSTE, PIERRE FRANÇOIS HENRI (1801-1875), French architect-engineer **9** 144

LACAN, JACQUES (1901-1981), French psychoanalyst **9** 145-147

LACHAISE, GASTON (1882-1935), French-born American sculptor **9** 147

LACHAPELLE, MARIE (1769-1821), French obstetrician and teacher **21** 245-247

LACOMBE, ALBERT (1827-1916), Canadian missionary priest **9** 147-148

LACORDAIRE, JEAN BAPTISTE HENRI (1802-1861), French Dominican preacher **9** 148

LACY, SAM (Samuel Harold Lacy; 1903-2003), African American journalist **26** 207-209

LADD, WILLIAM (1778-1841), American pacifist **9** 149

LADD-FRANKLIN, CHRISTINE (1847-1930), American logician and psychologist **23** 202-204

LAENNEC, RENÉ (René-Théophile-Hyacinthe Laënnec; 1781-1826), French physician and inventor **21** 247-249

LAFAYETTE, MARQUIS DE (Marie Joseph Paul Yves Roch Gilbert du Motier; 1757-1834), French general and statesman **9** 151-152

LAFONTAINE, SIR LOUIS-HIPPOLYTE (1807-1864), Canadian politician **9** 157-158

LAFONTAINE, OSKAR (born 1943), German politician **9** 158-160

LAFORGUE, JULES (1860-1887), French poet **9** 160-161

LAGERFELD, KARL (born 1938), German-French designer of high fashion **9** 161-162

LAGERKVIST, PÄR FABIAN (born 1891), Swedish author **9** 162-163

LAGERLÖF, SELMA OTTILIANA LOVISA (1858-1940), Swedish author **9** 163-164

LAGOS, RICARDO (born 1938), president of Chile **27** 223-225

LAGRANGE, JOSEPH LOUIS (1736-1813), Italian-born French mathematician **9** 164-166

LAHR, BERT (Irving Lahrheim; 1895-1967), performer and comedian in burlesque, vaudeville, musical comedy, film, and television **9** 167-168

LAING, R. D. (1927-1989), Scottish psychiatrist and author **26** 209-211

LAIRD, MELVIN R. (born 1922), U.S. congressman and secretary of defense **9** 168-170

LAKSHMIBAI (Laksmi Bai; Rani of Jhansi; c.1835-1857), Indian queen and national hero **22** 41-42

LALIBELA (ruled circa 1181-circa 1221), Ethiopian king and saint **9** 170

LALIQUE, RENÉ (1860-1945), French glass and jewelry designer **26** 211-213

LAMAR, LUCIUS QUINTUS CINCINNATUS (1825-1893), American politician and jurist **9** 170-171

LAMARCK, CHEVALIER DE (Jean Baptiste Pierre Antoine de Monet; 1744-1829), French naturalist **9** 171-173

LAMARQUE, LIBERTAD (Libertad Lamarque Bouza; 1908-2000), Argentine entertainer **26** 213-215

LAMARR, HEDY (Hedwig Eva Marie Kiesler; 1913-2000), American actress and inventor **27** 225-227

LAMARTINE, ALPHONSE MARIE LOUIS DE (1790-1869), French poet and diplomat **9** 173-175

LAMAS, CARLOS SAAVEDRA (1878-1959), Argentine scholar, statesman, and diplomat **9** 175-176

LAMB, CHARLES (1775-1834), English author, critic, and minor poet **9** 176-177

LAMBSDORFF, OTTO GRAF (born 1926), West German minister of economics **9** 177-179

LAMENNAIS, HUGUES FÉLICITÉ ROBERT DE (1782-1854), French priest and political writer **9** 179

L'AMOUR, LOUIS (Louis Dearborn LaMoore; 1908-1988), American author of westerns **20** 213-215

LAMPMAN, ARCHIBALD (1861-1899), Canadian poet **9** 180-181

LAMPRECHT, KARL (1856-1915), German historian **9** 181

LAMY, JEAN BAPTISTE (1814-1888), French archbishop in the United States **9** 181-182

LANCASTER, BURT (Burton Stephen Lancaster; 1913-1994), American actor **20** 215-218

LANCASTER, JOSEPH (1778-1838), English educator **9** 182-183

LAND, EDWIN HERBERT (1909-1991), American physicist, inventor, and manufacturer **9** 183-184

LANDAU, LEV DAVIDOVICH (1908-1968), Soviet theoretical physicist **9** 184-185

Landers, Ann
see Lederer, Esther Pauline

LANDINI, FRANCESCO (circa 1335-1397), Italian composer and poet **9** 185-186

LANDIS, KENESAW MOUNTAIN (1866-1944), American baseball commissioner **22** 285-287

LANDON, ALFRED MOSSMAN (1887-1987), American politician **22** 287-289

LANDOR, WALTER SAVAGE (1775-1864), English poet, essayist and critic **9** 186-187

LANDOWSKA, WANDA (1879-1959), Polish American harpsichordist and pianist **26** 215-218

LANDOWSKI, MARCEL (born 1915), French composer of lyric works **9** 187-188

LANDRY, TOM (Thomas Wade Landry; 1924-2000), American football coach **22** 290-292

LANDSTEINER, KARL (1868-1943), Austrian-born American immunologist **9** 188-189

LANE, DICK (Richard Lane; Dick "Night Train" Lane; 1928-2002), American football player **27** 227-229

LANE, FITZ HUGH (1804-1865), American marine painter **9** 189

LANFRANC (circa 1010-1089), Italian theologian, archbishop of Canterbury **9** 189-190

LOWIE, ROBERT HARRY (1883-1957), Austrian-born American anthropologist **10** 18

LOWRY, MALCOLM (1909-1957), English author **19** 209-211

LOZIER, CLEMENCE SOPHIA HARNED (1813-1888), American suffragist, reformer, and physician **25** 273-275

LU CHI (261-303), Chinese poet and critic **10** 24

LU CHIU-YUAN (Lu Hsiang-shan; 1139-1193), Chinese philosopher **10** 24-25

LU HSÜN (pen name of Chou Shu-jen; 1881-1936), Chinese author and social critic **10** 35-37

LUBITSCH, ERNST (1892-1947), German-American film director **10** 18-19

LUCARIS, CYRIL (1572-1637), Greek Orthodox patriarch and theologian **10** 20

LUCAS, GEORGE (born 1944), American filmmaker **19** 211-213

LUCAS VAN LEYDEN (1494-1533), Dutch engraver and painter **10** 20-21

LUCE, CLARE BOOTHE (1903-1987), playwright and U.S. congresswoman **10** 21-23

LUCE, HENRY ROBINSON (1898-1967), American magazine editor and publisher **10** 23-24

LUCIAN (circa 120-circa 200), Greek satirist **10** 25-26

LUCIANO, LUCKY (Charles Luciano, Salvatore Lucania; 1897-1962), Italian American mobster **19** 214-215

LUCID, SHANNON (born 1943), American astronaut **19** 215-217

LUCRETIUS (Titus Lucretius Carus; circa 94-circa 55 B.C.), Latin poet and philosopher **10** 26-27

LUDENDORFF, ERICH FRIEDRICH WILHELM (1865-1937), German general **10** 27-28

LUDLUM, ROBERT (a.k.a. Jonathan Ryder and Michael Shepherd; born 1927), American suspense novelist **10** 28-29

LUDWIG, DANIEL KEITH (1897-1992), American shipping magnate **10** 29-31

LUDWIG, KARL FRIEDRICH WILHELM (1816-1895), German physiologist **10** 31

LUGARD, FREDERICK JOHN DEALTRY (1st Baron Lugard; 1858-1945), British soldier and colonial administrator in Africa **10** 31-32

LUHAN, MABEL DODGE (1879-1962), American writer, salon hostess, and patron of artists, writers, and political radicals **10** 32-34

LUHMANN, NIKLAS (born 1927), German sociologist who developed a general sociological systems theory **10** 34-35

LUKÁCS, GYORGY (1885-1971), Hungarian literary critic and philosopher **10** 37-38

LUKE, SAINT (flourished A.D. 50), Evangelist and biblical author **10** 38

LUKENS, REBECCA (née Rebecca Webb Pennock; 1794-1854), American industrialist **25** 275-277

LUKS, GEORGE BENJAMIN (1867-1933), American painter **10** 38-39

LULA DA SILVA, LUIZ INÁCIO (Lula; born 1945), president of Brazil **27** 244-247

LULL, RAYMOND (1232/35-1316), Spanish theologian, poet, and missionary **10** 39-40

LULLY, JEAN BAPTISTE (1632-1687), Italian-born French composer **10** 40-41

LUMET, SIDNEY (born 1924), American filmmaker and television director **22** 305-307

LUMIÈRE BROTHERS (Auguste Marie Louis, 1862-1954, and Louis Jean, 1864-1948), French inventors **10** 41-43

LUMUMBA, PATRICE EMERY (1925-1961), Congolese statesman **10** 43-45

LUNDY, BENJAMIN (1789-1839), American journalist **10** 45-46

LUNS, JOSEPH (1911-2002), West European political leader **10** 46-47

LURIA, ISAAC BEN SOLOMON ASHKENAZI (1534-1572), Jewish mystic **10** 47-48

LUTHER, MARTIN (1483-1546), German religious reformer **10** 48-51

LUTHULI, ALBERT JOHN (1898-1967), South African statesman **10** 51-52

LUTOSLAWSKI, WITOLD (1913-1994), Polish composer **10** 52-53

LUTYENS, EDWIN LANDSEER (1869-1944), English architect **10** 54-55

LUXEMBURG, ROSA (1870-1919), Polish revolutionary **10** 55-56

LUZ, ARTURO ROGERIO (born 1926), Philippine painter and sculptor **10** 56-57

LUZHKOV, YURI MIKHAYLOVICH (born 1936), mayor of Moscow **18** 266-268

LUZZATO, MOSES HAYYIM (1707-1747), Jewish mystic and poet **10** 57-58

LUZZI, MONDINO DE' (circa 1265/70-1326), Italian anatomist **10** 58

LWOFF, ANDRÉ (1902-1994), French microbiologist and geneticist **10** 58-59

LY, ABDOULAYE (born 1919), Senegalese politician and historian **10** 60

LYAUTEY, LOUIS HUBERT GONZALVE (1854-1934), French marshal and colonial administrator **10** 60-61

LYDGATE, JOHN (circa 1370-1449/50), English poet **10** 61-62

LYELL, SIR CHARLES (1797-1875), Scottish geologist **10** 62-63

LYND, HELEN MERRELL (1896-1982), American sociologist and educator **10** 63-64

LYND, ROBERT STAUGHTON (1892-1970), American sociologist **10** 64-65

LYND, STAUGHTON (born 1929), historian and peace militant **10** 65-66

LYNDSAY, SIR DAVID (circa 1485-1555), Scottish poet and courtier **10** 66-67

LYON, MARY (1797-1849), American educator, religious leader, and women's rights advocate **10** 67-69

LYONS, JOSEPH ALOYSIUS (1879-1939), Australian statesman, prime minister 1932-39 **10** 69-70

LYSANDER (died 395 B.C.), Spartan military commander and statesman **10** 70

LYSENKO, TROFIM DENISOVICH (1898-1976), Soviet agronomist and geneticist **10** 71

M

MA, YO-YO (born 1955), American cellist **20** 232-234

MAAS, PETER (1929-2001), American author **27** 248-251

MAATHAI, WANGARI MUTA (born 1940), Kenyan environmental activist **18** 269-271

MABILLON, JEAN (1632-1707), French monk and historian **10** 72

MABINI, APOLINARIO (1864-1903), Filipino political philosopher **10** 72-73

statesman, president 1919-1935 **10** 314-315

MASINISSA, KING OF NUMIDIA (240 B.C. - 148 B.C.), prince of the Massylians who consolidated the Numidian tribes to form a North African kingdom **10** 315-317

MASIRE, QUETT KETUMILE (born 1925), a leader of the fight for independence and president of Botswana **10** 318-319

MASON, BRIDGET (Biddy Mason; 1818-1891), African American nurse, midwife, and entrepreneur **22** 312-314

MASON, GEORGE (1725-1792), American statesman **10** 319-320

MASON, JAMES MURRAY (1796-1871), American politician and Confederate diplomat **10** 320-321

MASON, LOWELL (1792-1872), American composer and music educator **10** 321-322

MASSASOIT (1580-1661), Native American tribal chief **10** 322-324 Samoset **27** 316-319

MASSEY, VINCENT (Charles Vincent Massey, 1887-1967), Canadian governor-general **24** 246-248

MASSEY, WILLIAM FERGUSON (1856-1925), New Zealand prime minister 1912-1925 **10** 324

MASSINGER, PHILIP (1583-1640), English playwright **10** 324-325

MASSYS, QUENTIN (1465/66-1530), Flemish painter **10** 325-326

MASTERS, EDGAR LEE (1869-1950), American author and lawyer **10** 326-327

MASTERS, WILLIAM HOWELL (born 1915), American psychologist and sex therapist **10** 327-328

MASUDI, ALI IBN AL- HUSAYN AL- (died 956), Arab historian **10** 328-329

MASUR, KURT (born 1927), German conductor and humanist **20** 246-248

MATA HARI (Margaretha Geertruida Zelle; 1876-1917), Dutch spy **21** 279-282

MATAMOROS, MARINO (1770-1814), Mexican priest and independence hero **10** 329-330

Mathematics
Poincaré conjecture
Perelman, Grigory **27** 288-290

MATHER, COTTON (1663-1728), American Puritan clergyman and historian **10** 330-332

MATHER, INCREASE (1639-1723), American Puritan clergymen, educator, and author **10** 332-333

MATHEWSON, CHRISTY (Christopher Mathewson; 1880-1925), American baseball player **21** 282-284

MATHIAS, BOB (Robert Bruce Mathias; 1930-2006), American track and field star **21** 284-286

MATHIEZ, ALBERT (1874-1932), French historian **10** 333-334

MATILDA OF TUSCANY (ca. 1046-1115), Italian countess **10** 334-336

MATISSE, HENRI (1869-1954), French painter and sculptor **10** 336-337

MATLIN, MARLEE (born 1965), American actress **19** 228-230

MATLOVICH, LEONARD (1943-1988), American gay rights activist **20** 248-250

MATSUNAGA, SPARK MASAYUKI (1916-1990), Asian American U.S. senator **18** 279-281

MATSUSHITA, KONOSUKE (1918-1989), Japanese inventor and businessman **19** 230-232

MATTA ECHAURREN, ROBERTO SEBASTIAN ANTONIO (Matta, 1911-2002), Chilean artist **24** 248-250

MATTEI, ENRICO (1906-1962), Italian entrepreneur **10** 337-339

MATTEOTTI, GIACOMO (1885-1924), Italian political leader **10** 339-340

MATTHAU, WALTER (Walter Matthow; Walter Matuschanskayasky; 1920-2000), American Actor **22** 314-316

MATTHEW, SAINT (flourished Ist century), Apostle and Evangelist **10** 340-341

MATTHEW PARIS (circa 1200-1259), English Benedictine chronicler **10** 341-342

MATTINGLY, GARRETT (1900-1962), American historian, professor, and author of novel-like histories **10** 342-344

MATZELIGER, JAN (1852-1889), American inventor and shoemaker **19** 232-234

MAUCHLY, JOHN (1907-1980), American computer entrepreneur **20** 250-252

MAUDSLAY, HENRY (1771-1831), British engineer and inventor **21** 286-288

MAUGHAM, WILLIAM SOMERSET (1874-1965), English author **10** 344-345

MAULBERTSCH, FRANZ ANTON (1724-1796), Austrian painter **10** 345

MAULDIN, BILL (1921-2003), cartoon biographer of the ordinary GI in World War II **10** 345-346

MAUPASSANT, HENRI RENÉ ALBERT GUY DE (1850-1893), French author **10** 347

MAURIAC, FRANÇOIS (1885-1970), French author **10** 347-348

MAURICE, JOHN FREDERICK DENISON (1805-1872), English theologian and Anglican clergyman **10** 349-350

MAURICE OF NASSAU, PRINCE OF ORANGE (1567-1625), Dutch general and statesman **10** 348-349

MAURRAS, CHARLES MARIE PHOTIUS (1868-1952), French political writer and reactionary **10** 350-351

MAURY, ANTONIA (1866-1952), American astronomer and conservationist **20** 252-254

MAURY, MATTHEW FONTAINE (1806-1873), American naval officer and oceanographer **10** 351-352

MAUSS, MARCEL (1872-1950), French sociologist and anthropologist **10** 352-353

MAWDUDI, ABU-I A'LA (1903-1979), Muslim writer and religious and political leader in the Indian sub-continent **10** 353-354

MAWSON, SIR DOUGLAS (1882-1958), Australian scientist and Antarctic explorer **10** 354-355

MAXIM, SIR HIRAM STEVENS (1840-1916), American-born British inventor **10** 355-356

MAXIMILIAN I (1459-1519), Holy Roman emperor 1493-1519 **10** 356-357

MAXIMILIAN II (1527-1576), Holy Roman emperor 1564-1576 **10** 357-358

MAXIMILIAN OF HAPSBURG (1832-1867), archduke of Austria and emperor of Mexico **10** 358-360

MAXWELL, IAN ROBERT (née Ludvik Hoch; 1923-1991), British publishing magnate **10** 360-361

MAXWELL, JAMES CLERK (1831-1879), Scottish physicist **10** 361-364

Maxwell Motor Co.
see Chrysler Corp.

MAY, KARL (1842-1912), German author **26** 248-250

MAYAKOVSKY, VLADIMIR VLADIMIROVICH (1893-1930), Russian poet **10** 364-365

MAYER, JEAN (born 1920), nutritionist, researcher, consultant to government and international organizations, and president of Tufts University **10** 365-366

MAYER, LOUIS BURT (Eliezer Mayer; 1885-1957), American motion picture producer **19** 234-235

MAYNARD, ROBERT CLYVE (1937-1993), African American journalist and publisher **10** 366-367

MAYO, WILLIAM J. (1861-1939) and CHARLES H. (1865-1939), American physicians **10** 367-369

MAYOR ZARAGOSA, FEDERICO (born 1934), Spanish biochemist who was director-general of UNESCO (United Nations Educational, Scientific, and Cultural Organization) **10** 369-371

MAYO-SMITH, RICHMOND (1854-1901), American statistician and sociologist **10** 371-372

MAYR, ERNST (1904-2005), American evolutionary biologist **10** 372-374

MAYS, BENJAMIN E. (1894-1984), African American educator and civil rights activist **10** 374-376

MAYS, WILLIE (William Howard Mays, Jr.; born 1931), African American baseball player **10** 376-379

MAZARIN, JULES (1602-1661), French cardinal and statesman **10** 379-380

MAZEPA, IVAN STEPANOVICH (circa 1644-1709), Ukrainian Cossack leader **10** 381

MAZZINI, GIUSEPPE (1805-1872), Italian patriot **10** 381-383

M'BOW, AMADOU-MAHTAR (born 1921), director general of UNESCO (United Nations Educational, Scientific, and Cultural Organization) **10** 383-384

MBOYA, THOMAS JOSEPH (1930-1969), Kenyan political leader **10** 384-385

MCADOO, WILLIAM GIBBS (1863-1941), American statesman **10** 385-386

MCAULIFFE, ANTHONY (1898-1975), American army officer **19** 236-239

MCAULIFFE, CHRISTA (nee Sharon Christa Corrigan; 1948-1986), American teacher **20** 254-257

MCCAIN, JOHN SIDNEY, III (born 1936), American politician **25** 285-287

MCCANDLESS, BRUCE (born 1937), American astronaut **23** 243-246

MCCARTHY, EUGENE JOSEPH (1916-2005), American statesman **10** 386-388

MCCARTHY, JOSEPH RAYMOND (1908-1957), American politician **10** 388-389

MCCARTHY, MARY T. (born 1912), American writer **10** 389-391

MCCARTHY, NOBU (nee Nobu Atsumi; 1934-2002), Japanese actress and model **26** 250-252

MCCARTNEY, PAUL (James Paul McCartney; born 1942), British musician **24** 250-253

MCCAY, WINSOR (Zenas Winsor McKay; 1871?-1934), American cartoonist and animator **21** 288-291

MCCLELLAN, GEORGE BRINTON (1826-1885), American general **10** 391-392

MCCLELLAN, JOHN LITTLE (1896-1977), U.S. senator from Arkansas **10** 392-393

MCCLINTOCK, BARBARA (1902-1992), geneticist and winner of the Nobel Prize in physiology **10** 393-394

MCCLINTOCK, SIR FRANCIS LEOPOLD (1819-1907), British admiral and Arctic explorer **10** 394-395

MCCLOSKEY, JOHN (1810-1885), American cardinal **10** 395

MCCLUNG, NELLIE LETITIA (1873-1951), Canadian suffragist, social reformer, legislator, and author **10** 396-397

MCCLURE, SIR ROBERT (1807-1873), English explorer and navy officer **10** 398-399

MCCLURE, SAMUEL SIDNEY (1857-1949), American editor and publisher **10** 398-399

MCCORMACK, JOHN WILLIAM (1891-1980), U.S. congressman and Speaker of the House **10** 399-400

MCCORMICK, CYRUS HALL (1809-1884), American inventor, manufacturer, and philanthropist **10** 400-401

MCCORMICK, ROBERT RUTHERFORD (1880-1955), American publisher **10** 401-402

MCCOSH, JAMES (1811-1894), Scottish-American minister, philosopher, and college president **10** 402-403

MCCOY, ELIJAH (1843-1929), American engineer and inventor **19** 239-241

MCCOY, ISAAC (1784-1846), American Indian agent and missionary **10** 403

MCCOY, JOSEPH GEITING (1837-1915), American cattleman **10** 403-404

MCCULLERS, CARSON (Lula Carson Smith; 1917-1967), American novelist and playwright **18** 281-283

MCCULLOCH, HUGH (1808-1895), American banker and lawyer **10** 404-405

MCDANIEL, HATTIE (1898-1952), African American actress **10** 405-408

MCDUFFIE, GEORGE (1790-1851), American statesman **10** 408

MCENROE, JOHN PATRICK, JR. (born 1959), American tennis player **10** 408-411

MCGILL, RALPH EMERSON (1898-1969), American journalist **10** 411-412

MCGILLIVRAY, ALEXANDER (circa 1759-1793), American Creek Indian chief **10** 412

MCGOVERN, GEORGE STANLEY (born 1922), American statesman **10** 412-414

MCGUFFEY, WILLIAM HOLMES (1800-1873), American educator **10** 414-415

MCINTIRE, SAMUEL (1757-1811), American builder and furniture maker **10** 415

MCKAY, CLAUDE (1890-1948), African American poet and novelist **10** 416

MCKAY, DONALD (1810-1880), American ship builder **10** 416-417

MCKIM, CHARLES FOLLEN (1847-1909), American architect **10** 417-418

MCKINLEY, WILLIAM (1843-1901), American statesman, president 1897-1901 **10** 418-420

MCKISSICK, FLOYD B., (1922-1991), African American civil rights leader **10** 420-422

MCLAREN, NORMAN (1914-1987), Canadian filmmaker **25** 287-289

MCLEAN, JOHN (1785-1861), American jurist and politician **10** 422-423

MCLOUGHLIN, JOHN (1784-1857), Canadian pioneer and trader **10** 423-424

MCLUHAN, MARSHALL (Herbert Marshall McLuhan; 1911-1980), Canadian professor of literature and culture **10** 424-426

MENDOZA, ANTONIO DE (1490-1552), Spanish viceroy in Mexico and Peru **10** 494-495

MENDOZA, DANIEL (1764-1836), English boxer **20** 261-263

MENELIK II (born Sahle Mariam; 1844-1913), Ethiopian emperor 1889-1913 **10** 495-497

MENEM, CARLOS SÁUL (born 1930), Peronist president of Argentina **10** 497-499

MENÉNDEZ DE AVILÉS, PEDRO (1519-1574), Spanish seaman and colonizer **10** 499-500

MENES (King of Egypt; ca. 3420 B.C. - 3345 B.C.), unifier of Egypt **10** 500-502

MENGELE, JOSEF (1911-1979), German physician and war criminal **10** 502-503

MENGISTU HAILE MARIAM (born 1937), head of state of Ethiopia **10** 503-505

MENGS, ANTON RAPHAEL (1728-1779), German painter **10** 505

MENKEN, ALAN (born 1949), American composer **20** 263-266

MENNO SIMONS (circa 1496-1561), Dutch reformer **10** 505-506

MENOCAL, MARIO GARCIA (1866-1941), Cuban statesman, president 1913-1921 **10** 506-507

MENON, VENGALIL KRISHNAN KRISHNA (born 1897), Indian statesman **10** 507-509

MENOTTI, GIAN CARLO (1911-2007), Italian-born American composer **10** 509-510

MENTEN, MAUD L. (1879-1960), Canadian biochemist **24** 259-260

MENUHIN, YEHUDI (1916-1999), American and British violinist and conductor **20** 266-268

MENZIES, SIR ROBERT GORDON (born 1894), Australian statesman **10** 510-511

MENZIES, WILLIAM CAMERON (1896-1957), American film director, producer, and set designer **21** 291-293

MERCATOR, GERHARDUS (1512-1594), Flemish cartographer **10** 511-512

MERCHANT, ISMAIL (Ismail Noor Mohammed Abdul Rehman; 1936-2005), Indian filmmaker **26** 252-254

MEREDITH, GEORGE (1828-1909), English novelist and poet **10** 512-513

MEREDITH, JAMES H. (born 1933), African American civil rights activist and politician **10** 514-515

MEREZHKOVSKY, DMITRY SERGEYEVICH (1865-1941), Russian writer and literary critic **10** 515-516

MERGENTHALER, OTTMAR (1854-1899), German-American inventor of the Linotype **10** 516-517

MERIAN, MARIA SIBYLLA (1647-1717), German artist and entomologist **20** 268-269

MERICI, ANGELA (St. Angela; 1474-1530), Italian nun and educator **21** 293-295

MÉRIMÉE, PROSPER (1803-1870), French author **10** 517

MERLEAU-PONTY, MAURICE (1908-1961), French philosopher **10** 518

MERMAN, ETHEL (Ethel Agnes Zimmermann; 1909-1984), American singer and actress **21** 295-297

MERRIAM, CHARLES EDWARD (1874-1953), American political scientist **10** 518-519

MERRILL, CHARLES E. (1885-1956), founder of the world's largest brokerage firm **10** 519-520

MERRILL, JAMES (1926-1995), American novelist, poet, and playwright **10** 521-522

MERTON, ROBERT K. (1910-2003), American sociologist and educator **10** 522-523

MERTON, THOMAS (1915-1968), Roman Catholic writer, social critic, and spiritual guide **10** 523-525

MERULO, CLAUDIO (1533-1604), Italian composer, organist, and teacher **10** 525-526

Mescalero Apache Indians (North America) Chino, Wendell **27** 86-88

MESMER, FRANZ ANTON (1734-1815), German physician **10** 526-527

MESSALI HADJ (1898-1974), founder of the Algerian nationalist movement **10** 527-528

MESSERSCHMITT, WILLY (Wilhelm Emil Messerschmitt; 1898-1978), German aircraft designer and manufacturer **25** 291-293

MESSIAEN, OLIVIER (1908-1992), French composer and teacher **10** 528-529

MESSNER, REINHOLD (born 1944), Austrian mountain climber and author **22** 316-318

METACOM (a.k.a. King Philip; 1640-1676), Wampanoag cheiftain **10** 529-531

Metastasio (Pietro Antonio Domenico Bonaventura Trapassi; 1698-1782), Italian Martinez, Marianne **27** 256-258

METCALFE, CHARLES THEOPHILUS (1st Baron Metcalfe; 1785-1846), British colonial administrator **10** 531-532

METCHNIKOFF, ÉLIE (1845-1916), Russian physiologist and bacteriologist **10** 532-533

Meteorology (science) Fujita, Tetsuya **27** 135-137

METHODIUS, SAINT (825-885), Greek missionary and bishop **4** 362-363

Metro-Goldwyn-Mayer (film studio) Kerkorian, Kirk **27** 201-203 Lamarr, Hedy **27** 225-227

Metropolitan Opera Company (New York City) Arroyo, Martina **27** 23-25 Farrell, Eileen **27** 119-121

METTERNICH, KLEMENS VON (1773-1859), Austrian politician and diplomat **10** 533-536

Mexican literature Anaya, Rudolfo Alfonso **27** 17-19

MEYERBEER, GIACOMO (1791-1864), German composer **10** 536-537

MEYERHOF, OTTO FRITZ (1884-1951), German biochemist **10** 537-539

MEYERHOLD, VSEVOLOD EMILIEVICH (1874-1942?), Russian director **10** 539

MFUME, KWEISI (born Frizzell Gray; born 1948), African American civil rights activist and congressman **10** 539-542

MGM *see* Metro-Goldwyn-Mayer

MI FEI (1051-1107), Chinese painter, calligrapher, and critic **11** 12-13

MICAH (flourished 8th century B.C.), prophet of ancient Israel **10** 542-543

MICHAEL VIII (Palaeologus; 1224/25-1282), Byzantine emperor 1259-1282 **11** 1-2

MICHELANGELO BUONARROTI (1475-1564), Italian sculptor, painter, and architect **11** 2-5

MICHELET, JULES (1798-1874), French historian **11** 5-6

MICHELOZZO (circa 1396-1472), Italian architect and sculptor **11** 6-7

MITCHELL, MARGARET (Munnerlyn; 1900-1949), American author of Gone With the Wind **11** 59-60

MITCHELL, MARIA (1818-1889), American astronomer and educator **11** 61

MITCHELL, WESLEY CLAIR (1874-1948), American economist **11** 61-62

MITRE, BARTOLOMÉ (1821-1906), Argentine historian and statesman, president 1862-1868 **11** 62-63

MITTERRAND, FRANÇOIS (born 1916), French politician and statesman and president (1981-1990) **11** 63-66

MIYAKE, ISSEY (born 1938), Japanese fashion designer **25** 297-299

MIZOGUCHI, KENJI (1898-1956), Japanese film director **23** 248-250

MIZRAHI, ISAAC (born 1961), American designer **11** 66-67

MLADIC, RATKO (born 1943), Bosnian Serb military leader **11** 68-69

MOBUTU SESE SEKO (Joseph Désiré Mobuto; 1930-1997), Congolese president **11** 69-71

MODEL, LISETTE (nee Lisette Seyberg; 1906?-1983), American photographer and educator **19** 254-256

MODERSOHN-BECKER, PAULA (1876-1907), German painter **11** 71-72

MODIGLIANI, AMEDEO (1884-1920), Italian painter and sculptor **11** 72-73

MODIGLIANI, FRANCO (1918-2003), Italian American economist **24** 265-267

MOFFETT, WILLIAM ADGER (1869-1933), American naval officer **21** 299-301

MOFOLO, THOMAS (1876-1948), Lesothoan author **11** 74

MOGILA, PETER (1596/1597-1646), Russian Orthodox churchman and theologian **11** 74-75

MOHAMMAD REZA SHAH PAHLAVI (1919-1980), king of Iran **11** 75-76

MOHAMMED (circa 570-632), founder of Islam **11** 76-78

MOHAMMED V (Mohammed Ben Youssef; 1911-1961), king of Morocco **11** 79-81

MOHAMMED ALI (1769-1849), Ottoman pasha of Egypt 1805-1848 **11** 81-82

MOHOLY-NAGY, LÁSZLÓ (1895-1946), Hungarian painter and designer **11** 82-83

MOI, DANIEL ARAP (born Daniel Toroitich arap Moi; born 1924), president of Kenya **11** 83-86

MOLIÈRE (1622-1673), French dramatist **11** 86-88

MOLINARI, SUSAN K. (born 1958), American newscaster **18** 289-291

MOLINOS, MIGUEL DE (1628-1696), Spanish priest **11** 88-89

MOLOTOV, VYACHESLAV MIKHAILOVICH (1890-1986), Soviet statesman **11** 89-90

MOLTKE, COUNT HELMUTH KARL BERNARD VON (1800-1891), Prussian military leader **11** 90-91

MOLTMANN, JÖURGEN (born 1926), German Protestant theologian **11** 91-92

MOMADAY, N. SCOTT (born 1934), Native American author **11** 92-94

MOMMSEN, THEODOR (1817-1903), German historian and philologist **11** 94-95

MOMPOU, FREDERIC (Federico Mompou i Dencausse; 1893-1987), Spanish composer **26** 261-263

MONAGHAN, TOM (Thomas Stephen Monaghan; born 1937), American businessman and philanthropist **19** 256-258

MONASH, JOHN (1865-1931), Australian soldier, engineer, and administrator **11** 95-96

MONCK, GEORGE (1st Duke of Albemarle; 1608-1670), English general and statesman **11** 96-97

MONDALE, WALTER F. (Fritz; born 1928), United States senator and vice president **11** 97-99

MONDAVI, ROBERT (born 1913), American winemaker **19** 258-260

MONDLANE, EDUARDO CHIVAMBO (1920-1969), Mozambican educator and nationalist **11** 100-101

MONDRIAN, PIET (1872-1944), Dutch painter **11** 101-102

MONET, CLAUDE (1840-1926), French painter **11** 102-104

MONGKUT (Rama IV; 1804-1868), king of Thailand 1851-1868 **11** 104

MONK, MEREDITH (born 1942), American composer, entertainer, and critic **26** 263-265

MONK, THELONIOUS (1917-1982), African American jazz musician **11** 104-108

MONMOUTH AND BUCCLEUGH, DUKE OF (James Scott; 1649-1685), English claimant to the throne **11** 108-109

MONNET, JEAN (1888-1979), French economist and diplomat **11** 109-110

MONOD, JACQUES (1910-1976), French biologist who discovered messenger RNA **11** 110-111

MONROE, JAMES (1758-1831), American diplomat and statesman, president 1817-1825 **11** 111-113

MONROE, MARILYN (Norma Jean Baker; 1926-1962), film actress **11** 113-114

MONTAGNIER, LUC (born 1932), French virologist **11** 114-116

MONTAGU, ASHLEY (Israel Ehrenberg; 1905-1999), British-born American anthroplogist and author **22** 320-322

MONTAGU, JOHN, FOURTH EARL OF SANDWICH (1718-1792), English politician and first lord of the admiralty **21** 301-303

MONTAGU, MARY WORTLEY (1689-1762), English poet **18** 291-293

MONTAIGNE, MICHEL EYQUEM DE (1533-1592), French essayist **11** 116-117

MONTALE, EUGENIO (1896-1981), Italian poet and critic **11** 117-118

MONTALEMBERT, COMTE DE (Charles Forbes; 1810-1870), French political writer **11** 118-119

MONTALVO, JUAN MARÍA (1832-1889), Ecuadorian writer **11** 119-120

MONTANA, JOE (born 1956), American football player **11** 120-121

MONTANUS (flourished 2nd century), Early Christian founder of schismatic sect **11** 122

MONTCALM DE SAINT-VÉRAN, MARQUIS DE (1712-1759), French general in Canada **11** 122-123

MONTEFIORE, MOSES (1784-1885), English Zionist and philanthropist **20** 272-274

MONTES, ISMAEL (Ismael Montes Gamboa; 1861-1933), president of Bolivia **24** 267-270

MONTESQUIEU, BARON DE (Charles Louis de Secondat; 1689-1755), French man of letters **11** 123-125

MONTESSORI, MARIA (1870-1952), Italian educator and physician **11** 125-126

MONTEVERDI, CLAUDIO GIOVANNI ANTONIO (1567-1643), Italian composer **11** 126-128

MONTEZUMA I (Motecuhzoma I; Moctezuma I; 1397-1469), Aztec ruler **22** 322-324

MONTEZUMA II (1466?-1520), Aztec emperor 1502-1520 **11** 128-129

MONTEZUMA, CARLOS (born Wassaja; ca. 1865-1923), Native American physician and political leader **11** 129-132

MONTFORT, SIMON DE (6th Earl of Leicester; 1208-1265), English statesman and soldier **11** 132-133

MONTGOLFIER, JACQUES ÉTIENNE (1745-1799), French inventor and industrialist **11** 133-134

MONTGOLFIER, JOSEPH MICHEL (1740-1810), French inventor and industrialist **11** 133-134

MONTGOMERY, BERNARD LAW (1st Viscount Montgomery of Alamein; born 1887), English field marshal **11** 135-136

MONTGOMERY, LUCY MAUD (1874-1942), Canadian author **11** 136-138

MONTGOMERY, RICHARD (1736-1775), colonial American general **11** 138-139

MONTREUIL, PIERRE DE (flourished circa 1231-1266/67), French architect **11** 139

MONTT TORRES, MANUEL (1809-1880), Chilean statesman, president 1851-1861 **11** 139-140

MOODIE, SUSANNA (1803-1885), Canadian poet, novelist, and essayist **11** 140-141

MOODY, DWIGHT L. (1837-1899), American evangelist **11** 141-142

MOOG, ROBERT (1934-2005), American inventor **26** 265-267

MOON, SUN MYUNG (born 1920), founder of the Unification Church **11** 142-143

MOORE, CHARLES WILLARD (1925-1993), American architect and educator **11** 143-145

MOORE, CHARLOTTE E. (1898-1990), American astrophysicist **11** 145-146

MOORE, GEORGE EDWARD (1873-1958), English philosopher **11** 146

MOORE, HENRY (1898-1986), English sculptor **11** 146-148

MOORE, MARIANNE (1887-1972), American poet and translator **11** 148-149

MOORE, MICHAEL (born 1954), American author and filmmaker **25** 299-302

MORAES, VINICIUS DE (Marcus Vinicius da Cruz de Mello Moraes; 1913-1980), Brazilian songwriter and author **26** 268-269

MORALES, LUIS DE (circa 1519-1586), Spanish painter **11** 150

MORALES-BERMÚDEZ CERRUTI, FRANCISCO (born 1921), president of Peru (1975-1980) **11** 150-151

MORAN, THOMAS (1837-1926), American painter and graphic artist **11** 151-152

MORANDI, GIORGIO (1890-1964), Italian painter of still lifes **11** 152-153

MORAVIA, ALBERTO (1907-1990), Italian author **11** 153-155

MORAZÁN, JOSÉ FRANCISCO (1792-1842), Central American general and statesman **11** 155

MORE, SIR THOMAS (1478-1535), English humanist and statesman **11** 156-157

MOREAU, GUSTAVE (1826-1898), French artist and professor **22** 324-326

MORELOS, JOSÉ MARÍA (1765-1815), Mexican priest and revolutionary leader **11** 157-158

MORENO, MARIANO (1778-1811), Argentine revolutionary **20** 274-275

MORGAGNI, GIOVANNI BATTISTA (1682-1771), Italian anatomist **11** 158-159

MORGAN, ANN HAVEN (Anna Haven Morgan; 1882-1966), American ecologist and teacher **24** 270-271

MORGAN, CONWAY LLOYD (1852-1936), English psychologist **11** 159-160

MORGAN, DANIEL (circa 1735-1802), American soldier and tactician **11** 160-161

MORGAN, GARRETT A. (1877-1963), African American inventor and publisher **11** 161-162

MORGAN, JOHN (1735-1789), American physician **11** 162-163

MORGAN, JOHN PIERPONT (1837-1913), American banker **11** 163-165

MORGAN, JOHN PIERPONT, II (1867-1943), American banker **11** 165

MORGAN, JULIA (1872-1957), American architect **11** 165-166

MORGAN, JUNIUS SPENCER (1813-1890), American banker **11** 166-167

MORGAN, LEWIS HENRY (1818-1881), American anthropologist **11** 167-168

MORGAN, ROBIN (born 1941), feminist writer, editor, poet, and political activist **11** 168-170

MORGAN, THOMAS HUNT (1866-1945), American zoologist and geneticist **11** 170-171

MORGENTHAU, HANS J. (1904-1979), American political scientist **11** 171-172

MORGENTHAU, HENRY, JR. (1891-1967), American statesman **11** 172-173

MORIN, PAUL (1889-1963), French-Canadian poet **11** 174

MORÍNIGO, HIGINIO (1897-1985), Paraguayan statesman **11** 174-175

MORISON, SAMUEL ELIOT (1887-1976), American historian and biographer **11** 175-176

MORISOT, BERTHE (1841-1895), French painter **21** 303-305

MORITA, AKIO (born 1921), Japanese industrial leader **11** 176-178

MORLEY, JOHN (Viscount Morley of Blackburn; 1838-1923), English statesman and author **11** 178-179

MORLEY, THOMAS (circa 1557-1602/08), English composer and organist **11** 179-180

MORO, ALDO (1916-1978), leader of Italy's Christian Democratic Party **11** 180-181

MORRICE, JAMES WILSON (1865-1924), Canadian painter **11** 181-182

MORRILL, JUSTIN SMITH (1810-1898), American legislator **11** 182

MORRIS, GOUVERNEUR (1752-1816), American statesman and diplomat **11** 182-183

MORRIS, LEWIS (1671-1746), American colonial official **11** 183-184

MORRIS, MARK (born 1956), American choreographer **11** 184-185

MORRIS, ROBERT (1734-1806), American financer and statesman **11** 185-187

MORRIS, WILLIAM (1834-1896), English man of letters, artist, and politician **11** 187-188

PLAATJE, SOLOMON TSHEKISHO (1878-1932), South African writer **12** 341-342

PLANCK, MAX KARL ERNST LUDWIG (1858-1947), German physicist **12** 342-344

PLATH, SYLVIA (1932-1963), American poet and novelist **12** 344-345

PLATO (428-347 B.C.), Greek philosopher **12** 345-347

PLATT, THOMAS COLLIER (1833-1910), American politician **12** 347-348

PLAUTUS (circa 254-circa 184 B.C.), Roman writer **12** 348-350

PLAZA LASSO, GALO (1906-1987), Ecuadorian statesman **12** 350-351

PLEKHANOV, GEORGI VALENTINOVICH (1856-1918), Russian revolutionist and social philosopher **12** 351-352

PLENTY COUPS (c. 1848-1932), Native American tribal leader and Crow chief **12** 352-355

PLINY THE ELDER (23/24-79), Roman encyclopedist **12** 355-356

PLINY THE YOUNGER (circa 61-circa 113), Roman author and administrator **12** 356

PLISETSKAYA, MAYA MIKHAILOVNA (born 1925), Russian ballet dancer **12** 356-358

PLOMER, WILLIAM (William Charles Franklyn Plomer; 1903-1973), South African/British author **24** 312-313

PLOTINUS (205-270), Greek philosopher, founder of Neoplatonism **12** 358-359

PLOTKIN, MARK (born 1955), American ethnobotanist and environmentalist **23** 308-310

PLUTARCH (circa 46-circa 120), Greek biographer **12** 359-360

Plymouth Colony (New England) Native American assistance Samoset **27** 316-319

PO CHÜ-I (772-846), Chinese poet **12** 362-363

POBEDONOSTSEV, KONSTANTIN PETROVICH (1827-1907), Russian statesman and jurist **12** 360-361

POCAHONTAS (circa 1595-1617), American Indian princess **12** 361-362

POE, EDGAR ALLAN (1809-1849), American writer **12** 363-365

POINCARÉ, JULES HENRI (1854-1912), French mathematician **12** 365-366 Perelman, Grigory **27** 288-290

POINCARÉ, RAYMOND (1860-1934), French statesman **12** 366-368

POIRET, PAUL (1879-1944), French fashion designer **19** 291-293

POITIER, SIDNEY (born 1927), African American actor and director **12** 368-370

POL POT (1928-1998), Cambodian Communist and premier of Democratic Kampuchéa (1976-1979) **12** 382-384

POLANSKI, ROMAN (born 1933), Polish filmmaker and director **23** 310-312

POLANYI, JOHN CHARLES (born 1929), Canadian scientist and Nobel Prize winner **12** 370-372

POLANYI, KARL (1886-1964), Hungarian economic historian **12** 372

POLANYI, MICHAEL (1891-1976), Hungarian medical doctor, physical chemist, social thinker, and philosopher **12** 372-373

Polish literature Lem, Stanislaw **27** 238-240 Mickiewicz, Adam Bernard **27** 263-265

POLITKOVSKAYA, ANNA (Anna Stepanova Politkovskaya; 1958-2006), Russian journalist **27** 292-294

POLIZIANO, ANGELO (Politian; 1454-94), Italian poet **12** 373-374

POLK, JAMES KNOX (1795-1849), American statesman, president 1845-49 **12** 374-376

POLK, LEONIDAS LAFAYETTE (1837-1892), American agrarian crusader and editor **12** 376-377

Polka Hall of Fame Floren, Myron **27** 131-133

POLKE, SIGMAR (born 1941), German painter **23** 312-315

POLLAIUOLO, ANTONIO (circa 1432-98), Italian painter, sculptor, goldsmith, and engraver **12** 377-378

POLLARD, ALBERT FREDERICK (1869-1948), English historian **12** 378

POLLOCK, JACKSON (1912-1956), American painter **12** 379-380 abstract expressionism Kamrowski, Gerome **27** 197-199

POLO, MARCO (circa 1254-circa 1324), Venetian traveler and writer **12** 380-382

POLYBIOS (circa 203-120 B.C.), Greek historian **12** 384-385

POLYKLEITOS (flourished circa 450-420 B.C.), Greek sculptor **12** 385-386

POMBAL, MARQUÊS DE (Sebastião José de Carvalho e Mello; 1699-1782), Portuguese statesman **12** 386-387

POMPEY (106-48 B.C.), Roman general and statesman **12** 387-389

POMPIDOU, GEORGES (1911-1974), second president of the French Fifth Republic (1969-1974) **12** 389-390

POMPONAZZI, PIETRO (1462-1525), Italian Aristotelian philosopher **12** 390-391

PONCE DE LEÓN, JUAN (1460?-1521), Spanish conqueror and explorer **12** 391-392

PONIATOWSKA, ELENA (born 1933), Mexican journalist, novelist, essayist, and short-story writer **12** 392-393

PONTIAC (circa 1720-69), Ottawa Indian chief **12** 393-394

PONTOPPIDAN, HENRIK (Rusticus; 1857-1943), Danish author **25** 336-338

PONTORMO (1494-1556), Italian painter **12** 394-395

POOL, JUDITH GRAHAM (1919-1975), American physiologist **23** 315-316

POPE, ALEXANDER (1688-1744), English poet and satirist **12** 395-397

POPE, JOHN RUSSELL (1874-1937), American architect in the classical tradition **12** 397-399

Popeye the Sailor Man (cartoon character) Questel, Mae **27** 299-301

POPHAM, WILLIAM JAMES (born 1930), American educator active in educational test development **12** 399-401

POPOVA, LIUBOV SERGEEVNA (1889-1924), Russian and Soviet avant-garde artist **12** 401-402

POPPER, SIR KARL RAIMUND (1902-1994), Austrian philosopher **12** 402

PORRES, MARTÍN DE, SAINT (1579-1639), Peruvian patron saint of universal brotherhood **27** 295-297

PORSCHE, FERDINAND SR. (1875-1951), Austrian German automobile designer and engineer **19** 293-295

PORTA, GIACOMO DELLA (circa 1537-1602), Italian architect **12** 402-403

PORTA, GIAMBATTISTA DELLA (1535-1615), Italian scientist and dramatist **12** 403-404

PORTALES PLAZAZUELOS, DIEGO JOSÉ VÍCTOR (1793-1837), Chilean statesman **12** 404

PORTER, COLE ALBERT (1891-1964), American composer **12** 405-406

PORTER, EDWIN STRATTON (1870-1941), American filmmaker **20** 299-301

PORTER, KATHERINE ANNE (1890-1980), American writer **12** 406-407

PORTINARI, CÂNDIDO (1903-1962), Brazilian painter **12** 407-408

PORTOLÁ, GASPAR DE (circa 1723-1784), Spanish explorer and colonial governor **12** 408

PORTUONDO, OMARA (born 1930), Cuban singer **26** 302-304

PORTZAMPARC, CHRISTIAN DE (born 1944), French architect **18** 324-326

POSEY, ALEXANDER LAWRENCE (1873-1908), Native American author and politician **26** 304-306

POST, CHARLES WILLIAM (1854-1914), American pioneer in the manufacture and mass-marketing of breakfast cereals **12** 408-409

POST, EMILY PRICE (1873-1960), American authority on etiquette **12** 409-410

Postmasters general
see Statesmen, American

POTEMKIN, GRIGORI ALEKSANDROVICH (1739-1791), Russian administrator and field marshal **12** 411-412

POTOK, CHAIM (Herman Harold Potok; Chaim Tzvi; 1929-2002), American author **25** 338-341

POTTER, BEATRIX (Helen Beatrix Potter; 1866-1943), English author and illustrator **18** 326-328

POTTER, DAVID M. (1910-1971), American historian **12** 412

POTTER, DENNIS (1935-1994), British essayist, playwright, screenwriter, and novelist **12** 412-414

POULENC, FRANCIS (1899-1963), French composer **12** 414-415

POUND, EZRA LOOMIS (1885-1972), American poet, editor, and critic **12** 415-417

POUND, ROSCOE (1870-1964), American jurist and botanist **12** 417-418

POUSSAINT, ALVIN FRANCIS (born 1934), African American psychiatrist **24** 313-316

POUSSIN, NICOLAS (1594-1665), French painter **12** 418-420

POWDERLY, TERENCE VINCENT (1849-1924), American labor leader **12** 420-421

POWELL, ADAM CLAYTON, JR. (1908-1972), African American political leader and Baptist minister **12** 421-422

POWELL, ANTHONY (1905-2000), English novelist **12** 422-423

POWELL, COLIN LUTHER (born 1937), African American chairman of the Joint Chiefs of Staff **12** 424-425

POWELL, JOHN WESLEY (1834-1902), American geologist, anthropologist, and explorer **12** 425-426

POWELL, LEWIS F., JR. (1907-1998), U.S. Supreme Court justice (1972-1987) **12** 426-428

POWERS, HIRAM (1805-1873), American sculptor **12** 428-429

POWHATAN (circa 1550-1618), Native American tribal chief **12** 429-430

POZZO, BROTHER ANDREA, S.J. (1642-1709), Italian artist and architect **25** 341-342

PRADO UGARTECHE, MANUEL (1889-1967), Peruvian statesman **12** 430-431

PRAETORIUS, MICHAEL (circa 1571-1621), German composer and theorist **12** 431-432

PRAN, DITH (born 1942), Cambodian American journalist and activist **18** 328-331

PRANDTAUER, JAKOB (1660-1726), Austrian baroque architect **12** 432

PRASAD, RAJENDRA (1884-1963), Indian nationalist, first president of the Republic **12** 433

PRAXITELES (flourished circa 370-330 B.C.), Greek sculptor **12** 433-434

PREBISCH, RAÚL (1901-1986), Argentine economist active in the United Nations **12** 434-436

PREGL, FRITZ (1869-1930), Austrian physiologist and medical chemist **12** 436-437

PREM TINSULANONDA (born 1920), military leader and prime minister of Thailand (1979-1988) **12** 437

PREMADASA, RANASINGHE (born 1924), president of Sri Lanka (1988-) **12** 437-439

PREMCHAND (1880-1936), Indian novelist and short-story writer **12** 439

PREMINGER, OTTO (1895-1986), Austrian filmmaker and theater producer/director **18** 331-332

PRENDERGAST, MAURICE BRAZIL (1859-1924), American painter **12** 440

Presbyterianism (religion)
missions
Sheppard, William Henry **27** 325-327

PRESCOTT, WILLIAM HICKLING (1796-1859), American historian **12** 440-441

PRESLEY, ELVIS ARON (1935-1977), American singer and actor **12** 441-442

PRESTES, LUIZ CARLOS (1898-1990), Brazilian revolutionary and Communist leader **12** 442-444

PRETORIUS, ANDRIES (1798-1853), South African politician and general **12** 444-445

PRÉVERT, JACQUES (Jacques Henri Marie Prevert; 1900-1977), French poet and filmmaker **27** 297-298

PREVIN, ANDRE (Andreas Ludwig Priwin; born 1929), German American composer and conductor **18** 333-334

PRÉVOST, ABBÉ (1697-1763), French novelist, journalist, and cleric **12** 445-446

PRICE, FLORENCE BEATRICE (nee Florence Beatrice Smith; 1887-1953), African American composer and music educator **26** 306-308

PRICE, LEONTYNE (Mary Leontyne Price; born 1927), American prima donna soprano **12** 446-447

PRICE, RICHARD (1723-1791), English Nonconformist minister and political philosopher **12** 447-448

PRICHARD, DIANA GARCÍA (born 1949), Hispanic American chemical physicist **12** 448-449

PRIDE, CHARLEY FRANK (born 1938), African American musician **23** 317-319

PRIDI PHANOMYONG (1901-1983), Thai political leader **12** 449

PRIEST, IVY MAUDE BAKER (1905-1975), treasurer of the United States (1953-1960) **12** 450-451

PRIESTLEY, J(OHN) B(OYNTON) (1894-1984), English author of novels, essays, plays, and screenplays **12** 451-452

PRIESTLEY, JOSEPH (1733-1804), English clergyman and chemist **12** 452-453

PRIMATICCIO, FRANCESCO (1504-1570), Italian painter, sculptor, and architect **12** 453-454

PRIMO DE RIVERA Y ORBANEJA, MIGUEL (1870-1930), Spanish general, dictator 1923-30 **12** 454-455

R

RODINO, PETER WALLACE, JR. (born 1909), Democratic U.S. representative from New Jersey **13** 238-239

RODNEY, GEORGE BRYDGES (1st Baron Rodney; 1718-92), British admiral **13** 239-240

RODÓ, JOSÉ ENRIQUE (1872-1917), Uraguayan essayist and literary critic **13** 240-241

RODRÍGUEZ DE TÍO, LOLA (1834-1924), Puerto Rican/Cuban poet and nationalist **23** 345-346

ROEBLING, JOHN AUGUSTUS (1806-1869), German-born American engineer **13** 241-242

ROEBLING, WASHINGTON AUGUSTUS (1837-1926), American engineer and manufacturer **13** 243

ROETHKE, THEODORE (1908-1963), American poet and teacher **13** 243-244

ROGER II (1095-1154), king of Sicily 1130-54 **13** 244-245

ROGERS, CARL RANSOM (1902-1987), American psychotherapist **13** 245-247

ROGERS, EDITH NOURSE (1881-1960), U.S. congresswoman from Massachusetts **13** 247-248

ROGERS, FRED ("Mr." Rogers; 1928-2003), American television host **18** 352-354

ROGERS, JOHN (1829-1904), American sculptor **13** 248

ROGERS, RICHARD (born 1933), British architect **13** 248-250

ROGERS, ROBERT (1731-1795), American frontiersman and army officer **13** 250-251

ROGERS, WILL (1879-1935), American actor, humorist, journalist, and performer **13** 251-252

ROH TAE WOO (born 1932), president of the Republic of Korea **13** 253-255

ROHDE, RUTH BRYAN OWEN (1885-1954), U.S. congresswoman **13** 252-253

ROHRER, HEINRICH (Born 1933), Swiss physicist **25** 358-360

ROJAS PINILLA, GUSTAVO (1900-1975), Colombian general and politician **13** 255-256

ROLAND, MADAME (Marie-Jeanne Phlipon; 1754-1793), French author and revolutionary **13** 256-259

ROLDÁN, LUISA IGNACIA (circa 1650-circa 1704), Spanish sculptor **26** 322-324

ROLFE, JOHN (1585-1622), English colonist in Virginia **13** 259-260

ROLLAND, ROMAIN (1866-1944), French writer **13** 260

ROLLE OF HAMPOLE, RICHARD (circa 1290-1349), English prose and verse writer **13** 260-261

ROLLING STONES, THE (formed in 1963), rock and roll band **13** 261-264

ROLLINS, CHARLEMAE HILL (1897-1979), African American librarian and author **23** 346-348

ROLLO (Rolf; circa 860-circa 932), Viking adventurer **13** 264-265

RÖLVAAG, OLE EDVART (1876-1931), Norwegian-American writer **13** 265

Roman Catholic Church
  missionary work
    Baraga, Frederic **27** 33-35
  Peru
    Porres, Martín de, Saint **27** 295-297

ROMANOV, ANASTASIA NICHOLAIEVNA (1901-1918), Russian grand duchess **18** 354-357

ROMBAUER, IRMA VON STARKLOFF (1877-1962), American cookbook author **26** 324-326

ROMERO, ARCHBISHOP OSCAR (1917-1980), archbishop of San Salvador **13** 265-267

ROMERO BARCELÓ, CARLOS (born 1932), Puerto Rican political leader and governor **13** 267-268

ROMILLY, SAMUEL (1757-1818), English legal reformer **23** 348-351

ROMMEL, ERWIN (1891-1944), German field marshal **13** 268-269

ROMNEY, GEORGE (1734-1802), English painter **13** 269-270

ROMNEY, GEORGE (1907-1995), American businessman and politician **20** 313-316

RÓMULO, CARLOS P. (1899-1985), Filipino journalist and diplomat **13** 270-271

RONDON, CANDIDO MARIANO DA SILVA (1865-1958), Brazilian militarist **13** 271

RONSARD, PIERRE DE (1524-1585), French poet **13** 271-273

RÖNTGEN, WILHELM CONRAD (1845-1923), German physicist **13** 273-275

ROOSEVELT, ANNA ELEANOR (1884-1962), American lecturer and author, first lady 1933-45 **13** 275-277

ROOSEVELT, FRANKLIN DELANO (1882-1945), American statesman, president 1933-45 **13** 277-280

ROOSEVELT, THEODORE (1858-1919), American statesman, president 1901-09 **13** 280-283

ROOT, ELIHU (1845-1937), American statesman **13** 283-284

ROOT, JOHN WELLBORN (1850-1891), American architect **21** 372-374

ROREM, NED (born 1923), American composer of art songs **13** 284-286

RORSCHACH, HERMANN (1884-1922), Swiss psychiatrist **13** 286-288

RORTY, RICHARD (born 1931), American philosopher and man of letters **13** 288-289

ROSA, SALVATOR (1615-1673), Italian painter and poet **13** 289-290

ROSAS, JUAN MANUEL DE (1793-1877), Argentine dictator 1829-52 **13** 290-291

ROSE, PETE (Peter Edward Rose; born 1941), American baseball player **21** 374-376

ROSEBUD YELLOW ROBE (Rosebud yellow Robe-Frantz; 1907-1992), Native American author and educator **26** 390-392

ROSENBERG, JULIUS AND ETHEL (died 1953), Americans executed for atomic espionage **13** 291-293

ROSENWALD, JULIUS (1862-1932), American retailer and philanthropist **13** 293

ROSENZWEIG, FRANZ (1886-1929), Jewish philosopher and writer **13** 294

ROS-LEHTINEN, ILEANA (born 1952) Hispanic American U.S. congresswoman **13** 294-296

ROSMINI-SERBATI, ANTONIO (1797-1855), Italian philosopher and priest **13** 296-297

ROSS, BETSY (Elizabeth Griscom; 1752-1836), American upholsterer who made the first U.S. flag **13** 297-298

ROSS, DIANA (born 1944), African American singer **13** 298-300

ROSS, EDWARD ALSWORTH (1866-1951), American sociologist **13** 300

ROSS, HAROLD (Harold Wallace Ross; 1892-1951), founder and editor of the *New Yorker* magazine **13** 300-302

ROSS, SIR JAMES CLARK (1800-1862), English admiral and polar explorer **13** 302-303

STEIN, GERTRUDE (1874-1946), American writer **14** 414-415

STEIN, BARON HEINRICH FRIEDRICH KARL VOM UND ZUM (1757-1831), Prussian statesman **14** 415-416

STEINBECK, JOHN ERNST (1902-1968), American author **14** 416-417

STEINEM, GLORIA (born 1934), American feminist and journalist **14** 418-419

STEINER, JAKOB (1796-1863), Swiss mathematician **23** 380-382

STEINER, RUDOLF (1861-1925), Austrian philosopher and educator **27** 331-333

STEINITZ, WILHELM (1836-1900), Bohemian American chess player **20** 343-346

STEINMETZ, CHARLES PROTEUS (Karl August Rudolf Steinmetz; 1865-1923), German-born American mathematician and electrical engineer **14** 419-420

STELLA, FRANK (born 1936), American painter **14** 420-422

STELLA, JOSEPH (1877-1946), Italian-born American painter **14** 422

STENDHAL (Marie Henri Beyle; 1783-1842), French author **14** 422-425

STENGEL, CASEY (Charles Dillon Stengel; 1890-1975), American baseball player and manager **19** 361-363

STENO, NICOLAUS (Niels Stensen; 1638-86), Danish naturalist **14** 425-426

STEPHEN (1096?-1154), king of England 1135-54 **14** 426-427

STEPHEN I (c. 973-1038), king of Hungary **14** 427-428

STEPHEN, SIR LESLIE (1832-1904), English historian **14** 429

STEPHEN HARDING, ST. (died 1134), English abbot and monastic reformer **14** 428-429

STEPHENS, ALEXANDER HAMILTON (1812-1883), American statesman **14** 429-430

STEPHENS, HELEN (1918-1994), American athlete **19** 363-365

STEPHENS, JAMES (1882-1950), Irish novelist and poet **14** 430-431

STEPHENS, URIAH (1821-1882), American labor leader **14** 431-432

STEPHENSON, GEORGE (1781-1848), English railway engineer **14** 432-433

STEPHENSON, ROBERT (1803-1859), English railway engineer **14** 432-433

STEPINAC, ALOJZIJE (1898-1960), Croatian nationalist, Catholic, and anti-Communist **14** 433-435

STEPTOE, PATRICK (1913-1988), British physician **20** 346-348

STERN, ISAAC (born 1920), American violinist **19** 365-367

STERN, OTTO (1888-1969), German-born American physicist **14** 435

STERNE, LAURENCE (1713-1768), British novelist **14** 435-437

STETTINIUS, EDWARD R., JR. (1900-1949), American industrialist and statesman **14** 437-438

STEUBEN, BARON FREDERICK WILLIAM AUGUSTUS VON (1730-1794), German officer in the American Revolution **14** 438-439

STEVENS, GEORGE COOPER (1904-1975), American Film Director and Producer **22** 401-403

STEVENS, JOHN (1749-1838), American engineer and inventor **14** 439-440

STEVENS, JOHN PAUL (born 1920), U.S. Supreme Court justice **14** 440-441

STEVENS, NETTIE MARIA (1861-1912), American biologist and geneticist **14** 441-442

STEVENS, THADDEUS (1792-1868), American politician **14** 442-443

STEVENS, WALLACE (1879-1955), American poet **14** 443-445

STEVENSON, ADLAI EWING (1900-1965), American statesman and diplomat **14** 445-446

STEVENSON, ROBERT LOUIS (1850-1894), Scottish novelist, essayist and poet **14** 446-448

STEVIN, SIMON (Simon Stevinus; 1548-1620), Dutch mathematician **21** 395-398

STEWARD, SUSAN MCKINNEY (nee Susan Marie Smith; 1847-1918), African American physician and activist **24** 390-392

STEWART, ALEXANDER TURNEY (1803-1876), American dry-goods merchant **14** 448-449

STEWART, DUGALD (1753-1828), Scottish philosopher **14** 449

STEWART, ELLEN (born 1920), African-American theater founder and director **20** 348-352

STEWART, JACKIE (John Young Stewart; born 1939), Scottish race car driver **24** 392-395

STEWART, JIMMY (James Maitland Stewart; 1908-1997), American actor **18** 385-386

STEWART, MARIA W. MILLER (1803-1879), African American author and activist **24** 395-397

STEWART, MARTHA (nee Martha Kostyra; born 1941), American author, entertainer, and businesswoman **19** 367-369

STEWART, POTTER (1915-1985), liberal U.S. Supreme Court justice **14** 449-451

STIEGEL, HENRY WILLIAM (1729-1785), German born American iron founder and glassmaker **14** 451

STIEGLITZ, ALFRED (1864-1946), American photographer, editor, and art gallery director **14** 451-452

STILICHO, FLAVIUS (died 408), Roman general **14** 452-453

STILL, CLYFFORD (1904-1980), American Abstract Expressionist artist **14** 453-454

STILL, WILLIAM (1821-1902), African American abolitionist, philanthropist, and businessman **14** 454-455

STILL, WILLIAM GRANT (born 1895), African American composer **14** 455-456

STILWELL, JOSEPH WARREN (1883-1946), American general **14** 456-457

STIMSON, HENRY LEWIS (1867-1950), American lawyer and statesman **14** 457-458

STIRLING, JAMES (1926-1992), British architect and city planner **14** 458-459

STIRNER, MAX (1806-1856), German philosopher **14** 459-460

STOCKHAUSEN, KARLHEINZ (born 1928), German composer **14** 460-461

STOCKTON, ROBERT FIELD (1795-1866), American naval officer and politician **14** 461-462

STODDARD, SOLOMON (1643-1728/29), American colonial Congregational clergyman **14** 462-463

STOKER, BRAM (Abraham Stoker; 1847-1912), Irish author **14** 463-464

STOKES, CARL B. (1927-1996), African American politician **14** 464-465

STOLYPIN, PIOTR ARKADEVICH (1862-1911), Russian statesman and reformer **14** 465-466

T

THIERS, LOUIS ADOLPHE (1797-1877), French journalist, historian, and statesman **15** 181-182

THIEU, NGUYEN VAN (1923-2001), South Vietnamese president **15** 182-183

THOMAS, ALMA WOODSEY (1891-1978), African American artist **23** 401-403

THOMAS, CLARENCE (born 1948), U.S. Supreme Court justice **15** 186-188

THOMAS, DAVE (R. David Thomas; 1932-2002), American businessman **18** 389-397

THOMAS, DYLAN MARLAIS (1914-1953), British poet **15** 188-190

THOMAS, GEORGE HENRY (1816-1870), American general **15** 190-191

THOMAS, HELEN (born 1920), American journalist **19** 381-384

THOMAS, NORMAN MATTOON (1884-1968), American Socialist politician, author, and lecturer **15** 191-192

THOMAS, THEODORE (1835-1905), American orchestral conductor **15** 192-193

THOMAS, WILLIAM ISAAC (1863-1947), American sociologist and educator **15** 193

THOMAS AQUINAS, SAINT (circa 1224-74), Italian philosopher and theologian **15** 183-186

THOMASIUS (1655-1728), German philosopher and jurist **15** 193-194

THOMPSON, DALEY (Francis Ayodele Thompson; born 1958), English track and field athlete **20** 368-370

THOMPSON, DAVID (1770-1857), Canadian explorer, cartographer, and surveyor **15** 194-195

THOMPSON, DOROTHY (1894-1961), conservative American journalist **15** 195-196

THOMPSON, EMMA (born 1959), British author and actress **27** 338-340

THOMPSON, HUNTER STOCKTON (born 1939), American journalist **15** 196-198

THOMPSON, TOMMY (born 1941), American politician **25** 413-415

THOMSON, SIR GEORGE PAGET (1892-1975), English atomic physicist **15** 198-199

THOMSON, JAMES (1700-1748), British poet **15** 199-200

THOMSON, SIR JOSEPH JOHN (1856-1940), English physicist **15** 200-201

THOMSON, KENNETH (1923-2006), Canadian print and broadcast journalism magnate **15** 201-202

THOMSON, TOM (1877-1917), Canadian painter **15** 202

THOMSON, VIRGIL (1896-1989), American composer, critic, and conductor **15** 202-203

THOREAU, HENRY DAVID (1817-1862), American writer and transcendentalist **15** 203-205

THOREZ, MAURICE (1900-1964), headed the French Communist Party from 1930 to 1964 **15** 206-207

THORN, GASTON (born 1928), prime minister of Luxembourg **15** 207-208

THORNDIKE, EDWARD LEE (1874-1949), American psychologist and educator **15** 208-209

THORNDIKE, SYBIL (Dame Agnes Sybil Thorndike; 1882-1976), English actress and manager **24** 415-417

THORPE, JIM (James Francis Thorpe; 1888-1953), American track star and professional football and baseball player **15** 209-211

THORVALDSEN, BERTEL (Albert Bertel Thorvaldsen; 1770-1848), Danish sculptor **23** 403-406

THUCYDIDES (circa 460-circa 401 B.C.), Greek historian **15** 211-212

THUKU, HARRY (1895-1970), Kenyan politician **15** 212-213

THURBER, JAMES GROVE (1894-1961), American writer and artist **15** 213-214

THURMOND, JAMES STROM (born 1902), American lawyer and statesman **15** 214-215

THURSTONE, LOUIS LEON (1887-1955), American psychologist **15** 215-216

THUTMOSE III (1504-1450 B.C.), Egyptian king **15** 216-217

TIBERIUS JULIUS CAESAR AUGUSTUS (42 B.C.-A.D. 37), emperor of Rome 14-37 **15** 217-218

TIECK, LUDWIG (1773-1853), German author **15** 218-219

TIEPOLO, GIOVANNI BATTISTA (1696-1770), Italian painter **15** 219-220

TIFFANY, LOUIS COMFORT (1848-1933), American painter and designer **15** 220-221

TIGLATH-PILESER III (ruled 745-727 B.C.), king of Assyria **15** 221-222

TILBERIS, ELIZABETH (Elizabeth Jane Kelly; Liz Tilberis; 1947-1999), British journalist **27** 340-342

TILDEN, BILL (William Tatem Tilden II; 1893-1953), American tennis player **20** 370-372

TILDEN, SAMUEL JONES (1814-1886), American politician **15** 222-223

TILLEY, SIR SAMUEL LEONARD (1818-1896), Canadian statesman **15** 223-224

TILLEY, VESTA (Matilda Alice Victoria Powles; 1864-1852), British entertainer **26** 359-361

TILLICH, PAUL JOHANNES (1886-1965), German-American Protestant theologian and philosopher **15** 224-225

TILLMAN, BENJAMIN RYAN (1847-1918), American statesman and demagogue **15** 225-226

TILLY, GRAF VON (Johann Tserclaes; 1559-1632), Flemish general **20** 372-374

TIMERMAN, JACOBO (1923-1999), Argentine journalist and human rights advocate **15** 226-228

TINBERGEN, JAN (1903-1994), Dutch economist **15** 228-229

TINBERGEN, NIKOLAAS (1907-1988), English ethologist and zoologist **15** 229-230

TING, SAMUEL CHAO CHUNG (born 1936), American nuclear physicist **23** 406-408

TINGUELY, JEAN (1925-1991), Swiss sculptor **15** 230-232

TINTORETTO (1518-1594), Italian painter **15** 232-234

TIPPETT, MICHAEL KEMP, SIR (1905-1998), English composer and conductor **15** 234-235

TIPPU TIP (Hamed bin Mohammed bin Juma bin Rajab el Murjebi; circa 1840-1905), Zanzibari trader **15** 235-236

TIPU SULTAN (1750-1799), Moslem ruler of Mysore **15** 236

TIRADENTES (José Joaquim da Silva Xavier; 1748-92), Brazilian national hero **15** 237

TIRPITZ, ALFRED VON (1849-1930), German admiral and politician **20** 374-376

TIRSO DE MOLINA (1584-1648), Spanish dramatist **15** 237-238

TISCH BROTHERS (1923-), real estate developers **15** 238-240

VALDEZ, LUIS (born 1940), Hispanic American playwright and filmmaker **15** 399-400

VALDIVIA, PEDRO DE (circa 1502-53), Spanish conquistador and professional soldier **15** 400-401

VALENS, RITCHIE (Richard Steven Valenzuela; 1941-1959), Hispanic American musician **22** 415-417

VALENTI, JACK JOSEPH (born 1921), presidential adviser and czar of the American film industry **15** 401-403

VALENTINO, RUDOLPH (Rodolfo Alfonso Raffaelo Pierre Filibert de Valentina d'Antonguolla Guglielmi; 1895-1926), Italian/American actor **20** 388-390

VALENZUELA, LUISA (born 1938), Argentine author **23** 421-423

VALERA Y ALCALÁ GALIANO, JUAN (1824-1905), Spanish novelist and diplomat **15** 403

VALERIAN (Publius Licinius Valerianus; circa 200-circa 260), Roman emperor 253-260 **15** 404-405

VALÉRY, PAUL AMBROISE (1871-1945), French poet, philosopher, and critic **15** 405-406

VALLA, LORENZO (circa 1407-57), Italian humanist **15** 406

VALLANDIGHAM, CLEMENT LAIRD (1820-1871), American politician **15** 406-407

VALLE INCLÁN, RAMÓN MARIA DEL (circa 1866-1936), Spanish novelist, playwright, and poet **15** 407-408

VALLEJO, CÉSAR ABRAHAM (1892-1938), Peruvian poet **15** 408-409

VAN BUREN, MARTIN (1782-1862), American statesman, president 1837-41 **15** 410-411

Van Dahorst, Anthonis Mor
see Moro, Antonio

VAN DER GOES, HUGO (flourished 1467-82), Flemish painter **15** 416-417

VAN DIEMEN, ANTHONY MEUZA (1593-1645), Dutch colonial official and merchant **15** 420

VAN DOESBURG, THEO (1883-1931), Dutch painter **15** 421

VAN DONGEN, KEES (Cornelis Theodorus Marie Van Dongen; 1877-1968), Fauvist painter, portraitist, and socialite **15** 421-422

VAN DUYN, MONA (1921-2004), first woman to be appointed poet laureate of the United States **15** 422-423

VAN DYCK, ANTHONY (1599-1641), Flemish painter **15** 423-425

VAN DYKE, DICK (Richard Wayne Van Dyke; born 1925), American actor, author, and producer **25** 416-418

VAN EEKELEN, WILLEM FREDERIK (born 1931), Dutch secretary-general of the Western European Union **15** 426-427

VAN GOGH, VINCENT (1853-1890), Dutch painter **15** 427-429

VAN HORNE, SIR WILLIAM CORNELIUS (1843-1915), American-born Canadian railroad entrepreneur **15** 429-430

VAN PEEBLES, MELVIN (Melvin Peebles; born 1932), American film director and producer, actor, author, and musician **21** 414-416

VAN RENSSELAER, KILIAEN (circa 1580-1643), Dutch merchant and colonial official in America **15** 430-431

VAN VECHTEN, CARL (1880-1964), American writer and photographer **18** 400-402

VAN VLECK, JOHN HASBROUCK (1899-1980), American physicist **25** 418-420

VANBRUGH, SIR JOHN (1664-1726), English architect and dramatist **15** 409-410

VANCE, CYRUS R. (1917-2002), American secretary of the army and secretary of state **15** 411-413

VANCE, ZEBULON BAIRD (1830-1894), American politician **15** 413-414

VANCOUVER, GEORGE (1758-1798), English explorer and navigator **15** 414-415

VANDER ZEE, JAMES (1886-1983), photographer of the people of Harlem **15** 418-419

VANDERBILT, CORNELIUS (1794-1877), American financier, steamship and railroad builder **15** 415-416

VANDERBILT, GLORIA (born 1924), American designer, artist, and author **19** 395-397

VANDERLYN, JOHN (1775-1852), American painter **15** 417

VANDROSS, LUTHER (1951-2005), American singer **26** 364-366

VANE, SIR HENRY (1613-1662), English statesman **15** 425-426

VAN'T HOFF, JACOBUS HENDRICUS (1852-1911), Dutch physical chemist **15** 431-432

VARDHAMANA MAHAVIRA (circa 540-470 B.C.), Indian ascetic philosopher **10** 135-137

VARÈSE, EDGARD (1883-1965), French-American composer **15** 432-433

VARGAS, GETULIO DORNELLES (1883-1954), Brazilian political leader **15** 433-434

VARGAS LLOSA, MARIO (born 1936), Peruvian novelist, critic, journalist, screenwriter, and essayist **15** 434-436

VARMUS, HAROLD ELIOT (born 1939), medical research expert and director of the National Institutes of Health (1993-) **15** 436-437

VARNHAGEN, FRANCISCO ADOLFO DE (1816-1878), Brazilian historian **15** 437-438

VARRO, MARCUS TERENTIUS (116-27 B.C.), Roman scholar and writer **15** 438-439

VARTHEMA, LUDOVICO DI (circa 1470-circa 1517), Italian traveler and adventurer **15** 439-440

VASARELY, VICTOR (1908-1997), Hungarian-French artist **15** 440-442

VASARI, GIORGIO (1511-1570), Italian painter, architect, and author **15** 442-443

VASCONCELOS, JOSÉ (1882-1959), Mexican educator and author **15** 443-444

VAUBAN, SEBASTIEN LE PRESTRE DE (1633-1707), French military engineer **18** 402-404

VAUDREUIL-CAVAGNAL, MARQUIS DE (Pierre Françsois de Regaud; 1698-1778), Canadian-born governor of New France **15** 444

VAUGHAN, HENRY (1621/22-95), British poet **15** 444-445

VAUGHAN, SARAH LOIS (1924-1990), jazz singer **15** 445-446

VAUGHAN WILLIAMS, RALPH (1872-1958), English composer **15** 446-447

VAUGHT, WILMA L. (born 1930), U.S. Air Force officer **24** 427-429

VAVILOV, NIKOLAI IVANOVICH (1887-1943), Russian botanist and geneticist **15** 447-448

VÁZQUEZ, HORACIO (1860-1936), president of the Dominican Republic 1903-04 and 1924-30 **15** 448-449

VÁZQUEZ ARCE Y CEBALLOS, GREGORIO (1638-1711), Colombian artist **23** 423-425